KV-418-992

STAFFORDSHIRE
COUNTY COUNCIL
LIBRARY
STOKE-ON-TRENT

Statutory Instruments 1987

PART III

SECTION 1

Published by Authority

LONDON

HER MAJESTY'S STATIONERY OFFICE

1989

© *Crown Copyright 1989*

ISBN 0 11 840285 4

HMSO publications are available from:

HMSO Publications Centre
(Mail and telephone orders only)
PO Box 276, London, SW8 5DT
Telephone orders 01-873 9090
General enquiries 01-873 0011
(queuing system in operation for both numbers)

HMSO Bookshops
49 High Holborn, London, WC1V 6HB   01-873 0011 (Counter service only)
258 Broad Street, Birmingham, B1 2HE   021-643 3740
Southey House, 33 Wine Street, Bristol, BS1 2BQ   (0272) 264306
9-21 Princess Street, Manchester, M60 8AS   061-834 7201
80 Chichester Street, Belfast, BT1 4JY   (0232) 238451
71 Lothian Road, Edinburgh, EH3 9AZ   031-228 4181

HMSO's Accredited Agents
(see Yellow Pages)

and through good booksellers

Price for three sections £240 net

STAFFORDSHIRE
COUNTY
LIBRARY

A5.490
C

Printed in the United Kingdom for Her Majesty's Stationery Office
Dd8051786 11/89 C7 G409 10170

Contents of the Edition

PART I

SECTION 1

SECTION 2

PART II

SECTION 1

SECTION 2

PART III

SECTION 1

SECTION 2

SECTION 3

List of Instruments in Part III

STATUTORY INSTRUMENTS

STATUTORY INSTRUMENTS

1987 No. 1525

LANDLORD AND TENANT

The Assured Tenancies (Approved Bodies) (No. 4) Order 1987

Made - - - -	*26th August 1987*
Laid before Parliament	*10th September 1987*
Coming into force	*1st October 1987*

The Secretary of State for the Environment, as respects England, and the Secretary of State for Wales, as respects Wales, in exercise of the powers conferred upon them by section 56(4) of the Housing Act 1980(**a**), and of all other powers enabling them in that behalf, hereby make the following Order:

1. This Order may be cited as the Assured Tenancies (Approved Bodies) (No. 4) Order 1987 and shall come into force on 1st October 1987.

2. The bodies named in the Schedule to this Order are hereby specified for the purposes of Part II of the Housing Act 1980.

SCHEDULE

BODIES SPECIFIED FOR THE PURPOSES OF PART II OF THE HOUSING ACT 1980

1. Albion Mills Housing Co-operative Limited.
2. Anglia Housing Association Limited.
3. Belmont Housing Association Limited.
4. Broadcasting Employees Housing Development Association Limited.
5. CCHA (Sunbourne Court) Limited.
6. Collingwood Housing Association.
7. Croydon Churches Housing Association Limited.
8. Derwent Housing Society Limited.
9. Donald Halliday and Joyce Mary Halliday trading as Homefinders.
10. Equity Housing Association Limited.
11. Fairlake Third Housing Association Limited.
12. Four Rivers Housing Limited.
13. G H Ball Limited.
14. Grosvenor Housing Association Limited.
15. "Johnnie" Johnson Housing Association Limited.
16. Liver Housing Association Limited.
17. Martha Mockford Limited.
18. Merseyside Housing Association Limited.

(**a**) 1980 c.51.

19. Mid-Wales Housing Association Limited.
20. Monmouth & Llandaff Housing Association Limited.
21. Nationwide Anglia Building Society.
22. North Wales Housing Association Limited.
23. Orbit Housing Developments Limited.
24. Parklands Housing Society Limited.
25. Richmond-upon-Thames Leasehold Housing Association Limited.
26. Stepnell Developments Limited.
27. Stepnell Estates Limited.
28. Swansea Hillside Housing Association Limited.
29. Swansea Housing Association Limited.
30. The Cambridge Housing Society Limited.
31. The Corporation of the Dean and Chapter of the Cathedral Church of Christ in Liverpool.
32. The Railway Housing Association and Benefit Fund.
33. The Sutton (Hastoe) Housing Association Limited.
34. Wessex Housing Society Limited.
35. Westland Homes Housing Society Limited.

Signed by authority of the Secretary of State   *Marion Roe*
20th August 1987   Parliamentary Under Secretary of State,
                                                  Department of the Environment

                                                            Peter Walker
26th August 1987   Secretary of State for Wales

EXPLANATORY NOTE

(This note is not part of the Order)

Assured tenancies are tenancies which would otherwise have been protected tenancies or housing association tenancies under the Rent Act 1977 (c. 42), and which meet certain other conditions. Such tenancies are subject to Part II of the Landlord and Tenant Act 1954 (c. 56), as modified by Schedule 5 to the Housing Act 1980. They can only be granted by bodies approved under section 56 of the 1980 Act.

This Order approves thirty-five bodies for the purposes of section 56.

STATUTORY INSTRUMENTS

1987 No. 1529 (S.112)

TOWN AND COUNTRY PLANNING, SCOTLAND

The Town and Country Planning (Listed Buildings and Buildings in Conservation Areas) (Scotland) Regulations 1987

Made - - - -		*28th August 1987*
Laid before Parliament		*10th September 1987*
Coming into force		*1st October 1987*

ARRANGEMENT OF REGULATIONS

Schedule 3 - Notice that a building has become, or ceased to be, listed.

Schedule 4 - Application of enactments to buildings in conservation areas.

The Secretary of State, in exercise of the powers conferred on him by sections 52(5), 54D, 160(2), 161(1), 162(3), 179(1), 257, 262A(8) and (9), 273(1) and (3), and 275(1) of, and paragraphs 1(1A), 1(1A) as applied by section 54D,2(1), 7(1), 8 and 11(2) of Schedule 10 to, the Town and Country Planning (Scotland) Act 1972(**a**) and section 1(5)(**b**) and (c), as read with section 6(4), of the Town and Country Planning Act 1984(**b**), and of all other powers enabling him in that behalf, hereby makes the following Regulations:

Citation and commencement

1.   These Regulations may be cited as the Town and Country Planning (Listed Buildings and Buildings in Conservation Areas) (Scotland) Regulations 1987 and shall come into force on 1st October 1987.

Interpretation

2.—(1) Any reference in these Regulations to a numbered regulation or to a numbered Schedule is, unless otherwise expressly provided or the context otherwise requires, a reference to the regulation or Schedule bearing that number in these Regulations and a reference in a regulation to a numbered paragraph is a reference to the paragraph bearing that number in that regulation.

(2) In these Regulations, unless the context otherwise requires–

"the Act" means the Town and Country Planning (Scotland) Act 1972;

"the appropriate authority" has the meaning assigned to it by section 253(7) of the Act;

"building in a conservation area" means an unlisted building within a conservation area to which listed building control is applied by sections 262A(8) and (9) of the Act;

"conservation area consent" means consent required by section 262A(2) of the Act;

"Crown land" and "Crown interest" have the meanings assigned to them by section 253(7) of the Act;

"listed building" has the meaning assigned to it by section 52(7) of the Act;

"listed building consent" means the consent required by sections 53(2) and 53(2A)(**c**) of the Act in respect of works for the demolition, extension or alteration of a listed building.

Applications for listed building consent and conservation area consent

3.—(1) An application to a planning authority for listed building consent or for conservation area consent shall be made on a form issued by the planning authority and obtainable from that authority and shall contain–

(a) sufficient particulars to identify the building to which it relates, including a plan,

(b) such other plans and drawings as are necessary to describe fully the works which are the subject of the application, and

(c) such information relating to those works as the planning authority may reasonably require,

(**a**) 1972 c.52; section 54D was inserted by the Housing and Planning Act 1986 (c.63), Schedule 9, paragraph 17; section 257 was substituted by the Town and Country Amenities Act 1974 (c.32), section 7(2); section 262A was inserted by the Town and Country Amenities Act 1974 (c.32), section 2(1); section 262A(8) was amended by the Local Government and Planning (Scotland) Act 1982 (c.43), Schedule 2, paragraph 38(a) and (b); paragraph (1A) of Schedule 10 was inserted by the Housing and Planning Act 1986 (c.63), Schedule 9, paragraph 22; sections 52(5), 160(2), 161(1), 162(3) and 179(1) and paragraphs 1, 2,7(1) and 8 of Schedule 10 were amended by the Local Government (Scotland) Act 1973 (c.65), section 172(2); section 275(1) contains a definition of "prescribed" relevant to the exercise of the statutory powers under which these Regulations are made.
(**b**) 1984 c.10.
(**c**) Section 53(2A) was inserted by the Housing and Planning Act 1986 (c.63), Schedule 9, paragraph 14(2).

and shall be lodged with the planning authority together with such documents or certificates as may be required in accordance with regulations 6 and 7 and two further copies of the form, plans and drawings.

(2) The planning authority may by a direction in writing addressed to the applicant require him to provide such further information, in addition to that given in the application, as may be requisite to enable them to determine the application, or to produce to them such evidence as they may reasonably call for to verify any particulars of information given to them.

(3) Where an application under paragraph (1) above has been received by the planning authority, the period within which the planning authority shall give notice to an applicant of their decision or of the reference of an application to the Secretary of State shall be two months from the date of receipt of the application by the planning authority and, in any case where the planning authority have asked for additional information or evidence, two months from the latest date of receipt thereof or such extended period as may at any time (except where the applicant has already given notice of appeal to the Secretary of State) be agreed upon in writing between the applicant and the planning authority.

(4) Every notice by a planning authority of their decision or of reference of an application to the Secretary of State shall be in writing and, where the planning authority decide to grant listed building consent or conservation area consent subject to conditions or to refuse it, they shall state their reasons in writing and send with the decision a notification in the terms (or substantially in the terms) set out in Part I of Schedule 1.

Applications to vary or discharge conditions attached to listed building consent and conservation area consent

4.—(1) An application to a planning authority by a person interested in a building for the variation or discharge of conditions attached to a listed building consent or conservation area consent granted in respect of that building, shall be made on a form issued by the planning authority and obtainable from that authority, and shall

(a) give particulars of that person's interest in the building,

(b) indicate what variation or discharge of conditions is applied for,

(c) contain sufficient particulars to identify the building to which it relates, including a plan,

(d) contain such other particulars as may be required by the planning authority, and

(e) be lodged with the planning authority together with such certificates or documents as may be required in accordance with regulations 6 or 7 and two further copies of the form, plans and drawings.

(2) Paragraphs (2) to (4) of regulation 3 shall have effect in relation to an application under this regulation as they have effect in relation to an application under regulation 3(1), except that for the reference in regulation 3(4) to a notification in the terms set out in Part I of Schedule 1, there shall be substituted a reference to a notification in the terms set out in Part II of that Schedule.

Advertisement of applications

5.—(1) Where an application for listed building consent, for conservation area consent or to vary or discharge conditions attached to a listed building consent or a conservation area consent is made to a planning authority in respect of any building, the planning authority shall–

(a) publish in the Edinburgh Gazette and in a local newspaper circulating in the locality in which the building is situated a notice indicating the nature of the works which are the subject of the application, naming a place within that locality where a copy of the application, and of all plans and other documents submitted with it, will be open to inspection by the public at all reasonable hours during the period of 21 days beginning with the date of publication of the notice and stating that representations may be made in writing to the planning authority within that period; and

(b) for not less than 7 days display on or near the said building a notice containing the same particulars as are required to be contained in the notice to be published in accordance with sub-paragraph (a) of this paragraph.

(2) No application for listed building consent, for conservation area consent, or to vary or discharge conditions attached to a listed building consent or a conservation area consent

shall be determined by the planning authority before the following periods have elapsed, namely–

(a) the period of 21 days referred to in sub-paragraph (a) of paragraph (1) of this regulation, and where the date of publication of the notice in the Edinburgh Gazette and the date of publication of the notice in a local newspaper are not the same the above mentioned period of 21 days will be taken to commence on whichever is the later of the two dates of publication; and

(b) the period of 21 days beginning with the date on which the notice required by sub-paragraph (b) of paragraph (1) of this regulation was first displayed;

and in determining the application the planning authority shall take into account any representations relating to the application which are received by them before these periods have elapsed.

Certificates to accompany applications and appeals

6.—(1) A planning authority shall not entertain any application (which in this regulation means an application for listed building consent, for conservation area consent, or to vary or discharge conditions attached to a listed building consent or a conservation area consent) unless it is accompanied either by one or both of the documents described in regulation 7 or by one or other of the following certificates signed by or on behalf of the applicant, that is to say–

(a) a certificate stating that, in respect of the building or any part of the building to which the application relates, at the beginning of the period of 21 days ending with the date of the application no person other than the applicant was the owner;

(b) a certificate stating that the applicant has given the requisite notice of the application to all persons (other than the applicant) who, at the beginning of the period of 21 days ending with the date of the application, were owners of the building to which the application relates, and setting out the names of those persons, the addresses at which notice of the application was given to them respectively, and the date on which each notice was served;

(c) a certificate stating that the applicant is unable to issue a certificate in accordance with either of the preceding sub-paragraphs, that he has given the requisite notice of the application to such one or more of the persons mentioned in the last preceding sub-paragraph as are specified in the certificate (setting out their names, the addresses at which notice of the application was given to them respectively, and the date on which each notice was served), that he has taken such steps as are reasonably open to him (specifying them) to ascertain the names and addresses of the remainder of those persons and that he has been unable to do so;

(d) a certificate stating that the applicant is unable to issue a certificate in accordance with sub-paragraph (a) above, that he has taken such steps as are reasonably open to him (specifying them) to ascertain the names and addresses of the persons mentioned in sub-paragraph (b) of this paragraph and that he has been unable to do so.

(2) Any such certificate as is mentioned in sub-paragraph (c) or sub-paragraph (d) of paragraph (1) shall also contain a statement that the requisite notice of the application, as set out in the certificate, has on a date specified in the certificate (being a date not earlier than the beginning of the period mentioned in sub-paragraph (b) of paragraph (1)) been published in a local newspaper circulating in the locality in which the building is situated.

(3) Where an application is accompanied by such a certificate as is mentioned in sub-paragraphs (b), (c) or (d) of paragraph (1)–

(a) the planning authority shall not determine the application before the end of the period of 21 days beginning with the date appearing from the certificate to be the latest of the dates on which notices were served as mentioned in the certificate, or the date of publication of a notice as therein mentioned, whichever is the later;

(b) the planning authority–

(i) in determining the application, shall take into account any representations relating thereto which are made to them, before the end of the period specified in sub-paragraph (a) of this paragraph, by any person who satisfies them that he is an owner of the building or any part thereof to which the application relates, and

(ii) shall give notice of their decision to every person who has made representations which they were required to take into account in accordance with the preceding head.

(4) For the purposes of this regulation, "owner" in relation to any building means any person who under the Lands Clauses Acts would be enabled to sell and convey the land to the promoters of an undertaking (that is to say the proprietor of the *dominium utile* or, in relation to a building situated on land not held on feudal tenure, the proprietor thereof), and any person entitled to possession of the building as lessee under a lease the unexpired period of which is not less than seven years.

(5) The provisions of this regulation shall apply, with any necessary modifications, in relation to an application which is referred to the Secretary of State under paragraph 4 of Schedule 10 to the Act or in relation to an appeal to the Secretary of State under paragraph 7 or paragraph 8 of that Schedule or in relation to those provisions as applied to buildings in conservation areas by section 262A(8) of the Act, as they apply in relation to an application which falls to be determined by the planning authority.

(6) Certificates issued for the purposes of this regulation shall be in the forms set out in Part I of Schedule 2 or in forms substantially to the like effect.

(7) The requisite notices for the purposes of the provisions of this regulation in relation to applications shall be in the forms set out in Part II of Schedule 2 or in forms substantially to the like effect.

(8) The requisite notices for the purposes of the provisions of this regulation in relation to appeals shall be in the forms set out in Part III of Schedule 2 or in forms substantially to the like effect.

Documents to accompany applications for listed building consent and conservation area consent in respect of Crown land and notification of disposal to planning authority

7.—(1) Where an application is made to a planning authority in respect of Crown land in accordance with section 1(2) of the Town and Country Planning Act 1984 by the appropriate authority or by a person authorised by that authority in writing for listed building consent or conservation area consent, and where there is no interest in the land which is for the time being held otherwise than by or on behalf of the Crown, the planning authority shall not entertain such application unless it is accompanied by the following documents namely—

(a) a statement that there is for the time being no private interest in the land; and

(b) where the application is made by a person authorised by the appropriate authority, a copy of the relevant authorisation.

(2) The appropriate authority shall, as soon as may be after disposing of an interest in any Crown land in respect of which an application has been made under section 1(2) of the said 1984 Act, give notice in writing to the planning authority of such disposal.

Appeals

8.—(1) Any person who desires to appeal—

(a) against a decision of a planning authority—

(i) refusing listed building consent or conservation area consent or granting such consent subject to conditions, or

(ii) refusing to vary or discharge the conditions attached to a listed building consent or conservation area consent or adding new conditions consequential upon any such variation or discharge, or

(iii) refusing to approve details of the works which were reserved for subsequent approval by a condition of a listed building consent,

(b) on the failure by a planning authority to give notice of their decision or of the reference of the application to the Secretary of State,

shall give notice of appeal to the Secretary of State (on a form obtained from the Secretary of State) within six months of notice of the decision or of the expiry of the appropriate period allowed under regulation 3(3) as the case may be, or such longer period as the Secretary of State may at any time allow.

(2) Any such person shall also furnish to the Secretary of State a copy of the following documents:–

(a) the application made to the planning authority;

(b) all relevant plans, drawings, particulars or documents submitted with the application, including a copy of the certificate given in accordance with regulation 6 or of the documents lodged in accordance with regulation 7, as the case may be;

(c) the notice of the decision, if any; and

(d) all other relevant correspondence with the planning authority.

Claims for compensation and listed building purchase notices

9.—(1) This regulation applies to–

(a) a claim for compensation made to a planning authority under–

(i) section 160 of the Act (compensation for refusal of consent to the alteration or extension of a listed building);

(ii) section 161 of the Act (compensation where listed building consent is revoked or modified);

(iii) section 161 of the Act as applied to buildings in conservation areas by section 262A(8) of the Act;

(iv) section 162 of the Act (compensation for loss or damage caused by the service of a building preservation notice); and

(b) a listed building purchase notice served on a planning authority under section 179 of the Act; and

(c) a listed building purchase notice served on a planning authority under section 179 of the Act, as applied to buildings in conservation areas by section 262A(8) of the Act.

(2) Any such claim or notice as is mentioned in paragraph (1) of this regulation shall be in writing and shall be served on the planning authority by sending it, addressed to them, by recorded delivery post, or by delivering it to their offices.

(3) The time within which any such claim or notice as is mentioned in paragraph (1) of this regulation shall be served shall be–

(a) in the case of a claim for compensation, 6 months; and

(b) in the case of a listed building purchase notice, 12 months from the date of the decision in respect of which the claim or notice is made or given, or such longer period as the Secretary of State may allow in any particular case.

Advertisement of unopposed revocation or modification order

10. Where, by virtue of the provisions of paragraph 11(2) of Schedule 10 to the Act as also applied to buildings in conservation areas by section 262A(8) of the Act (advertisement of unopposed order revoking or modifying listed building consent or conservation area consent), the making of an order under paragraph 9 of Schedule 10 to the Act in respect of works to or demolition of a building is required to be advertised, the planning authority shall publish in the Edinburgh Gazette and in a local newspaper circulating in the area in which the building is situated an advertisement stating that the order has been made and specifying the periods required by paragraph 11(2) of Schedule 10 to the Act as also applied as aforesaid to be specified.

Applications for listed building consent and conservation area consent by planning authorities

11.—(1) In relation to applications by planning authorities relating to the execution of works for the demolition, alteration or extension of listed buildings, or for conservation area consent for the demolition of unlisted buildings in conservation areas, the provisions of the Act referred to in Part IV of Schedule 19 to the Act shall have effect subject to the exceptions and modifications prescribed by this regulation.

(2) Where a planning authority require listed building consent for the demolition, alteration or extension of any listed building in their area, or conservation area consent for the demolition of unlisted buildings in conservation areas in their area, the authority shall make application to the Secretary of State for that consent.

(3) Any such application shall—

(a) be made in the form of an application to the planning authority;

(b) be published and displayed by the planning authority in the same manner as an application made to them for listed building consent and in accordance with the provisions of regulation 5(1) of these Regulations; and

(c) be deemed to have been referred to the Secretary of State under paragraph 4 of Schedule 10 to the Act;

and the provisions of paragraph 4 of Schedule 10 to the Act shall apply to the determination of the application by the Secretary of State.

(4) In relation to a listed building, or an unlisted building in a conservation area, belonging to a local authority and in respect of which they are the planning authority, the Secretary of State may serve any notice authorised to be served by a planning authority in relation to a listed building or an unlisted building in a conservation area.

Form of notice that a building has become, or ceased to be, listed

12. The forms set out in Schedule 3 hereto (or forms substantially to the like effect) are the prescribed forms of notice for the purposes of section 52(5) of the Act (service of notice that a building has become, or has ceased to be, listed).

Application of listed building control to buildings in conservation areas

13. Without prejudice to the general application of provisions in respect of buildings in conservation areas contained in section 262A(8) of the Act, the provisions of the Act relating to listed building control which are set out in column (1) of Schedule 4 to these Regulations shall have effect in their application to buildings in conservation areas subject to the exceptions and modifications set out opposite such provisions in column (2) of the said Schedule.

Revocation and savings

14.—(1) There are hereby revoked:—

(a) the Town and Country Planning (Listed Buildings and Buildings in Conservation Areas) (Scotland) Regulations 1975(**a**);

(b) the Town and Country Planning (Listed Buildings and Buildings in Conservation Areas) (Scotland) Amendment Regulations 1977(**b**);

(c) the provisions contained in the Town and Country Planning (Crown Land Applications) (Scotland) Regulations 1984(**c**) insofar as they relate to regulation 6 of the said 1975 Regulations and to applications for listed building consent and for conservation area consent.

(2) Anything done under or by virtue of any regulation revoked by these Regulations shall be deemed to have been done under or by virtue of the corresponding provision of these Regulations and anything begun under any such regulation may be continued under these Regulations as if begun under these Regulations.

(3) So much of any document, drawing or plan as refers expressly or by implication to any regulation revoked by these Regulations shall, if and so far as the context permits, be construed as referring to the corresponding provision of these Regulations.

James Douglas-Hamilton
New St. Andrew's House, Edinburgh   Parliamentary Under Secretary of State,
28th August 1987   Scottish Office

(**a**) S.I. 1975/2069.
(**b**) S.I. 1977/255.
(**c**) S.I. 1984/996.

Regulations 3 and 4 ## SCHEDULE 1

PART I

NOTIFICATION TO BE SENT TO APPLICANT ON REFUSAL OF LISTED BUILDING CONSENT OR CONSERVATION AREA CONSENT OR GRANT OF SUCH CONSENT SUBJECT TO CONDITIONS

1. If the applicant is aggrieved by the decision of the planning authority to refuse listed building consent or conservation area consent for the proposed works, or to grant such consent subject to conditions, he may, by notice served within 6 months of the receipt of this notice, appeal to the Secretary of State for Scotland (on a form obtainable from him on application to the Secretary, Scottish Development Department, New St Andrew's House, St James Centre, Edinburgh EH1 3SZ) in accordance with paragraph 7 of Schedule 10 to the Town and Country Planning (Scotland) Act 1972, as also applied to buildings in conservation areas by section 262A(8) of that Act (as substituted by section 2(1) of the Town and Country Amenities Act 1974 and amended by (1) Schedule 2, paragraph 38(a) of the Local Government and Planning (Scotland) Act 1982, and (2) Schedule 9, paragraph 21 of the Housing and Planning Act 1986). The Secretary of State has power to allow a longer period for the giving of a notice of appeal, but he will not normally be prepared to exercise this power unless there are special circumstances which excuse the delay in giving notice of appeal.

2. If listed building consent or conservation area consent is refused, or granted subject to conditions, whether by the planning authority or by the Secretary of State, and the owner of the land claims that the land has become incapable of reasonably beneficial use in its existing state and cannot be rendered capable of reasonably beneficial use by the carrying out of any works which have been or would be permitted, he may serve on the planning authority in whose district the land is situated a listed building purchase notice requiring that authority to purchase his interest in the land in accordance with the provisions of section 179 of the Town and Country Planning (Scotland) Act 1972, as also applied to buildings in conservation areas by section 262A(8) of that Act.

3. In certain circumstances a claim may be made against the planning authority for compensation where permission is refused or granted subject to conditions by the Secretary of State on appeal or on a reference of an application to him. The circumstances in which such compensation is payable are set out in section 160 of the Town and Country Planning (Scotland) Act 1972.

PART II

NOTIFICATION TO BE SENT TO APPLICANT ON REFUSAL TO VARY OR DISCHARGE CONDITIONS ATTACHED TO A LISTED BUILDING CONSENT OR A CONSERVATION AREA CONSENT OR ON THE ADDITION OF NEW CONDITIONS CONSEQUENTIAL UPON VARIATION OR DISCHARGE

If the applicant is aggrieved by the decision of the planning authority to refuse to vary or discharge the conditions attached to a listed building consent or conservation area consent or to add new conditions consequential upon any such variation or discharge, he may by notice served within 6 months of the receipt of this notice appeal to the Secretary of State for Scotland (on a form obtainable from him on application to the Secretary, Scottish Development Department, New St Andrew's House, St James Centre, Edinburgh EH1 3SZ) in accordance with paragraph 7 of Schedule 10 to the Town and Country Planning (Scotland) Act 1972, as also applied to buildings in conservation areas by section 262A(8) of that Act (as substituted by section 2(1) of the Town and Country Amenities Act 1974, and amended by (1) Schedule 2, paragraph 38(a) of the Local Government and Planning (Scotland) Act 1982, and (2) Schedule 9, paragraph 21 of the Housing and Planning Act 1986). The Secretary of State has power to allow a longer period for the giving of a notice of appeal, but he will not normally be prepared to exercise this power unless there are special circumstances which excuse the delay in giving notice of appeal.

SCHEDULE 2   Regulation 6

PART I

TOWN AND COUNTRY PLANNING (SCOTLAND) ACT 1972

Certificate under paragraph 2 of Schedule 10.

Certificate A* I hereby certify that:–

No person other than **myself/the applicant/the appellant* was an owner(a) of any part of the building to which the **application/appeal* relates at the beginning of the period of 21 days ending with the date of the accompanying **application/appeal*;

or

Certificate B* I hereby certify that:–

**I have/the applicant has/the appellant has* given the requisite notice to all the persons other than **myself/the applicant/the appellant* who, at the beginning of the period of 21 days ending with the date of the accompanying **application/appeal*, were owners (a) of the building or any part thereof to which the **application/appeal* relates, viz:–

Name of Owner   Address   Date of Service of Notice.

or

Certificate C* I hereby certify that:–

1.   **I am/the applicant is/the appellant is* unable to issue a certificate in accordance with either sub-paragraph (a) or sub-paragraph (b) of regulation 6(1) of the Town and Country Planning (Listed Buildings and Buildings in Conservation Areas) (Scotland) Regulations 1987 in respect of the accompanying **application/appeal* dated ....

2.   **I have/the applicant has/the appellant has* given the requisite notice to the following persons other than **myself/the applicant* who, at the beginning of the period of 21 days ending with the date of the **application/appeal*, were owners (a) of the building or any part thereof, to which the **application/appeal* relates, viz:–

Name of Owner   Address   Date of Service of Notice.

3.   **I have/the applicant has/the appellant has* taken the steps listed below, being steps reasonably open to **me/him* to ascertain the names and addresses of the [other] owners(a) of the building or any part thereof and **have/has* been unable to do so:

(b)   ....

4.   Notice of the **application/appeal* as set out below has been published in the(c) .... on (d) ....

Copy of notice as published.

or

Certificate D* I hereby certify that:–

1.   **I am/the applicant is/the appellant is* unable to issue a certificate in accordance with sub-paragraph (a) of regulation 6(1) of the Town and Country Planning (Listed Buildings and Buildings in Conservation Areas) (Scotland) Regulations 1987 in respect of the accompanying **application/-appeal* dated ....

**I have/He has* taken the steps listed below, being steps reasonably open to **me/him*, to ascertain the names and addresses of all the persons other than **myself/himself*, who at the beginning of the period of 21 days ending with the date of the **application/appeal* were owners of the building or any part thereof to which the **application/appeal* relates and **have/has* been unable to do so:

(b)   ....

2. Notice of the *application/appeal as set out below has been published in the (c)
.... on (d) ....

Copy of notice as published.

Signed

*[on behalf of   ]

Date

*Delete where inappropriate

Notes

(a) "Owner" means the proprietor of the *dominium utile* or, in relation to a building situated on land not held on feudal tenure, the proprietor thereof, or a lessee under a lease the unexpired term of which was not less than 7 years.

(b) Insert description of steps taken.

(c) Insert name of the local newspaper (circulating in the locality in which the land is situated) in which the notice has been published.

(d) Insert date of publication (the notice must not be published on a date earlier than 21 days before and ending with the date of the application or appeal).

PART II

TOWN AND COUNTRY PLANNING (SCOTLAND) ACT 1972

*Notice of application for *[listed building consent] [variation or discharge of conditions of listed building consent] [conservation area consent]*

[Notice for service on individuals]

Proposal to carry out works in respect of *[demolishing] [altering] [extending] [varying or discharging conditions] ....(a).

TAKE NOTICE that application is being made to the ....(b) Council by
....(c) for *[listed building consent] [conservation area consent] [variation or discharge of conditions] to ....(d).

If you wish to make representations about the application, you should make them in writing to the Council at ....(e) not later than ....(f).

Signed

*[on behalf of   ]

Date

TOWN AND COUNTRY PLANNING (SCOTLAND) ACT 1972

*Notice of application for *[listed building consent] [variation or discharge of conditions of listed building consent] [conservation area consent]*

[Notice for publication in local newspaper in accordance with regulation 5(1) of the Town and Country Planning (Listed Buildings and Buildings in Conservation Areas) Regulations 1987]

Proposal to carry out works in respect of *[demolishing] [altering] [extending] [varying or discharging conditions] ....(a).

Notice is hereby given that application is being made to the ....(b) Council by ....(c) for *[listed building consent] [conservation area consent] [variation or discharge of conditions] ....(d).

Representations to the council about the application may be made to them in writing to ....(e) not later than ....(f) by any owner of the building(s) or any part thereof(g).

Signed

*[on behalf of   ]

Date

*Delete where inappropriate

Notes

(a) Insert name, address, or location, of building with sufficient precision to ensure identification of it.

(b) Insert name of planning authority.

(c) Insert name of applicant.

(d) Insert description of proposed works or proposed variation or discharge and name, address, or location of building affected.

(e) Insert address of planning authority.

(f) Insert date not less than 21 days from and including the date on which the notice is served or published.

(g) "Owner" means the proprietor of the *dominium utile* or, in relation to a building situated on land not held on feudal tenure, the proprietor thereof, or a lessee under a lease the unexpired term of which was not less than 7 years.

PART III
TOWN AND COUNTRY PLANNING (SCOTLAND) ACT 1972

Notice of appeal against refusal, etc. of [listed building consent] [variation or discharge of conditions of listed building consent] [conservation area consent]

[Notice for service on individuals]

Proposal to carry out works in respect of *[demolishing] [altering] [extending] [varying or discharging conditions] ....(a).

TAKE NOTICE that an appeal is being made to the Secretary of State by ....(b).

*(i) against the decision of the ....(c) Council

*(ii) on the failure of the ....(c) Council to give a decision

on an application to ....(d).

If you wish to make representations to the Secretary of State about the appeal you should make them in writing not later than ....(e) to the Secretary, Scottish Development Department, New St. Andrew's House, St. James Centre, Edinburgh, EH1 3SZ.

Signed

*[on behalf of   ]

Date

TOWN AND COUNTRY PLANNING (SCOTLAND) ACT 1972

*Notice of appeal against refusal, etc. of *[listed building consent] [variation or discharge of conditions of listed building consent] [conservation area consent]*

[Notice for publication in local newspaper]

Proposal to carry out works in respect of *[demolishing] [altering] [extending] [varying or discharging conditions] ....(a).

Notice is hereby given that an appeal is being made to the Secretary of State by ....(b).

   *(i) against the decision of the ....(c) Council

   *(ii) on the failure of the ....(c) Council to give a decision

on an application to ....(d).

Representations to the Secretary of State about the appeal may be made in writing to the Secretary, Scottish Development Department, New St. Andrew's House, St. James Centre, Edinburgh, EH1 3SZ not later than ....(e) by any owner(f) of the buildings or any part thereof.

Signed

*[on behalf of   ]

Date

Notes

(a) Insert name, address or location, of building with sufficient precision to ensure identification of it.

(b) Insert name of appellant.

(c) Insert name of planning authority.

(d) Insert description of proposed works or proposed variation or discharge and name, address or location of building affected.

(e) Insert date not less than 21 days from and including the date on which the notice is served or published.

(f) "Owner" means the proprietor of the *dominium utile* or, in relation to a building situated on land not held on feudal tenure, the proprietor thereof, or a lessee under a lease the unexpired term of which was not less than 7 years.

Delete where inappropriate

SCHEDULE 3   Regulation 12

Notice that a building has become listed

IMPORTANT - This communication affects YOUR PROPERTY

TOWN AND COUNTRY PLANNING (SCOTLAND) ACT 1972

Buildings of Special Architectural or Historic Interest

To:

NOTICE IS HEREBY GIVEN that the building known as .... situated in the .... has been included in the list of buildings of special architectural or historic interest in that area compiled by the Secretary of State under section 52 of the Town and Country Planning (Scotland) Act 1972 on .... 19.......

Dated...................................... 19........

.... *(Signature of Authorised Officer)*

Explanatory Note

Listing of Buildings of Special Architectural or Historic Interest

It is understood that you are the owner, lessee, or occupier of the building named in the accompanying notice. This notice is to let you know that the building has been included in one of the lists of buildings of special architectural or historic interest which it is the Secretary of State's duty to compile under section 52 of the Town and Country Planning (Scotland) Act 1972.

This notice does not call for any action on your part unless you propose at any time to demolish the building or to do any works (either to the exterior or to the interior) which would affect its character. In that event you will need to seek "listed building consent", that is to say, the consent of the planning authority (the .... Council) to the work you wish to do.

Certain buildings are exempt from this requirement, notably ecclesiastical buildings in use for the time being for ecclesiastical purposes, but it should also be noted that this exemption may be restricted or excluded by an order of the Secretary of State under section 56AA of the Town and Country Planning (Scotland) Act 1972.

It is an offence if you execute or cause to be executed any works for which listed building consent is necessary without such consent, but it is a defence to prove the following matters–

(a) that the works were urgently necessary in the interests of safety or of health, or to preserve the building;

(b) that it was not practicable to secure safety or health or the preservation of the building by works of repair or works for affording temporary support or shelter;

(c) that the works carried out were limited to the minimum measures immediately necessary; and

(d) that notice in writing justifying in detail the carrying out of the works was given to the planning authority as soon as reasonably practicable.

There is no right of appeal as such against the listing of a building but, if the planning authority should refuse consent for the carrying out of any proposed works, section 54(6) of the Town and Country Planning (Scotland) Act 1972 as read with paragraph 7 of Schedule 10 to that Act provides a right of appeal against the refusal to the Secretary of State. One of the statutory grounds of appeal is that the building is not of special architectural or historic interest. You are not precluded from writing at any time to the Secretary of State claiming that the building should cease to be listed on the ground that it is not in fact of special architectural or historic interest; and any such claim, with the evidence supporting it, will be carefully considered.

A fuller explanation of the consequences of the listing of a building is enclosed with this notice. If at any time you propose to take any action which may affect the character of your building, you would be well advised to refer to Part IV of, and Schedule 10 to, the Town and Country Planning (Scotland) Act 1972 and to the Town and Country Planning (Listed Buildings and Buildings in Conservation Areas) (Scotland) Regulations 1987.

Notice that a building has ceased to be listed

IMPORTANT - This communication affects YOUR PROPERTY

TOWN AND COUNTRY PLANNING (SCOTLAND) ACT 1972

Buildings of Special Architectural or Historic Interest

To:

NOTICE IS HEREBY GIVEN that the building known as .... situated in the .... has, by an amendment made by the Secretary of State under section 52 of the Town and Country Planning (Scotland) Act 1972 on .... 19 ...., been excluded from the list of buildings of special architectural or historic interest in that area compiled by the Secretary of State on .... 19 ....

Dated...................................... 19........

.... *(Signature of Authorised Officer)*

Explanatory Note

The building referred to in the above notice has been excluded from the list because*

**Insert reason for exclusion*

SCHEDULE 4   Regulation 13

APPLICATION OF ENACTMENTS TO BUILDINGS IN CONSERVATION AREAS

Column (1) *Provisions of the Act relating to listed building control*	Column (2) *Exceptions and modifications*
Section 53	1. In subsection (1) omit the words "or for its alteration or extension in any manner which would affect its character as a building of special architectural or historic interest". 2. In subsection (2)– (i) omit the words "or for its alteration or extension"; (ii) omit paragraph (b). 3. In subsection 2A omit the words "alteration or extension". 4. Omit subsection (3). 5. For subsection (3A) substitute the following subsection– "3A. Consent under subsection (2) or (2A) of this section is referred to in this part of this Act as "conservation area consent"."
Section 54(3) and (4)	1. In subsection (3)– (i) omit the words from the beginning to "its setting, and"; (ii) for the words "the desirability of preserving the building or its setting or any features of special architectural or historic interest which it possesses", substitute the words "the desirability of preserving the character or appearance of the conservation area". 2. In subsection (4) the words "in respect of any building" shall be inserted before the words "subject to conditions".
Section 54C	In subsection (1) omit paragraph (b).
Section 56AA	In subsection (1) for the words "sections 54(1) and 56(2)" substitute "section 54(1)".
Section 92	1. In subsection (1) for the words "the character of the building as one of special architectural or historic interest", substitute the words "the character or appearance of the conservation area in which the building is situated". 2. In subsection (1A), in paragraph (b) in place of sub-paragraphs (i) and (ii) substitute the following– "the character or appearance of the conservation area in which the building is situated".
Section 93	1. In subsection (1)– (i) substitute the following paragraph for paragraph (a)– "(a) that retention of the building is not necessary in the interests of preserving the character or appearance of the conservation area in which it is situated;"; (ii) omit paragraph (h); (iii) in paragraph (k) for the words "listed building control" substitute "conservation area control". 2. In subsection (5) omit paragraph (c).
Section 257	Omit the words "alteration or extension".
Schedule 10, Part I	In part I omit paragraphs 6 and 7(2) and (3)(b).
Schedule 19, Part IV	The exceptions and modifications referred to in regulation 13 and specified in the above column shall have effect in relation to the appropriate provisions in Part IV of Schedule 19.

EXPLANATORY NOTE

(This note is not part of the Regulations)

These Regulations revoke and re-enact with amendments the Town and Country Planning (Listed Buildings and Buildings in Conservation Areas) (Scotland) Regulations 1975 to take account of the provisions of the Town and Country Planning Act 1984 and the Housing and Planning Act 1986.

The changes of substance are:–

  (i) provision of a definition of "conservation area consent" which follows the precedent set in respect of Crown land applications in the Town and Country Planning Act 1984 (regulation 2(2));

 (ii) removal of the requirement that listed building consent and conservation area consent applications be made on a form prescribed by the Secretary of State (regulation 3);

(iii) provision of procedures for applications and appeals in respect of the power to vary or discharge conditions attached to a listed building consent or conservation area consent introduced in Schedule 9, paragraph 17 of the 1986 Act (regulations 4 and 8);

 (iv) incorporation in these Regulations of provisions in respect of Crown land applications formerly contained in the Town and Country Planning (Crown Land Applications) (Scotland) Regulations 1984 (regulations 7 and 14);

  (v) amendment of the notice of listing sent to owners to take into account amendments to the Town and Country Planning (Scotland) Act 1972 made by paragraphs 15 and 18 of Schedule 9 to the 1986 Act (Schedule 3); and

 (vi) amendment of the application of section 262A(8) of the Town and Country Planning (Scotland) Act 1972 to take account of amendments made in Schedule 9, paragraph 21 of the 1986 Act (Schedule 4).

The Regulations make procedural provision for applications for listed building consent, for consent to demolish certain buildings in conservation areas, for the variation or discharge of conditions attached to listed building consents, and for appeals in respect of these matters. The Regulations also prescribe the manner in which and the time within which claims are to be made for compensation arising from the application of statutory control to listed buildings and buildings in conservation areas, the serving of listed building purchase notices, the advertising of unopposed orders revoking or modifying listed building consent, or the execution of works under listed building enforcement procedure.

STATUTORY INSTRUMENTS

1987 No. 1531 (S.114)

TOWN AND COUNTRY PLANNING, SCOTLAND

The Town and Country Planning (Determination of Appeals by Appointed Persons) (Prescribed Classes) (Scotland) Regulations 1987

Made - - - -	*28th August 1987*
Laid before Parliament	*10th September 1987*
Coming into force	*1st October 1987*

The Secretary of State, in exercise of the powers conferred on him by sections 273 and 275(1) of, and paragraph 1 of Schedule 7 to, the Town and Country Planning (Scotland) Act 1972(**a**) and of all other powers enabling him in that behalf, hereby makes the following Regulations:

Application, citation and commencement

1.—(1) These Regulations may be cited as the Town and Country Planning (Determination of Appeals by Appointed Persons) (Prescribed Classes) (Scotland) Regulations 1987 and shall come into force on 1st October 1987.

(2) Subject to regulation 6 below, these Regulations apply to appeals within the classes prescribed in regulation 3 of which notice is given on or after the date when they come into force.

Interpretation

2.—(1) In the Regulations, unless the context otherwise requires–

"the Act" means the Town and Country Planning (Scotland) Act 1972;

"the 1984 Act" means the Town and Country Planning Act 1984(**b**);

"statutory undertakers" means persons authorised by any enactment to carry on any railway, light railway, tramway, road transport, water transport, canal, inland navigation, dock, harbour, pier or lighthouse undertaking or any undertaking for the supply of electricity, hydraulic power or water and includes the British Airports Authority, the Civil Aviation Authority, the Post Office and companies which are deemed to be statutory undertakers by virtue of section 141(2) of the Transport Act 1968(**c**), telecommunications code system operators within the meaning of the Telecommunications Act 1984(**d**) and public gas suppliers within the meaning of Part I of the Gas Act 1986(**e**).

(2) Any reference to a numbered regulation or to a numbered Schedule is, unless otherwise expressly provided or the context otherwise requires, a reference to the regulation or Schedule bearing that number in these Regulations.

(**a**) 1972 c.52; section 275(1) contains a definition of "prescribed" relevant to the exercise of the statutory powers under which these Regulations are made.
(**b**) 1984 c.10.
(**c**) 1968 c.73; section 141(2) was relevantly amended by the Town and Country Planning (Scotland) Act 1972 (c.52), Schedule 21, Part II.
(**d**) 1984 c.12.
(**e**) 1986 c.44.

Classes of appeal for determination by appointed persons

3. Subject to the provisions of regulation 4, the classes of appeal specified in Schedule 1 are prescribed for the purposes of paragraph 1(1) of Schedule 7 to the Act as appeals to be determined by a person appointed by the Secretary of State for the purpose instead of by the Secretary of State.

Classes of appeal reserved for determination by the Secretary of State

4. The classes of case specified in Schedule 2 are prescribed for the purposes of paragraph 1(1) of Schedule 7 to the Act as appeals which are not to be determined in the manner set out in that paragraph.

Publicity for directions under paragraph 1(1) of Schedule 7 to the Act

5. On the making by the Secretary of State of a direction under paragraph 1(1) of Schedule 7 to the Act, he may by notice in writing enclosing a copy of the direction require the planning authority for every area in respect of which the direction has effect to publish as soon as may be a notice in at least one newspaper circulating in the area; and such notice shall contain a concise statement of the effect of the direction and shall specify the place or places where a copy of the direction may be seen at all reasonable hours.

Revocation and saving

6. The Town and Country Planning (Determination of Appeals by Appointed Persons) (Prescribed Classes) (Scotland) Regulations 1980(**a**) are hereby revoked and any appeal to which those Regulations applied, but in respect of which a person had not been appointed to determine the appeal before the coming into force of these Regulations, shall be determined under and in accordance with the provisions of these Regulations.

James Douglas-Hamilton
Parliamentary Under Secretary of State,
Scottish Office

New St. Andrew's House, Edinburgh
28th August 1987

(**a**) S.I. 1980/1675.

SCHEDULE 1

Regulation 3

CLASSES OF APPEALS FOR DETERMINATION BY APPOINTED PERSONS

Appeals under–

(1) section 33 of the Act (appeals against planning decisions) or under that section as applied by section 34 of the Act (appeals in default of planning decisions) or by section 51 of the Act (appeals against determinations as to whether a use or operation constitutes or involves development) or appeals under any of these provisions as applied by section 1 of the 1984 Act, or as applied to any application for consent under an order made under section 58 of the Act or under section 58 of the Act and section 2 of the 1984 Act (appeals against refusal of consent or conditional consent in respect of the felling of trees subject to a tree preservation order) or as applied by section 179 of the Local Government (Scotland) Act 1973(a) (appeals against decisions by regional planning authorities referred to them);

(2) section 63A of the Act (appeals against notices under section 63 of the Act);

(3) section 85 of the Act (appeals against enforcement notices) or under section 85 as applied by section 3 of the 1984 Act (appeals against special enforcement notices);

(4) section 91 of the Act (appeals against refusals of established use certificates);

(5) section 93 of the Act (appeals against listed building enforcement notices) or under that section as applied by section 262A (appeals against enforcement notices in respect of the demolition of buildings in conservation areas);

(6) section 99 of the Act (appeals against an enforcement notice requiring the replacement of trees);

(7) paragraph 7 of Schedule 10 to the Act (appeals against refusal of or conditional consent to applications for listed building consent or against refusal of approval required by a condition), or under that paragraph as applied by paragraph 8 of Schedule 10 to the Act (appeals in default of decision on application for listed building consent or for approval required by a condition), or under either of those provisions as applied by section 54D of the Act (applications for variation or discharge of conditions) or by section 262A of the Act (control of demolition of buildings in conservation areas), or appeals under any of these provisions as applied by section 1 of the 1984 Act.

SCHEDULE 2

Regulation 4

CLASSES OF APPEALS RESERVED FOR DETERMINATION BY THE SECRETARY OF STATE

Appeals by statutory undertakers (in relation to land to which section 214(2) of the Act applies) under section 33 or section 85 of the Act or under either of these provisions as applied by section 1 and section 3 respectively of the 1984 Act.

EXPLANATORY NOTE

(This note is not part of the Regulations)

These Regulations re-enact with amendments the provisions of the Town and Country Planning (Determination of Appeals by Appointed Persons) (Prescribed Classes) (Scotland) Regulations 1980. They prescribe the classes of appeal which are to be determined by persons appointed for the purpose by the Secretary of State instead of being determined by the Secretary of State and they also prescribe certain classes of appeal within those prescribed classes which are to continue to be determined by the Secretary of State. They provide for publication by planning authorities of any direction made by the Secretary of State specifying classes of case within the prescribed classes which are to be determined by the Secretary of State.

The change of substance is the extension of the classes of delegated appeal to cover the determination of appeals against refusal of listed building consent, consent to demolish buildings in conservation areas and enforcement notices related to such cases.

(a) 1973 c.65.

STATUTORY INSTRUMENTS

1987 No. 1532 (S.115)

TOWN AND COUNTRY PLANNING, SCOTLAND

The Town and Country Planning (Simplified Planning Zones) (Scotland) Regulations 1987

Made - - - -	*28th August 1987*
Laid before Parliament	*10th September 1987*
Coming into force	*1st October 1987*

The Secretary of State, in exercise of the powers conferred on him by sections 273(1) and 275(1) of, and paragraphs 1, 5(2), 7(2), 7(3), 7(4), 10(3) and 12 of Schedule 6A to, the Town and Country Planning (Scotland) Act 1972(**a**) and of all other powers enabling him in that behalf, hereby makes the following Regulations:

Citation and commencement

1.   These Regulations may be cited as the Town and Country Planning (Simplified Planning Zones) (Scotland) Regulations 1987 and shall come into force on 1st October 1987.

Interpretation

2.—(1) In these Regulations–
   "document" includes a map, diagram, illustration or other descriptive matter in any form and also includes, where appropriate, a copy of a document;
   "local advertisement" means an advertisement on at least one occasion in each of two successive weeks in a local newspaper circulating in the area likely to be affected by the proposed simplified planning zone scheme or, as the case may be, by the proposed alteration to an existing scheme; and
   "Schedule 6A" means Schedule 6A to the Town and Country Planning (Scotland) Act 1972.

(2) A regulation referred to in these Regulations only by number means the regulation so numbered in these Regulations, and references to "the Schedule" are to the Schedule to these Regulations.

Prescribed period for making representations

3.   The period within which representations may be made about proposals to make or alter a simplified planning zone scheme is a period of four weeks commencing with such date as the planning authority specify when giving publicity to their proposals in accordance with paragraph 5(2) of Schedule 6A.

Consultation

4.   A planning authority who propose to make or alter a simplified planning zone scheme shall, without prejudice to any other steps which they take to secure the matters described in paragraph 5(2) of Schedule 6A–

(**a**) 1972 c.52; section 275(1) contains a definition of "prescribed" relevant to the exercise of the statutory powers under which these Regulations are made; Schedule 6A was inserted by section 26(2) of, and Part III of Schedule 6 to, the Housing and Planning Act 1986 (c.63).

(a) consult the following–
    (i) any local authority whose area or any parts thereof are comprised within the area to which the scheme relates;
    (ii) where the area to which the scheme relates includes land within the area of a New Town, the New Town Development Corporation;
    (iii) where the area to which the scheme relates includes an area of coal working or former or proposed coal working notified to the planning authority by the British Coal Corporation, the British Coal Corporation;
    (iv) where the area to which the scheme relates includes or is affected by or is likely to be affected by an installation of a type or at a location notified to the planning authority by the Health and Safety Executive, the Health and Safety Executive; and
    (v) such other authorities or bodies as the planning authority think appropriate;
(b) afford the authorities and bodies consulted under paragraph (a) above an opportunity to express their views; and
(c) take such views into consideration.

Objections to a proposed scheme etc.

5. The period specified in the statement referred to in paragraph 5(4) of Schedule 6A as the period within which objections to a proposed scheme or proposals to alter an existing scheme may be made shall be a period of six weeks from the date on which the proposed scheme or alteration is first made available for inspection in accordance with paragraph 5(3)(a) of that Schedule.

Title

6. A simplified planning zone scheme shall be given a title which shall include the name of the planning authority making the scheme and an indication of the area to which the scheme relates; and each document contained in a simplified planning zone scheme shall bear the title of the scheme.

Reconciliation of contradictions in simplified planning zone schemes

7. In the case of any contradiction between the written statement and any other document forming part of a simplified planning zone scheme, the provisions of the written statement shall prevail.

Notice that documents containing proposals to make or alter a scheme are available for inspection

8. When a planning authority make copies of a proposed simplified planning zone scheme or a proposed alteration to an existing scheme available for inspection in accordance with paragraph 5(3) of Schedule 6A, they shall publish a notice in the Edinburgh Gazette and by local advertisement stating–
(a) the area affected by the proposed scheme or, as the case may be, by the proposed alteration;
(b) the general nature of the proposed scheme or alteration;
(c) the place and times at which copies of the proposed scheme or alteration may be inspected by the public;
(d) that any objections to the proposed scheme or alteration should be made in writing; and
(e) the time within which such objections must be made and the address to which they should be sent.

Modification of a proposed scheme or of an alteration to an existing scheme

9.—(1) Where a planning authority intend to modify their proposals for the making or alteration of a simplified planning zone scheme, whether to conform with a direction given by the Secretary of State under paragraph 8(3) of Schedule 6A or otherwise, they shall, unless they are satisfied that the proposed modifications would not materially affect the content of the proposed scheme or alteration–

(a) prepare a list of the proposed modifications with their reasons for proposing them;

(b) publish a notice by local advertisement in form 1 in the Schedule or a form substantially to the like effect;

(c) serve a notice in similar form on every person who has duly made objection to the proposed scheme or alteration and not withdrawn his objection and on such other persons as they think fit;

(d) subject to any direction given by the Secretary of State, decide whether to afford any person who duly makes objection to the proposed modifications and does not withdraw his objections an opportunity of appearing before and being heard by a person appointed by the authority for the purpose at a local inquiry or other hearing; and

(e) where a local inquiry or other hearing is held, afford an opportunity to such other persons as they think fit to appear before and be heard by the person appointed to hold it.

(2) Without prejudice to any other provision as to the time at which a proposed simplified planning zone scheme or a proposed alteration to an existing scheme may be adopted, a planning authority shall not proceed to adopt proposals for the making or alteration of a scheme with modifications until–

(i) the period for making objections to the proposed modifications has expired; and

(ii) where objections were duly made within that period, the objections so made have been considered.

Appointment of persons to hold local inquiries or other hearings

10.—(1) A planning authority intending to hold a local inquiry or other hearing to consider objections to proposals to make or alter a simplified planning zone scheme shall appoint a person from a list of persons specified by the Secretary of State to hold the inquiry or hearing.

(2) Subject to any direction given by the Secretary of State, the planning authority shall pay to any person appointed under this regulation such remuneration and allowances as they think fit.

Local inquiries and other hearings

11.—(1) A planning authority intending to hold a local inquiry to consider objections to proposals to make or alter a simplified planning zone scheme, or to proposed modifications to such proposals, shall, at least four weeks before the inquiry is due to open–

(a) give notice by local advertisement of the time and place at which the inquiry is to open and of the purpose of the inquiry; and

(b) serve a notice in similar terms on every person who has duly made objection (other than an objector who has indicated in writing that he does not wish to appear or be represented at any inquiry) and on such other persons as they think fit.

(2) A planning authority intending to hold a hearing to consider such objections as are mentioned in paragraph (1) shall, at least 4 weeks before the date of the hearing, notify every person who has made objection as aforesaid (other than an objector who has indicated in writing that he does not wish to appear or be represented at any hearing) and every other person whom they consider should be given notice of the hearing of the time and place at which the hearing is to be held and of the purpose of the hearing.

(3) Copies of all objections to proposals to make or alter a simplified planning zone scheme or to proposed modifications to such proposals which are to be considered at a local inquiry or other hearing shall be made available for inspection at the office of the planning authority; and the authority shall include notice of their availability for inspection in the notices given or served under paragraphs (1) and (2).

(4) A local inquiry held for the purpose mentioned in paragraph (1) shall be a public local inquiry.

Report of local inquiry or other hearing

12.—(1) Where a local inquiry or other hearing is held for the purpose mentioned in regulation 11, the planning authority shall, after considering the report of the person appointed to hold the inquiry or hearing, prepare a statement of–

(a) the decisions they have reached in the light of the report and any recommendations contained in it; and

(b) the reasons for those decisions.

(2) A copy of the report and of the statement of decisions and reasons mentioned in paragraph (1) shall be made available by the planning authority for public inspection from the date on which notice is first given under regulation 13(1) or, where it is proposed to modify the proposed scheme or alteration and regulation 9(1) applies, from the date on which the document mentioned in regulation 9(1)(a) is made available for public inspection.

Action prior to adopting proposals to make or alter a scheme

13.—(1) Where a planning authority are disposed to adopt proposals for the making or alteration of a simplified planning zone scheme, they shall, before adopting the proposals–

(a) publish by local advertisement a notice in form 2 in the Schedule or a form substantially to the like effect; and

(b) serve a notice in similar form on every person who has duly made objection to the proposed scheme or alteration (or duly objected to any proposed modifications thereto) and not withdrawn his objection, and on any other person whom they consider should be given notice.

(2) The planning authority shall, after complying with paragraph (1), send to the Secretary of State–

(a) a certificate that they have so complied;

(b) two copies of the simplified planning zone scheme or alteration to an existing scheme which they are disposed to adopt;

(c) particulars of any modifications that have been made to the original proposals; and

(d) where the Secretary of State has given a direction under paragraph 8(3) of Schedule 6A, a statement explaining how any relevant modifications meet the requirements of the direction or, where such requirements are not met, of the reasons why the authority considers it inappropriate to meet them.

(3) Without prejudice to paragraph 8(4) of Schedule 6A and paragraph (5) of this regulation, a planning authority shall not adopt proposals to make or alter a simplified planning zone scheme until at least 28 days after the date on which the certificate referred to in paragraph (2)(a) is sent.

(4) Where, after a planning authority has complied with paragraph (1), the relevant proposals are modified in consequence of a direction given by the Secretary of State under paragraph 8(3) of Schedule 6A, the authority shall comply with paragraphs (1) and (2) in relation to the modified proposals before adopting them.

(5) If, before the planning authority have adopted proposals for the making or alteration of a simplified planning zone scheme, the Secretary of State directs them not to adopt those proposals until he has decided whether to give them a direction under paragraph 9(1) of Schedule 6A in relation to the proposals, they shall not adopt the proposals until he has notified them of his decision.

Notice of adoption of a simplified planning zone scheme etc.

14.—(1) Where a planning authority adopt proposals for the making of a simplified planning zone scheme or the alteration of an existing scheme, they shall give notice in the Edinburgh Gazette and by local advertisement in form 3 in the Schedule or a form substantially to the like effect and shall serve a notice in similar form on such persons as they think fit; and a copy of the notice and a copy of the scheme or alteration to which it relates shall be made available for inspection at every place at which copies of the proposed scheme or alteration were made available for public inspection.

(2) The planning authority shall, not later than the date on which notice is first given by advertisement in accordance with paragraph (1), send two copies of the scheme or alteration to the Secretary of State.

Withdrawal of a proposed scheme etc.

15.—(1) Subject to paragraph (2), a planning authority who have brought forward proposals for the making or alteration of a simplified planning zone scheme may withdraw those proposals at any time prior to their adoption.

(2) A planning authority who are acting in accordance with a simplified planning zone direction given by the Secretary of State under paragraph 3 of Schedule 6A may not withdraw proposals for the making or alteration of a simplified planning zone scheme unless the Secretary of State withdraws the direction.

(3) Where a planning authority determine to withdraw proposals for the making or alteration of a simplified planning zone scheme they shall–

(a) give notice of such withdrawal by publishing a notice in the Edinburgh Gazette and by local advertisement; and

(b) serve a notice in similar terms on any person who has duly made objection to the proposed scheme or alteration and on any other person whom they consider should be given notice.

Notice of an inquiry or hearing on behalf of the Secretary of State

16.—(1) Where, under paragraph 10(3) of Schedule 6A, the Secretary of State causes a local inquiry to be held for the purpose of considering objections to proposals for the making or alteration of a simplified planning zone scheme submitted to him under paragraph 9(1) of that Schedule, he shall, at least four weeks before the inquiry is due to open–

(a) give notice by local advertisement of the time and place at which the inquiry is to open and of the purpose of the inquiry; and

(b) serve a notice in similar terms on every person who has duly made objection (other than an objector who has indicated in writing that he does not wish to appear or be represented at any inquiry) and on such other persons as he thinks fit.

(2) Where the Secretary of State intends to hold a hearing for the purpose mentioned in paragraph (1), he shall, at least 4 weeks before the date of the hearing, notify every person who has made objection as aforesaid (other than an objector who has indicated in writing that he does not wish to appear or be represented at any hearing) and every other person whom he considers should be given notice of the hearing of the time and place at which the hearing is to be held and of the purpose of the hearing.

Modifications to a proposed scheme etc. by the Secretary of State

17.—(1) Subject to paragraph (2), where the Secretary of State is minded to approve with modifications proposals for the making or alteration of a simplified planning zone scheme which have been submitted to him in accordance with paragraph 9(1) of Schedule 6A, the planning authority, on being notified by him of the modifications he proposes to make, shall -

(a) give notice by local advertisement in form 4 in the Schedule or a form substantially to the like effect; and

(b) comply with any direction which the Secretary of State has served on them requiring notice to be given in similar form to the persons named in the direction.

(2) Paragraph (1) shall not apply where the Secretary of State is satisfied that either–

(a) the proposed modifications will not materially affect the content of the proposed scheme or alteration; or

(b) the planning authority have previously advertised the proposed modifications and considered any objections to them in accordance with regulation 9.

Notice of approval by the Secretary of State of a simplified planning zone scheme etc.

18. Where the Secretary of State approves, either with or without modifications, proposals for the making or alteration of a simplified planning zone scheme which have been submitted to him in accordance with paragraph 9(1) of Schedule 6A, the planning authority, on being notified by him of his approval, shall give notice in the Edinburgh Gazette and by local advertisement in form 3 in the Schedule (subject to the necessary modifications) or a form substantially to the like effect and shall serve a notice in similar form on such persons as the Secretary of State may direct; and a copy of the notice and a copy of the scheme or alteration to which it relates shall be made available for inspection at every place at which copies of the proposed scheme or alteration were made available for public inspection.

Availability of documents referred to in notices

19. Where a planning authority gives or serves a notice under these Regulations which indicates that a document is available for inspection by the public, the authority shall make that document available for inspection at their office and at such other place or places within their area as they think fit having regard to convenience to the public and to the area likely to be affected by the proposed simplified planning zone scheme or, as the case may be, by the proposed alteration to an existing scheme.

Documents to be sent to the Secretary of State

20. In addition to the certificates and other documents sent in accordance with regulations 13(2) and 14(2), the planning authority shall send to the Secretary of State—

(a) at the time of first publication, a copy of any notice given by local advertisement in accordance with the requirements of these Regulations; and

(b) any other document relating to proposals by the authority to make or alter a simplified planning zone scheme which the Secretary of State requests them to supply to him.

Reproduction and sale of documents

21.—(1) A planning authority who propose to make or alter a simplified planning zone scheme shall provide, on request, subject to payment of a reasonable charge, copies of any document which they have made available for inspection by members of the public under these Regulations.

(2) Where a simplified planning zone scheme has been adopted by a planning authority under paragraph 8(1) of Schedule 6A or has been approved by the Secretary of State under paragraph 10(1) of that Schedule, the planning authority shall—

(a) arrange for its reproduction, incorporating any modifications made to it, as soon as possible after the date on which it takes effect;

(b) arrange for its reproduction to take into account any alteration to it as soon as possible after the date on which the alteration takes effect;

(c) make available for sale to the public on payment of a reasonable charge copies of the scheme as reproduced.

Preparation of simplified planning zone schemes etc. by the Secretary of State

22.—(1) These Regulations apply with any necessary modifications to action taken by the Secretary of State in connection with the making or alteration of a simplified planning zone scheme by him under paragraph 11 of Schedule 6A as they apply to the making or alteration of a scheme by a planning authority.

(2) The Secretary of State may require the planning authority concerned to give, in relation to any proposals by him to make or alter a simplified planning zone scheme or any scheme or alterations so made, any notice or notification required to be given by these Regulations in their application by virtue of paragraph (1).

New St. Andrew's House, Edinburgh
28th August 1987

James Douglas-Hamilton
Parliamentary Under Secretary of State,
Scottish Office

SCHEDULE

Regulation 9   FORM 1

*Form of notice of proposed modifications to a proposed simplified planning zone scheme or to a
proposed alteration to such a scheme*

NOTICE OF PROPOSED MODIFICATIONS TO [A PROPOSED] [PROPOSALS FOR THE ALTERATION OF A] (1) SIMPLIFIED PLANNING ZONE SCHEME

Town and Country Planning (Scotland) Act 1972
(Title of scheme)

(2) are disposed to make modifications to [the above-named proposed scheme] [the proposed alteration to the above-named scheme] (1) which was made available for public inspection at (3).

[Some of the] [The] (1) modifications are intended to implement a direction given by the Secretary of State on (4).]

[A copy of the Secretary of State's direction, and a] [A] (1) list of the proposed modifications and of the reasons for proposing them together with a copy of the original proposals have been deposited at (5).

The deposited documents are available for inspection free of charge (6).

Objections to any of the proposed modifications may be made in writing. They should be sent to (7) on or before (8).

Objections should state the name and address of the objector, the matters to which they relate and the grounds on which they are made.

.... 19........

.... (Signature of the responsible officer of the authority)

(1) Use whichever form is appropriate.

(2) Insert the name of the planning authority.

(3) Insert the address of the planning authority's office and of the other places at which the original documents were deposited and the period during which they were available for public inspection.

(4) Delete if no direction has been given. If the paragraph is included, insert the date of the direction.

(5) Insert the address of the planning authority's office and of the other places at which the documents have been deposited.

(6) Specify the days and hours during which the deposited documents are available for public inspection.

(7) Insert the name and address of the planning authority.

(8) Insert a date six weeks after the date of first publication of the notice.

FORM 2   Regulation 13

Form of notice of disposition to adopt proposals for the making or alteration of a simplified planning zone scheme

NOTICE OF DISPOSITION TO ADOPT [AN ALTERATION TO] (1) A SIMPLIFIED PLANNING ZONE SCHEME

Town and Country Planning (Scotland) Act 1972
(Title of scheme)

(2) .... are disposed to adopt [an alteration to] (1) the above-named scheme [as modified by them] (1) on or after (3) ...., unless, before the [scheme] [alteration] (4) has been adopted, the Secretary of State directs that the [scheme] [alteration] (4) shall be submitted to him for his approval.

Copies of the [scheme] [alteration] (4) [together with copies of the report of the [local inquiry] [hearing] (4) held and of the council's statement prepared following consideration of that report] (1) have been desposited at (5) ....

The deposited documents are available for inspection free of charge (6) ....

.... 19......

.... (Signature of the responsible officer of the authority)

(1) Omit the words in square brackets if irrelevant.

(2) Insert the name of the planning authority.

(3) Insert a date allowing for the period which must intervene to comply with regulation 13(3).

(4) Use whichever form is appropriate.

(5) Insert the address of the planning authority's office and of the other places at which the documents have been deposited.

(6) Specify the days on which, and the hours during which, the deposited documents are available for public inspection.

Regulations 14 and 18   FORM 3

Form of notice of adoption of proposals for the making or alteration of a simplified planning zone scheme

NOTICE OF ADOPTION OF [AN ALTERATION TO] (1) A SIMPLIFIED PLANNING ZONE SCHEME

Town and Country Planning (Scotland) Act 1972
(Title of scheme)

On .... 19...... .... (2) adopted [an alteration to] (1) the above-named scheme [as modified by them] (1).

Copies of the [scheme] [alteration] (3) [together with copies of the report of the [local inquiry] [hearing] (3) held and of the council's statement prepared following consideration of that report] (1) have been deposited at (4) ....

The deposited documents are available for inspection free of charge (5) ....

The [scheme] [alteration] (3) became operative on (6) ...., but if any person aggrieved by the [scheme] [alteration] (3) desires to question its validity on the ground that it is not within the powers conferred by the Town and Country Planning (Scotland) Act 1972, as amended, or that any requirement of that Act or of any regulation made under it has not been complied with in relation to the adoption of the [scheme] [alteration] (3), he may, within six weeks from (7) ...., make an application to the Court of Session under section 232 of that Act.

.... 19........

.... (Signature of the responsible officer of the authority)

(1) Omit the words in square brackets if irrelevant.

(2) Insert the date of adoption and the name of the planning authority.

(3) Use whichever form is appropriate.

(4) Insert the address of the planning authority's office and of the other places at which the documents have been deposited.

(5) Specify the days on which, and the hours during which, the deposited documents are available for public inspection.

(6) Insert the operative date.

(7) Insert the date of first publication of this notice by local advertisement.

FORM 4   Regulation 17

Form of notice of proposed modifications by the Secretary of State to proposals for the making or alteration of a simplified planning zone scheme

NOTICE OF PROPOSED MODIFICATIONS BY THE SECRETARY OF STATE TO A PROPOSED [ALTERATION TO A] (1) SIMPLIFIED PLANNING ZONE SCHEME

Town and Country Planning (Scotland) Act 1972
(Title of Scheme)

T he Secretary of State proposes to modify [the alteration to] (1) the above-named scheme proposed by (2) ....

Copies of the [scheme] [alteration] (3) and of the list of proposed modifications subject to which the Secretary of State is minded to approve it have been deposited at (4) ....

The deposited documents are available for inspection free of charge (5) ....

Objections to the proposed modifications should be sent in writing to the Secretary of State (6) ....

Objections should state the name and address of the objector, the matters to which they relate and the grounds on which they are made.

.... 19........

.... (Signature of the responsible officer of the authority)

(1) Omit the words in square brackets if irrelevant.

(2) Insert the name of the planning authority.

(3) Use whichever form is appropriate.

(4) Insert the address of the planning authority's office and of the other places at which the documents have been deposited.

(5) Specify the days on which, and the hours during which, the deposited documents are available for public inspection.

(6) Insert the address notified by the Secretary of State and a date six weeks after the date of first publication of the notice by local advertisement.

EXPLANATORY NOTE

(This note is not part of the Regulations)

Sections 21A - 21E of, and Schedule 6A to, the Town and Country Planning (Scotland) Act 1972 (as inserted by section 26 of the Housing and Planning Act 1986) impose upon district and general planning authorities a duty to consider whether it would be desirable to establish simplified planning zones in their area and, where they decide that it would be beneficial to do so, to make schemes establishing such zones. These Regulations make further provision as to the procedures to be followed in the making or alteration of a simplified planning zone scheme.

1987 No. 1534

INDUSTRIAL TRAINING

The Industrial Training Levy (Clothing and Allied Products) Order 1987

Made - - - -	*27th August 1987*
Laid before Parliament	*9th September 1987*
Coming into force	*30th September 1987*

Whereas proposals made by the Clothing and Allied Products Industry Training Board for the raising and collection of a levy have been submitted to, and approved by, the Manpower Services Commission under section 11(1) of the Industrial Training Act 1982(**a**) ("the 1982 Act") and have thereafter been submitted by the said Commission to the Secretary of State under that sub-section;

And whereas in pursuance of section 11(3) of the 1982 Act the said proposals include provision for the exemption from the levy of employers who, in view of the small number of their employees, ought in the opinion of the Secretary of State to be exempted from it;

And whereas the Secretary of State estimates that the amount which, disregarding any exemptions, will be payable by virtue of this Order by any employer in the clothing and allied products industry, does not exceed an amount which the Secretary of State estimates is equal to one per cent. of the relevant emoluments, being the aggregate of the emoluments and payments intended to be disbursed as emoluments which have been paid or are payable by any such employer to or in respect of persons employed in the industry, in respect of the period specified in the said proposals as relevant, that is to say the period hereafter referred to in this Order as "the eighteenth base period";

Now, therefore, the Secretary of State in exercise of the powers conferred on him by sections 11(2), 12(3) and 12(4) of the 1982 Act and of all other powers enabling him in that behalf hereby makes the following Order:–

Citation and commencement

1. This Order may be cited as the Industrial Training Levy (Clothing and Allied Products) Order 1987 and shall come into force on 30th September 1987.

Interpretation

2.—(1) In this Order unless the context otherwise requires:–
   (a) "agriculture" has the same meaning as in section 109(3) of the Agriculture Act 1947(**b**) or, in relation to Scotland, as in section 86(3) of the Agriculture (Scotland) Act 1948(**c**);
   (b) "assessment" means an assessment of an employer to the levy;
   (c) "the Board" means the Clothing and Allied Products Industry Training Board;
   (d) "business" means any activities of industry or commerce;

(**a**) 1982 c. 10.
(**b**) 1947 c. 48.
(**c**) 1948 c. 45.

(e) "charity" has the same meaning as in section 360 of the Income and Corporation Taxes Act 1970(**a**);

(f) "clothing and allied products establishment" means an establishment in Great Britain engaged in the eighteenth base period wholly or mainly in the clothing and allied products industry for a total of twenty-seven or more weeks or, being an establishment that commenced to carry on business in the eighteenth base period, for a total number of weeks exceeding one half of the number of weeks in the part of the said period commencing with the day on which business was commenced and ending on the last day thereof;

(g) "the clothing and allied products industry" does not include any activities which have been transferred from the industry of the Board to the industry of another industrial training board by one of the transfer orders but save as aforesaid means any one or more of the activities which, subject to the provisions of paragraph 2 of Schedule 1 to the industrial training order, are specified in paragraph 1 of that Schedule as the activities of the clothing and allied products industry or, in relation to an establishment whose activities have been transferred to the industry of the Board by one of the transfer orders, any activities so transferred;

(h) "emoluments" means all emoluments assessable to income tax under Schedule E of the Income and Corporation Taxes Act 1970 (other than pensions), being emoluments from which tax under that Schedule is deductible, whether or not tax in fact falls to be deducted from any particular payment thereof;

(i) "employer" means a person who is an employer in the clothing and allied products industry at any time in the eighteenth levy period;

(j) "the industrial training order" means the Industrial Training (Clothing and Allied Products Board) Order 1969(**b**);

(k) "the levy" means the levy imposed by the Board in respect of the eighteenth levy period;

(l) "notice" means a notice in writing;

(m) "the transfer orders" means

    (i) the Industrial Training (Transfer of the Activities of Establishments) (No. 3) Order 1976(**c**), and

    (ii) the Industrial Training (Transfer of the Activities of Establishments) Order 1977(**d**);

(n) "the eighteenth base period" means the period of twelve months that commenced on 6th April 1986;

(o) "the eighteenth levy period" means the period commencing with the day upon which this Order comes into force and ending on 31st March 1988.

(2) Any reference in this Order to persons employed at or from a clothing and allied products establishment shall in any case where the employer is a company be construed as including a reference to any director of the company (or any person occupying the position of director by whatever name he was called) who was, at the material time, in receipt of a salary from the company.

(3) Any reference in this Order to an establishment that commences to carry on business or that ceases to carry on business shall not be taken to apply where the location of the establishment is changed but its business is continued wholly or mainly at or from the new location, or where the suspension of activities is of a temporary or seasonal nature.

Imposition of the levy

3.—(1) The levy to be imposed by the Board on employers in respect of the eighteenth levy period shall be assessed in accordance with the provisions of this article.

(2) Subject to the provisions of this article, the levy shall be assessed by the Board in respect of each employer and the amount thereof shall be equal to 0.1 per cent. of the sum of the emoluments of all the persons employed by the employer at or from the relevant establishment

---

(**a**) 1970 c. 10.
(**b**) S.I. 1969/1375, amended by S.I. 1982/920.
(**c**) S.I. 1976/2110.
(**d**) S.I. 1977/1951.

or establishments (that is to say the clothing and allied products establishment or establishments of the employer other than one which is an establishment of an employer who is exempted by virtue of paragraph (3) of this article) in the eighteenth base period.

(3) There shall be exempt from the levy:–

    (a) an employer in respect of whom the sum of the emoluments of the persons mentioned in the last foregoing paragraph is less than £68,250;

    (b) a charity.

(4) Where any persons whose emoluments are taken into account for the purposes of this article were employed at or from an establishment that ceases to carry on business in the eighteenth levy period, the sum of the emoluments of those persons shall be reduced for such purposes in the same proportion as the number of days between the commencement of the said levy period and the date of cessation of business (both dates inclusive) bears to the number of days in the said levy period.

(5) For the purposes of this article, no regard shall be had to the emoluments of any person wholly engaged:–

    (a) in agriculture; or

    (b) in the supply of food or drink for immediate consumption.

Assessment notices

4.—(1) The Board shall serve an assessment notice on every employer assessed to the levy.

(2) The amount of an assessment shall be rounded down to the nearest £1.

(3) An assessment notice shall state the Board's address for the service of a notice of appeal or of an application for an extension of time for appealing.

(4) An assessment notice may be served on the person assessed to the levy either by delivering it to him personally or by leaving it, or sending it to him by post, at his last known address or place of business in the United Kingdom or, if that person is a corporation, by leaving it, or sending it by post to the corporation, at such address or place of business or at its registered or principal office.

Payment of the levy

5.—(1) Subject to the provisions of this article and of articles 6 and 7, the amount of the assessment payable under an assessment notice served by the Board shall be due and payable to the Board one month after the date of the notice.

(2) The amount of an assessment shall not be recoverable by the Board until there has expired the time allowed for appealing against the assessment by article 7(1) of this Order and any further period or periods of time that the Board or an industrial tribunal may have allowed for appealing under paragraph (2) or (3) of that article or, where an appeal is brought, until the appeal is decided or withdrawn.

Withdrawal of assessment

6.—(1) The Board may, by a notice served on the person assessed to the levy in the same manner as an assessment notice, withdraw an assessment if that person has appealed against that assessment under the provisions of article 7 of this Order and the appeal has not been entered in the Register of Appeals kept under the appropriate Regulations specified in paragraph (5) of that article.

(2) The withdrawal of an assessment shall be without prejudice to the power of the Board to serve a further assessment notice on the employer.

Appeals

7.—(1) A person assessed to the levy may appeal to an industrial tribunal against the assessment within one month from the date of the service of the assessment notice or within any further period or periods of time that may be allowed by the Board or an industrial tribunal under the following provisions of this article.

(2) The Board by notice may for good cause allow a person assessed to the levy to appeal to an industrial tribunal against the assessment at any time within the period of four months

from the date of the service of the assessment notice or within such further period or periods as the Board may allow before such time as may then be limited for appealing has expired.

(3) If the Board shall not allow an application for extension of time for appealing, an industrial tribunal shall upon application made to the tribunal by the person assessed to the levy have the like powers as the Board under the last foregoing paragraph.

(4) In the case of an assessment that has reference to an establishment that ceases to carry on business in the eighteenth levy period on any day after the date of the service of the assessment notice, the foregoing provisions of this article shall have effect as if for the period of four months from the date of the service of the assessment notice mentioned in paragraph (2) of this article there were substituted the period of six months from the date of the cessation of business.

(5) An appeal or an application to an industrial tribunal under this article shall be made in accordance with the Industrial Tribunals (England and Wales) Regulations 1965(**a**) except where the assessment has reference to persons employed at or from one or more establishments that are wholly in Scotland and to no other persons, in which case the appeal or application shall be made in accordance with the Industrial Tribunals (Scotland) Regulations 1965(**b**).

(6) The powers of an industrial tribunal under paragraph (3) of this article may be exercised by the President of the Industrial Tribunals (England and Wales) or by the President of the Industrial Tribunals (Scotland) as the case may be.

Evidence

8.—(1) Upon the discharge by a person assessed to the levy of his liability under an assessment the Board shall if so requested issue to him a certificate to that effect.

(2) The production in any proceedings of a document purporting to be certified by the Secretary of the Board to be a true copy of an assessment or other notice issued by the Board or purporting to be a certificate such as is mentioned in the foregoing paragraph of this article shall, unless the contrary is proved, be sufficient evidence of the document and of the facts stated therein.

Signed by order of the Secretary of State

John Lee
Parliamentary Under Secretary of State,
27th August 1987   Department of Employment

EXPLANATORY NOTE

(*This note is not part of the Order*)

This Order, which comes into force on 30th September 1987 gives effect to proposals of the Clothing and Allied Products Industry Training Board which were submitted to and approved by the Manpower Services Commission and thereafter submitted by the Manpower Services Commission to the Secretary of State. The proposals are for the imposition of a levy on employers in the Clothing and Allied Products industry for the purpose of raising money towards meeting the expenses of the Board.

The levy is to be imposed in respect of the eighteenth levy period commencing with the day upon which this Order comes into force and ending on 31st March 1988. The levy will be assessed by the Board and there will be a right of appeal against an assessment to an industrial tribunal.

(**a**) S.I. 1965/1101, amended by S.I. 1967/301, 1977/1473.
(**b**) S.I. 1965/1157, amended by S.I. 1967/302, 1977/1474.

STATUTORY INSTRUMENTS

1987 No. 1535

PUBLIC PASSENGER TRANSPORT

The London Taxi Sharing Scheme Order 1987

Made - - - -	*1st September 1987*
Laid before Parliament	*7th September 1987*
Coming into force -	*28th September 1987*

The Secretary of State for Transport, in exercise of the powers conferred by section 10(4), (5), (6) and (10) of the Transport Act 1985**(a)**, and of all other enabling powers, hereby makes the following Order:

    1.   This Order may be cited as the London Taxi Sharing Scheme Order 1987 and shall come into force on 28th September 1987.

    2.   The Secretary of State hereby makes the London Taxi Sharing Scheme as set out in the Annex to this Order.

    3.   The Heathrow Taxi Sharing Scheme Order 1987**(b)** and the London (British Rail) Taxi Sharing Scheme Order 1987**(c)** are hereby revoked.

Signed by authority of the Secretary of State

David Mitchell
Minister of State,
1st September 1987   Department of Transport

ANNEX

The London Taxi Sharing Scheme 1987

Designation of authorised places and interpretation

    1.—(1) There is hereby designated as an authorised place every place at which a taxi may lawfully ply for hire.

    (2) In this Scheme–

      "authorised place" means any place designated in paragraph 1(1) from which taxis may be hired under the terms of the Scheme;

(a) 1985 c.67.
(b) S.I. 1987/784.
(c) S.I. 1987/839.

"exclusive service" means a service other than at separate fares;

"shared service" means a service at separate fares;

"taxi" means a vehicle licensed under section 6 of the Metropolitan Public Carriage Act 1869(a); and, except where otherwise stated, any reference to a numbered paragraph or Schedule is a reference to the paragraph or Schedule bearing that number in this Scheme.

Application

2.—(1) The requirements of this Scheme shall apply to taxis standing for hire or hired at separate fares under this Scheme for a journey from an authorised place.

(2) Any taxi may at the option of the holder of the licence for that vehicle be used for the carriage of passengers at separate fares under the terms of this Scheme.

(3) When a taxi is hired in accordance with this Scheme, the provisions of this Scheme applying to the journey for which it is hired shall apply to any part of that journey outside the London taxi area as they apply to any part within that area.

Availability

3. A taxi shall be available for hire under this Scheme when it is standing at an authorised place and displaying a notice containing the words specified in paragraph 4.

Signs on vehicles

4. There shall be displayed on any taxi standing for hire under this Scheme (in addition to any other sign, mark or notice which is required to be displayed on the taxi) a notice containing the words "Shared Taxi".

Fares

5.—(1) The taxi meter shall be set in motion only when the taxi leaves the authorised place and shall display the fare for an exclusive service payable under paragraphs 40 and 41(2) of the London Cab Order 1934(b);

(2) The maximum amount payable by a passenger sharing a service shall be the aggregate of:–

    (a) the amount calculated in accordance with the conversion table set out in Schedule 1 as at the time when the passenger is set down and according to the number of passengers who arranged the shared service; and

    (b) any charge for luggage payable under paragraph 41(1) of the London Cab Order 1934(c).

(3) No fare shall be charged for any child under the age of two years, and no such child shall be counted when calculating the number of people sharing the vehicle.

(4) For the purpose of computing fares, each child over the age of two years but under the age of ten years shall be charged at half fare and when calculating the number of people sharing the vehicle–

    (a) if an even number of children are being carried, one half of that number shall be counted; and

    (b) if an odd number of such children are being carried, one half of the even number immediately following that odd number shall be counted.

Fare tables

6.—(1) The driver of a taxi to which this Scheme applies shall at all times carry in his taxi–

    (a) a copy of the conversion table set out in Schedule 1; and

    (b) a copy of the fare table set out in Schedule 2.

(a) 1869 c.115.

(b) S.R & O. 1934/1346; paragraph 40 was substituted by S.I. 1987/999; paragraph 41 was substituted by S.I. 1980/588 and paragraph 41(2) was amended by S.I. 1982/610, 1983/653, 1984/707 and 1987/999.

(c) Paragraph 41(1) was amended by S.I. 1982/610 and 1984/707.

(2) The driver shall produce the tables specified in paragraph 6(1) to any passenger who asks to see them or either of them.

Obligatory hirings

7. The driver of a taxi available for hire under this Scheme who–
   (a) is not waiting with a person seeking a shared service for another person to offer to share the taxi; and
   (b) would, apart from the Licensed Taxis (Hiring at Separate Fares) (London) Order 1986**(a)**, be required to accept the hiring,

shall not without reasonable excuse refuse a hiring to two or more persons seeking a shared service to the same destination; but he may, with the agreement of those persons, wait for a reasonable period for further passengers to share the hiring.

Arrangements for a shared service

8.—(1) If a person seeks to hire for a shared service a taxi available for hire under this Scheme and the driver is unable to find at least one other person to share the hiring within a reasonable time, then no fare or other charge shall be payable and the driver shall be free to seek an alternative hiring provided that the driver and the first mentioned person may continue to wait for another person to offer to share the taxi for so long as they both agree to do so.

(2) The driver of a taxi available for hire under this Scheme may refuse to accept as a passenger for a shared service any person on the grounds that his intended destination could not be reached without an excessive or unreasonable addition to the length or duration of the journey of any passenger previously accepted for a journey, but shall not refuse to carry a person already accepted by him as a passenger because his destination is not on such grounds compatible with that of a person who subsequently seeks a shared service.

(3) Before the commencement of any journey from the authorised place by a taxi for the purpose of a shared service, any person may (notwithstanding any earlier agreement) decide not to be carried as a passenger and no fare or other charge shall be payable by that person.

Cessation of availability

9. If–
   (a) a person at any time seeks to hire for an exclusive service a taxi available for hire under this Scheme;
   (b) the driver is not waiting with a person seeking a shared service for another person to offer to share the taxi; and
   (c) the driver either–
      (i) would, apart from the Licensed Taxis (Hiring at Separate Fares) (London) Order 1986, be required to accept the hiring; or
      (ii) accepts the hiring although not required to do so,

then that taxi shall thereupon cease to be available for hire under this Scheme until the expiry of that hiring.

Luggage

10. The driver shall not refuse to carry in his taxi the luggage of a passenger if the luggage can be accommodated safely within the luggage compartment of the taxi with the luggage of other passengers already accepted by him.

Route to be followed

11. The route taken by the taxi and the order in which passengers are set down shall be determined by the driver, but he shall not unreasonably prolong the journey of any passenger.

(a) S.I. 1986/1387.

SCHEDULE 1

Paragraph 5

CONVERSION TABLE FOR USE IN CALCULATING SHARED FARES
Maximum amount payable by each passenger:

Fare displayed on meter	NUMBER SHARING				Fare displayed on meter	NUMBER SHARING			
	2	3	4	5		2	3	4	5
80p	50p	40p	40p	30p	£5.60	£3.60	£3.10	£2.50	£2.20
£1.00	70p	60p	50p	40p	£5.80	£3.80	£3.20	£2.60	£2.30
£1.20	80p	70p	50p	50p	£6.00	£3.90	£3.30	£2.70	£2.40
£1.40	90p	80p	60p	60p	£6.20	£4.00	£3.40	£2.80	£2.50
£1.60	£1.00	90p	70p	60p	£6.40	£4.20	£3.50	£2.90	£2.60
£1.80	£1.20	£1.00	80p	70p	£6.60	£4.30	£3.60	£3.00	£2.60
£2.00	£1.30	£1.10	90p	80p	£6.80	£4.40	£3.70	£3.10	£2.70
£2.20	£1.40	£1.20	£1.00	90p	£7.00	£4.60	£3.90	£3.20	£2.80
£2.40	£1.60	£1.30	£1.10	£1.00	£7.20	£4.70	£4.00	£3.20	£2.90
£2.60	£1.70	£1.40	£1.20	£1.00	£7.40	£4.80	£4.10	£3.30	£3.00
£2.80	£1.80	£1.50	£1.30	£1.10	£7.60	£4.90	£4.20	£3.40	£3.00
£3.00	£2.00	£1.70	£1.40	£1.20	£7.80	£5.10	£4.30	£3.50	£3.10
£3.20	£2.10	£1.80	£1.40	£1.30	£8.00	£5.20	£4.40	£3.70	£3.20
£3.40	£2.20	£1.90	£1.50	£1.40	£8.20	£5.30	£4.40	£3.70	£3.30
£3.60	£2.30	£2.00	£1.60	£1.40	£8.40	£5.50	£4.60	£3.80	£3.40
£3.80	£2.50	£2.10	£1.70	£1.50	£8.60	£5.60	£4.70	£3.90	£3.40
£4.00	£2.60	£2.20	£1.80	£1.60	£8.80	£5.70	£4.80	£4.00	£3.50
£4.20	£2.70	£2.30	£1.90	£1.70	£9.00	£5.90	£5.00	£4.10	£3.60
£4.40	£2.90	£2.40	£2.00	£1.80	£9.20	£6.00	£5.10	£4.20	£3.70
£4.60	£3.00	£2.50	£2.10	£1.80	£9.40	£6.10	£5.20	£4.20	£3.80
£4.80	£3.10	£2.60	£2.20	£1.90	£9.60	£6.20	£5.30	£4.30	£3.80
£5.00	£3.30	£2.80	£2.30	£2.00	£9.80	£6.40	£5.40	£4.40	£3.90
£5.20	£3.40	£2.90	£2.30	£2.10	£10.00	£6.50	£5.50	£4.50	£4.00
£5.40	£3.50	£3.00	£2.40	£2.20					

Where the fare displayed on the meter exceeds £10, the shared fare shall be calculated by repeated use of the conversion table for each multiple of £10 and for any sum by which the fare displayed exceeds the highest multiple of £10.

Paragraph 6   # SCHEDULE 2

FARE TABLE FOR SHARED SERVICE

Total fare

1. At any time when the taxi is shared the fare payable by each passenger shall be the sum of the basic fare specified in paragraph 2 of this Table and the permitted luggage charge.

Basic fare

2. The basic fare shall be calculated by applying the conversion table carried by the driver to the sum displayed on the meter when the passenger leaves the taxi.

Sum displayed on the meter

3. The meter will be started when the taxi leaves the authorised place and will operate at the normal rate for an exclusive service. It may include any additional charges that would apply to an exclusive service, with the exception of the charges for additional passengers and for luggage.

Number sharing

4. The basic fare is calculated from the sum displayed on the meter according to the number of passengers sharing the taxi when it leaves the authorised place.

Child fares

5. Children under the age of 2 years are carried free, and those aged between 2 and 10 years will be charged half fare. For the purpose of calculating the number of people sharing the taxi, children under the age of 2 years are not counted and, for children aged between 2 and 10 years–
    (a) 1 or 2 children count as 1 person;
    (b) 3 or 4 children count as 2 persons; and
    (c) 5 or 6 children count as 3 persons.

EXPLANATORY NOTE

(This note is not part of the Order)

This Order contains in its Annex the London Taxi Sharing Scheme. The Scheme applies to taxis standing for hire or hired at the authorised places designated in paragraph 1(1) of the Scheme.

Taxis available for hire under the Scheme are to display a sign containing the words 'Shared Taxi' (paragraphs 3 and 4). The fares payable are specified in paragraph 5 and Schedules 1 and 2.

Paragraphs 6 to 11 contain supplementary provisions relating to fare and conversion tables, obligatory hirings, arrangements for a shared service, cessation of availability for hire, luggage, and route to be followed.

The Order also revokes the Heathrow and London (British Rail) Taxi Sharing Scheme Orders.

STATUTORY INSTRUMENTS

1987 No. 1536

SEA FISHERIES

COMMUNITY RESTRICTIONS

The Sea Fishing (Enforcement of Community Control Measures) (Amendment) Order 1987

Made - - - -	*27th August 1987*
Laid before Parliament	*2nd September 1987*
Coming into force	*3rd September 1987*

The Minister of Agriculture, Fisheries and Food and the Secretaries of State respectively concerned with sea fishing in Scotland, Wales and Northern Ireland, in exercise of the powers conferred on them by section 30(2) of the Fisheries Act 1981(**a**), and all other powers enabling them in that behalf, hereby make the following Order:

Title and commencement

1. This Order may be cited as the Sea Fishing (Enforcement of Community Control Measures) (Amendment) Order 1987 and shall come into force on 3rd September 1987.

Amendment of the Sea Fishing (Enforcement of Community Control Measures) Order 1985

2. The Sea Fishing (Enforcement of Community Control Measures) Order 1985 (**b**) shall be amended in accordance with the following provisions of this Order.

3. In article 2 (interpretation) for the definition of "the Council Regulation" there shall be substituted the following definition—

'"the Council Regulation" means Council Regulation (EEC) No. 2241/87 establishing certain control measures for fishing activities(**c**)'.

4. In article 3(2) (offences) for the words "article 3, 6, 7 or 8" there shall be substituted the words "article 5, 6, 7 or 8".

5.—(1) In article 4(1) (penalties) for the words "article 2(2), 10(3) or 11" there shall be substituted the words "article 2(2), 11(3) or 13".

(2) In article 4(2) for the words "article 2(2), 10(3) or 11" there shall be substituted the words "article 2(2), 11(3) or 13".

(3) In article 4(3) for the words "article 3, 6, 7 or 8" there shall be substituted the words "article 5, 6, 7 or 8".

(**a**) 1981 c. 29.
(**b**) S.I. 1985/487, amended by S.I. 1986/926.
(**c**) O.J. No. L207, 29.7.87, p.l.

6.—(1) In article 8(a) (powers of British sea-fishery officers to seize fish and nets) for the words "article 10(3)" there shall be substituted the words "article 11(3)".

(2) In article 8(b) for the words "article 11" there shall be substituted the words "article 13".

(3) In article 8(c)(i) for the words "article 11" there shall be substituted the words "article 13".

(4) In article 8(c)(ii) for the words "article 10(3)" there shall be substituted the words "article 11(3)".

7.   In article 12 (admissibility in evidence of logbooks and landing or trans-shipment declarations) for the words "article 3" there shall be substituted the words "article 5".

8.   In the Schedule (Community provisions contravention of which constitutes an offence) in column 1 (provision of the Council Regulation), there shall be substituted—

(a) in paragraph 2 for the words "Article 3" the words "Article 5";

(b) in paragraph 5 for the words "Article 10(3)" the words "Article 11(3)";

(c) in paragraph 6 for the words "Article 11" the words "Article 13".

In witness thereof the official Seal of the Minister of Agriculture, Fisheries and Food is hereunto affixed on 27th August 1987.

John Selwyn Gummer
Minister of State,
Ministry of Agriculture, Fisheries and Food

27th August 1987

Sanderson of Bowden
Minister of State, Scottish Office

26th August 1987

Ian Grist
Parliamentary Under Secretary of State, Welsh Office

27th August 1987

Tom King
Secretary of State for Northern Ireland

EXPLANATORY NOTE

(This note is not part of the Order)

This Order amends the Sea Fishing (Enforcement of Community Control Measures) Order 1985 as amended ("the 1985 Order"), in consequence of the consolidation and repeal of Council Regulation (EEC) No. 2057/82 as amended, by Council Regulation (EEC) No. 2241/87 establishing certain control measures for fishing activities.

In consequence of the consolidation the 1985 Order is amended—

(a) by substituting a new definition of "the Council Regulation" (article 3); and

(b) by replacing references to numbered articles where the article numbers of the consolidating Regulation differ from the numbers of corresponding articles of the Regulation repealed (articles 4 to 8).

STATUTORY INSTRUMENTS

1987 No. 1537 (S.116)

POLICE

The Police (Common Police Services) (Scotland) Order 1987

Made - - - -	*28th August 1987*
Laid before Parliament	*9th September1987*
Coming into force	*1st October 1987*

The Secretary of State, in exercise of the powers conferred on him by sections 36(5) and 48(3) of the Police (Scotland) Act 1967(**a**), and of all other powers enabling him in that behalf, and after consultations in accordance with section 36(5) of that Act with such bodies or associations as appear to him to be representative of police authorities, hereby makes the following Order:

1. This Order may be cited as the Police (Common Police Services) (Scotland) Order 1987 and shall come into force on 1st October 1987.

2. The Police (Common Police Services) (Scotland) Order 1975(**b**) is hereby revoked.

3. Section 36(4) of the Police (Scotland) Act 1967 (which provides for the recovery by the Secretary of State from police authorities and joint police committees of one half of the expenses incurred by the Secretary of State in establishing and maintaining any central training institution) shall apply to the expenses incurred by the Secretary of State for the purposes of police forces generally, on or in connection with–

(a) the Police (Scotland) Examinations Board;

(b) police representative and negotiating machinery;

(c) the Scottish Criminal Record Office;

(d) attendance at meetings of the International Criminal Police Organisation (provincial representation) and other international police co-operation;

(e) attendance of officers at the Police College for England and Wales;

(f) the National Forensic Science Laboratory for Scotland;

(g) the Standard Entrance Examination for entry to police forces in Scotland;

(h) central recruitment publicity;

(i) the Police National Computer;

(j) the National Drugs Intelligence Unit;

(k) the Scottish Crime Squad;

(l) the National Co-ordinator of Ports Policing.

(**a**) 1967 c.77.
(**b**) S.I. 1975/1254.

New St. Andrew's House, Edinburgh
28th August 1987

James Douglas-Hamilton
Parliamentary Under Secretary of State,
Scottish Office

EXPLANATORY NOTE

(This note is not part of the Order)

Section 36(4) and (5) of the Police (Scotland) Act 1967 provides for one half of the expenses incurred by the Secretary of State in establishing and maintaining any central police training institution and in providing other common services to be recovered from police authorities and joint police committees. This Order revokes and re-enacts with amendments the Police (Common Police Services) (Scotland) Order 1975 which specified the services which fall within the classification of Common Police Services in Scotland. The only change of substance is the addition of the National Co-ordinator of Ports Policing to the range of services.

STATUTORY INSTRUMENTS

1987 No. 1538

WEIGHTS AND MEASURES

The Weights and Measures (Quantity Marking and Abbreviations of Units) Regulations 1987

Made - - -	*1st September 1987*
Laid before Parliament	*14th September 1987*
Coming into force -	*1st January 1988*

Whereas the Secretary of State pursuant to section 86(2) of the Weights and Measures Act 1985**(a)** has consulted such organisations as appear to him to be representative of interests substantially affected by these Regulations:

Now, therefore, the Secretary of State, in exercise of powers conferred on him by sections 15(1)(g), 23(1)(a), (d), 48(1)(a), (1A), 66, 68(1), (1A) (a), 86(1) and 94(1) of the Weights and Measures Act 1985 and of all other powers enabling him in that behalf, hereby makes the following Regulations:

PART I

PRELIMINARY

Citation, commencement, revocation and interpretation

1.—(1) These Regulations may be cited as the Weights and Measures (Quantity Marking and Abbreviations of Units) Regulations 1987 and shall come into force on 1st January 1988.

(2) The Weights and Measures (Marking of Goods and Abbreviations of Units) Regulations 1975**(b)**, the Weights and Measures (Marking of Goods and Abbreviations of Units) (Amendment) Regulations 1977**(c)** and the Weights and Measures (Marking of Goods and Abbreviations of Units) (Amendment) Regulations 1980**(d)** are hereby revoked.

(3) In these Regulations, "the Act" means the Weights and Measures Act 1985.

(a) 1985 c. 72; section 68(1) defines "regulations", sections 48(1A) and 68(1A) have effect by virtue of the modifications to Part V of the Act made by paragraphs 2(b) and 8(b) of Part II of Schedule 3 to the Weights and Measures (Packaged Goods) Regulations 1986 (S.I. 1986/2049) and section 94(1) defines "prescribed".
(b) S.I. 1975/1319.
(c) S.I. 1977/1683.
(d) S.I. 1980/8.

PART II

QUANTITY MARKING OF CONTAINERS AND UNITS OF MEASUREMENT TO BE USED IN MARKING

Application

2.—(1) Subject to paragraph (2) below, this Part of these Regulations shall apply in respect of–

    (a) the manner of the marking of any container required by or under Part IV of the Act or section 48(1) or (1A) or 68(1A) to be marked with information as to quantity; and

    (b) the units of measurement to be used in marking any container required by or under Part IV of the Act to be marked with information as to quantity by measurement.

(2) Regulations 5 and 6 shall not apply in relation to any catchweight product.

(3) In this regulation "catchweight product" means any product which is not pre-packed according to a pre-determined fixed weight pattern, but is pre-packed in varying quantities.

Marking with quantity by measurement

3.—(1) Subject to paragraph (2) below, the marking of any container with information as to quantity by measurement shall comprise the numerical value of the unit of measurement expressed in words or figures and a reference to that unit expressed either in words or by means of the relevant symbol or abbreviation which may lawfully be used for trade in relation to that unit under Part III of these Regulations.

(2) Where the numerical value of the unit of measurement is expressed in words, the reference to that unit shall be expressed in words and not by means of a symbol or abbreviation.

(3) Any marking with information as to quantity by gross weight shall include the word "gross" or the words "including container" or other words which indicate that the marked weight includes the weight of the container.

(4) No abbreviation of the word "net" or "gross" shall be used in the marking.

(5) Subject to paragraphs (6) and (7) below, a metric quantity used in the marking shall not be expressed as a vulgar fraction.

(6) For a period of 6 months after these Regulations come into force a metric quantity used in the marking may be expressed as one of the following vulgar fractions namely one half or $\frac{1}{2}$, or one quarter or $\frac{1}{4}$, of the unit of measurement.

(7) For a period of 1 year after these Regulations come into force a person shall not be guilty of an offence under section 25(2) of the Act by reason only of–

    (a) having in his possession for sale, or

    (b) having in his possession for delivery after sale, or

    (c) causing or suffering any other person to have in his possession for sale or for delivery after sale,

any goods pre-packed or otherwise made up in or on a container for sale, or for delivery after sale, where a metric quantity used in the marking is expressed as one of the said vulgar fractions.

Legibility and position of marking

4.—(1) Any marking of a container with information as to quantity–

    (a) shall be easy to understand, clearly legible and indelible;

    (b) shall be easily visible to an intending purchaser under normal conditions of purchase;

    (c) shall not in any way be hidden, obscured or interrupted by any other written or pictorial matter; and

(d) if it is not on the actual container or on a label securely attached to the container, shall be so placed that it cannot be removed without opening the container.

(2) Where, pursuant to regulation 7(3) below, the words "metric pack" are included in any marking, those words shall appear within a surrounding line or on a panel which is clearly distinguished in colour from its surroundings and within which or on which there is no other written and no pictorial matter.

Size of marking

5.—(1) Subject to regulation 2(2) above, where in any marking of any container the quantity by number or the numerical value of a unit of measurement is expressed in figures, all the relevant figures shall be at least the height specified in the second column of the Table set out in Schedule 1 to these Regulations in relation to–

(a) where the marking is of mass or weight, capacity or volume, the range of quantity specified in the first column of that Table, appropriate to the measurement being marked, within which the quantity of goods made up in or on that container falls, (or where the goods are made up in an imperial quantity, within which the metric equivalent of that quantity falls); or

(b) where the marking is of area, length or number, the range of size of container so specified within which the size of the container in or on which the goods are made up falls, being a size calculated in accordance with the provisions of that Schedule.

(2) Where, pursuant to regulation 7(3) below, the words "metric pack" are included in any marking, those words shall appear in capital letters of at least the height referred to in paragraph (1) above.

(3) The numerator and denominator together indicating a vulgar fraction of a unit of measurement shall appear one on top of the other and for the purposes of paragraph (1) above shall be treated as a single figure.

Imperial and metric units of measurement

6.—(1) Subject to regulation 2(2) above and paragraph (2) below, the marking of any container with information as to quantity by measurement shall be in metric units of measurement but may, in addition, be in imperial units.

(2) In the case of any goods required by or under Part IV of the Act to be pre-packed or otherwise made up in or on a container for sale, or for delivery after sale, only if made up either in specified imperial or metric quantities or in specified imperial quantities only, the marking of quantity shall be in both metric and imperial units.

7.—(1) Where the marking of quantity is in both metric and imperial units of measurement, the following provisions of this regulation shall apply.

(2) The marking shall indicate the quantity in terms of the same measurement in the imperial system of units as in the metric system.

(3) In the case of any goods required by or under Part IV of the Act to be pre-packed or otherwise made up in or on a container for sale, or for delivery after sale, only if made up in specified quantities, the marking shall–

(a) first indicate the quantity in which they are made up; and

(b) if the quantity in which they are made up is in metric units, include the words "metric pack".

(4) In any other case the marking may indicate the quantity first in either imperial or metric units.

(5) The indications of quantity in imperial and metric units shall be of equal size and shall be distinct but in close proximity to each other and nothing shall be inserted between them.

(6) Notwithstanding anything in regulation 10 of the Weights and Measures

(Packaged Goods) Regulations 1986**(a)**, in the case of cows' milk and goats' milk any marking of any quantity in imperial units shall be entirely in terms of the pint, quart or gallon.

(7) In paragraph (6) above, "cows' milk" means cows' milk in any liquid form other than that of condensed milk within the meaning of the Condensed Milk and Dried Milk Regulations 1977**(b)** (including evaporated milk) or of cream.

Units of measurement to be used in marking

8. Subject to regulation 7(6) above, the units of measurement to be used in marking any container with information as to quantity by measurement are those set out in Columns 2 and 3 of Schedule 2 to these Regulations, appropriate to the measurement being marked set out in Column 1.

Amendment of the Weights and Measures (Packaged Goods) Regulations 1986

9.—(1) Regulation 10 of the Weights and Measures (Packaged Goods) Regulations 1986 shall be amended as follows:–

(a) subject to paragraph (2) below, in paragraph (1)–

   (i) for "Paragraphs (2) to (7) of this Regulation have" there shall be substituted "This regulation has"; and

   (ii) the words "and the manner in which the statement is to be marked" shall be deleted;

(b) in paragraph (2)(a) for "the Weights and Measures (Marking of Goods and Abbreviations of Units) Regulations 1975" there shall be substituted "the Weights and Measures (Quantity Marking and Abbreviations of Units) Regulations 1987"; and

(c) subject to paragraph (2) below, paragraphs (7) and (8) shall be deleted.

(2) In the case of packages containing poultry, but not including part only of any poultry:

(a) paragraph (1)(c) above shall not apply; and

(b) for paragraph 1(B)(c)(ii) of Part I of Schedule 3 to the Weights and Measures (Packaged Goods) Regulations 1986 there shall be substituted "for Regulation 10(7) there were substituted the words "In the case of packages other than packages marked with the EEC mark the principal Regulations shall apply as if Regulations 3(3) and (4), 5 and 7(3) to (7) and Schedule 1 were omitted and as if in Regulation 6(1) for the words "metric units" onwards there were substituted "imperial or metric units or in both imperial and metric units" ".".

PART III

USE FOR TRADE OF ABBREVIATIONS OF, OR SYMBOLS FOR, UNITS OF MEASUREMENT

10. This Part of these Regulations shall apply as respects the use for trade (other than for the purpose of marking weighing or measuring equipment) of abbreviations of, or symbols for, units of measurement.

11.—(1) Only those symbols or abbreviations set out in Column 2 of Schedule 3 to these Regulations may be used for trade to indicate the relevant unit of measurement set out in Column 1 of that Schedule.

(2) In the case only of an abbreviation of an imperial unit so set out, the letter 's' may be added to it, when appropriate, to indicate the plural.

Francis Maude
Parliamentary Under-Secretary of State,
Department of Trade and Industry

1st September 1987

(a) S.I. 1986/2049.
(b) S.I. 1977/928, to which there are amendments not relevant to these Regulations.

Regulation 5   **SCHEDULE 1**

TABLE OF SIZE OF FIGURES IN QUANTITY MARKING OF CONTAINERS

1 *Mass or weight of goods*	2 *Minimum height of figures*
Not exceeding 50 g	2 mm
Exceeding 50 g but not exceeding 200 g	3 mm
Exceeding 200 g but not exceeding 1 kg	4 mm
Exceeding 1 kg	6 mm
Capacity of goods	
Not exceeding 5 cl	2 mm
Exceeding 5 cl but not exceeding 20 cl	3 mm
Exceeding 20 cl but not exceeding 1 L	4 mm
Exceeding 1 L	6 mm
Volume of goods	
Not exceeding 200 cm³	3 mm
Exceeding 200 cm³ but not exceeding 1000 cm³	4 mm
Exceeding 1000 cm³	6 mm
Not exceeding 5 cl	2 mm
Exceeding 5 cl but not exceeding 20 cl	3 mm
Exceeding 20 cl but not exceeding 1 L	4 mm
Exceeding 1 L	6 mm
Area, length and number	
Size of container	
Not exceeding 12 cm	2 mm
Exceeding 12 cm but not exceeding 30 cm	3 mm
Exceeding 30 cm but not exceeding 45 cm	4 mm
Exceeding 45 cm	6 mm

For the purposes of this Schedule, the size of a container shall be treated as equal–

(a) in the case of a rectilinear or approximately rectilinear container, to its height, length or width whichever is the greatest;

(b) in the case of a container with curvilinear or approximately curvilinear cross section, its height or maximum diameter, whichever is the greater.

SCHEDULE 2

Regulation 8

UNITS OF MEASUREMENT TO BE USED IN QUANTITY MARKING

1 *Measurement*	2 *Metric unit*	3 *Imperial unit*
Length	metre centimetre millimetre	yard foot inch
Area	square metre square decimetre square centimetre	square yard square foot
Volume	cubic metre cubic centimetre litre centilitre millilitre	
Capacity	litre centilitre millilitre	gallon quart pint fluid ounce
Mass or weight	kilogram gram	pound ounce

SCHEDULE 3

Regulation 11

SYMBOLS FOR AND ABBREVIATIONS OF UNITS OF MEASUREMENT WHICH MAY BE USED FOR TRADE

PART I

METRIC UNITS

1 *Unit of measurement*	2 *Symbol*
metre	m
centimetre	cm
millimetre	mm
square metre	m^2
square decimetre	dm^2
square centimetre	cm^2
cubic metre	m^3
cubic centimetre	cm^3
litre	l or L
decilitre	dl or dL
centilitre	cl or cL
millilitre	ml or mL
tonne	t
kilogram	kg
hectogram	hg
gram	g
milligram	mg

PART II

IMPERIAL UNITS

1 *Unit of measurement*	2 *Abbreviation*
yard	yd
foot	ft
inch	in
square yard	sq yd
square foot	sq ft
gallon	gal
quart	qt
pint	pt
fluid ounce	fl oz
pound	lb
ounce	oz

EXPLANATORY NOTE

(This note is not part of the Regulations)

These Regulations consolidate with amendments the Weights and Measures (Marking of Goods and Abbreviations of Units) Regulations 1975, as amended. Part II makes provision as to the manner in which quantities are to be marked on those containers of goods which are required to be marked under the Weights and Measures Act 1985 with information as to quantity. They also make provision for the units of measurement to be used in marking the containers required to be marked under Part IV of the Act. Part III makes provision with respect to the abbreviations of (or symbols for) units of measurement which may lawfully be used for trade, other than for the purpose of marking weighing or measuring equipment.

A number of detailed provisions in the 1975 Regulations have been omitted as to the manner of quantity marking having regard to the provisions for legibility and position of marking which has to be easy to understand, clearly legible and indelible and easily visible under normal conditions of purchase. Detailed restrictions on the use of fractions of imperial and metric units of measurement have also been omitted.

The separate provisions in regulation 10(7) and (8) of the Weights and Measures (Packaged Goods) Regulations 1986, which prescribed the manner in which quantity marking statements are marked on packages sold by weight or volume under the system commonly known as "the average system", are now replaced by these Regulations. Consequential amendments to certain other provisions of regulation 10 of the 1986 Regulations are also made.

STATUTORY INSTRUMENTS

1987 No. 1553

PUBLIC HEALTH, ENGLAND AND WALES

PUBLIC HEALTH, SCOTLAND

PUBLIC HEALTH, NORTHERN IRELAND

CONTAMINATION OF FOOD

The Food Protection (Emergency Prohibitions) (Wales) (No. 3) Amendment Order 1987

Made - - - -	*3rd September 1987*
Laid before Parliament	*4th September 1987*
Coming into force	*7th September 1987*

Whereas the Secretary of State is of the opinion, as mentioned in section 1(1)(a) of the Food and Environment Protection Act 1985 **(a)**, that there has been or may have been an escape of substances of such descriptions and in such quantities and such circumstances as are likely to create a hazard to human health through human consumption of food;

And wheareas the Secretary of State is of the opinion, as mentioned in section 1(1)(b) of the said Act, that in consequence of the said escape of substances food which is or may be in the future in the areas described in the Schedule to the Food Protection (Emergency Prohibitions) (Wales) (No. 3) Order 1987 **(b)**, or which is derived or may be in the future derived from anything in those areas, is, or may be, or may become, unsuitable for human consumption;

Now, therefore, the Secretary of State, in exercise of the powers conferred on him by the said section 1(1), (2), 24(1) and (3) of the said Act, and of all other powers enabling him in that behalf, hereby makes the following Order:—

Title and commencement

1. This Order may be cited as the Food Protection (Emergency Prohibitions) (Wales) (No. 3) Amendment Order 1987 and shall come into force on 7th September 1987.

Partial revocation and amendment

2. The Food Protection (Emergency Prohibitions) (Wales) (No. 3) Order 1987 is revoked to the extent that it imposes prohibitions on—

    (a) the slaughter of a sheep which—

      (i) was moved from a place in accordance with a consent given under section 2(1)

(a) 1985 c.48.
(b) S.I. 1987/1515.

of the Food and Environment Protection Act 1985 which consent was subject to the condition that the sheep to which it applies should be marked with a green mark; and

(ii) has been examined and marked with an ear-tag by a person authorised in that behalf by one of the Ministers; and

(b)   the supply or having in possession for supply of meat, or food containing meat, derived from such a sheep,

and accordingly that Order is further amended in accordance with the following provisions of this Order.

3.   In article 6, for paragraph (2) there shall be substituted the following paragraph—

"(2) Paragraph (1) above shall not apply in the case of—

(a) any sheep which was moved to a market in accordance with a consent given under section 2(1) of the Act which consent did not require that the sheep to which it applies should be marked in a manner specified therein—

(b) any sheep which was moved from any place in accordance with a consent given under the said section 2(1) which consent was subject to the condition that the sheep to which it applies should be marked with a blue mark; or

(c) any sheep which—

(i) was moved from any place in accordance with a consent given under the said section 2(1) which consent was subject to the condition that the sheep to which it applies should be marked with a red mark, with an apricot mark or with a green mark; and

(ii) has been examined and marked with an ear-tag by a person authorised in that behalf by one of the Ministers".

Peter Walker
3rd September 1987   Secretary of State for Wales

EXPLANATORY NOTE

(This note is not part of the Order)

The Food Protection (Emergency Prohibitions) (Wales) (No. 3) Order 1987 contains emergency prohibitions restricting various activities in order to prevent human consumption of food which has been or which may have been rendered unsuitable for that purpose in consequence of the escape of radioactive substances from a nuclear reactor situated at Chernobyl in the USSR.

This Order excepts from the prohibition on slaughter throughout the United Kingdom any sheep, and from the prohibition on supply throughout the United Kingdom any meat derived from such a sheep, identified by a green paint mark which have been examined and subsequently marked with an ear-tag by a person authorised by the Minister of Agriculture, Fisheries and Food, the Secretary of State for Scotland or the Secretary of State for Wales (article 3).

STATUTORY INSTRUMENTS

1987 No. 1554(C.47)

HOUSING, ENGLAND AND WALES
HOUSING, SCOTLAND

The Housing and Planning Act 1986 (Commencement No. 6) Order 1987

Made - - - - *1st September 1987*

The Secretary of State for the Environment, as respects England, the Secretary of State for Wales, as respects Wales, and the Secretary of State for Scotland, as respects Scotland, in exercise of the powers conferred on them by section 57(2) of the Housing and Planning Act 1986(**a**), and of all other powers enabling them in that behalf, hereby make the following Order:

1. This Order may be cited as the Housing and Planning Act 1986 (Commencement No. 6) Order 1987.

2. Section 24(1) of the Housing and Planning Act 1986 insofar as it relates to paragraph 8 (grants for affording tax relief to housing associations) of Schedule 5 to that Act shall come into force on 22nd September 1987.

25th August 1987

Nicholas Ridley
Secretary of State for the Environment

Signed by authority of
the Secretary of State
27th August 1987

Ian Grist
Parliamentary Under Secretary of State,
Welsh Office

1st September 1987

Malcolm Rifkind
Secretary of State for Scotland

(**a**) 1986 c.63.

EXPLANATORY NOTE

(This note is not part of the Order)

This Order brings into force on 22nd September 1987 paragraph 8 of Schedule 5 to the Housing and Planning Act 1986. This amends section 62 of the Housing Associations Act 1985(c.69) which provides for grants for affording tax relief to housing associations whose functions consist of or include providing or maintaining accommodation for letting. The effect of the amendment is to include the grant of a shared ownership lease (or in Scotland disposal under a shared ownership agreement) within the meaning of "letting".

NOTE AS TO EARLIER COMMENCEMENT ORDERS

(This note is not part of the Order)

The following provisions of the Housing and Planning Act 1986 have been brought into force by commencement orders made before the date of this Order –

Provision	Date of commencement	S.I. No.
ss. 1 to 4	7th January 1987	1986/2262
ss. 10 to 14		
ss.16 and 17		
ss. 19 and 20		
ss.22 and 23		
ss. 24 (partially)		
Part III (ss. 27 to 29)		
Part VI (partially)		
s.49 (partially)	2nd March 1987	1987/304
s.40	1st April 1987	1987/348
s.49 (partially)		
s. 9	13th May 1987	1987/754

STATUTORY INSTRUMENTS

1987 No. 1555

PUBLIC HEALTH, ENGLAND AND WALES
PUBLIC HEALTH, SCOTLAND
PUBLIC HEALTH, NORTHERN IRELAND

CONTAMINATION OF FOOD

The Food Protection (Emergency Prohibitions) (England) (No. 2) Amendment No. 4 Order 1987

Made - - -	*4th September 1987*
Laid before Parliament	*4th September 1987*
Coming into force	*7th September 1987*

Whereas the Minister of Agriculture, Fisheries and Food is of the opinion, in accordance with section 1(1)(a) of the Food and Environment Protection Act 1985 **(a)**, that there has been or may have been an escape of substances of such descriptions and in such quantities and such circumstances as are likely to create a hazard to human health through human consumption of food;

And whereas the said Minister is of the opinion, in accordance with section 1(1)(b) of the said Act, that in consequence of the said escape of substances food which is or may be in the future in the area described in Schedule 1 to the Food Protection (Emergency Prohibitions) (England) (No. 2) Order 1986 **(b)**, or which is derived or may be in the future derived from anything in that area, is, or may be, or may become, unsuitable for human consumption;

Now, therefore, the said Minister, in exercise of the powers conferred on him by the said section 1(1) and section 24(3) of the said Act, and of all other powers enabling him in that behalf, hereby makes the following Order:—

Title and commencement

1. This Order may be cited as the Food Protection (Emergency Prohibitions) (England) (No. 2) Amendment No. 4 Order 1987 and shall come into force on 7th September 1987.

Partial revocation and amendment

2. The Food Protection (Emergency Prohibitions) (England) (No. 2) Order 1986 is revoked to the extent that it imposes prohibitions on—

(a) the slaughter of a sheep which—

(i) was moved from a place in accordance with a consent given under section 2(1) of the Food and Environment Protection Act 1985 which consent was

---

(a) 1985 c. 48.
(b) S.I. 1986/1689, amended by S.I. 1986/2208, 1987/153, 249 and 906.

subject to the condition that the sheep to which it applies should be marked with a green mark; and

     (ii) has been examined and marked with an ear-tag by a person authorised in that behalf by one of the Ministers; and

  (b) the supply or having in possession for supply of meat, or food containing meat, derived from such a sheep,

and accordingly that Order is further amended in accordance with the following provisions of this Order.

3.   In article 6, for paragraph (2) there shall be substituted the following paragraph—

"(2) Paragraph (1) above shall not apply in the case of—

  (a) any sheep which was moved to a market in accordance with a consent given under section 2(1) of the Act which consent did not require that the sheep to which it applies should be marked in a manner specified therein;

  (b) any sheep which was moved from any place in accordance with a consent given under the said section 2(1) which consent was subject to the condition that the sheep to which it applies should be marked with a blue mark; or

  (c) any sheep which—

     (i) was moved from any place in accordance with a consent given under the said section 2(1) which consent was subject to the condition that the sheep to which it applies should be marked with a red mark, with an apricot mark or with a green mark; and

     (ii) has been examined and marked with an ear-tag by a person authorised in that behalf by one of the Ministers.".

In witness whereof the Official Seal of the Minister of Agriculture, Fisheries and Food is hereunto affixed on 4th September 1987.

John Selwyn Gummer
Minister of State,
Ministry of Agriculture, Fisheries and Food

EXPLANATORY NOTE

(This note is not part of the Order)

The Food Protection (Emergency Prohibitions) (England) (No. 2) Order 1986 contains emergency prohibitions restricting various activities in order to prevent human consumption of food which has been or which may have been rendered unsuitable for that purpose in consequence of the escape of radioactive substances from a nuclear reactor situated at Chernobyl in the USSR.

This Order excepts from the prohibition on slaughter throughout the United Kingdom any sheep, and from the prohibition on supply throughout the United Kingdom any meat derived from such a sheep, identified by a green paint mark which have been examined and subsequently marked with an ear-tag by a person authorised by the Minister of Agriculture, Fisheries and Food or the Secretary of State for Scotland or Wales.

STATUTORY INSTRUMENTS

1987 No. 1556

ROAD TRAFFIC

The Motor Vehicles (Type Approval and Approval Marks) (Fees) (Amendment) (No. 2) Regulations 1987

Made - - - -	*2nd September 1987*
Laid before Parliament	*10th September 1987*
Coming into force	*1st October 1987*

The Secretary of State for Transport, in exercise of the powers conferred by section 50(1) of the Road Traffic Act 1972(**a**), now vested in him(**b**), and of the powers conferred by section 56(1) and (2) of the Finance Act 1973(**c**) with the consent of the Treasury, and of all other enabling powers, and, in relation to the exercise of the powers conferred by section 50(1) of the Road Traffic Act 1972, after consultation with representative organisations in accordance with section 199(2) of that Act, hereby makes the following Regulations:

1. These Regulations may be cited as the Motor Vehicles (Type Approval and Approval Marks) (Fees) (Amendment) (No. 2) Regulations 1987 and shall come into force on 1st October 1987.

2. The Motor Vehicles (Type Approval and Approval Marks) (Fees) Regulations 1984(**d**) are hereby further amended in accordance with the following provisions of these Regulations.

3. In Schedule 1–

   (a) in the Note at the head of the Schedule the following words shall be added after the word "Schedule" where it appears for the third time–

      "with the exception of Directive 80/780/EEC(**e**), which appears opposite fee no 9100W, the particulars for which may be found in Schedule 4 to the Motor Vehicles (Designation of Approval Marks) Regulations 1979(**f**) as amended.";

   (b) the fee numbers and the information shown against each fee number specified in the Schedule to these Regulations shall be inserted in the appropriate places according to numerical order;

   (c) in column 2(b) opposite fee number 0100G there shall be added after the words "Great Britain Regulations" the words "in so far as it relates to the entry immediately above this entry".

   (d) in relation to those fee numbers which are listed in column 1 of the Table there shall be substituted for the existing fees listed in column 2 the new fees listed in column 3.

(**a**) 1972 c.20, amended by section 10 of, and Schedule 2 to, the Road Traffic Act 1974 (c.50).
(**b**) S.I. 1979/571 and 1981/238.
(**c**) 1973 c.51.
(**d**) S.I. 1984/1404, as amended by S.I. 1985/1656 and 1987/315.
(**e**) O.J. L229, 30.8.80, p. 49.
(**f**) S.I. 1979/1088, as amended by S.I. 1981/1732.

TABLE

(1) Fee No	(2) Existing Fee	(3) New Fee
0500H	420	550
0501E	500	650
4411D	1510	1600
4412A	1570	1760
4413X	1400	1440
4421R	1510	1600
4422N	1570	1760
4423K	1400	1440

Signed by authority of the Secretary of State.

Peter Bottomley
Parliamentary Under Secretary of State,
Department of Transport

24th August 1987

We consent to the making of these Regulations to the extent that they are made in exercise of the powers conferred by section 56(1) and (2) of the Finance Act 1973.

Peter Lloyd
Michael Neubert
2nd September 1987   Two of the Lords Commissioners of Her Majesty's Treasury

SCHEDULE

THE NEW FEE NUMBERS AND INFORMATION INSERTED IN SCHEDULE 1 TO THE 1984 REGULATIONS

(1) Fee No.	(2) Approval Requirements		(3) Particulars of type of examination, vehicle or vehicle part where not uniform in relation to each approval requirement	(4) Amount of fee for examination	
	(a) Subject Matter	(b) Document in which requirement is specified		(a) £	(b) £
0120H	Headlamps emitting an asymmetrical passing beam or a driving beam or both	ECE Regulation 1 as revised on 18th March 1986 or Item 6 in Schedule 1 to the Great Britain Regulations insofar as it relates to the above entry		940	
0720X	Lamps – Side, Rear and Stop		Single lamp function	450	
0721U		ECE Regulation 7 as revised on 15th August 1985 or	Single lamp function comprising an assembly of two lamps	690	
0722Q		Item 7A in Schedule 1 to the Great Britain Regulations	Additional fee for each extra single lamp function in a grouped rear light to Regulation 7.01	190	
0723M			Additional fee for each extra function comprising an assembly of 2 lamps to Regulation 7.01	430	
0820D	Headlamps emitting an asymmetrical passing beam or a driving beam	ECE Regulation 8 as revised on 6th May 1974 and corrected on 2nd	Type HR	860	
0821A	or both and equipped with halogen filament lamps (H1, H2 and H3 lamps) and the filament	May 1977 and 21st June 1978 and amended on 6th July 1986	Type HCR	940	
0822X	lamps	or Item 6 in Schedule 1 of the Great Britain Regulations	Filament Lamp	540	
1305H	Brakes	Directive 71/320/EEC of 26th July 1971, as amended by Directive 74/132/EEC of 11th February 1974, Directive 75/524/EEC of 25th July 1975, Directive 79/489/EEC of 18th April 1979, as corrected on 26th July	Trailers of category 01 not fitted with brakes	290	410
1306E		1979 and Directive 85/	Trailers fitted only with overrun brakes– compatibility	960	—

(1) Fee No.	(2) Approval Requirements		(3) Particulars of type of examination, vehicle or vehicle part where not uniform in relation to each approval requirement	(4) Amount of fee for examination	
	(a) Subject Matter	(b) Document in which requirement is specified		(a) £	(b) £
1307B		647/EEC of 23rd	control device	1,400	—
1308Y		December 1985, but	foundation brake	1,000	—
1309V		excluding the requirements of Annexes X, XI and XII	Other trailers	4,150	—
		or			
1325J		ECE Regulation 13 as	M1, N2 and N1 vehicles	2,790	1,800
1326F		revised on 4th January 1979 amended on 11th August 1981 and 26th November 1984 but excluding the requirements of Annexes 13, 14 and 15	M3, N2 and N3 vehicles, excluding those vehicles covered in fee number 1333D below	5,030	2,490
1327C			L5 vehicles	1,570	660
1328Z			N3 vehicles heavier than 50 tonnes or having individual axle weights over 11 tonnes	7,060	—
1329W	Brakes	Directive 71/320/EEC of 26th July 1971, as amended by Directive 74/132/EEC of 11th February 1974, Directive 75/524/EEC of 25th July 1975, Directive 79/489/EEC of 18th April 1979, as corrected on 26th July 1979 and Directive 85/	Trailers, except those of category 01 and those fitted with overrun brakes	3,980	—
1345K		647/EEC of 23rd December 1985 but excluding the requirements of Annexes XI and XII	M1, M2 and N1 vehicles	3,420	2,620
		or			
		ECE Regulation 13 as revised on 4th January 1979 amended on 11th August 1981 and 26th November 1984 but excluding the requirements of Annexes 14 and 15			
		or			
1346G		Items 6F, 6G, 6H, 6I and 6J in Schedule 1 to the Great Britain Regulations for Goods Vehicles	M3, N2 and N3 vehicles	5,910	4,560

(1) Fee No.	(2) Approval·Requirements		(3) Particulars of type of examination, vehicle or vehicle part where not uniform in relation to each approval requirement	(4) Amount of fee for examination	
	(a) Subject Matter	(b) Document in which requirement is specified		(a) £	(b) £
1347D 1348A 1349X 1365L	Brakes	ECE Regulation 13 as revised on 4th January 1979 amended on 11th August 1981 and 26th November 1984	Motorcycle brake test– L1 vehicles L1 vehicles with driver supplied by applicant L2, L3 and L4 vehicles L2, L3 and L4 vehicles with driver supplied by applicant	2,380 1,540 2,930 1,940	990 — 1,320 —
1366H 1367E 1368B	Brakes	Annex 13 of ECE Regulation 13 and Annex X of Directive 85/647/EEC as mentioned above or Items 13E, 13F and 13G in Schedule 1 to the Great Britain Regulations or Items 6F, 6G, 6H, 6I and 6J in Schedule 1 to the Great Britain Regulations for Goods Vehicles	Anti-lock devices for– trailers, except those of overrun brakes M1 and N1 vehicles M2, M3, N2 and N3 vehicles	1,130 1,110 1,690	— 990 1,650
1369Y	Brakes	Annex 14 of ECE Regulation 13 and Annex XI of Directive 85/647/EEC as mentioned above or Items 13E, 13F and 13G in Schedule 1 to the Great Britain Regulations or Items 6F, 6G, 6H, 6I and 6J in Schedule 1 to the Great Britain Regulations for Goods Vehicles	Electric brakes on Type 02 trailers	3,550	—
1385M	Brakes	Annex 15 of ECE Regulation 13 and Annex XII of Directive 85/647/EEC as mentioned above or Items 13E, 13F and 13G in Schedule 1 to	Inertia dynamometer test for brake linings	—	750

(1) Fee No.	(2) Approval Requirements		(3) Particulars of type of examination, vehicle or vehicle part where not uniform in relation to each approval requirement	(4) Amount of fee for examination	
	(a) Subject Matter	(b) Document in which requirement is specified		(a) £	(b) £
		the Great Britain Regulations			
		or			
		Items 6F, 6G, 6H, 6I and 6J in Schedule 1 to the Great Britain Regulations for Goods Vehicles			
1391N	Brakes	Item 6E in Schedule 1 to the Great Britain Regulations for Goods Vehicles	Slow vehicles and public works vehicles	—	190
2020K	Headlamps emitting an asymmetrical passing beam or a driving beam or both and equipped with halogen filament lamps (H4 lamps) and the filament lamps	ECE Regulation 20 as revised on 15th August 1976 and amended on 3rd July 1986	Type HR	900	—
2021G			Type HCR	980	—
2022D		or	Type HC	920	—
2023A		Item 6A in Schedule 1 of the Great Britain Regulations	Filament Lamp	680	—
3620D	Public service vehicles	ECE Regulation 36 of 12th November 1975 as amended on 8th February 1982 and 7th September 1986	Rigid vehicles	1,960	2,360
3621A			Articulated vehicles	2,380	2,920
3622X			Additional tests to prove compliance with paragraph 5.6.4.5 (per set of retractable steps)	170	170
4309H	Safety glass	ECE Regulation 43 of 15th February 1981, as amended on 14th October 1982 and 4th April 1986	Windscreen toughened	1,110	—
4310A			Windscreen laminated	1,430	—
4311X			Windscreen, treated and laminated	1,490	—
4312U		or Item 15B in Schedule 1 to the Great Britain Regulations	Windows other than windscreens, toughened	670	—
4313Q			Windows other than windscreens, laminated	770	—
4314M			Additional test on plastic coated glass	220	—
4315J			Additional test on double-glazed units	280	—

EXPLANATORY NOTE

(This note is not part of the Regulations)

1. These Regulations further amend the Motor Vehicles (Type Approval and Approval Marks) (Fees) Regulations 1984 in the following ways–

(a) Regulation 3(a) corrects an omission from the Note at the head of Schedule 1. The particulars of Directive 80/780/EEC are to be found in the Motor Vehicles (Designation of Approval Marks) Regulations 1979 as amended(**a**).

(b) Regulation 3(b) inserts new entries in Schedule 1 as a consequence of new or amended ECE Regulations: 1, 7, 8, 13, 20, 36 and 43.

(c) One of the requirements for fee number 0100G, Item 6 to Schedule 1 to the Great Britain Regulations (the Motor Vehicles (Type Approval) (Great Britain) Regulations 1984(**b**)) has been defined as relating to the requirement immediately preceding it in the Schedule, ECE Regulation 1 as revised and corrected up to 30th June 1985. This distinguishes fee number 0100G from fee number 0120H where item 6 to Schedule 1 to the Great Britain Regulations is defined as relating to ECE Regulation 1 as revised on 18th March 1986.

(d) Regulation 3(d) substitutes new fees for certain fees listed in Schedule 1 following re-calculation of the number of man-hours required for the tests listed.

2. Copies of the ECE Regulations and EEC Directives referred to in these Regulations may be obtained from Her Majesty's Stationery Office.

(**a**) S.I. 1979/1088, as amended by S.I. 1980/582 and 2027, 1981/126 and 1732, 1982/1479, 1983/1602, 1985/113 and 1986/369.
(**b**) S.I. 1984/981, as amended by S.I. 1984/1401 and 1761, 1985/1651, 1986/739 and 1987/1509.

STATUTORY INSTRUMENTS

1987 No. 1564

SEA FISHERIES

CONSERVATION OF SEA FISH

The Herring and White Fish (Specified Manx Waters) Licensing (Variation) Order 1987

Made - - - -	*4th September 1987*
Laid before Parliament	*7th September 1987*
Coming into force	*8th September 1987*

The Minister of Agriculture, Fisheries and Food and the Secretaries of State respectively concerned with the sea fishing industry in Scotland, Wales and Northern Ireland, acting jointly, in exercise of the powers conferred on them by sections 4, 15(3) and 20(1) of the Sea Fish (Conservation) Act 1967(**a**), and of all other powers enabling them in that behalf, hereby make the following Order:

Title and commencement

1. This Order may be cited as the Herring and White Fish (Specified Manx Waters) Licensing (Variation) Order 1987, and shall come into force on 8th September 1987.

Variation of the Herring and White Fish (Specified Manx Waters) Licensing Order 1983

2. The Herring and White Fish (Specified Manx Waters) Licensing Order 1983(**b**) is hereby varied–

(a) in article 3 thereof (prohibition of fishing without licence and exception thereto) by substituting for the words "Isle of Man Board of Agriculture and Fisheries" the words "Department of Agriculture, Fisheries and Forestry, the Isle of Man";

(b) by substituting for article 4 thereof (retention on board of fish) the following article–

"4. Notwithstanding the provisions of section 4(9A)(b) of the Sea Fish (Conservation) Act 1967 (return to the sea of fish the fishing for which is prohibited), there may be retained on board any fishing boat to which this Order applies a quantity of sea fish consisting of one or more of the specified white fish of the following species, namely cod (*Gadus morhua*), plaice (*Pleuronectes platessa*) and whiting (*Merlangius merlangus*), the fishing for which is for the time being prohibited by or under this Order, which–

(a) has been taken on board that fishing boat in the area of sea described in Schedule 2 to this Order in the course of fishing in that area for other

---

(**a**) 1967 c.84; section 4 was amended by the Fishery Limits Act 1976 (c.86), section 3 and by the Fisheries Act 1981 (c.29), section 20; section 15(3) was amended by the Sea Fisheries Act 1968 (c.77), Schedule 1, paragraph 38(3) and by the Fishery Limits Act 1976, Schedule 2, paragraph 16(1); section 4 was applied in relation to British fishing boats registered in the Isle of Man and any of the Channel Islands by the Sea Fish (Conservation) (Manx Boats) Order 1978 (S.I. 1978/281) and the Sea Fish (Conservation) (Channel Islands Boats) Order 1978 (S.I. 1978/280); section 22(2)(a) which contains a definition of "the Ministers" for the purposes of sections 4 and 15(3) was amended by the Fisheries Act 1981, sections 19(2)(d) and 45(b).
(**b**) S.I. 1983/1204, varied by S.I. 1983/1879 and 1986/1439.

specified white fish or any other description of sea fish the fishing for which is not for the time being prohibited by or under this Order or any other enactment; and

(b) does not exceed 10 per cent. by weight of the total catch of sea fish on board that fishing boat.".

In witness whereof the Official Seal of the Minister of Agriculture, Fisheries and Food is hereunto affixed on 4th September 1987.

John Selwyn Gummer
Minister of State,
Ministry of Agriculture, Fisheries and Food

1st September 1987

Ian Lang
Minister of State, Scottish Office

28th August 1987

Ian Grist
Parliamentary Under Secretary of State,
Welsh Office

29th August 1987

Brian S. Mawhinney
Parliamentary Under Secretary of State,
Northern Ireland Office

EXPLANATORY NOTE

(This note is not part of the Order)

This Order varies the Herring and White Fish (Specified Manx Waters) Licensing Order 1983 as varied ("the 1983 Order") which prohibits fishing for herring and for descriptions of white fish specified in the Order within the twelve-mile belt around the Isle of Man but outside territorial waters without a licence.

The reference to the Isle of Man Board of Agriculture and Fisheries is replaced by a reference to the Department of Agriculture, Forestry and Fisheries, the Isle of Man (article 2(a)).

Article 4 of the 1983 Order permits the retention on board a fishing boat of a quantity of one or more of the descriptions of white fish specified therein, the fishing for which is for the time being prohibited, when caught as a by catch not exceeding ten per cent. by weight of the total catch of sea fish on board the fishing boat in the course of lawful fishing for another description of sea fish.

This Order replaces that article and restricts the scope of the new article 4 to a by catch of cod, plaice and whiting, in consequence of which fish of any other description of white fish specified in the 1983 Order, the fishing for which is for the time being prohibited under article 3 thereof, must in all circumstances be returned to the sea forthwith in accordance with the provisions of section 4 (9A) of the Sea Fish (Conservation) Act 1967 (inserted by section 20(4) of the Fisheries Act 1981) (article 2(b)).

STATUTORY INSTRUMENTS

1987 No. 1565

SEA FISHERIES

CONSERVATION OF SEA FISH

The Sea Fish Licensing (Variation) Order 1987

Made - - - -	*4th September 1987*
Laid before Parliament	*7th September 1987*
Coming into force	*8th September 1987*

The Minister of Agriculture, Fisheries and Food, and the Secretaries of State respectively concerned with the sea fishing industry in Scotland, Wales and Northern Ireland, acting jointly, in exercise of the powers conferred on them by sections 4, 15(3) and 20(1) of the Sea Fish (Conservation) Act 1967(a), and of all other powers enabling them in that behalf, hereby make the following Order:

Title and commencement

1. This Order may be cited as the Sea Fish Licensing (Variation) Order 1987 and shall come into force on 8th September 1987.

Variation of the Sea Fish Licensing Order 1983

2. The Sea Fish Licensing Order 1983(b) is hereby varied in accordance with the following provisions of this Order.

3. In article 3(1) thereof (prohibition of fishing without a licence and exceptions thereto), for the words "Isle of Man Board of Agriculture and Fisheries" there shall be substituted the words "Department of Agriculture, Fisheries and Forestry, the Isle of Man".

(a) 1967 c.84; section 4 was amended by the Fishery Limits Act 1976 (c.86), section 3 and by the Fisheries Act 1981 (c.29), section 20; section 15(3) was amended by the Sea Fisheries Act 1968 (c.77), Schedule 1, paragraph 38(3) and by the Fishery Limits Act 1976, Schedule 2, paragraph 16(1); section 4 was applied in relation to British fishing boats registered in the Isle of Man and any of the Channel Islands by the Sea Fish (Conservation) (Manx Boats) Order 1978 (S.I. 1978/281) and the Sea Fish (Conservation) (Channel Islands Boats) Order 1978 (S.I. 1978/280); section 22(2)(a) which contains a definition of "the Ministers" for the purposes of sections 4 and 15(3) was amended by the Fisheries Act 1981, sections 19(2)(d) and 45(b).
(b) S.I. 1983/1206, varied by S.I. 1983/1881 and 1986/1438.

4. In article 3(2)(b) thereof after paragraph (v) the word "or" shall be omitted and after paragraph (vi) there shall be inserted the following –

"; or

(vii) in the Firth of Clyde, that is to say the area of sea which lies landward of a line drawn from a point on the mainland of Scotland at 55°17′.9 north latitude and 5°47′.8 west longitude (Mull of Kintyre) to a point on the mainland of Scotland at 55°00′.5 north latitude and 5°09′.4 west longitude (Corsewall Point)".

5. For article 4 thereof (retention on board of fish) there shall be substituted the following article –

"Retention on board of fish

4. Notwithstanding the provisions of section 4(9A)(b) of the Sea Fish (Conservation) Act 1967 (return to the sea of fish the fishing for which is prohibited), there may be retained on board any fishing boat to which this Order applies a quantity of sea fish consisting of one or more of the descriptions of sea fish specified in an entry in column 2 of Schedule 4 to this Order, the fishing for which is for the time being prohibited by or under this Order, and which –

(a) has been taken on board that fishing boat in a statistical division of ICES VII specified in column 1 of that Schedule opposite that entry, in the course of fishing in that statistical division of ICES VII for any description of sea fish the fishing for which is not for the time being prohibited by or under this Order or any other enactment; and

(b) does not exceed 10 per cent by weight of the total catch of sea fish on board that fishing boat.".

6. After Schedule 3 thereof (orders revoked) there shall be inserted the Schedule to this Order.

In witness whereof the Official Seal of the Minister of Agriculture, Fisheries and Food is hereunto affixed on 4th September 1987.

L.S.

John Selwyn Gummer
Minister of State,
Minister of Agriculture, Fisheries and Food

Ian Lang
1st September 1987   Minister of State, Scottish Office

Ian Grist
Parliamentary Under Secretary of State,
28th August 1987   Welsh Office

Brian S. Mawhinney
Parliamentary Under Secretary of State,
29th August 1987   Northern Ireland Office

Article 6   SCHEDULE

CONTAINING NEW SCHEDULE 4 TO THE SEA
FISH LICENSING ORDER 1983

"SCHEDULE 4   Article 4

AREAS OF SEA AND DESCRIPTIONS OF SEA FISH CAUGHT
THEREIN TO WHICH RETENTION ON BOARD PROVISIONS APPLY

(1) *Area of sea*	(2) *Description of sea fish*
ICES VIIa*	Cod, plaice, whiting
ICES VIIb, c	Whiting
ICES VIId	Plaice, sole, whiting
ICES VIIe*	Plaice, sole, whiting
ICES VIIf to k	Plaice, sole, whiting

Note: Where an entry in column 1 of this Schedule is marked with an asterisk the following waters are excluded from the area of sea referred to in that entry –

Waters lying within 12 miles of the baselines from which the breadth of the territorial sea adjacent to the Isle of Man and the Channel Islands respectively is measured, but not extending beyond a line every point of which is equidistant from the nearest points of such baselines and the corresponding baselines adjacent to the United Kingdom and France respectively."

EXPLANATORY NOTE

(This note is not part of the Order)

This Order varies the Sea Fish Licensing Order 1983, as varied, ("the 1983 Order"), which requires a licence to be obtained for fishing by British fishing boats in specified areas of sea for the principal species of sea fish. Boats not more than ten metres long, other than when fishing for herring in specified areas, are excepted from that requirement; this Order removes from that exception such boats fishing for herring in the Firth of Clyde (article 4).

The Order replaces article 4 of the 1983 Order (retention on board of fish) and adds a new Schedule 4 thereto to provide for the retention on board a fishing boat of a quantity of one or more of the descriptions of sea fish specified in that Schedule not exceeding ten per cent by weight of the total catch of sea fish on board the fishing boat, the fishing for which is for the time being prohibited, caught in a specified statistical division of ICES VII as a by-catch in the course of lawful fishing for another description of sea fish. In consequence fish of descriptions not so specified, the fishing for which is for the time being prohibited under article 3 of the 1983 Order, must in all circumstances be returned to the sea forthwith in accordance with the provisions of section 4(9A) of the Sea Fish (Conservation) Act 1967 (inserted by section 20(4) of the Fisheries Act 1981) (articles 5 and 6).

STATUTORY INSTRUMENTS

1987 No. 1566

SEA FISHERIES

CONSERVATION OF SEA FISH

The Sea Fishing (Specified Western Waters) (Restrictions on Landing) Order 1987

Made - - - -	*4th September 1987*
Laid before Parliament	*7th September 1987*
Coming into force -	*8th September 1987*

The Minister of Agriculture, Fisheries and Food and the Secretaries of State respectively concerned with the sea fishing industry in Scotland, Wales and Northern Ireland, acting jointly, in exercise of the powers conferred on them by sections 6(1), (2) and (3), 15(3) and 20(1) of the Sea Fish (Conservation) Act 1967(a), and of all other powers enabling them in that behalf, after consultation with the Secretary of State for Trade and Industry, hereby make the following Order:

Title and commencement

1. This Order may be cited as the Sea Fishing (Specified Western Waters) (Restrictions on Landing) Order 1987 and shall come into force on 8th September 1987.

Interpretation

2. In this Order–

"British fishing boat" means a fishing boat which is registered in the United Kingdom, the Isle of Man or any of the Channel Islands or which, not being so registered, is British-owned;

"Channel Island waters" means the waters within 12 miles from the baselines from which the breadth of the territorial sea adjacent to any of the Channel Islands is measured but not extending beyond a line every point of which is equidistant from the nearest points of such baselines and the corresponding baselines of France;

"ICES" followed by a roman numeral with or without a letter shall be construed as a reference to whichever of the statistical sub-areas and divisions of the International Council for the Exploration of the Sea(b) described in Schedule 1 or specified in Schedule 3 to this Order is identified therein by that roman numeral or that roman numeral and letter as the case may be;

(a) 1967 c.84; section 6(1) is to be read with the Secretary of State for Trade and Industry Order 1970 (S.I. 1970/1537), Schedule 2, paragraph 10, the Secretary of State (New Departments) Order 1974 (S.I. 1974/692), Schedule I, Part III and the Transfer of Functions (Trade and Industry) Order 1983 (S.I. 1983/1127), article 2(1); section 15(3) was substituted by paragraph 38(3) of Schedule 1 to the Sea Fisheries Act 1968 (c.77) and amended by paragraph 16(1) of Schedule 2 to the Fishery Limits Act 1976 (c.86); section 22(2)(a), which contains a definition of "the Ministers" for the purposes of sections 6(1) and 15(3), was amended by the Fisheries Act 1981 (c.29), sections 19(2)(d) and 45(b).
(b) Cmnd. 2586.

"length" means the length by reference to which the tonnage of a British fishing boat is calculated for the purpose of registration under Part IV of the Merchant Shipping Act 1894(a);

"specified sea fish" means the descriptions of sea fish set out in Schedule 2 to this Order.

Prohibition on landing

3. Subject to article 4 below, the landing in the United Kingdom of any of the specified sea fish caught in ICES VII or VIII is prohibited.

Exceptions from prohibition

4. The prohibition imposed by article 3 above is subject to the following exceptions:–

(a) the landing of specified sea fish caught by any fishing boat which is not a British fishing boat;

(b) the landing of specified sea fish caught by any British fishing boat whose length is not more than 10 metres;

(c) the landing of specified sea fish caught under the authority of a licence granted by or on behalf of one of the Ministers or the Department of Agriculture, Fisheries and Forestry, the Isle of Man;

(d) the landing of any of the specified sea fish caught in any part of ICES VIId or ICES VIIe respectively which is within Channel Island waters, if fishing for that description of sea fish in the remainder of the relevant ICES division is for the time being authorised by a licence granted by or on behalf of one of the Ministers;

(e) the landing of a quantity of sea fish consisting of one or more of the descriptions of sea fish referred to in an entry in column 2 of Schedule 3 to this Order which–

(i) has been caught in a division of ICES VII referred to in column 1 of that Schedule opposite that entry by the fishing boat landing that quantity otherwise than under the authority of a licence granted by or on behalf of one of the Ministers or the Department of Agriculture, Fisheries and Forestry, the Isle of Man, in the course of fishing in that division of ICES VII for another description of sea fish the fishing for which is not prohibited or being prohibited is authorised by such a licence; and

(ii) does not exceed 10 per cent by weight of the landed catch.

Powers of British sea-fishery officers in relation to fishing boats

5.—(1) For the purpose of the enforcement of this Order a British sea-fishery officer may exercise in relation to any British fishing boat anywhere the powers conferred by paragraphs (2) to (4) of this article.

(2) He may go on board the boat, with or without persons assigned to assist him in his duties, and for that purpose may require the boat to stop and do anything else which will facilitate the boarding of the boat.

(3) He may require the attendance of the master and other persons on board the boat and may make any examination and inquiry which appears to him to be necessary for the purpose mentioned in paragraph (1) of this article and, in particular–

(a) may examine any fish on the boat and the equipment of the boat, including the fishing gear, and require persons on board the boat to do anything which appears to him to be necessary for facilitating the examination; and

(b) may require any person on board the boat to produce any document relating to the boat, to its fishing operations or other operations ancillary thereto or to the persons on board which is in his custody or possession and may take copies of any such document;

(c) for the purpose of ascertaining whether the master, owner or charterer of the boat has committed an offence under section 6(5) of the Act as read with this

(a) 1894 c.60.

Order, may search the boat for any such document and may require any person on board the boat to do anything which appears to him to be necessary for facilitating the search;

(d) where the boat is one in relation to which he has reason to suspect that such an offence has been committed, may seize and detain any such document produced to him or found on board for the purpose of enabling the document to be used as evidence in proceedings for the offence;

but nothing in subparagraph (d) above shall permit any document required by law to be carried on board the boat to be seized and detained except while the boat is detained in a port.

(4) Where it appears to a British sea-fishery officer that an offence under this Order has at any time been committed within British fishery limits, he may–

(a) require the master of the boat in relation to which the offence took place to take, or may himself take, the boat and its crew to the port which appears to him to be the nearest convenient port; and

(b) detain or require the master to detain the boat in the port;

and where such an officer detains or requires the detention of a boat he shall serve on the master a notice in writing stating that the boat will be or is required to be detained until the notice is withdrawn by the service on the master of a further notice in writing signed by a British sea-fishery officer.

Revocation

6. The Orders specified in Schedule 4 to this Order are hereby revoked.

In witness whereof the Official Seal of the Minister of Agriculture, Fisheries and Food is hereunto affixed on 4th September 1987.

John Selwyn Gummer
Minister of State,
Minister of Agriculture, Fisheries and Food

Ian Lang
1st September 1987   Minister of State, Scottish Office

Ian Grist
Parliamentary Under Secretary of State,
28th August 1987   Welsh Office

Brian S. Mawhinney
Parliamentary Under Secretary of State,
29th August 1987   Northern Ireland Office

Article 2   SCHEDULE 1

STATISTICAL SUB-AREAS AND DIVISIONS OF THE INTERNATIONAL
COUNCIL FOR THE EXPLORATION OF THE SEA

ICES Statistical Sub-Area VII (Irish Sea, West of Ireland and Porcupine Bank, South Coast of Ireland, Bristol Channel and English Channel)

The waters bounded by a line beginning at a point on the west coast of the Republic of Ireland in 54°30′ north latitude; thence due west to 18°00′ west longitude; thence due south to 48°00′ north latitude; thence due east to the coast of France; thence in a northerly and north-easterly direction along the coast of France to a point in 51°00′ north latitude; thence due west to the south-east coast of England; thence in a westerly and northerly direction along the coasts of England, Wales and Scotland to a point on the West coast of Scotland in 55°00′ north latitude; thence due west to the coast of Northern Ireland; thence in a northerly and westerly direction along the coasts of Northern Ireland and the Republic of Ireland to the point of beginning.

ICES Statistical Division VIIa (Irish Sea)

The waters bounded by a line beginning at a point on the west coast of Scotland in 55°00′ north latitude; thence due west to the coast of Northern Ireland; thence in a southerly direction along the coasts of Northern Ireland and Ireland to a point on the south-east coast of the Republic of Ireland in 52°00′ north latitude; thence due east to the coast of Wales; thence in a north-easterly and northerly direction along the coasts of Wales, England and Scotland to the point of beginning.

ICES Statistical Division VIIb, c (West of Ireland and Porcupine Bank)

The waters bounded by a line beginning at a point on the west coast of Ireland in 54°30′ north latitude; thence due west to 18°00′ west longitude; thence due south to 52°30′ north latitude; thence due east to the coast of Ireland; thence in a northerly direction along the west coast of Ireland to the point of beginning.

ICES Statistical Division VIId (Eastern English Channel)

The waters bounded by a line beginning at a point on the west coast of France in 51°00′ north latitude; thence due west to the coast of England; thence in a westerly direction along the south coast of England to 2°00′ west longitude; thence south to the coast of France at Cape de la Hague; thence in a north-easterly direction along the coast of France to the point of beginning.

ICES Statistical Division VIIe (Western English Channel)

The waters bounded by a line beginning at a point on the south coast of England in 2°00′ west longitude; thence in a southerly and westerly direction along the coast of England to a point on the south-west coast in 50°00′ north latitude; thence due west to 7°00′ west longitude; thence due south to 49°30′ north latitude; thence due east to 5°00′ west longitude; thence due south to 48°00′ north latitude; thence due east to the coast of France; thence in a northerly and north-easterly direction along the coast of France to Cape de la Hague; thence due north to the point of beginning.

ICES Statistical Division VIIf (Bristol Channel)

The waters bounded by a line beginning at a point on the south coast of Wales in 5°00′ west longitude; thence due south to 51°00′ north latitude; thence due west to 6°00′ west longitude; thence due south to 50°30′ north latitude; thence due west to 7°00′ west longitude; thence due south to 50°00′ north latitude; thence due east to the coast of England; thence along the south-west coast of England and the south coast of Wales to the point of beginning.

ICES Statistical Division VIIg (South-east of Ireland)

The waters bounded by a line beginning at a point in 9°00′ west longitude on the south coast of Ireland; thence due south to 50°00′ north latitude; thence due east to 7°00′ west longitude; thence due north to 50°30′ north latitude; thence due east to 6°00′ west longitude; thence due north to 51°00′ north latitude; thence due east to 5°00′ west longitude; thence due north to the south coast of Wales; thence in a north-westerly direction along the coast of Wales to a point in 52°00′ north latitude; thence due west to the south-east coast of the Republic of Ireland; thence in a south-westerly direction along the coast of the Republic of Ireland to the point of beginning.

ICES Statistical Division VIIh (Little Sole Bank)

The waters bounded by a line beginning at a point in 50°00′ north latitude 7°00′ west longitude; thence due west to 9°00′ west longitude; thence due south to 48°00′ north latitude; thence due east to 5°00′ west longitude; thence due north to 49°30′ north latitude; thence due west to 7°00′ west longitude; thence due north to the point of beginning.

ICES Statistical Division VIIj (Great Sole Bank)

The waters bounded by a line beginning at a point in 52°30′ north latitude on the west coast of the Republic of Ireland; thence due west to 12°00′ west longitude; thence due south to 48°00′ north latitude; thence due east to 9°00′ west longitude; thence due north to the south coast of the Republic of Ireland; thence in a westerly and northerly direction along the coast of the Republic of Ireland to the point of beginning.

ICES Statistical Division VIIk (West of Great Sole Bank)

The waters bounded by a line beginning at a point in 52°30′ north latitude; 12°00′ west longitude; thence due west to 18°00′ west longitude; thence due south to 48°00′ north latitude; thence due east to 12°00′ west longitude; thence due north to the point of beginning.

ICES Statistical Sub-Area VIII (Bay of Biscay)

The waters bounded by a line beginning at a point on the coast of France in 48°00′ north latitude; thence due west to 18°00′ west longitude; thence due south to 43°00′ north latitude; thence due east to the coast of Spain; thence in a northerly direction along the coasts of Spain and France to the point of beginning.

SCHEDULE 2 Articles 2 and 3

SPECIFIED SEA FISH

Anglerfish (*Lophius spp*)
Cod (*Gadus morhua*)
Haddock (*Melanogrammus aeglefinus*)
Hake (*Merluccius spp*)
Herring (*Clupea harengus*)
Mackerel (*Scomber scombrus*)
Megrim (*Lepidorhombus whiffiagonis*)
Norway lobster (*Nephrops norvegicus*)
Plaice (*Pleuronectes platessa*)
Pollack (*Pollachius pollachius*)
Saithe (*Pollachius virens*)
Sole (*Solea solea*)
Sprat (*Sprattus sprattus*)
Whiting (*Merlangius merlangus*)

SCHEDULE 3 Articles 2 and 4(3)

STATISTICAL DIVISIONS OF ICES VII AND DESCRIPTIONS OF SEA FISH CAUGHT THEREIN TO WHICH EXCEPTION FROM LANDING PROHIBITION APPLIES

(1) *Statistical division*	(2) *Description of sea fish*
ICES VIIa	Cod, plaice, whiting
ICES VIIb, c	Whiting
ICES VIId to k	Plaice, sole, whiting

Article 6

SCHEDULE 4

REVOCATIONS

(1) Order revoked	(2) References
The Sea Fishing (Specified Western Waters) (Restrictions on Landing) Order 1980	S.I. 1980/335
The Sea Fishing (Specified Western Waters) (Restrictions on Landing) (Variation) Order 1983	S.I. 1983/1205
The Sea Fishing (Specified Western Waters) (Restrictions on Landing) (Variation) Order 1984	S.I. 1984/92
The Sea Fishing (Specified Western Waters) (Restrictions on Landing) (Variation) Order 1986	S.I. 1986/1437

EXPLANATORY NOTE

(This note is not part of the Order)

This Order consolidates with changes the provisions of the Sea Fishing (Specified Western Waters) (Restrictions on Landing) Order 1980 as varied ("the 1980 Order"). The Order prohibits, with exceptions, the landing in the United Kingdom of sea fish of descriptions specified in Schedule 2 to the Order caught in ICES sub-areas VII or VIII (article 3).

The provisions of this Order differ from those of the 1980 Order which it replaces in the following respects:–

(a) fishing boats registered in the Isle of Man or any of the Channel Islands are included in the definition of a "British fishing boat" (article 2);

(b) the enforcement powers conferred on British sea-fishery officers in relation to fishing boats are included in the text, their powers on land being set out in section 15(2A) of the Sea Fish (Conservation) Act 1967 (article 5);

(c) all of the statistical sub-areas and divisions of the International Council for the Exploration of the Sea to which the prohibition of landing provisions and exceptions thereto apply are described (Schedule 2);

(d) those descriptions of sea fish caught in particular divisions of ICES VII otherwise than under the authority of a licence as a by catch not exceeding 10 per cent by weight of the landed catch in the course of lawful fishing for another description sea fish, which by virtue of article 4(e) of the Order may be landed in the United Kingdom as an exception to the prohibition on landing provisions, are listed (Schedule 3).

STATUTORY INSTRUMENTS

1987 No. 1567

PUBLIC HEALTH, ENGLAND AND WALES
PUBLIC HEALTH, SCOTLAND
PUBLIC HEALTH, NORTHERN IRELAND

CONTAMINATION OF FOOD

The Food Protection (Emergency Prohibitions) Amendment Order 1987

Made - - - -	*4th September 1987*
Laid before Parliament	*7th September 1987*
Coming into force	*7th September 1987*

Whereas the Secretary of State is of the opinion, as mentioned in section 1(1)(a) of the Food and Environment Protection Act 1985(**a**), that there has been or may have been an escape of substances of such descriptions and in such quantities and such circumstances as are likely to create a hazard to human health through human consumption of food;

And whereas he is of the opinion, as mentioned in section 1(1)(b) of the said Act, that in consequence of the said escape of substances, food which is, or may be in the future, in the areas described in the Schedule to the principal Order or which is, or may be in the future, derived from anything in those areas, is, or may be, or may become, unsuitable for human consumption;

Now, therefore, in exercise of the powers conferred on him by sections 1(1) and (2) and 24(1) and (3) of the said Act(**b**), and of all other powers enabling him in that behalf, he hereby makes the following Order:

Title, commencement and interpretation

1.—(1) This Order may be cited as the Food Protection (Emergency Prohibitions) Amendment Order 1987 and shall come into force on 7th September 1987.

(2) In this Order the "principal Order" means the Food Protection (Emergency Prohibitions) Order 1987(**c**).

(**a**) 1985 c.48.
(**b**) Section 24(1) contains a definition of "the Ministers" relevant to the exercise of the statutory powers under which this Order is made.
(**c**) S.I. 1987/1165.

Designated incident

2. In the opinion of the Secretary of State, food in the areas described in the Schedule to the principal Order, or which is derived from anything in those areas, is or may be unsuitable for human consumption in consequence of the following escape of substances:–

the escape on or after 26th April 1986 of radioactive substances from a nuclear reactor situated at Chernobyl in the Ukraine, USSR.

Amendment of the principal Order

3.—(1) Article 4 of the principal Order shall be re-numbered article 4(1) and after that paragraph there shall be inserted the following paragraph:–

"(2) Paragraph (1) above shall not apply in the case of any sheep which–

(a) was moved from any place in accordance with a consent given under section 2(1) of the Food and Environment Protection Act 1985 which consent was subject to the condition that the sheep to which it applies should be marked with an apricot mark, or with a green mark; and

(b) has been examined and marked with an ear-tag by a person authorised in that behalf by one of the Ministers.".

(2) Article 5 of the principal Order shall be re-numbered article 5(1) and after that paragraph there shall be inserted the following paragraph:–

"(2) Paragraph (1) above shall not apply in the case of any sheep which was moved from any place in accordance with a consent given under section 2(1) of the said Act which consent was subject to the condition that the sheep to which it applies should be marked with an apricot mark, or with a green mark.".

(3) Article 6 of the principal Order shall be re-numbered article 6(1) and after that paragraph there shall be inserted the following paragraph:–

"(2) Paragraph (1) above shall not apply in the case of any sheep which–

(a) has been moved in accordance with a consent given under section 2(1) of the said Act which consent was subject to the condition that the sheep to which it applies should be marked with an apricot mark, or with a green mark; and

(b) has been examined and marked with an ear-tag by a person authorised in that behalf by one of the Ministers.".

New St. Andrew's House, Edinburgh
4th September 1987

J.W.L. Lonie
Assistant Secretary,
Scottish office

EXPLANATORY NOTE

(This note is not part of the Order)

The Food Protection (Emergency Prohibitions) (No. 2) Order 1987 ("the principal Order") contains emergency prohibitions restricting various activities in order to prevent human consumption of food which has been or which may have been rendered unsuitable for that purpose in consequence of the escape of radioactive substances from a nuclear reactor situated at Chernobyl in the Ukraine, USSR.

This Order excepts certain sheep from the following prohibitions imposed by the principal Order:–

   (a) the prohibition on slaughter of sheep in any of the designated areas (article 3(1));
   (b) the prohibition on movement (article 3(2));
   (c) the prohibition applying throughout the United Kingdom on the slaughter of, and the supply of meat derived from, sheep which have been in the designated areas (article 3(3)).

In article 3(2) an exception is made in respect of sheep which have been marked with an apricot or a green mark. In article 3(1) and (3) exceptions are made in respect of sheep which have been so marked and which have in addition been examined and marked with an ear-tag by a person authorised by the Minister of Agriculture, Fisheries and Food or the Secretary of State for Scotland or Wales.

STATUTORY INSTRUMENTS

1987 No. 1568

PUBLIC HEALTH, ENGLAND AND WALES
PUBLIC HEALTH, SCOTLAND
PUBLIC HEALTH, NORTHERN IRELAND

CONTAMINATION OF FOOD

The Food Protection (Emergency Prohibitions) (No. 2) Amendment Order 1987

Made - - - -	*4th September 1987*
Laid before Parliament	*7th September 1987*
Coming into force	*7th September 1987*

Whereas the Secretary of State is of the opinion, as mentioned in section 1(1)(a) of the Food and Environment Protection Act 1985(**a**), that there has been or may have been an escape of substances of such descriptions and in such quantities and such circumstances as are likely to create a hazard to human health through human consumption of food;

And whereas he is of the opinion, as mentioned in section 1(1)(b) of the said Act, that in consequence of the said escape of substances, food which is, or may be in the future, in the areas described in the Schedule to the principal Order, or which is, or may be in the future, derived from anything in those areas, is, or may be, or may become, unsuitable for human consumption;

Now, therefore, in exercise of the powers conferred on him by sections 1(1) and (2), and 24(1) and (3) of the said Act(**b**), and of all other powers enabling him in that behalf, he hereby makes the following Order:

Title, commencement and interpretation

1.—(1) This Order may be cited as the Food Protection (Emergency Prohibitions) (No. 2) Amendment Order 1987 and shall come into force on 7th September 1987.

(2) In this Order the "principal Order" means the Food Protection (Emergency Prohibitions) (No. 2) Order 1987(**c**).

(**a**) 1985 c.48.
(**b**) Section 24(1) contains a definition of "the Ministers" relevant to the exercise of the statutory powers under which this Order is made.
(**c**) S.I. 1987/1450.

Designated incident

2. In the opinion of the Secretary of State, food in the areas described in the Schedule to the principal Order, or which is derived from anything in those areas, is or may be unsuitable for human consumption in consequence of the following escape of substances:–

the escape on or after 26th April 1986 of radioactive substances from a nuclear reactor situated at Chernobyl in the Ukraine, USSR.

Amendment of the principal Order

3.—(1) Article 4 of the principal Order shall be re-numbered article 4(1) and after that paragraph there shall be inserted the following paragraph:–

"(2) Paragraph (1) above shall not apply in the case of any sheep which–

(a) was moved from any place in accordance with a consent given under section 2(1) of the Food and Environment Protection Act 1985 which consent was subject to the condition that the sheep to which it applies should be marked with an apricot mark, or with a green mark; and

(b) has been examined and marked with an ear-tag by a person authorised in that behalf by one of the Ministers.".

(2) Article 5 of the principal Order shall be re-numbered article 5(1) and after that paragraph there shall be inserted the following paragraph:–

"(2) Paragraph (1) above shall not apply in the case of any sheep which was moved from any place in accordance with a consent given under section 2(1) of the said Act which consent was subject to the condition that the sheep to which it applies should be marked with an apricot mark, or with a green mark.".

(3) Article 6 of the principal Order shall be re-numbered article 6(1) and after that paragraph there shall be inserted the following paragraph:–

"(2) Paragraph (1) above shall not apply in the case of any sheep which–

(a) has been moved in accordance with a consent given under section 2(1) of the said Act which consent was subject to the condition that the sheep to which it applies should be marked with an apricot mark, or with a green mark; and

(b) has been examined and marked with an ear-tag by a person authorised in that behalf by one of the Ministers.".

New St. Andrew's House, Edinburgh
4th September 1987

J. W. L. Lonie
Assistant Secretary,
Scottish Office

EXPLANATORY NOTE

(This note is not part of the Order)

The Food Protection (Emergency Prohibitions) Order 1987 ("the principal Order") contains emergency prohibitions restricting various activities in order to prevent human consumption of food which has been or which may have been rendered unsuitable for that purpose in consequence of the escape of radioactive substances from a nuclear reactor situated at Chernobyl, in the Ukraine, USSR.

This Order excepts certain sheep from the following prohibitions imposed by the principal Order:–

(a) the prohibition on slaughter of sheep in any of the designated areas (article 3(1));

(b) the prohibition on movement (article 3(2));

(c) the prohibition applying throughout the United Kingdom on the slaughter of, and the supply of meat derived from, sheep which have been in the designated areas (article 3(3)).

In article 3(2) an exception is made in respect of sheep which have been marked with an apricot or a green mark. In article 3(1) and (3) exceptions are made in respect of sheep which have been so marked and which have in addition been examined and marked with an ear-tag by a person authorised by the Minister of Agriculture, Fisheries and Food or the Secretary of State for Scotland or Wales.

STATUTORY INSTRUMENTS

1987 No. 1578

CONSUMER CREDIT

The Consumer Credit (Exempt Agreements) (No. 2) (Amendment) Order 1987

Made - - - -	*7th September 1987*
Laid before Parliament	*10th September 1987*
Coming into force	*1st October 1987*

The Secretary of State, after consulting in accordance with section 16(3) and (9) of the Consumer Credit Act 1974(**a**) the persons therein referred to, in exercise of the powers conferred on him by sections 16(1) and (4) and 182(2) and (4) of that Act and of all other powers enabling him in that behalf, hereby makes the following Order:

1. This Order may be cited as the Consumer Credit (Exempt Agreements) (No. 2) (Amendment) Order 1987 and shall come into force on 1st October 1987.

2. The Consumer Credit (Exempt Agreements) (No. 2) Order 1985(**b**) is hereby amended as follows–

    (a) in Article 2(2) by inserting, after the words "a building society authorised under the Building Societies Act 1986", the words "or an authorised institution under the Banking Act 1987 or a wholly-owned subsidiary of such an institution";

    (b) in Part I of the Schedule, in the list of Insurance Companies–

        (i) by omitting the name "World-Wide Assurance Company Limited" and substituting therefor the name "World-Wide Reassurance Company Limited"; and

        (ii) by inserting, at the appropriate place in alphabetical order, the name "National House-Building Council";

    (c) in the said Part I of the Schedule, in the list of Friendly Societies, by inserting at the appropriate place in alphabetical order the name "Independent Order of Oddfellows Kingston Unity Friendly Society"; and

    (d) in Part II of the Schedule, in the list of bodies corporate named or specifically referred to in a public general Act (United Kingdom) by omitting the entries relating to–

(**a**) 1974 c.39; section 16 was amended by the Employment Protection Act 1975 (c.71), Schedule 18, the Telecommunications Act 1984 (c.12), Schedule 4, paragraph 60, the Building Societies Act 1986 (c.53), Schedule 18, the Housing and Planning Act 1986 (c.63), section 22 and the Banking Act 1987 (c.22), section 88.
(**b**) S.I. 1985/757, amended by S.I. 1985/1736, 1918, 1986/1105, 2186.

Barclays Bank PLC
Coutts Finance Co.
The Royal Bank of Scotland p.l.c.
TSB England & Wales public limited company
TSB Northern Ireland public limited company
TSB Scotland public limited company

Francis Maude
Parliamentary Under-Secretary of State,
7th September 1987   Department of Trade and Industry

EXPLANATORY NOTE

(This note is not part of the Order)

This Order further amends the Consumer Credit (Exempt Agreements) (No. 2) Order 1985 ("the principal Order") insofar as it provides for the exemption of certain consumer credit agreements secured on land where the creditor is a body specified in the Schedule to the principal Order or a building society authorised under the Building Societies Act 1986. The Order

(a) provides for the exemption of certain agreements made by an authorised institution within the meaning of the Banking Act 1987, or a wholly-owned subsidiary of such an institution (Article 2(a)), consequent upon the coming into force of relevant provisions of the Banking Act 1987;

(b) amends the list of insurance companies in Part I of the Schedule to the principal Order by adding one name and amending another (Article 2(b));

(c) amends the list of friendly societies in Part I of the Schedule by adding one name (Article 2(c)); and

(d) amends the entries in Part II of the Schedule by omitting the names of six companies which are authorised institutions (Article 2(d)).

1987 No. 1579

LOCAL GOVERNMENT, ENGLAND AND WALES

The Local Government Reorganisation (Pensions etc.) (Greater Manchester and Merseyside) Order 1987

Made - - - -	*7th September 1987*
Laid before Parliament	*10th September 1987*
Coming into force	*1st October 1987*

The Secretary of State for the Environment, in exercise of the powers conferred on him by section 67(3) of the Local Government Act 1985(**a**), and of all other powers enabling him in that behalf, to effect transfers proposed to him under section 67(1)(a) of that Act, hereby makes the following Order:

Citation, commencement and interpretation

1.—(1) This Order may be cited as the Local Government Reorganisation (Pensions etc.) (Greater Manchester and Merseyside) Order 1987 and shall come into force on 1st October 1987.

(2) In this Order –

"the Act" means the Local Government Act 1985;

"transferor authority" means a body from which matters are transferred by article 2; and

"transferee authority" means a body to which matters are transferred by article 2.

Transfer of pension and other functions

2. On 1st October 1987 –

(a) the functions, property, rights and liabilities of the Greater Manchester Residuary Body which are specified in the Schedule shall become the functions, property, rights and liabilities of the council of the borough of Tameside; and

(b) the functions, property, rights and liabilities of the Merseyside Residuary Body which are specified in the Schedule shall become the functions, property, rights and liabilities of the council of the borough of Wirral.

(**a**) 1985 c.51.

Reimbursement

3.—(1) The total for any financial year of the expenditure described in paragraph (2) of a transferee authority shall be apportioned between all the district councils in the county in which the authority is situated in proportion to the population of their districts, as that population is certified for the making of levies with respect to that year under section 74(2) of the Act (levies by residuary bodies); and the appropriate portions shall be recoverable by the authority from each of the other district councils.

(2) The expenditure referred to in paragraph (1) is the expenditure of the transferee authority with respect to the matters mentioned in paragraph 1(b) and (c) of the Schedule (including the costs of the authority incidental to the making of any payments in connection with those matters) less –

(a) any amounts received by the authority with respect to those matters in consequence of this Order, and

(b) any amount of such expenditure as would have fallen to be met by the authority (otherwise than under section 74 of the Act) apart from this Order.

(3) In the event of a dispute between a transferee authority and another council as to the amount of any expenditure referred to in paragraph (2), as between the authority and that council the amount is to be determined by an arbitrator appointed by the Secretary of State; and section 31 of the Arbitration Act 1950**(a)** shall have effect in relation to the arbitration as if it were an arbitration to which that section applies.

(4) Notwithstanding any winding up of a transferor authority pursuant to section 67 of the Act, the functions of the Registrar General and the Secretary of State under section 74(2) of the Act shall continue with respect to the certification of population for the purposes of the reimbursement of a transferee authority under this article.

Continuity of the exercise of functions

4.—(1) Anything done by or in relation to (or having effect as if done by or in relation to) a transferor authority in the exercise of or in connection with a matter transferred by article 2 shall, so far as is required for continuing its effect on or after 1st October 1987, have effect as if done by or in relation to the transferee authority to which that matter is transferred.

(2) Without prejudice to the generality of paragraph (1), that paragraph applies to the making of any application, decision, or determination, to the giving of any notice, to the entering into of any agreement or other instrument, and to the bringing of any action or proceeding; but it shall not be construed as transferring any employee of a transferor authority to the employment of a transferee authority.

(3) Any pending action or proceeding may be amended in such manner as may be necessary or proper in consequence of this Order.

Other supplementary provision

5.—(1) The Local Government Superannuation Regulations 1986**(b)** are amended as follows –

(a) 1950 c.27; section 31 was repealed in part by the Arbitration Act 1975 (c.3), section 8(2), and amended by the Arbitration Act 1979 (c.42), section 7(1).
(b) S.I. 1986/24, amended by S.I. 1986/380 and 1987/293.

(a) in regulation C1(7A), by substituting for the Table the following Table –

"TABLE

(1)	(2)
Greater Manchester	Tameside
Merseyside	Wirral
Tyne and Wear	South Tyneside
West Midlands	Wolverhampton
West Yorkshire	Bradford

";

(b) in regulation P1(1), by substituting for the words "section 66" the words "sections 66 or 67".

(2) Without prejudice to the generality of article 4 (continuity of the exercise of functions) –

(a) any admission agreement within the meaning of the Local Government Superannuation Regulations 1986 in force immediately before 1st October 1987 whereby employees of any body were, or could become, admitted employees participating in the benefits of a superannuation fund maintained under those Regulations by a transferor authority shall be of full force and effect in favour of, or against, the transferee authority to which that fund is transferred by article 2;

(b) where a person has ceased to contribute to such a fund and has not become a contributor to any other superannuation fund maintained under those Regulations, the transferred fund shall on and after 1st October 1987 be deemed to be the fund to which he was last a contributor; and

(c) the transferee authority maintaining a superannuation fund transferred by article 2 is to be treated as being the previous fund authority for the purposes of Part Q of those Regulations in place of the transferor authority from which it was transferred.

(3) Section 61(5) of the Act shall continue to have effect, so that no liability to reimburse a transferee authority in respect of any payment made by it shall attach to the Secretary of State, the Arts Council of Great Britain or the Historic Buildings and Monuments Commission for England where no liability to reimburse the transferor authority would have attached to them if this Order had not been made and the payments concerned had been made by the transferor authority; and paragraphs 64A and 64B of Schedule 2 to the Pensions (Increase) Act 1971(a) shall continue to have effect as if references to a pension payable by a residuary body included references to a pension payable by a transferee authority.

Nicholas Ridley

7th September 1987 Secretary of State for the Environment

(a) 1971 c.56; paragraphs 64A and 64B of Schedule 2 were inserted by the Local Government Act 1985 (c.51), section 61(2).

Article 2

SCHEDULE

FUNCTIONS, PROPERTY, RIGHTS AND LIABILITIES TRANSFERRED

1. Subject to paragraph 3, the functions, property, rights and liabilities which are transferred by article 2 are –

    (a) the functions of the Greater Manchester Residuary Body and the Merseyside Residuary Body as administering authority under the Local Government Superannuation Regulations 1986, together with the superannuation fund maintained by those bodies and all property, rights and liabilities of those bodies in respect of it;

    (b) the functions, rights and liabilities of those bodies in respect of pensions payable by them otherwise than under those Regulations; and

    (c) without prejudice to the foregoing, the functions, rights and liabilities which are vested in or fall to be discharged by those bodies under or by virtue of section 61 of the Act (payment of pensions increases).

2. In paragraph 1(b), references to pensions include references to –

    (a) allowances, grants or other benefits in respect of past service, death, injury or disease (whether of the pensioner or another person);

    (b) compensation under regulations made under section 24 of the Superannuation Act 1972(**a**); and

    (c) any other such compensation as is mentioned in section 8(1)(b) of the Pensions (Increase) Act 1971.

3.—(1) There shall not transfer under article 2 the functions of the Greater Manchester Residuary Body or the Merseyside Residuary Body in crediting a person with a period of additional service under regulation 5 of the Local Government (Compensation for Premature Retirement) Regulations 1982(**b**).

(2) There shall not transfer under article 2 any matter relating to the payment of compensation for loss of employment or loss or diminution of emoluments arising with respect to an employment with the Greater Manchester Residuary Body or the Merseyside Residuary Body unless that compensation is –

    (a) compensation under the Local Government (Compensation for Premature Retirement) Regulations 1982 payable in consequence of a person having been credited by one of those bodies with a period of additional service under regulation 5 of those Regulations;

    (b) compensation under Part II of the Local Government Reorganisation (Compensation) Regulations 1986(**c**) payable in consequence of a person being treated as having been credited with a period of additional service under regulation 3(2)(b)(i) of those Regulations, or compensation under Part III of those Regulations; or

    (c) compensation under rights preserved by section 53(3) of the Act which falls to be calculated by reference to a person having been credited with a period of additional service.

(3) There shall not transfer under article 2 any matter relating to the payment of compensation for loss of employment or loss or diminution of emoluments arising with respect to an employment with a body other than the Greater Manchester Residuary Body or the Merseyside Residuary Body if that compensation is –

(**a**) 1972 c.11.
(**b**) S.I. 1982/1009, amended by S.I. 1984/740 and 1986/151.
(**c**) S.I. 1986/151.

(a) compensation under Part VI of the Employment Protection (Consolidation) Act 1978(a) (including that Part as applied by section 59 of the Act) or Part II of the Local Government (Compensation for Redundancy and Premature Retirement) Regulations 1984(b);

(b) compensation under Part II of the Local Government Reorganisation (Compensation) Regulations 1986 which is not payable in consequence of a person being treated as having been credited with a period of additional service under regulation 3(2)(b)(i) of those Regulations; or

(c) compensation under rights preserved by section 53(3) of the Act, or under rights arising by virtue of section 59(4) of the Act, which does not fall to be calculated by reference to a person having been credited with a period of additional service.

(4) There shall not transfer under article 2 any matter relating to the making of payments under a scheme made pursuant to section 59(3) of the Act.

(5) There shall not transfer under article 2 any matter relating to the payment of compensation under paragraph 3(3) of Schedule 13 to the Act.

(6) There shall not transfer under article 2 any rights of the Greater Manchester Residuary Body to recover sums paid unlawfully by the Greater Manchester County Council to any of its employees or former employees.

(7) There shall not transfer under article 2 any matter mentioned in paragraph 1(c) of this Schedule (payment of pensions increases) in cases where the functions of the Greater Manchester Residuary Body or the Merseyside Residuary Body with respect to the payment of the pension by reference to which the relevant increase is payable are not transferred under that article.

EXPLANATORY NOTE

(This note is not part of the Order)

This Order gives effect to proposals made by the Greater Manchester Residuary Body and the Merseyside Residuary Body for the transfer of the responsibility for pension and certain related compensation functions from those bodies to the councils of the boroughs of Tameside and Wirral respectively (article 2 and the Schedule). Subject to certain exceptions (paragraph 3 of the Schedule), the compensation matters transferred concern compensation for loss of office or employment and loss or diminution of emoluments. The costs which will fall on those councils and which are not otherwise recoverable by them are to be shared with the councils of the other districts in each county (article 3).

Article 4 makes supplementary and transitional provision for the continuity of the exercise of the transferred functions. Further supplementary provision is made by article 5, including necessary amendments to the Local Government Superannuation Regulations 1986.

(a) 1978 c.44; Part VI was amended by the Employment Act 1980 (c.42), Schedule 2, by the Employment Act 1982 (c.46), Schedule 2, paragraph 6, Schedule 3, paragraph 2 and Schedule 4, and by the Wages Act 1986 (c.48), section 27 and Schedule 4, paragraph 8; it also has effect in certain cases as modified by the Redundancy Payments (Local Government) (Modification) Order 1983 (S.I. 1983/1160, amended by S.I. 1985/1872).
(b) S.I. 1984/740.

STATUTORY INSTRUMENTS

1987 No. 1583

LOCAL GOVERNMENT, ENGLAND AND WALES

The Local Government (Prescribed Expenditure) (Works) Regulations 1987

Made - - - -	*7th September 1987*
Laid before Parliament	*10th September 1987*
Coming into force	*1st October 1987*

The Secretary of State for the Environment and the Secretary of State for Transport, as respects England, and the Secretary of State for Wales, as respects Wales, in exercise of the powers conferred on them by sections 80A(7) and 84 of the Local Government, Planning and Land Act 1980(**a**) and of all other powers enabling them in that behalf, hereby make the following Regulations:

Citation and commencement

1. These Regulations may be cited as the Local Government (Prescribed Expenditure) (Works) Regulations 1987 and shall come into force on 1st October 1987.

Interpretation

2. In these Regulations–

"the Act" means the Local Government, Planning and Land Act 1980;

"dwelling-house" shall be construed in accordance with section 112 of the Housing Act 1985(**b**) but shall not include any hostel or lodging-house as defined in sections 622 and 56 of that Act respectively; and references to a dwelling-house shall include references to any outhouses and appurtenances belonging to the dwelling-house or usually enjoyed with it;

"housing authority" means a district council, a London borough council, the Common Council of the City of London or the Council of the Isles of Scilly;

"long lease" shall be construed in accordance with section 458 of the Housing Act 1985;

"new town corporation" means a development corporation established by an order made, or having effect as if made, under the New Towns Act 1981(**c**), or the Commission for the New Towns;

"project" means the aggregate of the works included in a single contract or in two or more contracts where the works are to be carried out on the same or adjacent sites;

"public body" means a housing authority, a county council, a new town corporation, an urban development corporation or the Development Board for Rural Wales;

"shared ownership lease" shall be construed in accordance with section 622 of the Housing Act 1985;

(**a**) 1980 c. 65; section 80A was inserted by, and section 84 amended by, section 1 of the Local Government Act 1987 (c. 44). The functions of the Minister of Transport under section 84(5) of the Local Government, Planning and Land Act 1980 were transferred to the Secretary of State for Transport by article 2(1)(b) of the Transfer of Functions (Transport) Order 1981 (S.I. 1981/238).
(**b**) 1985 c. 68.
(**c**) 1981 c. 64.

"subsidiary" shall be construed in accordance with section 736 of the Companies Act 1985(**a**).

Cases to which section 80A(1) of the Act does not apply

3. (1) Subject to paragraph (2), section 80A(1) of the Act shall not apply in relation to any works carried out for any authority on or after 1st October 1987 which comprise or form part of a project which is estimated to cost three million pounds or less at the date on which the contract relating to it or, if more than one, the first such contract is made (a "qualifying project").

(2) Paragraph (1) shall not exclude the application of section 80A(1) to a second or further qualifying project carried out for the same authority unless there is an interval of at least sixty consecutive months between the commencement of works on that project and the last previous qualifying project.

(3) Subject to paragraph (4), section 80A(1) of the Act shall not apply in relation to works for the construction, preparation, conversion, improvement, renewal or replacement of a dwelling-house carried out for a housing authority on or after 23rd July 1986 pursuant to an agreement whereby the authority retains its interest in the land on which the works are carried out if that agreement provides (or that agreement and any other agreement or arrangement made in connection with that agreement or any variation or extension of those agreements or arrangements together provide) for–

(a) the sale or the grant of a long lease of the dwelling-house by the authority to a person other than–

(i) a public body, or

(ii) a company which is under the control of a public body; or

(b) the retention of the dwelling-house by the authority for the sole purpose of enabling the authority to grant a shared ownership lease.

(4) Paragraph (3) shall not apply if the authority does anything that has the effect of releasing it from its obligations to sell or grant a lease of the dwelling-house as mentioned in paragraph 3(a) or (b).

(5) A company shall be treated for the purposes of paragraph (3) as under the control of a public body if at the time of the agreement, arrangement, variation or extension either–

(a) it is a subsidiary of a single public body; or

(b) if two or more public bodies who are members of the company were a single body corporate, it would be a subsidiary of that body corporate.

Prescribed expenditure

4. Where works to which section 80A(1) does not apply by virtue of regulation 3 are carried out for an authority, the authority shall be taken for the purposes of Part VIII of the Act (capital expenditure of local authorities etc.) to make payments in respect of expenditure on the works when and as they are actually made.

Nicholas Ridley
Secretary of State for the Environment

7th September 1987

Paul Channon
Secretary of State for Transport

2nd September 1987

Signed by authority of the Secretary of State

Wyn Roberts
Minister of State, Welsh Office

28th August 1987

(**a**) 1985 c. 6.

EXPLANATORY NOTE

(This note is not part of the Regulations)

Section 72(3) of the Local Government, Planning and Land Act 1980 limits the prescribed expenditure of a local authority and other bodies to which Part VIII of the Act applies. "Prescribed expenditure" is essentially expenditure of a capital nature. Section 80A of the Local Government, Planning and Land Act 1980 (inserted by the Local Government Act 1987) regulates the amount of prescribed expenditure that authorities and other bodies are taken to have incurred when capital works are carried out for them and the time at which it is treated as incurred.

These Regulations provide two exemptions. The first exemption relates to projects which are estimated to cost not more than three million pounds. It is restricted to one project in any period of 60 consecutive months (regulation 3(1)). The second exemption relates to projects carried out for housing authorities which consist of the construction and improvement of dwelling-houses. In order to qualify for this exemption the authority must retain its interest in the land on which the works are carried out and provision must be made in the arrangements relating to the project for the sale or grant of a long lease of the dwelling-house to a person other than a public body or a company which is under the control of a public body, or for the grant by the authority of a shared ownership lease (regulation 3(3)).

The first exemption applies to works which are carried out on or after 1st October 1987. The second exemption applies to works carried out on or after 23rd July 1986 (the relevant date for the purposes of the prescribed expenditure arrangements contained in section 80A of the Act).

Where the exemptions apply, authorities will be treated as incurring prescribed expenditure of amounts equal to the payments which they make in relation to the exempt works at the times when those payments are made (regulation 4).

STATUTORY INSTRUMENTS

1987 No. 1590

SOCIAL SECURITY

The Social Security (Contributions) Amendment (No.3) Regulations 1987

Made - - - -	4th September 1987
Laid before Parliament	15th September 1987
Coming into force -	6th October 1987

The Secretary of State for Social Services, in exercise of powers conferred upon him by sections 3(2) and (3) and 168(1) of, and Schedule 20 to, the Social Security Act 1975(a) and of all other powers enabling him in that behalf, after reference to the Social Security Advisory Committee(b), hereby makes the following Regulations:–

Citation, commencement and interpretation

1.—(1) These Regulations may be cited as the Social Security (Contributions) Amendment (No.3) Regulations 1987 and shall come into force on 6th October 1987.

(2) In these Regulations "the principal Regulations" means the Social Security (Contributions) Regulations 1979(c).

Amendment of regulation 19 of the principal Regulations

2. In regulation 19 of the principal Regulations (payments to be disregarded) sub-paragraph (e) of paragraph (1) shall be omitted.

Insertion of regulation 19A in the principal Regulations

3. After regulation 19 of the principal Regulations there shall be inserted the following regulation:–

"Certain payments by trustees to be disregarded

19A.—(1) For the purposes of earnings-related contributions, there shall be excluded from the computation of a person's earnings in respect of any employed earner's employment any payment, or any part of a payment,–

    (a) which is made by trustees before 6th April 1990,

    (b) the amount of which is or may be dependent upon the exercise by the trustees of a discretion or the performance by them of a duty arising under the trust,

    (c) not being a sickness payment which by virtue of section 3(1A) of the Act is treated as remuneration derived from an employed earner's employment,

---

(a) 1975 c.14; *see* definitions of "prescribe" and "regulations" in Schedule 20.
(b) *See* sections 9 and 10 of the Social Security Act 1980 (c.30).
(c) S.I. 1979/591; the relevant amending instrument is S.I. 1983/395.

and in respect of which either the condition contained in paragraph (2) or the conditions contained in paragraph (3) of this regulation is or are satisfied.

(2) The condition referred to in paragraph (1) of this regulation as being contained in this paragraph is that the trust under which the payment is made was created before 6th April 1985.

(3) The conditions referred to in paragraph (1) of this regulation as being contained in this paragraph are–
  (a) that the trust under which the payment is made was created on or after 6th April 1985,
  (b) that that trust took effect immediately on the termination of a trust created before 6th April 1985,
  (c) that the person to whom the payment is made either
    (i) was a beneficiary under the earlier trust, or
    (ii) would have been such a beneficiary if while the earlier trust was subsisting, he had held the employment in respect of which the payment is made,
  (d) that there were or are payments under the earlier trust which–
    (i) in the case of payments made before 6th October 1987, were excluded from the computation of the earnings of the person or persons to whom they were made by virtue of regulation 19(1)(e) of these Regulations as in force immediately before that date,
    (ii) in the case of payments made on or after 6th October 1987, are payments made in circumstances to which sub-paragraphs (a), (b) and (c) of this paragraph apply".

Signed by authority of the Secretary of State for Social Services.

Nicholas Scott
Minister of State,
Department of Health and Social Security

4th September 1987

EXPLANATORY NOTE

(This note is not part of the Regulations)

These Regulations further amend the Social Security (Contributions) Regulations 1979.

They revoke regulation 19(1)(e) and insert regulation 19A. The new regulation provides for the disregard, for the purposes of earnings-related contributions, of certain payments made by trustees before 6th April 1990.

The principal conditions for the exclusion of these payments from the computation of a person's earnings in respect of employed earner's employment are either that the trust was created before 6th April 1985 or, if it was created on or after that date, that it took effect immediately on termination of a trust created before 6th April 1985, some payments under which were or are excluded from the computation of earnings of those to whom they were or are made, and that the person now receiving payment was a beneficiary under the replaced trust or meets a specified requirement in relation to it.

STATUTORY INSTRUMENTS

1987 No. 1591

MERCHANT SHIPPING

SAFETY

The Merchant Shipping (Smooth and Partially Smooth Waters) Regulations 1987

Made - - - -	*8th September 1987*
Laid before Parliament	*17th September 1987*
Coming into force	*8th October 1987*

The Secretary of State for Transport, after consulting with the persons referred to in section 22(2) of the Merchant Shipping Act 1979(**a**) in exercise of the powers conferred on him by sections 21(1)(a) and (b) and 22(3)(a) of that Act and of all other powers enabling him in that behalf, hereby makes the following Regulations:

1. These Regulations may be cited as the Merchant Shipping (Smooth and Partially Smooth Waters) Regulations 1987 and shall come into force on 8th October 1987.

2. The Merchant Shipping (Smooth and Partially Smooth Waters) Rules 1977(**b**), the Merchant Shipping (Smooth and Partially Smooth Waters) (Amendment) Rules 1977(**c**), the Merchant Shipping (Smooth and Partially Smooth Waters) (Amendment) Rules 1978(**d**) and the Merchant Shipping (Smooth and Partially Smooth Waters) (Amendment) Rules 1984(**e**) are hereby revoked.

3.—(1) This regulation applies to instruments in force on the making of these Regulations being–

(a) regulations made pursuant to section 21(1) of the Merchant Shipping Act 1979; or

(b) rules or regulations made pursuant to any other provision of the Merchant Shipping Acts 1894 to 1977 in which the expression "smooth waters" or "partially smooth waters" or any cognate expression occurs.

(2) For the purposes of any instrument to which this regulation applies and notwithstanding anything therein–

(a) "smooth waters" shall mean (a) the waters specified in column 2 of the Schedule and (b) any other waters which are neither partially smooth waters nor the sea;

(b) "partially smooth waters" shall mean, as respects any period specified in the Schedule hereto, the waters of any of the areas specified in column 3 of that Schedule in relation to that period.

and cognate expressions (including, in particular, "smooth and partially smooth waters" and "smooth or partially smooth waters") shall be construed accordingly.

(**a**) 1979 c.39. (**b**) S.I. 1977/252. (**c**) S.I. 1977/632.
(**d**) S.I. 1978/801. (**e**) S.I. 1984/955.

Paul Channon
8th September 1987   Secretary of State for Transport

SCHEDULE

LIMITS OF SMOOTH WATER AND PARTIALLY SMOOTH WATER AREAS

(1) The outer limits of the smooth water areas specified in column 2 of this Schedule shall be taken to be the corresponding inner limits of the partially smooth water areas specified in column 3 of this Schedule.

(2) Unless otherwise indicated, these limits apply to all times of the year. In this Schedule "summer" means the months of April to October, inclusive, and "winter" means the months of November to March, inclusive.

(1) *District*	(2) *Smooth Water Areas*	(3) *Partially Smooth Water Areas*
SHETLAND ISLES:		
Blue Mull Sound	No smooth waters	Between Gutcher and Belmont
Yell Sound	No smooth waters	Between Tofts Voe and Ulsta
Sullom Voe	No smooth waters	Within a line from the north-east point of Gluss Island to the northern point of Calback Ness
Dales Voe	No smooth waters	In winter within a line from the north point of Kebister Ness to the Coast of Breiwick at Longitude 1° 10.8′W. In summer as for Lerwick.
Lerwick	No smooth waters	In winter within the area bounded to the northward by a line from Scottle Holm to Scarfi Taing on Bressay and to the southward by a line from Twageos Point Lighthouse to Whalpa Taing on Bressay. In summer within the area bounded to the northward by a line from Brim Ness to the north east corner of Inner Score and to the southward by a line from the south end of Ness of Sound to Kirkabisterness.
ORKNEY ISLANDS:		
Kirkwall	No smooth waters	Between Kirkwall and Rousay not east of a line between Point of Graand (Egilsay) and Galt Ness (Shapinsay) or between Head of Work (Mainland) through Helliar Holm light to the shore of Shapinsay; not north west of the south east tip of Eynhallow Island, or north of the southern tip of Holm of Scockness.

(1) *District*	(2) *Smooth Water Areas*	(3) *Partially Smooth Water Areas*
Stromness	No smooth waters	To Scapa but not outside Scapa Flow.
Scapa Flow	Within an area bounded by lines drawn from Wharth on the island of Flotta to the Martello Tower on South Walls, and from Point of Cletts on the island of Hoy to Thomson's Hill triangulation point on the island of Fara and thence to Gibraltar Pier on the island of Flotta.	Within an area bounded by lines drawn from Point of Cletts on the island of Hoy to Thomson's Hill triangulation point on the island of Fara and thence to Gibraltar Pier on the island of Flotta; from St. Vincent Pier on the island of Flotta to the westernmost point of Calf of Flotta; from the easternmost point of Calf of Flotta to Needle Point on the island of South Ronaldsay, and from the Ness on Mainland to Point of Oxan lighthouse on the island of Graemsay and thence to Bu Point on the island of Hoy.

EAST OF SCOTLAND:

Cromarty Firth	Within a line between North Sutor and South Sutor.	Within a line from North Sutor to Nairn Breakwater.
Inverness	Within a line from Fort George to Chanonry Point to Fort William.	Within a line from North Sutor to Nairn Breakwater.
Aberdeen	Within a line from South Jetty to Abercromby Jetty.	No partially smooth waters.
Dundee	Within a line from the tidal basin (fish dock) Dundee to Craig Head, East Newport	Within a line from Broughty Castle to Tayport.
Queensferry, North and South	Within the Firth of Forth but not east of the Forth railway bridge.	Within a line from Kirkcaldy to Portobello.
Leith	Within the Breakwaters.	Within a line from Kirkcaldy to Portobello.

NORTH EAST OF ENGLAND:

Berwick on Tweed	Within a line from Spittal Point to the inner end of the northern Breakwaters.	No partially smooth waters.
Amble	Within the Breakwaters.	No partially smooth waters.
Blyth	Within the outer Blyth Pier Heads.	No partially smooth waters.
Newcastle, North and South Shields	Within the Tyne Pier Heads.	No partially smooth waters.
Hartlepool	Within a line from Middleton Jetty to Old Pier Head.	No partially smooth waters.
Middlesbrough	Within a line extending due west from Government Jetty.	No partially smooth waters.
Whitby	Within Whitby Pier Heads.	No partially smooth waters.
Seaham Harbour	Within the Breakwaters.	No partially smooth waters.
Sunderland	Within the outer Sunderland Pier Heads.	No partially smooth waters.

(1) *District*	(2) *Smooth Water Areas*	(3) *Partially Smooth Water Areas*
EAST OF ENGLAND:		
Hull	No smooth waters.	In winter within a line from New Holland to Paull.
		In summer a line from Cleethorpes Pier to Patrington Church.
Goole	Within a line from North Ferriby to South Ferriby.	In winter within a line from New Holland to Paull.
		In summer within a line from Cleethorpes Pier to Patrington Church.
Grimsby	No smooth waters.	In winter no partially smooth waters.
		In summer within a line from Cleethorpes Pier to Patrington Church.
Boston	Inside the New Cut.	No partially smooth waters.
LONDON:		
Wisbech	Inside Wisbech Cut.	No partially smooth waters.
King's Lynn	Inside Lynn Cut.	No partially smooth waters.
Yarmouth and Lowestoft	Within the Harbour Entrances at Yarmouth or Lowestoft.	No partially smooth waters.
Woodbridge	On the River Deben to the Mouth.	No partially smooth waters.
Harwich, Ipswich, Felixstowe–River Orwell and River Stour	Within a line from Blackmans Head Breakwater to Landguard Point.	No partially smooth waters.
Maldon – River Blackwater	Within a line from the south western extremity of Mersea Island to Sales Point.	In winter within a line from Colne Point to Whitstable.
		In summer within a line from Clacton Pier to Reculvers.
Burnham on Crouch – River Crouch	Within a line from Hollywell Point to Foulness Point.	In winter within a line from Colne Point to Whitstable.
		In summer within a line from Clacton Pier to Reculvers.
London–River Thames	Westward of a North/South line through PHA Isolation Hospital, Gravesend.	In winter within a line from Colne Point to Whitstable.
		In summer within a line from Clacton Pier to Reculvers.
Rochester, Chatham, Sheerness, Whitstable–River Medway and The Swale	Within a line from Garrison Point to the Grain Tower and within a line from Whitstable to Warden Point.	In winter within a line from Colne Point to Whitstable.
		In summer within a line from Clacton Pier to Reculvers.
Dover	Within a line drawn across the east and west entrances to the harbour.	No partially smooth waters.
Rye–River Rother	Within the area above the tidal signal station at Camber.	No partially smooth waters.

(1) District	(2) Smooth Water Areas	(3) Partially Smooth Water Areas
Littlehampton – River Arun	Within the area above Littlehampton Pier.	No partially smooth waters.

S & SW OF ENGLAND:

District	Smooth Water Areas	Partially Smooth Water Areas
Chichester	Within a line drawn between Eastoke point and the church spire, West Wittering.	Inside the Isle of Wight within an area bounded by lines drawn between the church spire, West Wittering, to Trinity Church, Bembridge, to the eastward and the Needles and Hurst Point to the westward.
Langstone Harbour	Within a line drawn between Eastney Point and Gunner Point.	Inside the Isle of Wight within an area bounded by lines drawn between the church spire, West Wittering, to Trinity Church, Bembridge, to the eastward, and the Needles and Hurst Point to the westward.
Portsmouth	Within a line drawn across the harbour entrance from Fort Blockhouse to the Round Tower.	Inside the Isle of Wight within an area bounded by lines drawn between the church spire, West Wittering, to Trinity Church, Bembridge, to the eastward, and the Needles and Hurst Point to the westward.
Bembridge, Isle of Wight	Within Brading Harbour	Inside the Isle of Wight within an area bounded by lines drawn between the church spire, West Wittering, to Trinity Church, Bembridge, to the eastward, and the Needles and Hurst Point to the westward.
Cowes, Isle of Wight	The River Medina within a line from the Breakwater Light on the east bank to the Watch House Light on the west bank.	Inside the Isle of Wight within an area bounded by lines drawn between the church spire, West Wittering, to Trinity Church, Bembridge, to the eastward, and the Needles and Hurst Point to the westward.
Southampton	Within a line from Calshot Castle to Hook Beacon.	Inside the Isle of Wight within an area bounded by lines drawn between the church spire, West Wittering to Trinity Church, Bembridge, to the eastward, and the Needles and Hurst Point to the westward.
Beaulieu	Within Beaulieu River not eastward of a North/South line through Needs Oar Point.	Inside the Isle of Wight within an area bounded by lines drawn between the church spire, West Wittering to Trinity Church, Bembridge, to the eastward and the Needles and Hurst Point to the westward.
Keyhaven Lake	Within a line drawn due north from Hurst Point Low Light to Keyhaven Marshes.	No partially smooth waters.
Christchurch	Within Christchurch Harbour excluding the Run.	No partially smooth waters.

(1) *District*	(2) *Smooth Water Areas*	(3) *Partially Smooth Water Areas*
Poole	Within the line of the Chain Ferry between Sandbanks and South Haven Point.	No partially smooth waters.
Weymouth	No smooth waters.	Within Portland Harbour and between the River Wey and Portland Harbour.
Exeter	Within a line from Warren Point to the coastguard flag staff at Exmouth.	No partially smooth waters.
Teignmouth	Within the Harbour.	No partially smooth waters.
Dartmouth – River Dart	Within a line from Kettle Point to Battery Point.	No partially smooth waters.
Salcombe and Kingsbridge – River Salcombe	Within a line from Splat Point to Limebury Point.	No partially smooth waters.
Plymouth	Within a line from Mount Batten Pier to Raveness Point through Drake's Island. The River Yealm within a line from Warren Point to Misery Point.	Within a line from Cawsand to the Breakwater to Staddon Pier.
Fowey	Inside the Harbour	No partially smooth waters.
Falmouth	Within a line from St. Anthony Head to Pendennis Point.	In winter within a line from St. Anthony Head to Rosemullion Point. In summer within a line from St. Anthony Head to Nare Point.
Padstow – River Camel	Within a line from Gun Point to Brea Hill.	Within a line from Stepper Point to Trebetherick Point.
Barnstaple and Bideford – Rivers Taw and Torridge	Within a line bearing 200° from the lighthouse on Crow Point to the shore at Skern Point.	No partially smooth waters.

BRISTOL CHANNEL:

Bridgwater	South of a line running due east from Stert Point (51° 13.0′N)	Within the Bar
Bristol	Within a line from Avonmouth Pier to Wharf Point.	In winter within a line from Blacknore Point to Caldicot Pill, Portskewett. In summer within a line from Barry Dock Pier to Steepholm thence to Brean Down.
Gloucester	North of a line running due west from Sharpness Point (51° 43.4′N).	In winter within a line from Blacknore Point to Caldicot Pill, Portskewett. In summer within a line from Barry Dock Pier to Steepholm thence to Brean Down.
Chepstow	The River Wye at Chepstow North of latitude 51° 38.0′N.	In winter within a line from Blacknore Point to Caldicot Pill, Portskewett. In summer within a line from Barry Dock Pier to Steepholm thence to Brean Down.

(1) District	(2) Smooth Water Areas	(3) Partially Smooth Water Areas
Newport	North of the overhead power cables crossing at Fifoots Points.	In winter no partially smooth waters.
		In summer within a line from Barry Dock Pier to Steepholm thence to Brean Down.
Cardiff	Within a line from South Jetty to Penarth Head.	In winter no partially smooth waters.
		In summer within a line from Barry Dock Pier to Steepholm thence to Brean Down.
Barry	Within a line joining the seaward ends of the breakwaters.	In winter no partially smooth waters.
		In summer within a line from Barry Dock Pier to Steepholm thence to Brean Down.
Port Talbot	(i) Within enclosed Docks.	No partially smooth waters.
	(ii) Within a line joining the seaward ends of the breakwaters.	No partially smooth waters.
Neath	Within a line running due north from the seaward end of Baglan Bay Tanker Jetty (51° 37.2′N, 3° 50.5′W).	No partially smooth waters.
Swansea	Within the enclosed docks.	Within a line joining the seaward ends of the East and West breakwaters.
Llanelli and Burry Port	Within an area bounded by a line drawn from Burry Port Western Pier to Whiteford Point.	No partially smooth waters.
Milford Haven	Within a line from South Hook Point to Thorn Point.	No partially smooth waters.
Fishguard	Within a line joining the seaward ends of the North and East breakwaters.	No partially smooth waters.
Cardigan	Within the Narrows at Pen-Yr-Ergyd.	No partially smooth waters.
Aberystwyth	Within the seaward ends of the breakwaters.	No partially smooth waters.
Aberdyfi	Within a line from Aberdyfi Railway Station to Twyni Bach Beacon.	No partially smooth waters.
LIVERPOOL:		
Barmouth	Within a line from Barmouth Railway Station to Penrhyn Point.	No partially smooth waters.
Portmadoc	Within a line from Harlech Point to Graig Ddu.	No partially smooth waters.
Holyhead	Within an area bounded by the main breakwater and a line drawn from the head of the breakwater to Brynglas Point, Towyn Bay.	No partially smooth waters.

(1) District	(2) Smooth Water Areas	(3) Partially Smooth Water Areas
Caernarvon, Bangor	Within the Menai Straits between a line joining Aber Menai Point to Belan Point and a line joining Beaumaris Pier to Pen-y-Coed Point.	Within the Menai Straits from a line joining Llanddwyn Island Light to Dinas Dinlleu and lines joining the South end of Puffin Island to Trwyn Du Point and Llanfairfechan Railway Station.
Conway	Within a line from Mussel Hill to Tremlyd Point.	No partially smooth waters.
Chester	River Dee not below Connah's Quay.	In winter within a line from Hilbre Point to Point of Air.
		In summer within a line from Formby Point to Point of Air.
Liverpool	Within a line between the Rock Lighthouse and the North West Gladstone Dock Tower.	In winter no partially smooth waters.
		In summer within a line from Formby Point to Point of Air.
Preston	Within a line from Lytham to Southport.	Within a line from Southport to Blackpool inside the banks.
Fleetwood	Within a line from Low Light to Knott End Pier.	In winter no partially smooth waters.
		In summer within a line from Rossal Point to Humphrey Head.
Lancaster	Within a line from Sunderland Point to Chapel Hill.	In winter no partially smooth waters.
		In summer within a line from Rossal Point to Humphrey Head.
Heysham	No smooth waters.	In winter no partially smooth waters.
		In summer from within a line from Rossal Point to Humphrey Head.
Morecambe	No smooth waters.	In winter no partially smooth waters.
		In summer within a line from Rossal Point to Humphrey Head.
Barrow	Within a line joining Haws Point, Isle of Walney to Roa Island Slipway.	No partially smooth waters.
Douglas, Isle of Man	Within a line from Princess Alexandra Pier to Victoria Pier.	No partially smooth waters.
Carlisle	Within a line joining Port Carlisle to Torduff Point.	Within a line from Southerness Point to Silloth.
WEST OF SCOTLAND:		
Dumfries	Within a line from Airds Point to Scar Point.	Within a line from Southerness Point to Silloth.
Stranraer	Within a line from Cairn Ryan to Kirkcolm Point.	Loch Ryan within a line from Finnart's Point to Milleur Point.
Ayr	Inside the Bar.	No partially smooth waters.

(1) *District*	(2) *Smooth Water Areas*	(3) *Partially Smooth Water Areas*
Glasgow	Above partially smooth waters.	Outer limit: a line from Skipness to a position one mile south of Garroch Head thence to Farland Head. Inner Limit in winter: a line from Cloch Lighthouse to Dunoon Pier. Inner limit in summer: a line from Bogany Point, Isle of Bute to Skelmorlie Castle and a line drawn from Ardlamont Point to the southern extremity of Etterick Bay, inside the Kyles of Bute. Note: The above inner summer limit is extended between 5th June and 5th September (both dates inclusive) by a line drawn from a point two miles off the Ayrshire coast at Skelmorlie Castle to Tomont End, Cumbrae, and a line drawn from Portachur Point, Cumbrae to Green Point Ayrshire.
Colintraive	Between Colintraive and Rhudhabodach.	No partially smooth waters.
Cambeltown Harbour	Within a line from Macringan's Point to Ottercharach Point.	No partially smooth waters.
Oban	No smooth waters.	Within an area bounded on the north by a line from Dunollie Point Light to Ard na Chruidh and to the south by a line from Rudha Seanach to Ard na Cuile.
Loch Etive	Within Loch Etive above the Falls of Lora.	No partially smooth waters.
Ballachulish	Within Loch Leven and not outside Peter Straits.	No partially smooth waters.
Fort William	In Loch Linnhe north of Corran Point Light, and including Loch Eil and the Canal to Inverness.	No partially smooth waters.
Kyle of Lochalsh	Within Kyle Akin not westward of Eilean Ban Light or eastward of Eileanan Dubha.	Through Loch Alsh to the Head of Loch Duich.
Strome	Between Stromemore and Strome Ferry.	No partially smooth waters.
Ullapool – Loch Broom	Within a line drawn between Ullapool Point Light and Aultnaharrie.	No partially smooth waters.
Kylesku	Across Loch Cairnbawn in the area between the eastern-most point of Garbh Eilean and the western-most point of Eilean na Rainich.	No partially smooth waters.
Stornoway Harbour	Within a line from Arnish Point to Sandwick Bay Lighthouse, north-west side.	No partially smooth waters.
The Sound of Scalpay	Not east of Berry Cove and not west of Croca Hoin on Harris.	No partially smooth waters.

(1) District	(2) Smooth Water Areas	(3) Partially Smooth Water Areas
North Harbour, Scalpay and Tarbert Harbour	Within one mile from the shore of the Island of Harris.	No partially smooth waters.
NORTHERN IRELAND:		
Carlingford Lough	Within a line from Greenore to Greencastle Point.	No partially smooth waters.
Strangford Lough	Within Strangford Lough but not seaward of Rue Point.	No partially smooth waters.
Larne	Within a line from Larne Pier to the ferry pier on Island Magee.	No partially smooth waters.
Belfast	Within a line from Holywood to Macedon Point.	In winter no partially smooth waters. In summer within a line from Carrick-fergus to Bangor.
Lough Erne	Upper or Lower Lough Erne.	No partially smooth waters.
Lough Neagh	Within two miles of the shore.	At a greater distance than two miles from the shore.
Londonderry	Within a line from Magilligan Point to Greencastle.	No partially smooth waters.

EXPLANATORY NOTE

(This note is not part of the Regulations)

These Regulations replace the Merchant Shipping (Smooth and Partially Smooth Waters) Rules 1977 as amended in 1977, 1978 and 1984. They extend the winter and summer partially smooth water limits for Lerwick to the northward and specify a new winter area of partially smooth waters in Dales Voe and a new area of smooth waters at Aberystwyth. In other respects the limits of smooth and partially smooth waters remain unchanged.

Smooth and partially smooth waters are referred to in 14 sets of rules and regulations now in force made under the Merchant Shipping Acts 1894–1979.

STATUTORY INSTRUMENTS

1987 No. 1594 (C.48) (S.117)

CRIMINAL LAW, SCOTLAND

The Criminal Justice (Scotland) Act 1987 (Commencement No. 2) Order 1987

Made - - - - *7th September 1987*

The Secretary of State, in exercise of the powers conferred on him by section 72(2) of the Criminal Justice (Scotland) Act 1987(**a**) and of all other powers enabling him in that behalf, hereby makes the following Order:

1. This Order may be cited as the Criminal Justice (Scotland) Act 1987 (Commencement No. 2) Order 1987.

2. The provisions of the Criminal Justice (Scotland) Act 1987 referred to in Column 1 of the Schedule to this Order (which relate to the matters described in Column 2 of that Schedule) shall come into force on 1st October 1987.

New St. Andrew's House, Edinburgh
7th September 1987

James Douglas-Hamilton
Parliamentary Under Secretary of State,
Scottish Office

_____

(**a**) 1987 c.41.

Article 2

SCHEDULE

*Provisions of the Criminal Justice (Scotland) Act 1987 coming into force on
1st October 1987*

Column 1 *Provisions of the Act*	Column 2 *Subject matters of provisions*
Section 48	Detention and questioning by customs officers.
Section 49	Right to have someone informed when detained.
Section 60	Transcript of police interview sufficient evidence.
Section 64	Aiding and abetting.
Section 69	Interpretation.
Section 70 to the extent necessary to give effect to the provisions of Schedules 1 and 2 specified below.	Amendments and repeals.
In Schedule 1 the paragraphs specified in Column 1 of Appendix A hereto (which amend the enactments specified in Column 2 of that Appendix).	Minor and consequential amendments.
Schedule 2 to the extent specified in Appendix B hereto.	Repeals.

APPENDIX A

*Provisions of Schedule 1 to the Criminal Justice (Scotland) Act 1987 coming into force on 1st
October 1987*

Column 1 *Provisions of Schedule 1*	Column 2 *Enactment amended*
Paragraph 3	The Road Traffic Act 1972 (c.20).
Paragraphs 10(b) and 11 to 14	The Criminal Procedure (Scotland) Act 1975 (c.21).
Paragraphs 16 to 18	The Criminal Justice (Scotland) Act 1980 (c.62).
Paragraph 19	The Contempt of Court Act 1981 (c.49).

APPENDIX B

*Repeals in Schedule 2 to the Criminal Justice (Scotland) Act 1987 taking effect on
1st October 1987*

Chapter	*Short title*	*Extent of repeal*
1974 c.50.	The Road Traffic Act 1974.	In Schedule 3, paragraph 10(4).
1975 c.21.	The Criminal Procedure (Scotland) Act 1975.	In section 263(2), the words ", or on any point arising on the case,".

EXPLANATORY NOTE

(This note is not part of the Order)

This Order brings into force on 1st October 1987 the provisions of the Criminal Justice (Scotland) Act 1987 which are referred to in Column 1 of the Schedule to the Order.

NOTE AS TO EARLIER COMMENCEMENT ORDERS

(This note is not part of the Order)

The following provisions of the Act have been brought into force by Commencement Order made before the date of this Order:–

Provisions	Date of commencement	S.I. No.
Sections 57, 70 (partially), Schedule 1 (partially) and Schedule 2 (partially)	1 September 1987	1987/1468

STATUTORY INSTRUMENTS

1987 No. 1601

ANIMALS

ANIMAL HEALTH

The Warble Fly (England and Wales) (Amendment) Order 1987

Made - - - -	*10th September 1987*
Coming into force	*11th September 1987*

The Minister of Agriculture, Fisheries and Food, in relation to England, and the Secretary of State, in relation to Wales, in exercise of the powers conferred on them by sections 1, 8(1) and 86(1) of the Animal Health Act 1981(**a**) and of all other powers enabling them in that behalf, hereby Order as follows:

Title and commencement

1. This Order may be cited as the Warble Fly (England and Wales) (Amendment) Order 1987 and shall come into force on 11th September 1987.

Amendment

2. The Warble Fly (England and Wales) Order 1982(**b**) shall be amended as follows–
  (a) in paragraphs (1), (3) and (4) of article 5 (veterinary enquiry and service of notices) after the word "affected" there shall be inserted the words "or suspected";
  (b) in article 6 (contents and effects of notices)–
    (i) in paragraph (1)(a), (c) and (d) for the word "shall" there shall be substituted the word "may";
    (ii) in paragraph (1)(a) after the words "within the autumn period" there shall be inserted the words "or between such dates in the autumn period as may be specified in it."; and
    (iii) after paragraph (2) there shall be inserted the following paragraph–

      "(3) Where a notice in Form A prohibits the movement of any animal in accordance with paragraph (1)(d) above but does not impose any other requirement, a veterinary inspector may by a further notice in writing amend that notice so as to impose any one or more of the requirements mentioned in paragraph (1) above".;
  (c) for article 7 (autumn treatment) there shall be substituted the following article–

      "7.   If a veterinary inspector knows or has reasonable grounds for suspecting that, at any time during the current calendar year before the beginning of the autumn period,–
      (a) any animal was affected;
      (b) an affected animal was present on any premises; or

(**a**) 1981 c.22.
(**b**) S.I. 1982/234, amended by S.I. 1985/328.

(c) an animal which has or which may have been exposed to infection by warble fly was present on any premises,

he may, at any time after the end of the spring period and before the end of the autumn period in that year, serve a notice in Form A on the owner or person in charge of the animal, or of any animal on the premises, as the case may be; and in this case the notice in Form A shall require the treatment to be carried out during the autmn period or between such dates in the autumn period as may be specified in it."; and

(d) for Form A in the Schedule there shall be substituted the following Form–

"FORM A
ANIMAL HEALTH ACT 1981
Warble Fly (England and Wales) Order 1982 (as amended)
(Articles 5, 6 and 7)
NOTICE OF MOVEMENT RESTRICTIONS AND TREATMENT

To ....

of ....

....

I, the undersigned, being a veterinary inspector of the Ministry of Agriculture, Fisheries and Food, hereby give you notice in accordance with the provisions of the above Order that–

*(1) No animal to which this notice applies may be moved until this notice has been cancelled by a notice in Form E except–

(a) under the authority of a licence (Form D) issued by a veterinary inspector, and

(b) in the case of an animal which has been treated and in which the presence of the warble fly can be seen or felt, where accompanied by a declaration in Form C or a declaration of treatment under the Warble Fly (Scotland) Order 1982 made in respect of it.

(2) You are required, as the owner/person in charge of the animals to which the notice applies,–

(a) to treat or have treated the animals to which this notice applies by using a dressing licensed for systemic use against warble fly, such treatment to be carried out

* within 10 days,
* between the following dates .... and ....,
* during the period 15th September to 30 November inclusive,
* in the presence of, and to the satisfaction of, an appropriate officer;

(b) to give me written notification of the date and time on which the treatment is to be carried out, such notice to be delivered or sent by post so as to be received at least 3 clear days before the treatment is to be carried out;

(c) to deliver or to send to me by post a Declaration of Treatment in Form B within 7 days of the treatment being carried out.

The animals to which this notice applies are:

*(1) all cattle in your ownership or charge present on the premises specified below at the time of service of this notice, other than cattle exempted from treatment under article 15 of the Order and calves aged less than 12 weeks.

Description of premises
Full postal address

* Delete if inappropriate

*(2) the cattle specified in the table below–

Official Identity number	Description of cattle e.g. Breed Sex Age

Signed .... Dated ....
     (Veterinary Inspector)
Name in block letters ....
Official address ....
....

Notes

  1. Animals are exempted from treatment under article 15 of the Order if:–

    (a) it is not reasonable to treat them because of sickness, because treatment other than for warble fly has been administered to them or because of some other veterinary reason and it has not been reasonable to treat them at any time since the requirement to treat them arose; or

    (b) a veterinary inspector has issued a certificate of exemption under article 15(2) in respect of them; or

    (c) they are at a slaughterhouse.

  2. An appropriate officer is, in respect of premises in England, an inspector of the Ministry of Agriculture, Fisheries and Food or any other officer of the Ministry and, in respect of premises in Wales, an officer of the Secretary of State for Wales."

In Witness whereof the Official Seal of the Minister of Agriculture, Fisheries and Food is hereunto affixed on 10th September 1987.

John MacGregor
Minister of Agriculture, Fisheries and Food

24th August 1987

Peter Walker
Secretary of State for Wales

* Delete if inappropriate

EXPLANATORY NOTE

(This note is not part of the Order)

This Order further amends the Warble Fly (England and Wales) Order 1982 by adding provisions which–

(1) enable a veterinary inspector, where there are on any premises cattle which are suspected of being infected with warble fly, to serve a notice in Form A prohibiting the movement of any cattle from the premises or requiring them to be treated in respect of warble fly (article 2(a) and (b)(i));

(2) enable a veterinary inspector, where he serves a notice in Form A on any person requiring him to treat cattle in respect of warble fly to require the treatment to be carried out between such dates during the autumn period (the period from 15th September to 30th November inclusive in any year) as may be specified in the notice (article 2(b)(ii));

(3) enable a veterinary inspector, where a notice in Form A has been served on any person prohibiting the movement of cattle from any premises, to serve a further notice on such person requiring the cattle to be treated in respect of warble fly (article 2(b)(iii)); and

(4) enable a veterinary inspector, where he knows or suspects that at any time during the current calendar year before the beginning of the autumn period any cattle which have, or may have been, exposed to infection by warble fly were present on any premises to serve a notice in Form A requiring any cattle on those premises to be treated in respect of warble fly (article 2(c)).

STATUTORY INSTRUMENTS

1987 No. 1603

MERCHANT SHIPPING

SAFETY

The Merchant Shipping (Submersible Craft Operations) (Amendment) Regulations 1987

Made - - - -	*10th September 1987*
Laid before Parliament	*21st September 1987*
Coming into force	*12th October 1987*

The Secretary of State for Transport, in exercise of his powers under section 17 of, and Schedule 5 to, the Merchant Shipping Act 1974(**a**) and of all other powers enabling him in that behalf, hereby makes the following Regulations:

Citation and commencement

1. These Regulations may be cited as the Merchant Shipping (Submersible Craft Operations) (Amendment) Regulations 1987 and shall come into force on 12th October 1987.

2. The Merchant Shipping (Submersible Craft Operations) Regulations 1987(**b**) shall be amended as follows:–

    (a) for regulation 7(1)(b) there shall be substituted the following:–

        "there is produced to him a valid safety certificate issued by the Certifying Authority under the Merchant Shipping (Submersible Craft Construction and Survey) Regulations 1981(**c**) in respect of the submersible craft and its supporting equipment;

    (b) in paragraphs I and II of Schedule 5, for "1986" there shall be substituted "1987".

10th September 1987

Paul Channon
Secretary of State for Transport

EXPLANATORY NOTE

(This note is not part of the Regulations)

These Regulations make minor amendments to the Merchant Shipping (Submersible Craft Operations) Regulations 1987, principally to bring one provision into line with an amendment to the Merchant Shipping (Submersible Craft Construction and Survey) Regulations 1981 made by the Merchant Shipping Submersible Craft (Amendment) Regulations 1987.

(**a**) 1974 c. 43.
(**b**) 1987/311.
(**c**) S.I. 1981/1098, amended by S.I. 1987/306.

STATUTORY INSTRUMENTS

1987 No. 1607 (C.49) (S.118)

TOWN AND COUNTRY PLANNING, SCOTLAND

The Housing and Planning Act 1986 (Commencement No. 7) (Scotland) Order 1987

Made - - - - *10th September 1987*

The Secretary of State, in exercise of the powers conferred on him by section 57(2) of the Housing and Planning Act 1986(**a**), and of all other powers enabling him in that behalf, hereby makes the following Order:

1. This Order may be cited as the Housing and Planning Act 1986 (Commencement No. 7) (Scotland) Order 1987.

2. The following provisions of the Housing and Planning Act 1986 shall come into force on 1st October 1987:–

  (a) section 26 (simplified planning zones in Scotland) and Parts III and IV of Schedule 6;

  (b) section 50 (listed buildings and conservation areas) and Part II of Schedule 9; and

  (c) section 51 (grants for repair of buildings in town schemes).

James Douglas-Hamilton
New St. Andrew's House, Edinburgh   Parliamentary Under Secretary of State,
10th September 1987   Scottish Office

(**a**) 1986 c.63.

EXPLANATORY NOTE

(This note is not part of the Order)

This Order brings into force on 1st October 1987 sections 26, 50 and 51 of, and Parts III and IV of Schedule 6 and Part II of Schedule 9 to, the Housing and Planning Act 1986.

Section 26 inserts into the Town and Country Planning (Scotland) Act 1972 new sections 21A - 21E and a new Schedule 6A which impose upon district and general planning authorities a duty to consider whether it would be desirable to establish simplified planning zones in their area and, where they decide that it would be beneficial to do so, to make schemes establishing such zones. They also prescribe some of the procedures to be followed in the making or alteration of a simplified planning zone scheme. Certain other provisions of the Town and Country Planning (Scotland) Act 1972 are amended to take account of the introduction of simplified planning zones.

Section 50 amends enactments relating to listed buildings and conservation areas with respect to the matters listed in that section and provided for in detail in Part II of Schedule 9.

Section 51 sets out the procedure under which the Secretary of State may give grants towards the cost of repairing buildings comprised in town schemes (ie. repair schemes in certain conservation areas jointly funded by the Secretary of State and the local authority).

NOTE AS TO EARLIER COMMENCEMENT ORDERS

(This note is not part of the Order)

The following provisions of the Housing and Planning Act 1986 have been brought into force by Commencement Orders made before the date of this Order:–

Provision	Date of Commencement	S.I. No.
ss. 1 to 4	7th January 1987	1986/2262
ss. 10 to 14		
ss. 16 and 17		
ss. 19 and 20		
ss. 22 and 23		
s. 24 (partially)		
ss. 27 to 29		
ss. 44 to 48		
s. 49 (partially)		
s. 53 (partially)		
ss. 54 and 55		
s. 49 (partially)	2nd March 1987	1987/304
s. 40	1st April 1987	1987/348
s. 49 (partially)		
s. 9	13th May 1987	1987/754
s. 24 (partially)	22nd September 1987	1987/1554

STATUTORY INSTRUMENTS

1987 No. 1612

POWERS OF ATTORNEY

The Enduring Powers of Attorney (Prescribed Form) Regulations 1987

Made - - - -	*1st September 1987*
Laid before Parliament	*23rd September 1987*
Coming into force	*1st November 1987*

The Lord Chancellor, in exercise of the powers conferred on him by section 2(2) of the Enduring Powers of Attorney Act 1985(a), hereby makes the following Regulations:

Citation and commencement

1. These Regulations may be cited as the Enduring Powers of Attorney (Prescribed Form) Regulations 1987 and shall come into force on 1st November 1987.

Prescribed Form

2.—(1) Subject to paragraphs (2) and (3) of this regulation and to regulation 4, an enduring power of attorney must be in the form set out in the Schedule to these Regulations and must include all the explanatory information headed "About using this form" in Part A of the Schedule and all the relevant marginal notes to Parts B and C. It may also include such additions or restrictions as the donor may decide.

(2) In completing the form of enduring power of attorney, the donor shall exclude (either by omission or deletion) one and only one of any pair of alternatives. When one of a pair of alternatives is omitted or deleted, the corresponding marginal note may be omitted or deleted.

(3) The form of execution by an attorney of an enduring power of attorney may be adapted to provide for sealing by a trust corporation with its common seal.

(4) Subject to paragraphs (1), (2) and (3) of this regulation and to regulation 4, an enduring power of attorney which seeks to exclude any provision contained in these Regulations is not a valid enduring power of attorney.

Execution

3. An enduring power of attorney in the form set out in the Schedule to these Regulations shall be executed by both the donor and the attorney, although not necessarily at the same time, in the presence of a witness, but not necessarily the same witness, who shall give his full name and address. The donor and an attorney shall not witness the signature of each other nor one attorney the signature of another. Where more than one attorney is appointed and they are to act jointly and severally, then at least one of the attorneys so appointed must execute the instrument for it to take effect as an enduring power of attorney, but only those attorneys who have executed the instrument shall be able to act under the enduring power of attorney in the event of the donor's mental incapacity or of the registration of the power, whichever first occurs.

(a) 1985 c.29.

Revocation

4. The Enduring Powers of Attorney (Prescribed Form) Regulations 1986(a) are hereby revoked, except that a power executed in the form prescribed by those Regulations and executed before 1st July 1988 shall be capable of being a valid enduring power of attorney.

Dated 1st September 1987   *Havers*, C.

(a) S.I. 1986/126.

SCHEDULE   Regulations 2 and 3

Enduring Power of Attorney

Part A : About using this form

You may choose one attorney or more than one. If you choose more than one, you must decide whether they are to be able to act:

- Jointly (that is, they must all act together and cannot act separately) or
- Jointly and severally (that is, they can all act together but they can also act separately if they wish).

On the form, at the place marked **1**, show what you have decided by crossing out one of the alternatives.

If you give your attorney(s) general power in relation to all your property and affairs, it means that they will be able to deal with your money or property and may be able to sell your house.

If you don't want your attorney(s) to have such wide powers, you can include any restrictions you like. For example, you can include a restriction that your attorney(s) must not act on your behalf until they have reason to believe that you are becoming mentally incapable; or a restriction that your attorney(s) may not sell your house. Any restrictions you choose must be written or typed on the form in the place marked **2**.

Unless you put in a restriction preventing it your attorney(s) will be able to use any of your money or property to benefit themselves or other people by doing what you yourself might be expected to do to provide for their needs. Your attorney(s) will also be able to use your money to make gifts, but only for reasonable amounts in relation to the value of your money and property.

5. **Your attorney(s) can recover the out-of-pocket expenses** of acting as your attorney(s). If your attorney(s) are professional people, for example solicitors or accountants, they may be able to charge for their professional services as well.

6. **If your attorney(s) have reason in the future to believe** that you have become or are becoming mentally incapable of managing your affairs, your attorney(s) will have to apply to the Court of Protection for registration of this power.

7. **Before applying to the Court of Protection for registration** of this power, your attorney(s) must give written notice that that is what they are going to do, to you and your nearest relatives as defined in the Enduring Powers of Attorney Act 1985. You or your relatives will be able to object if you or they disagree with registration.

8. **This is a simplified explanation** of what the Enduring Powers of Attorney Act 1985 and the Rules and Regulations say. If you need more guidance, you or your advisers will need to look at the Act itself and the Rules and Regulations. The Rules are the Court of Protection (Enduring Powers of Attorney) Rules 1986 (Statutory Instrument 1986 No 127). The Regulations are the Enduring Powers of Attorney (Prescribed Form) Regulations 1987 (Statutory Instrument 1987 No 1612).

9. **Note to Attorney(s)**
After the power has been registered the attorney(s) should notify the Court of Protection if the donor dies or recovers.

You can cancel this power at any time before it has to be registered

Part B: To be completed by the 'donor' (the person appointing the attorney(s))

Don't sign this form unless you understand what it means

Please read the notes in the margin

I_____

of _____

Donor's name and address

Donor's date of birth

born on _____

Attorney(s) name(s) and address(es)

appoint _____

See note 1 on the front of this form. If you are appointing only one attorney you should cross out everything between the square brackets

of _____

● [and _____

   of _____

Cross out the one which does not apply (see note 1 on the front of this form)

1. ● jointly
   ● jointly and severally]

to be my attorney(s) for the purpose of the Enduring Powers of Attorney Act 1985

Cross out the one which does not apply (see note 2 on the front of this form)

● with general authority to act on my behalf
● with authority to do the following on my behalf:

If you don't want the attorney(s) to have general power, you must give details here of what authority you are giving the attorney(s)

in relation to

Cross out the one which does not apply

● all my property and affairs
● the following property and affairs:

Part B: continued

Please read the notes
in the margin

If there are restrictions or
conditions, insert them
here; if not, cross out these
words (See note 3 on the
front of this form)

2 ● subject to the following restrictions and conditions :

I intend that this power shall continue even if I become
mentally incapable.

I have read or have had read to me the notes in Part A which are
part of, and explain, this form.

Your signature

Signed, sealed and
delivered by me _____ (L.S.)

Date

on _____

Someone must witness
your signature

Signature of witness

In the presence of _____

Your attorney(s) cannot be
your witness. If you are
married it is **not** advisable
for your husband or wife to
be your witness

Full name of witness _____

Address of witness _____

_____

_____

_____

Part C: To be completed by the attorney(s)

Note   • This form may be adapted to provide for sealing by a corporation with its common seal

      • If there are more than two attorneys attach an additional **Part C**

Don't sign this form before the donor has signed Part B

I understand that I have a duty to apply to the Court for the registration of this form under the Enduring Powers of Attorney Act 1985 when the donor is becoming or has become mentally incapable.

I also understand my limited power to use the donor's property to benefit persons other than the donor.

   I am not a minor

Signature of attorney

Signed, sealed and delivered by me _____ (L.S.)

Date

on _____

Signature of witness

in the presence of _____

Full name of witness _____

Each attorney must sign the form and each signature must be witnessed. The donor may not be the witness and one attorney may not witness the signature of the other

Address of witness _____

_____

_____

To be completed only if there is a second attorney

I understand that I have a duty to apply to the Court for the registration of this form under the Enduring Powers of Attorney Act 1985 when the donor is becoming or has become mentally incapable.

I also understand my limited power to use the donor's property to benefit persons other than the donor.

I am not a minor.

Signature of attorney

Signed, sealed and delivered by me _____ (L.S.)

Date

on _____

Signature of witness

in the presence of _____

Full name of witness _____

Each attorney must sign the form and each signature must be witnessed. The donor may not be the witness and one attorney may not witness the signature of the other

Address of witness _____

_____

_____

EXPLANATORY NOTE

(This note is not part of the Regulations)

These Regulations prescribe a revised form of an enduring power of attorney, the explanatory information endorsed on it and the manner in which it is to be executed.

1987 No. 1613

TRANSPORT

The Bus Companies (Dissolution) Order 1987

Made - - - -	*14th September 1987*
Laid before Parliament	*23rd September 1987*
Coming into force	*14th October 1987*

The Secretary of State for Transport, in exercise of the powers conferred by section 47(12) and (13) of the Transport Act 1985 (**a**), and of all other enabling powers, hereby makes the following Order:

Citation and commencement

1. This Order may be cited as the Bus Companies (Dissolution) Order 1987 and shall come into force on 14th October 1987.

Dissolution of companies

2. The Cheltenham District Traction Company, the Gosport and Fareham Omnibus Company and the Mansfield District Traction Company (which are all subsidiaries of the National Bus Company and all incorporated by local Act or by an order under the Light Railways Act 1896 (**b**)) are hereby dissolved.

Rights and Liabilities

3. All rights vested in and liabilities binding upon any of the companies named in article 2 of this Order, including (without prejudice to the generality of the foregoing) the obligation to provide services contained in the Gosport and Fareham Omnibus Services Act 1929 (**c**), are hereby extinguished.

Signed by authority of the Secretary of State.

David B. Mitchell
14th September 1987   Minister of State, Department of Transport

---

(**a**) 1985 c.67.   (**b**) 1896 c.48.   (**c**) 1929 c.1xv.

EXPLANATORY NOTE

(This note is not part of the Order)

This Order dissolves the Cheltenham District Traction Company, the Gosport and Fareham Omnibus Company and the Mansfield District Traction Company, which are all subsidiaries of the National Bus Company and all incorporated by local Act or by an order under the Light Railways Act 1896.

STATUTORY INSTRUMENTS

1987 No. 1628

NORTHERN IRELAND

The Enduring Powers of Attorney (Northern Ireland Consequential Amendment) Order 1987

Made - - - - *15th September 1987*

Coming into force in accordance with Article 1(b)

At the Court at Balmoral, the 15th day of September 1987

Present,

The Queen's Most Excellent Majesty in Council

Whereas a draft of this Order has been approved by resolution of each House of Parliament:

Now, therefore, Her Majesty, in exercise of the powers conferred by section 38(2) of the Northern Ireland Constitution Act 1973**(a)** as extended by paragraph 1(7) of Schedule 1 to the Northern Ireland Act 1974**(b)**, and of all other powers enabling Her in that behalf, is pleased, by and with the advice of Her Privy Council, to order, and it is hereby ordered as follows:–

Title, commencement and extent

1. This Order–

(a) may be cited as the Enduring Powers of Attorney (Northern Ireland Consequential Amendment) Order 1987;

(b) shall come into force on the day appointed under Article 1(2) of the Enduring Powers of Attorney (Northern Ireland) Order 1987**(c)** for the coming into operation of that Order, and

(c) extends to the whole of the United Kingdom.

Amendment of Enduring Powers of Attorney Act 1985

2. In section 7(3) of the Enduring Powers of Attorney Act 1985**(d)**, after the words "under this Act" there shall be inserted the words "or under the Enduring Powers of Attorney (Northern Ireland) Order 1987".

G. I. de Deney
Clerk of the Privy Council

(a) 1973 c. 36; section 38 was amended by paragraph 6 of Schedule 2 to the Northern Ireland Act 1982 (c.38).
(b) 1974 c. 28.
(c) S.I. 1987/1627 (N.I. 16).
(d) 1985 c.29.

EXPLANATORY NOTE

(This note is not part of the Order)

Section 7(3) of the Enduring Powers of Attorney Act 1985 provides that an office copy of an instrument registered under that Act is to be evidence in any part of the United Kingdom of the contents of the instrument and of the fact that it has been registered.

This Order, which is made in consequence of the Enduring Powers of Attorney (Northern Ireland) Order 1987, extends section 7(3) to instruments registered under that Order.

STATUTORY INSTRUMENTS

1987 No. 1634 (S.119)

NATIONAL HEALTH SERVICE, SCOTLAND

The National Health Service (General Dental Services) (Scotland) Amendment Regulations 1987

Made - - - -	*15th September 1987*
Laid before Parliament	*17th September 1987*
Coming into force	*1st October 1987*

The Secretary of State, in exercise of powers conferred on him by sections 25(1), (2) and(5), 105(7) and 108(1) of the National Health Service (Scotland) Act 1978(**a**), and of all other powers enabling him in that behalf, hereby makes the following Regulations:

Citation and commencement

1.—(1) These Regulations may be cited as the National Health Service (General Dental Services) (Scotland) Amendment Regulations 1987 and shall come into force on 1st October 1987.

(2) In these Regulations, "the principal Regulations" means the National Health Service (General Dental Services) (Scotland) Regulations 1974(**b**).

Amendment of the principal Regulations

2. After Part VII of the principal Regulations there shall be inserted the following Part:–

"Part VIII

PAYMENTS IN CONSEQUENCE OF SUSPENSION

Interpretation of Part VIII

33. In this Part of these Regulations, unless the context otherwise requires–

(a) "claimant" means a person claiming to be entitled to, or receiving, a payment;

"erasure" means the erasure of a person's name from the register;

"fees" does not include remuneration by way of salary;

"Health Committee" means the Committee of that name being a Committee of the General Dental Council and constituted in accordance with section 2(4) of the Dentists Act 1984(**c**);

"immediate suspension" means suspension by virtue of an order under section 30(3) of the Dentists Act 1984 except such a suspension terminated by the court under section 30(6) of that Act;

(**a**) 1978 c.29; section 25(2) was amended by S.I. 1981/432; section 25(5) was inserted by the Health and Social Services and Social Security Adjudications Act 1983 ("the 1983 Act") (c.41), section 16(a); section 105(7) was amended by the Health Services Act 1980 (c.53), Schedule 6, paragraph 5, and Schedule 7, and by the 1983 Act, Schedule 9, paragraph 24; *see* section 108(1) for definition of "regulations".

(**b**) S.I. 1974/505; the relevant amending instrument is S.I. 1986/1571.

(**c**) 1984 c.24.

"interim suspension order" means an order under section 32 of the Dentists Act 1984;

"payment" means a payment under Part VIII of these Regulations;

"register" means the dentists register referred to in section 14(1) of the Dentists Act 1984, and "registration" means registration in that register;

"suspension date" means the date on which suspension of a person's registration takes effect;

(b) a reference to a direction or order of the Health Committee is a reference to a direction or order of that Committee under the Dentists Act 1984.

Entitlement to payment

34.—(1) A dentist whose registration is suspended by an interim suspension order or by a direction or an order of the Health Committee shall be entitled to payment in accordance with this Part of these Regulations.

(2) Entitlement as provided for by paragraph (1) shall cease in the event of erasure or of termination of the said suspension.

(3) No payment shall be made to a person–

(a) whose registration has been suspended by a direction or order of the Health Committee after he has received total payments in accordance with this Part covering twelve months of such suspension, whether in respect of one or more periods of suspension, and whether or not those twelve months were consecutive;

(b) in respect of any part of a third or subsequent period of suspension by a direction or order of the Health Committee, no account being taken of any period of such suspension before 1st October 1987; or

(c) in respect of any part of a period of suspension, where in the two years immediately preceding the suspension date he received no fees for the provision of general dental services.

(4) No payment shall be made to a person for any part of a period of suspension–

(a) earlier than 1st October 1987;

(b) earlier than 8 weeks before the date on which an application for payment is received by the Health Board, unless that Board is satisfied that the lateness of the application is due to illness or other reasonable cause;

(c) during which his name is not included in the dental list of any Health Board;

(d) during which he is absent from the United Kingdom;

(e) for which he is entitled to any benefit under a contract of insurance against the risk of the suspension of his registration, or of the circumstances which led to it, or for which the Health Board is satisfied he could have been so entitled but for his failure to enter into such a contract or to pay any premium due under such a contract;

(f) during which he is serving a term of imprisonment;

(g) during which he is remanded in custody in connection with a criminal offence for which he is subsequently convicted; or

(h) during which he is in breach of any condition of bail in connection with a criminal offence for which he is subsequently convicted.

Application for payment

35.—(1) An application for payment shall be made to the Health Board in whose dental list the claimant's name was included immediately before the suspension date; and where his name was then included in the list of more than one Health Board, the application shall be made to the Health Board by which the larger or largest total amount of fees was payable to him in the two years immediately preceding that date.

(2) An application for payment shall–

(a) be in writing;

(b) be made by the claimant or, where he is incapable of applying, on his behalf; and

(c) contain or be supported by such information as the Health Board may reasonably require for the purpose of establishing the claimant's entitlement to payment.

(3) Where the claimant's name was immediately before the suspension date on the dental list of one or more Health Boards and on that of one or more Family Practitioner Committees, the application for payment shall be made to whichever of those bodies by which the larger or largest total amount of fees was payable to him in the two years immediately preceding that date.

Amounts and times of payment

36.—(1) The Health Board to whom an application for payment is made in accordance with regulation 35, shall, if satisfied that, having made such enquiries as it considers relevant, the claimant is eligible for payment by virtue of regulation 34, determine that he shall in respect of any period for which he is so entitled receive payment which, subject to paragraphs (2) to (6) below, shall be calculated as follows:–

(a) where his registration is suspended by a direction or order of the Health Committee–

(i) £1,935 per month for each of the first six months for which he is entitled to payment, whether in respect of one or more periods of such suspension and whether or not those six months are consecutive, and

(ii) £967 per month thereafter;

(b) where his registration is suspended by an interim suspension order–

(i) where the period of interim suspension ends with an order for erasure or immediate suspension, £967 per month for the period of interim suspension, and

(ii) in any other case, £1,935 per month.

(2) Where in the period of two years immediately preceding the suspension date the total amount of fees received by the claimant for the provision of general dental services was less than £107,103, payment made to him shall (subject to any further reduction under paragraph (3)) be in the same proportion to the amount otherwise payable in accordance with paragraph (1) as that total amount of fees is to £107,103.

(3) Where the claimant's name was included in the dental list of the Health Board to which the application is made for a period of less than two years immediately preceding the suspension date, payment made to him shall be in the same proportion to the amount otherwise payable in accordance with paragraph (1) or paragraph (2) as the number of complete months in that lesser period is to 24.

(4) Subject to regulation 34(3)(b), where the claimant's registration has been suspended by an interim suspension order or by a direction or order of the Health Committee within a period of two years after the expiry of a previous period of such suspension, the references in paragraphs (2) and (3) above to the suspension date shall be taken as references to the suspension date applicable to that previous period.

(5) Where the Health Board has to make a determination as to payment at a time when it does not know whether or not the period of a person's interim suspension will end with an order for erasure or immediate suspension, or whether or not he will be convicted of a criminal offence, it shall make that determination as though his period of suspension did so end or he was convicted of the offence; but it shall review that determination and make appropriate adjustment as to past payment, if subsequently that period does not so end or he is not convicted of the offence.

(6) Any payment shall, so far as is reasonably practicable, be made by the Health Board at the end of each month in arrears, and an appropriate proportion of the monthly amount shall be paid where the claimant is entitled to a payment for part only of a month.

Changes in circumstances

37.—(1) A claimant shall notify the Health Board in writing immediately of any changes in his circumstances which he might reasonably consider might affect his entitlement to, or the amount of, any payment made or to be made to him in terms of this Part, and in particular of erasure, immediate suspension or termination of suspension of his registration.

(2) Where the Health Board considers, whether or not following a notification under paragraph (1), that there has been a change of circumstances affecting a claimant's entitlement to payment, it shall make such adjustment to payment as it considers to be appropriate.

Overpayments

38. Where the Health Board considers that a payment has been made to a claimant in error or in circumstances where he was not entitled to it, it shall, except to the extent that the Secretary of State on the Health Board's application directs otherwise, draw the fact of overpayment to the attention of the claimant and–

(a) where he agrees that the overpayment has occurred; or

(b) where he does not so agree but, the matter having been referred under regulation 7(1)(a) of the National Health Service (Service Committees and Tribunal) (Scotland) Regulations 1974(**a**) for investigation, the Health Board, or the Secretary of State on appeal, decides that there has been an overpayment,

the overpayment shall be recoverable either by deduction from the fees to which the claimant is otherwise entitled or in some other manner.".

3. In Part I of Schedule 1 to the principal Regulations (terms of service) paragraph 9A(**b**) shall be deleted and the following substituted:—

"**Preventive treatment**

9A. A dentist may undertake the application of topical fluoride preparations or fissure sealants to persons under the age of 16 where necessary to maintain dental health.".

Michael B Forsyth
New St. Andrew's House, Edinburgh   Parliamentary Under Secretary of State,
15th September 1987   Scottish Office

(**a**) S.I. 1974/504, to which there are amendments not relevant to these Regulations.
(**b**) Paragraph 9A was inserted by S.I. 1986/1571.

EXPLANATORY NOTE

(This note is not part of the Regulations)

These Regulations amend the National Health Service (General Dental Services) (Scotland) Regulations 1974 ("the principal Regulations") by the insertion, by way of regulation 2, of a new Part VIII (comprising regulations 33-38) into the principal Regulations. The new Part VIII makes provision for payments to be made to dentists whose registration under the Dentists Act 1984 is suspended by an interim suspension order or by a direction or order of the Health Committee. Under section 25(4) of the National Health Service (Scotland) Act 1978 a dentist with whom arrangements have been made for the provision of general dental services and whose registration is so suspended is not permitted to provide those services in person during the suspension, although the suspension does not result in termination of the arrangements.

In particular provision is made in the new Part VIII for the following matters:–

    (a) entitlement to payment (regulation 34 of the principal Regulations), including restrictions on entitlement (regulation 34(3) and (4));

    (b) application for payment (regulation 35);

    (c) amounts and times of payment (regulation 36); two different rates of payment depending upon the circumstances of the suspension, subject also to a reduction in cases where the dentist has low earnings or has been on the dental list of a Health Board for less than two years;

    (d) changes in circumstances (regulation 37);

    (e) overpayments (regulation 38).

Regulation 3 of these Regulations amends Schedule 1 to the principal Regulations so as to enable dentists to provide fissure sealants as preventive treatment to persons under 16.

STATUTORY INSTRUMENTS

1987 No. 1635

NATIONAL DEBT

The National Savings Stock Register (Amendment) Regulations 1987

Made - - - -	*15th September 1987*
Laid before Parliament	*18th September 1987*
Coming into force	*9th October 1987*

The Treasury, in exercise of the powers conferred on them by section 3 of the National Debt Act 1972**(a)** and of all other powers enabling them in that behalf, hereby make the following Regulations:

1. These Regulations may be cited as the National Savings Stock Register (Amendment) Regulations 1987 and shall come into force on 9th October 1987.

2. The National Savings Stock Register Regulations 1976**(b)** shall be amended as follows –

(a) by inserting in regulation 5(2) after the word "shall" the words ", unless made in accordance with paragraph (3) of this Regulation,";

(b) by inserting after regulation 5(2) the following new paragraphs –

"(3) Application to subscribe for stock of any issue to which this paragraph applies may be made to the Bank of England in accordance with the terms of the prospectus for that issue.

(4) Paragraph (3) of this Regulation shall apply to an issue of stock –

(i) which is of a description corresponding to stock and securities transferable in the books of the Bank of England, and

(ii) the prospectus for which contains a statement that the stock concerned may be registered in the register.

(5) The Director of Savings shall, following receipt by him of an application in writing in the approved form to register in the register stock subscribed for under paragraph (3) of this Regulation (not being stock which has been previously registered in the books of the Bank of England or the Bank of Ireland or in the register), and subject to regulation 5A of these Regulations, cause entries relating to such stock to be made in the register in accordance with regulation 4(1) of these Regulations."

(a) 1972 c.65   **(b)** S.I. 1976/2012, to which there are amendments not relevant to these Regulations.

(c) by inserting after regulation 5 the following new regulation –

"Limit on amount of stock which may be registered under Regulation 5(5)

5A (1) No person shall be entitled to have registered in his name under regulation 5(5) of these Regulations stock of any one issue exceeding £10,000 in nominal value.

(2) The limitation imposed by paragraph (1) of this Regulation shall not apply where the stock is to be registered –

(a) in the name of a registered friendly society or a branch thereof within the meaning of the Friendly Societies Act 1974**(a)**;

(b) in the name of a society incorporated or deemed to be incorporated under the Building Societies Act 1986**(b)**;

(c) in the name of a society registered or deemed to be registered under the Industrial and Provident Societies Act 1965**(c)**;

(d) with the approval of the Commissioners, and subject to such conditions as they may require, in the names of the trustees or treasurers or any charitable or provident institution or society or of any penny savings bank;

(e) in the name of the Public Trustee;

(f) with the approval of the Director of Savings, and subject to such conditions as he may require, by a responsible officer of any government department or office in his official capacity;

(g) in the name of the registrar of a county court in England, a sheriff clerk in Scotland, or a Clerk of the Crown and Peace in Northern Ireland, by virtue of or in pursuance of any enactment in that behalf; or

(h) in the name of the Accountant General of the Supreme Court.

(3) If application shall be made under regulation 5(5) to have registered in the name of any person stock of any one issue exeeding £10,000 in nominal value and paragraph (2) of this Regulation does not apply, the Director of Savings may arrange for the excess amount of the stock to be registered in that name in the books of the Bank of England or the Bank of Ireland.

(4) If not withstanding paragraph (1) of this Regulation the Director of Savings registers in the name of any person under regulation 5(5) of these Regulations stock of any one issue exceeding £10,000 in nominal value and paragraph (2) of this Regulation does not apply –

(a) Regulation 53(1) of these Regulations shall apply as if the registration of the excess amount of stock had been in accordance with these Regulations, and

(b) the Director of Savings may arrange for the excess amount of the stock to be transferred from the register and registered in that name in the books of the Bank of England or the Bank of Ireland."; and

(d) by deleting in regulation 8(1) the words "Regulation 7" and "substituting the words "Regulations 5A and 7".

Michael Neubert
David Lightbown
Two of the Lords Commissioners
of Her Majesty's Treasury

15th September 1987

(a) 1974 c.46.   **(b)** 1986 c.53.   **(c)** 1965 c.12.

EXPLANATORY NOTE

(This note is not part of the Regulations)

These Regulations amend the National Savings Stock Register Regulations 1976 to enable persons who apply to the Bank of England to subscribe for certain issues of stock to have the stock registered in the National Savings Stock Register. The issues of stock to which the Regulations apply are those of stock which is transferable in the books of the Bank of England and the prospectus for which contains a statement that the stock may be registered in the National Savings Stock Register. The Regulations impose a limit of £10,000 in nominal value on the amount of stock of any one issue which a person is entitled to have registered in his name under the Regulations, subject to certain exceptions, and make provision in relation to holdings in excess of that amount.

1987 No. 1636

CRIMINAL LAW, ENGLAND AND WALES

The Crown Prosecution Service (Witnesses' Allowances) (Amendment No. 5) Regulations 1987

Made - - - -	*15th September 1987*
Laid before Parliament	*16th September 1987*
Coming into force	*7th October 1987*

The Attorney General, in exercise of the powers conferred upon him by section 14(1)(b) and (2) of the Prosecution of Offences Act 1985(**a**), and with the approval of the Treasury, hereby makes the following Regulations:

1. These Regulations may be cited as the Crown Prosecution Service (Witnesses' Allowances) (Amendment No. 5) Regulations 1987 and shall come into operation on 7th October 1987.

2. In these Regulations "the principal Regulations" means the Crown Prosecution Service (Witnesses' Allowances) Regulations 1986(**b**).

3. In Schedule 1 to the principal Regulations, in Column 3 of the Table, which sets out relevant amounts in relation to allowances payable under those Regulations –

(a) for the sum of £25.40 in the entry for regulation 6(a) (financial loss allowance in respect of certain expenditure incurred by a witness who attends to give evidence other than professional or expert evidence) there shall be substituted £27.50; and

(b) for the sums of £12.70 and £25.40 in the entry for regulation 6(b) (financial loss allowance in respect of certain losses suffered by such a witness) there shall be substituted £13.75 and £27.50 respectively.

4. In Schedule 2 to the principal Regulations, which makes provision as to mileage rates etc. in respect of journeys by private motor vehicles –

(a) in the Table in Part I (standard mileage rate), for the sums of 10.2p, 14.3p, 19.6p and 31.8p there shall be substituted 11p, 15.3p, 21.3p and 34.4p respectively; and

(b) in the Table in Part II (public transport mileage rates), for the sums of 10.2p, 14.3p and 14.5p (in both places where it appears) there shall be substituted 11p, 15.3p and 15.6p respectively.

(**a**) 1985 c.23. (**b**) S.I. 1986/405, amended by S.I. 1986/842, 1250 and 1818 and 1987/902.

5. The Crown Prosecution Service (Witnesses' Allowances) (Amendment) Regulations 1986**(a)** and regulation 5 of the Crown Prosecution Service (Witnesses' Allowances) (Amendment No. 3) Regulations 1986**(b)** are hereby revoked.

P. B. B. Mayhew
Her Majesty's Attorney General

2nd September 1987

We approve

Michael Neubert
David Lightbown
Two of the Lords Commissioners
of Her Majesty's Treasury

15th September 1987

EXPLANATORY NOTE

(This note is not part of the Regulations)

These Regulations increase the maximum financial loss allowances payable under regulation 6 of the Crown Prosecution Service (Witnesses' Allowances) Regulations 1986 to a witness other than a professional or expert witness who, at the instance of the Crown Prosecution Service, attends court to give evidence and thereby incurs certain expenditure or suffers certain loss as described in that regulation. They also increase the mileage rates payable to all categories of witnesses.

(a) S.I. 1986/842.   **(b)** S.I. 1986/1818.

STATUTORY INSTRUMENTS

1987 No. 1637

HOVERCRAFT

The Hovercraft (Fees) Regulations 1987

Made - - - -	*15th September 1987*	
Coming into force	*15th October 1987*	

The Secretary of State for Transport, in exercise of powers conferred on him by article 35 of the Hovercraft (General) Order 1972(**a**) and of all other powers enabling him in that behalf, and with the approval of the Treasury, hereby makes the following Regulations:

Citation and Commencement

1. The Regulations may be cited as the Hovercraft (Fees) Regulations 1987 and shall come into force on 15th October 1987.

Interpretation and Revocation

2.—(1) In these Regulations, unless the context otherwise requires –

"costs of making an investigation" means any costs incurred by the CAA in making an investigation;

"hoverplatform" means a hovercraft with no installed means of propulsion or directional control and where any external agency providing propulsion or directional control is not itself a hovercraft;

"item" means an engine, propeller, fan, instrument, component, radio apparatus or equipment;

"maximum weight of the hovercraft" means the maximum total weight specified in the relevant application;

"the Order" means the Hovercraft (General) Order 1972;

"the weight of the type of hovercraft" means the maximum permissible weight specified in the Type Certificate.

(2) The Hovercraft (Fees) Regulations 1985(**b**) and the Hovercraft (Fees) (Amendment) Regulations 1987(**c**) are hereby revoked.

3. The provisions of the Schedule to these Regulations shall have effect with respect to the fees to be paid in connection with the Certificates and other documents and with tests, inspections, investigations, permissions and approvals, required by or for the purposes of the Order.

(**a**) S.I. 1972/674.   (**b**) S.I. 1985/1605.   (**c**) S.I. 1987/136.

4. For the purposes of these Regulations a variation of a document incorporated by reference in a Certificate shall be treated as variation of the Certificate itself.

Paul Channon
10th September 1987   Secretary of State for Transport

We approve the making of these Regulations.

Michael Neubert
David Lightbown
Two of the Lords Commissioners of
15th September 1987   Her Majesty's Treasury

THE SCHEDULE

Certificate of registration

1. The fee to be paid for the issue of a certificate of registration pursuant to Article 5(7) of the Order shall be £14.

Experimental Certificate

2. Where an application is made for the issue, variation, or renewal of an Experimental Certificate in respect of a hovercraft there shall be paid for any investigations required by the CAA in pursuance of Article 9 of the Order, a fee of an amount equal to the cost of making the investigations:

Provided that the fee shall not exceed, for the first period of 6 months or part thereof required for carrying out the investigations, £15,200 or 31.5p per kg. of the maximum weight of the hovercraft, whichever is the greater amount, and thereafter pro rata for every month or part thereof.

Type Certificates for types of hovercraft

3. Where an application is made for the issue or variation of a Type Certificate in respect of a type of hovercraft, there shall be paid, for any investigations required by the CAA in pursuance of Article 10 of the Order, a fee of an amount equal to the cost of making the investigations:

Provided that

(a) the fee shall not exceed, for the first period of 12 months or part thereof required for carrying out the investigations £36,500 or 75p per kg. of the maximum weight of the hovercraft, whichever is the greater amount, and thereafter pro rata for every month or part thereof;

(b) the cost of the investigations shall not include the cost of investigating any items for which the CAA requires separate type approval;

(c) the cost of the investigations shall not include the cost of any inspection of a craft which also serves as evidence leading to the first issue of a Safety Certificate for that craft.

Type Certificates for items

4. Where an application is made for the issue or variation of a Type Certificate in respect of a type of item, there shall be paid for any investigations required by the CAA in pursuance of Article 10 of the Order, a fee of an amount equal to the cost of making the investigations:

Provided that the fee shall not exceed for the first period of 12 months or part required for carrying out the investigations, £18,250 and thereafter pro rata for every month or part thereof.

Safety Certificates (Issue)

5.—(1) Where an application is made for the issue of a Safety Certificate, in pursuance of Article II of the Order, in respect of a hovercraft which has been used solely in accordance with the conditions of an Experimental Certificate issued by the CAA, the fee to be paid in respect thereof (including any investigations undertaken by the CAA in connection with the application) shall be, for each month or part thereof for which the Safety Certificate is to be in force, on the following scale –

Maximum weight of the Hovercraft	Fee per tonne or part thereof
For the first 10 tonnes	£6.30
For the next 10 tonnes	£4.75
For the next 10 tonnes	£3.15
For the next 10 tonnes	£1.60
For any excess over 40 tonnes	£1.05

plus in each case an amount equal to the fee for an additional 3 months.

(2) Where an application is made for the issue of a Safety Certificate, in pursuance of Article 11 of the Order, in respect of a hovercraft which has not been used solely in accordance with the conditions of an Experimental Certificate issued by the CAA, the fee to be paid in respect thereof shall be in accordance with the scale of sub-paragraph (1) of this paragraph together with a fee equal to the cost of any additional investigations deemed necessary in the circumstances by the CAA:

Provided that the total fee shall not exceed £18,250 or 36p per kg. of the maximum weight of the hovercraft, whichever is the greater amount, for the first period of 12 months or part thereof.

Safety Certificates (Renewal)

6.—(1) Where an application is made for the renewal of a Safety Certificate in pursuance of Article 12 of the Order in respect of a hovercraft, within a period of 7 days from the date of expiry of the previous Certificate and where there has been no change in the conditions affecting maintenance during that period, the fee to be paid in respect thereof (including any investigations undertaken by the CAA in connection with the application) shall be, for each month, or part thereof, for which the Certificate is to be renewed, on the following scale –

Maximum weight of the Hovercraft	Fee per tonne or part thereof
For the first 10 tonnes	£6.30
For the next 10 tonnes	£4.75
For the next 10 tonnes	£3.15
For the next 10 tonnes	£1.60
For any excess over 40 tonnes	£1.05

(2) Where an application for the renewal of a Safety Certificate is not in accordance with the conditions of sub-paragraph (1) of this paragraph or where the storage of the hovercraft has not been in accordance with arrangements having prior CAA approval, the fee to be paid shall be that specified in the scale of sub-paragraph (1) together with the cost of any additional investigations deemed necessary by the CAA:

Provided that the total fee shall not exceed for the first period of 12 months or part thereof £18,250 or 36p per kg. of the maximum weight of the hovercraft, whichever is the greater amount.

Variation of Safety Certificates

7. Where an application is made for the variation of a Safety Certificate there shall be paid for the investigations required by the CAA a fee equal to the cost of making the investigations:

Provided that the fee shall not exceed for any period of 12 months, or part thereof, required for carrying out the investigations £36,500 or 75p per kg. of the maximum weight of the hovercraft, whichever is the greater amount, and thereafter pro rata for every month or part of a month.

Approval of Persons

8.—(1) Subject to sub-paragraph (2) of this paragraph, the fee to be paid per annum by a person for the inspection of his organisation for the purposes of Article 14 of the Order shall, for each branch of the organisation which is separately inspected, be in accordance with the following tables –

A: HOVERCRAFT (EXCLUDING HOVERPLATFORMS)

Table 1: Design and construction

Purpose of approval	Fee per tonne of maximum weight of hovercraft for which approval is applied for and granted	Minimum Fee
Either or both of the following: Design and construction of hovercraft	£3.15	£95

Table 2: Maintenance, overhaul and repair

Purpose of approval	Fee per tonne of the weight of the type of hovercraft having the greatest weight of any types of hovercraft for which approval is applied for and granted	Minimum Fee
Any or all of the following: *Maintenance, overhaul and repair of hovercraft	£1.60	£47

B: ENGINES, PROPELLERS AND FANS

Table 3: Design and manufacture

Purpose of approval	Fee per maximum shaft h.p. of engine, propeller or fan for which approval is applied for and granted	Minimum Fee
Any or all of the following: Design and manufacturer of engines, propellers or fans	16p	£95

---

*1. No fee is payable under Table 2 by an organisation or branch approved for the purposes of construction in respect of approval for the purpose of maintenance, overhaul or repair of hovercraft constructed by that organisation.

2. For approval for the purposes of maintenance, overhaul or repair of hovercraft of which the applicant is the sole operator a fixed fee of £47 will be charged in place of any fees which might otherwise be payable in accordance with Tables 2, 4 or 5.

Table 4: Maintenance, overhaul and repair

Purpose of approval	Fee per shaft h.p. of the type of engine, propeller or fan having the greatest shaft h.p. of a type of engine propeller or fan for which approval is applied for and granted	Minimum Fee
Any or all of the following: †Maintenance, overhaul and repair of engines, propellers or fans	8p	£47

C: OTHER ITEMS
Table 5

Purpose of approval	Fee
Any or all of the following: Manufacture and design of items not referred to in Table 3	£95
Maintenance, overhaul and repair of such items	£47

Table 6

Purpose of approval	Fee
Design and construction of hoverplatforms	An amount equal to the cost of inspection of his organisation: Provided that the fee shall not exceed £3,150

(2) In the application of sub-paragraph (1) of this paragraph:

(a) Where a fee would otherwise be payable in respect of an organisation or branch under Table 1, and also under Tables 3 or 5 or both, a fee shall only be payable in accordance with Table 1.

(b) Where a fee would otherwise be payable in respect of an organisation or branch under Table 2, and also under Tables 4 or 5 or both, a fee shall only be payable in accordance with Table 2.

(c) Where a fee would be payable in respect of a branch or organisation under Table 3, and also under Table 5, a fee shall only be payable in accordance with Table 3.

(d) Where a fee would be payable in respect of a branch or organisation under Table 4, and also under Table 5, a fee shall only be payable in accordance with Table 4.

Maintenance

9.—(1)(a) Where an operator's organisation is not approved for maintenance, there shall be paid for any visits of inspection pursuant to Article 13 of the Order in excess of one per month made by the CAA to the said operator, a fee equal to the cost of making such visits:

Provided that such fee in no case exceed £315 per visit.

(b) Where the said unapproved operator obtains for the purpose of maintenance either goods or services or both from an organisation which is not approved by the CAA for such purpose, there shall be paid by the operator for any visits of inspection made to the suppliers of such goods or services or both, a fee equal to the cost of making such visits:

Provided that

(i) a total of one visit per month to the said operator or such suppliers shall not be subject to charges;

(ii) such fee shall in no case exceed £315 per visit.

---

†No fee is payable under Table 4 by an organisation or branch approved for the purpose of manufacture in respect of approval for the purpose of maintenance, overhaul or repair of engines, propellers or fans manufactured by that organisation or branch.

(2) In this paragraph the term "maintenance" shall be deemed to include the installation of a modification covered by a variation of a document incorporated by reference in a Type Certificate.

(3) In sub-paragraph (1) above "visits of inspection" means visits made to an organisation for the purpose of investigating and approving maintenance arrangements. A visit shall be any visit of twenty-four hours or less.

Operating Permits

10.—(1) The fees to be paid for the issue of an Operating Permit pursuant to Article 18(2) of the Order shall be determined by the amount of work involved (including any investigations carried out preparatory to the issue of the Permit) charged at an hourly rate of £45.50 for each type of hovercraft.

(2) The fee to be paid for amending, at the request of the operator:

(a) the area of operation of a type of hovercraft specified in an existing Operating Permit,

(b) a condition under which an existing Operating Permit has been issued other than that referred to in (a) above,

shall also be determined by the amount of work involved (including any investigations carried out preparatory to the amendment of the Permit) charged at an hourly rate of £45.50.

(3) Notwithstanding sub-paragraph (1) of this paragraph, no fee shall be payable for the issue of an Operating Permit in respect of hovercraft of a type and operating in an area specified in a permit to fly issued to the applicant pursuant to Article 7 of the Air Navigation Order 1985(a) or having effect as if made thereunder.

11. The fees to be paid for an exemption granted under Article 32 of the Order shall be determined by the amount of work involved, charged at an hourly rate of £45.50.

Payment of Fees

12.—(1) The fees specified in paragraphs 1, 10 and 11 of this Schedule shall be payable to the Secretary of State; and fees specified in paragraphs 2 to 9 shall be payable to the CAA.

(2) The fees specified in these Regulations shall be payable upon application being made for the certificate, other document or approval, as the case may be:
Provided that where the amount of the fee depends on the actual costs incurred by the CAA –

(i) they may require that the application shall be accompanied by payment of an amount up to 5 per cent. of the maximum of such fee;

(ii) the fee in respect of the investigations made during any month shall be payable at the end of that month, and any amount paid on application shall be deducted from the fee payable at the end of the final month of investigations.

EXPLANATORY NOTE

(This note is not part of the Regulations)

These Regulations revoke the Hovercraft (Fees) Regulations 1985 and the Hovercraft (Fees) (Amendment) Regulations 1987.

These Regulations prescribe an average increase of 5% in the fees to be paid to the Civil Aviation Authority for the issue of Type and Safety Certificates, and other matters under Part II (Certification and Maintenance) of the Hovercraft (General) Order 1972.

(a) S.I. 1985/1643, to which there is an amendment not relevant to these Regulations.

STATUTORY INSTRUMENTS

1987 No. 1638

PUBLIC HEALTH, ENGLAND AND WALES
PUBLIC HEALTH, SCOTLAND
PUBLIC HEALTH, NORTHERN IRELAND

CONTAMINATION OF FOOD

The Food Protection (Emergency Prohibitions) (Wales) (No. 4) Order 1987

Made - - - -	*17th September 1987*
Laid before Parliament	*17th September 1987*
Coming into force	*18th September 1987*

Whereas the Secretary of State is of the opinion, as mentioned in section 1(1)(a) of the Food and Environment Protection Act 1985(**a**), that there has been or may have been an escape of substances of such descriptions and in such quantities and such circumstances as are likely to create a hazard to human health through human consumption of food;

And whereas the Secretary of State is of the opinion, as mentioned in section 1(1)(b) of the said Act, that in consequence of the said escape of substances food which is or may be in the future in the areas described in the Schedule to the following Order, or which is derived or may be in the future derived from anything in those areas, is, or may be, or may become, unsuitable for human consumption;

Now, therefore, the Secretary of State, in exercise of the powers conferred on him by the said section 1(1) and (2) and section 24(1) and (3) of the said Act, and of all other powers enabling him in that behalf, hereby makes the following Order:

Title, commencement and interpretation

1.—(1) This Order may be cited as the Food Protection (Emergency Prohibitions) (Wales) (No. 4) Order 1987 and shall come into force on 18th September 1987.

(2) In this Order–

    (a) "the Act" means the Food and Environment Protection Act 1985,

    (b) "designated area" means an area described in the Schedule to this Order,

    (c) "sheep" means an animal of the genus *Ovis* of whatever age or sex.

Designated incident

2. In the opinion of the Secretary of State, food in the areas described in the Schedule to this Order, or which is derived or may be in the future derived from anything

---

(**a**) 1985 c.48.

in those areas, is, or may be, or may become unsuitable for human consumption in consequence of the following escape of substances:

the escape on or after 26th April 1986 of radioactive substances from a nuclear powered reactor situated at Chernobyl in the Ukraine, USSR.

Designated areas

3. The areas described in the Schedule to this Order are hereby designated for the purposes of Part I of the Act.

Activities prohibited in the designated areas

4.—(1) Subject to paragraph (2) below, no person shall in a designated area slaughter any sheep for human consumption or for use in the preparation of feeding stuffs.

(2) Paragraph (1) above shall not apply in the case of any sheep which–

(a) was moved from any place in accordance with a consent given under section 2(1) of the Act which consent was subject to the condition that the sheep to which it applies should be marked with a red mark; and

(b) has been examined and marked by an ear-tag by a person authorised in that behalf by one of the Ministers(**a**).

Restrictions on movement

5.—(1) No person shall move any sheep from a farm, holding or agricultural premises situated in a designated area.

(2) Subject to paragraph (3) below, no person shall move into a designated area any sheep which has been removed from a designated area or from an area which is from time to time designated by an order other than this Order under section 1 of the Act which refers to the escape of substances described in article 2 of this Order.

(3) Paragraph (2) above shall not apply in the case of any sheep which was moved from any place in accordance with a consent given under section 2(1) of the Act which was subject to the condition that the sheep to which it applies should be marked with a red mark.

Restrictions throughout the United Kingdom

6.—(1) Subject to paragraph (2) below, no person shall, in the United Kingdom–

(a) slaughter for human consumption or for use in the preparation of feeding stuffs any sheep that was–

(i) in any of the areas numbered 1, 2 and 3 of the designated areas detailed in the Schedule to this Order at any time after 11 a.m. on 20th June 1986; or

(ii) in the area numbered 4 of the designated areas detailed in the said Schedule at any time after 9th July 1987; or

(iii) in any of the areas numbered 5, 6, 7 and 8 of the designated areas detailed in the said Schedule at any time after 10th August 1987; or

(iv) in any of the areas numbered 9, 10, 11 and 12 of the designated areas detailed in the said Schedule at any time after 27th August 1987; or

(v) in any of the areas numbered 13, 14 and 15 of the designated areas detailed in the said Schedule at any time after 17th September 1987, or

(b) supply, or have in possession for supply, any meat derived from a sheep, or any food which contains any such meat, if that sheep was–

(i) in any of the areas numbered 1, 2 and 3 of the designated areas detailed in the Schedule to this Order at any time after 11 a.m. on 20th June 1986; or

(ii) in the area numbered 4 of the designated areas detailed in the said Schedule at any time after 9th July 1987; or

(iii) in any of the areas numbered 5, 6, 7 and 8 of the designated areas detailed in the said Schedule at any time after 10th August 1987; or

(iv) in any of the areas numbered 9, 10, 11 and 12 of the designated areas detailed in the said Schedule at any time after 27th August 1987; or

---

(**a**) The definition of "the Ministers" is in section 24(1) of the Food and Environment Protection Act 1985.

(v) in any of the areas numbered 13, 14 and 15 of the designated areas detailed in the said Schedule at any time after 17th September 1987.

(2) Paragraph (1) above shall not apply in the case of–

(a) any sheep which was moved to a market in accordance with a consent given under section 2(1) of the Act which consent did not require that the sheep to which it applies should be marked in a manner specified therein;

(b) any sheep which was moved from any place in accordance with a consent given under the said section 2(1) which consent was subject to the condition that the sheep to which it applies should be marked with a blue mark; or

(c) any sheep which–

(i) was moved from any place in accordance with a consent given under the said section 2(1) which consent was subject to the condition that the sheep to which it applies should be marked with a red mark, with an apricot mark or with a green mark; and

(ii) has been examined and marked with an ear-tag by a person authorised in that behalf by one of the Ministers.

Revocation

7.   The Food Protection (Emergency Prohibitions) (Wales) (No. 3) Order 1987 **(a)** and the Food Protection (Emergency Prohibitions) (Wales) (No. 3) Amendment Order 1987 **(b)** are hereby revoked.

17th September 1987

Peter Walker
Secretary of State for Wales

(a) S.I. 1987/1515.
(b) S.I. 1987/1553.

SCHEDULE

DESIGNATED AREAS

1. An area comprising that part of the County of Powys which lies within the following boundary–

From the meeting of the Afon Conwy with the Forestry Commission fence at OS map reference SH 999179 generally north-eastwards following the forest boundary fence to its junction with the farm fence at OS map reference SH 995188 then generally northwards following the farm fence to OS map reference SH 998199 and then generally north-westwards along the forest fence to where it crosses the stream at OS map reference SH 989204 and then generally following the course of the stream to where it joins Llyn Efyrnwy near the waterfall at OS map reference SH 995206 and then crossing Llyn Efyrnwy in a generally north-westwards direction to the forest boundary at OS map reference SH 988217 and then following the forestry boundary to its junction with the stream at OS map reference SH 993225 and then generally eastwards following the course of the stream through the forest to its junction with the stream at OS map reference SH 999222 and then generally north-eastwards following the course of the stream to where it meets the forestry boundary at OS map reference SJ 003224 and then generally north-eastwards following the forest boundary to where it joins the fenced Nant Coedwyr Boundary at OS map reference SJ 003226 and then generally north-eastwards, following the fenced Nant Coedwyr Boundary to where it joins the Severn-Trent Boundary at OS map reference SJ 013240 and then generally north-westwards along the Severn-Trent Boundary passing through OS map references SJ 004244 and SJ 003260 to where it joins the fence at the County Boundary at OS map reference SH 990280 at Cyrniau Nod; then westwards and then south-westwards along the fence following the County Boundary passing through OS map references SH 946270 and SH 916229; then generally southwards along the fence to the Severn-Trent Water Authority fence at OS map reference SH 928202 and thereafter as a Forestry Commission fence to a point near Drum Ddu at OS map reference 932166; then continuing generally eastwards along the Forestry Commission fence to where it meets a Forestry Commission fence along a footpath at OS map reference SH 975168; generally northwards following the fence along the footpath to where it meets a Forestry Commission fence at OS map reference SH 972177; generally south-eastwards then north-eastwards along the fence to where it meets the Afon Conwy at OS map reference SH 999179.

The area excludes any part of a road, footpath or body of water by reference to which its boundary is defined.

2. An area comprising that part of the County of Gwynedd which lies within the following boundary–

From where the mountain wall meets the railway line at Conwy at OS map reference SH 775779; generally westwards along the railway line to where it meets the boundary wall at OS map reference SH 744784 on the western side of Penmaen-bach Point; generally southwards along the boundary wall to where it meets the boundary fence at OS map reference SH 747769, generally south-westwards following the boundary fence passing through OS map references SH 730746, SH 728757, SH 703751, SH 703742, SH 711738, SH 700721, SH 693726, SH 693738, SH 683738, SH 689726, SH 680704, SH 660701, SH 656716, SH 636702 and SH 639696 to where it joins the unmarked road near Bryn Hall at OS map reference SH 633693; generally westwards along the unmarked road to the junction with the unmarked road to the north of Llanllechid at OS map reference SH 621690: generally southwards along the unmarked road passing through Llanllechid and Rachub to its junction with the A5(T) and B4366 roads; generally north-westwards along the B4366 road to its junction with an unmarked road at OS map reference SH 616664; generally south-westwards along the unmarked road through Hirdir and Tan-y-Bwlch to where it meets and unmarked road at OS map reference SH 593654; generally southwards along the unmarked road, past Pen-y-bwlch to its junction with the forest fence at OS map reference SH 594644, generally south-eastwards along the forest fence to a point at OS map reference SH 597638 to its junction with the farm fence, generally southwards along the line of the fence at OS map reference SH 597637, generally south-eastwards through a point at OS map reference SH 600635 to a point at OS map reference SH 604630 then generally eastwards along the fence to a point at OS map reference SH 606629, south-eastwards to a point at OS map reference SH 610626 and then north-westwards along the fence to OS map reference SH 606627, generally south-westwards to a point at OS map reference SH 603624 passing through OS map references SH 598620 and SH 597619, generally north-westwards to OS map reference SH 597620, generally south-westwards to OS map reference SH 595618, generally southwards passing through OS map reference SH 595615 to OS map reference SH 597613 on the quarry boundary; generally south-westwards along the line of the quarry incline passing through OS map references SH

596610, SH 592606, SH 590603 and SH 589602, continuing along the track of the quarry incline south-westwards to the unmarked road at OS map reference SH 587601; generally south-westwards along the unmarked road to its junction with the A4086 road at OS map reference SH 583598; generally southwards along the A4086 road to where it meets the boundary fence of the Snowdon Railway at OS map reference SH 583597; generally south-westwards along the boundary fence to where it meets a fence near Afon Hwch at OS map reference SH 578590; generally south-westwards along the fence following the course of Afon Hwch to where it meets Llyn Dwythwch at OS map reference SH 571582; generally southwards along the western edge of Llyn Dwythwch to where it meets a fence at OS map reference SH 568577; generally westwards along the fence to where it meets a fence at OS map reference SH 564576; generally north-westwards along the fence passing through OS map references SH 563578 and SH 560581 to where it meets a fence at OS map reference SH 558582; generally south-westwards along the fence to OS map reference SH 556577; generally north-westwards to OS map reference SH 554578; generally westwards to a disused mine at OS map reference SH 544578; generally south-westwards to OS map reference SH 539577; generally north-westwards along the old Waenfawr/Nant y Betws Parish Boundary to OS map reference SH 535579 where it meets the east bank of Afon Gwyrfai; following the east bank of Afon Gwyrfai northwards to where the disused tramway crosses Afon Gwyrfai at OS map reference SH 534583; south-westwards along the line of the disused tramway over Afon Gwyrfai to where it meets the A4085 road at OS map reference SH 532582; generally south-eastwards along the A4085 road to where it meets a fence near Plasisaf at OS map reference SH 547564; generally eastwards along the fence passing through OS map reference SH 550564 to OS map reference SH 552564; generally north-eastwards along the fence passing through OS map reference SH 553567 to OS map reference SH 555567; generally south-eastwards along the fence to OS map reference SH 557564; generally eastwards along the fence passing through OS map references SH 560564, SH567560 and SH 570599 to its junction with a fence at OS map reference SH 573559; generally south-eastwards along the fence passing through OS map references SH 575554 and SH 580554 to where it meets Afon Trewennydd at OS map reference SH 584548; generally south-westwards along the fence following the course of Afon Trewennydd to where it and Afon Gwyrfai are crossed by the A4085 road at OS map reference SH 568540; generally south-eastwards along the course of the Afon Gwyrfai to where it is crossed by the A4085 road at OS map reference SH 571532; generally south-eastwards along the A4085 road to its junction with the A498 road near Beddgelert at OS map reference SH 591481; generally north-eastwards following the A498 road to a point at OS map reference SH 613494 on the western side of Llyn Dinas then following the lake shore eastwards to join the fence at OS map reference SH 615493 then generally southwards following the mountain wall and field boundaries passing through OS map references SH 616490, SH 620492, SH 621494, SH 624491 and SH 623487 to join Afon Nanmor at OS map reference SH 627478 then generally south-westwards following the course of Afon Nanmor to a point at OS map reference SH 620468, then generally south-westwards following the boundary of Coed Caeddafydd passing through OS map reference SH 621460 and SH 619458 then south-eastwards to a point at OS map reference SH 620454, crossing Afon Dylif at OS map reference SH 621452 then eastwards to OS map reference SH 627452, then generally northwards to the junction of the fences at OS map reference SH 628457; generally eastwards along the fence passing through OS map references SH 630458, SH 635460, SH 639460, SH 640456, SH 644460 and SH 647462; generally southwards along the fence to where it meets Cwm Croesor at OS map reference SH 647459; generally eastwards along the fence following the course of Cwm Croesor to where it meets a disused tramway at OS map reference SH 654460; generally south-eastwards along the disused tramway to where it meets a fence at OS map reference SH 656455; generally south-westwards along the fence to OS map reference SH 650453; generally southwards along the fence passing through OS map references SH 649450 and SH 648449; generally eastwards along the fence to OS map reference SH 650449; generally south-eastwards along the fence to OS map reference SH 654444; generally south-westwards along the fence passing through OS map references SH 650444 and SH 643443 to where it joins a forest fence at OS map reference SH 639437; generally south-eastwards along the forest fence to the junction of the fences at OS map reference SH 641435; generally southwards along the fence to its junction with the forest fence at OS map reference SH 641431; generally south-eastwards along the forest fence passing through OS map references SH 650434, SH 656430, SH 667426 and SH 664420 to its junction with the fence along the Ffestiniog Railway at OS map reference SH 664417; generally eastwards then northwards along the fence following the Ffestiniog Railway to its junction at Blaenau Ffestiniog with Glanarwel road at OS map reference SH 695463; generally north-eastwards along Glanarwel road to its junction with the A470(T) road at OS map reference SH 697467; generally southwards along the A470(T) road to its junction with the A496 road at Blaenau Ffestiniog at OS map reference SH 698460; generally southwards along the A470(T) road to its junction with an unmarked road by Congl-y-wal at OS map reference SH 706444; generally south-westwards along the unmarked road to its junction with an unmarked road at OS map reference SH 697434; generally south-eastwards along the unmarked road to its junction with the A470(T) road at OS map reference SH 706427; generally southwards along the A470(T) road to its junction with the B4391 road at Ffestiniog at OS map reference SH 705418; generally eastwards along the B4391 road to where it meets a fence at OS map reference SH 736417; generally south-westwards along the fence passing through OS map reference SH 733416 to where it meets a fence alongside Afon Cynfal at OS map reference SH 732413; generally eastwards along the fence following the course of Afon Cynfal to its junction with the forest fence at OS map reference SH 734413; generally eastwards then westwards along the forest fence passing through OS map references SH 740408, SH 750410, SH 751409, SH 750405, SH 740398, SH 730397, SH 720397, SH 720395 and SH 715395 to where it meets a fence along a forest track at OS map reference SH 710399; generally south-westwards following the fence along the forest track through Sychnant to OS map reference SH 707398; generally south-westwards following the fence to a point north of Castell Tomen-y-Mur north of Trawsfynydd at OS map reference SH 708387 generally south-eastwards following field boundaries passing through OS map references SH 710387, SH 719380, SH 720379 and SH 724378 then north-eastwards passing through OS map references SH 727379 and SH 730378 then generally southwards passing through OS map references SH 729376, SH 726370 and SH 726366 then eastwards to Afon Llafar at OS map reference SH 733373 then southwards following the course of the river to the A4212 road at OS map reference SH 737363 then eastwards along the road to OS map reference SH 741363 and then following Afon Prysor westwards to its confluence with Nant Budr at OS map reference SH 737360 then following the course of Nant Budr south-eastwards to the fence at OS map reference SH 750347 and then following the line of the fence south-eastwards passing through OS map references SH 753344 and SH 755343 to Afon Gain at OS map reference SH 756339, then following the course of Afon Gain generally southwards to the forest fence at OS map reference SH 755336 then following the fence southwards to Pont y Gain at OS map reference SH 752328 where it meets an unmarked road; generally eastwards along the unmarked road to where it meets a fence at OS map reference SH 829325 near Buarthmeini; generally north-eastwards following the fence to where it meets the forest at OS map reference SH 832328; following the fence around the forest generally north to OS map reference SH 833343; generally north-westwards along the fence passing through OS map reference SH 830345 to OS map reference SH 823350; generally north-eastwards along the fence passing through OS map references SH 818352, SH 820353, SH 825360 and SH 826370 to OS map reference SH 830371; generally north-westwards along the fence passing through OS map reference SH 820379 to OS map reference SH 811381; generally southwards along the fence to OS map reference SH 812378; generally westwards along the fence to OS map reference SH 809378; generally northwards along the fence passing through OS map reference SH 811380 to where it joins Afon Tryweryn at OS map reference SH 808385; generally eastwards along the fence following the course of Afon Tryweryn to where it meets an unmarked road at OS map reference SH 817394; generally northwards along the unmarked road to its junction with the A4212 and B4391 roads at OS map reference SH 817395; generally north-westwards along the B4391 road to where it meets a fence at OS map reference SH 812397; generally north-eastwards along the fence passing through OS map references SH 814400 and SH 814403; generally eastwards along the fence passing through OS map references SH 820402, SH 830401 and SH 833405 to its junction with a forest fence at OS map reference SH 835403; generally south-eastwards along the forest fence to its junction with a fence at OS map reference SH 836401; generally south-eastwards along the fence to where it meets the A4212 road and a fence at OS map reference SH 837400; generally south-eastwards along the fence to where it meets Afon Tryweryn at OS map reference SH 838399; generally eastwards along the course of Afon Tryweryn to Llyn Celyn; generally eastwards along the southern bank at Llyn Celyn to where it meets the A4212 road at OS map reference SH 880404, generally south-eastwards along the A4212 road to its crossing of Afon Hesgyn at OS map reference SH 894401; generally north-westwards along the course of Afon Hesgyn passing through OS map references SH 890410, SH 885420 and OS map reference SH 884426 to where it meets a fence; generally eastwards along the fence to OS map reference SH 890425 and generally north-eastwards along the fence to OS map reference SH 895430; generally northwards along the fence to its junction with a stream at OS map reference SH 895437 then northwards along the fence to its junction with a stream at OS map reference SH 895442; generally north-eastwards along the fence to OS map reference SH 900450; generally eastwards along the fence to its junction with the unmarked road at OS map reference SH 908450; generally north-westwards along the unmarked road to where it meets a fence at OS map reference SH 907454; generally south-westwards along the fence to OS map reference SH 900452; generally north-westwards along the fence crossing Afon Nant-Fach at OS map reference SH 897454 to its junction with a fence along the County Boundary above Trum Nant-Fach at OS map reference SH 891458; generally south-westwards, north-westwards and north-eastwards along the fence following the County Boundary to where it meets a fence alongside Nant-y-Glychedd at OS map reference SH 868458; generally northwards along the fence following Nant-y-Glychedd then Nant Glan Gwrach to its Junction with a fence at OS map reference SH 866470; generally south-westwards and then north-westwards along the fence through OS map references SH

863467, SH 861470 and SH 860474 to its junction with Nant Adwy'r-llan at OS map reference SH 858474; generally south-westwards along the course of Nant Adwy'r-llan to its junction with a fence at OS map reference SH 844461; generally westwards and then south-westwards along the fence through OS map references SH 843460, SH 839458 and SH 840457; generally south-westwards along the fence along the bank of Afon Marddwr to its junction with the fence at OS map reference SH 836454; generally south-westwards along the fence through OS map reference SH 836450 and which continues alongside Afon Marddwr to OS map reference SH 830444; generally westwards along the fence through OS map references SH 826443, SH 824445, SH 820446 to its junction with Afon Serw at OS map reference SH 818447; generally northwards following the course of Afon Serw to its confluence with Afon Conwy at OS map reference SH 816455; generally south-westwards along the course of Afon Conwy to its junction with the fence at OS map reference SH 806453; generally northwards along the fence through OS map references SH 806457, SH 809470, SH 811484 and SH 812493 to its junctions with a fence at OS map reference SH 812499; generally north-eastwards along the fence to its junction with a fence at OS map reference SH 815506; generally westwards to its junction with a forest fence at OS map reference SH 814507; generally south-westwards along the forest fence passing through OS map reference SH 811500 to its junction with a forest fence at OS map reference SH 802492; generally north-westwards along the forest fence passing through OS map reference SH 798497 to OS map reference SH 794498; generally southwards along the forest fence to its junction with a fence at OS map reference SH 793474; generally north-westwards along the fence passing through OS map reference SH 790477 to OS map reference SH 787481; generally south-westwards along the fence passing through OS map reference SH 780477 to its junction with the forest fence at OS map reference SH 771473; generally southwards along the forest fence to its junction with a fence at OS map reference SH 771464; generally southwards along the fence to OS map reference SH 769457; generally westwards along the fence to its junction with a fence at OS map reference SH 764457; generally north-westwards along the fence to OS map reference SH 759464; generally westwards along the fence to OS map reference SH 750465 to its junction with the forest fence at OS map reference SH 747466; generally south-westwards along the forest fence passing near to a quarry to OS map reference SH 739453; generally north-westwards along the forest fence to its junction with a fence at OS map reference SH 735457; generally westwards along the fence passing through OS map reference SH 730459 to OS map reference SH 728458; generally north-eastwards along the fence passing through OS map references SH 731465 and SH 731470 to its junction with a forest fence at OS map reference SH 734477; generally north eastwards along the forest fence to its junction with a fence at OS map reference SH 738480; generally eastwards along the fence to its junction with a fence at OS map reference SH 739482; generally eastwards along the fence passing through OS map references SH 742483, SH 745482 and SH 750483, to where it meets a stream at OS map reference SH 753484; generally south-eastwards along the fence following the course of the stream passing through OS map reference SH 759477 to where it meets an unmarked road at OS map reference SH 761477; generally north-eastwards along the fence following the unmarked road to where it meets Afon Machno at OS map reference SH 764479; generally northwards along the course of Afon Machno to where it meets a forest fence at OS map reference SH 763482; generally westwards along the forest fence to OS map reference SH 755482; generally north-eastwards along the forest fence to OS map reference SH 756482; generally eastwards along the forest fence to OS map reference SH 759484; generally westwards along the forest fence passing through OS map reference SH 750485 to OS map reference SH 744487; generally south-westwards along the forest fence to its junction with a fence at OS map reference SH 742483; generally westwards along the fence to its junction with the forest fence at OS map reference SH 739482; generally northwards along the forest fence to its junction with the fence at OS map reference SH 744489; generally north-eastwards along the fence to OS map reference SH 749491; generally north-westwards along the fence to OS map reference SH 745497; generally north-eastwards along the fence passing through OS map references SH 748500, SH 750503 and SH 756506 to OS map reference SH 757510; generally northwards along the fence to OS map reference SH 757514; generally north-westwards along the fence to its junction with a forest fence at OS map reference SH 750516; generally north-westwards along the forest fence to where it meets an unmarked road at OS map reference SH 737521; generally northwards along the unmarked road to its junction with the A470(T) road at OS map reference SH 735524; generally north-eastwards along the A470(T) road to where it meets Afon Conwy at OS map reference SH 798547; generally eastwards then northwards along the A470(T) road to its junction with the A5(T) road at Waterloo Bridge near Betws y Coed; generally westwards along the A5(T) road to its junction with an unmarked road near Ty Hyll at OS map reference SH 756575; generally westwards along the unmarked road to where it meets a fence at OS map reference SH 754575; generally southwards along the fence to OS map reference SH 754570 then westwards along the fence to where it meets a stream at OS map reference SH 752570; generally southwards along the fence through OS map references SH 752569, SH 752565 and SH 752561; generally south-eastwards to OS map reference SH 754555; generally south-westwards through OS map references SH 750551 and SH 743548 to its junction with Afon Ystumiau at OS map reference SH 741547; generally westwards along the course of Afon Ystumiau to its junction with the fence at OS map reference SH 738546; generally north-westwards to its junction with the forest fence at OS map reference SH 737547; generally westwards along the forest fence to OS map reference SH 736546; generally north-westwards to OS map reference SH 733548; northwards to OS map reference SH 733550; generally generally north-eastwards through OS map references SH 737557 and SH 740560 to OS map reference SH 743567; in a generally anti-clockwise direction around the forest to OS map reference SH 743568; generally northwards through OS map reference SH 743569 to its junction with the Afon Llugwy at OS map reference SH 743573; generally westwards along the course of Afon Llugwy to the A4086 road and its junction with a fence at OS map reference SH 741572; generally north-westwards along the fence to OS map reference SH 738579; generally north-eastwards along the forest fence passing through OS map references SH 740583, SH 747588, SH 747590 and SH 748594 to where it meets Llyn Bychan at OS map reference SH 752594; generally north-eastwards along the bank of Llyn Bychan to where it meets a forest fence at OS map reference SH 753595; generally westwards along the forest fence passing through OS map reference SH 765596 to where it meets Llyn Bodgynydd at OS map reference SH 760594; generally southwards and north-eastwards along the bank of Llyn Bodgynydd to where it meets a forest fence at OS map reference SH 763595; generally north-eastwards along the forest fence to where it meets an unmarked road at OS map reference SH 768595; generally north-westwards along the unmarked road to where it meets a forest fence at OS map reference SH 764599; generally north-eastwards along the forest fence passing through OS map references SH 765602, SH 763603 and SH 765604 to where it meets Llyn Geirionydd at OS map reference SH 764605; generally northwards along the bank of Llyn Geirionydd to where it meets a forest fence at OS map reference SH 765612; generally eastwards along the forest fence to OS map reference SH 767612 then northwards along the forest fence to OS map reference SH 768618 then southwards along the forest fence to where it meets Llyn Geirionydd at OS map reference SH 766615; generally westwards along the bank of Llyn Geirionydd to where it meets a boundary fence at OS map reference SH 764614; generally north-westwards along the boundary fence passing through OS map references SH 762616, SH 760615 and SH 759619 to where it meets Afon Crafnant at OS map reference SH 757619; generally south-westwards along the western side of Llyn Crafnant to where it is met by a forest fence at OS map reference SH 748611; generally north-westwards along the forest fence to its junction with a fence at OS map reference SH 742620; generally northwards along the fence to OS map reference SH 742625; generally westwards along the fence passing through OS map reference SH 740624 to OS map reference SH 737624; generally northwards along the fence to where it meets Llyn Cowlyd Reservoir at OS map reference SH 737631; generally northwards along the edge of Llyn Cowlyd Reservoir to where it meets a fence along Afon Ddu at OS map reference SH 739633; generally north-eastwards along the fence along the course of Afon Ddu to where it meets a fence at OS map reference SH 757649; generally westwards along the fence to OS map reference SH 752649; generally north-westwards to OS map reference SH750653; generally north-eastwards to OS map reference SH 749660; generally north-westwards crossing Afon-Porth-Llwyd at OS map reference SH 743665 passing through OS map references SH 742670 and SH 743674 to where it meets Afon Dulyn at OS map reference SH 738677; generally south-westwards following the course of Afon Dulyn to OS map reference SH 730674; generally north-westwards along the fence passing through OS map references SH 725680, SH 720690, SH 710697 and SH 709698 where it meets the National Trust Boundary; generally northwards along the boundary to OS map reference SH 709700; generally north-westwards along the fence to OS map reference SH 707708; generally north-eastwards to OS map reference SH 709714; generally north-eastwards along the boundary wall passing through OS map references SH 716722, SH 739728, SH 749738, SH 745737, SH 747751, SH 753761, SH 761761, SH 762771 and SH 749772 to its junction with the railway line at OS map reference SH 77579 at Conwy.

The area excludes any part of a road, footpath or body of water by reference to which its boundary is defined.

3. An area comprising that part of the County of Gwynedd which lies within the following boundary–

From where the forest fence meets a fence at OS map reference SH 806288; generally southwards along the forest fence to its junction with a fence at OS map reference SH 796238; generally southwards along the fence to its junction with a fence at OS map reference SH 796234; generally north-eastwards along the fence to its junction with Afon Eiddon at OS map reference SH 807239; generally north-eastwards following the course of Afon Eiddon to where it meets a fence at OS map reference SH 814248; generally eastwards along the fence to its junction with a fence at OS map reference SH 815248; generally southwards along the fence passing through OS map references SH 815244 and SH 815240 to OS map reference SH 814237; generally westwards along the fence to OS map reference SH 813237; generally southwards along the fence passing through OS map references SH 812234 and SH 810232 to

SH 809229; generally south-eastwards along the fence to OS map reference SH 811227; generally south-westwards along the fence to OS map reference SH 809225; generally south-eastwards along the fence to where it meets the A494(T) road at OS map reference SH 810224; generally north-eastwards along the A494(T) road to where it meets the Afon Wnion at OS map reference SH 812225; generally westwards along the course of Afon Wnion to its confluence with Nant Terfyn at OS map reference SH 809218; generally southwards along the course of Nant Terfyn to where it meets a forest fence at OS map reference SH 809217; generally south-eastwards then westwards along the fence around the forest to where it meets Nant Terfyn at OS map reference SH 811215; generally southwards along the course of Nant Terfyn to where it meets the forest fence at OS map reference SH 812214; generally westwards, then south eastwards, then southwards along the fence passing through OS map references SH 801209, SH 809206, SH 813210 and SH 814200 to where it meets a stream at OS map reference SH 822192; generally south eastwards along the course of the stream to where it meet a forest fence at OS map reference SH 826187 along the Parish boundary; generally north-eastwards following the fence along the Parish boundary passing by Glasgwm at OS map reference SH 845196, by Drws Bach at OS map reference SH 862213, turning eastwards about Creiglyn Dyfiant at OS map reference SH 865230 to its junction with Cwm Llwydd at OS map reference SH 872229; generally north-eastwards along the course of Cwm Llwydd to join Cwm Ffynnon at OS map reference SH 874238; generally south-westwards along the course of Cwm Ffynnon to its junction with the fence at OS map reference SH 872238; generally northwards along the fence to OS map reference SH 874247; generally eastwards along the fence to OS map reference SH 875246; generally north-eastwards along the fence passing through OS map reference SH 879250 to its junction with Llyn Lliwbran at OS map reference SH 878255; along the south bank of Llyn Lliwbran generally westwards to its junction with the fence at OS map reference SH 874256; generally westwards along the fence to OS map reference SH 870256; generally northwards along the fence to Craig y Geifr at OS map reference SH 872269; generally westwards along the fence to a forest plantation at OS map reference SH 865268; generally southwards along the fence following the forest plantation's eastern boundary to its junction with the fence at OS map reference SH 865261; generally westwards then north-westwards along the fence to its junction with a forest plantation near Llechwedd-Fwyalchen at OS map reference SH 859272; generally westwards along the fence following the southern boundary of the forest plantation near Llechwedd-Fwyalchen at OS map reference SH 859276; generally westwards along the fence to its junction with the A494(T) road at OS map reference SH 852276; generally south-westwards along the A494(T) road to its crossing of Afon Mynach at OS map reference SH 832246; generally north-westwards following the course of Afon Mynach to where it meets a fence at OS map reference SH 824254; generally north-westwards along the fence to OS map reference SH 822257; generally north-eastwards along the fence to OS map reference SH 823258; generally north-westwards along the fence passing through OS map references SH 821260 and SH 820261 to OS map reference SH 818263; generally north-eastwards along the fence to OS map reference SH 820266; generally south-eastwards along the fence to OS map reference SH 823264; generally north-eastwards along the fence to its junction with a forest fence alongside Afon Dyfrdwy at OS map reference SH 826269; generally north-westwards along the fence passing through OS map references SH 820274 and SH 815280 to where it meets a fence at OS map reference SH 817287; generally westwards along the fence passing through map references, SH 810287 and SH 809291 to where it meets a forest fence at OS map reference SH 806288;

The area excludes any part of a road, footpath or body of water by reference to which its boundary is defined.

4. An area comprising that part of the County of Gwynedd which lies within the following boundary–

From where the unmarked road meets a forest fence at OS map reference SH 792333 generally south and south-eastwards along the forest fence to OS map reference SH 803314; generally south-westwards along the forest fence to where it meets Afon Bryn-lliw-fawr at OS map reference SH 773297; generally southwards along Afon Bryn-lliw-fawr to its confluence with Afon Mawddach at OS map reference SH 771293; generally south-westwards along Afon Mawddach to where it is crossed by an unmarked roat at Pont Aber-Geirw at OS map reference SH 768292; generally southwards along the unmarked road to its junction with an unmarked road at OS map reference SH 768286; generally south-westwards along the unmarked road to where it meets a forest fence at OS map reference SH 766284; generally south-westwards along the forest fence to OS map reference SH 763278; generally south-eastwards to OS map reference SH 768276; generally north-eastwards to meet Afon Ceirw at OS map reference SH 774281; generally south-eastwards along the fence following the course of Afon Ceirw to OS map reference SH 776276; generally westwards along the fence to OS map reference SH 771275; generally south-eastwards to where the fence meets the mountain wall at OS map reference SH 772265; generally eastwards along the mountain wall passing through OS map reference SH 774268, SH 778269 and SH 780266 to where it meets a fence at OS map reference SH 782264; generally eastwards along the fence to OS map reference SH 782265 to where it meets Nant yr Helyg at OS map reference SH 792267; generally north-eastwards along the fence following Nant yr Helyg then Afon Mawddach to its junction with the forest fence at OS map reference SH 806288; generally eastwards along the fence passing through OS map references SH 809291 and SH 810287 to where it meets a forest fence at OS map reference SH 817287; generally eastwards along the forest fence passing through OS map references SH 823290, SH 840290 and SH 850295 to OS map reference SH 866299 where it meets an unmarked road; generally north-eastwards along the unmarked road to its junction with the A494(T) road at OS map reference SH 872303; generally northwards along the A494(T) road to its junction with an unmarked road at OS map reference SH 872306; generally westwards along the unmarked road to its junction with an unmarked road at OS map reference SH 852308; generally north-eastwards along the unmarked road crossing Afon Lliw to its junction with an unmarked road at OS map reference SH 853309; generally north-westwards along the unmarked road passing by Ty'n-y-bwlch to its meeting with an unmarked road at OS map reference SH 829325 near Buarthmeini; generally westwards along the unmarked road to where it meets a forest fence at OS map reference SH 792333;

The area excludes any part of a road, footpath or body of water by reference to which its boundary is defined.

5. An area comprising that part of the County of Gwynedd which lies within the following boundary–

From the junction of the B5113 road and the unmarked road at OS map reference SH 837621 near Gorswen generally eastwards along the unmarked road to where it meets a fence on the County boundary at OS map reference SH 853623; generally southwards along the fence following the County boundary to where it meets an unmarked road at OS map reference SH 858599; generally westwards along the unmarked road to its junction with the B5113 road at OS map reference SH 838588; generally northwards along the B5113 road to its junction with the unmarked road at OS map reference SH 837621 near Gorswen.

The area excludes any part of a road, footpath or body of water by reference to which its boundary is defined.

6. An area comprising that part of the County of Gwynedd which lies within the following boundary–

From where two fences at OS map reference SH 811487 generally eastwards along the fence to where it meets a fence at OS map reference SH 815488 at Afon Rhydyrhalen; generally north eastwards along the fence following Afon Rhydyrhalen to where it meets a fence at the confluence of the Afon Rhydyrhalen and Afon Eidda at OS map reference SH 827495; generally southwestwards along the fence passing through OS map reference SH 826491 to where it meets an unmarked road at OS map reference SH 825488; generally westwards along the unmarked road to where it meets a fence at Afon Eidda at OS map reference SH 823489; generally southwestwards along the fence to where it meets a fence at OS map reference SH 819486; generally southwestwards along the fence passing through OS map references SH 816486 and SH 813484 to where it meets a fence at OS map reference SH 810484; generally northwards along the fence to where it meets a fence at OS map reference SH 811487.

The area excludes any part of a road, footpath or body of water by reference to which its boundary is defined.

7. An area comprising that part of the County of Gwynedd which lies within the following boundary–

From where a fence meets Nant Adwy'r-Llan at OS map reference SH 858474 generally northwards follows the course of Nant Adwy'r-Llan to where it meets a fence at OS map reference SH 859476; generally northwestwards along the fence passing through OS map references SH 857479, SH 859482, SH 855485, SH 854487 and SH 850489 to where it meets an unmarked road at OS map reference SH 848491; generally northwards along the unmarked road to where it meets a fence at OS map reference SH 849492; generally northwestwards along the fence to where it meets Afon Conwy at OS map reference SH 848495; generally northeastwards following the course of Afon Conwy to where it meets a fence at its confluence with Afon Caletwr at OS map reference SH 854501; generally southeastwards along the fence following Afon Caletwr to where it meets an unmarked road at OS map reference SH 857494; generally northeastwards along the unmarked road to where it meets a fence on the County boundary at OS map reference SH 861497; generally southeastwards then southwestwards along the fence following the County boundary to where it meets a fence near Nant-y-Glychedd at OS map reference SH 868460; generally northwards along the fence following Nant-y-Glychedd then Nant Glan Gwrach to its junction with a fence at OS map reference SH 866470; generally southwestwards and then northwestwards along the fence through OS map references SH 863467, SH 861470 and SH 860470 to where it meets Nant Adwy'r-Llan at OS map reference SH 858474.

The area excludes any part of a road, footpath or body of water by reference to which its boundary is defined.

8. An area comprising that part of the County of Gwynedd which lies within the following boundary–

From where the forest fence meets a forest fence at OS map reference SH 811500 generally southwestwards along the forest fence to where it meets a forest fence at OS map reference SH 804496; generally northwards along the forest fence to where it meets a fence by Nant y Parc at OS map reference SH 803499; generally northwards along the fence following Nant y Parc passing through OS map references SH 803500 and SH 805507 to where it meets a fence at the confluence of Nant y Parc and Nant Ffridd Wen at OS map reference SH 806510 generally southeastwards along the fence following Nant Ffridd Wen to where it meets a forest fence at OS map reference SH 808508; generally southeastwards then southwards along the forest fence passing through OS map references SH 812508 and SH 811505 to where it meets a forest fence at OS map reference SH 811500.

The are excludes any part of a road, footpath or body of water by reference to which its boundary is defined.

9. An area comprising that part of the County of Gwynedd which lies within the following boundary–

From where the fence meets Llyn Crafnant at OS map reference SH 751614, generally south-westwards along the edge of Llyn Crafnant to where it is met by a forest fence at OS map reference SH 748611; generally north-westwards along the forest fence to its junction with a fence at OS map reference SH 742620; generally northwards along the fence to OS map reference SH 742625; generally westwards along the fence passing through OS map reference SH 740624 to OS map reference SH 737624; generally northwards along the fence to where it meets Llyn Cowlyd Reservoir at OS map reference SH 737631; generally northwards along the edge of Llyn Cowlyd Reservoir to where it meets a fence along the Afon Ddu at OS map reference SH 739633; generally north-eastwards along the fence along the course of the Afon Ddu passing through OS map references SH 757649 and SH 759651; and continuing along the course of the Afon Ddu to the bridge on the B5106 at OS map reference SH 775663; generally southwards along the B5106 passing through OS map references SH 779652, SH 780644 and SH 780639 to the junction of the B5106 with an unmarked road at OS map reference SH 780636; southwards along the unmarked road to the junction with the unmarked roads at OS map reference SH 779632; westwards along an unmarked road passing through OS map reference SH 778632 to OS map reference SH 769631; then generally south-westwards to where the unmarked road meets the Afon Crafnant at OS map reference SH 757620; then south-westwards along the course of the Afon Crafnant to where it meets the Llyn Crafnant at OS map reference SH 753616 and then along the western edge of Llyn Crafnant to where it meets with the fence at OS map reference SH 751614.

The area excludes any part of a road, footpath or body of water by reference to which its boundary is defined.

10. An area comprising that part of the County of Gwynedd which lies within the following boundary–

From where the weir of Llyn Celyn and a track meet at OS map reference SH 877398 generally southwards along the track to OS map reference SH 880394 then southwards along the fence passing through OS map references SH 878390 and SH 879387; generally north-westwards and westwards along the fence passing through OS map references SH 878387, SH 877390, SH 876391, SH 875390 and SH 874389; generally south-westwards along the fence to OS map reference SH 875387; generally westwards along the fence passing through OS map references SH 872385, SH 870385, SH 867384, SH 867383 to SH 864384; generally south-westwards along the fence crossing an unmarked road at OS map reference SH 864383 and crossing Nant Aberbleidoyn at OS map reference SH 863382 and passing through OS map reference SH 863380 to OS map reference SH 861374; generally south-eastwards along the fence to OS map reference SH 865370; generally south-westwards along the fence passing through OS map references SH 865369, SH 864367 and SH 863366; generally westwards along the fence passing through OS map reference SH 858367 to where it meets Nant Hir at OS map reference SH 853367; generally westwards along the fence following the course of Nant Hir then Pistyll Gwyn through OS map references SH 850369 and SH 846367 to its junction with a fence at OS map reference SH 845367; generally southwards along the fence passing through OS map references SH 848365 and SH 847360 to where it meets the Afon

Llafar at OS map reference SH 847353; generally westwards along the fence following the course of Afon Llafar to its junction with a fence at OS map reference SH 845353; generally southwards along the fence passing through OS map references SH 844352, SH 844350, SH 845348, SH 843346, SH 844346 and SH 842344; generally westwards along the fence passing through OS map reference SH 840344 to its junction with a fence at OS map reference SH 833343.

The area excludes any part of a road, footpath or body of water by reference to which its boundary is defined.

11. An area comprising that part of the County of Clwyd which lies within the following boundary–

From where the fence meets the County Boundary at OS map reference SH 881482 south-eastwards along the fence to OS map reference SH 884478; along the fence in a north-easterly direction to OS map reference SH 888480; southwards to where the fence meets the Nant Tyr'nyr-erw at OS map reference SH 889479; eastwards along the fence to OS map reference SH 893479; southwards along the fence to OS map reference SH 894477; generally south-eastwards, passing through OS map references SH 895477, SH 896476 and SH 898476 to where the fence meets the unmarked road at OS map reference SH 898475; south-westwards along the unmarked road to the junction with another unmarked road near Tyn-y-rhos; generally south-eastwards along the unmarked road to where it meets the fence on the County Boundary at OS map reference SH 903467; generally south-westwards along the fence following the County Boundary to OS map reference SH 871446; north-westwards following the fence on the County Boundary to OS map reference SH 867451; generally north-eastwards along the fence following the County Boundary to where it meets the fence at OS map reference SH 871482 near Copa Ceiliog.

The area excludes any part of a road, footpath or body of water by reference to which its boundary is defined.

12. An area comprising that part of the County of Clwyd which lies within the following boundary–

From where the fence meets the County Boundary and unmarked road at OS map reference SH 861497; generally north-eastwards to the junction of the unmarked road with an unmarked mountain road and gate at OS map references SH 862499, continuing along the track in a north-easterly direction to OS map reference SH 867499; generally southwards along the track to where it meets with a fence at OS map reference SH 868496; generally south-eastwards along the fence to OS map reference SH 877487; south-westwards to where the fence meets the County Boundary at OS map reference SH 875485 near Copa Ceiliog; generally north-westwards following the fence on the County Boundary to where it meets an unmarked road at OS map reference SH 861497.

The area excludes any part of a road, footpath or body of water by reference to which its boundary is defined.

13. An area comprising that part of the County of Gwynedd which lies within the following boundary–

From the confluence of the Afon Prysor with Nant Budr at OS map reference SH 737360; following the course of Nant Budr south-eastwards to the fence at OS map reference SH 750347; following the line of the fence south-eastwards to Afon Gain at OS map reference SH 756339; following the course of the Afon Gain generally southwards to the forest fence at OS map reference SH 755336; following the fence southwards to Pont y Gain at OS map reference SH 752328 then following the Afon Gain to where it meets an unmarked road near Pont-y-Llyn-du at OS map reference SH 731306; generally north-westwards along the unmarked road until it meets the A470(T) at OS map reference SH 711349, generally southwards along the A470(T) passing through OS map reference SH 712318, SH 714301 and SH 715291 until it meets a fence and public footpath at OS map reference SH 715287 near Gelli-goch; along the public footpath in a generally north-westwards direction to a ford at the confluence of the Afon Eden and Afon Crawcwellt at OS map reference SH 712290; westwards along the course of the Afon Crawcwellt to where it meets a fence at a ford at OS map reference SH 693289; generally south-westwards along the fence which forms the eastern boundary to the forest known as Coed y Brenin Forest to OS map reference SH 679278; along the forest boundary fence in a north-westwards direction to OS map reference SH 672286, then continuing in a south-westwards direction to the junction with a path at OS map reference SH 670288; following the path in a south-westwards direction to the fence at OS map reference SH 665282; along the fence in a generally south-westwards direction passing through OS map references SH 658280 and SH 644269, to where the fence meets the Afon Cwmnantcol at OS map reference SH 637263; along the course of the Afon Cwmnantcol in a generally west-north-westwards direction passing through OS map references SH 625267, SH

615569 and SH 610265 to the reservoir at OS map reference SH 604269; along the northern edge of the reservoir to the dam at OS map reference SH 603269 and continuing along the Afon Cwmnantcol to where it meets with an unmarked road at OS map reference SH 600274; along the road in a north-eastwards direction to its junction with another unmarked road near Werngron at OS map reference SH 609283; north-westwards along this road passing by Maesyraelfor and Cefnfilltir to its junction with the B4573, also known as Stryd Fawr, Harlech at OS map reference SH 582311; along the B4573 in a generally north-eastwards direction to the junction with the A496 at OS map reference SH 606349; along the A496 in a north-eastwards direction to the junction with the Afon Prysor at Pont Felinrhyd-fawr at OS map reference SH 653396; along the course of the Afon Prysor in a south-eastwards direction until it meets Llyn Trawsfynydd at OS map reference SH 674377; following the south-western boundary of the lake passing through OS map references SH 689359 and SH 701349 until it meets the Afon Prysor at OS map reference SH 708349 then following the Afon Prysor in a north-eastwards direction passing through OS map references SH 711350 and SH 727352 to where it meets with Nant Budr at OS map reference SH 737360.

The area excludes any part of a road, footpath or body of water by reference to which its boundary is defined.

14. An area comprising that part of the County of Gwynedd which lies within the following boundary–

From the junction of the A5(T) with an unmarked road near Ty Hyll at OS map reference SH 756575; generally westwards along the unmarked road to where it meets a fence at OS map reference SH 754575; generally southwards along the fence to OS map reference SH 754570 then westwards along the fence to where it meets a stream at OS map reference SH 752570; generally southwards along the fence through OS map references SH 752569, SH 752565 and SH 752561; generally south-eastwards to OS map reference SH 754555; generally south-westwards through OS map references SH 750551 and SH 743548 to its junction with Afon Ystumiau at OS map reference SH 741547; generally westwards along the course of Afon Ystumiau to its junction with the fence at OS map reference SH 738546; generally north-westwards to its junction with the forest fence at OS map reference SH 737547; generally westwards along the forest fence to OS map reference SH 736546; generally north-westwards to OS map reference SH 733548; northwards to OS map reference SH 733550; generally north-eastwards through OS map references SH 737557 and SH 740560 to OS map reference SH 743567; in a generally anti-clockwise direction around the forest to the unmarked road at OS map reference SH 743568; along the unmarked road to the junction of the A5(T) with an unmarked road near Ty Hyll at OS map reference SH 756575.

The area excludes any part of a road, footpath or body of water by reference to which its boundary is defined.

15. An area comprising that part of the County of Gwynedd which lies within the following boundary–

From the forest fence at OS map reference SH 802496 generally north-westwards along the forest fence to the junction with an unmarked road at OS map reference SH 798497 north-westwards along the unmarked road to the junction with another unmarked road at OS map reference SH 795502; then northwards along the road to the junction with the B4406 at OS map reference SH 795511; then north-eastwards along the B4406 to where it meets with Nant Caddugen at OS map reference SH 800518; following the course of the Nant Caddugen in a generally south-eastwards direction to where it meets with the Nant y Parc at OS map reference SH 808513; then southwards following the course of the Nant y Parc to where it meets with a fence at the confluence of the Nant y Parc with the Nant Ffridd Wen at OS map reference SH 806510 then generally southwards along the fence to where it meets with a track at SH 802496.

The area excludes any part of a road, footpath or body of water by reference to which its boundary is defined.

EXPLANATORY NOTE

(This note is not part of the Order)

This Order replaces in relation to areas of land in Wales the Food Protection (Emergency Prohibitions) (Wales) (No. 3) Order 1987 ("the preceding order"). It contains emergency prohibitions restricting various activities in order to prevent human consumption of food which has been or which may have been rendered unsuitable for that purpose in consequence of the escape of radioactive substances from a nuclear reactor situated at Chernobyl in the USSR.

The Order designates areas of land in Wales affected by the escape from which the movement of sheep, and in which the slaughter of sheep, are prohibited (articles 3, 4, 5(1) and the Schedule). These areas comprise the areas designated by the preceding order together with three other areas. All these other areas are in the County of Gwynedd and are respectively numbered 13, 14 and 15 in the Schedule. The prohibition on slaughter in the designated areas does not apply to any sheep identified by a red paint mark which have been examined and subsequently marked by an ear-tag by a person authorised by the Minister of Agriculture, Fisheries and Food or the Secretary of State (article 4(2)). Movement into a designated area of sheep which have been removed from it or from a similarly designated area elsewhere in the United Kingdom (other than sheep which have been identified by a red paint mark, and moved, in accordance with a Ministerial consent) is prohibited (article 5(2)).

Restrictions on the slaughter of sheep which were–

(a) in any of the designated areas numbered 1, 2 and 3 in the Schedule after 11 a.m. on 20th June 1986;

(b) in the designated area numbered 4 in the Schedule after 9th July 1987;

(c) in any of the designated areas numbered 5, 6, 7 and 8 in the Schedule after 10th August 1987;

(d) in any of the designated areas numbered 9, 10, 11 and 12 in the Schedule after 27th August 1987; and

(e) in any of the designated areas numbered 13, 14 and 15 in the Schedule after 17th September 1987,

and the supply of meat derived from such sheep, extend throughout the United Kingdom (article 6(1)). This order replaces restrictions which–

(a) as regards the areas mentioned in (a) above have been in force since 11 a.m. on 20th June 1986,

(b) as regards the area mentioned in (b) above have been in force since 10th July 1987,

(c) as regards the areas mentioned in (c) above have been in force since 11th August 1987, and

(d) as regards the areas mentioned in (d) above have been in force since 28th August 1987.

The said restrictions on slaughter and supply imposed by article 6(1) shall not apply to any sheep–

(a) which have been moved unmarked to a market in accordance with a Ministerial consent;

(b) identified by a blue paint mark and which have been moved in accordance with a Ministerial consent; or

(c) identified by a red, apricot or green paint mark which have been examined and subsequently marked with an ear-tag by a person authorised by the Minister of Agriculture, Fisheries and Food or the Secretary of State and which have been moved in accordance with a Ministerial consent (article 6(2)).

Under Section 21 of the Food and Environment Protection Act 1985 the penalty for contravening an emergency prohibition is–

(a) on summary conviction, a fine of an amount not exceeding the statutory maximum (at present £2,000);

(b) on conviction on indictment, an unlimited fine, or imprisonment for a term of not more than two years or both.

Powers of enforcement in relation to emergency prohibitions are conferred by section 4 of, and Schedule 2 to, the 1985 Act. Obstruction of enforcement officers is an offence under paragraph 10 of that Schedule.

Maps showing the designated areas are available for inspection during normal office hours at the offices of the Welsh Office Agriculture Department at Penrallt, Caernarfon, Gwynedd LL55 1EP; Government Buildings, Spa Road East, Llandrindod Wells, Powys LD1 5HA; Station Road, Ruthin, Clwyd LL15 1BP and Cathays Park, Cardiff, South Glamorgan CF1 3NQ.

STATUTORY INSTRUMENTS

1987 No. 1664(C.50)

BANKS AND BANKING

The Banking Act 1987 (Commencement No. 2) Order 1987

Made - - - -		*21st September 1987*

The Treasury, in exercise of the powers conferred upon them by section 110(2) of the Banking Act 1987(**a**), hereby make the following Order:

1. This Order may be cited as the Banking Act 1987 (Commencement No. 2) Order 1987.

2. All the provisions of the Banking Act 1987 which are not already in force, except those specified in the Schedule to this Order, shall come into force on 1st October 1987.

Michael Neubert
Tony Durant
Two of the Lords Commissioners
of Her Majesty's Treasury

21st September 1987

SCHEDULE

Article 2

Provisions of the Act	*Subject matter of provisions*
Section 38.	Reports of large exposures.
The entry in Part I of Schedule 7 relating to section 193 of the Financial Services Act 1986(**b**) (which contains an exemption from the statutory control of deposit-taking) and section 108(2) in so far as it relates to that entry.	Repeals.

(**a**) 1987 c.22.   (**b**) 1986 c.60.

EXPLANATORY NOTE

(This note is not part of the Order)

This Order brings into force on 1st October 1987 all the provisions of the Banking Act 1987 which are not already in force, except those specified in the Schedule.

NOTE AS TO EARLIER COMMENCEMENT ORDER

(This note is not part of the Order)

The following provisions of the Act were brought into force on 15th July 1987 by the Banking Act 1987 (Commencement No. 1) Order 1987 (S.I. 1987/1189):

> Part V
> s.   102
> s.   106
> ss.   107 and 108, Schs. 5, 6 and 7 (partially)
> ss.   109 and 110.

1987 No. 1670

BUILDING SOCIETIES

The Building Societies (Banking Institutions) Order 1987

Made - - - -	*21st September 1987*
Laid before Parliament	*23rd September 1987*
Coming into force	*1st October 1987*

The Building Societies Commission, in exercise of the powers conferred on it by sections 7(9), 15(2) and 34(2) of the Building Societies Act 1986**(a)** and of all other powers enabling it in that behalf, and with the consent (except in so far as this Order is made under section 34(2) of that Act) of the Treasury, hereby makes the following Order:

Citation and commencement

1. This Order shall be cited as the Building Societies (Banking Institutions) Order 1987 and shall come into force on 1st October 1987.

Amendment of provisions of the Building Societies Act 1986

2. The Building Societies Act 1986 shall be amended as follows:

(a) in section 7(4) (which identifies non-retail funds and deposits), for paragraph (bb) there shall be substituted the following paragraph:

"(bb) sums deposited otherwise than in excepting circumstances with the society by, or by a trustee for, an institution which is –

(i) an authorised institution, for the purposes of, or

(ii) an overseas institution for the purposes of Part IV of,

the Banking Act 1987**(b)**;"; and

(b) in Schedule 8 (services), in paragraph 7(a) of Part III, for the words "recognised bank or licensed institution" there shall be substituted the words "authorised institution".

Amendment of the Building Societies (Mobile Home Loans) Order 1986

3. The Building Societies (Mobile Home Loans) Order 1986**(c)** shall be amended as follows:

(a) 1986 c.53; section 7 was amended by S.I. 1987/378 and Schedule 8 was amended by S.I. 1987/172.
(b) 1987 c.22.
(c) S.I. 1986/1877.

(a) in article 2 (interpretation) –

   (i) after the definition of "the Act" there shall be inserted the following definition:

      ""authorised institution" means an institution which is an authorised institution for the purposes of the Banking Act 1987;"; and

   (ii) the definitions of "licensed deposit taker" and "recognised bank" and the word "and" immediately before the latter definition shall be omitted; and

(b) in article 3 (security for mobile home loans) –

   (i) in paragraph (c)(ii), for the words "society, recognised bank or licensed deposit taker" there shall be substituted the words "society or authorised institution"; and

   (ii) in paragraph (d), for the words "a recognised bank or licensed deposit taker" there shall be substituted the words "an authorised institution".

In witness whereof the common seal of the Building Societies Commission is hereunto fixed, and is authenticated by me, a person authorised under paragraph 14 of Schedule 1 to the Building Societies Act 1986, on 18th September 1987.

Gerald Watson
Deputy Chairman of the Commission

We consent to this Order,

Michael Neubert
Tony Durant
21st September 1987   Two of the Lords Commissioners
of Her Majesty's Treasury

EXPLANATORY NOTE

(This note is not part of the Order)

This Order amends provisions of legislation relating to building societies by replacing references to bodies which were recognised banks and licensed institutions under the Banking Act 1979 (c.37) by references to authorised institutions under the Banking Act 1987 (which among other things gives deemed authorisation to those bodies).

STATUTORY INSTRUMENTS

1987 No. 1671

BUILDING SOCIETIES

The Building Societies (Residential Use) Order 1987

Made - - - -	*15th September 1987*
Laid before Parliament	*30th September 1987*
Coming into force -	*1st April 1988*

The Building Societies Commission, with the consent of the Treasury, in exercise of the powers conferred on it by section 12(1) and (2) of the Building Societies Act 1986(a) and of all other powers enabling it in that behalf hereby makes the following Order:

Citation and commencement

1. This Order may be cited as the Building Societies (Residential Use) Order 1987 and shall come into force on 1st April 1988.

Interpretation

2. In this Order–

"the Act" means the Building Societies Act 1986;

"the borrower", in this article and in articles 3 and 4, includes a dependant of the borrower;

"a dependant" has the meaning given in article 8;

"gross external area" has the meaning given in the Schedule;

"grounds" means land which either has not been built on or contains outbuildings but no other buildings;

"outbuilding" means a building or a structure which either–

    (a) is required to be excluded from the gross external area calculation in accordance with paragraph 4 of the Schedule; or

    (b) is a shed, greenhouse, summerhouse or other similar building or structure;

"relevant grounds" means grounds which are not for the residential use of the borrower;

"residential area" means the internal floor area of those rooms in a building which are for the residential use of the borrower;

"society" means a building society;

"total area" has the meaning given in the Schedule; and

"valuer" means a person who is competent to value the land on which an advance is to be secured and who would not be disqualified under section 13 of the Act (which makes provision as to the valuation of security) from making a report on that land under that section.

(a) 1986 c.53.

Residential use

3. For the purposes of section 11(2)(b) of the Act (which requires land upon which a class 1 advance is secured to be for the residential use of the borrower), land is for the residential use of the borrower if either of the following requirements is satisfied–

(a) that all of the land is for the residential use of the borrower; or

(b) that the residential area within that land is not less than forty per cent of the total area of that land.

Future occupation

4. Where–

(a) land fails to satisfy one of the requirements of article 3 solely because by reason of the borrower's occupation he is required either–

(i) to work outside the United Kingdom; or

(ii) to live in accommodation provided by his employer,

and is thereby prevented from residing on the land, and

(b) the borrower intends to reside on the land upon his ceasing to work outside the United Kingdom or his ceasing to live in accommodation provided by his employer, as the case may be,

the land shall be treated as satisfying that requirement.

Evidence of residential use under article 3(a)

5. A society shall be entitled to be satisfied (in the absence of evidence to the contrary) that the requirement in article 3(a) is satisfied by a statement supported by the signature of the borrower which relates to the land on which the advance is to be secured and states that all of that land is for the residential use of the borrower or a dependant of his.

Evidence of residential use under article 3(b)

6. A society shall be entitled to be satisfied (in the absence of evidence to the contrary) that the requirement in article 3(b) is satisfied if it receives both–

(a) a statement supported by the signature of the borrower which relates to the land on which the advance is to be secured and states–

(i) which rooms of the buildings he or his dependant intends to reside in;

(ii) the intended use of the remaining rooms;

(iii) the intended use of the grounds; and

(b) a valuer's certificate stating that the residential area within that land (as indicated by the borrower's statement) is not less than forty per cent of the total area of that land.

Evidence of future occupation

7. A society shall be entitled to be satisfied (in the absence of evidence to the contrary) that the land on which the advance is to be secured falls within article 4 by receipt of–

(a) a statement, supported by the signature of the borrower, under article 5 or article 6,

(b) a declaration so supported that–

(i) the borrower is, by reason of his occupation, required either to work outside the United Kingdom or to live in accommodation provided by his employer and is thereby prevented from residing on the land, and

(ii) the borrower intends, upon ceasing to work outside the United Kingdom or (as the case may be) ceasing to live in accommodation provided by his employer, to reside upon the land in accordance with that statement,

or (where that statement relates to a dependant of the borrower) that the dependant is subject to that requirement and has that intention, and

(c) where that statement is made under article 6, a valuer's certificate in accordance with paragraph (b) of that article.

Prescribed dependants

8.—(1) For the purposes of section 11(2)(b) of the Act, a person is a dependant of a borrower if he both–

(a) is a relative of the borrower; and

(b) is wholly or partly maintained by the borrower.

(2) A person is a relative of the borrower if he is–

(a) the borrower's spouse;

(b) the borrower's brother, sister, ancestor or descendant;

(c) the borrower's spouse's brother, sister, ancestor or descendant; or

(d) the spouse of any person classified, by virtue of sub-paragraph (b) or (c) of this paragraph, as a relative of the borrower.

(3) In this article–

"ancestor" means a parent or a parent's parent;

"brother" includes a half-brother and a step-brother;

"child" includes a step-child;

"descendant" means a child or a child's child;

"parent" includes a step-parent;

"relative" includes a relative by adoption;

"sister" includes a half-sister and a step-sister; and

"spouse" includes a former spouse.

In witness whereof the common seal of the Building Societies Commission is hereunto fixed, and is authenticated by me, a person authorised under paragraph 14 of Schedule 1 to the Building Societies Act 1986, on 3rd September 1987.

D. B. Severn
Secretary to the Commission

We consent to this Order,

Michael Neubert
David Lightbown

15th September 1987   Two of the Lords Commissioners of Her Majesty's Treasury

---

SCHEDULE   Article 2

1.   The total area is the sum of the gross external area and the relevant grounds.

2.   The gross external area is the sum of the areas of each floor of a building (other than an outbuilding), being measured so as to include the features listed in paragraph 3 and to exclude the features listed in paragraph 4.

3.   The features to be included when measuring the area of a floor in accordance with paragraph 2 are:

(a) perimeter wall thicknesses and external projections;

(b) areas occupied by internal walls and partitions;

(c) columns, piers, chimney-breasts, stairwells, lift-wells and similar structures;

(d) lift rooms, plant rooms, tank rooms and fuel stores;

(e) garages (whether detached or not) and open-sided covered parking areas; and

(f) outside water or earth closets.

4. The features to be excluded when measuring the area of a floor in accordance with paragraph 2 are–

    (a) open balconies;

    (b) open fire escapes;

    (c) open covered ways or minor canopies;

    (d) open vehicle parking areas, terraces and similar areas;

    (e) domestic coal houses; and

    (f) areas with a headroom of less than five feet.

EXPLANATORY NOTE

(This note is not part of the Order)

The requirements which must be satisfied in order for an advance to be classified as a class 1 advance are in section 11(2) of the Building Societies Act 1986. One of these requirements is that the land is for the residential use of the borrower or a dependant of his of a prescribed description.

This Order specifies the circumstances in which land is for a person's residential use, who are to be a person's dependants and the evidence upon which a building society is entitled (in the absence of evidence to the contrary) to be satisfied as to these matters.

This Order comes into force on 1 April 1988. Before that date the classification of land according to residential use is governed by article 5 of the Building Societies Act 1986 (Powers and Miscellaneous Transitional Provisions) Order 1986 (S.I. 1986/2169), which treats land on any of which a borrower or his dependant resides as being for the residential use of the borrower. This Order instead applies a test of residential use of forty per cent of the land and sets the criteria for how that forty per cent is measured.

STATUTORY INSTRUMENTS

1987 No. 1679

PLANT HEALTH

The Import and Export (Plant Health) (Great Britain) (Amendment)(No. 2) Order 1987

Made - - - -	*22nd September 1987*
Laid before Parliament	*24th September 1987*
Coming into force	*3rd October 1987*

The Minister of Agriculture, Fisheries and Food in relation to England, the Secretary of State for Scotland in relation to Scotland and the Secretary of State for Wales in relation to Wales, in exercise of the powers conferred by sections 2 and 3(1) and (2) of the Plant Health Act 1967(a), and now vested in them(b), and of all other powers enabling them in that behalf, hereby make the following Order:

Title, extent and commencement

1. This Order may be cited as the Import and Export (Plant Health) (Great Britain) (Amendment) (No. 2) Order 1987, shall apply to Great Britain and shall come into force on 3rd October 1987.

Amendment of principal Order

2. The Import and Export (Plant Health) (Great Britain) Order 1980(c) shall be amended as follows –

(1) After paragraph (h) of article 5 (prohibition of landing of certain plants etc.) there shall be inserted the following paragraph –
> "(i) any raw vegetables, intended for consumption or processing, from plants of beets (*Beta* L.), carrot (*Daucus* L.), celery or celeriac (*Apium* L.), leek (*Allium* L.), turnip or swede, (*Brassica* L.) if the consignment contains more than 1% by weight of soil.".

(2) In Part IIIA of Schedule 2, in item 45(7), (soil tolerance in a consignment of potatoes), for "2%" there shall be substituted "1%".

(a) 1967 c.8; sections 2(1) and 3(1) and (2) were amended by the European Communities Act 1972 (c.68), section 4(1) and Schedule 4, paragraph 8.   (b) In the case of the Secretary of State for Wales by virtue of S.I. 1978/272.
(c) S.I. 1980/420; relevant amending instruments are S.I. 1985/873, 1230, 1986/195, 1135.

In Witness whereof the Official Seal of the Minister of Agriculture, Fisheries and Food is hereunto affixed on 22nd September 1987.

John MacGregor
Minister of Agriculture, Fisheries and Food

22nd September 1987

James Douglas-Hamilton
Parliamentary Under-Secretary of State, Scottish Office

22nd September 1987

Peter Walker
Secretary of State for Wales

EXPLANATORY NOTE

(This note is not part of the Order)

This Order amends the Import and Export (Plant Health) (Great Britain) Order 1980 –

(a) by prohibiting the landing in Great Britain of consignments of certain vegetables if they contain more than 1% by weight of soil, and

(b) by reducing the soil tolerance in consignments of potatoes from 2% to 1% (article 2).

STATUTORY INSTRUMENTS

1987 No. 1680 (C.51)

CONSUMER PROTECTION

The Consumer Protection Act 1987 (Commencement No. 1) Order 1987

Made	-	-	-	-	*23rd September 1987*

The Secretary of State, in exercise of the powers conferred upon him by section 50(2), (4) and (5) of the Consumer Protection Act 1987(**a**), hereby makes the following Order:

1. This Order may be cited as the Consumer Protection Act 1987 (Commencement No. 1) Order 1987.

2. In this Order–
"the 1961 Act" means the Consumer Protection Act 1961(**b**);
"the 1965 Act" means the Consumer Protection Act (Northern Ireland) 1965(**c**);
"the 1987 Act" means the Consumer Protection Act 1987;
"the existing Regulations" means Regulations made under the 1961 Act or the 1965 Act which are in force on 1st October 1987, including, for the avoidance of doubt, the Regulations referred to in section 6(2) of the 1961 Act.

3. The following provisions of the 1987 Act shall come into force on 1st October 1987–
  (a) Part II (consumer safety);
  (b) Part IV (enforcement) in so far as it has effect for the purposes of or in relation to Part II;
  (c) Part V (miscellaneous and supplemental) sections 37 to 47 in so far as they have effect for the purposes of or in relation to Part II;
  (d) section 48(1) (minor and consequential amendments) in so far as it relates to the paragraphs of Schedule 4 mentioned in paragraph (j) below;
  (e) section 48(2)(b) (repeal of Fabrics (Misdescription) Act 1913);
  (f) section 48(3) (repeals) in so far as it gives effect to the repeals in Schedule 5 mentioned in paragraph (k) below;
  (g) section 49 (Northern Ireland);
  (h) section 50 (short title, commencement and transitional provision);
  (i) Schedule 2 (prohibition notices and notices to warn);
  (j) Schedule 4 (minor and consequential amendments) paragraphs 1, 2, 4, 6, 7, 9, 10, 11 and 13;
  (k) Schedule 5 (repeals) the repeals set out in Part I of the Schedule to this Order.

4. The following provisions of the 1987 Act shall come into force on 1st March 1988–
  (a) Part I (product liability);
  (b) section 36 (amendments of Part I of the Health and Safety at Work etc. Act 1974(**d**));

(**a**) 1987 c.43.   (**b**) 1961 c.40.   (**c**) 1965 c.14 (N.I.).
(**d**) 1974 c.37.

(c) sections 41(2) and (6) (civil proceedings), 45 (interpretation) and 46 (meaning of "supply") in so far as they have effect for the purposes of or in relation to Part I;

(d) section 48(1) (minor and consequential amendments) in so far as it relates to the paragraphs of Schedule 4 mentioned in paragraph (h) below.;

(e) section 48(3) (repeals) in so far as it gives effect to the repeals in Schedule 5 mentioned in paragraph (i) below;

(f) Schedule 1 (limitation of actions under Part I);

(g) Schedule 3 (amendments of Part I of the Health and Safety at Work etc. Act 1974);

(h) Schedule 4 (minor and consequential amendments) paragraphs 5, 8 and 12;

(i) Schedule 5 (repeals) the repeals set out in Part II of the Schedule to this Order.

5. The following provisions of this Order shall come into force on 1st October 1987.

6. The existing Regulations shall have effect as if they had been made under section 11 of the 1987 Act, subject to the following provisions of this Order, and references in those Regulations to either the 1961 Act or the 1965 Act or to any provision of those Acts shall be construed as references to the 1987 Act or to the corresponding provision of that Act.

7. Any provisions of the existing Regulations concerning the application of section 2 of the 1961 Act or section 2 of the 1965 Act shall cease to have effect.

8. The existing Regulations shall be treated for all purposes as including a provision prohibiting any person from supplying, or from offering to supply, agreeing to supply, exposing for supply or possessing for supply goods in respect of which any of the requirements of the Regulations are not satisfied, except where that person reasonably believes that the goods will not be used in the United Kingdom.

9. For the avoidance of doubt, the provision referred to in article 8 above shall have effect irrespective of the date of manufacture of the goods to which that provision applies.

John Butcher
Parliamentary Under-Secretary of State,
Department of Trade and Industry

23rd September 1987

SCHEDULE   articles 3(k) and 4(i)

PART I

REPEALS COMING INTO FORCE ON 1st OCTOBER 1987

Short title	Extent of repeal
The Fabrics (Misdescription) Act 1913(**a**).	The whole Act.
The Criminal Justice Act 1967(**b**).	In Part I of Schedule 3, the entry relating to the Fabrics (Misdescription) Act 1913.
The Fines Act (Northern Ireland) 1967(**c**).	In Part I of the Schedule, the entry relating to the Fabrics (Misdescription) Act 1913.
The Local Government Act 1972(**d**).	In Part II of Schedule 29, paragraph 18(1).
The Local Government (Scotland) Act 1973(**e**).	In Part II of Schedule 27, paragraph 50.
The Explosives (Age of Purchase etc.) Act 1976(**f**).	In section 1, in subsection (1), the words from "and for the word" onwards and subsection 2.
The Consumer Safety Act 1978(**g**)	The whole Act.
The Magistrates' Courts Act 1980(**h**)	In Schedule 7, paragraphs 172 and 173.
The Telecommunications Act 1984 (**i**).	In section 101(3)(f), the word "and".
The Food Act 1984(**j**).	In Schedule 10, paragraph 32.
The Consumer Safety (Amendment) Act 1986(**k**).	The whole Act.
The Airports Act 1986(**l**).	In section 74(3)(g), the word "and".
The Gas Act 1986(**m**).	In section 42(3), paragraphs (a) and (g) and, in paragraph (h), the word "and".

PART II

REPEALS COMING INTO FORCE ON 1st MARCH 1988

Short title	Extent of repeal
The Prescription and Limitation (Scotland) Act 1973(**n**).	Section 23.
The Health and Safety at Work etc. Act 1974(**o**).	In section 53(1), the definition of "substance for use at work".

(**a**) 1913 c.17.	(**b**) 1967 c.80.	(**c**) 1967 c.29 (N.I.).
(**d**) 1972 c.70.	(**e**) 1973 c.65.	(**f**) 1976 c.26.
(**g**) 1978 c.38.	(**h**) 1980 c.43.	(**i**) 1984 c.12.
(**j**) 1984 c.30.	(**k**) 1986 c.29.	(**l**) 1986 c.31.
(**m**) 1986 c.44.	(**n**) 1973 c.52.	(**o**) 1974 c.37.

EXPLANATORY NOTE

(This note is not part of the Order)

This Order brings into force most of the provisions of the Consumer Protection Act 1987 on 1st October 1987 and 1st March 1988. The main provisions not brought into force by the Order are those of Part III (misleading price indications) and that repealing the Trade Descriptions Act 1972 (c.34), which relates to origin marking.

The provisions brought into force on 1st October 1987 are–

Part II (consumer safety);

Part IV (enforcement) for the purposes of Part II;

Part V (miscellaneous and supplemental) sections 37 to 47 for the purposes of Part II; section 48(1) and (3) in relation to the minor and consequential amendments (Schedule 4) and repeals (Schedule 5) mentioned below; section 48(2)(b) (repeal of the Fabrics (Misdescription) Act 1913); section 49 (Northern Ireland); and section 50 (short title, commencement and repeals);

Schedule 2 (prohibition notices and notices to warn);

Schedule 4 (minor and consequential amendments) paragraph 1 (amendment of the Explosives Act 1875 (c.17)), paragraphs 2, 4, 6, 7, 9, 10 and 11 (relating to Part II) and paragraph 13 (amendment of the Motor Cycle Noise Act 1987 (c.34));

Schedule 5 (repeals) the repeals set out in Part I of the Schedule to the Order (article 3).

The provisions brought into force on 1st March 1988 are–

Part I (product liability);

Part V (miscellaneous and supplemental) section 36 (amendment of Part I of the Health and Safety at Work etc. Act 1974); and sections 41(2) and (6) (civil proceedings), 45 (interpretation) and 46 (meaning of "supply") for the purposes of Part I;

Schedule 1 (limitation of actions under Part I);

Schedule 3 (amendment of Part I of the Health and Safety at Work etc. Act 1974);

Schedule 4 (minor and consequential amendments) for the purposes of Part I (product liability);

Schedule 5 (repeals) the repeals set out in Part II of the Schedule to the Order (article 4).

The Order also makes provision, coming into force on 1st October 1987, for regulations made under the Consumer Protection Act 1961 and the Consumer Protection Act (Northern Ireland) 1965 to be treated as though they had been made under section 11 of the Consumer Protection Act 1987 (article 6).

The regulations are to be treated as including a provision prohibiting any person from supplying the goods in question, offering or agreeing to supply them, or exposing or possessing them for supply, except where that person reasonably believes that the goods will not be used in the United Kingdom. The prohibition will apply no matter when the goods were manufactured (articles 8 and 9).

"Supply" is defined by section 46 of the Consumer Protection Act 1987 and includes supply as an agent.

STATUTORY INSTRUMENTS

1987 No. 1681(C.52)

CONSUMER PROTECTION

The Consumer Safety Act 1978 (Commencement No. 3) Order 1987

Made	-	-	-	*23rd September 1987*

The Secretary of State, in exercise of the powers conferred upon him by section 12(2) of the Consumer Safety Act 1978**(a)**, hereby makes the following Order:

1. This Order may be cited as the Consumer Safety Act 1978 (Commencement No. 3) Order 1987.

2. Subsection (1) of section 10 of, and Schedule 3 to, the Consumer Safety Act 1978 shall come into force on 1st October 1987 for the purpose of repealing, in so far as they are not already so repealed, the enactments mentioned in the first and second columns of that Schedule to the extent specified in the third column of that Schedule.

John Butcher
Parliamentary Under-Secretary of State,
23rd September 1987   Department of Trade and Industry

(a) 1978 c.38.

EXPLANATORY NOTE

(This note is not part of the Order)

This Order brings into force on 1st October 1987 section 10(1) of, and Schedule 3 to, the Consumer Safety Act 1978 for the purpose of completing the repeal of the legislation set out in Schedule 3 to the 1978 Act.

The principal repeals brought into force are those of the Consumer Protection Act 1961 (c.40) and the Consumer Protection Act (Northern Ireland) 1965 (c.14 (N.I.)).

The previous Commencement Orders were (i) the Consumer Safety Act 1978 (Commencement No. 1) Order 1978 (S.I. 1978/1445), which brought into force on 1st November 1978 all the provisions of the 1978 Act, with the exception of section 10(1) and Schedule 3, and (ii) the Consumer Safety Act 1978 (Commencement No. 2) Order 1986 (S.I. 1986/1297) which brought into force on 8th August 1986 that section and Schedule for the purpose of repealing section 3(2A) and (2B) of the 1961 Act and section 3(3) and (4) of the 1965 Act (together with legislation amending those provisions).

This Order therefore completes the bringing into force of the 1978 Act.

It should be noted that the 1978 Act is itself repealed on 1st October 1987 by section 48 of, and Schedule 5 to, the Consumer Protection Act 1987. The relevant Commencement Order is the Consumer Protection Act 1987 (Commencement No. 1) Order 1987 (S.I. 1987/1680).

STATUTORY INSTRUMENTS

1987 No. 1682

PUBLIC HEALTH, ENGLAND AND WALES
PUBLIC HEALTH, SCOTLAND
PUBLIC HEALTH, NORTHERN IRELAND

CONTAMINATION OF FOOD

The Food Protection (Emergency Prohibitions) (Wales) (No. 4) Amendment Order 1987

Made - - - - -	*24th September 1987*
Laid before Parliament - -	*24th September 1987*
Coming into force - - -	*28th September 1987*

Whereas the Secretary of State is of the opinion, as mentioned in section 1(1)(a) of the Food and Environment Protection Act 1985(a), that there has been or may have been an escape of substances of such descriptions and in such quantities and such circumstances as are likely to create a hazard to human health through human consumption of food;

And whereas the Secretary of State is of the opinion, as mentioned in section 1(1)(b) of the said Act, that in consequence of the said escape of substances food which is or may be in the future in the areas described in the Schedule to the Food Protection (Emergency Prohibitions) (Wales) (No. 4) Order 1987(b), or which is derived or may be in the future derived from anything in those areas, is, or may be, or may become, unsuitable for human consumption;

Now, therefore, the Secretary of State, in exercise of the powers conferred on him by the said section 1(1) and (2) and section 24(1) and (3) of the said Act, and of all other powers enabling him in that behalf, hereby makes the following Order:—

Title and commencement

1. This Order may be cited as the Food Protection (Emergency Prohibitions) (Wales) (No. 4) Amendment Order 1987 and shall come into force on 28th September 1987.

Partial revocation and amendment

2. The Food Protection (Emergency Prohibitions) (Wales) (No. 4) Order 1987 is revoked to the extent that it imposes prohibitions on—

(a) the slaughter of a sheep which was moved from any place in accordance with a consent given under section 2(1) of the Food and Environment Protection Act 1985 on or before 26th July 1987 which consent was subject to the condition that the sheep to which it applies should be marked with an apricot mark; and

(b) the supply or having in possession for supply of meat, or food containing meat, derived from such a sheep,

and accordingly that Order is amended in accordance with the following provisions of this Order.

(a) 1985 c.48.
(b) S.I. 1987/1638.

3.   In article, 6, for paragraph (2) there shall be substituted the following paragraph—

"(2) Paragraph (1) above shall not apply in the case of—

(a) any sheep which was moved to a market in accordance with a consent given under section 2(1) of the Act which consent did not require that the sheep to which it applies should be marked in a manner specified therein;

(b) any sheep which was moved from any place in accordance with a consent given under the said section 2(1) on or before 21st December 1986 which consent was subject to the condition that the sheep to which it applies should be marked with a blue mark;

(c) any sheep which was moved from any place in accordance with a consent given under the said section 2(1) on or before 26th July 1987 which consent was subject to the condition that the sheep to which it applies should be marked with an apricot mark; or

(d) any sheep which—

(i) was moved from any place in accordance with a consent given under the said section 2(1) which consent was subject to the condition that the sheep to which it applies should be marked with a red mark or with a green mark; and

(ii) has been examined and marked with an ear-tag by a person authorised in that behalf by one of the Ministers.".

Peter Walker
24th September 1987   Secretary of State for Wales

EXPLANATORY NOTE

(This note is not part of the Order)

The Food Protection (Emergency Prohibitions) (Wales) (No. 4) Order 1987 contains emergency prohibitions restricting various activities in order to prevent human consumption of food which has been or which may have been rendered unsuitable for that purpose in consequence of the escape of radioactive substances from a nuclear reactor situated at Chernobyl in the USSR.

This Order excepts from the prohibition on slaughter throughout the United Kingdom any sheep, and from the prohibition on supply throughout the United Kingdom any meat derived from such a sheep, identified by an apricot paint mark which are no longer required to be examined and marked with an ear-tag by a person authorised by the Minister of Agriculture, Fisheries and Food, the Secretary of State for Scotland or the Secretary of State for Wales (article 3).

The Order also limits the scope of the existing exception from those prohibitions in respect of sheep identified by a blue paint mark to sheep for the movement of which a consent was given on or before 21st December 1986 (article 3).

STATUTORY INSTRUMENTS

1987 No. 1683

SOCIAL SECURITY

The Social Security (Hospital In-Patients) Amendment (No. 2) Regulations 1987

Made - - - -	*23rd September 1987*
Laid before Parliament	*28th September 1987*
Coming into force	
Regulations 1, 2(1), 2(2)(a)(i), (ii) and (iii) and (b) and 2(13)(c)	*2nd November 1987*
for all other purposes	*11th April 1988*

The Secretary of State for Social Services, in exercise of the powers conferred upon him by sections 81(4)(d), 82(6)(b) and 85(1) of and Schedule 20 to the Social Security Act 1975(**a**) and of all other powers enabling him in that behalf, after reference to the Social Security Advisory Committee(**b**), hereby makes the following Regulations:

Citation, interpretation and commencement

1. These Regulations, which may be cited as the Social Security (Hospital In-Patients) Amendment (No. 2) Regulations 1987, amend the Social Security (Hospital In-Patients) Regulations 1975(**c**) ("the principal Regulations") and shall come into force in the case of this regulation and regulation 2(1), 2(2)(a)(i), (ii) and (iii) and (b) and 2(13)(c) on 2nd November 1987 and in the case of the remainder of the Regulations on 11th April 1988.

Amendment of the principal Regulations

2.—(1) The principal Regulations shall be amended in accordance with the following provisions of this regulation.

(2) In regulation 2 (interpretation)–

  (a) in paragraph (1)–

    (i) for the definition of "basic component" there shall be substituted the following definition–

    " "basic pension" means the higher weekly rate of basic pension specified in section 6(1)(a) of the Social Security Pensions Act 1975(**d**) "

(**a**) 1975 c.14. Schedule 20 is cited because of the meaning ascribed to the word "Regulations".

(**b**) *See* sections 9 and 10 of the Social Security Act 1980. Section 10 was amended by paragraph 98 of Schedule 10 to the Social Security Act 1986 (c.50).

(**c**) S.I. 1975/555; relevant amending instruments are S.I. 1977/342, 956, 1693, 1979, 1984/1699, 1986/903 and 1987/31.

(**d**) 1975 c.60; section 6(1)(a) was amended by article 3 of the Social Security Benefits Up-rating Order 1987 (S.I. 1987/45).

and for any reference to "basic component" wherever that expression occurs in the principal Regulations there shall be substituted a reference to "basic pension"(**a**);

  (ii) in the definition of "the Overlapping Benefits Regulations" for the words "Social Security (Overlapping Benefits) Regulations 1975" there shall be substituted the words "Social Security (Overlapping Benefits) Regulations 1979"(**b**);

  (iii) in the definition of "personal benefit" the words from "but does not include" to the end shall be omitted;

  (iv) after the definition of "40% of the basic pension" the following definition shall be inserted–

  "60% of the basic pension means an amount equal to 3 times 20% of the basic pension;";

(b) in paragraph (2) for the words from "National Health" to "1947 to 1976" there shall be substituted the words "National Health Service Act 1977(**c**) or the National Health Service (Scotland) Act 1978(**d**)" and for the words from "and a person shall not be regarded" to the end of the paragraph there shall be substituted the words–

  "and such a person shall be regarded as being maintained free of charge in such a hospital or similar institution for any period unless his accommodation and services are provided under section 65 of the National Health Service Act 1977 or section 58 of the National Health Service (Scotland) Act 1978.".

(3) In regulation 4 (circumstances in which personal benefit is to be adjusted)–

(a) in paragraphs (a) and (c) for the reference to "8 weeks" there shall be substituted a reference to "6 weeks";

(b) in paragraph (d) the words "and before the 105th week" shall be omitted;

(c) paragraph (e) shall be omitted.

(4) In regulation 4A(1) (provision for adjusting benefit for part of a week) for the reference to "5, 6 or 7" there shall be substituted a reference to "5 or 6".

(5) For regulation 5 there shall be substituted the following regulation–

"Adjustment of personal benefit after 6 weeks in hospital

5.   For any part of the period to which regulation 4(c) applies during which–

(a) the beneficiary has a dependant, the weekly rate of the personal benefit shall be reduced by 20% of the basic pension;

(b) he has no dependant, it shall be reduced by 40% of the basic pension,

so however that where such a reduction would reduce the weekly rate to less than 20% of the basic pension, the reduction shall be such as will reduce it to that 20%.".

(6) In regulation 6 (adjustment of personal benefit after 52 weeks in hospital)–

(a) paragraph (1)(b) for the reference to "20%" there shall be substituted a reference to "40%";

(b) paragraph (1)(c) for the reference to "40%" there shall be substituted a reference to "60%";

(c) for paragraph (2) there shall be substituted the following paragraph–

  "(2) Where a person to whom regulation 4(d) applies has no dependant or has a dependant but has not made an application to the Secretary of State in accordance with paragraph (5) of this regulation, the weekly rate of his personal benefit shall be adjusted so that 20% of the basic pension is payable to him.";

(d) in paragraph (3) the words "and regulation 7" and "or, as the case may be, regulation 7" shall be omitted.

(7) Regulation 7 (adjustment of benefit after 104 weeks in hospital) shall be omitted.

(8) In regulation 9(b) (circumstances in which dependency benefit is to be adjusted) for the reference to "8 weeks" there shall be substituted a reference to "6 weeks".

(9) In regulation 11 (adjustment of dependency benefit where dependant is husband or wife of beneficiary and is in hospital)–

(a) in paragraph (1)–

   (i) for the words "Subject to the following paragraphs" there shall be substituted the words "Subject to paragraph (3)";

   (ii) in paragraph (1)(a) for the reference to "8 weeks" there shall be substituted a reference to "6 weeks" and for a reference to "105th week" there shall be substituted a reference to "53rd week";

   (iii) in paragraph (1)(b) for the reference to "104th week" there shall be substituted a reference to "52nd week";

(b) for paragraph 3 there shall be substituted the following paragraph–

"(3) Where both the dependant and the beneficiary are in-patients and each has been an in-patient for a period of not less than 52 weeks, for any part of the period of free in-patient treatment received by the beneficiary which occurs after the 52nd week of that treatment and during that part of the period during which the dependant is an in-patient which occurs after the 52nd week of the dependant's treatment, the dependency benefit which has been adjusted in accordance with paragraph (1)(b) shall not be payable unless the beneficiary makes an application to the Secretary of State which complies with regulation 12 to pay that benefit on his behalf to that dependant or some other person mentioned in regulation 12(b)."

(10) In regulation 12 (application to the Secretary of State for the purposes of regulations 10 and 11)–

(a) in paragraph (a) the words from "except that" to "of that regulation" shall be omitted;

(b) in paragraph (b), for the reference to "regulation 11(3)(a)" there shall be substituted a reference to "regulation 11(3)".

(11) Regulation 15 (benefit payable on discharge from a hospital or similar institution) shall be omitted.

(12) In regulation 16 (adjustment or further adjustment of benefit in certain cases after 52 weeks in hospital) the words in parenthesis in paragraph (1)(b) and paragraphs (5) and (6) shall be omitted.

(13) In regulation 17 (calculation of periods)–

(a) in paragraph (1) for the words "Parts II and III" to the end of the paragraph there shall be substituted the words "Parts II, III and IV of these Regulations" and the words "and regulation 20" shall be omitted;

(b) for paragraph (3) the following paragraph shall be substituted–

"(3) Where a person to whom paragraph (2) applies has ceased to reside–

(a) in prescribed accommodation in premises managed by a voluntary organisation; or

(b) in prescribed accommodation in a home which–

   (i) is registered under Part I of the Registered Homes Act 1984 (a) including a home which but for section 1(4) of that Act would be registered; or

   (ii) is managed or provided by a body constituted by Act of Parliament or incorporated by Royal Charter; or

   (iii) in Scotland, is registered under section 61 of the Social Work (Scotland) Act 1968(b) or, being an establishment provided by a housing association, registered with the Housing Corporation

---

(a) 1984 c.23.

(b) 1968 c.49; section 61 was amended by the Criminal Procedure (Scotland) Act 1975 (c.21), section 289E (as inserted by the Criminal Justice Act 1982 (c.48), section 54).

established by the Housing Act 1964(**a**)which provides care equivalent to that given in residential accommodation provided under Part IV of the Social Work (Scotland) Act 1968,

paragraphs (2) and (4) shall not apply unless and until he has received free in-patient treatment for a continuous period exceeding 6 weeks.";

(c) in paragraph (5) for the words "Social Security (Contributions) Regulations 1975" there shall be substituted the words "Social Security (Contributions) Regulations 1979(**b**)" and for the reference to Schedule 5 there shall be substituted a reference to Schedule 3;

(d) after paragraph (5) there shall be added the following paragraph–

"(6) For the purposes of this regulation "prescribed accommodation" means in relation to any person–

(a) any hospital accommodation or similar accommodation in which that person is residing or has resided either as a patient or inmate or as a person in need of care and attention wholly or partly at the cost of the Secretary of State or any body exercising functions on behalf of the Secretary of State under the National Health Service Act 1977(**c**) or the National Health Service (Scotland) Act 1978(**d**); or

(b) residential accommodation provided to that person under section 27 of the National Health Service (Scotland) Act 1947(**e**), sections 21 to 24 and 26 of the National Assistance Act 1948(**f**) or section 7 of the Mental Health (Scotland) Act 1984(**g**);

(c) residential accommodation provided for that person under section 21(1) of and paragraph 1 or 2 of Schedule 8 to the National Health Service Act 1977(**h**) or, in Scotland, section 59 of the Social Work (Scotland) Act 1968 in both cases where board is available to that person,

but does not include any such accommodation for any period for which he is or was receiving free in-patient treatment.".

(14) Regulation 20 (transitional provisions), which is spent, is revoked.

Transitional provisions

3.—(1) Where resettlement benefit under regulation 15 of the principal Regulations is being paid to a person discharged from a hospital or similar institution on or before 11th April 1988, any benefit which has not been paid on that date shall be paid to that person in one sum.

(**a**) 1964 c.56.
(**b**) S.I. 1979/591, to which there are amendments not relevant to these Regulations.
(**c**) 1977 c.49.
(**d**) 1978 c.29.
(**e**) 1947 c.27 (10 & 11 Geo.6); section 27 was amended by the Local Government and Miscellaneous Financial Provisions (Scotland) Act 1958 (c.64), Schedule 5 paragraph 9; the Mental Health (Scotland) Act 1960 (c.61), Schedule 5; the Health Services and Public Health Act 1968 (c.46), Schedule 4; and saved for the purposes of section 1(4) of the Social Work (Scotland) Act 1968 (c.49) by the National Health Service (Scotland) Act 1978 (c.29), Schedule 15 paragraph 15.
(**f**) 1948 c.29; section 21 was amended by the Local Government Act 1972 (c.70), Schedule 23 paragraphs 1 and 2 and Schedule 30; the National Health Service Reorganisation Act 1973 (c.32), Schedule 4 paragraph 44 and Schedule 5; the Housing (Homeless Persons) Act 1977 (c.48), Schedule; the National Health Service Act 1977 (c.49), Schedule 15 paragraph 5; the Health Services Act 1980 (c.53), Schedule 1 Part I paragraph 5. Section 22 was amended by the Social Work (Scotland) Act 1968 (c.49), section 87(4) and Schedule 9 Part I; the Supplementary Benefits Act 1976 (c.71), Schedule 7 paragraph 3; the Housing (Homeless Persons) Act 1977 (c.48), Schedule; the Social Security Act 1980 (c.30), section 20, Schedule 4 paragraph 2(1) and Schedule 5 Part II and the Health and Social Services and Social Security Adjudications Act 1983 (c.41), section 20(1)(a). Section 24 was amended by the National Assistance (Amendment) Act 1959 (c.30), section 1(1); the National Health Service (Scotland) Act 1972 (c.58), Schedule 6 paragraph 82; the Local Government Act 1972 (c.70), Schedule 23 paragraph 2; the National Health Service Reorganisation Act 1973 (c.32), Schedule 4 paragraph 45 and the Housing (Homeless Persons) Act 1977 (c.48), Schedule. Section 26 was amended by the Health Services and Public Health Act 1968 (c.46), section 44 and Schedule 4 and the Social Work (Scotland) Act 1968 (c.49), Schedule 9 Part I and applied by section 87(3); the Local Government Act 1972 (c.70), Schedule 23 paragraph 2; the Housing (Homeless Persons) Act 1977 (c.48), Schedule and the Health and Social Services and Social Security Adjudications Act 1983 (c.41), section 20(1)(b).
(**g**) 1984 c.36.
(**h**) 1977 c.49; paragraph 2 of Schedule 8 was amended by the Mental Health Act 1983 (c.20), Schedule 4 paragraph 47.

(2) Subject to paragraphs (3) and (4) where a person (the payee) has been in a hospital or similar institution before, and is in a hospital or similar institution after, 11th April 1988 any resettlement benefit which would have been payable to him had he been discharged on 10th April 1988 shall be payable to him notwithstanding the revocation of regulation 15 of the principal Regulations.

(3) Any resettlement benefit which is payable in accordance with paragraph (2) shall be paid in one sum upon the payee's discharge where–

(a) his discharge from the hospital or similar institution was effected by and with the approval of a person authorised or empowered to discharge him, and

(b) he is neither receiving free in-patient treatment nor residing in prescribed accommodation

except where, having regard to the circumstances of any particular case, the Secretary of State decides that payment shall be made by specified instalments.

(4) "Free in-patient treatment" has the meaning ascribed to it in regulation 2(2) of the principal Regulations and in this regulation "prescribed accommodation" means accommodation to which regulation 2(13)(d) of these Regulations refers.

Signed by authority of the Secretary of State for Social Services.

Michael Portillo
Parliamentary Under-Secretary of State,
Department of Health and Social Security

23rd September 1987

EXPLANATORY NOTE

(This note is not part of the Regulations)

These Regulations amend the Social Security (Hospital In-Patients) Regulations 1975 (the principal Regulations). The circumstances in which a person is not to be regarded as maintained free of charge while receiving treatment as an in-patient are amended by regulation 2(2)(b). Where social security benefits are payable to or in respect of a person who has been undergoing continuous medical or other treatment as an in-patient in a hospital or similar institution, those periods after which the rates of benefit are reduced are provided by regulation 2(3) to be 6 weeks for the first reduction of benefit and 52 weeks for the second reduction. New rates of reductions to be made from benefits are specified in regulation 2(6). Resettlement benefit is abolished by regulation 2(11) except where a person becomes entitled to the benefit before 11th April 1988 (regulation 3).

The Report of the Social Security Advisory Committee dated 29th April 1987 on the draft of these Regulations which had been referred to them together with a statement showing why the Regulations do not give effect to the Committee's recommendations is contained in Command Paper No. 215 published by Her Majesty's Stationery Office.

S T A T U T O R Y   I N S T R U M E N T S

1987 No. 1687

PUBLIC HEALTH, ENGLAND AND WALES
PUBLIC HEALTH, SCOTLAND
PUBLIC HEALTH, NORTHERN IRELAND

CONTAMINATION OF FOOD

The Food Protection (Emergency Prohibitions) (England) (No. 2) Amendment No. 5 Order 1987

Made - - - -	*24th September 1987*
Laid before Parliament	*25th September 1987*
Coming into force	*28th September 1987*

Whereas the Minister of Agriculture, Fisheries and Food is of the opinion, in accordance with section 1(1)(a) of the Food and Environment Protection Act 1985(a), that there has been or may have been an escape of substances of such descriptions and in such quantities and such circumstances as are likely to create a hazard to human health through human consumption of food;

And whereas the said Minister is of the opinion, in accordance with section 1(1)(b) of the said Act, that in consequence of the said escape of substances food which is or may be in the future in the area described in Schedule 1 to the Food Protection (Emergency Prohibitions) (England) (No. 2) Order 1986(b), or which is derived or may be in the future derived from anything in that area, is, or may be, or may become, unsuitable for human consumption;

Now, therefore, the said Minister, in exercise of the powers conferred on him by the said section 1(1) and section 24(3) of the said Act, and of all other powers enabling him in that behalf, hereby makes the following Order:

Title and commencement

1. This Order may be cited as the Food Protection (Emergency Prohibitions) (England) (No. 2) Amendment No. 5 Order 1987 and shall come into force on 28th September 1987.

Partial revocation and amendment

2. The Food Protection (Emergency Prohibitions) (England) (No. 2) Order 1986 is revoked to the extent that it imposes prohibitions on –

(a) the slaughter of a sheep which was moved from any place in accordance with a consent given under section 2(1) of the Food and Environment Protection Act 1985 on or before 26th July 1987 which consent was subject to the condition that the sheep to which it applies should be marked with an apricot mark; and

---

(a) 1985 c.48.   (b) S.I. 1986/1689, amended by S.I. 1986/2208, 1987/153, 249, 906 and 1555.

(b) the supply or having in possession for supply of meat, or food containing meat, derived from such a sheep,

and accordingly that Order is further amended in accordance with the following provisions of this Order.

3. In article 6, for paragraph (2) there shall be substituted the following paragraph –

"(2) Paragraph (1) above shall not apply in the case of –

(a) any sheep which was moved to a market in accordance with a consent given under section 2(1) of the Act which consent did not require that the sheep to which it applies should be marked in a manner specified therein;

(b) any sheep which was moved from any place in accordance with a consent given under the said section 2(1) on or before 21st December 1986 which consent was subject to the condition that the sheep to which it applies should be marked with a blue mark;

(c) any sheep which was moved from any place in accordance with a consent given under the said section 2(1) on or before 26th July 1987 which consent was subject to the condition that the sheep to which it applies should be marked with an apricot mark; or

(d) any sheep which –

(i) was moved from any place in accordance with a consent given under the said section 2(1) which consent was subject to the condition that the sheep to which it applies should be marked with a red mark or with a green mark; and

(ii) has been examined and marked with an ear-tag by a person authorised in that behalf by one of the Ministers.".

In witness whereof the Official Seal of the Minister of Agriculture, Fisheries and Food is hereunto affixed on 24th September 1987.

(L.S.)

Donald Thompson
Parliamentary Secretary,
Ministry of Agriculture, Fisheries and Food

EXPLANATORY NOTE

(This note is not part of the Order)

The Food Protection (Emergency Prohibitions) (England) (No. 2) Order 1986 contains emergency prohibitions restricting various activities in order to prevent human consumption of food which has been or which may have been rendered unsuitable for that purpose in consequence of the escape of radioactive substances from a nuclear reactor situated at Chernobyl in the USSR.

This Order excepts from the prohibition on slaughter throughout the United Kingdom any sheep, and from the prohibition on supply throughout the United Kingdom any meat derived from such a sheep, identified by an apricot paint mark which are no longer required to be examined and marked with an ear-tag by a person authorised by the Minister of Agriculture, Fisheries and Food or the Secretary of State for Scotland or Wales.

The Order also limits the scope of the existing exception from those prohibitions in respect of sheep identified by a blue paint mark to sheep for the movement of which a consent was given on or before 21st December 1986.

STATUTORY INSTRUMENTS

1987 No. 1689

SPORTS GROUNDS AND SPORTING EVENTS

The Safety of Sports Grounds (Designation) Order 1987

Made - - - -	*24th September 1987*
Laid before Parliament	*1st October 1987*
Coming into force	*31st October 1987*

In exercise of the powers conferred upon me by section 1(1) of the Safety of Sports Grounds Act 1975(**a**), and after such consultation as is mentioned in section 18(4) of that Act, I hereby make the following Order:

1. This Order may be cited as the Safety of Sports Grounds (Designation) Order 1987 and shall come into force on 31st October 1987.

2. The sports stadium at The Athletic Ground, Seamer Road, Scarborough, North Yorkshire (being a stadium which in the opinion of the Secretary of State has accommodation for more than 10,000 spectators) is hereby designated as a stadium requiring a safety certificate under the Safety of Sports Grounds Act 1975.

Douglas Hurd
Home Office   One of Her Majesty's Principal Secretaries of State
24th September 1987

EXPLANATORY NOTE

(This note is not part of the Order)

By this Order the Secretary of State designates the sports stadium referred to in article 2 of it as a stadium requiring a safety certificate under the Safety of Sports Grounds Act 1975.

(**a**) 1975 c.52; section 1(1) was amended by Schedule 2 to the Fire Safety and Safety of Places of Sport Act 1987 (c.27) but the amendments are not yet in force.

1987 No. 1692

SOCIAL SECURITY

The Social Security (Widow's Benefit) Transitional Regulations 1987

Made - - - -	*25th September 1987*
Laid before Parliament	*1st October 1987*
Coming into force -	*11th April 1988*

The Secretary of State for Social Services, in exercise of the powers conferred upon him by sections 84(1) and 89(1) of the Social Security Act 1986**(a)** and of all other powers enabling him in that behalf, by this instrument, which contains only provisions consequential on section 36 of the Act of 1986 and which is made before the end of a period of 12 months from the commencement of that enactment, makes the following Regulations:

Citation, commencement and interpretation

1.—(1) These Regulations may be cited as the Social Security (Widow's Benefit) Transitional Regulations 1987 and shall come into force on 11th April 1988.

(2) In these Regulations–
"the 1975 Act" means the Social Security Act 1975**(b)**;
"the 1986 Act" means the Social Security Act 1986.

Widow's Allowance

2. In the case of a woman whose husband died before 11th April 1988, the provisions of the 1975 Act relating to widow's allowance shall continue to apply to her as though–

(a) the following provisions of the 1986 Act had not been enacted, that is to say, section 36(1) and (2) and section 86 in so far as it relates to Schedule 10, paragraphs 63 and 66, and

(b) the following provisions of the 1975 Act had not been repealed–

  (i) in section 12(2), the words "and widow's allowance";

  (ii) in section 13(1), the entry relating to widow's allowance;

  (iii) in section 25(3) the words "and for which she is not entitled to widow's allowance";

  (iv) in section 26(3) the words "a widow's allowance or";

  (v) section 41(2)(e);

  (vi) in Schedule 3, Part II, the words in paragraph 8(2)(a) "other than widow's allowance" and in paragraphs 9 and 10 the words "(other than widow's allowance)"; and

  (vii) in Schedule 4, Part I, paragraph 5, and in Part IV, paragraph 4.

(a) 1986 c.50; section 84(1) is cited because of the meaning ascribed to the word "regulations".
(b) 1975 c.14.

Widow's Pension

3.—(1) Subject to paragraph (2) below, where

    (a) a widow's pension is payable to a woman for a period which includes the whole or part of the week ending 10th April 1988, or would have been so payable but for any of the following provisions of the 1975 Act, that is to say, the proviso to section 26(3) (widow's pension not payable after remarriage), section 82(5)(b) (benefit not payable while person is imprisoned) or section 85 (overlapping benefits) or the regulations made thereunder; and

    (b) the woman was under the age of 55 either at her husband's death or at the time she ceased to be entitled to a widowed mother's allowance,

section 26 of the 1975 Act shall apply to her as though section 36(3) of the 1986 Act had not been enacted.

(2) Where on or after 11th April 1988 widow's pension ceases to be payable to a woman mentioned in paragraph (1) above because entitlement to a widowed mother's allowance arises in her case, that paragraph shall not thereafter apply to her.

Signed by authority of the Secretary of State for Social Services.

Michael Portillo
Parliamentary Under-Secretary of State,
Department of Health and Social Security

25th September 1987

EXPLANATORY NOTE

(This note is not part of the Regulations)

These Regulations are made under section 89(1) of the Social Security Act 1986 ("the 1986 Act"). They are consequential upon the coming into force of section 36 of the 1986 Act. As they are made earlier than 12 months from the commencement of that provision, they are exempted by section 61(5)(b) of the 1986 Act from reference to the Social Security Advisory Committee and are made without being so referred.

Section 36 of the 1986 Act provides for the replacement of widow's allowance (a weekly benefit) with a widow's payment (a lump sum payment), and for widow's pension to be payable from a later age.

These Regulations contain savings for existing beneficiaries to both widow's allowance and widow's pension.

STATUTORY INSTRUMENTS

1987 No. 1696

PUBLIC HEALTH, ENGLAND AND WALES
PUBLIC HEALTH, SCOTLAND
PUBLIC HEALTH, NORTHERN IRELAND

CONTAMINATION OF FOOD

The Food Protection (Emergency Prohibitions) Amendment No.2 Order 1987

Made - - - -	*25th September 1987*
Laid before Parliament	*28th September 1987*
Coming into force	*28th September 1987*

Whereas the Secretary of State is of the opinion, as mentioned in section 1(1)(a) of the Food and Environment Protection Act 1985(**a**), that there has been or may have been an escape of substances of such descriptions and in such quantities and such circumstances as are likely to create a hazard to human health through human consumption of food;

And whereas he is of the opinion, as mentioned in section 1(1)(b) of the said Act, that in consequence of the said escape of substances, food which is, or may be in the future, in the areas described in the Schedule to the principal Order or which is, or may be in the future, derived from anything in those areas, is, or may be, or may become, unsuitable for human consumption;

Now, therefore, in exercise of the powers conferred on him by sections 1(1) and (2) and 24(1) and (3) of the said Act(**b**), and of all other powers enabling him in that behalf, he hereby makes the following Order:

Title, commencement and interpretation

1.—(1) This Order may be cited as the Food Protection (Emergency Prohibitions) Amendment No.2 Order 1987 and shall come into force on 28th September 1987.

(2) In this Order "the principal Order" means the Food Protection (Emergency Prohibitions) Order 1987(**c**).

(**a**) 1985 c.48.
(**b**) Section 24(1) contains a definition of "the Ministers" relevant to the exercise of the statutory powers under which this Order is made.
(**c**) S.I. 1987/1165, amended by S.I. 1987/1567.

Designated incident

2.   In the opinion of the Secretary of State, food in the areas described in the Schedule to the principal Order, or which is derived from anything in those areas, is or may be unsuitable for human consumption in consequence of the following escape of substances:–

the escape on or after 26th April 1986 of radioactive substances from a nuclear reactor situated at Chernobyl in the Ukraine, USSR.

Amendment of the principal Order

3.—(1) In article 4 of the principal Order for paragraph (2) there shall be substituted the following paragraph:–

"(2) Paragraph (1) above shall not apply in the case of–

(a) any sheep which was moved from any place in accordance with a consent given under section 2(1) of the Food and Environment Protection Act 1985 which consent was subject to the condition that the sheep to which it applies should be marked with an apricot mark; or

(b) any sheep which–

(i) was moved from any place in accordance with a consent given under section 2(1) of the said Act which consent was subject to the condition that the sheep to which it applies should be marked with a green mark or with a blue mark, and

(ii) has been examined and marked with an ear-tag by a person authorised in that behalf by one of the Ministers.".

(2) In article 5 of the principal Order for paragraph (2) there shall be substituted the following paragraph:–

"(2) Paragraph (1) above shall not apply in the case of any sheep which was moved from any place in accordance with a consent given under section 2(1) of the said Act which consent was subject to the condition that the sheep to which it applies should be marked with an apricot mark or with a green mark or with a blue mark.".

(3) In article 6 of the principal Order for paragraph (2) there shall be substituted the following paragraph:–

"(2) Paragraph (1) above shall not apply in the case of—

(a) any sheep which was moved from any place in accordance with a consent given under section 2(1) of the said Act which consent was subject to the condition that the sheep to which it applies should be marked with an apricot mark; or

(b) any sheep which–

(i) was moved from any place in accordance with a consent given under section 2(1) of the said Act which consent was subject to the condition that the sheep to which it applies should be marked with a green mark or with a blue mark, and

(ii) has been examined and marked with an ear-tag by a person authorised in that behalf by one of the Ministers.".

New St Andrew's House, Edinburgh   *D.J. Essery*
25th September 1987   Under Secretary, Scottish Office

EXPLANATORY NOTE

(This note is not part of the Order)

The Food Protection (Emergency Prohibitions) (No.2) Order 1987 ("the principal Order") contains emergency prohibitions restricting various activities in order to prevent human consumption of food which has been or which may have been rendered unsuitable for that purpose in consequence of the escape of radioactive substances from a nuclear reactor situated at Chernobyl in the Ukraine, USSR.

The Food Protection (Emergency Prohibitions) (No.2) Amendment Order 1987 made certain exceptions to the following prohibitions imposed by articles 4, 5 and 6 of the principal Order:–

    (a) the prohibition on slaughter of sheep in any of the designated areas;

    (b) the prohibition on movement of sheep;

    (c) the prohibition applying throughout the United Kingdom on the slaughter of, and the supply of meat derived from, any sheep which has been in the designated areas.

This Order revises these exceptions as follows:–

    (a) to except from the said prohibitions on slaughter, and from the said prohibition on the supply of meat, any sheep which has been marked (in accordance with a condition attached to a consent given under section 2(1) of the Food and Environment Protection Act 1985) with an apricot paint mark without the necessity of such sheep having been examined and marked with an ear-tag by a person authorised by the Minister of Agriculture, Fisheries and Food or the Secretary of State for Scotland or Wales (article 3(1) and (3));

    (b) to except from the said prohibition on movement any sheep which has been so marked with a blue paint mark (article 3(2));

    (c) to except from the said prohibitions on slaughter, and from the said prohibition on the supply of meat, any sheep which has been so marked with a blue paint mark where any such sheep has been examined and marked with an ear-tag by a person authorised by the Minister of Agriculture, Fisheries and Food or the Secretary of State for Scotland or Wales (article 3(1) and (3)).

The exceptions from the said prohibition on movement of any sheep which has been so marked with an apricot or with a green paint mark, remain unchanged.

The exceptions from the said prohibitions on slaughter of sheep, and from the said prohibition on the supply of meat, where any such sheep has been so marked with a green paint mark, and where any such sheep has been examined and marked by an ear-tag by a person authorised by the Minister of Agriculture, Fisheries and Food or the Secretary of State for Scotland or Wales, also remain unchanged.

STATUTORY INSTRUMENTS

1987 No. 1697

PUBLIC HEALTH, ENGLAND AND WALES
PUBLIC HEALTH, SCOTLAND
PUBLIC HEALTH, NORTHERN IRELAND

CONTAMINATION OF FOOD

The Food Protection (Emergency Prohibitions) (No.2) Amendment No.2 Order 1987

Made - - - -	*25th September 1987*
Laid before Parliament	*28th September 1987*
Coming into force	*28th September 1987*

Whereas the Secretary of State is of the opinion, as mentioned in section 1(1)(a) of the Food and Environment Protection Act 1985(**a**), that there has been or may have been an escape of substances of such descriptions and in such quantities and such circumstances as are likely to create a hazard to human health through human consumption of food;

And whereas he is of the opinion, as mentioned in section 1(1)(b) of the said Act, that in consequence of the said escape of substances, food which is, or may be in the future, in the areas described in the Schedule to the principal Order or which is, or may be in the future, derived from anything in those areas, is, or may be, or may become, unsuitable for human consumption;

Now, therefore, in exercise of the powers conferred on him by sections 1(1) and (2) and 24(1) and (3) of the said Act(**b**), and of all other powers enabling him in that behalf, he hereby makes the following Order:

Title, commencement and interpretation

1.—(1) This Order may be cited as the Food Protection (Emergency Prohibitions) (No.2) Amendment No.2 Order 1987 and shall come into force on 28th September 1987.

(2) In this Order the "principal Order" means the Food Protection (Emergency Prohibitions) (No.2) Order 1987(**c**).

(**a**) 1985 c.48.
(**b**) Section 24(1) contains a definition of "the Ministers" relevant to the exercise of the statutory powers under which this Order is made.
(**c**) S.I. 1987/1450, amended by S.I. 1987/1568.

Designated incident

2. In the opinion of the Secretary of State, food in the areas described in the Schedule to the principal Order, or which is derived from anything in those areas, is or may be unsuitable for human consumption in consequence of the following escape of substances:–

the escape on or after 26th April 1986 of radioactive substances from a nuclear reactor situated at Chernobyl in the Ukraine, USSR.

Amendment of the principal Order

3.—(1) In article 4 of the principal Order for paragraph (2) there shall be substituted the following paragraph:–

"(2) Paragraph (1) above shall not apply in the case of–

(a) any sheep which was moved from any place in accordance with a consent given under section 2(1) of the Food and Environment Protection Act 1985 which consent was subject to the condition that the sheep to which it applies should be marked with an apricot mark; or

(b) any sheep which–

(i) was moved from any place in accordance with a consent given under section 2(1) of the said Act which consent was subject to the condition that the sheep to which it applies should be marked with a green mark or with a blue mark, and

(ii) has been examined and marked with an ear-tag by a person authorised in that behalf by one of the Ministers.".

(2) In article 5 of the principal Order for paragraph (2) there shall be substituted the following paragraph:–

"(2) Paragraph (1) above shall not apply in the case of any sheep which was moved from any place in accordance with a consent given under section 2(1) of the said Act which consent was subject to the condition that the sheep to which it applies should be marked with an apricot mark or with a green mark or with a blue mark.".

(3) In article 6 of the principal Order for paragraph (2) there shall be substituted the following paragraph:–

"(2) Paragraph (1) above shall not apply in the case of–

(a) any sheep which was moved from any place in accordance with a consent given under section 2(1) of the said Act which consent was subject to the condition that the sheep to which it applies should be marked with an apricot mark; or

(b) any sheep which–

(i) was moved from any place in accordance with a consent given under section 2(1) of the said Act which consent was subject to the condition that the sheep to which it applies should be marked with a green mark or with a blue mark, and

(ii) has been examined and marked with an ear-tag by a person authorised in that behalf by one of the Ministers.".

New St Andrew's House, Edinburgh
25th September 1987

D.J. Essery
Under Secretary, Scottish Office

EXPLANATORY NOTE

(This note is not part of the Order)

The Food Protection (Emergency Prohibitions) Order 1987 ("the principal Order") contains emergency prohibitions restricting various activities in order to prevent human consumption of food which has been or which may have been rendered unsuitable for that purpose in consequence of the escape of radioactive substances from a nuclear reactor situated at Chernobyl in the Ukraine, USSR.

The Food Protection (Emergency Prohibitions) Amendment Order 1987 made certain exceptions to the following prohibitions imposed by articles 4, 5 and 6 of the principal Order:–

(a) the prohibition on slaughter of sheep in any of the designated areas;

(b) the prohibition on movement of sheep;

(c) the prohibition applying throughout the United Kingdom on the slaughter of, and the supply of meat derived from, any sheep which has been in the designated areas.

This Order revises these exceptions as follows:–

(a) to except from the said prohibitions on slaughter, and from the said prohibition on the supply of meat, any sheep which has been marked (in accordance with a condition attached to a consent given under section 2(1) of the Food and Environment Protection Act 1985) with an apricot paint mark without the necessity of such sheep having been examined and marked with an ear-tag by a person authorised by the Minister of Agriculture, Fisheries and Food or the Secretary of State for Scotland or Wales (article 3(1) and (3));

(b) to except from the said prohibition on movement any sheep which has been so marked with a blue paint mark (article 3(2));

(c) to except from the said prohibitions on slaughter, and from the said prohibition on the supply of meat, any sheep which has been so marked with a blue paint mark where any such sheep has been examined and marked with an ear-tag by a person authorised by the Minister of Agriculture, Fisheries and Food or the Secretary of State for Scotland or Wales (article 3(1) and (3)).

The exceptions from the said prohibition on movement of any sheep which has been so marked with an apricot or with a green paint mark, remain unchanged.

The exceptions from the said prohibitions on slaughter of sheep, and from the said prohibition on the supply of meat, where any such sheep has been so marked with a green paint mark, and where any such sheep has been examined and marked by an ear-tag by a person authorised by the Minister of Agriculture, Fisheries and Food or the Secretary of State for Scotland or Wales, also remain unchanged.

1987 No. 1698 (S.120)

POLICE

The Special Constables (Injury Benefit) (Scotland) Regulations 1987

Made - - - -	*18th September 1987*
Laid before Parliament	*5th October 1987*
Coming into force	*28th October 1987*

The Secretary of State, in exercise of the powers conferred on him by section 26 of the Police (Scotland) Act 1967(**a**), as read with section 1(2) of the Police Pensions Act 1961(**b**) and as extended by sections 12 and 15(5)(c) of the Superannuation Act 1972(**c**), and of all other powers enabling him in that behalf, and after submitting a draft of the following Regulations to and considering any representations made by the Joint Central Committee and such bodies and associations as are mentioned in section 26(9)(b) of the said Act of 1967, hereby makes the following Regulations:

Citation and commencement

1.—(1) These Regulations may be cited as the Special Constables (Injury Benefit) (Scotland) Regulations 1987.

(2) These Regulations shall come into force on 28th October 1987 and shall have effect as from 25th November 1982.

Interpretation

2.—(1) Subject to the following provisions of these Regulations, these Regulations shall be construed as one with the Special Constables (Pensions) (Scotland) Regulations 1973(**d**) (hereinafter referred to as "the principal Regulations").

(2) Notwithstanding regulation 3(3) of the principal Regulations, in these Regulations "totally disabled" means incapable by reason of the disablement in question of earning any money in any employment and "total disablement" shall be construed accordingly.

(3) Notwithstanding any enactment applied by regulation 3(2) of the principal Regulations, the reference in regulation 3(1)(a) of these Regulations to a person being totally and permanently disabled is to be taken as a reference to that person being totally disabled at the time when the question arises for decision and to that total disablement being at that time likely to be permanent.

Injury benefit

3.—(1) The Police (Injury Benefit) Regulations 1987(**e**) shall apply, subject to the necessary modifications, in relation to—

(**a**) 1967 c.77; section 26 was amended by section 4(8) of the Police Act 1969 (c.63), by section 2(4) of the Police Negotiating Board Act 1980 (c.10), and by section 111 of the Police and Criminal Evidence Act 1984 (c.60).
(**b**) 1961 c.35; section 1(2) was amended by the Police Pensions Act 1976 (c.35), Schedule 2, paragraph 3(b).
(**c**) 1972 c.11.
(**d**) S.I. 1973/433, amended by S.I. 1974/1630, 1979/784, 1980/1411.
(**e**) S.I. 1987/156, amended by S.I. 1987/256 and 341.

(a) a person who—

    (i) receives or received an injury without his own default and in the execution of his duty, whether before, on or after 25th November 1982; and

    (ii) on or after that date ceases or has ceased to serve as a special constable; and

    (iii) within 12 months of so receiving that injury, becomes or became totally and permanently disabled as a result thereof; and

(b) a special constable who—

    (i) receives or received an injury without his own default and in the execution of his duty, whether before, on or after 25th November 1982; and

    (ii) was serving as a special constable on or after that date; and

    (iii) within 12 months of so receiving that injury, dies or has died as a result thereof;

as they apply in the case of a person such as is mentioned in regulation 4(1) or, as the case may be, regulation 5(1) of those Regulations.

(2) For the purposes of paragraph (1) any references in the Police (Injury Benefit) Regulations 1987(**a**) to any of the provisions of the Police Pensions Regulations 1973(**b**) or, as the case may be, the Police Pensions Regulations 1987(**c**) shall include references to those provisions as applied in relation to special constables by the principal Regulations.

Michael B. Forsyth

New St. Andrew's House, Edinburgh   Parliamentary Under Secretary of State,
18th September 1987   Scottish Office

EXPLANATORY NOTE

(This note is not part of the Regulations)

These Regulations, which apply to special constables appointed in Scotland, make provision for enhanced benefits in cases of death or total disablement resulting from an injury received by a special constable in the execution of his duty, similar to that made in relation to members of police forces by the Police (Injury Benefit) Regulations 1987.

These Regulations come into force on 28th October 1987 and have effect as from 25th November 1982. (Retrospective effect is authorised by sections 12 and 15 of the Superannuation Act 1972).

(**a**) These Regulations were amended by S.I. 1987/256, with effect from 1st April 1987, so as to substitute for references to the Police Pensions Regulations 1973 (S.I. 1973/428) references to the Police Pensions Regulations 1987 (S.I. 1987/257).

(**b**) S.I. 1973/428, to which there are amendments not relevant to these Regulations, revoked at 1st April 1987 by S.I. 1987/256.

(**c**) S.I. 1987/257, brought into force at 1st April 1987 by S.I. 1987/256.

STATUTORY INSTRUMENTS

1987 No. 1699 (S.121)

POLICE

The Police Cadets (Pensions) (Scotland) Amendment Regulations 1987

Made - - - -	*18th September 1987*
Laid before Parliament	*5th October 1987*
Coming into force	*28th October 1987*

The Secretary of State, in exercise of the powers conferred on him by section 27 of the Police (Scotland) Act 1967(**a**), as extended by section 13 of the Superannuation (Miscellaneous Provisions) Act 1967(**b**) and sections 12 and 15(5)(d) of the Superannuation Act 1972(**c**), and of all other powers enabling him in that behalf, and after consultation with the Police Negotiating Board for the United Kingdom in accordance with section 2(3) of the Police Negotiating Board Act 1980(**d**), hereby makes the following Regulations:

Citation and commencement

1.—(1) These Regulations may be cited as the Police Cadets (Pensions) (Scotland) Amendment Regulations 1987.

(2) These Regulations shall come into force on 28th October 1987 and shall have effect as from 25th November 1982.

Amendment of principal Regulations

2. In the Police Cadets (Pensions) (Scotland) Regulations 1973(**e**), after regulation 7 there shall be inserted the following regulation:–

"Dependent relative's special pension

7A.—(1) This regulation shall apply where a police cadet dies or has died as the result of an injury received without his own default and in the execution of his duty as a police cadet and, in such case, shall apply–

(a) to a parent or (without prejudice to the following sub-paragraph) to a brother or sister of the police cadet who had attained the age of 19 years before the police cadet's death, or

(b) subject to his having attained the age of 19 years, to any child of the police cadet, whether or not he had attained that age before the police cadet's death,

being a person who was substantially dependent on the police cadet immediately before his death (hereinafter referred to in this regulation as a dependent relative).

(**a**) 1967 c.77; section 27(3) was amended by section 4(8) of the Police Act 1969 (c.63), and by section 111(2) of the Police and Criminal Evidence Act 1984 (c.60).
(**b**) 1967 c.28; section 13 was amended by the Police (Scotland) Act 1967, Schedule 4, by the Social Security Act 1973 (c.38), Schedule 27, paragraph 72, and by the Social Security (Consequential Provisions) Act 1975 (c.18), Schedule 1, Part I.
(**c**) 1972 c.11.
(**d**) 1980 c.10.
(**e**) S.I. 1973/434, to which there are amendments not relevant to these Regulations.

(2) A dependent relative to whom this regulation applies may be granted a special pension if the police authority, having regard to all the circumstances of the case, in their discretion so determine, and regulations 36(3) and Part XIII of the principal Regulations(**a**), or, as the case may be, regulations E1(3) and E9 of the Police Pensions Regulations 1987(**b**), shall apply subject to the necessary modifications as if the police cadet had been a regular policeman at the time when he received the injury.".

New St. Andrew's House, Edinburgh
18th September 1987

Michael B. Forsyth
Parliamentary Under Secretary of State,
Scottish Office

EXPLANATORY NOTE

(This note is not part of the Regulations)

These Regulations amend the Police Cadets (Pensions) (Scotland) Regulations 1973 with effect from 25th November 1982 (retrospection is authorised by sections 12 and 15 of the Superannuation Act 1972). They provide for the payment, at the discretion of the police authority, of a dependent relative's special pension in cases of death resulting from an injury received by a police cadet in the execution of his duty, similar to that payable in the case of a regular policeman under the Police Pensions Regulations 1973 or, after 1st April 1987, the Police Pensions Regulations 1987.

(**a**) The Police Pensions Regulations 1973 (S.I. 1973/428), to which there are amendments not relevant to these Regulations, revoked at 1st April 1987 by S.I. 1987/256.
(**b**) S.I. 1987/257, brought into force at 1st April 1987 by S.I. 1987/256.

STATUTORY INSTRUMENTS

1987 No. 1700 (S.122)

POLICE

The Police Cadets (Injury Benefit) (Scotland) Regulations 1987

Made - - - -	*18th September 1987*
Laid before Parliament	*5th October 1987*
Coming into force	*28th October 1987*

The Secretary of State, in exercise of the powers conferred on him by section 27 of the Police (Scotland) Act 1967(a), as extended by section 13 of the Superannuation (Miscellaneous Provisions) Act 1967(b) and sections 12 and 15(5)(d) of the Superannuation Act 1972(c), and of all other powers enabling him in that behalf, and after consultation with the Police Negotiating Board for the United Kingdom in accordance with section 2(3) of the Police Negotiating Board Act 1980(d), hereby makes the following Regulations:

Citation and commencement

1.—(1) These Regulations may be cited as the Police Cadets (Injury Benefit) (Scotland) Regulations 1987.

(2) These Regulations shall come into force on 28th October 1987 and shall have effect as from 25th November 1982.

Interpretation

2.—(1) Subject to the following provisions of these Regulations, these Regulations shall be construed as one with the Police Cadets (Pensions) (Scotland) Regulations 1973(e) (hereinafter referred to as "the principal Regulations").

(2) Notwithstanding regulation 3(4) of the principal Regulations, in these Regulations "totally disabled" means incapable by reason of the disablement in question of earning any money in any employment and "total disablement" shall be construed accordingly.

(3) Notwithstanding any enactment applied by regulation 3(2) of the principal Regulations, the reference in regulation 3(1)(a) of these Regulations to a person being totally and permanently disabled is to be taken as a reference to that person being totally disabled at the time when the question arises for decision and to that total disablement being at that time likely to be permanent.

(a) 1967 c.77; section 27(3) was amended by section 4(8) of the Police Act 1969 (c.63), and by section 111(2) of the Police and Criminal Evidence Act 1984 (c.60).
(b) 1967 c.28; section 13 was amended by the Police (Scotland) Act 1967, Schedule 4, by the Social Security Act 1973 (c.38), Schedule 27, paragraph 72, and by the Social Security (Consequential Provisions) Act 1975 (c.18), Schedule 1, Part I.
(c) 1972 c.11.
(d) 1980 c.10.
(e) S.I. 1973/434, amended by S.I. 1974/1629, 1979/783, 1980/1410, 1982/1660, 1987/1699.

Injury benefit

3.—(1) The Police (Injury Benefit) Regulations 1987(**a**) shall apply, subject to the necessary modifications, in relation to–

(a) a person who–

(i) receives or received an injury without his own default and in the execution of his duty, whether before, on or after 25th November 1982; and

(ii) on or after that date ceases or has ceased to serve as a police cadet; and

(iii) within 12 months of so receiving that injury, becomes or became totally and permanently disabled as a result thereof; and

(b) a police cadet who–

(i) receives or received an injury without his own default and in the execution of his duty, whether before, on or after 25th November 1982; and

(ii) was serving as a police cadet on or after that date; and

(iii) within 12 months of so receiving that injury, dies or has died as a result thereof;

as they apply in the case of a person such as is mentioned in regulation 4(1) or, as the case may be, regulation 5(1) of those Regulations.

(2) For the purposes of paragraph (1) any references in the Police (Injury Benefit) Regulations 1987(**b**) to any of the provisions of the Police Pensions Regulations 1973(**c**) or, as the case may be, the Police Pensions Regulations 1987(**d**) shall include references to those provisions as applied in relation to police cadets by the principal Regulations.

(3) These Regulations shall have effect in relation to a police cadet notwithstanding regulation 4(3) of the principal Regulations; and accordingly there shall be inserted therein after the words "any enactment" the words "other than the Police Cadets (Injury Benefit) (Scotland) Regulations 1987".

New St. Andrew's House, Edinburgh
18th September 1987

Michael B. Forsyth
Parliamentary Under Secretary of State,
Scottish Office

EXPLANATORY NOTE

(This note is not part of the Regulations)

These Regulations make provision for enhanced benefits in cases of death or total disablement resulting from an injury received by a police cadet in the execution of his duty, similar to that made in relation to members of police forces by the Police (Injury Benefit) Regulations 1987.

The Regulations come into force on 28th October 1987 and have effect as from 25th November 1982. (Retrospective effect is authorised by sections 12 and 15 of the Superannuation Act 1972).

(**a**) S.I. 1987/156, amended by S.I. 1987/256 and 341.

(**b**) These Regulations were amended by S.I. 1987/256, with effect from 1st April 1987, so as to substitute for references to the Police Pensions Regulations 1973 (S.I. 1973/428) references to the Police Pensions Regulations 1987 (S.I. 1987/257).

(**c**) S.I. 1973/428, to which there are amendments not relevant to these Regulations, revoked at 1st April 1987 by S.I. 1987/256.

(**d**) S.I. 1987/257, brought into force at 1st April 1987 by S.I. 1987/256.

STATUTORY INSTRUMENTS

1987 No. 1706

ROAD TRAFFIC

The Traffic Signs General (Amendment) Directions 1987

Made	-	-	-	-	*24th September 1987*
Coming into force		-			*15th October 1987*

The Secretary of State for Transport, the Secretary of State for Scotland and the Secretary of State for Wales, acting jointly in exercise of the powers conferred by section 65(1) of the Road Traffic Regulation Act 1984**(a)**, and of all other enabling powers, hereby give the following Directions:–

1. These Directions may be cited as the Traffic Signs General (Amendment) Directions 1987 and shall come into force on 15th October 1987.

2. The Traffic Signs General Directions 1981**(b)** shall be further amended in accordance with the following provisions of these Directions.

3. In the directions specified in column (1) of the Schedule to these Directions, for the words specified in column (2) there shall be substituted the words specified in column (3).

4. In direction 36, after paragraph (3) there shall be inserted the following new paragraph–

"(4) The front of any backing board for a sign mounted otherwise than as described in sub-paragraph (a) of paragraph (1) shall be coloured either grey or yellow.".

5. In direction 41, after paragraph (3) there shall be inserted the following new paragraph–

"(4) When a traffic sign to which this paragraph applies is not in use, it shall display a plain grey or black face.".

15th September 1987

Paul Channon
Secretary of State for Transport

21st September 1987

Malcolm Rifkind
Secretary of State for Scotland

24th September 1987

Peter Walker
Secretary of State for Wales

(a) 1984 c.27.
(b) S.I. 1981/859; the relevant amending instruments are S.I. 1982/1880 and 1983/1086.

Direction 3

SCHEDULE

(1)	(2)	(3)
Direction	*Existing words*	*Substituted words*
12	547.1 to 547.4	547.1 to 547.5
14	diagram 638 640	diagram 638, 640 or 646
34(6), 35 and 36(1)(b)	grey	grey or black

EXPLANATORY NOTE

(This note is not part of the Directions)

These Directions amend the Traffic Signs General Directions 1981. The changes are–

(a) to direction 12, to provide for the use of the traffic sign for humped zebra crossings, introduced by the Traffic Signs (Amendment) Regulations 1986 (S.I. 1986/1859);

(b) to direction 14, to correct an error in an earlier instrument (S.I. 1982/1880);

(c) to directions 34(6), 35 and 36(1)(b), to provide for black as well as grey posts for traffic signs and signals, and for black as well as grey for the backs of signs;

(d) to direction 36, to allow the use of grey or yellow faced backing boards for traffic signs; and

(e) to direction 41, to require certain traffic signs not continuously in use to display a plain grey or black face when not in use.

STATUTORY INSTRUMENTS

1987 No. 1712

VALUE ADDED TAX

The Value Added Tax (Supplies by Retailers) (Amendment) Regulations 1987

Made - - - -	*28th September 1987*
Laid before the House of Commons	*7th October 1987*
Coming into force	*30th October 1987*

The Commissioners of Customs and Excise, by virtue of the powers conferred upon them by paragraph 2(3) of Schedule 7 to the Value Added Tax Act 1983(**a**) and of all other powers enabling them in that behalf, hereby make the following Regulations:

1.—(1) These Regulations may be cited as the Value Added Tax (Supplies by Retailers) (Amendment) Regulations 1987 and shall come into force on 30th October 1987.

(2) In these Regulations the "principal regulations" means the Value Added Tax (Supplies by Retailers) Regulations 1972(**b**).

2. For regulation 3 of the principal regulations there shall be substituted the following:

"**3.** The Commissioners may refuse to permit the value of taxable supplies to be determined in accordance with a scheme if it appears to them—

(a) that the use of any particular scheme does not produce a fair and reasonable valuation during any period; or

(b) that it is necessary to do so for the protection of the revenue; or

(c) that the retailer could reasonably be expected to account for tax in accordance with Regulations made under paragraph 2(1) of Schedule 7 to the Value Added Tax Act 1983.".

King's Beam House
Mark Lane
London EC3R 7HE
28th September 1987

Colin C. Finlinson
Commissioner of Customs and Excise

(**a**) 1983 c.55.
(**b**) S.I. 1972/1148, to which there are amendments not relevant to these Regulations.

EXPLANATORY NOTE

(This note is not part of the Regulations)

These Regulations make minor amendments to regulation 3 of the Value Added Tax (Supplies by Retailers) Regulations 1972 and clarify the Commissioners' powers to refuse the use of a retail scheme method for determining the value of taxable supplies.

STATUTORY INSTRUMENTS

1987 No. 1730

PUBLIC HEALTH, ENGLAND AND WALES
PUBLIC HEALTH, SCOTLAND

The Control of Noise (Code of Practice for Construction and Open Sites) Order 1987

Made - - - -	*25th September 1987*
Laid before Parliament	*7th October 1987*
Coming into force	*28th October 1987*

The Secretary of State for the Environment as respects England, the Secretary of State for Wales as respects Wales and the Secretary of State for Scotland as respects Scotland, in exercise of the power conferred by sections 71 and 104(1) of the Control of Pollution Act 1974(**a**), and of all other powers enabling them in that behalf, hereby make the following Order:

Citation and commencement

1. This Order may be cited as the Control of Noise (Code of Practice for Construction and Open Sites) Order 1987 and shall come into force on 28th October 1987.

Approval of Code of Practice

2. The Code of Practice for noise control applicable to piling operations published by the British Standards Institution numbered BS 5228: Part 4: 1986(**b**) which came into effect on 31st January 1986 (and which is concerned amongst other things with the carrying out of works to which section 60 of the Control of Pollution Act 1974 applies) is approved as being suitable for giving guidance on appropriate methods of minimising noise.

	Nicholas Ridley
22nd September 1987	Secretary of State for the Environment
	Peter Walker
22nd September 1987	Secretary of State for Wales
	Malcolm Rifkind
25th September 1987	Secretary of State for Scotland

(**a**) 1974 c.40.
(**b**) The International Standard Book Number (ISBN) in respect of BS 5228: Part 4: 1986 is 0 580 14922 6.

EXPLANATORY NOTE

(This note is not part of the Order)

Under section 71 of the Control of Pollution Act 1974 the Secretary of State may give guidance on appropriate methods for minimising noise by approving codes of practice. He is required to approve a code for the carrying out of works to which section 60 of the Act applies. These include building and roadworks, demolition, dredging and other works of engineering construction.

This Order approves the code mentioned in article 2.

The Codes of Practice contained in Parts 1 and 3 of the British Standards Institution publication "Noise Control on Construction and Open Sites" (BS 5228) were approved in relation to England and Wales by the Control of Noise (Codes of Practice for Construction and Open Sites) Order 1984 (S.I. 1984/1992) and in relation to Scotland by the Control of Noise (Codes of Practice for Construction and Open Sites) (Scotland) Order 1985 (S.I. 1985/145 (S.8)).

The approved Codes of Practice are available separately and may be obtained from any of the sales outlets of the British Standards Institution or by post from the British Standards Institution, Linford Wood, Milton Keynes, MK14 6LE (Telephone number: Milton Keynes (STD 0908) 320033).

STATUTORY INSTRUMENTS

1987 No. 1732

HOUSING, ENGLAND AND WALES

The Housing (Extension of Right to Buy) Order 1987

Made - - - -	*30th September 1987*	
Laid before Parliament	*2nd October 1987*	
Coming into force	*23rd October 1987*	

The Secretary of State, in exercise of the powers conferred on him by section 171 of the Housing Act 1985(**a**) and of all other powers enabling him in that behalf, hereby makes the following Order —

Citation and commencement

1. This Order may be cited as the Housing (Extension of Right to Buy) Order 1987 and shall come into force on 23rd October 1987.

Interpretation

2. In this Order, unless the contrary intention appears, a reference to a numbered section, Part or Schedule, without more, is a reference to the section, Part or Schedule bearing that number in the Housing Act 1985.

Extension of the right to buy

3.—(1) Where there are in a dwelling-house let on a secure tenancy one or more interests all of which are interests to which this article applies, and the dwelling-house is a house, Part V (the right to buy) has effect with the modifications specified in the Schedule to this Order being modifications to enable a secure tenant to acquire the freehold of the dwelling-house.

(2) This article applies to an interest held by –

a local authority,
a new town corporation,
an urban development corporation,
the Development Board for Rural Wales,
the Housing Corporation, or
a registered housing association, other than one excepted from the right to buy by Schedule 5, paragraph 1 (charities), 2 (co-operatives) or 3 (associations which have not received grant),

which is immediately superior to the interest of the landlord or to another interest to which this article applies.

(**a**) 1985 c.68.

Consequential, supplementary and transitional provisions

4.—(1) In a case where a secure tenant, at a time when this Order did not apply, has served, in relation to the dwelling-house, a notice under section 122(1) (tenant's notice claiming to exercise right to buy), this Order does not apply while that notice remains in force.

(2) Where, in pursuance of Part V as modified by this Order, a secure tenant has served a notice under section 122(1) (notice claiming to exercise right to buy) then in the event of the interest of the landlord, an intermediate landlord or the freeholder in the dwelling-house passing to a person not being an authority or body to which article 3(2) applies, the freeholder shall as soon as practicable serve on the tenant a notice in writing telling him that he is no longer entitled to acquire the freehold of the dwelling-house.

Nicholas Ridley
30th September 1987   One of Her Majesty's Principal Secretaries of State

Article 3   SCHEDULE

                          MODIFICATIONS OF PART V

1. In section 118 (the right to buy), for subsection (1) substitute –

"(1) A secure tenant has the right to buy, that is to say, the right, in the circumstances and subject to the conditions and exceptions stated in the following provisions of this Part, to acquire the freehold of the dwelling-house.".

2. In section 122 (tenant's notice claiming to exercise right to buy), omit subsection (3).

3. After section 122 (tenant's notice claiming to exercise right to buy) insert –

"**122A**—(1) Where a notice under section 122(1) (notice claiming to exercise right to buy) is served by the tenant, the landlord shall, as soon as practicable –

    (a) serve a copy of the notice on the authority or body which is its landlord in relation to the dwelling-house, and

    (b) serve on the tenant a notice in writing that this has been done and of the name and address of that authority or body.

(2) If the authority or body referred to in subsection (1)(a) is an intermediate landlord, it shall in turn serve a copy of the notice on the authority or body which is its immediate landlord in relation to the dwelling-house (and so on, if that authority or body is also an intermediate landlord).

(3) The landlord and each of the intermediate landlords (if any) shall, at the same time as it serves on its landlord the copy of the tenant's notice, notify that authority or body whether to its knowledge there are any reasons for denying the tenant's right to buy and, if there are, state those reasons.

(4) When an intermediate landlord, in accordance with subsection (3), notifies its immediate landlord whether there are any reasons for denying the tenant's right to buy, it shall send with that notification the notification or notifications under that subsection which it has received from the landlord or from any other intermediate landlord or landlords.

(5) An authority or body which serves a copy of the tenant's notice on another authority or body in accordance with subsection (2) shall at the same time notify the landlord and the tenant that this has been done and of the name and address of the other authority or body.".

4. In section 123 (claim to share right to buy with members of family), in paragraph (b) of subsection (2), for the reference to the landlord substitute a reference to the freeholder.

5. For section 124 (landlord's notice admitting or denying right to buy) substitute –

"**124.**—(1) Where a notice under section 122 (notice claiming to exercise right to buy) has been served by the tenant, the freeholder shall, unless the notice has been withdrawn, serve on the tenant, within eight weeks of service under section 122A on the freeholder of the copy of the tenant's notice, a written notice either –

(a) admitting his right, or

(b) denying it and stating the reasons why in its opinion the tenant does not have the right to buy.

(2) The freeholder shall, as soon as practicable, serve a copy of the notice on the landlord and on each of the intermediate landlords (if any).".

6. After section 124 insert –

"Withdrawal **124A**—(1) If the tenant wishes to withdraw a notice served under section of tenant's 122(1) (notice claiming to exercise right to buy) before he has received the notice freeholder's notice under section 124(1) (notice admitting or denying right to buy), he may do so by notice in writing served on the landlord.

(2) Where the landlord receives the tenant's notice of withdrawal under subsection (1) after it has served a copy of the tenant's notice under section 122(1) (notice claiming to exercise right to buy) on its landlord, it shall, as soon as practicable, serve on its landlord a copy of the notice of withdrawal.

(3) An intermediate landlord shall, in turn, similarly serve a copy of the tenant's notice of withdrawal on its immediate landlord.

(4) If the tenant wishes to withdraw his notice claiming to exercise the right to buy after he has received the freeholder's notice admitting or denying the right, he may do so by a notice in writing served on the freeholder.

(5) Where the tenant serves a notice of withdrawal on the freeholder, the freeholder shall, as soon as practicable, inform the landlord and the intermediate landlords (if any) of this fact.".

7. In section 125 (landlord's notice of purchase price and other matters) –

(a) for subsection (1) substitute –

"(1) Where a secure tenant has claimed to exercise the right to buy and that right has been established (whether by the freeholder's admission or otherwise), the freeholder shall within twelve weeks serve on the tenant a notice complying with this section.";

(b) in subsection (2) –

(i) for the reference to the landlord substitute a reference to the freeholder, and

(ii) omit the words "or, as the case may be, the lease granted to him";

(c) in subsection (3) –

(i) for the reference to the landlord substitute a reference to the freeholder, and

(ii) omit the words "or grant";

(d) in subsection (4)(**a**) –

(i) for the words "the landlord" substitute the words "the freeholder, an intermediate landlord or the landlord",

(ii) omit the words ", or (b) improvement contributions,", and

(iii) omit the words "or 125B (improvement contributions)";

(e) in subsection (4A)(**b**) –

(i) for the reference to the landlord substitute a reference to the freeholder, and

(ii) omit the words "or lease"; and

(f) in subsection (5) –

(i) at the end of paragraph (b) add the word "and",

(ii) in paragraph (c), for the words "landlord's notices" substitute the words "freeholder's notices", and

(iii) omit the word "and" at the end of paragraph (c) and omit paragraph (d).

8. In section 125A(**c**) (estimates and information about service charges) –

(a) in subsection (1) –

(i) for the references to landlord substitute references to freeholder, and

---

(**a**) Section 125(4) was substituted by section 4(1) of the Housing and Planning Act 1986 (c.63). (**b**) Section 125(4A) was inserted by paragraph 3 of Schedule 5 to the Housing and Planning Act 1986. (**c**) Section 125A was inserted by section 4(2) of the Housing and Planning Act 1986.

(ii) omit the words "(excluding, in the case of a flat, charges to which subsection (2) applies)"; and

(b) omit subsections (2) and (3).

9. Omit section 125B**(a)** (estimates and information about improvement contributions).

10. In section 125C**(a)** (reference period for purpose of s.125A) –

(a) in subsection (1) –

(i) omit the words "or 125B",

(ii) in paragraph (a), for the reference to the landlord substitute a reference to the freeholder and omit the words "or the lease granted", and

(iii) in paragraph (b), omit the words "or lease" and the words "or improvement contribution"; and

(b) in subsection (2), omit the words "or the lease granted".

11. In section 126 (purchase price) –

(a) in subsection (1), omit the words "or grant"; and

(b) omit subsection (2).

12. In section 127 (value of dwelling-house) –

(a) in subsection (1) –

(i) for paragraph (a) substitute –

"(a)   on the assumptions stated in subsection (2),", and

(ii) in paragraph (c)**(b)**, omit the words "or improvement contributions" and for the words "landlord's notice" substitute the words "freeholder's notice";

(b) in subsection (2), omit the words "For a conveyance"; and

(c) omit subsection (3).

13.—(1)   In section 128 (determination of value by district valuer) –

(a) in subsections (2) to (5), for references to landlord, other than the third reference in subsection (2), substitute references to freeholder; and

(b) in subsection (2), for the third reference to landlord substitute the words "freeholder, an intermediate landlord or the landlord".

(2) In section 129**(c)** (discount), in subsection (2), in paragraph (a) omit the words "in the case of a house", and omit paragraph (b).

(3) In section 130 (reduction of discount where previous discount given) –

(a) in subsection (2), in paragraph (b), after the words "Schedule 8" insert "to this Act without taking into account the modifications made by the Housing (Extension of Right to Buy) Order 1987"; and

(b) in subsection (3) in paragraph (a), after the words "right to buy" insert "(whether or not taking into account the modifications made by the Housing (Extension of Right to Buy) Order 1987)".

14. In section 132 (the right to a mortgage) for subsection (1) substitute –

"(1) A secure tenant who has the right to buy has the right, subject to the following provisions of this Part, to have the whole or part of the aggregate amount mentioned in section 133(1) advanced to him, on the security of a first mortgage of the dwelling-house, by the freeholder or if the freeholder is a housing association by the Housing Corporation; and in this Act that right is referred to as "the right to a mortgage.".

15. In section 133 (the amount to be secured) –

(a) in subsection (1) –

(i) omit the words "leave outstanding, or" and omit the comma after the word "him", and

(ii) for the references to the landlord substitute references to the freeholder;

(b) in subsection (2), omit the words "leave outstanding or";

(c) for subsection (4) substitute –

(a) Sections 125B and 125C were inserted by section 4(2) of the Housing and Planning Act 1986.   **(b)** Section 127(1)(c) was inserted by section 4(3) of the Housing and Planning Act 1986.   **(c)** Section 129 was amended by section 2(1) of the Housing and Planning Act 1986.

"(4) Where the amount which a secure tenant is entitled to have advanced to him by the freeholder on the security of the dwelling-house is reduced by the limit imposed by this section, the freeholder may, if it thinks fit and the tenant agrees, treat him as entitled to have advanced on that security such amount exceeding the limit, but not exceeding the aggregate mentioned in subsection (1), as the freeholder may determine."; and

(d) in subsection (5), omit the words "leave outstanding or".

16. In section 134 (tenant's notice claiming to exercise right to a mortgage), throughout for references to the landlord substitute references to the freeholder.

17. In section 135 (landlord's notice of amount and terms of mortgage) –

(a) in subsections (1) and (4), for references to the landlord substitute references to the freeholder; and

(b) in subsection (1), in paragraph (a), omit the words "leave outstanding or"; and

(c) omit subsection (3).

18. In section 136 (change of secure tenant after notice claiming right to buy) –

(a) in subsections (2), (4) and (5), for references to the landlord substitute references to the freeholder; and

(b) after subsection (1), insert –

"(1A) On becoming aware of the change of secure tenant the landlord shall forthwith notify its landlord in writing of this fact.

(1B) An intermediate landlord so notified shall, in turn, similarly notify its immediate landlord.".

19. In section 137(**a**) (change of landlord after notice claiming right to buy or right to a mortgage) –

(a) for subsection (1) substitute –

"(1) Where, after the tenant has served a notice –
(a) under section 122(1) (notice claiming to exercise right to buy), or
(b) under section 134(1) (notice claiming to exercise right to a mortgage),

the interest of the landlord, an intermediate landlord or the freeholder in the dwelling-house passes from that authority or body to another person, or the interest comes to an end –

(i) the landlord, intermediate landlord or freeholder, as the case may be, shall forthwith notify its tenant of the change and the landlord and intermediate landlord shall similarly notify its landlord,

(ii) an intermediate landlord so notified by its tenant shall, in turn, similarly notify its immediate landlord or, if so notified by its landlord, shall similarly notify its tenant, and

(iii) all parties shall be in the same position as if the change had occurred before the notice under section 122(1) or section 134(1), as the case may be, was served and all other notices served had been served by or on the appropriate parties and all steps had been taken by them."; and

(b) in subsection (2), in paragraph (b), for the reference to the landlord substitute a reference to the freeholder.

20. In section 138 (duty of landlord to convey freehold) –

(a) for subsection (1) substitute –

"(1) Where a secure tenant has claimed to exercise the right to buy and that right has been established, then, as soon as all matters relating to the grant and to the amount to be advanced on the security of the dwelling-house have been agreed or determined, the freeholder shall make to the tenant a grant of the dwelling-house for an estate in fee simple absolute, in accordance with the following provisions of this Part."; and

(b) in subsections (2) and (3), for the references to the landlord substitute references to the freeholder.

21. After section 138 insert –

"**138A.**—(1) On completion the freeholder shall pay –

(a) to the landlord and to an intermediate landlord (if any), and

---

(**a**) Section 137 was amended by paragraph 4 of Schedule 5 to the Housing and Planning Act 1986.

  (b) to the rent owner of a rentcharge charged on or issuing out of the lease of the landlord or an intermediate landlord,

an amount calculated in accordance with the formula –

$$A = \frac{R}{V} \times P$$

where –

  A is the amount payable to the landlord, intermediate landlord or rent owner;

  R is the amount which, under this section, is to be taken to be the value immediately before completion of the lease of the landlord or intermediate landlord (as the case may be) or of the rentcharge charged on or issuing out of such a lease;

  P is the price payable for the dwelling-house by the tenant; and

  V is the amount which is the sum of the values, immediately before completion, of the interests in the dwelling-house of –

   the landlord,
   intermediate landlords (if any),
   rent owners as mentioned in subsection (1)(b) (if any), and
   the freeholder.

  (2) Where the whole or any part of any discount obtained by the tenant is recovered by the freeholder (whether by the receipt of a payment determined by reference to the discount or by a reduction so determined of any consideration given by the freeholder or in any other way), the freeholder shall pay to the authority or body which immediately before completion was the landlord or an intermediate landlord and to the rent owner of a rentcharge which was then charged on or issued out of the lease of any such authority or body, an amount calculated in accordance with the formula –

$$A = \frac{R}{V} \times D$$

where –

  A is the amount payable to the authority or body or rent owner;

  R is the amount which, under this section, is to be taken to be the value immediately before completion of the lease of the authority or body or of the rentcharge charged on or issuing out of such a lease;

  D is the amount of the discount recovered by the freeholder; and

  V is the amount which is the sum of the values, immediately before completion, of the interests in the dwelling-house of –

   the landlord
   intermediate landlords (if any),
   rent owners as mentioned in subsection (1)(b) (if any), and
   the freeholder.

  (3) For the purposes of this section –

  (a) the value of an interest immediately before completion shall be taken to be the price which, at that time, it would realise if sold on the open market, free from any mortgage, by a willing vendor on the assumption that this Part did not apply, and

  (b) where a lease or a rentcharge includes property other than the dwelling-house the value of the interest shall be taken to be that part of the value which is attributable to the dwelling-house.

  (4) No payment shall be made under subsection (1) or (2) in relation to a lease of the dwelling-house if it is (or was) a lease for a term certain and the residue of the term unexpired immediately before completion is (or was) a period of less than twelve months or if it is (or was) a periodic tenancy.

  (5) In this section "rentcharge" and "rent owner" have the same respective meanings as in the Rentcharges Act 1977(a).".

22. In section 139 (terms and effect of conveyance and mortgage) –

  (a) in subsection (1), omit the words "a grant of a lease so executed shall conform with Parts I and III of that Schedule;";

(a) 1977 c.30.

(b) after subsection (1) insert –

"(1A) The freeholder shall –

(a) execute the conveyance on its own behalf and in the names of the landlord and the intermediate landlord or landlords (if any) and it shall be binding on those authorities or bodies, and

(b) secure that the conveyance states that it is a conveyance to which this subsection applies"; and

(c) for subsection (2) substitute –

"(2) The secure tenancy, the lease of the landlord and the lease of each of the intermediate landlords (if any), in so far as any such lease relates to the dwelling-house, come to an end and are extinguished on the grant to the tenant of an estate in fee simple in pursuance of the right to buy; and if there is then a subtenancy deriving out of the secure tenancy section 139 of the Law of Property Act 1925(**a**) (effect of extinguishment of reversion) applies as on a merger or surrender.".

23. In section 140(**b**) (freeholder's first notice to complete) –

(a) throughout for references to landlord substitute references to freeholder; and

(b) in subsection (5), omit the words "left outstanding or".

24. In section 141 (freeholder's second notice to complete) and section 142 (when tenant is entitled to defer completion), for references throughout to landlord substitute references to freeholder.

25. Omit sections 143 to 153 and Schedules 8 and 9 (the right to a shared ownership lease).

26. In section 154 (registration of title) –

(a) for subsection (1) substitute –

"(1) Where the freeholder's title to the dwelling-house is not registered, section 123 of the Land Registration Act 1925(**c**) (compulsory registration of title) applies in relation to the conveyance of the freehold in pursuance of this Part whether or not the dwelling-house is in an area in which an Order in Council under section 120 of that Act is for the time being in force (areas of compulsory registration).";

(b) in subsection (2), for references to the landlord substitute references to the freeholder and omit the words "or make the grant" and the words "or grant";

(c) omit subsection (3);

(d) in subsections (4) and (5), for the references to the landlord substitute references to the freeholder;

(e) after subsection (5) insert –

"(5A) Where the lease of the landlord or of any intermediate landlord is registered, the freeholder shall use his best endeavours to obtain (and if obtained shall produce to the Chief Land Registrar) that lease and its appropriate land or charge certificate."; and

(f) omit subsection (6).

27. In section 155(**d**) (repayment of discount on early disposal) –

(a) in subsection (1), for the words from the beginning to "no discount)" substitute the words "A conveyance of the freehold in pursuance of this Part shall contain (unless there is no discount)";

(b) in subsection (2) –

(i) omit the words "In the case of a conveyance or grant in pursuance of the right to buy,",

(ii) for the reference to the landlord substitute a reference to the freeholder, and

(iii) omit the words "or grant" in the remaining place in which those words occur; and

(c) omit subsection (3).

(**a**) 1925 c.20. (**b**) Section 140 was amended by paragraph 5(1) of Schedule 5 to the Housing and Planning Act 1986. (**c**) 1925 c.21. (**d**) Section 155 was amended by section 2(3) of the Housing and Planning Act 1986.

28.   In section 156 (liability to repay is a charge on the premises) –

(a) in subsection (2) –

   (i)   for paragraph (a) substitute –

      "(a) advanced to the tenant by the freeholder for the purpose of enabling him to exercise the right to buy, or", and

   (ii)   for the reference to the landlord substitute a reference to the freeholder; and

(b) in subsection (3A)(**a**) omit the words "or grant" and the words "to authorise a forfeiture or".

29.   In section 157 (restriction on disposal of dwelling-houses in National Parks, etc.) –

(a) in subsections (1), (2) and (4), for the references to the landlord substitute references to the freeholder;

(b) in subsection (1), omit the words "or grant" in both places in which those words occur; and

(c) in subsection (4) –

   (i)   omit the words "or grant", and

   (ii)   in paragraph (a), omit the words "or as the case may be surrender the lease".

30.   In section 158 (consideration for reconveyance under s.157) –

(a) in subsection (1) –

   (i)   omit the words "or surrender", and

   (ii)   for the reference to the landlord substitute a reference to the freeholder;

(b) in subsection (2) –

   (i)   omit the words "or surrendered", and

   (ii)   omit the word "and" at the end of paragraph (a) and omit paragraph (b);

(c) in subsection (3), for the reference to the landlord substitute a reference to the freeholder; and

(d) in subsection (4)(**b**), omit the words "or surrender".

31.   In section 159 (relevant disposals), in subsection (1)(a) omit the words "or an assignment of the lease".

32.   In section 160 (exempted disposals), in subsection (1)(a) omit the words "or an assignment of the lease".

33.   In section 164 (Secretary of State's general power to intervene) –

(a) in subsection (1) –

   (i)   after the words "particular landlord" insert the words "intermediate landlord or freeholder",

   (ii)   after the words "description of landlords" insert the words "intermediate landlords or freeholders", and

   (iii)   omit the words "or the right to be granted a shared ownership lease";

(b) in subsection (2), after the words "landlord or landlords" insert the words ", intermediate landlord or intermediate landlords or freeholder or freeholders";

(c) for subsection (4) substitute –

     "(4) Where a notice under this section has been given to a landlord or landlords, intermediate landlord or intermediate landlords or freeholder or freeholders, no step taken by any such authority or body while the notice is in force or before it was given has any effect in relation to the exercise by a secure tenant of the right to buy or the right to a mortgage, except in so far as the notice otherwise provides.";

(d) in subsection (5) –

   (i)   for the words "the landlord or landlords" substitute the words "the landlord or landlords, intermediate landlord or intermediate landlords or freeholder or freeholders",

   (ii)   after the words "the right to buy" insert the word "and" and omit the words "and the right to be granted a shared ownership lease", and

   (iii)   for the words "the landlord" in the second place in which those words occur substitute the words "the landlord, intermediate landlord or freeholder"; and

(e) in subsection (6) for both of the references to landlord substitute references to freeholder.

(**a**) Section 156(3A) was inserted by paragraph 1(2) of Schedule 5 to the Housing and Planning Act 1986. (**b**) Section 158(4) was inserted by paragraph 1(3) of Schedule 5 to the Housing and Planning Act 1986.

34. In section 165 (vesting orders for purposes of s.164) –

(a) in subsection (1) –

(i) omit the words "or granting a lease", and

(ii) for the reference to the landlord substitute a reference to the freeholder;

(b) in subsection (2) –

(i) omit the words "or grant", and

(ii) for the words "the landlord and its successors in title" substitute the words "the freeholder, the intermediate landlords (if any) and the landlord and its or their successors in title";

(c) in subsection (3) –

(i) for the words "the landlord's title" substitute the words "the freeholder's title", and

(ii) omit the words "or grant made";

(d) in subsection (4), in paragraph (a), omit the words "or as the case may require a good leasehold title";

(e) in subsection (5) –

(i) for the words "the landlord's title" substitute the words "the title of the freeholder, an intermediate landlord or the landlord", and

(ii) omit the words "or the right to be granted a shared ownership lease"; and

(f) in subsection (6), omit the words "from landlord".

35. In section 166 (other provisions supplementary to s.164) –

(a) in subsection (1), for the words "a particular landlord" substitute the words "a particular freeholder, intermediate landlord or landlord";

(b) in subsection (2), for the words "the landlord" –

(i) where the words first occur substitute the words "the freeholder, intermediate landlord or landlord", and

(ii) where those words occur for the second time substitute the words "that authority or body";

(c) in subsection (3) –

(i) for the words "a landlord" substitute the words "a freeholder, intermediate landlord or landlord", and

(ii) for the words "the landlord" in both places where those words occur substitute the words "that authority or body";

(d) in subsection (4) –

(i) for paragraph (b) substitute –

"(b) certify a sum as representing those costs and the freeholder, intermediate landlord or landlord by which those costs (or such proportion thereof as he may specify) are to be borne;", and

(ii) for the words "the landlord" substitute the words "the authority or body concerned";

(e) in subsection (5), for the words "the landlord" –

(i) where those words first occur substitute the words "the freeholder, intermediate landlord or landlord", and

(ii) where those words occur for the second time substitute the words "that authority or body"; and

(f) in subsection (6), for the words "references to a landlord" substitute the words "references to a freeholder".

36. After section 166 (other provisions supplementary to s.164) insert –

"**166A**. The Secretary of State, on giving to a freeholder, intermediate landlord or landlord –

(a) a notice under section 164 (notice of intention to intervene), or

(b) a further notice under section 166 (notice withdrawing previous notice),

shall, as soon as practicable, send a copy of the notice to any other authority or body which is, to his knowledge, a freeholder, intermediate landlord or landlord of any dwelling-house affected by the notice.".

37. In section 167 (power to give directions as to covenants and conditions), in subsection (1) –

(a) omit the words "or grants" in both places where those words occur,

(b) at the end of paragraph (a), omit the word "or" and omit paragraph (b), and

(c) for the references to landlords substitute references to freeholders.

38. In section 168 (effect of direction under s.167 on existing covenants and conditions) –

(a) in subsection (1), in paragraphs (a) and (b), omit the words "or grant";

(b) in subsection (3) –

  (i) for the reference to the landlord substitute a reference to the freeholder, and

  (ii) omit the words "or grant"; and

(c) in subsection (4), for the references to the landlord substitute references to the freeholder.

39. In section 169 (power to obtain information, etc.) –

(a) in subsection (1), for the words "a landlord" substitute the words "a freeholder, intermediate landlord or landlord";

(b) in subsection (2), for the words "the landlord" –

  (i) where those words first occur substitute the words "the freeholder, intermediate landlord or landlord", and

  (ii) where those words occur for the second time substitute the words "that authority or body"; and

(c) in subsection (3) –

  (i) for the references to a landlord substitute references to a freeholder, and

  (ii) omit the words "or grant".

40. In section 170 (power to give assistance in connection with legal proceedings) –

(a) in subsection (1), in paragraph (b), omit the words "or grant", and

(b) in subsection (2) –

  (i) in paragraph (a), omit the words "or the right to be granted a shared ownership lease", and

  (ii) in paragraph (b), for the words "either of those rights" substitute the words "that right".

41. Omit sections 171 (power to extend right to buy etc.) and 172 to 175 (modifications or Leasehold Reform Act 1967).

42. In section 176 (notices), in subsections (2) and (4), after the word "landlord" in each place in which that word occurs insert the words "or freeholder".

43. In section 177 (errors and omissions in notices) –

(a) in subsection (2) –

  (i) in paragraphs (a) and (b), for the references to the landlord substitute references to the freeholder,

  (ii) in paragraph (a), omit the words "or the right to be granted a shared ownership lease" and the words "or 146", and

  (iii) after the words "the parties" insert the words "(including the landlord and an intermediate landlord)"; and

(b) in subsection (3), omit the references to section 147, paragraph 1(3) of Schedule 8 and paragraph 5 of Schedule 9.

44. After section 177 insert –

"Assistance to freeholder.

177A. The landlord and any intermediate landlord shall –

(a) on written request give the freeholder such information and assistance as it may reasonably require in order to give effect to the provisions of this Part; and

(b) ensure that all deeds and other documents in its possession or under its control to which the tenant is entitled or reasonably requires on the conveyance to him of the freehold of the dwelling-house are available for this purpose, including in the case of registered land the land certificate and any other documents which would be necessary to perfect the tenant's title if the title were not to be registered.".

45. In section 178 (costs) –

(a) for subsection (1) substitute –

"(1) An agreement between –

(a) the landlord, an intermediate landlord or the freeholder and a tenant claiming to exercise the right to buy, or

(b) the landlord, an intermediate landlord, the freeholder, or, as the case may be, the Housing Corporation and a tenant claiming to exercise the right to a mortgage,

is void in so far as it purports to oblige the tenant to bear any part of the costs incurred by the landlord, intermediate landlord, freeholder or Housing Corporation in connection with the tenant's exercise of that right."; and

(b) in subsection (2) –

(i) omit the words from "or such a right" to "(right to further advances)", and

(ii) for the reference to the landlord substitute a reference to the freeholder.

46. In section 179 (provisions restricting right to buy, etc. of no effect) omit subsection (1).

47. In section 180 (statutory declarations), for the word "landlord" in both places where that word occurs substitute the words "freeholder, intermediate landlord, landlord".

48. In section 181 (jurisdiction of county court), in subsection (1) –

(a) in paragraph (b), omit the words "or under a shared ownership lease granted in pursuance of this Part", and

(b) in the words following paragraph (b), omit the words "and paragraph 11 of Schedule 8".

49. In section 184 (land let with or used for purposes of dwelling-house) –

(a) for subsection (1) substitute –

"(1) For the purposes of this Part land owned by the freeholder in fee simple –

(a) which is let by the freeholder to the landlord or to an intermediate landlord,

(b) in respect of which each of the intermediate landlords (if any) is an authority or body specified in article 3(2) of the Housing (Extension of Right to Buy) Order 1987, and

(c) which is let to the tenant together with the dwelling-house,

shall be treated as part of the dwelling-house, unless the land is agricultural land (within the meaning set out in section 26(3)(a) of the General Rate Act 1967**(a)**) exceeding two acres.";

(b) in subsection (2) –

(i) after the words "any land" insert the words "owned by the freeholder in fee simple", and

(ii) for paragraphs (a) and (b) substitute –

"(a) the leases of the land (if any), other than any granted by way of security, are held by authorities or bodies which hold a lease of the dwelling-house and which are authorities or bodies specified in article 3(2) of the Housing (Extension of Right to Buy) Order 1987,

(b) the tenant, by a written notice served on the landlord or the freeholder (as the case may be) at any time before he exercises the right to buy requires the land to be included in the dwelling-house, and

(c) it is reasonable in all the circumstances that the land should be so included.";

(c) in subsection (3) –

(i) for the words "the landlord" substitute the words "the landlord or the freeholder (as the case may be)", and

(ii) omit the words "or the right to be granted a shared ownership lease";

(a) 1967 c.9.

(d) after subsection (3) insert –

"(3A) A notice under subsection (2) or (3), if served before the freeholder serves on the tenant a notice under section 124 (notice admitting or denying right to buy), shall be served on the landlord and in any other case shall be served on the freeholder.

(3B) On receiving any notice served by the tenant under this section, the landlord shall, as soon as practicable –

(a) serve a copy of the notice on the authority or body which is its landlord in relation to the dwelling-house, and

(b) serve on the tenant notice in writing that this has been done and of the name and address of that authority or body.

(3C) If the authority or body referred to in subsection (3B)(a) is an intermediate landlord, it shall in turn serve a copy of the notice on the authority or body which is its immediate landlord in relation to the dwelling-house (and so on, if that authority or body is also an intermediate landlord).

(3D) An authority or body which serves a copy of the tenant's notice on another authority or body in accordance with subsection (3C) shall at the same time notify the landlord and the tenant that this has been done and of the name and address of the other authority or body.

(3E) On receiving a notice served on it by the tenant under this section, the freeholder shall, as soon as possible, serve a copy of the notice on each authority or body which, to its knowledge, has a leasehold interest in the dwelling-house and notify the tenant that this has been done."; and

(e) in subsection (4), omit from the first set of brackets the word "landlord's".

50. In section 187 (minor definitions), omit the definitions of "improvement contribution" and "total share", and at the appropriate places insert –

""freeholder" means the owner of the freehold of the dwelling-house;"

""intermediate landlord" means the owner of a lease of the dwelling-house (other than one created by way of security) which is immediately superior to the lease of the landlord or to the lease of another intermediate landlord;".

51. In section 188 (index of defined expressions: Part V) –

(a) omit from the first column of the Table the following expressions together with the corresponding entries in the second column –

"additional share" etc.,
"effective discount" etc.,
"initial share" etc.,
"prescribed percentage" etc.,
"right to be granted a shared ownership lease",
"right to further advances",
"total share" etc.; and

(b) at the appropriate places in the Table insert –

"freeholder   section 187"

"intermediate   section 187".
landlord

52. In Schedule 5 (exceptions to the right to buy) –

(a) omit paragraph 4 (landlord with insufficient interest in the property);

(b) in paragraph 5(1)(a) and (b) (dwelling-houses let in connection with employment), after the words "the landlord" insert the words "an intermediate landlord or the freeholder";

(c) in paragraphs 7(a), 8 and 9(1)(a) (certain dwelling-houses for the disabled), after the words "the landlord" in each place in which those words occur, insert the words "an intermediate landlord or the freeholder";

(d) in paragraph 10(1)(b) (certain dwelling-houses for persons of pensionable age), after the words "the landlord" insert the words "an intermediate landlord or the freeholder";

(e) in paragraph 11(a) (certain dwelling-houses for persons of pensionable age) –

(i) in sub-paragraph (1)(a)(ii), for the words "the landlord" substitute the words "the landlord, an intermediate landlord, the freeholder", and

---

(a) Paragraph 11 was substituted by section 1 of the Housing and Planning Act 1986.

(ii) in sub-paragraph (2), omit head (c); and

(f) omit paragraph 12 (dwelling-houses held on Crown tenancies).

53. In Schedule 6 (conveyance of freehold and grant of lease in pursuance of right to buy) –

(a) in Part 1 (common provisions) –

(i) in paragraphs 1, 2(1) and (3), 3, 4 and 5 omit the words "or grant";

(ii) in paragraphs 1, 2(2)(a), 3, 4 and 6 for references to the landlord substitute references to the freeholder;

(iii) in paragraph 3 (rights of way), omit the word "and" at the end of sub-paragraph (a), in sub-paragraph (b) for the words "or by the person then entitled to the reversion on the tenancy." substitute the words "or by the person then entitled to the freehold; and", and after sub-paragraph (b) insert –

"(c) such provisions (if any) as the freeholder may require for the purpose of making the dwelling-house subject to rights of way which to the knowledge of the freeholder are necessary for the reasonable enjoyment of other property, being property in which at the relevant time the landlord or an intermediate landlord has an interest, or to rights of way, of which the freeholder has knowledge, granted or agreed to be granted before the relevant time by the landlord or an intermediate landlord or by the person then entitled to the reversion on the tenancy or an intermediate tenancy, other than such right of way which falls within sub-paragraph (b).";

(iv) after paragraph 4 (covenants and conditions) insert –

"**4A.** Where the freeholder is aware of an obligation relating to the dwelling-house breach of which may expose the landlord or an intermediate landlord to liability to another person, the freeholder shall include in the conveyance such provision (if any) as may be reasonable in the circumstances to relieve the landlord or intermediate landlord (as the case may be) from, or to indemnify him against, that liability.";

(v) in paragraph 5 (reasonable covenants and conditions may be included), for the words "Parts II and III" substitute the words "Part II";

(vi) in paragraph 6 (no charge to be made for landlord's consent or approval), omit the words "or lease"; and

(vii) in paragraph 7, in paragraph (a) in the definition of "tenant's incumbrance", for the word "reversion" substitute the words "freehold reversion".

(b) in Part II (conveyance of freehold), in paragraphs 8 and 10, for the references to the landlord substitute references to the freeholder;

(c) omit Part III (leases); and

(d) in Part IV (charges) –

(i) omit paragraph 20 (grant of lease),

(ii) in paragraph 21 (conveyance of freehold), in sub-paragraphs (2), (3) and (4), for the references to the landlord substitute references to the freeholder, and

(iii) after paragraph 21 insert –

"**21A**—(1) This paragraph applies to a charge (however created or arising) on a lease (including the secure tenancy) extinguished by section 139(2) (terms and effect of conveyance and mortgage) when the freehold is conveyed in pursuance of the right to buy.

(2) The extinguishment of the lease does not affect the personal liability of the landlord or intermediate landlord (as the case may be) or of any other person in respect of any obligation which the charge was created to secure.".

54. In Schedule 7 (mortgage in pursuance of right to a mortgage), in paragraph 2(1), omit the word "or" at the end of sub-paragraph (a) and omit sub-paragraph (b).

EXPLANATORY NOTE

(This note is not part of the Order)

This Order extends the right to buy (Part V of the Housing Act 1985) by enabling a secure tenant to buy the freehold of his dwelling-house in cases where –

(a) the dwelling-house is a house (i.e. not a flat),

(b) the secure tenant's landlord has a lease of the dwelling-house, and

(c) the freeholder and each intermediate landlord (should there be any) is an authority or body which would be subject to the right to buy were it the secure tenant's immediate landlord.

The Schedule contains modifications to Part V of the Housing Act 1985 to meet these circumstances. Apart from certain changes in the procedure, the principal modifications are that the freeholder (and not the landlord) or, where the freeholder is a housing association, the Housing Corporation is required to grant the secure tenant a mortgage and the secure tenant does not have the right to a shared ownership lease.

STATUTORY INSTRUMENTS

1987 No. 1738 (S.123)

LICENSING (LIQUOR)

The Liquor Licensing (Fees) (Scotland) Order 1987

Made - - - -		*24th September 1987*
Coming into force		*1st January 1988*

The Secretary of State, in exercise of the powers conferred on him by sections 8(1) and 135 of the Licensing (Scotland) Act 1976(**a**) and of all other powers enabling him in that behalf, hereby makes the following Order:

1.—(1) This Order may be cited as the Liquor Licensing (Fees) (Scotland) Order 1987 and shall come into force on 1st January 1988.

(2) In this Order "the Act" means the Licensing (Scotland) Act 1976.

2. The fee payable by any applicant to a licensing board in respect of any matter described in column 1 of the Schedule to this Order and arising under the provision of the Act specified in column 2 of that Schedule shall be the amount specified in the corresponding entry in column 3 thereof.

3. The Liquor Licensing (Fees) (Scotland) Order 1977(**b**) is revoked.

New St Andrew's House, Edinburgh
24th September 1987

James Douglas-Hamilton
Parliamentary Under Secretary of State,
Scottish Office

(**a**) 1976 c.66.
(**b**) S.I. 1977/1085.

Article 2   SCHEDULE

Column 1 *Matter to which fee relates*	Column 2 *Relevant provision of the Act*	Column 3 *New fee* £	Column 4 *Old fee*(a) £
(a) Application in respect of a seamen's canteen under Part III of the Act for–			
Licence under Part III	Section 40	75	50
Provisional licence	Section 41(5)	60	40
Declaration of finality of provisional licence	Section 41(5)	15	10
Renewal of licence	Section 42(2)	37.50	25
Transfer of licence	Section 43(2)	7.50	5
Occasional extension of permitted hours	Section 64(1)	7.50	5
Regular extension of permitted hours	Section 64(1)	37.50	25
(b) Application in respect of a registered club for–			
Occasional licence	Section 33(2)	7.50	5
Declaration of satisfaction with adaptation and use of premises	Section 57(1) or 58(1)	7.50	5
Occasional extension of permitted hours	Section 64(5)	7.50	5
Regular extension of permitted hours	Section 64(5)	37.50	25
Revocation of restriction order	Section 65(5)	15	10
(c) Other applications under the Act for–			
Licence under Part II	Section 9	75	50
Provisional grant of licence	Section 26(1) or (2)	60	40
Affirmation of provisional grant of licence	Section 26(2)	15	10
Declaration of finality of provisional grant	Section 26(4)	15	10
Renewal of licence	Section 9 as read with definition of "grant" in section 139(1)	37.50	25
Transfer of licence to new tenant or occupant	Section 25(1)	51.75	34.50
Transfer of licence to executors etc.	Section 25(2)	6.75	4.50
Endorsement of transferred licence	Section 25(5)	0.75	0.50
Substitution in licence of name of another employee or agent	Section 25(3)	7.50	5
Provisional licence	Section 27	60	40
Occasional licence	Section 33(1)	7.50	5
Occasional permission	Section 34(1)	3.75	2.50
Declaration of satisfaction with adaptation and use of premises	Section 57(1) or 58(1) or 59(1)	7.50	5
Occasional extension of permitted hours	Section 64(1)	7.50	5
Regular extension of permitted hours	Section 64(1)	37.50	25
Sunday opening (unaccompanied by application for new licence or renewal)	Section 53(2)	37.50	25
Revocation of restriction order	Section 65(5)	15	10
Revocation of Sunday restriction order	Section 65(5) as applied by Schedule 4, Part II, paragraph 22	15	10
Cancellation of a closure order	Section 32(5)	15	10
Cancellation of suspension order	Section 36(6)	15	10
Consent to reconstruction etc.	Section 35(1)	7.50	5

(a) The fees in column 4 are the fees previously payable in terms of the Liquor Licensing (Fees) (Scotland) Order 1977 revoked by this Order.

EXPLANATORY NOTE

(This note is not part of the Order)

This Order amends the fees payable from 1st January 1988 under the Licensing (Scotland) Act 1976 by an applicant to a licensing board in respect of the matters listed in the Schedule to the Order. The fees are increased by 50 per cent.

STATUTORY INSTRUMENTS

1987 No. 1749

INCOME TAX

The Occupational Pension Schemes (Additional Voluntary Contributions) Regulations 1987

Made - - - -	*5th October 1987*
Laid before the House of Commons	*5th October 1987*
Coming into force	*26th October 1987*

ARRANGEMENT OF REGULATIONS

The Commissioners of Inland Revenue, in exercise of the powers conferred on them by paragraph 10 of Schedule 5 to the Finance Act 1970(a), hereby make the following Regulations:

Citation and commencement

1. These Regulations may be cited as the Occupational Pension Schemes (Additional Voluntary Contributions) Regulations 1987 and shall come into force on 26th October 1987.

(a) 1970 c.24; paragraph 10 was extended by paragraph 6A(4) which was inserted by the Finance (No.2) Act 1987 (c.51), Schedule 3, paragraph 12.

Interpretation

2.—(1) In these Regulations unless the context otherwise requires –

"the Board" means the Commissioners of Inland Revenue;

"scheme administrator" means the administrator of a scheme;

"scheme member" means a member of a scheme;

"section" means a section of the Finance Act 1970;

"tax month" means a period beginning on the 6th day of any month and ending on the 5th day of the following month;

"the Schedule" means Part II of Schedule 5 to the Finance Act 1970;

"year of assessment" means a year beginning with 6th April in any year and ending with 5th April in the following year.

(2) The Table below indexes other definitions in these Regulations –

Term defined	Regulation
annual claim	6
interim claim	6
scheme	4

Prescribed cases and conditions: introductory

3. Regulations 4 and 5 respectively prescribe the cases in which, and the conditions subject to which, relief under section 21(4)**(a)** shall be given in accordance with sub-paragraphs (2) and (3) of paragraph 6A**(b)** of the Schedule.

Prescribed cases

4. The prescribed cases are cases where a retirement benefits scheme ("scheme") is –

(a) one to which the employer of a scheme member is not a contributor and which provides benefits in addition to those provided by a scheme to which he is a contributor; and

(b) an "exempt approved scheme" within the meaning of section 21(1).

Prescribed conditions

5.—(1) The prescribed conditions are that a scheme member shall –

(a) at or before the time at which he first pays a contribution from which he deducts an amount equal to income tax at the basic rate on the contribution; and

(b) without prejudice to the condition in sub-paragraph (a), within 30 days of being so required to do by notice in writing given by the scheme administrator;

furnish to the scheme administrator in writing the particulars specified in paragraph (2).

(a) Subsection (4) was amended by the Finance (No.2) Act 1987 (c.51), Schedule 3, paragraph 4(1) and subsection (4A) was added by that paragraph.   **(b)** Paragraph 6A (2) and (3) was inserted by the Finance (No.2) Act 1987, Schedule 3, paragraph 12. A relevant amendment was made to paragraph 6 by the Finance (No.2) Act 1987, Schedule 3, paragraph 11.

(2) The particulars specified in this paragraph are –

(a) his full name and address;

(b) his national insurance number and tax office reference;

(c) an estimate of his remuneration for the year of assessment;

(d) the full name and address of his employer who makes contributions to a retirement benefits scheme approved under section 20(a);

(e) the full name and address of the scheme administrator of any retirement benefits scheme referred to in sub-paragraph (d) and the full name or title of any such scheme.

Claims: introductory

6.—(1) Amounts recoverable by a scheme administrator under paragraph 6A(3)(b) of the Schedule shall be recovered on a claim made to the Board for the purpose of these Regulations.

(2) Subject to paragraph (3), a claim shall be for a year of assessment ("annual claim").

(3) A claim may also be made in accordance with regulation 7 for a tax month ("interim claim").

(4) Notwithstanding the provisions of any other enactment, the Board shall not be under an obligation to make any payment under regulation 7 or 8 earlier than the end of the month following the month in which the claim is received.

Interim claims

7.—(1) Subject to paragraph (3), an interim claim for a tax month may be made by a scheme administrator within 6 months after the end of the tax month for which it is made.

(2) A claim under this regulation may not be based on an estimate but may only be made to recover an amount deducted in respect of contributions paid in the tax month.

(3) An interim claim may not be made for the tax month ending 5th October or any subsequent month until the annual claim for the preceding year of assessment has been made by the scheme administrator and received by the Board.

(4) If the amount claimed is established to the Board's satisfaction they shall pay the amount to the claimant; if they are not so satisfied they shall pay to the claimant any lesser amount established to their satisfaction.

(5) Where a scheme administrator discovers that an amount paid to him under paragraph (4) was excessive he shall bring into account in the interim claim made by him next after the discovery (in this regulation referred to as "the subsequent claim") the amount of the excess; and if that amount exceeds the amount deducted in respect of the tax month for which the subsequent claim is made –

(a) the scheme administrator shall repay the amount of the excess to the Board with the claim; and

(b) if he fails so to do that amount shall immediately be recoverable by the Board in the same manner as tax charged by an assessment on the scheme administrator which has become final and conclusive.

(a) Subsection (1) was amended by the Finance (No.2) Act 1987 (c.51), Schedule 3, paragraph 3(2); subsection (2) was amended by the Finance Act 1971 (c.68), section 21(4), by the Finance Act 1981 (c.35), section 32(1), and by the Finance (No.2) Act 1987, Schedule 3, paragraph 3(3) and (4); subsection (2A) was inserted by the Finance Act 1981, section 32(2); and subsections (4), (5) and (6) were added by the Finance (No.2) Act 1987, Schedule 3, paragraph 3(5).

Annual claims

8.—(1) An annual claim for a year of assessment may, subject to paragraph (2), be made at any time within 6 years after the end of the year of assessment.

(2) Where in relation to any year of assessment a scheme administrator has received and not repaid in full any amount on an interim claim he shall within 6 months after the end of the year of assessment make an annual claim.

(3) A claim under this regulation –

(a) may not be based on an estimate but may only be made to recover an amount deducted in respect of contributions paid in the year of assessment, and

(b) shall bring into account payments made in respect of the year of assessment; and for the purpose of this regulation "aggregate interim payments" means the aggregate of payments made (and not repaid) on interim claims.

(4) Where the aggregate interim payments shown by an annual claim exceeds the amount deducted for the year of assessment –

(a) the scheme administrator shall repay the amount of the excess to the Board with the claim; and

(b) if he fails so to do, that amount shall immediately be recoverable by the Board in the same manner as tax charged by an assessment on the scheme administrator which has become final and conclusive.

(5) If a scheme administrator fails to make an annual claim under paragraph (2) within the time limited by that paragraph, the Board may issue a notice to the scheme administrator showing the aggregate interim payments for the year, and stating that the Board are not satisfied that the amount due to the scheme administrator for the year of assessment exceeds the lower amount stated in the notice.

(6) If an annual claim is not delivered to the Board within 14 days after the issue of a notice under paragraph (5), the amount of the difference between the aggregate amount and the amount stated in the notice shall immediately be recoverable by the Board in the same manner as tax charged by an assessment on the scheme administrator which has become final and conclusive.

(7) Where an annual claim has been made and the scheme administrator subsequently discovers that an error or mistake has been made in the claim the scheme administrator may make a supplementary claim within the time limited by paragraph (1).

Claims: supplementary provisions

9.—(1) Section 42 of the Taxes Management Act 1970(a) (procedure for making claims) shall not apply to a claim under these Regulations.

(2) No appeal shall lie from the Board's decision on an interim claim.

(3) An appeal shall be to the Special Commissioners from the Board's decision on an annual claim, and the appeal shall be brought by giving written notice to the Board within 30 days of receipt of written notice of the decision.

(4) No payment made or other thing done on or in relation to an interim claim shall prejudice the decision on an annual claim.

(5) Part V of the Taxes Management 1970(b) (appeals and other proceedings) shall apply to an appeal under paragraph (3), and on an appeal the Special Commissioners may vary the decision appealed against whether or not the variation is to the advantage of the appellant.

(a) 1970 c.9.   (b) Relevant amendments were made to section 45 by the Finance Act 1984 (c.43), section 127 and Schedule 22, paragraph 2, and by section 128(6), and Schedule 23, Part XIII; to section 48 by the Finance (No.2) Act 1975 (c.45), section 45(4); to section 50 by the Finance (No.2) Act 1975, section 67(2); to section 53 by the Finance Act 1972 (c.41), section 129(1); to section 56 by the Finance (No.2) Act 1975, section 45(3). Section 56A was inserted by the Finance Act 1984 (c.43), section 127 and Schedule 22, paragraph 7; and section 57B by the Finance Act 1984, section 127 and Schedule 22, paragraph 4.

(6) All such assessments, payments and repayments shall be made as are necessary to give effect to the Board's decision on an annual claim, or to any variation of that decision on appeal.

(7) Claims under these Regulations –

    (a) shall contain such information and be in such form as the Board may prescribe (and forms prescribed for annual claims may require a report to be given by the scheme administrator's auditor);

    (b) shall contain declarations to the effect that –

        (i) sufficient records in respect of the scheme are maintained so as to enable the requirements of these Regulations to be satisfied, and

        (ii) the information contained in the claim (including the declaration referred to in paragraph (i)) is correct; and

    (c) shall be signed by the scheme administrator or by an authorised representative in the service of the scheme administrator.

Recovery on withdrawal of approval of schemes

10. Where a scheme administrator furnishes to the Board information in accordance with regulation 12(2) he shall at the time that he furnishes the information –

    (a) pay to the Board the amount (if any) referred to in regulation 12(3)(d); and

    (b) if he fails so to do, that amount shall immediately be recoverable by the Board in the same manner as tax charged by an assessment on the scheme administrator which has become final and conclusive.

Recovery of amounts by assessment

11.—(1) Section 30 of the Taxes Management Act 1970(a) (recovery of overpayment of tax, etc) shall apply in relation to the payment by the Board of an amount –

    (a) paid under these Regulations to which a scheme administrator was not entitled, or

    (b) recoverable from a scheme administrator under regulation 7(5), regulation 8(4) or (6) or regulation 10,

as if it had been income tax repaid to the scheme administrator to which he was not entitled.

(2) An assessment made by virtue of this regulation shall be made by the Board and, subject to the provisions of these Regulations, the Taxes Management Act 1970 shall apply as if the assessment were an assessment to tax for the year of assessment in respect of which the amount was paid or is recoverable.

Information

12.—(1) The Board may by notice in writing require any person who is, or who at any time has been, –

    (a) a scheme administrator to whom contributions have been paid under paragraph 6A(2) and (3) of the Schedule, or

    (b) a scheme member who has paid such contributions,

to furnish to them within such time (not being less than 14 days) as may be provided in the notice such information and in such form as may be prescribed in the notice.

(2) If the Board by notice under section 19(3)(b) withdraw their approval of a scheme in relation to which contributions have been paid under paragraph 6A(2) and (3) of the Schedule, the scheme administrator shall within 30 days furnish to the Board in relation to that scheme the information prescribed in paragraph (3).

(a) Section 30 was substituted by the Finance Act 1982 (c.39), section 149(1).   (b) Subsection (3) was amended by the Finance (No.2) Act 1987 (c.51), Schedule 3, paragraph 2(1).

(3) The information prescribed in this paragraph is –

(a) the full name, address, national insurance number and tax office reference of each scheme member who has paid contributions after the date specified in the notice (in this regulation referred to as "the relevant contributions");

(b) the amount of the relief obtained under section 21(4) by means of the relevant contributions;

(c) the amount of such relief actually due; and

(d) the difference between the relief referred to in sub-paragraph (b) and that referred to in sub-paragraph (c).

(4) If a scheme member who has paid contributions under paragraph 6A(2) and (3) of the Schedule fails to comply with the requirements of regulation 5(1)(b), the scheme administrator to whom such contributions have been made shall within 30 days furnish to the Board the information prescribed in paragraph (5).

(5) The information prescribed in this paragraph is –

(a) the full name, address, national insurance number and tax office reference of the scheme member;

(b) the amount of relief obtained by him under section 21(4) by means of such contributions;

(c) the amount of such relief actually due; and

(d) the difference between the relief referred to in sub-paragraph (b) and that referred to in sub-paragraph (c).

Inspection of records

13.—(1) Every scheme administrator to whom contributions have been paid under paragraph 6A(2) and (3) of the Schedule shall, whenever required so to do, make available for inspection by a person authorised by the Board for that purpose all books, documents and other records (including all particulars furnished under regulation 5) in his possession or under his control relating to –

(a) such contributions paid to him,

(b) the scheme to which the contributions relate, and

(c) the scheme member who paid the contributions.

(2) Where records are maintained by computer the scheme administrator shall provide the person making the inspection with all facilities necessary to obtain information from them.

(3) Subject to paragraph (4) all books, documents and records referred to in paragraph (1), shall be preserved by the scheme administrator in such manner as may be approved by the Board so as to be available for inspection under this regulation for a period of three years following the termination of the scheme to which they relate.

(4) All particulars furnished under regulation 5 shall be so preserved for a period of three years following the date on which the scheme member to whom they relate ceased to be a member of a scheme.

A. J. G. Isaac
B. Pollard
Two of the Commissioners of Inland Revenue

5th October 1987

EXPLANATORY NOTE

(This note is not part of the Regulations)

These Regulations supplement paragraph 6A of Schedule 5 to the Finance Act 1970 (which was inserted by paragraph 12 of Schedule 3 to the Finance (No.2) Act 1987) which provides for relief by deduction from contributions made to approved occupational schemes to which employees, but not their employers, are contributors and which provide benefits additional to benefits provided by schemes to which their employers are contributors.

Paragraph 6A(2) provides that an employee who is entitled to relief under section 21(4) of the Finance Act 1970 in respect of a contribution may deduct from the contribution when he pays it, and may retain, an amount equal to income tax at the basic rate. Paragraph 6A(3) provides that the administrator of a scheme shall accept the amount paid after deduction in discharge of an employee's liability to the same extent as if the deduction had not been made, and may recover an amount equal to the deduction from the Commissioners of Inland Revenue ("the Commissioners").

Regulation 1 provides for citation and commencement and regulation 2 for interpretation.

Regulation 3 introduces regulations 4 and 5 which, respectively, prescribe the cases in which, and the conditions subject to which, relief shall be given in accordance with paragraph 6A(2) and (3).

Regulation 6 introduces regulations 7 and 8 which, respectively, provide a system of interim and annual claims by which scheme administrators may recover from the Commissioners amounts equal to those deducted under paragraph 6A(2) of the Schedule. Regulation 9 contains supplementary provisions including a right of appeal against decisions on annual claims.

Regulation 10 provides that when, following the withdrawal of approval of a scheme, the scheme administrator furnishes information to the Commissioners he shall at the same time pay to them the difference between the amount (if any) of relief obtained under section 21(4) of the Finance Act 1970 by means of contributions paid under paragraph 6A(2) and (3) of the Schedule to that Act and the amount of such relief actually due.

Regulation 11 provides for the recovery by assessment from administrators of schemes of amounts paid to them by the Commissioners to which they are not entitled, which are recoverable in default or which are recoverable following the withdrawal of approval of a scheme.

Regulation 12 provides that the Commissioners may require a present, or former, administrator of a scheme, or an employee who has contributed to a scheme, to furnish them with information. In addition, the regulation provides that if the Commissioners withdraw their approval of a scheme, or if a member of a scheme fails to comply with regulation 5(1)(b), the administrator of that scheme shall furnish information to them.

Regulation 13 provides for the inspection by a person authorised by the Commissioners of books, documents and records.

STATUTORY INSTRUMENTS

1987 No. 1750

TOWN AND COUNTRY PLANNING, ENGLAND AND WALES

The Town and Country Planning (Simplified Planning Zones) Regulations 1987

Made - - - -		*1st October 1987*
Laid before Parliament		*12th October 1987*
Coming into force		*2nd November 1987*

The Secretary of State for the Environment as respects England and the Secretary of State for Wales as respects Wales in exercise of the powers conferred upon them by sections 287(1) and 290(1) of, and paragraphs 5(2), 6(4) and 13 of Schedule 8A to, the Town and Country Planning Act 1971(a), and all other powers enabling them in that behalf, hereby make the following Regulations:

Citation, commencement and application

1.—(1) These Regulations may be cited as the Town and Country Planning (Simplified Planning Zones) Regulations 1987 and shall come into force on 2nd November 1987.

(2) These Regulations extend throughout England and Wales.

Interpretation

2. In these Regulations–

"local advertisement" means an advertisement on at least one occasion in each of two successive weeks in a local newspaper circulating in the area likely to be affected by the proposed simplified planning zone scheme or where the scheme to be altered has effect, as the case may be; and

"Schedule 8A" means that Schedule to the Town and Country Planning Act 1971.

Prescribed period for making representations

3. The period for making representations about proposals to make or alter a simplified planning zone scheme is a period of six weeks beginning with such date as the local planning authority specify when giving publicity to their proposals in accordance with paragraph 5(2) of Schedule 8A or, where the authority are proceeding under paragraph 6 as respects proposed alterations, a period of six weeks beginning with the date on which the alterations are first made available for inspection in accordance with paragraph 6(2).

(a) 1971 c.78. As to section 290(1), *see* the definition of "prescribed". Schedule 8A is set out in Schedule 6 to the Housing and Planning Act 1986 (c.63).

Objections to a proposed scheme etc.

4. Objections to a proposed scheme or proposals to alter an existing scheme shall be made in writing within a period of six weeks beginning with the date on which the proposed scheme or alterations are first made available for inspection in accordance with paragraph 5(3) or 6(2) of Schedule 8A, as the case may be.

Notice that documents containing proposals to make or alter a scheme are open to inspection

5.—(1) When a local planning authority make copies of a proposed simplified planning zone scheme or proposed alterations to an existing scheme available for public inspection in accordance with paragraphs 5(3) or 6(2) of Schedule 8A they shall publish a notice in the London Gazette and by local advertisement stating–

(a) the area affected by the proposed scheme or the scheme which it is proposed to alter, as the case may be;

(b) the general nature of the proposed scheme or alterations;

(c) the place and times at which copies of the proposed scheme or alterations may be inspected by the public;

(d) that any objections to the proposed scheme or alterations, and in a case where the authority is acting pursuant to paragraph 6 any representations about the alterations, should be made in writing;

(e) the time within which such objections and representations must be made and the address to which they must be sent; and

(f) that any person making an objection may ask to be notified of the local planning authority's decision in writing at such address as he specifies.

(2) Where a local planning authority comply with paragraph (1) above in relation to copies of proposed alterations made available for inspection in accordance with paragraph 6(2), they shall notify any persons who in their opinion may be expected to wish to make representations about the proposed alterations that they are entitled to do so and inform them of the matters specified in heads (a) to (e) of paragraph (1) as they apply to those proposed alterations.

Advertisement of the withdrawal of a scheme etc.

6. A local planning authority withdrawing copies of a proposed scheme or alterations (or of proposed modifications) whether in accordance with paragraph 7(4)(a) of Schedule 8A or on their own initiative shall give notice of the withdrawal in the London Gazette and by local advertisement. They shall also notify any person who has duly objected to the proposed scheme or alterations or to the proposed modifications of the withdrawal and any other person whom they consider should be notified.

Modification of a proposed scheme or of alterations to an existing scheme

7.—(1) Where the local planning authority intend to modify their proposals for a simplified planning zone scheme or for the alteration of an existing scheme, whether to comply with a direction given by the Secretary of State under paragraph 9(3) of Schedule 8A or on their own initiative, they shall unless they are satisfied that the proposed modifications will not materially affect the content of the scheme or the alterations:-

(a) prepare a list of the proposed modifications with their reasons for proposing them;

(b) publish a notice in Form 1 in the Schedule hereto by local advertisement;

(c) serve a notice in similar form on any person who has duly objected to the scheme or alteration and not withdrawn his objection and on any other person whom they consider should be given notice;

(d) subject to any direction of the Secretary of State, decide whether to afford any person who duly makes objection to the proposed modifications and does not withdraw his objections an opportunity of appearing before, and being heard by, a person appointed by the Secretary of State for the purpose; and

(e) where a local inquiry or other hearing is held, afford an opportunity to such other persons as they think fit to appear before, and be heard by, the person appointed.

(2) Without prejudice to any other provision as to the time at which a proposed simplified planning zone scheme or proposed alterations to such a scheme may be adopted, a local planning authority shall not proceed to adopt proposals for the making or alteration of a scheme with modifications until–

(i) the period for making objections to the modifications has expired; and

(ii) where objections were duly made within that period, the objections so made have been considered; and

(iii) where a direction has been given by the Secretary of State under paragraph 9(3) of Schedule 8A, details of the modifications it is proposed to incorporate in the scheme or alterations and the reasons for proposing them have been sent to the Secretary of State and he has notified the authority that he is satisfied with the modifications or he has withdrawn the direction.

Local inquiries and other hearings

8.—(1) A local planning authority intending to hold a local inquiry to consider objections to proposals to make or alter a simplified planning zone scheme or to proposed modifications to such proposals shall at least six weeks before the inquiry is due to open–

(a) give notice by local advertisement of the time and place at which the inquiry is to open and of the purpose of the inquiry; and

(b) notify every person who has duly made objection (other than an objector who has indicated in writing that he does not wish to appear at any inquiry or hearing), and any other person whom they consider should be given notice, of the matters mentioned in sub-paragraph (a) above.

(2) A local planning authority intending to hold a hearing to consider such objections as are mentioned in paragraph (1) shall at least six weeks before the date of the hearing notify every person who has made objection as aforesaid and every other person whom they consider should be given notice of the hearing of the time and place at which the hearing is to be held and of the purpose of the hearing.

(3) A local inquiry held for the purpose mentioned in paragraph (1) shall be held in public.

9.—(1) If a local inquiry or other hearing is held for the purpose mentioned in regulation 8, the local planning authority shall after considering the report of the person appointed to hold the inquiry or hearing prepare a statement of—

(a) the decisions they have reached in the light of the report and any recommendations as to the action to be taken (or not to be taken) contained in the report; and

(b) of the reasons for those decisions.

(2) A copy of the report and of the statement of decisions and reasons mentioned in paragraph (1) shall be made available by the local planning authority for public inspection—

(a) from the date on which notice is first given under regulation 10(1) or,

(b) where a list of proposed modifications or further proposed modifications to the proposed scheme or alterations is made available for public inspection after the statement mentioned in paragraph (1) has been prepared, from the date on which that list is made available for public inspection,

until the date on which the scheme is, or alterations are, adopted, approved, withdrawn or rejected.

Action prior to adopting a scheme or alterations

10.—(1) Where a local planning authority are disposed to adopt proposals for the making or alteration of a simplified planning zone scheme, they shall before adopting the proposals—

(a) publish a notice in Form 2 in the Schedule hereto by local advertisement; and

(b) serve a notice in similar form on any person who has duly objected to the scheme or alteration or to any proposed modifications thereto and not withdrawn his objection and on any other person whom they consider should be given notice.

(2) The local planning authority shall after complying with paragraph (1) send the Secretary of State—

(a) a certificate that they have so complied; and

(b) particulars of any modifications that have been made to the original proposal otherwise than in consequence of the giving by him of a direction under paragraph 9(3) of Schedule 8A.

(3) Without prejudice to paragraph 9(4) of Schedule 8A and paragraph (5) of this regulation, a local planning authority shall not adopt proposals to make or alter a simplified planning zone scheme until at least 28 days after complying with paragraph (1).

(4) Where after a local planning authority have complied with paragraph (1), the relevant proposals are modified in consequence of a direction by the Secretary of State under paragraph 9(3) of Schedule 8A, the authority shall comply with sub-paragraphs (1) and (2) in relation to the modified proposals before adopting them.

(5) If before the local planning authority have adopted proposals for the making or alteration of a simplified planning zone scheme, the Secretary of State directs them not to adopt those proposals until he has decided whether to give them a direction under paragraph 10(1) of Schedule 8A in relation to the proposals, they shall not adopt the proposals until he has notified them of his decision.

Notice of adoption of a simplified planning zone scheme etc.

11.—(1) Where a local planning authority adopt proposals for a simplified planning zone scheme or the alteration of such a scheme they shall give notice in Form 3 in the Schedule hereto in the London Gazette and by local advertisement and shall serve a notice in similar form on any interested person who has asked the authority to notify him of their decision; and a copy of the notice and a copy of the scheme or alteration to which it relates shall be made available for inspection at every place at which the copies of the proposed scheme or alteration were made available for public inspection.

(2) The local planning authority shall, not later than the date on which notice is first given by advertisement in accordance with paragraph (1), send two copies of the scheme or alteration to the Secretary of State.

Notice of an inquiry or hearing on behalf of the Secretary of State

12. Where under paragraph 11(3) of Schedule 8A, the Secretary of State causes a local inquiry or other hearing to be held for the purpose of considering objections to proposals for the making or alteration of a simplified planning zone scheme submitted to him under paragraph 10(1) of that Schedule, he shall give such notice and notification as is mentioned in regulations 8(1) (a) and (b) or (2), as appropriate.

Modifications as to a proposed scheme etc. by the Secretary of State

13. Where the Secretary of State is minded to approve with modifications proposals for the making or alteration of a simplified planning zone scheme which have been submitted to him in accordance with paragraph 10 of Schedule 8A, the local planning authority on being notified by him of the modifications he proposes to make shall—

(i) give notice by local advertisement in Form 4 in the Schedule hereto and

(ii) comply with any direction which the Secretary of State has served on them requiring notice to be given in similar form to the persons named in the direction.

Documents to be sent to the Secretary of State

14. The local planning authority shall send to the Secretary of State at the time of first publication, a copy of any notice given by local advertisement in accordance with the requirements of these Regulations.

Preparation of simplified planning zone schemes etc. by the Secretary of State

15.—(1) These Regulations apply so far as practicable and with any necessary modifications to action taken by the Secretary of State in connection with the making or alteration of a simplified planning zone scheme by him under paragraph 12 of Schedule 8A as they apply to the making of a scheme or alteration by a local planning authority.

(2) The Secretary of State may require the local planning authority concerned to give in relation to any proposals by him to make or alter a simplified planning zone scheme or any scheme or alterations so made any notice or notification required to be given by these Regulations in their application by virtue of paragraph (1).

Nicholas Ridley
1st October 1987   Secretary of State for the Environment

Peter Walker
1st October 1987   Secretary of State for Wales

SCHEDULE

FORM 1   Regulation 7

Form of notice of proposed modifications to a proposed simplified planning zone scheme or to proposed alterations to such a scheme

NOTICE OF PROPOSED MODIFICATIONS
TO [A PROPOSED] [PROPOSALS FOR THE ALTERATION OF A] (1)
SIMPLIFIED PLANNING ZONE SCHEME

Town and Country Planning Act 1971
(Title of scheme)

The .... (2) are disposed to make modifications to [the above named proposed scheme] [the proposed alterations to the above named scheme] (1) which [was] [were] made available for public inspection at .... (3).

[The modifications are intended to implement a direction given by the Secretary of State for [the Environment] [Wales] (1) on .... (4)]

[A copy of the Secretary of State's direction, and a] [A] (1) list of the proposed modifications and of the reasons for making them together with the original proposals have been deposited at .... (5).

The deposited documents are available for inspection free of charge on .... (6).

Objections to any of the proposed modifications may be made in writing. They must be sent to .... (7) on or before .... (8).

If any objections that are duly made are not withdrawn the local planning authority may decide to cause a public local inquiry or other hearing to be held.

19   (Signature of a responsible officer of the authority)

Notes

(1) Use whichever words are appropriate.

(2) Insert the name of the local planning authority.

FORM 1 – *continued*

(3) Insert the address of the local planning authority and of any other places at which the original documents were deposited and the period during which they were available for inspection.

(4) Delete if no direction has been given. If the paragraph is included, insert the date of the direction.

(5) Insert the address of the local planning authority's office and of any other places where the documents are being made available for inspection.

(6) Specify the days on which, and hours during which, the deposited documents are available for public inspection.

(7) Insert the name and address of the planning authority.

(8) Insert such date as allows a period of six weeks beginning with the date of first publication of the notice by local advertisement for objections to be lodged.

Regulation 10   FORM 2

Form of notice of disposition to adopt a simplified planning zone scheme or alterations to an existing scheme

NOTICE OF DISPOSITION TO ADOPT [ALTERATIONS TO] (1) A SIMPLIFIED PLANNING ZONE SCHEME

Town and Country Planning Act 1971
(Title of scheme)

.... (2) are disposed to adopt the above-named scheme .... (3) [as modified by them] (1) on or after .... (4), unless, before the scheme has been adopted, the Secretary of State directs that the scheme shall not be adopted until further notice, or that the scheme shall be submitted to him for his approval.

Copies of the scheme [together with copies of the report of the [local inquiry] [hearing] held and of the council's statements prepared following the consideration of that report] have been deposited at .... (5).

The deposited documents are available for inspection free of charge .... (6).

19   (Signature of the responsible officer of the authority)

Notes

(1) Omit these words and other words in square brackets, if irrelevant.

(2) Insert the name of the local planning authority.

(3) When this form is to be used in connection with proposals to alter an existing scheme, references to a scheme should be appropriately changed.

(4) Insert a date allowing for the period which must intervene to comply with Regulation 10(3).

(5) Insert the address of the local planning authority's office and of any other places at which the documents are available for inspection.

(6) Specify the days on which, and the hours during which, the deposited documents are available for public inspection.

FORM 3   Regulation 11

Form of notice of adoption of simplified planning zone scheme or of alterations to an existing scheme

NOTICE OF ADOPTION OF [ALTERATIONS TO] (1) A SIMPLIFIED PLANNING ZONE SCHEME

Town and Country Planning Act 1971
(Title of scheme)

On   19   (2) adopted the above-named scheme .... (3) [as modified by that authority] .... (1).

Copies of the scheme [together with a copy of the report of the [local inquiry] [hearings] held and of the council's statements prepared following the consideration of that report] have been deposited at .... (4).

The deposited documents are available for inspection free of charge .... (5).

The scheme became operative on .... (6), but if any person aggrieved by the scheme desires to question its validity on the ground that it is not within the powers conferred by the Town and Country Planning Act 1971, or that any requirement of that Act or of any regulation made under it has not been complied with in relation to the adoption of the scheme, he may, within six weeks from .... (7), make an application to the High Court under section 244 of that Act.

19   (Signature of the responsible officer of the authority)

Notes

(1) Omit these words and other words in square brackets, if irrelevant.

(2) Insert the date of adoption and the name of the local planning authority.

(3) Where the form is to be used in connection with the alteration of an existing scheme, all references to a scheme should be changed appropriately.

(4) Insert the address of the local planning authority's office and of other places at which the documents are deposited.

(5) Specify the days on which, and the hours during which, the deposited documents are available for public inspection.

(6) Insert the operative date.

(7) Insert the date of first publication of the this notice by local advertisement.

FORM 4   Regulation 13

Form of notice of proposed modifications by the Secretary of State to a proposed simplified planning zone scheme or to proposed alterations to such a scheme

NOTICE OF PROPOSED MODIFICATIONS BY THE SECRETARY OF STATE TO [A PROPOSED] [PROPOSED ALTERATIONS TO A] (1) SIMPLIFIED PLANNING ZONE SCHEME

Town and Country Planning Act 1971
(Title of scheme)

The Secretary of State for [the Environment] [Wales] (1) proposes to modify [the alterations to] (2) the above-named scheme proposed by .... (3)

Copies of the [scheme] [alterations] (1) and of the list of proposed modifications subject to which the Secretary of State is minded to approve the [scheme] [alterations] have been deposited at .... (4).

The deposited documents are available for inspection free of charge.

FORM 4 – *continued*

Objections to the proposed modifications should be sent in writing to the Secretary of State at .... by .... (5).

Objections should state the matters to which they relate and the grounds on which they are made. A person making objections may write to .... (6) requesting that they be notified of the Secretary of State's decision at such address as they mention.

19   (Signature of the responsible officer of the authority)

Notes

(1) Use whichever wording is appropriate.

(2) Delete if inapplicable.

(3) Insert the name of the local planning authority.

(4) Insert the address of the local planning authority's office and of other places at which the documents are available for inspection and the days on which, and the hours within which, the documents are available for public inspection.

(5) Insert the address notified by the Secretary of State and such date as allows a period of six weeks beginning with the date of first publication of the notice by local advertisement for objections to be lodged.

(6) Insert the name and address of the local planning authority.

EXPLANATORY NOTE

(This note is not part of the Regulations)

The Housing and Planning Act 1986 amends the Town and Country Planning Act 1971 to empower local authorities to make simplified planning zone schemes. Such a scheme provides planning permission within the area covered by the scheme for development in accordance with the scheme, without the need for specific application.

These Regulations, which apply throughout England and Wales, are concerned with the procedure for making and altering such schemes. They are made under, and supplement the provision made by, Schedule 8A to the 1971 Act (which is set out in Schedule 6 to the 1986 Act). They prescribe the periods within which representations and objections must be made (regulations 3 and 4) and lay down a procedure for the consideration by the local planning authority of any reports occasioned by objections (regulation 9) and for the modification of proposals to make or alter a scheme (regulations 7 and 13). They also specify the content or form of certain notices to be given by the authority (regulations 5, 6, 10 and 11).

Regulation 15 generally applies the regulations with necessary modifications where the Secretary of State intervenes to make or alter a scheme himself.

STATUTORY INSTRUMENTS

1987 No. 1753

POLICE

The Police (Amendment) Regulations 1987

Made - - - -	*5th October 1987*
Laid before Parliament	*12th October 1987*
Coming into force	*16th November 1987*

In exercise of the powers conferred on me by section 33 of the Police Act 1964**(a)**, and after taking into account the recommendations made by the Police Negotiating Board for the United Kingdom and furnishing the said Board with a draft of the Regulations in accordance with section 2(1) of the Police Negotiating Board Act 1980**(b)**, I hereby make the following Regulations:

1.   These Regulations may be cited as the Police (Amendment) Regulations 1987.

2.   These Regulations shall come into force on 16th November 1987 and shall have effect for the purposes of regulation 3(a), as from 1st July 1986, for the purposes of regulation 3(b), as from 1st February 1987, for the purposes of regulation 4(b) to (f), as from 15th June 1987, and for the purposes of regulation 4(h) and (j), as from 1st September 1987.

3.   The Police Regulations 1979**(c)** (as they continue to have effect in relation to the period prior to their revocation by the Police Regulations 1987**(d)**) shall be deemed to have been amended as follows –

   (a) in regulation 36 (London weighting) and paragraph 3(2) of Schedule 4 (university scholars) for the words "£885" there shall be deemed to have been substituted the words "£945";

   (b) in regulation 48(3)(a) and (b) (supplementary rent allowance) for the words "£8.33" there shall be deemed to have been substituted the words "£13.92".

4.   The Police Regulations 1987**(d)** shall be amended as follows –

   (a) in regulation 5(1) (meanings assigned to certain expressions), in the definition of the expression "public holiday", after the words "Christmas Day" there shall be inserted the words "the 26th December (if it falls on a Saturday or a Sunday), the 1st January (if it so falls),";

   (b) in regulation 39 (London weighting) and in paragraph 3(2) of Schedule 4 (university scholars) for the words "£885" there shall be substituted the words "£945";

(a) 1964 c.48.   **(b)** 1980 c.10.   **(c)** S.I. 1979/1470; the relevant amending instruments are S.I. 1980/405, 803, 1981/41, 1982/271, 1983/160, 812, 1985/885, 1986/784.   **(d)** S.I. 1987/851.

(c) in regulation 41(2)(a) (reckoning by constables of service in certain constabularies) after the words "Ministry of Defence Police Act 1987(**a**)" there shall be inserted the words "or, before the coming into force of that Act, comprising constables appointed under section 3 of the Special Constables Act 1923(**b**) on the nomination of the Defence Council or, before 1st April 1964, of the Admiralty, Army Council or Air Council";

(d) in regulation 43 (reckoning by constables of overseas police service) after paragraph (4) there shall be added the following provision –

"(5) A certificate given by or on behalf of –

(a) the Secretary for Technical Co-operation before 27th November 1964, or

(b) the Minister of Overseas Development on or after that date but before 12th November 1970,

shall be treated for the purposes of paragraph (2) as if it had been given by or on behalf of the Secretary of State.";

(e) in regulation 44(1)(a) (deductions from pay of social security benefits and statutory sick pay) for the words "1982" there shall be substituted the words "1986";

(f) in regulation 50(3)(a) and (b) (supplementary rent allowance) for the words "£8.33" there shall be substituted the words "£13.92";

(g) in regulation 53(1)(d) (removal allowance) for the word "13" in the second place where it occurs there shall be substituted the word "39";

(h) in Schedule 5 for tables A and B there shall be substituted respectively the tables set out in the Appendix to these Regulations;

(j) in paragraph 1 of Schedule 11 (dog handler's allowance) for the words "£567" in sub-paragraph (a) there shall be substituted the words "£612", and for the words "£771" in sub-paragraph (b) there shall be substituted the words "£831".

Douglas Hurd

Home Office   One of Her Majesty's Principal Secretaries of State
5th October 1987

(**a**) 1987 c.4.   (**b**) 1923 c.11.

APPENDIX

TABLES SUBSTITUTED FOR TABLES IN SCHEDULE 5 TO THE POLICE REGULATIONS 1987 WITH EFFECT FROM 1ST SEPTEMBER 1987

Table A

Rank	Service in Rank	Annual Pay	
		London	Provinces
		£	£
Chief Superintendent	Less than 1 year	26,262	26,262
	After 1 year	26,637	26,637
	After 2 years	27,234	27,234
	After 3 years	27,885	27,885
Superintendent	Less than 1 year	24,225	23,622
	After 1 year	24,699	24,225
	After 2 years	25,170	24,825
	After 3 years	25,650	25,650
Chief Inspector	Less than 1 year	18,195	17,364
	After 1 year	18,645	17,850
	After 2 years	19,122	18,336
	After 3 years	19,635	18,825
	After 4 years	20,142	19,317
Inspector	Less than 1 year	16,116	15,294
	After 1 year	16,566	15,771
	After 2 years	17,151	16,392
	After 3 years	17,679	16,875
	After 4 years	18,195	17,364
Sergeant	Less than 1 year	13,332	13,332
	After 1 year	13,938	13,938
	After 2 years	14,427	14,427
	After 3 years	14,907	14,907
	After 4 years	15,294	15,294

Table B

ANNUAL PAY OF CONSTABLES

Reckonable service	Annual Pay
	£
Before completing 1 year of service	8,352
After 1 year of service	8,931
After 2 years of service	10,512
After 3 years of service	10,761
After 4 years of service	11,118
After 5 years of service	11,499
After 6 years of service	11,868
After 7 years of service	12,234
After 8 years of service	12,597
After 12 years of service	13,332
After 15 years of service	13,938

EXPLANATORY NOTE

(This note is not part of the Regulations)

These amending Regulations have effect, as provided by regulation 2, for the purposes of regulation 3(a), as from 1st July 1986, for the purposes of regulation 3(b), as from 1st February 1987, for the purposes of regulation 4(b) to (f), as from 15th June 1987, for the purposes of regulation 4(h) and (j) as from 1st September 1987 (retrospection is authorised by section 33(4) of the Police Act 1964) and, for all other purposes, as from 16th November 1987.

Under regulation 3 the Police Regulations 1979 have deemed to have been amended for the purpose of increasing London weighting and the supplementary pay of university scholars in the City and the metropolitan police district (regulation 3(a)) and the supplementary rent allowance (regulation 3(b)).

Regulation 4 amends the Police Regulations 1987.

Regulation 4(a) designates as public holidays for the purposes of the 1987 Regulations 26th December or 1st January where either of those dates falls on a Saturday or a Sunday.

Regulation 4(b) increases London weighting and the supplementary pay of university scholars in the City and the metropolitan police district.

Regulation 4(c) to (e) make good certain minor defects and omissions in the consolidation of the 1987 Regulations.

Regulation 4(f) increases the supplementary rent allowance.

Regulation 4(g) increases the period in respect of which additional removal expenses may be paid at the discretion of the police authority.

Regulation 4(h) increases pay.

Regulation 4(j) increases the dog handler's allowance.

STATUTORY INSTRUMENTS

1987 No. 1754

POLICE

The Police Cadets (Amendment) Regulations 1987

Made - - - -	*5th October 1987*
Laid before Parliament	*12th October 1987*
Coming into force - -	*16th November 1987*

In exercise of the powers conferred upon me by section 35 of the Police Act 1964**(a),** and after taking into consideration the recommendations made by the Police Negotiating Board for the United Kingdom and furnishing the said Board with a draft of the Regulations in accordance with section 2(1) of the Police Negotiating Board Act 1980**(b),** I hereby make the following Regulations:

1. These Regulations may be cited as the Police Cadets (Amendment) Regulations 1987.

2. These Regulations shall come into force on 16th November 1987 and shall have effect for the purposes of regulation 3(a) and (c) as from 1st September 1986.

3. The Police Cadets Regulations 1979**(c)** shall be amended as follows—

(a) in regulation 13 for the words " in Schedule 2 hereto " there shall be substituted the words—

" (a) in respect of the period beginning with 1st September 1986 and ending with 31st August 1987, in Part I of the Table in Schedule 2 hereto and,

(b) in respect of the period thereafter, in Part II of the said Table ";

(b) in regulation 17, for the words " £0·50 " in paragraph (1) there shall be substituted the words " £1·27 ", and for the words " £36 " in paragraph (2) there shall be substituted the words " £92 ";

(c) for the Table in Schedule 2 (scales of pay) there shall be substituted the following Table—

" Table

Age	London	Provinces
Part I—Pay from 1st September 1986 to 31st August 1987		
Under 17 years	£3,582 a year	£3,015 a year
17 years	£3,762 a year	£3,195 a year
18 years or over	£4,125 a year	£3,558 a year
Part II—Pay from 1st September 1987		
Under 17 years	£3,762 a year	£3,195 a year
17 years	£3,954 a year	£3,387 a year
18 years or over	£4,338 a year	£3,771 a year "

(d) for paragraph 2 of Schedule 3 (charge for board and lodging) there shall be substituted the following paragraph—

" 2.   The annual rate of charge shall be—

(a) in the case of a police cadet attached to the City of London or Metropolitan Police force, £480;

(b) in any other case, £444.".

Douglas Hurd
Home Office   One of Her Majesty's Principal Secretaries of State
5th October 1987

(a) 1964 c.48.   **(b)** 1980 c.10.
(c) S.I. 1979/1727; the relevant amending instruments are S.I. 1985/1909 and 1986/2033.

EXPLANATORY NOTE

(This note is not part of the Regulations)

These Regulations amend the Police Cadets Regulations 1979 with effect, save as otherwise provided, from 16th November 1987.

Regulation 3(a) and (c) increase the pay of cadets from 1st September 1986 to 31st August 1987 and, again, from 1st September 1987 (retrospective effect is authorised by section 33(4), as applied by section 35(2), of the Police Act 1964).

Regulation 3(b) increases the maximum and minimum levels of travel allowance payable to cadets.

Regulation 3(d) increases charges payable by cadets for board and lodging provided by police authorities.

STATUTORY INSTRUMENTS

1987 No. 1755

PUBLIC PASSENGER TRANSPORT

ROAD TRAFFIC

The Road Transport (International Passenger Services) (Amendment) Regulations 1987

Made - - - -	*3rd October 1987*
Laid before Parliament	*9th October 1987*
Coming into force	*1st November 1987*

The Secretary of State for Transport, being a Minister designated(**a**) for the purposes of section 2(2) of the European Communities Act 1972(**b**) in relation to the international carriage of passengers by road, in exercise of the powers conferred by that section, section 60(1) and (1A) of the Public Passenger Vehicles Act 1981(**c**) and, with the consent of the Treasury, in exercise of the powers conferred by section 56(1) of the Finance Act 1973(**d**) and of all other enabling powers and (in respect of the Regulations insofar as made under the said Act of 1981), after consultation with representative organisations in accordance with section 61(2) of the said Act of 1981, hereby makes the following Regulations:

1. These Regulations may be cited as the Road Transport (International Passenger Services) (Amendment) Regulations 1987 and shall come into force on 1st November 1987.

2.—(1) The Road Transport (International Passenger Services) Regulations 1984(**e**) shall be amended in accordance with the following provisions of this regulation.

(2) In regulations 5(2) and 6(2)

(a) after the words "Act of 1981" where they first occur there shall be inserted the words "and Parts I and II of the Transport Act 1985"; and

(b) in paragraph (b) for the words "section 30 of the Act of 1981 there shall be substituted the following section" there shall be substituted "section 6 of the Transport Act 1985 there shall be substituted the following section and section 35 of that Act shall be omitted" and in the fourth line for "30" there shall be substituted "6".

(**a**) S.I. 1972/1811, 1979/571 and 1981/238.   (**b**) 1972 c.68.   (**c**) 1981 c.14; sections 60 and 61 are extended by sections 134 and 135 of the Transport Act 1985 (c.67).   (**d**) 1973 c.51.   (**e**) S.I. 1984/748.

(3) In regulation 14 –

  (a) in paragraph (3) for the words "section 30 of the Public Passenger Vehicles Act 1981" there shall be substituted the words "section 6 of the Transport Act 1985" and for "£110" there shall be substituted "£125"; and

  (b) in paragraph (4) for the words "when the application is made" there shall be substituted the words "before the authorisation is issued".

3rd October 1987

David B. Mitchell
Minister of State,
Department of Transport

EXPLANATORY NOTE

(This note is not part of the Regulations)

These Regulations amend the Road Transport (International Passenger Services) Regulations 1984. They provide that

  (a) the fee of £110 prescribed by regulation 14(3) payable on application for an authorisation under the Regulations shall be increased to £125, and

  (b) the fee of £25 prescribed by regulation 14(4) in respect of each year of validity of a regular, or special regular, service authorisation shall be payable before the authorisation is issued rather than when the application for the authorisation is made.

They also amend the 1984 Regulations for the avoidance of doubt as consequence of the coming into force by virtue of the Transport Act 1985 (Commencement No. 6) Order 1986 (S.I. 1986/1794 (C.63)) of the repeal of section 30 of the Public Passenger Vehicles Act 1981 by section 139(3) of the Transport Act 1985. The requirement of section 30 of the 1981 Act was replaced by the requirement of section 6 of the 1985 Act for the registration of certain local services outside London.

STATUTORY INSTRUMENTS

1987 No. 1757

TERMS AND CONDITIONS OF EMPLOYMENT

The Guarantee Payments (Exemption) (No. 23) Order 1987

Made - - - -		*5th October 1987*
Coming into force		*12th November 1987*

Whereas the National Agreements for the Wire and Wire Rope Industries are collective agreements which make provision whereby employees to whom the said agreements relate have a right to guaranteed remuneration;

And whereas the parties to the said collective agreements (whose descriptions are set out in Schedule 1 to this Order) all made application to the Secretary of State under section 18 of the Employment Protection (Consolidation) Act 1978 (**a**) ("the Act");

And whereas the Secretary of State, having regard to the provisions of the agreements (which so far as are material are set out in Schedule 2 to this Order) is satisfied that section 12 of the Act should not apply to those employees;

And whereas the said agreements comply with the provisions of section 18(4) of the Act;

Now, therefore, the Secretary of State in exercise of the powers conferred on him as the appropriate Minister under section 18(1) and 18(5) of the Act and of all other powers enabling him in that behalf, hereby makes the following Order:

Citation and commencement

1. This Order may be cited as the Guarantee Payments (Exemption) (No. 23) Order 1987 and shall come into force on 12th November 1987.

Interpretation

2. The "exempted agreements" mean the National Agreements for the Wire and Wire Rope Industries.

Exemption

3. Section 12 of the Act shall not apply to any person who is an employee to whom the exempted agreements relate.

4. The Guarantee Payments (Exemption) (No. 4) Order 1977 (**b**) is revoked.

(**a**) 1978 c.44.   (**b**) S.I. 1977/208.

Signed by order of the Secretary of State.

Patrick Nicholls
Parliamentary Under Secretary of State,
Department of Employment

5th October 1987

SCHEDULE 1

PARTIES TO THE COLLECTIVE AGREEMENTS

1. *Representing Employers* the Wire and Wire Rope Employers' Association (formerly the British Steel Wire Industries Association and the Institute of Iron and Steel Wire Manufacturers).

2. *Representing Employees* the Wire Workers Union; the General Municipal Boilermakers and Allied Trades Union; the Transport and General Workers Union.

SCHEDULE 2

MATERIAL PROVISIONS OF THE EXEMPTED AGREEMENTS

A. GUARANTEED PAYMENT AGREEMENT

1. This Agreement supersedes the Guaranteed Payment Agreement dated 25th April 1985. Throughout this Agreement the expression "Minimum Datal Rate" includes any supplements payable under the Minimum Datal Rate Agreement currently in force.

2. It is agreed that in the event of short-time working or temporary lay off, each employee will be paid the J.I.C. minimum datal rate for each day up to a maximum of TEN days in any period of twenty-six consecutive weeks. The amount to be paid in respect of each day will be a fifth of the J.I.C. minimum datal rate per standard working week of thirty-nine hours.

3. The guarantee shall apply only provided that during the period of the guarantee, the employee has been continuously employed by the same employer for not less than FOUR weeks, is capable of, available for, and willing to perform according to his/or her capabilities, the work associated with his/or her usual occupation, or reasonable alternative work when his/or her normal work is not available. When he/or she undertakes such alternative employment within the company, payment shall be made at the rate applicable to that alternative employment or his/or her company datal rate, whichever is the greater.

4. The guarantee shall not apply
   (a) at any plant or unit of plant
      (i) when that plant or unit is laid idle through avoidable absenteeism or failure of any employee to take reasonable action to keep the plant in operation.
      (ii) when by custom and practice, or by mutual agreement between the employer and employees, it is decided that a shift, or part shift at the commencement or resumption of holiday periods shall be an unpaid holiday.
   (b) to any individual employee who has been summarily dismissed without notice or has been suspended for disciplinary reasons.
   (c) to any employee who refuses to accept reasonable alternative employment when his/or her normal work is not available.

5. The guarantee shall be suspended automatically in the event of dislocation of work as a result of strike action or irregular action short of strike action within any company which is a party to the agreements of the J.I.C. for the wire and wire rope industries.

6. The guarantee shall be reduced in the case of a holiday recognised by agreement or custom and practice in respect of the standard working week in which the holiday takes place in the same proportion as the normal working days or shifts are reduced in that standard working week.

7. Any difference arising in relation to this agreement which cannot otherwise be resolved shall be reported to the Joint Secretaries of the Joint Industrial Council and will be dealt with under the J.I.C. procedure for settling differences and disputes or, if the claimant is not a member of a trade union party to this Agreement, it may be referred to an industrial tribunal.

8. This Agreement may be cancelled by either party giving three months' notice in writing.

B. AGREEMENT ON PROCEDURE FOR SETTLING DIFFERENCES AND DISPUTES

14.

(i) In the event of any questions arising in relation to wages and/or working conditions which cannot be resolved by domestic procedure, the matter shall, in the first instance, be dealt with between the management of the employer and the area official(s) of the Trade Union(s) concerned.

Failing a settlement, status quo* shall apply until the following procedure has been exhausted.

(ii) The parties to the dispute shall define the dispute and forward their written submissions as quickly as possible to the Joint Secretaries. Any problems of definition shall be referred to the Chairman of the Joint Industrial Council. Within 14 days of notification, the Joint Secretaries will notify to the parties the date of a meeting of a Dispute Panel.

(iii) The Dispute Panel will comprise two representatives appointed by each of the Employer and Trade Union Panels of the Joint Industrial Council under the Chairmanship, in a non-voting capacity, of the Chairman of the Joint Industrial Council, or in his absence the Vice-Chairman.

(iv) The decision of the Dispute Panel will be binding on both parties. In the event of a Dispute Panel being unable to reach a decision, the matter shall be referred to arbitration arranged through A.C.A.S., the decision of which shall be binding on both parties.

(v) The parties to a dispute shall pay the expenses of their respective sides of any committee to which the Dispute is referred, and shall share equally any other expenses which arise from the reference.

**i.e., Work shall be continued on the terms and conditions of employment in force prior to the question being raised.

EXPLANATORY NOTE

(This note is not part of the Order)

This Order excludes from the operation of section 12 of the Employment Protection (Consolidation) Act 1978 employees to whom the National Agreements of the Wire and Wire Rope Industries relate. It supersedes the Guarantee Payments (Exemption) (No. 4) Order 1977 which is revoked by this Order. The present Order has been made to take account of the revised National Agreements the material provisions of which are set out in Schedule 2. These differ from the provisions in Schedule 2 to the previous Order in that the standard working week has been reduced to 39 hours and the procedure for settling disputes has been simplified. In addition paragraph 4(a)(ii) of Schedule 2 to the previous Order (dealing with short-time working) has been omitted.

Copies of the Agreements are available for inspection between 10 am and noon and 2 pm and 5 pm on any week-day (except Saturdays) at the offices of the Department of Employment, Caxton House, Tothill Street, London SW1H 9NF.

STATUTORY INSTRUMENTS

1987 No. 1758

PLANT HEALTH

The Plant Health (Great Britain) Order 1987

Made - - - -	*5th October 1987*
Laid before Parliament	*9th October 1987*
Coming into force -	*1st November 1987*

ARRANGEMENT OF ARTICLES

PART I

Introductory

PART III

Additional measures to prevent spread of particular plant pests

Colorado Beetle

Red core disease of strawberries

Fire blight disease

Potato cyst nematode

Wart disease of potatoes

Beet cyst nematode

Progressive wilt disease

PART IV
General

42. Licences.
43. The Customs Act.
44. Powers of an officer of Customs and Excise.
45. Information to be given.
46 & 47. Offences.

ARRANGEMENT OF SCHEDULES

SCHEDULE

1. PLANT PESTS

PART I

Plant pests which may not be landed and which may not be kept etc. unless specified in Part III and which must be notified unless specified in Part III.

PART II

Plants which may not be landed if carrying or infected with plant pests specified and which may not be kept etc. if carrying or infected with plant pests specified unless specified in Part III, and plant pests which may not be kept etc. unless specified in Part III and which must be notified unless specified in Part III.

PART III

Plant pests specified in Parts I and II which, insofar as they are of a subspecies or strain normally present in Great Britain, may be kept etc. whether or not in association with plants and need not be notified.

2. PLANTS, AGRICULTURAL MACHINERY, SOIL AND GROWING MEDIUM WHICH MAY NOT BE LANDED IF THEY ORIGINATE IN CERTAIN COUNTRIES

PART I

General types of plants.

PART II

Families of plants.

PART III

Genera of plants.

PART IV

Agricultural machinery.

PART V

Soil and growing medium.

3. CONDITIONS SUBJECT TO WHICH PLANTS, SOIL AND GROWING MEDIUM MAY BE LANDED UNLESS OTHERWISE PROHIBITED UNDER ARTICLE 4

PART I

Conditions subject to which soil and growing medium may be landed.

PART II

Conditions subject to which rooted plants, planted or intended for planting, and rooted vegetative propagating material other than tubers of potato and seeds may be landed.

    A.   General types of plants.
    B.   Families of plants.
    C.   Genera of plants.

PART III

Conditions subject to which tubers of potato may be landed.

PART IV

Conditions subject to which seeds of beet, of the families Cruciferae and Gramineae and of the genus *Trifolium* L. and of lettuce, lucerne, pea, tomato and of the genus *Rubus* L. may be landed.

PART V

Conditions subject to which raw fruit may be landed.

    A.   General conditions.
    B.   Additional conditions applying in the case of raw fruit of the genera: *Citrus, Cydonia, Malus, Prunus* and *Pyrus.*
    C.   Additional conditions applying in the case of raw fruit of the genera: *Fragaria, Ribes, Rubus, Vaccinium* and *Vitis.*

PART VI

Conditions subject to which particular raw vegetables may be landed.

PART VII

Conditions subject to which cut flowers and parts of plants for decoration may be landed.

- A. General conditions.
- B. Additional conditions applying in the case of cut flowers and parts of plants for decoration of statice and of the genera: *Dendranthema, Dianthus, Gladiolus, Gypsophila, Protea, Prunus, Rosa, Salix, Syringa* and *Vitis*.

4. EXPORTS OF PLANTS AND GROWING MEDIUM TO MEMBER STATES

PART I

Plants and growing medium to be accompanied by a phytosanitary certificate or a reforwarding phytosanitary certificate issued in Great Britain when exported or re-exported to a Member State, and by a phytosanitary certificate issued in the country of origin when re-exported to a Member State.

PART II

Plants to be accompanied by a phytosanitary certificate issued in the country of origin when re-exported to a Member State.

5. INSTRUMENTS AMENDING COUNCIL DIRECTIVE 77/93/EEC

6. FORM OF PHYTOSANITARY CERTIFICATE

7. FORM OF REFORWARDING PHYTOSANITARY CERTIFICATE

8. PLANT PESTS IN RESPECT OF WHICH PREMISES MAY BE DECLARED INFECTED

9. REVOCATIONS

The Minister of Agriculture, Fisheries and Food in relation to England, the Secretary of State for Scotland in relation to Scotland and the Secretary of State for Wales in relation to Wales, in exercise of the powers conferred by sections 2, 3 and 4(1) of the Plant Health Act 1967(a), as read with section 20 of the Agriculture (Miscellanous Provisions) Act 1972(b) and now vested in them(c) and of all other powers enabling them in that behalf, hereby make the following Order:

PART I

INTRODUCTORY

Title, extent and commencement

1. This Order may be cited as the Plant Health (Great Britain) Order 1987, shall apply to Great Britain and shall come into force on 1st November 1987.

Revocation of previous Orders

2. The Orders specified in column 1 of Schedule 9 are revoked.

Interpretation

3.—(1) In this Order, unless the context otherwise requires–

"appropriate Minister" means in the application of this Order to England the Minister of Agriculture, Fisheries and Food, in its application to Scotland the Secretary of State for Scotland and in its application to Wales the Secretary of State for Wales;

"approved immune variety" means a variety of potatoes approved for the time being by the appropriate Minister as being immune from wart disease of potatoes;

"approved resistant variety" means a variety of potatoes approved for the time being by the appropriate Minister as being resistant to one or more pathotypes of potato cyst nematode;

"authorised officer" means–

    (a) in relation to a certificate, translation or copy issued in Great Britain, an inspector or other officer of the appropriate Minister, and

    (b) in relation to a certificate, translation or copy issued in a place other than Great Britain, a representative of the Plant Protection Service of the country in which the certificate, translation or copy was issued;

"beet cyst nematode" means the cyst forming nematode *Heterodera schachtii* Schmidt;

"Central America" means the geographical area comprising Belize, Costa Rica, El Salvador, Guatemala, Honduras, Nicaragua, Panama and the islands commonly known as the West Indies;

"chrysanthemum" means plants (other than seeds) of those species, cultivars and hybrids of the genus *Dendranthema* (DC.) Des Moulins commonly known as the florists' chrysanthemum;

"Colorado Beetle" means the insect *Leptinotarsa decemlineata* (Say);

"Customs Act" means the Customs and Excise Management Act 1979(d);

(a) 1967 c.8; sections 2(1), 3(1) and (2) and 4(1) were amended by the European Communities Act 1972 (c.68), section 4(1) and Schedule 4, paragraph 8; section 3(4) was substituted by section 42 of the Criminal Justice Act 1982 (c.48) and is to be read with S.I. 1984/447, 526.

(b) 1972 c.62.

(c) In the case of the Secretary of State for Wales by virtue of S.I. 1978/272.

(d) 1979 c.2.

"Directive 77/93/EEC" means Council Directive of 21st December 1976 on protective measures against the introduction into the Member States of harmful organisms of plants or plant products(a) as amended by the instruments listed in Schedule 5;

"the Euro-Mediterranean area" means the geographical area comprising Europe, Algeria, Cyprus, Egypt, Israel, Jordan, Lebanon, Libya, Malta, Morocco, Syria, Tunisia and Turkey;

"Europe" includes the Canary Islands, but does not include Cyprus, Turkey or the following regions of the Union of Soviet Socialist Republics, namely the Kazakh, Kirghiz, Tadzhik, Turkmen and Uzbek Soviet Socialist Republics and the following regions of the Russian Soviet Federal Socialist Republic, namely the Buryat, Yakut and Tuva Autonomous Soviet Socialist Republics, the Altai, Khabarovsk, Krasnoyarsk and Maritime Krais and the Amur, Chita, Irkutsk, Kamchatka, Kemerovo, Kurgan, Magadan, Novosibirsk, Omsk, Sakhalin, Tomsk and Tyumen Oblasts;

"farm" means the whole of the land which is occupied as a unit for agricultural purposes;

"genetically manipulated material" means material derived from any activity which has involved genetic manipulation and which has resulted or, in the opinion of the appropriate Minister, is likely to result in the production of a plant pest, or any activity which has involved genetic manipulation of a plant pest, and includes material which contains a plant pest which has been genetically manipulated;

"genetic manipulation" means the formation of new combinations of heritable material by the insertion of nucleic acid molecules, produced by whatever means outside the cell, into any virus, bacterial plasmid, or other vector system so as to allow their incorporation into a host organism in which they do not naturally occur but in which they are capable of continued propagation;

"growing medium" means material, intended to sustain the life of plants, which consists wholly or partly of soil or peat (whether used or unused) or of any other solid substance;

"importer" in relation to any plant pest, genetically manipulated material, plant, plant product, agricultural machinery, soil or growing medium includes–

(a) any person who, (whether as owner, consignor, consignee, agent, broker or otherwise), is in possession of or in any way entitled to the custody or control of the plant pest, genetically manipulated material, plant, plant product, agricultural machinery, soil or growing medium; and

(b) any person by whose action the plant pest, genetically manipulated material, plant, plant product, agricultural machinery, soil or growing medium is likely to be or has been landed in Great Britain;

"inspector" means a person appointed by the appropriate Minister to be an inspector for the purposes of this Order;

"landed" includes imported by post and "landing" shall be construed accordingly;

"Member State" means a Member State of the European Community other than the United Kingdom and does not include the Isle of Man or any of the Channel Islands or the French overseas departments, the Canary Islands, Ceuta or Melilla;

"North America" means the geographical area comprising Canada, Mexico and the United States of America (except the state of Hawaii);

"nursery" means any premises wholly or partly used for the cultivation or keeping of plants for the purpose of transplantation or removal to other premises;

"official" in relation to any testing or any other procedure required by this Order to be carried out in respect of any plant, soil or growing medium means carried out by or under the supervision of the Plant Protection Service of the country in which the testing or other procedure is carried out and "officially" shall be construed accordingly;

"phytosanitary certificate" means a certificate duly completed either in the form set out in Schedule 6 or the equivalent in a language other than English;

"place of production" means any premises, normally worked as a unit, together with any contiguous uncultivated land;

(a) OJ No. L26, 31.1.77, p.20.

"plant" means a living plant or living part of a plant, including any tree, shrub, bush or seed and includes, where the context so admits, any growing medium, packing material and container attached thereto or associated therewith, and "living part of a plant" shall be considered to include–

(i) raw fruit,

(ii) raw vegetables,

(iii) tubers, corms, bulbs or rhizomes,

(iv) cut flowers,

(v) branches with foliage,

(vi) cut trees retaining foliage, and

(vii) plants in tissue culture;

"plant in tissue culture" means a plant growing in a clear liquid or clear solid aseptic culture medium in a closed transparent container;

"plant pest" means a pathogen, or any living organism other than a vertebrate animal in any stage of its existence, which is injurious to any plant and includes a culture of such pathogen or organism;

"plant product" means a product of plant origin, which is unprocessed or has undergone simple preparation insofar as it is not a plant and includes any packing material and container associated therewith;

"potato" means any tuber or true seed or any other plant of *Solanum tuberosum* L. or other tuber-forming species or hybrid of the genus *Solanum* L.;

"potato cyst nematode" means cyst-forming nematodes of the genus *Globodera* Skarbilovich (Behrens) that infest and multiply on potatoes and includes all strains and pathotypes thereof;

"premises" includes any land, building, vehicle, vessel, aircraft, hovercraft or freight container;

"progressive wilt disease" means either the disease of hop plants which is caused by strains of *Verticillium albo-atrum* Reinke and Berth. and is known as progressive wilt disease of hops or progressive verticillium wilt of hops or any strain of the fungus *Verticillium albo-atrum* Reinke and Berth. causing that disease as the context may require;

"raw fruit" does not include dried, dehydrated, lacquered or deep-frozen fruit, and "raw" in relation to fruit of any particular description shall be construed accordingly;

"raw vegetables" does not include potatoes and does not include any other kind of vegetable which has been dried, dehydrated, lacquered, brined, pickled or deep-frozen and "raw" in relation to vegetables of any particular description shall be construed accordingly;

"red core disease of strawberries" means either the disease of strawberry plants which is caused by the fungus *Phytophthora fragariae* Hickman and is known as red core disease of strawberries or that fungus as the context may require;

"re-forwarding phytosanitary certificate" means a certificate duly completed either in the form set out in Schedule 7 or the equivalent written in a language other than English;

"seed" means seed in the botanical sense, other than seed not intended for planting;

"soil" means material wholly or partly derived from the upper layer of the earth's crust which is capable of sustaining plant life and which contains solid organic substances such as parts of plants, humus, peat or bark, but does not include material composed entirely of unused peat;

"South America" means the geographical area comprising Argentina, Bolivia, Brazil, Chile, Colombia, Ecuador, French Guiana, Guyana, Paraguay, Peru, Surinam, Uruguay and Venezuela;

"third country" means a country or territory other than a Member State, the United Kingdom, the Isle of Man or any of the Channel Islands;

"wart disease of potatoes" means either the disease of potatoes which is caused by the fungus *Synchytrium endobioticum* (Schilb.) Perc. and is known as wart disease of potatoes or that fungus as the context may require.

(2) Any reference in this Order to a particular plant pest shall be construed as a reference to that pest in any stage of its existence.

(3) Any reference in this Order to premises declared infected with any particular plant pest shall be construed as a reference to premises declared infected with that plant pest by a notice served or having effect as if served under article 15(4) and for the time being in force.

(4) Any reference in this Order to a Member State, third country, Great Britain, Northern Ireland, the Channel Islands or the Isle of Man includes reference to a state, province or region within that Member State, third country, Great Britain, Northern Ireland, the Channel Islands or the Isle of Man.

(5) Any reference in this Order to a numbered article or a numbered Schedule shall be construed as a reference to the article or Schedule so numbered in this Order.

PART II

MEASURES TO PREVENT INTRODUCTION, SPREAD OR CONVEYANCE OF PLANT PESTS

Prohibition on the landing of plant pests, plants, etc.

4.—(1) Subject to paragraph (2) of this article, the landing in Great Britain of the following is prohibited, namely–

(a) any plant pest of a description specified in Part I of Schedule 1;

(b) any plant, plant product, soil or growing medium carrying or infected with a plant pest of a description specified in Part I of Schedule 1;

(c) any plant of a description specified in column 3 of Part II of Schedule 1 carrying or infected with a plant pest of a description specified in column 2 of that Part opposite the reference to such plant;

(d) any plant, agricultural machinery, soil or growing medium of a description specified in column 2 of Schedule 2 which originates in a country (other than Northern Ireland, the Channel Islands or the Isle of Man) specified in column 3 of that Schedule opposite the reference to such plant, agricultural machinery, soil or growing medium;

(e) any plant, soil or growing medium of a description specified in column 2 of Schedule 3 if any of the conditions specified in column 3 of that Schedule opposite the reference to such plant, soil or growing medium are not complied with;

(f) any genetically manipulated material;

(g) any plant pest not associated with a consignment of plants, plant products, agricultural machinery, soil or growing medium (except insofar as such plants, plant products, soil or growing medium are necessary to enable such plant pest to be landed or to sustain its life) being a plant pest which is not normally present in Great Britain and which is injurious to plants in Great Britain.

(2) Notwithstanding paragraph (1)(b) to (d) of this article, a person may land raw fruit, cut flowers and parts of plants for decoration if they are of a description specified in column 2 of Parts V and VII of Schedule 3 and the conditions specified in column 3 of those Parts opposite the reference to such raw fruit, cut flowers and parts of plants for decoration are complied with.

Prohibition on the keeping etc. of plant pests, plants, etc.

5.—(1) Subject to the provisions of this Order, no person shall–

(a) knowingly keep, sell, plant, release, deliver, or otherwise dispose of, or knowingly cause or permit to be kept, sold, planted, released, delivered, or otherwise disposed of–

(i) any plant pest of a description specified in Part I or column 2 of Part II of Schedule 1, except a pest of a description specified in Part III of that Schedule,

(ii) any plant, plant product, soil or growing medium carrying or infected with a plant pest of a description specified in Part I of Schedule 1, except a pest of a description specified in Part III of that Schedule,

(iii) any plant of a description specified in column 3 of Part II of Schedule 1 carrying or infected with a plant pest of a description specified in column 2 of that Part opposite the reference to such plant, except a pest of a description specified in Part III of that Schedule,

(iv) any plant, agricultural machinery, soil or growing medium landed in contravention of article 4(1)(d) or (e),

(v) any genetically manipulated material,

(vi) any plant pest not associated with plants, plant products, soil or growing medium (except insofar as such plants, plant products, soil or growing medium are necessary to sustain the life of such plant pest) being a plant pest which is not normally present in Great Britain and which is injurious to plants in Great Britain;

(b) engage in any activity which involves genetic manipulation of a plant pest or engage in any activity which to his knowledge involves genetically manipulated material.

(2) Nothing in paragraph (1)(a) of this article shall prohibit the destruction, or the delivery to an inspector, of any such plant pest, genetically manipulated material, plant, plant product, agricultural machinery, soil or growing medium referred to in that paragraph.

Phytosanitary certificates for imported plants etc.

6.—(1) Subject to paragraphs (2) and (3) of this article, where by virtue of article 4 the landing of any plant, soil or growing medium is prohibited unless that plant, soil or growing medium is accompanied by a phytosanitary certificate, the phytosanitary certificate shall have been issued in the country in which that plant was grown, or that soil or growing medium originated.

(2) A phytosanitary certificate which relates to plants which are directly consigned to Great Britain from a Member State and are–

(a) bulbs or corms for planting other than corms of gladiolus and bulbs of tulip and narcissus; or

(b) raw fruit of a description specified in column 2 of Part VB of Schedule 3; or

(c) of a description specified in column 2 of Part VIIB of Schedule 3 (certain cut flowers and parts of plants for decoration) other than cut flowers and parts of plants for decoration of *Protea* L. and *Limonium* Mill.;

shall have been issued

(i) in the Member State from which they were so consigned, or

(ii) where the plants to which it relates had been consigned from any other country before being consigned from that Member State to Great Britain, in that Member State or in one of the countries from which it had previously been consigned.

(3) Where any plant, soil or growing medium following its export from Great Britain is re-imported into Great Britain, the phytosanitary certificate shall have been issued in the country from which the plant, soil or growing medium was directly consigned to Great Britain.

Reforwarding phytosanitary certificates for imported plants etc.

7.—(1) Where, after a phytosanitary certificate has been issued, the consignment to which that certificate relates has been stored, repacked or split up in a country other than that in which the certificate was issued, that certificate shall be accompanied by a reforwarding phytosanitary certificate issued in that other country.

(2) Where the address of the consignee shown on a phytosanitary certificate is not in Great Britain and, in the case of a consignment direct from a Member State, the consignment contains tubers of potato or raw vegetables with foliage of the following genera: *Apium* L., *Beta* L., *Brassica* L., *Cichorium* L., *Daucus* L., *Lactuca* L., *Petroselinum* L. or *Spinacia* L., that phytosanitary certificate shall be accompanied by a reforwarding phytosanitary certificate issued in each country from which it has been consigned subsequent to the issue of that phytosanitary certificate before being landed in Great Britain.

Exception from requirement of phytosanitary certification

8.   The requirements of article 4(1)(e) shall not apply to–
  (a) any plants which–
    (i) are landed in Great Britain in the baggage of a passenger or other traveller, and
    (ii) are not intended for use in the course of a trade or business, and
    (iii) have been grown in the Euro-Mediterranean area or, in the case of citrus fruit, in the Euro-Mediterranean area or North America, and
    (iv) are not in any of the following categories, namely
      (A) plants intended for planting or propagation of *Beta* L.
      (B) plants intended for planting or propagation, other than seeds, of the family Gramineae or of the genera *Cydonia* Mill., *Malus* Mill., *Prunus* L., *Pyrus* L. and *Vitis* L.
      (C) potatoes
      (D) cut flowers of gladiolus and plants of chrysanthemum, and
    (v) are in one of the following categories, not exceeding the stated quantities–
      (A) raw fruit and raw vegetables, together 2 kilograms
      (B) cut flowers and any parts of plants together forming a single bouquet, 1 bouquet
      (C) seeds, 5 retail packets, that is to say packets in which the seed in question is normally sold to the consumer (other than for use in the course of a trade or business) or packets of a similar size
      (D) bulbs, corms, tubers and rhizomes, free of soil, together 2 kilograms
      (E) other plants, 5 plants, or
  (b) any plants, soil or growing medium which are directly consigned to Great Britain from Northern Ireland, the Channel Islands or the Isle of Man and which–
    (i) originate in any of those countries, or
    (ii) were landed in the country from which they are directly consigned to Great Britain in accordance with the plant health requirements of that country.

Official Statements in respect of imported plants etc.

9.   Any official statement required to be made in accordance with column 3 of Schedule 3 in respect of a plant, soil or growing medium shall, except where the said column 3 requires such a statement to appear on a phytosanitary certificate, be deemed to have been made by the issue of a phytosanitary certificate to accompany that plant, soil or growing medium in accordance with this Order.

General provisions relating to certificates

10.—(1) Where a phytosanitary certificate or a reforwarding phytosanitary certificate is issued in a third country in a language other than English it shall incorporate or be accompanied by a translation into the English language, which translation, if it is a document separate from the certificate, shall be completed and signed by an authorised officer.

(2) Subject to paragraph (3) of this article, where a consignment of plants, soil or growing medium has been consigned between two or more countries before being

consigned to Great Britain it may be accompanied in the place of any certificate required by this Order by a copy of such certificate issued in the country from which the consignment has been directly consigned to Great Britain and certified as a true copy of the original or a true copy of a certified copy of the original, as the case may be, by an authorised officer.

(3) Paragraph (2) of this article shall not apply in the case of a reforwarding phytosanitary certificate issued in the country from which the consignment was directly consigned to Great Britain, in which case the original reforwarding phytosanitary certificate issued in that country shall accompany the consignment.

(4) A certificate issued by or on behalf of a state, provincial or other regional or local government authority of part of a country, or by or on behalf of any department, service or other organ of such authority shall not be deemed to be a valid phytosanitary certificate or a valid reforwarding phytosanitary certificate for the purposes of this Order unless such authority is the only one empowered to issue, in relation to such part of the country, phytosanitary certificates or reforwarding phytosanitary certificates to accord with the requirements of this Order.

(5) Except in the case of consignments imported into Great Britain by post, any phytosanitary certificate and reforwarding phytosanitary certificate shall be delivered to the proper officer at the same time as, and together with, the entry relating to the consignment. In this paragraph the expression "proper officer" has the like meaning as in the Customs Act and the reference to the entry shall be construed as reference to the entry, delivery of which is to be made in accordance with the provisions of that Act.

(6) In the case of a consignment imported into Great Britain by post any phytosanitary certificate and reforwarding phytosanitary certificate shall be affixed to the outside of the package comprising the consignment or, if the consignment consists of more than one package, such certificate shall be affixed to the outside of one of the packages and copies thereof affixed to the outside of each of the remaining packages.

(7) All phytosanitary certificates and reforwarding phytosanitary certificates produced when plants, soil or growing medium are landed in Great Britain shall be stamped or otherwise endorsed by an officer of Customs and Excise showing the date on which the plant, soil or growing medium is cleared from Customs charge.

Period during which inspections are to be made and certificates issued

11.—(1) Except for an inspection which is required to be carried out for the purposes of making an official statement in accordance with a condition referred to in column 3 of Schedule 3, an inspection carried out for the purposes of issuing a phytosanitary certificate or a reforwarding phytosanitary certificate shall be carried out not more than 14 days, and in the case of a phytosanitary certificate accompanying a consignment of chrysanthemums (not being a consignment of chrysanthemum cut flowers) not more than 48 hours, before the date of the despatch of the consignment to which the inspection relates.

(2) A phytosanitary certificate or a reforwarding phytosanitary certificate shall not be valid for the purposes of this Order unless it has been completed and signed by an authorised officer not more than 14 days, and in the case of a phytosanitary certificate accompanying a consignment of chrysanthemums (not being a consignment of chrysanthemum cut flowers) not more than 48 hours, before the date of despatch of the consignment which it is to accompany and after the carrying out of any inspection referred to in paragraph (1) of this article which relates to that consignment.

Exports of plants etc. to Member States

12.—(1) Subject to paragraph (6) of this article, no person shall export from Great Britain to a Member State any consignment of plants or growing medium of a description specified in column 2 of Part I of Schedule 4 unless the consignment is accompanied by–

    (a) a phytosanitary certificate issued by an authorised officer; or

(b) in the case of a consignment to which this sub-paragraph applies (and without prejudice to paragraph (4) of this article), a reforwarding phytosanitary certificate issued by an authorised officer.

(2) No phytosanitary certificate shall be issued for the purposes of paragraph (1)(a) of this article unless the entire consignment or a representative sample taken from it, its packaging (and, where necessary, the vehicle in which it is carried) have been examined by an inspector in order to ensure that the consignment complies with such requirements of the Member State concerned as are adopted in accordance with the provisions of Directive 77/93/EEC.

(3) Paragraph (1)(b) of this article applies to a consignment which–

(a) is imported from a Member State or a third country;

(b) is to be re-exported to a Member State; and

(c) when imported, was accompanied by a phytosanitary certificate.

(4) No person shall export from Great Britain to a Member State any consignment of plants or growing medium which–

(a) is of a description specified in Schedule 4, and

(b) originated in another Member State or a third country

unless the consignment is accompanied by a phytosanitary certificate issued in the country of origin or by a certified copy of that certificate.

(5) Applications for phytosanitary certificates or reforwarding phytosanitary certificates shall be made to the appropriate Minister in such form and manner, and giving such information, as he may require.

(6) Paragraph (1) of this article does not apply to the export from Great Britain of any consignment of plants or growing medium which is imported from a Member State or third country and re-exported to a Member State without being stored, repacked or split up in Great Britain.

Notification of the presence or suspected presence of certain plant pests

13.—(1) The occupier or other person in charge of any premises who knows or suspects that any plant pest to which this article applies or any genetically manipulated material is present on the premises or any other person who, in the course of his duties or business, becomes aware or suspicious of the presence of such plant pest or genetically manipulated material on any premises, shall immediately give notice to the appropriate Minister of the presence or suspected presence of such plant pest or genetically manipulated material and shall as soon as reasonably practicable after giving such notice confirm it in writing.

(2) This article applies to any plant pest–

(a) which is of a description specified in Part I or column 2 of Part II of Schedule 1 other than a plant pest of a description specified in Part III of that Schedule; or

(b) which is mentioned in column 3 of Schedule 3; or

(c) which is not normally present in Great Britain and which is injurious to plants in Great Britain.

Notification of the likely entry into, or presence in, a free zone of plant pests, plants etc.

14.—(1) The responsible authority for a free zone who knows or suspects that any plant pest, genetically manipulated material, plant, soil or growing medium to which this article applies is likely to enter, or is present in, the free zone for which he is the responsible authority, shall immediately give notice of that fact to the appropriate Minister and shall as soon as reasonably practicable after giving such notice confirm it in writing.

(2) This article applies to any–

(a) plant pests;

(b) genetically manipulated material;

(c) plants, planted or intended for planting other than tubers of potato and seeds;

(d) seeds of a description specified in column 2 of Schedule 2 or in column 2 of Part IV of Schedule 3;

(e) tubers of potato;

(f) cut flowers;

(g) raw fruit and raw vegetables; and

(h) soil and growing medium

which have been, or are likely to be, landed in Great Britain, and have not been cleared from Customs charge.

(3) In this article "the responsible authority" and "free zone" have the same meaning as in the Customs Act(a).

Actions which may be taken by an inspector

15.—(1) If an inspector has reasonable grounds for suspecting that any plant pest, genetically manipulated material, plant, plant product, agricultural machinery, soil or growing medium is likely to be, or has been, landed in Great Britain in contravention of this Order, he may by notice in writing served on the importer or any person in charge of the vessel, aircraft, vehicle, hovercraft or freight container from which such plant pest, genetically manipulated material, plant, plant product, agricultural machinery, soil or growing medium is likely to be, or has been landed–

> (i) prohibit the landing;
>
> (ii) specify the manner in which the landing is to be carried out and the precautions which are to be taken during and subsequent to the landing;
>
> (iii) require the plant pest, genetically manipulated material, plant, plant product, agricultural machinery, soil or growing medium to be treated, re-exported, destroyed or otherwise disposed of in such manner and within such reasonable time as may be specified in the notice;
>
> (iv) prohibit the removal of the plant pest, genetically manipulated material, plant, plant product, agricultural machinery, soil or growing medium from premises specified in the notice;
>
> (v) require the removal of the plant pest, genetically manipulated material, plant, plant product, agricultural machinery, soil or growing medium to premises specified in the notice in such manner and within such reasonable time as may be so specified;
>
> (vi) require the taking of such other steps, specified in the notice, as appear to the inspector to be necessary to prevent the introduction or spread of any plant pest or genetically manipulated material in such manner and within such reasonable time as may be specified in the notice.

(2) If an inspector has reasonble grounds for suspecting that there is present or there is likely to be present on any premises–

(a) any plant, plant product, soil, hop pole or hop picking machine as a consequence of the contravention of articles 21, 26, 29 to 32, 34 or 36 to 41;

(b) any plant pest of a description specified in Part I or column 2 of Part II of Schedule 1 (other than a plant pest of a description specified in Part III of that Schedule) or which is mentioned in column 3 of Schedule 3;

(c) any plant pest which is not normally present in Great Britain and in respect of which there is in the opinion of an inspector an imminent danger of its spreading or being spread in Great Britain;

(d) any plant, plant product, soil or growing medium which is carrying or infected with, or which may be carrying or infected with, a plant pest mentioned in sub-paragraphs (b) or (c) of this paragraph;

(e) any genetically manipulated material;

he may by notice in writing served on the occupier or other person in charge of the premises or of any of the things mentioned in sub-paragraph (a) to (e) of this paragraph–

(a) See section 100A of the Customs Act which was inserted by the Finance Act 1984 (c.43), section 8 and Schedule 4, Part I.

(i) require any of the things so mentioned to be treated, destroyed or otherwise disposed of in such manner and within such reasonable time as may be specified in the notice;

(ii) prohibit the removal of those things or impose such other prohibitions as appear to the inspector to be necessary to prevent the spread of any plant pest or genetically manipulated material;

(iii) require the removal of those things to premises specified in the notice in such manner and within such reasonable time as may be so specified;

(iv) require the taking of such other steps, specified in the notice, as appear to the inspector to be necessary to prevent the spread of any plant pest or genetically manipulated material in such manner and within such reasonable time as may be specified in the notice.

(3) If an inspector has reasonable grounds for believing that it is necessary for the purpose of preventing the spread of any plant pest or genetically manipulated material from the premises mentioned in paragraph (2) of this article, he may by notice in writing served on the occupier or other person in charge of any other premises impose such prohibitions and require the taking of such reasonable steps, specified in the notice, as appear to him to be necessary for that purpose, such steps to be taken in such manner and within such reasonable time as may be specified in the notice.

(4) If an inspector has reasonable grounds for suspecting that any plant pest of a description specified in Schedule 8 other than potato cyst nematode is present on any premises, or if, in consequence of the examination of a sample of soil taken from any premises for the purpose of preventing the spread of potato cyst nematode or for any other purpose of this Order, it appears to an inspector that those premises are infected with potato cyst nematode, he may by notice in writing served on the occupier or other person in charge of such premises declare the premises infected with the appropriate plant pest for the purposes of Part III of this Order, the provisions of which shall be without prejudice to the provisions of this article.

(5) An inspector may serve on the occupier or other person in charge of premises which surround, adjoin or are in close proximity to premises declared infected with wart disease of potatoes a notice declaring the first mentioned premises to be a safety zone.

(6) Any notice served under paragraph (4) or (5) of this article may define by reference to a map or plan or otherwise the extent of the premises declared in the notice to be infected, or to be a safety zone, as the case may be.

Miscellaneous provisions as to notices

16.—(1) A notice served under paragraph (1) or (2) of article 15 may specify one or more requirements or alternative requirements.

(2) A notice served under paragraph (1)(iii) or paragraph (2)(i) of article 15 requiring any plant pest, genetically manipulated material, plant, plant product, soil or growing medium to be destroyed or otherwise disposed of, may contain provisions deferring the destruction or disposal for such period and subject to such conditions, if any, as may be specified in the notice.

(3) Where the destruction or disposal of any plant pest, genetically manipulated material, plant, plant product, soil or growing medium has been deferred under paragraph (2) of this article, the person on whom the notice is served shall be permitted, within the period specified in the notice, to destroy or dispose of the plant pest, genetically manipulated material, plant, plant product, soil or growing medium. If the person on whom the notice is served fails to destroy or dispose of the plant pest, genetically manipulated material, plant, plant product, soil or growing medium within the period specified in the notice to the satisfaction of an inspector, the destruction or disposal required by the notice shall be carried out by that person within two days following the expiry of the period specified in the notice or within such shorter or longer period as may be specified in writing by an inspector.

(4) Any treatment, re-exportation, destruction or disposal required by a notice served under article 15 shall be carried out by the person on whom the notice is served to the

satisfaction of an inspector from or at a place designated by an inspector and, except with the written authority of an inspector or any other officer of the appropriate Minister, none of the plant pests, genetically manipulated material, plants, plant products, agricultural machinery, soil, growing medium, hop poles or hop picking machines shall be moved otherwise than directly to such a place.

(5) An inspector may amend or withdraw a notice served by an inspector under this Order or having effect as if so served by a further notice served on the person on whom the original notice was served or on the person who is the occupier or in charge of the premises in respect of which the further notice is intended to be served. The amendment or withdrawal of a notice may be subject to such conditions, if any, as the inspector considers expedient to impose for the purpose of preventing the introduction or spread of any plant pest or re-infection with the plant pest to which the original notice relates.

(6)(a) A notice under this Order may be served on any person either–
    (i) by delivering it to him personally, or
    (ii) by leaving it for him at his last known place of abode or business, or
    (iii) by sending it through the post addressed to him at his last known place of abode or business.
(b) A notice may–
    (i) in the case of a body corporate, be served on the secretary or clerk of that body at the address of the registered or principal office of that body,
    (ii) in the case of a partnership, be served on a partner or person having the control or management of the partnership business or in Scotland, the firm at the principal office of the partnership.

Examination, sampling and marking

17.—(1) Subject to article 20, an inspector may, on production if so required of his authority–
(a) at all reasonable times for the purpose of ascertaining whether any plant pest of a description specified in Part I or column 2 of Part II of Schedule 1, or which is mentioned in column 3 of Schedule 3 or in Schedule 8, or a plant pest which is not normally present in Great Britain and which is injurious to plants in Great Britain, exists on any premises, or for any other purpose of this Order, enter any premises and examine and mark any part of the premises or any objects on the premises and examine, take samples of and mark any plant pests, genetically manipulated material, plants, plant products, soil or growing medium and any container or other package which has been or may have been in contact therewith;
(b) for the purposes of the examinations referred to in paragraph (a) of this article, open or authorise any person to open on his behalf or require the importer or any person in charge of any such container or other package to open, in such manner as the inspector may specify, that container or other package;
(c) if and insofar as is necessary for the purposes of the examinations referred to in paragraph (1)(a) of this article, prohibit entirely, or to such extent as he may indicate, the movement of any plant pests, genetically manipulated material, plants, plant products, soil, growing medium, container, or other package or of any material or object by means of which in his opinion a plant pest may spread.

(2) An inspector entering any premises under paragraph (1) of this article may take with him such persons, equipment and vehicles as are necessary for the purpose of facilitating the exercise of his powers under that paragraph.

Information as to compliance with notices

18.—(1) The person on whom a notice has been served under this Order, or under an Order revoked by this Order, shall, if so required by an inspector, immediately inform the inspector whether the requirements of the notice have been complied with and, if they have been complied with, of the details of the steps taken in order to comply with those requirements.

(2) Any information given under this article shall not be used as evidence against the person giving the information in any prosecution, except in respect of an alleged failure to comply with this article.

Failure to comply with a notice

19.—(1) Subject to article 20, if any person fails to comply with the requirements of a notice served, or having effect as if served, under this Order then, without prejudice to any proceedings consequent upon such failure, an inspector may, on production if so required of his authority, at all reasonable times for the purposes of this Order enter any premises on which the plant pest, genetically manipulated material, plant, plant product, agricultural machinery, soil, growing medium, hop pole or hop picking machine to which the notice relates may be present or in respect of which a notice under article 28 has been served and take or cause to be taken such steps as appear to him to be necessary either to ensure compliance with the requirements of the notice or to remedy the consequences of the failure to carry them out, and all reasonable costs of taking such steps shall be recoverable by the appropriate Minister as a civil debt from the person on whom the notice was served.

(2) An inspector entering any premises under paragraph (1) of this article may take with him such persons, equipment and vehicles as are necessary for the purpose of facilitating the exercise of his powers under that paragraph.

Power to enter premises used wholly or mainly as a dwelling

20.—(1) The power to enter premises conferred by articles 17, 19 and 27 of this Order may be exercised by an inspector to enter premises used wholly or mainly as a dwelling only if he has been granted a warrant by–

    (a) in England and Wales, a justice of the peace; or

    (b) in Scotland, a sheriff or a justice of the peace.

(2) A justice of the peace or sheriff may grant a warrant under paragraph (1) of this article only if he is satisfied–

    (a) that admission to any premises has been refused, or is likely to be refused, or that the case is one of urgency, or that a request for admission might prejudice the purpose of the entry; and

    (b) that there is reasonable ground for entry under articles 17, 19 or 27, as the case may be.

(3) A warrant granted under paragraph (1) of this article shall remain in force–

    (a) for one month; or

    (b) until the purpose for which the warrant is granted has been fulfilled,

whichever period is the shorter.

Restriction on the planting of imported potatoes

21.—(1) Without prejudice to article 22, no person shall plant or knowingly cause or permit to be planted in Great Britain any potatoes which have been grown in any place outside Great Britain, Northern Ireland, the Channel Islands, the Isle of Man, a Member State (other than Denmark or the Federal Republic of Germany), Austria or Switzerland.

(2) Potatoes referred to in paragraph (1) of this article shall include any potatoes which have been derived from such potatoes.

(3) This article shall not apply to any potatoes which have been landed in Great Britain under and in accordance with the conditions of a licence granted under article 42 or which have been derived from potatoes which have been so landed.

Restriction on the movement to and planting of potatoes in the protected region

22.—(1) For the purposes of this article "the protected region" means the whole of Scotland and the following parts of England, namely, the county of Northumberland excluding the district of Blyth Valley and Wansbeck, and the county of Cumbria excluding the districts of Barrow-in-Furness and South Lakeland.

(2) The provisions of this article shall have effect for the purpose of preventing the spread of plant pests to or in the protected region.

(3) No person shall plant or knowingly cause or permit to be planted in the protected region any potatoes which have been grown in any place outside that region and no person shall bring or knowingly cause to be brought into the protected region any such potatoes for planting in that region.

(4) Where the appropriate Minister has reason to believe that potatoes have been planted in or brought into the protected region contrary to the provisions of paragraph (3) of this article, he may by notice in writing served on any person who appears to him to be in charge of or in possession of such potatoes or of any potatoes derived from such potatoes prohibit the planting thereof in that region or the removal thereof from any premises specified in the notice otherwise than in accordance with such conditions as may be so specified and may by such notice require the treatment or destruction thereof or the removal thereof to any other place so specified, by such person in such manner and in accordance with such conditions and within such reasonable time as may be specified in the notice and to the satisfaction of an inspector.

PART III

ADDITIONAL MEASURES TO PREVENT SPREAD OF PARTICULAR PLANT PESTS

Colorado Beetle

Display of notices

23.   Every person who is the occupier or other person in charge of premises declared infected with Colorado Beetle shall, if so required by an inspector, display and keep displayed so long as the notice by which the premises were declared so infected is in force, in prominent positions on the infected premises, such number of copies of that notice, or any other notice or sign indicating that the premises are infected, as the inspector shall supply to him for the purpose.

Restriction on entry to infected premises

24.   No person other than the occupier or other person in charge of premises declared infected with Colorado Beetle, or the servants or agents of such occupier or other person in charge, shall enter such premises except with the authority of an inspector, and the occupier or other person in charge of such premises shall take all reasonable steps to prevent any unauthorised person from entering.

Restriction on planting on infected premises

25.   No person shall plant any crop on premises declared infected with Colorado Beetle without the written authority of an inspector.

Restriction on removal of crops from infected premises

26.   No person shall, without the authority of an inspector, remove or knowingly cause or permit to be removed from any premises declared infected with Colorado Beetle any potatoes, or any other plants of the family Solanaceae, and the occupier of any such premises shall take all reasonable steps to prevent removal in contravention of this article.

Actions which may be taken by an inspector

27.—(1) Subject to article 20, an inspector may, on production if so required of his authority, at all reasonable times enter any premises declared infected with Colorado Beetle and any premises to which, in the opinion of the inspector, Colorado Beetle may spread and treat such premises and treat, remove or destroy or otherwise dispose of, or cause to be treated, removed, destroyed or otherwise disposed of, any crop growing or stored on such premises and may take or cause to be taken such other steps as the inspector may think expedient for preventing the spread of Colorado Beetle.

(2) Nothing in paragraph (1) of this article shall authorise the destruction of any crop growing on premises which have not been declared infected with Colorado Beetle.

(3) An inspector entering any premises mentioned in paragraph (1) of this article may take with him such persons, equipment and vehicles as are necessary for the purpose of facilitating the exercise of his powers under that paragraph.

(4) The owner of the crop and the occupier or other person in charge of premises mentioned in paragraph (1) of this article, shall give all reasonable assistance for the purpose of facilitating the exercise of the powers conferred by this article.

(5) Without prejudice to paragraphs (1) to (4) of this article, the appropriate Minister may treat or cause to be treated by aerial spray any premises mentioned in paragraph (1) of this article or any crop growing or stored on such premises.

28. An inspector may, by notice in writing served on the occupier or other person in charge of any premises declared infected with Colorado Beetle, require him in any year to plant or cause to be planted within such reasonable time as may be specified in the notice, and to grow or cause to be grown on the premises, potatoes of such varieties and in such quantities as the inspector may determine.

Red core disease of strawberries

Restriction on the sale, delivery and planting of infected strawberry plants

29.—(1) No person shall–
(a) sell or deliver to any other person; or
(b) plant or knowingly cause or permit to be planted on any premises other than premises declared infected with red core disease of strawberries,
any strawberry plant runner or other strawberry plant (other than fruit) which he knows or suspects to be infected with red core disease of strawberries or which he knows or suspects to have been grown on premises declared infected with red core disease of strawberries.

(2) Paragraph (1) of this article shall not apply to Scotland.

Fire blight disease

Prevention of the spread of fire blight disease

30.—(1) No person shall bud or graft, or knowingly cause or permit to be budded or grafted, any tree or rootstock with any bud or scion of the pear variety Laxton's Superb or otherwise propagate, or knowingly cause or permit to be propagated, any pear tree of that variety.

(2) No person shall plant on any premises a tree which is wholly or partly of the pear variety Laxton's Superb.

(3) For the purposes of Part III of Schedule 1 "the fire blight free region" means the region comprising Scotland and the counties of Northumberland, Cumbria, Tyne and Wear, Durham, Cleveland and North Yorkshire (except the district of Selby and the Borough of York).

Potato cyst nematode

Restriction on the planting, sale etc. of potatoes

31.—(1) No person shall plant or knowingly cause or permit to be planted any potatoes on any premises in his occupation or under his charge declared infected with potato cyst nematode.

(2) No person shall remove for transplanting elsewhere from any premises declared infected with potato cyst nematode any plants which have been grown or stored on those premises.

32.—(1) If in consequence of the examination of a sample of the soil taken from any premises by an inspector for the purposes of this Order those premises appear not to be infected with potato cyst nematode, an inspector may issue a written certificate to that effect in relation to those premises.

(2) Unless previously amended or withdrawn, such a certificate shall remain in force until the expiration of 48 months from the taking of the sample mentioned in the certificate or until potatoes are planted on the premises to which the certificate relates, whichever is the earlier.

(3) No person shall sell, offer or expose for sale, deliver or knowingly cause or permit to be delivered or otherwise pass from his possession any potatoes grown by him and intended for planting unless immediately before the planting of the potatoes from which those potatoes were produced there was in force in relation to the premises on which they were grown a written certificate issued or having effect as if issued in accordance with paragraph (1) of this article.

Prohibition of misdescription of potatoes

33.—(1) No person shall sell or offer or expose for sale or knowingly cause or permit to be sold or offered or exposed for sale as being of approved resistant varieties any potatoes which are not of approved resistant varieties.

(2) A person shall not be liable to conviction for a failure to comply with, or a contravention of, conditions of a licence granted or having effect as if granted under this Order relating to the planting of approved resistant varieties if he proves to the satisfaction of the court that the potatoes were sold to him as potatoes of approved resistant varieties and that he did not know that the potatoes were not of approved resistant varieties.

Wart disease of potatoes

Restrictions on the planting, sale etc. of potatoes

34.—(1) No person shall plant or knowingly cause or permit to be planted any potatoes on any premises in his occupation or under his charge declared infected with wart disease of potatoes.

(2) Subject to paragraph (3) of this article, no person shall plant or knowingly cause or permit to be planted on any premises in his occupation or under his charge–

    (a) which have been declared a safety zone by a notice served or having effect as if served under article 15(5); or

    (b) as respects premises in England or Wales, in respect of which a notification of the presence or apparent presence of wart disease of potatoes was given before the commencement of the Wart Disease of Potatoes Order 1958(a) by the then occupier or other person then in charge of the premises or by the Minister of Agriculture, Fisheries and Food,

any potatoes which are not of an approved immune variety, or, in the case of any

---

(a) S.I. 1958/308.

premises which surround, adjoin or are in close proximity to premises on which wart disease of potatoes of any race other than the common European race is present and in respect of which an inspector so directs by notice in writing served on that person, any potatoes whatsoever except such variety or varieties, if any, as an inspector may authorise in writing to be planted on those premises.

(3) The provisions of paragraph (2) of this article shall not apply as respects any premises of a kind described in paragraph (2)(b) of this article if an inspector has served on the occupier or other person in charge of those premises a notice in writing declaring that the provisions of that paragraph shall not apply as respects those premises.

(4) No person shall remove for transplanting elsewhere from any premises declared infected with wart disease of potatoes any plants which have been grown or stored on those premises.

(5) No person shall sell or offer or expose for sale for planting or deliver or knowingly cause or permit to be sold, offered or exposed for sale for planting or delivered for planting or knowingly cause or permit to be planted any potatoes from a crop grown on premises declared infected with wart disease of potatoes.

Prohibition of misdescription of potatoes

35.—(1) No person shall sell or offer or expose for sale or knowingly cause or permit to be sold or offered or exposed for sale as potatoes of an approved immune variety any potatoes which are not of an approved immune variety.

(2) A person shall not be liable to conviction for a contravention of article 34(2) if he proves to the satisfaction of the court that the potatoes were sold to him as potatoes of an approved immune variety and that he did not know that the potatoes were not of an approved immune variety.

Restriction on the removal of soil from infected premises

36. No person shall remove, or knowingly cause or permit to be removed, any soil from any premises declared infected with wart disease of potatoes, so that it may be used or disposed of where that disease is not present.

Beet cyst nematode

Restriction on the planting of certain plants

37. No person shall sow or plant or knowingly cause or permit to be sown or planted any seed or other plant of the families Chenopodiaceae and Cruciferae including sugar beet, fodder beet, spinach beet, Swiss chard (also known as seakale beet), red beet, mangel, cabbage, kale, cauliflower, broccoli, calabrese, Brussels sprout, turnip, swede, rape or coleseed (including turnip rape and swede rape), mustard, cress or kohl-rabi on any premises declared infected with beet cyst nematode.

Progressive wilt disease

Destruction of dead and dying bines and leaves of hop plants etc.

38. The occupier or other person in charge of any farm who knows or suspects that progressive wilt disease exists thereon, shall with all practicable speed from time to time destroy by fire on the farm all dead and dying bines and leaves of hop plants which may be present there.

Restriction on the movement of hop plants etc.

39. No person shall move or knowingly cause or permit to be moved any hop plant (other than a hop cone), used hop pole or used hop picking machine from or into any farm in England or Wales.

Restriction on the planting or movement for planting of hop plants grown in certain counties

40. Subject to article 39, no person shall–
   (a) plant or knowingly cause or permit to be planted outside Kent, East Sussex or West Sussex any hop plant grown in those counties;
   (b) plant or knowingly cause or permit to be planted outside Surrey, Hampshire, Oxfordshire, Kent, East Sussex, or West Sussex any hop plant grown in Surrey, Hampshire or Oxfordshire; or
   (c) plant or knowingly cause or permit to be planted outside Hereford and Worcester, Shropshire, Surrey, Hampshire, Oxfordshire, Kent, East Sussex or West Sussex any hop plant grown in Hereford and Worcester or Shropshire.

Restriction on the planting or sale for planting of certain hop plants

41.—(1) For the purposes of this article "the specified area" means the area comprising the counties of–
   (a) East Sussex,
   (b) West Sussex except that part which lies west of the A24 road, and
   (c) Kent except that part which lies east of a line following the A20 road from Folkestone to Maidstone, the A229 road from Maidstone to Rochester, the A2 road from Rochester to Strood, the A228 road from Strood and the B2001 road to Grain.

(2) No person shall–
   (a) plant or knowingly cause or permit to be planted outside the specified area; or
   (b) sell, in the knowledge that such plant is intended for planting outside the specified area,

any hop plant other than a hop plant of one of the following varieties, namely

Brewers Gold	Male 24/68/103	Wye Challenger
Bullion	Northern Brewer	Wye Northdown
Fuggle	Omega	Wye Target
Male 1/63/45	Silks B	Wye Viking
Male 12/97/91	Silks C	Wye Yeoman
Male 24/68/8	True Golding varieties	Zenith

PART IV
GENERAL

Licences

42. Notwithstanding the provisions of this Order any plant pest, genetically manipulated material, plant, plant product, soil or growing medium may be landed, kept, released, delivered, sold, planted or otherwise disposed of in Great Britain, and any other thing prohibited by this Order may be done, under the authority of a licence, whether general or specific, granted by the appropriate Minister and in accordance with the conditions, if any, of that licence.

The Customs Act

43. The provisions of this Order shall apply without prejudice to the Customs Act.

Powers of an officer of Customs and Excise

44.—(1) An inspector may request an officer of Customs and Excise (either orally or in writing) to prohibit the removal of any plant pest, genetically manipulated material, plant, plant product, agricultural machinery, soil or growing medium which has not been cleared from Customs charge until it has been examined by an inspector and such request may identify the plant pest, genetically manipulated material, plant, plant product, agricultural machinery, soil or growing medium in any way. A request made orally under this paragraph shall be confirmed in writing.

(2) Where a request has been made under paragraph (1) of this article, the officer of Customs and Excise shall, by notice in writing served upon the importer, require that, until the plant pest, genetically manipulated material, plant, plant product, agricultural machinery, soil or growing medium has been examined by an inspector, it shall not be removed from the place specified in the notice and he shall at the same time inform an inspector of the contents of the notice.

(3) An inspector shall, without undue delay, examine any plant pest, genetically manipulated material, plant, plant product, agricultural machinery, soil or growing medium in respect of which a notice has been served by an officer of Customs and Excise under this article and shall advise that officer in writing of the terms of any notice issued and of any other action taken by the inspector in accordance with this Order.

(4) Where an officer of Customs and Excise has served a notice under paragraph (2) of this article prohibiting removal of any plant pest, genetically manipulated material, plant, plant product, agricultural machinery, soil or growing medium, nothing to which the notice relates shall be removed by any person except with the written authority of either the said officer or an inspector.

Information to be given

45.—(1) Any person who–
  (a) is the owner or occupier or other person in charge of premises in respect of which a notice has been served or which has effect as if it has been served under paragraph (4) or (5) of article 15, or on which an inspector knows or has reason to suspect that hop plants, hop plant products or hop poles are or have been present; or
  (b) has or has had, or is reasonably suspected by an inspector or any other officer of the appropriate Minister to have or have had in his possession or under his charge,
    (i) any potatoes, hop plants, hop plant products or hop poles, or
    (ii) any plant pest which is of a description specified in Part I or column 2 of Part II of Schedule 1 or which is mentioned in column 3 of Schedule 3, or
    (iii) any plant pest which is not normally present in Great Britain and which is injurious to plants in Great Britain, or
    (iv) any plant, plant product, soil or growing medium carrying or infected with a plant pest mentioned in paragraph (1)(b)(ii) or (iii) of this article, or
    (v) any plant, plant product, agricultural machinery, soil or growing medium which an inspector or any other officer of the appropriate Minister knows to have been landed or suspects has been landed in, or exported from, Great Britain, or
    (vi) any genetically manipulated material; or
  (c) as auctioneer, salesman or otherwise, has sold or offered for sale any of the things mentioned in sub-paragraph (b) of this article;
shall, if so required by an inspector or any other officer of the appropriate Minister by notice in writing, give to the said inspector or officer within such reasonable time as may be specified in that notice, any information he may possess as to crops grown at any time on the premises mentioned in sub-paragraph (a) of this article, as to any of the things mentioned in sub-paragraphs (a) or (b) of this article and as to the persons who have or have had or are likely to have or have had any of the last mentioned things in their possession or under their charge, and shall produce for examination by the inspector any licences, declarations, certificates, records, invoices or other documents relating to such things.

(2) Any information given under this article shall not be used as evidence against the person giving the information in any prosecution, except in respect of an alleged failure to comply with this article.

Offences

46.—(1) Subject to paragraph (4) of this article, no person shall contravene, or fail to comply with, a provision of this Order or a provision or condition of a notice served or having effect as if served or a licence granted or having effect as if granted in accordance with the provisions of this Order.

(2) No person shall for the purpose of procuring the issue of a phytosanitary certificate or a reforwarding phytosanitary certificate under article 4 or of a licence under article 42–

    (a) make a statement which he knows to be false in a material particular;

    (b) recklessly make a statement which is false in a material particular; or

    (c) intentionally fail to disclose any material particular.

(3) No person shall intentionally obstruct an inspector or any person authorised by an inspector in the exercise of his powers given by or under this Order.

(4) Paragraph (1) of this article shall not apply to the landing in Great Britain of articles of any description in contravention of a prohibition imposed by or under this Order.

47. A person shall be guilty of an offence who, without reasonable excuse, proof of which shall lie on him, contravenes or fails to comply with any provision of article 46 and shall be liable on summary conviction to a fine not exceeding £2,000.

In witness whereof the Official Seal of the Minister of Agriculture, Fisheries and Food is hereunto affixed on 5th October 1987.

John MacGregor
Minister of Agriculture, Fisheries and Food

5th October 1987

Sanderson of Bowden
Minister of State, Scottish Office

5th October 1987

Peter Walker
Secretary of State for Wales

Articles 4(1) and 5(1)   **SCHEDULE 1**

                                        PLANT PESTS

                                        PART I

                                   PLANT PESTS WHICH

(1) MAY NOT BE LANDED
(2) MAY NOT BE KEPT etc. UNLESS SPECIFIED IN PART III
(3) MUST BE NOTIFIED UNLESS SPECIFIED IN PART III

A.   *Live organisms of the animal kingdom at all stages of their existence*

1. *Amauromyza maculosa* (Malloch) – an American leafminer

2. *Cacoecimorpha pronubana* (Hübner) – Carnation Tortrix Moth

3. *Ceratitis capitata* (Wiedemann) – Mediterranean Fruit Fly

4. *Comstockaspis perniciosa* (Comstock) (syn. *Quadraspidiotus perniciosus* (Comstock)) – San José Scale

5. *Conotrachelus nenuphar* (Herbst) – Plum Curculio (a weevil)

6. *Epichoristodes acerbella* (Walker) – African Carnation Tortrix Moth

7. *Frankliniella occidentalis* (Pergande) – Western Flower Thrips

8. *Globodera rostochiensis* (Wollenweber) Behrens and *Globodera pallida* (Stone) Behrens – Potato Cyst Nematodes

9. *Helicoverpa armigera* (Hübner) and *H. zea* (Boddie) – Old and New World Bollworms

10. *Hyphantria cunea* (Drury) – Fall Webworm

11. *Leptinotarsa decemlineata* (Say) – Colorado Beetle

12. *Liriomyza huidobrensis* (Blanchard), *L. sativae* Blanchard and *L. trifolii* (Burgess) – American Leafminers

13. *Phthorimaea operculella* (Zeller) – Potato Tuber Moth

14. *Popillia japonica* Newman – Japanese Beetle

15. *Rhagoletis cerasi* (L.) – European Cherry Fruit Fly

16. *Spodoptera littoralis* (Boisduval) – Mediterranean Climbing Cutworm

17. *Spodoptera litura* (Fabricius) – Asian and Pacific Cutworm

18. Trypetidae (non-European):
    (a) *Rhagoletis cingulata* (Loew) – North American Cherry Fruit Fly
    (b) *Rhagoletis completa* Cresson – Walnut Husk Fly
    (c) *Rhagoletis fausta* (Osten Sacken) – Black Cherry Fruit Fly
    (d) *Rhagoletis pomonella* (Walsh) – Apple Fruit Fly
    (e) *Anastrepha fraterculus* (Wied.) – South American Fruit Fly
    (f) *Anastrepha ludens* (Loew) – Mexican Fruit Fly
    (g) *Anastrepha mombinpraeoptans* Sein – West Indian Fruit Fly
    (h) *Ceratitis rosa* Karsch – Natal Fruit Fly
    (i) *Dacus cucurbitae* (Coq.) – Melon Fly
    (j) *Dacus dorsalis* Hendel – Oriental Fruit Fly
    (k) Other harmful Trypetidae in so far as they do not exist in Europe.

B. *Bacteria*

1. *Clavibacter michiganense* pv. *sepedonicum* (Spieck. and Kotth.) Davis *et al.* (syn. *Corynebacterium sepedonicum* (Spieck. and Kotth.) Skapt. and Burkh.), the cause of Potato Ring Rot.

2. *Erwinia amylovora* (Burr.) Winslow *et al.,* the cause of Fire Blight of Rosaceae.

C. *Cryptogams*

1. *Angiosorus solani* Thirum. and O'Brien, the cause of Potato Smut.

2. *Synchytrium endobioticum* (Schilb.) Perc., the cause of Wart Disease of Potatoes.

D. *Viruses and Virus-Like Pathogens*

1. Harmful viruses and virus-like pathogens of the genera *Cydonia* Mill., *Fragaria* L., *Malus* Mill., *Prunus* L., *Pyrus* L., *Ribes* L. and *Rubus* L.:–
   (a) Apple Proliferation Disease mycoplasm
   (b) Apricot Chlorotic Leaf Roll Disease mycoplasm
   (c) Cherry Rasp Leaf virus (American)
   (d) Peach Mosaic virus (American)
   (e) Peach Phony rickettsia
   (f) Peach Rosette Disease mycoplasm
   (g) Peach Yellows Disease mycoplasm
   (h) Pear Decline Disease mycoplasm
   (i) Plum Line Pattern virus (American)
   (j) Plum Pox (Sharka) virus
   (k) Raspberry Leaf Curl viruses (American)
   (l) Strawberry Latent 'C' virus
   (m) Strawberry Vein Banding virus
   (n) Strawberry Witches' Broom Disease mycoplasm
   (o) X Disease mycoplasm.
   (p) Other harmful viruses and virus-like pathogens of the genera *Cydonia* Mill., *Fragaria* L., *Malus* Mill., *Prunus* L., *Pyrus* L., *Ribes* L. and *Rubus* L. which are not known to occur within the Member States.

2. Harmful viruses and virus-like pathogens of potato:–
   (a) Potato Yellow Dwarf virus
   (b) Potato Yellow Vein virus
   (c) Other harmful viruses and virus-like pathogens of potato which are not known to occur within the Member States.

3. Rose Wilt Disease complex (syn. Rose Dieback, Rose Leaf Curl, Rose Proliferation, Rose Spring Dwarf and Rose Stunt).

4. Potato Spindle Tuber viroid.

5. Tomato Ring Spot virus.

6. Harmful viruses and virus-like pathogens of grapevine (*Vitis* L.).

7. Beet Necrotic Yellow Vein virus–the cause of Beet Rhizomania Disease.

SCHEDULE 1 *(cont.)*

PART II

(1) PLANTS WHICH MAY NOT BE LANDED IF CARRYING OR INFECTED WITH THE PLANT PESTS SPECIFIED

(2) PLANTS WHICH MAY NOT BE KEPT etc. IF CARRYING OR INFECTED WITH THE PLANT PESTS SPECIFIED UNLESS SPECIFIED IN PART III

(3) PLANT PESTS WHICH MAY NOT BE KEPT etc. UNLESS SPECIFIED IN PART III

(4) PLANT PESTS WHICH MUST BE NOTIFIED UNLESS SPECIFIED IN PART III

A.   *Live organisms of the animal kingdom, at all stages of their existence*

Item (1)	Description of plant pests (2)	Description of plants (3)
1.	*Anarsia lineatella* Zeller – Peach Twig Borer	Plants of *Cydonia* Mill., *Malus* Mill., *Prunus* L., *Pyrus* L. other than fruit and seeds
2.	*Rhopalomyia chrysanthemi* (Ahlberg) (syn. *Diarthronomyia chrysanthemi* Ahlb.) – Chrysanthemum Gall Midge	Plants of chrysanthemum (*Chrysanthemum* L. partim) other than seeds
3.	*Ditylenchus destructor* Thorne – Potato Tuber Nematode	Flower bulbs and tubers of potato (*Solanum tuberosum* L.)
4.	*Ditylenchus dipsaci* (Kühn) Filipjev – Stem Nematode	Seeds and bulbs of *Allium cepa* L., *Allium porrum* L. and *Allium schoenoprasum* L. intended for planting, seeds of lucerne (*Medicago sativa* L.) and flower bulbs
5.	*Caloptilia azaleella* (Brants) (syn. *Gracillaria azaleella* Brants) – Azalea Leafminer	Plants of azalea (*Rhododendron* L. partim)
6.	*Merodon equestris* (Fabricius) (syn. *Lampetia equestris* Fabricius) – Large Narcissus Fly	Flower bulbs and flower corms
7.	*Laspeyresia molesta* (Busck) – Oriental Fruit Moth	Plants of *Cydonia* Mill., *Malus* Mill., *Prunus* L. and *Pyrus* L., other than fruit and seeds
8.	*Radopholus citrophilus* Huettel, Dickson and Kaplan – a Burrowing Nematode	Plants of Araceae, *Citrus* L., *Fortunella* Swingle, Marantaceae, Musaceae, *Persea americana* Mill., *Poncirus* Raf., Strelitziaceae, rooted or with growing medium attached or associated
9.	*Radopholus similis* (Cobb) Thorne – a Burrowing Nematode	Plants of Araceae, Marantaceae, Musaceae, Strelitziaceae, rooted or with growing medium attached or associated
10.	*Daktulosphaira vitifoliae* (Fitch) (syn. *Viteus vitifolii* (Fitch)) – Grape phylloxera	Plants of *Vitis* L. other than fruit and seeds

B. *Bacteria*

Item (1)	Description of plant pests (2)	Description of plants (3)
1.	*Clavibacter michiganense* subsp. *insidiosum* (McCulloch) Davis *et al.* (syn. *Corynebacterium insidiosum* (McCulloch) Jensen) – Bacterial Wilt of Lucerne	Seeds of lucerne (*Medicago sativa* L.)
2.	*Clavibacter michiganense* subsp. *michiganense* (E.F. Smith) Davis *et al.* (syn. *Corynebacterium michiganense* (E.F. Smith) Jensen) – Bacterial Canker of Tomato	Plants of tomato (*Lycopersicon lycopersicum* L.) Karsten ex Farwell (syn. *Solanum lycopersicum* L.), other than fruit
3.	*Erwinia chrysanthemi* Burkh. *et al.* – Slow Wilt of Carnation and Bacterial Blight of Chrysanthemum	Plants of carnation (*Dianthus* L.) and plants of *Dendranthema* (DC.) Des Moulins including florists' chrysanthemum, other than cut flowers and seeds
4.	*Pseudomonas caryophylli* (Burkh.) Starr and Burkh. – Bacterial Wilt of Carnation	Plants of carnation (*Dianthus* L.) other than cut flowers and seeds
5.	*Pseudomonas gladioli* pv. *gladioli* Severini (syn. *Pseudomonas gladioli* Severini) (syn. *Pseudomonas marginata* McCulloch Stapp) – Gladiolus Scab and Neck Rot	Corms of gladiolus (*Gladiolus* L.) and corms of freesia (*Freesia* Klatt)
6.	*Pseudomonas syringae* pv. *pisi (Sackett)* Young *et al.* (syn. *Pseudomonas pisi* Sackett) – Bacterial Blight of Pea	Seeds of pea (*Pisum sativum* L.)
7.	*Pseudomonas solanacearum* (E.F. Smith) Jensen – Potato Brown Rot	Plants (other than fruit and seeds) of tomato (*Lycopersicon lycopersicum* L.) Karsten ex Farwell (syn. *Solanum lycopersicum* L.) and aubergine (*Solanum melongena* L.), and plants of potato (*Solanum tuberosum* L.)
8.	*Pseudomonas andropogonis* (E.F. Smith) Stapp (syn. *Pseudomonas woodsii* (E.F. Smith) Stev.) – Carnation Bacterial Leaf Spot	Plants of carnation (*Dianthus* L.) other than cut flowers and seeds
9.	*Xanthomonas campestris* pv. *pruni* (E.F. Smith) Dye – Bacterial Spot of Prunus	Plants of *Prunus* L., intended for planting, other than seeds
10.	*Xanthomonas fragariae* Kennedy and King – Strawberry Angular Leafspot	Plants of *Fragaria* L., intended for planting, other than seeds
11.	*Xanthomonas campestris* pv. *vesicatoria* (Doidge) Dye (syn. *Xanthomonas vesicatoria* (Doidge) Dowson) – Bacterial Spot of Pepper and Tomato	Plants of tomato (*Lycopersicon lycopersicum* L.) Karsten ex Farwell (syn. *Solanum lycopersicum* L.) other than fruit

SCHEDULE 1
PART II (*cont.*)

C.   *Cryptogams*

Item (1)	Description of plant pests (2)	Description of plants (3)
1.	*Didymella chrysanthemi* (Tassi) Garibaldi and Gullino (syn. *Mycosphaerella ligulicola* Baker *et al.*) – Chrysanthemum Ray Blight	Plants of chrysanthemum (*Chrysanthemum* L. sensu lato including *Dendranthema* (DC.) Des Moulins)
2.	*Fusarium oxysporum* Schlecht. f.sp. *gladioli* (Massey) Snyder and Hansen – Fusarium Yellows and Corm Rot	Corms of freesia (*Freesia* Klatt), gladiolus (*Gladiolus* L.), and crocus (*Crocus* L.) and bulbs of iris (*Iris* L.)
3.	*Guignardia baccae* (Cav.) Jacz. – Vine Black Rot	Plants of *Vitis* L. other than fruit and seeds
4.	*Ovulinia azaleae* Weiss – Rhododendron Petal Blight	Plants of azalea (*Rhododendron* L.)
5.	*Phialophora cinerescens* (Wollenw.) V. Beyma – a Carnation Wilt (previously known as Verticillium Wilt of Carnation)	Plants of carnation (*Dianthus* L.) other than cut flowers and seeds
6.	*Phytophthora fragariae* Hickman – Red Core Disease of Strawberries	Plants of strawberry (*Fragaria* L.) other than fruit and seeds
7.	*Puccinia horiana* P. Henn. – Chrysanthemum White Rust	Plants of chrysanthemum (*Chrysanthemum* L. sensu lato including *Dendranthema* (DC.) Des Moulins)
8.	*Puccinia pelargonii-zonalis* Doidge – Pelargonium Rust	Plants of pelargonium (*Pelargonium* L'Hérit. partim)
9.	*Sclerotinia bulborum* (Wakk.) Rehm – Hyacinth Black Slime	Flower bulbs
10.	*Sclerotinia convoluta* Drayt. – Botrytis Rot of Iris	Rhizomes of iris (*Iris* L.)
11.	*Septoria gladioli* Passer. – Gladiolus Hard Rot	Flower bulbs and flower corms
12.	*Stromatinia gladioli* (Drayt.) Whet. – Gladiolus Dry Rot	Flower bulbs and flower corms
13.	*Uromyces* spp. – Gladiolus Rust	Plants of gladiolus (*Gladiolus* L.)
14.	*Verticillium albo-atrum* Reinke and Berth. – Verticillium Wilt of Hop and Lucerne (including Progressive Wilt Disease of Hops)	Plants of hop (*Humulus lupulus* L.) and seeds of lucerne (*Medicago sativa* L.)

D.   *Viruses and Virus-Like Pathogens*

Item (1)	Description of plant pests (2)	Description of plants (3)
1.	Arabis Mosaic virus	Plants of strawberry (*Fragaria* L.), blackberry and raspberry (*Rubus* L. partim), intended for planting, other than seeds

Item (1)	Description of plant pests (2)	Description of plants (3)
2.	Beet Curly Top virus	Plants of *Beta* L., intended for planting, other than seeds
3.	Beet Leaf Curl virus	Plants of Beet (*Beta vulgaris* L.), intended for planting, other than seeds
4.	Black Raspberry Latent virus	Plants of *Rubus* L., intended for planting
5.	Cherry Leaf Roll virus	Plants of *Rubus* L., intended for planting
6.	Cherry Necrotic Rusty Mottle virus	Plants of sweet cherry (*Prunus avium* L.), intended for planting, other than seeds
7.	Chrysanthemum Stunt viroid	Plants of chrysanthemum (*Chrysanthemum* L. partim), other than seeds and cut flowers
8.	Little Cherry pathogen	Plants of morello cherry (*Prunus cerasus* L.), sweet cherry (*Prunus avium* L.), ornamental cherries (*Prunus incisa* Thunb.; *Prunus sargentii* Rehd.; *Prunus serrula* Franch.; *Prunus serrulata* Lindl.; *Prunus speciosa* (Koidz.) Ingram; *Prunus subhirtella* Miq.; *Prunus* x *yedoensis* Matsum.), intended for planting, other than seeds, originating in countries outside Europe
9.	Prunus Necrotic Ring Spot virus	Plants of *Rubus* L., intended for planting
10.	Raspberry Ring Spot virus	Plants of strawberry (*Fragaria* L.), blackberry and raspberry (*Rubus* L. partim), intended for planting, other than seeds
11.	Stolbur Disease mycoplasm	Plants of the family Solanaceae, intended for planting, other than fruit and seeds
12.	Strawberry Crinkle virus	Plants of strawberry (*Fragaria* L.), intended for planting, other than seeds
13.	Strawberry Latent Ring Spot virus	Plants of strawberry (*Fragaria* L.), blackberry and raspberry (*Rubus* L. partim), intended for planting, other than seeds
14.	Strawberry Yellow Edge virus	Plants of strawberry (*Fragaria* L.), intended for planting, other than seeds
15.	Tomato Black Ring virus	Plants of strawberry (*Fragaria* L.), blackberry and raspberry (*Rubus* L. partim), intended for planting, other than seeds
16.	Tomato Spotted Wilt virus	Plants of potato (*Solanum tuberosum* L.)

SCHEDULE 1 (*cont.*)

PART III

PLANT PESTS SPECIFIED IN PARTS I AND II WHICH, INSOFAR AS THEY ARE OF A SUBSPECIES OR STRAIN NORMALLY PRESENT IN GREAT BRITAIN, MAY BE KEPT etc. (WHETHER OR NOT IN ASSOCIATION WITH PLANTS) AND NEED NOT BE NOTIFIED

A.   *Live organisms of the animal kingdom at all stages of their existence*

1. *Cacoecimorpha pronubana* (Hübner) – Carnation Tortrix Moth

2. *Rhopalomyia chrysanthemi* (Ahlberg) – (syn. *Diarthronomyia chrysanthemi* Ahlb.) – Chrysanthemum Gall Midge

3. *Ditylenchus destructor* Thorne – Potato Tuber Nematode

4. *Ditylenchus dipsaci* (Kühn) Filipjev – Stem Nematode

5. *Caloptilia azaleella* (Brants) (syn. *Gracillaria azaleella* Brants) – Azalea Leafminer

6. *Globodera rostochiensis* (Wollenweber) Behrens and *Globodera pallida* (Stone) Behrens – Potato Cyst Nematodes

7. *Merodon equestris* (Fabricius) (syn. *Lampetia equestris* Fabricius) – Large Narcissus Fly

B.   *Bacteria*

1. *Clavibacter michiganense* subsp. *insidiosum* (McCulloch) Davis *et al.* (syn. *Corynebacterium insidiosum* (McCulloch) Jensen) – Bacterial Wilt of Lucerne

2. *Erwinia chrysanthemi* Burkh. *et al.* – Slow Wilt of Carnation and Bacterial Blight of Chrysanthemum

3. *Erwinia amylovora* (Burr.) Winslow *et al.*, the cause of Fire Blight of Rosaceae, other than in the fire blight free region and other than on nurseries outside that region.

4. *Pseudomonas gladioli* pv. *gladioli* Severini (syn. *Pseudomonas gladioli* Severini) (syn. *Pseudomonas marginata* (McCulloch Stapp)) – Gladiolus Scab and Neck Rot, on gladiolus (*Gladiolus* L.) and freesia (*Freesia* Klatt.)

C.   *Cryptogams*

1. *Didymella chrysanthemi* (Tassi) Garibaldi and Gullino (syn. *Mycosphaerella ligulicola* Baker *et al.*) – Chrysanthemum Ray Blight

2. *Fusarium oxysporum* Schlecht. f.sp. *gladioli* (Massey) Snyder and Hansen – Fusarium Yellows and Corm Rot

3. *Ovulinia azaleae* Weiss – Rhododendron Petal Blight

4. *Phialophora cinerescens* (Wollenw.) V. Beyma – a Carnation Wilt (previously known as Verticillium Wilt of Carnation)

5. *Phytophthora fragariae* Hickman – Red Core Disease of Stawberries, in Scotland

6. *Puccinia pelargonii-zonalis* Doidge – Pelargonium Rust

7. *Sclerotinia bulborum* (Wakk.) Rehm – Hyacinth Black Slime

8. *Stromatinia gladioli* (Drayt.) Whet. – Gladiolus Dry Rot

9. *Verticillium albo-atrum* Reinke and Berth. – Verticillium Wilt of Hops and Lucerne other than strains causing Progressive Wilt Disease of Hops

D.   *Viruses and Virus-Like Pathogens*

1. Arabis Mosaic virus

2. Cherry Necrotic Rusty Mottle virus

3. Chrysanthemum Stunt viroid

4. Plum Pox (Sharka) virus, other than on nurseries

5. Raspberry Ring Spot virus

6. Rose Proliferation and Dieback (part of the Rose Wilt Disease complex)

7. Strawberry Crinkle virus

8. Strawberry Latent Ring Spot virus

9. Strawberry Yellow Edge virus

10. Tomato Black Ring virus

Article 4(1)

SCHEDULE 2

PLANTS, AGRICULTURAL MACHINERY, SOIL AND GROWING MEDIUM WHICH MAY NOT BE LANDED IF THEY ORIGINATE IN CERTAIN COUNTRIES

PART I: GENERAL TYPES OF PLANTS

Item (1)	Description of plants (2)	Country of origin (3)
1.	Annual and biennial plants for planting other than seeds.	Countries outside the Euro-Mediterranean area.
2.	Plants of herbaceous perennials for planting of the families:– Caryophyllaceae except carnation (*Dianthus caryophyllus* L.) Compositae except *Dendranthema* (DC.) Des Moulins (including florists' chrysanthemum) and *Dahlia* Cav. Cruciferae Leguminosae and Rosaceae (except *Fragaria* L.) other than seeds.	Countries outside the Euro-Mediterranean area.
3.	Plants of trees and shrubs for planting other than (1) seeds and (2) plants of the following families intended for use as indoor or glasshouse ornamentals:– Araucariaceae Agavaceae Araceae Araliaceae Bromeliaceae Cycadaceae Gesneriaceae Haemodoraceae Palmae Polypodiaceae Strelitziaceae and Zingiberaceae	Countries outside the Euro-Mediterranean area other than Canada and Continental States of the USA and other than as specified in column 2 of Schedule 3, Items 8 and 11.

PART II: FAMILIES OF PLANTS

Item (1)	Description of plants (2)	Country of origin (3)
4.	Plants of the family Gramineae for planting other than seeds.	Third countries other than as specified in column 2 of Schedule 3, Item 11.
5.	Plants of the family Solanaceae for planting other than plants of potato and other than seeds.	Countries outside the Euro-Mediterranean area.

PART III: GENERA OF PLANTS

Item (1)	Description of plants (2)	Country of origin (3)
6.	Plants of the genus *Beta* L. for planting other than seeds and other than plants of beet (*Beta vulgaris* L.)	Third countries.
7.	Plants of beet (*Beta vulgaris* L.) other than:– (i) seeds of red beet or beetroot, spinach beet, leaf beet or chard; (ii) plants of red beet or beetroot, spinach beet, leaf beet or chard for consumption as food; (iii) seeds of genetically monogerm varieties which have been cleaned free from soil and other debris and have been rubbed or ground to remove the outer layers of the perianth and graded to between 3.00 and 4.50 mm.	All countries.
8.	Raw vegetables from plants of:– beets (*Beta* L.) carrot (*Daucus* L.) celery and celeriac (*Apium* L.) leek (*Allium* L.) turnip and swede (*Brassica* L.) intended for consumption or processing, where the consignment contains more than 1% by weight of soil.	All countries.
9.	Plants of *Citrus* L., *Fortunella* Swingle and *Poncirus* Raf. other than fruit, seeds and parts of plants for decoration.	USA (the States of Florida, Louisiana and Hawaii).
10.	Plants of the genera *Cydonia* Mill., *Malus* Mill., *Prunus* L. and *Pyrus* L. for planting other than seeds.	Third countries other than:– Algeria Canada Egypt Finland Israel Lebanon Libya Morocco Norway Sweden Syria Tunisia USA.
11.	Plants of *Dendranthema* (DC.) Des Moulins (including florists' chrysanthemum), *Leucanthemella serotina* (L.) Tzvelev and *Nipponanthemum nipponicum* (Franch. ex Maxim.) Kitamura for planting other than seeds.	Third countries other than Malta and the Canary Islands.
12.	Plants of the genus *Fragaria* L. (including cultivars of strawberry) for planting other than seeds.	Countries outside Europe and Africa other than:– Australia Canada

SCHEDULE 2
PART III (*cont.*)
GENERA OF PLANTS

Item (1)	Description of plants (2)	Country of origin (3)
		Cyprus Israel Lebanon Malta New Zealand Syria Turkey Continental States of the USA.
13.	Seeds of lucerne (*Medicago sativa* L.).	Third countries where *Clavibactor michiganense* subsp. *insidiosum* (McCulloch) Davis *et al.* (syn. *Corynebacterium insidiosum* (McCulloch) Jensen) is known to occur other than:– Australia Austria Canada Czechoslovakia Finland The German Democratic Republic Israel Poland Romania Republic of South Africa Sweden New Zealand USA.
14.	Seeds of pea (*Pisum sativum* L.) for use as Breeder's Pre-Basic or Basic or Certified Seed of the First Generation within the meaning of the Fodder Plant Seeds Regulations 1985**(a)**.	All countries.
15.	Plants of tuber-forming species or hybrids of the genus *Solanum* L. other than tubers of potato but including true seed of potato and tubers of potato in tissue culture.	All countries.
16.	Tubers of potato for planting.	Denmark Federal Republic of Germany Third countries other than:– Austria Switzerland.
17.	Tubers of potato other than tubers of potato for planting.	Denmark Federal Republic of Germany Third countries other than:– Algeria Austria Cyprus

(a) S.I. 1985/975.

Item (1)	Description of plants (2)	Country of origin (3)
		Egypt
		Israel
		Libya
		Malta
		Morocco
		Switzerland
		Tunisia.

PART IV: AGRICULTURAL MACHINERY

Item (1)	Description of agricultural machinery (2)	Country of origin (3)
18.	Used agricultural machinery which has not been cleaned immediately prior to despatch so as to remove all particles of soil and other debris.	All countries.

PART V: SOIL AND GROWING MEDIUM

Item (1)	Description of soil and growing medium (2)	Country of origin (3)
19.	Soil.	Third countries.
20.	Used growing medium not attached to or associated with plants.	Third countries.

Article 4

SCHEDULE 3

CONDITIONS SUBJECT TO WHICH PLANTS, SOIL AND GROWING MEDIUM MAY BE LANDED UNLESS OTHERWISE PROHIBITED UNDER ARTICLE 4

PART I

CONDITIONS SUBJECT TO WHICH SOIL AND GROWING MEDIUM MAY BE LANDED

Item (1)	Description of soil and growing medium (2)	Conditions of landing (3)
1.	Soil not attached to or associated with plants.	The consignment shall be accompanied by a phytosanitary certificate and, as appropriate, one or more re-forwarding phytosanitary certificates.
2.	Growing medium not attached to or associated with plants and containing organic substances, other than that composed entirely of unused peat.	The consignment shall be accompanied by a phytosanitary certificate and, as appropriate, one or more re-forwarding phytosanitary certificates.
3.	Growing medium attached to or associated with plants other than that attached to or associated with plants in tissue culture.	(1) The consignment shall be accompanied by a phytosanitary certificate and, as appropriate, one or more re-forwarding phytosanitary certificates. (2) Where the growing medium originates in a country outside the Euro-Mediterranean area, in addition to complying with the requirement specified in paragraph (1) of this Item, an official statement shall have been made that:– (a) the growing medium at the time of planting was:– (i) either free from soil and organic matter; or (ii) subjected to appropriate treatment to ensure freedom from plant pests; or (iii) subjected to appropriate examination or testing and found free from plant pests; and (b) since planting:– (i) either the growing medium has been kept free from soil, and –either appropriate measures have been taken to ensure that it has been maintained free from plant pests, or –within 14 days prior to despatch of the consignment the plants were freed from the medium in which they were grown, leaving the minimum amount necessary to sustain the life of the plants during transport and, if replanted, the growing medium used for the purpose was free from plant pests and soil; or (ii) within 14 days prior to despatch of the consignment the plants were freed from the medium in which they were grown and, if replanted, the growing medium used for the purpose was free from plant pests and soil.

PART II

CONDITIONS SUBJECT TO WHICH ROOTED PLANTS, PLANTED OR
INTENDED FOR PLANTING AND UNROOTED VEGETATIVE PROPAGATING
MATERIAL OTHER THAN TUBERS OF POTATO AND SEEDS MAY BE LANDED

PART IIA: GENERAL TYPES OF PLANTS

Item (1)	Description of plants (2)	Conditions of landing (3)
4.	Rooted plants, planted or intended for planting, and all unrooted vegetative propagating material including bulbs, corms, tubers, cuttings, scions, budwood and plants in tissue culture, but excluding (1) warm-temperate, subtropical or tropical plants originating in a Member State, intended for use in temperature-controlled water tanks and (2) plants of the genera:– *Abies* Mill. *Castanea* Mill. *Larix* Mill. *Picea* A. Dietr. *Pinus* L. *Pseudotsuga* Carrière *Quercus* L. *Tsuga* Carrière *Zelkova* Spach. the landing of which genera in Great Britain is subject to the provisions of The Import and Export of Trees, Wood and Bark (Health) (Great Britain) Order 1980**(a)**.	The consignment shall be accompanied by a phytosanitary certificate and, as appropriate, one or more reforwarding phytosanitary certificates.
5.	Rooted plants, planted or intended for planting, grown in the open air.	An official statement shall have been made that the plants were grown on land:– (a) which is free from Potato Ring Rot (*Clavibacter michiganense* pv. *sepedonicum* (Spieck. and Kotth.) Davies *et al.* (syn. *Corynebacterium sepedonicum*) (Spieck. and Kotth.) Skapt. and Burkh.) and Wart Disease of Potatoes (*Synchytrium endobioticum* (Schilb.) Perc.); and (b) which has been officially sampled and the samples found to be free from Potato Cyst Nematodes (*Globodera pallida* (Stone) Behrens and *G. rostochiensis* (Wollenweber) Behrens).
6.	Plants of trees, shrubs and bushes other than plants in tissue culture.	Where the consignment originates in a third country:– (a) it shall be free from plant debris; and (b) where the plants comprising it originate outside the Euro-Mediterranean area they shall have undergone effective treatment for

(a) S.I. 1980/449.

SCHEDULE 3
PART IIA (*cont.*)
GENERAL TYPES OF PLANTS

Item (1)	Description of plants (2)	Conditions of landing (3)
		the control of insect and mite pests and the method of treatment shall be declared in the phytosanitary certificate accompanying the plants.
7.	Plants of deciduous trees and shrubs other than plants in tissue culture.	Where the consignment originates in a country outside the Euro-Mediterranean area the plants shall be dormant and free from leaves and fruit.
8.	Plants of trees and shrubs grown in and directly consigned to Great Britain from New Zealand other than bonsai and other than plants of the genera:– *Camellia* L. *Chaenomeles* Lindl. *Crataegus* L. *Cydonia* Mill. *Eriobotrya* Lindl. *Malus* Mill. *Prunus* L. *Pyrus* L. and any other host of Fruit Brown Rot (*Sclerotinia fructicola* (Wint.) Rehm (syn. *Monilinia fructicola* (Wint.) Honey)) the landing of which is prohibited under Item 3 of Schedule 2.	(1) An official statement shall have been made that the plants were officially examined at least once since the beginning of the last complete cycle of vegetation and found free from the plant pests specified in Parts I and II of Schedule 1 and substantially free from other plant pests.

(2) An official statement shall have been made that the plants were derived directly from parent and, where applicable, stock plants which were officially examined at least twice since the beginning of the last complete cycle of vegetation and found free from symptoms of viruses and virus-like organisms, and substantially free from other plant pests.

(3) In the case of evergreen plants, they shall have been freed from fruit prior to export.

(4) In the case of plants of the genus *Phormium* J.R. and G. Forster, they shall:–

    (a) have been treated immediately prior to export to ensure freedom from the Flax Mealy Bug, *Trionymus diminutus* Leonardi and the method of treatment shall be declared in the phytosanitary certificate accompanying the plants; and

    (b) be free from the fungi *Phaeoseptoria* sp. and *Gloeosporium phormii* (P. Henn.) Bubák.

(5) In the case of plants of the genus *Photinia* Lindl., they shall have been found free from Photinia Leaf Scorch (*Pestalotia photiniae* Thüm.) and the phytosanitary certificate shall bear an additional declaration stating how this condition has been met.

(6) An official statement shall have been made that the plants were grown in a sterile soil free medium which has not been in contact with soil.

(7) Plants of the genera *Acacia* Mill., *Acer* L., *Amelanchier* Medik., *Euonymus* L., *Fagus* L., *Juglans* L., *Ligustrum* L., *Maclura* Nutt., *Populus* L., *Ptelea* L., *Salix* L., *Syringa* L., *Tilia* L. and *Vitis* L.:–

    (a) shall not have been consigned between 16 October and 31 March (both dates inclusive);

    (b) between 1 April and 15 October shall have been fumigated in accordance with a method approved by the appropriate Minister.

SCHEDULE 3 (*cont.*)

PART IIB: FAMILIES OF PLANTS

Item (1)	Description of plants (2)	Conditions of landing (3)

9.	Plants of:–
	 Araceae
	 Marantaceae
	 Musaceae
	 Strelitziaceae
	 and of the genera:
	   Citrus L.
	   Fortunella Swingle
	   Persea Mill.
	   Poncirus Raf.
	 rooted or with growing medium attached other than plants in tissue culture.
		Where the consignment has been directly consigned to Great Britain from a third country or the plants comprising it were grown in a third country an official statement shall have been made:–
		 (a) either that the plants were grown in and directly consigned from countries known to be free from the Burrowing Nematodes (*Radopholus citrophilus* Huttel, Dickson and Kaplan and *R. similis* (Cobb) Thorne); or
		 (b) that representative samples of growing medium and roots from the place of production of the plants comprising it were subjected to official nematological testing and found to be free from at least *R. citrophilus* and *R. similis* since the beginning of the last complete cycle of vegetation.

10.	Plants of the families:– Araceae Marantaceae Musaceae Strelitziaceae rooted or with growing medium attached, other than plants in tissue culture.	Where the consignment has been directly consigned to Great Britain from a Member State and the plants comprising it were grown in a Member State an official statement shall have been made:– (a) either that no symptoms of the Burrowing Nematode (*Radopholus similis* (Cobb) Thorne) have been observed at the place of production of the plants comprising it since the beginning of the last complete cycle of vegetation; or (b) that growing medium and roots from suspect plants taken from the place of production of the plants comprising it have been subjected to official nematological testing and found to be free from at least *R. similis* since the beginning of the last complete cycle of vegetation.
11.	Plants of the following genera of the family Gramineae grown in and directly consigned to Great Britain from New Zealand:– *Arundinaria* Michx. *Bambusa* Schreb. *Chimonobambusa* Mak. *Dendrocalamus* Nees *Phyllostachys* Siebold and Zucc. *Pleioblastus* Nakai *Pseudosasa* Mak. ex Nakai *Sasa* Mak. and Shib. *Semiarundinaria* Mak. ex Nakai *Shibataea* Mak. ex Nakai *Sinarundinaria* Ohwi (Bamboo) and plants of *Cortaderia selloana* (J.A. and J.H. Schultes) Asch. and Graebn. and its cultivars and *Pennisetum setaceum* (Forssk.) Chiov. (syn. *P. rupelli* Steud.)	(1) Conditions (1), (2) and (6) specified in column 3 of Schedule 3, Item 8, shall apply. (2) The condition specified in column 3 of Schedule 3, Item 6, shall apply.

SCHEDULE 3
PART IIB (*cont.*)
FAMILIES OF PLANTS

Item (1)	Description of plants (2)	Conditions of landing (3)

12.	Plants of the family Solanaceae other than plants of potato.	An official statement shall have been made:–
		
		 (a) either that the plants were grown at a place of production at which no symptoms of Stolbur Disease mycoplasm have been observed during at least one official inspection carried out since the beginning of the last complete cycle of vegetation; or
		
		 (b) where the consignment is of plants in tissue culture, that the plants were derived from plants which:–
		
		   (i) either comply with the requirement specified in sub-paragraph (a) of this Item; or
		
		   (ii) were tested and found free from Stolbur Disease mycoplasm.

PART IIC: GENERA OF PLANTS

Item (1)	Description of plants (2)	Conditions of landing (3)
13.	Plants of the genus *Allium* L.	(1) Where the consignment originates in a third country it shall be free from:– (a) Allium Leaftip Dieback (*Mycosphaerella schoenoprasi* (Auersw.) Schroet); (b) Onion Smut (*Ustilago allii* McAlpine). (2) Where the consignment has been directly consigned to Great Britain from a third country, in addition to complying with the requirements specified in paragraph (1) of this Item, it shall be free from Corticium Rot (*Corticium rolfsii* Curzi (syn. *Sclerotium rolfsii* Sacc.)).

14.	Plants of the genera:–
	 Amelanchier Medik.
	 Cercidiphyllum Sieb. and Zucc.
	 Euonymus L.
	 Fagus L.
	 Juglans L.
	 Ligustrum L.
	 Lonicera L.
	 Populus L.
	 Ptelea L.
	 Pyracantha M. Roem.
	 Rosa L.
	 Salix L.
	 Spiraea L.
	 Syringa L.
	 Tilia L.
	 Ulmus L.
	 other than plants in tissue culture.
		Where the consignment has been directly consigned to Great Britain from, or the plants comprising it were grown in, a country in which San José Scale (*Comstockaspis perniciosa* (Comstock)) is known to occur an official statement shall have been made:–
		
		 (a) either that the plants were grown in a Member State in accordance with Council Directive 69/466/EEC(a); and
		
		   (i) that the plants were grown at a place of production at which and in the immediate vicinity of which no evidence of *C. perniciosa* has been observed during at least one official inspection carried out in each of the last two complete cycles of vegetation; and
		
		   (ii) in the case of plants of the genus *Rosa* L., that they were fumigated in accordance with a method approved by the appropriate Minister; or

(a) OJ No.L323, 24.12.69, p.5 (OJ/SE 1969 (II) p.565).

Item (1)	Description of plants (2)	Conditions of landing (3)

(b) that the plants were grown at a place of production at which and in the immediate vicinity of which no evidence of *C. perniciosa* has been observed during at least one official inspection carried out in each of the last two complete cycles of vegetation and the plants were fumigated in accordance with a method approved by the appropriate Minister.

15.   Plants of the genera:–

Apium L.
Beta L.
Brassica L.
Cichorium L.
Daucus L.
Lactuca L.
Petroselinum L.
Spinacia L.

with foliage, consigned between 1 April and 14 October (both dates inclusive) other than plants in tissue culture.

(1) An official statement shall have been made:–

(a) either that the plants were grown under permanent structures of glass or plastic; or

(b) that the plants were grown in a region known to be free from Colorado Beetle (*Leptinotarsa decemlineata* (Say)) since the beginning of the last complete cycle of vegetation; or

(c) that the plants were grown in a region in which intensive measures were taken to control *L. decemlineata* at least on:–
  (i) potatoes and egg plants (*Solanum melongena* L.) grown in the immediate vicinity of the plants; and
  (ii) the plants themselves, where potatoes or egg plants were grown as the immediately preceding crop;

unless no evidence of *L. decemlineata* has been observed on the plants during at least two official inspections carried out since the beginning of the last complete cycle of vegetation.

(2) An official statement shall have been made that the plants have been cleaned, packed and transported in a manner such as to avoid any contamination with *Leptinotarsa decemlineata*.

16.   Plants of:–

Apium graveolens L.
Capsicum annuum L.
Chrysanthemum L.
  Dendranthema (DC.)
  Des Moulins
Dianthus caryophyllus L.
Gerbera L.
Gypsophila L.
Lycopersicon lycopersicum
(L.) Karsten ex Farwell
other than plants in tissue culture.

(1) Where the plants comprising the consignment were grown in a Member State where the American Leafminer *Liriomyza trifolii* (Burgess) is known to occur an official statement shall have been made:–

(a) either that the plants or, in the case of cuttings, the stock plants were grown at a place of production at which no evidence of *L. trifolii* has been observed during official inspections carried out at least monthly during the three months prior to harvesting; or

(b) that the plants or, in the case of cuttings, the stock plants have been subjected to an officially approved and officially supervised control regime, including appropriate treatment, aimed at eradicating *L. trifolii* from those plants.

(2) Where the plants comprising the consignment were grown in a third country an official statement shall have been made that the plants or, in the case of cuttings, the stock plants were grown at a place of production at which no evidence of the American

SCHEDULE 3
PART IIC (*cont.*)
GENERA OF PLANTS

Item (1)	Description of plants (2)	Conditions of landing (3)
		Leafminers (*Amauromyza maculosa* (Malloch), *Liriomyza huidobrensis* (Blanchard), *L. sativae* Blanchard or *L. trifolii* (Burgess)) has been observed during official inspections carried out at least monthly during the three months prior to harvesting.
17.	Plants of the genus *Beta* L.	(1) An official statement shall have been made:–
		(a) either that the plants were grown in a country in which Beet Leaf Curl virus is not known to occur; or
		(b) that the plants were grown in a region in which Beet Leaf Curl virus is not known to occur and at a place of production at which and in the immediate vicinity of which no symptoms of Beet Leaf Curl virus have been observed since the beginning of the last complete cycle of vegetation.
		(2) An official statement shall have been made that no symptoms of Beet Curly Top virus have been observed at the place of production since the beginning of the last complete cycle of vegetation.
18.	Plants of the genus *Camellia*.	(1) Where the consignment originates in a third country it shall:–
		(a) be free from Camellia Petal Blight (*Ciborinia camelliae*) Kohn, and
		(b) except for plants in tissue culture, an official statement shall have been made that the plants were grown at a place of production at which no symptoms of *C. camelliae* have been observed in the flowers of the plants during at least one official inspection carried out since the beginning of the last complete cycle of vegetation.
		(2) Where the consignment has been directly consigned to Great Britain from a third country, in addition to complying with the requirements specified in paragraph (1) of this Item, it shall:–
		(a) be free from Camellia Canker and Dieback (*Glomerella cingulata* (Stonem.) Spauld. and Schrenk); and
		(b) an official statement shall have been made that the plants:–
		(i) were, except for plants in tissue culture, grown at a place of production at which and in the immediate vicinity of which no symptoms of *Glomerella cingulata* have been observed during at least two official inspections carried out during each of the last two complete cycles of vegetation;
		(ii) were, except for plants in tissue culture, treated with officially approved fungicides to protect the plants from *Glomerella cingulata;* and
		(iii) were derived from stock plants in which no symptoms of *Glomerella cingulata* have been observed.

Item (1)	Description of plants (2)	Conditions of landing (3)
19.	Plants of carnation (*Dianthus caryophyllus* L.)	(1) An official statement shall have been made that the plants were:–

(a) directly derived from stock plants which have been found to be free from Carnation Wilts (*Erwinia chrysanthemi* Burkh. *et al.*, *Phialophora cinerescens* (Wollenw.) V. Beyma and *Pseudomonas caryophylli* (Burkh.) Starr and Burkh.) in officially approved tests carried out within the last two complete cycles of vegetation and which during the same period, have been examined and found to be free from Carnation Bacterial Leaf Spot (*Pseudomonas andropogonis* (E.F. Smith Stapp)); and

(b) except for plants in tissue culture, grown at a place of production at which no symptoms of *E. chrysanthemi, P. cinerescens, Ps. andropogonis* and *Ps. caryophylli* have been observed during at least one official inspection carried out since the beginning of the last complete cycle of vegetation.

(2) Where the consignment has been directly consigned to Great Britain from a third country, in addition to complying with the requirements specified in paragraph (1) of this Item, it shall be free from Carnation Wilt (*Fusarium oxysporum* Schlecht.).

| **20.** | Plants of the genera:– *Chaenomeles* Lindl. *Cornus* L. *Cotoneaster* Medik. *Crataegus* L. *Cydonia* Mill. *Malus* Mill. *Mespilus* L. *Prunus* L. *Pyrus* L. *Ribes* L. *Sorbus* L. *Symphoricarpos* Duhamel other than plants in tissue culture. | (1) Between 16 April and 30 September (both dates inclusive) in the case of the Northern Hemisphere and between 16 October and 31 March (both dates inclusive) in the case of the Southern Hemisphere, the consignment shall not have been directly consigned from, and the plants shall not have been grown in any of the following countries or parts of countries, namely:– |

(a) Third countries:

Albania, Austria, Bulgaria, Czechoslovakia, Germany – Democratic Republic, Hungary, Poland, Romania, Switzerland, USSR, Yugoslavia, China, India, Iran, Iraq, Japan, Korea, Lebanon, Nepal, Pakistan, Syria, Turkey, Algeria, Kinshasa, Republic of South Africa, Zaire, Zimbabwe, Australia, New Zealand, Canada, Mexico, USA, Cuba, Argentina, Bolivia, Chile, Peru, Uruguay, Venezuela and any other third country in which San José Scale (*Comstockaspis perniciosa* (Comstock)) is known to occur.

(b) Member States:

France: departments of l'Ain, l'Ardèche, Bouches du Rhône, Côte d'Or, Drôme, Indre, Isère, Loire, Nievre, Pyrenées Orientales, Bas Rhin, Rhône, Saone et Loire, Savoie, Haute Savoie, Vaucluse.

Federal Republic of Germany: states of Baden-Württtenberg, Hessen, Rhineland Pfalz.

Greece.

SCHEDULE 3
PART IIC (*cont.*)
GENERA OF PLANTS

Item (1)	*Description of plants* (2)	*Conditions of landing* (3)

		Italy: all provinces except Calabria, Sicily and Sardinia.
		
		Portugal.
		
		Spain: mainland and Balearic Islands.
		
		except those regions declared free from *C. perniciosa* in accordance with the procedure laid down in article 16 of Directive 77/93/EEC**(a)**.
		
		(2) Where the consignment has been directly consigned to Great Britain from, or the plants comprising it grown in, a country or region specified in paragraph (1)(a) or (b) of this Item an official statement shall have been made:–
		
		(a) that the plants were grown in accordance with Council Directive 69/466/EEC; and
		
		(b) that:–
		
		   (i) either the plants were grown in a Member State in a region other than a region specified in paragraph (1)(b) of this Item at a place of production at which and in the immediate vicinity of which no evidence of *C. perniciosa* has been observed during at least one official inspection carried out in each of the last two complete cycles of vegetation; or
		
		   (ii) if grown in a third country or in a region of a Member State specified in paragraph (1)(b) of this Item the plants were grown at a place of production at which and in the immediate vicinity of which no evidence of *C. perniciosa* has been observed during at least one official inspection carried out in each of the last two complete cycles of vegetation and the plants were fumigated in accordance with a method approved by the appropriate Minister.

21.	Plants of the genera:–
	   Chaenomeles Lindl.
	   Cotoneaster Medic.
	   Crataegus L.
	   Cydonia Mill.
	   Malus Mill.
	   Pyracantha M. Roem.
	   Pyrus L.
	   Sorbus L. other than
	   Sorbus intermedia (Ehrh.) Pers.
	   Stranvaesia Lindl.
		An official statement shall have been made that the plants:
		
		(a) either were grown in a country or, in the case of a Member State, a region known to be free from Fireblight (*Erwinia amylovora* (Burr.) Winslow *et al.*); or
		
		(b) were grown at a place of production at which and in the immediate vicinity of which no symptoms of *E. amylovora* have been observed during at least one official inspection carried out since the beginning of the last complete cycle of vegetation; or
		
		(c) where the plants are in tissue culture, were derived from plants which were: –
		
		   (i) either officially inspected and found free from *E. amylovora;* or

(a) OJ No. L26, 31.1.77, p.20.

Item (1)	Description of plants (2)	Conditions of landing (3)
		(ii) grown at a place of production at which, and in the immediate vicinity of which, no symptoms of *E. amylovora* have been observed during at least one official inspection carried out since the beginning of the last complete cycle of vegetation prior to the taking of the culture.
22.	Plants of the genera:– *Chaenomeles* Lindl. *Crataegus* L. *Cydonia* Mill. *Eriobotrya* Lindl. *Malus* Mill. *Prunus* L. *Pyrus* L.	Where the consignment originates in a third country it shall:– (a) be free from:– (i) Oriental Peach Moth (*Carposina niponensis* Walsingham (syn. *Carposina sasakii* Matsumura)); (ii) Cherry Fruit Worm (*Enarmonia packardi* (Zeller)); (iii) Lesser Apple Worm (*E. prunivora* (Walsh)); (iv) Asian Fruit Moth (*Grapholita inopinata* (Heinrich)); (v) Fruit Brown Rot (*Sclerotinia fructicola* (Wint.) Rehm); and (vi) Apple Curculio (*Tachypterellus quadrigibbus* (Say)); (b) except for plants in tissue culture, if the plants comprising it were grown in Egypt, the Republic of South Africa, any country in Central America or North America or in any other country in which *Sclerotinia fructicola* is known to occur, an official statement shall have been made that the plants were grown in a region in which *S. fructicola* is not known to occur.
23.	Plants of:– *Chrysanthemum* L. *Dendranthema* (DC.) Des Moulins *Dianthus caryophyllus* L. *Pelargonium* L'Hérit; other than plants in tissue culture.	(1) Where the consignment originates in a Member State an official statement shall have been made:– (a) either that the plants were grown at a place of production which is known to have been free, since the beginning of the last complete cycle of vegetation, from African Carnation Tortrix (*Epichoristodes acerbella* (Walker)), Old World Bollworm (*Helicoverpa armigera* (Hübner)), Asian and Pacific Cutworm (*Spodoptera litura* (Fabricius)) and Mediterranean Climbing Cutworm (*S. littoralis* (Boisduval)); or (b) that the plants have been treated in accordance with officially approved methods for the eradication of *E. acerbella*, *H. armigera*, *S. litura* and *S. littoralis*. (2) Where the consignment originates in a third country:– (a) except for the plants to which paragraph (5) of column 3 of Item 26 applies: – (i) either an official statement shall have been made that the plants comprising it were grown in a country which is known

SCHEDULE 3
PART IIC (*cont.*)
GENERA OF PLANTS

Item (1)	Description of plants (2)	Conditions of landing (3)
		to be free from *Helicoverpa armigera*, *Spodoptera littoralis* and *S. litura;* or
		(ii) the plants comprising it shall have been subject to cold storage at 1.5°C for not less than 10 days immediately prior to export and this shall be declared on the phytosanitary certificate accompanying the plants; and
		(b) an official statement shall have been made
		(i) either that the plants comprising it were grown in a country which is known to be free from *Epichoristodes acerbella;* or
		(ii) the stock plants from which the plants comprising it were taken were subjected to regular official inspection during the three months prior to the date on which the consignment was despatched and were found free, in those inspections from *E. acerbella;* and
		(c) an official statement shall have been made that the plants comprising it were officially examined prior to export and found to be free from:
		(i) American Corn Earworm (*Helicoverpa zea* (Boddie));
		(ii) Fall Armyworm (*Spodoptera frugiperda* (Smith));
		(iii) Southern Armyworm (*Spodoptera eridania* (Cramer)).
24.	Plants of the genera *Cydonia* Mill., *Malus* Mill. and *Pyrus* L.	An official statement shall have been made: –
		(a) either that the plants were grown in a country in which viruses, or virus-like pathogens of a description specified in paragraph (1)(p) of Part ID of Schedule 1 are not known to occur in *Cydonia, Malus* or *Pyrus;* or
		(b) that the plants were grown at a place of production at which no symptoms of viruses, or virus-like pathogens of a description specified in paragraph (1)(p) of Part ID of Schedule 1 have been observed during at least one official inspection carried out since the beginning of the last complete cycle of vegetation.
25.	Plants of dahlia. (*Dahlia* Cav.)	Where the consignment has been directly consigned to Great Britain from a third country:–
		(a) any tubers in the consignment shall be in a dormant state; and
		(b) an official statement shall have been made that the plants comprising it have been directly derived from plants which were officially tested and found free from plant viruses.

Item (1)	Description of plants (2)	Conditions of landing (3)
26.	Plants of *Dendranthema* (DC.) Des Moulins, including florists' chrysanthemum and other hosts of Chrysanthemum White Rust (*Puccinia horiana* P. Henn.)	(1) An official statement shall have been made:–

(a) either that the plants are of no more than third generation stock derived from material which has been found to be free from Chrysanthemum Stunt viroid in officially approved tests; or

(b) that the plants have been directly derived from material of which a representative sample of at least 30 plants or 10% of the plants, whichever is the greater, has been found to be free from Chrysanthemum Stunt viroid during an official inspection carried out at the time of flowering.

(2) Where the consignment has been directly consigned to Great Britain from a third country, in addition to complying with the requirements specified in paragraphs (1) and (3) of this Item:–

(a) it shall be free from Chrysanthemum Chlorotic Mottle viroid; and

(b) an official statement shall have been made that the requirements specified in paragraph (1) of this Item relating to Chrysanthemum Stunt viroid have also been complied with for Chrysanthemum Chlorotic Mottle viroid.

(3) An official statement shall have been made that the plants were grown:–

(a) at a place of production which has been officially inspected, at least monthly, during the three months prior to the despatch of the plants and has been found to be free from Chrysanthemum White Rust (*Puccinia horiana* P. Henn.); and

(b) except for plants in tissue culture, in an area within which during the three months prior to the despatch of the plants there has been no occurrence of *P. horiana* within 800 metres of the place of production.

(4) Except for plants in tissue culture, an official statement shall have been made that:–

(a) in the case of unrooted cuttings, no symptoms of Chrysanthemum Ray Blight (*Didymella chrysanthemi* (Tassi) Garibaldi and Gullino) have been observed either in the cuttings or in the plants from which the cuttings were taken; or

(b) in the case of rooted cuttings, no symptoms of *D. chrysanthemi* have been observed either in the cuttings or in the rooting bed.

(5) Where the consignment is of cuttings and has been directly consigned to Great Britain from Malta or the Canary Islands, in addition to complying with the requirements specified in paragraphs (1), (2) and (3) of this Item an official statement shall have been made that:–

(a) the cuttings comprising it were directly derived from stock plants which, at the time

SCHEDULE 3
PART IIC (*cont.*)
GENERA OF PLANTS

Item (1)	Description of plants (2)	Conditions of landing (3)

the cuttings were taken, were not more than 15 months old since initial propagation from nuclear stock produced at a source approved by the appropriate Minister, which stock was tested and found free from chrysanthemum viroids including Chrysanthemum Stunt viroid and Chlorotic Mottle viroid;

(b) all other chrysanthemums being grown at the approved nursery specified under (a) when the cuttings were taken were derived from nuclear stock material which was tested and found free from all chrysanthemum viroids, including Chrysanthemum Stunt viroid and Chlorotic Mottle viroid;

(c) the stock plants from which the cuttings were taken were inspected at least monthly during the three months prior to the despatch of the cuttings and found free in these inspections from Bacterial Blight (*Erwinia chrysanthemi* Burkh. *et al.*) and Chrysanthemum Ray Blight (*Didymella chrysanthemi* (Tassi) Garibaldi and Gullino); and

(d) the cuttings comprising it were either:–

(i) subjected to cold storage at 1.5°C for not less than 10 days; or

(ii) fumigated in accordance with a method approved by the appropriate Minister.

The method of treatment shall be declared in the phytosanitary certificate accompanying the consignment. If the American Leafminer (*Liriomyza trifolii* (Burgess)) has occurred on the place of production within the previous 2 years the second method of treatment shall have been used.

(6) Where the consignment is of pot plants originating in the Netherlands, in addition to complying with the requirements specified in paragraphs (1) and (3) of this Item:–

(a) the plants shall have been produced in nurseries which meet the following requirements:

(i) the nurseries shall have been officially approved for producing plants for the purposes of Commission Decision 84/58/EEC(a) upon official statement:

–that no symptoms of *Puccinia horiana* have been observed on plants grown or stored there, in at least two official inspections, the first carried out following the application for approval and the second carried out one month after the first, and

–that any earlier approval has not

(a) OJ No. L35, 7.2.84, p.20.

Item (1)	Description of plants (2)	Conditions of landing (3)

ceased within two months prior to the application for approval; and

(ii) no symptoms of *Puccinia horiana* have been observed on plants grown or stored on the nurseries in regular official inspections carried out as frequently as necessary in the light of the seasonal risk of infection; and

(iii) the nurseries have not automatically ceased to be officially approved by virtue of paragraph (2) of Article 1 of Commission Decision 84/58/EEC.

(b) the plants shall since their production have been continuously kept separate from plants of chrysanthemum produced on nurseries other than those complying with the requirements of sub-paragraph (a) above in such a way as to avoid any risk of contamination with *Puccinia horiana* through such material;

(c) the plants shall have been maintained under a fungicidal regime appropriate to ensure freedom from *Puccinia horiana* having regard to the cultivars and in the light of the seasonal risk of infection;

(d) the plants shall have been packed on arrival at the first place of public sale at the latest, in boxes each of which was marked with a sign indicating that no symptoms of *Puccinia horiana* were found, in appropriate examination carried out by qualified persons, on the plants packed in the box;

(e) the examination provided for in Article 6 of Directive 77/93/EEC shall have been made on samples taken from each lot in accordance with the requirements of the Plant Protection Organisation of the Netherlands with regard to the size of the lot and in the light of the seasonal risk of infection; for the purposes of this paragraph, "lot" means a consignment consisting of a single variety of chrysanthemums produced by a single grower;

(f) the examination referred to in sub-paragraph (e) above shall also ascertain whether the conditions in sub-paragraphs (a) to (d) above were complied with;

(g) each of the boxes or other packing units into which the plants have been packed for export shall have been marked with the number of the phytosanitary certificate or another mark or marks enabling authorised officers of the Plant Protection Services of the Netherlands and Great Britain to identify the nursery or nurseries on which the plants packed in the box or packing unit were produced; and

SCHEDULE 3
PART IIC (*cont.*)
GENERA OF PLANTS

Item (1)	Description of plants (2)	Conditions of landing (3)
		(h) the phytosanitary certificate shall state under "Additional Declaration": "The consignment meets the requirements laid down in Commission Decision 84/58/EEC".
27.	Plants of the genus *Fragaria* L. (including cultivars of strawberry).	(1) The consignment shall be free from:– (a) Strawberry Latent 'C' virus; (b) Strawberry Vein Banding virus; (c) Strawberry Witches' Broom Disease mycoplasm; (d) Strawberry Crinkle virus; (e) Strawberry Yellow Edge virus; (f) Arabis Mosaic virus; (g) Raspberry Ring Spot virus; (h) Strawberry Latent Ring Spot virus; (i) Tomato Black Ring virus; (j) Strawberry Angular Leafspot (*Xanthomonas fragariae* Kennedy and King); and (k) Red Core Disease of Strawberries (*Phytophthora fragariae* Hickman).
		(2) An official statement shall have been made:– (a) either that the plants were grown in a country in which the harmful organisms specified in paragraph (1)(f) to (k) of this Item and viruses or virus-like pathogens of a description specified in paragraph (1)(p) of Part ID of Schedule 1 are not known to occur in *Fragaria;* or (b) that the plants were grown at a place of production at which no symptoms of the harmful organisms specified in paragraph (1)(f) to (k) of this Item and viruses or virus-like pathogens of a description specified in paragraph (1)(p) of Part ID of Schedule 1 have been observed during at least one official inspection carried out since the beginning of the last complete cycle of vegetation.
		(3) An official statement shall have been made:– (a) either that the plants were grown in a country in which the viruses and mycoplasm specified in paragraph (1)(a) to (e) of this Item are not known to occur; or (b) (i) that the plants, other than those raised from seed, were either officially certified under a certification scheme requiring them to be derived in a direct line from material which has been maintained under appropriate conditions and subjected to regular official testing for at least the

Item (1)	Description of plants (2)	Conditions of landing (3)

viruses and mycoplasm specified in paragraph (1)(a) to (e) of this Item using appropriate indicators or equivalent methods and has been found free, in those tests, from those viruses and that mycoplasm; or were derived in a direct line from material which has been maintained under appropriate conditions and which has been subjected, within the last three complete cycles of vegetation, at least once, to official testing for at least the viruses and mycoplasm specified in condition (1)(a) to (e) of this Item using appropriate indicators or equivalent methods and has been found free, in those tests from those viruses and that mycoplasm; and

(ii) that no symptoms of the viruses and mycoplasm specified in paragraph (1)(a) to (e) of this Item have been observed in the plants comprising it or in other susceptible plants at the place of production or in its immediate vicinity during at least one official inspection carried out since the beginning of the last complete cycle of vegetation.

(4) Where the consignment originates in a third country, in addition to complying with the requirements specified in paragraphs (1), (2) and (3) of this Item:–

(a) it shall be free from dead leaves and plant debris; and

(b) an official statement shall have been made that the plants comprising the consignment, if they were grown elsewhere than in Europe, shall have been grown in a region which is known to be free from Strawberry Weevils *Anthonomus signatus* (Say) and *Anthonomus bisignifer* Schenkling.

(5) Where the consignment has been directly consigned to Great Britain from a third country, in addition to complying with the requirements specified in paragraphs (1)–(4) of this Item, it shall be free from Strawberry Black Spot (*Colletotrichum acutatum* Simmonds) and an official statement shall have been made that the plants were:–

(i) derived in a direct line from mother plants which have been officially inspected and found to be free from *Phytophthora fragariae* and Strawberry Black Spot (*Colletotrichum acutatum* Simmonds); and

(ii) except for plants in tissue culture, grown at a place of production:–

–in respect of which records have been maintained for not less than thirty years which records show that *Phytophthora fragariae* has not occurred on that land during that period; or

–which tests have shown to be free from *Phytophthora fragariae;* and

SCHEDULE 3
PART IIC (cont.)
GENERA OF PLANTS

Item (1)	Description of plants (2)	Conditions of landing (3)
		(iii) except for plants in tissue culture, grown at a place of production:–
		–at which no symptoms of *Colletotrichum acutatum* were observed on the plants or on any plants within at least 30 metres of the plants during at least two official inspections carried out since the beginning of the last complete cycle of vegetation; and
		–at which all plants of *Fragaria* and other host plants of *Colletotrichum acutatum* have been subjected to a fungicidal regime approved by the plant protection service of the exporting country for the control of *Colletotrichum acutatum*.
		(6) Where the consignment has been directly consigned to Great Britain from New Zealand, in addition to complying with the requirements specified in paragraphs (1)–(5) of this Item, conditions (1), (2), (3) and (6) specified at Item 8 in column 3 shall apply.
28.	Plants of fuchsia (*Fuchsia* L.)	Where the consignment has been directly consigned to Great Britain from a third country it shall be free from Fuchsia Gall Mite (*Aculops fuchsiae* Keifer).
29.	Plants of the genus *Gladiolus* L.	An official statement shall have been made:–
		(a) either that the plants originate in a country known to be free from Gladiolus Rust (*Uromyces* spp.); or
		(b) that the plants were grown at a place of production at which no symptoms of *Uromyces* spp. have been observed during at least one official inspection carried out since the beginning of the last complete cycle of vegetation.
30.	Plants of hop (*Humulus lupulus* L.)	(1) An official statement shall have been made that the plants, the stock plants from which they were taken and the place of production at which they were grown have been officially inspected at least once since the beginning of the last complete cycle of vegetation and found to be free from symptoms of Verticillium Wilt of Hop (*Verticillium albo-atrum* Reinke and Berth.).
		(2) Where the consignment has been directly consigned to Great Britain from a third country, in addition to complying with the requirement specified in paragraph (1) of this Item, that requirement shall also be complied with in respect of Hop Wilt (*Verticillium dahliae* Kleb.) and it shall be free from:
		(i) Hop Stunt viroid;
		(ii) American Hop Latent virus; and
		(iii) dead leaves and plant debris.
31.	Plants of the genera *Iris* L. and *Ornithogalum* L.	Where the consignment has been directly consigned to Great Britain from a third country:–
		(a) it shall be free from Corticium Rot (*Corticium rolfsii* Curzi (syn. *Sclerotium rolfsii* Sacc.));
		(b) for plants other than plants in tissue culture, an official statement shall have been made

Item (1)	Description of plants (2)	Conditions of landing (3)
		that the plants were taken from a crop in which no symptoms of *C. rolfsii* have been observed during at least one official inspection carried out since the beginning of the last complete cycle of vegetation.
32.	Plants of the genus *Juniperus* L.	Where the consignment has been directly consigned to Great Britain from a third country it shall be free from Juniper Pear Rust (*Gymnosporangium asiaticum* Miyabe) and other non-European *Gymnosporangium* spp.
33.	Plants of lettuce (*Lactuca sativa* L.) and cucumber (*Cucumis sativus* L.).	Where the consignment has been directly consigned to Great Britain from a third country it shall be free from Beet Pseudo Yellows virus.
34.	Plants of the genus *Malus* Mill.	(1) An official statement shall have been made:–

(a) either that the plants were grown in a country in which neither Cherry Rasp Leaf virus (American) nor Tomato Ring Spot virus is known to occur in the genus *Malus* L.; or

(b) (i)–either that the plants were officially certified under a certification scheme requiring them to be derived in a direct line from material which has been maintained under appropriate conditions and subjected to regular official testing for at least Cherry Rasp Leaf virus (American) and Tomato Ring Spot virus using appropriate indicators or equivalent methods and has been found free, in those tests, from those viruses; or

–that the plants were derived in a direct line from material which has been maintained under appropriate conditions and which has been subjected, within the last three complete cycles of vegetation, at least once, to official testing for at least Cherry Rasp Leaf virus (American) and Tomato Ring Spot virus using appropriate indicators or equivalent methods and has been found free, in those tests, from those viruses; and

(ii) that no symptoms of Cherry Rasp Leaf virus (American) or Tomato Ring Spot virus have been observed in the plants or in other susceptible plants at the place of production or its immediate vicinity during at least one official inspection carried out in each of the last three complete cycles of vegetation.

(2) Where the consignment originates in a third country, in addition to complying with the requirements specified in paragraph (1) of this Item, it shall be free from:–

(a) Alternaria Blotch of Apple (*Alternaria alternata* (Fr.) Keissler (apple pathotype) (syn. *Alternaria mali* Roberts));

(b) Apple Fruit Canker *Guignardia piricola* (Nose) Yamamoto.

SCHEDULE 3
PART IIC (*cont.*)
GENERA OF PLANTS

Item (1)	Description of plants (2)	Conditions of landing (3)
		(3) Where the consignment has been directly consigned to Great Britain from a third county, in addition to complying with the requirements specified in paragraphs (1) and (2) of this Item, it shall be
		(a) free from Tobacco Ring Spot virus; and
		(b) an official statement shall have been made that the requirements specified in paragraph (1) of this Item relating to Tomato Ring Spot virus have also been complied with for Tobacco Ring Spot virus.
35.	Plants of *Malus pumila* Mill.	An official statement shall have been made:–
		(a) either that the plants were grown in a region which is known to be free from Apple Proliferation Disease mycoplasm; or
		(b) (i)–either that the plants, other than those raised from seed, were officially certified under a certification scheme requiring them to be derived in a direct line from material which has been maintained under appropriate conditions and subjected to regular official testing for at least Apple Proliferation Disease mycoplasm using appropriate indicators or equivalent methods and has been found free, in those tests, from that disease; or
		–that the plants, other than those raised from seed, were directly derived from material which has been maintained under appropriate conditions and which has been subjected, within the last six complete cycles of vegetation, at least once, to official testing for at least Apple Proliferation Disease mycoplasm using appropriate indicators or equivalent methods and has been found free, in those tests, from that disease; and
		(ii) that no symptoms of Apple Proliferation Disease mycoplasm have been observed in the plants or in other susceptible plants at the place of production and in its immediate vicinity during at least one official inspection carried out in each of the last three complete cycles of vegetation.
36.	Plants of pelargonium (species, hybrids and cultivars of *Pelargonium* L'Hérit.)	(1) Where the plants comprising the consignment were grown in a country in which Tomato Ring Spot virus is known to occur but in which the nematode *Xiphinema americanum* Cobb or other vectors of Tomato Ring Spot virus are not known to occur an official statement shall have been made:–
		(a) either that the plants have been directly derived from a place of production known to be free from Tomato Ring Spot virus on the basis of official tests on samples taken from all pelargonium stock clones at the place of production; or
		(b) that the plants are of no more than fourth

Item (1)	Description of plants (2)	Conditions of landing (3)

generation stock derived from pelargonium plants which have been found to be free from Tomato Ring Spot virus in officially approved tests.

(2) Where the plants were grown in a country in which Tomato Ring Spot virus is known to occur and in which the nematode *Xiphinema americanum* Cobb or other vectors of Tomato Ring Spot virus are known to occur an official statement shall have been made:–

  (a) that the plants were grown at a place of production at which Tomato Ring Spot virus is not known to occur in the soil or elsewhere; and

  (b) that the plants are of no more than second generation stock which has been derived from pelargonium plants which have been found to be free from Tomato Ring Spot virus in officially approved tests;

  (c) for plants in tissue culture, that the plant cultures were derived from plants which were tested and found free from Tomato Ring Spot virus.

(3) Where the consignment has been directly consigned to Great Britain from a third country, in addition to complying, as appropriate, with the requirements specified in paragraph (1) or (2) of this Item:

  (a) it shall be free from Tobacco Ring Spot virus; and

  (b) an official statement shall have been made that the requirements specified, as appropriate, in paragraph (1) or (2) of this Item relating to Tomato Ring Spot virus have also been complied with for Tobacco Ring Spot virus.

---

37.   Plants of the genus *Prunus* L.

(1) The consignment shall be free from:–

  (a) Cherry Rasp Leaf virus (American);

  (b) Peach Mosaic virus (American);

  (c) Peach Phony rickettsia;

  (d) Peach Rosette Disease mycoplasm;

  (e) Peach Yellows Disease mycoplasm;

  (f) Plum Line Pattern virus (American);

  (g) X Disease mycoplasm; and

  (h) Tomato Ring Spot virus.

(2) An official statement shall have been made:–

  (a) either that the plants were grown in a country in which Apricot Chlorotic Leaf Roll Disease mycoplasm, Bacterial Spot (*Xanthomonas campestris* pv. *pruni* (E.F. Smith) Dye) and viruses, or virus-like pathogens, of a description specified in paragraph (1) of Part ID of Schedule 1 are not known to occur on *Prunus;* or

  (b) that the plants were:–

    (i) grown at a place of production at which

SCHEDULE 3
PART IIC (*cont.*)
GENERA OF PLANTS

Item (1)	Description of plants (2)	Conditions of landing (3)

no symptoms of Apricot Chlorotic Leaf Roll Disease mycoplasm, *Xanthomonas campestris* pv. *pruni* and viruses, or virus-like pathogens of a description specified in paragraph (1)(p) of Part ID of Schedule 1 have been observed on *Prunus* during at least one official inspection carried out since the beginning of the last complete cycle of vegetation; and

(ii)–either officially certified under a certification scheme requiring them to be derived in a direct line from material which has been maintained under appropriate conditions and which has been subjected to regular official testing for at least the virus and virus-like pathogens specified in paragraph 1(a) to (h) of this Item using appropriate indicators or equivalent methods and has been found free, in those tests, from those viruses and virus-like pathogens; or

–were derived in a direct line from material which has been maintained under appropriate conditions and which has been subjected, within the last three complete cycles of vegetation, at least once, to official testing for at least the virus and virus-like pathogens specified in paragraph 1(a) to (h) of this Item using appropriate indicators or equivalent methods and has been found free, in those tests from those viruses and virus-like pathogens; and

(iii) officially inspected at least once in each of the last three complete cycles of vegetation and no symptoms of the virus and virus-like pathogens specified in paragraph 1(a) to (h) of this Item have been observed in the plants or in other susceptible plants at the place of production or in its immediate vicinity.

(3) Where the consignment has been directly consigned to Great Britain from a third country, in addition to complying with the requirements specified in paragraphs (1) and (2) of this Item:–

(a) it shall be free from:–

(i) Prunus Black Knot (*Apiosporina morbosa* (Schwein.) von Arx (syn. *Dibotryon morbosum* (Schwein.) Thiessen and Sydow)); and

(ii) Tobacco Ring Spot virus;

(b) an official statement shall have been made that the requirements specified in paragraph (2) of this Item relating to Tomato Ring Spot virus have also been complied with for Tobacco Ring Spot virus; and

(c) an official statement shall have been made

Item (1)	Description of plants (2)	Conditions of landing (3)

that the plants have been grown at a place of production at which and in the immediate vicinity of which no symptoms of *Apiosporina morbosa* have been observed during at least one official inspection carried out in the last complete cycle of vegetation.

(4) Where the consignment originates in a third country, in addition to complying with the requirements specified in paragraphs (1)–(3) of this Item, it shall be free from:–

(a) Western Cherry Fruit Fly (*Rhagoletis indifferens* Curran);

(b) Japanese Cherry Fruit Fly (*Euphranta japonica* (Ito) (syn. *Rhacochlaena japonica* Ito)).

38. Plants of:

Prunus armeniaca L.
Prunus x *blireana* André
Prunus brigantina Vill.
Prunus cerasifera Ehrh.
Prunus x *cistena* (Hansen) Koehne
Prunus domestica L. subsp. *domestica*
Prunus x *domestica* L. subsp. *institia* (L.) C.K. Schneider (syn. *Prunus domestica* subsp. *italica* (Borkh.) Hegi)
Prunus dulcis (Mill.) D.A. Webb (syn. *Prunus amygdalus* Batsch.)
Prunus glandulosa Thunb.
Prunus holosericea Batal.
Prunus hortulana Bailey
Prunus kurdica Fenzl ex Fritsch
Prunus japonica Thunb.
Prunus mandschurica (Maxim.) Koehne
Prunus maritima Marsh
Prunus mume Sieb. and Zucc.
Prunus nigra Ait.
Prunus persica (L.) Batsch
Prunus salicina Lindl.
Prunus sibirica L.
Prunus simonii Carr.
Prunus spinosa L.
Prunus tomentosa Thunb.
Prunus triloba Lindl. and other *Prunus* species susceptible to plum pox virus.

An official statement shall have been made:–

(a) either that the plants were grown in a country in which Plum Pox virus is not known to occur; or

(b) (i)–either that the plants, other than those raised from seed, were officially certified under a certification scheme requiring them to be derived in a direct line from material which has been maintained under appropriate conditions and subjected to regular official virological testing for at least Plum Pox virus using appropriate indicators or equivalent methods and has been found free, in those tests, from that virus; or

–that the plants, other than those raised from seed, were derived in a direct line from material which has been maintained under appropriate conditions and which has been subjected, within the last three complete cycles of vegetation, at least once, to official virological testing for at least Plum Pox virus using appropriate indicators or equivalent methods and has been found free, in those tests, from that virus; and

(ii) that no symptoms of Plum Pox virus have been observed in the plants or in other susceptible plants at the place of production and in its immediate vicinity during at least one official inspection carried out in each of the last three complete cycles of vegetation; and

(iii) that the plants were grown at a place of production at which since the beginning of the last complete cycle of vegetation all plants which have shown symptoms of infection with any virus or virus-like pathogen other than Plum Pox virus have been removed.

39. Plants of sweet cherry (*Prunus avium* L.).

An official statement shall have been made that the plants were grown at a place of production at which no symptoms of Cherry Necrotic Rusty Mottle virus have

SCHEDULE 3
PART IIC (*cont.*)
GENERA OF PLANTS

Item (1)	Description of plants (2)	Conditions of landing (3)
		been observed during at least one official inspection carried out since the beginning of the last complete cycle of vegetation.
40.	Plants of sour cherry (*Prunus cerasus* L.) sweet cherry (*Prunus avium* L.) and ornamental cherries (*Prunus incisa* Thunb., *Prunus sargentii* Rehd., *Prunus serrula* Franch., *Prunus serrulata* Lindl., *Prunus speciosa* (Koidz.) Ingram, *Prunus subhirtella* Miq., *Prunus* x *yedoensis* Matsum.) and hybrids and cultivars thereof.	Where the plants were grown in a country outside Europe in which Little Cherry Disease pathogen is known to occur:– (a) they shall be free from Little Cherry Disease pathogen; and (b) an official statement shall have been made:– (i)–either that the plants were officially certified under a certification scheme requiring them to be derived in a direct line from material which has been maintained under appropriate conditions and subjected to regular official testing for at least Little Cherry Disease pathogen using appropriate indicators or equivalent methods and has been found free, in those tests, from that pathogen; or –that the plants were derived in a direct line from material which has been maintained under appropriate conditions and has been subjected, within the last three complete cycles of vegetation, at least once, to official testing for at least Little Cherry Disease pathogen using appropriate indicators or equivalent methods and has been found free, in those tests, from that pathogen; and (ii) that no symptoms of Little Cherry Disease pathogen have been observed in the plants or in other susceptible plants at the place of production during at least one official inspection carried out in each of the last three complete cycles of vegetation.
41.	Plants of the genera *Pyrus* L. and *Cydonia* Mill.	(1) Where the consignment has been directly consigned to Great Britain from a third country it shall be free from:– (a) Pear Black Spot (*Alternaria alternata* (Fr.) Keissler (pear pathotype) (syn. *Alternaria kikuchiana* Tanaka)); (b) Apple Fruit Canker (*Guignardia piricola* (Nose) Yamamoto); and (c) Asian Pear Bud Borer (*Ectomyelois pyrivorella*, (Matsumura) syn. *Nephopteryx pyrivorella* (Matsumura)). (2) Where the consignment has been directly consigned to Great Britain from a third country an official statement shall have been made that the plants comprising it were grown:– (a) either in a country which is known to be free from Pear Decline Disease mycoplasm; or (b) at a place of production at which and in the immediate vicinity of which upon official inspection all plants which have shown

Item (1)	*Description of plants* (2)	*Conditions of landing* (3)
		symptoms of Pear Decline Disease mycoplasm have been removed during each of the last three complete cycles of vegetation that the plants were at that place.
42.	Plants of pear (*Pyrus communis* L.) and quince (*Cydonia oblonga* Mill.).	An official statement shall have been made that the plants were grown:– (a) either in a country which is known to be free from Pear Decline Disease mycoplasm; or (b) at a place of production at which and in the immediate vicinity of which upon official inspection all plants which have shown symptoms of Pear Decline Disease mycoplasm have been removed during each of the last three complete cycles of vegetation that the plants were at that place.
43.	Plants of the genus *Rhododendron* L.	Where the consignment has been directly consigned to Great Britain from a third country:– (a) it shall be free from Rhododendron Powdery Mildew (*Oidium* spp.); (b) an official statement shall have been made that the plants comprising it were grown at a place of production at which no symptoms of *Oidium* spp. have been observed on the plants during at least one official inspection carried out since the beginning of the last complete cycle of vegetation.
44.	Plants of the genus *Ribes* L. (including cultivars of gooseberry, blackcurrant and redcurrant).	(1) An official statement shall have been made:– (a) either that the plants were grown in a country in which viruses or virus-like pathogens of a description specified in paragraph (1)(p) of Part ID of Schedule 1 are not known to occur in *Ribes;* or (b) that the plants were grown at a place of production at which no symptoms of viruses or virus-like pathogens of a description specified in paragraph (1)(p) of Part ID of Schedule 1 have been observed during at least one official inspection carried out since the beginning of the last complete cycle of vegetation. (2) Where the consignment originates in a third country, in addition to complying with the requirement specified in paragraph (1) of this Item, it shall be free from the Currant Fruit Flies (*Epochra canadensis* (Loew) and *Rhagoletis ribicola* Doane). (3) Where the consignment has been directly consigned to Great Britain from New Zealand, in addition to complying with the requirements specified in paragraphs (1) and (2) of this Item:– (a) conditions (1), (2), (3) and (6) specified at Item 8 in column 3 shall apply;

Item (1)	Description of plants (2)	Conditions of landing (3)
		(b) the plants shall have been derived directly from parent and, where applicable, stock plants which have been tested and found free from viruses.
45.	Plants of rose (species, hybrids and cultivars of *Rosa* L.).	An official statement shall have been made:– (a) either that the plants were grown in a country in which Rose Wilt Disease complex is not known to occur; or (b) that the plants were taken from a crop in which no symptoms of Rose Wilt Disease complex have been observed during at least one official inspection carried out since the beginning of the last complete cycle of vegetation.
46.	Plants of the genus *Rubus* L. (including cultivars and hybrids of raspberry and blackberry).	(1) The consignment shall be free from:– (a) Raspberry Leaf Curl viruses (American); (b) Tomato Ring Spot virus; (c) Cherry Leaf Roll virus; (d) Black Raspberry Latent virus; (e) Prunus Necrotic Ring Spot virus; (f) Arabis Mosaic virus; (g) Raspberry Ring Spot virus; (h) Strawberry Latent Ring Spot virus; and (i) Tomato Black Ring virus. (2)(a) Either an official statement shall have been made that the plants were grown in a country in which the viruses specified in paragraph (1)(a) to (e) of this Item are not known to occur in plants of the genus *Rubus* L.; or (b) the consignment shall be free from aphids and aphid eggs (Aphididae) and an official statement shall have been made:– (i)–either that the plants were officially certified under a certification scheme requiring them to be derived in a direct line from material which has been maintained under appropriate conditions and subjected to regular official testing for at least the viruses specified in paragraph (1)(a) to (e) of this Item using appropriate indicators or equivalent methods and has been found free, in those tests, from those viruses; or –that the plants were derived in a direct line from material which has been maintained under appropriate conditions and which has been subjected, within the last three complete cycles of vegetation, at least once, to official testing for at least the viruses specified in paragraph (1)(a) to (e) of this Item using appropriate indicators or equivalent methods and has been found free, in those tests, from those viruses; and

Item (1)	Description of plants (2)	Conditions of landing (3)
		(ii) that no symptoms of the viruses specified in paragraph (1)(a) to (e) of this Item have been observed in the plants or in other plants of the genus *Rubus* L. at the place of production or in its immediate vicinity during at least one official inspection carried out in each of the last three complete cycles of vegetation.

(3) An official statement shall have been made:–

(a) either that the plants were grown in a country in which the viruses specified in paragraph (1)(f) to (i) of this Item and viruses or virus-like pathogens of a description specified in paragraph (1)(p) of Part ID of Schedule 1 are not known to occur in *Rubus;* or

(b) that the plants were grown at a place of production at which no symptoms of the viruses specified in paragraph (1)(f) to (i) of this Item and viruses, or virus-like pathogens of a description specified in paragraph (1)(p) of Part ID of Schedule 1 have been observed during at least one official inspection carried out since the beginning of the last complete cycle of vegetation.

(4) Where the consignment has been directly consigned to Great Britain from a third country, in addition to complying with the requirements specified in paragraphs (1), (2) and (3) of this Item:–

(a) it shall be free from:–

(i) Raspberry Bud Moth (*Carposina adreptella* (Walker));

(ii) Raspberry Bushy Dwarf virus; and

(iii) Tobacco Ring Spot virus;

(b) an official statement shall have been made that the requirements specified in paragraph (2) of this Item relating to Tomato Ring Spot virus have also been complied with for Tobacco Ring Spot virus.

(5) Where the consignment has been directly consigned to Great Britain from New Zealand, in addition to complying with the requirements specified in paragraphs (1)–(4) of this Item, Conditions (1), (2), (3) and (6) specified at Item 8 in column 3 shall apply.

47.	Plants of tomato (*Lycopersicon lycopersicum* (L.) Karsten ex Farwell and hybrids and cultivars thereof).	(1) Where the consignment has been directly consigned to Great Britain from a third country, it shall be free from Tomato Bacterial Speck (*Pseudomonas syringae* pv. *tomato* (Okabe) Young, Dye and Wilkie).

(2) Where the consigment originates in a third country, in addition to complying with the requirement specified in paragraph (1) of this Item, an official statement shall have been made that the plants were grown:–

(a) either in a region which is known to be free from Potato Spindle Tuber viroid; or

(b) at a place of production at which no symptoms of Potato Spindle Tuber viroid have

SCHEDULE 3
PART IIC (*cont.*)
GENERA OF PLANTS

Item (1)	Description of plants (2)	Conditions of landing (3)
		been observed in plants during at least one official inspection carried out since the beginning of the last complete cycle of vegetation.
48.	Bulbs of the genera *Tulipa* L. and *Narcissus* L.	Except for plants in tissue culture an official statement shall have been made that the plants were taken from a crop in which no symptoms of Stem Nematode (*Ditylenchus dipsaci* (Kühn) Filipjev) have been observed during at least one official inspection carried out since the beginning of the last complete cycle of vegetation.
49.	Plants of the genus *Vaccinium* L. (including cultivars of blueberry).	(1) Where the consignment originates in a third country it shall be free from Blueberry Fruit Fly (*Rhagoletis mendax* Curran). (2) Where the consignment has been directly consigned to Great Britain from a third country, in addition to complying with the requirement specified in paragraph (1) of this Item:– (a) the plants shall be free from symptoms of Blueberry Canker and Dieback (*Diaporthe vaccinii* Shear); and (b) an official statement shall have been made that the plants were grown at a place of production at which no symptoms of *Diaporthe vaccinii* have been observed during at least one official inspection carried out since the beginning of the last complete cycle of vegetation.
50.	Plants of the genus *Vitis* L. (including cultivars of grapevine).	(1) An official statement shall have been made that the plants were grown at a place of production at which no symptoms of harmful viruses and virus-like pathogens of grapevine have been observed during at least one official inspection carried out since the beginning of the last complete cycle of vegetation. (2) Where the consignment originates in a third country, in addition to complying with the requirement specified in paragraph (1) of this Item:– (a) it shall be free from:– (i) Vine Black Rot (*Guignardia bidwellii* (Ellis) Viala and Ravaz); and (ii) Canker of Grapevine (*Xanthomonas ampelina* Panogopoulos); and (b) an official statement shall have been made that the plants were grown at a place of production at which no symptoms of Vine Black Rot caused by *Guignardia baccae* (Cav.) Jacz or *Guignardia bidwellii* and *Xanthomonas ampelina* have been observed in plants during at least one official inspection carried out since the beginning of the last complete cycle of vegetation.

PART III

CONDITIONS SUBJECT TO WHICH TUBERS OF POTATO MAY BE LANDED

Item (1)	Description of plants (2)	Conditions of landing (3)
51.	Tubers of potato (*Solanum tuberosum* L.).	(1) The consignment shall be accompanied by a phytosanitary certificate and, as appropriate, one or more re-forwarding phytosanitary certificates.

(2) The potatoes comprising the consignment shall have been directly derived from potatoes which were certified as seed potatoes in the United Kingdom, the Isle of Man, any of the Channel Islands, a Member State (other than Denmark or the Federal Republic of Germany) or in one of the following third countries:–

Algeria;
Austria;
Cyprus;
Egypt;
Israel;
Libya;
Malta;
Morocco;
Switzerland;
Tunisia.

(3) An official statement shall have been made:–

(a) either that the potatoes were grown in an area within which during the last complete cycle of vegetation there has been no occurrence of Colorado Beetle (*Leptinotarsa decemlineata* (Say)) within 25 km of the place of production; or

(b) that the potatoes were grown at a place of production at which all potatoes have been treated under official supervision during the growing season with an insecticide specifically to control *Leptinotarsa decemlineata* so as to prevent contamination of the harvested crop with that plant pest.

(4) An official statement shall have been made:–

(a) that, prior to export to Great Britain, the potatoes comprising it were riddled, brushed or washed and packed in an officially approved packing station in such a manner as to remove any *Leptinotarsa decemlineata* and to prevent re-infestation therewith; and

(b) that, in the case of potatoes which have been stored prior to export to Great Britain:–

(i) the potatoes were riddled, brushed or washed in the manner described in sub-paragraph (a) of this paragraph before they were stored; or

(ii) the potatoes have been freed from soil and officially examined to ensure freedom from *Leptinotarsa decemlineata* within the tubers.

(5) The consignment shall contain not more than 1% by weight of soil.

(6) Where the packages or containers in which the consignment of potatoes is packed are not new they shall:–

SCHEDULE 3
PART III (*cont.*)
TUBERS OF POTATO

Item (1)	Description of plants (2)	Conditions of landing (3)

(a) be constructed in such manner and of such materials that they are capable of being effectively cleaned; and

(b) have been cleaned in accordance with an officially approved method.

(7) The consignment shall have been transported from the packing station to the place from which the consignment left the territory of the exporting country in containers which were closed in such a manner as to prevent the entry of plant pests.

(8) Where the potatoes were grown in a Member State, in addition to complying with the requirements specified in paragraphs (1)–(7) of this Item, an official statement shall have been made that the potatoes:–

(a) were grown in accordance with Council Directive 69/464/EEC(a); and

(b) were grown in a country which is known to be free from Potato Ring Rot (*Clavibacter michiganense* pv. *sepedonicum* (Spieck. and Kotth.) Davis *et al.* (syn. *Corynebacterium sepedonicum* (Spieck. and Kotth.) Skapt. and Burkh.)).

(9) Where the potatoes were grown in a third country, in addition to complying with the requirements specified in paragraphs (1)–(7) of this Item, an official statement shall have been made that the potatoes were grown:–

(a) in a country known to be free from *Clavibacter michiganense* pv. *sepedonicum* and from races of *Synchytrium endobioticum* other than the common European race thereof;

(b) at a place of production at which and in the immediate vicinity of which no symptoms of *Synchytrium endobioticum* have been observed during the 30 years prior to the date on which the phytosanitary certificate accompanying the consignment was issued; and

(c) in a country in which Potato Spindle Tuber viroid is not known to occur.

(10) Where the consignment was directly consigned to Great Britain from a third country, in addition to complying with the requirements specified in paragraphs (1)–(7) and (9) of this Item, it shall be free from:–

(a) the Potato Flea Beetles (*Epitrix cucumeris* (Harris); *E. subcrinita* (Le Conte); and *E. tuberis* Gentner);

(b) the North American Chafer Beetles (*Phyllophaga anxia* (Le Conte); *P. errans* (Le Conte); and *P. fusca* (Froelich)).

(a) OJ No. L323, 24.12.69, p.1. (OJ/SE 1969 (II) p.561).

Item (1)	Description of plants (2)	Conditions of landing (3)
52.	Tubers of potato for planting.	An official statement shall have been made:–

(a) that the potatoes were certified under any official certification scheme which complies with Council Directive 66/403/EEC**(a)**;

(b) that the potatoes were grown at a place of production at which no symptoms of Stolbur Disease mycoplasm have been observed on plants of potato and other plants of the family Solanaceae during at least one official inspection carried out since the beginning of the last complete cycle of vegetation; and

(c) that, on the basis of official soil sampling carried out not more than two years before the planting of the crop from which the potatoes comprising the consignment were derived but after the date of the harvest of the preceding potato crop, if any, grown on the same land, the land on which the potatoes comprising the consignment were grown is believed to be free from Potato Cyst Nematodes (*Globodera rostochiensis* (Wollenweber) Behrens and *G. pallida* (Stone) Behrens); and

(d) that on the basis of official sampling of the potatoes and growing medium, the consignment is believed to be free from *G. rostochiensis* and *G. pallida*; and

(e) that the potatoes were grown in a region recognised as being free from Beet Necrotic Yellow Vein virus, the cause of Beet Rhizomania Disease.

| **53.** | Tubers of potato for planting of varieties other than those accepted for marketing in one or more Member State pursuant to Council Directive 70/457/EEC**(a)** landed under a licence granted under article 42. | An official statement shall have been made:– |

(a) that the potatoes belong to breeders' advanced selections; and

(b) that the potatoes were grown in a Member State other than Denmark or the Federal Republic of Germany; and

(c) that the potatoes were either:–

(i) derived in a direct line from plants which have been officially tested and found free from at least Potato Ring Rot (*Clavibacter michiganense* pv. *sepedonicum* (Spieck. and Kotth.) Davis *et al.* (syn. *Corynebacterium sepedonicum* (Spieck. and Kotth.) Skapt. and Burkh.)), Andean strains of Potato virus S and Potato Spindle Tuber viroid; or

(ii) derived in a direct line from plants which have been certified under an official certification scheme which complies with Council Directive 66/403/EEC and which includes routine testing for at least *Clavibacter michiganense* pv. *sepedonicum,* Potato Spindle Tuber

---

(a) OJ No. 125, 11.7.66, p.2320 (OJ/SE 1965–66 p.154).
(b) OJ No. L225, 12.10.70, p.1.

SCHEDULE 3
PART III *(cont.)*
TUBERS OF POTATO

Item (1)	Description of plants (2)	Conditions of landing (3)
		viroid and Andean strains of Potato virus S; and
		(d) that since the testing specified in paragraph (c) of this Item, the potatoes and all plants from which they were derived have been maintained under appropriate conditions to ensure freedom from at least the plant pests specified in Schedule 1.

PART IV

CONDITIONS SUBJECT TO WHICH SEEDS OF BEET, OF THE FAMILIES CRUCIFERAE AND GRAMINEAE AND OF THE GENUS *TRIFOLIUM* L. AND OF LETTUCE, LUCERNE, PEA, TOMATO AND OF THE GENUS *RUBUS* L. MAY BE LANDED

Item (1)	Description of plants (2)	Conditions of landing (3)
54.	Seeds of:– Red beet or beetroot, spinach beet, leaf beet or chard (*Beta vulgaris* L.).	(1) The consignment shall be accompanied by a phytosanitary certificate and, as appropriate, one or more re-forwarding phytosanitary certificates. (2) An official statement shall have been made:– (a) that the seeds were taken from a crop which was:– (i) grown in a region of production in which Beet Rhizomania Disease (caused by Beet Necrotic Yellow Vein virus) is known not to occur; and (ii) officially inspected at least once during the year of sowing and at least once during the year of harvest and found free in those inspections from symptoms of Beet Rhizomania Disease (caused by Beet Necrotic Yellow Vein virus); and (b) that the consignment contains less than 1% by weight of inert matter.
55.	Seeds from plants of the families:– Cruciferae and Gramineae and of the genus *Trifolium* L.	Where the consignment originates in Argentina, Australia or New Zealand it shall:– (a) be accompanied by a phytosanitary certificate and, as appropriate, one or more re-forwarding phytosanitary certificates; and (b) be free from the Stem Weevil (*Listronotus bonariensis* (Kuschel) (syn. *Hyperodes bonariensis* Kuschel)).
56.	Seeds of:– lettuce (*Lactuca sativa* L.); lucerne (*Medicago sativa* L.); pea (*Pisum sativum* L.); species of *Rubus* L. and tomato (*Lycopersicon lycopersicum* (L.) Karsten ex Farwell and hybrids and cultivars thereof).	The consignment shall be accompanied by a phytosanitary certificate and, as appropriate, one or more re-forwarding phytosanitary certificates.

Item (1)	Description of plants (2)	Conditions of landing (3)
57.	Seeds of lettuce (*Lactuca sativa* L.)	Where the consignment originates in a third country, an official statement shall have been made that:–

(a) either the seeds comprising it were taken from a crop which was found to be substantially free from Lettuce Mosaic virus at one or more official inspections carried out during the last complete cycle of vegetation; or

(b) in a representative sample of the seeds comprising it no Lettuce Mosaic virus was found when:–

    (i) not less than 3,000 seedlings were grown under officially approved conditions; or

    (ii) not less than 5,000 seeds were inoculated to suitable indicator plants or were tested by equivalent methods.

58. Seeds of lucerne (*Medicago sativa* L.)

(1) An official statement shall have been made:–

(a) either that the seeds were fumigated prior to export for the control of Stem Nematode (*Ditylenchus dipsaci* (Kühn) Filipjev) in accordance with a method of fumigation approved by the appropriate Minister; or

(b) that the seeds were taken from a crop grown at a place of production at which since the beginning of the last complete cycle of vegetation no symptoms of *Ditylenchus dipsaci* have been observed and were found to be free from *D. dipsaci* in laboratory tests on a representative sample of the seed.

(2) An official statement shall have been made:–

(a) either that the seeds were taken from a crop which was grown in a country in which Bacterial Wilt of Lucerne (*Clavibacter michiganense* subsp. *insidiosum* (McCulloch) Davis *et al.* (syn. *Corynebacterium insidiosum* (McCulloch) Jensen)) is not known to occur; or

(b) that:–

    (i) the seeds were taken from a crop which was grown at a place of production at which and in the immediate vicinity of which *C. michiganense* subsp. *insidiosum* is not known to have occurred during the 10 years prior to the date on which the phytosanitary certificate accompanying the consignment was issued;

    (ii) the seeds were taken from a crop which had not yet started its fourth complete cycle of vegetation from sowing and from which not more than one preceding seed harvest had been taken from the crop;

    (iii) the seeds were grown at a place of production at which and in the immediate vicinity of which no symptoms of *C. michiganense* subsp. *insidiosum* have been observed during an official inspection made during the last complete cycle

SCHEDULE 3
PART IV (*cont.*)
SEEDS

Item (1)	Description of plants (2)	Conditions of landing (3)

of vegetation or, where appropriate, the last two cycles of vegetation; and

(iv) the seeds were grown on land on which no lucerne has been grown during the three years immediately prior to the crop having been sown.

(3) Where the consignment originates in a third country, in addition to complying with the requirements specified in paragraphs (1) and (2) of this Item, an official statement shall have been made that the seeds were taken from a crop which was grown at a place of production at which no symptoms of Verticillium Wilt of Lucerne (*Verticillium albo-atrum* Reinke and Berth.) have been observed during at least one official inspection carried out since the beginning of the last complete cycle of vegetation.

59. Seeds of pea (*Pisum sativum* L.)

An official statement shall have been made:–

(a) that the seeds were taken from a crop which was grown in a region of production in which *Pseudomonas syringae* pv. *pisi* has not been known to occur during the period of 10 years prior to the date on which the phytosanitary certificate accompanying the consignment was issued; or

(b) that the seeds were grown at a place of production at which no symptoms of *Pseudomonas syringae* pv. *pisi* have been observed during at least one official inspection carried out since the beginning of the last complete cycle of vegetation.

60. Seeds from plants of the genus *Prunus* L.

(1) An official statement shall have been made:–

(a) either that the seeds were taken from plants which were grown in a country in which Tomato Ring Spot virus is not known to occur in plants of the genus *Prunus;* or

(b) (i) that the seeds were taken from plants which:–

–either were certified under a certification scheme requiring them to be directly derived from material which has been maintained under appropriate conditions and subjected to regular official testing for at least Tomato Ring Spot virus and has been found free in those tests, from that virus; or

–were directly derived from material which has been maintained under appropriate conditions and which has been subjected within the last three complete cycles of vegetation, at least once, to official testing for at least Tomato Ring Spot virus and has been found free, in those tests, from this virus; and

(ii) that no symptoms of Tomato Ring Spot virus have been observed in the plants from which the seeds were taken or in

Item (1)	Description of plants (2)	Conditions of landing (3)
		other plants of the genus *Prunus* at the place of production or in its immediate vicinity during at least one official inspection carried out in each of the last three complete cycles of vegetation.
		(2) Where the consignment has been directly consigned to Great Britain from a third country, in addition to complying with the requirement specified in paragraph (1) of this Item:–
		(a) it shall be free from Tobacco Ring Spot virus; and
		(b) an official statement shall have been made that the requirements specified in paragraph (1) of this item relating to Tomato Ring Spot virus have also been complied with for Tobacco Ring Spot virus.
61.	Seeds from plants of the genus *Rubus* L.	(1) The consignment shall be free from:–
		(a) Tomato Ring Spot virus;
		(b) Black Raspberry Latent virus;
		(c) Cherry Leaf Roll virus; and
		(d) Prunus Necrotic Ring Spot virus.
		(2) An official statement shall have been made:–
		(a) either that the seeds were taken from plants which were grown in a country in which the viruses specified in paragraph (1) of this Item are not known to occur in plants of the genus *Rubus* L.; or
		(b) (i) that the seeds were taken from plants which:–
		–either were certified under a certification scheme requiring them to be directly derived from material which has been maintained under appropriate conditions and subjected to regular official testing for at least the viruses specified in paragraph (1) of this Item and has been found free, in those tests, from those viruses; or
		–were directly derived from material which has been maintained under appropriate conditions and which has been subjected, within the last three complete cycles of vegetation, at least once, to official testing for at least the viruses specified in paragraph (1) of this Item and has been found free, in those tests, from those viruses; and
		(ii) that no symptoms of the viruses specified in paragraph (1) of this Item have been observed in the plants from which the seeds were taken or in other plants of the genus *Rubus* L. at the place of production, or in its immediate vicinity during at least one official inspection carried out in each of the last three complete cycles of vegetation.

SCHEDULE 3
PART IV (*cont.*)
SEEDS

Item (1)	Description of plants (2)	Conditions of landing (3)
		(3) Where the consignment has been directly consigned to Great Britain from a third country, in addition to complying with the requirements specified in paragraphs (1) and (2) of this Item:– (a) it shall be free from 　(i) Tobacco Ring Spot virus; 　(ii) Raspberry Bushy Dwarf virus; and (b) an official statement shall have been made that the requirements specified in paragraph (2) of this Item relating to Tomato Ring Spot virus have also been complied with for Tobacco Ring Spot virus.
62.	Seeds of tomato (*Lycopersicon lycopersicum* (L.) Karsten ex Farwell and hybrids and cultivars thereof).	(1) An official statement shall have been made:– (a) that the seeds were extracted by an officially approved acid extraction method; and (b) that:– 　(i) either the seeds were taken from plants which were grown in a region in which Potato Spindle Tuber viroid, Bacterial Canker of Tomato (*Clavibacter michiganense* subsp. *michiganense* (E.F. Smith) Davis *et al.* (syn. (*Corynebacterium michiganense* (E.F. Smith) Jensen)) and Tomato Bacterial Spot (*Xanthomonas campestris* pv. *vesicatoria* (Doidge) Dye (syn. *Xanthomonas vesicatoria* (Doidge) Dowson)) are not known to occur; or 　(ii) the seeds were taken from plants which were grown at a place of production at which no symptoms of Potato Spindle Tuber viroid, *Clavibacter michiganense* subsp. *michiganense* and *Xanthomonas campestris* pv. *vesicatoria* have been observed in any plants during at least one official inspection carried out since the beginning of the last complete cycle of vegetation. (2) Where the consignment has been directly consigned to Great Britain from a third country, in addition to complying with the requirement specified in paragraph (1) of this Item, it shall be free from Tomato Bacterial Speck (*Pseudomonas syringae* pv. *tomato* (Okabe) Young, Dye and Wilkie).

PART V

CONDITIONS SUBJECT TO WHICH RAW FRUIT MAY BE LANDED

PART VA

GENERAL CONDITIONS

Item (1)	Description of plants (2)	Conditions of landing (3)
63.	Raw fruit.	(1) The consignment shall be free from the plant pests specified in Part I of Schedule 1 other than San José Scale (*Comstockaspis perniciosa* (Comstock)) and, where appropriate, from the plant pests specified in Part II of that Schedule.
		(2) The consignment shall be substantially free from *Comstockaspis perniciosa* during the period 16 September to 30 April (both dates inclusive) and free from at least the young and mobile stage of that plant pest during the period 1 May to 15 September (both dates inclusive).

PART VB

ADDITIONAL CONDITIONS APPLYING IN THE CASE OF RAW FRUIT OF THE GENERA *CITRUS, CYDONIA, MALUS, PRUNUS* AND *PYRUS*

Item (1)	Description of plants (2)	Conditions of landing (3)
64.	Raw fruit from plants of the genera: *Cydonia* Mill. *Malus* Mill. *Prunus* L. *Pyrus* L. *Citrus* L. other than lemons (*Citrus limon* (L.) Burm.) and citrons (*Citrus medica* L.).	The consignment shall be accompanied by a phytosanitary certificate and, as appropriate, one or more re-forwarding phytosanitary certificates.
65.	Raw fruit from plants of the genera:– *Cydonia* Mill. *Malus* Mill. *Prunus* L. *Pyrus* L.	(1) Where the consignment has been directly consigned to Great Britain from a third country and the fruit comprising it was grown in North America, Egypt or Japan, an official statement shall have been made that the fruit has been officially examined and found to be free from Fruit Brown Rot (*Sclerotinia fructicola* (Wint.) Rehm (syn. *Monilinia fructicola* (Wint.) Honey)).
		(2) Where the consignment has been directly consigned to Great Britain from a third country and the fruit comprising it was grown in Central America, South America, the Republic of South Africa, Australia or New Zealand, an official statement shall have been made:–
		(a) either that the fruit originates in an area known to be free from *Sclerotinia fructicola;* or
		(b) that no symptoms of *Sclerotinia fructicola* have been observed on plants at the place of production or on the fruit during at least one official inspection carried out since the beginning of the last complete cycle of vegetation.

SCHEDULE 3
PART VB (*cont.*)
RAW FRUIT

Item (1)	Description of plants (2)	Conditions of landing (3)
		(3) Where the consignment originates in a third country, in addition to complying with the requirements specified in paragraph (1) or (2) of this Item, it shall be free from:–
		(a) Oriental Peach Moth (*Carposina niponensis* Walsingham (syn. *Carposina sasakii* Matsumura));
		(b) Asian Fruit Moth (*Grapholita inopinata* Heinrich);
		(c) Apple Fruit Worm (*Enarmonia prunivora* (Walsh));
		(d) Cherry Fruit Worm (*Enarmonia packardi* (Zeller)); and
		(e) Apple Curculio (*Tachypterellus quadrigibbus* (Say)).

66.	Raw fruit of apple (*Malus* Mill. and cultivars thereof).	Where the consignment originates in a third country it shall be free from:–
		    (a) Apple Fruit Canker (*Guignardia piricola* (Nose) Yamamoto); and
		    (b) Alternaria Blotch of Apple (*Alternaria alternata* (Fr.) Keissler (apple pathotype) (syn. *Alternaria mali* Roberts)).

67.	Raw fruit of cherry (*Prunus avium* L., *Prunus cerasus* L., and hybrids and cultivars thereof).	Where the consignment originates in a third country and the fruit comprising it was grown in North America or Japan it shall be free from:–
		    (a) Western Cherry Fruit Fly (*Rhagoletis indifferens* Curran); and
		    (b) Japanese Cherry Fruit Fly (*Euphranta japonica* (Ito) (syn. *Rhacochlaena japonica* Ito)).

68.	Raw fruit of pear (*Pyrus* L. and cultivars thereof).	Where the consignment originates in a third country it shall be free from:–
		    (a) Pear Black Spot (*Alternaria alternata* (Fr.) Keissler (pear pathotype) (syn. *Alternaria kikuchiana* Tanaka)); and
		    (b) Asian Pear Bud Borer (*Ectomyelois pyrivorella* (Matsumura) syn. *Nephopteryx pyrivorella* (Matsumura)).

PART VC

ADDITIONAL CONDITIONS APPLYING IN THE CASE OF RAW FRUIT OF THE GENERA *FRAGARIA, RIBES, RUBUS, VACCINIUM* AND *VITIS*

Item (1)	Description of plants (2)	Conditions of landing (3)

69.	Raw fruit from plants of the genera:–
	    Fragaria L.
	    Ribes L.
	    Rubus L.
	    Vaccinium L.
	    Vitis L.
		Where the consignment originates in a third country:–
		    (a) it shall be accompanied by a phytosanitary certificate and, as appropriate, one or more re-forwarding phytosanitary certificates; and
		    (b) it shall be free from plant debris, leaves and leaf pieces.

Item (1)	Description of plants (2)	Conditions of landing (3)
70.	Raw fruit of strawberry (species, hybrids and cultivars of *Fragaria* L.).	Where the consignment has been directly consigned to Great Britain from a third country it shall be free from Strawberry Black Spot (*Colletotrichum acutatum* Simmonds).
71.	Raw fruit from plants of the genus *Ribes* L.	Where the consignment originates in a third country it shall be free from the Currant Fruit Flies (*Epochra canadensis* (Loew); and *Rhagoletis ribicola* Doane).
72.	Raw fruit from plants of the genus *Vaccinium* L.	(1) Where the consignment originates in a third country it shall be free from Blueberry Fruit Fly (*Rhagoletis menda* Curran). (2) Where the consignment has been directly consigned to Great Britain from a third country, in addition to complying with the requirement specified in paragraph (1) of this Item, it shall be free from Blueberry Canker and Dieback (*Diaporthe vaccinii* Shear).
73.	Raw fruit of grape vine (species, hybrids and cultivars of *Vitis* L.).	Where the consignment originates in a third country it shall be free from Vine Black Rot (*Guignardia bidwellii* (Ellis) Viala and Ravaz).

PART VI

CONDITIONS SUBJECT TO WHICH PARTICULAR RAW VEGETABLES MAY BE LANDED

Item (1)	Description of plants (2)	Conditions of landing (3)
74.	Raw vegetables from plants of:– celery (*Apium* L.) beets (*Beta* L.) cabbage, cauliflower, broccoli, turnip and other related vegetables (*Brassica* L.) chicory (*Cichorium* L.) carrot (*Daucus* L.) lettuce (*Lactuca* L.) parsley (*Petroselinum* L.) spinach (*Spinacia* L.) with foliage.	During the period 1 April to 14 October (both dates inclusive):– (a) the consignment shall be accompanied by a phytosanitary certificate and, as appropriate, one or more re-forwarding phytosanitary certificates; (b) an official statement shall have been made that the vegetables comprising it were either:– (i) grown under permanent structures of glass or plastic; or (ii) grown in a region known to be free from Colorado Beetle (*Leptinotarsa decemlineata* (Say)) since the beginning of the last complete cycle of vegetation; or (iii) grown in a region in which intensive measures were taken to control *L. decemlineata*, at least on:– –potatoes and egg plants (*Solanum melongena*) grown in the immediate vicinity of the vegetables; and –the vegetables, where potatoes or egg plants were grown as the immediately preceding crop;

SCHEDULE 3
PART VI (*cont.*)
RAW VEGETABLES

Item (1)	Description of plants (2)	Conditions of landing (3)
		unless no evidence of *L. decemlineata* has been observed on the vegetables during at least two official inspections carried out since the beginning of the last complete cycle of vegetation; and
		(c) an official statement shall have been made that the vegetables comprising it have been cleaned, packed and transported in a manner such as to avoid any contamination with *L. decemlineata*.
75.	Raw vegetables from plants of:– onion, leek (*Allium* L.) celery (*Apium* L.) beets (*Beta* L.) cabbage, cauliflower, broccoli, turnip and other related vegetables (*Brassica* L.) carrot (*Daucus* L.) lettuce (*Lactuca* L.) parsnip (*Pastinaca* L.) peas (*Pisum* L.) radish (*Raphanus* L.) spinach (*Spinacia* L.) and beans (*Vicia* L. and *Phaseolus* L.).	Where the consignment has been directly consigned to Great Britain from a third country it shall:– (a) be accompanied by a phytosanitary certificate and, as appropriate, one or more reforwarding phytosanitary certificates; (b) be free from Corticium Rot (*Corticium rolfsii* Curzi (syn. *Sclerotium rolfsii* Sacc.)); and (c) be free from soil.

PART VII

CONDITIONS SUBJECT TO WHICH CUT FLOWERS AND PARTS OF PLANTS FOR DECORATION MAY BE LANDED

PART VIIA

GENERAL CONDITIONS

Item (1)	Description of plants (2)	Conditions of landing (3)
76.	All cut flowers and parts of plants for decoration.	(1) The consignment shall be free from the plant pests specified in Part I of Schedule 1 other than Carnation Tortrix Moth (*Cacoecimorpha pronubana* (Hübner)) and African Carnation Tortrix Moth (*Epichoristodes acerbella* (Walker)) and, where appropriate, from the plant pests specified in Part II of that Schedule. (2) The consignment shall be substantially free from *Cacoecimorpha pronubana* and *Epichoristodes acerbella* during the period 16 October to 30 April (both dates inclusive) and free from those plant pests during the period 1 May to 15 October (both dates inclusive).

PART VIIB

ADDITIONAL CONDITIONS APPLYING IN THE CASE OF CUT FLOWERS AND PARTS OF PLANTS FOR DECORATION OF STATICE AND OF THE GENERA *DENDRANTHEMA, DIANTHUS, GLADIOLUS, GYPSOPHILA, PROTEA, PRUNUS, ROSA, SALIX, SYRINGA* AND *VITIS*

Item (1)	Description of plants (2)	Conditions of landing (3)
77.	Cut flowers and parts of plants for decoration of the genera *Dendranthema* (DC.) Des Moulins (including florists' chrysanthemum) *Dianthus* L. *Gladiolus* L. *Gypsophila* L. *Prunus* L. *Rosa* L. *Salix* L. *Syringa* L. *Vitis* L.	The consignment shall be accompanied by a phytosanitary certificate and, as appropriate, one or more re-forwarding phytosanitary certificates.
78.	Cut flowers of *Dendranthema* (DC.) Des Moulins (including florist's chrysanthemum)	(1) Where the consignment is of cut flowers originating in the Netherlands:– (a) the crop from which the flowers were taken shall have been produced in nurseries which meet the following requirements:– (i) the nurseries shall have been officially approved for producing plants upon official statement –that no symptoms of Chrysanthemum White Rust (*Puccinia horiana* P. Henn) have been observed on plants grown or stored there, in at least two official inspections, the first carried out following the application for approval and the second carried out one month after the first, and –that any earlier approval has not ceased within two months prior to the application for approval; and (ii) no symptoms of *Puccinia horiana* have been observed on plants grown or stored in the nurseries during regular official inspections carried out as frequently as necessary in the light of the seasonal risk of infection; and (iii) the nurseries have not automatically ceased to be officially approved by virtue of paragraph 2 of Article 1 of Commission Decision 84/58/EEC(a); (b) the cut flowers shall since their production have been continuously kept separate from plants of chrysanthemum produced in nurseries other than those complying with the requirements of sub-paragraph (a) above in such a way as to avoid any risk of contami-

---

(a) OJ No. L35, 7.2.84, p.20.

SCHEDULE 3
PART VIIB (*cont.*)
CUT FLOWERS ETC.

Item (1)	Description of plants (2)	Conditions of landing (3)
		nation with *Puccinia horiana* through such material;
		(c) the plants shall have been maintained under a fungicidal regime appropriate to ensure freedom from *Puccinia horiana* having regard to the cultivars and in the light of the seasonal risk of infection;
		(d) the flowers shall have been packed, on arrival at the first place of public sale at the latest, in boxes each of which was marked with a sign indicating that no symptoms of *Puccinia horiana* were found, in appropriate examination carried out by qualified persons, on the flowers packed in the box;
		(e) the examination provided for in Article 6 of Directive 77/93/EEC(a) shall have been made on samples taken from each lot in accordance with the requirements of the Plant Protection Organisation of the Netherlands, with regard to the size of the lot and in the light of the seasonal risk of infection; for the purposes of this paragraph, "lot" means a consignment consisting of a single variety of chrysanthemums produced by a single grower;
		(f) the examination referred to in sub-paragraph (e) above shall also have been carried out for the purpose of ascertaining whether the conditions in sub-paragraphs (a) to (d) above were complied with;
		(g) each of the boxes or other packing units into which the flowers were packed for export shall have been marked with the number of the phytosanitary certificate or another mark or marks enabling an authorised officer of the Plant Protection Services of the Netherlands and Great Britain to identify the nursery or nurseries in which the flowers packed in the box or packing unit were produced; and
		(h) the phytosanitary certificate shall state under "Additional Declaration": "The consignment meets the requirements laid down in Commission Decision 84/58/EEC".
		(2) Where the consignment originates in a third country, an official statement shall have been made:–
		(a) either that the crop from which the flowers were taken was grown in a country in which *Puccinia horiana* is not known to occur; or
		(b) that the crop from which the flowers were taken was officially inspected and found to be free from *P. horiana*.

(a) OJ No. L26, 31.1.77, p.20.

Item (1)	Description of plants (2)	Conditions of landing (3)
79.	Cut flowers of gladiolus (*Gladiolus* L.).	(1) Where the consignment has been directly consigned to Great Britain from a Member State an official statement shall have been made:– (a) either that the plants comprising it were grown in a country which is known to be free from Gladiolus Rust (*Uromyces* spp.); or (b) that the plants comprising it were grown at a place of production at which no symptoms of *Uromyces* spp. have been observed during at least one official inspection carried out since the beginning of the last complete cycle of vegetation. (2) Where the consignment has been directly consigned to Great Britain from a third country:– (a) either an official statement shall have been made that the plants comprising it were grown in a country which is known to be free from *Uromyces* spp.; or (b) it shall be landed in Great Britain during the period 1 November to 30 April (both dates inclusive) and an official statement shall have been made that the plants comprising it were grown at a place of production at which no symptoms of *Uromyces* spp. have been observed during at least one official inspection carried out since the beginning of the last complete cycle of vegetation.
80.	Cut flowers of statice (*Limonium* Mill.).	Where the consignment has been directly consigned to Great Britain from a third country it shall:– (a) be accompanied by a phytosanitary certificate and, as appropriate, one or more re-forwarding phytosanitary certificates; and (b) be free from Limonium Leaf Spot (*Cercospora insulana* (Sacc.) Vassilijevesky).
81.	Cut flowers of the genus *Protea* L.	Where the consignment has been directly consigned to Great Britain from a third country it shall be accompanied by a phytosanitary certificate and, as appropriate, one or more re-forwarding phytosanitary certificates.

Article 12

SCHEDULE 4

EXPORTS OF PLANTS AND GROWING MEDIUM TO MEMBER STATES

PART I

PLANTS AND GROWING MEDIUM TO BE ACCOMPANIED BY A PHYTOSANITARY CERTIFICATE OR A REFORWARDING PHYTOSANITARY CERTIFICATE ISSUED IN GREAT BRITAIN WHEN EXPORTED OR RE-EXPORTED TO A MEMBER STATE, AND BY A PHYTOSANITARY CERTIFICATE ISSUED IN THE COUNTRY OF ORIGIN WHEN RE-EXPORTED TO A MEMBER STATE

Item (1)	Description of plants and growing medium (2)
1.	Plants planted or intended for planting other than seeds and aquarium plants.
2.	Seeds of lucerne (*Medicago sativa* L.), peas (*Pisum sativum* L.), tomato (*Lycopersicon lycopersicum* (L.) Karsten ex Farwell and hybrids and cultivars thereof) and of the genera *Rubus* L. and *Prunus* L.
3.	Cut flowers and other parts of plants intended to be used for decoration derived from plants of the genera:– *Chrysanthemum* L. *Dendranthema* (DC.) Des Moulins (including florists' chrysanthemum) *Dianthus* L. *Gladiolus* L. *Gypsophila* L. *Prunus* L. *Rosa* L. *Salix* L. *Syringa* L. *Vitis* L.
4.	Raw fruit from plants of the genera:– *Citrus* L., other than lemons (*Citrus limon* (L.) Burm.) and citron (*Citrus medica* L.) *Cydonia* Mill. *Malus* Mill. *Prunus* L. *Pyrus* L.
5.	Tubers of potato.
6.	(a) Soil and growing medium not attached to or associated with plants, other than that composed entirely of inorganic substances or unused peat; and (b) soil and growing medium:– (i) attached to or associated with plants; and (ii) originating in countries outside the Euro-Mediterranean area.

PART II

PLANTS TO BE ACCOMPANIED BY A PHYTOSANITARY CERTIFICATE ISSUED IN THE COUNTRY OF ORIGIN WHEN RE-EXPORTED TO A MEMBER STATE

Seeds of soya bean (*Glycine max* (L.) Merrill) for planting, for export to Greece, Spain, France, Italy or Portugal; seeds of cotton (*Gossypium* L.) for planting, for export to Greece or Spain.

SCHEDULE 5   Article 3

MEANING OF "DIRECTIVE 77/93/EEC"

INSTRUMENTS AMENDING COUNCIL DIRECTIVE 77/93/EEC

Instrument	*Reference*
Act concerning the conditions of accession of the Hellenic Republic and the adjustment of the Treaties	OJ No. L291, 19.11.79, p.86.
Council Directive 80/392/EEC	OJ No. L100, 17.4.80, p.32.
Council Directive 80/393/EEC	OJ No. L100, 17.4.80, p.35.
Council Directive 81/7/EEC	OJ No. L14, 16.1.81, p.23.
Council Directive 84/378/EEC	OJ No. L207, 2.8.84, p.1.
Council Directive 85/173/EEC	OJ No. L65, 6.3.85, p.23.
Council Regulation (EEC) No. 3768/85	OJ No. L362, 31.12.85, p.8.
Council Directive 85/574/EEC	OJ No. L372, 31.12.85, p.25.
Commission Directive 86/545/EEC	OJ No. L323, 18.11.86, p.14.
Commission Directive 86/547/EEC	OJ No. L323, 18.11.86, p.21.
Council Directive 86/651/EEC	OJ No. L382, 31.12.86, p.13.
Council Directive 87/298/EEC	OJ No. L151, 11.6.87, p.1.

Article 3

SCHEDULE 6

FORM OF PHYTOSANITARY CERTIFICATE

1 Name and address of exporter	2 PHYTOSANITARY CERTIFICATE No EEC / /
3 Declared name and address of consignee	4 Plant Protection Organization of to Plant Protection Organization(s) of
	5 Place of origin
6 Declared means of conveyance	
7 Declared point of entry	

8 Distinguishing marks: number and description of packages; name of produce; botanical name of plants	9 Quantity declared

10 This is to certify that the plants or plant products described above
  – have been inspected according to appropriate procedures, and
  – are considered to be free from quarantine pests and practically free from other injurious pests; and
  – are considered to conform with the current phytosanitary regulations of the importing country

11 Additional declaration

DISINFESTATION AND/OR DISINFECTION TREATMENT	Place of issue
12 Treatment	Date Name and signature of authorized officer Stamp of Organization
13 Chemical (active ingredient) 14 Duration and temperature	
15 Concentration 16 Date	
17 Additional information	

Note: The certificate shall be completed in typescript or in block capitals.

SCHEDULE 7   Article 3

FORM OF RE-FORWARDING PHYTOSANITARY CERTIFICATE

1 Name and address of exporter	2 PHYTOSANITARY CERTIFICATE No EEC / /
3 Declared name and address of consignee	4 Plant Protection Organization of to Plant Protection Organization(s) of
	5 Place of origin
6 Declared means of conveyance	
7 Declared point of entry	

8 Distinguishing marks: number and description of packages; name of produce; botanical name of plants	9 Quantity declared

10 This is to certify that the plants or plant products described above
    – have been inspected according to appropriate procedures, and
    – are considered to be free from quarantine pests and practically free from other injurious pests; and
    – are considered to conform with the current phytosanitary regulations of the importing country

11 Additional declaration

DISINFESTATION AND/OR DISINFECTION TREATMENT		Place of issue
12 Treatment		
13 Chemical (active ingredient)	14 Duration and temperature	Date Name and signature of authorized officer Stamp of Organization
15 Concentration	16 Date	
17 Additional information		

Note: The certificate shall be completed in typescript or in block capitals.

Article 15

SCHEDULE 8

PLANT PESTS IN RESPECT OF WHICH PREMISES MAY BE DECLARED INFECTED

Globodera rostochiensis (Wollenweber) Behrens, *Globodera pallida* (Stone) Behrens, Potato Cyst Nematodes.

Leptinotarsa decemlineata (Say), Colorado Beetle.

Phytophthora fragariae Hickman, the cause of Red Core Disease of Strawberries, other than in Scotland.

Synchytrium endobioticum (Schilb.) Perc., the cause of Wart Disease of Potatoes.

Heterodera schachtii Schmidt, Beet Cyst Nematode.

SCHEDULE 9

Article 2

REVOCATIONS

Orders revoked	References
The Silver Leaf (Scotland) Order of 1922	S.R.&O. 1922/112.
The Colorado Beetle Order of 1933	S.R.&O. 1933/830.
The Colorado Beetle (Scotland) Order 1933	S.R.&O. 1933/838.
The Narcissus Pests (Cornwall) Order of 1935	S.R.&O. 1935/1328.
The Cabbage Aphis (Bedfordshire, Cambridgeshire and Huntingdonshire) Order of 1936	S.R.&O. 1936/120.
The Woolly Aphis (Scotland) Order 1947	S.R.&O. 1947/1065.
The Blackcurrant Mite (Scotland) Order 1947	S.R.&O. 1947/2304.
The Colorado Beetle (Amendment) Order 1950	S.I. 1950/411.
The Colorado Beetle (Amendment) (Scotland) Order 1950	S.I. 1950/964.
The Blackcurrant Reversion (Scotland) Order 1952	S.I. 1952/225.
The Red Core Disease of Strawberry Plants Order 1957	S.I. 1957/753.
The Fire Blight Disease Order 1958	S.I. 1958/1814.
The Fire Blight Disease (Amendment) Order 1960	S.I. 1960/1557.
The Fire Blight Disease (Amendment) Order 1966	S.I. 1966/162.
The Examination of Seed Potatoes (Scotland) Order 1970	S.I. 1970/1287.
The Potato Cyst Eelworm (Great Britain) Order 1973	S.I. 1973/1059.
The Wart Disease of Potatoes (Great Britain) Order 1973	S.I. 1973/1060.
The Prevention of Spread of Pests (Seed Potatoes) (Great Britain) Order 1974	S.I. 1974/1152.
The Wart Disease of Potatoes (Great Britain) (Amendment) Order 1974	S.I. 1974/1159.
The Mediterranean Carnation Leaf Roller (Great Britain) Order 1975	S.I. 1975/1842.
The Plum Pox (Sharka Disease) Order 1975	S.I. 1975/2225.
The Beet Cyst Nematode Order 1977	S.I. 1977/988.
The Progressive Wilt Disease of Hops Order 1978	S.I. 1978/505.
The Import and Export (Plant Health) (Great Britain) Order 1980	S.I. 1980/420.
The Plant Pests (Great Britain) Order 1980	S.I. 1980/499.
The Progressive Wilt Disease of Hops (Amendment) Order 1981	S.I. 1981/1170.
The Vegetable Produce (Temporary Prohibition on Landing) (Great Britain) Order 1982	S.I. 1982/599.
The Progressive Wilt Disease of Hops (Amendment) Order 1983	S.I. 1983/1485.

SCHEDULE 9
REVOCATIONS (*cont.*)

Orders revoked	References
The Import and Export (Plant Health) (Great Britain) (Amendment) Order 1984	S.I. 1984/306.
The Parsley (Temporary Prohibition on Landing) (Great Britain) Order 1984	S.I. 1984/416.
The Import and Export (Plant Health) (Great Britain) (Amendment) (No. 2) Order 1984	S.I. 1984/839.
The Chrysanthemum (Temporary Prohibition on Landing) (Great Britain) Order 1984	S.I. 1984/1871.
The Fire Blight Disease (Scotland) Order 1985	S.I. 1985/637.
The Import and Export (Plant Health) (Great Britain) (Amendment) Order 1985	S.I. 1985/873.
The Import and Export (Plant Health) (Great Britain) (Amendment) (No. 2) Order 1985	S.I. 1985/1230.
The Plant Pests (Great Britain) (Amendment) Order 1986	S.I. 1986/194.
The Import and Export (Plant Health) (Great Britain) (Amendment) Order 1986	S.I. 1986/195.
The Import and Export (Plant Health) (Great Britain) (Amendment) (No. 2) Order 1986	S.I. 1986/1135.
The Potatoes (Prohibition on Landing) (Great Britain) Order 1987	S.I. 1987/19.
The Import and Export (Plant Health) (Great Britain) (Amendment) Order 1987	S.I. 1987/428.
The Import and Export (Plant Health) (Great Britain) (Amendment) (No. 2) Order 1987	S.I. 1987/1679.

EXPLANATORY NOTE

(This note is not part of the Order)

This Order, which applies to Great Britain, revokes and supersedes the Import and Export (Plant Health) (Great Britain) Order 1980, the Plant Pests (Great Britain) Order 1980 and various other Orders listed in Schedule 9. The Order (together with Orders made by the Forestry Commission) implements Council Directive 77/93/EEC (as amended by the instruments listed in Schedule 5) on protective measures against the introduction into the Member States of organisms harmful to plants or plant products, Council Directive 69/465/EEC (OJ No. L323, 24.12.69, p.3) (OJ/SE 1969 (II), p.563) on the control of potato cyst eelworm and Council Directive 69/464/EEC (OJ No. L323, 24.12.69, p.1) (OJ/SE 1969 (II), p.561) on the control of potato wart disease. The Order also imposes controls in respect of the import of agricultural machinery, genetically manipulated material and plants in tissue culture, in respect of direct trade in plants etc. with countries other than Member States and contains additional provisions to prevent the spread of plant pests in Great Britain.

The Order–

(a) prohibits the landing of certain plant pests, plants, plant products, agricultural machinery, soil, growing medium and genetically manipulated material and specifies conditions under which other polants etc. may be landed (article 4);

(b) prohibits the keeping, sale, planting, release, delivery or other disposal of certain plant pests, plants etc. and prohibits work involving genetic manipulation of a plant pest or genetically manipulated material (article 5);

(c) contains various provisions concerning phytosanitary certificates and re-forwarding phytosanitary certificates (articles 3 and 6 to 11);

(d) provides that certain plants etc. may be landed without a phytosanitary certificate if they are landed in the baggage of passengers or if they are directly consigned to Great Britain from Northern Ireland, the Channel Islands or the Isle of Man (article 8);

(e) requires that certain plants and growing medium when exported to a Member State are to be accompanied by a phytosanitary certificate or a re-forwarding phytosanitary certificate (article 12);

(f) requires notification of the presence of certain plant pests, plants etc. (articles 13 and 14);

(g) enables plant health inspectors to take remedial or precautionary action where certain plant pests, plants etc. are or are likely to be landed in contravention of the Order or where certain plant pests, plants etc. are or are likely to be present on premises (article 15);

(h) enables plant health inspectors to declare premises infected with certain plant pests and, in the case of wart disease of potatoes, to declare premises a safety zone (article 15(4) and (5));

(i) enables plant health inspectors to enter premises, carry out examinations and take samples and to take remedial action where the requirements of notices served under the Order have not been complied with (articles 17 and 19);

(j) restricts the planting and movement of potatoes (articles 21 and 22);

(k) contains additional provisions to prevent spread of Colorado Beetle, red core disease of strawberries, fire blight disease, potato cyst nematode, wart disease of potatoes, beet cyst nematode and progressive wilt disease (articles 23 to 41);

(l) provides that anything prohibited by the Order may be done under the authority of a licence (article 42);

(m) provides that officers of the Customs and Excise may detain plants, plant products etc. for examination by a plant health inspector (article 44);

(n) enables a plant health inspector to seek information in respect of certain plant pests, plants, plant products etc. (article 45);

(o) provides that the contravention of, or failure to comply with, any provisions of the Order (other than those relating to landing) shall be an offence punishable by a fine not exceeding £2,000 (articles 46 and 47). (Any person who lands articles in contravention of a prohibition imposed by this Order with intent to evade such prohibition is guilty of an offence under section 50(2) of the

Customs and Excise Management Act 1979 (c.2) and may be detained. A person guilty of such offence is liable, on summary conviction, to a penalty of £2,000 or of three times the value of the goods, whichever is the greater, or to imprisonment for a term not exceeding 6 months, or to both, and, on conviction on indictment, to a penalty of any amount, or to imprisonment for a term not exceeding 2 years, or to both.)

In addition to numerous minor and drafting amendments, the Order makes the following changes of substance–

1. the provisions of the Order as to imports of certain plants, plant products etc. apply not only where they are directly consigned to Great Britain from a third country but also where they reach Great Britain via a Member State (article 4 and Schedules 2 and 3);

2. the conditions as regards imports of certain trees and shrubs from New Zealand, of chrysanthemum cuttings from Malta and Canary Islands and of dahlias from third countries have been set out in the Order as opposed to the previous practice of setting them out in licences (articles 4 and Schedule 3, Parts IIB and IIC);

3. import controls on pea seeds have been extended to Certified Seed of the First Generation (article 4 and Schedule 2, Part III);

4. the import requirement that rooted plants etc. should have been grown at a place of production free from Western Flower Thrips has been removed although plants etc. (whether imported or not) are still required to be free from that pest (articles 4 and 5 and Schedule 1, Part I);

5. revised controls have been introduced in respect of the import of plants in tissue culture (articles 3 and 4 and Schedules 2 and 3);

6. Scotland and certain counties in the north of England have been designated as the fire blight free region so as to provide protection in that region against fire blight (articles 5, 13 and 30 and Schedule 1, Part III);

7. the provisions concerning plants and plant products which may be landed in a passenger's baggage without a phytosanitary certificate have been revised (article 8);

8. re-exports of certain plants etc. to Member States are now required to be accompanied by the phytosanitary certificate issued in the country of origin as well as a re-forwarding phytosanitary certificate (article 12 and Schedule 4);

9. the requirement to notify the presence of plant pests has been extended to persons who become aware of such presence in the course of their duties or business (article 13);

10. notification by the responsible authority is required of the likely entry into, or presence in, a free zone of imported plant pests, plants etc. (article 14);

11. entry to private dwellings may be obtained only under the authority of a warrant granted by a justice of the peace or sheriff (article 20);

12. the planting of the hop varieties Omega, Wye Target and Wye Yeoman outside "the specified area" is no longer prohibited (article 41);

13. the maximum fine which may be imposed for an offence under the Order has been increased to £2,000 (article 47) (the provision enabling the imposition of 3 months imprisonment for offences relating to Colorado Beetle has not been re-enacted);

14. generally, the protection afforded by the Order has been strengthened and its import controls have been extended to additional plants and to give protection against numerous additional plant pests (details of the changes may be obtained, free of charge, from Plant Health Division, Ministry of Agriculture, Fisheries and Food, Great Westminster House, Horseferry Road, London SW1P 2AE; Potatoes and Plant Health Branch, Department of Agriculture and Fisheries for Scotland (DAFS), Chesser House, 500 Gorgie Road, Edinburgh EH11 3AW; the plant health inspectorate in England and Wales and DAFS area offices in Scotland).

STATUTORY INSTRUMENTS

1987 No. 1759 (C.53)

TOWN AND COUNTRY PLANNING, ENGLAND AND WALES

The Housing and Planning Act 1986 (Commencement No. 8) Order 1987

Made - - - -	*1st October 1987*

The Secretary of State for the Environment, as respects England, and the Secretary of State for Wales, as respects Wales, in exercise of the powers conferred on them by section 57(2) of the Housing and Planning Act 1986(**a**), and of all other powers enabling them in that behalf, hereby make the following Order:

1.   This Order may be cited as the Housing and Planning Act 1986 (Commencement No. 8) Order 1987.

2.   The provisions of the Housing and Planning Act 1986 listed below shall come into force on 2nd November 1987–

section 25

section 41(1) and (2)

section 41(3)

section 49(1) (insofar as it relates to paragraphs 15, 23, 26 and 27 of Schedule 11 to that Act)

section 49(2) (insofar as it relates to the repeals specified in the Schedule to this Order).

Transitional provisions

3.—(1) Section 11A(7)(a) of the Town and Country Planning Act 1971(**b**) shall not apply in relation to proposals for the making, alteration, repeal or replacement of a local plan where the local planning authority have taken steps to prepare those proposals before the coming into force of that provision.

(2) Any direction given by the Secretary of State under section 15A(6) of the Town and Country Planning Act 1971 in force immediately before the making of this Order shall continue in force so far as it requires modifications to be made to the local plan or to proposals for the alteration, repeal or replacement of such a plan.

(**a**) 1986 c.63.   (**b**) 1971 c.78.

1st October 1987

Nicholas Ridley
Secretary of State for the Environment

1st October 1987

Peter Walker
Secretary of State for Wales

Article 2

SCHEDULE
ENACTMENTS REPEALED

Chapter	Short title	Extent of repeal
1972 c.70.	Local Government Act 1972.	Section 183(2). In Schedule 16, paragraphs 1 to 3.
1980 c.65.	Local Government, Planning and Land Act 1980.	Section 88.
1982 c.30.	Local Government (Miscellaneous Provisions) Act 1982.	In Schedule 6, in the table in paragraph 7(b), the entries relating to sections 15 and 15A of the Town and Country Planning Act 1971.

EXPLANATORY NOTE

(This note is not part of the Order)

This Order brings into force on 2nd November 1987 certain provisions of the Housing and Planning Act 1986.

In Part II of the 1986 Act, section 25 (simplified planning zones in England and Wales) is brought into force together with Parts I and II of Schedule 6 to which the section gives effect. The Town and Country Planning (Simplified Planning Zones) Regulations 1987 (S.I. 1987/1750) come into force on the same date.

In Part VI of the 1986 Act, the following provisions are brought into force–

section 41(1) and (2) which with Part I of Schedule 10 substitute (except in Greater London) new provisions for sections 10C to 15B of the Town and Country Planning Act 1971 (procedure relating to development plans);

section 41(3) which with Part II of Schedule 10 amends the Local Government Act 1985 (c.51) (unitary development plans);

section 49(1) and (2) so far as they make certain amendments and repeals consequential on the other provisions brought into force by this Order.

Article 3 makes transitional provision for local plans.

NOTE AS TO EARLIER COMMENCEMENT ORDERS

(This note is not part of the Order)

The following provisions of the Act have been brought into force by commencement orders made before the date of this Order–

Provision	Date of commencement	S.I. No.
sections 1 to 4 sections 10 to 14 sections 16 and 17 sections 19 and 20 sections 22 and 23 sections 24 (partially) Part III (ss. 27–29) Part VI (partially)	7th January 1987	1986/2262
section 49 (insofar as it relates to paragraph 8 of Schedule II and certain repeals)	2nd March 1987	1987/304
section 40 section 49(2)	1st April 1987	1987/348
section 9	13th May 1987	1987/754
section 24(1) (in so far as it relates to paragraph 8 of Schedule 5)	1st September 1987	1987/1554
sections 26, 50 and 51	1st October 1987	1987/1607

1987 No. 1760

TOWN AND COUNTRY PLANNING, ENGLAND AND WALES

The Town and Country Planning (Structure and Local Plans) (Amendment) Regulations 1987

Made - - - -	*1st October 1987*
Laid before Parliament	*12th October 1987*
Coming into force	*2nd November 1987*

The Secretary of State for the Environment, as respects England, and the Secretary of State for Wales, as respects Wales, in exercise of the powers conferred on them by sections 12A(4), 18, 287(1) and 290(1) of the Town and Country Planning Act 1971(a), and of all other powers enabling them in that behalf, hereby make the following Regulations:

Citation and commencement

1. These Regulations may be cited as the Town and Country Planning (Structure and Local Plans) (Amendment) Regulations 1987 and shall come into force on 2nd November 1987.

Amendment of existing Regulations

2. The Town and Country Planning (Structure and Local Plans) Regulations 1982 (b) shall have effect subject to the amendments set out in the Schedule.

1st October 1987

Nicholas Ridley
Secretary of State for the Environment

1st October 1987

Peter Walker
Secretary of State for Wales

(a) 1971 c.78; new sections 11 to 15B were substituted by section 41(1) of, and Part I of Schedule 10 to, the Housing and Planning Act 1986 (c.63). As to section 290(1), *see* the definition of "prescribed".
(b) S.I. 1982/555, as amended by S.I. 1986/443.

SCHEDULE

AMENDMENT OF THE TOWN AND COUNTRY PLANNING (STRUCTURE AND LOCAL PLANS) REGULATIONS 1982

1. Subject to the following provisions of this Schedule, for any existing reference to a subsection specified in the first column substitute a reference to the corresponding subsection specified in the second column–

Existing reference	Substituted reference
11(3)	11(1)
11(4A)	11(5)
12(1)	12(2)
12(2)	12(4)
12(3)	12B(1)
12(4)	12B(3)
12(5)	12B(4)
14(1A)	14(6)
14(3)	14A(1)
14(3A)	14A(3)
14(5)	15(2)

2. In regulation 29(2), insert at the end "or, if applicable, regulation 32A(2).".

3. In regulation 30(1), omit from "by" to "Act".

4. In regulation 31(1), after "modify it", insert "whether in response to a direction under section 14(4) of the Act (direction to reconsider proposals) or otherwise,".

5. After regulation 31, insert a new regulation 31A–

"Procedure where direction under section 14(4) is given

31A. Where the Secretary of State has given the authority a direction under section 14(4) of the Act, they shall send to the Secretary of State a statement of the modifications made to conform with the direction and the reasons for them or, as the case may be, a statement of their reasons for not modifying the plan.".

6. In regulation 32(2), for "14(1A)" substitute "14(5) and (6)".

7. After regulation 32 insert–

"Procedure where direction under section 14(4) is subsequent to certificate

32A.—(1) This regulation applies where, after receiving the certificate mentioned in regulation 32(2) and before the local plan is adopted, the Secretary of State has given the local planning authority a direction under section 14(4) of the Act and the authority have sent to the Secretary of State a statement of the modifications made to conform with the direction and the reasons for them or, as the case may be, a statement of their reasons for not modifying the plan.

(2) When the Secretary of State notifies the authority that he is satisfied that they have made the modifications necessary to conform with the direction, or the direction is withdrawn, they shall, before adopting the plan, again comply with regulation 32(1) and (2); and they shall, when again giving notice under regulation 32(1), make certified copies of the direction, the statement sent pursuant to regulation 31A and the Secretary of State's notification available for inspection.".

8. In regulation 36(1), for "12(2)" substitute "12(4) or (5)".

9. In regulation 39(1)(b) omit "as applied by section 15(3)".

10. For regulation 41 substitute–

"**Alteration, repeal or replacement of local plans**

    41.   These Regulations apply–

      (a) in relation to proposals for the alteration, repeal or replacement of a local plan as they apply to a local plan, with such modifications as are necessary, and

      (b) in relation to proposals to alter, repeal or replace a local plan made in accordance with section 12A of the Act (short procedure for certain alterations etc) with the following additional modifications and provisions–

         (i) any reference to a provision of section 12 or 12B(1) of the Act shall be treated as a reference to the corresponding provision of section 12A or 12B(2), as the case may be;

        (ii) an explanation of the local authority's reasons for proceeding in accordance with section 12A shall be included in the statement required to be sent to the Secretary of State by section 12B(2);

      (iii) the notice to be given in Form 7 shall include an invitation to make representations about the authority's proposals within the prescribed period and a notice in similar terms shall be given to persons who may be expected to make such representations;

      (iv) the prescribed period for the purposes of section 12A(4) shall be a period of six weeks beginning with the day on which notice in Form 7 is first published in a local newspaper.".

    11.   In the Schedule, for Form 12, substitute–

"FORM 12

Form of notice of disposition to adopt local plan

NOTICE OF DISPOSITION TO ADOPT LOCAL PLAN

Town and Country Planning Act 1971

(Title of local plan)

[To:] (8)

    (1) are disposed to adopt the above-named local plan [as modified by them] (3) on or after (11), unless, before the plan has been adopted, the Secretary of State for [the Environment] [Wales] (3) directs that the plan shall not be adopted until further notice or shall not have effect unless approved by him, or he [further] (3) directs the council to consider modifying the proposals in the plan.

    Certified copies of the plan [together with certified copies of the reports of all local inquiries or other hearings held] (12) and of the council's statements prepared following the consideration of [such reports] [objections] (3) have been deposited at (4).

    [The Secretary of State for [the Environment] [Wales] directed (1) to consider modifying the proposals in the plan. Certified copies of the direction and of the council's statement prepared following consideration of the direction and of the notification from the Secretary of State have also been deposited at (4).] (12)

    The deposited documents are available for inspection free of charge (5).

    .... 19 ...   . (Signature)".

EXPLANATORY NOTE

(This note is not part of the Regulations)

    These Regulations amend the Town and Country Planning (Structure and Local Plans) Regulations 1982 to take into account the provisions of the Housing and Planning Act 1986. The Act allows simplified procedures to be followed where a local planning authority propose to alter, repeal or replace a local plan and it appears to them that the issues involved are not of sufficient importance to warrant the full procedure set out in section 12 of the Town and Country Planning Act 1971, and permits the Secretary of State to direct a local planning authority to consider modifying local plan proposals. The amendments made take account of these changes and also amend the 1982 Regulations to reflect the re-numbering of sections of the 1971 Act brought about by the 1986 Act.

STATUTORY INSTRUMENTS

1987 No. 1762 (C. 54)

FIRE PRECAUTIONS
SPORTS GROUNDS AND SPORTING EVENTS

The Fire Safety and Safety of Places of Sport Act 1987 (Commencement No. 1) Order 1987

Made -	-	-	*6th October 1987*

In exercise of the powers conferred on me by section 50(2) of the Fire Safety and Safety of Places of Sport Act 1987**(a)**, I hereby make the following Order:

1. This Order may be cited as the Fire Safety and Safety of Places of Sport Act 1987 (Commencement No. 1) Order 1987.

2. The provisions of the Fire Safety and Safety of Places of Sport Act 1987 specified in the Schedule to this Order shall come into force on 1st January 1988.

Home Office
6th October 1987

Douglas Hurd
One of Her Majesty's Principal Secretaries of State

SCHEDULE

Article 2

PROVISIONS OF THE FIRE SAFETY AND SAFETY OF PLACES OF SPORT ACT 1987 COMING INTO FORCE ON 1st JANUARY 1988

Provisions of the Act	*Subject matter of provisions*
In Part I:	
Section 3	Charges for fire certification work
Section 4	Means of escape: scope of regulation
Section 8	Duties as regards safety pending determination of applications for fire certificates
Section 9	Special procedure in case of serious risk: prohibition notices
Section 11	Disclosure of information obtained in premises
Section 12	Civil and other liability
Section 13	Removal of exemption for premises used for public religious worship

(a) 1987 c.27.

Provisions of the Act	*Subject matter of provisions*
Section 14	Breaches of fire certificate requirements: restriction of defence
In section 16, subsection (1), subsection (2) to the extent necessary to give effect to the provisions of Schedule 1 specified in this Schedule, and subsection (3)	Special provision for certain premises
Section 17	Extension of power to apply the Fire Precautions Act 1971(a)
In section 18, so much of subsections (1), (2) and (3) as amends section 40 of the Fire Precautions Act 1971 by providing–	Application to the Crown
(a) that in subsection (1)(a) of that section after "4" there shall be inserted "5(2A)"; and	
(b) that in subsection (1)(b) of that section after "8" there shall be inserted "8B" and after "10" there shall be inserted "10B"	
Part II	Safety of sports grounds
In Part V:	
Section 46	Entertainment licences: fees for variation
Section 49, to the extent necessary to give effect to such of the repeals in Schedule 4 and provisions of Schedule 5 as are specified in this Schedule and the Appendix to this Schedule	Repeals and transitional and saving provisions
In section 50, subsections (1), (2) and (3) and so much of subsections (4) to (7) as has effect in relation to Part II of the Act	Short title, commencement and extent
In Schedule 1, Part I of Schedule 2 to the Fire Precautions Act 1971 and, in Part II of Schedule 2 to that Act, in paragraph 3, sub-paragraphs (1) and (2) and so much of sub-paragraph (3) as has effect in relation to the references to the occupier in sections 5(2A), 7(3A), 7(4) and 8B(1) of that Act	Fire precautions: special provision for certain premises
Schedule 2	Extension of application of Safety of Sports Grounds Act 1975(b) to sports grounds
In Schedule 4, so much of the entries as is specified in the Appendix to this Schedule	Repeals
In Schedule 5, paragraphs 1, 3, 4, 5, 6, 7 and 9	Transitional and saving provisions

(a) 1971 c.40.   (b) 1975 c.52.

APPENDIX TO THE SCHEDULE

REPEALS TAKING EFFECT ON 1st JANUARY 1988

Chapter	Short title	Extent of repeal
1971 c.40	Fire Precautions Act 1971	In section 2, the words from "of any of the following" to "any premises" where last occurring
		In section 12(1), the words "other than paragraph (d)"
		In section 43(1), in the definition of "the court", the words "and the Schedule thereto"
		Section 43(2)
1975 c.52	Safety of Sports Grounds Act 1975	Section 5(4), (6), (7) and (8)
		In section 7, in subsection (3), the words ", subject to subsection (4) below," and subsections (4) and (5)
		In section 12(2), the words "stadium or other"
		Section 15
		In section 17(1), the definition of "sports stadium"

EXPLANATORY NOTE

(This note is not part of the Order)

This Order brings into force on 1st January 1988 the provisions of the Fire Safety and Safety of Places of Sport Act 1987 specified in the Schedule to the Order.

1987 No. 1765

PENSIONS

The Personal Pension Schemes (Provisional Approval) Regulations 1987

Made - - - - - -	*8th October 1987*
Laid before the House of Commons	*8th October 1987*
Coming into force - - -	*29th October 1987*

The Commissioners of Inland Revenue, in exercise of the powers conferred on them by section 56(2) of the Finance (No. 2) Act 1987(a), hereby make the following Regulations:

Citation and commencement

1. These Regulations may be cited as the Personal Pension Schemes (Provisional Approval) Regulations 1987 and shall come into force on 29th October 1987.

Interpretation

2. In these Regulations unless the context otherwise requires–
   "Act" means the Finance (No. 2) Act 1987;
   "the Board" means the Commissioners of Inland Revenue;
   "scheme" means a personal pension scheme.

Provisional approval: conditions

3. Where an application to the Board for their approval of a scheme under section 19 of the Act is made before 1st August 1989 and is accompanied by–
   (a) written undertakings by the scheme administrator that–
      (i) to the best of his belief the application for approval, and the documents which accompany it, are in such form and contain such information that the scheme may be approved,
      (ii) the scheme does not make provision for any benefit other than those mentioned in sections 21 to 26 of the Act and that no member of the scheme will have a beneficial interest in the assets of the scheme, and
      (iii) the scheme will be administered in accordance with the provisions contained in Chapter II of Part I of the Act and any regulations made thereunder; and
   (b) a written undertaking by the person who has power to amend the rules of the scheme that he will comply with a notice given by the Board under regulation 4;
the Board may grant approval of the scheme provisionally notwithstanding that they have not satisfied themselves that the scheme complies with sections 20 to 30 of the Act.

(a) 1987 c.51.

Amendment of rules

4. If on examination of the application for approval, and the documents which accompany it, the Board are not satisfied that the scheme complies with the requirements of sections 20 to 30 of the Act the Board shall give written notice to the person who has power to amend the rules of the scheme requiring him within a period of 6 months from the date of the notice (or such further time as the Board may allow) to amend the rules of the scheme so that it complies with the requirements of those sections of the Act with effect as from the date of approval of the scheme.

Withdrawal of approval

5.—(1) If at the expiration of the period specified in regulation 4 (or at the end of such further time as the Board may have allowed) the Board are not satisfied that a scheme complies with sections 20 to 30 of the Act, the Board shall give written notice to the applicant for approval of the withdrawal of approval as from the date of approval of the scheme.

(2) A notice under paragraph (1) shall state the grounds on which approval is withdrawn.

Appeals

6.—(1) Where the Board withdraw an approval by notice under regulation 5(1) the applicant for approval may appeal to the Special Commissioners against the withdrawal.

(2) An appeal under this regulation shall be made by written notice stating the grounds for the appeal and given to the Board before the end of the period of 30 days beginning with the day on which notice of withdrawal was given to the appellant.

(3) The bringing of an appeal under this regulation shall not affect the validity of the withdrawal pending the determination of the proceedings.

(4) Part V of the Taxes Management Act 1970**(a)** (appeals and other proceedings) shall apply to an appeal under this regulation.

A. J. G. Isaac
D. B. Rogers
8th October 1987   Two of the Commissioners of Inland Revenue

---

EXPLANATORY NOTE

(This note is not part of the Regulations)

Section 19 of the Finance (No. 2) Act 1987 gives the Commissioners of Inland Revenue power on application to them to approve personal pension schemes established under Chapter II of Part I of that Act, and section 56(2) provides that the Commissioners may by regulations make provisions for the provisional approval of such schemes where applications are made before 1st August 1989 notwithstanding that the Commissioners have not satisfied themselves that the schemes comply with sections 20 to 30 of the Act.

Regulation 1 provides for commencement and citation, and regulation 2 for interpretation.

(a) 1970 c.9; relevant amendments were made to section 45 by the Finance Act 1984 (c.43), section 127 and Schedule 22, paragraph 2, and by section 128(6), and Schedule 23, Part XIII; to section 48 by the Finance (No. 2) Act 1975 (c.45), section 45(4); to section 50 by the Finance (No. 2) Act 1975, section 67(2); to section 53 by the Finance Act 1972 (c.41), section 129(1); to section 56 by the Finance (No. 2) Act 1975, section 45(3). Section 56A was inserted by the Finance Act 1984 (c.43), section 127 and Schedule 22, paragraph 7; and section 57B by the Finance Act 1984, section 127 and Schedule 22, paragraph 4.

Regulation 3 provides conditions subject to which provisional approval may be granted, and regulation 4 provides that in the circumstances there mentioned the Commissioners shall by notice, given to the person who has power to amend the rules of the scheme, require the rules of a scheme be amended so that it complies with sections 20 to 30 of the Act.

Regulation 5 provides that if at the expiration of the period specified in regulation 4 the Commissioners are not satisfied that a scheme complies with sections 20 to 30 of the Act, the Commissioners shall give notice to the applicant for approval of withdrawal of approval of the scheme as from the date of approval thereof; and regulation 6 provides a right of appeal against a notice under regulation 5.

STATUTORY INSTRUMENTS

1987 No. 1771

TRACTORS

The Agricultural or Forestry Tractors and Tractor Components (Type Approval) (Amendment) Regulations 1987

Made - - - -	*4th October 1987*
Laid before Parliament	*15th October 1987*
Coming into force	*5th November 1987*

The Minister of Agriculture, Fisheries and Food and the Secretary of State, being Ministers designated (a) for the purposes of section 2(2) of the European Communities Act 1972(b) in relation to any type approval scheme for agricultural or forestry tractors and their components, acting jointly, in exercise of the powers conferred on them by the said section 2(2), and of all their other enabling powers, hereby make the following Regulations:–

Title, commencement and interpretation

1.—(1) These Regulations may be cited as the Agricultural or Forestry Tractors and Tractor Components (Type Approval) (Amendment) Regulations 1987 and shall come into force on 5th November 1987.

(2) In these Regulations "the principal Regulations" means the Agricultural or Forestry Tractors and Tractor Components (Type Approval) Regulations 1979(c).

Amendment of the principal Regulations

2.—(1) Regulation 3(1) shall be amended by the substitution for the definition of "agricultural or forestry tractor" of the following definition–

" "agricultural or forestry tractor" means a tractor (whether or not equipped to carry a load of passengers) which–

(a) is a motor vehicle fitted with wheels and pneumatic tyres and having at least two axles, and

(b) is specially designed to tow, push, carry or power tools, machinery or trailers intended for agricultural or forestry use, and

(c) is designed so as to have a maximum speed of not less than 6, and not more than 30, kilometres per hour;

except that–

(i) in relation to the approval of a tractor in respect of its passenger seats, "agricultural or forestry tractor" means a tractor as defined above having a track width of at least 1,250 mm;

(ii) in relation to the approval of a tractor other than a narrow-track tractor in respect of its roll-over protection structure, "agricultural or forestry tractor" means a tractor as defined above–

(a) S.I. 1975/427.
(b) 1972 c. 68.
(c) S.I. 1979/221, amended by S.I. 1981/669, 1983/709.

   (aa) having clearance beneath the rear axle of not more than 1,000 mm,

   (ab) having a fixed or minimum adjustable track width of one of the driving axles of at least 1,150 mm,

   (ac) being capable of being fitted with a multipoint coupling device for detachable tools and a draw bar, and

   (ad) having a mass of 800 kilograms or more corresponding to the unladen weight of the tractor as defined in item 2.4 of Annex I to Council Directive 74/150/EEC(**a**) including the roll-over protection structure fitted in accordance with Council Directive 79/622/EEC(**b**) and tyres of the largest size recommended by the manufacturer; and

  (iii) in relation to the approval of a narrow-track tractor in respect of its roll-over protection structure, "agricultural or forestry tractor" means a tractor as defined above–

   (aa) having ground clearance of not more than 600 mm measured beneath the lowest points of the front or rear axles, allowing for the differential,

   (ab) having a fixed or minimum adjustable track width of one of the two axles of less than 1,150 mm,

   (ac) having the axles so set that the distance between the outer edges of the tyres on an axle with a fixed or minimum adjustable track width of less than 1,150 mm is never exceeded by the distance between the outer edges of the tyres on the other axle, and

   (ad) having a mass greater than 600 kilograms and corresponding to the unladen weight of the tractor as defined in item 2.4 of Annex I to Directive 74/150/EEC including the roll-over protection structure fixed in accordance with Council Directive 86/298/EEC(**c**) and tyres of the largest size recommended by the manufacturer;".

 (2) For Schedule 2 to the principal Regulations there shall be substituted the Schedule set out in the Schedule to these Regulations.

In witness whereof the Official Seal of the Minister of Agriculture, Fisheries and Food is hereunto affixed on 4th October 1987.

                 John MacGregor
           Minister of Agriculture, Fisheries and Food

                Sanderson of Bowden
30th September 1987   Minister of State, Scottish Office

(**a**) OJ No. L84, 28.3.74, p. 10; relevant amending instruments are Council Directives 79/694/EEC (OJ No. L205, 13.8.79, p. 17) and 82/890/EEC (OJ No. L378, 31.12.82, p. 45).

(**b**) OJ No. L179, 17.7.79, p. 1; the relevant amending instrument is Commission Directive 82/953/EEC (OJ No. L386, 31.12.82, p. 31).

(**c**) OJ No. L186, 8.7.86, p. 26.

SCHEDULE

Regulation 2(2)

SCHEDULE TO BE SUBSTITUTED FOR SCHEDULE 2 TO THE PRINCIPAL REGULATIONS

SCHEDULE 2

Regulation 3(1)

PART A

THE COMMUNITY DIRECTIVES WITH RESPECT TO THE DESIGN, CONSTRUCTION, EQUIPMENT AND MARKING OF TRACTORS.

(1) *Community reference number*	(2) *Date of directive*	(3) *Subject matter*	(4) *Official Journal reference*
74/151/EEC(**a**)	4th March 1974	The maximum permissible laden weight, location/fitting of rear registration plates, fuel tanks, ballast weights, audible warning devices, and permissible sound level/silencer.	OJ No. L84 (28.3.74) p. 25
74/152/EEC(**a**)	4th March 1974	Maximum design speeds and load platforms.	OJ No. L84 (28.3.74) p. 33
74/346/EEC(**a**)	25th June 1974	Rear view mirrors.	OJ No. L191 (15.7.74) p. 1
74/347/EEC(**a**)(**b**)	25th June 1974	Field of vision and windscreen wipers.	OJ No. L191 (15.7.74) p. 5
75/321/EEC(**a**)	20th May 1975	Steering equipment.	OJ No. L147 (9.6.75) p. 24
75/322/EEC(**a**)	20th May 1975	Radio interference suppressors.	OJ No. L147 (9.6.75) p. 28
76/432/EEC(**a**)	6th April 1976	Braking devices.	OJ No. L122 (8.5.76) p. 1
76/763/EEC(**a**)	27th July 1976	Passenger seats.	OJ No. L262 (27.9.76) p. 135
77/311/EEC(**a**)	29th March 1977	Driver-perceived noise level.	OJ No. L105 (28.4.77) p. 1
77/536/EEC	28th June 1977	Roll-over protection structures.	OJ No. L220 (29.8.77) p. 1
77/537/EEC(**a**)	28th June 1977	Emission of pollutants from diesel engines.	OJ No. L220 (29.8.77) p. 38
78/764/EEC(**a**)(**c**)	25th July 1978	Driver's seats.	OJ No. L255 (18.9.78) p. 1
78/933/EEC(**a**)	17th October 1978	Lighting and light signalling devices.	OJ No. L325 (20.11.78) p. 16
79/533/EEC(**a**)	17th May 1979	Coupling device and reverse.	OJ No. L145 (13.6.79) p. 20
79/622/EEC(**d**)	25th June 1979	Roll-over protection structures (static testing).	OJ No. L179 (17.7.79) p. 1
80/720/EEC(**a**)	24th June 1980	Operating space, access to driving position and doors and windows.	OJ No. L194 (28.7.80) p. 1

(**a**) As amended by 82/890/EEC of 17 December 1982 (OJ No. L378, 31.12.82, p. 45).
(**b**) As amended by 79/1073/EEC of 22 November 1979 (OJ No. L331, 27.12.79, p. 20).
(**c**) As amended by 83/190/EEC of 28 March 1983 (OJ No. L109, 26.4.83, p. 13).
(**d**) As amended by 82/953/EEC of 15 December 1982 (OJ No. L386, 31.12.81, p. 31).

(1) Community reference number	(2) Date of directive	(3) Subject matter	(4) Official Journal reference
86/297/EEC, with the exception of item 5.2 of Annex I	26th May 1986	Power take-offs.	OJ No. L186 (8.7.86) p. 19
86/298/EEC	26th May 1986	Roll-over protection structures ("narrow-track" tractors).	OJ No. L186 (8.7.86) p. 26
86/415/EEC	24th July 1986	Installation, location, operation and identification of controls.	OJ No. L240 (26.8.86) p. 1

PART B

THE COMMUNITY DIRECTIVES WITH RESPECT TO THE DESIGN, CONSTRUCTION, EQUIPMENT AND MARKING OF TRACTOR COMPONENTS.

(1) Community reference number	(2) Date of directive	(3) Subject matter	(4) Official Journal reference
77/536/EEC	28th June 1977	Roll-over protection structures.	OJ No. L220 (29.8.77) p. 1
78/764/EEC(a)(b)	25th July 1978	Driver's seats.	OJ No. L255 (18.9.78) p. 1
79/532/EEC(a)	17th May 1979	Lighting and light signalling devices.	OJ No. L145 (13.6.79) p. 16
79/622/EEC(c)	25th June 1979	Roll-over protection structures (static testing).	OJ No. L179 (17.7.79) p. 1
86/298/EEC	26th May 1986	Roll-over protection structures ("narrow track" tractors).	OJ No. L186 (8.7.86) p. 26

EXPLANATORY NOTE

(This note is not part of the Regulations)

These Regulations amend the Agricultural or Forestry Tractors and Tractor Components (Type Approval) Regulations 1979, which provide for the type approval of certain agricultural or forestry tractors and tractor components.

They implement Council Directives 86/297/EEC (OJ No. L186, 8.7.86, p. 19) on the approximation of the laws of the Member States relating to the power take-offs of tractors and their protection, 86/298/EEC (OJ No. L186, 8.7.86, p. 26) on rear-mounted roll-over protection structures of narrow-track tractors, and 86/415/EEC (OJ No. L240, 26.8.86, p. 1) on the installation, location, operation and identification of the controls of tractors.

These Regulations amend the definition of "agricultural or forestry tractor" so as to cover roll-over protection structures of narrow-track tractors, and amend Schedule 2 so as to include references to the Council Directives mentioned above.

(a) As amended by 82/890/EEC of 17 December 1982 (OJ No. L378, 31.12.82, p. 45).
(b) As amended by 83/190/EEC of 28 March 1983 (OJ No. L109, 26.4.83, p. 13).
(c) As amended by 82/953/EEC of 15 December 1982 (OJ No. L386, 31.12.81, p. 31).

STATUTORY INSTRUMENTS

1987 No. 1781

CUSTOMS AND EXCISE

The Customs Duties (Temporary Importation) (Revocation) Regulations 1987

Made - - - -	*12th October 1987*
Laid before Parliament	*20th October 1987*
Coming into force	*10th November 1987*

The Commissioners of Customs and Excise, in exercise of the powers conferred upon them by section 48 of the Customs and Excise Management Act 1979 (**a**) and of all other powers enabling them in that behalf, hereby make the following Regulations:

1. These Regulations may be cited as the Customs Duties (Temporary Importation) (Revocation) Regulations 1987 and shall come into force on 10th November 1987.

2. The Statutory Instruments mentioned in the Schedule to these Regulations are hereby revoked but shall continue to have effect in relation to goods imported prior to 1st January 1986.

King's Beam House,
Mark Lane,
London, EC3R 7HE
12th October 1987

Philip Nash
Commissioner of Customs and Excise

(**a**) 1979 c.2.

Regulation 2

SCHEDULE

(1) *Regulations Revoked*	(2) *References*
The Commercial Samples (Temporary Importation) Regulations 1955.	S.I. 1955/814.
The Tourist Publicity Materials (Temporary Importation) Regulations 1955.	S.I. 1955/1346.
The Films (Temporary Importation) Regulations 1958.	S.I. 1958/2141.
The Temporary Importation (Process and Films) (Amendment) Regulations 1962.	S.I. 1962/918.
The Temporary Importation (Goods for Exhibition) Regulations 1963.	S.I. 1963/1.
The Temporary Importation (Professional Effects) Regulations 1963.	S.I. 1963/2.
The Tourist Publicity Materials (Amendment) Regulations 1965.	S.I. 1965/2041.
The Temporary Importation (Technical Examination and Standards Testing) Regulations 1967.	S.I. 1967/940.
The Temporary Importation (Equipment on Hire or Loan) Regulations 1970.	S.I. 1970/423.
The Temporary Importation (Magnetic Tapes) Regulations 1971.	S.I. 1971/1356.
The Temporary Importation (Packings) Regulations 1976.	S.I. 1976/1099.

EXPLANATORY NOTE

(This note is not part of the Regulations)

These Regulations provide for the revocation of various statutory instruments relating to relief from duty on goods temporarily imported. The position is now governed by Council Regulation (EEC) No. 3599/82 (OJ No. L376, 31.12.82, p.1).

1987 No.1782

PUBLIC HEALTH, ENGLAND AND WALES
PUBLIC HEALTH, SCOTLAND

The Control of Pollution (Exemption of Certain Discharges from Control) (Variation) Order 1987

Made - - - -	*12th October 1987*
Laid before Parliament	*14th October 1987*
Coming into force	*15th October 1987*

The Secretary of State for the Environment as respects England, the Secretary of State for Wales as respects Wales and the Secretary of State for Scotland as respects Scotland, in exercise of the powers conferred by sections 32(3)(b) and 104(1)(a) of the Control of Pollution Act 1974(**a**) and of all other powers enabling them in that behalf, hereby make the following Order:

Citation and commencement

1.   This Order may be cited as the Control of Pollution (Exemption of Certain Discharges from Control) (Variation) Order 1987 and shall come into force on 15th October 1987.

Amendment of the Control of Pollution (Exemption of Certain Discharges from Control) (Variation) Order 1986

2.   The Control of Pollution (Exemption of Certain Discharges from Control) (Variation) Order 1986(**b**) shall be varied by inserting after article 3 the following article –

"**4.**   Where an application for consent in pursuance of section 34 of the Control of Pollution Act 1974(**c**) in respect of any discharge is duly made by a water authority to the Secretary of State before 15th October 1987 and the discharge in question is substantially a continuation of a previous discharge which during the year ending on 14th October 1987 was by virtue of article 3 of the 1983 Order lawfully made without such consent (any reduction of the temperature, volume or rate of the discharge as compared with that of the previous discharge being disregarded), the Secretary of State shall be deemed to have given unconditionally the consent applied for until he actually gives consent or refuses consent.".

(**a**) 1974 c.40.   (**b**) S.I. 1986/1623.   (**c**) Section 34 is modified in relation to discharges by a water authority by S.I. 1984/1200.

12th October 1987

Nicholas Ridley
Secretary of State
for the Environment

6th October 1987

Peter Walker
Secretary of State for Wales

8th October 1987

James Douglas-Hamilton
Parliamentary Under Secretary of State,
Scottish Office

EXPLANATORY NOTE

(This note does not form part of the Order)

This Order varies the Control of Pollution (Exemption of Certain Discharges from Control) (Variation) Order 1986.

Section 32(1) of the Control of Pollution Act 1974 makes certain discharges of trade or sewage effluent unlawful if made without consent.

The Control of Pollution (Exemption of Certain Discharges from Control) Order 1983 (S.I. 1983/1182) permitted certain discharges authorised by earlier statutes to be continued without consent after section 32(1) came into force. The 1986 Order withdraws many of these exemptions from 15th October 1987.

This Order adds a further transitional provision to the 1986 Order dealing with discharges by water authorities which places them in a similar position to other dischargers to whom the existing transitional provision applies. If an application for consent is made to the Secretary of State by a water authority (in Scotland, a river purification board or an islands council) before 15th October 1987 and certain other conditions are satisfied, the discharge to which the application relates can lawfully be continued pending the determination of the application by the Secretary of State.

STATUTORY INSTRUMENTS

1987 No. 1783

AGRICULTURE

The Olive Oil (Marketing Standards) Regulations 1987

Made - - - -	*6th October 1987*
Laid before Parliament	*19th October 1987*
Coming into force	*1st November 1987*

The Minister of Agriculture, Fisheries and Food and the Secretary of State, being Ministers designated(**a**) for the purposes of section 2(2) of the European Communities Act 1972(**b**) in relation to the common agricultural policy of the European Economic Community, acting jointly in exercise of the powers conferred upon them by the said section 2(2) and of all other powers enabling them in that behalf, hereby make the following Regulations:

Title, extent and commencement

1. These Regulations, which extend to Great Britain, may be cited as the Olive Oil (Marketing Standards) Regulations 1987 and shall come into force on 1st November 1987.

Interpretation

2.—(1) In these Regulations–

"the Council Regulation" means Regulation No. 136/66/EEC of the Council(**c**) on the establishment of a common organisation of the market in oils and fats as amended in particular by Council Regulation (EEC) No. 1915/87(**d**);

"enforcement authority" shall be construed in accordance with regulation 3 of these Regulations;

"oil" means any of the descriptions of olive oils and olive-pomace oils referred to in Article 35 of the Council Regulation and described in the Annex to that Regulation.

(2) Other expressions used in these Regulations have, in so far as the context admits, the same meaning as in the Council Regulation.

(3) References in these Regulations to the sale of oil by a person include references to his offering or exposing oil for sale and to his having oil in his possession for sale, and references to cognate expressions shall be construed accordingly.

Enforcement

3. These Regulations shall be enforced–

(a) in relation to imports, in England and Wales by the relevant port health authority, and in Scotland by a district or islands council within the meaning of section 26 of the Food and Drugs (Scotland) Act 1956(**e**);

(**a**) S.I. 1972/1811.
(**b**) 1972 c. 68; section 2 is subject to Schedule 2 to that Act and is to be read, as regards England and Wales, with sections 37, 40 and 46 of the Criminal Justice Act 1982 (c. 48); and as regards Scotland, with sections 289F and 289G of the Criminal Procedure (Scotland) Act 1975 (c. 21), as inserted by section 54 of the Criminal Justice Act 1982, and with S.I. 1984/526.
(**c**) OJ No. 172, 30.8.66, p. 3025/66 (OJ/SE 1965–66 p. 221).
(**d**) OJ No. L183, 3.7.87, p. 7.
(**e**) 1956 c. 30.

(b) at the retail stage, by the food and drugs authority as defined as respects England and Wales in section 71 of the Food Act 1984(**a**), and as respects Scotland by the above-mentioned district or islands councils;

(c) at all other stages, in England by the Minister of Agriculture, Fisheries and Food and in Scotland and Wales by the Secretary of State.

Offences relating to the marketing of oil

4.—(1) Subject to paragraph (2) of this regulation, a person who in selling any oil contravenes Article 35.1 of the Council Regulation (which provides that certain descriptions and definitions of oil shall, in relation to the marketing of oil, be compulsory) as read with the Annex thereto commits an offence under this regulation.

(2) Before 1st January 1990 it shall not be an offence under this regulation–

(a) in relation to sale in Great Britain, to use a description or definition of oil which is in commercial use in the United Kingdom immediately before these Regulations come into force, or

(b) in relation to the sale of oil referred to in point 3 of that Annex, being oil which is intended for export from the United Kingdom, to use the description "pure olive oil".

(3) A person who sells by retail any oil other than oil referred to in points 1(a) and (b), 3 and 6 of the Annex to the Council Regulation in contravention of Article 35.2 of that Regulation (which provides that only oil satisfying certain definitions shall be marketed at the retail stage) as read with that Annex commits an offence under this regulation.

(4) Where the commission by any person of an offence under this regulation is due to the act or default of some other person that other person shall be guilty of the offence, and a person may be charged with and convicted of the offence by virtue of this regulation whether or not proceedings are taken against the first-mentioned person.

(5) In proceedings against any person for an offence under this regulation it shall be a defence for that person to prove that he took all reasonable steps and exercised all due diligence to avoid committing the offence.

(6) A person guilty of an offence under this regulation shall be liable on summary conviction to a fine not exceeding £2,000.

Powers of authorised officers of enforcement authorities

5.—(1) For the purpose of enforcing these Regulations an authorised officer of an enforcement authority, on producing, if so required, some duly authenticated document showing his authority, may–

(a) at all reasonable times enter any premises (other than premises used only as a dwelling) on which he reasonably suspects that oil is being, or has been, sold; and

(b) inspect and take samples of oil and inspect and remove any container of oil found on the premises.

(2) Any person who intentionally obstructs an authorised officer of an enforcement authority acting in pursuance of these Regulations shall be guilty of an offence under this regulation and shall be liable on summary conviction to a fine not exceeding £400.

Offences by bodies corporate

6. Where an offence under any provision of these Regulations which has been committed by a body corporate is proved to have been committed with the consent or connivance of, or to be attributable to any neglect on the part of, any director, manager, secretary or similar officer of the body corporate or any person who was purporting to act in any such capacity, he as well as the body corporate shall be deemed to be guilty of that offence and shall be liable to be proceeded against and punished accordingly.

(**a**) 1984 c. 30.

In Witness whereof the Official Seal of the Minister of Agriculture, Fisheries and Food is hereunto affixed on 6th October 1987.

John MacGregor
Minister of Agriculture, Fisheries and Food

Sanderson of Bowden
Minister of State, Scottish Office

5th October 1987

EXPLANATORY NOTE

(This note is not part of the Regulations)

These Regulations make provision for the enforcement of Article 35 of Regulation No. 136/66/EEC of the Council on the establishment of a common organisation of the market in oils and fats ("the Council Regulation") (OJ No. 172, 30.8.66, p. 3025/66; OJ/SE 1965–66 p. 221) as amended by Council Regulation (EEC) No. 1915/87 (OJ No. L183, 3.7.87, p. 7). They apply in Great Britain and come into force on 1st November 1987.

Article 35 of the Council Regulation makes the use of prescribed descriptions and definitions of olive oils and olive-pomace oils (formerly known as olive residue oils) compulsory for the purposes of trade, and prohibits the marketing by retail of certain categories of such oil. These descriptions and definitions are set out in the Annex to the Council Regulation. There are transitional measures (applicable until 31st December 1989) permitting the continued use of definitions and descriptions of olive oil and olive-pomace oil in use in Member States and allowing the expression "pure olive oil" to be used for exports of olive oil as defined in point 3 of the Annex to the Council Regulation.

In implementation of Article 35 of the Council Regulation, these Regulations–

    (a) designate the authorities who are to enforce Article 35 of the Council Regulation (regulation 3);

    (b) prescribe offences and penalties for contravention of Article 35 of the Council Regulation, and provide for certain defences (regulations 4 and 6);

    (c) create powers of entry, inspection and sampling (regulation 5).

STATUTORY INSTRUMENTS

1987 No. 1785

CUSTOMS AND EXCISE

The Import Duty Reliefs (Revocation) Order 1987

Made - - -	*12th October 1987*
Laid before the House of Commons	*20th October 1987*
Coming into force	*10th November 1987*

The Secretary of State, in exercise of the powers conferred on him by sections 1 and 4 of the Customs and Excise Duties (General Reliefs) Act 1979(**a**) and of all other powers enabling him in that behalf, hereby makes the following Order:

1. This Order may be cited as the Import Duty Reliefs (Revocation) Order 1987 and shall come into force on 10th November 1987.

2. The Import Duty Reliefs Order 1970(**b**) is hereby revoked.

3. This Order does not restrict any relief from customs duty otherwise than in pursuance of a Community obligation.

Lord Young of Graffham
Secretary of State,
12th October 1987   Department of Trade and Industry

EXPLANATORY NOTE

(This note is not part of the Order)

This Order provides for the revocation of an Order relating to the relief from import duty of certain goods imported for use or demonstration at exhibitions or other events held in the United Kingdom. The position is now governed by Title XX of Council Regulation (EEC) No.918/83 (O.J. No. L105, 23.4.83, p.1.).

(**a**) 1979 c.3.   (**b**) S.I. 1970/380.

STATUTORY INSTRUMENTS

1987 No. 1801 (S.126)

EDUCATION, SCOTLAND

The Education (Grants for Further Training of Teachers and Educational Psychologists) (Scotland) Amendment Regulations 1987

Made - - - -	*8th October 1987*
Laid before Parliament	*22nd October 1987*
Coming into force	*1st December 1987*

The Secretary of State, in exercise of the powers conferred on him by sections 73(a) and (c) and 74(1) of the Education (Scotland) Act 1980(**a**), and of all other powers enabling him in that behalf, hereby makes the following Regulations:

Citation and commencement

1.   These Regulations may be cited as the Education (Grants for Further Training of Teachers and Educational Psychologists) (Scotland) Amendment Regulations 1987 and shall come into force on 1st December 1987.

Amendment of principal Regulations

2.   For regulation 3(b) of the Education (Grants for Further Training of Teachers and Educational Psychologists) (Scotland) (No. 2) Regulations 1987(**b**) there shall be substituted the following:–

"(b)   educational psychologists in respect only of training consisting of either–

(i)   the preparation of, or engagement in, a project approved as suitable by the Secretary of State, on the advice of an assessor, or

(ii)   attendance at a course leading to a post-graduate degree in educational psychology.".

Michael B. Forsyth
Parliamentary Under Secretary of State,
Scottish Office

New St. Andrew's House, Edinburgh
8th October 1987

(**a**)   1980 c.44.
(**b**)   S.I. 1987/644.

EXPLANATORY NOTE

(This note is not part of the Regulations)

These Regulations amend the Education (Grants for Further Training of Teachers and Educational Psychologists) (Scotland) (No. 2) Regulations 1987 so as to provide that grants may be paid in respect of educational psychologists who attend a course leading to a post-graduate degree in educational psychology.

STATUTORY INSTRUMENTS

1987 No. 1802

PUBLIC HEALTH, ENGLAND AND WALES
PUBLIC HEALTH, SCOTLAND
PUBLIC HEALTH, NORTHERN IRELAND

CONTAMINATION OF FOOD

The Food Protection (Emergency Prohibitions) (Wales) (No. 4) Amendment No. 2 Order 1987

Made - - - -	*15th October 1987*
Laid before Parliament	*15th October 1987*
Coming into force	*19th October 1987*

Whereas the Secretary of State is of the opinion, as mentioned in section 1(1)(a) of the Food and Environment Protection Act 1985(**a**), that there has been or may have been an escape of substances of such descriptions and in such quantities and such circumstances as are likely to create a hazard to human health through human consumption of food;

And whereas the Secretary of State is of the opinion, as mentioned in section 1(1)(b) of the said Act, that in consequence of the said escape of substances food which is or may be in the future in the areas described in the Schedule to the Food Protection (Emergency Prohibitions) (Wales) (No. 4) Order 1987(**b**), or which is derived or may be in the future derived from anything in those areas, is, or may be, or may become, unsuitable for human consumption;

Now, therefore, the Secretary of State, in exercise of the powers conferred on him by the said section 1(1) and (2) and section 24(1) and (3) of the said Act, and of all other powers enabling him in that behalf, hereby makes the following Order: –

Title and commencement

1. This Order may be cited as the Food Protection (Emergency Prohibitions) (Wales) (No. 4) Amendment No. 2 Order 1987 and shall come into force on 19th October 1987.

Partial revocation and amendment

2. The Food Protection (Emergency Prohibitions) (Wales) (No. 4) Order 1987 is revoked to the extent that it imposes prohibitions on –

    (a) the slaughter of a sheep which –

        (i) was moved from a place in accordance with a consent given under section 2(1) of the Food and Environment Protection Act 1985 on or after 28th September 1987 which consent was subject to the condition that the sheep to which it applies should be marked with a blue mark; and

---

(**a**) 1985 c.48.   (**b**) S.I. 1987/1638, amended by S.I. 1987/1682.

    (ii) has been examined and marked with an ear-tag by a person authorised in that behalf by one of the Ministers; and

  (b) the supply or having in possession for supply of meat, or food containing meat, derived from such a sheep,

and accordingly that Order is further amended in accordance with the following provisions of this Order.

3.   In article 6, for paragraph (2) there shall be substituted the following paragraph –

"(2) Paragraph (1) above shall not apply in the case of –

  (a) any sheep which was moved to a market in accordance with a consent given under section 2(1) of the Act which consent did not require that the sheep to which it applies should be marked in a manner specified therein;

  (b) any sheep which was moved from any place in accordance with a consent given under the said section 2(1) on or before 21st December 1986 which consent was subject to the condition that the sheep to which it applies should be marked with a blue mark;

  (c) any sheep which was moved from any place in accordance with a consent given under the said section 2(1) on or before 26th July 1987 which consent was subject to the condition that the sheep to which it applies should be marked with an apricot mark; or

  (d) any sheep which –

    (i) was moved from any place in accordance with a consent given under the said section 2(1) which consent was subject to the condition that the sheep to which it applies should be marked with a red mark or with a green mark; or

    (ii) was moved from any place in accordance with such a consent given on or after 28th September 1987 which consent was subject to the condition that the sheep to which it applies should be marked with a blue mark;

and which, in either case, has been examined and marked with an ear-tag by a person authorised in that behalf by one of the Ministers.".

15th October 1987   *Peter Walker*
Secretary of State for Wales

EXPLANATORY NOTE

(This note is not part of the Order)

The Food Protection (Emergency Prohibitions) (Wales) (No. 4) Order 1987 contains emergency prohibitions restricting various activities in order to prevent human consumption of food which has been or which may have been rendered unsuitable for that purpose in consequence of the escape of radioactive substances from a nuclear reactor situated at Chernobyl in the USSR.

This Order excepts from the prohibition on slaughter throughout the United Kingdom any sheep, and from the prohibition on supply throughout the United Kingdom any meat derived from such a sheep, identified by a blue paint mark on or after 28th September 1987 which have been examined and marked with an ear-tag by a person authorised by the Minister of Agriculture, Fisheries and Food, the Secretary of State for Scotland, the Secretary of State for Wales or the Department of Agriculture for Northern Ireland (article 3).

STATUTORY INSTRUMENTS

1987 No. 1803

PUBLIC HEALTH, ENGLAND AND WALES
PUBLIC HEALTH, SCOTLAND
PUBLIC HEALTH, NORTHERN IRELAND

CONTAMINATION OF FOOD

The Food Protection (Emergency Prohibitions) (England) (No.2) Amendment No.6 Order 1987

Made - - - -	*15th October 1987*
Coming into force	*19th October 1987*
Laid before Parliament	*19th October 1987*

Whereas the Minister of Agriculture, Fisheries and Food is of the opinion, in accordance with section 1(1)(a) of the Food and Environment Protection Act 1985(**a**), that there has been or may have been an escape of substances of such descriptions and in such quantities and such circumstances as are likely to create a hazard to human health through human consumption of food;

And whereas the said Minister is of the opinion, in accordance with section 1(1)(b) of the said Act, that in consequence of the said escape of substances food which is or may be in the future in the area described in Schedule 1 to the Food Protection (Emergency Prohibitions) (England) (No.2) Order 1986(**b**), or which is derived or may be in the future derived from anything in that area, is, or may be, or may become, unsuitable for human consumption;

Now, therefore, the said Minister, in exercise of the powers conferred on him by the said section 1(1) and section 24(3) of the said Act, and of all other powers enabling him in that behalf, hereby makes the following Order:–

Title and commencement

1. This Order may be cited as the Food Protection (Emergency Prohibitions) (England) (No.2) Amendment No.6 Order 1987 and shall come into force on 19th October 1987.

Partial revocation and amendment

2. The Food Protection (Emergency Prohibitions) (England) (No.2) Order 1986 is revoked to the extent that it imposes prohibitions on–

    (a) the slaughter of a sheep which–

        (i) was moved from a place in accordance with a consent given under section 2(1) of the Food and Environment Protection Act 1985 on or after 28th September 1987 which consent was subject to the condition that the sheep to which it applies should be marked with a blue mark; and

        (ii) has been examined and marked with an ear-tag by a person authorised in that behalf by one of the Ministers; and

---

(**a**) 1985 c. 48.
(**b**) S.I. 1986/1689, amended by S.I. 1986/2208, 1987/153, 249, 906, 1555 and 1687.

(b) the supply or having in possession for supply of meat, or food containing meat, derived from such a sheep,

and accordingly that Order is further amended in accordance with the following provisions of this Order.

3.   In article 6, for paragraph (2) there shall be substituted the following paragraph–

"(2) Paragraph (1) above shall not apply in the case of–

(a) any sheep which was moved to a market in accordance with a consent given under section 2(1) of the Act which consent did not require that the sheep to which it applies should be marked in a manner specified therein;

(b) any sheep which was moved from any place in accordance with a consent given under the said section 2(1) on or before 21st December 1986 which consent was subject to the condition that the sheep to which it applies should be marked with a blue mark;

(c) any sheep which was moved from any place in accordance with a consent given under the said section 2(1) on or before 26th July 1987 which consent was subject to the condition that the sheep to which it applies should be marked with an apricot mark; or

(d) any sheep which–

(i) was moved from any place in accordance with a consent given under the said section 2(1) which consent was subject to the condition that the sheep to which it applies should be marked with a red mark or with a green mark; or

(ii) was moved from any place in accordance with such a consent given on or after 28th September 1987 which consent was subject to the condition that the sheep to which it applies should be marked with a blue mark,

and which, in either case, has been examined and marked with an ear-tag by a person authorised in that behalf by one of the Ministers.".

In witness whereof the Official Seal of the Minister of Agriculture, Fisheries and Food is hereunto affixed on 15th October 1987.

John MacGregor
Minister of Agriculture, Fisheries and Food

EXPLANATORY NOTE

(This note is not part of the Order)

The Food Protection (Emergency Prohibitions) (England) (No.2) Order 1986 contains emergency prohibitions restricting various activities in order to prevent human consumption of food which has been or which may have been rendered unsuitable for that purpose in consequence of the escape of radioactive substances from a nuclear reactor situated at Chernobyl in the USSR.

This Order excepts from the prohibition on slaughter throughout the United Kingdom any sheep, and from the prohibition on supply throughout the United Kingdom any meat derived from such a sheep, identified by a blue paint mark on or after 28th September 1987 which have been examined and marked with an ear-tag by a person authorised by the Minister of Agriculture, Fisheries and Food, the Secretary of State for Scotland or Wales or the Department of Agriculture for Northern Ireland.

STATUTORY INSTRUMENTS

1987 No. 1804

CUSTOMS AND EXCISE

The Customs Duties (ECSC) (No.2) (Amendment No.10) Order 1987

Made - - - -	*14th October 1987*
Laid before the House of Commons	*21st October 1987*
Coming into force	*25th October 1987*

The Treasury, by virtue of the powers conferred on them by section 5(1) and (3) of, and paragraph 4 of Schedule 2 to, the European Communities Act 1972(**a**) and of all other powers enabling them in that behalf, on the recommendation of the Secretary of State, hereby make the following Order:

1. This Order may be cited as the Customs Duties (ECSC) (No. 2) (Amendment No. 10) Order 1987 and shall come into force on 25th October 1987.

2. Up to and including 31st December 1987, article 6(1) of the Customs Duties (ECSC) (No. 2) Order 1985(**b**) (which exempts from duty goods to which that Order applies originating in certain countries) shall not apply to goods which fall within heading 73.13 which originate in Yugoslavia.

Tony Durant
David Lightbown
Two of the Lords Commissioners of
Her Majesty's Treasury

14th October 1987

(**a**) 1972 c.68; section 5(3) and Schedule 2 were amended by the Customs and Excise Duties (General Reliefs) Act 1979 (c.3), Schedule 2, paragraphs 3 and 5.   (**b**) S.I. 1985/1630, amended by S.I. 1985/2020, 1986/348, 813, 1352, 2179, 1987/973, 1053, 1125, 1218.

EXPLANATORY NOTE

(This note is not part of the Order)

This Order, which comes into force on 25th October 1987, continues in effect the provisions formerly contained in the Customs Duties (ECSC) (No.2) (Amendment No. 8) Order 1987.

This Order reimposes duties on goods falling within heading 73.13 which originate in Yugoslavia.

This Order implements a reintroduction of duty up to the end of 1987 made pursuant to Article 1, paragraph 3 of a decision 86/642/ECSC of the representatives of the governments of Member States of the European Coal and Steel Community meeting within the Council on 22nd December 1986 (OJ No. L380, 31.12.1986, p.59). Decision 86/642/ECSC of 22nd December 1986 established ceilings for imports of certain ECSC goods originating in Yugoslavia. These ceilings have now been reached on goods falling within the above heading.

The Commission communication to Member States giving notice of the reintroduction of customs duties is published in OJ No. C172 of 30.6.1987.

STATUTORY INSTRUMENTS

1987 No. 1805

LOCAL GOVERNMENT, ENGLAND AND WALES
LOCAL GOVERNMENT, SCOTLAND

The Housing Benefits (Subsidy) Order 1987

Made - - -	*16th October 1987*
Laid before Parliament	*26th October 1987*
Coming into force -	*16th November 1987*

The Secretary of State for Social Services, with the consent of the Treasury, in exercise of the powers conferred upon him by section 32(2) of the Social Security and Housing Benefits Act 1982(a), and of all other powers enabling him in that behalf, after consultation in accordance with section 36(1) of that Act with organisations appearing to him to be representative of authorities concerned, hereby makes the following Order:

Citation, commencement and interpretation

1.—(1) This Order, which may be cited as the Housing Benefits (Subsidy) Order 1987, shall come into force on 16th November 1987.

(2) In this Order, unless the context otherwise requires–

"the Act" means the Social Security and Housing Benefits Act 1982;

"scheme" means either a statutory scheme in accordance with section 28 of the Act or a local scheme in accordance with section 30 thereof;

"subsidy" means rate rebate subsidy, rent rebate subsidy or rent allowance subsidy under section 32 of the Act;

"the Regulations" means the Housing Benefits Regulations 1985(b),

and other expressions have the same meaning as in the Regulations.

Amount of subsidy

2. The amount of an authority's subsidy for the year beginning 1st April 1987 shall be calculated, for the purposes of section 32(2) of the Act (subsidies to authorities), by adding together the amounts in articles 3, 4 and 6 of this Order.

Rebates or allowances

3. The amount of subsidy for the year in relation to an authority listed in column (1) of the Schedule to this Order shall include an amount calculated by reference to the rebates or allowances granted by that authority being–

(a) in the case of an authority granting rebates or allowances under the statutory scheme during the year or any part of it, the percentage specified in relation to that authority in column (2) or (3) of the said Schedule, as may be appropriate, of the total of rebates or allowances so granted; or

---

(a) 1982 c.24, as amended by section 22 of the Social Security Act 1985 (c.53).
(b) S.I. 1985/677, as amended by S.I. 1985/1100, 1244, 1445, 1986/84, 852, 1009, 1156 and 2183.

(b) in the case of an authority granting rebates or allowances under a local scheme within the meaning of section 30 of the Act (local schemes) during the year or any part of it, the percentage specified in relation to that authority in column (2) or (3) of the said Schedule, as may be appropriate, of the total of rebates or allowances which would have been granted under the statutory scheme,

less, in either case, any deductions specified in article 5 of this Order which fall to be made from that total.

Administration costs

4. An authority's subsidy for the year shall include an amount calculated by reference to the costs of administering rebates or allowances being–

(a) for a new town corporation, the Scottish Special Housing Association, or the Development Board for Rural Wales, 100%; and

(b) for an authority other than one specified in paragraph (a) of this article–

　(i) in England, 60%,

　(ii) in Scotland, 65%,

　(iii) in Wales, 70%,

of costs reasonably incurred by the authority during the year in administering its scheme.

Deductions from subsidy in respect of rebates or allowances

5. The deductions referred to in article 3 of this Order are deductions of the following amounts:

(a) where a tenant of an authority is or, if he were not in receipt of a rent rebate, would be able to choose whether or not to be provided with any services, facilities or rights or to choose whether or not to provide those services, facilities or rights for himself (whether or not in return for an award or grant from the appropriate authority) while continuing to occupy, or, as the case may be, when entering into occupation of, a dwelling as his home either under his existing tenancy agreement or by entering into a new agreement, the amounts attributable to those items (whether or not those amounts form part of the sum fixed as rent or are otherwise reserved as rent);

(b) where a person is, will be, or may become, entitled to a rent-free period which does not fall to be taken into account in calculating the amount of rent rebate to which he is entitled in accordance with the Regulations, the amount of rebate which is payable to him for the period beginning with the date of the award and equal to the length of the award;

(c) where a person in respect of whom a certificate issued under regulation 9 of the Regulations (person on supplementary benefit) is for the time being in force is charged a rent higher than that charged to any of the authority's other tenants in respect of a similar dwelling and is so charged for a reason relating to the fact that regulation 9 of the Regulations applies to him, the amount of rebate to which he is entitled by reference to the additional amount of the rent;

(d) any amounts awarded by an authority under regulation 25 of the Regulations (additional amount of benefit in exceptional cases);

(e) where an authority makes an award to one of its tenants in receipt of housing benefit in the form of a payment of money or money's worth, a credit to the person's rent account, or in some other form, and whether or not the person is immediately entitled to the award, the amount of the award, but no such deduction shall be made in respect of an award–

　(i) made to a tenant for a reason unrelated to the fact that he is a tenant,

　(ii) made under a statutory obligation,

　(iii) for a purpose specified in or under statute made in exercise of a discretion where the circumstances in which that discretion may be exercised are also specified as aforesaid,

　(iv) made as reasonable compensation for work actually carried out by the tenant in carrying out reasonable repairs or redecoration which the authority would otherwise have carried out or be required to carry out,

　(v) of a reasonable amount made as compensation for loss, damage or inconvenience of a kind which occurs only irregularly suffered by the tenant by virtue of his occupation of his home.

Overpayment of rebates or allowances

6.—(1) Where an authority makes an overpayment of housing benefit during the year, its subsidy for the year shall include any amount which may be payable in accordance with paragraph (2) of this article.

(2) Subject to paragraph (3), subsidy under paragraph (1) of this article shall be payable in certificated cases only, and in such a case the amount of subsidy shall be the following percentage of the difference between the amount of the overpayment and the amount, if any, of the overpayment recovered by the authority–

(a) in respect of an overpayment caused by an error of the authority making the payment, 100%; and

(b) in respect of any other overpayment–

(i) in the case of an authority referred to in paragraph 1 or 2 of the Schedule to this Order, 100%, and

(ii) in the case of an authority referred to in paragraph 3 of the Schedule to this Order, 100.6%.

(3) The total amount of subsidy payable to an authority for the year in respect of an overpayment to which paragraph (2)(a) of this article applies shall not exceed 0.19% of the aggregate of–

(a) the total of rebates and allowances granted by that authority during the year in certificated cases, and

(b) the total of any overpayments made by that authority to which paragraph (2)(b) of this article applies less any amount of those overpayments recovered by that authority.

(4) In this article "overpayment" means any amount paid by way of housing benefit to which there was no entitlement under the Regulations, including any excess of housing benefit actually paid over the amount to which there was in fact entitlement under the Regulations and including any amount in excess of the amount, if any, of benefit which would have been due had a certificate under regulation 9 of the Regulations not been issued or, as the case may be, had such a certificate been cancelled.

Signed by authority of the Secretary of State for Social Services.

Michael Portillo
Parliamentary Under-Secretary of State,
Department of Health and Social Security

6th October 1987

We consent,

T. Durant
D. Lightbown
Two of the Lords Commissioners of
Her Majesty's Treasury

16th October 1987

Article 3

SCHEDULE

PERCENTAGE OF REBATES OR ALLOWANCES PAYABLE FOR WHICH SUBSIDY IS PAYABLE

(1) *Authority granting rebates or allowances*	(2) *Percentage payable in certificated cases*	(3) *Percentage payable in cases other than those specified in column (2)*
1. The Scottish Special Housing Association or a new town corporation in Scotland.	1. 100%	1. 100%
2. A new town corporation in England or Wales or the Development Board for Rural Wales.	2. 100%	2. 90%
3. Any authority other than one specified in paragraph 1 or 2	3. 100.6%	3. 90%

EXPLANATORY NOTE

(This note is not part of the Order)

This Order sets out the manner in which the subsidy payable under section 32 of the Social Security and Housing Benefits Act 1982 to authorities who grant rate rebates, rent rebates or rent allowances under that Act is to be calculated in respect of the year beginning 1st April 1987.

Articles 3 and 5 and the Schedule set out the basis on which the subsidy in respect of rebates and allowances is to be calculated and article 4 the basis of calculating the amount of subsidy in respect of administration costs. The amount included in respect of rebates and allowances is to be the percentage (set out in the Schedule) of the rebates or allowances granted by an authority under the statutory scheme less the deductions set out in article 5. The amount included in respect of administration costs is to be the percentage (set out in article 4) of the costs reasonably incurred by an authority. Article 6 sets out the amount included in respect of overpayments of benefit in certain cases.

STATUTORY INSTRUMENTS

1987 No. 1806

VALUE ADDED TAX

The Value Added Tax (Tour Operators) Order 1987

Made - - -	*14th October 1987*
Laid before the House of Commons - - -	*21st October 1987*
Coming into force -	*1st April 1988*

The Treasury, in exercise of the powers conferred on them by sections 3(3), 6(6), 16(4), 37A(1) and (2) and 48(6) of the Value Added Tax Act 1983(a) and of all other powers enabling them in that behalf, hereby make the following Order:

Citation and Commencement

1. This Order may be cited as the Value Added Tax (Tour Operators) Order 1987 and shall come into force on 1st April 1988.

Supplies to which this Order applies

2. This Order shall apply to any supply of goods or services by a tour operator where the supply is for the benefit of travellers.

Meaning of "designated travel service"

3.—(1) Subject to paragraphs (2), (3) and (4) of this article, a "designated travel service" is a supply of goods or services–

(a) acquired for the purposes of his business; and

(b) supplied for the benefit of a traveller without material alteration or further processing;

by a tour operator in a member State of the European Community in which he has established his business or has a fixed establishment.

(2) The supply of one or more designated travel services, as part of a single transaction, shall be treated as a single supply of services.

(3) The Commissioners of Customs and Excise may on being given notice by a tour operator that he is a person who to the order of a taxable person–

(a) acquires goods or services from another taxable person; and

(b) supplies those goods or services, without material alteration or further processing, to the taxable person who ordered the supply for use in the United Kingdom by that person for the purpose of that person's business other than by way of re-supply–

treat supplies within sub-paragraph (b) as not being designated travel services.

(a) 1983 c.55; section 37A was inserted by section 16 of the Finance Act 1987 (c.16).

(4) The supply of goods and services of such description as the Commissioners of Customs and Excise may specify shall be deemed not to be a designated travel service.

Time of supply

4.—(1) Sections 4 and 5 of the Value Added Tax Act 1983 shall not apply to any supply comprising in whole or in part a designated travel service.

(2) Subject to paragraphs (3) and (4) of this article, all supplies comprising in whole or in part a designated travel service shall, at the election of the tour operator making the supplies, be treated as taking place either–

(a) when the traveller commences a journey or occupies any accommodation supplied, whichever is the earlier; or

(b) when any payment is received by the tour operator in respect of that supply which, when aggregated with any earlier such payment, exceeds 20% of the total consideration, to the extent covered by that and any earlier such payment, save insofar as any earlier such payment has already been treated as determining the time of part of that supply.

(3) Save as the Commissioners of Customs and Excise may otherwise allow, all supplies comprising in whole or in part a designated travel service made by the same tour operator shall, subject to paragraph (4) of this article, be treated as taking place at the time determined under one only of the methods specified in paragraph (2) of this article.

(4) Where–

(a) a tour operator uses the method specified in paragraph (2)(b) to determine the time of a supply; and

(b) payment is not received in respect of all or part of the supply;

notwithstanding paragraph (3), the time of any part of that supply, which has not already been determined under paragraph (2)(b), shall be determined in accordance with paragraph (2)(a).

Place of supply

5.—(1) The application of sections 6 and 8 of the Value Added Tax Act 1983 in relation to a supply of services or of a designated travel service shall be modified in accordance with the provisions of this article.

(2) A designated travel service shall be treated as supplied in the member State of the European Community in which the tour operator has established his business or, if the supply was made from a fixed establishment, in the member State in which the fixed establishment is situated and in no other place.

(3) Any supply by a tour operator, not being a designated travel service, of transport of persons or their effects shall be treated as being made:

(a) in the country in which the services are performed to the extent that they are performed in that country; or

(b) wholly in the country in which the services are performed or partly performed notwithstanding that they may be partly performed outside the territorial jurisdiction of that country, provided that they are not also partly performed in any other country.

(4) Any supply by a tour operator, not being a designated travel service, of cultural, artistic, sporting, entertainment, educational, scientific or related services or of the right of attendance at conferences, shall be treated as being made in the place where the services are performed.

(5) Any supply by a tour operator, not being a designated travel service, of accommodation, or of facilities for camping in tents and caravans, or for parking vehicles, shall be treated as being made in the place where the accommodation or facilities are provided.

(6) Any supply by a tour operator by way of hire of any means of transport which, apart from this paragraph, would be treated as being made outside the European

Community, shall be treated as being made within the United Kingdom where the means of transport is used within the United Kingdom.

6. The Value Added Tax (Place of Supply) Order 1984**(a)** shall be amended as follows:

(a) by deleting article 4 and substituting the following:

"**4.** This Order applies to the supply of services of or incidental to the provision of a course of formal instruction in the United Kingdom other than such a supply made as a designated travel service or as part of such a service."; and

(b) by deleting article 5 and substituting the following:

"**5.** A "designated travel service" has the same meaning as in the Value Added Tax (Tour Operators) Order 1987.".

Value of a designated travel service

7. Subject to articles 8 and 9 of this Order, the value of a designated travel service shall be determined by reference to the difference between sums paid or payable to and sums paid or payable by the tour operator in respect of that service, calculated in such manner as the Commissioners of Customs and Excise shall specify.

8.—(1) Where–

(a) a supply of goods or services is acquired for a consideration in money by a tour operator, for the purpose of supplying a designated travel service, and

(b) the value of the supply is (apart from this article) greater than its open market value, and

(c) the person making the supply and the tour operator to whom it is made are connected,

the Commissioners of Customs and Excise may direct that the value of the supply shall be deemed to be its open market value for the purpose of calculating the value of the designated travel service.

(2) A direction under this article shall be given by notice in writing to the tour operator acquiring the supply, but no direction may be given more than three years after the time of the supply.

(3) A direction given to a tour operator under this paragraph, in respect of a supply acquired by him, may include a direction that the value of any supply–

(a) which is acquired by him after the giving of the notice, or after such later date as may be specified in the notice, and

(b) as to which the conditions in sub-paragraph (a) to (c) of paragraph (1) above are satisfied,

shall be deemed to be its open market value for the purpose of calculating the value of the designated travel service.

(4) For the purposes of this article any question whether a person is connected with another shall be determined in accordance with section 533 of the Income and Corporation Taxes Act 1970**(b)**.

9.—(1) Where–

(a) goods and services have been acquired prior to the commencement of this Order; and

(b) input tax credit has been claimed in respect of those goods and services; and

(c) the goods and services are supplied as a designated travel service or as part of a designated travel service after the commencement of this Order;

article 7 of this Order shall not apply in determining the value of that part of a designated travel service referable to goods and services on which input tax has been claimed.

(a) S.I. 1984/1685.
(b) 1970 c.10.

(2) The value of that part of the designated travel service to which, by virtue of paragraph (1) of this article, article 7 of this Order does not apply shall be calculated in accordance with section 10 of the Value Added Tax Act 1983.

Tax chargeable on zero-rated and exempt designated travel services

10.—(1) Where a tour operator acquires goods or services of a description for the time being specified in Schedule 5 of the Value Added Tax Act 1983, in order to supply them as a designated travel service or as part of such a service, the rate at which tax shall be charged shall be nil on that portion of the value of the designated travel service supplied which is attributable to the goods and services specified in the Schedule.

(2) Where a tour operator acquires goods or services of a description for the time being specified in Schedule 6 to the Value Added Tax Act 1983, in order to supply them as a designated travel service, or part of such a service, no tax shall be chargeable on that portion of the value of the designated travel service supplied, which is attributable to the goods and services specified in the Schedule.

Amendment of zero-rating provisions

11.—(1) Schedule 5 to the Value Added Tax Act 1983 shall be varied by the addition of a new item to Group 10, after item 12, as follows–

"13. The supply of a designated travel service to be enjoyed outside the European Community, to the extent to which the supply is so enjoyed.".

(2) Schedule 5 to the Value Added Tax Act 1983 shall be varied by the addition of a new Note to Group 10 as follows–

"(7) "Designated travel service" has the same meaning as in the Value Added Tax (Tour Operators) Order 1987.".

Disallowance of input tax

12. Input tax on goods or services acquired by a tour operator for re-supply as a designated travel service shall be excluded from credit under sections 14 and 15 of the Value Added Tax Act 1983.

Disqualification from membership of group of companies

13. A tour operator shall not be eligible to be treated as a member of a group for the purposes of section 29 of the Value Added Tax Act 1983 if any other member of the proposed or existing group–

  (a) has an overseas establishment;
  (b) makes supplies outside the United Kingdom which would be taxable supplies if made within the United Kingdom; and
  (c) supplies goods or services which will become, or are intended to become, a designated travel service.

Option not to treat supply as designated travel service

14.—(1) Where a tour operator supplies a designated travel service he may treat that supply as not being a designated travel service if:

  (a) there are reasonable grounds for believing that the value of all such supplies in the period of one year then beginning will not exceed one per cent of all supplies made by him during that period; and
  (b) he makes no supplies of designated travel services consisting of accommodation or transport.

(2) For the purposes of this article the value of any supplies shall be calculated in accordance with section 10 of the Value Added Tax Act 1983.

Tony Durant
David Lightbown
14th October 1987   Two of the Lords Commissioners of Her Majesty's Treasury

EXPLANATORY NOTE

(This note is not part of the Order)

This Order introduces with effect from 1 April 1988 a special VAT scheme for supplies by tour operators. The vires for such a scheme under UK law lie principally in section 37A of the Value Added Tax Act 1983. The scheme is a requirement under Article 26 of the Council Directive No. 77/388/EEC. (OJ No. L145, 13.6.77, p. 1).

Articles 2 and 3 of the Order define the supplies affected by the scheme.

Articles 4, 7, 8 and 9 vary the normal rules on time of supply and tax value to fit in with the general requirements of the scheme.

Articles 10 and 11 provide reliefs, the latter introducing into Group 10 of Schedule 5 to the Value Added Tax Act 1983 an additional item which will allow supplies of services made under the scheme which are to be enjoyed outside the European Community to be zero-rated.

Article 12 prohibits the deduction of input tax in respect of supplies made under the scheme.

Article 13 is designed to prevent avoidance of tax under the scheme by amending the Value Added Tax Act 1983 provisions which deal with group registration.

Article 14 introduces an option for tour operators not to use the scheme for certain de minimis supplies.

Articles 5 and 6 are made under section 6 of the Value Added Tax Act 1983. Article 5 has two purposes:

(a) to specify the place of supply of services/supplies made by tour operators under the scheme; and

(b) to specify the place of supply of certain services of a type made by tour operators but not made under the scheme because they are made "in-house" rather than acquired from any other person.

Article 6 amends the Value Added Tax (Place of Supply) Order 1984 to exclude therefrom any supplies made under the scheme introduced by this Order.

STATUTORY INSTRUMENTS

1987 No. 1807

INDUSTRIAL DEVELOPMENT

The Industry Act 1972 (Amendment) Regulations 1987

Made - - - -	*14th October 1987*
Laid before Parliament	*21st October 1987*
Coming into force	*11th November 1987*

The Secretary of State, being a Minister designated(**a**) for the purposes of section 2(2) of the European Communities Act 1972(**b**) in relation to the provision of guarantees, grants and loans in respect of the financing of the construction of ships and mobile offshore installations and their equipment, in exercise of the powers conferred on him by that section and of all his other enabling powers, hereby makes the following Regulations: –

1. These Regulations may be cited as the Industry Act 1972 (Amendment) Regulations 1987 and shall come into force on 11th November 1987.

2. Section 10(1) of the Industry Act 1972(**c**) is hereby amended by the substitution for the words "in the United Kingdom" of the words "in any member State".

Robert Atkins
Parliamentary Under Secretary of State,
14th October 1987 Department of Trade and Industry

EXPLANATORY NOTE

(This note is not part of the Regulations)

These Regulations amend section 10(1) of the Industry Act 1972, which provides for guarantees of payments in connection with the financing of orders for the construction of ships and mobile offshore installations and their equipment. The Regulations provide that the guarantees can be made in connection with the construction in any member State of the European Communities instead of in the United Kingdom only.

(**a**) S.I. 1987/448.   (**b**) 1972 c.68.   (**c**) 1972 c.63.

STATUTORY INSTRUMENTS

1987 No. 1808

ANIMALS

ANIMAL HEALTH

The Export of Sheep (Prohibition) (No. 2) Order 1987

<table>
<tr><td>Made - - - -</td><td>18th October 1987</td></tr>
<tr><td>Coming into force</td><td>19th October 1987</td></tr>
</table>

The Minister of Agriculture, Fisheries and Food, in exercise of the power conferred by section 11 of the Animal Health Act 1981(**a**) and of all other powers enabling him in that behalf, hereby makes the following Order: –

Title and commencement

1. This Order may be cited as the Export of Sheep (Prohibition) (No. 2) Order 1987 and shall come into force on 19th October 1987.

Prohibition of export of sheep

2.—(1) No person shall export from Great Britain to a member State any sheep to which this Order applies.

(2) Subject to paragraphs (3) and (4) below, this Order applies to any sheep which –

  (a) was moved from a place situated in an area which is a designated area for the purposes of Part I of the Food and Environment Protection Act 1985(**b**) by virtue of –

  (i) article 3 of the Food Protection (Emergency Prohibitions) (England) (No. 2) Order 1986(**c**);

  (ii) article 3 of the Food Protection (Emergency Prohibitions) (Wales) (No. 4) Order 1987(**d**);

  (iii) article 3 of the Food Protection (Emergency Prohibitions) Order 1987(**e**) and of the Food Protection (Emergency Prohibitions) (No. 2) Order 1987(**f**); or

  (iv) article 3 of the Food Protection (Emergency Prohibitions) Order (Northern Ireland) 1987(**g**),

  in accordance with the terms of a consent under section 2(1) of that Act (consent to the doings of things prohibited by an emergency order under section 1 of that Act) which required that the sheep to which it applies should be marked in a manner specified therein; or

---

(**a**) 1981 c.22.   (**b**) 1985 c.48.   (**c**) S.I. 1986/1689, amended by S.I. 1986/2208, 1987/153, 249, 906, 1555 and 1687.   (**d**) S.I. 1987/1638, amended by S.I. 1987/1682.   (**e**) S.I. 1987/1165, amended by S.I. 1987/1567 and 1696.   (**f**) S.I. 1987/1450, amended by S.I. 1987/1568 and 1697.
(**g**) S.R. (N.I.) 1987 No. 367.

(b) was moved from such an area in contravention of a prohibition on its movement imposed by an order made under section 1(1) of that Act (which empowers the making of emergency orders) which applied to that sheep at the time it was moved.

(3) This Order applies to a sheep only for so long as the area from which it has been moved remains a designated area for the purposes of any of the orders referred to in paragraph (2)(a) above.

(4) Paragraph (2)(a) above shall not apply in the case of –

(a) any sheep which has been examined and marked with an ear-tag by a person authorised in that behalf by the appropriate Minister or the Department of Agriculture for Northern Ireland; or

(b) any sheep which was marked with a blue mark or with an apricot mark as a condition of the granting of a consent under section 2(1) of that Act to its removal from a designated area given on or before 21st December 1986 or 26th July 1987 respectively.

Enforcement

3. This Order shall be executed and enforced by local authorities.

Revocation

4. The Export of Sheep (Prohibition) Order 1987**(a)** and the Export of Sheep (Prohibition) (Amendment) Order 1987**(b)** are hereby revoked.

In witness whereof the Official Seal of the Minister of Agriculture, Fisheries and Food was hereunto affixed on 18th October 1987.

John MacGregor
Minister of Agriculture, Fisheries and Food

(a) S.I. 1987/211.   **(b)** S.I. 1987/248.

EXPLANATORY NOTE

(This note is not part of the Order)

The Orders mentioned in article 2(2) ("emergency orders") among other things designate areas which have been affected by an accident at a nuclear reactor at Chernobyl in the USSR ("designated areas").

This Order (which revokes and re-enacts the Export of Sheep (Prohibition) Order 1987 as amended) prohibits the export from Great Britain to a member State of the European Communities of sheep moved from a place in such a designated area in the circumstances described in article 2. The principal changes are that the present Order includes within its scope designated areas in Northern Ireland, but does not apply in the case of sheep which were marked with an apricot mark on or before 26th July 1987 as a condition of the granting of a consent under section 2(1) of the Food and Environment Protection Act 1985 to its removal from a designated area (article 2(2) and 2(4)(b)).

Export of a sheep is prohibited only for so long as the area from which it is was moved continues to be a designated area. The prohibition extends to sheep which have been moved in accordance with a Ministerial consent which required that the sheep to which it applies should be marked in a specified manner and to sheep which have been moved in contravention of a restriction, but it does not apply to those sheep which have been examined and subsequently marked with an ear-tag by an officer authorised by the Minister of Agriculture, Fisheries and Food or the Secretary of State for Scotland or Wales or the Department of Agriculture for Northern Ireland, or which were marked with a blue mark or with an apricot mark as a condition of the granting of a consent referred to in the preceding paragraph given on or before 21st December 1986 or 26th July 1987 respectively.

STATUTORY INSTRUMENTS

1987 No. 1809

HOUSING, ENGLAND AND WALES

The Home Purchase Assistance (Recognised Lending Institutions) (No. 2) Order 1987

Made - - - -	*14th October 1987*
Coming into force	*4th November 1987*

The Secretary of State, in exercise of the powers conferred on him by section 447(2) of the Housing Act 1985(**a**), and of all other powers enabling him in that behalf, and with the consent of the Treasury, hereby makes the following Order:

1. This Order may be cited as the Home Purchase Assistance (Recognised Lending Institutions) (No. 2) Order 1987 and comes into force on 4th November 1987.

2. The bodies named in the Schedule to this Order are hereby specified for the purposes of section 447(2) of the Housing Act 1985.

Nicholas Ridley
One of Her Majesty's Principal Secretaries of State

29th September 1987

We Consent,

Tony Durant
David Lightbown
14th October 1987   Two of the Lords Commissioners of Her Majesty's Treasury

SCHEDULE

BODIES SPECIFIED FOR THE PURPOSES OF SECTION 447 OF THE HOUSING ACT 1985

1. Abbey Life Executive Mortgages Limited.

2. Abbey Life Funding Limited.

(**a**) 1985 c.68.

EXPLANATORY NOTE

(This note is not part of the Order)

This Order specifies two additional bodies for the purposes of section 447 of the Housing Act 1985. Bodies recognised as lending institutions for the purposes of section 447 may receive advances from the Secretary of State to enable them to provide assistance to first-time purchasers of house property (the "Homeloan" Scheme).

STATUTORY INSTRUMENTS

1987 No. 1810

HOUSING, ENGLAND AND WALES

The Housing (Right to Buy) (Priority of Charges) (No. 2) Order 1987

Made - - - -	*14th October 1987*
Coming into force	*4th November 1987*

The Secretary of State for the Environment, as respects England, and the Secretary of State for Wales, as respects Wales, in exercise of the powers conferred on them by section 156(4) of the Housing Act 1985 (**a**), and of all other powers enabling them in that behalf, and with the consent of the Treasury, hereby make the following Order:

1. This Order may be cited as The Housing (Right to Buy) (Priority of Charges) (No. 2) Order 1987 and shall come into force on 4th November 1987.

2. The bodies named in the Schedule to this Order are hereby specified for the purposes of section 156(4) of the Housing Act 1985.

29th September 1987

Nicholas Ridley
Secretary of State for the Environment

30th September 1987

Peter Walker
Secretary of State for Wales

We consent,

14th October 1987

Tony Durant
David Lightbown
Two of the Lords Commissioners of Her Majesty's Treasury

(**a**) 1985 c.68.

SCHEDULE

BODIES SPECIFIED FOR THE PURPOSES OF SECTION 156(4) OF THE HOUSING ACT 1985

1. Abbey Life Executive Mortgages Limited.

2. Abbey Life Funding Limited.

EXPLANATORY NOTE

(This note is not part of the Order)

Under the Housing Act 1985 ("the 1985 Act") liability to repay discount following the exercise of the right to buy is secured by a charge on the dwelling-house. Such charges do not have priority over certain charges securing advances by bodies falling within section 156(4) of the 1985 Act.

This Order specifies two additional bodies for the purposes of section 156(4) of the 1985 Act. These two bodies are also approved lending institutions for the purposes of section 36(4) of the 1985 Act and paragraph 2(4) of Schedule 2 to the Housing Associations Act 1985 (c.69) dealing with voluntary disposals at a discount by local authorities and housing associations respectively.

STATUTORY INSTRUMENTS

1987 No. 1811

HOUSING, ENGLAND AND WALES

The Mortgage Indemnities (Recognised Bodies) (No.2) Order 1987

Made - - - -	*14th October 1987*
Coming into force	*4th November 1987*

The Secretary of State, in exercise of the powers conferred on him by section 444(1) of the Housing Act 1985(**a**), and all other powers enabling him in that behalf, and with the consent of the Treasury, hereby makes the following Order:

1. This Order may be cited as the Mortgage Indemnities (Recognised Bodies) (No.2) Order 1987 and shall come into force on 4th November 1987.

2. The bodies named in the Schedule to this Order are hereby specified for the purposes of section 444 of the Housing Act 1985.

Nicholas Ridley
One of Her Majesty's Principal Secretaries of State

29th September 1987

We consent,

Tony Durant
David Lightbown
14th October 1987   Two of the Lords Commissioners of Her
Majesty's Treasury

(**a**) 1985 c.68.

SCHEDULE

BODIES SPECIFIED FOR THE PURPOSES OF SECTION 444 OF THE HOUSING ACT 1985

1. Abbey Life Executive Mortgages Limited.

2. Abbey Life Funding Limited.

3. Bretton Financial Services Limited.

EXPLANATORY NOTE

(This note is not part of the Order)

This Order specifies three additional bodies for the purposes of section 444 of the Housing Act 1985 ("the 1985 Act"). The bodies specified become recognised bodies for the purposes of sections 442 and 443 of the 1985 Act. Local authorities may, with the approval of the Secretary of State, enter into agreements with recognised bodies providing for indemnities, where such bodies make advances secured by way of mortgage, on dwelling-houses bought from the public sector landlords listed in section 444(4) of the 1985 Act.

STATUTORY INSTRUMENTS

1987 No. 1812

CIVIL AVIATION

The Rules of the Air and Air Traffic Control (Fourth Amendment) Regulations 1987

Made - - - -	*20th October 1987*
Coming into force	*17th December 1987*

The Secretary of State for Transport, in exercise of his powers under article 64(1) of the Air Navigation Order 1985(a) and of all other powers enabling him in that behalf, hereby makes the following Regulations –

1. These Regulations may be cited as the Rules of the Air and Air Traffic Control (Fourth Amendment) Regulations 1987 and shall come into force on 17th December 1987.

2. The Schedule to the Rules of the Air and Air Traffic Control Regulations 1985(b) shall be amended as follows:–

(1) In rule 5(1)(a)(i) after the words "in the event of failure of a power unit" there shall be inserted the following –

"and if such an aircraft is towing a banner such height shall be calculated on the basis that the banner shall not be dropped within the congested area".

(2) In rule 5(1)(d)(ii), after the words "in the event of the failure of a power unit" there shall be inserted the following –

"and if such an aircraft is towing a banner such height shall be calculated on the basis that the banner shall not be dropped within 3000ft of the assembly".

(3) For rule 9 there shall be substituted the following –

"Display of lights by aircraft

9—(1)(a) By night an aircraft shall display such of the lights specified in these Rules as may be appropriate to the circumstances of the case, and shall not display any other lights which might obscure or otherwise impair the visibility of, or be mistaken for, such lights.

(b) By day an aircraft fitted with an anti-collision light shall display such a light in flight.

(2) A flying machine on a United Kingdom aerodrome shall:–

(a) display by night either the lights which it would be required to display when flying or the lights specified in rule 11(2)(c) of these Rules unless it is stationary on the apron or part of the aerodrome provided for the maintenance of aircraft;

(a) S.I. 1985/1643, to which there are amendments not relevant to these Regulations.   (b) S.I. 1985/1714, as amended by S.I. 1986/544, 2121 and 1987/1145.

(b) display when stationary on the apron by day or night with engines running a red anti-collision light, if fitted.

(3) Notwithstanding the provisions of this section of these Rules the commander of an aircraft may switch off or reduce the intensity of any flashing light fitted to the aircraft if such a light does or is likely to :

(a) adversely affect the performance of the duties of any member of the flight crew; or

(b) subject an outside observer to unreasonable dazzle.".

(4) For rule 10 there shall be substituted the following –

"Failure of navigation and anti-collision lights

10—(1) In the United Kingdom, in the event of the failure of any light which is required by these Rules to be displayed at night, if the light cannot be immediately repaired or replaced the aircraft shall not depart from the aerodrome and, if in flight, shall land as soon as in the opinion of the commander of the aircraft it can safely do so, unless authorised by the appropriate air traffic control unit to continue its flight.

(2) In the United Kingdom, in the event of a failure of an anti-collision light when flying by day, an aircraft may continue to fly by day provided that the light is repaired at the earliest practicable opportunity.".

(5) For rule 11(1) there shall be substituted the following –

"**11**—(1) A flying machine when flying at night shall display lights as follows :–

(a) in the case of a flying machine registered in the United Kingdom having a maximum total weight authorised of more than 5700kg or any other flying machine registered in the United Kingdom which conforms to a type first issued with a type certificate on or after 1st April 1988 the system of lights in paragraph (2)(b) of this rule;

(b) in the case of a flying machine registered in the United Kingdom which conforms to a type first issued with a type certificate before 1st April 1988 having a maximum total weight authorised of 5700kg or less, any one of the following systems of lights :–

(i) that specified in paragraph (2)(a) of this rule, or that specified in paragraph (2)(b); or

(ii) that specified in paragraph (2)(d), excluding sub-paragraph (ii);

(c) in the case of any other flying machine one of the systems of lights specified in paragraph (2) of this rule.".

(6) For rule 11(2)(a) there shall be substituted the following –

"(a)(i) a steady green light of at least five candela showing to the starboard side through an angle of 110 degrees from dead ahead in the horizontal plane; and

(ii) a steady red light of at least five candela showing to the port side through an angle of 110 degrees from dead ahead in the horizontal plane; and

(iii) a steady white light of at least three candela showing through angles of 70 degrees from dead astern to each side in the horizontal plane.".

(7) For rule 15(1) there shall be substituted the following –

"(1) Except as provided in paragraph (2) of this rule, an airship while flying at night shall display the following lights :–

(a) a steady white light of at least five candela showing through angles of 110 degrees from dead ahead to each side in the horizontal plane;

(b) a steady green light of at least five candela showing to the starboard side through an angle of 110 degrees from dead ahead in the horizontal plane;

(c) a steady red light of at least five candela showing to the port side through an angle of 110 degrees from dead ahead in the horizontal plane;

(d) a steady white light of at least five candela showing through angles of 70 degrees from dead astern to each side in the horizontal plane; and

(e) an anti-collision light.".

(8) In rule 15(3) for the words "An airship, while moored within the United Kingdom by night, shall display the following lights" shall be substituted the words "An airship, while moored within the United Kingdom by night, shall display the following steady lights".

(9) In rule 21 prior to the words "In relation to flights" there shall be inserted the words "Subject to Rule 21A of these Rules".

(10) After rule 21 there shall be inserted the following new rule –

"Flight by gliders in notified airspace

21A. Rule 21 of these Rules shall not apply to the commander of a glider which is flying in controlled airspace notified for the purposes of this rule if the glider is flown in accordance with conditions such as may also be notified for the purposes of this rule in respect of that controlled airspace.".

(11) In Column 1 of the Table to rule 36(1) immediately below "Aberdeen" there shall be inserted "Belfast/Aldergrove" and in Column 2 adjacent thereto there shall be inserted "(3)(a) and (b)".

(12) In rule 50 for the words "article 66(1)(a)(iii)" there shall be substituted the words "article 69(1)(a)(iii)".

Peter Bottomley

Signed by authority of the Secretary of State   Parliamentary Under Secretary of State,
20th October 1987   Department of Transport

EXPLANATORY NOTE

(This note is not part of the Regulations)

These Regulations amend the Rules of the Air and Air Traffic Control Regulations 1985. The principal changes are :

(1) Rule 5 is amended so that when calculating the ability of an aircraft to alight clear of a congested area or an assembly in the open air of more than 1000 persons, if the aircraft is towing a banner, the calculation must be done on the basis that the banner will not be jettisoned whilst over the congested area or within 3000ft of such an assembly (regulation 2(1) and (2)).

(2) Rule 9 is amended to require aircraft fitted with an anti-collision light to display such a light in flight by day, to require an aircraft to display specified lights at night whilst on the ground unless it is stationary in a specified part of an aerodrome, to require an aircraft to display an anti-collision light when stationary on the apron of an aerodrome with its engines running and to permit any flashing light to be switched off or reduced in intensity if it may adversely affect members of the flight crew or outside observers (regulation 2(3)).

(3) Rule 10 is amended to permit an aircraft to continue to fly by day when its anti-collision light has failed subject to a specified condition (regulation 2(4)).

(4) Rule 11 is amended to impose the requirements previously applying to aircraft having a maximum total weight authorised of more than 5700kg also on any other flying machine of a type first certified on or after 1st April 1988 (regulation 2(5) and (6)).

(5) Rule 15 is amended to require an airship to display an anti-collision light while flying at night (regulation 2(7)).

(6) A new rule 21A is added to permit gliders to enter specified airspace which is notified for the purpose of rule 21 without complying with the provision of rule 21 subject to compliance with such conditions as may be notified for the purpose of rule 21A (regulation 2(10)).

(7) Rule 36 is amended to establish Special Rules Airspace at Belfast/Aldergrove Airport (regulation 2(11)).

STATUTORY INSTRUMENTS

1987 No. 1823

CHARITIES

The Exempt Charities Order 1987

Made - - - - *21st October 1987*

At the Court of Saint James, the 21st day of October 1987

Present,

The Counsellors of State in Council

Whereas Her Majesty, in pursuance of the Regency Acts 1937 to 1953, was pleased, by Letters Patent dated the 17th day of September 1987, to delegate to the six Counsellors of State therein named or any two or more of them full power and authority during the period of Her Majesty's absence from the United Kingdom to summon and hold on Her Majesty's behalf Her Privy Council and to signify thereat Her Majesty's approval for anything for which Her Majesty's approval in Council is required:

Now, therefore, His Royal Highness The Prince Andrew Duke of York and Her Royal Highness The Princess Royal, being authorised thereto by the said Letters Patent, and in pursuance of paragraph (c) of Schedule 2 to the Charities Act 1960(a), and by and with the advice of Her Majesty's Privy Council, do on Her Majesty's behalf order, and it is hereby ordered, as follows:—

1. This Order may be cited as the Exempt Charities Order 1987.

2. The Institute of Education, University of London, a college of the University of London, is hereby declared to be an exempt charity for the purposes of the Charities Act 1960.

G. I. de Deney
Clerk of the Privy Council

EXPLANATORY NOTE

(This note is not part of the Order)

This Order declares the Institute of Education, University of London, to be an " exempt charity " within the meaning of the Charities Act 1960.

Exempt charities are not required to be registered with the Charity Commissioners and the Commissioners cannot exercise any of their powers under the Act of 1960 in relation to an exempt charity except at that charity's request.

(a) 1960 c.58.

STATUTORY INSTRUMENTS

1987 No. 1824

ARCHITECTS

The Architects' Qualifications (EEC Recognition) Order 1987

Made - - - -	*21st October 1987*
Laid before Parliament	*29th October 1987*
Coming into force	*19th November 1987*

At the Court of Saint James, the 21st day of October 1987

Present,

The Counsellors of State in Council

Whereas Her Majesty, in pursuance of the Regency Acts 1937 to 1953, was pleased, by Letters Patent dated the 17th day of September 1987, to delegate to the six Counsellors of State therein named or any two or more of them full power and authority during the period of Her Majesty's absence from the United Kingdom to summon and hold on Her Majesty's behalf Her Privy Council and to signify thereat Her Majesty's approval for anything for which Her Majesty's approval in Council is required:

Now, therefore, His Royal Highness The Prince Andrew Duke of York and Her Royal Highness The Princess Royal being authorised thereto by the said Letters Patent, and in pursuance of the powers conferred on Her Majesty by section 2(2) of the European Communities Act 1972(**a**), and all other powers enabling Her Majesty, and by and with the advice of Her Majesty's Privy Council, do on Her Majesty's behalf order, and it is hereby ordered, as follows:—

Citation and commencement

1. This Order may be cited as the Architects' Qualifications (EEC Recognition) Order 1987 and shall come into force on 19th November 1987.

Interpretation

2. In this Order–

"the 1931 Act" means the Architects (Registration) Act 1931(**b**); and
"the 1938 Act" means the Architects Registration Act 1938(**c**).

3. At the end of section 2 of the 1931 Act there shall be inserted the following definitions–

O.J. No. L. 223/15.
"The expression "the Directive" means European Communities Council Directive No. 85/384/EEC on the mutual recognition of diplomas, certificates and other evidence of formal qualifications in architecture, as

---

(**a**) 1972 c. 68.
(**b**) 1931 c. 33.
(**c**) 1938 c. 54.

O.J. No. L. 376/1.
O.J. No. L. 27/71.

amended by European Communities Council Directives Nos. 85/614/EEC and 86/17/EEC.

The expression "competent authority", in relation to a member State, means an authority or body designated by the member State in accordance with the Directive.

The expression "national" in relation to a member State means the same as in the Community Treaties, but does not include a person who, by virtue of article 2 of Protocol No. 3 (Channel Islands and Isle of Man) to the Treaty of Accession is not to benefit from Community provisions relating to the free movement of persons and services.

The expression "disqualifying decision in another member state" in relation to any person means a decision made by a competent authority of a member State other than the United Kingdom which–

(a) is expressed to be made on the ground that he has committed a criminal offence or has misconducted himself in a professional respect; and

(b) has in that State the effect that he is no longer registered or otherwise officially recognised as an architect or that he is prohibited from practising as an architect there.".

Recognition of European Community architectural qualifications

4. In section 5(2)(a) and (b) and (3) of the 1931 Act the words "in pursuance of section 6" shall be inserted after the word "Act".

5. After section 6 of the 1931 Act there shall be inserted the following section–

"European qualifications.

6A.—(1) Subject to the provisions of this Act, a national of a member State who satisfies any of the requirements set out in subsection (2) shall on application made to the Council in the prescribed manner and on payment of the prescribed fee be entitled to be registered in pursuance of this section.

(2) The requirements are that a person–

(a) holds a qualification listed in the Fourth Schedule or, where the course of study leading to that qualification has been started no later than the beginning of the first academic year beginning after 5th August 1987, Part I of the Fifth Schedule to this Act, together with a certificate issued by a competent authority of a member State, in accordance with Article 23 of the Directive, stating that he has gained at least two years practical training experience in that member State under the supervision of a person established as an architect in that member State;

(b) holds a qualification listed in Part II of the Fifth Schedule to the Act where the course of study leading to that qualification has been started no later than the beginning of the first academic year beginning after 5th August 1987, together with a certificate issued by a competent authority of the Federal Republic of Germany, in accordance with Article 4(1) of the Directive, stating that he has gained at least four years appropriate professional experience in the Federal Republic of Germany;

(c) holds a certificate issued by a competent authority of a member State, in accordance with Article 12 of the Directive, stating that he has been, no later than the date on which that member State implemented the Directive, authorised in that member State to use the title of architect and that he has pursued activities in the field of architecture effectively for at least three consecutive years during the five years preceding the issue of the certificate;

(d) holds a certificate issued by a competent authority of a member State, in accordance with Article 5 of the Directive, stating that he is, by reason of his distinguished achievements in the field of architecture, entitled to use the title of architect.

(3) Where a person holds a certificate issued by a competent authority of the Federal Republic of Germany stating that a qualification awarded to that person by an institution in the German Democratic Republic after 8th May 1945 is of equivalent effect to a qualification listed in the Fourth or the Fifth Schedule to this Act, that person shall, for the purposes of this Act, be deemed to hold a qualification listed in the Fourth or, as the case may be, the Fifth Schedule to this Act.

(4) The Council may refuse to register a person in pursuance of this section if they are aware that there is a disqualifying decision in another member State in force in respect of that person.

(5) The Council shall cause a written notice of their decision on any application for registration in pursuance of this section to be served on the applicant within three months of his application being duly made.

(6) If, in pursuance of Article 17(4) or 18(2) of the Directive, the Council consult a member State in respect of an application under this section, the period mentioned in subsection (5) shall be extended by such period as may elapse between initiating the consultation and the receipt by the Council of a final reply from that member State.

(7) A person who is registered in pursuance of this section shall, when using his academic title or any abbreviations of it, express such title or abbreviation in the language or one of the languages of the member State in which the body conferring the title is located and shall follow the title or any abbreviation of it with the name and location of the body conferring the title.".

6. There shall be inserted after the Third Schedule to the 1931 Act the Schedules set out in the Schedule to this Order.

7. After section 7 of the 1931 Act there shall be inserted the following section–

"Removal of name from Register: disqualification in another member State.

7A.—(1) If a person's name was entered on the Register in pursuance of section 6A of this Act at a time when there was a disqualifying decision in another member State in force in respect of that person, and if at that time the Council were unaware of that fact, the Council, on being satisfied that the person was at that time and still is subject to that disqualifying decision, may cause his name to be removed from the Register.

(2) If a person who is registered under this Act in pursuance of section 6A becomes subject to a disqualifying decision in another member State expressed to be made on the ground that he has committed a criminal offence he shall be deemed for the purposes of section 7 of this Act, to have been convicted of that offence.".

Visiting EEC architects

8. After section 1 of the 1938 Act there shall be inserted the following section–

"Visiting EEC architects.

1A.—(1) A national of a member State who is established as an architect in a member State other than the United Kingdom may practise or carry on business under a name, style or title containing the word "architect" while visiting the United Kingdom without being a person registered under the principal Act during the period, and in respect of the services, for which his enrolment on the list of visiting EEC architects is effective.

(2) Before so practising or carrying on business the person concerned shall supply to the Council–

(a) a declaration in writing giving particulars of the services to be provided and the period or periods for which he expects to provide them; and

    (b) a certificate (or certificates), issued not more than 12 months previously by the competent authority of a member State in which he is established as an architect, showing that–

        (i) he is lawfully pursuing activities in the field of architecture in a member State other than the United Kingdom; and

        (ii) he satisfies any of the requirements set out in section 6A(2) of the principal Act.

(3) Where a person complies with the requirements of subsection (2), the Council shall enrol his name on the list of visiting EEC architects maintained for the purposes of this section for such period or periods and in respect of such services as they consider appropriate having regard to the particulars given in the declaration referred to in subsection (2)(a).

(4) The Council shall maintain, for the purposes of this section, in addition to the Register, a list of the names of visiting EEC architects enrolled from time to time under this section, with their qualifications and the periods for which and the services in respect of which their respective enrolments are effective; and the Council shall permit any person to inspect the list during normal working hours.

(5) No fee shall be charged for enrolment under this section as a visiting EEC architect.

(6) A person shall not be enrolled as a visiting EEC architect at a time when he is subject to–

    (a) a disqualifying decision in another member State; or

    (b) a period of disqualification from registration imposed by the Council under the principal Act.

(7) A person's name shall be removed from the list of visiting EEC architects if–

    (a) he becomes established as an architect in the United Kingdom;

    (b) he renders services in the United Kingdom otherwise than in accordance with a declaration made by him under subsection (2)(a); or

    (c) he may no longer lawfully pursue activities in the field of architecture in the member State referred to in subsection (2)(b)(i).

(8) Section 7 of the principal Act and regulations made under section 13 of that Act for the regulation of disciplinary proceedings shall apply to a person who is or has been enrolled under this section as a visiting EEC architect as if that person had been registered under section 6 of that Act, and references to the Register and registration under this Act shall be construed accordingly.

(9) A person enrolled on the list of visiting EEC architects shall, when using his title or any abbreviation of it, express such title or abbreviation in the language or one of the languages of the member State in which the body conferring the title is located and shall follow the title or any abbreviation of it with the name and location of the body conferring the title.".

G.I. de Deney
Clerk of the Privy Council

SCHEDULE

Article 6

NEW SCHEDULES TO BE INSERTED IN THE 1931 ACT.

"FOURTH SCHEDULE

Section 6A

EUROPEAN COMMUNITY QUALIFICATIONS IN ARCHITECTURE

Belgium

1. The diplomas awarded by the higher national schools of architecture or the higher national institutes of architecture (architecte-architect).

2. The diplomas awarded by the higher provincial school of architecture of Hasselt (architect).

3. The diplomas awarded by the Royal Academies of Fine Arts (architecte-architect).

4. The diplomas awarded by the 'écoles Saint-Luc' (architecte-architect).

5. The civil engineering/architecture diplomas and architecture/engineering diplomas awarded by the faculties of applied sciences of the universities and by the Polytechnical Faculty of Mons (ingénieur-architecte, ingénieur-architect).

Denmark

1. The diploma awarded by the Danish State School of Architecture in Aarhus.

Ireland

1. The degree of Bachelor of Architecture awarded by the National University of Ireland (B. Arch (NUI)) to architecture graduates of University College, Dublin.

2. The diploma of degree standard in architecture awarded by the College of Technology, Bolton Street, Dublin (Dip. Arch).

3. The Certificate of Associateship of the Royal Institute of Architects of Ireland (ARIAI).

4. The Certificate of Membership of the Royal Institute of Architects of Ireland (MRIAI).

Portugal

1. The Diploma 'diploma licenciatura em arquitectura' awarded by the Department of Architecture of the Technical University of Lisbon.

2. The Diploma 'diploma licenciatura em arquitectura' awarded by the Department of Architecture of the University of Porto.

FIFTH SCHEDULE

Section 6A

ESTABLISHED EUROPEAN COMMUNITY RIGHTS

PART I

Belgium

1. University diplomas in civil engineering, accompanied by a traineeship certificate awarded by the association of architects entitling the holder to hold the professional title of architect (architecte-architect).

2. The diplomas in architecture awarded by the central or State examining board for architecture (architecte-architect).

Denmark

1. The diplomas awarded by the National Schools of Architecture in Copenhagen and Åarhus (arkitekt).

2. The certificate of registration issued by the Board of Architects pursuant to Law No. 202 of 28th May 1975 (registreret arkitekt).

3. Diplomas awarded by the Higher Schools of Civil Engineering (bygningskonstruktør), accompanied by a certificate from the competent authorities to the effect that the person concerned has passed a test of his formal qualifications in accordance with Article 13 of the Directive.

France

1. The Government architect's diploma awarded by the Ministry of Education until 1959, and subsequently by the Ministry of Cultural Affairs (architecte DPLG).

2. The diplomas awarded by the 'Ecole spećiale d'architecture' (architecte DESA).

3. The diplomas awarded since 1955 by the department of architecture of the 'Ecole nationale supérieure des Arts et Industries de Strasbourg' (formerly the 'Ecole nationale d'ingénieurs de Strasbourg' (architecte ENSAIS).

Germany

1. The diplomas awarded by higher institutes of fine arts (Dipl.-Ing., Architekt (HfbK)).

2. The diplomas awarded by the departments of architecture (Architektur/Hochbau) of 'Technische Hochschulen', of technical universities, of universities and, in so far as these institutions have been merged into 'Gesamthochschulen', of 'Gesamthochschulen' (Dipl.-Ing., and any other title which may be laid down later for holders of these diplomas).

3. The diplomas awarded by the departments of architecture (Arkitechtur/Hochbau) of 'Fachhochschulen' and, in so far as these institutions have been merged into 'Gesamthochschulen', by the departments of architecture (Architektur/Hochbau) of 'Gesamthochschulen', where the period of study leading to that diploma is at least four years (Ingenieur grad. and any other title which may be laid down later for holders of these diplomas).

4. The diplomas (Prüfungszeugnisse) awarded before 1st January 1973 by the departments of architecture of 'Ingenieurschulen' and of 'Werkkunstschulen', accompanied by a certificate from the competent authorities to the effect that the person concerned has passed a test of his formal qualifications in accordance with Article 13 of the Directive.

Greece

1. The engineering/architecture diplomas awarded by the METSOVION POLYTECHNION of Athens, together with a certificate issued by Greece's Technical Chamber conferring the right to pursue activities in the field of architecture.

2. The engineering/architecture diplomas awarded by the ARISTOTELION PANEPISTIMION of Thessaloniki, together with a certificate issued by Greece's Technical Chamber conferring the right to pursue activities in the field of architecture.

3. The engineering/civil engineering diplomas awarded by the METSOVION POLYTECHNION of Athens, together with a certificate issued by Greece's Technical Chamber conferring the right to pursue activities in the field of architecture.

4. The engineering/civil engineering diplomas awarded by the ARISTOTELION PANEPISTIMION of Thessaloniki, together with a certificate issued by Greece's Technical Chamber conferring the right to pursue activities in the field of architecture.

5. The engineering/civil engineering diplomas awarded by the PANEPISTIMION THRAKIS, together with a certificate issued by Greece's Technical Chamber conferring the right to pursue activities in the field of architecture.

6. The engineering/civil engineering diplomas awarded by the PANEPISTIMION PATRON, together with a certificate issued by Greece's Technical Chamber conferring the right to pursue activities in the field of architecture.

Italy

1. 'Laurea in architettura' diplomas awarded by universities, polytechnic institutes and the higher institutes of architecture of Venice and Reggio Calabria, accompanied by the diploma entitling the holder to pursue independently the profession of architect, awarded by the Minister for Education after

the candidate has passed before a competent board the State examination entitling him to pursue independently the profession of architect (dott. Architetto).

2. 'Laurea in ingegneria' diplomas in building construction ('sezione costenzione civile') awarded by universities and polytechnic institutes, accompanied by the diploma entitling the holder to pursue independently a profession in the field of architecture, awarded by the Minister for Education after the candidate has passed before a competent board the State examination entitling him to pursue the profession independently (dott. Ing. Architetto or dott. Ing. in ingegneria civile).

Netherlands

1. The certificate stating that its holder has passed the degree examination in architecture awarded by the departments of architecture of the technical colleges of Delft or Eindhoven (bouwkundig ingenieur).

2. The diplomas awarded by State-recognised architectural academies (architect).

3. The diplomas awarded until 1971 by the former architectural colleges (Hoger Bouwkunstonder-richt) (architect HBO).

4. The diplomas awarded until 1970 by the former architectural colleges (Voortgezet Bouwkunston-derricht) (architect VBO).

5. The certificate stating that the person concerned has passed an examination organised by the Architects Council of the 'Bond van Nederlandse Architecten' (Order of Dutch Architects, BNA) (architect).

6. The diploma of the 'Stichting Instituut voor Architectuur' ('Institute of Architecture' Foundation) (IVA) awarded on completion of a course organised by this foundation and extending over a minimum period of four years (architect), accompanied by a certificate from the competent authorities to the effect that the person concerned has passed a test of his formal qualifications in accordance with Article 13 of the Directive.

7. A certificate issued by the competent authorities to the effect that, before 5th August 1985 the person concerned passed the degree examination of 'Kandidaat in de bouwkunde' organised by the technical colleges of Delft or Eindhoven and that, over a period of at least five years immediately prior to that date, he pursued architectural activities the nature and importance of which, in accordance with Netherlands requirements, guarantee that he is competent to pursue those activities (architect).

8. A certificate issued by the competent authorities only to persons who have reached the age of 40 years before 5th August 1985 certifying that, over a period of at least five years immediately prior to that date, the person concerned had pursued architectural activities the nature and importance of which, in accordance with Netherlands requirements, guarantee that he is competent to pursue those activities (architect).

Note

The certificates referred to in paragraphs 7 and 8 need no longer be recognised as from the date of entry into force of laws and regulations in the Netherlands governing the taking up and pursuit of architectural activities under the professional title of architect, in so far as under such provisions those certificates do not authorise the taking up of such activities under that professional title.

Portugal

1. The Diploma 'diploma do curso especial de arquitectura' awarded by the Schools of Fine Arts of Lisbon and of Porto.

2. The Architects Diploma 'diploma de arquitecto' awarded by the Schools of Fine Arts of Lisbon and of Porto.

3. The Diploma 'diploma do curso de arquitectura' awarded by the Higher Schools of Fine Arts of Lisbon and Porto.

4. The Diploma 'diploma de licenciatura em arquitectura' awarded by the Higher School of Fine Arts of Lisbon.

5. The university diploma in civil engineering awarded by the Higher Technical Institute of the Technical University of Lisbon (Licenciatura em engenharia civil).

6. The university diploma in civil engineering awarded by the Faculty of Engineering (Engenharia) of the University of Porto (Licenciatura em engenharia civil).

7. The university diploma in civil engineering awarded by the Faculty of Science and Technology of the University of Coimbra (Licenciatura em engenharia civil).

8. The university diploma in civil engineering (production) awarded by the University of Minho (Licenciatura em engenharia civil (producão)).

Spain

The official formal qualification of an architect (titulo oficial de arquitecto) awarded by the Ministry of Education and Science or by the universities.

PART II
SPECIAL PROVISIONS FOR GERMANY

The diplomas awarded by the departments of architecture (Architektur/Hochbau) of 'Fachhochschulen' and, in so far as these institutions have been merged into 'Gesamthochschulen', by the departments of architecture (Architektur/Hochbau) of 'Gesamthochschulen', where the period of study leading to that diploma is less than four years but at least three years (Ingenieur grad. and any other title which may be laid down later for holders of these diplomas).

EXPLANATORY NOTE

(This note is not part of the Order)

This Order under section 2 of the European Communities Act 1972 comes into force on 19th November 1987. It implements European Communities Council Directives relating to the mutual recognition of qualifications in architecture. The Order amends the Architects (Registration) Act 1931 ("the 1931 Act") and the Architects Registration Act 1938 ("the 1938 Act").

The Order gives architects with defined European qualifications the right to be registered under the 1931 Act (articles 5 and 6, which insert new sections 6A and 7A and two new Schedules into the 1931 Act). In consequence, the role of the Board of Architectural Education and the Admission Committee in relation to European qualifications is abolished (article 4). Disqualification in another member State may lead to removal of an architects name from the register (article 7, which inserts a new section 7A into the 1931 Act).

A form of temporary registration is provided for architects established in other member States who wish to provide services while visiting the United Kingdom and such visiting architects are made subject to disciplinary provisions (article 8, which inserts a new section 1A into the 1938 Act).

STATUTORY INSTRUMENTS

1987 No. 1825

CHILDREN AND YOUNG PERSONS

The Child Abduction and Custody (Parties to Conventions) (Amendment) (No. 2) Order 1987

Made - - - - *21st October 1987*

At the Court of Saint James, the 21st day of October 1987

Present,

The Counsellors of State in Council

Whereas Her Majesty in pursuance of the Regency Acts 1937 to 1953, was pleased, by Letters Patent dated the 17th day of September 1987, to delegate to the six Counsellors of State therein named or any two or more of them full power and authority during the period of Her Majesty's absence from the United Kingdom to summon and hold on Her Majesty's behalf Her Privy Council and to signify thereat Her Majesty's approval for anything for which Her Majesty's approval in Council is required:

Now, therefore, His Royal Highness The Prince Andrew Duke of York and Her Royal Highness The Princess Royal, being authorised thereto by the said Letters Patent, and in pursuance of the powers conferred by section 2 of the Child Abduction and Custody Act 1985(**a**) and all other powers enabling Her Majesty, and by and with the advice of Her Majesty's Privy Council, do on Her Majesty's behalf order, and it is hereby ordered, as follows:

1.—(1) This Order may be cited as the Child Abduction and Custody (Parties to Conventions) (Amendment) (No. 2) Order 1987.

(2) The Child Abduction and Custody (Parties to Conventions) (Amendment) Order 1987(**b**) is revoked.

2. The Child Abduction and Custody (Parties to Conventions) Order 1986(**c**) is amended by deleting Schedule 1 thereto(**d**) and substituting therefor the following –

(**a**) 1985 c.60.
(**b**) S.I. 1987/163.
(**c**) S.I. 1986/1159.
(**d**) Schedule 1 to S.I. 1986/1159 was substituted by S.I. 1987/163.

"SCHEDULE 1 Article 2

CONVENTION ON THE CIVIL ASPECTS OF INTERNATIONAL CHILD ABDUCTION, THE HAGUE, 25th OCTOBER 1980

Contracting States to the Convention	Territories specified in Declarations under Article 39 or 40 of the Convention	Date of Coming into Force as between the United Kingdom and the State or Territory
Australia	Australian States and mainland Territories	1st January 1987
Canada	Ontario	1st August 1986
	New Brunswick	1st August 1986
	British Columbia	1st August 1986
	Manitoba	1st August 1986
	Nova Scotia	1st August 1986
	Newfoundland	1st August 1986
	Prince Edward Island	1st August 1986
	Quebec	1st August 1986
	Yukon Territory	1st August 1986
	Saskatchewan	1st November 1986
	Alberta	1st February 1987
The French Republic	—	1st August 1986
The Hungarian People's Republic	—	1st September 1986
The Grand Duchy of Luxembourg	—	1st January 1987
The Portuguese Republic	—	1st August 1986
Spain	—	1st September 1987
The Swiss Confederation	—	1st August 1986 "

G. I. de Deney
Clerk of the Privy Council

EXPLANATORY NOTE

(This note is not part of the Order)

This Order amends the Child Abduction and Custody (Parties to Conventions) Order 1986 in order to specify that the Convention on the Civil Aspects of International Child Abduction, The Hague, 25th October 1980 (Cm.33) has entered into force for Spain.

STATUTORY INSTRUMENTS

1987 No. 1826

COPYRIGHT

The Copyright (Taiwan) (Extension to Territories) Order 1987

Made - - - -	*21st October 1987*
Laid before Parliament	*29th October 1987*
Coming into force	*20th November 1987*

At the Court of Saint James, the 21st day of October 1987

Present,

The Counsellors of State in Council

Whereas Her Majesty in pursuance of the Regency Acts 1937 to 1953, was pleased, by Letters Patent dated the 17th day of September 1987, to delegate to the six Counsellors of State therein named or any two or more of them full power and authority during the period of Her Majesty's absence from the United Kingdom to summon and hold on Her Majesty's behalf Her Privy Council and to signify thereat Her Majesty's approval for anything for which Her Majesty's approval in Council is required;

Now, therefore, His Royal Highness The Prince Andrew Duke of York and Her Royal Highness The Princess Royal, being authorised thereto by the said Letters Patent, and in pursuance of the powers conferred by sections 31 and 47 of the Copyright Act 1956 (a) and all other powers enabling Her Majesty, and by and with the advice of Her Majesty's Privy Council, do on Her Majesty's behalf order, and it is hereby ordered, as follows:

1. This Order may be cited as the Copyright (Taiwan) (Extension to Territories) Order 1987 and shall come into force on 20th November 1987.

2. The Copyright (Taiwan) Order 1985 (b) shall extend to the countries mentioned in the Schedule to this Order, except that article 2 of that Order shall have effect as part of the law of any country to which it extends as if for the references to the United Kingdom there were substituted references to the country in question.

G. I. de Deney
Clerk of the Privy Council

(a) 1956 c.74.   (b) S.I. 1985/1777.

SCHEDULE

COUNTRIES TO WHICH THE COPYRIGHT (TAIWAN) ORDER 1985 EXTENDS

Bermuda
British Indian Ocean Territory
British Virgin Islands
Cayman Islands
Falkland Islands
Gibraltar
Montserrat
St. Helena
St. Helena Dependencies (Ascension, Tristan da Cunha)
South Georgia and the South Sandwich Islands

EXPLANATORY NOTE

(This note is not part of the Order)

This Order provides for the extension of the Copyright (Taiwan) Order 1985 to the countries listed in the Schedule to the Order.

STATUTORY INSTRUMENTS

1987 No. 1827

MERCHANT SHIPPING

The Merchant Shipping (Confirmation of Legislation) (Falkland Islands) Order 1987

Made - - - -	*21st October 1987*
Laid before Parliament	*29th October 1987*
Coming into force	*20th November 1987*

At the Court of Saint James, the 21st day of October 1987

Present,

The Counsellors of State in Council

Whereas Her Majesty, in pursuance of the Regency Acts 1937 to 1953, was pleased, by Letters Patent dated the 17th day of September 1987, to delegate to the six Counsellors of State therein named or any two or more of them full power and authority during the period of Her Majesty's absence from the United Kingdom to summon and hold on Her Majesty's behalf Her Privy Council and to signify thereat Her Majesty's approval for anything for which Her Majesty's approval in Council is required;

Now therefore, His Royal Highness The Prince Andrew Duke of York and Her Royal Highness The Princess Royal, being authorised thereto by the said Letters Patent, and in pursuance of the power conferred by section 735(1) of the Merchant Shipping Act 1894(**a**) and all other powers enabling Her Majesty, and by and with the advice of Her Majesty's Privy Council, do on Her Majesty's behalf order, and it is hereby ordered, as follows:

1.   This Order may be cited as the Merchant Shipping (Confirmation of Legislation) (Falkland Islands) Order 1987 and shall come into force on 20th November 1987.

2.   The Merchant Shipping (Registry) Ordinance, 1987(**b**) is hereby confirmed.

G. I. de Deney
Clerk of the Privy Council

(**a**)   1894 c.60.
(**b**)   Ordinance No. 7 of 1987 of the Falkland Islands.

EXPLANATORY NOTE

(This note is not part of the Order)

This Order, made under section 735(1) of the Merchant Shipping Act 1894, confirms a Law enacted by the Legislature of the Falkland Islands which repeals, in relation to the registration of ships in the Falkland Islands, certain provisions of Part I of the Merchant Shipping Act 1894 regarding such registration and in relation to fishing boats Part IV of that Act as it applies to the Islands.

STATUTORY INSTRUMENTS

1987 No. 1828

PRISONERS

The Repatriation of Prisoners (Overseas Territories) (Amendment) Order 1987

Made - - - -	*21st October 1987*
Coming into force	*16th November 1987*

At the Court of Saint James, the 21st day of October 1987

Present,

The Counsellors of State in Council

Whereas Her Majesty in pursuance of the Regency Acts 1937 to 1953, was pleased, by Letters Patent dated the 17th day of September 1987, to delegate to the six Counsellors of State therein named or any two or more of them full power and authority during the period of Her Majesty's absence from the United Kingdom to summon and hold on Her Majesty's behalf Her Privy Council and to signify thereat Her Majesty's approval for anything for which Her Majesty's approval in Council is required:

Now, therefore, His Royal Highness The Prince Andrew Duke of York and Her Royal Highness The Princess Royal, being authorised thereto by the said Letters Patent, and in pursuance of the powers conferred by section 9(4) of the Repatriation of Prisoners Act 1984(**a**) and all other powers enabling Her Majesty, and by and with the advice of Her Majesty's Privy Council, do on Her Majesty's behalf order, and it is hereby ordered, as follows:

1. This Order may be cited as the Repatriation of Prisoners (Overseas Territories) (Amendment) Order 1987 and shall come into force on 16th November 1987.

2. The Repatriation of Prisoners (Overseas Territories) Order 1986(**b**) shall be amended as follows:

(a) the following shall be substituted for paragraph 1(3)(a) of Schedule 1 to that Order:

"that person is a British citizen or a British Dependent Territories citizen or a British National (Overseas);"

(b) Hong Kong shall be added to the Territories specified in Schedule 2 to that Order.

G. I. de Deney
Clerk of the Privy Council

(**a**) 1984 c.47.   (**b**) S.I. 1986/2226.

EXPLANATORY NOTE

(This note is not part of the Order)

This Order extends the provisions of the Repatriation of Prisoners Act 1984, subject to exceptions, adaptations and modifications, to Hong Kong, and includes British Nationals (Overseas) as a specific category of persons in respect of whom warrants under the Repatriation of Prisoners (Overseas Territories) Order 1986 may be issued.

STATUTORY INSTRUMENTS

1987 No. 1829

CARIBBEAN AND NORTH ATLANTIC TERRITORIES

The Turks and Caicos Islands (Constitution) (Interim Amendment) (No. 3) Order 1987

Made - - - -	*21st October 1987*
Laid before Parliament	*29th October 1987*
Coming into force in accordance with section 1(3)	

At the Court of Saint James, the 21st day of October 1987

Present,

The Counsellors of State in Council

Whereas Her Majesty in pursuance of the Regency Acts 1937 to 1953, was pleased, by Letters Patent dated the 17th day of September 1987, to delegate to the six Counsellors of State therein named or any two or more of them full power and authority during the period of Her Majesty's absence from the United Kingdom to summon and hold on Her Majesty's behalf Her Privy Council and to signify thereat Her Majesty's approval for anything for which Her Majesty's approval in Council is required;

Now, therefore, His Royal Highness The Prince Andrew Duke of York and Her Royal Highness The Princess Royal, being authorised thereto by the said Letters Patent, and in pursuance of the powers conferred by section 5 of the West Indies Act 1962 (a) and all other powers enabling Her Majesty, and by and with the advice of Her Majesty's Privy Council, do on Her Majesty's behalf order, and it is hereby ordered, as follows:

1.—(1) This Order may be cited as the Turks and Caicos Islands (Constitution) (Interim Amendment) (No. 3) Order 1987 and shall be construed as one with the Turks and Caicos Islands (Constitution) Order 1976 (b), which Order is hereinafter referred to as "the principal Order". *(Citation, construction and commencement.)*

(2) This Order and the principal Order may be cited together as the Turks and Caicos Islands (Constitution) Orders 1976 to 1987.

(3) This Order shall come into force on 20th November 1987:

Provided that sections 2 and 3 of this Order shall come into force on the date of the first dissolution of the Legislative Council after the commencement of this Order.

2. Part IV of the principal Order shall be amended in the manner set out in Schedule 1 to this Order. *(Amendment of Part IV of principal Order.)*

(a) 1962 c.19.
(b) S.I. 1976/1156, amended by S.I. 1979/919, 1982/1075, 1986/1157, 1987/934 and 1271.

New electoral
districts.

3. For the purposes of elections to the Legislative Council, the Islands shall be divided into the five electoral districts specified in Column 1 of Schedule 2 to this Order which shall comprise the islands or component parts specified in relation thereto in Column 2 of that Schedule, and each electoral district shall return to the Legislative Council the number of members specified in relation thereto in Column 3 of that Schedule.

Electoral Reg-
ulations.

4.—(1) The Governor may, acting in his discretion, by regulations published in the *Gazette*, make provision for the holding of elections, the registration of electors and for the procedure for the election of members of the Legislative Council; and such regulations shall have effect as if they were a law made under section 28 of the principal Order.

(2) Regulations made under this section may be made and brought into force, and all necessary preparations for elections to be held in accordance with such regulations and with the principal Order as amended by this Order may be commenced, in anticipation of the coming into force of sections 2 and 3 of this Order:

Provided that no provisions of such regulations shall be brought into force before the coming into force of the said sections 2 and 3 except those provisions relating to the registration of electors, the compilation of electoral lists, and all matters connected therewith.

G. I. de Deney
Clerk of the Privy Council

SCHEDULE 1   article 2

AMENDMENTS TO PART IV OF PRINCIPAL ORDER

1. Section 19(b) of the principal Order shall be amended by substituting the word "thirteen" for the word "eleven".

2. Section 21 of the principal Order shall be amended by the deletion of subsection (2).

3. Section 22 of the principal Order shall be replaced by the following–

"Qualifications for elected membership.
    22. Subject to section 25 of this Order, a person shall be qualified to be elected as a member of the Legislative Council if, and shall not be qualified to be so elected unless, he–

    (a) has attained the age of twenty-one years; and

    (b) is, on the date of his nomination for election, resident in the Islands and has been so resident for not less than twelve months, in the aggregate, out of the two years immediately preceding that date; and

    (c) falls into one of the following categories, that is to say–

        (i) he was born in the Islands; or

        (ii) he was born outside the Islands of a father or mother either of whom was born in the Islands; or

        (iii) he has, under the law in force in the Islands regulating immigration, the status of "Belonger"."

4. Section 26(3) of the principal Order shall be amended by the deletion of paragraph (c).

5. Section 27 of the principal Order shall be amended by substituting for subsection (1) the following–

"(1) Subject to the provisions of subsection (2) of this section, a person shall be qualified to be registered as an elector for the purpose of the election of members of the Legislative Council if, and shall not be so qualified unless, on the qualifying date–

    (a) he has attained the age of eighteen years; and

    (b) he is resident in the Islands and has been so resident for not less than twelve months, in the aggregate, out of the two years immediately preceding the qualifying date; and

    (c) he falls into one of the following categories, that is to say–

        (i) he was born in the Islands; or

        (ii) he was born outside the Islands of a father or mother either of whom was born in the Islands; or

        (iii) he has, under the law in force in the Islands regulating immigration, the status of "Belonger"."

6. Section 28(2) of the principal Order shall be amended by the deletion of paragraph (b).

article 3

SCHEDULE 2

ELECTORAL DISTRICTS

Column 1 *Electoral District*	Column 2 *Islands or Component Parts*	Column 3 *Number of Members to be Returned*
First District (Grand Turk North)	That part of the island of Grand Turk bounded on the south by a line drawn from west to east across the island at the Prison.	3
Second District (Grand Turk South and Salt Cay)	That part of the island of Grand Turk bounded on the north by a line drawn from west to east across the island at the Prison, and the island of Salt Cay.	3
Third District (South Caicos)	The island of South Caicos.	2
Fourth District (North and Middle Caicos)	The islands of North Caicos, Middle (or Grand) Caicos, and Parrot Cay.	3
Fifth District (Providenciales)	The islands of Providenciales, Pine Cay and West Caicos.	2

EXPLANATORY NOTE

(This note is not part of the Order)

This Order establishes new electoral districts for the purpose of elections to the Legislative Council of the Turks and Caicos Islands, and enables the Governor to make electoral regulations. It also amends certain provisions of the Constitution of the Islands relating to elections.

STATUTORY INSTRUMENTS

1987 No. 1830

SOCIAL SECURITY

The Social Security (Austria) Order 1987

Made - - - -	*21st October 1987*
Coming into force	*1st November 1987*

At the Court of Saint James, the 21st day of October 1987

Present,

The Counsellors of State in Council

Whereas Her Majesty, in pursuance of the Regency Acts 1937 to 1953, was pleased, by Letters Patent dated the 17th day of September 1987, to delegate to the six Counsellors of State therein named or any two or more of them full power and authority during the period of Her Majesty's absence from the United Kingdom to summon and hold on Her Majesty's behalf Her Privy Council and to signify thereat Her Majesty's approval for anything for which Her Majesty's approval in Council is required:

And, whereas on 22nd July 1980 a Convention on social security between the Government of the United Kingdom of Great Britain and Northern Ireland and the Government of the Republic of Austria (hereinafter referred to as "the Convention")(a) was signed on behalf of those Governments and effect was given thereto by the Social Security (Austria) Order 1981(b) (hereinafter referred to as "the Principal Order"):

And Whereas at London on the 9th day of December 1985 the Convention was amended by a Supplementary Convention(c) signed on behalf of those Governments (which Supplementary Convention is set out in the Schedule to this Order):

And Whereas by Article III(2) thereof it is provided that the Supplementary Convention shall enter into force on the first day of the third month following the month in which the instruments of ratification are exchanged:

And Whereas the Supplementary Convention has been ratified by the said Governments and the instruments of ratification were exchanged on 5th August 1987:

And Whereas by section 143 of the Social Security Act 1975(d) it is provided that Her Majesty may by Order in Council make provision for modifying or adapting the said Social Security Act in its application to cases affected by agreements with other Governments providing for reciprocity in matters specified in that section:

And Whereas by virtue of section 166(4) of the Social Security Act 1975 any Order in Council made under the said section 143 may be varied by a subsequent Order in Council made under that section:

(a) Cmnd. 8048.   (b) S.I. 1981/605.   (c) Cmnd. 9749.   (d) 1975 c.14; subsection (1A) of section 143 was inserted by section 6(1) of the Social Security Act 1981 (c.33).

Now, therefore, His Royal Highness The Prince Andrew Duke of York and Her Royal Highness The Princess Royal, being authorised thereto by the said Letters Patent, and in pursuance of the powers conferred by the said section 143 and of all other powers enabling Her Majesty, and by and with the advice of Her Majesty's Privy Council, do on Her Majesty's behalf order, and it is hereby ordered, as follows:–

Citation and commencement

1. This Order may be cited as the Social Security (Austria) Order 1987 and shall come into force on 1st November 1987.

Amendment of Principal Order and Modification of the Social Security Act 1975

2. The Schedule to the Principal Order shall be amended in accordance with, and accordingly the Social Security Act 1975 shall be modified to such extent as may be required to give effect to, the provisions contained in the Supplementary Convention set out in the Schedule to this Order, so far as the same relate to England, Wales and Scotland.

G. I. de Deney
Clerk of the Privy Council

Article 2   SCHEDULE

SUPPLEMENTARY CONVENTION ON SOCIAL SECURITY BETWEEN THE UNITED KINGDOM OF GREAT BRITAIN AND NORTHERN IRELAND AND THE REPUBLIC OF AUSTRIA

Her Majesty The Queen of the United Kingdom of Great Britain and Northern Ireland and of Her other Realms and Territories, Head of the Commonwealth (hereinafter referred to as "Her Britannic Majesty") and the Federal President of the Republic of Austria;

Desiring to amend and supplement the Convention of 22 July 1980 on social security;

Have resolved to conclude a supplementary Convention and for that purpose have appointed as their Plenipotentiaries:

Her Britannic Majesty:

For the United Kingdom of Great Britain and Northern Ireland:

The Rt. Hon. The Baroness Young
Minister of State for Foreign and Commonwealth Affairs

The Federal President of the Republic of Austria:

For the Republic of Austria:

Dr Reginald Thomas
Ambassador Extraordinary and Plenipotentiary of the Republic of Austria to the United Kingdom of Great Britain and Northern Ireland.

The Plenipotentiaries, having communicated to each other their full powers, found in good and due form, have agreed as follows:

Article I

For the purposes of this supplementary Convention, "Convention" means the Convention on Social Security between the United Kingdom of Great Britain and Northern Ireland and the Republic of Austria which was signed at Vienna on 22 July 1980.

Article II

(1) (a) In sub-paragraph (5) of paragraph (1) of Article 1 of the Convention the words "the Federal Minister for Finance" shall be replaced by the words "the Federal Minister for Family, Youth and Consumer Protection".

      (b) Sub-paragraph (17) of paragraph (1) of Article 1 of the Convention shall be deleted and the following substituted:

> "17. "invalidity pension" means, in relation to the territory of the United Kingdom, invalidity benefit payable under the legislation of that Party, and, in relation to Austria, benefit payable under the pension insurance legislation of Austria in the case of reduced working capacity or permanent loss of earning capacity;"

(2) To Article 6 of the Convention a paragraph (3) with the following wording shall be added:

> "(3) A person employed as a member of the non-travelling personnel of an undertaking engaged in the international transport of passengers or goods by railway, road, or air, whether for a third party or on its own account, having its principal place of business in the territory of one Party, shall remain subject to the legislation of that Party when he is sent by that undertaking to work in the territory of the other Party."

(3) To Article 9 of the Convention a paragraph (4) with the following wording shall be added:

> "(4) Where in accordance with the provisions of paragraph (1) of this Article and of Articles 6 and 8 of this Convention a person is subject to the legislation of any part of the territory of the United Kingdom while he is gainfully occupied in the territory of Austria he shall be entitled to contribute voluntarily to sickness insurance under the legislation of Austria as if he were permanently resident in its territory."

(4) Sub-paragraph (b) of paragraph (1) of Article 10 of the Convention shall be deleted and the following substituted:

> "(b) for each week beginning in a relevant tax year under the legislation of the United Kingdom, the whole of which week is an equivalent period completed as an employed person under the legislation of Austria, as having completed an equivalent period under the legislation of the United Kingdom."

(5) Article 12 of the Convention shall be deleted.

(6) Paragraph (2) of Article 16 of the Convention shall be deleted and the following substituted:

> "(2) Where a person is entitled to an old age pension (other than the basic component of a Category B retirement pension payable to a married woman) under the legislation of any one part of the territory of the United Kingdom without the application of the provisions of paragraph (1) of this Article, that pension shall be paid and the provisions of paragraph (1) of Article 17 of this Convention shall not be applied under that legislation. Where the old age pension payable is the basic component of a Category B retirement pension payable to a married woman, her pension entitlement shall be determined in accordance with the provisions of Article 17, if this is to her advantage."

(7) Paragraph (2) of Article 17 of the Convention shall be deleted and the following substituted:

> "(2) For the purposes of the calculation in paragraph (1) of this Article:
>
> (a) where all the insurance periods completed by any person under the legislation of:
>
>   (i) either Great Britain, Northern Ireland or the Isle of Man amount to less than one reckonable or, as the case may be, qualifying year, or relate only to periods before 6 April 1975 and in aggregate amount to less than 50 weeks; or
>
>   (ii) Jersey amount to less than an annual contribution factor of 1.00; or
>
>   (iii) Guernsey amount to less than 50 weeks;

those periods shall be treated as if they had been completed under the legislation of any other part of the territory of the United Kingdom under which a pension is, or if such periods were taken into account would be, payable, or, where two such pensions are or would be payable, under the legislation of that part which, at the date on which entitlement first arose or arises, is paying or would pay the greater amount. Where, notwithstanding the foregoing, no old age pension is payable under the legislation of any part of the territory of the United Kingdom such periods shall be treated as if they had been completed under the legislation of Austria;

(b) where all the insurance periods completed by any person under the legislation of Austria amount to less than twelve months, no pension shall be payable under that legislation and those periods shall be treated as if they had been completed under the legislation of that part of the territory of the United Kingdom under which a pension is, or if such periods were taken into account would be payable, or, where such a pension is or would be payable under the legislation of two or more parts of the territory of the United Kingdom, as if they had been completed under the legislation of that part which, at the date on which entitlement first arose or arises, is paying or would pay the greater or greatest amount."

(8) Paragraph (4) of Article 20 of the Convention shall be deleted and the following substituted:

"(4) for the purpose of applying the provisions of paragraph (1) of Article 16 and of Article 17 of this Convention periods during which a person was entitled to receive an invalidity pension or an old age pension under the legislation of any part of the territory of the United Kingdom shall be treated as if they were neutral periods under the legislation of Austria;"

(9)   (a) In the German text of paragraph (2) of Article 22 of the Convention the words "Artikel 2 Absatz 1 Buchstabe a Ziffer 1" shall be replaced by the words "Artikel 2 Absatz 1 Buchstabe b Ziffer 1".

(b) Paragraph (3) of Article 22 of the Convention shall be deleted and the following substituted:

"(3) Where a woman is entitled to an old age pension under the legislation of any part of the territory of the United Kingdom instead of a widow's benefit under that legislation, then for the purpose of calculating a widow's pension under the legislation of Austria paragraph (1) of this Article shall be applied as if the woman were entitled to widow's benefit under the legislation of any part of the territory of the United Kingdom."

(10)   (a) Paragraph (1) of Article 23 of the Convention shall be deleted and the following substituted:

"(1) If a person has completed insurance periods under the legislation of both High Contracting Parties, then for the purpose of any claim to invalidity pension under the legislation of one Party any insurance period or period of entitlement to sickness benefit or invalidity pension completed under the legislation of the other Party shall be treated as if it were respectively an insurance period or period of entitlement to sickness benefit or invalidity pension under the legislation of the former Party."

(b) The wording of paragraph (3) of Article 23 of the Convention shall become sub-paragraph (a) of paragraph (3) and a sub-paragraph (b) of paragraph (3) with the following wording shall be added:

"(b) for the purpose of a claim for invalidity pension by virtue of this Convention under the legislation of Austria, the provisions of Articles 17 to 21 of this Convention shall apply *mutatis mutandis* subject to the provisions of paragraphs (4) and (5) of this Article."

(11) Paragraph (3) of Article 43 of the Convention shall be deleted and the following substituted:

"(3) This Convention shall not diminish any right to benefit acquired under the legislation of either High Contracting Party before its date of entry into force, except to the extent to which such right to benefit would have to be determined afresh had the Conventions specified in paragraph (1) of this Article remained in force."

(12) In paragraph (a) of Article 1 of the Protocol to the Convention concerning benefits in kind after the words "under the National Health Service of the United Kingdom" the words "or the Isle of Man" shall be inserted.

Article III

(1) This supplementary Convention shall be ratified and the instruments of ratification shall be exchanged at Vienna as soon as possible.

(2) This supplementary Convention shall enter into force on the first day of the third month following the month in which the instruments of ratification are exchanged.

In witness whereof the above named Plenipotentiaries have signed this supplementary Convention.

Done in duplicate at London this 9th day of December 1985 in the English and German languages, both texts being equally authoritative.

For Her Britannic Majesty: For the Federal President of the Republic of Austria:
Baroness Young *Dr Reginald Thomas (Ambassador)*

EXPLANATORY NOTE

(This note is not part of the Order)

This Order makes provision for modification of the Social Security Act 1975 so as to give effect in England, Wales and Scotland to the Supplementary Convention (set out in the Schedule) which amends the Convention on social security signed at Vienna on 22nd July 1980 between the Government of the United Kingdom of Great Britain and Northern Ireland and the Government of the Republic of Austria.

The changes (which do not affect the Convention insofar as family allowances are concerned) take account of amendments in the legislation of both Contracting Parties; the pension provisions have been simplified and a new provision has been included which allows persons employed in Austria but insured under United Kingdom legislation to contribute voluntarily to the Austrian scheme for purposes of sickness insurance. The provision dealing with maternity grant (Article 12) has been removed from the Convention.

STATUTORY INSTRUMENTS

1987 No. 1831

SOCIAL SECURITY

The Social Security (Portugal) Order 1987

Made - - - -	*21st October 1987*
Coming into force	*22nd October 1987*

At the Court of Saint James, the 21st day of October 1987

Present,

The Counsellors of State in Council

Whereas Her Majesty, in pursuance of the Regency Acts 1937 to 1953, was pleased, by Letters Patent dated the 17th day of September 1987, to delegate to the six Counsellors of State therein named or any two or more of them full power and authority during the period of Her Majesty's absence from the United Kingdom to summon and hold on Her Majesty's behalf Her Privy Council and to signify thereat Her Majesty's approval for anything for which Her Majesty's approval in Council is required:

And whereas at London on 15th November 1978 a Convention on social security between the Government of the United Kingdom of Great Britain and Northern Ireland and the Government of Portugal (hereinafter referred to as "the Convention") was signed on behalf of those Governments and effect was given thereto by the Social Security (Portugal) Order 1979(a):

And Whereas at London on the 28th day of September 1987 Notes were exchanged on behalf of the said Governments amending the Convention and the terms of the Note from the Secretary of State for Foreign and Commonwealth Affairs were reproduced in the Note from the Portuguese Ambassador to the Court of St James' which is set out in the Schedule to this Order:

And Whereas by section 143 of the Social Security Act 1975(b) and section 15(1) of the Child Benefit Act 1975(c) it is provided that Her Majesty may by Order in Council make provision for modifying or adapting the said Social Security Act and for modifying the provisions of Part I of the said Child Benefit Act and regulations made under it in their application to cases affected by agreements with other governments providing for reciprocity in matters specified in those sections:

And Whereas by virtue of section 166(4) of the Social Security Act 1975 any Order in Council made under the said section 143 may be varied by a subsequent Order in Council made under that section:

And Whereas by virtue of section 22(8) of the Child Benefit Act 1975 any power conferred by that Act to make an Order in Council includes a power to vary or revoke a previous Order:

(a) S.I. 1979/921.   (b) 1975 c.14; subsection (1A) of section 143 was inserted by section 6(1) of the Social Security Act 1981 (c.33).   (c) 1975 c.61; subsection (1A) of section 15 was inserted by section 6(2) of the Social Security Act 1981.

Now, therefore, His Royal Highness The Prince Andrew Duke of York and Her Royal Highness The Princess Royal, being authorised thereto by the said Letters Patent, and in pursuance of the powers conferred by the said section 143 and the said section 15(1), and of all other powers enabling Her Majesty, and by and with the advice of Her Majesty's Privy Council, do on Her Majesty's behalf order, and it is hereby ordered, as follows:

Citation and commencement

1. This Order may be cited as the Social Security (Portugal) Order 1987 and shall come into force on 22nd October 1987.

Modification of Acts and Variation of Order

2. The Social Security Act 1975 and the Child Benefit Act 1975 and any regulations made under it shall be modified and the Social Security (Portugal) Order 1979 shall be varied so as to give effect to the Agreement made on 28th September 1987 the terms of which are contained in the Note from the Portuguese Ambassador to the Court of St James to the Secretary of State for Foreign and Commonwealth Affairs which is set out in the Schedule to this Order, so far as the same relate to England, Wales and Scotland.

G. I. de Deney
Clerk of the Privy Council

SCHEDULE   Article 2

NOTE FROM THE PORTUGUESE AMBASSADOR TO THE COURT OF ST JAMES TO THE SECRETARY OF STATE FOR FOREIGN AND COMMONWEALTH AFFAIRS

28th September 1987

Sir,

I have the honour to acknowledge receipt of your Note of 14th August 1987 which reads as follows –

" I have the honour to refer to the Convention on Social Security between the Government of the United Kingdom of Great Britain and Northern Ireland and the Government of Portugal, which was signed at London on 15 November 1978 (hereinafter referred to as "the Convention"), and to recent correspondence between the Department of Health and Social Security of the United Kingdom and the Departamento de Relações Internacionais e Convenções de Segurança Social of Portugal concerning the need to amend the Convention to introduce revised family allowance provisions, to take account of changes made in United Kingdom social security legislation, and to make other minor modifications.

I now have the honour to propose the following amendments to the said Convention:

    (a) in Article 11 the existing paragraph (4) shall be renumbered (5) and the following paragraph inserted after paragraph (3):

"(4) Where a person is employed in the territory of one Party and the legislation of the other Party applies to him in accordance with any of the provisions of Articles 5 to 9 of this Convention, he shall be treated under that legislation for the purpose of any claim to sickness benefit or maternity allowance as if he were in the territory of the latter Party."

    (b) Article 12 shall be amended by inserting after paragraph (2) the following new paragraph (3):

"(3) Where a woman is confined on or after 4 July 1982 in Great Britain, Northern Ireland or the Isle of Man (other than a woman who is treated as having been confined there by virtue of Article 12(1)), periods during which she was present in the territory of Portugal shall be treated for the purpose of a claim by her for maternity grant under the legislation of the Party in whose territory the confinement occurred as if they were periods during which she was present in that territory."

(c) Article 26 shall be deleted and the following provision substituted –

"*Article 26*

(1) Subject to the provisions of paragraph (9) of this Article, where a person (other than a self-employed person) is employed in the territory of one Contracting Party and the legislation of the other Party applies to him in accordance with any of the provisions of Articles 5 to 9 of this Convention he shall be treated, for the purpose of any claim to receive family allowance under that legislation –

(a) as if he were in the territory of the latter Party and employed in that territory;

(b) as if his children or other dependants were in the territory of the latter Party, if they are in the territory of the former Party.

(2) Subject to the provisions of paragraphs (1), (3), (4) and (9) of this Article, a person (other than a self-employed person) subject to the legislation of one Party in respect of his employment shall be entitled to the family allowance provided for by the legislation of that Party for members of his family residing in the territory of the other Party, as though they were residing in the territory of the former Party.

(3) Subject to the provisions of paragraphs (4), (5) and (9) of this Article, a person resident in the territory of either Party (other than a self-employed person), who is in receipt of maternity allowance or benefit for unemployment, old age, total incapacity for work whether permanent or otherwise however caused, or survivor's benefit whether arising from industrial accident or industrial disease or otherwise under the legislation of one Party shall be entitled to the family allowance provided for by the legislation of that Party for members of his family residing in, or present in, as the case may be, the territory of the other Party, as though they were residing in, or present in, the territory of the former Party.

(4) The provisions of paragraph (3) of this Article shall not apply if there is entitlement to any of the benefits mentioned in that paragraph under the legislation of the Party in whose territory the member of the family is resident.

(5) Where there is entitlement to family allowance under the legislation of the territory of the United Kingdom otherwise than by virtue of this Convention and at the same time entitlement to family allowance for the same members of the family under the legislation of Portugal in accordance with paragraphs (1) or (2) of this Article, entitlement to benefit under the legislation of the territory of the United Kingdom shall be suspended so long as entitlement to benefit under the legislation of Portugal continues. Where, however, a person is subject to the legislation of Portugal and his spouse, having entitlement to family allowance under the legislation of the territory of the United Kingdom by virtue of this Convention or otherwise, is gainfully occupied in the territory of the United Kingdom, the right to family allowance under the legislation of Portugal shall be suspended and only family allowance under the legislation of the territory of the United Kingdom shall be paid.

(6) If the legislation of the territory of the United Kingdom relating to entitlement to family allowance is applicable to a person, he shall be treated, for the purpose of entitlement to family allowance, as if he had been present in the territory of the United Kingdom prior to his application for family allowance during any period when he was insured or employed within the territory or under the legislation of Portugal.

(7) For the purpose of any claim to family allowance under the legislation of Guernsey, a person whose place of birth is in the territory of Portugal shall be treated as if his place of birth were in the Islands of Guernsey, Alderney, Herm or Jethou.

(8) Where, but for the provisions of this paragraph, family allowance would be payable under the legislation of both Parties for the same children, family allowance shall be paid only under the legislation of the Party in whose territory the children concerned are ordinarily resident.

(9) Entitlement to family allowance under the legislation of Jersey shall exist only if the children are ordinarily resident in Jersey."

(d) Article 37 of the Convention shall be deleted.

If the foregoing proposals are acceptable to the Government of Portugal I have the honour to propose that this Note and Your Excellency's reply to that effect shall constitute an Agreement between our two Governments which shall enter into force on the date of your Excellency's reply.

I avail myself of this opportunity to renew to Your Excellency the assurance of my highest consideration."

I have the honour to inform you that these proposals are acceptable to the Government of Portugal, and that they agree that Your Note and this reply shall constitute an Agreement between our two Governments which shall enter into force on the 1st October 1987.

I avail myself of this opportunity to renew to you, Sir, the assurance of my highest consideration.

Joao Hall Themido
for the Government of Portugal

EXPLANATORY NOTE

(This note is not part of the Order)

This Order makes provision for the modification of the Social Security Act 1975 and the Child Benefit Act 1975 so as to give effect in England, Wales and Scotland to the agreement (set out in the Schedule) contained in Notes exchanged between the Government of the United Kingdom of Great Britain and Northern Ireland and the Government of Portugal amending the Convention contained in the Social Security (Portugal) Order 1979.

The amendments relating to sickness and maternity benefit enable those benefits to be paid to persons who, whilst employed in one country, contribute to the social security scheme of the other country, and to take account of changes in the conditions for the award of maternity grant. The principal amendment relating to family allowances enables persons employed in one country to be paid benefit in respect of members of their family who are resident in the other country.

1987 No. 1833

COPYRIGHT

The Copyright (Taiwan Order) (Isle of Man Extension) Order 1987

Made - - - -	*21st October 1987*
Laid before Parliament	*29th October 1987*
Coming into force -	*21st November 1987*

At the Court of Saint James, the 21st day of October 1987

Present,

The Counsellors of State in Council

Whereas Her Majesty in pursuance of the Regency Acts 1937 to 1953, was pleased, by Letters Patent dated the 17th day of September 1987, to delegate to the six Counsellors of State therein named or any two or more of them full power and authority during the period of Her Majesty's absence from the United Kingdom to summon and hold on Her Majesty's behalf Her Privy Council and to signify thereat Her Majesty's approval for anything for which Her Majesty's approval in Council is required:

Now, therefore, His Royal Highness The Prince Andrew Duke of York and Her Royal Highness The Princess Royal, being authorised thereto by the said Letters Patent, and in pursuance of section 31 of the Copyright Act 1956**(a)**, and by and with the advice of Her Majesty's Privy Council, do on Her Majesty's behalf order, and it is hereby ordered, as follows:

1. This Order may be cited as the Copyright (Taiwan Order) (Isle of Man Extension) Order 1987 and shall come into force on 21st November 1987.

2.—(1) The Copyright (Taiwan) Order 1985**(b)** shall extend to the Isle of Man subject to the following modifications.

(2) References in that Order to the Copyright Act 1956 shall be construed as references to that Act as extended to the Isle of Man by the Copyright (Isle of Man) Order 1986**(c)**.

(3) In article 2–
   (a) in paragraph (a), for the words "United Kingdom" there shall be substituted "Isle of Man"; and
   (b) in paragraph (c), for the words "any part of the United Kingdom" there shall be substituted "the Isle of Man".

(a) 1956 c.74.   **(b)** S.I. 1985/1777.   **(c)** S.I. 1986/1299.

(4) In article 5, for the words "commencement of this Order", in each place where those words occur, there shall be substituted "extension of this Order to the Isle of Man".

G. I. de Deney
Clerk of the Privy Council

EXPLANATORY NOTE

(This note is not part of the Order)

This Order extends to the Isle of Man, subject to the modifications specified in article 2, the Copyright (Taiwan) Order 1985 so as to provide for the copyright protection in the Isle of Man of works and other subject matter originating in the territory of Taiwan.

STATUTORY INSTRUMENTS

1987 No. 1834

CONTROL OF FUEL AND ELECTRICITY

The Fuel and Electricity (Control) Act 1973 (Continuation) (Jersey) Order 1987

Made - - - -	*21st October 1987*
Coming into force -	*30th November 1987*

At the Court of Saint James, the 21st day of October 1987

Present,

The Counsellors of State in Council

Whereas Her Majesty, in pursuance of the Regency Acts 1937 to 1953, was pleased, by Letters Patent dated the 17th day of September 1987, to delegate to the six Counsellors of State therein named or any two or more of them full power and authority during the period of Her Majesty's absence from the United Kingdom to summon and hold on Her Majesty's behalf Her Privy Council and to signify thereat Her Majesty's approval for anything for which Her Majesty's approval in Council is required:

Now, therefore, His Royal Highness The Prince Andrew Duke of York and Her Royal Highness The Princess Royal, being authorised thereto by the said Letters Patent, and in pursuance of section 10(3) of the Fuel and Electricity (Control) Act 1973(a), by and with the advice of Her Majesty's Privy Council, do on Her Majesty's behalf order, and it is hereby ordered, as follows:–

1. This Order may be cited as the Fuel and Electricity (Control) Act 1973 (Continuation) (Jersey) Order 1987 and shall come into force on 30th November 1987.

2. Sections 1 to 8 of the Fuel and Electricity (Control) Act 1973, as it has effect in the Bailiwick of Jersey, shall continue in force for a period of one year beyond 30th November 1987, being the date on which they would otherwise expire.

G.I. *de Deney*
Clerk of the Privy Council

(a) 1973 c.67, as extended to the Bailiwick of Jersey by the Fuel and Electricity (Control) Act 1973 (Jersey) Order 1973 (S.I. 1973/2160); the Act was repealed by Part I of Schedule 4 to the Energy Act 1976 (c.76) subject to the saving in Part II thereof that it remains in force in its application to Jersey so far as it extends there by virtue of the 1973 Order (which itself continues in force by virtue of Part III of Schedule 4).

EXPLANATORY NOTE

(This note is not part of the Order)

This Order continues provisions of the Fuel and Electricity (Control) Act 1973 in force in the Bailiwick of Jersey for one year from 30th November 1987 (being the date to which those provisions were continued in force by the Fuel and Electricity (Control) Act 1973 (Continuation) (Jersey) Order 1986 (S.I. 1986/1885).

STATUTORY INSTRUMENTS

1987 No.1835

HOVERCRAFT

The Hovercraft (Civil Liability) (Amendment) Order 1987

Made - - - -	*21st October 1987*
Coming into force	*1st December 1987*

At the Court of Saint James, the 21st day of October 1987

Present,

The Counsellors of State in Council

Whereas Her Majesty in pursuance of the Regency Acts 1937 to 1953, was pleased, by Letters Patent dated the 17th day of September 1987, to delegate to the six Counsellors of State therein named or any two or more of them full power and authority during the period of Her Majesty's absence from the United Kingdom to summon and hold on Her Majesty's behalf Her Privy Council and to signify thereat Her Majesty's approval for anything for which Her Majesty's approval in Council is required:

And, whereas a draft of this Order has been approved by a resolution of each House of Parliament in accordance with section 1(4) of the Hovercraft Act 1968(**a**):

Now, therefore, His Royal Highness, The Prince Andrew Duke of York and Her Royal Highness, The Princess Royal, being authorised thereto by the said Letters Patent, in pursuance of the powers conferred by section 1(1)(*i*), and section 1(3)(*f*) and (*g*) of the Hovercraft Act 1968, and of all other powers enabling Her Majesty, and by and with the advice of Her Majesty's Privy Council, do on Her Majesty's behalf order, and it is hereby ordered, as follows:

1. This Order may be cited as the Hovercraft (Civil Liability) (Amendment) Order 1987 and shall come into force on 1st December 1987.

2. The Hovercraft (Civil Liability) Order 1986(**b**) shall be amended as follows –

(a) in Schedule 1, Part B, in paragraph (14), for "£34,412" there shall be substituted "£80,009"; and

(b) in Schedule 4, in the First Schedule to the Carriage by Air Act 1961(**c**) set out therein as modified, in article 22 in paragraph (1) for "£34,412" there shall be substituted "£80,009".

G. I. de Deney
Clerk of the Privy Council

(**a**) 1968 c.59.   (**b**) S.I. 1986/1305.   (**c**) 1961 c.27, amended by 1963 c.47, 1964 c.1 (N.1), 1978 c.47 and 1979 c.28.

EXPLANATORY NOTE

(This note is not part of the Order)

This Order increases the limit of liability of carriers of passengers by hovercraft to £80,009 for loss of life or personal injury.

1987 No. 1836

PARLIAMENT

The Ministerial and other Salaries Order 1987

Made - - - -		*21st October 1987*
Coming into force		*1st January 1988*

At the Court of Saint James, the 21st day of October 1987

Present,

The Counsellors of State in Council

Whereas Her Majesty in pursuance of the Regency Acts 1937 to 1953, was pleased, by Letters Patent dated the 17th day of September 1987, to delegate to the six Counsellors of State therein named or any two or more of them full power and authority during the period of Her Majesty's absence from the United Kingdom to summon and hold on Her Majesty's behalf Her Privy Council and to signify thereat Her Majesty's approval for anything for which Her Majesty's approval in Council is required:

And whereas a draft of this Order has been approved by resolution of each House of Parliament:

Now, therefore, His Royal Highness The Prince Andrew Duke of York and Her Royal Highness The Princess Royal, being authorised thereto by the said letters Patent, and in pursuance of section 1(4) of the Ministerial and other Salaries Act 1975(a), and by and with the advice of Her Majesty's Privy Council, do on Her Majesty's behalf order, and it is hereby ordered, as follows:

Citation, commencement and revocation

1.—(1) This Order may be cited as the Ministerial and other Salaries Order 1987.

(2) This Order shall come into force on 1st January 1988.

(3) The Ministerial and other Salaries Order 1983(b) is hereby revoked.

Increase of Ministerial salaries

2. For the annual amount, or the maximum or minimum annual amount, of salary specified in Parts I, II, III and IV of Schedule 1 to the Ministerial and other Salaries Act 1975 ("the 1975 Act") in relation to each of the offices specified in the first column of Schedule 1 to this Order there shall be substituted the amount, or the maximum or minimum amount, of salary specified in relation to that office in the second column of that Schedule.

Increase of salaries of Opposition Leaders and Whips

3. For the annual amount of salary specified in Part I of Schedule 2 to the 1975 Act in relation to each of the positions specified in the first column of Schedule 2 to this Order there shall be substituted the amount specified in relation to that position in the second column of that Schedule.

(a) 1975 c. 27.   (b) S.I. 1983/1128.

Increase of the Speaker's salary

4. For the annual amount specified in section 1(3) of the 1975 Act as the salary of the Speaker of the House of Commons there shall be substituted £35,887.

G. I. de Deney
Clerk of the Privy Council

SCHEDULE 1
Article 2

MINISTERIAL SALARIES

PART I

Office	Salary £
Prime Minister and First Lord of the Treasury	45,787
Chancellor of the Exchequer	
Secretary of State	
Minister of Agriculture, Fisheries and Food	40,438
Any of the following offices for so long as the holder is a member of the Cabinet—	

(a) Lord President of the Council;
(b) Lord Privy Seal;
(c) Chancellor of the Duchy of Lancaster;
(d) Paymaster General;
(e) Chief Secretary to the Treasury;
(f) Parliamentary Secretary to the Treasury;
(g) Minister of State.

PART II

Office	Salary £
1. Any of the offices listed at (a) to (g) in Part I above for so long as the holder is not a member of the Cabinet	
2. Minister in charge of a public department of Her Majesty's Government in the United Kingdom who is not a member of the Cabinet, and whose office is not specified elsewhere in this Schedule	23,887 – 34,688
3. Financial Secretary to the Treasury	

PART III

Office	Salary £
Attorney General	36,357
Lord Advocate	40,508
Solicitor General	29,637
Solicitor General for Scotland	34,956

PART IV

Office	Salary £
Captain of the Honourable Corps of Gentlemen-at-Arms	34,688
Treasurer of Her Majesty's Household	23,887
Parliamentary Secretary other than Parliamentary Secretary to the Treasury .	28,688
Captain of the Queen's Bodyguard of the Yeoman of the Guard	28,688
Lord in Waiting	25,618
Comptroller of Her Majesty's Household	
Vice-Chamberlain of Her Majesty's Household	14,827
Junior Lord of the Treasury	
Assistant Whip, House of Commons	

Article 3

SCHEDULE 2

OPPOSITION LEADERS AND WHIPS

Position	Salary £
In the House of Commons –	
Leader of the Opposition	31,237
Chief Opposition Whip	23,887
Assistant Opposition Whip	14,827
In the House of Lords –	
Leader of the Opposition	28,688
Chief Opposition Whip	25,618

EXPLANATORY NOTE

(This note is not part of the Order)

This Order increases salaries payable under the Ministerial and other Salaries Act 1975 to Ministers, to salaried Members of the Opposition and to the Speaker of the House of Commons. The amounts specified in Schedule 1 to this Order are the maximum salaries payable. The actual salaries in payment may therefore be below these levels.

1987 No. 1837

PUBLIC HEALTH, ENGLAND AND WALES
PUBLIC HEALTH, SCOTLAND
PUBLIC HEALTH, NORTHERN IRELAND

CONTAMINATION OF FOOD

The Food Protection (Emergency Prohibitions) (No.3) Order 1987

Approved by both Houses of Parliament

Made - - - -	*21st October 1987*
Laid before Parliament	*22nd October 1987*
Coming into force	*22nd October 1987*

Whereas the Secretary of State is of the opinion, as mentioned in section 1(1)(a) of the Food and Environment Protection Act 1985(**a**), that there has been or may have been an escape of substances of such descriptions and in such quantities and such circumstances as are likely to create a hazard to human health through human consumption of food;

And whereas he is of the opinion, as mentioned in section 1(1)(b) of the said Act, that in consequence of the said escape of substances, food which is, or may be in the future, in the areas described in the Schedule to the following Order, or which is, or may be in the future, derived from anything in those areas, is, or may be, or may become, unsuitable for human consumption;

Now, therefore, in exercise of the powers conferred on him by sections 1(1) and (2), and 24(1) and (3) of the said Act(**b**), and of all other powers enabling him in that behalf, he hereby makes the following Order:

Title, commencement and interpretation

1.—(1) This Order may be cited as the Food Protection (Emergency Prohibitions) (No.3) Order 1987 and shall come into force on 22nd October 1987.

(2) In this Order–

(a) "designated area" means one of the areas described in the Schedule to this Order;

(b) "sheep" means an animal of the genus *Ovis* of whatever age or sex.

(**a**) 1985 c.48.
(**b**) Section 24(1) contains a definition of "the Ministers" relevant to the exercise of the statutory powers under which this Order is made.

Designated incident

2. In the opinion of the Secretary of State food in the areas described in the Schedule to this Order, or which is derived from anything in those areas, is or may be unsuitable for human consumption in consequence of the following escape of substances:–

the escape on or after 26th April 1986 of radioactive substances from a nuclear reactor situated at Chernobyl in the Ukraine, USSR.

Designated areas

3. The areas described in the Schedule to this Order are hereby designated for the purposes of Part I of the Food and Environment Protection Act 1985.

Activities prohibited in the designated areas

4.—(1) No person shall in any of the designated areas slaughter any sheep for human consumption or for use in the preparation of feeding stuffs.

(2) Paragraph (1) above shall not apply in the case of–

(a) any sheep which was moved on or after 7th September 1987 from any place in accordance with a consent given under section 2(1) of the Food and Environment Protection Act 1985 which consent was subject to the condition that the sheep to which it applies should be marked with an apricot mark; or

(b) any sheep which–

(i) was moved on or after 7th September 1987 from any place in accordance with a consent given under section 2(1) of the said Act which consent was subject to the condition that the sheep to which it applies should be marked with a green mark, or

(ii) was moved on or after 28th September 1987 from any place in accordance with a consent given under section 2(1) of the said Act which consent was subject to the condition that the sheep to which it applies should be marked with a blue mark,

and which in either case has been examined and marked with an ear-tag by a person authorised in that behalf by one of the Ministers.

Restrictions on movement

5.—(1) No person shall move any sheep from any farm, agricultural holding, agricultural premises, or holding in any of the designated areas.

(2) Paragraph (1) above shall not apply in the case of–

(a) any sheep which was moved on or after 7th September 1987 from any place in accordance with a consent given under section 2(1) of the said Act which consent was subject to the condition that the sheep to which it applies should be marked with an apricot mark;

(b) any sheep which was moved on or after 7th September 1987 from any place in accordance with a consent given under section 2(1) of the said Act which consent was subject to the condition that the sheep to which it applies should be marked with a green mark;

(c) any sheep which was moved on or after 28th September 1987 from any place in accordance with a consent given under section 2(1) of the said Act which consent was subject to the condition that the sheep to which it applies should be marked with a blue mark.

Restrictions throughout the United Kingdom

6.—(1) No person shall in the United Kingdom–

(a) slaughter for human consumption or for use in the preparation of feeding stuffs any sheep which was in a designated area at any time after 8th July 1987; or

(b) supply, or have in possession for supply, any meat derived from a sheep or any food which contains any such meat, if that sheep was in a designated area at any time after 8th July 1987.

(2) Paragraph (1) above shall not apply in the case of–

(a) any sheep which was moved on or after 7th September 1987 from any place in accordance with a consent given under section 2(1) of the said Act which consent was subject to the condition that the sheep to which it applies should be marked with an apricot mark; or

(b) any sheep which–

(i) was moved on or after 7th September 1987 from any place in accordance with a consent given under section 2(1) of the said Act which consent was subject to the condition that the sheep to which it applies should be marked with a green mark, or

(ii) was moved on or after 28th September 1987 from any place in accordance with a consent given under section 2(1) of the said Act which consent was subject to the condition that the sheep to which it applies should be marked with a blue mark,

and which in either case has been examined and marked with an ear-tag by a person authorised in that behalf by one of the Ministers.

Revocation

7. The Food Protection (Emergency Prohibitions) Order 1987(**a**), the Food Protection (Emergency Prohibitions) Amendment Order 1987(**b**) and the Food Protection (Emergency Prohibitions) Amendment No.2 Order 1987(**c**) are hereby revoked.

New St. Andrew's House, Edinburgh
21st October 1987

W. A. P. Weatherston
Under Secretary,
Scottish Office

(**a**) S.I. 1987/1165.
(**b**) S.I. 1987/1567.
(**c**) S.I. 1987/1696.

SCHEDULE

Article 3

THE DESIGNATED AREAS

Dumfries and Galloway

1. The area of land within Nithsdale District comprising that part of the Parish of Ruthwell bounded as follows:–

On the north-west and north from the point where the Black Grain Burn meets the Lochar Water running in an easterly direction along the Black Grain Burn and the Kirkshiel Burn until it meets the western boundary of Stragglingwath Plantation; on or towards the east by the ditch leading to Longbridgemuir, the Longbridgemuir access road to Peter's Plantation and along the line of the watercourse southwards to Dockridding Wood; on or towards the southwest and south in a north-westerly and westerly direction by the northern boundary of Dockridding Wood until it meets the Willow Burn; on the east in a southerly direction by the Willow Burn until it meets the eastern boundary of Cockpool Plantation and on the south by the northern boundary of Cockpool Plantation in a westerly direction until it meets the eastern boundary of Longbridgemuir Plantation; then in a westerly direction by the southern boundary of Longbridgemuir Plantation to the point national grid reference NY046681; then in a south-westerly direction to the point national grid reference NY042673 on Lochar Water; on the south-west and west in a northerly direction by the Lochar Water until it meets the Black Grain Burn.

2. The area of land within Nithsdale District comprising that part of the Parish of New Abbey bounded as follows:–

On the north by the Glensone Burn running in an easterly direction until it meets the weir below the junction of the Glensone Burn and the Kinharvie Burn; on the east by the Kinharvie Plantation and the Kinharvie Burn running in a southerly direction until Hawkhill; on the south by Hayfield Knowe, part of the Kinharvie Plantation, in a westerly direction until the Cullendeugh Plantation; and on the west running in a north-westerly direction by the Cullendeugh Plantation and the Drungans Plantation until the Drungans Plantation meets the Glensone Burn.

3. The area of land within Stewartry District comprising that part of the Parish of Kirkgunzeon bounded as follows:–

On the north-west by the fence from Bargrug Cottage in a north-easterly direction to Bargrug Plantation; on the west and south by the eastern and northern boundaries of Bargrug Plantation and then in a westerly direction to the point national grid reference NX865637 on the unclassified road from Congeith to Auchenskeoch Lodge; on the west in a northerly direction along the said unclassified road to the point national grid reference NX865642 and then on the south in a north-westerly direction by the ditch leading to Kirkgunzeon Lane; on the north-west and north by Kirkgunzeon Lane in a north-easterly direction until Mossfoot bridge; and then in a north-easterly direction along the Road A711 to Toll Bar Cottage; on the east by the Glaisters Burn running in a southerly direction until it meets Plascow Rig Plantation and then on the east following generally the western boundary of Plascow Rig Plantation until it meets the unclassified road from Congeith to Auchenskeoch Lodge; and on the south-west by the unclassified road running in a north-westerly direction until Bargrug Cottage.

EXPLANATORY NOTE

(This note is not part of the Order)

This Order revokes and substantially re-enacts the provisions of the Food Protection (Emergency Prohibitions) Order 1987, as amended.

This Order continues the emergency prohibitions imposed by that Order restricting various activities in order to prevent human consumption of food rendered unsuitable for that purpose in consequence of the escape in April 1986 of radioactive substances from a nuclear reactor situated at Chernobyl in the Ukraine, USSR.

The Order designates again areas in Scotland affected by the escape from which the movement of sheep and in which the slaughter of sheep are prohibited (articles 3, 4(1) and 5(1) and the Schedule). Restrictions on the slaughter of sheep from the designated areas, and the supply of meat derived from such sheep, extend throughout the United Kingdom (article 6(1)).

The Order continues the following exceptions to the prohibitions referred to in articles 4, 5 and 6:–

(a) an exception from the said prohibition on slaughter in any of the designated areas in respect of–

   (i) any sheep which was moved on or after 7th September 1987 from any place in accordance with a consent given under section 2(1) of the Food and Environment Protection Act 1985 which consent was subject to the condition that the sheep to which it applies should be marked with an apricot paint mark (article 4(2)(a));

   (ii) any sheep which was moved from any place on or after 7th September 1987 or on or after 28th September 1987 in accordance with a consent given under section 2(1) of the said Act which consent was subject to the condition that the sheep to which it applies should be marked with a green paint mark or with a blue paint mark respectively and which in either case has been examined and marked with an ear-tag by a person authorised by the Minister of Agriculture, Fisheries and Food, the Secretary of State for Scotland or Wales, or the Department of Agriculture for Northern Ireland (article 4(2)(b));

(b) an exception from the said prohibition on movement in respect of any sheep which

   (i) was moved on or after 7th September 1987, in accordance with a consent given under section 2(1) of the said Act which consent was subject to the condition that the sheep to which it applies should be marked with an apricot paint mark or with a green paint mark; (article 5(2)(a) and (b));

   (ii) was moved on or after 28th September 1987 in accordance with a consent given under section 2(1) of the said Act which consent was subject to the condition that the sheep to which it applies should be marked with a blue paint mark; (article 5(2)(c));

(c) an exception from the said prohibition on slaughter, and from the said prohibition on supply of meat in respect of–

   (i) any sheep which was moved on or after 7th September 1987 from any place in accordance with a consent given under section 2(1) of the Food and Environment Protection Act 1985 which consent was subject to the condition that the sheep to which it applies should be marked with an apricot paint mark (article 6(2)(a));

   (ii) any sheep which was moved from any place on or after 7th September 1987 or on or after 28th September 1987 in accordance with a consent given under section 2(1) of the said Act which consent was subject to the condition that the sheep to which it applies should be marked with a green paint mark or with a blue paint mark respectively and which in either case has been examined and marked with an ear-tag by a person authorised by the Minister of Agriculture, Fisheries and Food, the Secretary of State for Scotland or Wales, or the Department of Agriculture for Northern Ireland (article 6(2)(b));

Under section 21 of the Food and Environment Protection Act 1985 the penalty for contravening an emergency prohibition is–

(a) on summary conviction, a fine of an amount not exceeding the statutory maximum (at present £2,000);

(b) on conviction on indictment, an unlimited fine or imprisonment for a term of not more than two years, or both.

Powers of enforcement in relation to emergency prohibitions are conferred by section 4 of, and Schedule 2 to, the 1985 Act. Under paragraph 10 of that Schedule obstruction of enforcement officers is an offence.

STATUTORY INSTRUMENTS

1987 No. 1838 (C.55) (S.127)

COURT OF SESSION, SCOTLAND

SHERIFF COURT, SCOTLAND

The Debtors (Scotland) Act 1987 (Commencement No.1) Order 1987

Made	-	-	-	*19th October 1987*

The Lord Advocate, in exercise of the powers conferred on him by section 109(2) of the Debtors (Scotland) Act 1987(**a**), and of all other powers enabling him in that behalf, hereby makes the following Order:

1. This Order may be cited as the Debtors (Scotland) Act 1987 (Commencement No.1) Order 1987.

2. The following provisions of the Debtors (Scotland) Act 1987 shall come into force on 2nd November 1987:–

(a) section 75 (Power of Court of Session to make rules in relation to Messengers-at-Arms and Sheriff Officers);

(b) section 76 (Advisory Council on Messengers-at-Arms and Sheriff Officers); and

(c) section 97 (Power of Court of Session to make rules as to representation of parties in Sheriff Court proceedings).

26/27 Royal Terrace, Edinburgh   *G. Murray*
19th October 1987   Director, Scottish Courts Administration

EXPLANATORY NOTE

(This note is not part of the Order)

This Order brings into force on 2nd November 1987 sections 75, 76 and 97 of the Debtors (Scotland) Act 1987. Section 75 confers power on the Court of Session to make rules in relation to Messengers-at-Arms and Sheriff Officers. Section 76 establishes the Advisory Council on Messengers-at-Arms and Sheriff Officers. Section 97 extends the power of the Court of Session to make rules as to representation of parties in Sheriff Court proceedings under the Act.

(**a**) 1987 c.18.

STATUTORY INSTRUMENTS

1987 No. 1841

ACQUISITION OF LAND

COMPENSATION

The Acquisition of Land (Rate of Interest after Entry) (No. 3) Regulations 1987

Made - - - -	*21st October 1987*
Laid before Parliament	*26th October 1987*
Coming into force	*16th November 1987*

The Treasury, in exercise of the powers conferred upon them by section 32(1) of the Land Compensation Act 1961(**a**) , and of all other powers enabling them in that behalf, hereby make the following Regulations:

1. These Regulations may be cited as the Acquisition of Land (Rate of Interest after Entry) (No. 3) Regulations 1987, and shall come into force on 16th November 1987.

2. The rate of interest on any compensation in respect of the compulsory acquisition of an interest in any land on which entry has been made before the payment of the compensation shall be 11 per cent. per annum.

3. The Acquisition of Land (Rate of Interest after Entry) (No. 2) Regulations 1987(**b**) are hereby revoked.

Peter Lloyd
Mark Lennox-Boyd
21st October 1987   Two of the Lords Commissioners of Her Majesty's Treasury

EXPLANATORY NOTE

(This note is not part of the Regulations)

These Regulations increase from 10 per cent. to 11 per cent. per annum, in respect of any period after the coming into force of these Regulations, the rate of interest payable where entry is made, before payment of compensation, on land in England and Wales which is being purchased compulsorily, and revoke the Acquisition of Land (Rate of Interest after Entry) (No. 2) Regulations 1987.

(**a**) 1961 c.33.   (**b**) S.I. 1987/889.

STATUTORY INSTRUMENTS

1987 No. 1842

ACQUISITION OF LAND

COMPENSATION

The Acquisition of Land (Rate of Interest after Entry) (Scotland) (No. 3) Regulations 1987

Made - - - -	*21st October 1987*
Laid before Parliament	*26th October 1987*
Coming into force	*16th November 1987*

The Treasury, in exercise of the powers conferred upon them by section 40(1) of the Land Compensation (Scotland) Act 1963(**a**), and of all other powers enabling them in that behalf, hereby make the following Regulations:

1. These Regulations may be cited as the Acquisition of Land (Rate of Interest after Entry) (Scotland) (No. 3) Regulations 1987, and shall come into force on 16th November 1987.

2. The rate of interest on any compensation in respect of the compulsory acquisition of an interest in any land on which entry has been made before the payment of the compensation shall be 11 per cent. per annum.

3. The Acquisition of Land (Rate of Interest after Entry) (Scotland) (No. 2) Regulations 1987(**b**) are hereby revoked.

Peter Lloyd
Mark Lennox-Boyd
21st October 1987 Two of the Lords Commissioners of Her Majesty's Treasury

EXPLANATORY NOTE

(This note is not part of the Regulations)

These Regulations increase from 10 per cent. to 11 per cent. per annum, in respect of any period after the coming into force of these Regulations, the rate of interest payable where entry is made, before payment of compensation, on land in Scotland which is being purchased compulsorily, and revoke the Acquisition of Land (Rate of Interest after Entry) (Scotland) (No. 2) Regulations 1987.

(**a**) 1963 c.51.   (**b**) S.I. 1987/890.

STATUTORY INSTRUMENTS

1987 No. 1843

AGRICULTURE

The Common Agricultural Policy (Wine) Regulations 1987

Made - - - -	*18th October 1987*
Laid before Parliament	*30th October 1987*
Coming into force	*20th November 1987*

The Minister of Agriculture, Fisheries and Food and the Secretary of State, being Ministers designated(**a**) for the purposes of section 2(2) of the European Communities Act 1972(**b**) in relation to the common agricultural policy of the European Economic Community, acting jointly in exercise of the powers conferred upon them by the said section and of all other powers enabling them in that behalf, hereby make the following Regulations:

Title and commencement

1. These Regulations may be cited as the Common Agricultural Policy (Wine) Regulations 1987 and shall come into force on 20th November 1987.

Interpretation and revocation

2.—(1) In these Regulations, unless the context otherwise requires–

"the Commissioners" means the Commissioners of Customs and Excise;

"Community provision" means any provision of any regulation of the European Communities which is referred to in Schedule 1 to these Regulations, or of the treaties relating to the accession to the European Communities, respectively, of the Hellenic Republic signed at Athens on 28th May 1979(**c**) and of the Kingdom of Spain and the Portuguese Republic signed, respectively, at Madrid and Lisbon on 12th June 1985(**d**);

"manufacturing" means using wine, for the purpose of a trade or business (other than a catering business), in the composition, manufacture or preparation of any product;

"the Minister" means, in relation to England, the Minister of Agriculture, Fisheries and Food and, in relation to Scotland, Northern Ireland or Wales, the Secretary of State;

(**a**) S.I. 1972/1811.
(**b**) 1972 c.68; section 2 is subject to Schedule 2 to that Act and is to be read, as regards England and Wales, in relation to offences triable only summarily, with sections 37, 40 and 46 of the Criminal Justice Act 1982 (c.48), in relation to offences triable on indictment or summarily, with section 32 of the Magistrates' Courts Act 1980 (c.43), and, in each case, with S.I. 1984/447; as regards Scotland, in relation to offences triable only summarily with sections 289F and 289G of the Criminal Procedure (Scotland) Act 1975 (c.21), as inserted by section 54 of the Criminal Justice Act 1982, in relation to offences triable on indictment or summarily, with section 289B of the Criminal Procedure (Scotland) Act 1975, as inserted by paragraph 5 of Schedule 11 to the Criminal Law Act 1977 (c.45) and amended by section 55 of the Criminal Justice Act 1982, and, in each case, with S.I. 1984/526; and, as regards Northern Ireland, with S.I. 1984/703 (N.I. 3), S.R. (N.I.) 1984 No. 253.
(**c**) OJ No. L291, 19.11.79, p.17.
(**d**) OJ No. L302, 15.11.85, p.23.

"relevant Community provision" means any Community provision referred to in Column 1 or Column 2 of Schedule 2 to these Regulations, the subject matter of which is described in Column 3 thereof;

"retail sale" means any sale to a person buying otherwise than for the purpose of resale but does not include a sale to a caterer in the course of his catering business or to a manufacturer in the course of his manufacturing business;

(2) The Common Agricultural Policy (Wine) Regulations 1982(**a**) and the Common Agricultural Policy (Wine) (Amendment) Regulations 1983(**b**) are hereby revoked.

Enforcement

3.—(1) Subject to the provisions of this regulation, local authorities, the Minister, the Commissioners and the Wine Standards Board are hereby designated competent authorities or agencies for the purpose of Community provisions.

(2) Each local authority shall secure the enforcement and execution of the relevant Community provisions in so far as they relate to the retail sale of wine within its area.

(3) The Minister, the Commissioners and the Wine Standards Board shall secure the enforcement and execution of the relevant Community provisions in so far as they relate to the importation and exportation of wine to or from the United Kingdom.

(4) The Minister and the Wine Standards Board shall secure the enforcement and execution of the relevant Community provisions in so far as they relate to any matter not mentioned in paragraphs (2) or (3) of this regulation.

(5) Nothing in this regulation shall be taken as authorising in the United Kingdom the Wine Standards Board or the Commissioners, or in relation to Scotland only, the Minister or a local authority, to institute proceedings for an offence.

(6) In this regulation–
(a) "local authority" means–
(i) as respects England and Wales, a food and drugs authority for the purposes of the Food Act 1984(**c**) ;
(ii) as respects Scotland, an islands or district council which is the enforcement authority for the purposes of the Food and Drugs (Scotland) Act 1956(**d**);
(iii) as respects Northern Ireland, a district council for the purposes of section 29 of the Food and Drugs Act (Northern Ireland) 1958(**e**) ;
(b) "the Wine Standards Board" means the Wine Standards Board of The Vintners' Company.

(7) The provisions of this regulation are without prejudice to the duties of such local authorities under the provisions of the respective Acts referred to in paragraph (6) of this regulation.

Exemptions

4. The relevant Community provisions relating to the information required on labels of the products mentioned in Article 1 of Council Regulation (EEC) No. 355/79(**f**) shall not apply to–
(a) unlabelled products which are transported between two or more establishments or between vineyards and wine making plants, in either case belonging to the same undertaking and situated in the same local authority area;
(b) unlabelled quantities of grape musts and wines not exceeding 15 litres per batch and not intended for sale;
(c) unlabelled quantities of grape musts and wines intended for the domestic consumption of the producer and his employees.

(**a**) S.I. 1982/578.   (**b**) S.I. 1983/1042.   (**c**) 1984 c.30.
(**d**) 1956 c.30.   (**e**) 1958 c.27 (N.I.).   (**f**) OJ No. L54, 5.3.79, p.99.

5. The provisions of Article 13(1) of Council Regulation (EEC) No. 347/79(**a**) relating to the prohibition of the planting, field grafting and double-grafting of vine varieties not listed in the classification referred to in Article 1 of that Regulation shall not apply where the purpose of the planting is one of the purposes set out in the first subparagraph of Article 13(2) thereof.

Offences and penalties

6.—(1) If any person contravenes or fails to comply with any of the relevant Community provisions referred to in Columns 1 or 2 of Parts I, II, III or V of Schedule 2 to these Regulations, he shall be guilty of an offence and liable on summary conviction to a fine not exceeding £2,000, or on conviction on indictment to a fine.

(2) If any person–

(a) contravenes or fails to comply with any of the relevant Community provisions referred to in Columns 1 or 2 of Parts IV, VI or VII of Schedule 2 to these Regulations, or

(b) discloses to any other person any information obtained by him in pursuance of his duties under these Regulations, unless the disclosure is made in, or for the purposes of, the performance by him or any other person of any functions under these Regulations, or in pursuance of a Community obligation,

he shall be guilty of an offence and liable on summary conviction to a fine not exceeding £1,000.

(3) In any proceedings against any person for an offence under these Regulations, it shall be a defence for that person to prove that he took all reasonable precautions and exercised all due diligence to avoid committing the offence.

(4) Where an offence under these Regulations which has been committed by a body corporate is proved to have been committed with the consent or connivance of, or to be attributable to any neglect on the part of any director, manager, secretary or a similar officer of the body corporate, or any person who was purporting to act in any such capacity, he as well as the body corporate shall be deemed to be guilty of that offence and shall be liable to be proceeded against and punished accordingly.

In Witness whereof the Official Seal of the Minister of Agriculture, Fisheries and Food is hereunto affixed on 18th October 1987.

John MacGregor
Minister of Agriculture, Fisheries and Food

Sanderson of Bowden
Minister of State, Scottish Office

12th October 1987

(**a**)   OJ No. L54, 5.3.79, p.75.

SCHEDULE 1   Regulation 2(1)

COMMUNITY PROVISIONS

Measures containing Community provisions	*Official Journal of the European Communities: Reference*
1. Commission Regulation (EEC) No. 1594/70 on the notification, carrying out and control of the processes of enriching, acidifying and deacidifying wine, as amended by Commission Regulation (EEC) No. 2531/77 (OJ No. L294, 18.11.77, p.10) and by the Act of Accession of the Hellenic Republic (OJ No. L291, 19.11.79, p.17), and by Commission Regulation (EEC) No. 632/80 (OJ No. L69, 15.3.80, p.33), and by Commission Regulation (EEC) No. 418/86 (OJ No. L48, 26.2.86, p.8)	OJ No. L173, 6.8.70, p.23 (OJ/SE 1970 (II) p.558)
2. Commission Regulation (EEC) No. 1618/70 on measures for controlling the sweetening of table wines and of quality wines produced in specified regions	OJ No. L175, 8.8.70, p.17 (OJ/SE 1970 (II) p.562)
3. Commission Regulation (EEC) No. 2314/72 on certain measures for examining the suitability of certain vine varieties for cultivation, as amended by Commission Regulation (EEC) No. 3296/80 (OJ No. L344, 19.12.80, p.13)	OJ No. L248, 1.11.72, p.53 (OJ/SE 1972 (November) p.11)
4. Commission Regulation (EEC) No. 2247/73 on the control of quality wines produced in specified regions, as amended by the Act of Accession of the Hellenic Republic (OJ No. L291, 19.11.79, p. 17), and by Commission Regulation (EEC) No. 418/86 (OJ No. L48, 26.2.86, p.8)	OJ No. L230, 18.8.73, p.12
5. Commission Regulation (EEC) No. 2805/73 laying down certain transitional provisions relating to the percentage of sulphur dioxide in wines produced before 1 October 1973, as amended by Commission Regulation (EEC) No. 3548/73 (OJ No. L361, 29.12.73, p.35), and by Commission Regulation (EEC) No. 2160/75 (OJ No. L220, 20.8.75, p.7), and by Commission Regulation (EEC) No. 1455/76 (OJ No. L163, 24.6.76, p.12), and by Commission Regulation (EEC) No. 966/77 (OJ No. L115, 6.5.77, p.7)	OJ No. L289, 16.10.73, p.21
6. Commission Regulation (EEC) No. 1153/75 prescribing the form of accompanying documents for wine products and specifying the obligations of wine producers and traders other than retailers, as amended by Commission Regulation (EEC) No. 2617/77 (OJ No. L304, 29.11.77, p.33), and by the Act of Accession of the Hellenic Republic (OJ No. L291, 19.11.79, p.17), and by Commission Regulation (EEC) No. 3203/80 (OJ No. L333, 11.12.80, p.18), and by Commission Regulation (EEC) No. 418/86 (OJ No. L48, 26.2.86, p.8)	OJ No. L113, 1.5.75, p.1
7. Commission Regulation (EEC) No. 2152/75 on detailed rules for the application of Council Regulations (EEC) Nos. 358/79 and 823/87 in respect of sparkling wines (**a**)	OJ No. L219, 19.8.75, p.7

(**a**)   The title of this Regulation as published in the edition of the Official Journal referred to is Commission Regulation (EEC) No. 2152/75 on detailed rules for the application of Council Regulations (EEC) Nos. 2893/74 and 2894/74 in respect of sparkling wines. Regulations (EEC) Nos. 2893/74 and 2894/74 have been superseded by Council Regulations (EEC) Nos. 358/79 and 823/87 respectively.

Measures containing Community provisions	Official Journal of the European Communities: Reference
8. Commission Regulation (EEC) No. 643/77 laying down rules for coupage and wine making in free zones on the geographical territory of the Community in respect of wine products originating in third countries, as amended by Commission Regulation (EEC) No. 3203/80 (OJ No. L333, 11.12.80, p.18), and by Commission Regulation (EEC) No. 418/86 (OJ No. L48, 26.2.86, p.8)	OJ No. L81, 30.3.77, p.7
9. Commission Regulation (EEC) No. 1972/78 laying down detailed rules on oenological practices, as amended by Commission Regulation (EEC) No. 45/80 (OJ No. L7, 11.1.80, p.12)	OJ No. L226, 17.8.78, p.11
10. Council Regulation (EEC) No. 347/79 on general rules for the classification of vine varieties, as amended by the Act of Accession of the Hellenic Republic (OJ No. L291, 19.11.79, p.17), and by Council Regulation (EEC) No. 3805/85 (OJ No. L367, 31.12.85, p.39)	OJ No. L54, 5.3.79, p.75
11. Council Regulation (EEC) No. 351/79 concerning the addition of alcohol to products in the wine sector, as amended by Council Regulation (EEC) No. 2817/79 (OJ No. L320, 15.12.79, p.7), and by the Act of Accession of the Hellenic Republic (OJ No. L291, 19.11.79, p.17), and by Council Regulation (EEC) No. 3196/80 (OJ No. L333, 11.12.80, p.6), and by Council Regulation (EEC) No. 3658/81 (OJ No. L366, 22.12.81, p.1), and by Council Regulation (EEC) No. 3267/82 (OJ No. L347, 7.12.82, p.1), and by Council Regulation (EEC) No. 3518/83 (OJ No. L352, 15.12.83, p.1), and by Council Regulation (EEC) No. 3689/84 (OJ No. L341, 29.12.84, p.7), and by Council Regulation (EEC) No. 3581/85 (OJ No. L343, 20.12.85, p.6), and by Council Regulation (EEC) No. 255/87 (OJ No. L26, 29.1.87, p.2)	OJ No. L54, 5.3.79, p.90
12. Council Regulation (EEC) No. 353/79 laying down the conditions for coupage and wine making in the free zones on Community territory for wine products originating in third countries	OJ No. L54, 5.3.79, p.94
13. Council Regulation (EEC) No. 354/79 laying down general rules for the import of wines, grape juice and grape musts, as amended by the Act of Accession of the Hellenic Republic (OJ No. L291, 19.11.79, p.17), and by Council Regulation (EEC) No. 2633/85 (OJ No. L251, 20.9.85, p.3), and by Council Regulation (EEC) No. 3805/85 (OJ No. L367, 31.12.85, p.39)	OJ No. L54, 5.3.79, p.97
14. Council Regulation (EEC) No. 355/79 laying down general rules for the description and presentation of wines and grape musts, as amended by the Act of Accession of the Hellenic Republic (OJ No. L291, 19.11.79, p.17), and by Council Regulation (EEC) No. 461/80 (OJ No. L57, 29.2.80, p.36), and by Council Regulation (EEC) No. 1016/81 (OJ No. L103, 15.4.81, p.7), and by Council Regulation (EEC) No. 3685/81 (OJ No. L369, 24.12.81, p.1), and by Council Regulation (EEC) No. 2056/84 (OJ No. L191, 19.7.84, p.3), and by Council Regulation (EEC) No. 3490/84 (OJ No. L327, 14.12.84, p.2), and by Council Regulation (EEC) No. 1898/85 (OJ No. L179, 11.7.85, p.1), and by Council Regulation (EEC) No. 3805/85 (OJ No. L367, 31.12.85, p.39), and by Council Regulation (EEC) No. 1625/86 (OJ No. L144, 29.5.86, p.1), and by Council Regulation (EEC) No. 537/87 (OJ No. L55, 25.2.87, p.3)	OJ No. L54, 5.3.79, p.99

Measures containing Community provisions	Official Journal of the European Communities: Reference
15. Council Regulation (EEC) No. 357/79 on statistical areas under vines, as amended by Council Regulation (EEC) No. 1992/80 (OJ No. L195, 29.7.80, p.10), and by Council Regulation (EEC) No. 3719/81 (OJ No. L373, 29.12.81, p.5), and by Council Regulation (EEC) No. 3768/85 (OJ No. L362, 31.12.85, p.8), and by Council Regulation (EEC) No. 490/86 (OJ No. L54, 1.3.86, p.22)	OJ No. L54, 5.3.79, p.124
16. Council Regulation (EEC) No. 358/79 on sparkling wines produced in the Community and defined in item 15 of Annex I to Council Regulation (EEC) No. 822/87, as amended by Council Regulation (EEC) No. 2383/79 (OJ No. L274, 31.10.79, p.8), and by the Act of Accession of the Hellenic Republic (OJ No. L291, 19.11.79, p.17), and by Council Regulation (EEC) No. 3456/80 (OJ No. L360, 31.12.80, p.18), and by Council Regulation (EEC) No. 3686/84 (OJ No. L341, 29.12.84, p.3), and by Council Regulation (EEC) No. 3310/85 (OJ No. L320, 29.11.85, p.19), and by Council Regulation (EEC) No. 3805/85 (OJ No. L367, 31.12.85, p.39) **(a)**	OJ No. L54, 5.3.79, p.130
17. Act concerning the conditions of accession of the Hellenic Republic and the adjustments to the Treaties amending various Regulations concerning wine, as a result of the accession of Greece, signed on 28th May 1979	OJ No. L291, 19.11.79, p.17
18. Council Regulation (EEC) No. 2585/79 authorising, in the Gigondas registered designated area, the additional acidification of certain products from the 1979 wine harvest	OJ No. L296, 23.11.79, p.19
19. Council Regulation (EEC) No. 2903/79 on the downgrading of quality wines produced in specified regions, as amended by Council Regulation (EEC) No. 418/86 (OJ No. L48, 26.2.86, p.8)	OJ No. L326, 22.12.79, p.14
20. Council Regulation (EEC) No. 2931/80 on certain quality wines originating in the Republic of Austria	OJ No. L305, 14.11.80, p.2
21. Commission Regulation (EEC) No. 997/81 laying down detailed rules for the description and presentation of wines and grape musts, as amended by Commission Regulation (EEC) No. 2628/81 (OJ No. L258, 11.9.81, p.10), and by Commission Regulation (EEC) No. 1224/83 (OJ No. L134, 21.5.83, p.1), and by Commission Regulation (EEC) No. 1011/84 (OJ No. L101, 13.4.84, p.17), and by Commission Regulation (EEC) No. 2337/84 (OJ No. L215, 11.8.84, p.9), and by Commission Regulation (EEC) No. 2397/84 (OJ No. L224, 21.8.84, p.19), and by Commission Regulation (EEC) No. 418/86 (OJ No. L48, 26.2.86, p.8), and by Commission Regulation (EEC) No. 63/87 (OJ No. L8, 10.1.87, p.38), and by Commission Regulation (EEC) No. 689/87 (OJ No. L66, 11.3.87, p.5)	OJ No. L106, 16.4.81, p.1

(a) The title of this Regulation as published in the edition of the Official Journal referred to is Council Regulation (EEC) No. 358/79 on sparkling wines produced in the Community and defined in item 13 of Annex II to Council Regulation (EEC) No. 337/79. Regulation (EEC) No. 337/79 has been superseded by Council Regulation (EEC) No. 822/87.

Measures containing Community provisions	*Official Journal of the European Communities: Reference*
22. Commission Regulation (EEC) No. 3800/81 determining the classification of vine varieties, as amended by Commission Regulation (EEC) No. 1469/82 (OJ No. L159, 10.6.82, p.21), and by Commission Regulation (EEC) No. 2060/83 (OJ No. L202, 26.7.83, p.15), and by Commission Regulation (EEC) No. 3582/83 (OJ No. L356, 20.12.83, p.18), and by Commission Regulation (EEC) No. 1871/85 (OJ No. L175, 5.7.85, p.9), and by Commission Regulation (EEC) No. 2599/85 (OJ No. L248, 17.9.85, p.5), and by Commission Regulation (EEC) No. 418/86 (OJ No. L48, 26.2.86, p.8), and by Commission Regulation (EEC) No. 416/87 (OJ No. L42, 12.2.87, p.18), and by Commission Regulation (EEC) No. 1467/87 (OJ No. L138, 28.5.87, p.44)	OJ No. L381, 31.12.81, p.1
23. Council Regulation (EEC) No. 3826/81 on the conclusion of the Agreement between the European Economic Community and the Republic of Austria on the control and reciprocal protection of quality wines and certain wines bearing a geographical ascription	OJ No. L389, 31.12.81, p.1
24. Council Regulation (EEC) No. 1873/84 authorising the offer or disposal for direct human consumption of certain imported wines which may have undergone oenological processes not provided for in Council Regulation (EEC) No. 822/87 **(a)**	OJ No. L176, 3.7.84, p.6
25. Commission Regulation (EEC) No. 2102/84 on harvest, production and stock declarations relating to wine sector products, as amended by Commission Regulation (EEC) No. 2459/84 (OJ No. L231, 29.8.84, p.5), and by Commission Regulation (EEC) No. 2391/85 (OJ No. L225, 23.8.85, p.13), and by Commission Regulation (EEC) No. 2467/86 (OJ No. L211, 1.8.86, p.17), and by Commission Regulation (EEC) No. 2528/87 (OJ No. L240, 22.8.87, p.11)	OJ No. L194, 24.7.84, p.1
26. Commission Regulation (EEC) No. 2394/84 laying down conditions of use of ion exchange resins and detailed implementing rules for the preparation of rectified concentrated grape must, as amended by Commission Regulation (EEC) No. 888/85 (OJ No. L96, 3.4.85, p.14), and by Commission Regulation (EEC) No. 2751/86 (OJ No. L253, 5.9.86, p.11)	OJ No. L224, 21.8.84, p.8
27. Commission Regulation (EEC) No. 1907/85 on the list of vine varieties and regions providing imported wine for the making of sparkling wines in the Community	OJ No. L179, 11.7.85, p.21
28. Commission Regulation (EEC) No. 3190/85 authorising, in the Châteauneuf-du-Pape and Gigondas registered designation areas, the additional acidification of certain products from the 1985 wine harvest	OJ No. L301, 15.11.85, p.29
29. Act concerning the conditions of accession of the Kingdom of Spain and the Portuguese Republic and the adjustments to the Treaties, signed on 12th June 1985	OJ No. L302, 15.11.85, p.23

(a) The title of this Regulation as published in the edition of the Official Journal referred to is Council Regulation (EEC) No. 1873/84 authorising the offer or disposal for direct human consumption of certain imported wines which may have undergone certain oenological processes not provided for in Council Regulation (EEC) No. 337/79. Regulation (EEC) No. 337/79 has been superseded by Council Regulation (EEC) No. 822/87.

Measures containing Community provisions	Official Journal of the European Communities: Reference
30. Council Regulation (EEC) No. 3309/85 laying down general rules for the description and presentation of sparkling wines and aerated sparkling wines, as amended by Council Regulation (EEC) No. 3805/85 (OJ No. L367, 31.12.85, p.39), and by Council Regulation (EEC) No. 1626/86 (OJ No. L144, 29.5.86, p.3), and by Council Regulation (EEC) No. 538/87 (OJ No. L55, 25.2.87, p.4)	OJ No. L320, 29.11.85, p.9
31. Commission Regulation (EEC) No. 3590/85 on the certificate and analysis report required for the importation of wine, grape juice and grape must, as amended by Commission Regulation (EEC) No. 1614/86 (OJ No. L142, 28.5.86, p.22)	OJ No. L343, 20.12.85, p.20
32. Council Regulation (EEC) No. 3805/85 adapting, on account of the accession of Spain and Portugal, certain Regulations relating to the wine sector	OJ No. L367, 31.12.85, p.39
33. Commission Regulation (EEC) No. 305/86 on the maximum total sulphur dioxide content of wine originating in the Community produced before 1 September 1986 and, for a transitional period, imported wine	OJ No. L38, 13.2.86, p.13
34. Commission Regulation (EEC) No. 418/86 amending various Regulations concerning wine as a result of the accession of Spain and Portugal	OJ No. L48, 26.2.86, p.8
35. Commission Regulation (EEC) No. 479/86 determining the exceptional cases in which coupage of red Spanish wines with red wines of the other Member States, derived from certain varieties of grape and originating in certain regions of the Community, shall be allowed	OJ No. L54, 1.3.86, p.1
36. Council Regulation (EEC) No. 1627/86 laying down rules for the description of special wines with regard to the indication of alcoholic strength	OJ No. L144, 29.5.86, p.4
37. Commission Regulation (EEC) No. 1781/86 laying down certain detailed rules for authorising the coupage with Spanish red wines of certain red wines of other Member States	OJ No. L155, 10.6.86, p.6
38. Commission Regulation (EEC) No. 1888/86 on the maximum total sulphur dioxide content of certain sparkling wines originating in the Community and prepared before 1 September 1986, and, for a transitional period, of imported sparkling wines	OJ No. L163, 19.6.86, p.19
39. Commission Regulation (EEC) No. 2094/86 laying down detailed rules for the use of tartaric acid for the de-acidification of specified wine products in certain regions of Zone A, as amended by Commission Regulation (EEC) No. 2736/86 (OJ No. L252, 4.9.86, p.15)	OJ No. L180, 4.7.86, p.17
40. Council Regulation (EEC) No. 2392/86 establishing a Community vineyard register	OJ No. L208, 31.7.86, p.1
41. Commission Regulation (EEC) No. 2707/86 laying down detailed rules for the description and presentation of sparkling and aerated sparkling wines, as amended by Commission Regulation (EEC) No. 3378/86 (OJ No. L310, 5.11.86, p.5), and by Commission Regulation (EEC) No. 2249/87 (OJ No. L207, 29.7.87, p.26)	OJ No. L246, 30.8.86, p.71

Measures containing Community provisions	Official Journal of the European Communities: Reference
42. Commission Regulation (EEC) No. 649/87 laying down detailed rules for the establishment of a Community vineyard register	OJ No. L62, 5.3.87, p.10
43. Council Regulation (EEC) No. 822/87 on the common organisation of the market in wine, as amended by Council Regulation (EEC) No. 1390/87 (OJ No. L133, 22.5.87, p.3), and by Council Regulation (EEC) No. 1972/87 (OJ No. L184, 3.7.87, p.26)	OJ No. L84, 27.3.87, p.1
44. Council Regulation (EEC) No. 823/87 laying down special provisions relating to quality wines produced in specified regions	OJ No. L84, 27.3.87, p.59
45. Commission Regulation (EEC) No. 1069/87 laying down detailed rules as regards the indication of alcoholic strength on the labelling of special wines	OJ No. L104, 16.4.87, p.14

Regulation 2(1)

SCHEDULE 2

RELEVANT COMMUNITY PROVISIONS

PART I
ACCOMPANYING DOCUMENTS

Column 1	Column 2	Column 3
Relevant Community provisions	*Supplementing provisions*	*Subject matter*
1. Regulation 822/87: Article 71(1) and (2)	Regulation 1153/75: all Articles except 2, 4, 18, 22, 23, 25, 26, 27 and 28, as amended by Regulation 2617/77: Articles 1 and 2 and by Regulation 3203/80: Article 1(1) and by Regulation 418/86: Article 5(2) and (3)	Requirements relating to accompanying documents and turnover records
2. Regulation 822/87: Article 70(1)	Regulation 354/79: Article 1 as amended by Regulation 2633/85: Article 1(1) and (2) and Regulation 3590/85: Articles 1, 3, 4, 5, 6 and 8	Accompanying documents required for the importation of wines and other products

PART II
QUALITY WINES PRODUCED IN SPECIFIED REGIONS

Column 1	Column 2	Column 3
Relevant Community provisions	*Supplementing provisions*	*Subject matter*
1. Regulation 823/87: Article 15(1), (2), (4), (5) and (7)	Regulation 2247/73: Article 2 and Act of Accession of the Kingdom of Spain and the Portuguese Republic: Article 129	General provisions relating to the use of the expression 'quality wine psr' and other expressions traditionally used by Member States to designate particular quality wines
2. Regulation 823/87: Article 15(3)		Restrictions on use of the term 'quality sparkling wine psr' and other traditionally equivalent terms
3. Regulation 823/87: Article 15(8)	Regulation 2903/79: Articles 3 and 4	Provisions relating to downgraded quality wine psr

PART III
DESCRIPTION AND PRESENTATION

Column 1	Column 2	Column 3
Relevant Community provisions	*Supplementing provisions*	*Subject matter*
1. Regulation 355/79: all Articles except 1, 2(1)(b), 2(2)(i), 12(1)(c), 12(2)(u), 22(1)(c), 22(2)(d), 27(1)(b), 27(2)(h), 28(1)(b), 28(2)(r), 29(1)(c), 39, 47, 48 and 49 as amended by Act of Accession of the Hellenic Republic: Article 21 and Annex I, Part IIB, (n) 18 and Regulation 461/80: Articles 1 and 2 and by Regulation 1016/81: all Articles except 1 and 7 and by Regulation 3685/81: Article 1 and by Regulation 2056/84: Article 1 and by Regulation 3490/84: Article 1 and by Regulation 1898/85: Article 1 and by Regulation 3805/85: Article 6 and by Regulation 1625/86: Article 1 and by Regulation 537/87: Article 1	Regulation 997/81: all Articles except 24 and 25 as amended by Regulation 2628/81: Article 1(1) and by Regulation 1224/83: Article 1 and by Regulation 1011/84: Article 1 and by Regulation 2337/84: Article 1 and by Regulation 2397/84: Article 1 and by Regulation 418/86: Article 1 and by Regulation 63/87: Article 1 and by Regulation 689/87: Article 1	General rules and particular requirements relating to the description and presentation of wines and other products (except those relating to the indication of nominal volume)

Column 1	Column 2	Column 3
Relevant Community provisions	*Supplementing provisions*	*Subject matter*
2. Regulation 3309/85: all Articles except 16, 17 and 18 as amended by Regulation 3805/85: Article 10 and by Regulation 1626/86: Article 1 and by Regulation 538/87: Article 1	Regulation 2707/86: all Articles except 11 as amended by Regulation 3378/86: Article 1 and by Regulation 2249/87: Article 1	General rules and particular requirements relating to the description and presentation of sparkling wines and aerated sparkling wines
3. Regulation 1627/86: Article 1(1)	Regulation 1069/87: Articles 1 and 2	General rules and particular requirements relating to the indication of alcoholic strength on the labelling of liqueur wines, semi-sparkling wines and aerated semi-sparkling wines

PART IV
PRODUCTION AND CONTROL OF PLANTING

Column 1	Column 2	Column 3
Relevant Community provisions	*Supplementing provisions*	*Subject matter*
1. Regulation 822/87: Article 3(1), (2) and (3)	Regulation 2102/84: Articles 1(1), 2(1) and (2), 3, 4, 5, 11, 12, 13 as amended by Regulation 2391/85: Article 1(1), (2), (4), (9) and (10) and by Regulation 2528/87: Article 1(1) and (2)	Harvest, production and stock declarations
2. Regulation 822/87: Articles 13(2) and 69	Regulation 347/79: Article 13(1)	Restrictions on the use of certain vine varieties

PART V
OENOLOGICAL PROCESSES AND CONDITIONS FOR RELEASE TO THE MARKET

Column 1	Column 2	Column 3
Relevant Community provisions	*Supplementing provisions*	*Subject matter*
1. Regulation 822/87: Articles 18(1) and (2) and 19(1) to (7)		Conditions for increasing alcoholic strength
2. Regulation 822/87: Article 21(1) and (3)	Regulation 1594/70: Article 4 and Regulation 2585/79: Article 1 and Regulation 3190/85: Article 1 and Regulation 2094/86: Article 1 as amended by Regulation 2736/86: Article 1	Conditions for acidification and deacidification of wine

Column 1	Column 2	Column 3
Relevant Community provisions	*Supplementing provisions*	*Subject matter*
3. Regulation 822/87: Article 22(1) and (2)		Conditions for sweetening table wines and imported wines
4. Regulation 1618/70: Articles 1, 2, 3 and 4		Notifications and keeping of turnover records in relation to sweetening operations
5. Regulation 822/87: Article 23(1), (2) and (3)	Regulation 1594/70: Articles 5, 6, 7 and 8	Conditions for carrying out authorised processes (including notification and keeping of register)
6. Regulation 822/87: Article 16(2)		Restriction on mixing certain products with products suitable for yielding table wines
7. Regulation 822/87: Article 35(1)		Prohibition of the over pressing of grapes and the pressing of wine lees
8. Regulation 822/87: Article 25(1)	Regulation 351/79: Articles 1, 2 and 3 as amended by Act of Accession of the Hellenic Republic: Article 21 and Annex I, Part IIB, (n) 16 and by Regulation 3196/80: Article 1 and by Regulation 3267/82: Article 1 and by Regulation 3518/83: Article 1 and by Regulation 3689/84: Article 1 and by Regulation 3581/85: Article 1 and by Regulation 255/87: Article 1(1) and (2)	Addition of alcohol
9. Regulation 822/87: Article 16(3) to (7)	Regulation 479/86: Article 1 and Regulation 1781/86: Article 1	Permitted methods for the production of table wine by coupage
10. Regulation 353/79: Article 4	Regulation 643/77: Article 3	Description of wine produced in free zones of the Community
11. Regulation 822/87: Article 65(1) and (2)	Regulation 2805/73: Article 2 and Regulation 305/86: Article 1	Maximum permissible sulphur dioxide content of wine
12. Regulation 822/87: Articles 15(1), (3) and (4), 16(1) and (2), 17(1), (2) and (3) and 66	Regulation 2394/84: Articles 1(1) and 2 as amended by Regulation 2751/86: Article 1(1)	Permitted oenological practices and processes

Column 1	Column 2	Column 3
Relevant Community provisions	*Supplementing provisions*	*Subject matter*
13. Regulation 822/87: Article 67(1)		Wine and certain grape musts that may be offered for direct human consumption
14. Regulation 822/87: Articles 13(4) and 67(2) to (7)		Restrictions relating to certain wines and other products originating in the Community
15. Regulation 822/87: Article 68		Restrictions relating to the use of wine originating in third countries in the production of sparkling wine
16. Regulation 822/87: Article 70(3) to (6)		Restrictions on the use of products originating in third countries
17. Regulation 2931/80: Article 1	Regulation 3826/81	Rules relating to quality wines originating in the Republic of Austria
18. Regulation 822/87: Article 73(1)	Regulation 1873/84: Article 1	General rules relating to release of wine products for human consumption
19. Regulation 358/79: Articles 2, 4, 5(1) to (4), 6(1) and (2), 7(2), 8(1) and (2), 10, 11, 12(1), 13, 14, 15, 16(1), 17(1) and (2), 18 and 22 as amended by Regulation 2383/79: Article 1 and by Regulation 3456/80: Article 1 and by Regulation 3686/84: Article 1(1), (3), (4) and (5) and by Regulation 3310/85: Article 1(1) to (4)	Regulation 2152/75: Article 1 Regulation 1888/86: Article 1	Rules for the preparation and marketing of sparkling wines
20. Regulation 3590/85: Article 8(1)		Conditions for release for human consumption of products originating in third countries
21. Regulation 1972/78: Articles 1, 2, and 4a as amended by Regulation 45/80: Article 1		Restrictions relating to the holding of unfit wine and the use of oenological substances

PART VI
SPECIFICATION

Column 1	Column 2	Column 3
Relevant Community provisions	*Supplementing provisions*	*Subject matter*
1. Regulation 822/87: Article 72(1)		Use of the term 'table wine'
2. Regulation 355/79: Article 45	Regulation 997/81: Article 20	Use of the term 'wine'

PART VII
VINEYARD REGISTER

Column 1	Column 2	Column 3
Relevant Community provisions	*Supplementing provisions*	*Subject matter*
1. Regulation 2392/86: Article 3(2)		Establishment of a vineyard register

EXPLANATORY NOTE

(This note is not part of the Regulations)

These Regulations, which apply throughout the United Kingdom and come into force on 20th November 1987, provide for the enforcement of EEC regulations (as specified in Schedules 1 and 2) concerned with the production and marketing of wine and related products.

The Regulations, which revoke and re-enact with amendments the provisions of the Common Agricultural Policy (Wine) Regulations 1982 and the Common Agricultural Policy (Wine) (Amendment) Regulations 1983–

   (a) designate competent authorities for the purposes of enforcement (regulation 3);
   (b) exempt certain products from provisions relating to information required on labels (regulation 4);
   (c) provide for an exemption permitting the planting for certain purposes of vine varieties whose planting would otherwise be prohibited (regulation 5);
   (d) prescribe offences and penalties (regulation 6).

The Regulations differ from the Common Agricultural Policy (Wine) Regulations 1982, as amended by the Common Agricultural Policy (Wine) (Amendment) Regulations 1983 in that–

   (a) an exemption has been provided for permitting the planting for certain purposes of otherwise prohibited vine varieties (regulation 5);
   (b) the penalties for offences have been increased (regulation 6);
   (c) offences contrary to Part V of Schedule 2, relating to wine making processes, have been added to the offences contrary to Parts I, II and III of that Schedule which are punishable on summary conviction to a fine not exceeding £2,000 and on conviction on indictment to a fine (regulation 6(1));
   (d) an exception in the case of disclosure in pursuance of a Community obligation has been included in the provision creating the offence of disclosure of information (regulation 6(2)(b));
   (e) a provision has been added which deems various officers of a body corporate to be guilty in certain circumstances of an offence committed by that body corporate (regulation 6(4));
   (f) the Schedules have been revised and brought up to date so as to include references to relevant Regulations of the European Communities which have been adopted since the Common Agricultural Policy (Wine) (Amendment) Regulations 1983 came into force and to delete references to Regulations which have been repealed or superseded or have become redundant.

In Schedule 1 each Regulation is given the title which appears in the Official Journal, except in cases where the title refers to a Regulation that has been repealed or superseded. In such a case the title given in Schedule 1 refers to the superseding Regulation and the title in the Official Journal is given in a footnote.

STATUTORY INSTRUMENTS

1987 No. 1848

BUILDING SOCIETIES

The Building Societies (Provision of Services) (No. 2) Order 1987

Made - - - -	*19th October 1987*
Laid before Parliament	*23rd October 1987*
Coming into force	*15th November 1987*

The Building Societies Commission, in exercise of the powers conferred on it by section 34(2) and (8) of the Building Societies Act 1986**(a)** and of all other powers enabling it on that behalf, hereby makes the following Order:

Citation and commencement

1. This Order may be cited as the Building Societies (Provision of Services) (No. 2) Order 1987 and shall come into force on 15th November 1987.

Variation of Schedule 8 to the Building Societies Act 1986

2. Schedule 8 to the Building Societies Act 1986 (provision of services) shall be varied by the following amendments –

(a) in paragraph 7(a) of Part III, after the words "authorised institution" there shall be inserted the words "or building society";

(b) in paragraph 7(c) of Part III, after the words "other body" there shall be inserted the words "or description of body"; and

(c) in paragraph 7 of Part IV, in the definition of "mortgage investments", for the words "advances secured on land" there shall be substituted the words "secured lending where the security comprises or includes land".

In witness whereof the common seal of the Building Societies Commission is hereto fixed, and is authenticated by me, a person authorised under paragraph 14 of Schedule 1 to the Building Societies Act 1986, on 19th October 1987.

D. B. Severn
Secretary to the Commission

(a) 1986 c.53; Schedule 8 was amended by S.I.1987/172 and 1670.

EXPLANATORY NOTE

(This note is not part of the Order)

The Order varies Schedule 8 to the Building Societies Act 1986 in relation to the power of building societies to manage the mortgage investments of others and arrange for the provision of credit by others. Article 2(a) includes other building societies among the bodies for which a particular building society may arrange credit. Article 2(b) provides for the approval by the Building Societies Commission of descriptions of bodies (as well as individual bodies) for the purposes of arranging the provision of credit. Article 2(c) relates to the power to manage mortgage investments, which is found in paragraph 4 of Part I of Schedule 8. In Part IV "mortgage investments" are defined as meaning rights arising out of advances secured on land, a term which, in the context of the Act, means an advance of a particular nature by a building society, and accordingly the power is limited to the power to act on behalf of another society. Article 2(c), by changing the definition, removes that restriction.

STATUTORY INSTRUMENTS

1987 No. 1850 (S.128)

PENSIONS

The Local Government Superannuation (Scotland) Regulations 1987

Made - - - -	*19th October 1987*
Laid before Parliament	*30th November 1987*
Coming into force	*21st December 1987*

ARRANGEMENT OF REGULATIONS

PART A

PRELIMINARY

PART B

PENSIONABLE EMPLOYMENT

PART C

PAYMENTS BY EMPLOYEES

PART D

SERVICE

PART E

BENEFITS

PART F

WAR SERVICE

PART S

MISCELLANEOUS AND SUPPLEMENTAL

S1.   Periods of time

S2.   Application to benefits in respect of former employments

S3.   Revocations

SCHEDULES

The Secretary of State, in exercise of the powers conferred on him by sections 7, 8(3) and 12 of the Superannuation Act 1972(**a**), and by section 110 of the National Insurance Act 1965(**b**) as the appropriate Minister of the Crown under that section, and of all other powers enabling him in that behalf, after consultation with such associations of local authorities as appeared to him to be concerned and such representatives of other persons likely to be affected by the Regulations as appeared to him to be appropriate in accordance with section 7(5) of the said Act of 1972 and not having considered consultation with any individual local authority desirable, hereby makes the following Regulations:

PART A

PRELIMINARY

Citation and commencement

A1. These Regulations may be cited as the Local Government Superannuation (Scotland) Regulations 1987 and shall come into force on 21st December 1987.

Interpretation

A2.—(1) Schedule 1 contains a glossary of expressions and in these Regulations, unless the context otherwise requires, any expression listed in column 1 of that Schedule has the meaning given against it in column 2 of that Schedule or is to be construed in accordance with directions given against it in column 2 of that Schedule.

(2) In these Regulations, unless the context otherwise requires—

(a) any reference to a numbered regulation, Part or Schedule is to be construed as a reference to the regulation, Part or Schedule, as the case may be, which bears that number in these Regulations, and any reference to a numbered paragraph in a regulation of, or a Schedule to, these Regulations is to be construed as a reference to the paragraph bearing that number in that regulation or, as the case may be, that Schedule;

(b) any reference to, or to things done or falling to be done under or for the purposes of, any provision of these Regulations is, if and so far as the nature of the reference permits, to be construed as including, in relation to circumstances or purposes in relation to which the corresponding provision in the 1974 Regulations has or had effect, a reference to, or as the case may be to things done or falling to be done under or for the purposes of, that corresponding provision;

(c) any reference to—

(i) any enactment applying to Scotland listed in the table in paragraph 5 of Schedule 7 to the Act of 1972, or

(ii) any instrument (including a scheme) made under any enactment so listed, or

(iii) any provision of any such enactment or instrument,

is to be construed as a reference to that enactment, instrument or provision as having effect by virtue of sub-paragraph (1) of that paragraph and as amended by the Miscellaneous Provisions Regulations.

(3) Where these Regulations require anything to be done within a specified period after or from a specified day or event, the period begins immediately after the specified day or, as the case may be, the day on which the specified event occurs.

Application of the Regulations to the Scottish Special Housing Association and its employees

A3. Subject to the modifications set out in Schedule 2, these Regulations and any other Regulations having effect as if made under section 7 of the Act of 1972 shall apply to the

---

(**a**) 1972 c.11.

(**b**) 1965 c.51; section 110 was continued in force by regulation 3 of, and Schedule 1 to, the National Insurance (Non-participation—Transitional Provisions) Regulations 1974 (S.I. 1974/2057).

Scottish Special Housing Association and its employees as though it were a body described in Part I of Schedule 3 and an administering authority.

Transfers from England and Wales to Scotland

A4.—(1) In this regulation "previous local government employment" means employment or employments in England and Wales–

    (a) in relation to any time before 1st April 1974, as a contributory employee within the meaning of the Local Government Superannuation Act 1937(**a**) or as a local Act contributor within the meaning of that Act, and

    (b) in relation to any time after 31st March 1974, in which the person was or was deemed to be a pensionable employee within the meaning of the Local Government Superannuation Regulations 1974(**b**) or by virtue of which the person was a contributor to the local Act Superannuation Fund within the meaning of the Local Government Superannuation (City of London) Regulations 1977(**c**).

(2) This regulation shall apply to a person who was in previous local government employment and to whom Part II of the Local Government Superannuation (England and Scotland) Regulations 1948 to 1970(**d**) did not apply and who–

    (a) entered employment with a scheduled body on or after 1st April 1974, or

    (b) had ceased to be in previous local government employment on or after 1st April 1972, and more than a year after so ceasing became a contributing employee or local Act contributor.

(3) Where this regulation applies–

    (a) "appointed day" for the purposes of the 1974 Regulations shall be 1st April 1974;

    (b) these Regulations shall apply as if any period of previous local government employment was service with a scheduled body;

    (c) except in regulation A5, any reference in these Regulations to an enactment, rule or regulation shall be deemed to include a reference to the corresponding provisions which applied or which apply in England and Wales.

Transfers from Scotland to England and Wales

A5.—(1) This regulation shall apply to a person–

    (a) who on or after 31st March 1972 ceases to be employed in a local government employment;

    (b) who subsequently enters employment with a scheduled body within the meaning of the Local Government Superannuation Regulations 1974 or the Local Government Superannuation Regulations 1986(**e**) (hereinafter referred to as "the new employment"); and

    (c) to whom Part III of the Local Government Superannuation (England and Scotland) Regulations 1948 did not apply.

(2) Part Q of these Regulations shall apply to a person to whom this regulation applies as if on the date of entry to the new employment he had become employed by a scheduled body and any references to "new local government employment" and "new fund authority" in that Part of these Regulations shall be treated as if they included a reference to the corresponding terms in Part Q of the Local Government Superannuation Regulations 1986.

Payment of benefits

A6. Except where the contrary intention appears any benefit payable under these Regulations shall be paid out of the appropriate superannuation fund.

(**a**) 1937 c.68.
(**b**) S.I. 1974/520; the relevant amending instruments are 1977/1341, 1978/822 and 1979/1534.
(**c**) S.I. 1977/1341.
(**d**) S.I. 1948/1131, 1949/631, 1954/1250, 1970/1126.
(**e**) S.I. 1986/24.

PART B

PENSIONABLE EMPLOYMENT

Pensionable employees

B1.—(1) Paragraphs (2) to (10) have effect subject to paragraphs (11) and (12).

(2) A whole-time officer of a body described in Part I of Schedule 3 ("a Part I scheduled body") is a pensionable employee.

(3) A whole-time manual worker employed by a Part I scheduled body is a pensionable employee if he–

(a) has completed 12 months continuous employment with that body, or

(b) has entered or re-entered the employment of that body–

    (i) less than 12 months after completing at least 12 months continuous employment with a Part I scheduled body, or

    (ii) after having been in other local government employment and without having applied for a return of the whole of his contributions, or

(c) satisfies the requirements of Part III of Schedule 3.

(4) A variable-time employee of a Part I scheduled body who is also a pensionable employee in a whole-time employment with any such body–

(a) is a pensionable employee in the variable-time employment, and

(b) if he ceases to hold the whole-time employment, remains a pensionable employee while he continues without break of service in the variable-time employment.

(5) An employee described in Part II of Schedule 3 is a pensionable employee if the body employing him have by a statutory resolution–

(a) specified him as a pensionable employee, or

(b) specified a class of employees, to which he belongs, as pensionable employees.

(6) A whole-time member of a passenger transport executive is a pensionable employee if that executive have, with the consent of the passenger transport authority for which they are the executive, by a statutory resolution specified him as a pensionable employee.

(7) A whole-time director of a subsidiary of a passenger transport executive is a pensionable employee if that executive have by a statutory resolution specified him as a pensionable employee.

(8) A person who immediately before 16th May 1974–

(a) was a member of a passenger transport executive or a director of a subsidiary of a passenger transport executive, and

(b) was in that position a contributory employee,

is a pensionable employee while he continues without break in service in that position.

(9) A person who immediately before 21st December 1987 was a pensionable employee by virtue of regulation B2(1)(g) of the 1974 Regulations (certain former contributory employees continuously employed by same body) is a pensionable employee while he continues without break in service in employment with the same body.

(10) Subject to regulation B4, every pensionable employee employed by a scheduled body who before 1st April 1986 ceased to be a whole-time employee but who continued without a break of service in the employment of that body in the same post and who was, notwithstanding the provisions of the Local Government Superannuation (Scotland) Regulations 1974-86 in force before that date, regarded as a pensionable employee by that scheduled body and, where the body was not an administering authority, by the administering authority is a pensionable employee.

(11) A Part I scheduled body may resolve that a person who falls within paragraph (2), (3) or (4), or regulation B2 or B3 shall not become a pensionable employee unless he has undergone a medical examination to their satisfaction; and a resolution under this paragraph may apply to any specified person or to any specified class of persons.

(12) Notwithstanding anything in paragraphs (2) to (11), the following are not pensionable employees–

(a) subject to regulation B2, a person who elected under paragraph 3 of Schedule 4 to the Act of 1937 not to become a contributory employee and whose election did not cease to have effect before 16th May 1974, so long as he continues as a manual worker in employment with the body to whom he gave notice of the election;

(b) a person who elected under regulation 23 of the Miscellaneous Provisions Regulations not to become a contributory employee and whose election did not cease to have effect before 16th May 1974, so long as he continues in employment with the body to whom he gave notice of the election;

(c) a person who has not attained the age of 18 years;

(d) a person who has attained the age of 65 years and has completed not less than 45 years' reckonable service;

(e) any other person who has attained the age of 65 years, unless–

(i) there has become payable to him a pension which is liable to be reduced or suspended under regulation E15, an ill-health lump sum retiring allowance under regulation E4, or a short service grant under the Benefits Regulations, or

(ii) if he were to become a pensionable employee, he would immediately become entitled to reckon any period as reckonable service or qualifying service, or

(iii) under any enactment he has received or is entitled to receive compensation for loss of employment or loss or diminution of emoluments attributable to the provisions of an enactment, and the compensation is liable to be reduced or suspended, in consequence of his taking up employment with a scheduled body, in the like manner and to the like extent as it would have been reduced or suspended if he had remained subject to the pension scheme to which he was subject immediately before suffering the loss;

(f) a person who is, in the same employment, entitled to participate in the benefits of any other superannuation scheme provided by or under any enactment (including an enactment in a local Act), other than section 7 of the Act of 1972;

(g) an employee of a scheduled body in respect of whom contributions to the Merchant Navy Officers Pension Fund are made;

(h) a person who may elect under regulation B3 to become entitled to participate in the benefits of the appropriate superannuation fund.

(13) In this regulation "statutory resolution" means, in relation to a scheduled body, a resolution passed in the manner in which an ordinary resolution of the body may be passed, except that 28 days' notice of the meeting at which the resolution is passed and of the terms of the resolution and of the fact that it is to be proposed at that meeting must have been given in the manner in which notice for convening ordinary meetings of the body may be given.

Persons who may elect to be pensionable employees – persons who made election under paragraph 3 of Schedule 4 to the Act of 1937

B2.　A person who–

(a) elected under paragraph 3 of Schedule 4 to the Act of 1937 not to become a contributory employee, and

(b) had he not so elected, would be a pensionable employee by virtue of regulation B1(3),

may at any time, notwithstanding anything in regulation B1(3), by notice in writing to the body by whom he is employed elect to become a pensionable employee from the date on which the notice is given.

Other persons who may elect to be pensionable employees

B3.—(1) Subject to paragraph (6) and regulation B4, a person who is in a relevant employment as defined in paragraph (2) may elect to become entitled in relation to that employment to participate in the benefits of the appropriate superannuation fund maintained under these Regulations.

(2) In this regulation and in regulation B4, "relevant employment" means, subject to paragraphs (3) and (4), employment by a scheduled body in which in every period of 12 months–

(a) the contractual weeks are 35 or more but fewer than 45 and the contractual hours are 30 or more, or

(b) the contractual weeks are 35 or more and the contractual hours are 15 or more but fewer than 30.

(3) If a person is in two or more employments under a single scheduled body, and–

(a) none of those employments is an employment falling within paragraph (2)(b), but

(b) in each of the employments the contractual weeks in every period of 12 months are 35 or more, and

(c) the total of the contractual hours in all the employments is 15 or more,

then each of the employments is a relevant employment, but an election under this regulation in respect of any one of them is of no effect unless elections are made in respect of all of them.

(4) If a person is in two or more employments under a single scheduled body of which–

(a) one at least is an employment falling within paragraph (2)(b), and

(b) one at least is an employment in which the contractual weeks in every period of 12 months are 35 or more but the contractual hours are fewer than 15,

then every employment falling within sub-paragraph (b) is a relevant employment, but an election under this regulation in respect of such an employment is of no effect unless an election is made in respect of an employment falling within sub-paragraph (a).

(5) In paragraphs (2), (3) and (4), "the contractual weeks" means the number of weeks the employee is regularly or usually required to work by the scheduled body, and "the contractual hours" means the number of hours the employee is regularly or usually required to work by the scheduled body in each of those weeks.

(6) Paragraph (1) shall not apply to–

(a) a person who falls within regulation B1(12)(a) to (g), or

(b) a person who–

(i) was on 15th May 1974 a contributory employee or local Act contributor, and

(ii) on 16th May 1974 became a pensionable employee,

if there has since been no period of a day or more during which he was not a pensionable employee, or

(c) any other person who was a pensionable employee on 31st March 1986 if there has since been no period of a day or more during which he was not a pensionable employee, or

(d) a manual worker, unless–

(i) he has completed 12 months' continuous employment with his employing body, or

(ii) he entered or re-entered the employment of that body less than 12 months after completing at least 12 months' continuous employment with a scheduled body, or

(iii) he has commenced relevant employment following the termination of non-local government employment, and within 12 months of commencing such relevant employment he elected, by notice in writing to the appropriate administering authority for that employment, to become a pensionable employee, and within that 12 months, he has undertaken to apply to have his pension rights relating to his non-local government scheme transferred to such administering authority or preserved in the non-local government scheme on becoming a pensionable employee, or

(e) an employee of a scheduled body who are not a body specified in Part I of Schedule 3, unless they have by a statutory resolution as defined in regulation B1(13) specified him as a person, or specified a class of persons to which he belongs as a class of persons, to whom paragraph (1) is to apply, or

(f) a part-time member of a fire brigade maintained under the Fire Services Act 1947(a).

(7) An election under this regulation may be made at any time by giving notice in writing to the employing authority, and–

(a) 1947 c.41.

(a) subject to paragraphs (3) and (4), has effect from the date on which it is made, and

(b) subject to regulation B4, continues to have effect so long as the person who made it remains in the employment in respect of which it was made.

(8) An election made under regulation B2A of the 1974 Regulations shall continue to have effect as if it were an election under this regulation.

Other elections as to pensionability

B4.—(1) A person may by notice in writing to the employing authority elect to cease to be a pensionable employee if–

(a) he is in a relevant employment as defined in regulation B3(2) or relevant employments, and

(i) he was a pensionable employee on 31st March 1986,

(ii) there has since been no period of a day or more during which he was not a pensionable employee, and

(iii) he is not a person who falls within regulation B3(6)(b), or

(b) he has made an election under regulation B2A of the 1974 Regulations or regulation B3 while in a relevant employment falling within regulation B3(2)(a), and–

(i) is in a single relevant employment falling within regulation B3(2)(b) of that definition and is not in any relevant employment falling within regulation B3(4)(b), or

(ii) is in relevant employments falling within regulation B3(3).

(2) An election under paragraph (1) has effect from the date on which it is made, and for so long as the person who made it continues to be in a relevant employment or relevant employments.

(3) While an election under paragraph (1) has effect the person who made it is not entitled–

(a) under regulation B1 to be a pensionable employee in any superannuation fund maintained under these Regulations, or

(b) to make any election under regulation B3.

(4) If–

(a) a person became entitled by virtue of an election or elections under regulation B3 to participate in the benefits of the appropriate superannuation fund in relation to one or more employments, and

(b) the contractual hours, or as the case may be the total of the contractual hours, have become fewer than 15, or the contractual weeks have become fewer than 35,

he may elect to cease to be a pensionable employee.

(5) An election under paragraph (4) must be made in writing to the employing authority within 6 months from the date on which the contractual hours or as the case may be the total of the contractual hours became fewer than 15, or the contractual weeks became fewer than 35.

(6) For the purposes of these Regulations other than regulation C12 a person who makes an election under paragraph (1) or paragraph (4) shall be treated as if he had, on the date on which the election was made, ceased to hold the employment or employments in which he was a pensionable employee.

Persons deemed to be employees of a scheduled body

B5. For the purposes of these Regulations a person of a class described in column 1 of the Table below shall be deemed to be an officer or manual worker, whichever is appropriate, in employment with the body described opposite that class in column 2.

TABLE

(1) Class	(2) Deemed employing body
Registration officer	The regional council or the islands council who are the local registration authority for the purposes of section 5 of the Registration of Births, Deaths and Marriages (Scotland) Act 1965(**a**) and by whom he was appointed or deemed to have been appointed under section 7 of that Act
Rent officer	Any local authority with whom the Secretary of State has made arrangements under section 43 of the Rent (Scotland) Act 1984(**b**) to provide for the superannuation of the officer
Employees of a passenger transport authority	The relevant passenger transport executive
Members of passenger transport executives and directors of subsidiaries of passenger transport executives falling within regulation B1(6), (7) or (8)	The relevant passenger transport executive
Employees of a subsidiary of a passenger transport executive	The relevant passenger transport executive
Officers and manual workers of Trinity Hospital	City of Edinburgh District Council
Officers and manual workers of– (a) Heriot Watt College, (b) Heriot Watt University, (c) the Forth Road Bridge Joint Board and (d) Edinburgh College of Art	Lothian Regional Council.

Power to admit employees of other bodies

B6.—(1) Subject to paragraphs (3) to (6), an administering authority may make an agreement ("an admission agreement") with any body specified in paragraph (8) providing for employees of that body ("the employing body") to participate in the benefits of the superannuation fund or further fund maintained by the authority.

(2) In relation to an employee participating in the benefits of a fund by virtue of an admission agreement ("an admitted employee") these Regulations have effect as if he were a pensionable employee and the employing body were a scheduled body.

(3) Subject to paragraph (4), an admission agreement may provide for members of any specified class or classes of employees of the employing body to become admitted employees.

(4) An admission agreement may not provide for any person who–

(a) has not attained the age of 18 years, or

(b) has attained the age of 65 years and does not fall within regulation B1(12)(e),

to become an admitted employee.

(5) Except as provided in paragraph (6), an admission agreement cannot confer any greater or lesser rights or liabilities on any admitted employee than those he would have had if he had become a pensionable employee by virtue of regulation B1.

(6) An admission agreement may–

(a) provide that any previous period of employment of an admitted employee by the employing body is to be reckonable as reckonable service to such extent as may be specified in the agreement,

---

(**a**) 1965 c.49; section 5 was amended by the Local Government (Scotland) Act 1973 (c.65), section 166(2)(a).
(**b**) 1984 c.58.

(b) where the employing body is a development corporation established under the New Towns (Scotland) Act 1968(**a**), provide that a percentage, not exceeding 4.4%, of the remuneration of an admitted employee shall, if he is an employee of a description specified for the purpose in the agreement, be treated as not being remuneration for the purposes of these Regulations, and

(c) in the case of an employee of a body specified in column (1) of Schedule 20 who is admitted to participate in the benefits of a superannuation fund or further fund on or after the date in column (2) of Schedule 20 appropriate to the body by reason of an agreement made under this regulation or regulation B4 of the 1974 Regulations, contain a provision providing for the termination of the agreement and where an agreement is so terminated then for the purposes of these Regulations other than regulation C12 that person shall be treated as if he had on the day on which the agreement terminated ceased to hold the employment or employments in respect of which he was admitted to participate in the benefits of the superannuation fund or further fund.

(7) On making an admission agreement an administering authority shall forthwith inform the Secretary of State of the name of the employing body and the date from which the agreement takes effect.

(8) The bodies mentioned in paragraph (1) are–

(a) a voluntary organisation engaged in the provision of services–

(i) under Part III of the National Health Service (Scotland) Act 1978(**b**); or

(ii) under Part III of the National Assistance Act 1948(**c**); or

(iii) under the Disabled Persons (Employment) Act 1958(**d**); or

(iv) under the Mental Health (Scotland) Act 1984(**e**); or

(v) under section 14 of the Social Work (Scotland) Act 1968(**f**);

(b) a body representative of local authorities or of local authorities and officers of local authorities or a body representative of officers of local authorities formed for the purpose of consultation as to the common interests of those authorities and the discussion of matters relating to local government;

(c) a body authorised by any enactment to carry on any railway, light railway, tramway, road transport, water transport, canal, inland navigation, dock, harbour, pier, lighthouse or airport undertaking or any undertaking for the supply of electricity, gas, hydraulic power or water;

(d) a body approved for the purposes of this regulation by the Secretary of State who are primarily engaged in carrying on any undertaking of a kind mentioned in sub-paragraph (c) though not authorised by any enactment to carry on any such undertaking;

(e) a body who provide a public service in the United Kingdom otherwise than for the purposes of gain;

(f) a body to whose funds any local authority contribute or to whom any grant is made out of monies provided by Parliament;

(g) a development corporation established under the New Towns (Scotland) Act 1968.

(9) Any agreement made under regulation B4 of the 1974 Regulations, or continued in force by regulation J4 of the 1974 Regulations as if so made, continues in force as if it were an admission agreement made under this regulation.

Treatment of certain additional duties

B7.—(1) This regulation applies where the duties of an officer who is in a whole-time employment of a scheduled body include the additional duty of a returning officer or counting officer at any election or referendum authorised by Act of Parliament in circumstances where fees are paid.

(**a**) 1968 c.16.
(**b**) 1978 c.29.
(**c**) 1948 c.29.
(**d**) 1958 c.33.
(**e**) 1984 c.36.
(**f**) 1968 c.49.

(2) Where–
   (a) the officer became a pensionable employee under the 1974 Regulations on 16th May 1974, and
   (b) immediately before that date he was in the whole-time employment and his duties in it included one or both of the additional duties,

then unless the context otherwise requires these Regulations apply to him in relation to each additional duty as if it were a separate variable-time employment with a scheduled body other than the body with whom he is in the whole-time employment.

(3) In any other case these Regulations apply to the officer, unless the context otherwise requires–
   (a) where there is one additional duty, in relation to that duty as if it were, or
   (b) where there are more than one additional duty, in relation to them as if they were,

a separate variable-time employment with a scheduled body other than the body with whom he is in the whole-time employment.

Treatment of certain separate employments

B8. Where a person holds two or more separate employments under one scheduled body, then unless the context otherwise requires these Regulations apply in relation to each of those employments as if the other or others were held by him under another scheduled body.

Deemed employments

B9. In these Regulations, unless the context otherwise requires, references to employees of a scheduled body shall be construed as including references to persons who are deemed for the purposes of these Regulations to be in the employment of a scheduled body, and other provisions relating to employment by or under a scheduled body shall be construed accordingly.

Age of compulsory retirement

B10. When a pensionable employee attains the age of 65 years he shall cease to hold his employment, except that the employing authority may, with his consent, extend his services for one year or any lesser period, and so from time to time as they deem expedient.

PART C

PAYMENTS BY EMPLOYEES

Appropriate superannuation fund

C1.—(1) In relation to a pensionable employee of an administering authority the appropriate superannuation fund is the fund administered by that authority.

(2) In relation to a pensionable employee of an employing authority who are a party to an admission agreement or an agreement under regulation B6 made with an admitting authority the appropriate superannuation fund shall be the fund or further fund administered by the admitting authority.

(3) In relation to the pensionable employees of the Western Isles Islands Council the appropriate superannuation fund shall be the fund maintained by Highland Regional Council.

(4) In relation to the pensionable employees of the Central Scotland Water Development Board the appropriate superannuation fund shall be the fund maintained by Strathclyde Regional Council.

(5) Subject to paragraph (6), in relation to a pensionable employee whose case does not fall within paragraphs (1) to (4) the appropriate superannuation fund is the fund maintained by the administering authority within whose area his employing authority or the greater part of the area of his employing authority lies.

(6) Where paragraph (5) applies to any pensionable employees of a scheduled body the Secretary of State may, after consultation with the bodies appearing to him to be concerned,

by direction substitute as the appropriate superannuation fund in relation to those employees or any of them the fund maintained by some other administering authority ("the substituted fund").

(7) A direction under paragraph (6) shall, if the Secretary of State deems it necessary–

(a) require the making of financial adjustments between the funds, whether by way of a payment to the substituted fund or of a transfer of assets or both, or

(b) contain provision as to the transfer of liabilities to the substituted fund, and any other consequential and incidental matters.

Payment and amount of employee's contributions

C2.—(1) Subject to paragraph (3), a pensionable employee shall, at such intervals as the appropriate administering authority may determine, make contributions to the appropriate superannuation fund in respect of every employment in which he is a pensionable employee.

(2) The amount of the contribution to be made for any period is–

(a) in the case of a manual worker, 5%, and

(b) in the case of an officer, 6%,

of his remuneration in the employment.

(3) A pensionable employee shall not make contributions in respect of any employment in relation to which he is entitled to reckon 45 years' reckonable service.

(4) For the purposes of paragraph (3) reckonable service beyond a total of 40 years before attaining the age of 60 years shall be disregarded.

(5) In the case of an officer who–

(a) is a designated employee, and

(b) has not had a disqualifying break of service, and

(c) has not, before entering the employment in which he is a pensionable employee, ceased to hold another local government employment, and–

(i) has become entitled to benefits otherwise than under regulation E2(1)(c) of the 1974 Regulations or of these Regulations, or

(ii) having become entitled under regulation E2(1)(c) of the 1974 Regulations or of these Regulations, has given notice under regulation E2(9)(c) of these Regulations,

the amount of the contribution to be made for any period is 5% of his remuneration in the employment.

Leave of absence from duty

C3.—(1) A pensionable employee who is on leave of absence from duty in an employment, otherwise than by reason of illness or injury, with reduced remuneration or without remuneration, shall not make any contribution under regulation C2 in respect of the employment for the period of his absence.

(2) Such employee shall for a period of 30 days beginning on the first day of the leave of absence, or for the period of absence if shorter, make contributions to the appropriate superannuation fund of amounts equal to the contributions he would have been required to make under regulation C2 on the remuneration he would have received during that period but for the leave of absence.

(3) If the employee gives notice in writing to the employing authority within the period of 30 days beginning on–

(a) the day on which he returns to duty, or

(b) the day on which he ceases to be employed by that authority,

whichever is the earlier, he shall make such contributions as are mentioned in paragraph (2) for the period beginning with the day after the expiration of the period mentioned in paragraph (2) and ending 36 months from the day before the date on which he went on leave of absence, or for the period of leave of absence if shorter.

(4) Where the leave of absence was given to enable the employee to serve on a jury in Scotland before any court there, and the absence continues after the expiration of the period

of 30 days mentioned in paragraph (2), the employee shall be deemed to have given such a notice as is mentioned in paragraph (3).

Absence due to trade dispute

C4.—(1) This regulation applies to a person who—
  (a) has been absent from duty, otherwise than on leave of absence, for a period of one or more days during and in consequence of a trade dispute, and
  (b) immediately before—
    (i) the period of absence, or
    (ii) where two or more periods of absence occurred in consequence of a single trade dispute, the first of those periods,
  was a pensionable employee.

(2) For the purposes of paragraph (1)—
  (a) a person whose contract of employment is terminated in consequence of a trade dispute is, notwithstanding the termination, to be treated as having been absent from duty after the termination if, not later than the day after the end of the trade dispute, he again becomes a pensionable employee of the same scheduled body, and
  (b) it is immaterial whether or not—
    (i) the person was participating in or financing or otherwise directly interested in the trade dispute, or
    (ii) the employing authority were a party to the trade dispute.

(3) Subject to paragraphs (4), (5) and (7), if notice in writing is given for the purpose by—
  (a) a person to whom this regulation applies, or
  (b) the executors of a person to whom this regulation applies who has died before the end of the period of 3 months specified in paragraph (5)(a) without giving such notice (referred to in this regulation as a "deceased employee"),
the amount specified in paragraph (6) is payable in respect of a relevant contribution period to the authority to whom notice was given.

(4) Where all or part of more than one relevant contribution period is included in a relevant absence or relevant absences which occurred in consequence of a single trade dispute, notice given for the purpose mentioned in paragraph (3) in respect of any one of those periods is of no effect unless notice is given in respect of all those periods.

(5) Notice for the purpose mentioned in paragraph (3) must be given in writing to the authority who are or were the employing authority in relation to the person concerned—
  (a) within the period of 3 months beginning—
    (i) on the day after the last day of the relevant contribution period, or
    (ii) where paragraph (4) applies the day after the last day of the relevant contribution periods, or
  (b) in the case of a deceased employee within the period of 12 months beginning on the date of the death of the employee, or
  (c) within such longer period as the employing authority may allow.

(6) The amount mentioned in paragraph (3) is an amount equal to 16% of the difference between—
  (a) the person's remuneration (if any) for the relevant contribution period, and
  (b) the remuneration he would have received for that period if it had not included any relevant absence or part of a relevant absence.

(7) Notwithstanding anything in regulation C11, but without prejudice to the power of the appropriate administering authority under that regulation to deduct from any payment by way of benefits under these Regulations any sum remaining due on account of an amount payable under this regulation—
  (a) an employing authority shall not accept from a pensionable employee, or deduct from his remuneration, and
  (b) an administering authority shall not recover from a pensionable employee,
in any period of 12 months ending with 5th April, by way of full or part payment of so much of any amount payable under this regulation as is attributable to any relevant absence during

that period, any sum which, when aggregated with any such amounts as are mentioned in Schedule 8, would exceed 15% of his remuneration for that period.

(8) In this regulation, unless the context otherwise requires–

"relevant absence" means a period for which a person to whom this regulation applies was absent from duty as mentioned in paragraph (1) excluding any part of such period as would result in his reckonable service exceeding 45 years and disregarding reckonable service before attaining the age of 60 years beyond a total of 40 years;

"relevant contribution period" means a period which–

(a) is co-extensive with one of the intervals at which a person to whom this regulation applies was required under regulation C2(1) to contribute to the appropriate superannuation fund, and

(b) includes all or part of a relevant absence;

"remuneration" does not include any guarantee payment under Part II of the Employment Protection (Consolidation) Act 1978(a); and

"trade dispute" has the meaning given by section 29 of the Trade Union and Labour Relations Act 1974(b).

Lump sum payment to increase reckonable service

C5.—(1) Subject to paragraph (3), a pensionable employee may, by notice in writing given to the appropriate administering authority within 12 months after having first become a pensionable employee under these Regulations or the 1974 Regulations, elect to make a payment into the appropriate superannuation fund in order to become entitled under regulation D4 to reckon an additional period as reckonable service in relation to an employment in which he is a pensionable employee.

(2) The length of the period is not to exceed the maximum length determined in accordance with Schedule 4, the amount of the payment is to be calculated in accordance with Part I of Schedule 5, and the payment is to be made within the period of 1 month beginning on the date on which notice is given.

(3) An employee may not make an election under this regulation if he has attained the age of 65 years.

Periodical payments to increase reckonable service

C6.—(1) Subject to paragraph (4), a pensionable employee may, by notice in writing given to the appropriate administering authority, elect to make additional contributions to the appropriate superannuation fund in order to become entitled under regulation D5 to reckon an additional period as reckonable service in relation to an employment in respect of which he is a pensionable employee.

(2) The length of the period is not to exceed the maximum calculated in accordance with Schedule 4 and the additional contributions are to be calculated in accordance with Part II of Schedule 5.

(3) The additional contributions–

(a) are payable, at such intervals as the appropriate administering authority may determine, from the employee's birthday next following the date of the election, and

(b) subject to paragraph (5), cease to be payable on the day immediately before the birthday at which, or as the case may be his last birthday before, the employee attains pensionable age.

(4) An employee may not make an election under this regulation if–

(a) he has attained the age of 64 years, or

(b) he was precluded by regulation D13(6)(b) of the 1974 Regulations from making an election under that regulation, or

---

(a) 1978 c.44.
(b) 1974 c.52; section 29 was amended by the Trade Union and Labour Relations (Amendment) Act 1976 (c.7), section 1(d), by the Criminal Law Act 1977 (c.45), Schedule 13 and by the Employment Act 1982 (c.46), section 18.

(c) the appropriate administering authority have resolved that he should undergo a medical examination (at his own expense) and he has not done so to their satisfaction.

(5) Payment in accordance with paragraph (3) may be discontinued if the employee satisfies the appropriate administering authority that its continuance would cause financial hardship.

Payment by manual worker in respect of previous service

C7.—(1) A whole-time manual worker who becomes a pensionable employee by virtue of regulation B1(3)(c) may make a payment into the appropriate superannuation fund in order to become entitled under regulation D9 to reckon as reckonable service in relation to the employment in which he is a pensionable employee the period (hereinafter referred to as "the additional period") during which he was in that employment before becoming a pensionable employee.

(2) The amount of the payment shall be an amount equal to the contributions which he would have been required to make under regulation C2 if he had, throughout the additional period, been a pensionable employee, and the payment shall be made, unless the employing authority allow a longer period, within the period of 6 months beginning on the date on which he becomes a pensionable employee.

(3) The payment shall be treated for the purposes of these Regulations as if it were contributions made under regulation C2 in respect of employment in which the person was a pensionable employee.

Payments to avoid reduction of retiring allowance and death gratuity

C8.—(1) This regulation applies to a pensionable employee whose retiring allowance or death gratuity would be subject to reduction under regulation E3(7) or (8) (reduction in respect of reckonable service before 1st April 1972 etc.) or E11 (death gratuity) respectively.

(2) Subject to paragraphs (3) to (9), a person to whom this regulation applies may, by notice in writing given to the appropriate administering authority, elect to make payment to the appropriate superannuation fund in order to avoid all or part of the reduction in his retiring allowance, or any death gratuity that may become payable under regulation E11.

(3) A notice under paragraph (2) must specify whether the reckonable service in respect of which the reduction is to be avoided is the whole, and if not what part it is, of his reckonable service before, as the case may be–

(a) 1st April 1972, or

(b) in the case of a male employee, any earlier date on which he became a widower or was judicially separated from his wife or on which his marriage was dissolved.

(4) An election may not be made in respect of a period of reckonable service of less than one year unless the period that will be reduced under regulation E3(7) or (8) amounts to less than one year.

(5) A notice under paragraph (2) must specify whether payment is to be made–

(a) by a lump sum, or

(b) by instalments, or

(c) by way of additional contributions.

(6) An election by the pensionable employee to make payment by a lump sum or by instalments must be made within 12 months after first becoming a person to whom this regulation applies.

(7) An election to make payment by a lump sum may not be made by the pensionable employee after attaining the age of 65 years.

(8) An election by a pensionable employee to make payment by instalments may not be made–

(a) before attaining the age of 60 years or after attaining the age of 65 years, or

(b) after making an election to make payment by way of additional contributions, or

(c) if in the particular case the appropriate administering authority so resolve, without having, at his own expense, undergone a medical examination to their satisfaction.

(9) Elections to make payment by way of additional contributions may be made from time to time, but not–

(a) after attaining the age of 64 years, or

(b) after making an election to make payment by instalments, or

(c) if in the particular case the appropriate administering authority so resolve, without having at his own expense undergone a medical examination to their satisfaction.

(10) Subject to paragraph (11) and to Part IV of Schedule 6, payment is to be made—

(a) in the case of an election to make payment by a lump sum, in accordance with Part I of Schedule 6,

(b) in the case of an election to make payment by instalments, in accordance with Part II of that Schedule, and

(c) in the case of an election to make payment by way of additional contributions, in accordance with Part III of that Schedule.

(11) Payment in accordance with paragraph (10) may be discontinued if the employee satisfies the appropriate administering authority that its continuance would cause financial hardship.

Continuation of certain payments

C9.—(1) Where immediately before 21st December 1987 any payments remained to be made under a provision of the 1974 Regulations specified in column 1 of the table below, they shall be deemed to be payments due under the corresponding provision of these Regulations specified in column 2.

TABLE

(1) *(1974 Regulations)*	(2) *(These Regulations)*
Regulation C1A (trade disputes)	Regulation C4
Regulation C2A (avoidance of reduction of retiring allowance etc.)	Regulation C8
Regulation D12 (increase of reckonable service on lump sum payment)	Regulation C5
Regulation D13 (increase of reckonable service on periodical payments)	Regulation C6
Regulation D14A (whole-time manual workers)	Regulation C7

(2) Where immediately before 21st December 1987 any payments remained to be made under a provision of the 1974 Regulations specified in paragraph (3), they remain payable notwithstanding the revocation of the 1974 Regulations by these Regulations.

(3) The payments mentioned in paragraph (2) are payments under regulations D6 (non-contributing service), D7 (previous employment treated as non-contributing service), D8 (additional contributory payments under former Regulations), D10 (added years) and D11 (payments under former Regulations for added years) of the 1974 Regulations.

(4) Schedule 7 applies in relation to any payments under regulation D6, D7 or D8 of the 1974 Regulations which remain payable by virtue of paragraph (2) and, in relation to any payments under regulation D10 or D11 of those Regulations which remain so payable, Schedule 5 to those Regulations shall be deemed to have continued to have effect.

Statement of remuneration received otherwise than from employing authority

C10.—(1) A pensionable employee who receives any part of his remuneration otherwise than from the employing authority shall provide the employing authority with half-yearly statements of his receipts in respect of that part.

(2) The statements are to relate to the periods 1st April to 30th September and 1st October to 31st March, and are to be provided not later than 31st October and 30th April respectively.

(3) As soon as is reasonably practicable after receiving a request in writing from the employing authority the employee shall provide them with a statutory declaration verifying the correctness of any statement specified in the request.

Deduction and recovery of employee's contributions

C11.—(1) An employing authority may deduct from the remuneration payable by them to a pensionable employee–

(a) contributions payable under regulations C2 or C3,

(b) any amount payable under regulation C4, and

(c) any instalments or additional contributions payable to the appropriate superannuation fund.

(2) If and so far as deductions are not made under paragraph (1), the appropriate administering authority may recover any sum remaining due–

(a) in any court of competent jurisdiction, or

(b) by deducting it from any payment by way of benefits under these Regulations.

Return of employee's contributions in certain cases

C12.—(1) Subject to paragraphs (3) and (12), and regulation C13, this regulation applies to a pensionable employee of an employing authority who–

(a) before becoming entitled to any benefit under these Regulations, other than a retirement pension under regulation E2(2), ceases to be employed by that authority; and

(b) does not, within one month after ceasing to be so employed, enter further employment with any scheduled body and within that period become in that further employment a pensionable employee; and

(c) is entitled to reckon an aggregate of less than 5 years' reckonable service and qualifying service.

(2) Subject to paragraph (3), a person to whom this regulation applies shall be entitled to receive a refund of contributions calculated in accordance with paragraph (4).

(3) This regulation shall not apply to a person–

(a) who is entitled to a pension under regulation E2(1)(d) in respect of any period of service in contracted-out employment; or

(b) who is entitled to be paid, or has been paid, an ill-health lump sum retiring allowance under regulation E4.

(4) A person to whom this regulation applies shall be entitled–

(a) if he so ceases to be employed by reason of his voluntary resignation, or his resignation or dismissal in consequence of inefficiency or an offence of a fraudulent character or misconduct (not being such an offence or grave misconduct in connection with his employment), to receive out of the appropriate superannuation fund a sum equal to the aggregate amount of his contributions to the fund;

(b) if he so ceases to be employed for any reason not specified in paragraph (a), to receive out of the appropriate superannuation fund a sum equal to the aggregate amount of his contributions to the fund, together with compound interest thereon, calculated to the date on which he ceased to hold his employment–

(i) for any period before 1st April 1972, at the rate of 3 per cent per annum with half-yearly rests,

(ii) for any period between 1st April 1972 and 31st March 1980, at the rate of 4 per cent per annum with yearly rests, and

(iii) for any period after 31st March 1980, at the rate of 9 per cent per annum with yearly rests.

(5) Subject to paragraph (6), where a person to whom this regulation applies ceases to be employed as mentioned in paragraph (1)(a) in consequence of an offence of a fraudulent character or of grave misconduct, being such an offence or such misconduct in connection with his employment, the employing authority may, if they think fit, direct the return to him out of the appropriate superannuation fund of a sum equal to the whole or a part of the aggregate amount of his contributions to the fund or, if he so ceases to be employed in consequence of such an offence of a fraudulent character as aforesaid, the payment out of that fund of an equivalent sum to his spouse or any dependant of his.

(6) In the case of a person to whom paragraph (5) applies and who ceases to be employed in the circumstances mentioned in regulation E2(1)(c), the power of the employing authority

under this paragraph shall apply only in respect of any contributions relating to a period of service in respect of which the employing authority has given a direction as to forfeiture under regulation M1.

(7) No return of contributions shall be payable to a person under paragraph (4)–

(a) before the expiration of a year from the date on which he ceases to be employed, or

(b) until a claim for payment made not earlier than 1 month and two days after the date on which he ceases to be employed as mentioned in paragraph (1)(a) has been made to them,

whichever event first occurs.

(8) No payment shall be made under paragraph (7)(a) where the person has given a written notice to the administering authority requesting postponement of such payment.

(9) On making any repayment of contributions (with or without interest) under this regulation, the administering authority shall deduct from the repayment any tax to which they may become chargeable under paragraph 2 of Part II of Schedule 5 to the Finance Act 1970(a) (which relates to charge to tax on repayment of employee's contributions).

(10) For the purposes of this regulation a pensionable employee who–

(a) ceases to be employed in the circumstances mentioned in regulation E2(1)(c) (other than a person who elects under regulation E2(6) to receive benefits from the date on which he so ceased or to whom, on so ceasing, regulation E2(6)(c) applies), or

(b) satisfies the requirements of regulation E2(1)(d) (other than a person who elects under regulation E2(8)(a)),

shall be treated as not being entitled to any benefit under these Regulations.

(11) Subject to paragraph (13) references in this regulation to the aggregate amount of an employee's contributions to a superannuation fund include references to–

(a) any contributions paid by him to any superannuation fund–

(i) under regulation C2 or C3, or

(ii) under regulation C1 or C2 of the 1974 Regulations, or

(iii) under Part I of the Act of 1937, or

(iv) under the Act of 1922, or

(v) under a local Act scheme;

(b) any contributions which, if the former Regulations had not been revoked by the 1974 Regulations and he had immediately before ceasing to be employed as mentioned in paragraph (1)(a) been a contributory employee, he would, by virtue of interchange rules, have been deemed to have made to the appropriate superannuation fund within the meaning of the Act of 1937;

(c) any amount–

(i) which, if the former Regulations had not been revoked as aforesaid and he had immediately before so ceasing been a contributory employee, would, by virtue of interchange rules, have been included in any amount which would, on his so ceasing, have become payable to him by way of a return of contributions under section 10 of the Act of 1937; or

(ii) by which, if the former Regulations had not been revoked as aforesaid and he had, immediately before so ceasing, been a contributory employee, the last-mentioned amount would, by virtue of interchange rules, have been deemed to have been increased;

(d) any sum paid by him into a superannuation fund under an old modification scheme made in accordance with section 28(3) of the Widows', Orphans' and Old Age Contributory Pensions Act 1936(b);

(e) any sum paid by him by way of additional contributory payments or under regulation C4;

(f) any amount paid by him by way of added period payments; and

---

(a) 1970 c.24; paragraph 2 was substituted by the Finance Act 1971 (c.68), Schedule 3, paragraph 7.
(b) 1936 c.33.

(g) any amount paid by him under regulation C8, but only in so far as any such contribution, sum or amount–

   (i) has not been returned to the person or, if it has been returned, has subsequently been repaid by him;

   (ii) is attributable to service which might have been reckoned under Part D in relation to the employment he has ceased to hold; and

   (iii) is not attributable to any earlier period or service in respect of which a benefit under Part E has been paid.

(12) The foregoing paragraphs shall apply to a person who is entitled to reckon an aggregate of not less than 5 years reckonable service and qualifying service, where–

(a) part of the service of that person is attributable to a period prior to 6th April 1975,

(b) the person elects that this regulation applies in his case by notice in writing given to the appropriate authority not earlier than one month after the date he ceases to be employed but within 12 months of that date, and

(c) the person has not, before giving the notice referred to in paragraph (b), again become a pensionable employee and given notice under regulation E2(10),

subject to the modification that he shall only be entitled to receive a refund of contributions for any service prior to 6th April 1975.

(13) Where paragraph (12) applies paragraph (11) shall have effect as if sub-paragraphs (e) and (f) were omitted.

Effect of return to local government on right to a return of contributions

C13. A person's right to a payment under regulation C12 is extinguished if–

(a) he returns to local government employment after leaving previous local government employment with a right to such a payment, and

(b) on the date on which he returns to local government employment he has not received the payment, and

(c) he has not given, within 3 months after that date or such longer period as his previous fund authority and, if different, his new fund authority may allow, written notice to his previous fund authority that he wishes to receive an immediate payment.

Restoration of right to reckon service in transitional cases where there has been a return of contributions

C14.—(1) Notwithstanding regulation D3, service for which a return of contributions has been received shall be reckonable as reckonable service if the conditions in paragraph (2) are satisfied and the person makes the payment required by paragraph (3).

(2) The conditions are that–

(a) the person ceased to be employed in local government employment on or after 16th May 1974 and before 6th April 1978; and

(b) on the cessation of that employment the aggregate of his reckonable and qualifying service amounted to less than 5 years; and

(c) the return of contributions was made in relation to that employment; and

(d) he subsequently returns to local government employment.

(3) Within six months, or such longer period as may be provided in paragraph (4), of his return to local government employment the person must pay to his previous fund authority for the credit of their superannuation fund–

(a) a sum equal to the contributions returned to him (together with any increase under regulation J11 and any interest he was paid); and

(b) compound interest on that sum calculated in accordance with regulation J7 for the period beginning with the date on which he received the return of contributions and ending on the date of the payment of that sum.

(4) The previous fund authority may in any particular case extend the period mentioned in paragraph (3).

Reduction of returned contributions following payment in lieu of contributions

C15.—(1) Subject to the provisions of this regulation, where a pensionable employee leaves employment in circumstances–

(a) to which regulation 6 of the Transitional Provisions Regulations does not apply, and

(b) in which returned contributions are due and a payment in lieu of contributions has previously been made in respect of him in circumstances in which returned contributions were not due,

those returned contributions shall be reduced by a sum equal to the amount, or the aggregate of the amounts, by which under section 60(5) of the Insurance Act (which defines an employer's rights against an insured person in respect of payments in lieu of contributions) they could have been reduced if returned at the time when the previous payment in lieu of contributions was made.

(2) Paragraph (1) shall also apply for the reduction of returned contributions where a payment in lieu of contributions has been made under any insurance code in respect of any period of former employment which is reckonable as service as a pensionable employee if–

(a) that payment in lieu was made in circumstances not involving the return of any superannuation contributions made by him in that employment; and

(b) the transfer value payable in respect of that employment has been adjusted to take account of that payment in lieu;

and where no superannuation contributions were payable in that employment, any amount returnable in respect of contributions deemed to have been made therein shall be reduced by a sum equal to one half of that payment in lieu.

(3) No payment in lieu of contributions shall be taken into account for the purposes of paragraphs (1) and (2)–

(a) on more than one occasion; or

(b) if the payment is one which has been reduced under regulation 13 of the National Insurance (Non-participation – Assurance of Equivalent Pension Benefits) Regulations 1960(a) or any corresponding enactment in force in Northern Ireland or the Isle of Man.

(4) Where the employment of a pensionable employee comes to an end in circumstances to which regulation 6 of the Transitional Provisions Regulations applies, the amount of returned contributions to which he is entitled shall be reduced by any amount which, under section 60 of the Insurance Act as modified by the said regulation 6, the person who has made or is liable to make a payment in lieu of contributions in respect of such employee, or would be so liable had the employee not been assured of equivalent pension benefits, is entitled either to recover from the person liable for the returned contributions or to retain out of the returned contributions.

(5) Where returned contributions are due in the circumstances mentioned in paragraph (1) or paragraph (4) on the cessation of two or more concurrently held employments, the reduction required by that paragraph shall be made by such one of the authorities paying the returned contributions as they may agree or, in default of agreement, as is determined by the Secretary of State, and where those employments were held under the same employing authority, the reduction shall be made in relation only to such one of the employments as is determined by the authority.

(6) Where returned contributions are reduced under paragraph (1) or under section 60(5) of the Insurance Act or the said section 60(5) as modified by regulation 6 of the Transitional Provisions Regulations or under any corresponding provision of the Northern Ireland Act or the Isle of Man Act, any sum so deducted shall not form part of any amount payable to or in respect of him, either as returned contributions or as a benefit ascertained by reference to the amount of the contributions paid by him on the occasion of any later cessation of his employment.

(7) In this regulation "returned contributions" means an amount payable under regulation C12 to or in respect of a pensionable employee by way of a return of contributions.

Limitation of payments

C16.   Schedule 8 has effect for the limitation of payments under this Part.

(a) S.I. 1960/1103.

PART D

SERVICE

Reckonable service

D1.—(1) Reckonable service is time that counts both for the purpose of ascertaining entitlement to benefits under these Regulations and for the purpose of calculating them.

(2) Subject to paragraphs (3) and (4) and regulations D3 and D8, a pensionable employee is entitled to reckon as reckonable service, in relation to an employment in which he is a pensionable employee—

(a) any period for which he has paid contributions under regulation C2 or C3,

(b) any period which he became entitled to reckon as reckonable service by virtue of regulation D1(1)(b) to (g) of the 1974 Regulations, and

(c) any period which he is entitled to reckon as reckonable service by virtue of regulations D4 to D7 or Part F (war service).

(3) A period of absence from duty without remuneration, otherwise than on leave of absence, may not be reckoned as reckonable service unless—

(a) that period was a relevant absence, and

(b) the amount specified in regulation C4(6) has been paid in respect of every relevant contribution period all or part of which was included in that relevant absence.

(4) Where the amount specified in regulation C4(6) has been paid in respect of a relevant contribution period, so much of any relevant absence as was included in that period may be reckoned as reckonable service whether or not a contract of employment continued to subsist during the relevant absence or any part of it.

Qualifying service

D2.—(1) Qualifying service is time that counts for the purpose of ascertaining entitlement to benefits under these Regulations but not for the purpose of calculating them.

(2) Subject to regulation D3, a pensionable employee's qualifying service is—

(a) any period which he is entitled to reckon as qualifying service by virtue of regulations D10, D11, H8 or J9(1)(b); and

(b) in the case of a person who was at any time from 1st April 1974 until 31st March 1986 or, in the case of a manual worker, at any time from 1st April 1973 until 31st March 1986, in relevant employment as defined in regulation B3(2), any period of service during that time in which the employee was employed for at least 15 hours in a week except—

(i) any period of reckonable service,

(ii) where the employee's relevant employment was interrupted for 12 months or more, any period of relevant employment occurring before the interruption, and

(iii) in the case of a manual worker, the first 12 months of any period of relevant employment not otherwise excepted; and

(c) any period which he became entitled to reckon as qualifying service by virtue of regulation D2 of the 1974 Regulations.

Exclusion from reckonable service and qualifying service

D3.—(1) Subject to regulation E16 (combined benefits), a pensionable employee who—

(a) has entered the employment of a scheduled body after becoming entitled to receive payment in respect of any superannuation benefit other than a superannuation benefit under the Insurance Act, or

(b) has entered such employment after becoming entitled to a benefit under regulation E2(1)(c) and has given notice under regulation E2(9)(c) (retention of entitlement to preserved benefits), or

(c) by virtue of regulation K1 of the 1974 Regulations—

(i) became entitled to receive payment in respect of any benefit under those Regulations, or

(ii) became entitled to a benefit under paragraph (1)(c) of, and gave notice under paragraph (4)(e) of, regulation E2 of those Regulations,

is not entitled to reckon as reckonable service any period of which account has been taken for the purpose of determining whether he was entitled to that payment or benefit or of which account has been or is to be taken for the purpose of calculating its amount.

(2) Subject to regulation E16, a pensionable employee who–

(a) ceased after 5th April 1975 to hold a local government employment ("the first employment"), and

(b) after an interval not exceeding one month after ceasing to hold the first employment–

(i) entered the employment in which he is a pensionable employee, and

(ii) became in that employment a pensionable employee, and

(c) in respect of his ceasing to hold the first employment received a return of contributions under the 1974 Regulations,

is not entitled to reckon as reckonable service any period for which the return of contributions was made.

(3) Subject to regulation E16, a pensionable employee who–

(a) on ceasing to hold a local government employment became entitled to a benefit under regulation E2(1)(c) or (d), and

(b) in respect of his ceasing to hold that employment received a return of the whole of the aggregate amount of his contributions to the appropriate superannuation fund within the meaning of regulation C12,

is not entitled to reckon as reckonable service any period for which the return of contributions was made.

(4) Subject to regulation E16, a pensionable employee who–

(a) on ceasing to hold a local government employment became entitled to a benefit under regulation E2(1)(c) or (d), and

(b) in respect of his ceasing to hold that employment received a return of part of the aggregate amount mentioned in paragraph (3)(b), and

(c) has not given notice under regulation E2(9)(c),

is not entitled to reckon as reckonable service any period for which the return of contributions was made.

(5) Except where paragraphs (2), (3)(a) or (4)(a) and (c) apply, a pensionable employee who–

(a) before entering the employment in which he is a pensionable employee was in another local government employment ("the first employment"), and

(b) in respect of his ceasing to hold the first employment received a return of contributions under the 1974 Regulations or under these Regulations,

is not entitled to reckon either as reckonable service or as qualifying service any period for which the return of contributions was made.

(6) Where–

(a) before entering the employment in respect of which he is a pensionable employee he was in another local government employment ("the first employment"), and

(b) on his ceasing to hold the first employment a transfer value was paid to a body other than an administering authority, a body maintaining a superannuation fund under Part I of the Act of 1937 or a local Act authority,

a pensionable employee is not entitled to reckon either as reckonable service or as qualifying service any period in respect of which the transfer value was paid.

Increase of reckonable service on lump sum payment

D4. A pensionable employee who has made a payment in accordance with regulation C5 is entitled to reckon as reckonable service in relation to the relevant employment the period in respect of which the payment was made.

Increase of reckonable service on making periodical payments

D5. A pensionable employee is entitled to reckon as reckonable service in relation to the relevant employment–

   (a) if he completes payment of additional contributions in accordance with regulation C6(3), the additional period in respect of which payment was made, or

   (b) if he begins such payment but does not complete it, an additional period calculated in accordance with Schedule 9.

Increase of reckonable service on completion or cessation of payments under previous Regulations

D6.—(1) Where regulation C9(1) applies, on the making or, as the case may be, the completion or discontinuance of any payments deemed to be due under regulation C5, C6 or C7, a pensionable employee is entitled to reckon additional service in accordance, respectively, with regulation D4, D5 or D9.

(2) Where regulation C9(2) applies, on the making or as the case may be the completion or discontinuance of any payments of a kind there mentioned, a pensionable employee is entitled to reckon additional service to the same extent as if such making, completion or discontinuance had occurred before 21st December 1987.

Increase of reckonable service of certain late entrants at discretion of employing authority

D7.—(1) Subject to paragraphs (2) and (3), if the employing authority are satisfied that, having regard to the interests of the efficient exercise of their functions, there are exceptional reasons for doing so, they may resolve to add an additional period to a pensionable employee's reckonable service.

(2) A resolution under paragraph (1) may be passed not later than 6 months after the person becomes a pensionable employee in the authority's employment, but not after he has attained the age of 59 years unless he did so after becoming such an employee.

(3) The additional period is to be specified in the resolution and is not to exceed the maximum determined in accordance with Schedule 4.

(4) Where the employing authority have passed a resolution under paragraph (1) or under regulation D14 of the 1974 Regulations and the employee–

   (a) remains in his employment under that authority until he attains pensionable age, or

   (b) ceases to hold that employment, before attaining that age, on the ground that he is incapable of discharging efficiently the duties of the employment by reason of permanent ill-health or infirmity of mind or body, or

   (c) dies while in that employment,

he is entitled to reckon as reckonable service the additional period specified in the resolution.

(5) Where the employee leaves in any other circumstances and the employing authority have passed such a resolution mentioned in paragraph (1) the employee is entitled to reckon as reckonable service an additional period of $\dfrac{A \times T}{R}$, where–

A is the additional period specified in the resolution,

T is the period during which the employee has been in the employment of the authority who passed the resolution, and

R is the period during which the employee would have been in that employment if paragraph (4)(a) had applied.

Reduction of added years reckonable on payment as reckonable service

D8.—(1) This regulation applies where–

   (a) a consent–

      (i) was given under regulation D10 of the 1974 Regulations, or

      (ii) was given under regulation 12 of the Benefits Regulations in respect of a person who became a pensionable employee under the 1974 Regulations on 16th May 1974, and

   (b) the person in respect of whom the consent was given is a person in relation to whom regulation F3 applies, and

   (c) the notice of election under regulation R3 of the 1974 Regulations was given within the period of 6 months beginning on the relevant date specified in paragraph (2), or in the case of a deceased employee (within the meaning of Part F) who died during that period, within the period of 12 months beginning on the date of his death, and

(d) apart from this regulation some of the person's reckonable service would, or would if payments under regulation C9(2) were to continue up to the age specified in paragraph 1(a) or, as the case may be, paragraph 1(b) of Schedule 6 to the 1974 Regulations, be left out of account in accordance with regulation E30(1)(a)or (5).

(2) For the purposes of paragraph (1)(c) the relevant date–

(a) where regulation F3(2)(f) applies, is 5th September 1984, and

(b) in any other case, is 15th October 1982.

(3) Where this regulation applies, the consent shall be deemed always to have related not to the original number of added years but instead to the longest additional period that would not entail any such leaving out of account of reckonable service as is mentioned in paragraph (1)(d), and payments made and any remaining to be made are to be adjusted accordingly.

Previous service of certain whole-time manual workers

D9. A pensionable employee who has made a payment in accordance with regulation C7 is entitled to reckon as reckonable service, in relation to the employment in which he became a pensionable employee, the period during which he was in that employment before becoming a pensionable employee.

Previous service of certain variable-time employees

D10.—(1) This regulation applies to a person who–

(a) while a pensionable employee in the whole-time employment of a scheduled body becomes a variable-time employee of any scheduled body, and

(b) while remaining a pensionable employee in the whole-time employment becomes a pensionable employee in the variable-time employment.

(2) A person to whom this regulation applies is entitled to reckon as qualifying service in relation to the variable-time employment any period which, when he became a pensionable employee in the variable-time employment, he was entitled to reckon as reckonable service or qualifying service in relation to the whole-time employment.

Previous service of certain re-employed pensioners

D11.—(1) A person who–

(a) has become entitled to a retirement pension, otherwise than by virtue of regulation E2(2), and

(b) enters further employment with any scheduled body in which he becomes a pensionable employee,

is entitled to reckon as qualifying service the period in respect of which he became entitled to the retirement pension.

(2) A person–

(a) who is in receipt of a pension payable out of public funds or under a local Act scheme,

(b) who enters employment with any scheduled body in which he becomes a pensionable employee, and

(c) whose pension is on that account liable to be reduced or suspended,

is entitled to reckon as qualifying service the period in respect of which the pension was granted.

(3) A person who–

(a) after becoming entitled on ceasing to hold an employment ("the first employment") to a retirement pension by virtue of regulation E2(1)(c) enters further employment with any scheduled body in which he becomes a pensionable employee, and

(b) in respect of his ceasing to hold the first employment has received a return of the whole or a part of the aggregate amount of his contributions to the appropriate superannuation fund within the meaning of regulation C12,

is entitled to reckon as qualifying service the period in respect of which the return of contributions was made.

(4) In paragraph (1) "retirement pension" includes a short service grant under the Benefits Regulations, an ill-health lump sum retiring allowance under regulation E21 of the 1974 Regulations, an ill-health lump sum retiring allowance under regulation E4, a superannuation allowance under Part I of the Act of 1937, and an annual pension under the former Regulations.

PART E
BENEFITS

Guaranteed minimum pension for certain pensionable employees and their widows

E1.—(1) This regulation applies if the employment of a pensionable employee in any local government employment is contracted-out employment.

(2) Where this regulation applies it overrides any other provision of these Regulations that is inconsistent with it, except regulations E15 (reduction of retirement pension in the case of certain re-employed pensioners), E21 (power to compound certain small pensions) and M1 (forfeiture of rights).

(3) Where this regulation applies and the pensionable employee has a guaranteed minimum under section 35 of the Pensions Act, in relation to benefits under these Regulations–

(a) unless on ceasing to hold his local government employment he is entitled to a retirement pension at a higher rate, he is from the date on which he attains state pensionable age entitled to a pension at a weekly rate equal to that guaranteed minimum,

(b) if he attains state pensionble age while in local government employment, continues in the same employment for a further period of 5 years and does not then cease to hold it, he is (unless he consents to a postponement of the entitlement) entitled from the end of that period to so much of his retirement pension as equals that guaranteed minimum, and

(c) if he dies at any time and leaves a widow, unless she is entitled to a widow's pension at a higher rate she is, during any such period as is mentioned in section 36(6) of the Pensions Act, entitled to a pension at a weekly rate equal to half that guaranteed minimum.

Entitlement to retirement pension and retiring allowance

E2.—(1) Subject to paragraphs (3) to (10), when a person ceases to hold a local government employment he shall be entitled in relation to that employment to an annual retirement pension and a lump sum retiring allowance if–

(a) he has attained the age of 60 years and his reckonable service and any qualifying service when added together amount to not less than 25 years; or

(b) his reckonable service and any qualifying service when added together amount to not less than 5 years, and–

(i) he is incapable of discharging efficiently the duties of that employment by reason of permanent ill-health or infirmity of mind or body, or

(ii) he has attained the age of 65 years, or

(iii) he has attained the age of 50 years and one of the conditions in paragraph (4) is satisfied; or

(c) neither sub-paragraph (a) nor sub-paragraph (b) applies, and–

(i) his reckonable service and any qualifying service when added together amount to not less than 5 years, or

(ii) he is a person who by virtue of regulation B4(6) or J13(3) is to be treated as if he had ceased to be employed; or

(d) none of the preceding sub-paragraphs applies and he–

(i) has attained state pensionable age, or

(ii) would attain state pensionable age before the following 6th April.

(2) When a person ceases to hold a local government employment he shall be entitled in relation to that employment to an annual retirement pension if–

(a) he is not so entitled under paragraph (1)(a) to (c), or he is entitled under paragraph (1)(c) and receives a return of contributions (in which case he shall be treated as having ceased to hold the employment on the day before the date of receipt), and

(b) the whole or some part of his reckonable service was service in a non-participating employment or was reckonable service which relates to employment with a non-local government employer in a non-participating employment, and

(c) a period of his service in a non-participating employment came to an end by reason of the repeal of section 56(1) of the Insurance Act or by reason of the provisions of regulation 2(2) of the National Insurance (Non-participation – Assurance of Equivalent Pension Benefits) Regulations 1960 as modified by regulation 9(2)(a) or (b) of the Transitional Provisions Regulations, and

(d) no payment in lieu of contributions is made in respect of such service as is mentioned in sub-paragraphs (b) and (c).

(3) Where but for the revocation of the 1974 Regulations, regulation E2(2) of those Regulations (certain female nursing and other staff deemed to have satisfied regulation E2(1)(b)(iii) of those Regulations) would have applied to a person on her ceasing to hold a local government employment, she shall be deemed to have ceased to hold the employment in the circumstances mentioned in paragraph (1)(b)(iii).

(4) The conditions mentioned in paragraph (1)(b)(iii) are–

(a) that the employing authority certify that the person has ceased to hold the local government employment by reason of redundancy or in the interests of the efficient exercise of their functions, or

(b) that the person was one of the holders of a joint appointment and his appointment has been terminated because the other ceased to hold his appointment.

(5) Benefits to which a person is entitled by virtue of paragraph (1)(a) or (b) are payable immediately.

(6) Subject to paragraphs (9) to (11), preserved benefits become payable from the date on which the person attains pensionable age, or if earlier–

(a) from any date on which he becomes incapable by reason of permanent ill-health or infirmity of mind or body of discharging efficiently the duties of the employment he ceased to hold, or

(b) from any date after he has attained the age of 50 years from which the employing authority determine on compassionate grounds that the benefits are to become payable, or

(c) in the case of a woman, from the first date on which she is both–

    (i) at least 60 years old, and

    (ii) no longer in any employment,

unless he is a man who has attained the age of 60 years and has, on or after but not more than 3 months after the date of his attaining that age or of his ceasing to be employed, whichever is the later, by notice in writing to the employing authority, elected to receive payment from that date.

(7) Benefits to which a person has become entitled by virtue of paragraph (1)(d) are payable immediately if the person had attained the age of 65 years before he ceased to hold the employment.

(8) Subject to paragraph (11), benefits to which a person has become entitled by virtue of paragraph (1)(d) but which have not become payable by virtue of paragraph (7) and benefits to which a person was entitled by virtue of regulation E2(1)(d) of the 1974 Regulations immediately before 21st December 1987 which have not otherwise become payable, become payable–

(a) in the case of a man who has so elected by notice in writing given to the employing authority not later than 3 months after ceasing to hold the employment, as from the date on which he ceased to hold it, or

(b) in the case of a woman, from the first date (if earlier than the date mentioned in sub-paragraph (c)) on which she both–

    (i) has attained the age of 60 years, and

    (ii) is no longer in any employment, or

(c) in any other case, from the date on which the person attains the age of 65 years.

(9) A person who is entitled to preserved benefits ceases to be entitled to them–

    (a) if the whole of the aggregate amount of his contributions to the appropriate superannuation fund, within the meaning of regulation C12, has been returned to him under that regulation or under regulation C8 of the 1974 Regulations and, after receiving the return of contributions, he has no further right to reckon any reckonable service to which a transfer value accepted under regulation J8 relates, or

    (b) if rights in respect of the reckonable service he was entitled to reckon in relation to the employment he ceased to hold have been transferred to a non-local government scheme by virtue of the payment of a transfer value, or

    (c) if he re-enters local government employment, unless he elects to remain entitled to the preserved benefits.

(10) An election for the purposes of paragraph (9)(c) must be made by giving notice in writing to the appropriate administering authority, within 3 months after re-entering local government employment unless they, or where there is a change of fund the administering authorities of both funds, allow a longer period.

(11) A person may not make an election under paragraph (6) or (8)(a) if the retirement pension to which he has become entitled–

    (a) is a pension in relation to which he has a guaranteed minimum under section 35 of the Pensions Act, and

    (b) would, but for regulation E1(3)(a), be reduced under regulation E3(14) to less than his guaranteed minimum pension.

(12) A retirement pension to which a person has become entitled by virtue of paragraph (2) is payable from the first date on which he both–

    (a) has attained state pensionable age, and

    (b) is no longer in any local government employment.

Amount of retirement pension and retiring allowance

E3.—(1) Subject to paragraphs (2) and (12) to (16), and to regulation E30, the annual rate of a person's retirement pension is the amount obtained by multiplying one eightieth of his pensionable remuneration by the length in years of his reckonable service.

(2) In the case of a person who–

    (a) is entitled under regulation D4, D5, D6(1) or D7 to reckon an additional period as reckonable service, and

    (b) had at the appropriate time (as defined in paragraph 1(2) of Schedule 4) attained the age of 45 years,

the rate specified in paragraph (1) is increased by the amount obtained by multiplying one two hundred and fortieth of his pensionable remuneration by the length in years of that additional period.

(3) Subject to paragraphs (4) to (14) and to regulation E30, the amount of a person's retiring allowance is the amount obtained by multiplying three eightieths of his pensionable remuneration by the length in years of his reckonable service; but where paragraph (2) applies his reckonable service does not for the purposes of this paragraph include the additional period.

(4) Where but for the revocation of the 1974 Regulations regulation E3(4) of those Regulations (preservation of certain rights under former Regulations to increased retiring allowance) would have applied to a person on ceasing to hold a local government employment, the amount calculated in accordance with paragraph (3) is increased by the amount by which it would have been increased if that regulation had applied.

(5) For the purposes of paragraph (4)–

    (a) an additional period which a person has become entitled to reckon as reckonable service by virtue of, or of payments commenced under, regulation D10 of the 1974 Regulations shall be treated as reckonable service ending immediately before the date on which he first became a contributory employee or, if earlier, a local Act contributor, and

    (b) no account shall be taken of any period which a person has become entitled to reckon as reckonable service by virtue of regulation F6(1)(a) or (b) (war service).

(6) In the case of a person to whom regulation E19 of the 1974 Regulations applied but who made an election under paragraph (2) of that regulation, paragraph (4) of this regulation applies as if he had at no time been entitled as mentioned in paragraph (1)(b) of that regulation and had immediately before the time mentioned in that regulation been such a person as was mentioned in regulation 14(a) or (b) of the Benefits Regulations.

(7) Subject to paragraph (10), where the person is a married man and a widow's pension may become payable under regulation E5, the amount calculated in accordance with paragraphs (3) to (6) is reduced by the amount obtained by multiplying two eightieths of his pensionable remuneration by the length in years of any reckonable service before 1st April 1972.

(8) Subject to paragraphs (10) and (11), where–

(a) the person is a widower, or

(b) he and his wife are judicially separated, or

(c) his marriage has been dissolved,

and the death, separation or dissolution occurred after the relevant date specified in paragraph (9), the amount calculated in accordance with paragraphs (3) to (6) is reduced by two eightieths of his pensionable remuneration multiplied by the length in years of any reckonable service before 1st April 1972 or, if earlier, the date of the death, separation or dissolution.

(9) The relevant date for the purposes of paragraph (8) is–

(a) 30th September 1950, or

(b) if, but for the revocation of the 1974 Regulations, sub-paragraph (ii) of paragraph (6) of regulation E3 of those Regulations (certain cases where local Act provisions had applied before 16th May 1974) would have applied, the date that would have been the relevant date for the purposes of that paragraph.

(10) In calculating any reduction under paragraph (7) or (8), no account shall be taken of any reckonable service in respect of which payment under regulation C8 has or is to be treated as having been completed.

(11) No reduction is to be made under paragraph (8) where the person is a woman in relation to whom this regulation applies as provided in regulation E12 and who has not made any election under regulation E12(1)(b) or (2).

(12) Where regulation E2(1)(b)(i) (permanent ill-health etc.) applies, the person is to be treated for the purposes of this regulation as being entitled to reckon as reckonable service an additional period calculated in accordance with Schedule 10.

(13) Where a person has become entitled to preserved benefits and subsequently receives a return of contributions but regulation E2(9)(a) does not apply, for the purposes of this regulation his reckonable service shall be taken to be the reckonable service which he is entitled to reckon after he receives the return of contributions, excluding reckonable service to which the return of contributions relates.

(14) Subject to paragraph (15), where benefits have become payable–

(a) to a man by virtue of an election under regulation E2(6) or E2(8)(a), or

(b) to a woman by virtue of regulation E2(6)(c) or E2(8)(b),

the amounts calculated in accordance with paragraphs (1) to (13) are reduced in accordance with Schedule 11.

(15) A person's retirement pension is not to be reduced under paragraph (14)–

(a) to less than any minimum rate of equivalent pension benefits applicable under the Insurance Acts, or

(b) in the case of a woman, to less than the annual rate determined by multiplying one eightieth of her pensionable remuneration by the length in years of the whole period of her service in contracted-out employment.

(16) The rate of a retirement pension payable by virtue of regulation E2(2) is the rate of equivalent pension benefits applicable to the person in respect of any period of reckonable service in a non-participating employment or which relates to service with a non-local government employer in a non-participating employment.

Ill-health lump sum retiring allowance

E4.—(1) This paragraph applies to a person–

(a) who has at any time after 13th November 1978 ceased to hold a local government employment, and

(b) who when he ceased to hold that employment–

(i) was entitled to reckon an aggregate of one or more but less than 5 years' reckonable service and qualifying service, and

(ii) was incapable of discharging efficiently the duties of that employment by reason of permanent ill-health or infirmity of mind or body, and

(c) who did not cease to hold that employment in consequence of any such offence or misconduct as are mentioned in regulation C12(5), and

(d) who is not apart from this regulation entitled, whether by virtue of his having made a claim under regulation C12(7)(b) or otherwise, to any benefit under these Regulations, other than a return of contributions, and has not–

(i) received any return of contributions other than one in respect of which a payment was made under regulation E21(3) of the 1974 Regulations, or

(ii) been granted any gratuity under Part K, under Part T of the 1974 Regulations, under section 18 of the Act of 1953, or under any local Act, or

(iii) received an allowance under regulation E21 of the 1974 Regulations, and

(e) who if a return of contributions were made to him would receive a net amount smaller than that of an allowance calculated in accordance with paragraph (2).

(2) A person to whom paragraph (1) applies is, subject to paragraph (3), entitled to be paid an allowance ("an ill-health lump sum retiring allowance") of an amount equal to–

(a) one twelfth of his pensionable remuneration multiplied by the length in years of his reckonable service, or

(b) three eightieths of his pensionable remuneration multiplied by the length in years of the total period he would have been entitled to reckon as reckonable service if–

(i) he had continued in local government employment until he had attained the age of 65 years, and

(ii) any added period payments had been completed,

whichever is the lesser amount.

(3) A person to whom paragraph (1) applies–

(a) may, notwithstanding that he is for the time being entitled to an ill-health lump sum retiring allowance, at any time before such an allowance is paid to him be granted a gratuity under Part K, and

(b) on being so granted a gratuity under Part K he shall cease to be entitled to an ill-health lump sum retiring allowance.

(4) In the case of a person falling within paragraph (1)(a) to (c) who has ceased to hold his employment after 20th December 1987, the appropriate administering authority are, without prejudice to any subsequent decision under regulation N5 or N6, to notify him in writing, within 3 months after the date on which he ceased to hold his employment, of the amount of the ill-health retirement grant to which he would, subject to paragraph (3), be entitled if he were and remained a person to whom paragraph (1) applies.

Entitlement to widow's short-term and long-term pensions

E5.—(1) If at the time of his death a man–

(a) was entitled to receive payments in respect of a retirement pension, or

(b) would have been so entitled but for the operation of regulation E15 (reduction of certain retirement pensions), or

(c) was in a local government employment and–

(i) the total of his reckonable service and any qualifying service when added together amounted to not less than 5 years, or

(ii) he would if he had then ceased to be employed otherwise than by reason of his death have become entitled to benefits by virtue of regulation E2(1)(d), and he leaves a widow or widows she is, or as the case may be they are jointly, entitled, subject to paragraphs (3) to (5), to a widow's short-term pension for 3 months after his death and then to a widow's long-term pension.

(2) If at the time of his death a man was entitled to preserved benefits and he leaves a widow or widows she is, or as the case may be they are jointly, entitled, subject to paragraphs (3) to (5), to a widow's long-term pension.

(3) A widow is not entitled to any pension by virtue of paragraph (1) or (2) if when her husband died or became entitled to a retirement pension she was judicially separated from him.

(4) A widow is not entitled to any pension by virtue of paragraph (1)(a) or (b) or paragraph (2) if–

(a) she was not her husband's wife at some time while he was in local government employment after 31st March 1972 and before the date on which he became entitled to a retirement pension, or

(b) her husband became entitled to a retirement pension by virtue of regulation E2(2).

(5) Where but for paragraph (4)(a) a widow would have been entitled–

(a) under paragraph (1) to a widow's short-term pension and to a widow's long-term pension, or

(b) under paragraph (2) to a widow's long-term pension,

she is entitled, where sub-paragraph (a) applies to a short-term pension and a long-term pension and where sub-paragraph (b) applies to a long-term pension only, calculated in each case in accordance with regulation E6(4).

(6) A pension to which a widow is entitled by virtue of this regulation–

(a) is not payable to her during any subsequent marriage or any period of cohabitation outside marriage, and

(b) is payable from the end of any such marriage or period only if the appropriate administering authority in their discretion so decide.

Amount of widow's short-term and long-term pensions

E6.—(1) Subject to paragraphs (3) to (5), the annual rate of a widow's short-term pension is–

(a) where regulation E5(1)(a) or (b) applies and any new employment for the purposes of regulation E15 (re-employed pensioners) was not a local government employment, the annual rate of her husband's retirement pension immediately before the date of his death, disregarding any reduction under regulation E15, or

(b) where regulation E5(1)(c) applies and the local government employment was not a new employment for the purposes of regulation E15, a rate equal to his pensionable remuneration, or

(c) where regulation E5(1)(c) applies and the local government employment was such a new employment, a rate equal–

(i) if the retirement pension was not reduced under regulation E15, to the total of his pensionable remuneration in the new employment and the annual rate of the retirement pension, or

(ii) if the retirement pension was so reduced, to the total of his pensionable remuneration in the new employment and the annual rate, if any, at which the reduced retirement pension was payable.

(2) Subject to paragraphs (3) to (5), the annual rate of a widow's long-term pension is–

(a) where paragraph (1)(a) applies, half the annual rate of her husband's retirement pension immediately before the date of his death,

(b) where paragraph (1)(b) applies by virtue of regulation E5(1)(c)(i), one half of the annual rate of the retirement pension to which her husband would have been entitled if on the date of his death he had become entitled under regulation E2(1)(b)(i) (permanent ill-health, etc.),

(c) where paragraph (1)(b) applies by virtue of regulation E5(1)(c)(ii), one half of the annual rate of the retirement pension to which her husband would have been entitled if on the date of his death he had become entitled under regulation E2(1)(d),

(d) where paragraph (1)(c) applies, the greater of–

    (i) the total of half the annual rate of her husband's retirement pension and half the annual rate of the retirement pension to which he would have been entitled in respect of the new employment if on the date of his death he had become entitled under regulation E2(1)(b)(i), and

    (ii) half the annual rate of the retirement pension to which he would have been entitled if on the date of his death he had become entitled under regulation E2(1)(b)(i) and notice had been given under regulation E16, and

(e) where regulation E5(2) applies, half the annual rate of the retirement pension to which her husband would have been entitled if on the date of his death he had become entitled under regulation E2(1)(b)(ii).

(3) For the purposes of paragraph (2)–

(a) the retirement pension mentioned in paragraph (2)(a) is to be taken to be the pension that would have been payable but for–

    (i) any increase under regulation E3(2), (certain cases where additional service is reckonable),

    (ii) any reduction under regulation E3(14) (early payments) or E15 (re-employed pensioners) or E32 (National Insurance), and

    (iii) any surrender under regulation E20, and

(b) any retirement pension mentioned in paragraph (2)(b) or (d) is to be taken to be the pension that would have been payable but for any surrender under regulation E20, and if the pension would have been increased under regulation E3(2) or reduced under regulation E32 no account is to be taken of that increase or reduction.

(4) Where regulation E5(5) (post-retirement marriages) applies–

(a) the references in paragraphs (1)(a), (2)(a), (c), (d) and (e), and the second reference in paragraph (1)(c)(i), to the retirement pension are to be construed as references to, and

(b) for the purposes of paragraph (1)(c)(ii), any annual rate at which the retirement pension was payable is to be taken not to have exceeded the rate of,

the part of the pension attributable to the whole period of his service in respect of which the pension was payable which was in contracted-out employment.

(5) The annual rate of the pension payable under this regulation shall not be less than the amount determined by multiplying one one hundred and sixtieth of the pensionable remuneration of the deceased husband by the length in years of the whole period of his service in contracted-out employment.

Widow's special short-term pension

E7.—(1) If at the time of his death a man was in a local government employment and he leaves a widow or widows but neither of the conditions in regulation E5(1)(c) is satisfied, then she is, or as the case may be they are jointly, entitled to a widow's special short-term pension at an annual rate equal to his pensionable remuneration except that any widow's entitlement shall cease if she is–

(a) judicially separated from him, or

(b) cohabiting with another man.

(2) Where the deceased leaves no eligible child or there is no eligible child in the widow's care, the pension is payable for 3 months after the day of his death.

(3) While there is one eligible child in the widow's care, the pension is payable for $4\frac{1}{2}$ months after the day of his death.

(4) While there are two or more eligible children in the widow's care, the pension is payable for 6 months after the day of his death.

Entitlement to children's short-term and long-term pensions

E8.—(1) If at the time of his death a man–

(a) was entitled to receive payments in respect of a retirement pension, or

(b) would have been so entitled but for the operation of regulation E15 (re-employed pensioners), or

(c) was in a local government employment and the total of his reckonable service and any qualifying service when added together amounted to not less than 5 years,

and he leaves one or more eligible children, they are, subject to paragraphs (3) to (5), entitled to, or to the benefit of, a children's short-term pension for 3 months after the death and then a children's long-term pension.

(2) If at the time of his death a man was entitled to preserved benefits and he leaves one or more eligible children, they are, subject to paragraphs (4) and (5), entitled to, or to the benefit of, a children's long-term pension.

(3) No children's short-term pension is payable while a widow's short-term pension is payable under regulation E5.

(4) There is no entitlement to any pension by virtue of paragraph (1)(a) or (b) or paragraph (2) if the deceased became entitled to a retirement pension by virtue of regulation E2(2).

(5) Payments in respect of a pension under this regulation shall not be made to or for the benefit of a female eligible child–

(a) while she is married or during any period of cohabitation outside marriage, or

(b) from the end of any marriage or period of cohabitation outside marriage unless the appropriate administering authority in their discretion so decide.

Amounts of children's short-term and long-term pensions

E9.—(1) Subject to paragraph (2), the annual rate of a children's short-term pension is the rate at which a widow's short-term pension is or would have been payable by virtue of regulation E6(1).

(2) Where a widow's short-term pension is payable by virtue of regulation E5(5), the children's short-term pension rate specified in paragraph (1) is reduced by the rate of that pension.

(3) Subject to paragraphs (4) and (5), the annual amount of a children's long-term pension is–

(a) where there is one eligible child and he is in the care of a widow of the deceased person, one quarter of the deceased person's retirement pension,

(b) where there is one eligible child and he is not in the care of such a widow, one third of the retirement pension,

(c) where there are two or more eligible children and–

(i) half or more of them are in the care of such a widow, or

(ii) fewer than half of them are in the care of such a widow but a widow's pension under regulation E5 is for the time being payable,

one half of the retirement pension, and

(d) where there are two or more eligible children and fewer than half of them are in the care of such a widow and no such widow's pension is payable, two thirds of the retirement pension.

(4) For the purposes of paragraph (3)–

(a) the retirement pension of a deceased person who died while in local government employment shall be deemed to be the retirement pension to which he would have become entitled if regulation E2(1)(b)(i) (permanent ill-health, etc.) had applied,

(b) the retirement pension of a person who was entitled at the time of his death to preserved benefits shall be deemed to be the retirement pension to which he would have become entitled if regulation E2(1)(b)(ii) (retirement on or after pensionable age) had applied,

(c) the retirement pension of a person who was entitled at the time of his death to receive payments in respect of a retirement pension shall be deemed to be the retirement pension that would have been payable but for–

(i) any increase under regulation E3(2) (certain cases where additional service is reckonable),

(ii) any reduction under regulation E3(14) (early payments) or E15 (re-employed pensioners) or E32 (National Insurance), and

(iii) any surrender under regulation E20, and

(d) where a children's long-term pension is payable under paragraph (3)(b) or (d) and a widow's long-term pension is payable under regulation E5(5) the amount of the children's long-term pension shall not exceed an amount equal to the difference between–

    (i) the aggregate amount that would have been payable by way of widow's and children's long-term pensions had the post-retirement marriage been a pre-retirement marriage, and

    (ii) the long-term widow's pension payable under regulation E5(5),

and for the purposes of sub-paragraphs (a) and (b) it is to be assumed that the pension to which the person would have become entitled would not have been subject to any increase under regulation E3(2) or reduction under regulation E3(14), and that there has been no surrender under regulation E20.

(5) If a child in respect of whom a children's long-term pension is payable has attained the age of 17 years and is receiving remuneration in respect of full-time training for a trade, profession or calling at an annual rate in excess of the indexed training rate defined in paragraph (6),then–

(a) the annual rate of the pension is to be reduced by the amount of the excess, or

(b) the child is to be disregarded for the purpose of calculating the pension,

whichever results in the smaller reduction in its annual rate.

(6) In paragraph (5) "the indexed training rate" means the annual rate at which an official pension within the meaning of the Pensions (Increase) Act 1971(a) would for the time being be payable if it had begun on 1st June 1972 and had then been payable at an annual rate of £250.

(7) The appropriate administering authority may–

(a) apportion a children's pension among the eligible children in respect of whom it is for the time being payable in such shares as they think fit, and

(b) pay the pension or any part of it to a person other than an eligible child, to be applied in accordance with any directions they may give for the benefit of any eligible child or eligible children.

Children's special short-term pension

E10.—(1) If at the time of his death a man was in a local government employment and–

(a) the total of his reckonable service and any qualifying service is less than 5 years, and

(b) he leaves one or more eligible children, and

(c) any such child is in the care of a guardian,

a children's special short-term pension at an annual rate equal to the deceased's pensionable remuneration shall be paid to the guardian.

(2) In this regulation "guardian" means a person who is not entitled in respect of the deceased to either–

(a) a widow's special short-term pension by virtue of regulation E7, or

(b) a widow's short-term pension and a widow's long-term pension by virtue of regulation E5(1)(c)(ii).

(3) Where the deceased left a widow who is entitled as mentioned in paragraph (2)(a) or (b)–

(a) if there is no eligible child in the widow's care, the pension is payable to the guardian–

    (i) for 1½ months after the day of death if there is one eligible child in the care of the guardian, and

    (ii) for 3 months after the day of death if there are two or more eligible children in the care of the guardian, and

(b) if there is an eligible child in the widow's care, the pension is payable to the guardian for 1½ months after the day of death.

(4) Where the deceased did not leave a widow who is entitled as mentioned in paragraph (2)(a) or (b), the pension is payable to the guardian–

(a) 1971 c.56.

   (a) for 2 months after the day of death if there is one eligible child in the care of the guardian, and

   (b) for 4 months after the day of death if there are two or more eligible children in the care of the guardian.

Death gratuity

E11.—(1) Subject to paragraphs (9) to (11), if at the time of his death a person–

   (a) was in a local government employment, or

   (b) was entitled to receive payments in respect of a retirement pension in relation to which this paragraph applies, or

   (c) would have been so entitled but for the operation of regulation E15 (re-employed pensioners), or

   (d) was entitled to preserved benefits,

his executors are entitled to receive a lump sum death gratuity.

(2) Paragraph (1) applies in relation to a retirement pension if–

   (a) the reckonable service taken into account in calculating the pension amounted to less than 10 years and he had been entitled for less than 5 years to receive payments in respect of the pension, or

   (b) the reckonable service taken into account in calculating the pension amounted to 10 years or more.

(3) In paragraphs (4) to (11)–

A is the deceased's pensionable remuneration,

B is three eightieths of his pensionable remuneration,

C is the length in years of his reckonable service,

D is two eightieths of his pensionable remuneration multiplied by the length in years of any reckonable service before 1st April 1972 in respect of which a widow's pension is payable under regulation E5, other than service in respect of which a return of contributions has been made or payment under regulation C8 has been or is to be treated as having been completed,

E is the total of any payments made to him in respect of retirement pension and lump sum retiring allowance,

F is the length in years of the reckonable service he would have had on attaining pensionable age,

G is the annual rate of his retirement pension, and

H is the total of any payments made to him in respect of retirement pension.

(4) Subject to paragraphs (9) and (11), where–

   (a) paragraph (1)(a) applies, or

   (b) paragraph (1)(b) or (c) and paragraph (2)(b) apply and the deceased became entitled to the retirement pension otherwise than by virtue of regulation E2(1)(c),

the amount of the death gratuity is the greater of A and (B × C) but, where paragraph (1)(a) applies, C is to be treated as having included an additional period calculated as if Schedule 10 had applied.

(5) Where–

   (a) paragraph (1)(b) or (c) and paragraph (2)(b) apply and the deceased became entitled to the retirement pension by virtue of regulation E2(1)(c), or

   (b) paragraph (1)(b) or (c) and paragraph (2)(a) apply and the deceased–

     (i) became entitled to the retirement pension by virtue of regulation E2(1)(c), and

     (ii) would have had 10 years' or more reckonable service on attaining pensionable age,

the amount of the death gratuity is the greater of $(B \times C) - (D + E)$ or $\frac{C}{F} \times (A - (D + E))$.

(6) Subject to paragraph (10), where paragraph (1)(b) or (c) and paragraph (2)(a) apply and the deceased became entitled to the retirement pension otherwise than by virtue of regulation E2(1)(c) or (d), the amount of the death gratuity is $5 \times G$.

(7) Where paragraph (1)(b) or (c) and paragraph (2)(a) apply and the deceased–

(a) became entitled to the retirement pension by virtue of regulation E2(1)(c) and would have had less than 10 years' reckonable service on attaining pensionable age, or

(b) became entitled to the retirement pension by virtue of regulation E2(1)(d),

the amount of the death gratuity is $\frac{C}{F} \times ((5 \times G) - H)$.

(8) Subject to paragraph (9), where paragraph (1)(d) applies the amount of the death gratuity is B × C.

(9) Where–

(a) paragraph (1)(a) or (d) applies, or

(b) paragraph (1)(b) or (c) and paragraph (2)(b) apply and the deceased became entitled to the retirement pension otherwise than by virtue of regulation E2(1)(c),

and a widow's pension is payable under regulation E5, the amount of the death gratuity is reduced by D.

(10) Where paragraph (1)(b) or (c) and paragraph (2)(a) apply and the deceased became entitled to the retirement pension otherwise than by virtue of regulation E2(1)(c) or (d), the amount of the death gratuity is reduced–

(a) by H, or

(b) where the pension was reduced under regulation E15 or had been surrendered in part under regulation E20, by the amount which would have been paid in respect of the pension but for the reduction or surrender.

(11) Where paragraph (1)(b) or (c) and paragraph (2)(b) apply and the deceased became entitled to the retirement pension otherwise than by virtue of regulation E2(1)(c), the amount of the death gratuity is reduced–

(a) by E, or

(b) where the pension was reduced under regulation E15 or had been surrendered in part under regulation E20, by the amount which would have been paid in respect of retirement pension and retiring allowance but for the reduction or surrender.

(12) Subject to paragraph (13), for the purpose of calculating the amount of a death gratuity under the preceding provisions of this regulation no account shall be taken of reckonable service before attaining the age of 60 years beyond a total of 40 years.

(13) Where a death gratuity is reduced under paragraph (9), any reckonable service to be left out of account under paragraph (12) is to be taken from the beginning of the period of reckonable service.

Pensions of widowers etc.

E12.—(1) Where a woman who is a pensionable employee–

(a) has no husband but has a potentially eligible child or eligible children, or

(b) having a husband who is permanently incapacitated by reason of ill-health or infirmity of mind or body and wholly or mainly dependent on her, elects,

she will participate in the benefits provided by the Regulations as if she were a man and, where sub-paragraph (b) applies, as if her husband were a woman.

(2) Where a female pensionable employee makes an election under paragraph (1)(b) and thereafter she re-marries, the subsequent marriage and–

(i) the legitimate children of the subsequent marriage;

(ii) any adopted child of hers, adopted after re-marriage;

(iii) any legitimate child of hers, born after the expiration of one year after the date of the death of her former husband;

(iv) any step-child of hers, being a child of an earlier marriage of her husband by the subsequent marriage; and

(v) any adopted child of her husband by the subsequent marriage,

shall be left out of account for all the purposes of this Part unless her husband by the subsequent marriage is permanently incapacitated by reason of ill-health or infirmity of mind or body and wholly or mainly dependent on her, and she makes a further election under paragraph (1)(b).

(3) An election under paragraph (1)(b) or (2) is to be made by giving notice in writing to the appropriate administering authority.

(4) In this regulation "potentially eligible child" means a child who might become an eligible child on the woman's death.

Discretionary additional benefits for certain female nursing staff

E13.—(1) This regulation applies to a woman who–

(a) immediately before 16th May 1974 was a nurse, midwife or health visitor to whom section 16(1) of the Act of 1937 applied,

(b) became a pensionable employee on 16th May 1974,

(c) has not since had a disqualifying break of service,

(d) on or after attaining the age of 60 years, but before completing 40 years' reckonable service, becomes entitled, otherwise than by virtue of regulation E2(2), to a retirement pension, and

(e) immediately before becoming entitled to the pension was employed as a nurse, midwife or health visitor.

(2) The employing authority of a woman to whom this regulation applies may grant her an additional benefit not exceeding the difference between the benefit to which she is entitled and the benefit to which she would have been entitled if she had remained in their employment until she attained the age of 65 years receiving an annual remuneration equal to her pensionable remuneration.

Reduction of retirement pension in the case of certain former teachers

E14.—(1) Where a person becomes entitled to a retirement pension in the calculation of the amount of which account is taken of service which he was entitled to reckon under section 15 of the Act of 1937 (which related to teachers), the amount receivable by him in any year in respect of that pension shall be reduced by a sum equivalent to the amount (if any) which is receivable by him in that year by virtue of the Teachers Superannuation (Scotland) Regulations 1969 to 1976 or the Teachers' Superannuation (Scotland) Regulations 1977(a) (together in this regulation referred to as "the Teachers' Regulations"), or would have been so receivable by him in that year but for any reduction made under regulation 51 of the Teachers Superannuation (Scotland) Regulations 1969(b) or regulation 61 of the Teachers' Superannuation (Scotland) Regulations 1977.

(2) In computing the reduction to be made under paragraph (1), account shall be taken of any sum paid or payable at any time under the Teachers' Regulations which was or is in the nature of a capital payment or which represents a return of contributions in respect of a period of service which has been taken into account in calculating the amount of the retirement pension, in the following manner, that is to say–

(a) the amount of any sum paid under the Teachers' Regulations on or before the date on which the person became entitled to that retirement pension or becoming payable under the Teachers' Regulations at any time thereafter which was or is in the nature of a capital payment shall be divided by the factor shown in the following Table in relation to the class of the person and to his age at the date on which the sum was paid or becomes payable, and the resulting amount shall be treated as a sum receivable by him by virtue of the Teachers' Regulations in any year;

(b) the amount representing any balance of his contributions under the Teachers' Regulations which he has become entitled to be repaid at the date on which he became entitled to the retirement pension in respect of a period of service which has been taken into account in calculating the amount of the retirement pension shall be divided by the factor shown in the Table in relation to the class of the person and to his age at the date on which he became entitled to the retirement pension, and the resulting amount shall be treated as a sum receivable by him by virtue of the Teachers' Regulations in any year;

(a) S.I. 1977/1360.
(b) S.I. 1969/77.

(c) the amount representing any balance of his contributions under the Teachers' Regulations which he may become entitled to be repaid after the date on which he became entitled to the retirement pension in respect of a period of service which has been taken into account in calculating the amount of the retirement pension shall be divided by the factor shown in the Table in relation to the class of the person and to his age at the date on which he so becomes entitled to be repaid that balance of his contributions, and the resulting amount shall be treated as a sum receivable by him by virtue of the Teachers' Regulations in any year:

Provided that if, after the provisions of either sub-paragraph (b) or (c) have become applicable in relation to any person, an additional allowance under the Teachers' Regulations is granted to him then, if the aggregate amount of the deductions made from his retirement pension by reason of the previous operation of those provisions is less than the amount granted to him by way of additional allowance under the Teachers' Regulations, such latter amount for the purpose of the application of sub-paragraph (a) shall be deemed to be the difference between that amount and such aggregate amount as aforesaid and sub-paragraphs (b) and (c) shall cease to have any further effect in relation to him.

(3) If, after the provisions of either paragraph (2)(b) or (c) have become applicable in relation to any person, a repayment of the amount representing the balance of the person's contributions under the Teachers' Regulations is made to him, those provisions shall, in respect of the amount so repaid, continue to apply in the same manner as they had previously applied in relation to him for the purpose of computing the reduction to be made in his retirement pension in any year under paragraph (1) and no further account for that purpose shall be taken of that amount.

(4) If a person allocates or has allocated in accordance with Part VI of the Teachers Superannuation (Scotland) Regulations 1969, or the Teachers' Superannuation (Scotland) Regulations 1977, part of the annual allowance payable to him under the Teachers' Regulations, the annual allowance receivable in any year by virtue of the Teachers' Regulations shall for the purpose of paragraph (1) be deemed to be the annual allowance which would have been receivable by him in that year but for the allocation.

(5) Any reference in this regulation to the date on which a person becomes entitled to a retirement pension shall, in relation to a person who ceased to be employed in the circumstances mentioned in regulation E2(1)(c), be construed as a reference to the date on which he becomes entitled to receive payments in respect of that pension.

TABLE

Factor

Age	Men		Women	
	A.	B.	A.	B.
Under 60 years	10	–	12.5	–
60 years but under 61 years	10	11.6	12.5	13.4
61 years but under 62 years	10	11.2	12.5	13
62 years but under 63 years	10	10.8	12.5	
63 years but under 64 years	10	10.4	12.1	
64 years but under 65 years	10		11.7	
65 years but under 66 years	9.7		11.2	
66 years but under 67 years	9.3		10.8	
67 years but under 68 years	8.9		10.3	
68 years but under 69 years	8.5		9.9	
69 years but under 70 years	8.1		9.5	
70 years but under 71 years	7.7		9	

A. Applicable to persons who ceased to be employed in the circumstances mentioned in regulation E2(1)(b)(i).

B.   Applicable to persons who ceased to be employed in the circumstances mentioned in regulation E2(1), other than sub-paragraph (b)(i).

Reduction of retirement pension in the case of certain re-employed pensioners

E15.—(1) Subject to paragraph (12), this regulation applies to a person who, since becoming entitled to a retirement pension in relation to a former employment, has entered a new employment with any scheduled body, other than an employment by virtue of which he is entitled to participate in benefits provided under Regulations made under section 9 of the Act of 1972 (superannuation of teachers).

(2)(a) In paragraph (3)–

A is the annual rate of remuneration of the former employment,

B is the amount (if any) by which, immediately before the first day of the new employment, A would have been increased if it had been the rate of an official pension, within the meaning of the Pensions (Increase) Act 1971, the Pensions (Increase) Act 1974(**a**) or the Pensions Act, beginning on and payable from the day after the last day of the former employment,

C is the annual rate of remuneration of the new employment,

D is the reduced rate of the retirement pension, and

E is the amount (if any) by which D would, immediately before the first day of the new employment, have been increased under the Pensions (Increase) Act 1971, the Pensions (Increase) Act 1974 or the Pensions Act if it had been the rate of the retirement pension;

(b) in paragraph (5) A, B and C have the same meanings as in paragraph (2)(a), and–

F is the annual rate of remuneration of the concurrent employment on the last day of that employment, and

G is the amount (if any) by which, immediately before the first day of the new employment, F would have been increased if it had been the rate of an official pension, within the meaning of the Pensions (Increase) Act 1971, the Pensions (Increase) Act 1974 or the Pensions Act, beginning on and payable from the day after the last day of the concurrent employment.

(3) Subject to paragraphs (4), (5) and (11), while the person holds the new employment the annual rate of the retirement pension is reduced–

(a) if C equals or exceeds (A + B), to zero, and

(b) in any other case by the amount (if any) which is necessary to secure that C + D + E does not exceed A + B.

(4) This paragraph applies where within the last 12 months of the former employment the person held another concurrent employment with any scheduled body, former local authority or local Act authority, has ceased to hold the concurrent employment without becoming entitled in relation to it to a retirement pension, and–

(a) has–

(i) ceased to hold the concurrent employment before ceasing to hold the former employment, and

(ii) entered the new employment within 12 months after ceasing to hold the concurrent employment, or

(b) has ceased to hold the concurrent employment after ceasing to hold the former employment.

(5) Where paragraph (4) applies–

(a) if the person does not devote substantially more of his time to the new employment than he devoted to the concurrent employment during the 12 months before he ceased to hold it, the annual rate of the retirement pension is not reduced, and

(b) in any other case, the annual rate of the retirement pension is reduced by the amount (if any) by which the aggregate of that rate and C exceeds A + B + F + G.

(**a**) 1974 c.9.

(6) For the purposes of this regulation the annual rate of remuneration of the former employment is, subject to paragraph (7), to be ascertained in accordance with the Table below.

TABLE

Source of entitlement to the retirement pension	Annual rate of remuneration	
	Fixed-rate emoluments	Fees
These Regulations or the 1974 Regulations	Rate on last day of relevant period for the purposes of regulation E22.	Average rate during period by reference to which pensionable remuneration fell to be calculated under regulation E22(11).
Other	Rate on last day of employment.	Average rate during period, within last 3 years of employment, during which fees were receivable.

(7) For the purposes of paragraph (6), where the person's remuneration was at any material time reduced or discontinued by reason of his absence from duty, and either the absence was due to illness or injury or he made contributions or payments under section 6(5) of the Act of 1937 or regulation C3 or C4, then–

    (a) any reduction or discontinuance of fixed-rate emoluments is to be disregarded, and

    (b) any fees are to be averaged over a period of the same length as the period mentioned in the Table to paragraph (6) but ending immediately before the reduction or discontinuance.

(8) For the purposes of this regulation the annual rate of remuneration of the new employment is, subject to paragraph (9), to be ascertained in accordance with the Table below.

TABLE

Nature of remuneration	Annual rate of remuneration
Fixed-rate emoluments	Rate on first day of employment.
Fees	(1) Where fees were receivable in the former employment, the annual rate of those fees ascertained in accordance with paragraph (6). (2) Where no fees were receivable, a rate agreed by the person and the body employing him or, in default of agreement, determined by the Secretary of State.

(9) For the purposes of paragraph (8), if fees were receivable in the former employment and are receivable in the new employment and H is greater than J, where–

    H is the annual rate of remuneration of the former employment, and

    J is the annual rate of remuneration of the new employment ascertained in accordance with the Table,

the annual rate of the fees receivable in the new employment, ascertained in accordance with the table, is to be multiplied by $\dfrac{J}{H}$.

(10) If–

    (a) the person's contractual hours in a part-time new employment are altered, or

    (b) he is transferred to another post under the same employing body at an altered remuneration,

this regulation applies as if he had again entered a new employment.

(11) If this regulation applies to two or more retirement pensions, each is reduced in proportion to its amount.

(12) This regulation does not apply to a person who has become entitled to a retirement pension payable to him in respect of service rendered without a disqualifying break of service–

    (a) as a designated employee and a contributory employee, or

(b) as a designated employee, a contributory employee and a pensionable employee,

unless, within 3 months after entering his new employment, he elects by notice in writing to the employing authority that it is to apply to him.

(13) Where a person who has become entitled to a retirement pension proposes to accept any further employment with any scheduled body, he shall inform that body that he is so entitled and, if he enters their employment, shall forthwith give notice in writing that he is so employed to the body from whom he receives the pension.

(14) In this regulation, "retirement pension" includes an annual pension under the former Regulations and a retirement pension under the 1974 Regulations.

Combined benefits in the case of certain re-employed pensioners

E16.—(1) Subject to paragraph (7), where–

(a) a person has become entitled to a retirement pension other than one to which he became entitled under regulation E2(2) or one which is reduced under regulation E3(14) ("the first retirement pension"), and

(b) after becoming so entitled he entered further whole-time local government employment, and

(c) at any time while he held the further employment the first retirement pension was liable to be reduced or suspended under regulation E15, and

(d) he has ceased to hold the further employment and has become entitled, in relation to it, to a retirement pension which has become payable ("the second retirement pension"),

he may, by notice in writing given to the appropriate administering authority within 3 months after the date on which the second retirement pension became payable, elect that this regulation is to apply to him.

(2) Subject to paragraphs (4) to (7), a person to whom this regulation applies is to be treated as having, on the date on which the second retirement pension became payable–

(a) become entitled to payment of an annual retirement pension ("the annual pension") and a lump sum payment ("the lump sum") each calculated by reference to both his reckonable service in the further employment and the reckonable service taken into account in calculating the first retirement pension, and

(b) ceased to be entitled to the first retirement pension and the second retirement pension.

(3) In paragraph (2) "the reckonable service" includes any period by reference to which an additional benefit has been granted under regulation E13 or under regulation 13 of the Benefits Regulations (both of which concern additional benefits for certain female nursing staff).

(4) If in conjunction with the first retirement pension the person received a retiring allowance–

(a) in calculating the lump sum no account is to be taken of any additional period excluded in accordance with regulation E3(3) from the calculation of the retiring allowance,

(b) if the lump sum would be the same as or less than the retiring allowance, the person–

(i) is not entitled to payment of the lump sum, and

(ii) is not entitled to the annual pension unless, within 3 months after giving notice under paragraph (1), he pays to the appropriate administering authority the amount of any difference, and

(c) if the lump sum is greater than the retiring allowance, the lump sum is reduced by the amount of the allowance.

(5) If–

(a) the first retirement pension was, and

(b) the second retirement pension would not have been,

reduced under Part F of the 1974 Regulations or regulation E32, the annual pension is reduced by the same amount as the first retirement pension.

(6) If part of the first retirement pension was surrendered under regulation E20–

(a) the annual pension is to be treated as having been surrendered to the same extent, and

(b) any resulting pension becoming payable on the person's death is to be paid by the authority by whom the annual pension is payable.

(7) In relation to a person who–

(a) before 1st April 1972–

(i) became entitled to a superannuation allowance under Part I of the Act of 1937 or to an annual pension under the former Regulations, and

(ii) again became a contributory employee, and

(b) has not, since he again became a contributory employee, had a disqualifying break of service,

this regulation has effect as if references to the first retirement pension were references to that superannuation allowance or annual pension and references to a retiring allowance were references to a retirement grant under the former Regulations.

Separate benefits in the case of certain re-employed pensioners

E17.—(1) This regulation applies to a person who–

(a)(i) has become entitled to a retirement pension (a "previous pension"), and

(ii) after becoming so entitled entered further local government employment, and

(iii) has ceased to hold the further employment and has become entitled in relation to it to a retirement pension (an "additional pension"), and

(iv) has not become entitled to the annual pension mentioned in regulation E16 (combined benefits), or

(b) is subject to regulation E18.

(2) If–

(a) on the person's ceasing to hold an employment in relation to which he became entitled to a previous pension (a "previous employment") regulation E2(1)(b)(i) (permanent ill-health) applied, and

(b) he gave a notice under paragraph 4 of Schedule 10,

regulation E3(12) (additional reckonable service) does not apply on his ceasing to hold any further employment.

(3) If regulation E2(1)(b)(i) did not apply on the person's ceasing to hold a previous employment, but does apply on his ceasing to hold a further employment–

(a) sub-paragraph (1) of paragraph 2 of Schedule 10 applies with the substitution for the words from "the period specified" to the end of the sub-paragraph of the words "$6\frac{243}{365}$ years", and

(b) paragraph 4 of Schedule 10 does not apply.

(4) Subject to paragraph (5), if when the person dies paragraph (4) of regulation E11 (death gratuity) applies, it applies with the substitution for the words "is the greater of A and $(B \times C)$" of the words "is $(B \times C)$".

(5) If the person became entitled to a previous pension or to an additional pension by virtue of regulation E2(1)(c) or (d)–

(a) if P equals or exceeds Q, there is no entitlement under regulation E11 to a death gratuity in relation to the further employment, and

(b) if P is less than Q but $(P + R)$ is greater than Q, R is reduced by the amount of the excess.

(6) In paragraph (5)–

(a) P is the total of–

(i) every death gratuity payable in relation to any previous employment calculated in accordance with regulation E11,

(ii) payments made in respect of every previous pension,

(iii) every retiring allowance to which the person became entitled in conjunction with any previous pension,

(iv) any payments made in respect of the additional pension, and

(v) any retiring allowance to which the person became entitled in conjunction with the additional pension,

including in each case any increase under the Pensions (Increase) Act 1971;

(b) Q is the greater of–

(i) the aggregate obtained by taking for each previous pension the amount of the pensionable remuneration by reference to which it was calculated and the amount by which that amount would have been increased if it had been the rate of an official pension, within the meaning of that Act, beginning on and payable from the day after the last day of the relevant previous employment, and

(ii) the amount of the pensionable remuneration by reference to which the additional pension was calculated; and

(c) R is the amount of the death gratuity calculated in accordance with regulation E11 in relation to the further employment.

(7) In this regulation "retirement pension" includes–

(a) a superannuation allowance under Part I of the Act of 1937,

(b) an annual pension under the former Regulations,

(c) a pension under a local Act scheme, and

(d) a short service grant under regulation 9 of the Benefits Regulations.

Adjustment of superannuation rights on death of certain re-employed pensioners

E18.—(1) This paragraph applies where–

(a) a person was entitled to a retirement pension other than one which was reduced under regulation E3(14),

(b) after becoming so entitled he entered further local government employment,

(c) he dies in the further employment, and

(d) if he had then ceased to be employed otherwise than by reason of his death he would have been entitled to give notice under regulation E16 (combined benefits).

(2) Where paragraph (1) applies–

(a) any benefits payable in respect of the person (except any widow's short-term pension or children's short-term pension) are to be calculated, and

(b) any surrender of part of a retirement pension has effect,

as if immediately before his death he had become entitled to benefits under regulation E16 or E17, whichever is the more favourable to the person entitled to receive the benefits payable.

(3) Where–

(a) a person was entitled to a superannuation allowance under Part I of the Act of 1937 or an annual pension under the former Regulations or a pension under a local Act scheme,

(b) after becoming so entitled he entered further local government employment,

(c) the pension or allowance was on that account reduced or suspended, and

(d) he dies in the further employment,

any benefits payable in respect of him (except any widow's short-term pension or children's short-term pension) are to be calculated as if immediately before his death he had become entitled to benefits under regulation E17 (separate benefits).

Benefits of certain persons employed before 16th May 1974

E19. In relation to a pensionable employee who is a person to whom regulation E19 of the 1974 Regulations applied but who did not make an election under that regulation, this Part applies–

(a) if paragraph (1)(b)(i) of that regulation (no previous right to retiring allowance or widow's pension) applied to him, subject to the modifications set out in Parts I and III of Schedule 12, or

(b) if paragraph (1)(b)(ii) of that regulation (no previous right to widow's pension) applied to him, subject to the modifications set out in Parts II and III of Schedule 12.

Surrender of part of retirement pension

E20.—(1) This regulation has effect subject to Schedule 13.

(2) A person who–

(a) has become entitled to receive payments in respect of a retirement pension, or

(b) is a pensionable employee and has attained pensionable age,

may surrender as from the relevant date, in favour of his spouse or any dependant of his ("the beneficiary"), a part of the retirement pension which is or, as the case may be, may become payable to him.

(3) For the purposes of this regulation the relevant date is the date of becoming entitled to receive payments in respect of the retirement pension; and if the person dies while a pensionable employee he is to be treated as having become so entitled immediately before he died.

(4) An annual pension at a rate which is (according to tables to be prepared from time to time by the Government Actuary) actuarially equivalent at the relevant date to the value of the surrendered part of the retirement pension becomes payable to the beneficiary on the person's death.

(5) A person who has surrendered part of a retirement pension may surrender further parts of it.

Power to compound certain small pensions

E21.—(1) Where–

(a) a pensionable employee has become entitled to a retirement pension or pensions and has attained the age of 65 years in the case of a man or 60 years in the case of a woman; and

(b) the annual rate of that pension or the aggregate of the annual rates of those pensions, including the amount of any pensions increase payable thereon under the Pensions (Increase) Act 1971(**a**), the Pensions (Increase) Act 1974 or the Pensions Act, does not exceed £78,

the administering authority may discharge their liability in respect of–

(i) that pension or those pensions; and

(ii) if the pensionable employee is a male–

(A) the widow's long-term pension which, in the event of his dying leaving a widow, would be payable to her in respect of his reckonable service; and

(B) the children's long-term pension which, in the event of his dying leaving an eligible child or eligible children, would be payable to or for the benefit of his eligible child or eligible children in respect of his reckonable service,

by payment to the pensionable employee of a lump sum of such amount as represents the capital value of the pensions mentioned in sub-paragraphs (i) and (ii) above, calculated in accordance with tables prepared by the Government Actuary.

(2) For the purposes of paragraph (1) a pensionable employee who ceases to be employed in the circumstances mentioned in regulation E2(1)(c) or who satisfies the requirements of regulation E2(1)(d) shall not be treated as having become entitled to a retirement pension until the date (if any) on which he becomes entitled to receive payments in respect of that pension.

(3) Where the annual rate of the widow's long-term pension or pensions payable to a widow does not exceed in total £104, including the amount of any pensions increase payable thereon under the Pensions (Increase) Act 1971, the Pensions (Increase) Act 1974 or the Pensions Act, the administering authority may discharge their liability in respect of that pension or those pensions by payment to the widow of a lump sum of such amount as represents the capital value of that pension or pensions, calculated in accordance with the tables mentioned in paragraph (1).

(4) Where the annual amount of the children's long-term pension payable to or for the benefit of an eligible child or eligible children does not exceed £104, the administering authority

(**a**) 1971 c.56.

may discharge their liability in respect of that pension by payment of a lump sum of such amount as represents the capital value of that pension, calculated in accordance with the tables mentioned in paragraph (1).

Pensionable remuneration

E22.—(1) Subject to paragraphs (4) and (6) to (13) and regulations E23 (further provision as to pensionable remuneration) and G1 (certain former contributory employees), a person's pensionable remuneration in relation to a local government employment is his remuneration for so much of the relevant period as he is entitled to reckon as reckonable service in relation to that employment.

(2) Subject to paragraphs (3), (4) and (5), for the purposes of this regulation the relevant period is the year ending with the day on which the person ceases to hold the employment or, if earlier, the day on which he becomes entitled to reckon 45 years as reckonable service in relation to the employment, disregarding reckonable service before attaining the age of 60 years beyond a total of 40 years.

(3) Subject to paragraphs (4) and (5), where–
  (a) the person is not entitled to reckon the whole of the period specified in paragraph (2) as reckonable service because he has been absent from duty otherwise than by reason of illness or injury, and
  (b) this paragraph applies to him by virtue of a notice or determination,
the relevant period comprises the last 365 days which he is entitled to reckon as reckonable service.

(4) Where a person's remuneration has been reduced and the employing authority have certified under regulation E24 that the reduction in his remuneration was in consequence of a material change in his circumstances, then the relevant period is–
  (a) if the reduction occurred during the 13 years ending with the day mentioned in paragraph (2), either–
    (i) such one of the last 5 of those 13 years, or
    (ii) such consecutive 3 of those 13 years,
        as is specified in the notice or determination, or
  (b) if the reduction occurred during the last 5 of those 13 years, such one of those 5 years as is specified in the notice or determination;
and where by virtue of this paragraph the relevant period is a period of 3 consecutive years, the person's pensionable remuneration is the aggregate of his remuneration during that period divided by 3.

(5) Where–
  (a) the relevant period would otherwise be the period specified in paragraph (2), and
  (b) either one or each of the 2 immediately preceding years would yield a higher amount of pensionable remuneration, and
  (c) this paragraph applies to the person by virtue of a notice or determination,
the relevant period is the year which yields the highest amount.

(6) If during the 13 years ending with the day mentioned in paragraph (2) the person's remuneration was reduced or suspended during absence from duty by reason of illness or injury, he is for the purposes of this regulation to be treated as having received the remuneration which he would have received but for the reduction or suspension.

(7) If during the 13 years ending with the day mentioned in paragraph (2) the person's remuneration was reduced or discontinued during absence from duty otherwise than by reason of illness or injury and he–
  (a) made contributions under regulation C3 (leave of absence) or a payment under regulation C4 (absence due to trade dispute), or
  (b) contributed under section 6(5) of the Act of 1937 (leave of absence etc.),
he is for the purposes of this regulation to be treated as having received for any period in respect of which he made such contributions or payment the remuneration which he would have received but for the reduction or discontinuance.

(8) The remuneration of any period of part-time local government service shall be treated as being the remuneration the person would have received in respect of a single comparable whole-time employment except for–

(a) the purposes of calculating any benefit attributable to any added years or additional period reckonable under regulation D10 of the 1974 Regulations, or regulations D4 or D5,

(b) the purposes of regulation E6(1)(b) and (c), E7 and E10, or

(c) ascertaining the value of "A" for the purposes of regulation E11(4).

(9) Where immediately before ceasing to be a pensionable employee a person was in the employment in respect of which he was an employee and was required to serve for fewer than 45 weeks in every period of 12 months, his remuneration shall be deemed to be the remuneration which would have been paid for a single comparable whole-time employment in which remuneration was payable for 52 weeks in every period of 12 months except for–

(a) the purposes of calculating any benefit attributable to any added years or additional period reckonable under regulation D10 of the 1974 Regulations, or regulations D4 or D5,

(b) the purposes of regulation E6(1)(b) and (c), E7 and E10, or

(c) ascertaining the value of "A" for the purposes of regulation E11(4).

(10) Where–

(a) the person was at any time employed in a single local government employment ("the first employment"), and

(b) he becomes entitled to a benefit in relation to one of two or more concurrent local government employments ("the second employment"), and

(c) his remuneration in the first employment becomes material for the purposes of calculating that benefit,

that remuneration is for that purpose to be multiplied by $\frac{A}{B}$, where A is the annual rate of remuneration of the second employment at the date of cessation and B is the total of the annual rates of remuneration of all the concurrent employments at that date.

(11) Where the whole or a part of the person's remuneration consisted of fees, his pensionable remuneration in respect of them is the annual average of the fees earned by him–

(a) during the period of 3 years ending with the last day of the relevant period, or

(b) during such more favourable period, of more than 3 but not more than 5 years, as his last employing authority may allow, or

(c) if he was entitled to receive fees during part only of the period mentioned in sub-paragraph (a), during that part of the period.

(12) Where the person is entitled to reckon as reckonable service, in relation to the employment which he ceases to hold, only part of the period specified in paragraph (2), his pensionable remuneration is his remuneration during that part multiplied by $\frac{365}{A}$, where A is the number of days comprised in that part.

(13) Where–

(a) any part of the person's remuneration during the relevant period was determined in accordance with an agreement under regulation G3 (standard remuneration agreements), and

(b) his average weekly earnings from his local government employment in that period (other than payments for overtime and payments by way of bonus) exceed one and a half times the lower earnings limit, but do not exceed the upper earnings limit, in force under section 4(1) of the Social Security Act 1975(a) at the end of the period, and

(c) his pensionable remuneration would be greater if determined by reference to those earnings,

his pensionable remuneration is to be determined by reference to those earnings.

(a) 1975 c.14; section 4(1) was amended by the Social Security Pensions Act 1975 (c.60), Schedule 4, Part I, paragraph 36(a).

(14) References in this regulation to a notice are references to a notice in writing given by the person to the appropriate administering authority not later than one month after he is notified under regulation N7 of his entitlement to a benefit.

(15) References in this regulation to a determination are references to a determination given by the appropriate administering authority in respect of a person who has died while still in local government employment or without having given a notice.

Further provision as to pensionable remuneration

E23.—(1) This regulation applies to a person who has at any time after 31st March 1978 ceased to hold an employment in which he was a pensionable employee and who—

   (a) was at a material time a person whose remuneration fell to be determined by reference to the Scottish Teachers Salaries Memorandum 1978, as from time to time amended, or

   (b) was affected by a staging agreement.

(2) A person who has ceased to hold an employment as mentioned in paragraph (1) is affected by a staging agreement if—

   (a) there has been an agreement or award—

      (i) which, whether before or after he ceased to hold his employment, gave rise to rights enforceable by every member of a class or description of employees to which he belonged at a material time, and

      (ii) which, whether or not it entitled him to any interim increase, entitled him, or would if he had not ceased to hold his employment have entitled him, in that employment to the payment of remuneration from a specified date at an increased rate ("the final rate") which was either specified in or to be determined by a method or in a manner specified in the agreement or award, and

      (iii) under the terms of which either the final rate or any interim increase became payable on or before 1st January 1980;

   (b) but for considerations of economy the final rate would have been payable from a date ("the relevant date") earlier than the date mentioned in sub-paragraph (a)(ii); and

   (c) his remuneration at a material time was less than it would have been if the final rate had become payable from the relevant date.

(3) Subject to paragraph (4), where this regulation applies to a person the amount of any remuneration that is material for the purpose of regulation E22 shall for those purposes—

   (a) where paragraph (1)(a) applies, be taken to be what it would have been on the hypotheses set out in regulation 3(2) of the Teachers' Superannuation (Notional Salaries) (Scotland) Regulations 1982(a), and

   (b) where paragraph (1)(b) applies, be taken to be what it would have been if the final rate had become payable from the relevant date.

(4) Paragraph (3) does not apply to the calculation of a person's pensionable remuneration for the purposes of regulations E6(1)(b) or (c), E7 and E10.

(5) For the purposes of this regulation—

   (a) a material time is a time material for the purpose of calculating the person's pensionable remuneration under regulation E22,

   (b) in paragraph (1)(a) the reference to the Scottish Teachers Salaries Memorandum 1978 is a reference to the document published by Her Majesty's Stationery Office on 14th December 1978 under that title, and

   (c) a class or description of employees may include persons who neither are nor are deemed to be employees of a scheduled body.

(6) In relation to a person to whom regulation G1 applies, any reference in this regulation to regulation E22 is to be construed as a reference to regulation E22 as it has effect in relation to him by virtue of regulation G1.

(a) S.I. 1982/1302.

Certificates as to reduction in remuneration

E24.—(1) Where a pensionable employee other than a person who is a pensionable employee by virtue of an election under regulation B3 suffers a material change in circumstances (being a change resulting from his incapacity to continue to discharge efficiently the duties of his post or otherwise from circumstances beyond his control) which results in a reduction in the remuneration of an employment which he continues to hold, he shall, subject to paragraph (4), be entitled to be issued by the employing authority with a certificate to that effect.

(2) Subject to paragraph (3), a change in circumstances is material if, and only if, the employee's pensionable remuneration would be likely to be less if the relevant period were the period specified in regulation E22(2) than if it were a period mentioned in regulation E22(4).

(3) A change in circumstances is not material if–

(a) it did not result from circumstances beyond the employee's control, or

(b) it was temporary, or

(c) it consisted in the termination of, or a reduction in, a temporary increase in remuneration.

(4) The employing authority may issue a certificate without an application from the employee, but need not issue a certificate if he does not apply for one within 12 months after the date of the reduction.

(5) A certificate issued under this regulation is to specify the date of the material reduction and the authority are to keep, for 10 years from that date, a record of the certificate including such information as would be necessary for applying regulation E22(4).

Calculation of part-time service

E25. For the purposes of calculating the amount of any benefit which is or will become payable under these Regulations other than under regulation E3(4) to or in respect of a pensionable employee who–

(a) has served as a part-time employee, or

(b) who has made an election under regulation B3 but is not an employee whose contract of employment requires him to serve for less than 45 weeks in every period of 12 months,

the period of part-time service shall be treated as though it were whole-time service for a proportionately reduced period.

Calculation of service in certain other cases

E26.—(1) For the purposes of calculating the amount of any benefit under these Regulations which is or will become payable to or in respect of a pensionable employee, being an employee whose contract of employment requires him to serve for fewer than 45 weeks in every period of 12 months, the period of service in each income tax year during which he was a pensionable employee by virtue of an election under regulation B3 shall be multiplied by $\frac{A}{B}$, where–

A is the remuneration he would have received during the income tax year on the assumption that there had been no discontinuance or reduction of remuneration during any absence from duty owing to illness or injury, and

B is the remuneration that would, on that assumption, have been paid during the income tax year in respect of a single comparable whole-time employment under a scheduled body in which remuneration was payable for 52 weeks in every period of 12 months.

(2) For the purposes of paragraph (1) "service" includes any period of time covered by the contract of employment but not a period of absence without leave.

Counting of non-contributing service

E27.—(1) Subject to paragraph (3), any period which–

(a) is reckonable as reckonable service by virtue of its having been reckonable under the former Regulations as non-contributing service, and

(b) does not fall to be treated as having been reckonable as contributing service,

shall for the purposes of these Regulations be counted at half its full length.

(2) For the purposes of paragraph (1), the full length of a period of part-time non-contributing service is its length as calculated under regulation E25.

(3) This regulation does not apply for the purpose of–

(a) determining whether a person is entitled to, or to payment of, a benefit,

(b) ascertaining, where notice was given under Schedule 2 to the Benefits Regulations or regulation D6 or D7 of the 1974 Regulations, the maximum length of any additional period to which Schedule 4 applies, or

(c) ascertaining the length of the additional period where notice is given under paragraph 4 of Schedule 10.

Disregard of certain reckonable service in determining entitlement to benefits

E28. For the purpose of determining entitlement to any benefit, no account shall be taken of–

(a) any added years,

(b) any additional period reckonable as reckonable service by virtue of regulations D4 to D7,

(c) any period which by virtue of interchange rules became reckonable under the former Regulations only for the purpose of calculating the amount of benefits, or

(d) except in relation to regulation E2(2), any period reckonable by virtue of regulation J9(1)(a).

Counting of certain reckonable service and qualifying service in determining entitlement to benefits

E29. For the purpose of determining whether a person is entitled to, or to payment of, a benefit, any reckonable service and qualifying service which was reckonable for the purpose of determining entitlement to benefits under the former Regulations shall be counted at the same length as it would have been counted for the latter purpose.

Disregard of certain reckonable service in calculating amount of benefits

E30.—(1) For the purpose of calculating the amount of any benefit under regulation E3–

(a) subject to paragraphs (2) to (4), no account shall be taken of reckonable service before attaining the age of 60 years beyond a total of 40 years, and

(b) where an amount is recovered or retained under regulation M3, reckonable service shall be left out of account to the extent necessary to reduce the actuarial value referred to in regulation M3(2)(b) by that amount.

(2) For the purposes of paragraph (1)(a), a period which a person is entitled to reckon as reckonable service by virtue of regulation F6(1)(a) or (b) (war service) shall be treated as reckonable service before attaining the age of 60 years.

(3) Where a retiring allowance is to be reduced under regulation E3(7) or (8) (potential widow's pensions), any reckonable service to be left out of account by virtue of paragraph (1)(a) shall be taken from the beginning of the person's reckonable service.

(4) Where a retiring allowance is to be increased under regulation E3(4) (preservation of certain rights under former Regulations), any reckonable service to be left out of account by virtue of paragraph (1)(a) shall be taken from the end of the person's reckonable service.

(5) Where $A + B + C$ exceeds 45 years, for the purpose of calculating any benefit A is reduced by a period equal to the excess.

(6) In paragraph (5)–

A is the total length of the periods reckonable as reckonable service in relation to the relevant employment, excluding any service which is to be left out of account by virtue of paragraph (1)(a),

B is the length of any earlier period which was taken into account in the calculation of a retirement pension, an annual pension under the former Regulations, or a superannuation allowance under Part I of the Act of 1937, or in respect of which any pension was granted under a local Act scheme, and

C is the length of any period by reference to which an additional benefit has been granted under regulation E13 or under regulation 13 of the Benefits Regulations.

Counting of certain reckonable service in calculating amount of benefits

E31. For the purpose of calculating the amount of any benefit–

(a) any period which is reckonable as reckonable service by virtue of its having been reckonable under the former Regulations as contributing service shall, subject to regulations E25 and E27 (part-time and non-contributing service), be counted at the same length as it would have been counted for the purpose of calculating any benefit under the former Regulations, and

(b) such part (if any) of the reckonable service of an employee as does not amount to a number of complete years shall be counted as a fraction of a year, of which the denominator shall be 365 and the numerator shall be the number of completed days comprised in that part.

National Insurance

E32.—(1) Where but for the revocation of the 1974 Regulations the amount of a benefit would have fallen to be reduced under Part F of those Regulations, the amount shall be reduced as if that Part had not been revoked.

(2) No provision in these Regulations–

(a) for the surrender or assignation of a pension, or

(b) for the reduction, termination or suspension of a pension, where the provision is invoked for any cause other than one prescribed by Regulations made or deemed to have been made under section 57(1)(c) of the Insurance Act (which section describes equivalent pension benefits),

shall apply so as to reduce a pension payable in respect of any period of service to an employee who attains state pensionable age below the minimum rate of equivalent pension benefits applicable in respect of that period under the Insurance Acts.

(3) For the purposes of paragraph (2) "service" means service in a non-participating employment which is reckonable for the purposes of calculating any benefits payable to the employee, except any earlier period of such service in respect of which–

(a) a payment in lieu of contributions has been made, or

(b) equivalent pension benefits satisfying the requirements of the Insurance Acts had already been assured to him.

Benefits not assignable

E33. Every benefit, including a payment under regulation C12 (return of contributions)–

(a) is payable to, or in trust for, the person who is entitled to it under these Regulations, and

(b) is not assignable and is not chargeable with that person's debts or other liabilities.

Payment of benefits

E34. Payments in respect of annual benefits paid under these Regulations shall be made at such interval, not being longer than 3 months, as the appropriate administering authority may determine.

PART F
WAR SERVICE

Interpretation etc.

F1.—(1) In this Part, unless the context otherwise requires–

"deceased employee" means a person with war service who died after 31st March 1978 and in relation to whom the conditions specified in regulation F3(2) to (10) were or are deemed to have been satisfied when he died;

"excess remuneration" means, in relation to a retired officer of the armed forces of the Crown who is re-employed in those forces, any service pension drawn in respect of such period of re-employment, or any addition to the normal pay attaching to the post in which the officer is re-employed which is granted by reason of the officer's former employment in those forces;

"non-effective pay" includes naval, military and air force pensions, retired pay, and gratuities (other than war gratuities to which section 23 of the Finance (No.2) Act 1945(**a**), which exempted war gratuities from income tax, applies and gratuities paid to former members of the Palestine Police Force);

"occupational pension scheme" means any scheme or arrangement comprised in one or more instruments or agreements and having, or being capable of having, effect in relation to one or more descriptions or categories of employments so as to provide benefits, in the form of pensions or otherwise, payable on termination of service, or on death or retirement, to or in respect of earners with qualifying service in an employment of any such description or category;

and references to war service are to be construed in accordance with regulation F2.

(2) Where by virtue of a determination or determinations given under one or more of the following, that is to say section 12(6) of the Act of 1937, section 7(3) of the Act of 1953 and regulation D4 of the 1974 Regulations, a period comprising the whole or a part or parts of a person's indirect service was, or has fallen to be treated as having been, reckonable by him as non-contributing service for the purposes of the former Regulations, then–

(a) for the purposes of regulation F2(2)(b), the period shall be deemed to have been so reckonable only to the extent that its length exceeds that of his civilian indirect service, and

(b) if the period is not the whole of the indirect service–

(i) it shall for the purposes of regulation F3(2)(c) be deemed to have been a continuous period ending on the last day of the indirect service, and

(ii) none of the indirect service shall for the purposes of regulation F2(2)(d) be taken to be or to have been capable of being taken into account as there mentioned.

(3) For the purposes of paragraph (2)–

(a) a person's indirect service is the total of any service, employment and periods in respect of which determinations could have been given under any of the provisions mentioned in that paragraph, and

(b) a person's civilian indirect service is any of his indirect service that was not such whole-time service as is described in regulation F2(1).

War service

F2.—(1) For the purposes of this Part, a person's war service is, subject to paragraph (2), the period of his whole-time service at any time after 2nd September 1939 and before 30th June 1950, while 18 years old or older, in the armed forces of the Crown, in the merchant navy or the mercantile marine, or in any of the women's services specified in Schedule 14.

(2) Subject to regulation F1(2), a person's war service does not include–

(a) any period in respect of which any non-effective pay or excess remuneration has been received by him and not refunded,

(b) any period that was, or falls to be treated as having been, reckonable by him as non-contributing or contributing service, or a period of contribution, for the purposes of the former Regulations, or of a local Act scheme,

(c) any period that has at any time been taken into account (whether at its full length or otherwise) for the purpose of calculating any benefit under any other occupational pension scheme, or

(d) any period that is or has at any time been capable of being taken into account otherwise than under this Part (whether at its full length or otherwise) for the purpose of calculating any benefit under any occupational pension scheme; but in the case of a person to whom regulation F3(2)(f) applies "benefit" does not include a benefit under the war service provisions of a public service scheme.

(**a**) 1945 c.13 (9 & 10 Geo. 6).

Election as to war service

F3.—(1) A person with war service in relation to whom the conditions specified in paragraphs (2) to (10) are satisfied, or the executors of a deceased employee, may by notice given in accordance with regulation F5 elect that this regulation shall apply in relation to him.

(2) One at least of the following must be the case:–

(a) he became before 1st July 1950 entitled to participate in the benefits of a superannuation fund maintained under Part I of the Act of 1937 or under a local Act, or

(b) he became before 1st July 1950 a participant in a scheme which was a relevant policy scheme within the meaning of regulation P13 of the 1974 Regulations or a relevant scheme within the meaning of regulation G14 of the Local Government Superannuation Regulations 1974(**a**), and is a person to whom regulation P13 of the 1974 Regulations applied, or

(c) a period beginning before 1st July 1950 was, or falls to be treated as having been, reckonable by him otherwise than by virtue of interchange rules as non-contributing or contributing service, or a period of contribution, for the purposes of the former Regulations or of a local Act scheme, or

(d) if sub-paragraph (c) is not the case, and he is a person to whom regulation D4 of the 1974 Regulations applied, and–

(i) his period of previous employment (within the meaning of that regulation) began before 1st July 1950, and

(ii) an application was made by or in respect of him under regulation D4 of the 1974 Regulations, or

(e) he was on 30th June 1950 undergoing a full-time course of training for, and subsequently obtained, the Royal Sanitary Institute's Diploma in Public Health Inspection, and not later than 6 months after completing the course of training he became entitled to participate or was a participant as mentioned in sub-paragraph (a) or (b) respectively or, as the case may be, a period began which was reckonable, or falls to be treated as having been reckonable, as mentioned in sub-paragraph (c), or

(f) a transfer value was accepted and received in relation to him by an administering authority or a former local authority before 1st April 1978 and a scheme is designated under regulation F5(2)(b).

(3) He must on 1st April 1978 have been–

(a) an employee entitled to participate in the benefits of a superannuation fund maintained under the 1974 Regulations, or

(b) a participant in a scheme which was a relevant scheme within the meaning of regulation P13 of those Regulations, or

(c) entitled to receive payments in respect of an annual pension out of a superannuation fund maintained under those Regulations or would have been so entitled but for the operation of regulation E15 of those Regulations, or

(d) entitled to an annual pension under regulation E2(1)(c) of those Regulations.

(4) Except where paragraph (2)(e) or (f) is the case, there must not since the date specified in paragraph (11) have been a continuous period of 12 months or more throughout which none of the following was the case–

(a) he was entitled to participate or was a participant as mentioned in paragraph (2)(a) or (b), or

(b) the period mentioned in paragraph (2)(c) or (d)(i) was running, or

(c) he was undergoing such a course of training as is mentioned in paragraph (2)(e), or

(d) he was entitled to participate or was a participant as mentioned in paragraph (3), or

(e) he was entitled to receive payments in respect of a pension out of a superannuation fund mentioned in paragraph (2)(a), or

(f) he was a person to whom regulation E15, section 6 of the Act of 1953 or section 26 of the Act of 1937 applied.

(5) Where paragraph (2)(e) is the case, paragraph (4) applies–

(**a**) S.I. 1974/520; the relevant amending instrument is S.I. 1978/1739.

(a) with the substitution for the date specified in paragraph (11) of the date (being a date later than 30th June 1950) on which he became entitled to participate or was a participant as mentioned in paragraph (2)(a) or (b), or, as the case may be, a period began which was reckonable, or falls to be treated as having been reckonable, as mentioned in paragraph (2)(c), and

(b) with the substitution for the reference in paragraph (4)(b) to the period mentioned in paragraph (2)(c) or (d)(i) of a reference to such a period as is mentioned in sub-paragraph (a).

(6) Where paragraph (2)(f) is the case, paragraph (4) applies with the substitution for the date specified in paragraph (11) of the date (being a date later than 30th June 1950) on which he last became entitled to participate or was a participant as mentioned in paragraph (2)(a) or (b).

(7) If he is a person to whom regulation D1(2) of the 1974 Regulations applied in respect of any service after the end of his war service, he must have repaid to the appropriate administering authority the sum or amount there mentioned.

(8) If he is an employee entitled to participate in the benefits of a superannuation fund maintained under these Regulations, he must not be entitled to reckon more than 45 years' reckonable service, disregarding reckonable service before attaining the age of 60 years beyond a total of 40 years.

(9) If he has become entitled to receive payment in respect of an annual pension out of a superannuation fund maintained under these Regulations (including a pension which is for the time being subject to reduction or suspension under regulation E15), no more than 45 years' service must have been taken into account in calculating the amount of that pension.

(10) Where paragraph (2)(f) applies and the scheme designated under regulation F5(2)(b) is not a scheme specified in Schedule 15, war service is for the purposes of paragraph (1) to be assumed.

(11) The date mentioned in paragraph (4) is the date before 1st July 1950 and after the end of his war service when, as the case may be–

(a) he became entitled to participate or was a participant as mentioned in paragraph (2)(a) or (b), or

(b) the period mentioned in paragraph (2)(c) or (d)(i) began.

Modified application of regulation F3 in certain cases

F4.—(1) Regulation F3 applies in accordance with paragraphs (3) to (5) of this regulation in the cases specified in those paragraphs.

(2) In this regulation, unless the context otherwise requires, "service" means service or employment with any employer.

(3) In the case of a person to whom rule 11 of the Superannuation (Local Government and Overseas Employment) Interchange (Scotland) Rules 1969(a) applied otherwise than by virtue of rule 3(3)(c) of those Rules, or to whom rule 6 of the Superannuation (Local Government and Overseas Employment) Interchange (Scotland) Rules 1958(b), rule 3 of the Superannuation (Local Government, Commonwealth and Foreign Service) Interchange (Scotland) Rules 1952(c), or rule 3 of the Superannuation (Local Government and Colonial Service) (Scotland) Interchange Rules 1949(d) applied–

(a) service reckonable by virtue of the provisions of any of those Rules shall for the purposes of regulation F3(2)(c) be deemed to have been reckonable by him otherwise than by virtue of interchange rules, and

(b) the period between his leaving and re-entering local government employment shall be deemed not to be such a period as is mentioned in regulation F3(4).

(4) In the case of a person to whom regulation 4 of the Electricity (Pension Rights) Regulations 1948(e) applied, or to whom regulation 4 of the Gas (Pension Rights) Regulations

(a) S.I. 1969/1642.
(b) S.I. 1958/1402.
(c) S.I. 1952/433.
(d) S.I. 1949/1988.
(e) S.I. 1948/2172.

1950(**a**) applied as mentioned in paragraph (4) of that regulation, and who has re-entered local government employment not more than 12 months after ceasing to hold the employment by virtue of which the relevant regulation applied to him–

(a) any period of service beginning before 1st July 1950–

    (i) in respect of which a transfer value has been accepted under interchange rules, or has been accepted or fallen to be treated as if it had been accepted under Part J, or

    (ii) which he became entitled to reckon as reckonable service, or as non-contributing or contributing service or a period of contribution for the purposes of the former Regulations or of a local Act scheme,

shall be deemed to be such a period as is mentioned in regulation F3(2)(c), and

(b) the period between his leaving and re-entering local government employment shall be deemed not to be such a period as is mentioned in regulation F3(4).

(5) In the case of a person–

(a) who after the date specified in regulation F3(11) left local government employment and became entitled to participate in the benefits of another occupational pension scheme, and

(b) who re-entered local government employment not more than 12 months after ceasing to be entitled as mentioned in sub-paragraph (a) and became entitled in that employment to reckon a period at least equal in length to the whole of his service from the date specified in regulation F3(11)–

    (i) as reckonable service or qualifying service, or

    (ii) s non-contributing or contributing service, or a period of contribution, for the purposes of the former Regulations or of a local Act scheme, or

    (iii) a service material for the purposes of regulation H5(8),

the period between his leaving and re-entering local government employment shall be deemed not to be such a period as is mentioned in regulation F3(4).

Notice of election

F5.—(1) Notice of an election under regulation F3 is to be given in writing–

(a) in the case of a person who has, or a deceased employee who before he died had–

    (i) become entitled to receive payments in respect of any annual pension out of a superannuation fund maintained under these Regulations (including a pension subject for the time being to reduction or suspension under regulation E15), or

    (ii) become entitled to any annual pension under regulation E2(1)(c),

    to the administering authority maintaining the superannuation fund which is or was liable in respect of the pension or, where there is more than one pension, the first of them, or

(b) in the case of a person in respect of whom a transfer value has been paid after 31st March 1978, under Part J or under Part P of the 1974 Regulations, to the administering authority maintaining the superannuation fund out of which it was paid, or

(c) in any other case, to the appropriate administering authority.

(2) The person giving notice of an election under regulation F3–

(a) is to give the authority, in writing–

    (i) all information in his possession, and

    (ii) if the authority notify him in writing that they so require, any further information specified by them that he can reasonably be expected to obtain,

concerning the war service of the person to whom the notice relates and his past membership of any scheme designated under sub-paragraph (b), and

(b) is to designate in the notice the scheme, if any, which he believes complies with regulation F6(3), and

(c) may–

(**a**) S.I. 1950/1206.

(i) in that notice, or

(ii) at any time before he receives a notification of a decision or determination that the conditions specified in regulation F3(2) to (11) are satisfied in relation to the person to whom that notice relates by a further notice in writing to the same authority,

elect that regulation F6 shall apply with the substitution, in paragraph (1)(a) or (b) or (12) as the case may be, for "47 per cent" (or for any reduced percentage substituted under paragraph (13)) of any specified lesser percentage, and

(d) whether or not he has so elected, may at any time before he receives such a notification withdraw the notice given under regulation F3.

Reckonable service and benefits

F6.—(1) Subject to regulation F5(2)(c) and paragraphs (2) to (16), a person in relation to whom regulation F3 applies is entitled, or as the case may be shall be deemed to have been entitled–

(a) in the case of a person entitled on the relevant date–

(i) to participate in the benefits of a superannuation fund maintained under these Regulations, or

(ii) to a retirement pension,

other than a person to whom regulation P13 of the 1974 Regulations applied, to reckon as reckonable service a period equal to 47 per cent of his war service; or

(b) in the case of a person to whom on the relevant date regulation P13 of the 1974 Regulations applied, to have a period equal to 47 per cent of his war service treated as having been for the purposes of paragraph (4) of that regulation a period during which the whole of his relevant policies were fully maintained; or

(c) in the case of a person who, having become entitled to receive an annual pension under the former Regulations or a local Act scheme, was on the relevant date entitled to receive payments in respect of that pension out of a superannuation fund maintained under these Regulations or the 1974 Regulations, to receive, in respect of the service in respect of which that pension is payable, the additional benefits specified in paragraph (11).

(2) Where regulation F3(2)(f) applies and the scheme designated under regulation F5(2)(b) ("the designated scheme") is a scheme specified in Schedule 15, paragraph (1) applies only if that scheme complies with paragraph (3).

(3) A scheme complies with this paragraph if–

(a) it is the first public service scheme the war service provisions of which could have become applicable to the person if he had remained a member of it, and

(b) he is, or in the case of a deceased employee was, immediately before he died–

(i) entitled to reckon the employment in which he was subject to the scheme as reckonable service, or

(ii) entitled to a retirement pension in the calculation of which that employment was taken into account as reckonable service.

(4) Where the designated scheme is a scheme specified in Part I of Schedule 15 and complies with paragraph (3), this regulation applies with the substitution throughout for references to 47 per cent of references to $63\frac{2}{3}$ per cent.

(5) Where the designated scheme is a scheme specified in Part II of Schedule 15 and complies with paragraph (3), this regulation applies with the substitution throughout for references to 47 per cent of references to $46\frac{1}{2}$ per cent.

(6) Where the designated scheme is not a scheme specified in Schedule 15, paragraph (1) applies only if a transfer value, calculated in accordance with Part V of Schedule 16, is received in respect of the period that could have become reckonable under the war service provisions of that scheme.

(7) Where paragraph (1) applies by virtue of the acceptance of such a transfer value, this regulation applies with the substitution throughout for references to a period equal to 47 per cent of the person's war service of references to the period that could have become reckonable under the war service provisions of the designated scheme.

(8) Where the person was entitled on the relevant date to a retirement pension–

   (a) his entitlement under paragraph (1)(a) or (b), and to any resulting increase in the rate of his retirement pension, shall be taken to have arisen on–

      (i) 1st April 1978, or

      (ii) the date on which he ceased to hold his employment,

     whichever is the later, and

   (b) if regulation E3(9) of the 1974 Regulations applied to him before 15th October 1982–

      (i) any increase by virtue of paragraph (1)(a) or (b) in the amount of any benefit is not subject to reduction under regulation E3(14), and

      (ii) the period that he is entitled by paragraph (1)(a) or (b) to reckon as reckonable service is not to be taken into account in calculating the reduction of any benefit falling to be reduced under regulation E3(14),

     and for the purpose of this sub-paragraph any reference to regulation E3(14) shall be taken to include a reference to regulation 4 of the National Insurance (Modification of Local Government Superannuation Schemes) (Scotland) Regulations 1961(**a**) and regulation 36 of the National Insurance (Modification of Local Government Superannuation Schemes) (Scotland) Regulations 1970(**b**).

(9) The relevant date for the purposes of paragraphs (1) and (8) is the date of the election under regulation F3, except in the case of a deceased employee where it is the date of his death.

(10) Any period which a person is or is deemed to have been entitled to reckon as reckonable service by virtue of paragraph (1)(a) or (b) shall for the purposes of regulation E3(7) to (10) and of regulation E11(5) and (9) be deemed to be reckonable service before, as the case may be–

   (a) 1st April 1972, or

   (b) any earlier date on which he became a widower or was judicially separated from his wife or on which his marriage was dissolved.

(11) The additional benefits mentioned in paragraph (1)(c) are–

   (a) an additional pension, payable from–

      (i) 1st April 1978, or

      (ii) the date on which the person became entitled to receive payments in respect of a pension as mentioned in paragraph (1)(c),

     whichever is the later date, and

   (b) if the person has received or is entitled to receive payment of any lump sum of the same nature as a retiring allowance, an additional lump sum,

calculated in accordance with paragraph (12).

(12) Subject to regulation F5(2)(c) and paragraphs (13) and (16)–

   (a) the annual rate of an additional pension, and

   (b) the amount of an additional lump sum,

specified in paragraph (11) is the amount by which the annual rate of the corresponding original pension or, as the case may be, the amount of the corresponding original lump sum would have been increased if a period equal to 47 per cent of the person's war service had been service, or a period, of a kind which (however described) counted in full in the calculation of the original pension or lump sum.

(13) If a period of part-time service or employment falling to be treated under section 12(5) of the Act of 1937 or under regulation E25 or under regulation P13(4)(b) of the 1974 Regulations as though it were whole-time service or employment for a proportionately reduced period–

   (a) began before and ended on or after 1st July 1950, and

   (b) was not preceded, without any break, by a period of whole-time service or employment,

(**a**) S.I. 1961/206.
(**b**) S.I. 1970/1307.

paragraph (1)(a) or, as the case may be, paragraph (1)(b) or paragraphs (12) and (16) apply with the substitution for "47 per cent" of the percentage obtained by reducing 47 per cent in the same proportion.

(14) Where–

(a) before the date of notification of a decision or determination that he is entitled to reckon a period as reckonable service by virtue of paragraph (1)(a) or (b), a person in relation to whom regulation F3 applies has been credited with an additional period of service under–

(i) any provision made by an enactment or instrument for compensation for loss of employment or loss or diminution of emoluments or for early retirement in lieu of such compensation, or

(ii) regulation E3(12),

("the enhancement provision"), and

(b) A + B + C exceeds 40 years, where–

A is the period which would but for this paragraph be reckonable by him as reckonable service by virtue of paragraph (1)(a) or (b),

B is the remainder of his reckonable service, and

C is the additional period of service with which he has been credited under the enhancement provision,

the period which is reckonable by him as reckonable service by virtue of paragraph (1)(a) or (b) is the total of 40 – (B + C) and the amount, if any, by which (A + B + C) – 40 exceeds C; except that where the instrument referred to in sub-paragraph (a) above is the Local Government Re-organisation (Retirement of Chief Officers) (Scotland) Regulations 1974(a) for the figure "40" wherever it occurs in this sub-paragraph there shall be substituted the figure "45".

(15) Where a person who was entitled or deemed to be entitled to any additional benefit specified in paragraph (11) dies and there is payable in respect of him out of a superannuation fund maintained under these Regulations any benefit similar to a widow's pension, children's pension or death gratuity payable under Part E ("the death benefit"), the person entitled to receive the death benefit is entitled to receive, in respect of the service in respect of which the death benefit is payable, a corresponding additional benefit at any rate or, as the case may be, of any amount which bears the same proportion to the death benefit as the first additional benefit bears to the corresponding original benefit.

(16) The total of an additional benefit under paragraph (11) or (15) and the corresponding original benefit must not exceed the greatest original benefit that could have been paid if–

(a) the period equal to 47 per cent of the person's war service had been a period of service before he attained the age of 60 years, and

(b) no more than–

(i) 40 years' service before attaining that age, and

(ii) 45 years' service in all,

had been capable of counting in the calculation of the original benefit.

(17) In calculating a period equal to a percentage of a person's war service for any of the purposes of this regulation, the war service is to be counted as a number of days, arrived at by–

(a) multiplying the number of complete years of war service, if any, by 365, and

(b) counting any part of the war service that does not amount to a number of complete years at its actual length in days,

and any fraction of a day resulting from the calculation is to be excluded from the period.

Revision of certain elections

F7.—(1) Subject to paragraph (2), where–

(a) notice of one or more elections under regulation C8(2) or notice under regulation C2B(1) of the 1974 Regulations has been given by or in respect of a person in relation to whom regulation F3 applies, and

---

(a) S.I. 1974/1754.

(b) the service thereby specified amounts to the whole of his reckonable service before, as the case may be–

(i) 1st April 1972, or

(ii) any earlier date on which he became a widower or was judicially separated from his wife or on which his marriage was dissolved,

he or his executors may elect that the period which he is or is deemed to be entitled to reckon as reckonable service by virtue of regulation F6(1)(a) or (b) is to be treated as having been included in the service specified in the latest notice.

(2) An election under paragraph (1)–

(a) may not be made unless notice of election under regulation R3 of the 1974 Regulations was given within the period of 6 months beginning on the relevant date, or in the case of a deceased employee who died during that period within the period of 12 months beginning on the date of his death, and

(b) must, unless they allow a longer period, be made by giving notice in writing to the administering authority concerned within 3 months after the date of notification of a decision by that authority, or as the case may be a determination by the Secretary of State under regulation N8, that the person is or is deemed to be entitled to reckon such a period as is mentioned in paragraph (1).

(3) For the purposes of paragraph (2)(a) the relevant date–

(a) where regulation F3(2)(b) applies, is 5th September 1984 and

(b) in any other case, is 15th October 1982.

PART G

SPECIAL PROVISIONS FOR CERTAIN CASES

Preservation of rights and liabilities of persons to whom the provisions of a local Act scheme applied immediately before 16th May 1974

G1.—(1) This regulation applies to a person who–

(a) immediately before 16th May 1974 was a local Act contributor; and

(b) became on 16th May 1974 a pensionable employee under a scheduled body.

(2) Where any provision of the person's former local Act scheme which was similar to a provision of regulation C2, E2(1)(a) or E22 would have been more beneficial than the provision of such regulation, these Regulations have effect, for the appropriate period, as if the former provision had applied.

(3) The appropriate period for the purposes of this regulation is the period of application specified in the relevant provision of the person's former local Act scheme, or, if no period is so specified, the period during which he continues in the employment of the scheduled body mentioned in paragraph (1)(b) or of any successor body.

Modification of the Regulations in their application to employees previously subject to a local Act scheme

G2.—(1) Where an employee–

(a) was immediately before 16th May 1974 a local Act contributor; and

(b) became on that day a pensionable employee under a scheduled body,

these Regulations shall, so long as he remains in the employment of that body or of any successor body, have effect in relation to him as if–

(i) for any reference to a provision in the former Regulations there were substituted a reference to the corresponding or similar provision in the local Act scheme; and

(ii) for any reference to an expression in column 1 of the following Table (which lists certain expressions used in these Regulations) there were substituted a reference to the expression appearing opposite thereto in column 2.

TABLE

(1)	(2)
1. The Acts of 1937 to 1953 and the Regulations made thereunder.	The appropriate local Act scheme.
2. The appropriate superannuation fund within the meaning of the Act of 1937.	A superannuation fund maintained under the appropriate local Act scheme.
3. Contributory employee.	Local Act contributor.
4. (a) Contributing service, and (b) Non-contributing service, for the purposes of the former Regulations.	Service for the purposes of the appropriate local Act scheme.
5. The former Regulations.	The appropriate local Act scheme.

(2) In this regulation "the appropriate local Act scheme" means the local Act scheme to which an employee mentioned in paragraph (1) was subject immediately before 16th May 1974.

Standard remuneration agreements

G3. A scheduled body may from time to time enter into an agreement with the bodies or persons representative of any class or description of employee of that scheduled body specifying the method which shall for the duration of the agreement determine–

(a) an amount representing the whole of the remuneration, or

(b) such part of his remuneration as is specified in the agreement,

of a member of that class or employee of that description.

PART H

LOCAL GOVERNMENT REORGANISATION ETC.

Definitions

H1. In this Part unless the context otherwise requires–

"Health Service Regulations" means the National Health Service (Superannuation) (Scotland) Regulations 1961 to 1974(**a**);

"transferred employee" means–

(a) any person transferred on or after 16th May 1975 by or under an Order or Regulations made under the Local Government (Scotland) Act 1973(**b**) which, in accordance with the provisions of section 216 of that Act, contain a provision as to the transfer of that person;

(b) any person appointed by a local authority or a river purification board to hold any office or employment before or as from 16th May 1975, who, but for the appointment, would be transferred on that day under the said section 216; or

(c) any person who at 16th May 1975 remained in the employment of the same body as immediately before that date but who, in consequence of the Local Government (Scotland) Act 1973, or anything done thereunder or of the 1974 Regulations, became on that day entitled to participate in the benefits of a superannuation fund maintained under those Regulations by a body different from the body which maintained the superannuation fund in the benefits of which he was immediately before 16th May 1975 entitled to participate;

"new employment" means employment to which a person is so transferred or appointed; and

---

(**a**) S.I. 1961/1398, 1966/1522, 1972/1356, 1604, 1973/304, 746, 1713, 1974/441 and 1357.
(**b**) 1973 c.65.

"new employing body" means the body which becomes the employing authority in relation to a person so transferred or appointed;

and in relation to a person appointed as aforesaid his taking up the office or employment to which he is appointed shall for the purposes of this Part be deemed to be a transfer.

Continuity of employment and preservation of status

H2.—(1) Subject to paragraph (2)–

(a) any provision of these Regulations has effect, in relation to a transferred employee to whom it applies, as if his new employment and his former employment had been one continuous employment, and

(b) notwithstanding anything in these Regulations, a transferred employee who is transferred after 20th December 1987 and was a pensionable employee immediately before the date on which he is transferred continues in his new employment to be a pensionable employee.

(2) Paragraph (1) does not affect the operation of regulation H3 or of regulations Q1 to Q3.

Discretionary powers

H3. Where–

(a) a transferred employee has continued in the employment of his new employing body, and

(b) immediately before he was transferred (whether before or after the commencement of these Regulations) it was the prevailing practice of the body employing him, in relation to employees of that description, to exercise so as to secure the payment of, or of increased, gratuities, allowances or pensions any discretionary power exercisable by them by virtue of any enactment relating to pensions, and

(c) that or any corresponding power becomes exerciseable in relation to him,

the new employing body shall exercise the power in a way which is not less beneficial than the general character of that practice.

Contributions of transferred manual workers

H4. A transferred employee who immediately before he was transferred (whether before or after the commencement of these Regulations) was paying contributions at a rate appropriate to a manual worker shall continue to contribute at the like rate so long as he continues to be employed by his new employing body on duties reasonably comparable to those on which he was engaged immediately before he was transferred.

Persons transferred to scheduled bodies under an Order under section 34 of the Local Government (Scotland) Act 1975 or in consequence of section 1 of the Education (Mentally Handicapped Children) (Scotland) Act 1974

H5.—(1) This regulation applies to a person–

(a)(i) who was by or under an order made under section 34 of the Local Government (Scotland) Act 1975(a), or

(ii) who was in consequence of section 1 of the Education (Mentally Handicapped Children) (Scotland) Act 1974(b),

transferred to the employment of a scheduled body, and

(b) who immediately before he was so transferred was in an employment in which he was an officer within the meaning of the Health Service Regulations, and

(c) to whom neither paragraph (6) nor paragraph (8) applies.

(2) Subject to paragraph (8), a person to whom paragraph (1) applies is entitled to reckon–

(i) as reckonable service, any service which for the purposes of the Health Service Regulations he was entitled to reckon in relation to the employment mentioned in paragraph (1)(b) as, or as a period of, contributing service, and

(a) 1975 c.30.
(b) 1974 c.27.

(ii) as qualifying service, any service which for the purposes of those Regulations he was entitled to reckon in relation to that employment for the purpose of determining whether he was entitled to a benefit under those Regulations, but for no other purpose.

(3) Where, immediately before he was transferred, a person to whom paragraph (1) applies was in the process of making payments which were or were deemed to be payments under Schedule 2 to the Health Service Regulations, he is entitled–

    (a) to make the outstanding payments as if they had been instalments of an amount payable under regulation D6 of the 1974 Regulations, and

    (b) if he completes the payments in the manner provided in Schedule 7, to have the service in respect of which they were made counted for all the purposes of these Regulations at its full length.

(4) Where, immediately before he was transferred, a person to whom paragraph (1) applies was in the process of making payments in respect of added years under Schedule 8 to the Health Service Regulations, he is entitled–

    (a) to make the outstanding payments as if they had been payments of an amount payable under regulation D10 of the 1974 Regulations, and

    (b) in respect of the added years for which those payments are made he shall enjoy rights and be subject to liabilities as if those years were added years reckonable under regulation D6 in the employment to which he is so transferred.

(5) For the purposes of paragraph (2) any period of part-time service shall be treated as though it was whole-time service for a proportionately reduced period and, except for the purposes referred to in regulation E27(3), any service which was reckonable under the Health Service Regulations for all purposes (other than for the purpose of determining whether any benefit was payable) as a period of contributing service at half its length shall, subject to paragraph (3), be counted at half its length.

(6) Where, immediately before he was transferred, a person in relation to whom paragraph (1) is satisfied was a person in respect of whom the Secretary of State paid contributions under regulation 46 of the Health Service Regulations (persons subject to non-statutory superannuation schemes and arrangements) or carried out any such scheme or arrangements as are referred to in that regulation, that person shall not be subject to any provisions of these Regulations except those contained in this regulation, and the body to which that person was transferred shall–

    (a) where immediately before 16th May 1974 the Secretary of State was under regulation 46 of the Health Service Regulations paying in respect of that person the contributions authorised or required by the relevant scheme to be paid by the employer, pay those contributions, and

    (b) deduct from the person's remuneration the amount of any contribution required by the scheme or under the arrangements to be paid by the employee.

(7) A person to whom sub-paragraph (1)(a) of this regulation applies but who was not, immediately before he was so transferred, an officer within the meaning of the Health Service Regulations and who would otherwise have become a pensionable employee in terms of regulation B2 of the 1974 Regulations shall not become a pensionable employee in terms of regulation B1 without his agreement so long as he is employed without a disqualifying break of service by a scheduled body on duties reasonably comparable to those on which he was engaged immediately before he was so transferred.

(8) In relation to a person who gave notice under regulation N12(3)(e) of the 1974 Regulations that he did not wish to avail himself of the benefits provided under those Regulations, these Regulations have effect as if they conferred on him rights corresponding with those which he would have enjoyed if he had remained subject to the provisions of the Health Service Regulations, and continue so to apply so long as he is employed without a disqualifying break of service by a scheduled body on duties reasonably comparable to those on which he was engaged immediately before he was transferred.

(9)(a) Notwithstanding anything in paragraph (3) and subject to paragraph (6), regulations D3, D11, E5, E6, E15 and E33 shall have effect in relation to a pensionable employee who had given notice under regulation N12(3)(e) of the 1974 Regulations as if–

(i) any reference to reckonable service or qualifying service included a reference to service reckonable for the purpose of determining whether any benefit is payable to or in respect of him;

(ii) any reference to a retirement pension included a reference to a pension payable to him in terms of paragraph (8);

(iii) any reference to regulation E2(1)(c) included a reference to any right conferred upon him by virtue of paragraph (8) corresponding to regulation 10(1)(a)(iv) of the Health Service Regulations; and

(iv) in regulation D3(3)(b) the reference to the appropriate superannuation fund within the meaning of regulation C12 included a reference to the employing authority under the Health Service Regulations.

(b) In the case where the conditions of entitlement mentioned in regulation E5 or E6, as modified by sub-paragraph (a)(i), are satisfied, the widow's pension payable in terms of paragraph (8) shall be payable at an annual rate of not less than the amount determined by multiplying one one hundred and sixtieth of the pensionable remuneration of her deceased husband by the length of years of the whole period of his service in contracted-out employment.

(10)(a) Notwithstanding anything in paragraph (8), in the case of a pensionable employee who has given notice under regulation N12(3)(e) of the 1974 Regulations a refund of contributions shall not be payable–

(i) if his period of reckonable service and qualifying service after 5th April 1975 is not less than 5 years, in respect of any period of reckonable service and qualifying service after that date; or

(ii) if his period of reckonable service and qualifying service commenced before 6th April 1975 and is not less than 5 years, in respect of any period of reckonable service and qualifying service after 5th April 1975 of less than 5 years unless a payment is being or has been made in respect of the period of reckonable service and qualifying service before 6th April 1975; or

(iii) if he is entitled to any right conferred upon him by virtue of regulation N12(3)(e) of the 1974 Regulations corresponding to regulation 10(1)(a)(iv) of the Health Service Regulations,

and any reference in this paragraph to reckonable service and qualifying service shall include any service reckonable for the purpose of determining whether any benefit is payable to or in respect of him.

(b) Notwithstanding anything in paragraph (3)(e) of regulation N12 of the 1974 Regulations, a pensionable employee who has given notice in terms of that paragraph shall not surrender such part of his pension as would result in that pension being reduced to–

(i) an annual rate less than an annual rate determined by multiplying one eightieth of his pensionable remuneration by the length in years of the whole period of his service in contracted-out employment; and

(ii) if he has a guaranteed minimum under section 35 of the Pensions Act in relation to that pension, but for the provisions of regulation E1, less than his guaranteed minimum pension.

Gratuities etc. granted by former local authorities

H6.   Notwithstanding the revocation of the 1974 Regulations, an authority who became responsible under regulation N6(1)(a) of those Regulations for the continued payment of a gratuity or allowance remain so responsible as if the 1974 Regulations had not been revoked.

Policy schemes

H7.   Any agreement or trust deed which immediately before 21st December 1987 had effect as mentioned in regulation N7 of the 1974 Regulations continues so to have effect, and any policy of insurance held by a scheduled body immediately before that date for the purposes mentioned in that regulation shall continue to be held by them for those purposes.

Overseas employment

H8.—(1) This regulation applies–

(a) to a person who as at 31st March 1972 was subject to the Superannuation (Local Government and Overseas Employment) Interchange (Scotland) Rules 1969(a) (in this regulation referred to as the "Rules of 1969"); or

(b) to a person who had ceased to be a contributory employee or local Act contributor before 1st April 1972 and had become so subject before the appointed day;

and shall apply to such a person who left his overseas employment and entered other overseas employment, whether or not he gave notice of the change of employment to the first fund authority or there was a break of more than 12 months between the overseas employments and who had not–

(i) again become a contributory employee or a local Act contributor, or

(ii) received any benefit under rule 6 of the Rules of 1969.

(2) Subject to paragraph (3), where a person, to whom this regulation applies, becomes a pensionable employee then, notwithstanding that there may have been a break of more than 12 months between his ceasing his overseas employment and becoming a pensionable employee, he shall be entitled–

(a) to reckon as reckonable service–

(i) any service, employment or period which immediately before he ceased to be a contributory employee in the employment of a local authority or other body he was, or for the purposes of the Regulations is treated as having been, entitled under or by virtue of the former Regulations or any other enactment to reckon as or aggregate with service he was entitled to reckon as either contributing service in relation to his employment under that body or non-contributing service for the purposes of the former Regulations, or

(ii) any service, employment or period which he would have been entitled to reckon as service (or a period of contribution) for the purpose of calculating a benefit payable to him under a local Act scheme if at the date on which he ceased to be a local Act contributor he had been entitled to a benefit payable under that scheme;

(b) to reckon as qualifying service–

(i) any service, employment or period which immediately before he so ceased he was entitled under or by virtue of the former Regulations or any other enactment to reckon either for the purpose of determining whether he was entitled to receive a benefit under the former Regulations or, as the case may be, for the purpose of determining whether he was entitled to a benefit under a local Act scheme, but for no other purpose, and

(ii) any period of overseas employment;

(c) where he gives notice in writing to the new fund authority, to aggregate the service he is entitled to reckon as reckonable or qualifying service by virtue of this regulation with any other service he is entitled to reckon as reckonable or qualifying service respectively by reason of the employment in respect of which he became a pensionable employee for the first time; and

(d) for the purpose of these Regulations to be regarded as if he had ceased to be a contributory employee or a local Act contributor immediately before 16th May 1974 and became a pensionable employee on that day but, for the purpose of observing any time limit related to the appointed day of the 1974 Regulations, the appointed day shall be taken to be the date on which he became a pensionable employee for the first time:

Provided that nothing in this paragraph shall entitle any person to reckon as reckonable service any period between the date he ceased to be a contributory employee or a local Act contributor and became for the first time a pensionable employee, or to reckon as qualifying service any period between those dates other than service in overseas employment.

(3) Paragraph (2) shall not apply to a person who has received a return of contributions from the first fund authority on or after ceasing to hold his last overseas employment unless

(a) S.I. 1969/1642.

he pays to the new fund authority an amount equal to the returned contributions (other than voluntary contributions) and compound interest thereon at a rate of three per cent per annum with half-yearly rests for a period beginning either with the date 12 months after the date on which he left overseas employment or, where this is later, the date on which he received the return of contributions and ending on the date on which he pays the said amount.

(4) Where a person gives notice in terms of paragraph (2)(c) and pays any amount required by paragraph (3) and the first fund authority and the new fund authority are not the same authority, then the first fund authority shall pay to the new fund authority a transfer value in accordance with the provisions of regulation Q2(1).

(5) Where a person to whom this regulation applies does not become a pensionable employee, then where he is, or but for the revocation of the Rules of 1969 would be, entitled to a benefit under rule 6 of the Rules of 1969 he shall, notwithstanding the revocation of the Rules of 1969, continue to be entitled to that benefit and the said benefit shall become payable without any requirement that he ceases to be in his overseas employment, but nothing in this paragraph shall entitle a person to reckon any service as reckonable service under regulation D1.

(6) Where a person to whom this regulation applies–

(a) does not become a pensionable employee,

(b) would not under the former Regulations or appropriate local Act scheme and the Rules of 1969 have had an entitlement to a benefit (other than a refund of contributions),

(c) was when he ceased to be a contributory employee or a local Act contributor entitled under the former Regulations to reckon not less than 5 years' contributing service, or not less than 5 years' service (or a period of not less than 5 years' contributions) under a local Act scheme,

(d) has attained the age of 60 years, or any lesser age at which under the conditions of service applicable to him in his overseas employment he is required by reason of age to retire from that employment,

(e) gives notice to the first fund authority, and

(f) has not received a refund of contributions, or has received a refund of contributions and either previously repaid such a refund, or within one month of giving notice under this regulation makes payment to the first fund authority of an amount equal to the refunded contributions (other than voluntary contributions) together with a like sum of interest as he would have had to pay had the repayment of refunded contributions been made under paragraph (3) of this regulation,

he shall be entitled to receive a benefit (not being a refund of contributions) calculated on the basis of the former Regulations or the appropriate local Act scheme, and the Rules of 1969 as they applied to that person at the time he ceased to be a contributory employee or a local Act contributor, but nothing in this paragraph shall entitle a person to reckon any service as reckonable service under regulation D1.

(7) This regulation shall apply to any person to whom rule 16 of the Rules of 1969 applied as if, in any paragraph other than this paragraph, there were substituted for any reference to the Rules of 1969 a reference to the Superannuation (Local Government and Overseas Employment) Interchange (Scotland) Rules 1958 (a) and for any reference to rule 6 of the Rules of 1969 a reference to rule 5 of the said Rules of 1958.

(8) Notwithstanding regulation J2(5)(d) or Part Q, where before 5th September 1984 there was paid a transfer value under Part P or Part Q of the 1974 Regulations in respect of a person to whom this regulation applies and that transfer value took no account of any additional reckonable service to which that person is entitled by virtue of this regulation, an additional transfer value shall be paid in respect of that person as regards the said additional reckonable service calculated in accordance with the provisions of Part J or Part Q as the case may be.

(9) In this regulation–

"appointed day" means 16th May 1974;

(a) S.I. 1958/1402, as amended by S.I. 1961/1156.

"contributing service" and "non-contributing service" mean the service which a person to whom this regulation applies was entitled to reckon as contributing or non-contributing service within the meaning of the Act of 1937;

"first fund authority" means the successor to the local authority administering the superannuation fund to which the person last contributed before entering overseas employment;

"new fund authority" means the local authority administering the superannuation fund to which the person contributes after first becoming a pensionable employee;

"overseas employment" means employment in the service of–

(a) the central or local government of an overseas country or a government constituted for two or more overseas countries or any Authority established for the purpose of providing or administering services which are common to, or relate to matters of common interest to, two or more overseas countries;

(b) a university or college in an overseas country;

(c) a public institution or other organisation engaged in health, welfare, research or educational services in an overseas country;

(d) an organisation receiving grants from Her Majesty's Government in connection with functions overseas;

(e) the United Nations Organisation or any of its specialised agencies or any other inter-govenmental organisation to which Her Majesty's Government may be party; or

(f) the Overseas Development Administration or any predecessor body for service overseas, being employment which is either pensionable employment within the meaning of section 17(1) of the Superannuation (Miscellaneous Provisions) Act 1948(a) or employment undertaken with the approval of the first fund authority;

"voluntary contributions" means payments made voluntarily by a contributory employee for the purpose of securing benefits for his widow, children or other dependants and payments (other than payments made in respect of a liability which has been wholly discharged) of any of the following categories–

(a) additional contributory payments of the kind referred to in section 2(3) and (4) of the Act of 1953;

(b) any similar payments made under a local Act scheme as a condition of reckoning any period of employment as service or as a period of contribution for the purposes of the scheme or where the local Act scheme provides for the reckoning of non-contributing service for the purposes of the scheme;

(c) any payments made for the purpose of increasing the length at which any period of service or of contribution would be reckonable for the purpose of calculating a benefit under a local Act scheme;

(d) any payments made in respect of added years.

PART J

INTERCHANGE ETC.

Interpretation

J1. In this Part, unless the context otherwise requires–

"Communities' scheme" means the pension scheme provided for officials and other servants of the Communities in accordance with regulations adopted by the Council of the European Communities;

"Community institution" includes a body treated as one of the Community institutions for the purposes of the Communities' scheme;

"fund authority" means–

(a) in relation to a person who became, or ceased to be, employed in his local government employment before 16th May 1974, the local authority within the meaning of the

---

(a) 1948 c.33.

Act of 1937 maintaining the superannuation fund to which the person became a contributor after he ceased to be employed in non-local government employment or, as the case may be, was last a contributor before he became employed in approved non-local government employment; and

(b) in relation to a person who became, or ceased to be, employed in his local government employment on or after 16th May 1974, the scheduled body maintaining the superannuation fund to which the person became a contributor after he ceased to be employed in non-local government employment or, as the case may be, was last a contributor before he became employed in approved non-local government employment;

"local Act authority" and "local Act scheme" have–

(a) in relation to any time before 25th March 1972, the same meanings as in the Act of 1937, and

(b) in relation to any time on or after 25th March 1972, the same meanings as in section 8 of the Act of 1972;

"local government employer", in relation to a person who is, or has been, employed in local government employment, means the body which is, or is treated as being, the employing authority or former employing authority for the purposes of the Acts of 1937 to 1953, the local Act scheme or these Regulations, as the case may be;

"pension" does not include an allowance or gratuity; and

"service" means service or employment with any employer.

Outwards transfers

J2.—(1) Subject to paragraphs (5) and (6), a transfer value shall be paid in relation to a person who has ceased to be employed in local government employment and has become employed in approved non-local government employment if the conditions in paragraph (3) are satisfied.

(2) This regulation applies even if the cessation of the local government employment, or the commencement of the approved non-local government employment, or both the cessation and the commencement, occurred before 21st December 1987.

(3) The conditions are that–

(a) he has made a written request to his fund authority for the transfer value to be paid; and

(b) subject to paragraph (4), the request was made not later than 6 months after 21st December 1987 or, if later, 6 months after the date on which he became employed in his approved non-local government employment; and

(c) the scheme managers of his approved non-local government scheme have agreed to accept the transfer value; and

(d) in the case of a person who ceased to be employed in his local government employment before 31st March 1972, his local government employer has consented to the payment of the transfer value; and

(e) in the case of a person who received a return of contributions in relation to his local government employment (other than a person falling within paragraph (6)), he has within 3 months of making his request under sub-paragraph (a) paid his fund authority for the credit of their superannuation fund–

(i) a sum equal to the contributions returned to him (together with any interest which he was paid),

(ii) a sum equal to any deduction made on account of tax under section 378(2) of the Income Tax Act 1952(**a**) or section 209(2) of the Income and Corporation Taxes Act 1970(**b**); and

(iii) compound interest on both those sums calculated in accordance with regulation J7 for the period beginning with the date on which he received the return of contributions and ending on the date of his request under sub-paragraph (a) (but no interest is to be paid if that period is less than 6 months).

(**a**) 1952 c.10.
(**b**) 1970 c.10.

(4) The local government employer may in any particular case extend the period mentioned in paragraph (3)(b).

(5) A transfer value shall not be paid in relation to a person–

(a) who has received any benefit (other than a return of contributions) under the Acts of 1937 to 1953 and the Regulations made thereunder, the former Regulations, any local Act scheme, the 1974 Regulations or these Regulations in respect of his local government employment, or

(b) who ceased to be employed in local government employment on or after 6th April 1978 having reached state pensionable age, unless his accrued pension for the purposes of Schedule 16 relates solely to service after he reached state pensionable age, or

(c) who ceased to be employed in local government employment on or after 6th April 1978 and who has become employed in approved non-local government employment (other than employment with a Community institution) which is not contracted-out employment for the purposes of the Pensions Act, unless–

(i) the person is a married woman or widow who, by virtue of an election made or treated as made for the purposes of Regulations under section 3 of the Pensions Act, is either liable to pay primary Class 1 contributions or Class 2 contributions (within the meaning of the Social Security Act 1975(a) at a reduced rate prescribed by such Regulations or is exempt from liability to pay Class 2 contributions; or

(ii) the person's reckonable service and qualifying service amounts in aggregate to less than 5 years; or

(d) in respect of whom a transfer value has been paid by the fund authority or a predecessor of that authority since he ceased to be employed in his local government employment; or

(e) who, on becoming employed in approved non-local government employment, became entitled, without any condition as to receipt of a transfer value, to reckon service in his local government employment in relation to his approved non-local government employment; or

(f) if a direction has been made in relation to his service in his local government employment under regulation C12(5) or M1 or any corresponding provision of earlier legislation or a local Act scheme.

(6) In relation to a person who ceased to be employed in local government employment on or after 6th April 1978 and has received a return of contributions in relation to that employment, a transfer value may only be paid in relation to service in respect of which he is entitled to preserved benefits.

Additional transfer value for certain persons transferring to public service pension schemes

J3.—(1) Notwithstanding regulation J2(5)(d), where after 31st March 1978 and before 5th September 1984 there has been paid in respect of a person to whom regulation F3 applies a transfer value in the calculation of which the period that he became entitled by regulation F6(1)(a) or (b) to reckon as reckonable service was not taken into account, an additional transfer value shall be paid in respect of that period.

(2) Notwithstanding regulation J2(5)(d), where a transfer value has been paid before 1st April 1978 in respect of a person in relation to whom one of the conditions in regulation F3(2)(a) to (e) is satisfied and the conditions in regulation F3(4) to (9) were satisfied at the time of payment, an additional transfer value shall be paid if the conditions in paragraph (3) are satisfied.

(3) The conditions are that–

(a) the scheme managers of a public service scheme not specified in Schedule 15–

(i) have made a written request to the fund authority for the additional transfer value to be paid, and

(ii) have given them particulars of the service (being such whole-time service as is described in regulation F2(1)) to which it is to relate, and the rate or amount,

---

(a) 1975 c.14.

as the case may be, to be used in ascertaining C of the formula set out in Part V of Schedule 16, and

(b) on payment of the additional transfer value the service to which it relates will be reckonable as service in respect of which benefits are payable under the war service provisions of the scheme.

Amount of transfer value

J4.—(1) The amount of any transfer value payable under regulation J2 and of any additional transfer value payable under regulation J3(1) shall be calculated in accordance with the provisions of Parts I to III of Schedule 16.

(2) The amount of any additional transfer value payable under regulation J3(2) shall be calculated in accordance with Part V of Schedule 16.

(3) The transfer value or additional transfer value shall be paid to the scheme managers by the fund authority out of their superannuation fund.

(4) The fund authority shall provide the scheme managers and the person to whom the transfer value or additional transfer value relates with a written notice showing how it was calculated.

(5) A notice provided to a person under paragraph (4) shall include a statement of the kind required by regulation N7(2)(c).

Termination of right to payment out of fund authority's superannuation fund

J5.   Notwithstanding anything in the Acts of 1937 to 1953 and the Regulations made thereunder, the former Regulations, any local Act scheme, the 1974 Regulations or any other provision of these Regulations (excepting regulations H8(8), J3 and J6), where a transfer value is to be or has been paid under regulation J2 no other payment or transfer of assets shall, subject to regulations H8(8), J3 and J6, be made out of the superannuation fund on account of the service to which the transfer value relates.

Rights where a person transfers to the Communities' scheme and leaves without a right to either an immediate or prospective pension

J6.—(1) Where a person–

(a) became employed by a Community institution and became a participant in the Communities' scheme after having been employed in local government employment, and

(b) the scheme managers of the Communities' scheme were paid a transfer value under regulation J2 in relation to his previous service in local government employment, and

(c) he ceased to be employed in his employment with the Community institution without the right to an immediate or prospective pension, and

(d) his fund authority has been paid for the credit of their superannuation fund–

(i) a sum equal to the amount of the transfer value which the scheme managers received, and

(ii) compound interest on that sum calculated in accordance with regulation J7 for the period beginning with the date on which the transfer value was received by the scheme managers and ending on the date on which the fund authority was paid the sum required by (i) above (but no interest is to be paid if that period is less than 6 months),

the person and those claiming through him shall be entitled to the rights specified in paragraphs (2) and (3) below and nothing in regulation J5 shall apply to any such rights unless a transfer value under regulation J4 is subsequently paid.

(2) Where the person ceased to be employed in his local government employment before 31st March 1972, he and those claiming through him shall have the same rights (other than to a refund of contributions) as they would have had by virtue of the Acts of 1937 to 1953 and the Regulations made thereunder, the former Regulations, any local Act scheme and these Regulations (so far as applicable) if–

    (a) he had reached the age of 65 by the termination of his local government employment, and

    (b) he had been able to reckon 10 years' service, and

    (c) the payment of the transfer value had not been requested or made.

(3) Where the person ceased to be employed in his local government employment on or after 31st March 1972, he and those claiming through him shall be entitled to the like benefits (other than to a return of contributions) as those which–

    (a) if, on so ceasing, he had became entitled to benefits under Part E other than a pension under regulation E1 or E2(2)(a) or a local Act scheme, would have become payable to or in respect of him under that Part or that scheme in respect of service for which the transfer value mentioned in paragraph (1) above was paid if this Part had not applied to him, or

    (b) if, on so ceasing, he had not become so entitled, would have become payable to or in respect of him under Part E or a local Act scheme in respect of such service as aforesaid if, immediately before he ceased that employment, he had been entitled to reckon an aggregate of 5 years' reckonable service and qualifying service or 5 years' service for the purpose of determining whether he was entitled to a benefit under a local Act scheme and if this Part had not applied to him,

and such benefits shall be deemed to be benefits under regulation E2(1)(c).

(4) This regulation shall not confer any right to the payment of any benefit for any period ending on or before–

    (a) in relation to a person who ceased to be employed in his local government employment before 31st March 1972, the date on which he ceased to be employed in the service of the Community institution mentioned in paragraph (1) above or, where this is later, the earliest date at which, if he had remained in his local government employment without any break of service and become a pensionable employee on 16th May 1974, he would have become entitled, on ceasing to be employed, to a retirement pension by virtue of sub-paragraph (a) or, as the case may be, (b)(ii) of regulation E2(1); and

    (b) in relation to a person who ceased to be employed in his local government employment on or after 31st March 1972, the date on which he ceased to be employed in the service of the Community institution mentioned in paragraph (1) above or, where this is later, the date on which the benefits to which he became entitled on ceasing to be employed in his local government employment or, as the case may be, to which he would have become so entitled if, immediately before he ceased to be employed in that employment, he had been entitled to reckon an aggregate of 5 years' reckonable service and qualifying service would, if this Part had not applied to him, have become payable to him under Part E.

(5) For the purposes of this regulation references to those claiming through a person shall be construed as references to his widow, dependants, children and executors so far as is appropriate in his particular case.

Compound interest on certain sums

J7. Compound interest under regulations J2(3)(e)(iii) and J6(1)(d)(ii) and Parts I (paragraph 1(2)) and V of Schedule 16 is to be calculated–

    (a) at the rate of 6 per cent with yearly rests for each complete period of a year ending before 1st April 1977 (and any residual period of less than a year is to be ignored), and

    (b) at the rate of $2\frac{1}{4}$ per cent with 3-monthly rests for each complete period of 3 months beginning after 31st March 1977 (and any residual period of less than 3 months is to be ignored).

Inward transfers

J8.—(1) Subject to paragraphs (5) and (6), a transfer value offered to a person's fund authority by the scheme managers of his previous non-local government scheme shall be accepted by them and shall, together with the amount of any limited revaluation premium under section 45 of the Pensions Act repaid to the fund authority by the Secretary of State, be credited to their superannuation fund if the conditions specified in paragraph (3) are satisfied.

(2) This regulation applies even if the cessation of the non-local government employment, or the commencement of the local government employment, or both the cessation and commencement, occurred before 21st December 1987.

(3) The conditions are that–

(a) except where the transfer value is offered as mentioned in paragraph (5)(a) and is in respect of such a period as is mentioned in paragraph (5)(b), or relates only to service reckonable under the war service provisions of a public service scheme, he has made a written request to his fund authority for the transfer value to be accepted, and

(b) subject to paragraph (4), the request was made not later than 6 months after 21st December 1987 or, if later, 6 months after the date on which he became employed in his local government employment, and

(c) the transfer value is not offered on conditions which are inconsistent with the provisions of these Regulations, and

(d) his local government employer has consented to the transfer value being accepted, except in the case of a person who became employed in his local government employment on or after 6th April 1978 and who ceased to be employed in his non-local government employment on or after 31st March 1972, and

(e) in the case of a person who became employed in his local government employment before 31st March 1972, he was employed in local government employment on that date.

(4) The local government employer may in any particular case extend the period mentioned in paragraph (3)(b).

(5) A transfer value which–

(a) is offered by the scheme managers of a public service scheme in relation to a person in relation to whom a transfer value was accepted and received before 1st April 1978, and

(b) is in respect of a period which could, if he had not ceased to be employed in his non-local government employment, have become reckonable under the war service provisions of the scheme,

shall not be accepted unless it is one calculated in accordance with Part V of Schedule 16.

(6) A transfer value under paragraph (1) shall not be accepted in relation to a person if–

(a) his non-local government employment was contracted-out employment for the purposes of the Pensions Act, and

(b) his non-local government scheme was not a statutory scheme or a scheme which is to be treated for the purposes of Schedule 17 as being a statutory scheme, and

(c) the transfer value would not secure a resultant pension calculated under paragraph (7) at least equal to–

(i) the annual equivalent of his guaranteed minimum in respect of service to which the transfer value relates, and

(ii) where equivalent pension benefits were, but would not remain, assured by his non-local government scheme, the annual rate of those benefits.

(7) A person's resultant pension shall be calculated in accordance with the formula–

$$R = \frac{N}{80} \times S, \text{ where–}$$

R is the annual amount of the resultant pension,

N is the reckonable service (expressed in years and fractions of a year) which would, apart from paragraph (5), be credited to him under regulation J9(1)(a) if the transfer value were to be accepted by the fund authority, and

S is the annual rate of his remuneration on becoming employed in his local government employment (if he is paid weekly, the annual rate shall be calculated by multiplying the weekly rate by 52.18).

(8) A person's guaranteed minimum shall be calculated in accordance with section 35 of the Pensions Act and the annual equivalent shall be calculated by multiplying the guaranteed minimum by 52.18.

Right to reckon service

J9.—(1) Where a transfer value (other than one to which regulation J8(5) applies) has been accepted in relation to a person under regulation J8—

(a) he shall, subject to regulation J10, be entitled to reckon as reckonable service a period calculated in accordance with Schedule 17 for all purposes of these Regulations except that of determining whether there is any entitlement to benefit (other than any benefit under regulation E2(2)), and

(b) he shall be entitled to reckon as qualifying service any service to which the transfer value relates which would not otherwise be qualifying service.

(2) A period reckonable under paragraph (1)(a) shall be treated as reckonable service after 31st March 1972 for the purposes of making any calculation under these Regulations.

(3) Service reckonable under paragraph (1)(b) shall count at its actual length.

(4) The fund authority shall provide the person with a written notice stating the periods of service which he is entitled to reckon under paragraph (1)(a) and (b) and, in the case of a person who became employed in his local government employment before 1st April 1980, whether or not his retirement pension is subject to reduction under regulation J12.

(5) A notice under paragraph (4) shall contain a statement of the kind required by regulation N7(2)(c).

Adjustment to crediting of reckonable service and qualifying service on payment of refund of contributions

J10. Where a person on ceasing local government employment has received a return of contributions in relation to part only of the service which, but for the provisions of this regulation, he would be entitled to reckon as reckonable service under regulation J9, that reckonable service which he would otherwise be so entitled to reckon shall be reduced by X years, where X is a period expressed in years and fractions of a year in accordance with the following formula—

$$X = \frac{A}{B} \times C, \text{where}-$$

A is the length of service in the non-local government scheme which reckoned for the purpose of determining whether he was entitled to a benefit thereunder in respect of which contributions were returned by the fund authority on his ceasing local government employment;

B is the service which he is entitled to reckon under regulation J9(1)(b); and

C is the period he would, but for the provisions of this regulation, be entitled to reckon as reckonable service under regulation J9(1)(a).

Computation of contributions

J11.—(1) Where a person to whom regulation J8 applies ceases to be employed in his local government employment in circumstances in which there is payable to him under regulation C12(4) an amount by way of return of contributions (with or without interest), then, in calculating that amount, the amount of the contributions paid by him shall be deemed to be increased by the aggregate of the following two sums:—

(i) if his non-local government scheme contains provision for return of contributions, such sum as would have been payable by way of a return of contributions, including interest (if any), under his non-local government scheme at the date of payment of the transfer value received under regulation J8(1) had that transfer value not been paid, and

(ii) such sum as was paid by him by way of superannuation contributions during the period which has become reckonable as reckonable service under regulation J9 which has not been taken into account under sub-paragraph (i).

(2) Where under regulation C12(4) the amount payable by way of return of contributions is a sum equal to the amount of a person's contributions with compound interest thereon, compound interest shall also be payable on the amount by which those contributions are increased under paragraph (1) above, calculated in the manner described in regulation C12(4)(b) in respect of the period from the date of payment of the transfer value.

(3) Notwithstanding anything previously contained in this regulation, the sum by which contributions are increased under paragraph (1) above shall not include any sum in respect of contributions which were returned to and retained by the person who had paid them.

National Insurance modification

J12.—(1) The retirement pension of a person to whom regulation J9 applies shall be reduced in accordance with paragraph (2) where–

(a) he became employed in his local government employment before 1st April 1980, and

(b) on becoming employed in his local government employment he did not enjoy unmodified status for the purposes of Part F of the 1974 Regulations, and

(c) his retirement pension is calculated by reference to reckonable service which includes the period which he is entitled to reckon under regulation J9(1)(a).

(2) Regulation F7 of the 1974 Regulations shall be taken to have applied in relation to the period which he is entitled to reckon under regulation J9(1)(a) as if–

(a) during that period he had been a person within Case B of Part F of the 1974 Regulations, and

(b) that period were service after 31st August 1947.

(3) Where a person to whom paragraph (1)(a) applies was in his non-local government employment subject to a statutory scheme under which he was subject to a reduction of pension in connection with graduated retirement benefit under section 36 of the Insurance Act, any retirement pension payable to him at the termination of his local government employment shall be reduced by the amount by which his pension under that scheme would have been reduced in connection as aforesaid.

(4) The reduction shall take effect on the date when a retirement pension becomes payable unless the person has not then reached pensionable age within the meaning of the Social Security Act 1975, in which case the reduction shall take effect on the date on which he reaches that age.

Certain persons who become subject to certain other superannuation schemes

J13.—(1) Subject to the conditions in paragraph (2) being satisfied, this regulation applies to a person–

(a) who either–

(i) is in the employment of a passenger transport executive by virtue of which he is a pensionable employee; or

(ii) is in the employment of a body (other than a scheduled body) mentioned in regulation B5 by virtue of which he is deemed to be a pensionable employee; or

(iii) is in the employment of a body mentioned in paragraph (8) of regulation B6 and by virtue of an agreement made, or continued in force as if made, under that regulation is in that employment entitled to participate in the benefits of a superannuation fund maintained under Part P; and

(b) for whose superannuation in that employment that body can make other provision under an approved non-local government scheme.

(2) The conditions referred to in paragraph (1) are that–

(a) the person shall notify the body in whose employment he is as mentioned in paragraph (1)(a) and the appropriate administering authority in writing that he desires this regulation to apply to him; and

(b) that body and that authority shall consent to the application to him of this regulation.

(3) A person to whom this regulation applies–

(a) shall not, on and after the date on which he becomes subject in the employment mentioned in paragraph (1)(a) to an approved non-local government scheme, in that employment be liable to contribute to the appropriate superannuation fund; and

(b) shall be treated for the purposes of these Regulations (other than regulation C12 and, in the case of a person to whom regulation J14 applies, regulation J2) as if he had ceased to hold that employment on the day immediately before that date.

(4) In this regulation, for the purpose of giving on or after 21st December 1987 a notification under paragraph (2), "approved non-local government scheme" means such a scheme which is a contracted-out scheme within the meaning of the Pensions Act.

Transfer of rights of persons to whom regulation J13 applies

J14.—(1) Where–

(a) regulation J13 applies to a person; and

(b) on the date on which he becomes subject to the approved non-local government scheme he has not reached pensionable age within the meaning of the Social Security Act 1975(**a**); and

(c) he gives written notice to the appropriate administering authority that he wishes to transfer his rights under these Regulations to the approved non-local government scheme; and

(d) both the appropriate administering authority and the body by whom he is employed have given their consent,

the appropriate administering authority shall, subject to paragraphs (3), (4) and (5), pay to the scheme managers of the approved non-local government scheme out of the superannuation fund a transfer value calculated in accordance with Schedule 16.

(2) The appropriate administering authority shall not give their consent under paragraph (1)(d) unless they are satisfied that the person transferring his rights will acquire rights under the approved non-local government scheme at least equivalent to those which he would have obtained if a transfer value had been paid to the scheme managers under regulation J2 or J3.

(3) If–

(a) the number of persons transferring their rights under paragraph (1) from a particular superannuation fund to the same or a different approved non-local government scheme as part of the same transfer scheme is more than 9 but less than 100; and

(b) the superannuation fund's assets immediately before any transfer takes place are not adequate, or are more than adequate, to meet the accrued actuarial liabilities of the fund at that time,

the total payable under paragraph (1) (or, as the case may be, the respective totals) shall be adjusted by an actuary appointed by the administering authority to the extent he considers appropriate in the circumstances, subject to the agreement of that authority and the scheme managers.

(4) If the parties are unable to agree on the adjustment to be made under paragraph (3), the adjustment (if any) to be made shall be decided by an actuary appointed by the Secretary of State.

(5) If the number of persons transferring their rights under paragraph (1) from a particular superannuation fund to the same or a different approved non-local government scheme as part of the same transfer scheme is 100 or more–

(a) no payment shall be made under that paragraph; and

(b) the superannuation fund shall be apportioned in accordance with Schedule 18.

(6) Notwithstanding anything in the Acts of 1937 to 1953 and the Regulations made thereunder, the former Regulations, any local Act scheme, the 1974 Regulations or any provision of these Regulations, where a payment or transfer of assets is to be or has been made under this regulation or under Schedule 18, no other payment or transfer of assets shall be made out of the superannuation fund on account of service or employment to which the payment or transfer of assets under this regulation or under Schedule 18 relates.

(**a**) 1975 c.14.

(7) A person to whom this regulation applies shall be treated for the purposes of this regulation and of Schedule 18 as if a transfer value had been paid in terms of these Regulations on the day on which he becomes subject to the approved non-local government scheme.

(8) For the purposes of this regulation, a transfer scheme is a scheme, agreed between the scheme managers, the appropriate administering authority and, if different, the employing authority, providing for the transfer of rights under this regulation of a number of employees.

(9) In this regulation "accrued actuarial liabilities" means the actual and potential liabilities of the fund in connection with any service or employment before any transfer takes place.

PART K

GRATUITIES

Interpretation

K1. In this Part, unless the context otherwise requires–

"annual pay" means the remuneration received by an employee in respect of his employment with an employing authority during the final year of his employment, except that if the annual remuneration in either of the two consecutive preceding years was higher, then the pay received in either of those years, whichever is the greater, shall be deemed to be the annual pay received by the employee in the final year of his employment with an employing authority;

"benefits" means any allowance or lump sum payable under this Part;

"employing authority" means a scheduled body or the Scottish Special Housing Association in whose employment the employee was immediately before he ceased to be employed under the terms of regulation K2;

"lower earnings limit" means the lower earnings limit prescribed for the purposes of section 4(1) of the Social Security Act 1975(**a**) applying at the time the employee ceases to be employed or, if earlier, at the end of the period used to determine annual pay;

"relevant policy scheme" means the Federated Superannuation System for Universities or the Federated Superannuation Scheme for Nurses and Hospital Officers or a scheme which the Secretary of State approved for the purposes of regulation P13 of the 1974 Regulations or approved under rule 3 or 3A of the Superannuation (Policy and Local Government Schemes) Interchange (Scotland) Rules 1948 to 1971(**b**) or a scheme to which any person contributed by reason of regulation N12(2) of the 1974 Regulations;

"upper earnings limit" means the upper earnings limit prescribed for the purposes of section 4(1) of the Social Security Act 1975 applying at the time the employee ceases to be employed or, if earlier, at the end of the period used to determine annual pay;

"war service" means 50% of any period after 2nd September 1939 and before 30th June 1950 during which the employee concerned was over 18 years of age and was serving in the armed forces of the Crown, the merchant navy or mercantile marine, or in any of the women's services specified in Schedule 14 and after which the employee concerned before 1st July 1950 entered the employment of an employing authority and remained in the employment of such a body, without there having been a continuous period of 12 months or more during which he was not employed by an employing authority, but does not include any war service of a kind specified in regulation F2(1) or taken into account for the purposes of Part F of these Regulations.

Persons to whom Part K applies

K2.—(1) This Part shall apply to an employee who ceases to be employed by an employing authority and who–

(a) has not attained the age of 60 but has completed not less than 5 years' service; or

---

(**a**) Section 4(1) was amended by the Social Security Pensions Act 1975 (c.60), Schedule 4, Part I, paragraph 36(a).
(**b**) S.I. 1948/1462, 1955/982, 1971/1879.

(b) has not attained the age of 60 but has completed not less than one year's service and is incapable of discharging efficiently the duties of that employment by reason of permanent ill-health or infirmity of mind or body; or

(c) has attained age 60 and completed not less than one year's service;

and, where an employee dies while in the employment of an employing authority, to his widow or any other dependant provided that the employee was a person to whom this regulation would have applied had he remained in service to age 60, or where at the time of his death his age exceeded 60 and he had completed at least one year's service.

(2) With consent of the Secretary of State this Part may apply to a former employee of an employing authority or to the widow or any other dependant of such an employee.

Payment of benefit

K3.—(1) An employing authority may pay to any person to whom this Part applies a benefit of an amount not exceeding that determined in accordance with regulation K4.

(2) Any benefit payable under paragraph (1) may take the form of–

(a) a lump sum; or

(b) an annuity, the capital value of which does not exceed the amount payable under paragraph (1).

(3) Where an employing authority have granted a benefit to an employee under paragraph (1) by way of an annuity, and the employee dies before receiving an aggregate amount equal to the capital value of the annuity, the authority may grant a benefit to the widow or any other dependant of the employee and for that purpose regulation K2 shall have effect as if the employee had died while in the employment of the authority but as if for the amount specified in paragraph (2) there were substituted the difference between the capital value of the annuity and the aggregate amount of the payments made to the employee before his death.

Calculation of benefit

K4.—(1) Where an employing authority have granted a benefit in respect of an employee under regulation K3, subject to paragraph (2) the amount of that benefit shall not exceed the aggregate of–

(a) 5% of his annual pay for each year of service, including war service, prior to 1st April 1986 with an employing authority in respect of which he is not entitled to receive a benefit under a public service scheme; and

(b) 5% of either his annual pay or the lower earnings limit, whichever is the lower, for each year of service after 31st March 1986 with an employing authority in respect of which–

(i) he is not entitled to receive a benefit under a public service scheme; and

(ii) he, not having attained the age of 55 on 1st April 1986, could not have exercised an option under regulations B2, B3, B4(1) or B4(4); and

(c) 5% of the excess of his annual pay over the upper earnings limit for each year of service after 1st April 1986 with an employing authority in respect of which–

(i) he was not entitled to receive a benefit under a public service scheme; and

(ii) he, not having attained the age of 55 on 1st April 1986, could not have exercised an option under regulations B2, B3, B4(1) or B4(4).

(2) For the purposes of this regulation–

(a) no account shall be taken of service before the age of 18 and after attaining the age of 70;

(b) no account shall be taken of service for which a payment has been made under the Act of 1953, the former Regulations, the 1974 Regulations or this Part of these Regulations;

(c) no account shall be taken of service after 1st April 1986 for which a return of contributions under the terms of regulation C12 has been made;

(d) no account shall be taken of service for which the employee has rights in a relevant policy scheme;

(e) no account shall be taken of service exceeding 40 years in total and, where actual service exceeds 40 years, the period of service after 1st April 1986 shall be reduced by that excess; and

(f) no payment under this regulation shall exceed an amount equal to twice annual pay.

Financial

K5. Any benefit under this Part shall not be paid out of the superannuation fund.

PART L

INJURY ALLOWANCES ETC.

Interpretation

L1. In this Part, unless the context otherwise requires–

"benefits" means any allowance or lump sum payable under this Part;

"relevant body" has the meaning given by regulation L7; and

"relevant employment" has the meaning given by regulation L2(2).

Persons to whom Part L applies

L2.—(1) Subject to paragraph (4), this Part applies to a person employed in a relevant employment if he–

(a) sustains an injury, or

(b) contracts a disease,

as a result of anything he was required to do in carrying out his work.

(2) "Relevant employment" is employment, otherwise than as a teacher, with a body specified in Part I of Schedule 3 or in Part II of that Schedule or the predecessor of such a body, and for the purposes of this Part a police cadet appointed under section 8 of the Police (Scotland) Act 1967(**a**) shall be deemed to be in employment with the police authority who maintain the police force with which he is undergoing training.

(3) A person is to be treated for the purpose of paragraph (1) as having sustained an injury as mentioned in that paragraph if–

(a) he sustains the injury while travelling by vehicle as a passenger with the express or implied permission of his employer to or from his place of work, and

(b) at the time of the injury the vehicle was being operated, otherwise than in the course of a public transport service, by or on behalf of his employer or pursuant to arrangements made by his employer.

(4) This Part does not apply where the injury or disease is one in respect of which the person is entitled to an injury award under a scheme made in accordance with section 26 of the Fire Services Act 1947(**b**) or is entitled to injury benefits under Regulations made in accordance with section 27 of the Police (Scotland) Act 1967.

Loss of employment through permanent incapacity

L3.—(1) If, as a result of an incapacity which is likely to be permanent caused by the injury or disease, a person to whom this Part applies ceases to be employed in a relevant employment (whether or not it is the same employment as that in which the injury or disease was sustained or contracted), he shall be entitled to an annual allowance.

(2) The allowance is to be paid by the relevant body and is to be of such amount as the body may from time to time determine.

(**a**) 1967 c.77.
(**b**) 1947 c.41.

(3) The relevant body may suspend or discontinue the allowance if the person becomes capable of working again.

(4) The allowance shall not exceed 85 per cent of the person's annual rate of remuneration in respect of the employment when he ceased to be employed.

(5) In ascertaining for the purposes of paragraph (4) a person's annual rate of remuneration in respect of the employment when he ceased to be employed–

(a) the annual rate of any fluctuating element of his remuneration is to be estimated by reference to an average taken over a representative period;

(b) the annual rate of any benefit in kind included in his remuneration is to be the estimated annual value of the benefit in kind at the date on which he ceased to be employed;

(c) if at that date he had no remuneration or his remuneration was reduced because of absence from duty, the annual rate is to be taken to be the annual rate which would have applied if he had not been absent;

(d) if at that date he was entitled to an allowance under regulation L4 by reason of a reduction in his remuneration, whether as a result of the same or of some other injury or disease, the annual rate is to be taken to be the annual rate which would have applied if his remuneration had not been reduced;

(e) if his remuneration is retrospectively altered as a result of a pay award, the annual rate of his remuneration is to be based on the retrospective pay award; and

(f) if his remuneration is not calculated by reference to an annual rate but by reference to some other rate, the annual rate is to be derived from the applicable rate at the date on which he ceased to be employed.

(6) In determining the amount of the allowance the relevant body is to have regard to all the circumstances of the case, including the matters specified in regulation L8.

Reduction in remuneration

L4.—(1) If as a result of the injury or disease to a person to whom this Part applies that person suffers a reduction in his remuneration while he is employed in relevant employment (whether or not it is the same employment as that in which the injury or disease was sustained or contracted) and regulation L3 does not apply, he shall be entitled to an allowance while the reduction continues.

(2) A person's remuneration is to be treated for the purposes of paragraph (1) as reduced if at any time it is lower than it would have been but for the injury or disease.

(3) The allowance is to be paid by the relevant body and is to be of such amount as the body may from time to time determine.

(4) The amount of the allowance, together with the person's remuneration in the relevant employment, is not in any year to exceed the remuneration he would have been paid if he had not sustained or contracted the injury or disease.

(5) In determining the amount of an allowance under this regulation the relevant body is to have regard to all the circumstances of the case, including the matters specified in regulation L8.

Allowances for pensioners

L5.—(1) If on ceasing to be employed in a relevant employment a person becomes entitled under regulation E2 to receive payments in respect of an annual retirement pension and–

(a) immediately before ceasing to be so employed he was entitled to an allowance under regulation L4, and

(b) on ceasing to be so employed he does not become entitled to an allowance under regulation L3, and

(c) regulation E22(4) does not apply,

the relevant body may pay him an allowance under this regulation.

(2) An allowance under this regulation–

(a) is not in any year to exceed the amount by which the annual rate of the retirement pension falls short of what it would have been if the amount of the allowance paid under regulation L4 during the relevant period (within the meaning of regulation E22(2)) had been part of his remuneration in the relevant employment, and

(b) continues for such period as the relevant body may determine.

Death benefits

L6.—(1) If a person to whom this Part applies dies as a result of the injury or disease–

(a) if he leaves a widow who qualifies under paragraph (2), she shall be entitled to an annual allowance or lump sum, and

(b) if he leaves a dependant, the dependant shall be eligible for an annual allowance or lump sum.

(2) A widow qualifies for an annual allowance or lump sum unless–

(a) her marriage to the person in question took place after he ceased to be employed in relevant employment and he was not subsequently employed in such employment; or

(b) at the date of death she was judicially separated or cohabiting with another man.

(3) The allowance or lump sum is to be paid by the relevant body and is to be of such amount as the body may from time to time determine or, as the case may be, may determine.

(4) In determing the amount of any allowance or lump sum the relevant body is to have regard to all the circumstances of the case, including the matters specified in regulation L8.

(5) An allowance to a widow shall cease if she remarries or cohabits with another man, but if she again becomes a widow or the marriage is dissolved or she no longer cohabits with a man the relevant body may restore the allowance for such period as they may determine.

(6) An allowance to a dependant shall continue for such period as the relevant body may determine.

(7) This regulation shall apply with necessary modifications to a widower who at the date of his wife's death is permanently incapacitated by reason of ill-health or infirmity of mind or body and wholly or mainly dependent on her.

The relevant body

L7.—(1) The relevant body for the purposes of this Part is–

(a) the body by whom the person in question was employed immediately before he first qualifies for any benefit under this Part; or

(b) if he dies without qualifying for any benefit under this Part, the body which last employed him in a relevant employment before his death; or

(c) if the body specified in sub-paragraph (a) or (b) has ceased to exist, the body to which he would have been transferred if he had continued in the employment in question.

(2) Any question arising under paragraph (1)(c) as to the identity of the body to which the person would have been transferred shall be determined by the Secretary of State.

Rights and payments to be taken into account in determining amount of benefit

L8. In determining the amount of any benefit under this Part the relevant body is to have regard to–

(a) any right to benefit under Chapter IV or Chapter V of Part II of the Social Security Act 1975 or corresponding provisions of earlier enactments;

(b) any other statutory right to benefit or compensation:

(c) any right to receive superannuation benefit (whether payable under an enactment or otherwise) out of any fund to which any body which employed him in relevant employment has made any contributions in respect of him or out of any fund to which assets of any such fund were transferred; and

(d) any damages recovered, and any sum received by virtue of a contract of insurance.

Retrospective effect

L9.—(1) Subject to the following provisions of this regulation, this Part applies even if the injury or disease was sustained or contracted before 21st December 1987.

(2) Regulation L3, L4, L5 or L6, as the case may be, does not apply if the relevant event occurred before 31st March 1972 but, subject to the following provisions of this regulation, does apply if the relevant event occurred on or after that date and before 21st December 1987.

(3) For regulations L3 and L5 the relevant event is the cessation of the employment, for regulation L4 it is the reduction of remuneration and for regulation L6 it is the death of the employee.

(4) If adequate provision has already been made for the person in question under regulation 7 of the Benefits Regulations or the 1974 Regulations, this Part does not apply to him.

(5) If regulation L3, L4, L5 or L6 applies in any case by virtue of paragraph (2) and paragraph (4) does not apply, the relevant body shall decide what benefit, if any, is to be granted in accordance with the applicable regulation for any past or future period but in making that decision they shall take into account any allowance to which the person is or was entitled under regulation 7 of the Benefits Regulations.

(6) For the purpose of this Part any injury benefit payable under Part S of the 1974 Regulations shall be treated as if it had been paid under this Part.

Finance

L10. Benefits under this Part are not to be met out of any superannuation fund.

Appeals

L11. Regulation N8(3)(b) shall not apply to this Part.

Notice of decisions

L12. The relevant body shall give notice in writing of any decision relating to any benefit under this Part to the person affected and shall inform him about his right of appeal under regulation N8 and the time in which it must be exercised.

PART M

FORFEITURE ETC.

Forfeiture of rights

M1.—(1) If–
  (a) a person has been convicted of an offence in connection with an employment in which he was a pensionable employee, and
  (b) he has (whether before or after the conviction) ceased to hold that employment in consequence of that offence, and
  (c) on an application made within 3 months after the conviction by the body who were his employing authority in that employment, the Secretary of State has certified that the offence either was gravely injurious to the State or is liable to lead to serious loss of confidence in the public service,

that body may direct that all or any of the rights enjoyed by or in respect of him under these Regulations with respect to his previous service shall, subject to paragraphs (2) and (5), be forfeited.

(2) Unless the person ceased to hold his employment in consequence of–
  (a) an offence of treason, or
  (b) one or more offences under the Official Secrets Acts 1911 to 1939(**a**) for which he has been sentenced on the same occasion to a term of imprisonment of, or to two or more consecutive terms amounting in the aggregate to, at least 10 years,

---

(**a**) 1911 c.28, 1920 c.75, 1939 c.121.

no direction may be given under paragraph (1) which would deprive him of his guaranteed minimum pension or would, in the event of his leaving a widow, deprive her of her widow's guaranteed minimum pension.

(3) If–

(a) a person has ceased to hold an employment in which he was a pensionable employee in consequence of an offence in connection with his employment, and

(b) the body who were his employing authority have neither notified a decision under Part N on any question as to entitlement to a benefit nor given any direction under paragraph (1),

the appropriate administering authority shall if so directed by that body make interim payments to any person specified by them who would be entitled to receive payment of a benefit under these Regulations if no direction under paragraph (1) were given.

(4) Directions under paragraph (3) may be given from time to time and–

(a) must specify the amounts to be paid and the persons to whom they are to be paid,

(b) must not require any person to be paid more than he would for the time being be entitled to have been paid on the assumption that no direction under paragraph (1) were given, and

(c) do not constitute decisions under Part N as to any person's entitlement to a benefit.

(5) Payments made to a person in accordance with directions under paragraph (3) shall, notwithstanding any direction given under paragraph (1) or any decision under Part N as to entitlement, be deemed to have been payments in respect of a benefit to which he was entitled.

(6) A body making an application to the Secretary of State for a certificate under paragraph (1)(c) shall at the same time send copies of the application to the person concerned and to the appropriate administering authority.

Transfer of certain sums from the superannuation fund

M2.—(1) This regulation applies where–

(a) a person ("the former employee") has ceased to hold an employment in which he was a pensionable employee in consequence of–

(i) an offence of a fraudulent character, or

(ii) grave misconduct,

in connection with that employment, and

(b) the body who were his employing authority in that employment ("the former employing authority") have suffered direct financial loss by reason of the offence or misconduct.

(2) Where this regulation applies and the former employing authority are an administering authority, they may take out an appropriate amount from their superannuation fund.

(3) Where this regulation applies and the former employing authority are not an administering authority, the appropriate administering authority shall pay them an appropriate amount out of the superannuation fund if requested to do so.

(4) An appropriate amount is an amount which does not exceed the lesser of–

(a) the amount of the direct financial loss, or

(b) the amount of any contributions which could have, but have not, been returned to the former employee, or paid to his spouse or a dependant, under regulation C12(4)(a).

(5) If after making a payment under paragraph (3) the administering authority are required to pay a transfer value in respect of the former employee, the former employing authority shall repay them the amount of that payment if requested to do so.

Recovery or retention by employing authority of certain sums from the superannuation fund

M3.—(1) This regulation applies where a person ("the former employee")–

(a) has ceased to hold an employment, in which he was a pensionable employee, in consequence of a criminal, negligent or fraudulent act or omission on his part in connection with that employment, and

(b) has incurred some monetary obligation, arising out of that act or omission, to the body who were his employing authority in that employment ("the former employing authority").

(2) Where this regulation applies, the former employing authority may recover or retain out of the appropriate superannuation fund an amount which (subject to any different agreement in writing between them and the former employee) does not exceed the lesser of–

(a) the amount of the monetary obligation, or

(b) the actuarial value, at the time of the recovery or retention, of all rights enjoyed by or in respect of the former employee under these Regulations with respect to his previous service, other than rights enjoyed by virtue of the receipt of a transfer value from the scheme managers of a non-local government scheme.

(3) The former employing authority shall give the former employee not less than 3 months' notice of the amount to be recovered or retained under paragraph (2).

(4) The former employee is entitled to a certificate from the former employing authority showing the amount retained under paragraph (2), the manner in which it is calculated, and the effect of the recovery or retention on his benefits or prospective benefits.

(5) In the event of any dispute as to the amount to be recovered or retained under paragraph (2), the former employing authority are not entitled to recover or retain any amount except after the monetary obligation has become enforceable under an order of a competent court or the award of an arbiter.

PART N

DECISIONS AND APPEALS

Initial decisions

N1.—(1) Any question concerning–

(a) the rights or liabilities under these Regulations of an employee, or a person claiming to be treated as an employee, of a scheduled body, or

(b) the rights under these Regulations of a person who has been an employee of a scheduled body, or of his widow, dependants or executors, or

(c) the rights of any person under Part F (war service),

shall be decided in the first instance by the body concerned.

(2) Where the body by whom any such question falls to be decided is ascertainable by reference to regulations N2 to N6, that body is for the purposes of this regulation and of regulation N8 (appeals) the body concerned.

(3) A decision by the body concerned does not bind any other scheduled body or the Secretary of State.

Decisions by employing authorities as to status of employees

N2.—(1) In relation to every employment under them of each of their employees a scheduled body are to decide–

(a) whether the employee is an officer or a manual worker,

(b) whether he is a whole-time, a variable-time or a part-time employee,

(c) whether he has undergone to their satisfaction any medical examination required under regulation B1(11), and

(d) whether or not he is a pensionable employee.

(2) If the body decide that a person is a pensionable employee in any employment they shall also decide–

(a) which of his emoluments are remuneration on which contributions are payable, and

(b) if he is a part-time employee, the proportion which his contractual minimum hours of employment in each week bear to those of a comparable whole-time employee.

(3) The questions specified in paragraph (1) and, where applicable, paragraph (2) are to be decided–

- (a) within 3 months after the person enters the employment, and
- (b) as soon as is reasonably practicable after–
  - (i) any statutory resolution is passed by the body for the purposes of regulation B1(5),
  - (ii) any change occurs in the number of his regular or usual hours of employment, or
  - (iii) any other change occurs in or in relation to the employment,

  which is material for the purposes of these Regulations.

Decisions by administering authorities as to status of employees

N3.—(1) In relation to any employment in which a person is a pensionable employee the appropriate administering authority are to decide–

- (a) what previous service or employment (if any) he is entitled to reckon–
  - (i) as reckonable service, and
  - (ii) as qualifying service,
- (b) whether it includes any, and if so what, periods of service as a part-time employee,
- (c) what proportion of whole-time service his service during any such period represents,
- (d) whether a payment in lieu of contributions has been made or equivalent pension benefits have been assured under Part III of the Insurance Act in respect of any period of non-participating employment,
- (e) the amount of any payment in lieu of contributions,
- (f) what rate of contribution the employee is liable to pay to the appropriate superannuation fund, and
- (g) whether he is entitled to reckon as reckonable service–
  - (i) any, and if so how many, added years, or
  - (ii) any, and if so what, additional period.

(2) The questions specified in paragraph (1) are to be decided as soon as is reasonably practicable after the person becomes a pensionable employee in the relevant employment but not later than 6 months after that event.

Decisions by administering authorities as to war service

N4.—(1) Within 6 months after receiving notice of an election under regulation F3 (election as to war service) and the information mentioned in regulation F5(2)(a), an administering authority are to decide whether the conditions specified in regulation F3(2) to (9) are satisfied in relation to the person in respect of whom the notice was given.

(2) If they decide, or the Secretary of State determines under regulation N8, that those conditions are satisfied in relation to the person, the authority are, within 12 months after the date of notification of that decision or determination–

- (a) in the case of a person who is a pensionable employee or entitled to a retirement pension under regulation E2, to decide what period if any he is entitled, or is to be deemed to have been entitled, to reckon as reckonable service by virtue of regulation F6(1)(a) or (b), or
- (b) in any other case, to decide to which if any of the additional benefits specified in regulation F6(11) and (15) he or any other person is entitled.

(3) If the authority decide, or the Secretary of State determines under regulation N8, that a period is reckonable as mentioned in paragraph (2)(a), the authority are, within 3 months after the date of notification of that decision or determination, to decide whether regulation D8 applies.

Decisions by employing authorities as to benefits

N5.—(1) Any question whether a person is entitled to a benefit under these Regulations is to be decided by the employing authority employing the person in respect of whose employment the question arises.

(2) For the purposes of paragraph (1) "benefit" includes a return of contributions but does not include a benefit specified in Part L or regulation F6(11) or (15).

(3) Any such question as is mentioned in paragraph (1) is to be decided as soon as is reasonably practicable after the cessation of the employment or, as the case may be, the death of the employee.

Decisions by administering authorities as to the amount of benefits

N6.—(1) Where a person is entitled to a benefit which is or may become payable out of their superannuation fund, an administering authority are to decide the amount of the benefit.

(2) The amount of a benefit is to be decided as soon as is reasonably practicable after the person becomes entitled to it.

(3) For the purposes of this regulation "benefit" includes a return of contributions and a benefit specified in regulation F6(11) or (15).

Notification of decisions

N7.—(1) As soon as is reasonably practicable after deciding any question, the body concerned shall send a written notification of their decision to every person whose rights or liabilities the question concerns.

(2) The written notification shall include–

(a) in the case of a decision that the person is not entitled to a benefit, the grounds for the decision, and

(b) in the case of a decision as to the amount of a benefit, a statement showing how the amount is calculated, and

(c) in any case, a conspicuous statement directing the person's attention–

    (i) to the address from which he may obtain further information about the decision, including details of any calculation of service or benefits, and

    (ii) to his right of appeal under regulation N8 to the Secretary of State.

Appeals

N8.—(1) Where the body concerned have either decided or failed to decide any such question as is mentioned in regulation N1 and written notice of appeal is served on the Secretary of State, the question shall, subject to paragraph (2), be determined by him and his determination of it shall be final.

(2) The Secretary of State shall not under this regulation determine any question that fell to be decided by the body concerned in the exercise of a discretion conferred on them by these Regulations.

(3) Notice of appeal (which may be sent by post) may be served–

(a) by–

    (i) an employee of a scheduled body or a person claiming to be treated as such an employee who is dissatisfied with any decision made under these Regulations by the body concerned as to his rights or liabilities or with the body's failure to make any such decision; or

    (ii) a person who has been an employee of a scheduled body, his widow, any dependant or his executors who is or are dissatisfied with any decision made under these Regulations by the body concerned as to his or their rights or with the body's failure to make any such decision; or

    (iii) any other person who is dissatisfied with any decision made by the body concerned as to his rights under Part F or with the body's failure to make any such decision,

    within 3 months from the date on which he was notified of an authority's decision or 3 months after their failure to make a decision, and

(b) where the body concerned are not an administering authority, by the administering authority maintaining the superannuation fund to which the body pay employer's contributions, within the period of 3 months from the date of the employing authority's decision or their failure to make a decision.

(4) For the purpose of this regulation the body concerned shall be deemed to have failed to have made a decision if, after 3 months from the date on which they receive a written request from a person or administering authority that they decide a question, they have not decided that question.

(5) If the Secretary of State is satisfied that there are reasonable grounds for not serving the notice within the period specified in paragraph (3)(a), it may be extended by such longer period as the Secretary of State may allow.

PART P

SUPERANNUATION FUNDS AND PAYMENTS BY AUTHORITIES

Superannuation funds

P1.—(1) The superannuation fund, other than any further fund established under the Local Government Superannuation (Funds) (Scotland) Regulations 1986(**a**), maintained immediately before 21st December 1987 under the 1974 Regulations–

(a) by each regional council,

(b) by the Orkney Islands Council, and

(c) by the Shetland Islands Council,

shall be maintained by those bodies for the purposes of these Regulations and for the purposes of regulations P2, P3, P4 and P10 shall be known as "the fund".

(2) Any further fund established under the Local Government Superannuation (Funds) (Scotland) Regulations 1986 by a council mentioned in paragraph (1) immediately before 21st December 1987 shall subject to regulation P4 be maintained by those bodies for the purposes of these Regulations.

(3) Every regional council and islands council who by virtue of paragraph (1) is administering a superannuation fund and who enters into an admission agreement under regulation B6 may establish and administer for the purposes of these Regulations a further superannuation fund or funds which shall be known as the further fund or further funds respectively.

Apportionment of the fund

P2.—(1) Upon the establishment of a further fund the fund shall be apportioned and the provisions of Schedule 19 shall apply in all cases for the purposes of such apportionment and for the transfer of assets from the fund to the further fund as those provisions apply where such a change of employment occurs as is mentioned in regulation Q2(6); and as if–

(a) references to the previous fund to be apportioned under that Schedule were references to the fund, and references to the fund of the new fund authority were references to the further fund; and

(b) paragraph 7 of that Schedule and, in paragraph 8, the words "Subject to paragraph 7" were omitted.

(2) The administering authority shall bear the costs of the apportionment required by this regulation.

Pensions increase

P3.—(1) In respect of any employee of a body specified in column (1) of Schedule 20 who is a person admitted to the fund or a further fund, that fund shall bear the cost of increases of pensions, allowances and gratuities under the provisions of the Pensions (Increase) Act 1971(**b**) where and to such extent as those pensions, allowances and gratuities relate to service undertaken by the employee following the date referred to in column (2) of Schedule 20 in relation to his employing body or the date of his admission to the fund or a further fund, if later.

(**a**) S.I. 1986/1449.
(**b**) 1971 c.56.

(2) For the purposes of paragraph (1) above the costs of pensions increase attributable to any part of the pension, allowance or gratuity payable by virtue of–

(a) an election under regulation D12 or D13 of the 1974 Regulations or regulation C5 or C6;

(b) any increase in reckonable service made in accordance with the provisions of Schedule 9 to the 1974 Regulations or the provisions of Schedule 10; or

(c) a transfer value received under the provisions of Part P or Part Q of the 1974 Regulations or Part J or Part Q of these Regulations;

shall be borne by that fund to which the employee has been admitted.

(3) Where under the provisions of regulation P4 a further fund is dissolved, the fund shall subsequent to the date of such dissolution meet the cost of pensions increase so far as these costs would have been met by the further fund in respect of liabilities arising before the date of dissolution.

Dissolution of further funds

P4.—(1) The administering authority may if they think fit dissolve a further fund and transfer the assets thereof to the fund, and thereupon–

(a) any entitlement to participate in the benefits of the further fund shall become an entitlement to participate in the benefits of the fund; and

(b) the fund shall become the appropriate superannuation fund for those participants.

(2) The administering authority may not dissolve a further fund unless they have given notice of not less than 28 days to the bodies whose employees are entitled to participate in that fund of their intention to dissolve the fund.

Management of superannuation funds

P5.   Every administering authority shall in each year carry and credit to the appropriate superannuation funds–

(a) the amounts contributed during the year by pensionable employees entitled to participate in the benefits of that fund,

(b) the employer's contributions payable by scheduled bodies under regulation P12,

(c) all dividends and interest arising during the year out of the investment or use of that fund or any part thereof, and any capital moneys resulting from the realisation of investments or from the repayment of moneys used temporarily for other authorised purposes,

(d) the amount of any additional contributory payments received by the administering authority under these Regulations, and

(e) any other sum which the administering authority may become liable to carry to that fund under these Regulations.

Use and investment of superannuation funds' moneys

P6.—(1) Subject to paragraphs (3) to (7), an administering authority–

(a) shall invest any moneys forming part of the superannuation fund or funds maintained by them ("fund moneys") that are not for the time being required to meet payments to be made out of the funds under these Regulations, and

(b) may vary the manner in which any fund moneys are for the time being invested.

(2) For the purposes of this regulation and of regulation P5(c), investment includes–

(a) any contract which by virtue of section 45 of the Finance Act 1984(**a**) (extension of pension schemes' tax exemptions to dealings in financial futures and traded options) is to be regarded as an investment for the purposes of the enactments referred to in that section, and

(b) use by the administering authority for any purpose for which they have a statutory borrowing power.

(**a**) 1984 c.43.

(3) On the total of any fund moneys used by them and for the time being not repaid an administering authority shall pay interest to the fund at a rate no lower than the lowest rate at which that amount could have been borrowed by them at arm's length, otherwise than by way of overdraft from a bank, at 7 days' notice.

(4) An administering authority shall not–

(a) make any investment in securities of companies other than listed securities so as to cause the total value of such investments (except investments made in accordance with a scheme under section 11 of the Trustee Investments Act 1961(a) to exceed 10% of the value at the time of all investments of fund moneys, or

(b) make any investment, other than–

(i) an investment made in accordance with a scheme under section 11 of the Trustee Investments Act 1961, or

(ii) an investment falling within paragraph 1 of Part I or paragraph 1 or 2 of Part II of Schedule 1 to that Act, or

(iii) a deposit with an institution authorised for the purposes of section 3 of the Banking Act 1987(b) or with a person for the time being specified in Schedule 2 to that Act,

so as to result in more than 5% of the value at the time of all investments of any fund's moneys being represented by a single holding, or

(c) make any deposit falling within sub-paragraph (b)(iii) so as to bring the aggregate of any fund's moneys deposited with any one bank, institution or person other than the National Savings Bank to an amount which exceeds 10% of the value at the time of all investments of that fund's moneys, or

(d) lend to any person other than Her Majesty's Government in the United Kingdom or the Government of the Isle of Man, or use as mentioned in paragraph (2), or deposit with a person specified in paragraph 12 or 13 of Schedule 2 to the Banking Act 1987, any fund moneys so as to bring the aggregate of any fund's moneys so lent, used or deposited to an amount which exceeds 10% of the value at the time of all investments of that fund's moneys.

(5) For the purposes of paragraph (4)(d) moneys are not lent if they are invested in registered securities to which section 1 of the Stock Transfer Act 1963(c) applies or in listed securities.

(6) In the discharge of their functions under this regulation an administering authority shall have regard–

(a) to the need for diversification of investments of fund moneys,

(b) to the suitability of investments of any description of investment proposed and of any investment proposed as an investment of that description, and

(c) to proper advice, obtained at reasonable intervals.

(7) Paragraph (6)(c) does not apply where functions under this regulation are lawfully discharged, under arrangements made under section 56 of the Local Government (Scotland) Act 1973(d) or otherwise, by an officer who is competent to give proper advice.

(8) Where any fund moneys are used as mentioned in paragraph (2), sub-paragraphs (2) and (3) of paragraph 25 of Schedule 3 to the Local Government (Scotland) Act 1975(e) shall apply as they apply in the case of money so used under that paragraph; but except as aforesaid that paragraph shall not apply to a superannuation fund maintained under these Regulations.

(9) An administering authority may pay out of fund moneys any costs, charges and expenses incurred by them in the discharge of their functions under this regulation.

(10) For the purposes of this regulation–

"companies" includes companies established under the law of any territory outside the United Kingdom;

(a) 1961 c.62.
(b) 1987 c.22.
(c) 1963 c.18; section 1 was amended by virtue of the Interpretation Act 1889 (c.63), section 38(1), and by the Finance Act 1964 (c.49), Schedule 9, and the Post Office Act 1969 (c.48), section 108(1)(f).
(d) 1973 c.65; section 56 was amended by the Local Government and Planning (Scotland) Act 1982 (c.43), section 32.
(e) 1975 c.30.

"listed securities" means securities in respect of which a listing has been granted and not withdrawn–

(a) on a stock exchange in the United Kingdom which is a recognised stock exchange within the meaning of the Prevention of Fraud (Investments) Act 1958(**a**), or

(b) on a stock exchange outside the United Kingdom of international repute;

"local authority" means a local authority within the meaning of the Local Government (Scotland) Act 1973 or the Local Government Act 1972(**b**), the Common Council of the City of London, the Council of the Isles of Scilly, and a district council within the meaning of the Local Government (Northern Ireland) Act 1972(**c**);

"proper advice" means the advice of a person, including an officer of theirs, who is reasonably believed by the administering authority to be qualified by his ability in, and practical experience of, financial matters;

"securities" includes shares, stock and debentures;

"single holding" means investments–

(a) in securities of, or in units or other shares of the investments subject to the trusts of unit trust schemes managed by, or in loans to or deposits with, any one body, or

(b) in the acquisition, development or management of, or in any advance of money upon the security of, any separate interest in any one item of heritable property, or

(c) in the acquisition of any one item of moveable property;

and the value at any time of all investments of fund moneys is to be taken to include the amount of any fund moneys used as mentioned in paragraph (2) and for the time being not repaid.

Accounts and audit

P7. As soon as may be after an audit of any of their superannuation funds an administering authority shall send each body whose employees contribute to that fund copies of the revenue account and balance sheet of the fund and of any report by the auditor.

Periodical valuation of superannuation funds

P8.—(1) Every administering authority shall obtain an actuarial valuation of the assets and liabilities of each of their superannuation funds as at 31st March in the year 1990 and in every fifth year thereafter, together with a report by the actuary and shall for that purpose provide the actuary with the consolidated revenue account of each fund and such other information as he may require.

(2) Unless the Secretary of State allows an extended period, the valuation and report are to be obtained within 21 months from the date as at which the valuation is made.

(3) Forthwith upon receiving any such valuation and report an administering authority shall–

(a) send copies of them to the Secretary of State and to each body whose employees contribute to the fund,

(b) send the Secretary of State a copy of the consolidated revenue account with which the actuary was provided, and

(c) unless the report contains a summary of the assets of the fund at the date as at which the valuation was made, send the Secretary of State such a summary.

Actuary's certificates

P9.—(1) Every administering authority shall, as soon as is reasonably practicable after obtaining a valuation under regulation P8, obtain from the same actuary a certificate for each fund specifying–

(a) the common rate of employer's contribution, and

(b) any individual adjustments,

(**a**) 1958 c.45.
(**b**) 1972 c.70.
(**c**) 1972 c.9 (N.I.).

for each year of the period of 5 years beginning with 1st April third following the date as at which the valuation was made.

(2) The common rate of employer's contribution is the percentage of their pensionable employees' contributions to a fund during the year under regulation C2 or C3 which should in the actuary's opinion be paid to that fund, so as to ensure its solvency, by all bodies whose employees contribute to it, having regard to—

(a) the existing and prospective liabilities of the fund arising from circumstances common to all those bodies, and

(b) the desirability of maintaining as nearly constant a rate as possible.

(3) An individual adjustment is any percentage or amount by which in the actuary's opinion contributions at the common rate should in the case of a particular body be increased or reduced having regard to existing or prospective—

(a) liabilities of the fund, or

(b) benefits accruing to the fund,

arising from circumstances peculiar to that body.

(4) Forthwith upon receiving a certificate under this regulation an administering authority shall send a copy of it to the Secretary of State and to each body whose employees contribute to the fund.

(5) If—

(a) the common rate for the first year of the period to which an actuary's certificate relates ("the new rate") is less than the common rate for the last year of the period immediately preceding the period to which the certificate relates ("the preceding period"), and

(b) the certificate has been obtained more than 6 months before the end of the preceding period,

the new rate shall, if the actuary and the administering authority so agree, have effect for the whole or part of the last year of the preceding period.

Valuation and actuary's certificates for further funds

P10. The administering authority shall, upon the establishment of a further fund, obtain from an actuary a certificate in respect of that further fund in accordance with the requirements of regulation P9 but for the period specified in regulation P8(1) there shall be substituted the period beginning with the date of the establishment of the further fund until the date of coming into effect of the rate specified by the actuary under regulation P8 for each fund following the first actuarial valuation of the original fund after the establishment of the further fund.

Cost of pensions increase

P11. Where under the provisions of regulation P3 the cost of pensions increase is to be met by a fund, the actuary, when setting a contribution rate for the purposes of regulation P9 or P10 for an employer specified in column (1) of Schedule 20, shall set a rate which shall be sufficient to cover the cost of the liabilities to be met from that fund including the cost of pensions increase under the Pensions (Increase) Act 1971 insofar as the latter cost is not met by other payments received by the fund.

Employer's contributions

P12.—(1) A scheduled body shall contribute to the appropriate superannuation fund in each year of any period of 5 years for which a certificate is required under regulation P9 at the common rate increased or, as the case may be, reduced by any individual adjustment which has been specified for the year in respect of the employing authority under regulation P9(1)(b).

(2) A scheduled body shall pay the contributions required by paragraph (1) at the intervals determined under regulation P15.

(3) If all or part of any sum due under paragraph (1) remains unpaid at the end of the period of one month after the date on which it becomes due, or of any subsequent period of one month, the employing authority shall pay to the appropriate fund a further contribution equal

to one-twelfth of a year's interest, at 1% above what was the base rate at the end of the first day of that month or period, on the amount remaining unpaid.

(4) Interest paid under paragraph (3) shall be carried to the appropriate superannuation fund.

Employer's additional contributions

P13.—(1) Where immediately before 21st December 1987 any payments remained to be made by an employee under regulation D10 (added years) or D11 (payments under former Regulations for added years) of the 1974 Regulations, his employing authority shall, so long as he remains in their employment, pay to the appropriate superannuation fund—

    (a) contributions equal to the amounts payable by the employee under regulation C9(2), or

    (b) where the amounts payable by the employee—

        (i) were reduced under proviso (ii) to regulation 12(3) of the Benefits Regulations or the proviso to paragraph 1 of Schedule 6 to the 1974 Regulations, or

        (ii) were or are reduced by virtue of the payment of a lump sum under Schedule 4 to the 1974 Regulations or Schedule 8 to these Regulations,

    contributions equal to the amounts that would have been payable by the employee but for the reduction.

(2) Where on the employee's ceasing to hold his employment the employing authority agree to pay a sum under paragraph 2A of Schedule 5 to the 1974 Regulations and the employee pays the required amount for the purposes of that paragraph, the employing authority shall pay the agreed sum to the appropriate superannuation fund before the end of the period of one month beginning on the date of the payment by the employee.

(3) If all or part of any sum due under the provisions of this regulation remains unpaid at the end of the period of one month after the date on which it becomes due, or of any subsequent period of one month, the employing authority shall pay to the administering authority a further sum equal to one-twelfth of a year's interest, at 1 per cent above what was the base rate at the end of the first day of the period, on the amount remaining unpaid.

(4) Payments made in pursuance of paragraph (3) shall be paid into the appropriate superannuation fund.

(5) Where by virtue of paragraph 6 of Schedule 5 to the 1974 Regulations an election under regulation D10 of the 1974 Regulations continues to have effect, then for the purposes of this regulation the employing authority in whose employment the employee again became a pensionable employee shall be deemed from the date of his again becoming a pensionable employee to be the employing authority who gave consent to the election under regulation D10 of the 1974 Regulations.

Employer's further payments

P14. Any extra charge on the appropriate superannuation fund resulting from—

    (a) a determination under regulation D4 of the 1974 Regulations (previous employment under an officer to be treated as non-contributing service), or

    (b) a resolution under regulation D9 of the 1974 Regulations (non-contributing service to be treated as contributing service), or

    (c) a resolution under regulation D14 of the 1974 Regulations or regulation D7 of these Regulations (increase of reckonable service), or

    (d) an additional benefit granted under regulation E13 of the 1974 Regulations or regulation E13 of these Regulations (additional benefits for female nursing staff),

shall be repaid to that fund by the scheduled body concerned.

Payments by employing authorities to administering authorities

P15.—(1) Every scheduled body who are not an administering authority shall pay to the appropriate administering authority, at such intervals of not more than 12 months as that authority may determine—

    (a) all amounts from time to time deducted from the remuneration of their pensionable employees under these Regulations,

(b) any amounts received by them under regulation C4, by deduction from remuneration or otherwise, during the interval,

(c) any amount due under regulation P13(1) and (5),

(d) any extra charge payable under regulation P14, the amount of which has been notified to them by the administering authority during the interval, and

(e) a contribution towards the cost of the administration of the fund of which their pensionable employees are members.

(2) The annual amount of the contributions payable under paragraph (1)(e) is to be agreed between the body concerned and the administering authority or, in default of agreement, determined by the Secretary of State.

(3) Payments made in pursuance of, and interest paid under paragraph (6) on sums due under, paragraph (1)(a) to (d) shall be carried to the appropriate superannuation fund.

(4) Subject to paragraph (5), every payment under paragraph (1)(a) is to be accompanied by a statement showing–

(a) the name and remuneration of each of the pensionable employees in relation to whom the payment is made,

(b) the amounts comprised in the payment which represent deductions from the remuneration of each of those employees and the periods in respect of which the deductions were made,

(c) the amount of the remuneration of those employees from or in respect of whom deductions have not been made, and

(d) the names of any pensionable employees from whose remuneration no deductions have been made.

(5) An adminstering authority may direct that, instead of complying with paragraph (4), the bodies making payments to them under paragraph (1)(a) are to provide them with the information mentioned in paragraph (4) in such form, and at such intervals of not more than 12 months, as may be specified in the direction.

(6) If all or part of any sum due under the provisions of this regulation remains unpaid at the end of the period of one month after the date on which it becomes due, or of any subsequent period of one month, the employing authority shall pay to the administering authority a further sum equal to one-twelfth of a year's interest, at one per cent above what was the base rate at the end of the first day of the period, on the amount remaining unpaid.

Funds out of which combined benefits are to be paid

P16.—(1) Where under regulation E16 a person elects to receive a combined benefit, or where under regulation E18(1) the benefits in respect of any person fall to be calculated as a combined benefit in accordance with regulation E16, and the superannuation fund concerned is not the same in the case of the employments in respect of which the benefits become payable, then the fund authority maintaining the fund out of which the combined benefit has become payable (in this regulation referred to as the "second fund authority") shall intimate to the fund authority maintaining the fund out of which the retirement pension was payable (in this regulation referred to as the "first fund authority") that such a combined benefit has become payable.

(2) Where a first fund authority receives an intimation in terms of paragraph (1), that authority in lieu of any payments of benefits to or in respect of such a person shall make payments in accordance with paragraph (3) out of its superannuation fund to the second fund authority for the credit of its superannuation fund.

(3) The payments to be made for the purposes of paragraph (2) are to be equivalent in amount to the payments which would have been payable from the fund maintained by the first fund authority, but for the operation of either–

(a) regulation E16 in relation to the person who elected to receive combined benefits in terms of that regulation commencing with the date of his election, or

(b) regulation E18(1) in relation to the person or persons entitled to combined benefits in terms of that regulation commencing with the date of the death of the pensionable employee concerned in further pensionable employment,

and such payments (which shall comprise all sums due in respect of the period immediately prior to the date of payment) shall be made at quarterly intervals on the last day of March,

June, September and December respectively or at such longer intervals as the fund authorities concerned may agree.

(4) Whenever all or part of any payment due under the foregoing provisions of this regulation remains unpaid at the end of the period of one month after the date on which it becomes due, or any subsequent period of one month, the first fund authority shall pay to the second fund authority a further sum equal to one-twelfth of a year's interest, at one per cent above what was the base rate at the end of the first day of that period, on the amount remaining unpaid.

(5) Where after the combined benefit becomes payable the first fund authority make any payment in respect of the retirement pension to a person appearing to them to be entitled to it, the amount of that payment shall be deducted–

(a) by the second fund authority from the combined benefit payable to the pensioner, and

(b) by the first fund authority from the amount to be paid by them under paragraphs (2) and (3).

Provision as to protection of pension

P17. Any increase in a pension which is required by virtue of sections 41A to 41C (protection of pensions) of the Pensions Act shall be paid out of the appropriate superannuation fund.

PART Q

INTERFUND ADJUSTMENTS

Interpretation

Q1. For the purposes of this Part, unless the context otherwise requires–

"fund authority" means–

(a) in relation to a person's previous local government employment, the body maintaining the superannuation fund to which he was a contributor immediately before he ceased to be employed in his previous local government employment, or its successor body; and

(b) in relation to a person's new local government employment, the body maintaining the superannuation fund to which he became a contributor in his new local government employment or its successor body;

"new local government employment" has the same meaning as in regulation Q2(1)(a) and "new employing authority" is to be construed accordingly;

"pension" does not include an allowance or gratuity;

"previous local government employment" has the same meaning as in regulation Q2(1)(a) and "previous employing authority" is to be construed accordingly.

Change of local government employment and fund authority

Q2.—(1) Where–

(a) a person who has ceased to be employed in a local government employment ("the previous local government employment") subsequently becomes employed in some other local government employment ("the new local government employment"), and

(b) in his new local government employment the fund authority ("the new fund authority") is different from the fund authority ("the previous fund authority") in his previous local government employment, and

(c) in his new local government employment he is entitled to reckon any reckonable service which he was entitled to reckon in his previous local government employment, and

    (d) no direction has been made at any time in relation to his reckonable service in his previous local government employment under regulation M1, regulation L12 of the 1974 Regulations, or any corresponding provision of any earlier enactment,

the previous fund authority shall, subject to the following provisions of these Regulations, pay, out of a superannuation fund to which the person was a contributor to the new fund authority for the credit of their superannuation fund to which the person will be a contributor, a transfer value calculated in accordance with Part IV of Schedule 16.

    (2) Subject to paragraphs (3), (4) and (5), if the change of employment occurs as a result of an Order or Regulations made under the Local Government (Scotland) Act 1973 in accordance with section 216 of that Act (**a**) and the number of persons changing superannuation funds is more than 9 but less than 100, the transfer values payable under paragraph (1) shall be calculated as if they were payable under Part I of Schedule 16.

    (3) An adjustment shall be made to the total sum payable under paragraph (2) if the assets of the fund of the previous fund authority immediately before any change of employment occurs are not adequate, or are more than adequate, to meet the accrued actuarial liabilities of the fund at that time.

    (4) The total shall be adjusted to the extent that the actuaries of the funds concerned consider appropriate in the circumstances.

    (5) If any question arises as to the application of paragraphs (3) and (4) or the actuaries are unable to agree on the adjustment to be made, the adjustment (if any) to be made shall be decided by an actuary appointed by the Secretary of State.

    (6) If the change of employment occurs as a result of an Order or Regulations made under the Local Government (Scotland) Act 1973 in accordance with section 216 of that Act and the number of persons changing superannuation funds is 100 or more–

    (a) no payment shall be made under paragraph (1); and

    (b) the superannuation fund of the previous fund authority to which the persons were contributors shall be apportioned in accordance with Schedule 19.

    (7) "Accrued actuarial liabilities" means the actual and potential liabilities of the fund in connection with any service or employment before the change of employment takes place.

Partial forfeitures

Q3.—(1) Where–

    (a) a direction has been made in relation to any person under regulation M1, or any corresponding provision of any earlier enactment, and

    (b) any right to benefit under these Regulations, the 1974 Regulations or the former Regulations is retained, and

    (c) the conditions of regulation Q2(1) are satisfied with the exception of the conditions in sub-paragraph (d) of that regulation,

the previous fund authority shall pay out of their superannuation fund to which the person was a contributor a transfer value to the new fund authority for the credit of their superannuation fund.

    (2) The transfer value is to be an amount equal to the actuarial value of the remaining benefits.

PART R

MISCELLANEOUS POWERS AND DUTIES OF AUTHORITIES

Information to be supplied by certain employees

R1.—(1) Subject to paragraph (4)–

    (a) within 3 months after a person enters the employment of a scheduled body, and

---

(**a**) Section 216 was amended by the Local Government and Planning (Scotland) Act 1982 (c.43), Schedule 4, Part I.

    (b) within 6 months after any change which is material for the purposes of these Regulations occurs in or in relation to a person's employment under a scheduled body,

the body are to request the person in writing to provide them with the documents specified in paragraph (2).

    (2) The documents mentioned in paragraph (1) are–

    (a) a statement in writing of all his previous periods of employment (whether by a scheduled body or by any other person) and any national service and war service, and

    (b) copies of all notifications previously given to him under these Regulations, the 1974 Regulations, the Local Government Superannuation (Administration) (Scotland) Regulations 1954(**a**) or the Local Government Superannuation (Administration) (Scotland) Regulations 1938(**b**).

    (3) A request under paragraph (1) is to include a conspicuous statement directing the attention of the employee to the importance of his providing full and accurate information and warning him that any omission or inaccuracy may prejudice the ascertainment of his rights under these Regulations.

    (4) Paragraph (1) does not apply where the body are satisfied–

    (a) that the person is not a pensionable employee, or

    (b) that they, or the administering authority if different, already have a complete and accurate record of any previous service or employment which is relevant for the purposes of these Regulations.

Records to be kept by authorities

R2.—(1) A scheduled body are to keep, in such form as they think fit, a record of–

    (a) the name of, and

    (b) all their decisions under regulation N2 in relation to,

each of their pensionable employees.

    (2) An administering authority are to keep, in such form as they think fit, a record of–

    (a) the name of, and

    (b) all their decisions under regulation N3 or N4 in relation to,

every pensionable employee in relation to whom they are the appropriate administering authority.

Transmission of documents and information

R3.—(1) A scheduled body who are not an administering authority are to send the appropriate administering authority, as soon as is reasonably practicable–

    (a) copies of all documents provided under regulation R1,

    (b) copies of all notifications of decisions made under regulation N2 or N5,

    (c) copies of all statements and statutory declarations provided under regulation C10, and

    (d) such other documents and information as the administering authority may reasonably require for the purposes of discharging their functions under these Regulations.

    (2) A scheduled body who are not an administering authority–

    (a) on receiving from a pensionable employee notice of his intended retirement, or

    (b) on giving an employee notice to terminate his employment in circumstances in which he may become entitled to a return of contributions or to a benefit payable out of the appropriate superannuation fund, or

    (c) on becoming aware of any other circumstances which may necessitate any payment out of that fund,

are to comply, as soon as is reasonably practicable, with the requirements in paragraph (3).

(**a**) S.I. 1954/1243.
(**b**) S.R. & O. 1938/245.

(3) The requirements mentioned in paragraph (2) are to inform the appropriate administering authority of the notice or other circumstances and–

    (a) send them particulars of the employee's remuneration during the period that is relevant to a decision on the amount of the benefit that may become payable to or in respect of him, and

    (b) send them a copy of any relevant medical or death certificate and of any certificate issued by the body under regulation E24.

(4) An administering authority when notifying a person who is not in their employment of a decision under regulation N3 or N4 are to send a copy of the notification to the body, if any, who are the employing authority in relation to that person.

(5) If an administering authority decide, or the Secretary of State determines under regulation N8, that the conditions specified in regulation F3(2) to (9) are satisfied in relation to a person, and regulation F3(2)(f) applies and the scheme designated under regulation F5(2)(b) is not a scheme specified in Schedule 15, the authority shall as soon as is reasonably practicable–

    (a) inform the scheme managers of the designated scheme that on receipt by the authority of a transfer value (calculated in accordance with Part V of Schedule 16) regulation F6(1) (reckonable service and benefits in respect of war service) would apply to the person, and

    (b) inform them of the rate or amount, as the case may be, to be used in ascertaining C of the formula set out in that Part.

Provisions as to contributions equivalent premiums

R4.—(1) Where a scheduled body pay a contributions equivalent premium under Part III of the Pensions Act in respect of any pensionable employee, they are entitled to recover, or if they are an administering authority to retain, out of the appropriate superannuation fund a sum not exceeding the amount of that premium, less the amount (if any) which they could recover or retain under section 47 of that Act in respect of the premium.

(2) Where such a contributions equivalent premium is refunded under regulation 8(3)(c) of the Occupational Pension Schemes (Contracting-out) Regulations 1984(**a**), the authority to whom it is refunded shall pay to the superannuation fund to which the person involved has become a contributor a sum equal to the amount of the premium.

PART S

MISCELLANEOUS AND SUPPLEMENTAL

Periods of time

S1. Where a period of time specified in any Regulations revoked by these Regulations is current at the commencement of these Regulations, these Regulations have effect as if the corresponding provision of these Regulations had been in force when that period began to run.

Application to benefits in respect of former employments

S2.—(1) Subject to paragraph (2), these Regulations apply in relation to benefits which–

    (a) were before 21st December 1987 being paid, or

    (b) may on or after that date become payable,

to or in respect of persons who before that date ceased to hold, or died while in, a local government employment.

    (2) Where–

    (a) a provision of these Regulations ("the new provision") re-enacts with any modification a provision of any Regulations revoked by these Regulations ("the former provision"), and

---

(**a**) S.I. 1984/380, to which there are amendments not relevant to these Regulations.

(b) a person, to whom a benefit in relation to which the new provision applies was being paid, or may become payable, as mentioned in paragraph (1), is placed in a worse position by the new provision than he would have been in if the former provision had continued to have effect,

he may, by notice in writing given to the appropriate administering authority within 3 months after 21st December 1987, elect that the new provision shall apply in relation to the benefit as if it had re-enacted the former provision without modification.

(3) In this regulation "benefit" includes an allowance, a gratuity and a return of contributions.

Revocations

S3. The Regulations specified in Schedule 21 are revoked.

New St. Andrew's House, Edinburgh
19th October 1987

Michael B. Forsyth
Parliamentary Under Secretary of State,
Scottish Office

SCHEDULE 1

GLOSSARY OF EXPRESSIONS

(1) Expression	(2) Meaning
"The Act of 1922"	The Local Government and other Officers' Superannuation Act 1922(**a**).
"The Act of 1937"	The Local Government Superannuation (Scotland) Act 1937(**b**).
"The Act of 1953"	The Local Government Superannuation Act 1953(**c**).
"The Acts of 1937 to 1953"	The Local Government Superannuation (Scotland) Acts 1937 to 1953(**d**).
"The Act of 1972"	The Superannuation Act 1972(**e**).
"Actuary"	A Fellow of the Institute of Actuaries or of the Faculty of Actuaries in Scotland.
"Added period payment"	A payment made for the purposes of regulation C5 or C6, regulation D10 of the 1974 Regulations, or section 2(1) of the Act of 1953 or any similar provision contained in a local Act scheme.
"Added years"	An additional period which a person has become entitled to reckon as reckonable service by virtue of– (a) regulation D10 of the 1974 Regulations, or (b) regulation D6(2), or (c) regulation 12 of the Benefits Regulations, or (d) regulation 5 of the Local Government Superannuation (Reckoning of Service on Transfer) (Scotland) Regulations 1954(**f**), or (e) regulation 4(2)(b) of the Local Government Superannuation (England and Scotland) Regulations 1948 to 1954(**g**), or (f) any similar provision of a local Act scheme.
"Additional contributory payment"	A payment made under– (a) regulation D6 or D7 of the 1974 Regulations, or (b) regulation C9(2), or (c) section 2(3) of the Act of 1953 as originally enacted or as having effect as mentioned in regulation A2(2)(c), or (d) the Act of 1937 as originally enacted, the Act of 1922 or a local Act scheme, as a condition of being entitled to reckon any service either as service generally or as service of a particular character, or (e) proviso (ii) to section 8(2)(b) of the Act of 1937.
"Administering authority"	A body required to maintain a superannuation fund under these Regulations.
"Admission agreement"	An agreement made or continued in force as if made under regulation B6.
"Appropriate administering authority"	In relation to a pensionable employee and to the employing authority means the body maintaining the superannuation fund which is, in relation to him and to the employing authority, the appropriate superannuation fund.

(**a**) 1922 c.59.
(**b**) 1937 c.69.
(**c**) 1953 c.25.
(**d**) 1937 c.69, 1939 c.18, 1953 c.25.
(**e**) 1972 c.11.
(**f**) S.I. 1954/1241.
(**g**) S.I. 1948/1131, 1949/631, 1954/1250.

(1) *Expression*	(2) *Meaning*
"Appropriate superannuation fund"	Shall be construed in accordance with regulation C1.
"Approved non-local government employment"	Employment in which a person participates in an approved non-local government scheme.
"Approved non-local government scheme"	A non-local government scheme– (a) the fund of which is wholly approved under section 208 of the Income and Corporation Taxes Act 1970(a), or (b) which is approved under section 222 of that Act or under Chapter II of Part II of the Finance Act 1970(b), or (c) which is approved by the Commissioners of Inland Revenue for the purposes of these Regulations.
"Base rate"	The highest base rate for lending purposes fixed by the Governors and Company of the Bank of Scotland, Clydesdale Bank plc and The Royal Bank of Scotland plc.
"The Benefits Regulations"	The Local Government Superannuation (Benefits) (Scotland) Regulations 1954 and 1955(c).
"Child"	A person who– (a) has not attained the age of 17 years, or (b) has attained the age of 17 years and has since been receiving full-time education or undergoing a full-time course of training, of not less than 2 years' duration, for a trade, profession or calling, either– (i) continuously, or (ii) except during a period which the appropriate administering authority, being satisfied that his education or training ought not to be regarded as completed, have in their discretion decided to disregard, or (c) has attained the age of 17 years and is incapacitated by reason of ill-health or infirmity of mind or body which arose either before he attained that age or while receiving such full-time education or training.
"Contracted-out employment"	Shall be construed in accordance with section 30 of the Pensions Act.
"Contributory employee"	A person who was entitled to participate in the benefits of a superannuation fund maintained under Part I of the Act of 1937.
"Death gratuity"	A death gratuity payable under regulation E11.
"Disqualifying break of service"	A continuous period of 12 months or longer during no part of which was the person concerned a pensionable employee, contributory employee or local Act contributor or subject to the Act of 1922.
"Eligible child"	A child in relation to a person who has died after becoming entitled to a retirement pension is an eligible child if he is– (a) (i) a child of that person born within 12 months of the date on which he became entitled to that pension, or (ii) wholly or mainly dependent upon that person both before he became entitled to that pension and at the time of his death, (b) a child adopted by the person before he became entitled to the retirement pension, or (c) a child wholly or mainly dependent on the person both before he became entitled to the retirement pension and at the time of his death who is– (i) the person's step-child, or

(a) 1970 c.10.
(b) 1970 c.24.
(c) S.I. 1954/1059, 1955/1226.

(1) Expression	(2) Meaning
	(ii) an adopted child of a woman who married the person before he became entitled to the retirement pension, or
	(iii) a child accepted by the person as a member of the family.
	A child in relation to a person who has died in an employment in which he was a pensionable employee is an eligible child if he is—
	(a) the person's child born before the expiration of 12 months from the date of the person's death or an adopted child of that person, or
	(b) a child wholly or mainly dependent on the person at the time of his death who is—
	(i) the person's step-child, or
	(ii) an adopted child of a woman who has been married to the person, or
	(iii) a child accepted by the person as a member of the family.
"Employee"	An employee whether permanent or temporary, other than a person appointed to a post in a temporary capacity for a period of not more than 3 months or whose employment is of a casual nature.
"Employer's contribution"	A sum payable under regulation P12(1).
"Employing authority"	The body employing a pensionable employee.
"Employment"	Shall be construed as including office.
"Enactment"	Shall be construed as including any instrument made under an Act.
"Equivalent pension benefits"	Has the meaning given by section 57(1) of the Insurance Act.
"The former Regulations"	Those of the enactments and instruments referred to in paragraph 5 of Schedule 7 to the Act of 1972 as applying to Scotland that were in force immediately before 16th May 1974 and the Miscellaneous Provisions Regulations.
"A further fund"	Has the meaning given to it by regulation P1(3).
"Guaranteed minimum"	A guaranteed minimum under section 35 of the Pensions Act.
"Guaranteed minimum pension"	A guaranteed minimum pension under section 26 of the Pensions Act.
"The Insurance Act"	The National Insurance Act 1965(a).
"The Insurance Acts"	The National Insurance Acts 1965 to 1973(b).
"Insurance code"	The Insurance Act, the Northern Ireland Act or the Isle of Man Act.
"Interchange rules"	Rules made under section 2 of the Superannuation (Miscellaneous Provisions) Act 1948(c) (pensions of persons transferring to different employment) and any similar instrument made, or having effect as if made, under any other Act which makes similar provision.
"The Isle of Man Act"	The National Insurance (Isle of Man) Act 1961 (an Act of Tynwald).
"Judicially separated"	Judicially separated in circumstances in which the husband is not required by decree or order of any competent court to contribute to the support of his wife and is not in fact so contributing.

(a) 1965 c.51.
(b) 1965 c.51, 1966 c.6, 1969 c.44, 1971 c.50, 1972 c.57, 1973 c.42.
(c) 1948 c.33.

(1) *Expression*	(2) *Meaning*
"Local Act contributor"	A person who was entitled to participate in the benefits of a superannuation fund maintained under a local Act scheme.
"Local Act scheme"	Has the same meaning as in section 8 of the Act of 1972.
"Local government employment"	In relation to any time before 16th May 1974, the expression means employment by virtue of which the person employed was, or is deemed to have been, a contributory employee or a local Act contributor. In relation to any time after 15th May 1974, the expression means employment by virtue of which the person employed is, or is deemed to be, a pensionable employee.
"Manual worker"	An employee who is not an officer.
"The Miscellaneous Provisions Regulations"	The Local Government Superannuation (Miscellaneous Provisions) (Scotland) Regulations 1973(**a**).
"New fund authority"	Has the meaning given by regulation Q2(1)(**b**).
"The 1974 Regulations"	The Local Government Superannuation (Scotland) Regulations 1974(**b**).
"Non-local government employment"	Means employment in which the person participates in a non-local government scheme.
"Non-local government scheme"	A superannuation scheme or other arrangement for superannuation, other than– (a) the superannuation scheme provided in the Acts of 1937 to 1953 and the Regulations made thereunder, or in the Local Government Superannuation Acts 1937 to 1953(**c**) and the Regulations made thereunder, (b) a superannuation scheme provided in Regulations for the time being in force under section 7 of the Act of 1972, and (c) a local Act scheme.
"Non-participating employment"	Has the same meaning as in section 56(1) of the Insurance Act.
"The Northern Ireland Act"	The National Insurance Act (Northern Ireland) 1959(**d**).
"Officer"	An employee whose duties are wholly or mainly administrative, professional, technical or clerical.
"Part-time employee"	An employee who is neither a whole-time employee nor a variable-time employee.
"Passenger transport executive"	The Executive for a designated area within section 9(1) of the Transport Act 1968(**e**).
"Payment in lieu of contributions"	A payment in lieu of contributions under Part III of the Insurance Act.
"Pensionable age"	A person's pensionable age is the earliest age at which (assuming continuous local government employment) he could become entitled by virtue of regulation E2(1)(a) or (b)(ii) to a retirement pension.
"Pensionable employee"	In relation to any time before 21st December 1987, the expression means a person who was a pensionable employee under the 1974 Regulations. In relation to any time after 20th December 1987, the expression is to be construed in accordance with regulation B1.

(**a**) S.I. 1973/503.
(**b**) S.I. 1974/812, amended by S.I. 1975/638, 1978/425, 1378, 1794, 1926, 1980/198, 342, 1885, 1981/1892, 1982/385, 1303, 1983/1421, 1984/254, 1232, 1986/214, 1449.
(**c**) 1937 c.68, 1939 c.18, 1953 c.25.
(**d**) 1959 c.21 (N.I.).
(**e**) 1968 c.73.

(1) *Expression*	(2) *Meaning*
"Pensionable remuneration"	Shall be construed in accordance with regulation E22.
"The Pensions Act"	The Social Security Pensions Act 1975(**a**).
"Preserved benefits"	Benefits to which a person– (a) was entitled immediately before 21st December 1987 by virtue of regulation E2(1)(c) of the 1974 Regulations, or (b) has become entitled by virtue of regulation E2(1)(c), and which have not become payable.
"Previous fund authority"	Has the meaning given by regulation Q2(1)(b).
"Public service scheme"	The Universities' Superannuation Scheme and any occupational pension scheme which– (a) cannot come into force or be amended without the scheme or amendment being approved by a Minister of the Crown or government department, and (b) includes provisions for any such whole-time service as is described in regulation F2(1), rendered before becoming entitled to participate in the scheme, to be reckonable as service in respect of which benefits are payable under the scheme.
"Qualifying service"	Shall be construed in accordance with regulation D2.
"Reckonable service"	Shall be construed in accordance with regulation D1.
"Registration officer"	A person holding, or deemed to be holding, an appointment under section 7 of the Registration of Births, Deaths and Marriages (Scotland) Act 1965(**b**).
"Relevant absence" and "relevant contribution period"	The meanings given by regulation C4(8).
"Remuneration"	Except to the extent that any standard remuneration agreement has been agreed under regulation G3, the expression means all the salary, wages, fees, poundage and other payments paid or made to an employee as such for his own use and the money value of any apartments, rations or other allowances in kind appertaining to his employment. The expression does not include– (a) payments for non-contractual overtime, (b) any allowance paid to an employee to cover the cost of office accommodation or clerk's assistance, (c) any travelling or subsistence allowance or other moneys to be spent, or to cover expenses incurred by him, for the purposes of his employment, (d) any payment made to him on his ceasing to hold his employment in consideration of loss of holidays, or (e) any payment accepted by him in lieu of notice to terminate his contract of employment; and for the purposes of calculating any payment based on remuneration to be made by an employee under these Regulations any reduction in remuneration by reason of the actual or assumed enjoyment of any statutory entitlement by the employee during any period of absence from duty shall be disregarded.
"Rent officer" and "deputy rent officer"	Any person who has been appointed a rent officer under section 43 of the Rent (Scotland) Act 1984(**c**).
"Retirement pension"	A retirement pension payable under regulation E2.

(**a**) 1975 c.60.
(**b**) 1965 c.49.
(**c**) 1984 c.58.

(1) *Expression*	(2) *Meaning*
"Retiring allowance"	A retiring allowance payable under regulation E2.
"Scheduled body"	A body or the predecessor of a body described in Schedule 3.
"Scheme managers"	In relation to a statutory scheme, the expression means the Minister of the Crown or police or fire authority administering the scheme. In any other case, the expression means the person responsible for the management of a non-local government scheme.
"Service"	Except in Part J, where it has the meaning given by regulation J1, the expression means service rendered to a scheduled body. Service rendered by an employee of a scheduled body whose services are placed at the disposal of a Minister of the Crown or a government department in pursuance of any enactment is to be treated as service rendered to the scheduled body.
"State pensionable age"	In the case of a man, 65; in the case of a woman, 60.
"Statutory scheme"	A scheme established under– (a) section 1 of the Act of 1972, (b) arrangements for superannuation maintained in pursuance of Regulations made or having effect as if made under section 9 or 10 of that Act, (c) section 1 of the Police Pensions Act 1976(**a**), or (d) the Firemens' Pension Scheme made under the Fire Services Act 1947(**b**).
"Trade dispute"	Has the meaning given by regulation C4(8).
"The Transitional Provisions Regulations"	The National Insurance (Non-participation – Transitional Provisions) Regulations 1974(**c**).
"Variable-time employee"	An employee who has no contractual hours of employment.
"War service"	Shall be construed in accordance with regulation F2.
"War service provisions"	In relation to a public service scheme, means provisions of the kind specified in paragraph (b) of the definition of "public service scheme" in this Schedule.
"Water development board"	A board established under section 3 or 5 of the Water (Scotland) Act 1967(**d**).
"Whole-time"	A person is a "whole-time employee", and as the case may be a "whole-time officer" or a "whole-time manual worker", if his contractual minimum hours of employment regularly or usually amount to 30 hours or more in each week.

(**a**) 1976 c.35.
(**b**) 1947 c.41.
(**c**) S.I. 1974/2057.
(**d**) 1967 c.78.

Regulation A3

SCHEDULE 2

MODIFICATIONS TO THE REGULATIONS IN THEIR APPLICATION TO EMPLOYEES OF THE SCOTTISH SPECIAL HOUSING ASSOCIATION

1. Regulation C12(5) shall have effect as if it provided that any direction required by that regulation shall not have effect unless it has been approved by the Secretary of State.

2. For the purposes of Part D "service" rendered to the Association before 16th May 1945 shall not be construed as qualifying or reckonable service.

3. Regulation P6 shall have effect as if paragraph (2)(b) of that regulation were deleted.

4. Arrangements for actuarial valuations of, and reports on, the assets and liabilities of the fund administered by the Association and arrangements for making good any deficiency or for disposal of a disposable surplus disclosed by a valuation and report shall be made by the Secretary of State.

5. Where the General Manager of the Association elects by notice in writing given to the Association, a percentage, not exceeding 4.4%, of his remuneration shall be treated as not being remuneration for the purposes of these Regulations.

Regulation B1

SCHEDULE 3

PENSIONABLE EMPLOYEES

PART I

1. A regional council, an islands council or a district council.

2. A joint board or joint committee appointed under any enactment, order or scheme, all the constituent authorities of which are such councils as aforesaid.

3. A water development board.

4. A river purification board.

PART II

1. A variable-time employee of a body described in Part I who is also in the whole-time employment of such a body.

2. A whole-time employee or a variable-time employee of any other body to which section 270 of the Local Government (Scotland) Act 1947(a) applied.

3. A whole-time employee of a passenger transport executive.

PART III

1. The requirements to be satisfied in order that a whole-time manual worker employed by a body described in Part I may be a pensionable employee by virtue of regulation B1(3)(c) are that–
    (a) he became employed by that body as such a worker after ceasing to be employed in non-local government employment, and
    (b) he has, not later than 12 months after the date on which he became employed by that body as such a worker, elected to become a pensionable employee by notice in writing given to that body.

2. A notice under paragraph 1(b) must also contain a declaration by the worker that his pension rights under his non-local government scheme will be preserved or that he has applied, or will apply, for their transfer to the appropriate administering authority.

(a) 1947 c.43.

SCHEDULE 4 Regulations C5, C6, D7

MAXIMUM LENGTH OF ADDITIONAL PERIODS

1.—(1) Subject to paragraph 2, the maximum length of the period in respect of which payment may be made under regulation C5 or C6 or which may be specified in a resolution under regulation D7 is $A - B$, where–

A is the number of years specified in column (2) of the Table below against the age specified in column (1) which the person had attained at the appropriate time, and

B is the period he would otherwise be entitled to reckon as reckonable service in relation to his local government employment if he continued in it until he attained the age of 65 years.

TABLE

(1) Age attained	(2) Number of years
Any age less than 55	40
55	32
56	24
57	16
58	8
59	0

(2) Subject to sub-paragraph (3), the appropriate time is the first day of the earliest period that the person is entitled to reckon as reckonable service in relation to his local government employment.

(3) Where that period is one of service as an officer of a scheduled body or former local authority, or one during which the person was subject to a non-local government scheme other than one which was or became a statutory scheme, the appropriate time is the first day of the earliest period of local government employment that the person is entitled to reckon as mentioned in sub-paragraph (2).

2.—(1) In the case of a person who at the appropriate time was entitled to or had received superannuation benefits (including a return of contributions and any benefit by way of a lump sum payment) in respect of any local government employment or under any non-local government scheme, the number of years specified in column (2) of the Table in paragraph 1(1) is to be reduced, in accordance with the certificate of an actuary, to the extent necessary to ensure that–

(a) the aggregate annual amount of–

(i) the actuarial value, expressed as an annuity payable to him, of those superannuation benefits, and

(ii) the part of his retirement pension attributable to reckonable service before attaining pensionable age, and

(iii) the actuarial value, expressed as an annuity payable to him, of the part of his retiring allowance attributable to such reckonable service,

will not exceed two-thirds of his pensionable remuneration, and

(b) the aggregate amount of–

(i) his retiring allowance, and

(ii) any lump sum comprised in those superannuation benefits,

will not exceed one hundred and twenty eightieths of his pensionable remuneration.

(2) For the purposes of this paragraph–

(a) it is to be assumed that the person will, until he attains pensionable age, continue in the same local government employment and on the same scale of remuneration as at the material date,

(b) any reckonable service on or after the material date is to be disregarded,

(c) the material date is the date of, as the case may be, the election under regulation C5 or C6 or the resolution under regulation D7,

(d) a person who, when a scheduled body passed a resolution in respect of him under regulation D7, had not become a pensionable employee in their employment is to be treated as if he had on the date of the resolution become such an employee on the scale of remuneration at which the employment was offered to him, and

(e) regard is to be had to any Inland Revenue advice as to the calculation of the value of the earlier benefits.

SCHEDULE 5

AMOUNT TO BE PAID FOR ADDITIONAL PERIOD

PART I

LUMP SUM PAYMENT

1. The amount to be paid by an employee who has made an election under regulation C5 is $\dfrac{A \times B \times C}{100}$, where–

A is the length of the additional period, expressed in complete years and any fraction of a year,

B is his remuneration at the time when he made the election, and

C is the figure in Table I or II below appropriate to his age on his birthday next following the date of the election and to his pensionable age.

TABLE I

MALES

| Age on birthday next following election | Figure to be used by reference to the under-mentioned pensionable age | | | | | | | |
| | Employee to whom on retirement regulation E3(2) would apply | Others | | | | | | |
	65	60	Over 60 and under 61	61 and under 62	62 and under 63	63 and under 64	64 and under 65	65
26		22.20						
27		21.40						
28		20.80						
29		20.30						
30		19.90						
31		19.60						
32		19.30						
33		19.10						
34		18.90						
35		18.80						
36		18.70	18.50					
37		18.60	18.40	18.00				
38		18.60	18.40	17.90	17.50			
39		18.60	18.40	17.90	17.50	17.10		
40		18.60	18.40	17.90	17.50	17.10	16.70	
41		18.70	18.40	18.00	17.60	17.20	16.70	16.50
42		18.80	18.50	18.00	17.60	17.20	16.80	16.60
43		18.90	18.60	18.10	17.70	17.20	16.80	16.60
44		19.00	18.70	18.20	17.80	17.30	16.90	16.70
45		19.10	18.80	18.30	17.90	17.40	16.90	16.70
46	17.30	19.20	18.90	18.40	18.00	17.50	17.00	16.80
47	17.40	19.30	19.00	18.50	18.10	17.60	17.10	16.90
48	17.50	19.40	19.10	18.60	18.20	17.70	17.20	17.00
49	17.60	19.50	19.20	18.70	18.30	17.80	17.30	17.10
50	17.70	19.70	19.40	18.80	18.40	17.90	17.40	17.20
51	17.80	19.90	19.60	19.00	18.50	18.00	17.50	17.30
52	17.90	20.10	19.80	19.20	18.70	18.10	17.60	17.40
53	18.00	20.30	20.00	19.40	18.90	18.30	17.70	17.50
54	18.10	20.50	20.20	19.60	19.10	18.50	17.80	17.60
55	18.30	20.70	20.40	19.80	19.30	18.70	18.00	17.80
56	18.50	20.90	20.60	20.00	19.50	18.90	18.20	18.00
57	18.70	21.20	20.90	20.20	19.70	19.10	18.40	18.20
58	18.90	21.50	21.20	20.50	19.90	19.30	18.60	18.40
59	19.10	21.80	21.50	20.80	20.10	19.50	18.80	18.60
60	19.40			21.10	20.40	19.70	19.10	18.80
61	19.70				20.70	19.90	19.30	19.00
62	20.00					20.10	19.50	19.30
63	20.30						19.70	19.60
64	20.70							19.90

TABLE II

FEMALES

Age on birthday next following election	Figure to be used by reference to the under-mentioned pensionable age							
	Employee to whom on retirement regulation E3(2) would apply	Others						
	65	60	Over 60 and under 61	61 and under 62	62 and under 63	63 and under 64	64 and under 65	65
26		20.40						
27		19.80						
28		19.40						
29		19.00						
30		18.70						
31		18.60						
32		18.60						
33		18.70						
34		18.70						
35		18.80						
36		18.90	18.60					
37		19.00	18.70	18.20				
38		19.10	18.80	18.30	17.80			
39		19.30	19.00	18.40	17.90	17.30		
40		19.40	19.10	18.60	18.00	17.40	16.90	
41		19.60	19.30	18.70	18.10	17.50	17.00	16.70
42		19.70	19.40	18.80	18.20	17.60	17.10	16.80
43		19.80	19.50	18.90	18.30	17.80	17.20	16.90
44		19.90	19.60	19.00	18.40	17.90	17.30	17.00
45		20.10	19.70	19.10	18.50	18.00	17.40	17.10
46	18.80	20.20	19.90	19.20	18.60	18.10	17.50	17.20
47	18.90	20.40	20.00	19.40	18.80	18.20	17.60	17.30
48	19.00	20.50	20.20	19.50	18.90	18.30	17.70	17.40
49	19.10	20.60	20.30	19.60	19.00	18.40	17.80	17.50
50	19.20	20.80	20.40	19.80	19.20	18.60	17.90	17.60
51	19.30	21.00	20.60	19.90	19.30	18.70	18.00	17.70
52	19.40	21.10	20.80	20.10	19.40	18.80	18.20	17.90
53	19.50	21.30	21.00	20.30	19.60	19.00	18.30	18.00
54	19.60	21.50	21.20	20.40	19.80	19.10	18.40	18.10
55	19.80	21.70	21.40	20.60	19.90	19.20	18.60	18.20
56	20.00	21.90	21.60	20.80	20.10	19.40	18.70	18.30
57	20.20	22.10	21.80	21.00	20.30	19.60	18.80	18.50
58	20.40	22.30	22.00	21.20	20.50	19.80	19.00	18.70
59	20.60	22.60	22.20	21.40	20.70	20.00	19.20	18.90
60	20.80			21.70	20.90	20.20	19.40	19.10
61	21.10				21.20	20.40	19.60	19.30
62	21.40					20.50	19.80	19.50
63	21.70						20.00	19.80
64	22.00							20.10

PART II

PERIODICAL PAYMENTS

2. The amount to be paid by way of additional contributions by an employee who has made an election under regulation C6 is $\dfrac{A \times B \times C}{100}$, where–

A is the length of the additional period, expressed in complete years and any fraction of a year,

B is his remuneration for the time being, and

C is the figure in Table I or II below appropriate to his age on his birthday next following the date of the election and to his pensionable age.

TABLE I

MALES

Age on birthday next following election	Figure to be used by reference to the under-mentioned pensionable age							
	Employee to whom on retirement regulation E3(2) would apply	Others						
	65	60	Over 60 and under 61	61 and under 62	62 and under 63	63 and under 64	64 and under 65	65
26		0.58						
27		0.60						
28		0.62						
29		0.64						
30		0.66						
31		0.68						
32		0.71						
33		0.74						
34		0.77						
35		0.80						
36		0.84	0.83					
37		0.88	0.87	0.82				
38		0.93	0.91	0.86	0.81			
39		0.98	0.96	0.90	0.85	0.80		
40		1.03	1.01	0.95	0.90	0.84	0.80	
41		1.09	1.07	1.00	0.95	0.89	0.84	0.81
42		1.16	1.14	1.06	1.00	0.94	0.88	0.85
43		1.23	1.22	1.13	1.06	0.99	0.93	0.89
44		1.31	1.30	1.20	1.12	1.05	0.98	0.93
45		1.40	1.39	1.28	1.19	1.11	1.04	0.98
46	1.08	1.51	1.49	1.37	1.27	1.18	1.10	1.04
47	1.15	1.64	1.61	1.48	1.36	1.26	1.17	1.11
48	1.23	1.79	1.75	1.61	1.47	1.35	1.25	1.18
49	1.31	1.97	1.92	1.76	1.60	1.45	1.34	1.26
50	1.40	2.18	2.13	1.93	1.75	1.57	1.44	1.35
51	1.50	2.42	2.38	2.12	1.92	1.71	1.56	1.45
52	1.62	2.74	2.69	2.36	2.11	1.88	1.70	1.57
53	1.76	3.15	3.09	2.66	2.33	2.08	1.86	1.71
54	1.92	3.68	3.62	3.05	2.63	2.31	2.05	1.87
55	2.12	4.44	4.36	3.57	3.02	2.60	2.28	2.06
56	2.36	5.53	5.45	4.30	3.53	2.98	2.56	2.29
57	2.66	7.40	7.28	5.36	4.23	3.49	2.94	2.58
58	3.04	11.08	10.90	7.17	5.30	4.18	3.43	2.95
59	3.56	22.25	21.88	10.70	7.06	5.21	4.12	3.45
60	4.26			21.50	10.55	6.95	5.12	4.12
61	5.32				21.11	10.37	6.83	5.14
62	7.09					20.41	10.18	6.84
63	10.64						20.14	10.25
64	21.10							20.32

TABLE II

FEMALES

Age on birthday next following election	Figure to be used by reference to the under-mentioned pensionable age							
	Employee to whom on retirement regulation E3(2) would apply	Others						
	65	60	Over 60 and under 61	61 and under 62	62 and under 63	63 and under 64	64 and under 65	65
26		0.59						
27		0.61						
28		0.63						
29		0.65						
30		0.68						
31		0.71						
32		0.74						
33		0.77						
34		0.80						
35		0.83						
36		0.87	0.86					
37		0.91	0.90	0.85				
38		0.96	0.94	0.89	0.83			
39		1.01	0.99	0.93	0.87	0.82		
40		1.07	1.05	0.98	0.91	0.86	0.80	
41		1.13	1.11	1.03	0.96	0.90	0.84	0.80
42		1.20	1.18	1.09	1.01	0.93	0.88	0.84
43		1.28	1.26	1.16	1.07	1.00	0.93	0.88
44		1.37	1.34	1.23	1.14	1.06	0.98	0.93
45		1.46	1.43	1.31	1.21	1.12	1.04	0.98
46	1.14	1.57	1.54	1.40	1.29	1.19	1.11	1.04
47	1.21	1.70	1.67	1.51	1.38	1.27	1.18	1.11
48	1.29	1.85	1.82	1.64	1.49	1.36	1.26	1.18
49	1.38	2.03	1.99	1.79	1.62	1.46	1.35	1.26
50	1.48	2.24	2.20	1.96	1.77	1.58	1.45	1.35
51	1.59	2.50	2.46	2.17	1.94	1.72	1.57	1.45
52	1.72	2.83	2.78	2.42	2.14	1.89	1.71	1.57
53	1.87	3.24	3.19	2.73	2.38	2.09	1.87	1.71
54	2.05	3.80	3.73	3.13	2.69	2.33	2.06	1.87
55	2.26	4.58	4.50	3.67	3.08	2.63	2.30	2.06
56	2.52	5.73	5.64	4.40	3.60	3.02	2.59	2.30
57	2.84	7.66	7.53	5.51	4.33	3.54	2.96	2.59
58	3.24	11.47	11.26	7.36	5.40	4.24	3.47	2.96
59	3.79	22.86	22.45	11.05	7.20	5.30	4.15	3.46
60	4.53			22.15	10.79	7.05	5.17	4.14
61	5.65				21.64	10.59	6.89	5.17
62	7.52					20.72	10.24	6.87
63	11.28						20.34	10.29
64	22.44							20.46

3.—(1) For the purposes of paragraph 2, in relation to any additional contribution falling to be paid by an employee under regulation C6 his remuneration for the time being is, subject to sub-paragraph (2), the remuneration received by him for the interval (being an interval determined under regulation C6(3)(a)) at the end of which the additional contribution falls to be paid.

(2) For the purposes of sub-paragraph (1), an employee is to be taken to have received for any period for which, while a contract of employment subsisted, he was absent from duty with reduced remuneration or without remuneration, otherwise than by reason of illness or injury, the remuneration that he would have received but for his absence from duty.

Regulation C8

SCHEDULE 6

PAYMENT TO AVOID REDUCTION OF RETIRING ALLOWANCE

PART I

LUMP SUM PAYMENT

1. The amount to be paid by an employee who has under regulation C8 elected to make payment by a lump sum is $\dfrac{A \times B \times C}{100}$, where–

A is the length of the period of reckonable service specified in his notice of election, expressed in complete years and any fraction of a year,

B is his remuneration at the date of the election, and

C is, in the case of a man, the figure specified in column (2) of the Table below against his age as specified in column (1) on his birthday following the date of the election and, in the case of a woman, a figure to be specified by the Government Actuary.

TABLE

(1) Age on birthday next following election	(2) Figure to be used
25	2.76
26	2.61
27	2.51
28	2.44
29	2.39
30	2.35
31	2.31
32	2.28
33	2.25
34	2.23
35	2.21
36	2.20
37	2.18
38	2.17
39	2.16
40	2.15
41	2.14
42	2.13
43	2.12
44	2.11
45	2.10
46	2.09
47	2.08
48	2.08
49	2.09
50	2.10
51	2.12
52	2.14
53	2.16
54	2.18
55	2.20
56	2.22
57	2.24
58	2.26
59	2.28
60	2.30
61	2.31
62	2.32
63	2.33
64	2.34

2. The amount is to be paid within one month after the date of the election.

PART II

INSTALMENTS

3. The amount to be paid by an employee who has under regulation C8 elected to make payment by instalments is the amount he would have been required to pay under Part I if he had on the same date elected to make payment by a lump sum, increased by 5% for each complete year, and *pro rata* for any fraction of a year, during which, under paragraph 4, instalments are due to be paid.

4. The employee is to specify in his notice of election the date up to which instalments are to be paid, which may not be–

(a) later than his 65th birthday, or

(b) earlier than the date on which he would attain pensionable age.

5. Instalments are to be of equal amounts and to be paid at such intervals as the appropriate administering authority may determine, the first instalment being due to be paid not later than one month after the date of the election.

PART III

ADDITIONAL CONTRIBUTIONS

6. The amount to be paid by way of additional contributions by an employee who has under regulation C8 elected to make payment in that manner is $\dfrac{A \times B \times C}{100}$, where–

A is the length of the period of reckonable service specified in his notice of election, expressed in complete years and any fraction of a year,

B is his remuneration for the time being, and

C is in the case of a man, the figure in column (2), (3), (4), (5), (6) or (7) of the Table below appropriate to his age on his birthday next following the date of the election and to his specified birthday (within the meaning of paragraph 8), and, in the case of a woman, a figure to be specified by the Government Actuary.

TABLE

Age on birthday next following election	Figure to be used by reference to the under-mentioned specified age					
(1)	(2)	(3)	(4)	(5)	(6)	(7)
	60	61	62	63	64	65
25	0.07					
26	0.07					
27	0.07					
28	0.07					
29	0.08					
30	0.08					
31	0.08					
32	0.08					
33	0.09					
34	0.09					
35	0.09					
36	0.10					
37	0.10	0.10				
38	0.11	0.10	0.10			
39	0.12	0.11	0.10	0.09		
40	0.12	0.11	0.11	0.10	0.09	
41	0.13	0.12	0.11	0.10	0.10	0.09
42	0.14	0.13	0.12	0.11	0.10	0.10
43	0.14	0.13	0.12	0.12	0.11	0.10
44	0.15	0.14	0.13	0.12	0.11	0.11
45	0.16	0.15	0.14	0.13	0.12	0.11
46	0.17	0.16	0.15	0.14	0.13	0.12
47	0.19	0.17	0.16	0.15	0.14	0.13
48	0.21	0.19	0.17	0.16	0.15	0.14
49	0.23	0.21	0.18	0.17	0.16	0.15
50	0.25	0.23	0.20	0.18	0.17	0.16
51	0.28	0.25	0.22	0.20	0.18	0.17
52	0.32	0.28	0.25	0.22	0.20	0.18
53	0.37	0.32	0.28	0.24	0.22	0.20
54	0.43	0.36	0.31	0.27	0.24	0.22
55	0.52	0.42	0.36	0.31	0.27	0.24
56	0.65	0.51	0.42	0.35	0.30	0.27
57	0.87	0.63	0.50	0.41	0.34	0.30
58	1.30	0.84	0.62	0.49	0.40	0.35
59	2.62	1.26	0.83	0.61	0.48	0.41
60		2.53	1.24	0.82	0.60	0.48
61			2.48	1.22	0.80	0.60
62				2.40	1.20	0.80
63					2.37	1.21
64						2.39

7.—(1) For the purposes of paragraph 6, in relation to any additional contribution falling to be paid by an employee his remuneration for the time being is, subject to sub-paragraph (2), the remuneration received by him for the interval (being an interval determined under paragraph 9) at the end of which the additional contribution falls to be paid.

(2) For the purposes of sub-paragraph (1), an employee is to be taken to have received for any period for which, while a contract of employment subsisted, he was absent from duty with reduced remuneration or without remuneration, otherwise than by reason of illness or injury, the remuneration that he would have received but for his absence from duty.

8. An employee is to specify in his notice of election the birthday ("the specified birthday") up to which additional contributions are to be paid, which may be–

(a) his 65th birthday, or

(b) any earlier birthday falling on the date on which he would attain pensionable age, or

(c) the birthday immediately prior to the date on which he would attain pensionable age.

9. Additional contributions are to be paid, at such intervals as the appropriate administering authority may determine, from the employee's birthday next following the date of the election.

PART IV

UNCOMPLETED PAYMENTS

10. This Part applies where an employee has under regulation C8 elected to make payment by instalments or by way of additional contributions and has commenced payment, but before, as the case may be–

(a) the date specified under paragraph 4, or

(b) the birthday specified under paragraph 8,

a relevant event occurs.

11. The relevant events are–

(a) the discontinuance of payment under regulation C8(11), and

(b) where there has been no such discontinuance of payment–

(i) the employee's ceasing to hold his employment by reason of permanent ill-health or infirmity of mind or body,

(ii) the death of the employee while in local government employment, or

(iii) the employee's ceasing to hold his employment for any reason other than that specified in sub-paragraph (i) or (ii) above.

12. Where the relevant event is the discontinuance of payment under regulation C8(11), the period of reckonable service in respect of which the election was made is to be treated as having been $\frac{A \times B}{C}$, where–

A is the length of the period during which instalments or additional contributions have been paid,

B is the length of the period of reckonable service in respect of which the election was made, and

C is the length of the period during which, under Part II or Part III, instalments or additional contributions were to have been paid,

each period being expressed in complete years and any fraction of a year.

13. Where the relevant event is–

(a) the death of the employee, or

(b) his ceasing to hold his employment by reason of permanent ill-health or infirmity of mind or body,

he is to be treated as having completed payment in accordance with Part II or, as the case may be, Part III.

14.—(1) Where the relevant event is the employee's ceasing to hold his employment in any other circumstance, he may within 3 months of so ceasing elect to pay to the appropriate superannuation fund within the period specified in sub-paragraph (2) the actuarial equivalent of the balance of contributions or instalments outstanding and shall in that event be treated as having completed payment in accordance with Part II or, as the case may be, Part III.

(2) The period for making a payment under sub-paragraph (1) is the period of one month beginning on the date on which the person is notified by the appropriate administering authority of the amount calculated as mentioned in that sub-paragraph.

15.—(1) Where the employee ceases to hold his employment and neither paragraph 13(b) nor paragraph 14 applies, he is, unless sub-paragraph (2) applies, to be treated as if paragraph 12 (discontinuance of payment) had applied.

(2) This sub-paragraph applies where the employee–

(a) elected under regulation C8 to make payment by way of additional contributions, and

(b) has within 12 months after ceasing to hold his employment again entered local government employment, without having–

(i) become entitled in relation to the first employment to the payment of any benefit, or

(ii) elected to receive a payment under regulation C12(4) (return of contributions), or

(iii) made a request for earlier payment under regulation C12(7)(b), and

(c) has not made an election for the purposes of regulation E2(9)(c) (retention of right to preserved benefits), and

(d) within 3 months after his again entering local government employment pays to his new employing authority an amount equal to any additional contributions that would have been payable if he had not ceased to hold the first employment.

(3) Where sub-paragraph (2) applies, the election under regulation C8 continues to have effect as if the relevant event had not occurred.

SCHEDULE 7   Regulation C9(4)

OUTSTANDING PAYMENTS UNDER 1974 REGULATIONS

1. Paragraphs 2 to 7 apply while any amount is outstanding in respect of payments under regulation D6, D7 or D8 of the 1974 Regulations which remain payable by virtue of regulation C9(4) of these Regulations.

2. Compound interest, calculated at the rate of 3% per annum with half-yearly rests, is payable on the amount for the time being outstanding.

3. If a benefit calculated by reference to the length of the employee's reckonable service becomes payable to or in respect of him, the amount outstanding is to be recovered by deducting it from any amount payable by way of benefits.

4. If benefits become payable to or in respect of the employee under these Regulations but none of them is calculated by reference to the length of his reckonable service, the amount outstanding ceases to be payable.

5. Subject to paragraphs 6 and 7, if the employee ceases to hold his employment and no benefit becomes payable to him, the amount then outstanding ceases to be payable.

6. If the employee becomes entitled to preserved benefits and does not elect to receive a payment under regulation C12(4) (return of contributions), he may, by notice in writing given to his employing authority within 3 months after becoming entitled to those benefits, elect to pay in a lump sum to that authority the amount outstanding.

7.—(1) If the employee ceases to hold his employment and–
   (a) no benefit becomes payable to him, and
   (b) he has paid all the instalments due up to the date when he ceased to hold his employment, and
   (c) within 12 months afer that date he has again entered local government employment, without having–
      (i) elected to receive a payment under regulation C12(4), or
      (ii) made a request for earlier payment under regulation C12(7)(b),
he may, subject to sub-paragraphs (2) and (3), pay the amount outstanding as if he had not ceased to hold the first employment.

(2) The amount outstanding is payable to the new employing authority or, where there are more than one, among them in the proportions which the employee's remuneration in each of the employments bear to the aggregate of his remuneration in all the employments.

(3) An apportionment under sub-paragraph (2) takes effect as if the employee had entered all the employments to which it relates on the date on which he entered the first of them, and any payments made by him under this paragraph before the apportionment are to be adjusted accordingly.

SCHEDULE 8   Regulation C16

LIMITATION ON PAYMENT BY WAY OF ADDITIONAL CONTRIBUTIONS OR BY INSTALMENTS

1. If the amount payable by the pensionable employee by way of additional contributions in pursuance of a notice given under regulation D10 or D10A of the 1974 Regulations or an election made under regulation C6 or C8, or the amount of an instalment payable in pursuance of an election made under regulation C8, as the case may be, when aggregated with–
   (a) any other amounts payable by him under any of those regulations in addition to the first-mentioned amount; and
   (b) the amount payable by him by way of contributions under regulation C2,

exceeds 15% of his remuneration, he shall satisfy his liability in respect of the excess over 15% by payment in a lump sum of a sum–

    (i) in the case of an election under regulation C6 or, in the case of a male employee, an election under regulation C8 to pay by the method described in regulation C8(5)(c), determined in accordance with the formula in paragraph 2; and

    (ii) in any other case, calculated by the Government Actuary to represent the capital value of the excess.

2.   The formula mentioned in paragraph 1 is–

$$\frac{T \times R \times F}{100}, \text{ where–}$$

T is the length in years and fractions of a year of the period relating to the excess;

R is the remuneration of the employee at the time he made the election under regulation C6 or, in the case of a male employee, an election under regulation C8 to pay by the method described in regulation C8(5)(c);

F is the figure specified, opposite to the age of the employee on his birthday next following the date on which he made that election, in the relevant column of Table I or Table II in relation to an election under regulation C6 and Table III below in relation to an election under regulation C8 appropriate to his pensionable age as defined in paragraph 3.

TABLE I

MALES

Age on birthday next following election	Employee to whom on retirement regulation E3(2) would apply	Others						
	65	60	Over 60 and under 61	61 and under 62	62 and under 63	63 and under 64	64 and under 65	65
40		18.60	18.40	17.90	17.50	17.10	16.70	16.50
41		18.70	18.40	18.00	17.60	17.20	16.70	16.50
42		18.80	18.50	18.00	17.60	17.20	16.80	16.60
43		18.90	18.60	18.10	17.70	17.20	16.80	16.60
44		19.00	18.70	18.20	17.80	17.30	16.90	16.70
45		19.10	18.80	18.30	17.90	17.40	16.90	16.70
46	17.30	19.20	18.90	18.40	18.00	17.50	17.00	16.80
47	17.40	19.30	19.00	18.50	18.10	17.60	17.10	16.90
48	17.50	19.40	19.10	18.60	18.20	17.70	17.20	17.00
49	17.60	19.50	19.20	18.70	18.30	17.80	17.30	17.10
50	17.70	19.70	19.40	18.80	18.40	17.90	17.40	17.20
51	17.80	19.90	19.60	19.00	18.50	18.00	17.50	17.30
52	17.90	20.10	19.80	19.20	18.70	18.10	17.60	17.40
53	18.00	20.30	20.00	19.40	18.90	18.30	17.70	17.50
54	18.10	20.50	20.20	19.60	19.10	18.50	17.80	17.60
55	18.30	20.70	20.40	19.80	19.30	18.70	18.00	17.80
56	18.50	20.90	20.60	20.00	19.50	18.90	18.20	18.00
57	18.70	21.20	20.90	20.20	19.70	19.10	18.40	18.20
58	18.90	21.50	21.20	20.50	19.90	19.30	18.60	18.40
59	19.10	21.80	21.50	20.80	20.10	19.50	18.80	18.60
60	19.40			21.10	20.40	19.70	19.10	18.80
61	19.70				20.70	19.90	19.30	19.00
62	20.00					20.10	19.50	19.30
63	20.30						19.70	19.60
64	20.70							19.90

TABLE II

FEMALES

Age on birthday next following election	Figure to be used by reference to the under-mentioned pensionable age							
	Employee to whom on retirement regulation E3(2) would apply	Others						
	65	60	Over 60 and under 61	61 and under 62	62 and under 63	63 and under 64	64 and under 65	65
40		19.40	19.10	18.60	18.00	17.40	16.90	16.60
41		19.60	19.30	18.70	18.10	17.50	17.00	16.70
42		19.70	19.40	18.80	18.20	17.60	17.10	16.80
43		19.80	19.50	18.90	18.30	17.80	17.20	16.90
44		19.90	19.60	19.00	18.40	17.90	17.30	17.00
45		20.10	19.70	19.10	18.50	18.00	17.40	17.10
46	18.80	20.20	19.90	19.20	18.60	18.10	17.50	17.20
47	18.90	20.40	20.00	19.40	18.80	18.20	17.60	17.30
48	19.00	20.50	20.20	19.50	18.90	18.30	17.70	17.40
49	19.10	20.60	20.30	19.60	19.00	18.40	17.80	17.50
50	19.20	20.80	20.40	19.80	19.20	18.60	17.90	17.60
51	19.30	21.00	20.60	19.90	19.30	18.70	18.00	17.70
52	19.40	21.10	20.80	20.10	19.40	18.80	18.20	17.90
53	19.50	21.30	21.00	20.30	19.60	19.00	18.30	18.00
54	19.60	21.50	21.20	20.40	19.80	19.10	18.40	18.10
55	19.80	21.70	21.40	20.60	19.90	19.20	18.60	18.20
56	20.00	21.90	21.60	20.80	20.10	19.40	18.70	18.30
57	20.20	22.10	21.80	21.00	20.30	19.60	18.80	18.50
58	20.40	22.30	22.00	21.20	20.50	19.80	19.00	18.70
59	20.60	22.60	22.20	21.40	20.70	20.00	19.20	18.90
60	20.80			21.70	20.90	20.20	19.40	19.10
61	21.10				21.20	20.40	19.60	19.30
62	21.40					20.50	19.80	19.50
63	21.70						20.00	19.80
64	22.00							20.10

TABLE III

Age on birthday next following election	Figure to be used by reference to the under-mentioned pensionable age					
	60	61	62	63	64	65
25	2.76					
26	2.61					
27	2.51					
28	2.44					
29	2.39					
30	2.35					
31	2.31					
32	2.28					
33	2.25					
34	2.23					
35	2.21					
36	2.20					
37	2.19	2.11				
38	2.19	2.11	2.06			
39	2.19	2.11	2.06	2.01		
40	2.20	2.12	2.06	2.01	1.97	
41	2.20	2.12	2.07	2.02	1.97	1.95
42	2.21	2.12	2.07	2.02	1.98	1.95
43	2.22	2.13	2.08	2.03	1.98	1.96
44	2.23	2.14	2.09	2.04	1.99	1.96
45	2.24	2.15	2.10	2.05	2.00	1.97
46	2.25	2.16	2.11	2.06	2.01	1.98
47	2.27	2.17	2.12	2.07	2.02	1.99
48	2.29	2.19	2.13	2.08	2.03	2.00
49	2.31	2.21	2.15	2.09	2.04	2.01
50	2.33	2.23	2.17	2.10	2.05	2.02
51	2.35	2.25	2.19	2.12	2.06	2.03
52	2.37	2.27	2.21	2.14	2.07	2.04
53	2.39	2.29	2.23	2.16	2.09	2.06
54	2.41	2.31	2.25	2.18	2.11	2.08
55	2.44	2.33	2.27	2.20	2.13	2.10
56	2.47	2.35	2.29	2.22	2.15	2.12
57	2.50	2.38	2.31	2.24	2.17	2.14
58	2.53	2.41	2.34	2.26	2.19	2.16
59	2.56	2.44	2.37	2.29	2.21	2.18
60		2.48	2.40	2.32	2.24	2.21
61			2.43	2.35	2.27	2.24
62				2.38	2.30	2.27
63					2.33	2.30
64						2.34

3. In paragraph 2 "pensionable age" means the earliest age at which, if the employee were to remain a pensionable employee without any break of service, he would become entitled by virtue of regulation E2(1)(a) or (b)(ii), if he then ceased to be employed, to a retirement pension or, if at the birthday next following an election under regulation C8(5)(c) he satisfies the requirements of regulation E2(1)(a), the age at which he has indicated he intends to retire.

SCHEDULE 9

Regulation D5

UNCOMPLETED PAYMENT OF ADDITIONAL CONTRIBUTIONS

1. This Schedule applies where an employee has made an election under regulation C6 (periodical payments to increase reckonable service) and has commenced payment, but before he attains pensionable age a relevant event occurs and any payment made to him under regulation C12 (return of contributions) does not include the amount already paid by him under regulation C6(3).

2.   The relevant events are–
   (a) the discontinuance of payment under regulation C6(5), and
   (b) where there has been no such discontinuance of payment–
      (i) the employee's ceasing to hold his employment, and
      (ii) the death of the employee while in local government employment.

3.   Where the relevant event is the discontinuance of payment under regulation C6(5), the employee is entitled to reckon as reckonable service an additional period of $\dfrac{A \times B}{C}$, where–

   A is the length of the period during which additional contributions have been paid,
   B is the length of the additional period in respect of which the election was made, and
   C is the length of the period during which, under regulation C6(3), the additional contributions were to have been paid,

each period being expressed in complete years and any fraction of a year.

4.   Where the relevant event is–
   (a) the death of the employee, or
   (b) his ceasing to hold his employment by reason of permanent ill-health or infirmity of mind or body,

he is to be treated as having completed payment in accordance with regulation C6(3).

5.—(1) Where the relevant event is the employee's ceasing to hold his employment, and–
   (a) he then, by virtue of the satisfaction of condition (a) or (b) in regulation E2(4), becomes entitled to benefits under regulation E2(1)(b)(iii), and
   (b) he gives notice in writing for the purpose to the appropriate administering authority within the period of 3 months beginning on the day after the last day of his employment,

he may pay to the appropriate superannuation fund within the period specified in sub-paragraph (2) the actuarial equivalent of the balance of his contributions due, and shall in that event be treated as having completed payment in accordance with regulation C6(3).

(2) The period for making a payment under sub-paragraph (1) is the period of one month beginning on the date on which the person is notified by the appropriate administering authority of the amount calculated as mentioned in that sub-paragraph.

6.—(1) Where the relevant event is the employee's ceasing to hold his employment and neither paragraph 4(b) nor paragraph 5 applies, he is, unless sub-paragraph (2) applies, to be treated as if paragraph 3 (discontinuance of payment) had applied.

(2) This sub-paragraph applies where the employee–
   (a) has within 12 months after ceasing to hold his employment again entered local government employment, without having–
      (i) become entitled in relation to the first employment to the payment of any benefit, or
      (ii) received any payment under regulation C12(4) (return of contributions) which includes the amount already paid by him under regulation C6(3), or
      (iii) made a request for earlier payment under regulation C12(7)(b), and
   (b) has not made an election for the purposes of regulation E2(9)(c) (retention of right to preserved benefits), and
   (c) within 3 months after his again entering local government employment pays to his new employing authority an amount equal to any additional contributions that would have been payable if he had not ceased to hold the first employment.

(3) Where sub-paragraph (2) applies, the election under regulation C6 continues to have effect as if the relevant event had not occurred.

Regulation E3(12)   **SCHEDULE 10**

ADDITIONAL RECKONABLE SERVICE FOR ILL-HEALTH

1.   For the purposes of this Schedule–
   (a) a person's relevant service is so much of his contributing service and non-contributing service as did not consist of years added to his service–

(i) under regulation 12 of the Benefits Regulations or under that regulation as applied by or under any enactment, or

(ii) under a provision of a local Act scheme which has the same effect, and

(b) a person's relevant reckonable service is the total of–

(i) any relevant service which became reckonable service by virtue of regulation D1 of the 1974 Regulations, and

(ii) any subsequent reckonable service except additional periods purchased by lump sum or additional contributions.

2.—(1) Subject to sub-paragraph (2) and paragraphs 3 and 4, the additional period which a person is to be treated as being entitled to reckon as reckonable service under regulation E3(12) is the period specified in column (2) of the Table below appropriate to the length of the person's relevant reckonable service specified in column (1) of that Table.

TABLE

(1) Length of relevant reckonable service	(2) Additional period
Not exceeding 10 years	A period equal to the length of the relevant reckonable service
Exceeding 10 years but not exceeding 13 121/365 years	The period by which the length of the relevant reckonable service falls short of 20 years
Exceeding 13 121/365 years	6 243/365 years

(2) The additional period is not to exceed the period by which the person's reckonable service would have been increased if he had continued in the employment which he has ceased to hold–

(a) until he attained the age of 65 years, or

(b) until his reckonable service amounted to 40 years,

whichever would have occurred first.

3.—(1) Subject to paragraph 4, this paragraph applies where, before entering the employment which he has ceased to hold, the person had, on ceasing to hold a previous employment, become entitled to benefits under regulation E2(1)(b)(i) or under regulation 5(1)(a) of the Benefits Regulations.

(2) Where this paragraph applies, the person's relevant reckonable service is to be treated for the purposes of paragraph 2 as having included A – B, where–

A is the length of his relevant reckonable service or, as the case may be, his relevant service, in relation to the previous employment, and

B is the length of the additional period which became reckonable in relation to the previous employment by virtue of regulation E3(12) or, as the case may be, the period by which his relevant service in relation to that employment is by virtue of sub-paragraph (3) to be deemed to have been increased.

(3) For the purposes of sub-paragraph (2)–

(a) where the person's retirement pension in respect of the previous employment was calculated under regulation 5(3)(a) of the Benefits Regulations, his relevant service shall be deemed to have been increased by the period by which its length fell short of 20 years, and

(b) where that pension was calculated under regulation 5(3)(b) of the Benefits Regulations, his relevant service shall be deemed to have been increased by the period by which it would have been increased if he had continued in the previous employment until he reached the age of 65 years.

4.—(1) This paragraph applies where–

(a) the person either–

(i) was a contributory employee immediately before 16th May 1974 and became a pensionable employee on that day, or

(ii) became a pensionable employee within 12 months after having ceased to be a contributory employee, and

(b) the length of his relevant reckonable service is not less than 10 years, and

(c) notice that this paragraph is to apply is given in accordance with sub-paragraph (3) or (4).

(2) Where this paragraph applies, paragraphs 2 and 3 do not apply and the additional period is the shorter of–

(a) the period by which the person's reckonable service would have been increased if he had continued in the employment which he has ceased to hold until he attained the age of 65 years, and

(b) the period by which his reckonable service falls short of 20 years.

(3) Subject to sub-paragraph (4), notice that this paragraph is to apply must be given by the person to the appropriate administering authority, in writing, within one month after ceasing to hold his employment or such longer period as the authority may allow.

(4) If the person dies within the period allowed for giving notice without having given it, notice may be given–

(a) if the person was a man and has left a widow, by her, or

(b) if the person was a man and has not left a widow, or his widow has died without giving notice, by his executors, or

(c) if the person was a woman, by her executors,

within 6 months after the date of the person's death, or such longer period as the authority may allow.

Regulation E3(14)

SCHEDULE 11

REDUCTION OF BENEFITS ON EARLY PAYMENT

Where regulation E3(14) applies, benefits are reduced by the percentage shown in columns (2) and (3) of the Table below for the retirement pension for males and females respectively and column (4) of the Table for the retiring allowance opposite the period set out in column (1), being the period remaining from the date from which the person became entitled to receive benefits to the attainment of pensionable age; and where the period remaining is not an exact number of years the necessary interpolations are to be made in the Table.

TABLE

Period remaining (years)	Percentage reduction		Retiring allowance
	Retirement pension		
	Male	*Female*	*Both sexes*
(1)	(2)	(3)	(4)
0	0	0	0
1	8	7	2
2	15	13	5
3	22	18	7
4	28	23	9
5	33	27	11

Regulation E19

SCHEDULE 12

MODIFICATIONS TO PART E WHERE NO RIGHT TO RETIRING ALLOWANCE ETC.

PART I

1. In regulation E2(1), the words "and a lump sum retiring allowance" shall be deleted.

2. In regulation E3–

(a) in paragraph (1), for the words "one eighteenth" there shall be substituted "one sixtieth"; and

(b) paragraphs (2) to (11) shall be deleted.

3. In regulation E11–

(a) in paragraph (1)(b), after the word "pension" there shall be inserted the words ", other than a pension under regulation E2(2),"; and

(b) paragraph (11) shall be deleted.

4. In regulation E17, paragraph (6)(a)(iii) and (v) shall be deleted.

PART II

5. In regulation E3, paragraphs (4) to (11) shall be deleted.

6. In regulation E11, paragraph (10) shall be deleted.

PART III

7. In regulation E6, for paragraphs (2) to (4) there shall be substituted–

"(2) Subject to paragraphs (3) and (5), the annual rate of a widow's long-term pension is the aggregate of–

(a) one four hundred and eightieth of her husband's pensionable remuneration multiplied by the length in years of his reckonable service before 1st April 1972, and

(b) one one hundred and sixtieth of his pensionable remuneration multiplied by the length in years of his reckonable service after 31st March 1972, and

(c) in the case of a person to whom regulation E2(1)(b)(i) applied or who dies in employment in which he was a pensionable employee, the amount ascertained by multiplying one one hundred and sixtieth of his pensionable remuneration by the length in years of the additional period of reckonable service determined in accordance with Schedule 10 or, in the case of a person who dies in employment as aforesaid, an additional period of reckonable service determined as if at the date of his death he were a person to whom regulation E2(1)(b)(i) applied.

(3) For the purpose of calculating the rate of the pension under paragraph (2), no account shall be taken of reckonable service before attaining the age of 60 years beyond a total of 40 years, and any reckonable service which is accordingly to be left out of account shall be taken from the beginning of the period of reckonable service.".

8. In regulation E8–

(a) in paragraph (1), sub-paragraph (b) and the words "and then a children's long-term pension" shall be deleted;

(b) paragraph (2) shall be deleted; and

(c) in paragraph (4), the words "or (b) or paragraph (2)" shall be deleted.

9. In regulation E11–

(a) in paragraph (1)(b), the words "in relation to which this paragraph applies" shall be deleted;

(b) paragraph (2) shall be deleted;

(c) in paragraphs (4)(b) and (5)(a), for the words "and paragraph (2)(b) apply" there shall be substituted "applies";

(d) in paragraph (5)(b), for the words "and paragraph (2)(a) apply" there shall be substituted "applies";

(e) in paragraph (5), for the words from "the greater of" to the end of the paragraph there shall be substituted "the greater of $(B \times C) - E$ or $\dfrac{C}{F} \times (A - E)$";

(f) paragraphs (6), (7) and (9) shall be deleted;

(g) in paragraph (12), the words "Subject to paragraph (13)," shall be deleted; and

(h) paragraph (13) shall be deleted.

SCHEDULE 13   Regulation E20

SURRENDER OF PART OF RETIREMENT PENSION

PART I

LIMITS ON AMOUNT SURRENDERED

1.—(1) The part of the retirement pension surrendered on any occasion–

(a) must be an exact number of pounds, and

(b) must secure for the beneficiary a pension of at least £39 per annum.

(2) The surrendered part must not, together with any parts previously surrendered–

(a) exceed the lower of–

(i) the amount which would result in the reduction of the retirement pension to less than the rate of the pension which would become payable to the beneficiary under this Schedule, or

(ii) one third of the retirement pension, or where regulation E14 (former teachers) applies one third of the retirement pension receivable after reduction under that regulation, or

(b) be of an amount which would result in the reduction of the retirement pension to less than any minimum rate of equivalent pension benefits applicable under the Insurance Acts, or

(c) where the person's local government employment is or was contracted-out employment, be of an amount which would result in the retirement pension–

(i) becoming payable at an annual rate less than that obtained by multiplying one eightieth of his pensionable remuneration by the length in years of the whole period of his service in contracted-out employment, or

(ii) being, but for regulation E1(3), less than his guaranteed minimum if any.

2.   Where the person falls within regulation E20(2)(b), references in paragraph 1 to the retirement pension are references to the retirement pension which would become payable if he were to cease to hold his employment on the day on which the surrender takes effect.

PART II

PROCEDURE

3.   Upon a person's first becoming eligible to notify his wish to surrender part of his retirement pension the appropriate administering authority shall send him a notice stating that provision has been made by these Regulations for the surrender of part of a retirement pension to a spouse or dependant and informing the person to whom the notice is addressed that he may on application to the authority obtain further information on the subject.

4.   Where a person wishes to make a surrender he may–

(a) in the case of a pensionable employee who on ceasing to hold his employment becomes entitled to a retirement pension (in this Schedule referred to as "a retiring employee"), not more than 2 months before or within one month after the date on which he ceases to be employed; and

(b) in the case of a pensionable employee who would, if he were to retire from his employment, become entitled to a retirement pension (in this Schedule referred to as "a continuing employee"), within 2 months before or at any time after becoming a continuing employee and while he is still employed;

notify his desire to surrender a part of that retirement pension by completing a copy of the form specified at the end of this Schedule, or a form to the like effect, and sending it to the appropriate administering authority:

Provided that where the appropriate administering authority are satisfied that it has not been reasonably practicable for a retiring employee to notify his desire to surrender a part of a retirement pension within the time limit imposed by sub-paragraph (a) owing to circumstances beyond his control, they may at their discretion extend that limit to a date not more than 6 months after the date on which he ceases to be employed.

5.   On receipt by the appropriate administering authority of a notification given by a person under paragraph 4, that authority shall–

(a) forthwith arrange for the person to be examined by a registered medical practitioner nominated by them and for a report to be given to them by the practitioner stating whether, in his opinion, the person is in good health, regard being had to his age; and if the opinion stated in such report is that the person is not in good health, the appropriate administering authority shall notify him accordingly and offer him an opportunity of a further examination by some other registered medical practitioner nominated by them with a view to that practitioner reporting to them on the state of the person's health; and

(b) require the person to furnish at his own expense–

(i) a certificate of his birth, except where the date of birth has been duly recorded by the authority and is not disputed;

(ii) in respect of a beneficiary who is the person's spouse, a birth certificate and a marriage certificate;

(iii) in respect of a beneficiary who is a dependant, a birth certificate and such evidence as may be appropriate to prove dependency,

and any other information or evidence which the authority consider necessary:

Provided that, if for any reason a birth or marriage certificate cannot be supplied, the authority may accept such other evidence of birth or marriage as they think fit in order to determine the age or the question of marriage of the person concerned, as the case may be.

6. Any fee payable to a practitioner in respect of an examination and report under paragraph 5 shall be paid by the person examined at the time of the examination.

7.—(1) Subject to the provisions of this Schedule, unless the appropriate administering authority are of the opinion, on consideration of a report obtained by them under paragraph 5, that the person to whom the report relates is not in good health or they are of the opinion that the evidence produced in regard to marriage or dependency is not satisfactory, they shall allow the surrender of such part of the retirement pension as is specified in the person's notification and as is in conformity with this Schedule and shall grant to the beneficiary named in the notification a pension, payable in the event of the beneficiary's surviving the person and to be calculated in accordance with regulation E20(4):

Provided that a decision by an appropriate administering authority to allow a surrender by a retiring employee shall not be made before the date on which he ceases to be employed and a decision by an appropriate administering authority to allow a surrender by a continuing employee shall not be made before the date on which he becomes such an employee.

(2) Notwithstanding anything in sub-paragraph (1), the appropriate administering authority shall, if they are dissatisfied with the evidence of marriage, but are nevertheless satisfied on the evidence already before them or after making such further enquiries as they think necessary that a person named as spouse in the notification given under paragraph 4 is a dependant of the person who gave the notification, treat the notification as if the person named therein as spouse had been named as a dependant of the person giving the notification.

(3) As soon as is reasonably practicable after coming to a decision in regard to a notification given by a person, the appropriate administering authority shall notify him that they have allowed a surrender in favour of the person named in his notification or that they have decided not to allow a surrender of any part of the retirement pension, as the case may be, and if the appropriate administering authority have allowed a surrender they shall also furnish him with a statement as to the amount of the pension to which the beneficiary may become entitled after his death and, if the person who gave the notification under paragraph 4 is a retiring employee, with a statement as to the amount of the reduced retirement pension to which he is entitled.

(4) A notification of a decision not to allow a surrender shall state the grounds for the decision.

(5) A notification sent to an employee in pursuance of sub-paragraph (3) shall, if it has been posted in a prepaid envelope addressed to the employee by the appropriate administering authority, be deemed to have been received by the employee at the time at which a letter would be delivered in the ordinary course of post.

8. A person who has given a notification of his desire to surrender a part of his retirement pension under paragraph 4 may cancel or amend the notification by a notice in writing addressed to the appropriate administering authority and posted in a prepaid envelope to, or left at, the principal office of the authority at any time before he has received notification from the authority that his surrender has been allowed.

9.—(1) A notification given by a person under paragraph 4 shall become null and void if–

(a) the beneficiary dies before the person receives notification from the appropriate administering authority that his surrender has been allowed; or

(b) the person dies at any time before midnight on the day on which the appropriate administering authority decide to allow the surrender.

(2) Subject as aforesaid, a surrender allowed in pursuance of a notification given by a person shall have effect as from the date on which the person ceases to hold his employment.

FORM OF NOTIFICATION OF SURRENDER

LOCAL GOVERNMENT SUPERANNUATION (SCOTLAND) REGULATIONS

(Regulation E20 and Schedule 13)

SURRENDER OF PART OF RETIREMENT PENSION

To(**a**) ....

....

Name of employing authority or former employing authority

....

....

Particulars relating to person desiring to make the surrender

(a) Name in full...

(b) Date of birth..

(c) Address (private) ....

....

Particulars relating to beneficiary

(a) Name in full...

(b) Date of birth..

(c) Address (private) ....

....

(d) Sex ....

(e) Relationship of beneficiary to person desiring to make the surrender

....

(f) If the beneficiary is spouse of person desiring to make the surrender, date of marriage

....

A.(**b**) In pursuance of paragraph 4(a) of Schedule 13 to the above-mentioned Regulations, I hereby notify my desire to surrender in favour of the above-named beneficiary the under-mentioned part of the retirement pension to which, on .... 19...., I became/expect to become(**c**) entitled to receive payments in respect thereof.

B.(**b**) In pursuance of paragraph 4(b) of Schedule 13 to the above-mentioned Regulations, I hereby notify my desire to surrender in favour of the above-named beneficiary the under-mentioned part of the retirement pension to which, if I were to retire immediately/on .... 19....(**c**), I would become entitled.

	£	p
(1) Amount of retirement pension to be surrendered(**d**)		
(2) Amount of retirement pension expected after deduction of amount surrendered(**e**)		
(3) Pension to beneficiary expected in return for amount surrendered(**f**)		

Signature ....

Date ....

(**a**) Insert name of local authority administering the superannuation fund.
(**b**) Delete paragraph A or B, whichever does not apply.
(**c**) Delete the word or words which do not apply.
(**d**) This must be an exact number of pounds.
(**e**) This must not be less than the pension payable under the above-mentioned Regulations to the beneficiary.
(**f**) This must not be less than £39.

SCHEDULE 14   Regulations F2(1) and K1

WOMEN'S SERVICES

1. Member of Queen Alexandra's Royal Naval Nursing Service or any reserve thereof.

2. Member of the Women's Royal Naval Service.

3. Woman medical or dental practitioner serving in the Royal Navy or any Naval reserve.

4. Member of Queen Alexandra's Imperial Military Nursing Service or any reserve thereof or of Queen Alexandra's Royal Army Nursing Corps or any reserve thereof.

5. Member of the Territorial Army Nursing Service or any reserve thereof.

6. Member of the Auxiliary Territorial Service.

7. Woman employed with the Royal Army Medical Corps or the Army Dental Corps with relative rank as an officer.

8. Member of Princess Mary's Royal Air Force Nursing Service or any reserve thereof.

9. Member of the Women's Auxiliary Air Force.

10. Woman employed with the Medical Branch or the Dental Branch of the Royal Air Force with relative rank as an officer.

11. Member of the Voluntary Aid Detachments employed under the Admiralty, Army Council or Air Council.

SCHEDULE 15   Regulations F6 and J3(3)

PUBLIC SERVICE SCHEMES

PART I

1. Regulations from time to time in force under the Police Pensions Act 1948(a) or the Police Pensions Act 1976(b).

2. Orders and Regulations from time to time in force under the Constabulary Acts (Northern Ireland) 1922 to 1949(c) or section 25 of the Police Act (Northern Ireland) 1970(d).

3. The Firemen's Pension Scheme brought into operation under section 26 of the Fire Services Act 1947(e), as in force from time to time.

4. Orders from time to time in force under section 10 of the Fire Services (Amendment) Act (Northern Ireland) 1950(f) ("the Act of 1950") or section 17 of the Fire Services Act (Northern Ireland) 1969(g) ("the Act of 1969"), and schemes from time to time in force under section 13 of the Act of 1950 or section 26 of the Act of 1969.

(a) 1948 c.24.
(b) 1976 c.35.
(c) 1922 c.8 (N.I.), 1924 c.17 (N.I.), 1928 c.4 (N.I.), 1930 c.18 (N.I.), 1933 c.27 (N.I.), 1934 c.10 (N.I.), 1944 c.9 (N.I.), 1949 c.9 (N.I.).
(d) 1970 c.9 (N.I.); section 25 was amended by the Police (Northern Ireland) Order 1977 (S.I. 1977/53 (N.I. 2)), article 13.
(e) 1947 c.41.
(f) 1950 c.4 (N.I.); section 10 was amended by the Superannuation (Miscellaneous Provisions) Act (Northern Ireland) 1958 (c.21 (N.I.)), section 5.
(g) 1969 c.13 (N.I.); section 17 was amended by the Fire Services (Northern Ireland) Order 1973 (S.I. 1973/601 (N.I. 9)), articles 7 and 12.

PART II

5. The Teachers (Superannuation) Act 1925(**a**) and Rules from time to time in force under that Act, a Teachers' Superannuation Scheme within the meaning of section 145 (47) of the Education (Scotland) Act 1962(**b**), and Regulations from time to time in force under section 102 of that Act or under the Teachers' Superannuation Act 1965(**c**), the Teachers' Superannuation Act 1967(**d**), the Teachers' Superannuation (Scotland) Act 1968(**e**) or section 9 of the Act of 1972.

6. A 1923 Act scheme within the meaning of the Teachers' (Superannuation) Act (Northern Ireland) 1950(**f**), and Regulations from time to time in force under the Teachers' Superannuation Acts (Northern Ireland) 1950 to 1967(**g**) or article 11 of the Superannuation (Northern Ireland) Order 1972(**h**).

PART III

7. Provisions of or under the Local Government Superannuation Act 1937(**i**), the Act of 1953, section 7 of the Act of 1972, or a local Act scheme, as in force from time to time, being provisions relating to the payment of pensions, allowances or gratuities by local authorities or other bodies in England.

8. Regulations from time to time in force under section 67 of the National Health Service Act 1946(**j**), section 66 of the National Health Service (Scotland) Act 1947(**k**) or section 10 of the Act of 1972.

9. Regulations from time to time in force under section 61 of the Health Services (Northern Ireland) Act 1948(**l**) or article 12 of the Superannuation (Northern Ireland) Order 1972.

10. Regulations from time to time in force under section 2 of the Local Government (Superannuation) Act (Northern Ireland) 1950(**m**), or article 9 of the Superannuation (Northern Ireland) Order 1972.

Regulations F6(6),
J2 to J4, J8, J14 and Q2

SCHEDULE 16

CALCULATION OF TRANSFER VALUES

PART I

1. The transfer value payable under regulation J2, J3(1), J14 or Q2(2) in respect of any person is an amount equal to—

(1) the aggregate of the sums calculated in accordance with paragraph 2 below in respect of his accrued pension, accrued retiring allowance and, if the person is a man, his accrued widow's pension, less—

    (a) a sum (calculated in accordance with paragraph 2 below) in respect of accrued modification, and where a request has been received under regulation J2(3) his guaranteed minimum pension,

---

(**a**) 1925 c.59.
(**b**) 1962 c.47.
(**c**) 1965 c.83.
(**d**) 1967 c.12.
(**e**) 1968 c.12.
(**f**) 1950 c.33 (N.I.).
(**g**) 1950 c.33 (N.I.), 1951 c.28 (N.I.), Part I, 1956 c.22 (N.I.), 1963 c.7 (N.I.), 1967 c.3 (N.I.).
(**h**) S.I. 1972/1073 (N.I. 10).
(**i**) 1937 c.68.
(**j**) 1946 c.81; section 67 was amended by the National Health Service (Amendment) Act 1949 (c.93), Schedule, Part I, by the Local Government Superannuation Act 1953 (c.25), section 4(1)(c), and by S.I. 1968/1699; the 1946 Act was repealed by the National Health Service Act 1977 (c.49), Schedule 16.
(**k**) 1947 c.27; section 66 was amended by the National Health Service (Amendment) Act 1949, Schedule, Part II, by the Local Government Superannuation Act 1953, section 4(2)(c), and by S.I. 1968/1699; the 1947 Act was repealed by the National Health Service (Scotland) Act 1978 (c.29), Schedule 17.
(**l**) 1948 c.3 (N.I.); section 61 was amended by the Health Services Act (Northern Ireland) 1953 (c.6 (N.I.)), section 11, by the Health Service Act (Northern Ireland) 1958 (c.29 (N.I.)), section 8, by the Health Services (Amendment) Act (Northern Ireland) 1963 (c.20 (N.I.)), section 2, by the Administration of Estates (Small Payments) Act (Northern Ireland) 1967 (c.5 (N.I.)), section 1, and by the Health Services (Amendment) Act (Northern Ireland) 1969 (c.36 (N.I.)), sections 21 to 24.
(**m**) 1950 c.10 (N.I.).

(b) any additional contributory payments remaining unpaid when he ceased to be employed in his local government employment, and

(c) in the case of a person in relation to whom when he ceases to be employed in local government employment–

(i) a contributions equivalent premium is paid under section 42 of the Pensions Act, or

(ii) a limited revaluation premium is paid under section 45 of that Act otherwise than by the scheme managers of his approved non-local government scheme,

a sum equal to the amount of that premium,

together with–

(2) compound interest calculated in accordance with regulation J7 in respect of the period beginning immediately after the date on which the person ceased to be employed in his local government employment and ending with the date on which the transfer value is paid (but no interest is to be included in the transfer value if that period is less than 6 months).

2.—(1) The sums mentioned in paragraph 1 shall be calculated as follows–

(a) the accrued pension shall be multiplied by the pension factor,

(b) the accrued retiring allowance shall be multiplied by the retiring allowance factor,

(c) the accrued modification shall be multiplied by the modification factor, and

(d) the guaranteed minimum pension shall be multiplied by the guaranteed minimum pension factor,

such factors being the factors in the appropriate Table specified in sub-paragraph (3) in relation to the person's age at the date when he ceased to be employed in local government employment.

(2) The sum in respect of accrued widow's pension shall be calculated by multiplying the accrued widow's pension by 4 in the case of a transfer value payable under regulation J2 or J3(1), and by 2.4 in the case of a transfer value payable under regulation J14 or Q2(2).

(3) For the purposes of sub-paragraph (1) the appropriate Table shall be–

(a) in the case of a transfer value payable under regulation J2 or J3(1) the relevant Table in Part II, and

(b) in the case of a transfer value payable under regulation J14 or Q2(2) the relevant Table in Part III.

(4) The guaranteed minimum pension shall be the guaranteed minimum calculated in accordance with section 35 of the Pensions Act.

3. In this Schedule–

"accrued pension" means the annual retirement pension (however named) to which, having regard to regulations E1(3) and E32(2) and apart from any reduction falling to be made in that pension in connection with a retirement pension under section 30 of the Insurance Act or section 28 of the Social Security Act 1975 or graduated retirement benefit under section 36 of the Insurance Act, the person would have become entitled if, on the date when he ceased to be employed in his local government employment–

(a) he had attained the age of 65 years; and

(b) (i) where the person ceased to be employed in that employment before 31st March 1972, he had complied with any requirement as to a minimum period of qualifying service and, notwithstanding anything in any enactment–

(A) if in that employment he was a contributory employee within the meaning of the Act of 1937, for the purpose of calculating the amount of that pension his service had been calculated in accordance with regulation 4(1) to (1B) of the Benefits Regulations; and

(B) his entitlement to that pension had been calculated by reference to completed years and completed days;

(ii) where the person ceased to be employed in that employment on or after 31st March 1972, he had been entitled to reckon an aggregate of not less than 5 years' reckonable service and qualifying service; and

(c) he had completed any additional contributory payments;

"accrued retiring allowance" means the lump sum retiring allowance (however named) to which the person would have become entitled if, on the date when he ceased to be employed in his local government employment–

(a) he had attained the age of 65 years; and

(b) (i) where the person ceased to be employed in that employment before 31st March 1972, he had complied with any requirement as to a minimum period of qualifying service and, notwithstanding anything in any enactment–

(A) if in that employment he was a contributory employee within the meaning of the Act of 1937, for the purpose of calculating the amount of that allowance his service had been calculated in accordance with regulation 4(1) to (1B) of the Benefits Regulations; and

(B) his entitlement to that allowance had been calculated by reference to completed years and completed days;

(ii) where the person ceased to be employed in that employment on or after 31st March 1972, he had been entitled to reckon an aggregate of not less than 5 years' reckonable service and qualifying service; and

(c) he had completed any additional contributory payments; and

(d) if the person is a man, he had been married and he and his wife had not been judicially separated;

"accrued widow's pension" means the annual widow's pension (however named) which, after any initial period during which it might not have been payable, would have been payable in respect of the person if, on the date when he ceased to be employed in his local government employment–

(a) he had been married and he and his wife had not been judicially separated; and

(b) by virtue of his having attained the age of 65 years, he had been in receipt of a pension equivalent to his accrued pension; and

(c) he had died;

"accrued modification" means the amount by which the accrued pension would be reduced in connection with retirement pension under section 30 of the Insurance Act or section 28 of the Social Security Act 1975 or graduated retirement benefit under section 36 of the Insurance Act.

PART II

TABLE I — MEN

Age	Pension factor	Retiring allowance factor	Modification factor	Guaranteed minimum pension factor
Under 20	5.00	.60	.25	1.47
20	5.05	.60	.25	1.50
21	5.10	.61	.25	1.53
22	5.15	.61	.30	1.56
23	5.20	.61	.30	1.59
24	5.25	.62	.30	1.62
25	5.30	.62	.35	1.65
26	5.35	.63	.40	1.68
27	5.40	.63	.40	1.71
28	5.45	.63	.45	1.74
29	5.50	.64	.50	1.78
30	5.55	.64	.50	1.81
31	5.60	.65	.55	1.85
32	5.65	.66	.60	1.88
33	5.70	.66	.65	1.92
34	5.75	.67	.70	1.95
35	5.80	.67	.80	1.99
36	5.85	.68	.90	2.02
37	5.90	.68	1.00	2.06
38	5.95	.68	1.10	2.10
39	6.00	.69	1.20	2.14
40	6.05	.69	1.30	2.18
41	6.10	.70	1.40	2.22
42	6.15	.70	1.50	2.26
43	6.20	.71	1.60	2.30
44	6.25	.72	1.70	2.34
45	6.30	.72	1.80	2.39
46	6.40	.73	1.90	2.44
47	6.50	.74	2.00	2.48
48	6.60	.74	2.20	2.53
49	6.70	.75	2.40	2.58
50	6.80	.75	2.60	2.62
51	6.90	.76	2.90	2.67
52	7.10	.76	3.20	2.72
53	7.30	.77	3.50	2.78
54	7.50	.78	3.80	2.84
55	7.70	.79	4.20	2.90
56	8.00	.80	4.60	2.97
57	8.30	.81	5.00	3.04
58	8.60	.82	5.40	3.12
59	9.00	.84	5.80	3.20
60	9.50	.86	6.30	3.28
61	9.50	.88	6.80	3.36
62	9.50	.91	7.40	3.44
63	9.50	.94	8.10	3.53
64	9.50	.98	9.00	3.64
65	9.50	1.00	9.50	—

TABLE 2 – WOMEN

Age	Pension factor	Retiring allowance factor	Modification factor	Guaranteed minimum pension factor
Under 20	7.00	.60	.50	2.20
20	7.05	.60	.50	2.24
21	7.10	.61	.55	2.28
22	7.15	.61	.60	2.32
23	7.20	.61	.65	2.36
24	7.25	.62	.70	2.40
25	7.35	.62	.75	2.45
26	7.40	.63	.80	2.50
27	7.45	.63	.85	2.55
28	7.50	.63	.90	2.60
29	7.55	.64	.95	2.66
30	7.65	.64	1.05	2.71
31	7.70	.65	1.15	2.77
32	7.80	.66	1.25	2.82
33	7.90	.66	1.35	2.88
34	7.95	.67	1.45	2.93
35	8.05	.67	1.55	2.99
36	8.15	.68	1.65	3.05
37	8.25	.68	1.75	3.11
38	8.35	.681	.85	3.17
39	8.45	.69	1.95	3.24
40	8.55	.69	2.10	3.31
41	8.65	.70	2.25	3.38
42	8.75	.70	2.45	3.45
43	8.85	.71	2.65	3.52
44	8.95	.72	2.90	3.59
45	9.05	.73	3.15	3.66
46	9.15	.74	3.40	3.74
47	9.25	.75	3.70	3.82
48	9.35	.76	4.00	3.90
49	9.45	.77	4.35	3.98
50	9.55	.78	4.75	4.06
51	9.65	.79	5.15	4.15
52	9.80	.80	5.60	4.24
53	9.95	.81	6.10	4.33
54	10.10	.82	6.65	4.43
55	10.30	.83	7.25	4.53
56	10.50	.84	7.95	4.63
57	10.75	.85	8.75	4.74
58	11.05	.87	9.65	4.85
59	11.40	.89	10.65	4.97
60	11.75	.91	11.75	—
61	11.75	.93	11.75	—
62	11.75	.95	11.75	—
63	11.75	.97	11.75	—
64	11.75	.99	11.75	—
65	11.75	1.00	11.75	—

PART III

TABLE I – MEN

Age	Pension factor	Retiring allowance factor	Modification factor	Guaranteed minimum pension factor
Under 20	3.90	.60	.20	1.47
20	3.95	.60	.20	1.50
21	4.00	.61	.20	1.53
22	4.05	.61	.25	1.56
23	4.10	.61	.25	1.59
24	4.10	.62	.25	1.62
25	4.15	.62	.30	1.65
26	4.20	.63	.30	1.68
27	4.25	.63	.35	1.71
28	4.30	.63	.35	1.74
29	4.30	.64	.40	1.78
30	4.35	.64	.40	1.81
31	4.40	.65	.45	1.85
32	4.45	.66	.50	1.88
33	4.45	.66	.50	1.92
34	4.50	.67	.55	1.95
35	4.55	.67	.65	1.99
36	4.60	.68	.70	2.02
37	4.65	.68	.80	2.06
38	4.65	.68	.90	2.10
39	4.70	.69	.95	2.14
40	4.75	.69	1.05	2.18
41	4.80	.70	1.10	2.22
42	4.85	.70	1.20	2.26
43	4.85	.71	1.30	2.30
44	4.90	.72	1.35	2.34
45	4.95	.72	1.45	2.39
46	5.00	.73	1.50	2.44
47	5.10	.74	1.60	2.48
48	5.20	.74	1.75	2.53
49	5.25	.75	1.90	2.58
50	5.35	.75	2.10	2.62
51	5.45	.76	2.30	2.67
52	5.60	.76	2.55	2.72
53	5.75	.77	2.80	2.78
54	5.90	.78	3.05	2.84
55	6.05	.79	3.35	2.90
56	6.25	.80	3.65	2.97
57	6.50	.81	4.00	3.04
58	6.75	.82	4.30	3.12
59	7.05	.84	4.65	3.20
60	7.45	.86	5.05	3.28
61	7.45	.88	5.45	3.36
62	7.45	.91	5.85	3.44
63	7.45	.94	6.35	3.53
64	7.45	.98	7.05	3.64
65	7.45	1.00	7.45	—

TABLE 2 — WOMEN

Age	Pension factor	Retiring allowance factor	Modification factor	Guaranteed minimum pension factor
Under 20	5.20	.60	.40	2.20
20	5.20	.60	.40	2.24
21	5.25	.61	.40	2.28
22	5.30	.61	.45	2.32
23	5.35	.61	.50	2.36
24	5.40	.62	.50	2.40
25	5.45	.62	.55	2.45
26	5.50	.63	.60	2.50
27	5.55	.63	.65	2.55
28	5.60	.63	.65	2.60
29	5.65	.64	.70	2.66
30	5.70	.64	.80	2.71
31	5.75	.65	.85	2.77
32	5.80	.66	.95	2.82
33	5.85	.66	1.00	2.88
34	5.90	.67	1.10	2.93
35	6.00	.67	1.15	2.99
36	6.10	.68	1.25	3.05
37	6.15	.68	1.30	3.11
38	6.25	.68	1.35	3.17
39	6.30	.69	1.45	3.24
40	6.40	.69	1.55	3.31
41	6.45	.70	1.65	3.38
42	6.55	.70	1.80	3.45
43	6.60	.71	1.95	3.52
44	6.70	.72	2.15	3.59
45	6.80	.73	2.35	3.66
46	6.85	.74	2.55	3.74
47	6.95	.75	2.75	3.82
48	7.00	.76	3.00	3.90
49	7.10	.77	3.25	3.98
50	7.15	.78	3.55	4.06
51	7.25	.79	3.85	4.15
52	7.35	.80	4.15	4.24
53	7.45	.81	4.55	4.33
54	7.60	.82	4.95	4.43
55	7.75	.83	5.40	4.53
56	7.90	.84	5.90	4.63
57	8.10	.85	6.50	4.74
58	8.30	.87	7.20	4.85
59	8.60	.89	8.00	4.97
60	8.85	.91	8.85	—
61	8.85	.93	8.85	—
62	8.85	.95	8.85	—
63	8.85	.97	8.85	—
64	8.85	.99	8.85	—
65	8.85	1.00	8.85	—

PART IV

1. The transfer value payable under regulation Q2(1) in respect of a person is to be calculated in accordance with the following formula if the service he is entitled to reckon in his new local government employment which he was also entitled to reckon in his previous local government employment exceeds 182 days–

$$T = \frac{(F \times S \times R)}{100} - A, \text{ where–}$$

T is the amount of the transfer value;

F is the amount shown in column (2) of the following Table applicable to his age as set out in column (1) when he ceased to be employed in his previous local government employment,

TABLE

(1)	(2)
(Age on ceasing to be employed in previous local government employment)	*(Amount)*
	£
Under 30	11
30 to 39 (inclusive)	12
40 to 49 (inclusive)	13
50 and over	14;

S is the length of the reckonable service in complete years ignoring any residual period of 182 days or less and taking any residual period which exceeds 182 days as a complete year;

R is the annual rate of his remuneration of his previous local government employment at the date on which he ceased to be employed in that employment; and

A is the amount of any additional contributory payments remaining outstanding when he ceased to be employed in his previous local government employment.

2. In any case not falling within paragraph 1 the transfer value payable under regulation Q2(1) in respect of a person is to be calculated in accordance with the following formula–

T = 2 × C, where–

T is the amount of the transfer value; and

C is the amount of the employer's contributions in relation to the reckonable service,

but the amount of the transfer value shall be zero if the person becomes employed in his new local government employment on or after 1st October 1981.

3. In ascertaining for the purposes of this Part the length of reckonable service which a person is or was entitled to reckon, the reckonable service is to count at the length at which it would reckon in calculating the amount of a retirement pension under regulation E2(1)(b)(ii), except that–

(a) any period of reckonable service which was reckonable under section 15 of the Act of 1937 (which related to teachers) is to be ignored;

(b) it is to be assumed that he had completed the payment of any additional contributory payments; and

(c) if additional contributions under regulation D10 of the 1974 Regulations (or any corresponding provision of an earlier enactment) or regulation C6 have been paid but not all those for which he was originally liable, the apportionment formula in paragraph 3 of Schedule 9 is to be applied.

4. Subject to paragraph 5, in ascertaining for the purposes of this Part the annual rate of a person's remuneration at the date on which he ceased to be employed in his previous local government employment–

(a) the annual rate of any fluctuating element of his remuneration is to be estimated by reference to an average taken over a representative period;

(b) the annual rate of any benefit in kind included in his remuneration is to be the estimated annual value of the benefit in kind at the date on which he ceased to be employed;

(c) if at that date he had no remuneration or his remuneration was reduced because of absence from duty, the annual rate is to be taken to be the annual rate which would have applied if he had not been absent;

(d) if the annual rate of his remuneration is retrospectively altered as a result of a pay award promulgated by a national joint council or other negotiating body on or before the date on which he ceased to be employed, the annual rate of his remuneration is to be based on the retrospective pay award;

(e) if his remuneration is not calculated by reference to an annual rate but by reference to some other rate, the annual rate is to be derived from the applicable rate at the date on which he ceased to be employed;

(f) if his previous local government employment was part-time, the annual rate of remuneration of a single comparable whole-time employment is to be used; and

(g) if the annual rate of his remuneration exceeds £100 it is to be rounded down to the nearest £100.

5. If–

(a) during the 13 years ending on the cessation of the person's previous local government employment his remuneration was reduced; and

(b) his employing authority certified under regulation E24 that the reduction was in consequence of a material change in circumstances; and

(c) his annual rate of remuneration immediately before the reduction, ascertained on similar principles to those in paragraph 4, was greater than the annual rate of remuneration on the date on which he ceased to be employed in his previous local government employment,

it is to be assumed for the purposes of this Part that he was earning at the higher rate at the date on which he ceased to be employed in his previous local government employment.

6. Where the person has made a payment to his new fund authority under regulation D1(2) or J9(3) of the 1974 Regulations or H8(3) of these Regulations, the transfer value payable under regulation Q2(1) is to be reduced by an amount equal to that payment.

7. Compound interest calculated in accordance with regulation J7 is to be paid on the transfer value payable under regulation Q2(1) for the period beginning with the date on which the person ceased to be employed in his previous local government employment and ending on the date on which the transfer value is paid (but no interest is to be paid if that period is less than 6 months).

PART V

1. The additional transfer value payable under regulation J3(2) and the transfer value that may be accepted where regulation J8(5) applies is in each case $(A \times B \times C) + D$, where–

A is the period–

(a) which the person would have been entitled to reckon as reckonable service by virtue of regulation F6(1)(a) or (b), or

(b) which would have been taken into account in calculating additional benefits in accordance with regulation F6(12), or

(c) which he would have been entitled to reckon under the war service provisions of the public service scheme,

as the case may be;

B is the figure in column 2 or 3 of the Table below appropriate to the person's age on 1st April 1978 and sex;

C is either–

(a) the annual rate of the person's pensionable remuneration at 1st April 1978, or

(b) if on that date he was entitled to a pension, the amount of remuneration taken into account in calculating the pension, increased by the annual amount (if any) by which an annual pension at a rate equal to that amount of remuneration, and beginning on the same date as the person's pension, would by 1st April 1978 have been increased under the Pensions (Increase) Act 1971(a); and

D is compound interest on $(A \times B \times C)$, calculated, in the case of an additional transfer value payable under regulation J4(2), in accordance with regulation J7 in respect of the period beginning on 1st April 1978 and ending with the date on which the transfer or additional transfer value is paid.

2. For the purposes of paragraph 1, the annual rate of a person's pensionable remuneration shall be ascertained in accordance with the provisions of paragraphs 4 and 5 of Part IV of this Schedule.

(a) 1971 c.56.

TABLE

Age on last birthday before 1st April 1978	Men	Women
40	0.1009	0.1328
41	0.1018	0.1344
42	0.1024	0.1357
43	0.1031	0.1372
44	0.1038	0.1389
45	0.1045	0.1405
46	0.1058	0.1422
47	0.1073	0.1437
48	0.1085	0.1454
49	0.1099	0.1470
50	0.1111	0.1487
51	0.1125	0.1502
52	0.1150	0.1525
53	0.1176	0.1548
54	0.1203	0.1571
55	0.1229	0.1599
56	0.1267	0.1628
57	0.1306	0.1663
58	0.1345	0.1707
59	0.1397	0.1759
60	0.1463	0.1810
61	0.1465	0.1818
62	0.1469	0.1825
63	0.1473	0.1833
64	0.1478	0.1840
65	0.1480	0.1844
66	0.1436	0.1800
67	0.1392	0.1756
68	0.1355	0.1713
69	0.1311	0.1669
70	0.1267	0.1625
71	0.1230	0.1575
72	0.1190	0.1519
73	0.1144	0.1463
74	0.1106	0.1406
75	0.1063	0.1350
76	0.1019	0.1294
77	0.0981	0.1238
78	0.0938	0.1181
79	0.0900	0.1131
80	0.0854	0.1088
81	0.0815	0.1044
82	0.0775	0.1006
83	0.0735	0.0969
84	0.0698	0.0931
85	0.0661	0.0894
86	0.0623	0.0856
87	0.0585	0.0825
88	0.0554	0.0794
89	0.0525	0.0769
90	0.0496	0.0744
91	0.0467	0.0719
92	0.0440	0.0694
93	0.0419	0.0669
94	0.0398	0.0644
95	0.0377	0.0625
96	0.0356	0.0600
97	0.0342	0.0581
98	0.0321	0.0556
99	0.0306	0.0531

Age on last birthday before 1st April 1978	Men	Women

Regulation J9(1)(a)

SCHEDULE 17

CALCULATION OF RECKONABLE SERVICE TO BE CREDITED UNDER REGULATION J9(1)(a)

1.   Subject to the provisions of this Schedule, the period which a person is entitled to reckon as reckonable service by virtue of regulation J9(1)(a) is a period equal to the period of reckonable service which would enable the fund authority to pay under regulation J2 a transfer value (calculated in accordance with Schedule 16)–

(a) of the amount which that authority accepted in respect of him under regulation J8, or

(b) where–

(i) the person became employed in his local government employment after 4th April 1983, and

(ii) a limited revaluation premium was paid under section 45 of the Pensions Act and has been repaid to the fund authority by the Secretary of State,

of the total of the amount mentioned in sub-paragraph (a) and the amount of the premium.

2.   For the purposes of paragraph 1 above–

(1) in the case of a person who was subject in his non-local government employment to a statutory scheme or to any other scheme which is for the time being specified by the Secretary of State as a scheme which is to be treated as a statutory scheme for the purposes of this Schedule–

(a) the calculation of the period he is entitled to reckon as reckonable service is to be made by reference to his age, and to the rate of his pensionable pay, used in the calculation of the transfer value received,

(b) where in that calculation an amount of a person's pay has been disregarded in connection with a retirement pension under section 30 of the Insurance Act or section 28 of the Social Security Act 1975, the pensionable pay is to be increased by that amount, and

(c) any sum representing interest included in the transfer value accepted is to be ignored;

(2) in the case of a person who was subject in his non-local government employment to any other scheme–

(a) if he became employed in his local government employment before 8th May 1975–

(i) the calculation of the period he is entitled to reckon as reckonable service is to be made by reference to his age, and the annual rate of his remuneration, on 1st April 1972, or, if later, on the date when he became employed in his local government employment (here referred to as the "relevant date"); and

(ii) the sum to be used as the amount of the transfer value shall be the sum notified to the fund authority by the scheme managers as the sum which the fund authority would have received in respect of the person had the transfer value been calculated and paid on the relevant date;

(b) if he became employed in his local government employment on or after 8th May 1975 the calculation of the period he is entitled to reckon as reckonable service is to be made by reference to his age, and the annual rate of his remuneration, on the date when he became employed in his local government employment or, if the transfer value in respect of him is received by the fund authority more than one year after he became employed in his local government employment, on the date on which the transfer value is received;

(c) any sum representing interest which is included in the transfer value accepted is to be taken into account;

(3) the accrued pension in respect of the period last mentioned in paragraph 1 above shall be deemed–

(a) where the person is such a person as is mentioned in regulation J12(1), to be subject to that paragraph, and paragraph (2) of that regulation shall have effect for this purpose as if at the end there were added the following sub-paragraph:–

"(c) at the end of regulation F7(2) of the 1974 Regulations, there had been added the words "and a proportionate amount in respect of part of a year of such service".";

(b) where the person is such a person as is mentioned in regulation J12(3), to be subject to that paragraph;

(4)(a) where the pensionable pay mentioned in sub-paragraph (1) above relates to a period of part-time employment, the pensionable pay for that period shall be deemed to be the pensionable pay by reference to which the transfer value accepted would have been calculated had the person during that period been in a single comparable whole-time employment;

(b) where the remuneration mentioned in sub-paragraph (2) above relates to part-time employment, the annual rate of remuneration on the relevant date shall be deemed to be the annual rate of remuneration notified to the fund authority by his local government employer as the remuneration which would have been paid in respect of a single comparable whole-time employment;

(5) in the case of a person whose non-local government employment was not contracted-out employment, the calculation of the period he is entitled to reckon as reckonable service shall be made by reference to the transfer value which would have been payable under regulation J2 if Schedule 16 contained no reference to guaranteed minimum pension.

SCHEDULE 18

Regulation J14

FUND APPORTIONMENT WHERE 100 OR MORE TRANSFER THEIR PENSION RIGHTS UNDER REGULATION J14

PART I

1. This Part of this Schedule applies where the fund is to be apportioned under regulation J14(5) and all of the transfers under the transfer scheme are to take place on the same day.

2. The appropriate administering authority shall obtain a report from the fund's actuary specifying the apportionment fraction to be applied in apportioning the fund together with details of the calculation.

3. The apportionment fraction is–

$$\frac{\left[\frac{A}{B} \times (C + D)\right] - E}{C}, \text{ where–}$$

A is the value at the relevant date of the accrued actuarial liabilities of the fund which relate to the persons transferring their pension rights on that date to the approved non-local government scheme,

B is the value at the relevant date of all accrued actuarial liabilities of the fund,

C is the value at the relevant date of the transferable assets of the fund minus any sums then due from the fund,

D is the value at the relevant date of any adjustments to be made in consequence of a certificate under regulation P9(1)(b) to sums (other than sums then due to the fund) to be contributed to the fund under regulation P12(1), and

E is the value at the relevant date of the part (if any) of those adjustments that relate to the persons transferring their pension rights on that date to the approved non-local government scheme.

4. The relevant date is the date on which those transferring their pension rights become subject to the approved non-local government scheme.

5. The accrued actuarial liabilities of the fund are the actual and potential liabilities of the fund in connection with any service or employment before the relevant date and, for this purpose, it is to be assumed that the liabilities which relate to those transferring their pension rights remain liabilities of the fund notwithstanding regulation J14(6).

6. The transferable assets of the fund are the assets which belong to the fund at the relevant date.

7. The values of items D and E are to be agreed by the actuary and the scheme managers of the approved non-local government scheme or, if they are unable to agree, they are to be determined by an actuary appointed by the Secretary of State.

8. Subject to paragraph 7 above, valuations are to be made by the actuary.

9. Where more than one approved non-local government scheme is involved, separate apportionment fractions shall be specified in the actuary's report for the different schemes.

10. When the appropriate administering authority receive the actuary's report they shall provide the scheme managers of the approved non-local government scheme with a copy of it.

11. The value of the share of the fund to which the scheme managers of the approved non-local government scheme are entitled shall be calculated in accordance with the formula–

$$V = W \times (X - [Y + Z]), \text{ where–}$$

V is the value of the share of the fund to which the scheme managers are entitled,

W is the apportionment fraction specified in the actuary's report,

X is the value (determined by the fund's actuary) at the apportionment date of the transferable assets which still belong to the fund at that date and any other assets which belong to the fund at that date which represent in any form, or have accrued from, any transferable asset,

Y is the total of any sums due from the fund at the relevant date and still outstanding at the apportionment date, and

Z is the total of any sums due from the fund at the apportionment date (but not at the relevant date) in respect of any expenditure in connection with the transferable assets of the fund or assets representing, or accruing from, those assets.

12. The apportionment date is the date specified as such by the appropriate administering authority in a notice given to the scheme managers of the approved non-local government scheme.

13. Except with the agreement of the scheme managers of the approved non-local government scheme, the apportionment date shall not be later than six months after the date on which the appropriate administering authority receive the actuary's report.

14. Subject to paragraphs 15 to 17 below, immediately after the apportionment date the appropriate administering authority shall transfer to the scheme managers of the approved non-local government scheme assets of the fund of a value at the apportionment date equal to the value of the scheme managers' share of the fund and, unless the appropriate administering authority and the scheme managers otherwise agree, the composition of the assets to be transferred shall so far as possible reflect the composition of the transferable assets which still belong to the fund at the apportionment date and any other assets which belong to the fund at that date which represent in any form, or have accrued from, any transferable asset.

15. The appropriate administering authority and the scheme managers may agree to transfer assets in advance of the apportionment date.

16. The value of an advance under paragraph 15 shall not exceed such sum as the fund's actuary may specify as appropriate in the circumstances.

17. Where an advance is made under paragraph 15, the appropriate administering authority's liability under paragraphs 11 and 14 shall be reduced by an amount equal to–

$$\frac{L}{M} \times N, \text{ where–}$$

L is the value of the advance,

M is the value of the share of the fund to which the scheme managers would have been entitled under paragraph 11 if the apportionment date had been the date on which the advance was made, and

N is the value of the share of the fund to which the scheme managers would have been entitled under paragraph 11 if the advance had not been made.

18. The employing authority shall bear the costs of apportioning the fund or, if there is more than one employing authority involved, each shall bear such part of those costs as the fund's actuary determines.

19. The appropriate administering authority shall keep their accounts in a form which enables the calculations required in apportioning the fund to be made, and they shall also provide the fund's actuary with any information he requires in connection with the apportionment.

PART II

20. This Part of this Schedule applies where the fund is to be apportioned under regulation J14(5) and the transfers under the transfer scheme are to take place on different days.

21. The provisions of Part I of this Schedule are to apply to the apportionment as if the transfers had occurred on a single date, but suitable adjustments are to be made to the sums payable to the scheme managers to reflect the fact that the transfers take place on different dates.

22. Any adjustments to be made under paragraph 21 shall be determined by the fund's actuary, subject to the agreement of the appropriate administering authority and the scheme managers or, if they are unable to agree, by an actuary appointed by the Secretary of State.

SCHEDULE 19

Regulations P2(1)
and Q2(6)

FUND APPORTIONMENT FOR CHANGES OF FUND WITHIN LOCAL GOVERNMENT

PART I

1. This Part of this Schedule applies where the fund is to be apportioned under regulation Q2(6) and all of the persons who are changing funds do so on the same day.

2. The previous fund authority shall obtain a report from an actuary specifying the apportionment fraction to be applied in apportioning the fund together with details of the calculation.

3. The apportionment fraction is–

$$\frac{\left[\dfrac{A}{B} \times (C + D)\right] - E}{C}, \text{ where–}$$

A is the value at the relevant date of the accrued actuarial liabilities of the fund which relate to the persons changing funds on that date,

B is the value at the relevant date of all accrued actuarial liabilities of the fund,

C is the value at the relevant date of the transferable assets of the fund minus any sums then due from the fund,

D is the value at the relevant date of any adjustments to be made in consequence of a certificate under regulation P9(1)(b) to sums (other than sums then due to the fund) to be contributed to the fund under regulation P12(1), and

E is the value at the relevant date of the part (if any) of those adjustments which relates to the persons changing funds on that date.

4. The relevant date is the date on which the change of fund occurs.

5. The accrued actuarial liabilities of the fund are the actual and potential liabilities of the fund in connection with any service or employment before the relevant date and, for this purpose, it is to be assumed that the liabilities which relate to those changing funds remain liabilities of the fund.

6. The transferable assets of the fund are the assets which belong to the fund at the relevant date.

7. The values of items D and E are to be agreed between the fund's actuary and the actuary of the new fund authority or, if they are unable to agree, they are to be determined by an actuary appointed by the Secretary of State.

8. Subject to paragraph 7, valuations are to be made by the fund's actuary.

9. Where more than one new fund authority is involved, separate apportionment fractions shall be specified in the actuary's report for the different new fund authorities.

10. When the previous fund authority receive the actuary's report they shall provide the new fund authority with a copy of it.

11. The value of the share of the fund to which the new fund authority are entitled shall be calculated in accordance with the formula–

$$V = W \times (X - [Y + Z]), \text{ where–}$$

V is the value of the share of the fund to which the new fund authority are entitled,

W is the apportionment fraction specified in the actuary's report,

X is the value (determined by the fund's actuary) at the apportionment date of the transferable assets which still belong to the fund at that date and any other assets which belong to the fund at that date which represent in any form or have accrued from any transferable asset,

Y is the total of any sums due from the fund at the relevant date and still outstanding at the apportionment date, and

Z is the total of any sums due from the fund at the apportionment date (but not at the relevant date) in respect of any expenditure in connection with the transferable assets of the fund or assets representing, or accruing from, those assets.

12.   The apportionment date is the date specified as such by the previous fund authority in a notice given to the new fund authority.

13.   Except with the agreement of the new fund authority, the apportionment date shall not be later than six months after the date on which the previous fund authority receive the actuary's report.

14.   Subject to paragraphs 15 to 17, immediately after the apportionment date the previous fund authority shall transfer to the new fund authority assets of the fund of a value at the apportionment date equal to the value of the new fund authority's share of the fund and, unless the previous fund authority and new fund authority otherwise agree, the composition of the assets to be transferred shall so far as possible reflect the composition of the transferable assets which still belong to the fund at the apportionment date and any other assets which belong to the fund at that date whch represent in any form, or have accrued from, any transferable asset.

15.   The previous fund authority and the new fund authority may agree to transfer assets in advance of the apportionment date.

16.   The value of an advance under paragraph 15 shall not exceed such sum as the fund's actuary may specify as appropriate in the circumstances.

17.   Where an advance is made under paragraph 15, the previous fund authority's liability under paragraphs 11 and 14 shall be reduced by an amount equal to–

$$\frac{L}{M} \times N, \text{ where–}$$

L is the value of the advance,

M is the value of the share of the fund to which the new fund authority would have been entitled under paragraph 11 if the apportionment date had been the date on which the advance was made, and

N is the value of the share of the fund to which the new fund authority would have been entitled under paragraph 11 if the advance had not been made.

18.   The previous employing authority shall bear the costs of apportioning the fund or, if there is more than one previous employing authority involved, each shall bear such part of the costs as the fund's actuary determines.

19.   The previous fund authority shall keep their accounts in a form which enables the calculations required in apportioning the fund to be made, and they shall also provide the fund's actuary with any information he requires in connection with the apportionment.

PART II

20.   This Part of this Schedule applies where the fund is to be apportioned under regulation Q2(6) and the persons who are changing funds do so on different days.

21.   The provisions of Part I of this Schedule are to apply to the apportionment as if the changes of fund had occurred on a single date, but suitable adjustments are to be made to the sums payable to the new fund authority to reflect the fact that the changes of fund occur on different dates.

22.   If any question arises in connection with paragraph 21, it shall be determined by the fund's actuary and the actuary of the new fund authority or, if they are unable to agree, by an actuary appointed by the Secretary of State.

SCHEDULE 20

Regulations B6(6), P3
and P11

BODIES WHOSE EMPLOYEES ARE TO HAVE PENSIONS INCREASE PAID BY THE FUND OR FURTHER FUND

(1) *Body*	(2) *Date*
A public transport company established under the Transport Act 1985(a)	Date of incorporation

SCHEDULE 21

Regulation S3

REVOCATIONS

(1) *Instruments revoked*	(2) *References*
The Local Government Superannuation (Scotland) Regulations 1974	S.I. 1974/812
The Local Government Superannuation (Scotland) Amendment Regulations 1975	S.I. 1975/638
The Local Government Superannuation (Scotland) Amendment Regulations 1978	S.I. 1978/425
The Local Government Superannuation (Scotland) Amendment (No. 2) Regulations 1978	S.I. 1978/1378
The Local Government Superannuation (Scotland) Amendment (No. 3) Regulations 1978	S.I. 1978/1794
The Local Government Superannuation (Scotland) Amendment (No. 4) Regulations 1978	S.I. 1978/1926
The Local Government Superannuation (Scotland) Amendment Regulations 1980	S.I. 1980/198
The Local Government Superannuation (Scotland) Amendment (No. 2) Regulations 1980	S.I. 1980/342
The Local Government Superannuation (Scotland) Amendment (No. 3) Regulations 1980	S.I. 1980/1885
The Local Government Superannuation (Scotland) Amendment Regulations 1981	S.I. 1981/1892
The Local Government Superannuation (Scotland) Amendment Regulations 1982	S.I. 1982/385
The Local Government Superannuation (Scotland) Amendment (No. 2) Regulations 1982	S.I. 1982/1303
The Local Government Superannuation (Scotland) Amendment Regulations 1983	S.I. 1983/1421
The Local Government Superannuation (Scotland) Amendment Regulations 1984	S.I. 1984/254
The Local Government Superannuation (Scotland) Amendment (No. 2) Regulations 1984	S.I. 1984/1232
The Local Government Superannuation (Scotland) Amendment Regulations 1986	S.I. 1986/214
The Local Government Superannuation (Funds) (Scotland) Regulations 1986	S.I. 1986/1449

(a) 1985 c.67.

EXPLANATORY NOTE

(This note is not part of the Regulations)

These Regulations consolidate the provisions revoked by regulation S3 and Schedule 21, comprising the bulk of the Regulations applying to Scotland made, or having effect as if made, under section 7 of the Superannuation Act 1972.

The Appendix to this Explanatory Note has the corrections and minor amendments made in the consolidation.

Certain regulations in these Regulations have retrospective effect as authorised by section 12 of the Superannuation Act 1972.

Provision is made for opting out where rights in relation to ex-employees could be adversely affected (regulation S2).

APPENDIX TO EXPLANATORY NOTE

(Corrections and minor amendments)

Column (1) – Provision of consolidated Regulations.
Column (2) – Corresponding regulation in Local Government Superannuation (Scotland) Regulations 1974.
Column (3) – Effect of correction or amendment.

(1)	(2)	(3)
A3 and Schedule 2	G2 and Schedule 15	(a) Removes the need for the Scottish Special Housing Association to resolve to admit new categories of staff to the superannuation scheme. (b) Allows the Association to invest in "traded options" and "financial futures" on the same basis as local authorities.
B6(3)	—	To clarify that an admission agreement may cover a class of employee as well as individuals.
E9	E9	Corrects the starting date from 16th May 1974 to 1st June 1972 for the indexation of the prescribed amount (£250) for the reduction of children's pensions when they are also in receipt of remuneration.
F1	R1	Expands the definition of non-effective pay to show the effect of the Finance (No. 2) Act 1945.
J4(5)	—	To ensure that an employee transferring from local government employment is made aware of his right of appeal to the Secretary of State with regard to the transfer value.
N1(3)	—	Highlights the scope of decisions taken by scheduled bodies.
Schedule 1	A3	Amends the definition of "eligible child" to take account of the Law Reform (Parent and Child) (Scotland) Act 1986 (c.9), and removes differences in treatment between people which depend on whether or not their parents are or have been married to each other.

STATUTORY INSTRUMENTS

1987 No. 1851

CRIMINAL LAW, ENGLAND AND WALES

The Crown Prosecution Service (Witnesses' Allowances) (Amendment No. 6) Regulations 1987

Made - - - -	*22nd October 1987*
Laid before Parliament	*26th October 1987*
Coming into force -	*16th November 1987*

The Attorney General, in exercise of the powers conferred upon him by section 14(1)(b) and (2) of the Prosecution of Offences Act 1985(a), and with the approval of the Treasury, hereby makes the following Regulations:

1. These Regulations may be cited as the Crown Prosecution Service (Witnesses' Allowances) (Amendment No. 6) Regulations 1987 and shall come into force on 16th November 1987.

2. In Schedule 1 to the Crown Prosecution Service (Witnesses' Allowances) Regulations 1986(b), in Column 3 of the Table, which sets out relevant amounts in relation to allowances payable under those Regulations–

  (a) for the sums of £46.50 and £38.25 in the entry for regulation 5 (overnight subsistence allowance payable to professional or expert witness who attends to give evidence) there shall be substituted £49.50 and £40.95 respectively;

  (b) for the sums of £1.40, £2.65 and £5.85 in the entry for regulation 7(1) (day subsistence allowance payable to a witness other than a professional or expert witness who attends to give evidence) there shall be substituted £1.50, £2.85 and £6.25 respectively; and

  (c) for the sums of £52.35 and £44.10 in the entry for regulation 7(2) (overnight subsistence allowance payable to a witness other than a professional or expert witness who attends to give evidence) there shall be substituted £55.75 and £47.20 respectively.

3. Regulation 4 of the Crown Prosecution Service (Witnesses' Allowances) (Amendment No. 3) Regulations 1986(c) is hereby revoked.

P. B. B. Mayhew
Her Majesty's Attorney General

14th October 1987

(a) 1985 c.23.
(b) S.I. 1986/405, amended by S.I. 1986/842, 1250, 1818, 1987/902 and 1636.
(c) S.I. 1986/1818.

We approve.

Peter Lloyd
Mark Lennox Boyd
22nd October 1987   Two of the Lords Commissioners of Her Majesty's Treasury

EXPLANATORY NOTE

(This note is not part of the Regulations)

These Regulations increase the overnight subsistence allowances payable under regulation 5 of the Crown Prosecution Service (Witnesses' Allowances) Regulations 1986 to a professional or expert witness and under regulation 7(2) to any other witness who, at the instance of the Crown Prosecution Service, attends court to give evidence.

They also increase the day subsistence allowances payable under regulation 7(1) to witnesses other than professional or expert witnesses.

STATUTORY INSTRUMENTS

1987 No. 1852

WAGES COUNCILS

The Wages Councils (Notices) (No. 2) Regulations 1987

Made - - - -	23rd October 1987
Laid before Parliament	3rd November 1987
Coming into force	25th November 1987

The Secretary of State, in exercise of the powers conferred on him by sections 19(2) and (3) and 25 of and paragraphs 1 and 2 of Schedule 3 to the Wages Act 1986(**a**) and of all other powers enabling him in that behalf, hereby makes the following Regulations:

Citation, commencement and revocation

1.—(1) These Regulations may be cited as the Wages Councils (Notices) (No. 2) Regulations 1987 and shall come into force on 25th November 1987.

(2) The Wages Councils (Notices) Regulations 1987 (**b**) are hereby revoked.

Interpretation

2. In these Regulations, "the Act" means the Wages Act 1986.

Publication of notices of proposal to make an order

3.—(1) Before making an order under section 14 of the Act a wages council shall publish notice of any rate or limit which the council proposes to fix under subsection (1) of that section, and, subject to paragraph (2) that notice shall be published in the London and Edinburgh Gazettes.

(2) Where the issue of the London or Edinburgh Gazette in which the notice was expected to appear does not contain the notice, or where the council has reason to believe that the issue of the London or Edinburgh Gazette in which it wishes the notice to appear will not be published or will be published late, the council may publish the notice in an English national daily newspaper instead of the London Gazette or, as the case may be, in a Scottish national daily newspaper instead of the Edinburgh Gazette.

(3) The date to be taken for the purposes of the Act as the date of publication of a notice to which paragraph (1) refers shall be the first or only date on which the notice is published in England and Scotland or, if the notice is published on different dates in those countries, the date on which it is first published in the country in which it is published second.

Notice to employers of proposals

4.—(1) A wages council shall send to every employer appearing to the council to be affected by proposals it has made under paragraph 1 of Schedule 3 to the Act a notice fulfilling the requirements of paragraphs (2) and (3) below.

(**a**) 1986 c.48.
(**b**) S.I. 1987/863.

(2) The notice referred to in paragraph (1) shall–

  (a) set out the contents of the notice referred to in regulation 3;

  (b) state the date from which the council intends its proposals to come into force;

  (c) state the place where further copies of the proposals may be obtained;

  (d) state the period, being a period of not less than 28 days beginning with the date of publication of the notice referred to in regulation 3, within which written representations with respect to the proposals may be sent to the council;

  (e) state that the order will not apply to workers under the age of 21.

(3) (a) Subject to sub-paragraph (b), the notice referred to in paragraph (1) shall also give short and, so far as practicable having regard to that requirement, legally accurate explanations of–

    (i) the way in which any rate or limit which will have effect (or continue to have effect) if an order implementing the proposals is made, will apply to time workers under section 14(1) and (2) of the Act and, where the council operates in relation to piece workers, to piece workers under sections 14(3) and 15(1) and (2) of the Act;

    (ii) the effect of section 14(5) of the Act and, where the council operates in relation to piece workers, of section 15(4) of the Act on the way in which any such rate will apply to time to which that section or those sections apply, specifying separately, where the council operates in relation to homeworkers who are time workers, the effect of section 14(5) in relation to those workers and, where the council operates in relation to homeworkers who are piece workers, the effect of section 15(4) in relation to those workers;

    (iii) the requirement on employers contained in regulation 6(1) to post notices and, where the council operates in relation to homeworkers, the requirement on employers under regulation 6(2) to send notices.

  (b) No explanation as required by sub-paragraph (i) of paragraph (3)(a) shall be given where–

    (i) the council does not operate in relation to any piece workers; and

    (ii) no limit will have effect if an order implementing the proposals is made.

Notice to employers of orders made under section 14 of the Act.

5. As soon as a wages council has made an order under section 14 of the Act, the council shall send to every employer appearing to the council to be affected thereby a notice which, in addition to stating that the order has been made and describing its contents–

  (a) states that the order does not apply to workers under the age of 21;

  (b) contains explanations of the matters specified in paragraph (3)(a)(i), (ii) and (iii) of regulation 4 being explanations which, in relation to the matters specified in paragraph 3(a)(i), reflect where appropriate the exception in paragraph 3(b) of regulation 4, and which, in relation to the matters specified in paragraph 3(a)(i) and (ii), are framed by reference to the application of any rate or limit which has effect but otherwise comply with the requirements of paragraph 3(a);

  (c) where the order amends or partially revokes a previous order made by the council, contains particulars of the matters previously in force left unaffected by the amendment or revocation and indicates the matters amended or revoked.

Posting and sending of notice by employers.

6.—(1) An employer of any workers who are affected by any proposal under paragraph 1 of Schedule 3 to the Act, or order under section 14 of the Act, shall, on receipt of the notice referred to in regulation 4(1) or the notice referred to in regulation 5, post up and keep posted up at any place of business of his where any such workers work clear copies of the notice in such positions and numbers as will ensure that a copy can easily be seen and read by each such worker.

(2) An employer of any homeworker affected by any proposal under paragraph 1 of Schedule 3 to the Act, or order under section 14 of the Act, shall, on receipt of the notice referred to in regulation 4(1) or the notice referred to in regulation 5, send to each such homeworker at his last known address, a clear copy of that notice.

Signed by order of the Secretary of State.

Patrick Nicholls
Parliamentary Under-Secretary of State,
Department of Employment

23rd October 1987

EXPLANATORY NOTE

(This note is not part of the Regulations)

These Regulations require a wages council proposing to make an order under the Wages Act 1986 to publish notice of the proposals in the London and Edinburgh Gazettes and to send employers notice of the proposals and notice of the provisions of an order once it is made. The Regulations prescribe matters which must be contained in the notices and require employers to post copies of the notices sent to them at workplaces so that the notices can be read by workers affected and to send copies of the notices to homeworkers affected.

The Regulations revoke the Wages Councils (Notices) Regulations 1987.

STATUTORY INSTRUMENTS

1987 No. 1853 (C. 56)

SOCIAL SECURITY

The Social Security Act 1986 (Commencement No. 8) Order 1987

Made - - - - *23rd October 1987*

The Secretary of State for Social Services, in exercise of the powers conferred on him by section 88(1) of the Social Security Act 1986(**a**) and of all other powers enabling him in that behalf, hereby makes the following Order:

Citation and interpretation

1.—(1) This Order may be cited as the Social Security Act 1986 (Commencement No. 8) Order 1987.

(2) In this Order, unless the context otherwise requires, references to sections and Schedules are references to sections of and Schedules to the Social Security Act 1986.

Appointed days

2.—(1) The day appointed for the coming into force of the provisions of the Social Security Act 1986 which are specified in Part I of the Schedule to this Order, so far as they relate to housing benefit, is–

(a) in a case where rent is payable at intervals of one month or any other interval which is not a week or a multiple thereof, 1st April 1988;

(b) in a case where payments by way of rates are not made together with payments of rent at weekly intervals or multiples thereof, 1st April 1988;

(c) in any other case, 4th April 1988.

(2) The day appointed for the coming into force of the provisions of the Social Security Act 1986 which are specified in Part II of the Schedule to this Order is 11th April 1988.

Revocation

3. In the Social Security Act 1986 (Commencement No. 7) Order 1987(**b**), article 2(2) (child benefit claims and payments), article 2(3) (abolition of industrial death benefit), and the commencement in the Schedule to that Order of the repeal in Schedule 11 of sections 67, 68 and 70 to 75 of, and Schedule 9 to, the Social Security Act 1975(**c**)

(**a**) 1986 c.50.   (**b**) S.I. 1987/1096.   (**c**) 1975 c.14.

and section 86(2) so far as it relates to the repeal of those sections and Schedule, are hereby revoked.

Signed by authority of the Secretary of State for Social Services.

Nicholas Scott
Minister of State,
23rd October 1987   Department of Health and Social Security

SCHEDULE

Article 2

PART I

(PROVISIONS COMING INTO FORCE ON 1ST APRIL 1988 AND 4TH APRIL 1988)

Provisions of the Social Security Act 1986	Subject matter
Section 20(1), (7), (8), (9), (11) and (12), section 21(4) to (7), section 22, and sections 28, 29, 30(1) to (3) and (5) to (7), and section 31.	Housing benefit
The following paragraphs of Schedule 10 and section 86(1) so far as it relates to those paragraphs–	Minor and consequential amendments
paragraphs 44, 48, 49, 52, 53 and 58 to 60	(housing benefit)
The following repeals in Schedule 11 and section 86(2) so far as it relates to those repeals–	Repeals
Social Security Act 1980(**a**), in Schedule 3, in Part II, paragraph 15B	(housing benefit)
Social Security and Housing Benefits Act 1982(**b**)–	
(i) Part II,	
(ii) in section 45, in subsection (1), the words from "and any power" to the end, in subsection (2), paragraphs (b) and (c) and subsection (3),	
(iii) in section 47 in the definition of "benefit" the words "Part II and",	
(iv) in Schedule 4, paragraphs 5, 19, 27, 28, 35(1) and (2)	
Social Security Act 1985(**c**), section 22, and in section 32(2), the words "section 22(1)(b) and (c) and (2)"	

(**a**) 1980 c.30.   (**b**) 1982 c.24.   (**c**) 1985 c.53.

PART II
(PROVISIONS COMING INTO FORCE ON 11TH APRIL 1988)

Provisions of the Social Security Act 1986	Subject matter
Sections 20, 21 and 22 in so far as they are not brought into force in accordance with Part I of this Schedule	Income support and family credit
Section 23	Trade Disputes
Sections 24 to 26	Liability to maintain
Section 27 for all purposes for which it is not already in force	Prevention of duplication of payments
Section 32 in so far as it is not already in force and sections 33 to 35	Social Fund
Section 39 and Schedule 3 paragraph 8 in so far as they relate to section 67(2)(b) of the Social Security Act 1975	Industrial death benefit
Section 65(4)	Reciprocal arrangements
Section 77	Refreshments for school pupils
Section 79(3)	Crown employment and family credit
Schedule 7 paragraph 3 in so far as it is not already in force and section 73 so far as it relates to it	Claims and payments
The following paragraphs of Schedule 10 and section 86(1) so far as it relates to those paragraphs—	Minor and consequential amendments
paragraphs 32 to 43, 45 to 47, 48 for all purposes for which it is not already in force, 50, 51, 54 to 57 and 61	(income support and family credit)
paragraph 108 in so far as it is not already in force	(forfeiture)
The following repeals in Schedule 11 and section 86(2) so far as it relates to those repeals—	Repeals
National Assistance Act 1948(a), in section 43(6), the words ", whether before or after the commencement of the Supplementary Benefits Act 1976," in section 50(4), the words "or subsection (3)" and the words from "less" to the end, and section 53	(supplementary benefit)
Family Income Supplements Act 1970(b), in so far as it is not already repealed	(family income supplement)
Pensioners and Family Income Supplement Payments Act 1972(c), in so far as it is not already repealed	
National Insurance Act 1974(d), in section 6(1), the words "the Supplementary Benefits Act 1976, the Family Income Supplements Act 1970,"	(supplementary benefit and family income supplement)
Social Security Act 1975—	
(i) section 67(2)(b),	(industrial death benefit)
(ii) in section 143(1), the words "relating to social security"	(reciprocity with other countries)

(a)   11 and 12 Geo. 6 c.29.   (b) 1970 c.55.   (c) 1972 c.75.
(d)   1974 c.14.

Provisions of the Social Security Act 1986	Subject matter

Supplementary Benefits Act 1976 (**a**)–
  (i) sections 1 to 11,
  (ii) sections 13 to 19,
  (iii) section 21,
  (iv) sections 24, 25 and 27,
  (v) sections 31 to 34,
  (vi) Schedule 1,
  (vii) in Schedule 5, in paragraph 1(2), the words from the beginning to "and" in the first place where it occurs,
  (viii) in Schedule 7, paragraphs 1(b) and (d), 3(a), 5, 19, 21, 23, 24, 31, 33 and 37
	(supplementary benefit)

Social Security (Miscellaneous Provisions) Act 1977 (**b**), in section 18, in subsection (1) in paragraph (a) the words "and the Supplementary Benefits Act 1976", and in section 22, subsection (16)	(supplementary benefit and family income supplement)
Employment Protection (Consolidation) Act 1978 (**c**), in section 132, in subsection (6), the definition of "supplementary benefit"	(supplementary benefit)
Social Security Act 1979 (**d**), in Schedule 3, paragraphs 1, 2, and 24 to 27	(supplementary benefit and family income supplement)

Social Security Act 1980 (**e**)–
  (i) section 7,
  (ii) in section 8, in subsection (1), the words "or 7",
  (iii) in section 9(7), the words "the Family Income Supplements Act 1970" and the words "and the Supplementary Benefits Act 1976",
  (iv) in section 18, in subsection (1), the words "the Family Income Supplements Act 1970;", the words "the Supplementary Benefits Act 1976" and the word "and" immediately preceding them,
  (v) in Schedule 2, paragraphs 1 to 10, 12 to 18 and 22 to 30,
  (vi) in Schedule 3, in Part II, paragraphs 11 and 15	

Social Security (No. 2) Act 1980 (**f**) section 6	(supplementary benefit)
Social Security Act 1981 (**g**), section 4 and in Schedule 1, paragraphs 8 and 9	
Social Security and Housing Benefits Act 1982 (**h**) section 38, section 44(1)(a), and in Schedule 4, paragraphs 2, 4, and 23 to 25	(supplementary benefit and family income supplement)
Health and Social Services and Social Security Adjudications Act 1983 (**i**), section 19(2) and Schedule 8 Part III and Part IV, in so far as that Part is not already repealed	
Law Reform (Parent and Child) (Scotland) Act 1986 (**j**), in Schedule 1, paragraph 16 and in Schedule 2, the entry relating to the Supplementary Benefits Act 1976	(supplementary benefit)

(**a**) 1976 c.71.   (**b**) 1977 c.5.   (**c**) 1978 c.44.
(**d**) 1979 c.18.   (**e**) 1980 c.30.   (**f**) 1980 c.39.
(**g**) 1981 c.33.   (**h**) 1982 c.24.   (**i**) 1983 c.41.
(**j**) 1986 c.9.

EXPLANATORY NOTE

(This note is not part of the Order)

Article 2(1) of this Order brings into force the provisions of the Social Security Act 1986 relating to housing benefit which are specified in Part I of the Schedule, including consequential amendments and repeals–

(a) on 1st April 1988 where rent is payable at any interval which is not a week or a multiple thereof, or where payments by way of rates are not made together with payments of rent at weekly intervals or multiples thereof, and

(b) on 4th April 1988 in any other case.

Article 2(2) of the Order brings into force the provisions of the Social Security Act 1986 which are specified in Part II of the Schedule on 11th April 1988. Part II includes all those provisions concerned with income support, family credit and the social fund, in so far as they have not already been brought into force. Part II also covers industrial death benefit, reciprocal arrangements, refreshments for school pupils, claims and payments and consequential amendments and repeals.

Article 3 revokes articles 2(2) and 2(3) of the Social Security Act 1986 (Commencement No. 7) Order 1987 which respectively appointed 6th April 1988 as the day for the commencement of Schedule 10, paragraph 96 (child benefit claims and payments) and section 86(1) so far as it relates to it; and 10th April 1988 as the day for the commencement of Schedule 3 paragraphs 8, 9 and 10 (abolition of industrial death benefit) and section 39 so far as it relates to those paragraphs. Article 3 also revokes the consequential repeal in Schedule 11 of sections 67, 68 and 70 to 75 of, and Schedule 9 to, the Social Security Act 1975 and section 86(2) so far as it relates to those repeals.

NOTE AS TO EARLIER COMMENCEMENT ORDERS

(This note is not part of the Order)

Provisions	Date of Commencement	S.I. No.
s.1	4. 1.88	1987/543
s.2, Sch 1	1. 5.87	1987/543
s.3	4. 1.88	1987/543
s.4	4. 1.88	1987/543
s.5	4. 1.88	1987/543
s.6, Sch 2	6. 4.88	1987/543
s.7	6. 4.88	1987/543
s.8	1.11.86	1986/1719
s.9	6. 4.88	1987/543
s.10	6. 4.88	1987/543
s.11	6. 4.87	1986/1719
s.12 (in certain respects)	4. 1.88	1987/543
(in all other respects)	6. 4.88	1987/543
s.13	1. 5.87	1987/543
s.14	1. 5.87	1987/543
s.15 (in certain respects)	4. 1.88	1987/543
(in all other respects)	6. 4.88	1987/543
s.16	1.11.86	1986/1719
s.17	1. 5.87	1987/543
s.18(1)	6. 4.87	1987/354

Provisions	Date of Commencement	S.I. No.
s.18(2) to (6)	6. 4.88	1987/543
s.19	6. 4.88	1987/543
s.27 (partially)	6. 4.87	1986/1959
s.32 (partially)	6. 4.87	1986/1959
s.36	11. 4.88	1987/1096
s.38 (partially)	6. 4.87	1986/1959
s.39, Sch 3 (partially)	1.10.86	1986/1609
(partially)	6. 4.87	1987/354
(partially)	10. 4.88	1987/1096
(partially)	11. 4.88	1987/1096
ss.40 and 41	6. 4.87	1986/1959
s.42 (with saving)	5.10.86	1986/1609
ss. 43 and 44	5.10.86	1986/1609
s.46 (partially)	15. 3.87	1986/1959
(partially)	6. 4.87	1986/1959
ss. 47 and 48	6. 4.87	1986/1959
s.49, Sch 4 (partially)	15. 3.87	1986/1959
(partially)	6. 4.87	1986/1959
s.50	6. 4.87	1986/1959
s.51 (partially)	1.10.86	1986/1609
(partially)	6. 4.87	1986/1959
(partially)	11. 4.88	1987/1096
s.52, Sch 5 (with saving)	6. 4.87	1986/1958
ss. 53 to 60	6. 4.87	1986/1959
s.62	1.10.86	1986/1609
s.65 (partially)	11. 4.88	1987/1096
s.66, Sch 6	11. 4.88	1987/1096
s.67 (partially)	1.10.86	1986/1609
(partially)	6. 4.87	1986/1959
ss. 68 to 69	6. 4.87	1986/1959
s.71 (partially)	1.10.86	1986/1609
s.73, Sch 7 (partially)	6. 4.87	1986/1959
s.75, Sch 8	6. 4.87	1986/1959
s.78	11. 4.88	1987/1096
s.79 (partially)	6. 4.87	1986/1959
(partially)	1. 5.87	1987/543
s.80 (partially)	6. 4.87	1986/1959
(partially)	1. 5.87	1987/543
s.82, Sch 9	6. 4.87	1986/1958
s.86(1), Sch 10 (partially)	1.10.86	1986/1609
(partially)	1.11.86	1986/1719
(partially)	6. 4.87	1986/1719
(partially)	6. 4.87	1986/1959
(partially)	6. 4.87	1987/354
(partially)	1. 5.87	1987/543
(partially)	4. 1.88	1987/543
(partially)	6. 4.88	1987/543
(partially)	26. 6.87	1987/1096
(partially)	11. 4.88	1987/1096

Provisions	Date of Commencement	S.I. No.
s.86(2), Sch 11 (partially)	1.10.86	1986/1609
(partially)	5.10.86	1986/1609
(partially)	1.11.86	1986/1719
(partially)	6. 4.87	1986/1959
(partially)	7. 4.87	1986/1959
(partially)	6. 4.87	1987/354
(partially)	4. 1.88	1987/543
(partially)	6. 4.88	1987/543
(partially)	26. 6.87	1987/1096
(partially)	11. 4.88	1987/1096

STATUTORY INSTRUMENTS

1987 No. 1854

SOCIAL SECURITY

The Social Security (Widow's Benefit and Retirement Pensions) Amendment Regulations 1987

Made - - - -	*26th October 1987*
Laid before Parliament	*27th October 1987*
Coming into force	*11th April 1988*

The Secretary of State for Social Services, in exercise of powers conferred upon him by sections 29(5)(b), 39(4), 166(2) and 168(1) of, and Schedule 20 to, the Social Security Act 1975(**a**), section 12 of, and paragraph 3 of Schedule 1 to, the Social Security Pensions Act 1975(**b**) and section 89(1) of the Social Security Act 1986(**c**) and of all other powers enabling him in that behalf, after agreement by the Social Security Advisory Committee that proposals to make these Regulations should not be referred to it(**d**), hereby makes the following Regulations:

Citation, commencement and interpretation

1.—(1) These Regulations may be cited as the Social Security (Widow's Benefit and Retirement Pensions) Amendment Regulations 1987 and shall come into force on 11th April 1988.

(2) In these Regulations, "the principal Regulations" means the Social Security (Widow's Benefit and Retirement Pensions) Regulations 1979(**e**).

Amendment of Regulations

2.—(1) The principal Regulations shall be amended in accordance with the following provisions of this regulation.

(2) In regulation 5(1) for the words "section 124 of the Act" there shall be substituted the words "section 63 of the Social Security Act 1986"(**f**).

(3) In regulation 7(b) the words "a widow's allowance or" shall be omitted.

(4) In regulation 11–

(a) in paragraph (1)(c) for the reference to "40" there shall be substituted a reference to "45";

(b) in paragraph (3)(a) for the reference to "50" there shall be substituted a reference to "55".

(**a**) 1975 c.14; Schedule 20 is cited both because of the meaning ascribed to the words "prescribed" and "Regulations" and because of the power conferred in the meaning of the expression 'child', as inserted by the Child Benefit Act 1975 (c.61), section 2(1), Schedule 4, paragraph 3.
(**b**) 1975 c.60.
(**c**) 1986 c.50.
(**d**) *See* section 10(2)(b) of the Social Security Act 1980 (c.30).
(**e**) S.I. 1979/642, to which there are amendments not relevant to these Regulations.
(**f**) 1986 c.50.

(5) In regulation 13–

    (a) in paragraph (1)(a) for the reference to "40" there shall be substituted a reference to "45";

    (b) in paragraph (3) for the reference to "50" there shall be substituted a reference to "55".

(6) In regulation 16 for sub-paragraph (a) of paragraph (1) there shall be substituted the following sub-paragraph–

> "(a) any person under the age of 19 residing with the widow shall be deemed to be a child falling within section 25(2) of the Act if–
>
> > (i) the requirements of section 25(2)(a) are satisfied in his case and child benefit would have been payable in respect of him had he not been absent from Great Britain and had a claim for it been made in the manner prescribed under section 6 of the Child Benefit Act 1975 (a), or
> >
> > (ii) the requirements of section 25(2)(b) or (c) would have been satisfied, and child benefit would have been payable in respect of him continuously since the date of death of the late husband, had he not been absent from Great Britain and had a claim for child benefit been made in respect of him in the manner prescribed under section 6 of the Child Benefit Act 1975; and".

Widowed Mother's Allowance in respect of deaths before 11th April 1988

3.—(1) Where a widowed mother's allowance is payable to a woman by virtue of regulation 16(1) of the principal Regulations for a period which includes the whole or part of the week preceding 10th April 1988, or would have been so payable but for any of the provisions of the 1975 Act mentioned in paragraph (2) below, regulation 16(1) shall apply to her as though regulation 2(6) above had not been made.

(2) The provisions of the 1975 Act mentioned in paragraph (1) above are the proviso to section 25(3) (benefit not payable where a widow and a man to whom she is not married live together as husband and wife), section 82(5)(b) (benefit not payable while person is imprisoned) and section 85 (overlapping benefits).

Savings

4. In the case of a woman whose husband died before 11th April 1988, the following provisions of the principal Regulations, that is to say–

    (a) regulation 11(1) and (3), and

    (b) regulation 13(1) and (3),

shall continue to apply as though paragraph (4) or, as the case may be, paragraph (5) of regulation 2 above had not been made.

Signed by authority of the Secretary of State for Social Services.

Michael Portillo
Parliamentary Under-Secretary of State,
26th October 1987   Department of Health and Social Security

(a) 1975 c.61.

EXPLANATORY NOTE

(This note is not part of the Regulations)

These Regulations amend the Social Security (Widow's Benefit and Retirement Pensions) Regulations 1979 ("the principal Regulations"). Minor amendments are made to regulations 5(1) and 7(6) of the principal Regulations (regulation 2(2) and (3)). The age over which a widow is entitled to a Category C retirement pension and a benefit corresponding to a widow's pension is amended from 40 to 45 and the age under which a widow receives such a benefit at a reduced rate is amended from 50 to 55 (regulation 2(4) and (5)). Regulation 16 of the principal Regulations is modified so that widows with children under 19 who are not receiving full-time education are no longer entitled to widowed mother's allowance (regulation 2(5)).

Regulation 3 contains different provisions for those women entitled to widowed mother's allowance by virtue of regulation 16 of the principal Regulations where the date of death of the husband was before 11th April 1988.

Regulation 4 contains savings for existing beneficiaries of both Category C retirement pensions and benefit corresponding to widow's pension.

STATUTORY INSTRUMENTS

1987 No. 1871

BUILDING SOCIETIES

The Building Societies (Designation of Pension Companies) Order 1987

Made - - - - -	*26th October 1987*
Laid before Parliament	*30th October 1987*
Coming into force	*20th November 1987*

The Building Societies Commission, with the consent of the Treasury, in exercise of the powers conferred on it by section 18(2)(c) of the Building Societies Act 1986(**a**), and of all other powers enabling it in that behalf, hereby makes the following Order:

Title and commencement

1. This Order may be cited as the Building Societies (Designation of Pension Companies) Order 1987 and shall come into force on 20th November 1987.

Designation of pension companies

2.—(1) A pension company is designated for the purposes of section 18 of the Building Societies Act 1986 (power to invest in associated bodies) as a description of body corporate suitable for–

(a) investment and support, or

(b) support,

by a society for the purposes specified in paragraph (2) below.

(2) The purposes specified in this paragraph are the purposes of enabling the pension company to act as trustee in respect of a relevant pension scheme.

(3) In this Article–

"pension company" means a company the objects of which include acting as trustee in respect of pension schemes or descriptions of them;

"pension scheme" means–

(a) a retirement benefits scheme within the meaning of, and approved or capable of being approved by the Commissioners of Inland Revenue for the purposes of, Chapter II of Part II of the Finance Act 1970(**b**) (occupational pension schemes), or

(b) a personal pension scheme within the meaning of, and approved or capable of being approved by the Commissioners of Inland Revenue under, Chapter II of Part I of the Finance (No. 2) Act 1987 (**c**) (personal pension schemes); and

"relevant pension scheme" means a pension scheme which does not include a provision requiring the investment of any of the funds within the scheme in shares in or deposits with a building society of which the pension company which acts as trustee in respect of the scheme is a subsidiary.

(**a**) 1986 c.53.   (**b**) 1970 c.24.   (**c**) 1987 c.51.

In witness whereof the common seal of the Building Societies Commission is hereunto fixed, and is authenticated by me, a person authorised under paragraph 14 of Schedule 1 to the Building Societies Act 1986, on 22nd October 1987.

D. B. Severn
Secretary to the Commission

We consent to this Order.

Mark Lennox-Boyd
Tony Durant

26th October 1987   Two of the Lords Commissioners of Her Majesty's Treasury

---

EXPLANATORY NOTE

(This note is not part of the Order)

This Order designates companies acting as trustees in respect of pension schemes as bodies corporate which building societies may invest in (for example by acquiring shares) and for which they may provide supporting services. The purpose of investment and support of such a company must be to enable it to act as trustee of pension schemes which do not require the placing of any funds within the scheme with a building society of which the company is a subsidiary.

1987 No. 1872

BUILDING SOCIETIES

The Building Societies (Jersey) Order 1987

Made	-	-	-	*26th October 1987*
Laid before Parliament				*30th October 1987*
Coming into force				*20th November 1987*

The Building Societies Commission, with the consent of the Treasury, in exercise of the powers conferred on it by section 14 of the Building Societies Act 1986(**a**), and of all other powers enabling it in that behalf, hereby makes the following Order:

Citation and Commencement

1. This Order may be cited as the Building Societies (Jersey) Order 1987 and shall come into force on 20th November 1987.

Interpretation

2.—(1) In this Order –

"the Act" means the Buildings Societies Act 1986;

"relevant form of security" means the form of security to which paragraph 1 of Schedule 1 to this Order refers;

"relevant provision" means a provision of the Act which applies or has effect in relation to advances secured on land;

"society" means a building society;

"specified territory" means Jersey; and

"territory advance" means an advance which, by virtue of this Order, a society may make.

(2) For the purposes of this Order, a provision of the Act which applies or has effect in relation to advances fully secured on land shall be treated as one which applies or has effect in relation to advances secured on land.

Designation of specified territory

3.—(1) Subject to paragraph (2) below, the specified territory is designated as a territory as respects which advances under section 14 of the Act (power to make advances secured on land overseas) may be made secured on land.

(**a**) 1986 c.53.

(2) Schedule 1 to this Order shall have effect in respect of –

(a) the forms of security on land which may be taken for such advances,

(b) the circumstances in which such forms of security may be taken,

(c) the conditions subject to which such forms of security may be taken, and

(d) the classification of territory advances (and accordingly of the mortgage debts) as class 1 advances or class 2 advances for the purposes of the requirements of Part III of the Act for the structure of commercial assets,

in relation to the specified territory, and a society shall not have power to make advances secured on land in the specified territory except in accordance with Schedule 1 to this Order.

Availability of power

4. The power conferred by this Order is not available to a society which does not for the time being have a qualifying asset holding, but the cessation of its availability does not require the disposal of any property or rights.

Exercise of power without adoption

5. The power conferred by this Order shall not require adoption by a society in order to be exercisable by it.

Other security

6. Nothing in this Order is to be taken as precluding a society from taking other security for an advance classified as specified in Article 3(2)(d) above, but the value of the other security shall be disregarded for the purpose of that classification.

Application of relevant provisions

7. Subject to Schedule 2 to this Order, the relevant provisions shall apply or, as the case may be, have effect in relation to territory advances as they apply or have effect in relation to other advances secured on land and in any relevant provision –

(a) any reference to a mortgage shall be construed as including a reference to the relevant form of security, and

(b) any reference to a mortgage debt shall be construed accordingly.

In witness whereof the common seal of the Building Societies Commission is hereunto fixed, and is authenticated by me, a person authorised under paragraph 14 of Schedule 1 to the Building Societies Act 1986, on 22nd October 1987.

D. B. Severn
Secretary to the Commission

We consent to this Order.

Mark Lennox-Boyd
Tony Durant
26th October 1987   Two of the Lords Commissioners of Her Majesty's Treasury

Articles 2 and 3 # SCHEDULE 1

1. The form of security which may be taken for an advance under section 14 of the Act in relation to the specified territory is the form (known there as a hypotheque judiciaire or hypotheque conventionelle simple) –

    (a) acknowledging a mortgage debt and obliging (or referring to another document which obliges) the borrower to pay it, and

    (b) securing payment of that mortgage debt on land in the specified territory,

in respect of which the following provisions of this Schedule are satisfied.

2. Circumstances in which the relevant form of security may be taken for an advance –

    (a) do not, subject to Article 6 above, include circumstances in which payment of the mortgage debt is to be secured on any interest in land treated in the specified territory as moveable property or on a lease;

    (b) do not include circumstances in which provision is included as respects either the capital or the interest element in the mortgage debt that the amount due to the society may be adjusted by reference to any index of prices (whether housing prices or other prices) or to a share in the open market value of the land.

3.—(1) A territory advance shall be classified as a class 1 advance for the purposes of the requirements of Part III of the Act for the structure of commercial assets where the society at the time when it makes the advance is satisfied that –

    (a) the borrower is an individual,

    (b) the land comprising the security is exclusively for the residential use of –

        (i) the borrower, or

        (ii) the borrower and any person residing with the borrower;

    (c) the amount advanced will not exceed the value of the land comprising the security (after deducting from that value any mortgage debt of the borrower to the society outstanding under a relevant form of security relating to that land); and

    (d) the land comprising the security will not be security for any advance other than an advance by the society (except where that other advance is postponed to the society's advance).

(2) For the purposes of subparagraph (1)(d) above a right secured by the form of security known in the specified territory as a hypotheque legale shall, however arising, be treated as arising by virtue of an advance.

4. A territory advance shall be classified as a class 2 advance for the purposes of the requirements of Part III of the Act for the structure of commercial assets where the society at the time when it makes the advance is satisfied that the requirements of paragraph 3(1)(c) and (d) above are satisfied but is not satisfied that the requirements of paragraph 3(1)(a) and (b) above are satisfied.

5. If at any time when an advance treated by virtue of this Order as a class 1 advance or a class 2 advance for the purposes specified in paragraphs 3 and 4 above is outstanding the society is satisfied, on notice given to it by the borrower, that there has been a change in the use of the land comprising the security and is satisfied that, had the use been so changed before the making of the advance, the advance would instead have been a class 2 advance or a class 1 advance, as the case may be, for those purposes, the advance shall be reclassified accordingly as from that time.

6. Where a society, in exercise of its powers arising as a result of having taken the relevant form of security over land on which a territory advance is made, takes possession of the land, the land shall until sale be treated –

    (a) if the advance was most recently treated as a class 1 advance by virtue of this Order, as a class 1 asset, and

    (b) if the advance was most recently treated as a class 2 advance by virtue of this Order, as a class 2 asset,

for the purposes of the requirements of Part III of the Act for the structure of commercial assets.

7. The relevant form of security may only be taken for an advance under section 14 of the Act in circumstances in which the advance is classifiable as a class 1 advance under paragraph 3 above or a class 2 advance under paragraph 4 above.

SCHEDULE 2

Article 7

EXCLUSION OR MODIFICATION OF RELEVANT PROVISIONS

1. Section 10 of the Act (power to make advances secured on land) shall not apply to territory advances.

2. Subsections (1) to (7), (9) to (13) and (15) of section 11 of the Act (classification of advances made under section 10) shall not apply to territory advances.

3. Subsections (1) to (11) and (13) of section 12 of the Act (supplementary provisions) shall not apply to territory advances.

4. Section 13(7) of, and Schedule 4 to, the Act (sale of mortgaged property and discharge of mortgages) shall not apply to territory advances.

5. Section 18 of the Act (power to invest in associated bodies) shall have the effect in relation to territory advances so as to treat them, for the purposes of subsection (4) thereof, as if they were advances secured on land in the United Kingdom.

6. Section 69 of the Act (disclosure and record of income of related businesses) shall have effect in relation to territory advances as if, in subsection (17) thereof –

    (a) the definition of "conveyancing services" related additionally to land in the specified territory and included the preparation of conveyances, contracts and other documents in connection with, and other services ancillary to, the disposition or acquisition of interests in that land, and

    (b) the definition of "solicitor" included, in relation to the specified territory, an advocate and an ecrivain.

EXPLANATORY NOTE

(This note is not part of the Order)

This Order empowers building societies with commercial assets of at least £100 million to make advances on the security of land in Jersey, and provides for the classification of those advances within the asset classification provisions of the Building Societies Act 1986. By virtue of article 5 of this Order, the power to make such an advance does not require adoption by a special resolution of a society in order to be exercisable by it.

This Order provides (article 7 and Schedule 2) for the general treatment of those advances under the Building Societies Act 1986 to correspond to the treatment, under the Act, of advances secured on land in the United Kingdom.

STATUTORY INSTRUMENTS

1987 No. 1878 (S.129)

POLICE

The Police Cadets (Scotland) Amendment (No.2) Regulations 1987

Made - - - -		*27th October 1987*
Laid before Parliament		*6th November 1987*
Coming into force		*27th November 1987*

The Secretary of State, in exercise of the powers conferred upon him by section 27 of the Police (Scotland) Act 1967(**a**), and of all other powers enabling him in that behalf, and after taking into consideration the recommendations made by the Police Negotiating Board for the United Kingdom and furnishing the said Board with a draft of the Regulations in accordance with section 2(1) of the Police Negotiating Board Act 1980(**b**), hereby makes the following Regulations:

Citation

1. These Regulations may be cited as the Police Cadets (Scotland) Amendment (No.2) Regulations 1987.

Commencement

2. These Regulations shall come into force on 27th November 1987 and shall have effect for the purposes of regulation 5 as from 1st September 1987.

Interpretation

3. In these Regulations any reference to "the principal Regulations" is a reference to the Police Cadets (Scotland) Regulations 1968(**c**).

Amendment of the principal Regulations

4. In regulation 15 of the principal Regulations (which relates to travel allowances) for the sums "£0.50" and "£36" there are substituted the sums "£1.27" and "£92" respectively.

5. For the Table in Schedule 1 to the principal Regulations (which contains scales of pay) there is substituted the following Table:–

"TABLE

Age	Annual Pay
Under 17 years	£3,195
17 years	£3,387
18 years or over	£3,771".

(**a**) 1967 c.77; section 27 was amended by the Police and Criminal Evidence Act 1984 (c.60), section 111(2).
(**b**) 1980 c.10.
(**c**) S.I. 1968/208; the relevant amending instruments are S.I. 1976/621 and 1987/424.

6. In Schedule 2 to the principal Regulations (which relates to charges for board and lodging), for the sum "£420" there is substituted the sum "£444".

Revocation

7. The Police Cadets (Scotland) Amendment Regulations 1987(**a**) are revoked.

New St. Andrew's House, Edinburgh
27th October 1987

James Douglas-Hamilton
Parliamentary Under Secretary of State,
Scottish Office

EXPLANATORY NOTE

(This note is not part of the Regulations)

These Regulations further amend the Police Cadets (Scotland) Regulations 1968.

Regulation 4 increases the maximum travel allowance for cadets travelling to their parents or guardian outside the British Isles from £36 to £92 and increases the minimum cost below which no reimbursement is made from £0.50 to £1.27.

Regulation 5 increases the pay of police cadets with retrospective effect from 1st September 1987. Retrospection is authorised by section 27(2) of the Police (Scotland) Act 1967.

Regulation 6 increases the charges payable by cadets for board and lodging provided by police authorities from £420 per annum to £444 per annum with effect from 27th November 1987.

(**a**) S.I. 1987/424.

STATUTORY INSTRUMENTS

1987 No. 1886

MERCHANT SHIPPING

SAFETY

The Merchant Shipping (Passenger Ship Construction) (Amendment) Regulations 1987

Made - - - -	*3rd November 1987*
Laid before Parliament	*6th November 1987*
Coming into force -	*1st January 1988*

The Secretary of State, after consulting with the persons referred to in section 22(2) of the Merchant Shipping Act 1979(a), in exercise of the powers conferred on him by sections 21(1)(a) and (b) and (3) and 22(1) of that Act and of all other powers enabling him in that behalf, hereby makes the following Regulations:—

1. These Regulations may be cited as the Merchant Shipping (Passenger Ship Construction) (Amendment) Regulations 1987 and shall come into force on 1st January 1988.

2.—(1) The Merchant Shipping (Application of Construction and Survey Regulations to other ships) Regulations 1985(b) shall be amended as follows:—

(a) regulation 2 shall be omitted;

(b) in regulation 4, for " Notwithstanding regulations 2 and 3 of these Regulations, neither the Passenger Ship Regulations nor the Cargo Ship Regulations 1984 " there shall be substituted " Notwithstanding regulation 3 of these Regulations, the Cargo Ship Regulations 1984 shall not ".

(2) Regulation 3(2) of the Merchant Shipping (Passenger Ship Construction) (Amendment) Regulations 1985(c) is hereby revoked.

3. The Merchant Shipping (Passenger Ship Construction and Survey) Regulations 1984(d) shall be further amended as follows:—

(1) In regulation 1(2) after the definition of " Ro/ro cargo spaces " there shall be inserted the following definition:

" ' Ro/ro passenger ship ' means a passenger ship provided with cargo or vehicle spaces in which vehicles or cargo can be loaded or unloaded in a horizontal direction; ".

(a) 1979 c. 39.   (b) S.I. 1985/661.   (c) S.I. 1985/660.
(d) S.I. 1984/1216; relevant amendments are S.I. 1985/661, 1986/1074.

(2) Regulation 1(3) shall be replaced by the following:—

"(3) These Regulations apply:—

(i) to new United Kingdom passenger ships wherever they may be,

(ii) subject to the exceptions mentioned below in this paragraph, to other new passenger ships while they are within the United Kingdom or the territorial waters thereof, and

(iii) to the extent that the Secretary of State deems reasonable and practical, to any major repairs, alterations or modifications to existing United Kingdom passenger ships

except that

(a) regulations 16, 17 and 20 shall not apply to other new passenger ships; but such ships shall comply instead with regulations 16, 17 and 19 of the Merchant Shipping (Passenger Ship Construction) Regulations 1980(a), and

(b) Part VIA shall not apply to non-United Kingdom ro/ro passenger ships.".

(3) After regulation 80A the following new regulations shall be inserted:—

"PART VIA

MISCELLANEOUS: SHIPS WITH SPECIAL CATEGORY OR RO/RO CARGO SPACES

Application of Part VIA

80B   Subject to regulation 1(3)(b), this Part of these Regulations applies to every ro/ro passenger ship to which these Regulations apply.

Access opening indicator lights

80C   Indicators shall be provided for all shell doors, loading doors and other closing appliances fitted to openings which if left open or not properly secured could lead to major flooding of a special category space or ro/ro cargo space. The indicator system shall be a panel at the navigating bridge consisting of a green indicator light and a red indicator light for each access opening connected to suitable switches at the opening so that the green light will be illuminated on the panel for a particular opening only when the door or other closing appliance is both closed and secured. All switches or relays shall be connected so that if the door or appliance is not fully closed or properly secured the red light on the panel will illuminate. The power supply for the indicator system shall be independent of the power supply for operating and securing the doors or closing appliances.

Supplementary emergency lighting

80D   From 31st July 1988,

(i)   in addition to the emergency lighting required by Part IV of these Regulations, all passenger public spaces and alleyways shall be provided with supplementary electric lighting that can operate independently of the main and emergency and transitional sources of electric power for at least three hours when the ship is listed up to 90 degrees. The illumination provided shall be such that the approach to the means of escape from the space can be seen. The source of electric power for the lighting shall be accumulator batteries located within the lighting unit that are continuously charged, where practicable, from the emergency switchboard whilst the ship is in service. The lighting shall be of the maintained type so that any failure of the lamp will be immediately apparent. The accumulator batteries shall be replaced in accordance with the service life established by the manufacturer having regard to the ambient temperature to which they are subject in service.

(ii)   a portable rechargeable battery operated hand lamp shall be provided in every crew space alleyway, recreational space and every working space which is normally occupied unless supplementary emergency lighting as required by sub-paragraph (i) of this regulation is provided.

(a) S.I. 1980/535; relevant amendment is S.I. 1985/660.

Television Surveillance

80E   A television system shall be installed which shall be capable of transmitting reliable information to the navigating bridge on the condition (including position) of bow doors, stern doors or any other cargo or vehicle loading doors which if left open or not properly secured could lead to major flooding of a special category space or ro/ro cargo space. Special category spaces and ro/ro cargo spaces shall be continuously patrolled or shall be monitored by a television surveillance system during any voyage so that movement of vehicles in adverse weather or unauthorised entry by passengers can be observed. The system monitors shall be placed at a location that is continuously manned whilst the ship is underway.".

4. The Merchant Shipping (Passenger Ship Construction) Regulations 1980 shall be further amended as follows:—

(1) In regulation 1(2) after the definition of " Radiotelegraph room " there shall be inserted the following definitions:

" ' Ro/ro cargo spaces ' means spaces not normally subdivided in any way and extending to either a substantial length or the entire length of the ship in which goods (packaged or in bulk, in or on rail or road cars, vehicles (including road or rail tankers), trailers, containers, pallets, demountable tanks or in or on similar stowage units or other receptacles) can be loaded and unloaded normally in a horizontal direction;

' Ro/ro passenger ship ' means a passenger ship provided with cargo or vehicle spaces in which vehicles or cargo can be loaded or unloaded in a horizontal direction;".

(2) Regulation 1(3) shall be replaced by the following:

(3)(a) Subject to sub-paragraph (b) below these Regulations apply to United Kingdom passenger ships wherever they may be and to other passenger ships while they are within the United Kingdom or the territorial waters thereof except—

    (i) ships the keels of which were laid, or which were at a similar stage of construction, on or after 1st September 1984;

    (ii) ships which, although constructed before that date, were subsequently converted to passenger ships, such conversions having commenced on or after that date.

(b) Part VIIB shall not apply to non-United Kingdom ro/ro passenger ships.".

(3) After regulation 131 the following new regulations shall be inserted:—

"PART VIIB

MISCELLANEOUS: SHIPS WITH SPECIAL CATEGORY OR RO/RO CARGO SPACES

Application of Part VIIB

131A   Subject to regulation 1(3)(b), this Part of these regulations applies to every ro/ro passenger ship to which these Regulations apply.

Access opening indicator lights

131B   Indicators shall be provided for all shell doors, loading doors and other closing appliances fitted to openings which if left open or not properly secured could lead to major flooding of a special category space or ro/ro cargo space. The indicator system shall be a panel at the navigating bridge consisting of a green indicator light and a red indicator light for each access opening connected to suitable switches at the opening so that the green light will be illuminated on the panel for a particular opening only when the door or other closing appliance is both closed and secured. All switches or relays shall be connected so that if the door or appliance is not fully closed or properly secured the red light on the panel will illuminate. The power supply for the indicator system shall be independent of the power supply for operating and securing the doors or closing appliances.

Supplementary emergency lighting

131C   From 31st July 1988,

(i) in addition to the emergency lighting required by Parts IV and IVA of these Regulations, all passenger public spaces and alleyways shall be provided with supplementary electric lighting that can operate independently of the main, emergency and transitional sources of electric power for at least three hours when the ship is listed up to 90 degrees. The illumination provided shall be such that the approach to the means of escape from the space can be seen. The source of electric power for the lighting shall be accumulator batteries located within the lighting unit that are continuously charged, where practicable, from the emergency switchboard whilst the ship is in service. The lighting shall be of the maintained type so that any failure of the lamp will be immediately apparent. The accumulator batteries shall be replaced in accordance with the service life established by the manufacturer having regard to the ambient temperature to which they are subject in service.

(ii) a portable rechargeable battery operated hand lamp shall be provided in every crew space alleyway, recreational space and every working space which is normally occupied unless supplementary emergency lighting as required by sub-paragraph (i) of this regulation is provided.

Television Surveillance

131D   A television system shall be installed which shall be capable of transmitting reliable information to the navigating bridge by television on the condition (including position) of bow doors, stern doors or any other cargo or vehicle loading doors which if left open or not properly secured could lead to major flooding of a special category space or ro/ro cargo space. Special category spaces and ro/ro cargo spaces shall be continuously patrolled or shall be monitored by a television surveillance system during any voyage so that movement of vehicles in adverse weather, or unauthorised entry by passengers can be observed. The system monitors shall be placed at a location that is continuously manned whilst the ship is underway.".

3rd November 1987

Paul Channon
Secretary of State for Transport

EXPLANATORY NOTE

(This note is not part of the Regulations)

These Regulations further amend the Merchant Shipping (Passenger Ship Construction and Survey) Regulations 1984 and the Merchant Shipping (Passenger Ship Construction) Regulations 1980.

The amendments introduce requirements for access door indicating systems, supplementary emergency lighting and television systems on all United Kingdom ro/ro passenger ships. The requirements for access door indicating systems and television systems or equivalent arrangements shall be in force by 1st January 1988 and the requirements for supplementary emergency lighting shall be in force by 31st July 1988.

STATUTORY INSTRUMENTS

1987 No. 1887

OPTICIANS

The General Optical Council (Registration and Enrolment (Amendment) Rules) Order of Council 1987

Made - - - - *3rd November 1987*

At the Council Chamber, Whitehall, the 3rd day of November 1987

By the Lords of Her Majesty's Most Honourable Privy Council

Whereas in pursuance of section 7 of the Opticians Act 1958(a) the General Optical Council have made the Registration and Enrolment (Amendment) Rules 1987:

And whereas by subsection (5) of the said section such rules shall not come into force until approved by Order of the Privy Council:

Now, therefore, Their Lordships having taken the said rules into consideration, are hereby pleased to approve the same as set out in the Schedule to this Order.

This Order may be cited as the General Optical Council (Registration and Enrolment (Amendment) Rules) Order of Council 1987.

G. I. de Deney
Clerk of the Privy Council

SCHEDULE

THE REGISTRATION AND ENROLMENT (AMENDMENT) RULES 1987

In pursuance of their powers under section 7 of the Opticians Act 1958, the General Optical Council hereby make the following rules:—

1. These rules may be cited as the Registration and Enrolment (Amendment) Rules 1987.

2. The Appendix to the Registration and Enrolment Rules 1976 (scheduled to the General Optical Council (Registration and Enrolment Rules) Order of Council 1977(b) shall be further amended by replacing the figures £25, £13, and £6, on each occasion where they appear, by the figures £30, £16 and £10, respectively.

3. These rules shall come into operation on the 1st day of April 1988 and shall apply to applications for registration, enrolment, retention, restoration and transfer to take effect on or after the 1st day of April, 1988 whether made before, on or after that date.

(a) 1958 c.32.
(b) S.I. 1977/176, as amended by S.I. 1979/1638, 1980/1936, 1981/1821, 1983/1 and 1985/2024.

Sealed on the 17th September 1987.

Attested by:—

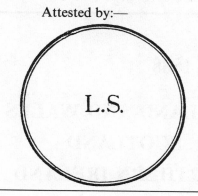

L.S.

Philip J. Cox
Chairman

J. P. Quilliam
Member of Council

R. D. Wilshin
Registrar

EXPLANATORY NOTE

(This note is not part of the Order)

The rules approved by this Order increase, with effect from the 1st April 1988, the fees payable to the General Optical Council by opthalmic and dispensing opticians and bodies corporate carrying on business as opticians for registration, enrolment, retention, restoration and transfer.

STATUTORY INSTRUMENTS

1987 No. 1888

PUBLIC HEALTH, ENGLAND AND WALES
PUBLIC HEALTH, SCOTLAND
PUBLIC HEALTH, NORTHERN IRELAND

CONTAMINATION OF FOOD

The Food Protection (Emergency Prohibitions) (No.4) Order 1987

Approved by both Houses of Parliament

Made - - - -		*3rd November 1987*
Laid before Parliament		*4th November 1987*
Coming into force		*4th November 1987*

Whereas the Secretary of State is of the opinion, as mentioned in section 1(1)(a) of the Food and Environment Protection Act 1985(**a**), that there has been or may have been an escape of substances of such descriptions and in such quantities and such circumstances as are likely to create a hazard to human health through human consumption of food;

And whereas he is of the opinion, as mentioned in section 1(1)(b) of the said Act, that in consequence of the said escape of substances, food which is, or may be in the future, in the areas described in the Schedule to the following Order, or which is, or may be in the future, derived from anything in those areas, is, or may be, or may become, unsuitable for human consumption;

Now, therefore, in exercise of the powers conferred on him by sections 1(1) and (2), and 24(1) and (3) of the said Act(**b**), and of all other powers enabling him in that behalf, he hereby makes the following Order:

Title, commencement and interpretation

1.—(1) This Order may be cited as the Food Protection (Emergency Prohibitions) (No.4) Order 1987 and shall come into force on 4th November 1987.

(2) In this Order–

(a) designated area" means one of the areas described in the Schedule to this Order;

(b) sheep" means an animal of the genus *Ovis* of whatever age or sex.

(**a**) 1985 c.48.
(**b**) Section 24(1) contains a definition of "the Ministers" relevant to the exercise of the statutory powers under which this Order is made.

Designated incident

2. In the opinion of the Secretary of State food in the areas described in the Schedule to this Order, or which is derived from anything in those areas, is or may be unsuitable for human consumption in consequence of the following escape of substances:–

the escape on or after 26th April 1986 of radioactive substances from a nuclear reactor situated at Chernobyl in the Ukraine, USSR.

Designated areas

3. The areas described in the Schedule to this Order are hereby designated for the purposes of Part I of the Food and Environment Protection Act 1985.

Activities prohibited in the designated areas

4.—(1) No person shall in any of the designated areas slaughter any sheep for human consumption or for use in the preparation of feeding stuffs.

(2) Paragraph (1) above shall not apply in the case of–

(a) any sheep which was moved from any place in accordance with a consent given under section 2(1) of the Food and Environment Protection Act 1985 which consent was subject to the condition that the sheep to which it applies should be marked with an apricot mark; or

(b) any sheep which

(i) was moved from any place in accordance with a consent given under section 2(1) of the said Act which consent was subject to the condition that the sheep to which it applies should be marked with a green mark, or

(ii) was moved from any place in accordance with a consent given on or after 28th September 1987 under section 2(1) of the said Act which consent was subject to the condition that the sheep to which it applies should be marked with a blue mark,

and which in either case has been examined and marked with an ear-tag by a person authorised in that behalf by one of the Ministers.

Restrictions on movement

5.—(1) No person shall move any sheep from any farm, agricultural holding, agricultural premises, or holding in any of the designated areas.

(2) Paragraph (1) above shall not apply in the case of–

(a) any sheep which was moved from any place in accordance with a consent given under section 2(1) of the said Act which consent was subject to the condition that the sheep to which it applies should be marked with an apricot mark;

(b) any sheep which was moved from any place in accordance with a consent given under section 2(1) of the said Act which consent was subject to the condition that the sheep to which it applies should be marked with a green mark;

(c) any sheep which was moved from any place in accordance with a consent given on or after 28th September 1987 under section 2(1) of the said Act which consent was subject to the condition that the sheep to which it applies should be marked with a blue mark.

Restrictions throughout the United Kingdom

6.—(1) No person shall in the United Kingdom–

(a) slaughter for human consumption or for use in the preparation of feeding stuffs any sheep which was in a designated area at any time after 12th August 1987; or

(b) supply, or have in possession for supply, any meat derived from a sheep or any food which contains any such meat, if that sheep was in a designated area at any time after 12th August 1987.

(2) Paragraph (1) above shall not apply in the case of -

(a) any sheep which was moved from any place in accordance with a consent given under section 2(1) of the said Act which consent was subject to the condition that the sheep to which it applies should be marked with an apricot mark; or

(b) any sheep which–

    (i) was moved from any place in accordance with a consent given under section 2(1) of the said Act which consent was subject to the condition that the sheep to which it applies should be marked with a green mark, or

    (ii) was moved from any place in accordance with a consent given on or after 28th September 1987 under section 2(1) of the said Act which consent was subject to the condition that the sheep to which it applies should be marked with a blue mark,

and which in either case has been examined and marked with an ear-tag by a person authorised in that behalf by one of the Ministers.

Revocation

7.   The Food Protection (Emergency Prohibitions) (No.2) Order 1987(**a**), the Food Protection (Emergency Prohibitions) (No.2) Amendment Order 1987(**b**) and the Food Protection (Emergency Prohibitions) (No.2) Amendment No.2 Order 1987(**c**) are hereby revoked.

N.E. Sharp
Assistant Secretary,
Scottish Office

New St. Andrew's House, Edinburgh
3rd November 1987

(**a**) S.I. 1987/1450.
(**b**) S.I. 1987/1568.
(**c**) S.I. 1987/1697.

SCHEDULE

Article 3

THE DESIGNATED AREAS

1. Dumfries and Galloway Region

a. The area of land within Stewartry District comprising that part of the Parishes of Glencairn and Dunscore bounded as follows:–

On the north from the point where the Walls Burn meets the boundary between Stewartry District and Nithsdale District running in an easterly direction through Craes Hill to Bogrie Hill and then in a southerly direction until the minor road north of Castramon Moor; then in a south-westerly direction to the Castramon Hill then in a westerly direction until the watercourse to the north of Craigenputtock Moor; then following the said watercourse in a westerly direction until it meets the Urr Water; then in a northerly direction following the Urr Water and the boundary between Stewartry District and Nithsdale District until the Walls Burn.

b. The area of land within Stewartry District comprising that part of the Parish of Kirkpatrick Durham bounded as follows:–

On the north from the point where the Craigenputtock Burn meets the Urr Water and running in a south-easterly direction to the Barr Hill plantation; then in a south-easterly direction following the western boundary of said plantation until it meets the Auchenhay Burn and then in a southerly direction by the said Burn to the point national grid reference NX773777; then in a westerly direction until Crogo Mill; and then following the Urr Water in a northerly direction until it meets the Craigenputtock Burn.

c. The area of land within Wigtown District comprising that part of the Parish of Minnigaff bounded as follows:–

On the north-west from the point where the Cross Burn meets the boundary between Dumfries and Galloway Region and Strathclyde Region running in an easterly direction following said boundary until it meets the boundary between Wigtown District and Stewartry Distict at the point national grid reference NX467873; then in a southerly direction following the western boundary of the forestry plantation and the boundary between Wigtown District and Stewartry District until it meets the River Dee to the south of Rig of Crow Nest; then following the eastern, northern and western boundaries of Ellergower Knowe plantation until it meets Loch Dee; then following round the western edge of Loch Dee to the point where it meets the White Laggan Burn; then in a westerly and then southerly direction following the boundary of White Laggan plantation until it again meets the White Laggan Burn; then in a south-easterly direction to Millfore Hill and continuing on to the Plantation south of Kirkloch; then following generally the western boundary of said plantation to the point where the Green Burn meets the Pulbae Burn; then in a northerly direction, following the boundary of the said plantation to the point national grid reference NX412711; then following the Coldstream Burn in a south-westerly direction until it meets the plantation south of Drannandow Farm; then in a northerly direction following the eastern boundary of Glentrool Forest passing to the south of Glenhead and Buchan steadings and following the boundary of Glentrool Forest to the south of Palgowan; then in a northerly direction following generally the eastern boundary of Glentrool Forest until the point where the Cross Burn meets the said Regional boundary.

d. The area of land within Nithsdale District comprising that part of the Parish of Kirkconnel bounded as follows:–

On the north from the point where the Polmarlach Burn meets the River Nith and running in an easterly direction by the River Nith to the point national grid reference NS693130; then in a southerly direction to, and crossing the Road A70 at the point national grid reference NS695125 and then continuing generally in a south-westerly direction through White Hill and south-westerly until the eastern boundary of the plantation at the point national grid reference NS682102 north of Polnagrie Hill; then following generally the eastern and northern boundaries of the said plantation until it meets the Polmarlach Burn; and then following the said Burn until it meets the River Nith.

2. Strathclyde Region

a. The area of land within Cumnock and Doon Valley District comprising that part of the Parishes of Dalmellington and Coylton bounded as follows:–

On the north from the point where the Burnhead Burn meets the boundary between the Parishes of Dalrymple and Dalmellington and running in a north-easterly direction by the said Burn and Parish boundary until the point where the boundaries of the Parishes of Dalrymple, Dalmellington and Coylton meet; and then in a northerly direction along the boundary between the Parishes of Dalrymple and Coylton to the point national grid reference NS458114; and then in a north-easterly direction until the western corner of the Kyle Forest Plantation; and then generally in a southerly direction following the western boundary of the said Plantation to the point national grid reference NS480094; and then generally in a south-westerly and south-south-westerly direction to the point where the path meets the unmetalled road at spot height 287; and then in a north-westerly direction along the said unmetalled road until it meets the Dunaskin Burn; and then in a westerly direction along the said Burn to the Castle at the point national grid reference NS450089; then in a north-easterly direction to where the path crosses the Burnhead Burn at the point national grid reference NS455092; and then following the said Burn in a northerly direction until the point where it meets the boundaries between the Parishes of Dalrymple and Dalmellington.

b. The area of land within Cumnock and Doon Valley District comprising that part of the Parish of Sorn bounded as follows:–

On the north from the point national grid reference NS540330 on the boundary between Cumnock and Doon Valley District and Kilmarnock and Loudoun District continuing in an easterly direction by the said boundary to the point national grid reference NS587325 on the said boundary; then in a south-westerly direction to the Road B7037 at the point national grid reference NS537302 and continuing in a north-westerly direction to where the said road crosses the Auchmannock Burn; then following the said Burn in a north-easterly direction to the point national grid reference NS542312 and continuing generally in a northerly direction to the boundary between Cumnock and Doon Valley District and Kilmarnock and Loudoun District at the point national grid reference NS540330.

c. The area of land within Cumnock and Doon Valley District comprising that part of the Parish of Dalmellington bounded as follows:–

On the north from the point national grid reference NS485029 continuing in an easterly direction by the southern boundary of the Bellsbank Plantation until it meets the Muck Water; then in a south-easterly direction by the Muck Water and the western boundary of another plantation to the point national grid reference NS511013; then in a southerly direction to the western edge of Loch Muck and continuing along the western and southern edges of said Loch to the boundary between Strathclyde Region and Dumfries and Galloway Region; and then continuing in a south-westerly direction by said boundary until it meets Loch Doon; and then continuing in a north-westerly direction by the north-eastern edge of said Loch until it meets the Eriff Plantation; then continuing along the eastern and northern boundaries of said Plantation until it again meets the eastern edge of Loch Doon; and then in a north-easterly direction to the point national grid reference NS485029.

d. The area of land within Cumnock and Doon Valley District comprising that part of the Parish of Auchinleck bounded as follows:–

On the north from the point national grid reference NS625249 in a north-easterly direction to the point national grid reference NS640257; then in a south-easterly direction to the course of the old railway at the point national grid reference NS644254 and continuing along the said course until it meets the boundary between the Parishes of Auchinleck and Muirkirk; then continuing generally in a south-easterly direction by the said Parish boundary until it meets the boundary between Cumnock and Doon Valley District and Clydesdale District; then continuing in a south-easterly direction by the said boundary until it meets the boundary of the Drummond Knowe Plantation; then following the western boundary of the said Plantation in a south-westerly direction until it meets the boundary between the Parishes of Auchinleck and New Cumnock; then continuing in a westerly direction by the said boundary and the boundary between the Parishes of Auchinleck and Old Cumnock to the point national grid reference NS636195 and continuing in a northerly direction to the point national grid reference NS636198, then continuing in a westerly direction to the small plantation and then continuing by the eastern and northern boundaries of the small plantation to the point national grid reference NS634202; and then in a north-westerly direction to the point national grid reference NS629215; then in a south-westerly direction to the western boundary of the small plantation at the point national grid reference NS627215 and following the northern and western boundaries of said plantation in a south-westerly direction then in a westerly direction to the point national grid reference NS618214; then following the eastern and northern boundaries of the said plantation and continuing generally in northerly direction from the north-western corner of the said plantation to the Road A70 at spot height 211; and then in a northerly direction to the point national grid reference NS625249.

e. The area of land within Cumnock and Doon Valley District comprising that part of the Parish of Muirkirk bounded as follows:–

On the north from the point national grid reference NS595310 and continuing generally in an easterly direction by the boundary between Cumnock and Doon Valley District and East Kilbride District until it meets the boundary between Cumnock and Doon Valley District and Clydesdale District and then continuing in a south-easterly direction by said lastmentioned boundary to the summit of Hare Craig; then in a southerly direction to the point national grid reference NS740304 and continuing generally in a westerly and southerly direction by the northern and western boundaries of the plantation until the western boundary meets the Ponesk Burn; then continuing in a south-westerly direction to the summit at spot height 368 and continuing in a north-westerly direction to Greenock Water at the point national grid reference NS701298; then in a south-westerly direction by Greenock Water to the point national grid reference NS670282 and continuing in a westerly and southerly direction by the northern and western boundaries of the Burnfoot Moor Plantation to the point national grid reference NS669274; then in a southerly direction to the point national grid reference NS668269 and continuing in a south-westerly direction by the south-eastern boundary of the Toll Plantation to the Road B743 at spot height 214; then continuing in a southerly direction to the River Ayr at the point national grid reference NS664262 and continuing generally in a north-easterly direction by said river to the point national grid reference NS720281; then in a south-easterly direction to the summit of Hawlk Hill and continuing in a south-easterly direction to the point national grid reference NS742262; then generally in a south-westerly direction by the boundary between Cumnock and Doon Valley District and Clydesdale District until it meets the boundary between the Parishes of Muirkirk and Auchinleck and continuing generally in a north-westerly direction by said boundary to the point national grid reference NS626270; then in a northerly direction to the point national grid reference NS629289 and continuing in a westerly direction to the point national grid reference NS611287; and then continuing generally in a north-westerly direction by the boundary between the Parishes of Muirkirk and Sorn to the point national grid reference NS595310.

f. The area of land within Cumnock and Doon Valley District comprising that part of the Parish of Old Cumnock bounded as follows:–

On the north from the point national grid reference NS628194 and continuing in a south-easterly direction by the boundary between the Parishes of Auchinleck and Old Cumnock until it meets the boundary between the Parishes of Old Cumnock and New Cumnock; then in a southerly then a north-westerly direction by said boundary to the point national grid reference NS628174 and continuing in a northerly direction to the point national grid reference NS629179; then generally in a northerly direction by the unnamed burn to the point national grid reference NS628194.

g. The area of land within Kyle and Carrick District comprising that part of the Parish of Straiton bounded as follows:–

On the north from the point national grid reference NS403059 continuing in an easterly direction along the southern boundary of the Lambdoughty Hill Plantation to the point national grid reference NS416062; then generally in a south-easterly direction by the Lambdoughty Burn and continuing in a south-easterly direction over the summit of Turgeny to the north-western corner of the Auldcraigoch Hill Plantation; then following the western boundary of said plantation to its western corner and continuing in a westerly direction to where the Chapel Burn runs into Baing Loch; then generally in a north-westerly direction to the point national grid reference NS410048 and continuing in a north-westerly direction by the watercourse to the point national grid reference NS403059.

h. The area of land within Kyle and Carrick District and comprising that part of the Parish of Straiton bounded as follows:–

On the north from the point national grid reference NS450025 continuing in a south-easterly direction over Rowantree Craig to the boundary between Kyle and Carrick District and Cumnock and Doon Valley District at the point national grid reference NS477015; then following the western edge of Loch Doon to the point where the Garpel Burn issues and continuing up said Burn in a westerly direction to the weir at the south-eastern end of Loch Finlas; then following generally the eastern edge of said Loch to its northern end and continuing in a north-westerly direction up the unnamed burn to the point national grid reference NX449998; then continuing in a north-westerly direction to the point national grid reference NS442015; then continuing in a north-easterly direction to Black Loch; and then continuing in a north-easterly direction to the point national grid reference NS450025.

i. The area of land on the Island of Arran within Cunninghame District comprising that part of the Parish of Kilbride bounded as follows:–

On the north from the point national grid reference NR969372 continuing in a north-easterly direction to the summit of Cul nan Creagan; then in a south-easterly direction to the western corner of the Torr Plantation and following the southern and eastern boundaries of said Plantation to the point national grid reference NR997372; then generally in a southerly direction to the point national grid reference NR999362 and continuing generally in a south-westerly direction to the boundary between the Parishes of Kilbride and Kilmory at the summit of Cnoc Dubh; then continuing in a north-westerly direction by the said boundary to the point national grid reference NR969372.

j. The area of land on the Island of Arran within Cunninghame District and comprising that part of the Parish of Kilmory bounded as follows:–

On the north from the point national grid reference NR955400 continuing in a south-easterly direction by the boundary between the Parishes of Kilmory and Kilbride until it meets the String Road; and then in a westerly direction by said road to the point national grid reference NR938348; then in a north-westerly direction to the summit of Garbh Thorr and continuing in a northerly direction over the summit of Beinn Tarsuinn to the point national grid reference NR939385; and then continuing in a north-easterly direction to the said Parish boundary at the point national grid reference NR955400.

k. The area of land within Kilmarnock and Loudoun District comprising that part of the Parish of Galston bounded as follows:–

On the north from the Glenoul Burn at the point national grid reference NS578360 continuing in a north-easterly direction to the point national grid reference NS588362; then generally in a southerly direction to the point national grid reference NS590355 and continuing along the watercourse in a south-easterly direction until it meets the Dubs Burn; then in a north-easterly direction by the said Burn to the point national grid reference NS597359 and continuing in a north-easterly direction and by a watercourse to the point national grid reference NS605369; then generally in a south-easterly direction to the boundary between Kilmarnock and Loudoun District and East Kilbride District at the point national grid reference NS618363 and following the said boundary in a south-westerly direction until it meets the boundary between Kilmarnock and Loudoun District and Cumnock and Doon Valley District; then following the said boundary in a northerly and westerly direction until it meets the Logan Burn; then continuing in a northerly direction by the said Burn until it meets the Glenoul Burn; and then continuing in a northerly direction by the Burn to the point national grid reference NS578360.

l. The area of land within Kilmarnock and Loudoun District comprising that part of the Parish of Fenwick bounded as follows:–

On the north from the point national grid reference NS475483 continuing in an easterly direction by the boundary between the Parishes of Fenwick and Stewarton and the Swinzie Burn to the point national grid reference NS492483; then in a northerly direction to the point national grid reference NS493487 and continuing in a south-easterly direction until the minor road at the point national grid reference NS502483; then in a south-westerly direction to the point national grid reference NS479466 and continuing in a north-westerly direction to the point national grid reference NS475471; then in a north-easterly direction to the point national grid reference NS478475 and continuing in a north-westerly direction to the point national grid reference NS475483.

m. The area of land within Kilmarnock and Loudoun District comprising that part of the Parish of Fenwick bounded as follows:–

On the north from the point national grid reference NS515471 and continuing in a north-easterly direction to the boundary between Kilmarnock and Loudoun District and Eastwood District; then in a north-easterly and south-easterly direction by said boundary until it meets the Rough Hill Plantation and continuing generally in a westerly direction by the northern boundary of said Plantation to the point national grid reference NS531459; then in a westerly direction to the boundary of the Flow Moss Plantation at the point national grid reference NS525459; then generally in a northerly direction by the eastern boundary of said Plantation to the point national grid reference NS515471.

n. The area of land within Kilmarnock and Loudoun District and comprising that part of the Parish of Galston bounded as follows:–

On the north from the point national grid reference NS615366 continuing in a north-easterly direction by the course of the old railway until it meets the boundary between East Kilbride District and Kilmarnock and Loudoun District; and then continuing in a south-easterly and westerly direction by said boundary to the point national grid reference NS619364 and continuing in a north-westerly direction to the point national grid reference NS618367; then in a south-westerly direction to the point national grid reference NS615366 and continuing in a north-westerly direction by the minor road until it meets the course of the old railway at the point national grid reference NS615366.

o. The area of land within East Kilbride District comprising that part of the Parish of Avondale bounded as follows:–

On the north from the point national grid reference NS625371 continuing in a south-easterly direction to the point national grid reference NS631368; then in a north-easterly direction to the point national grid reference NS635369 and continuing in a south-easterly direction to the point national grid reference NS646364; then generally in a northerly direction by the road until it meets the Road B745 and continuing in a north-westerly direction by said road until it meets the boundary of the small plantation to the east of the road; then generally in an easterly direction and by the southern boundary of the said plantation to the point national grid reference NS654374 and continuing in a south-easterly direction to the Road A723 at the point national grid reference NS657373; then in a south-easterly direction by said road until it meets the boundary between East Kilbride District and Cumnock and Doon Valley District and continuing generally in a south-westerly direction by said boundary to the point national grid reference NS602310; then in a north-easterly direction to the summit of Hart Hill; then in a north-easterly direction to the summit of Little Hartmidden; then in a north-easterly direction to the summit of Anderside Hill; then in a northerly direction to the point national grid reference NS616346 and continuing in a north-westerly direction to the point national grid reference NS611347; then generally in a north-easterly direction by the boundary between East Kilbride District and Kilmarnock and Loudoun District to the point national grid reference NS625371.

p. The area of land within Eastwood District comprising that part of the Parish of Eaglesham bounded as follows:–

On the north from the point national grid reference NS503502 and continuing in a north-easterly direction to the point national grid reference NS510504; then continuing in a south-easterly direction to the point national grid reference NS517503 and then in a north-easterly direction to the point national grid reference NS524509; then continuing in a north-westerly direction to the point national grid reference NS523516 and continuing in a north-easterly direction to the point national grid reference NS533523; then continuing generally in a northerly direction to the point national grid reference NS533526 and then in a north-easterly direction to the point national grid reference

NS547536; then in a south-easterly direction to the point national grid reference NS549534; then in a north-easterly direction by the unnamed burn until it meets the minor road between Mearns and Eaglesham, and then continuing in a south-easterly direction by said road to its junction with another minor road at the point national grid reference NS557537; then in a south-westerly direction by said road to the point national grid reference NS541520; then continuing in a south-easterly direction to the road B764 at the point national grid reference NS553508 and continuing in a south-westerly direction to the point national grid reference NS547501; and then continuing generally in an easterly direction by the Dunwan Burn to the point national grid reference NS569498; and then generally in a southerly direction to the point national grid reference NS572488 then in an easterly direction to the point national grid reference NS577488; then in a north-easterly direction to the point national grid reference NS587495 and continuing generally in a south-easterly direction to the point national grid reference NS592494; and then continuing in a south-easterly direction to the point national grid reference NS593491 then in a south-easterly direction to the point national grid reference NS595490; then continuing in a southerly direction to the point national grid reference NS596484 and in a south-easterly direction to the point national grid reference NS604482; then continuing generally in a south-westerly direction by the boundary between Eastwood District and East Kilbride District until it meets the boundary between Kilmarnock and Loudoun District and Eastwood District; and then continuing generally in a north-westerly direction by said District boundary to the point national grid reference NS503502.

3. Central Region

a. The area of land within Stirling District comprising that part of the Parish of Killin bounded s follows:–

On the north from the point national grid reference NN494391 continuing in an easterly and southerly direction along the boundary between Central Region and Tayside Region to the point national grid reference NN585354; then continuing in a westerly direction and following the northern and western boundaries of the plantation and the burn Allt na Ceardaich to where it meets the River Lochay; then in a southerly direction to the point national grid reference NN568338 and continuing generally in a southerly direction along the western boundary of the Monemore Plantation to the southernmost corner of said Plantation; then in a south-easterly direction to the Road A827 and continuing in a south-westerly direction by said road to its junction with the Road A85; then in a southerly direction following said road until it meets the boundary between the Parishes of Killin and Balquhidder; then continuing in a westerly direction by said boundary to the point national grid reference NN470250; then continuing in a north-westerly direction to the south-eastern corner of the Meall Thairbh Plantation and continuing along the eastern and northern boundaries of said Plantation to the point national grid reference NN444272; then continuing in a northerly direction to the plantation to the north of the River Dochart and continuing in a northerly direction along the eastern boundary of said Plantation and in a westerly direction by the Allt Essan Burn to the point national grid reference NN419286; and then continuing in a northerly direction to the summit of Beinn nan Imirean; and then continuing in a north-easterly direction to the summit of Meall Glas; then continuing in an easterly direction to the summit at spot height 908; then continuing in a north-easterly direction to the summit of Beinn Cheathaich then continuing in an easterly direction to the summit of Meall a Churain; then in a north-easterly direction to the summit at spot height 881; then in an easterly direction to the summit at spot height 864; then in a south-easterly direction to the summit at spot height 766; then continuing generally in a northerly direction to and by the Allt Dubhchlair burn until it meets the River Lochay; then continuing in a north-easterly direction to the road and in a westerly direction by the road to where the Allt Lebhain burn meets the River Lochay; and then continuing generally in a northerly direction to the boundary between Tayside Region and Central Region at the point national grid reference NN494391.

b. The area of land within Stirling District comprising that part of the Parish of Balquhidder bounded as follows:–

On the north from the point national grid reference NN532244 continuing generally in a north-easterly direction until it meets the boundary between the Parishes of Balquhidder and Kenmore; then continuing in a southerly direction by said boundary until it meets the boundary between Central Region and Tayside Region; then continuing in a southerly direction to the point where the Kendrum Burn flows into Loch Earn and continuing in a south-westerly direction by said burn until it meets the dismantled railway; and then in a southerly direction by said dismantled railway until it meets the Road A84 and continuing in a south-westerly direction by said road to its junction with the road to Balquhidder at Kingshouse Hotel; then in a north-westerly direction by said road to Balquhidder until it crosses a small burn; then in a south-westerly direction by said burn until it meets the River Balvag and continuing in a north-westerly direction by said river until it meets a small burn then in a northerly direction by said burn to the Auchtubhmore Hill Plantation and continuing by the southern, western and northern boundaries of said plantation to the point national grid reference NN559217; and then continuing in a north-westerly direction to the summit of Meall an t - Seallaidh and then continuing in a north-westerly direction to the point national grid reference NN532244.

c. The area of land within Stirling District comprising that part of the Parish of Balquhidder bounded as follows:–

On the north from the point national grid reference NN618230 continuing in a southerly direction by the boundary between Central Region and Tayside Region until it meets the boundary between the Parishes of Balquhidder and Callander; then continuing in a south-westerly direction by said Parish boundary until it meets the Strathyre Plantation; then in a northerly direction by the eastern boundary of said plantation to the point national grid reference NN578200; then continuing in an easterly direction to the Burn of Ample and then in a northerly direction by said burn until it meets the minor road at Falls of Edinample; then in an easterly direction by said road to the point national grid reference NN618230.

d. The area of land within Stirling District and comprising that part of the Parish of Callander bounded as follows:–

On the north from the point where the boundary between the Parishes of Callander and Balquhidder meets the boundary between Central Region and Tayside Region continuing in a south-easterly direction by said Regional boundary to the point national grid reference NN680134; then in a south-westerly direction along the Meall Leathan Dhail ridge to the spot height 452 and then in a south-westerly direction to the Tom Dubh Plantation; then in a south-westerly direction by the south-eastern boundary of said plantation to Keltie Water and continuing in a north-westerly direction by Keltie Water to the point national grid reference NN639094; then continuing in a south-westerly direction to the plantation and continuing generally in a south-westerly direction by the northern and western boundaries of the plantation and grounds of Leny House to the River Teith south of Kilmahog; then in a north-westerly direction by said river until it meets Loch Lubnaig and continuing in a northerly direction by the eastern edge of said Loch until it meets the boundary between the Parishes of Callander and Balquhidder; and then continuing in a north-easterly direction by said Parish boundary until it meets the boundary between Central Region and Tayside Region.

e. The area of land within Stirling District comprising that part of the Parish of Callander bounded as follows:–

On the north from the point national grid reference NN486144 continuing generally in an easterly direction by the boundary between the Parishes of Callander and Balquhidder to the point national grid reference NN558122; then in a southerly direction to the summit of Ben Ledi; then in a south-easterly direction to the point national grid reference NN580077; then continuing in an easterly direction to the burn west of Samson's Stone and continuing in a south-easterly direction by the said burn to the plantation south of the Eas Gobhain River; then continuing generally in an easterly direction by the western and southern boundaries of the plantation to the Road A81 and continuing in a southerly direction by said road to the point national grid reference NN633062; then in an easterly direction to the River Teith and continuing in a southerly direction by said river until it meets the boundary between the Parishes of Callander and Kilmadock; then continuing in a south-westerly direction along said boundary until it meets the boundary between the Parishes of Callander and Port-of-Menteith; then continuing in a westerly direction by said boundary until it meets the boundary between the Parishes of Callander and Aberfoyle and continuing in a north-westerly direction along said boundary until it meets the Trossachs Plantation; then in a north-westerly direction by the eastern and northern boundaries of said plantation to the point national grid reference NN481108; then continuing generally in a northerly direction to the point national grid reference NN486144.

EXPLANATORY NOTE

(This note is not part of the Order)

This Order revokes and re-enacts the provisions of the Food Protection (Emergency Prohibitions) (No.2) Order 1987, as amended.

This Order continues the emergency prohibitions imposed by that Order restricting various activities in order to prevent human consumption of food rendered unsuitable for that purpose in consequence of the escape in April 1986 of radioactive substances from a nuclear reactor situated at Chernobyl in the Ukraine, USSR.

The Order designates again areas in Scotland affected by the escape from which the movement of sheep and in which the slaughter of sheep are prohibited (articles 3, 4(1) and 5(1) and the Schedule). Restrictions on the slaughter of sheep from the designated areas, and the supply of meat derived from such sheep, extend throughout the United Kingdom (article 6(1)).

The Order continues the following exceptions to the prohibitions referred to in articles 4, 5 and 6:–

(a) an exception from the said prohibition on slaughter in any of the designated areas in respect of–

(i) any sheep which was moved from any place in accordance with a consent given under section 2(1) of the Food and Environment Protection Act 1985 which consent was subject to the condition that the sheep to which it applies should be marked with an apricot paint mark (article 4(2)(a));

(ii) any sheep which was moved from any place in accordance with a consent given under section 2(1) of the said Act which consent was subject to the condition that the sheep to which it applies should be marked with a green paint mark or, after 28th September 1987 with a blue paint mark and which in either case has been examined and marked with an ear-tag by a person authorised by the Minister of Agriculture, Fisheries and Food, the Secretary of State for Scotland or Wales, or the Department of Agriculture for Northern Ireland (article 4(2)(b));

(b) an exception from the said prohibition on movement in respect of any sheep which–

(i) was moved in accordance with a consent given under section 2(1) of the said Act which consent was subject to the condition that the sheep to which it applies should be marked with an apricot paint mark or with a green paint mark (article 5(2)(a) and (b));

(ii) was moved in accordance with a consent given on or after 28th September 1987 under section 2(1) of the said Act which consent was subject to the condition that the sheep to which it applies should be marked with a blue paint mark (article 5(2)(c));

(c) an exception from the said prohibition on slaughter, and from the said prohibition on supply of meat in respect of–

(i) any sheep which was moved from any place in accordance with a consent given under section 2(1) of the Food and Environment Protection Act 1985 which consent was subject to the condition that the sheep to which it applies should be marked with an apricot paint mark (article 6(2)(a));

(ii) any sheep which was moved from any place in accordance with a consent given under section 2(1) of the said Act which consent was subject to the condition that the sheep to which it applies should be marked with a green paint mark or, after 28th September 1987 with a blue paint mark respectively and which in either case has been examined and marked with an ear-tag by a person authorised by the Minister of Agriculture, Fisheries and Food, the Secretary of State for Scotland or Wales, or the Department of Agriculture for Northern Ireland (article 6(2)(b)).

Under section 21 of the Food and Environment Protection Act 1985 the penalty for contravening an emergency prohibition is–

(a) on summary conviction, a fine of an amount not exceeding the statutory maximum (at present £2,000);

(b) on conviction on indictment, an unlimited fine or imprisonment for a term of not more than two years, or both.

Powers of enforcement in relation to emergency prohibitions are conferred by section 4 of, and Schedule 2 to, the 1985 Act. Under paragraph 10 of that Schedule obstruction of enforcement officers is an offence.

STATUTORY INSTRUMENTS

1987 No. 1891

TRUSTEES

The Public Trustee (Custodian Trustee) Rules 1987

Made - - - -	*28th October 1987*
Laid before Parliament	*16th November 1987*
Coming into force	*1st January 1988*

The Lord Chancellor, in exercise of the powers conferred upon him by section 14(1) of the Public Trustee Act 1906(**a**), and with the concurrence of the Treasury, hereby makes the following Rules:

1. These Rules may be cited as the Public Trustee (Custodian Trustee) Rules 1987 and shall come into force on 1st January 1988.

2. Rule 30(1) of the Public Trustee Rules 1912(**b**) shall be amended by the addition of the following sub-paragraph after sub-paragraph *(j)*:

"*(k)* any corporation acting as trustee of the trusts of any pension scheme or pension fund established or maintained by the British Broadcasting Corporation, but only in relation to those trusts.".

Dated 23rd October 1987   *Havers*, C.

We concur,

David Lightbown
Mark Lennox-Boyd
Dated 28th October 1987   Two of the Lords Commissioners of Her Majesty's Treasury

EXPLANATORY NOTE

(This note is not part of the Rules)

These Rules amend rule 30 of the Public Trustee Rules 1912 so as to include as a corporation entitled to act as custodian trustee any corporation acting as trustee of trusts of any pension scheme or fund established or maintained by the British Broadcasting Corporation.

(**a**) 1906 c.55.
(**b**) S.R. & O. 1912/348; the relevant amending instruments are S.I. 1975/1189, 1976/836 and 1981/358.

STATUTORY INSTRUMENTS

1987 No. 1892

HALLMARK

The Hallmarking (International Convention) (Amendment) Order 1987

Made - - - -   *5th November 1987*

Coming into force   *3rd December 1987*

The Secretary of State, in exercise of his powers under sections 2(1)(c) and (3), 21(3) and 22(1) of the Hallmarking Act 1973(**a**) and of all other powers enabling him in that behalf, hereby makes the following Order:–

1.—(1) This Order may be cited as the Hallmarking (International Convention) (Amendment) Order 1987 and shall come into force on 3rd December 1987.

(2) The Hallmarking (International Convention) (Amendment) Order 1983(**b**) is hereby revoked.

2. Schedule 2 to the Hallmarking (International Convention) Order 1976(**c**) is hereby further amended by the substitution for the entry for Portugal of the entry set out in the Schedule hereto.

Francis Maude
Parliamentary Under Secretary of State,
Department of Trade and Industry

5th November 1987

(**a**) 1973 c. 43.
(**b**) S.I. 1983/1389.
(**c**) S.I. 1976/730; relevant amending instruments are S.I. 1981/559, 1983/1389.

Article 2

THE SCHEDULE

PORTUGAL

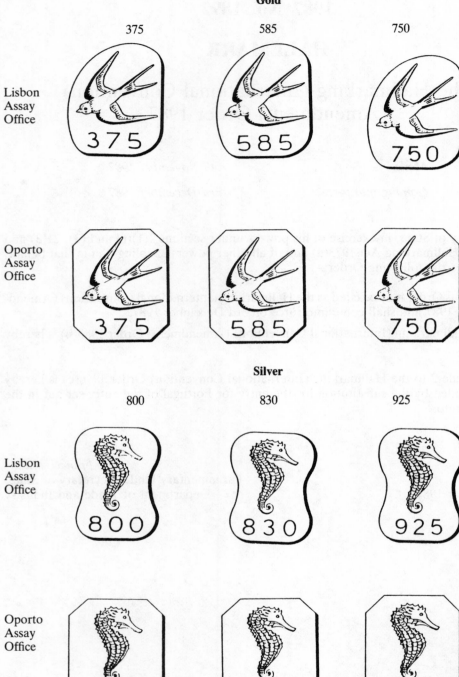

Gold

	375	585	750
Lisbon Assay Office			
Oporto Assay Office			

Silver

	800	830	925
Lisbon Assay Office			
Oporto Assay Office			

Platinum

950

Lisbon
Assay Office

Oporto
Assay Office

EXPLANATORY NOTE

(This note is not part of the Order)

This Order, which is made under the Hallmarking Act 1973, further amends Schedule 2 to the Hallmarking (International Convention) Order 1976 consequent upon the alteration of the Portuguese hallmarks for gold and silver, and the introduction of a mark for platinum, as notified by the authorised assay offices of Lisbon and Oporto in accordance with the Convention on the Control and Marking of Articles of Precious Metals done at Vienna on 15th November 1972 (Cmnd. 7219).

STATUTORY INSTRUMENTS

1987 No. 1893

PUBLIC HEALTH, ENGLAND AND WALES
PUBLIC HEALTH, SCOTLAND
PUBLIC HEALTH, NORTHERN IRELAND

CONTAMINATION OF FOOD

The Food Protection (Emergency Prohibitions) (England) Order 1987

Made - - - -	*5th November 1987*
Laid before Parliament	*5th November 1987*
Coming into force	*7th November 1987*

Whereas the Minister of Agriculture, Fisheries and Food is of the opinion, in accordance with section 1(1)(a) of the Food and Environment Protection Act 1985(**a**), that there has been or may have been an escape of substances of such descriptions and in such quantities and such circumstances as are likely to create a hazard to human health through human consumption of food;

And whereas the said Minister is of the opinion, in accordance with section 1(1)(b) of the said Act, that in consequence of the said escape of substances food which is or may be in the future in the area described in Schedule 1 to the following Order, or which is derived or may be in the future derived from anything in that area, is, or may be, or may become, unsuitable for human consumption;

Now, therefore, the said Minister, in exercise of the powers conferred on him by section 1(1) and section 24(3) of the said Act, and of all other powers enabling him in that behalf, hereby makes the following Order:

Title, commencement and interpretation

1.—(1) This Order may be cited as the Food Protection (Emergency Prohibitions) (England) Order 1987 and shall come into operation on 7th November 1987.

(2) In this Order–

    (a) "the Act" means the Food and Environment Protection Act 1985,

    (b) "designated area" means the area described in Schedule 1 to this Order,

    (c) "sheep" means an animal of the genus *Ovis* of whatever age or sex.

Designated incident

2. In the opinion of the Minister of Agriculture, Fisheries and Food, food in the area described in Schedule 1 to this Order, or which is derived or may be in the future derived

---

(**a**) 1985 c.48.

from anything in that area, is, or may be, or may become unsuitable for human consumption in consequence of the following escape of substances–

the escape on or after 26th April 1986 of radioactive substances from a nuclear powered reactor situated at Chernobyl in the Ukraine, USSR.

Designated area

3. The area described in Schedule 1 to this Order is hereby designated for the purposes of Part I of the Act.

Activities prohibited in the designated area

4.—(1) No person shall in the designated area slaughter any sheep for human consumption or for use in the preparation of feeding stuffs.

(2) Paragraph (1) above shall not apply in the case of any sheep which–

(a) was moved from any place in accordance with a consent given under section 2(1) of the Act which consent was subject to the condition that the sheep to which it applies should be marked with a red mark; and

(b) has been examined and marked with an ear-tag by a person authorised in that behalf by one of the Ministers.

Restrictions on movement

5.—(1) No person shall move any sheep from a farm, holding or agricultural premises situated in the designated area.

(2) Subject to paragraph (3) below, no person shall move into the designated area any sheep which has been removed from that area or from an area which is from time to time designated by an Order under section 1 of the Act which refers to the escape of substances described in article 2 of this Order.

(3) Paragraph (2) above shall not apply in the case of any sheep which was moved from any place in accordance with a consent given under section 2(1) of the Act which consent was subject to the condition that the sheep to which it applies should be marked with a red mark.

Restrictions throughout the United Kingdom

6.—(1) Subject to paragraph (2) below, no person shall, in the United Kingdom–

(a) slaughter for human consumption or for use in the preparation of feeding stuffs any sheep that was in the designated area at any time after 11 am on 20th June 1986; or

(b) supply, or have in possession for supply, any meat derived from a sheep, or any food which contains any such meat, if that sheep was in the designated area at any time after 11 am on 20th June 1986.

(2) Paragraph (1) above shall not apply in the case of–

(a) any sheep which was moved to a market in accordance with a consent given under section 2(1) of the Act which consent did not require that the sheep to which it applies should be marked in a manner specified therein;

(b) any sheep which was moved from any place in accordance with a consent given under the said section 2(1) on or before 21st December 1986 which consent was subject to the condition that the sheep to which it applies should be marked with a blue mark;

(c) any sheep which was moved from any place in accordance with a consent given under the said section 2(1) on or before 26th July 1987 which consent was subject to the condition that the sheep to which it applies should be marked with an apricot mark; or

(d) any sheep which–

(i) was moved from any place in accordance with a consent given under the said section 2(1) which consent was subject to the condition that the sheep to which it applies should be marked with a red mark or with a green mark; or

(ii) was moved from any place in accordance with such a consent given on or
after 28th September 1987 which consent was subject to the condition that
the sheep to which it applies should be marked with a blue mark,

and which, in either case, has been examined and marked with an ear-tag by a
person authorised in that behalf by one of the Ministers.

Revocation

7. The Orders specified in Schedule 2 to this Order are hereby revoked.

In witness whereof the Official Seal of the Minister of Agriculture, Fisheries and Food is
hereunto affixed on 5th November 1987.

John MacGregor
Minister of Agriculture, Fisheries and Food

Article 3   **SCHEDULE 1**

                            THE DESIGNATED AREA

Cumbria

The area comprising those parts of the county of Cumbria which lie within the following boundary–
From the junction of a minor road with a footpath at O.S. map ref. SD 216929, north on the
footpath to O.S. map ref. SD 218933; south east on the footpath to O.S. map ref. SD 225923;
north east on the footpath via Carter Ground to its junction with a footpath at O.S. map ref.
SD 232935; east and then north on the footpath via Stephenson Ground to its junction with
Walna Scar Road; east on Walna Scar Road to its junction with a footpath at O.S. map ref.
SD 258965; north east on the footpath via Dow Crag to its junction with a footpath at Cairn;
north on the footpath via Little How Crags and Great How Crags to its junction with a
footpath at O.S. map ref. NY 273000; north west and then north east on the footpath to its
junction with a minor road at O.S. map ref. NY 276027; east on the minor road via Fell Foot
to its junction with a minor road at O.S. map ref. NY 302030; north west along the minor road
to where it crosses Great Langdale Beck at O.S. map ref. NY 285060; north west along Great
Langdale Beck through Mickleden to Rossett Gill; north west along Rossett Gill to where it
meets a footpath at Rossett Pike (O.S. map ref. NY 248075); north west on the footpath to
Angle Tarn (O.S. map ref. NY 245078); north along the stream which leaves Angle Tarn to
Langstrath Beck; north east along Langstrath Beck to its confluence with Greenup Gill; north
west along Stonethwaite Beck to where it meets the road B5289 at Rosthwaite (O.S. map ref.
NY 258145); south west on the road B5289 to Seatoller; north west on the road B5289 via
Honister Pass and Gatesgarth to where it meets Buttermere (O.S. map ref. NY 191153);
through the centre of Buttermere to its north west corner (O.S. map ref. NY 173163); north
west along a river where it flows into Crummock Water; north through the middle of
Crummock Water to where the River Cocker flows out of it; north along the River Cocker to
where it is crossed by a minor road at O.S. map ref. NY 148215; west on the minor road to its
junction with a minor road at Fangs Brow Farm (O.S. map ref. NY 105228); south west on
the minor road via Lamplugh to its junction with a minor road at Croasdale (O.S. map ref.
NY 093174); north east on a minor road to O.S. map ref. NY 094176; north east following
field boundaries to O.S. map ref. NY 097177; south east following fell walls along the edge of
Banna Fell and Herdus Fell to O.S. map ref. NY 109165; south following field boundaries to
O.S. map ref. NY 112159; west following the boundary of Bowness Plantation to a track at
O.S. map ref. NY 110159; south on the track to its junction with a footpath at O.S. map ref.
NY 109154; north west on the footpath to Ennerdale Water at O.S. map ref. NY 106155;
north west along the edge of Ennerdale Water to a footpath at O.S. map ref. NY 091151; west
following the footpath to Cragg Farm; west following the forest boundary to O.S. map ref.
NY 072147; south following field boundaries to O.S. map ref. NY 067142; north west
following the forest boundary to O.S. map ref. NY 065145; south west following the forest
boundary to a minor road at O.S. map ref. NY 063144; south on the minor road via Blakeley

Raise and Cold Fell to its junction with a minor road at O.S. map ref. NY 047066; north east along the minor road to where it crosses the River Calder at O.S. map ref. NY 056068; north along the River Calder to O.S. map ref. NY 062078; south east following the field boundary to its junction with the minor road north east of High Prior Scales (O.S. map ref. NY 065075); east following the field boundary to where it meets a footpath at Farmery (O.S. map ref. NY 076071); south east following the footpath to O.S. map ref. NY 077072; south east along the boundary of Ponsonby Fell to O.S. map ref. NY 076061; east to the west corner of Blengdale Forest (O.S. map ref. NY 077062); south east following the edge of Blengdale Forest to O.S. map ref. NY 080057; north east following the edge of Blengdale Forest to O.S. map ref. NY 082062; follow the edge of Blengdale Forest to O.S. map ref. NY 086058; across the River Bleng and through Blengdale Forest in a direct line to the edge of the forest at O.S. map ref. NY 089058; north and then west following the edge of the Blengdale Forest to O.S. map ref. NY 093060; south east along the field boundaries to a minor road at O.S. map ref. NY 096053; north east along the field boundaries to where it meets Bolton Wood at O.S. map ref. NY 097054; south following the boundary of Bolton Wood and following the field boundaries along the east side of Scarbrow Wood to the Gosforth/Nether Wasdale minor road at O.S. map ref. NY 101043; east along the minor road to its junction with a minor road at O.S. map ref. NY 113047; east on the minor road to the road junction at O.S. map ref. NY 119049; north east on the minor road leading to Greendale and via Greendale to the edge of Wast Water at O.S. map ref. NY 151054; south west following the edge of Wast Water and across where the River Irt leaves Wast Water at O.S. map ref. NY 143038; west on a track to its junction with a footpath at Easthwaite (O.S. map ref. NY 136034); south on the footpath to where it meets Latterbarrow Wood at O.S. map ref. NY 135032; west along the north edge of the forest to a minor road at O.S. map ref. NY 118027; south west along the minor road to Santon Bridge (O.S. map ref. NY 111016); south east along a minor road to the railway station at Irton Road (O.S. map ref. SD 138999); south west along the Ravenglass and Eskdale Railway to the railway station at Muncaster Mill (O.S. map ref. SD 095978); south along the road A595(T) to its junction with a minor road at Broad Oak; south following the minor road to its junction with a minor road at O.S. map ref. SD 116923; south east on the minor road to the road Junction at O.S. map ref. SD 118921; south west on the minor road via Corney to its junction with the road A595(T) at Cross House (O.S. map ref. SD 107890); south on the road A595(T) to its junction with the road A5093 at Whicham; north east on the road A595(T) to its junction with a minor road at O.S. map ref. SD 180864; north on the minor road via Broadgate and Cragg Hall to its junction with a minor road at O.S. map ref. SD 177894; east along the minor road to its junction with a minor road at O.S. map ref. SD 186900; north west along the minor road to its junction with a track at Beckstones; north on the track via Ulpha Park to its junction with a minor road at O.S. map ref. SD 187924; north east on the minor road via Ulpha and The Crook and across the River Duddon to its junction with a minor road at O.S. map ref. SD 213953; south on the minor road via Far Kiln Bank to its junction with a footpath at O.S. map ref. SD 216929.

The area excludes any part of a road, track, footpath, railway or river by reference to which its boundary is defined.

Article 7

SCHEDULE 2

ORDERS REVOKED

Orders	References
1. The Food Protection (Emergency Prohibitions) (England) (No. 2) Order 1986.	S.I. 1986/1689.
2. The Food Protection (Emergency Prohibitions) (England) (No. 2) Amendment Order 1986.	S.I. 1986/2208.
3. The Food Protection (Emergency Prohibitions) (England) (No. 2) Amendment Order 1987.	S.I. 1987/153.
4. The Food Protection (Emergency Prohibitions) (England) (No. 2) Amendment No. 2 Order 1987.	S.I. 1987/249.
5. The Food Protection (Emergency Prohibitions) (England) (No. 2) Amendment No. 3 Order 1987.	S.I. 1987/906.
6. The Food Protection (Emergency Prohibitions) (England) (No. 2) Amendment No. 4 Order 1987.	S.I. 1987/1555.
7. The Food Protection (Emergency Prohibitions) (England) (No. 2) Amendment No. 5 Order 1987.	S.I. 1987/1687.
8. The Food Protection (Emergency Prohibitions) (England) (No. 2) Amendment No. 6 Order 1987.	S.I. 1987/1803.

EXPLANATORY NOTE

(This note is not part of the Order)

This Order replaces in relation to an area of land in England the Food Protection (Emergency Prohibitions) (England) (No. 2) Order 1986 as amended. It contains emergency prohibitions restricting various activities in order to prevent human consumption of food which has been or which may have been rendered unsuitable for that purpose in consequence of the escape of radioactive substances from a nuclear reactor situated at Chernobyl in the USSR.

The Order designates an area of land in England affected by the escape from which the movement of sheep, and in which the slaughter of sheep other than sheep identified by a red paint mark which have been examined and subsequently marked with an ear-tag, are prohibited (articles 3, 4 and 5(1) and Schedule 1). Movement into the designated area of sheep which have been removed from it or from a similarly designated area elsewhere in the United Kingdom (other than sheep which have been identified by a red paint mark, and moved, in accordance with a Ministerial consent) is prohibited (article 5(2)).

Restrictions on the slaughter of sheep from the designated area, and the supply of meat derived from such sheep, extend throughout the United Kingdom subject to exceptions (article 6(1)). Those exceptions permit the slaughter of, and the supply of meat derived from, such sheep moved unmarked to a market in accordance with a Ministerial consent or moved in accordance with such a consent which required the sheep to which it applied to be marked with a specified colour subject, in certain cases, to the sheep so identified having been subsequently examined and marked with an ear-tag by a person authorised in that behalf by the Minister of Agriculture, Fisheries and Food, the Secretary of State for Scotland or Wales or the Department of Agriculture for Northern Ireland (article 6(2)).

Under section 21 of the Food and Environment Protection Act 1985 the penalty for contravening an emergency prohibition is–

(a) on summary conviction, a fine of an amount not exceeding the statutory maximum (at present £2,000);

(b) on conviction on indictment, an unlimited fine, or imprisonment for a term of not more than two years or both.

Powers of enforcement in relation to emergency prohibitions are conferred by section 4 of, and Schedule 2 to, the Act. Obstruction of enforcement officers is an offence under paragraph 10 of that Schedule.

STATUTORY INSTRUMENTS

1987 No. 1894

PUBLIC HEALTH, ENGLAND AND WALES
PUBLIC HEALTH, SCOTLAND
PUBLIC HEALTH, NORTHERN IRELAND

CONTAMINATION OF FOOD

The Food Protection (Emergency Prohibitions) (Wales) (No. 5) Order 1987

Made - - - -	*5th November 1987*
Laid before Parliament	*5th November 1987*
Coming into force -	*7th November 1987*

Whereas the Secretary of State is of the opinion, as mentioned in section 1(1)(a) of the Food and Environment Protection Act 1985**(a)**, that there has been or may have been an escape of substances of such descriptions and in such quantities and such circumstances as are likely to create a hazard to human health through human consumption of food;

And whereas the Secretary of State is of the opinion, as mentioned in section1(1)(b) of the said Act, that in consequence of the said escape of substances food which is or may be in the future in the areas described in the Schedule to the following Order, or which is derived or may be in the future derived from anything in those areas, is, or may be, or may become, unsuitable for human consumption;

Now, therefore, the Secretary of State, in exercise of the powers conferred on him by the said section 1(1) and (2) and section 24(1) and (3) of the said Act, and of all other powers enabling him in that behalf, hereby makes the following Order:—

Title, commencement and interpretation

1.—(1) This Order may be cited as the Food Protection (Emergency Prohibitions) (Wales) (No. 5) Order 1987 and shall come into force on 7th November 1987.

(2) In this Order—

(a) "the Act" means the Food and Environment Protection Act 1985,

(b) "designated area" means an area described in the Schedule to this Order,

(c) "sheep" means an animal of the genus *Ovis* of whatever age or sex.

Designated incident

2. In the opinion of the Secretary of State, food in the areas described in the Schedule to this Order, or which is derived or may be in the future derived from anything in those areas, is, or may be, or may become unsuitable for human consumption in consequence of the following escape of substances:—

the escape on or after 26th April 1986 of radioactive substances from a nuclear powered reactor situated at Chernobyl in the Ukraine, USSR.

(a) 1985 c.48.

Designated areas

3. The areas described in the Schedule to this Order are hereby designated for the purposes of Part I of the Act.

Activities prohibited in the designated areas

4.—(1) Subject to paragraph (2) below, no person shall in a designated area slaughter any sheep for human consumption or for use in the preparation of feeding stuffs.

(2) Paragraph (1) above shall not apply in the case of any sheep which—

(a) was moved from any place in accordance with a consent given under section 2(1) of the Act which consent was subject to the condition that the sheep to which it applies should be marked with a red mark; and

(b) has been examined and marked by an ear-tag by a person authorised in that behalf by one of the Ministers(a).

Restrictions on movement

5.—(1) No person shall move any sheep from a farm, holding or agricultural premises situated in a designated area.

(2) Subject to paragraph (3) below, no person shall move into a designated area any sheep which has been removed from a designated area or from an area which is from time to time designated by an order other than this Order under section 1 of the Act which refers to the escape of substances described in article 2 of this Order.

(3) Paragraph (2) above shall not apply in the case of any sheep which was moved from any place in accordance with a consent given under section 2(1) of the Act which was subject to the condition that the sheep to which it applies should be marked with a red mark.

Restrictions throughout the United Kingdom

6.—(1) Subject to paragraph (2) below, no person shall, in the United Kingdom—

(a) slaughter for human consumption or for use in the preparation of feeding stuffs any sheep that was—

(i) in any of the areas numbered 1, 2 and 3 of the designated areas detailed in the Schedule to this Order at any time after 11 a.m. on 20th June 1986; or

(ii) in the area numbered 4 of the designated areas detailed in the said Schedule at any time after 9th July 1987; or

(iii) in any of the areas numbered 5, 6, 7 and 8 of the designated areas detailed in the said Schedule at any time after 10th August 1987; or

(iv) in any of the areas numbered 9, 10, 11 and 12 of the designated areas detailed in the said Schedule at any time after 27th August 1987; or

(v) in any of the areas numbered 13, 14 and 15 of the designated areas detailed in the said Schedule at any time after 17th September 1987, or

(b) supply, or have in possession for supply, any meat derived from a sheep, or any food which contains any such meat, if that sheep was—

(i) in any of the areas numbered 1, 2 and 3 of the designated areas detailed in the Schedule to this Order at any time after 11 a.m. on 20th June 1986; or

(ii) in the area numbered 4 of the designated areas detailed in the said Schedule at any time after 9th July 1987; or

(iii) in any of the areas numbered 5, 6, 7 and 8 of the designated areas detailed in the said Schedule at any time after 10th August 1987; or

(iv) in any of the areas numbered 9, 10, 11 and 12 of the designated areas detailed in the said Schedule at any time after 27th August 1987; or

(v) in any of the areas numbered 13, 14 and 15 of the designated areas detailed in the said Schedule at any time after 17th September 1987.

(a) The definition of "the Ministers" is in section 24(1) of the Food and Environment Protection Act 1985.

(2) Paragraph (1) above shall not apply in the case of—

    (a) any sheep which was moved to a market in accordance with a consent given under section 2(1) of the Act which consent did not require that the sheep to which it applies should be marked in a manner specified therein;

    (b) any sheep which was moved from any place in accordance with a consent given under the said section 2(1) on or before 21st December 1986 which consent was subject to the condition that the sheep to which it applies should be marked with a blue mark;

    (c) any sheep which was moved from any place in accordance with a consent given under the said section 2(1) on or before 26th July 1987 which consent was subject to the condition that the sheep to which it applies should be marked with an apricot mark; or

    (d) any sheep which—

        (i) was moved from any place in accordance with a consent given under the said section 2(1) which consent was subject to the condition that the sheep to which it applies should be marked with a red mark or with a green mark; or

        (ii) was moved from any place in accordance with such a consent given on or after 28th September 1987 which consent was subject to the condition that the sheep to which it applies should be marked with a blue mark;

    and which, in either case, has been examined and marked with an ear-tag by a person authorised in that behalf by one of the Ministers.

Revocation

7. The Food Protection (Emergency Prohibitions) (Wales) (No. 4) Order 1987**(a)**, the Food Protection (Emergency Prohibitions) (Wales) (No. 4) Amendment Order 1987**(b)** and the Food Protection (Emergency Prohibitions) (Wales) (No. 4) Amendment No. 2 Order 1987**(c)** are hereby revoked.

Peter Walker

5th November 1987   Secretary of State for Wales

Article 3   **SCHEDULE**

DESIGNATED AREAS

    1. An area comprising that part of the County of Powys which lies within the following boundary:—

From the meeting of the Afon Conwy with the Forestry Commission fence at OS map reference SH 999179 generally north-eastwards following the forest boundary fence to its junction with the farm fence at OS map reference SH 995188 then generally northwards following the farm fence to OS map reference SH 998199 and then generally north-westwards along the forest fence to where it crosses the stream at OS map reference SH 989204 and then generally following the course of the stream to where it joins Llyn Efyrnwy near the waterfall at OS map reference SH 995206 and then crossing Llyn Efyrnwy in a generally north-westwards direction to the forest boundary at OS map reference SH 988217 and then following the forestry boundary to its junction with the stream at OS map reference SH 993225 and then generally eastwards following the course of the stream through the forest to its junction with the stream at OS map reference SH 999222 and then generally north-eastwards following the course of the stream to where it meets the forestry boundary at OS map reference SJ 003224 and then generally north-eastwards following the forest boundary to where it joins the fenced Nant Coedwyr Boundary at OS map reference SJ 003226 and then generally north-eastwards, following the fenced Nant Coedwyr Boundary to where it joins the Severn-Trent Boundary at OS map reference SJ 013240 and then generally north-westwards along the Severn-Trent Boundary passing through OS map references SJ 004244 and SJ 003260 to where it joins the fence at the County Boundary at OS map reference SH 990280 at Cyrniau Nod; then westwards and then south-westwards along the fence following the County Boundary passing through OS map references SH 946270 and SH 916229; then generally southwards along the fence to the Severn-Trent Water Authority fence at OS map reference SH 928202 and thereafter as a Forestry Commission fence to a point near Drum Ddu at OS map reference SH 932166; then continuing generally eastwards along the Forestry Commission fence to where it meets a Forestry Commission fence

(a) S.I. 1987/1638.   **(b)** S.I. 1987/1682.   **(c)** S.I. 1987/1802.

along a footpath at OS map reference SH 975168; generally northwards following the fence along the footpath to where it meets a Forestry Commission fence at OS map reference SH 972177; generally south-eastwards then north-eastwards along the fence to where it meets the Afon Conwy at OS map reference SH 999179.

The area excludes any part of a road, footpath or body of water by reference to which its boundary is defined.

2. An area comprising that part of the County of Gwynedd which lies within the following boundary:—

From where the mountain wall meets the railway line at Conwy at OS map reference SH 775779; generally westwards along the railway line to where it meets the boundary wall at OS map reference SH 744784 on the western side of Penmaen-bach Point; generally southwards along the boundary wall to where it meets the boundary fence at OS map reference SH 747769, generally south-westwards following the boundary fence passing through OS map references SH 730746, SH 728757, SH 703751, SH 703742, SH 711738, SH 700721, SH 693726, SH 693738, SH 683738, SH 689726, SH 680704, SH 660701, SH 656716, SH 636702 and SH 639696 to where it joins the unmarked road near Bryn Hall at OS map reference SH 633693; generally westwards along the unmarked road to the junction with the unmarked road to the north of Llanllechid at OS map reference SH 621690; generally southwards along the unmarked road passing through Llanllechid and Rachub to its junction with the A5(T) and B4366 roads; generally north-westwards along the B4366 road to its junction with an unmarked road at OS map reference SH 616664; generally south-westwards along the unmarked road through Hirdir and Tan-y-Bwlch to where it meets an unmarked road at OS map reference SH 593654; generally southwards along the unmarked road, past Pen-y-bwlch to its junction with the forest fence at OS map reference SH 594644, generally south-eastwards along the forest fence to a point at OS map reference SH 597638 to its junction with the farm fence, generally southwards along the line of the fence at OS map reference SH 597637, generally south-eastwards through a point at OS map reference SH600635 to a point at OS map reference SH 604630 then generally eastwards along the fence to a point at OS map reference SH 606629, south-eastwards to a point at OS map reference SH 610626 and then north-westwards along the fence to OS map reference SH 606627, then generally south-westwards to a point at OS map reference SH 603624 passing through OS map references SH 598620 and SH 597619, generally north-westwards to OS map reference SH 597620, generally south-westwards to OS map reference SH 595618, generally southwards passing through OS map reference SH 595615 to OS map reference SH 597613 on the quarry boundary; generally south-westwards along the line of the quarry incline passing through OS map references SH 596610, SH 592606, SH 590603 and SH 589602, continuing along the track of the quarry incline south-westwards to the unmarked road at OS map reference SH 587601; generally south-westwards along the unmarked road to its junction with the A4086 road at OS map reference SH 583598; generally southwards along the A4086 road to where it meets the boundary fence of the Snowdon Railway at OS map reference SH 583597; generally south-westwards along the boundary fence to where it meets a fence near Afon Hwch at OS map reference SH 578590; generally south-westwards along the fence following the course of Afon Hwch to where it meets Llyn Dwythwch at OS map reference SH 571582; generally southwards along the western edge of Llyn Dwythwch to where it meets a fence at OS map reference SH 568577 generally westwards along the fence to where it meets a fence at OS map reference SH 564576; generally north-westwards along the fence passing through OS map references SH 563578 and SH 560581 to where it meets a fence at OS map reference SH 558582; generally south-westwards along the fence to OS map reference SH 556577; generally north-westwards to OS map reference SH 554578; generally westwards to a disused mine at OS map reference SH 544578; generally south-westwards to OS map reference SH 539577; generally north-westwards along the old Waenfawr/Nant y Betws Parish Boundary to OS map reference SH 535579 where it meets the east bank of Afon Gwyrfai; following the east bank of Afon Gwyrfai northwards to where the disused tramway crosses Afon Gwyrfai at OS map reference SH 534583; south-westwards along the line of the disused tramway over Afon Gwyrfai to where it meets the A4085 road at OS map reference SH 532582; generally south-eastwards along the A4085 road to where it meets a fence near Plasisaf at OS map reference SH 547564; generally eastwards along the fence passing through OS map reference SH 550564 to OS map reference SH 552564; generally north-eastwards along the fence passing through OS map reference SH 553567 to OS map reference SH 555567; generally south-eastwards along the fence to OS map reference SH 557564; generally eastwards along the fence passing through OS map references SH 560564, SH 567560 and SH 570599 to its junction with a fence at OS map reference SH 573559; generally south-eastwards along the fence passing through OS map references SH 575554 and SH 580554 to where it meets Afon Trewennydd at OS map reference SH 584548; generally south-westwards along the fence following the course of Afon Trewennydd to where it and Afon Gwyrfai are crossed by the A4085 road at OS map reference SH 568540; generally south-eastwards along the course of the Afon Gwyfrai to where it is crossed by the A4085 road at OS map reference SH 571532; generally south-eastwards along the A4085 road to its junction with the A498 road near Beddgelert at OS map reference SH 591481; generally north-eastwards following the A498 road to a point at OS map reference SH 613494 on the western side of Llyn Dinas then following the lake shore eastwards to join the fence at OS map reference SH 615493 then generally southwards following the mountain wall and field boundaries passing through OS map references SH 616490, SH 620492, SH 621494, SH 424491 and SH 623487 to join Afon Nanmor at OS map reference SH 627478 then generally south-westwards following the course of Afon Nanmor to a point at OS map reference SH 620468, then generally south-westwards following the boundary of Coed Caeddafydd passing through OS map references SH 621460 and SH 619458 then south-eastwards to a point at OS map reference SH 620454, crossing Afon Dylif at OS map reference SH 621452 then eastwards to OS map reference SH 627452, then generally northwards to the junction of the fences at OS map reference SH 628457; generally eastwards along the fence passing through OS map references SH 630458, SH 635460, SH 639460, SH 640456, SH 644460 and SH 647462; generally southwards along the fence to where it meets Cwm Croesor at OS map reference SH 647459; generally eastwards along the fence following the course of Cwm Croesor where it meets a disused tramway at OS map reference SH 654460; generally south-eastwards along the disused tramway to where it meets a fence at OS map reference SH 656455; generally south-westwards along the fence to OS map reference SH 650453; generally southwards along the fence passing through OS map references SH 649450 and SH 648449; generally eastwards along the fence to OS map reference SH 650449; generally south-eastwards along the fence to OS map reference SH 654444; generally south-westwards along the fence passing through OS map references SH 650444 and SH 643443 to where it joins a forest fence at OS map reference SH 639437; generally south-eastwards along the forest fence to the junction of the fences at OS map reference SH 641435; generally southwards along the fence to its junction with the forest fence at OS map reference SH 641431; generally south-eastwards along the forest fence passing through OS map references SH 650434, SH 656430, SH 667426 and SH 664420 to its junction with its fence along the Ffestiniog Railway at OS map reference SH 664417; generally eastwards then northwards along the fence following the Festiniog Railway to its junction at Blaenau Ffestiniog with Glanarwel road at OS map reference SH 695463; generally north-eastwards along Glanarwel road to its junction with the A470(T) road at OS map reference SH 697467; generally southwards along the A470(T) to its junction with the A496 road at Blaenau Ffestiniog at OS map reference SH 698460; generally southwards along the A470(T) road to its junction with an unmarked road by Congl-y-wal at OS map reference SH 706444; generally south-westwards along the unmarked road to its junction with an unmarked road at OS map reference SH 697434; generally south-eastwards along the unmarked road to its junction with the A470(T) road at OS map reference SH 706427; generally southwards along the A470(T) road to its junction with the B4391 road at Ffestiniog at OS map reference SH 705418; generally eastwards along the B4391 road to where it meets a fence at OS map reference SH 736417; generally south-westwards along the fence passing through OS map reference SH 733416 to where it meets a fence alongside Afon Cynfal at OS map reference SH 732413; generally eastwards along the fence following the course of Afon Cynfal to its junction with the forest fence at OS map reference SH 734413; generally eastwards then westwards along the forest fence passing through OS map references SH 740408, SH 750410, SH 751409, SH 750405, SH 740398, SH 730397, SH 720397, SH 720395 and SH 715395 to where it meets a fence along a forest track at OS map reference SH 710399; generally south-westwards following the fence along the forest track through Sychnant to OS map reference SH 707398; generally south-westwards following the fence to a point north of Castell Tomen-y-Mur north of Trawsfynydd at OS map reference SH 708387 generally south-eastwards following field boundaries passing through OS map references SH 710387, SH 719380, SH 720379 and SH 724378 then north-eastwards passing through OS map references SH 727379, and SH 730378 then generally southwards passing through SO map references SH 729376, SH 726370 and SH 726366 then eastwards to Afon Llafar at OS map reference SH 733373 then southwards following the course of the river to the A4212 road at OS map reference SH 737363 then eastwards along the road to SO map reference SH 741363 and then following Afon Prysor westwards to its confluence with Nant Budr at OS map reference SH 737360 then following the course of the Nant Budr south-eastwards to the fence at OS map reference SH 750347 and then following the line of the fence south-eastwards passing through OS map references SH 753344 and SH 755343 to Afon Gain at SO map reference SH 756339, then following the course of Afon Gain generally southwards to the forest fence at OS map reference SH 755336 then following the fence southwards to Pont y Gain at OS map reference SH 752328 where it meets an unmarked road; generally eastwards along the unmarked road to where it meets a fence at OS map reference SH 829325 near Buarthmeini; generally north-eastwards following the fence to where it meets the forest at OS map reference SH 832328; following the fence around the forest generally north to OS map reference SH 833343; generally north-westwards along the fence passing through OS map reference SH 830345 to OS map reference SH 823350; generally north-eastwards along the fence passing through OS map references SH 818352, SH 820353, SH 825360 and SH 826370 to OS map reference SH 830371; generally north-westwards along the fence passing through OS map reference SH 820379 to OS map reference SH 811381; generally southwards along the fence to OS map reference SH 812378; generally westwards along the fence to OS map reference SH 809378; generally northwards along the fence passing through OS map reference SH 811380 to where it joins Afon Tryweryn at OS map reference SH 808385; generally eastwards along the fence following the course of Afon Tryweryn to where it meets an unmarked road at OS map reference SH 817394; generally northwards along the unmarked road to its junction with the A4212 and B4391 roads at OS map reference SH 817395; generally north-westwards along the B4391 road to where it meets a fence at OS map reference SH 812397; generally north-eastwards along the fence passing through OS map references SH 814400 and SH 814403; generally eastwards along the fence passing through SO map references SH 820402, SH 830401 and

SH 833405 to its junction with a forest fence at OS map reference SH 835403; generally south-eastwards along the forest fence to its junction with a fence at OS map reference SH 836401; generally south-eastwards along the fence to where it meets the A4212 road and a fence at OS map reference SH 837400; generally south-eastwards along the fence to where it meets Afon Tryweryn at OS map reference SH 838399; generally eastwards along the course of Afon Tryweryn to Llyn Celyn; generally eastwards along the southern bank at Llyn Celyn to where it meets the A4212 road at OS map reference SH 880404, generally south-eastwards along the A4212 road to its crossing of Afon Hesgyn at OS map reference SH 894401; generally north-westwards along the course of Afon Hesgyn passing through OS map references SH 890410, SH 885420 and OS map reference SH 884426 to where it meets a fence; generally eastwards along the fence to OS map reference SH 890425 and generally north-eastwards along the fence to OS map reference SH 895430; generally northwards along the fence to its junction with a stream at OS map reference SH 895437 then northwards along the fence to its junction with a stream at OS map reference SH 895442; generally north-eastwards along the fence to OS map reference SH 900450; generally eastwards along the fence to its junction with the unmarked road at OS map reference SH 908450; generally north-westwards along the unmarked road to where it meets a fence at OS map reference SH 907454; generally south-westwards along the fence to OS map reference SH 900452; generally north-westwards along the fence crossing Afon Nant-Fach at OS map reference SH 897454 to its junction with a fence along the County Boundary above Trum Nant-Fach at OS map reference SH 891458; generally south-westwards, north-westwards and north-eastwards along the fence following the County Boundary to where it meets a fence alongside Nant-y-Glychedd at OS map reference SH 868458; generally northwards along the fence following Nant-y-Glychedd then Nant Glan Gwrach to its junction with a fence at OS map reference SH 866470; generally south-westwards and then north-westwards along the fence through OS map references SH 863467, SH 861470 and SH 860474 to its junction with Nant Adwy'r-llan at OS map reference SH 858474; generally south-westwards along the course of Nant Adwy'r-llan to its junction with a fence at OS map reference SH 844461; generally westwards and then south-westwards along the fence through OS map references SH 843460, SH 839458 and SH 840457; generally south-westwards along the fence along the bank of Afon Marddwr to its junction with the fence at OS map reference SH 836454; generally south-westwards along the fence through OS map reference SH 836450 and which continues alongside Afon Marddwr to OS map reference SH 830444; generally westwards along the fence through OS map references SH 826443, SH 824445, SH 820446 to its junction with Afon Serw at OS map reference SH 818447; generally northwards following the course of Afon Serw to its confluence with Afon Conwy at OS map reference SH 816455; generally south-westwards along the course of Afon Conwy to its junction with the fence at OS map reference SH 806453; generally northwards along the fence through OS map references SH 806457, SH 809470, SH 811484 and SH 812493 to its junction with a fence at OS map reference SH 812499; generally north-eastwards along the fence to its junction with a fence at OS map reference SH 815506; generally westwards to its junction with a forest fence at OS map reference SH 814507; generally south-westwards along the forest fence passing through OS map reference SH 811500 to its junction with a forest fence at OS map reference SH 802492; generally north-westwards along the forest fence passing through OS map reference SH 798497 to OS map reference SH 794498; generally southwards along the forest fence to its junction with a fence at OS map reference SH 793474; generally north–westwards along the fence passing through OS map reference SH 790477 to OS map reference SH 787481; generally south-westwards along the fence passing through OS map reference SH 780477 to its junction with the forest fence at OS map reference SH 771473; generally southwards along the forest fence to its junction with a fence at OS map reference SH 771464; generally southwards along the fence to OS map reference SH 769457; generally westwards along the fence to its junction with a fence at OS map reference SH 764457; generally north-westwards along the fence to OS map reference SH 759464; generally westwards along the fence to OS map reference SH 750465 to its junction with the forest fence at OS map reference SH 747466; generally south-westwards along the forest fence passing near to a quarry to OS map reference SH 739453; generally north-westwards along the forest fence to its junction with a fence at OS map reference SH 735457; generally westwards along the fence passing through OS map reference SH 730459 to OS map reference SH 728458; generally north-eastwards along the fence passing through OS map references SH 731465 and SH 731470 to its junction with a forest fence at OS map reference SH 734477; generally north-eastwards along the forest fence to its junction with a fence at OS map reference SH 738480; generally eastwards along the fence to its junction with a fence at OS map reference SH 739482; generally eastwards along the fence passing through OS map references SH 742483, SH 745482 and SH 750483, to where it meets a stream at OS map reference SH 753484; generally south-eastwards along the fence following the course of the stream passing through OS map reference SH 759477 to where it meets an unmarked road at OS map reference SH 761477; generally north-eastwards along the fence following the unmarked road to where it meets Afon Machno at OS map reference SH 764479; generally northwards along the course of Afon Machno to where it meets a forest fence at OS map reference SH 763482; generally westwards along the forest fence to OS map reference SH 755482; generally north-eastwards along the forest fence to OS map reference SH 756482; generally eastwards along the forest fence to OS map reference SH 759484; generally westwards along the forest fence passing through OS map reference SH 750485 to OS map reference SH 744487; generally south-westwards along the forest fence to its junction with a fence at OS map reference SH 742483; generally westwards along the fence to its junction with the forest fence at OS map reference SH 739482; generally northwards along the forest fence to its junction with the fence at OS map reference SH 744489; generally north-eastwards along the fence to OS map reference SH 749491; generally north-westwards along the fence to OS map reference SH 745497; generally north-eastwards along the fence passing through OS map references SH 748500, SH 750503 and SH 756506 to OS map reference SH 757510; generally northwards along the fence to OS map reference SH 757514; generally north-westwards along the fence to its junction with a forest fence at OS map reference SH 750516; generally north-westwards along the forest fence to where it meets an unmarked road at OS map reference SH 737521; generally northwards along the unmarked road to its junction with the A470(T) road at OS map reference SH 735524; generally north-eastwards along the A470(T) road to where it meets Afon Conwy at OS map reference SH 798547; generally eastwards then northwards along the A470(T) road to its junction with the A5(T) road at Waterloo Bridge near Betws y Coed; generally westwards along the A5(T) road to its junction with an unmarked road near Ty Hyll at OS map reference SH 756575; generally westwards along the unmarked road to where it meets a fence at OS map reference SH 754575; generally southwards along the fence to OS map reference SH 754570 then westwards along the fence to where it meets a stream at OS map reference SH 752570; generally southwards along the fence through OS map references SH 752569, SH 752565 and SH 752561; generally south-eastwards to OS map reference SH 754555; generally south-westwards through OS map references SH 750551 and SH 743548 to its junction with Afon Ystumiau at OS map reference SH 741547; generally westwards along the course of Afon Ystumiau to its junction at the fence at OS map reference SH 738546; generally north-westwards to its junction with the forest fence at OS map reference SH 737547; generally westwards along the forest fence to OS map reference SH 736546; generally north-westwards to OS map reference SH 733548; northwards to OS map reference SH 733550; generally north-eastwards through OS map references SH 737557 and SH 740560 to OS map reference SH 743567; in a generally anti-clockwise direction around the forest to OS map reference SH 743568; generally northwards through OS map reference SH 743569 to its junction with the Afon Llugwy at OS map reference SH 743573; generally westwards along the course of Afon Llugwy to the A4086 road and its junction with a fence at OS map reference SH 741572; generally north-westwards along the fence to OS map reference SH 738579; generally north-eastwards along the forest fence passing through OS map references SH 740583, SH 747588, SH 747590 and SH 748594 to where it meets Llyn Bychan at OS map reference SH 752594; generally north-eastwards along the bank of Llyn Bychan to where it meets a forest fence at OS map reference SH 753595; generally westwards along the forest fence passing through OS map reference SH 765596 to where it meets Llyn Bodgynydd at OS map reference SH 760594; generally southwards and north-eastwards along the bank of Llyn Bodgynydd to where it meets a forest fence at OS map reference SH 763595; generally north-eastwards along the forest fence to where it meets an unmarked road at OS map reference SH 768595; generally north-westwards along the unmarked road to where it meets a forest fence at OS map reference SH 764599; generally north-eastwards along the forest fence pasing through OS map references SH 765602, SH 763603 and SH 765604 to where it meets Llyn Geirionydd at OS map reference SH 764605; generally northwards along the bank of Llyn Geirionydd to where it meets a forest fence at OS map reference SH 765612; generally eastwards along the forest fence to OS map reference SH 767612 then northwards along the forest fence to OS map reference SH 768618 then southwards along the forest fence to where it meets Llyn Geirionydd at OS map reference SH 766615; generally westwards along the bank of Llyn Geirionydd to where it meets a boundary fence at OS map reference SH 764614; generally north-westwards along the boundary fence passing through OS map references SH 762616, SH 760615 and SH 759619 to where it meets Afon Crafnant at OS map reference SH 757619; generally south-westwards along the western side of Llyn Crafnant to where it is met by a forest fence at OS map reference SH 748611; generally north-westwards along the forest fence to its junction with a fence at OS map reference SH 742620; generally northwards along the fence to OS map reference SH 742625; generally westwards along the fence passing through OS map reference SH 740624 to OS map reference SH 737624; generally northwards along the fence to where it meets Llyn Cowlyd Reservoir at OS map reference SH 737631; generally northwards along the edge of Llyn Cowlyd Reservoir to where it meets a fence along Afon Ddu at OS map reference SH 739633; generally north-eastwards along the fence along the course of Afon Ddu to where it meets a fence at OS map reference SH 757649; generally westwards along the fence to OS map reference SH 752649; generally north-westwards to OS map reference SH 750653; generally north-eastwards to OS map reference SH 749660; generally north-westwards crossing Afon-Porth-Llwyd at OS map reference SH 743665 passing through OS map references SH 742670 and SH 743674 to where it meets Afon Dulyn at OS map reference SH 738677; generally south-westwards following the course of Afon Dulyn to OS map reference SH 730674; generally north-westwards along the fence passing through OS map references SH 725680, SH 720690, SH 710697 and SH 709698 where it meets the National Trust Boundary; generally northwards along the boundary to OS map reference SH 709700; generally north-westwards along the fence to OS map reference SH 707708; generally north-eastwards to OS map reference SH 709714; generally north-eastwards along the boundary wall passing through OS map references SH 716722, SH 739728, SH 749738, SH 745737, SH 747751, SH 753761, SH 761761, SH 762771 and SH 749772 to its junction with the railway line at OS map reference SH 775779 at Conwy.

The area excludes any part of a road, footpath or body of water by reference to which its boundary is defined.

3. An area comprising that part of the County of Gwynedd which lies within the following boundary:—

From where the forest fence meets a fence at OS map reference SH 806288; generally southwards along the forest fence to its junction with a fence at OS map reference SH 796238; generally southwards along the fence to its junction with a fence at OS map reference SH 796234; generally north-eastwards along the fence to its junction with Afon Eiddon at OS map reference SH 807239; generally north-eastwards following the course of Afon Eiddon to where it meets a fence at OS map reference SH 814248; generally eastwards along the fence to its junction with a fence at OS map reference SH 815248; generally southwards along the fence passing through OS map references SH 815244 and SH 815240 to OS map reference SH 814237; generally westwards along the fence to OS map reference SH 813237; generally southwards along the fence passing through OS map references SH 812234 and SH 810232 to SH 809229; generally south-eastwards along the fence to OS map reference SH 811227; generally south-westwards along the fence to OS map reference SH 809225; generally south-eastwards along the fence to where it meets the A494(T) road at OS map reference SH 810224; generally north-eastwards along the A494(T) road to where it meets the Afon Wnion at OS map reference SH 812225; generally westwards along the course of Afon Wnion to its confluence with Nant Terfyn at OS map reference SH 809218; generally southwards along the course of Nant Terfyn to where it meets a forest fence at OS map reference SH 809217; generally south-eastwards then westwards along the fence around the forest to where it meets Nant Terfyn at OS map reference SH 811215; generally southwards along the course of Nant Terfyn to where it meets the forest fence at OS map reference SH 812214; generally westwards, then south-eastwards, then southwards along the fence passing through OS map references SH 801209, SH 809206, SH 813210 and SH 814200 to where it meets a stream at OS map reference SH 822192; generally south eastwards along the course of the stream to where it meets a forest fence at OS map reference SH 826187 along the Parish boundary; generally north-eastwards following the fence along the Parish boundary passing by Glasgwm at OS map reference SH 845196, by Drws Bach at OS map reference SH 862213, turning eastwards about Creiglyn Dyfiant at OS map reference SH 865230 to its junction with Cwm Llwydd at OS map reference SH 872229; generally north-eastwards along the course of Cwm Llwydd to join Cwm Ffynnon at OS map reference SH 874238; generally south-westwards along the course of Cwm Ffynnon to its junction with the fence at OS map reference SH 872238; generally northwards along the fence to OS map reference SH 874247; generally eastwards along the fence to OS map reference SH 875246; generally north-eastwards along the fence passing through OS map reference SH 879250 to its junction with Llyn Lliwbran at OS map reference SH 878255; along the south bank of Llyn Lliwbran generally westwards to its junction with the fence at OS map reference SH 874256; generally westwards along the fence to OS map reference SH 870256; generally northwards along the fence to Craig y Geifr at OS map reference SH 872269; generally westwards along the fence to a forest plantation at OS map reference SH 865268; generally southwards along the fence following the forest plantation's eastern boundary to its junction with the fence at OS map reference SH 865261; generally westwards then north-westwards along the fence to its junction with a forest plantation near Llechwedd-Fwyalchen at OS map reference SH 859272; generally westwards along the fence following the southern boundary of the forest plantation near Llechwedd-Fwyalchen at OS map reference SH 859276; generally westwards along the fence to its junction with the A494(T) road at OS map reference SH 852276; generally south-westwards along the A494(T) road to its crossing of Afon Mynach at OS map reference SH 832246; generally north-westwards following the course of Afon Mynach to where it meets a fence at OS map reference SH 824254; generally north-westwards along the fence to OS map reference SH 822257; generally north-eastwards along the fence to OS map reference SH 823258; generally north-westwards along the fence passing through OS map references SH 821260 and SH 820261 to OS map reference SH 818263; generally north-eastwards along the fence to OS map reference SH 820266; generally south-eastwards along the fence to OS map reference SH 823264; generally north-eastwards along the fence to its junction with a forest fence alongside Afon Dyfrdwy at OS map reference SH 826269; generally north-westwards along the fence passing through OS map references SH 820274 and SH 815280 to where it meets a fence at OS map reference SH 817287; generally westwards along the fence passing through OS map references SH 810287 and SH 809291 to where it meets a forest fence at OS map reference SH 806288;

The area excludes any part of a road, footpath or body of water by reference to which its boundary is defined.

4. An area comprising that part of the County of Gwynedd which lies within the following boundary:—

From where the unmarked road meets a forest fence at OS map reference SH 792333 generally south and south-eastwards along the forest fence to OS map reference SH 803314; generally south-westwards along the forest fence to where it meets Afon Bryn-lliw-fawr at OS map reference SH 773297; generally southwards along Afon Bryn-lliw-fawr to its confluence with Afon Mawddach at OS map reference SH 771293; generally south-westwards along Afon Mawddach to where it is crossed by an unmarked road at Pont Aber-Geirw at OS map reference SH 768292; generally southwards along the unmarked road to its junction with an unmarked road at OS map reference SH 768286; generally south-westwards along the unmarked road to where it meets a forest fence at

OS map reference SH 766284; generally south-westwards along the forest fence to OS map reference SH 763278; generally south-eastwards to OS map reference SH 768276; generally north-eastwards to meet Afon Ceirw at OS map reference SH 774281; generally south-eastwards along the fence following the course of Afon Ceirw to OS map reference SH 776276; generally westwards along the fence to OS map reference SH 771275; generally south-eastwards to where the fence meets the mountain wall at OS map reference SH 772265; generally eastwards along the mountain wall passing through OS map references SH 774268, SH 778269 and SH 780266 to where it meets a fence at OS map reference SH 782264; generally eastwards along the fence to OS map reference SH 782265 to where it meets Nant yr Helyg at OS map reference SH 792267; generally north-eastwards along the fence following Nant yr Helyg then Afon Mawddach to its junction with the forest fence at OS map reference SH 806288; generally eastwards along the fence passing through OS map references SH 809291 and SH 810287 to where it meets a forest fence at OS map reference SH 817287; generally eastwards along the forest fence passing through OS map references SH 823290, SH 840290 and SH 850295 to OS map reference SH 866299 where it meets an unmarked road; generally north-eastwards along the unmarked road to its junction with the A494(T) road at OS map reference SH 872303; generally northwards along the A494(T) road to its junction with an unmarked road at OS map reference SH 872306; generally westwards along the unmarked road to its junction with an unmarked road at OS map reference SH 852308; generally north-eastwards along the unmarked road crossing Afon Lliw to its junction with an unmarked road at OS map reference SH 853309; generally north-westwards along the unmarked road passing by Ty'n-y-bwlch to its meeting with an unmarked road at OS map reference SH 829325 near Buarthmeini; generally westwards along the unmarked road to where it meets a forest fence at OS map reference SH 792333;

The area excludes any part of a road, footpath or body of water by reference to which its boundary is defined.

5. An area comprising that part of the County of Gwynedd which lies within the following boundary:—

From the junction of the B5113 road and the unmarked road at OS map reference SH 837621 near Gorswen generally eastwards along the unmarked road to where it meets a fence on the County boundary at OS map reference SH 853623; generally southwards along the fence following the County boundary to where it meets an unmarked road at OS map reference SH 858599; generally westwards along the unmarked road to its junction with the B5113 road at OS map reference SH 838588; generally northwards along the B5113 road to its junction with the unmarked road at OS map reference SH 837621 near Gorswen.

The area excludes any part of a road, footpath or body of water by reference to which its boundary is defined.

6. An area comprising that part of the County of Gwynedd which lies within the following boundary:—

From where two fences meet at OS map reference SH 811487 generally eastwards along the fence to where it meets a fence at OS map reference SH 815488 at Afon Rhydyrhalen; generally north eastwards along the fence following Afon Rhydyrhalen to where it meets a fence at the confluence of the Afon Rhydyrhalen and Afon Eidda at OS map reference SH 827495; generally south-westwards along the fence passing through OS map reference SH 826491 to where it meets an unmarked road at OS map reference SH 825488; generally westwards along the unmarked road to where it meets a fence at Afon Eidda at OS map reference SH 823489; generally south-westwards along the fence to where it meets a fence at OS map reference SH 819486; generally south-westwards along the fence passing through OS map references SH 816486 and SH 813484 to where it meets a fence at OS map reference SH 810484; generally northwards along the fence to where it meets a fence at OS map reference SH 811487.

The area excludes any part of a road, footpath or body of water by reference to which its boundary is defined.

7. An area comprising that part of the County of Gwynedd which lies within the following boundary:—

From where a fence meets Nant Adwy'r-Llan at OS map reference SH 858474 generally northwards follows the course of Nant Adwy'r-Llan to where it meets a fence at OS map reference SH 859476; generally north-westwards along the fence passing through OS map references SH 857479, SH 859482, SH 855485, SH 854487 and SH 850489 to where it meets an unmarked road at OS map reference SH 848491; generally northwards along the unmarked road to where it meets a fence at OS map reference SH 849492; generally north-westwards along the fence to where it meets Afon Conwy at OS map reference SH 848495; generally north-eastwards following the course of Afon Conwy to where it meets a fence at its confluence with Afon Caletwr at OS map reference SH 854501; generally south-eastwards along the fence following Afon Caletwr to where it meets an unmarked road at OS map reference SH 857494; generally north-eastwards along the unmarked road to where it meets a fence on the County boundary at OS map reference SH 861497; generally south-eastwards then south-westwards along the fence following the County boundary to where it meets a fence near Nant-y-Glychedd at OS map reference SH 868460; generally northwards along the fence following Nant-y-Glychedd then Nant Glan Gwrach to its junction with a fence at OS map reference SH 866470; generally south-westwards and then north-westwards along the fence through OS map references SH 863467, SH 861470 and SH 860470 to where it meets Nant Adwy'r-Llan at OS map reference SH 858474.

The area excludes any part of a road, footpath or body of water by reference to which its boundary is defined.

8. An area comprising that part of the County of Gwynedd which lies within the following boundary:—

From where the forest fence meets a forest fence at OS map reference SH 811500 generally south-westwards along the forest fence to where it meets a forest fence at OS map reference SH 804496; generally northwards along the forest fence to where it meets a fence by Nant y Parc at OS map reference SH 803499; generally northwards along the fence following Nant y Parc passing through OS map references SH 803500 and SH 805507 to where it meets a fence at the confluence of Nant y Parc and Nant Ffridd Wen at OS map reference SH 806510; generally south-eastwards along the fence following Nant Ffridd Wen to where it meets a forest fence at OS map reference SH 808508; generally south-eastwards then southwards along the forest fence passing through OS map references SH 812508 and SH 811505 to where it meets a forest fence at OS map reference SH 811500.

The area excludes any part of a road, footpath or body of water by reference to which its boundary is defined.

9. An area comprising that part of the County of Gwynedd which lies within the following boundary:—

From where the fence meets Llyn Crafnant at OS map reference SH 751614, generally south-westwards along the edge of Llyn Crafnant to where it is met by a forest fence at OS map reference SH 748611; generally north-westwards along the forest fence to its junction with a fence at OS map reference SH 742620; generally northwards along the fence to OS map reference SH 742625; generally westwards along the fence passing through OS map reference SH 740624 to OS map reference SH 737624; generally northwards along the fence to where it meets Llyn Cowlyd Reservoir at OS map reference SH 737631; generally northwards along the edge of Llyn Cowlyd Reservoir to where it meets a fence along the Afon Ddu at OS map reference SH 739633; generally north-eastwards along the fence along the course of the Afon Ddu passing through OS map references SH 757649 and SH 759651; and continuing along the course of the Afon Ddu to the bridge on the B5106 at OS map reference SH 775663; generally southwards along the B5106 passing through OS map references SH 779652, SH 780644 and SH 780639 to the junction of the B5106 with an unmarked road at OS map reference SH 780636; southwards along the unmarked road to the junction with the unmarked roads at OS map reference SH 779632; westwards along an unmarked road passing through OS map reference SH 778632 to OS map reference SH 769631; then generally south-westwards to where the unmarked road meets the Afon Crafnant at OS map reference SH 757620; then south-westwards along the course of the Afon Crafnant to where it meets the Llyn Crafnant at OS map reference SH 753616 and then along the western edge of Llyn Crafnant to where it meets with the fence at OS map reference SH 751614.

The area excludes any part of a road, footpath or body of water by reference to which its boundary is defined.

10. An area comprising that part of the County of Gwynedd which lies within the following boundary:—

From where the weir of Llyn Celyn and a track meet at OS map reference SH 877398 generally southwards along the track to OS map reference SH 880394 then southwards along the fence passing through OS map references SH 878390 and SH 879387; generally north-westwards and westwards along the fence passing through OS map references SH 878387, SH 877390, SH 876391, SH 875390 and SH 874389; generally south-westwards along the fence to OS map reference SH 875387; generally westwards along the fence passing through OS map references SH 872385, SH 870385, SH 867384, SH 867383 to SH 864384; generally south-westwards along the fence crossing an unmarked road at OS map reference SH 864383 and crossing Nant Aberbleidoyn at OS map reference SH 863382 and passing through OS map reference SH 863380 to OS map reference SH 861374; generally south-eastwards along the fence to OS map reference SH 865370; generally south-westwards along the fence passing through OS map references SH 865369, SH 864367 and SH 863366; generally westwards along the fence passing through OS map reference SH 858367 to where it meets Nant Hir at SH 853367; generally westwards along the fence following the course of Nant Hir then Pistyll Gwyn through OS map references SH 850369 and SH 846367 to its junction with a fence at OS map reference SH 845367; generally southwards along the fence passing through OS map references SH 848365 and SH 847360 to where it meets the Afon Llafar at OS map reference SH 847353; generally westwards along the fence following the course of Afon Llafar to its junction with a fence at OS map reference SH 845353; generally southwards along the fence passing through OS map references SH

844352, SH 844350, SH 845348, SH 843346, SH 844346 and SH 842344; generally westwards along the fence passing through OS map reference SH 840344 to its junction with a fence at OS map reference SH 833343.

The area excludes any part of a road, footpath or body of water by reference to which its boundary is defined.

11. An area comprising that part of the County of Clwyd which lies within the following boundary:—

From where the fence meets the County Boundary at OS map reference SH 881482 south-eastwards along the fence to OS map reference SH 884478; along the fence in a north-easterly direction to OS map reference SH 888480; southwards to where the fence meets the Nant Tyr'nyr-erw at OS map reference SH 889479; eastwards along the fence to OS map reference SH 893479; southwards along the fence to OS map reference SH 894477; generally south-eastwards, passing through OS map references SH 895477, SH 896476 and SH 898476 to where the fence meets the unmarked road at OS map reference SH 898475; south-westwards along the unmarked road to the junction with another unmarked road near Tyn-y-rhos; generally south-eastwards along the unmarked road to where it meets the fence on the County Boundary at OS map reference SH 903467; generally south-westwards along the fence following the County Boundary to OS map reference SH 871446; north-westwards following the fence on the County Boundary to OS map reference SH 867451; generally north-eastwards along the fence following the County Boundary to where it meets the fence at OS map reference SH 871482 near Copa Ceiliog.

The area excludes any part of a road, footpath or body of water by reference to which its boundary is defined.

12. An area comprising that part of the County of Clwyd which lies within the following boundary:—

From where the fence meets the County Boundary and unmarked road at OS map reference SH 861497; generally north-eastwards to the junction of the unmarked road with an unmarked mountain road and gate at OS map reference SH 862499, continuing along the track in a north-easterly direction to OS map reference SH 867499; generally southwards along the track to where it meets with a fence at OS map reference SH 868496; generally south-eastwards along the fence to OS map reference SH 877487; south-westwards to where the fence meets the County Boundary at OS map reference SH 875485 near Copa Ceiliog; generally north-westwards following the fence on the County Boundary to where it meets an unmarked road at OS map reference SH 861497.

The area excludes any part of a road, footpath or body of water by reference to which its boundary is defined.

13. An area comprising that part of the County of Gwynedd which lies within the following boundary:—

From the confluence of the Afon Prysor with Nant Budr at OS map reference SH 737360; following the course of Nant Budr south-eastwards to the fence at OS map reference SH 750347; following the line of the fence south-eastwards to Afon Gain at OS map reference SH 756339; following the course of the Afon Gain generally southwards to the forest fence at OS map reference SH 755336; following the fence southwards to Pont y Gain at OS map reference SH 752328 then following the Afon Gain to where it meets an unmarked road near Pont-y-Llyn-du at OS map reference SH 731306; generally north-westwards along the unmarked road until it meets the A470(T) at OS map reference SH 711349, generally southwards along the A470(T) passing through OS map references SH 712318, SH 714301 and SH 715291 until it meets a fence and public footpath at OS map reference SH 715287 near Gelli-goch; along the public footpath in a generally north-westwards direction to a ford at the confluence of the Afon Eden and Afon Crawcwellt at OS map reference SH 712290; westwards along the course of the Afon Crawcwellt to where it meets a fence at a ford at OS map reference SH 693289; generally south-westwards along the fence which forms the eastern boundary to the forest known as Coed y Brenin Forest to OS map reference SH 679278; along the forest boundary fence in a north-westwards direction to OS map reference SH 672286, then continuing in a south-westwards direction to the junction with a path at OS map reference SH 670288; following the path in a south-westwards direction to the fence at OS map reference SH 665282; along the fence in a generally south-westwards direction passing through OS map references SH 658280 and SH 644269, to where the fence meets the Afon Cwmnantcol at OS map reference SH 637263; along the course of the Afon Cwmnantcol in a generally west-north-westwards direction passing through OS map references SH 625267, SH 615569 and SH 610265 to the reservoir at OS map reference SH 604269; along the northern edge of the reservoir to the dam at OS map reference SH 603269 and continuing along the Afon Cwmnantcol to where it meets with an unmarked road at OS map reference SH 600274; along the road in a north-eastwards direction to its junction with another unmarked road near Werngron at OS map reference SH 609283; north-westwards along this road passing by Maesyraelfor and Cefnfilltir to its junction with the B4573, also known as Stryd Fawr, Harlech at OS map reference SH 582311; along the B4573 in a generally north-eastwards direction to the junction with the A496 at OS map reference SH 606349; along the A496 in a north-eastwards direction to the junction with the Afon Prysor at Pont Felinrhyd-fawr at OS map reference SH 653396; along the course of the Afon Prysor in a south-eastwards direction until it meets Llyn Trawsfynydd at OS map reference SH 674377; following the south-western boundary of the lake passing through OS map references SH 689359 and SH 701349 until it meets the Afon Prysor at OS map reference SH 708349 then following the Afon Prysor in a north-eastwards direction passing through OS map references SH 711350 and SH 727352 to where it meets with Nant Budr at OS map reference SH 737360.

This area excludes any part of a road, footpath or body of water by reference to which its boundary is defined.

14. An area comprising that part of the County of Gwynedd which lies within the following boundary:—

From the junction of the A5(T) with an unmarked road near Ty Hyll at OS map reference SH 756575; generally westwards along the unmarked road to where it meets a fence at OS map reference SH 754575; generally southwards along the fence to OS map reference SH 754570 then westwards along the fence to where it meets a stream at OS map reference SH 752570; generally southwards along the fence through OS map references SH 752569, SH 752565 and SH 752561; generally south-eastwards to OS map reference SH 754555; generally south-westwards through OS map references SH 750551 and SH 743548 to its junction with Afon Ystumiau at OS map reference SH 741547; generally westwards along the course of Afon Ystumiau to its junction with the fence at OS map reference SH 738546; generally north-westwards to its junction with the forest fence at OS map reference SH 737547; generally westwards along the forest fence to OS map reference SH 736546; generally north-westwards to OS map reference SH 733548; northwards to OS map reference SH 733550; generally north-eastwards through OS map references SH 737557 and SH 740560 to OS map reference SH 743567; in a generally anti-clockwise direction around the forest to the unmarked road at OS map reference SH 743568; along the unmarked road to the junction of the A5(T) with an unmarked road near Ty Hyll at OS map reference SH 756575.

The area excludes any part of a road, footpath or body of water by reference to which its boundary is defined.

15. An area comprising that part of the County of Gwynedd which lies within the following boundary:—

From the forest fence at OS map reference SH 802496 generally north-westwards along the forest fence to the junction with an unmarked road at OS map reference SH 798497 then north-westwards along the unmarked road to the junction with another unmarked road at OS map reference SH 795502; then northwards along the road to the junction with the B4406 at OS map reference SH 795551; then north-eastwards along the B4406 to where it meets with Nant Caddugen at OS map reference SH 800518; following the course of the Nant Caddugen in a generally south-eastwards direction to where it meets with the Nant y Parc at OS map reference SH 808513; then southwards following the course of the Nant y Parc to where it meets with a fence at the confluence of the Nant y Parc with the Nant Ffridd Wen at OS map reference SH 806510 then generally southwards along the fence to where it meets with a track at SH 802496.

The area excludes any part of a road, footpath or body of water by reference to which its boundary is defined.

EXPLANATORY NOTE

(This note is not part of the Order)

This Order revokes and re-enacts without modification the Food Protection (Emergency Prohibitions) (Wales) (No. 4) Order 1987 as amended by S.I. 1987/1682 and /1802. It contains emergency prohibitions restricting various activities in order to prevent human consumption of food which has been or which may have been rendered unsuitable for that purpose in consequence of the escape of radioactive substances from a nuclear reactor situated at Chernobyl in the USSR.

The Order designates areas of land in Wales affected by the escape from which the movement of sheep, and in which the slaughter of sheep, are prohibited (articles 3, 4, 5(1) and the Schedule). The prohibition on slaughter in the designated areas does not apply to any sheep identified by a red paint mark which have been examined and subsequently marked by an ear-tag by a person authorised by the Minister of Agriculture, Fisheries and Food, the Secretary of State for Scotland, the Secretary of State for Wales or the

Department of Agriculture for Northern Ireland (article 4(2)). Movement into a designated area of sheep which have been removed from it or from a similarly designated area elsewhere in the United Kingdom (other than sheep which have been identified by a red paint mark, and moved, in accordance with a Ministerial consent) is prohibited (article 5(2)).

Restrictions on the slaughter of sheep which were—

(a) in any of the designated areas numbered 1, 2 and 3 in the Schedule after 11 a.m. on 20th June 1986;

(b) in the designated area numbered 4 in the Schedule after 9th July 1987;

(c) in any of the designated areas numbered 5, 6, 7 and 8 in the Schedule after 10th August 1987;

(d) in any of the designated areas numbered 9, 10, 11 and 12 in the Schedule after 27th August 1987; and

(e) in any of the designated areas numbered 13, 14 and 15 in the Schedule after 17th September 1987,

and the supply of meat derived from such sheep, extend throughout the United Kingdom (article 6(1)). This order replaces restrictions which—

(a) as regards the areas mentioned in (a) above have been in force since 11 a.m. on 20th June 1986,

(b) as regards the area mentioned in (b) above have been in force since 10th July 1987,

(c) as regards the areas mentioned in (c) above have been in force since 11th August 1987,

(d) as regards the areas mentioned in (d) above have been in force since 28th August 1987, and

(e) as regards the areas mentioned in (e) above have been in force since 18th September 1987.

The said restrictions on slaughter and supply imposed by article 6(1) shall not apply to any sheep—

(a) which has been moved unmarked to a market in accordance with a Ministerial consent;

(b) identified by a blue paint mark and which has been moved in accordance with a Ministerial consent given on or before 21st December 1986;

(c) identified by an apricot paint mark and which has been moved in accordance with a Ministerial consent given on or before 26th July 1987; or

(d) identified by a red, green or blue paint mark which has been examined and subsequently marked with an ear-tag by a person authorised by the Minister of Agriculture, Fisheries and Food, the Secretary of State for Scotland, the Secretary of State for Wales or the Department of Agriculture for Northern Ireland and which has been moved in accordance with a Ministerial consent, in the case of sheep identified by a blue paint mark only if such a consent has been given on or after 28th September 1987 (article 6(2)).

Under Section 21 of the Food and Environment Protection Act 1985 the penalty for contravening an emergency prohibition is—

(a) on summary conviction, a fine of an amount not exceeding the statutory maximum (at present £2,000);

(b) on conviction on indictment, an unlimited fine, or imprisonment for a term of not more than two years or both.

Powers of enforcement in relation to emergency prohibitions are conferred by section 4 of, and Schedule 2 to, the 1985 Act. Obstruction of enforcement officers is an offence under paragraph 10 of that Schedule.

Maps showing the designated areas are available for inspection during normal office hours at the offices of the Welsh Office Agriculture Department at Penrallt, Caernarfon, Gwynedd LL55 1EP; Government Buildings, Spa Road East, Llandrindod Wells, Powys LD1 5HA; Station Road, Ruthin, Clwyd LL15 1BP and Cathays Park, Cardiff, South Glamorgan CF1 3NQ.

STATUTORY INSTRUMENTS

1987 No. 1897

INCOME TAX

The Income Tax (Cash Equivalents of Car Benefits) Order 1987

Made - - - - -	*5th November 1987*
Laid before the House of Commons	*17th November 1987*
Coming into force - - -	*6th April 1988*

The Treasury, in exercise of the powers conferred on them by section 64(4) of the Finance Act 1976**(a)**, hereby make the following Order:

1. This Order may be cited as the Income Tax (Cash Equivalents of Car Benefits) Order 1987 and shall come into force on 6th April 1988.

2. In Part I of Schedule 7 to the Finance Act 1976 (Tables of flat rate cash equivalents) for Tables A, B and C there shall be substituted the following Tables–

Table A

CARS WITH ORIGINAL MARKET VALUE UP TO £19,250 AND HAVING A CYLINDER CAPACITY

Cylinder capacity of car in cubic centimetres	Age of car at end of relevant year of assessment	
	Under 4 years	*4 years or more*
1,400 or less	£580	£380
More than 1,400, but not more than 2,000	£770	£520
More than 2,000	£1,210	£800

(a) 1976 c.40; relevant amendments to section 64 were made by section 51(2) of the Finance Act 1980 (c.48), section 68(3) of the Finance Act 1981 (c.35), and section 46(2) and (3) of the Finance Act 1982 (c.39).

Table B

CARS WITH ORIGINAL MARKET VALUE UP TO £19,250 AND NOT HAVING A CYLINDER CAPACITY

Original market value of car	Age of car at end of relevant year of assessment	
	Under 4 years	*4 years or more*
Less than £6,000	£580	£380
£6,000 or more, but less than £8,500	£770	£520
£8,500 or more, but not more than £19,250	£1,210	£800

Table C

CARS WITH ORIGINAL MARKET VALUE MORE THAN £19,250

Original market value of car	Age of car at end of relevant year of assessment	
	Under 4 years	*4 years or more*
More than £19,250, but not more than £29,000	£1,595	£1,070
More than £29,000	£2,530	£1,685

Peter Lloyd
Mark Lennox-Boyd

5th November 1987   Two of the Lords Commissioners of Her Majesty's Treasury

EXPLANATORY NOTE

(This note is not part of the Order)

Section 64 of the Finance Act 1976 provides that in certain circumstances a person employed in director's or higher-paid employment is chargeable to income tax in respect of the benefit of a car made available for private use by reason of his employment. The cash equivalent of such a benefit is, subject to the provisions of the section, to be ascertained from Tables A, B and C in Part I of Schedule 7 to that Act.

This Order, with effect from 6th April 1988, substitutes such Tables for those substituted by S.I. 1986/703.

1987 No. 1900

SEA FISHERIES

CONSERVATION OF SEA FISH

The Saithe (Specified Sea Areas) (Prohibition of Fishing) (Revocation) Order 1987

Made - - - -		*6th November 1987*
Laid before Parliament		*6th November 1987*
Coming into force -		*9th November 1987*

The Minister of Agriculture, Fisheries and Food and the Secretaries of State respectively concerned with the sea fishing industry in Scotland, Wales and Northern Ireland, acting jointly, in exercise of the powers conferred on them by sections 5(1), 15(3) and 20(1) of the Sea Fish (Conservation) Act 1967**(a)**, and of all other powers enabling them in that behalf, hereby make the following Order:

Title and commencement

1. This Order may be cited as the Saithe (Specified Sea Areas) (Prohibition of Fishing) (Revocation) Order 1987 and shall come into force on 9th November 1987.

Revocation

2. The Saithe (Specified Sea Areas) (Prohibition of Fishing) Order 1987**(b)** is hereby revoked.

In witness whereof the Official Seal of the Minister of Agriculture, Fisheries and Food is hereunto affixed on 5th November 1987.

John MacGregor
Minister of Agriculture, Fisheries and Food

5th November 1987

Sanderson of Bowden
Minister of State, Scottish Office

(a) 1967 c.84; section 5(1) was substituted by section 22(1) of the Fisheries Act 1981 (c.29) and, by virtue of S.I. 1973/238, section 5 applies in relation to British fishing boats registered in the Isle of Man as it applies in relation to British fishing boats registered in the United Kingdom; section 15(3) was substituted by paragraph 38(3) of Schedule 1 to the Sea Fisheries Act 1968 (c.77) and amended by paragraph 16(1) of Schedule 2 to the Fishery Limits Act 1976 (c.86); section 22(2)(a) which contains a definition of "the Ministers" for the purposes of sections 5 and 15(3) was amended by the Fisheries Act 1981, sections 19(2)(d) and 45(b).
(b) S.I. 1987/718.

6th November 1987

Wyn Roberts
Minister of State, Welsh Office

5th November 1987

Tom King
Secretary of State for Northern Ireland

EXPLANATORY NOTE

(This note is not part of the Order)

This Order revokes the Saithe (Specified Sea Areas) (Prohibition of Fishing) Order 1987 which prohibited, with an exception, fishing for saithe *(Pollachius virens)* by any British fishing boat registered in the United Kingdom, the Isle of Man or the Channel Islands within any part of a sea area specified in that Order with effect from 18th April 1987.

STATUTORY INSTRUMENTS

1987 No. 1902

CUSTOMS AND EXCISE

The Customs Duties (ECSC) (No.2) (Amendment No.11) Order 1987

Made - - - - -	*6th November 1987*
Laid before the House of Commons	*9th November 1987*
Coming into force - - -	*6th November 1987*

The Treasury, by virtue of the powers conferred on them by section 5(1) and (3) of, and paragraph 4 of Schedule 2 to, the European Communities Act 1972**(a)** and of all other powers enabling them in that behalf, on the recommendation of the Secretary of State, hereby make the following Order:

1. This Order may be cited as the Customs Duties (ECSC) (No.2) (Amendment No. 11) Order 1987.

2. Up to and including 31st December 1987, article 6(1) of the Customs Duties (ECSC) (No. 2) Order 1985**(b)** (which exempts from duty goods to which that Order applies originating in certain countries) shall not apply to goods which fall within headings 73.08, 73.11 AI, AIV a) 1 and 73.11B which originate in Yugoslavia.

Nigel Lawson
Peter Lloyd
6th November 1987   Two of the Lords Commissioners of Her Majesty's Treasury

---

(a) 1972 c.68; section 5(3) and Schedule 2 were amended by the Customs and Excise Duties (General Reliefs) Act 1979 (c.3), Schedule 2, paragraphs 3 and 5.

(b) S.I. 1985/1630, amended by S.I. 1985/2020, 1986/348, 813, 1352, 2179, 1987/973, 1053, 1125, 1218, 1804.

EXPLANATORY NOTE

(This note is not part of the Order)

This Order comes into operation on 6th November 1987. It replaces the provisions formerly contained in the Customs Duties (ECSC) (No. 2) (Amendment No. 9) Order 1987 which expired on 5th November 1987.

This Order reimposes duties on goods falling within headings 73.08, 73.11 AI AIV a) 1 and 73.11B which originate in Yugoslavia. Decision 86/642/ECSC of the representatives of the governments of the Member States of the European Coal and Steel Community meeting within the Council on 22nd December 1986 (OJ No. L380 of 31.12.1986, p.59) established ceilings for imports of certain ECSC products originating in Yugoslavia. These ceilings have now been reached on products falling within the above headings.

The Commission Communications to Member States giving notice of the reintroduction of customs duties were published in OJ No. C138 of 23.5.1987 and OJ No. C154 of 12.6.1987.

STATUTORY INSTRUMENTS

1987 No. 1903

DATA PROTECTION

The Data Protection (Subject Access Modification) (Health) Order 1987

Made - - -	*9th November 1987*
Coming into force	*11th November 1987*

Whereas a draft of this Order has been laid before and approved by a resolution of each House of Parliament:

Now, therefore, in exercise of the powers conferred upon me by section 29(1) and (3) of the Data Protection Act 1984(**a**) and after consultation with the Data Protection Registrar in accordance with section 40(3) of that Act, I hereby make the following Order:

1. This Order may be cited as the Data Protection (Subject Access Modification) (Health) Order 1987 and shall come into force on 11th November 1987.

2. In this Order—

"the Act" means the Data Protection Act 1984;

"care" includes examination, investigation and diagnosis;

"dental practitioner" and "medical practitioner" mean, respectively, a person registered under the Dentists Act 1984(**b**) and the Medical Act 1983(**c**);

"health authority" has the same meaning as in section 128(1) of the National Health Service Act 1977(**d**);

"Health Board" has the same meaning as in section 108(1) of the National Health Service (Scotland) Act 1978(**e**);

"Health and Social Services Board" has the same meaning as in Article 16 of the Health and Personal Social Services (Northern Ireland) Order 1972(**f**);

"health professional" means any person listed in the Schedule to this Order; and

"the subject access provisions" has the meaning which it has for the purposes of Part IV of the Act.

3.—(1) This Order applies to personal data consisting of information as to the physical or mental health of the data subject if—

(a) the data are held by a health professional; or

(**a**) 1984 c. 35.	(**b**) 1984 c. 24.	(**c**) 1983 c. 54.
(**d**) 1977 c. 49. This definition was amended by Schedule 3 to 1984 c. 48.	(**e**) 1978 c. 29.	(**f**) S.I. 1972/1265 (N.I. 14.).

(b) the data are held by a person other than a health professional but the information constituting the data was first recorded by or on behalf of a health professional.

(2) This Order is without prejudice to any exemption from the subject access provisions contained in any provision of the Act or of any Order made under the Act.

4.—(1) The subject access provisions shall not have effect in relation to any personal data to which this Order applies in any case where either of the requirements specified in paragraph (2) below is satisfied with respect to the information constituting the data and the obligations contained in paragraph (5) below are complied with by the data user.

(2) The requirements referred to in paragraph (1) above are that the application of the subject access provisions—

(a) would be likely to cause serious harm to the physical or mental health of the data subject; or

(b) would be likely to disclose to the data subject the identity of another individual (who has not consented to the disclosure of the information) either as a person to whom the information or part of it relates or as the source of the information or enable that identity to be deduced by the data subject either from the information itself or from a combination of that information and other information which the data subject has or is likely to have.

(3) Paragraph (2) above shall not be construed as excusing a data user—

(a) from suppling the information sought by the request for subject access where the only individual whose identity is likely to be disclosed or deduced as mentioned in sub-paragraph (b) thereof is a health professional who has been involved in the care of the data subject and the information relates to him or he supplied the information in his capacity as a health professional; or

(b) from supplying so much of the information sought by the request as can be supplied without causing serious harm as mentioned in sub-paragraph (a) thereof or enabling the identity of another individual to be disclosed or deduced as mentioned in sub-paragraph (b) thereof, whether by the omission of names or other particulars or otherwise.

(4) In relation to data to which this Order applies, section 21 of the Act shall have effect as if subsections (4)(b) and (5) were omitted and as if the reference in subsection (6) to the consent referred to in the said section 21(4)(b) were a reference to the consent referred to in paragraph (2)(b) above.

(5) A data user who is not a health professional shall not supply information constituting data to which this Order applies in response to a request under section 21 and shall not withhold any such information on the ground that one of the requirements specified in paragraph (2) above is satisfied with respect to the information unless the data user has first consulted the person who appears to the data user to be the appropriate health professional on the question whether either or both of those requirements is or are so satisfied.

(6) In paragraph (5) above "the appropriate health professional" means—

(a) the medical practitioner or dental practitioner who is currently or was most recently responsible for the clinical care of the data subject in connection with the matters to which the information which is the subject of the request relates; or

(b) where there is more than one such practitioner, the practitioner who is the most suitable to advise on the matters to which the information which is the subject of the request relates; or

(c) where there is no practitioner available falling within sub-paragraph (a) or (b) above, a health professional who has the necessary experience and qualifications to advise on the matters to which the information which is the subject of the request relates.

(7) Section 21(8) of the Act shall have effect, in relation to data to which this Order applies, as if the reference therein to a contravention of the foregoing provisions of that section included a reference to a contravention of the provisions contained in this Article.

Home Office

9th November 1987

Douglas Hurd

One of Her Majesty's Principal Secretaries of State

SCHEDULE

Article 2

HEALTH PROFESSIONALS

DESCRIPTION	STATUTORY DERIVATION *(where applicable)*
Registered medical practitioner	Medical Act 1983 (**a**), section 55.
Registered dentist	Dentists' Act 1984 (**b**), section 53(1).
Registered optician	Opticians Act 1958 (**c**), section 30(1).
Registered pharmaceutical chemist or druggist	Pharmacy Act 1954 (**d**), section 24(1). Pharmacy (Northern Ireland) Order 1976 (**e**), Article 6(1).
Registered nurse, midwife or health visitor	Nurses, Midwives and Health Visitors Act 1979 (**f**), section 10.
Registered chiropodist, dietician, occupational therapist, orthoptist or physiotherapist (subject to the Note below.)	Professions Supplementary to Medicine Act 1960 (**g**), section 1(2).
Clinical psychologist, child psychotherapist or speech therapist	
Art therapist or music therapist employed by a health authority, Health Board or Health and Social Services Board	
Scientist employed by such an authority or Board as a head of department	

Note This category shall be construed as not including any person belonging to a profession specified in the first column which, by virtue of an Order under section 10 of the Professions Supplementary to Medicine Act 1960, is for the time being treated as if it were not mentioned in section 1(2) of that Act and as including any person belonging to a profession not specified therein which is for the time being treated by virtue of such an Order as if it were mentioned therein.

(**a**) 1983 c.54.   (**b**) 1984 c.24.   (**c**) 1958 c.32.
(**d**) 1954 c.61.   (**e**) S.I. 1976/1213 (N.I.22).   (**f**) 1979 c.36.
(**g**) 1960 c.66; section 1(2) was amended by S.I. 1966/990 and 1986/630.

EXPLANATORY NOTE

(This note is not part of the Order)

This Order provides for the partial exemption from the provisions of the Data Protection Act 1984 which confer rights on data subjects to gain access to data held about them ("the subject access provisions") of data relating to the physical or mental health of the data subject held by any data user where the data are held by a health professional or the information constituting the data was first recorded by or on behalf of a health professional. Schedule 1 to the Order lists the persons who are health professionals for the purposes of the Order.

The subject access provisions are disapplied only where to supply the data subject with particulars of the information constituting the data would be likely to cause serious harm to his physical or mental health or lead to the identification of another person (other than a health professional who has been involved in the care of the data subject). Before deciding whether either of those criteria is met (and, accordingly, whether to grant or withhold subject access) a data user who is not a health professional is obliged by the Order to consult the medical practitioner or dental practitioner responsible for the clinical care of the data subject or, if there is more than one, the most suitable available medical or dental practitioner or if there is none available a health professional who has the necessary experience and qualifications to advise on the matters to which the information which is requested relates.

STATUTORY INSTRUMENTS

1987 No. 1904

DATA PROTECTION

The Data Protection (Subject Access Modification) (Social Work) Order 1987

Made - - - -	*9th November 1987*
Coming into force	*11th November 1987*

Whereas a draft of this Order has been laid before and approved by a resolution of each House of Parliament:

Now, therefore, in exercise of the powers conferred upon me by section 29(1), (2) and (3) of the Data Protection Act 1984(a) and after consultation with the Data Protection Registrar in accordance with section 40(3) of that Act, I hereby make the following Order:

1. This Order may be cited as the Data Protection (Subject Access Modification) (Social Work) Order 1987 and shall come into force on 11th November 1987.

2.—(1) In this Order –

"the Act" means the Data Protection Act 1984;

"education welfare officer" has the same meaning as in section 50 of the Education (No.2) Act 1986(b);

"health authority" has the same meaning as in the National Health Service Act 1977(c); and

"the subject access provisions" has the meaning which it has for the purposes of Part IV of the Act.

(2) Any reference in this Order to a local authority in relation to data held or formerly held by it includes a reference to the Council of the Isles of Scilly in relation to data held or formerly held by the Council in connection with any functions mentioned in article 3(1)(a)(i) below which are or have been conferred upon the Council by or under any enactment.

3.—(1) Subject to paragraph (3) below, this Order applies to personal data falling within any of the following descriptions:-

(a) data held by a local authority –

(a) 1984 c.35.   (b) 1986 c.61.   (c) 1977 c.49. This definition was amended by Schedule 3 to 1984 c.48.

(i) in connection with its social services functions within the meaning of the Local Authority Social Services Act 1970(a) or any functions which stand referred to a social work committee under the Social Work (Scotland) Act 1968(b), or

(ii) in the exercise of other functions but obtained or consisting of information obtained in connection with any of those functions;

(b) data held by a Health and Social Services Board established under Article 16 of the Health and Personal Social Services (Northern Ireland) Order 1972(c) in connection with the provision of personal social services within the meaning of that Order or held by the Board in the exercise of other functions but obtained or consisting of information obtained in connection with the provision of those services;

(c) data held by a district council in the exercise of its functions under Part II of Schedule 9 to the Health and Social Services and Social Security Adjudications Act 1983(d);

(d) data held by a probation committee established by Schedule 3 to the Powers of Criminal Courts Act 1973(e) or the Probation Board for Northern Ireland;

(e) data held by a local education authority or local authority for the purposes of any functions performed by education welfare officers;

(f) data relating to persons detained in a special hospital provided by the Secretary of State under section 4 of the National Health Service Act 1977 and held by a health authority in the exercise of any functions similar to any social services functions of a local authority;

(g) data held by the National Society for the Prevention of Cruelty to Children or the Royal Scottish Society for the Prevention of Cruelty to Children or by any other voluntary organization or other body designated under this sub-paragraph by the Secretary of State or the Department of Health and Social Services for Northern Ireland and appearing to the Secretary of State or the Department, as the case may be, to be held for the purposes of the provision of any service similar to a service provided in the exercise of any functions specified in sub-paragraphs (a)(i), (b) or (c) above;

(h) data held by –

(i) a health authority or a Family Practitioner Committee established under section 10 of the National Health Service Act 1977, or

(ii) a Health Board established under section 2 of the National Health Service (Scotland) Act 1978(f),

which were obtained or consisted of information which was obtained from any authority or body mentioned above or government department and which, whilst held by that authority or body or government department, fell within any sub-paragraph of this paragraph;

(i) data held by a government department and obtained or consisting of information obtained from any authority or body mentioned above and which, whilst held by that authority or body, fell within any of the preceding sub-paragraphs of this paragraph;

(j) data held for the purposes of the functions of the Secretary of State pursuant to section 80 of the Child Care Act 1980(g);

(k) data held by any person appointed for any purpose mentioned in section 103 of the Children Act 1975(h) or by a reporter appointed under section 36 of the Social Work (Scotland) Act 1968.

(a) 1970 c.42.   (b) 1968 c.49.   (c) S.I. 1972/1265(N.I.14).   (d) 1983 c.41.   (e) 1973 c.62. Schedule 3 was amended by 1982 c.48, Schedule 11.   (f) 1978 c.29.   (g) 1980 c.5.   (h) 1975 c.72. Section 103 was amended by 1980 c.5 and 1983 c.41.

(2) This Order applies to personal data held by a court and consisting of information supplied in a report or other evidence given to the court by a local authority, Health and Social Services Board, probation officer or other person in the course of any proceedings to which the Magistrates' Courts (Children and Young Persons) Rules 1970(a), the Magistrates' Courts (Children and Young Persons) (Northern Ireland) Rules 1969(b) or the Act of Sederunt (Social Work) Sheriff Court Procedure Rules 1971(c) apply where, in accordance with a provision of any of those Rules, the information may be withheld by the court in whole or in part from the data subject.

(3) This Order, except so far as it relates to any data mentioned in paragraph (2) above, does not apply –

(a) to any data consisting of information as to the physical or mental health of the data subject to which the Data Protection (Subject Access Modification) (Health) Order 1987(d) applies; or

(b) to any data which are exempted from the subject access provisions by an order made under section 34(2) of the Act,

and this Order is without prejudice to any exemption from the subject access provisions contained in any provision of the Act.

4.—(1) The subject access provisions shall not have effect in relation to any personal data to which this Order applies by virtue of article 3(2) above.

(2) So much of the subject access provisions as concerns the obligation in section 21(1)(b) of the Act to supply the data subject with a copy of the information constituting the data and any power of the Registrar in Part II thereof which is exercisable by reference to paragraph (a)(ii) of the seventh data protection principle shall not have effect in relation to any personal data to which this Order applies by virtue of article 3(1) above in any case where either of the requirements specified in paragraph (3) below is satisfied.

(3) The requirements referred to in paragraph (2) above are that the application of the provisions mentioned in that paragraph would be likely to prejudice the carrying out of social work by reason of the fact that –

(a) serious harm to the physical or mental health or emotional condition of the data subject or any other person would be likely to be caused; or

(b) the identity of another individual (who has not consented to the disclosure of the information) either as a person to whom the information or part of it relates or as the source of the information would be likely to be disclosed to or deduced by the data subject or any other person who is likely to obtain access to it either from the information itself or from a combination of that information and other information which the data subject or such other person has or is likely to have.

(4) Paragraph (3) above shall not be construed as excusing a data user –

(a) from supplying the information sought by the request for subject access where the only individual whose identity is likely to be disclosed or deduced as mentioned in sub-paragraph (b) thereof is a relevant person; or

(b) from supplying so much of the information sought by the request as can be supplied without causing serious harm as mentioned in sub-paragraph (a) thereof or enabling the identity of another individual to be disclosed or deduced as mentioned in sub-paragraph (b) thereof, whether by the omission of names or other particulars or otherwise.

(a) S.I. 1970/1792.   (b) S.R. & O.(N.I.) 1969 No. 221.   (c) S.I. 1971/92.   (d) S.I. 1987/1903.

(5) In paragraph (3) above "the carrying out of social work" shall be construed as including –

(a) the exercise of any functions specified in article 3(1)(a)(i), (c), (e), (f) or (j) above;

(b) the provision of any service mentioned in article 3(1) (b) or (g) above; and

(c) the exercise of the functions of any body mentioned in article 3(1)(d) above or any person mentioned in article 3(1)(k) above.

(6) A person is a relevant person for the purposes of paragraph (4)(a) above if he –

(a) is a person referred to in article 3(1)(k) above; or

(b) is or has been employed by any person or body referred to in the said article 3(1) in connection with functions which are or have been exercised in relation to the data consisting of the information; or

(c) has provided for reward a service similar to a service provided in the exercise of any functions specified in sub-paragraph (a)(i), (b), or (c) thereof,

and the information relates to him or he supplied the information in his official capacity or, as the case may be, in connection with the provision of that service.

(7) In relation to data to which this Order applies, section 21 of the Act shall have effect as if subsections (4)(b) and (5) were omitted and as if the reference in subsection (6) to the consent referred to in the said section 21(4)(b) were a reference to the consent referred to in paragraph (3)(b) above.

(8) Section 21(8) of the Act shall have effect, in its application to data to which this Order applies by virtue of article 3(1) above, as if the reference therein to a contravention of the foregoing provisions of that section included a reference to a contravention of the provisions contained in paragraphs (2) to (7) above.

Home Office
9th November 1987

Douglas Hurd
One of Her Majesty's Principal Secretaries of State

EXPLANATORY NOTE

(This note is not part of the Order)

This Order provides for the partial exemption from the provisions of the Data Protection Act 1984 which confer rights on data subjects to gain access to data held about them ("the subject access provisions") of certain data where the exercise of those rights would be likely to prejudice the carrying out of social work by causing serious harm to the health or emotional condition of the data subject or another person or lead to the identification of other individuals (except individuals employed or engaged for reward in social work). (The Order, except so far as it relates to information contained in certain court reports, does not apply to any data about a person's physical or mental health to which the Data Protection (Subject Access Modification) (Health) Order 1987 (S.I.1987/1903) applies.)

Except in the case of court reports in certain proceedings where information in the report may be withheld by the court, for which there is complete exemption from the subject access provisions, the Order only disapplies so much of those provisions which requires the data subject to be supplied with a copy of the information constituting the data.

The Order principally applies to data held by local authorities, in relation to their social services and education welfare functions, and health authorities to whom such data are passed and by probation committees and the National Society for the Prevention of Cruelty to Children. The Order also applies to data held for similar purposes by the corresponding bodies in Scotland and Northern Ireland. Data held by government departments for certain purposes connected with social work and by officers such as guardians ad litem and (in Scotland) reporters appointed to safeguard the interests of children in certain court proceedings are also within the scope of the Order. Provision is made enabling other voluntary organisations or other bodies to be added to the list of bodies whose data are subject to the provisions of the Order where the data are held for purposes similar to the social services functions (or in Scotland social work functions) of local authorities.

STATUTORY INSTRUMENTS

1987 No. 1905

DATA PROTECTION

The Data Protection (Regulation of Financial Services etc.) (Subject Access Exemption) Order 1987

Made - - - -	*9th November 1987*
Coming into force	*11th November 1987*

Whereas a draft of this Order has been laid before and approved by a resolution of each House of Parliament;

Now, therefore, in exercise of the powers conferred upon me by section 30(2) of the Data Protection Act 1984(**a**) and section 190 of the Financial Services Act 1986(**b**) and after consultation with the Data Protection Registrar in accordance with section 40(3) of the Act of 1984, I hereby make the following Order:

1. This Order may be cited as the Data Protection (Regulation of Financial Services etc.) (Subject Access Exemption) Order 1987 and shall come into force on 11th November 1987.

2. The functions designated for the purposes of section 30 of the Data Protection Act 1984 (exemption from subject access provisions of data held for the purpose of discharging designated functions relating to the regulation of financial services etc.) are–

(a) those specified in Schedule 1 to this Order being functions conferred by or under the enactments listed in column 1 of that Schedule and described in column 2 thereof; and

(b) those specified in Schedule 2 to this Order being functions of a type mentioned in paragraphs (a) to (c) of section 190 of the Financial Services Act 1986 and designated for the purposes of section 30 as if they were functions conferred by or under any enactment.

3. This Order is without prejudice to any exemption from the subject access provisions within the meaning of section 26(2) of the Data Protection Act 1984.

Douglas Hurd
Home Office
One of Her Majesty's Principal Secretaries of State
9th November 1987

(**a**) 1984 c.35.   (**b**) 1986 c.60.

SCHEDULE 1

Article 2(a)

FUNCTIONS DESIGNATED FOR THE PURPOSES OF SECTION 30 OF THE DATA PROTECTION ACT 1984 WHICH ARE CONFERRED BY OR UNDER ANY ENACTMENT

(1) Enactment by or under which function conferred	(2) Description of function
Lloyd's Acts 1871 to 1982(a)	Functions of organs of Lloyd's in relation to admission of persons to membership and regulation of insurance business.
Bankruptcy (Ireland) Amendment Act 1872(b)	Functions relating to control over trustee by Department of Economic Development under section 118.
Bankruptcy Act 1914(c)	Functions of Board of Trade under sections 19, 81 and 95 in relation to appointment, conduct and removal of trustees in bankruptcy.
	Functions of Board of Trade under sections 82 and 87 in relation to remuneration of and statement of proceedings by trustees in bankruptcy.
	Functions of official receivers in relation to conduct of bankrupts.
	Functions of trustees in bankruptcy in relation to conduct of bankrupts.
	Functions of deputy official receivers and officers of Board of Trade under section 71 in relation to functions of official receivers.
	Functions of the Lord Chancellor and Secretary of State under section 132 in relation to conduct of discharged or undischarged bankrupts.
Industrial Assurance Act 1923(d)	Functions of Industrial Assurance Commissioner under section 17 in relation to inspection of industrial assurance company and action taken consequent upon such inspection.
Prevention of Fraud (Investments) Act (Northern Ireland) 1940(e)	Functions of Department of Economic Development in relation to collection of data under powers conferred by Act.
Prevention of Fraud (Investments) Act 1958(f)	Functions conferred on Secretary of State and tribunal established under section 6 in relation to grant, refusal and revocation of licences.
	Functions conferred on Secretary of State in relation to making and revocation of orders exempting certain persons from licensing requirement, supervision or regulation of persons carrying on business of dealing in securities.
	Functions in relation to making and revocation of orders recognising stock exchanges and associations of dealers in securities and authorising unit trust schemes.
Industrial and Provident Societies Act 1965(g)	Functions of appropriate registrar under sections 16 and 17 in relation to cancellation or suspension of registration of society.
	Functions of appropriate registrar under section 56 in relation to petition for winding up society.
Industrial and Provident Societies Act (Northern Ireland) 1969(h)	Functions of Registrar of Friendly Societies under sections 15 and 16 in relation to cancellation or suspension of registration of society.
	Functions of Registrar of Friendly Societies under section 65 in relation to petition for winding up society.
Insolvency Service (Accounting and Investment) Act 1970(i)	Functions of Board of Trade in relation to Insolvency Services Account.

(a)   1871 c.xxi, 1911 c.lxii, 1925 c.xxvi, 1951 c.viii, 1982 c.xiv.
(b)   1872 c.58.

(c) 1914 c.59.	(d) 1923 c.8.	(e) 1940 c.9 (N.I.).
(f) 1958 c.45.	(g) 1965 c.12.	(h) 1969 c.24 (N.I.).
(i) 1970 c.8.		

(1) *Enactment by or under which function conferred*	(2) *Description of function*
Friendly Societies Act (Northern Ireland) 1970(**a**)	Functions of Registrar of Friendly Societies under section 77 in relation to investigation or winding up of societies or branches. Functions of Registrar of Friendly Societies under section 78 in relation to suspension of business of societies. Functions of Registrar of Friendly Societies under section 79 in relation to production of documents. Functions of Registrar of Friendly Societies under section 80 in relation to cancellation and suspension of registration of society. Functions of Registrar of Friendly Societies under section 84 in relation to dissolution by award of society. Functions of Registrar of Friendly Societies under sections 87 and 88 in relation to institution of proceedings and punishment of fraud.
Fair Trading Act 1973(**b**)	Functions of Director-General of Fair Trading under Part III in relation to the protection of consumers.
Powers of Criminal Courts Act 1973(**c**)	Functions of Official Petitioner under Schedule 2 in relation to criminal bankruptcies.
Consumer Credit Act 1974(**d**)	Functions of Director-General of Fair Trading under Part III in relation to licensing of businesses.
Friendly Societies Act 1974 (**e**)	Functions of Chief Registrar under section 87 in relation to inspection or winding up of societies or branches. Functions of Chief Registrar under section 88 in relation to suspension of business of societies. Functions of Chief Registrar under section 89 in relation to production of documents. Functions of Chief Registrar and assistant registrar for Scotland under section 91 in relation to cancellation and suspension of registration. Functions of Chief Registrar under section 95 in relation to dissolution by award of society. Functions of Chief Registrar and assistant registrars under sections 98 and 99 in relation to institution of proceedings and punishment of fraud.
Policyholders Protection Act 1975 (**f**)	Functions of Policyholders Protection Board exercisable in relation to policyholders and others prejudiced by inability of insurance companies to meet liabilities.
Insurance Brokers Registration Act 1977(**g**)	Functions of Insurance Brokers Registration Council relating to registration and training of insurance brokers and regulation of their professional standards.
Credit Unions Act 1979 (**h**)	Functions of Chief Registrar under section 18 in relation to inspection of credit unions and calling of special meetings. Functions of Chief Registrar under section 19 in relation to suspension of operations of credit unions. Functions of appropriate registrar under section 20 in relation to cancellation or suspension of registration and petition for winding up of credit union.
Industrial Assurance (Northern Ireland) Order 1979 (**i**)	Functions of Industrial Assurance Commissioner for Northern Ireland under Article 18 in relation to investigation of affairs of industrial assurance company and action taken consequent upon such investigation.

(**a**)	1970 c.31 (N.I.).	(**b**)	1973 c.41.	(**c**)	1973 c.62.
(**d**)	1974 c.39.	(**e**)	1974 c.46.	(**f**)	1975 c.75.
(**g**)	1977 c.46.	(**h**)	1979 c.34.	(**i**)	S.I. 1979/1574 (N.I.13).

(1) *Enactment by or under which function conferred*	(2) *Description of function*
Bankruptcy Amendment (Northern Ireland) Order 1980 (**a**)	Functions of Department of Economic Development under Articles 27 and 39 in relation to release of official assignee and trustees.
	Functions of official assignee in relation to examination of bankrupt and preparation of notes and reports under Articles 11, 28 and 30.
Insurance Companies Act 1982 (**b**)	Functions of Secretary of State under Part I in relation to authorisation and withdrawal of authorisation of insurance companies.
	Functions of Secretary of State conferred by or under Parts II to V in relation to regulation of insurance business and its conduct.
	Functions of Secretary of State or officer in relation to requirements, directions and powers under Companies Act 1967 (**c**) as saved by Schedule 4 to Act.
Bankruptcy Rules (Northern Ireland) 1983 (**d**)	Functions of official assignee in relation to examination of bankrupt and preparation of notes under Rules 77 and 78.
Companies Act 1985 (**e**)	Functions of Secretary of State under Chapter II of Part I in relation to names of companies and under section 694 in relation to names of oversea companies.
	Functions of Secretary of State under section 134.
	Functions of Secretary of State under section 179.
	Functions of Secretary of State under Part VI and section 456 and of Governor of Bank of England under section 216.
	Functions of Secretary of State under Part VII, Schedule 5, Schedule 7 and Schedule 9 in relation to accounts of companies and under Chapter II of Part XXIII in relation to accounts of oversea companies.
	Functions of registrar under section 244.
	Functions of Secretary of State under section 315 in relation to modification of provisions in relation to general meetings of companies for purpose of that section.
	Functions of Secretary of State under section 345 in relation to increase of financial limits for purpose of Part X.
	Functions of Secretary of State under section 367 in relation to calling of general meetings of companies.
	Functions of Secretary of State under sections 384 and 385 in relation to appointment and remuneration of auditors and under section 389 in relation to qualification and authorisation for appointment as auditor.
	Functions of following persons under Part XIV–
	Secretary of State or inspectors in relation to investigation powers and investigations conducted in exercise of these powers;
	Secretary of State or officer authorised by him under section 447 in relation to power to require production of documents;
	Secretary of State under section 440 in relation to winding up and under section 445 in relation to restrictions on shares and debentures.
	Functions of Secretary of State under section 460.
	Functions of Secretary of State under section 491 when appointed receiver in relation to companies being wound up by court.

(**a**)   S.I. 1980/561 (N.I.4).   (**b**)   1982 c.50.   (**c**)   1967 c.81.
(**d**)   S.R. 1983 No. 310.   (**e**)   1985 c.6.

(1) *Enactment by or under which function conferred*	(2) *Description of function*
Companies Act 1985 (contd.)	Functions of Secretary of State under section 548 in relation to committees of inspection.
	Functions of special managers under section 556 in relation to companies where official receiver is liquidator.
	Functions of Secretary of State under sections 584 and 594 in relation to holding of meetings.
	Functions of Secretary of State under Part XX in relation to conduct, accounts, records and release of liquidators and provisional liquidators.
	Functions of Secretary of State under Part XX in relation to Insolvency Services Account.
	Functions of liquidators under Part XX in relation to winding up of companies.
	Functions of provisional liquidators under Part XX in relation to companies in respect of which winding up petition is presented.
	Functions of official receivers under Part XX in relation to winding up of companies.
	Functions of Secretary of State under Chapters V and VII of Part XX in relation to winding up of companies.
	Functions of registrar under sections 652 and 653 in relation to striking off companies.
	Functions of registrar under section 713 in relation to enforcement of duty of companies to file with, deliver or send to registrar returns, accounts and other documents.
	Any functions of making available information for purposes of or otherwise in connection with any functions specified in this Schedule in relation to Act.
Bankruptcy (Scotland) Act 1985 (**a**)	Functions of Accountant in Bankruptcy under section 1 in relation to making of report to Lord Advocate.
	Functions of interim and permanent trustee under sections 2 and 3 in relation to making of reports to Accountant in Bankruptcy.
Credit Unions (Northern Ireland) Order 1985 (**b**)	Functions of Registrar of Friendly Societies under Article 58 in relation to inspection of credit unions and calling of special meetings.
	Functions of Registrar of Friendly Societies under Article 59 in relation to suspension of operation of credit unions.
	Functions of Registrar of Friendly Societies under Articles 60, 61 and 63 in relation to cancellation or suspension of registration and petition for winding up of credit union.
Insolvency Act 1986 (**c**)	Functions of administrators under Part II and Schedule 1 in relation to companies in respect of which an administration order has been made.
	Functions of official receivers under section 32 when appointed receiver in relation to companies being wound up by court.
	Functions of Secretary of State under sections 93 and 105 in relation to holding of meetings.
	Functions of Secretary of State under section 124 in relation to presentation of winding up petitions.
	Functions of Secretary of State under section 141 in relation to liquidation committees.
	Functions of special managers under section 177 in relation to companies in liquidation or where a provisional liquidator has been appointed.

(1)	(2)
Enactment by or under which function conferred	*Description of function*
Insolvency Act 1986 (contd).	Functions of Secretary of State under Part IV in relation to appointment, removal and release of liquidators and provisional liquidators.
	Functions of Accountant of Court under Part IV in relation to release of liquidators.
	Functions of provisional liquidators under Part IV and Schedule IV in relation to companies in respect of which winding up petition is presented.
	Functions of liquidators under Part IV and Schedule IV in relation to winding up of companies.
	Functions of official receivers under Part IV in relation to winding up of companies.
	Functions of Secretary of State under Chapter IX of Part IV in relation to dissolution of companies.
	Functions of Secretary of State under Chapter X of Part IV in relation to directors, shadow directors, officers or members of companies.
	Functions of official receivers and persons referred to as office-holders under Part VI in relation to companies which are insolvent or in liquidation,
	Functions of trustees in bankruptcy under Part IX and Schedule 5 in relation to conduct of bankrupts.
	Functions of official receivers under Part IX in relation to conduct of bankrupts.
	Functions of Secretary of State under Part IX in relation to appointment, removal and release of trustees in bankruptcy.
	Functions of Secretary of State under section 301 in relation to creditors' committee.
	Functions of Official Petitioner in relation to criminal bankruptcies.
	Functions of professional bodies recognised under section 391 in relation to insolvency practitioners.
	Functions of Secretary of State under Parts XIII and XV in relation to insolvency practitioners.
	Functions of Secretary of State in relation to Insolvency Practitioners Tribunal.
	Functions of Insolvency Practitioners Tribunal under Part XIII in relation to insolvency practitioners.
	Functions of deputy official receivers under section 401 in relation to cases of insolvency.
	Functions of Secretary of State under Part XIV in relation to Insolvency Services Account.
	Functions of Secretary of State, liquidators, provisional liquidators, special managers, official receivers and trustees in relation to insolvent partnerships, administration of insolvent estates of bankrupts and authorised and former authorised institutions within the meaning of the Banking Act 1987.
	Functions of Lord Chancellor, Secretary of State, Treasury and Bank of England under Part XV in relation to functions under Act specified in this Schedule or to functions under Company Directors Disqualification Act 1986 specified in this Schedule (a)
Company Directors Disqualification Act 1986 (b)	Functions of Secretary of State, official receivers, liquidators, administrators, administrative receivers and former liquidators conferred by or under Act in relation to conduct of persons and making of disqualification orders.

(a)   Part XV of 1986 c.45 was extended by s.21(2) of 1986 c.46 so as to apply to certain functions of the latter Act.
(b)   1986 c.46.

(1)	(2)
Enactment by or under which function conferred	*Description of function*
Building Societies Act 1986 (**a**)	Functions of Building Societies Commission under section 1(4) in promoting protection by each building society of investments of its shareholders and depositors and financial stability of building societies generally.
	Functions of Building Societies Commission under section 9 in relation to initial authorisation to raise funds and borrow money.
	Functions of Building Societies Investor Protection Board under Part IV in relation to administration of Investor Protection Scheme.
	Functions of Building Societies Commission under sections 36 to 51 in relation to powers of control over registered building societies.
	Functions of Building Societies Commission under sections 93 to 103 in relation to mergers and transfer of business.
	Functions of Building Societies Commission under section 107 in relation to restrictions on use of certain names and descriptions.
	Functions of Building Societies Commission under section 108 in relation to power to require building society to change misleading name.
Financial Services Act 1986 (**b**)	Functions of Secretary of State conferred by or under Chapter I of Part I.
	Functions of Secretary of State or designated agency under Chapter II of Part I in relation to injunctions and restitution orders.
	Functions of Secretary of State or designated agency under Chapter III of Part I in relation to authorisation, suspension of authorisation and withdrawal of authorisation.
	Functions of Secretary of State or designated agency under Chapter III of Part I in relation to self-regulating organisations and professional bodies.
	Functions of Secretary of State or designated agency under Chapter IV of Part I in relation to investment exchanges and clearing houses.
	Functions of Bank of England under section 43.
	Functions of Secretary of State under section 46.
	Functions of Secretary of State or designated agency under Chapter V of Part I in relation to–
	(a) conduct of investment business or any business carried on in connection with investment business or held out as being for the purpose of investment;
	(b) financial resources of persons carrying on investment business;
	(c) rescission of agreements entered into with persons carrying on investment business;
	(d) information to be notified or furnished by persons carrying on investment business;
	(e) indemnity and compensation;
	(f) money held by persons carrying on investment business;
	(g) unsolicited calls;
	(h) investment advertisements;
	(i) employment of persons in connection with investment business or investment business of particular description;

(**a**)   1986 c.53.   (**b**)   1986 c.60.

(1) *Enactment by or under which function conferred*	(2) *Description of function*
Financial Services Act 1986 (contd.)	(j) public statements as to misconduct by person who is or was authorised person under Act; (k) injunctions and restitution orders. Functions of Secretary of State or designated agency under Chapter VI of Part I in relation to powers of intervention. Functions of Secretary of State or designated agency under Chapter VII of Part I in relation to winding up and administration orders. Functions of Secretary of State under section 75(9) in relation to amendment of provisions of that section. Functions of Secretary of State or designated agency under section 76 in relation to promotion of collective investment schemes by authorised persons. Functions of Secretary of State or designated agency under section 76 in relation to schemes which are single property schemes for purposes of section 76(4). Functions of Secretary of State or designated agency under Chapter VIII of Part I in relation to authorisation, refusal of authorisation and revocation of authorisation of unit trust schemes. Functions of Secretary of State or designated agency under Chapter VIII of Part I in relation to recognition and revocation of collective investment schemes established outside United Kingdom. Functions of Secretary of State or designated agency under section 81. Functions of Secretary of State or designated agency under section 82 in relation to alteration of authorised unit trust scheme and changes of manager or trustee of such a scheme including functions under that section as applied by section 88(9). Functions of Secretary of State or designated agency under section 85 in relation to document referred to in that section as "scheme particulars" including functions under that section as it has effect by virtue of sections 87(5) and 88(10). Functions of Secretary of State or designated agency under section 86 in relation to collective investment scheme constituted in another member State including functions under that section as it has effect by virtue of paragraph 10 of Schedule 15. Functions of Secretary of State under section 87 in relation to designation and revocation of designation of countries or territories. Functions of Secretary of State or designated agency under section 90 in relation to facilities to be maintained in United Kingdom by operator of recognised collective investment and to explanatory information to be included in any advertisement issued or caused to be issued in United Kingdom by any such operator. Functions of Secretary of State or designated agency under sections 91 to 93 in relation to powers of intervention mentioned in those sections and to applications made to court under section 93. Functions of Secretary of State or designated agency under sections 60 and 61 as those sections to have effect by virtue of section 91(4). Functions of Secretary of State or designated agency under section 94. Functions of inspector appointed under section 94. Functions of Financial Services Tribunal.

(1)	(2)
Enactment by or under which function conferred	*Description of function*
Financial Services Act 1986 (contd.)	Functions of Secretary of State or designated agency in relation to Financial Services Tribunal.
	Functions of Secretary of State or designated agency under Chapter X of Part I in relation to register of authorised persons and recognised organisations etc to be maintained under that Chapter.
	Functions of Secretary of State or designated agency under section 104 in relation to requisition of information.
	Functions of Secretary of State or designated agency under sections 60 and 61 as they have effect by virtue of section 104(4).
	Functions of Secretary of State or designated agency under section 105 in relation to investigation powers and investigations conducted in exercise of those powers.
	Functions of any person authorised by Secretary of State or designated agency under section 106 to exercise on his or its behalf all or any of powers conferred by section 105.
	Functions of Secretary of State or designated agency under section 107.
	Functions of Secretary of State or designated agency under section 108 in relation to power to require a person authorised under section 25 or 31 to submit accounts or matters mentioned in section 108 for further examination.
	Functions of Secretary of State under section 109(2) and (3) in relation to circumstances in which matters are to be communicated to Secretary of State or designated agency.
	Functions of Secretary of State or designated agency under section 110 in relation to equivalence of qualifications, powers and duties mentioned in that section.
	Functions of Secretary of State under Chapter XIII of Part I in relation to transfer and resumption of functions.
	Functions of Secretary of State under Chapter XIV of Part I in relation to effect on competition of any of rules, guidance, arrangements or restrictions mentioned in that Chapter.
	Functions of Secretary of State under sections 129 to 134 and Schedule 10 in relation to regulation of insurance companies.
	Functions of Secretary of State under section 130 in relation to promotion of insurance contracts.
	Functions of Secretary of State under section 61 as it has effect by virtue of section 131(8).
	Functions of Secretary of State, Chief Registrar, Registrar of Friendly Societies for Northern Ireland and transferee body under sections 140 and 141 and Schedule 11 in relation to regulation of friendly societies.
	Functions of competent authority under Part IV in relation to listing rules.
	Functions of competent authority under Part IV in relation to admission or refusal of admission to and discontinuance or suspension of listing.
	Functions of competent authority under Part IV in relation to listing particulars and advertisements or other information of kind described in section 154(1).
	Functions under sections 148 and 165 in relation to exemption from disclosure.
	Functions of competent authority under section 152 in relation to certification of directors.
	Functions of Secretary of State under section 157 in relation to alteration of competent authority.

(1)	(2)
Enactment by or under which function conferred	*Description of function*

Financial Services Act 1986 (contd.)	Functions of Secretary of State under section 158 in relation to approval of exchanges and under section 162 in relation to directions in respect of rules of such exchanges.
	Functions of approved exchange under section 159 in relation to approval of prospectus.
	Functions of approved exchange under sections 159 and 161 in relation to certification respecting information.
	Functions of Secretary of State under section 160 in relation to exemption of advertisements from provisions of section 160(1).
	Functions of Secretary of State under section 161(4) in relation to disapplication of sections 159 and 160.
	Functions of Secretary of State under section 162 in relation to form and contents of prospectus.
	Functions of approved exchange under section 168 in relation to certification of directors.
	Functions of Secretary of State under section 169 in relation to terms upon which person may offer securities and regulation of such person's conduct.
	Functions of Secretary of State under section 170 in relation to advertisements.
	Functions of Secretary of State under section 177.
	Functions of inspector appointed under section 177.
	Functions of Secretary of State or designated agency under section 178 in relation to service or revocation of notice or giving or revocation of direction of kind described in section 178(3) or 178(5).
	Functions of Secretary of State under section 181.
	Functions of Secretary of State under section 191(3) in relation to scope of that section.
	Functions of Secretary of State under section 192.
	Functions of Secretary of State or designated agency under section 199 in relation to powers of entry.
	Functions of Secretary of State or designated agency under section 206 in relation to publication of information and giving of advice.
	Functions of Secretary of State or designated agency under paragraph 23 of Schedule 1 in relation to grant and withdrawal of permission under that paragraph.
	Functions of Secretary of State or designated agency under paragraph 23(5) of Schedule 1 in relation to information to be supplied by persons holding permissions granted under that paragraph.
	Functions of Secretary of State or designated agency under sections 61, 104 and 105 as they have effect by virtue of paragraphs 23(6) and (7) of paragraph 23 of Schedule 1.
	Functions of person authorised by Secretary of State or designated agency under section 106 to exercise on his or its behalf all or any of powers conferred by section 105 as it has effect by virtue of paragraph 23(7) of Schedule 1.
	Functions of Secretary of State or designated agency under paragraph 25 of Schedule 1 in relation to grant and revocation of certificates.
	Functions of Secretary of State or designated agency under paragraph 13 of Schedule 9 in relation to exchange of information.
	Functions of Secretary of State under paragraph 3(6) of Schedule 10 in relation to circumstances in which he may transfer functions in relation to regulated insurance company.

(1)	(2)
Enactment by or under which function conferred	*Description of function*
Financial Services Act 1986 (contd.)	Functions of designated agency under paragraph 6(3) of Schedule 10 in relation to notice to be given to Secretary of State under that paragraph.
	Functions of Secretary of State under paragraph 6(4) of Schedule 10 in relation to service of notice by Secretary of State.
	Functions under paragraph 6(3) and (4) of Schedule 10 as they apply by virtue of paragraph 6(5) of that Schedule.
	Functions under paragraph 8 of Schedule 10 in relation to termination of investment business authorisation of insurer established in another member State.
	Functions of Secretary of State and designated agency under paragraph 10 of Schedule 10.
	Functions under paragraph 1(4) of Schedule 15 in relation to making available information described in that paragraph.
	Functions of Secretary of State or designated agency under paragraph 4 of Schedule 15 in relation to making and extension of interim recognition orders.
	Functions of Secretary of State or designated agency under paragraph 5 of Schedule 15 in relation to interim authorisation by recognised professional body.
	Functions of Secretary of State under paragraph 6(4) of Schedule 15 in relation to statutory provisions relating to regulation of conduct, practice or discipline of member of recognised professional body.
	Functions of Secretary of State under paragraph 10(1) of Schedule 15 in relation to orders directing that schemes established in another member State are to be recognised schemes for purposes of Act.
	Functions of Secretary of State or designated agency under paragraph 11 of Schedule 13.
	Functions of Secretary of State under paragraph 15 of Schedule 15 in relation to requirements which may be imposed on person who has applied for permission under paragraph 23 of Schedule 1 before the day on which paragraph 3 of Act comes into force and whose application has not been determined before that day.
	Any functions of making available information for purposes of, or otherwise in connection with, any functions specified in this Schedule in relation to Act.
	Functions of Secretary of State or designated agency in relation to supervision or regulation of any person authorised, recognised or holding permission under Act or to supervision or regulation of any collective investment schemes.
	Functions of Secretary of State in relation to designated agency.
Companies (Northern Ireland) Order 1986 (a)	Functions of Department of Economic Development and official assignee under Articles 303, 308 and 309 and Schedule 12 in relation to making of disqualification orders.
	Functions of Department of Economic Development and official assignee under Article 481(4), (6) and (7) in relation to presentation of winding up petitions.
	Reporting functions of official assignee under Article 491.
	Functions of liquidators under Article 495 in relation to assisting official assignee perform his functions under Order.

(a)   S.I. 1986/1032 (N.I.6).

(1)	(2)
Enactment by or under which function conferred	*Description of function*
Companies (Northern Ireland) Order 1986 (contd.)	Functions of Department of Economic Development under Part XV in relation to investigation and winding up of companies.
	Functions of Department of Economic Development under Part XX in relation to control and release of liquidators.
Company Securities (Insider Dealing) (Northern Ireland) Order 1986(**a**)	Functions of Department of Economic Development under Order.
Banking Act 1987(**b**)	Functions of Bank of England under Part I in relation to regulation of deposit-taking business.
	Functions of Bank of England under Part III in relation to regulation of use of banking names and descriptions.
	Functions of Bank of England under Part IV in relation to regulation of overseas institutions with representative offices.
	Functions of members of Board of Banking supervision under section 2.
	Functions of Deposit Protection Board under Part II in relation to administration of Deposit Protection Scheme.

SCHEDULE 2

Article 2(b)

FUNCTIONS DESIGNATED FOR THE PURPOSES OF SECTION 30 OF THE DATA PROTECTION ACT 1984 AS IF THEY WERE FUNCTIONS CONFERRED BY OR UNDER ANY ENACTMENT

1. Functions of a recognised self-regulating organisation within the meaning of section 8(1) of the Financial Services Act 1986(**c**) in connection with the admission or expulsion of members, the supervision of a person's membership or the supervision or regulation of persons carrying on investment business by virtue of membership of the organisation.

2. Functions of a recognised professional body within the meaning of section 207(1) of that Act in connection with the issue of certificates for the purposes of Part I of the Act, the withdrawal and suspension of such certificates or the supervision or regulation of persons carrying on investment business by virtue of certification by that body.

3. Functions of a recognised self-regulating organisation for friendly societies within the meaning of paragraph 1 of Schedule 11 to that Act in connection with the supervision or regulation of its member societies.

(**a**)   S.I. 1986/1034 (N.I.8).   (**b**)   1987 c.22.   (**c**)   1986 c.60.

EXPLANATORY NOTE

(This note is not part of the Order)

Section 30 of the Data Protection Act 1984 provides that personal data held for the purpose of discharging statutory functions which are designated by the Secretary of State by an order made under that section shall be exempt from the subject access provisions of the Act in any case in which the application of those provisions to the data would be likely to prejudice the proper discharge of those functions. The functions that may be designated are those conferred by or under any enactment appearing to the Secretary of State to be designed for protecting members of the public against financial loss due to dishonesty, incompetence or malpractice by persons concerned in the provision of banking, insurance, investment or other financial services or in the management of companies or to the conduct of discharged or undischarged bankrupts.

Section 190 of the Financial Services Act 1986 provides that an order made under that section may designate certain additional functions for the purposes of section 30 as if they were functions conferred by or under an enactment, namely certain functions of recognised self-regulating organisations, recognised professional bodies and recognised self-regulating organisations of friendly societies.

This Order designates functions for the purposes of section 30. Schedule 1 sets out the designated functions which are conferred by or under an enactment and Schedule 2 sets out the designated functions which are of a type mentioned in section 190 of the Financial Services Act.

STATUTORY INSTRUMENTS

1987 No. 1906

DATA PROTECTION

The Data Protection (Miscellaneous Subject Access Exemptions) Order 1987

Made - - - -	*9th November 1987*	
Coming into force -	*11th November 1987*	

Whereas a draft of this Order has been laid before and approved by a resolution of each House of Parliament:

Now, therefore, in exercise of the powers conferred upon me by sections 34(2) and 40(2) of the Data Protection Act 1984(a) and after consultation with the Data Protection Registrar in accordance with section 40(3) of that Act, I hereby make the following Order:

1.—(1) This Order may be cited as the Data Protection (Miscellaneous Subject Access Exemptions) Order 1987 and shall come into force on 11th November 1987.

(2) In this Order "the subject access provisions" has the meaning which it has for the purposes of Part IV of the Data Protection Act 1984(a).

2. There shall be exempted from the subject access provisions any personal data consisting of information the disclosure of which is prohibited or restricted by the enactments and instruments listed in the Schedule to this Order, being enactments and instruments which impose prohibitions or restrictions on disclosure which ought to prevail over those provisions in the interests of data subjects or of other individuals.

Home Office
9th November 1987

Douglas Hurd
One of Her Majesty's Principal Secretaries of State

(a) 1984 c.35.

Article 2

SCHEDULE

EXEMPTIONS FROM SUBJECT ACCESS PROVISIONS

PART I

ENACTMENTS AND INSTRUMENTS EXTENDING TO ENGLAND AND WALES

(a) *Adoption records and reports*

Sections 50 and 51 of the Adoption Act 1976(a) (subject to the Note below).

Regulations 6 and 14 of the Adoption Agencies Regulations 1983(b), so far as they relate to records and other information in the possession of local authorities.

Rules 5, 6, 9, 17, 18, 21, 22 and 53 of the Adoption Rules 1984(c).

Rules 5, 6, 9, 17, 18, 21, 22 and 32 of the Magistrates' Courts (Adoption) Rules 1984(d).

Note Until the date of the coming into force of sections 50 and 51 of the Adoption Act 1976, the references above to those sections shall be construed as references, respectively, to sections 20 and 20A(e) of the Adoption Act 1958(f).

(b) *Statement of child's special educational needs*

Regulation 11 of the Education (Special Educational Needs) Regulations 1983(g).

PART II

ENACTMENTS AND INSTRUMENTS EXTENDING TO SCOTLAND

(a) *Adoption records and reports*

Section 45 of the Adoption (Scotland) Act 1978(h).

Regulation 24 of the Adoption Agencies (Scotland) Regulations 1984(i), so far as it relates to records and other information in the possession of local authorities.

Rule 230 of the Act of Sederunt (Rules of Court) (consolidation and amendment) 1965(j).

Paragraphs 9, 24 and 28 of the Act of Sederunt (Adoption of Children) 1984(k).

(b) *Information provided by reporter for children's hearing*

Rule 6 of the Children's Hearings (Scotland) Rules 1986(l).

(c) *Record of child or young person's special educational needs*

Section 60(4) of the Education (Scotland) Act 1980(m).

Proviso (bb) to Regulation 7(2) of the Education (Record of Needs) (Scotland) Regulations 1982(n).

(a) 1976 c.36.   (b) S.I. 1983/1964.   (c) S.I. 1984/265.
(d) S.I. 1984/611.   (e) Section 20A was inserted by section 26(2) of the Children Act 1975 (c.72).
(f) 1958 c.5.   (g) S.I. 1983/29.   (h) 1978 c.28.
(i) S.I. 1984/988.   (j) S.I. 1965/321. Rule 230 was inserted by S.I. 1984/997.
(k) S.I. 1984/1013.   (l) S.I. 1986/2291.
(m) 1980 c.44. Section 60 was amended by section 4 of the Education (Scotland) Act 1981 (c.58).
(n) S.I. 1982/1222.

PART III

ENACTMENTS AND INSTRUMENTS EXTENDING TO NORTHERN IRELAND

(a) *Adoption records and reports*

Section 23 of the Adoption Act (Northern Ireland) 1967**(a)**.

Any enactment contained in an Order in Council made under the Northern Ireland Act 1974**(b)** and making provision corresponding to section 51 of the Adoption Act 1976.

Rule 35 of the Rules of the Supreme Court (Northern Ireland) (No. 4) 1969**(c)**.

Rule 22 of the County Court (Adoption) Rules (Northern Ireland) 1980**(d)**.

(b) *Statement of child's special educational needs*

Regulation 11 of the Education (Special Educational Needs) Regulations (Northern Ireland) 1985**(e)**.

EXPLANATORY NOTE

(This note is not part of the Order)

This Order exempts from the provisions of the Data Protection Act 1984 which entitle individuals to gain access to personal data held about them ("the subject access provisions") data, the disclosure of which is prohibited or restricted by certain enactments and subordinate instruments, in the interests of protecting the subject of the data himself or some other individual. The subject access provisions are section 21 of the 1984 Act and the provisions of Part II which confer powers on the Data Protection Registrar to ensure observance of paragraph (a) of the seventh data protection principle contained in Schedule 1.

The data which are exempted by the Order from the subject access provisions concern information contained in adoption records and reports and statements and records of the special educational needs of children in England and Wales, Scotland and Northern Ireland and, in Scotland, information provided by reporters for the purposes of a children's hearing.

(a) 1967 c.35 (N.I.) **(b)** 1974 c.29. **(c)** S.R. & O. (N.I.) 1969 No. 288.
(d) S.R. (N.I.) 1980 No. 227. **(e)** S.R. (N.I.) 1985 No. 365.

STATUTORY INSTRUMENTS

1987 No. 1907

POLICE

The Police Pensions (War Service) (Transferees) (Amendment) Regulations 1987

Made - - - -	*5th November 1987*
Laid before Parliament	*16th November 1987*
Coming into force	*21st December 1987*

In exercise of the powers conferred upon me by sections 1, 3 and 4 of the Police Pensions Act 1976(**a**), and after consultation with the Police Negotiating Board for the United Kingdom, I hereby, with the consent of the Treasury(**b**), make the following Regulations:

1.—(1) These Regulations may be cited as the Police Pensions (War Service) (Transferees) (Amendment) Regulations 1987.

(2) These Regulations shall come into force on 21st December 1987 and shall have effect as from 1st April 1978.

2.—(1) The Police Pensions (War Service) (Transferees) Regulations 1985(**c**) shall be amended in accordance with the following provisions of this regulation.

(2) After regulation 9(2) there shall be inserted the following paragraph –

"(2A) In the case of a former policeman who, notwithstanding that no such transfer value as is mentioned in paragraph (2)(b) has been paid in respect of him, was on 1st April 1978, or immediately before his retirement or death, if earlier, entitled to reckon service as a member of a police force for the purposes of the 1978 scheme –

(a) paragraph (1)(b) shall have effect as if for the reference therein to paragraph (2) there were substituted a reference to paragraph (2)(a), and

(b) regulations 10 and 11 shall have effect as if such a transfer value had been paid.".

(**a**) 1976 c.35, as amended by section 2(3) of the Police Negotiating Board Act 1980 (c.10).
(**b**) Formerly the Minister for the Civil Service : *see* S.I. 1981/1670.
(**c**) S.I. 1985/2029, as amended by Schedule 4 to the Police Pensions (Supplementary Provisions) Regulations 1987 (S.I. 1987/256).

(3) For regulation 9(4) there shall be substituted the following paragraph –

"(4) In paragraph (3), "public service" means public service for the purposes of a public service pension scheme within the meaning of section 51(3)(b) of the Social Security Act 1973(a).".

Home Office
21st October 1987

Douglas Hurd
One of Her Majesty's Principal Secretaries of State

We consent
5th November 1987

Mark Lennox-Boyd
Peter Lloyd
Two of the Lords Commissioners of Her Majesty's Treasury

EXPLANATORY NOTE

(This note is not part of the Regulations)

These Regulations, which come into force on 21st December 1987, amend the Police Pensions (War Service) (Transferees) Regulations 1985 ("the 1985 Regulations") with effect from 1st April 1978 (the date as from which the 1985 Regulations had effect: retrospection is authorised by section 1(5) of the Police Pensions Act 1976).

Regulation 2(2) enlarges the categories of policemen specified in regulation 9 of the 1985 Regulations (in respect of whom an additional transfer value may be paid to permit war service to reckon in another scheme) so as to include a policeman in respect of whom no transfer value had been paid but who nevertheless was entitled to reckon service as a member of a police force for the purposes of the public service pension scheme to which he transferred.

Regulation 2(3) substitutes a new paragraph for regulation 9(4) of the 1985 Regulations in order to correct an error in the definition of "public service".

(a) 1973 c.38; section 51(3) was amended by section 4(1) of the Social Security Act 1980 (c.30).

STATUTORY INSTRUMENTS

1987 No. 1908

LIBRARIES

The Public Lending Right Scheme 1982 (Amendment) Order 1987

Made - - - -	*2nd November 1987*
Laid before Parliament	*18th November 1987*
Coming into force	*10th December 1987*

The Lord President of the Council, in exercise of powers conferred by section 3(7) of the Public Lending Right Act 1979(**a**) and now vested in him(**b**) and after consulting with representatives of authors and library authorities and of others who appear likely to be affected, hereby makes the following Order:–

1. This Order may be cited as the Public Lending Right Scheme 1982 (Amendment) Order 1987 and shall come into force on 10th December 1987.

2. Article 46 of the Public Lending Right Scheme 1982(**c**) (determination of the sum due in respect of public lending right) shall be amended in paragraph (1)(a) by substituting "1.12p." for "1.20p.".

3. The Public Lending Right Scheme 1982 (Amendment) Order 1986(**d**) is hereby revoked.

Whitelaw
2nd November 1987 Lord President of the Council

EXPLANATORY NOTE

(This note is not part of the Order)

This Order amends the provisions of the Public Lending Right Scheme under which the amount (if any) payable in respect of loans of a particular book from public libraries in a particular year is calculated. The sum attributed to each loan for the purpose of the calculation is changed from 1.20p to 1.12p.

(**a**) 1979 c. 10.
(**b**) S.I. 1979/907, 1981/207, 1983/879, 1984/1814, 1986/600.
(**c**) The Scheme is set out in the Appendix to S.I. 1982/719; the relevant amending instrument is S.I. 1986/2103.
(**d**) S.I. 1986/2103.

STATUTORY INSTRUMENTS

1987 No. 1909 (C. 57)

LAND SETTLEMENT, IRELAND

The Irish Sailors and Soldiers Land Trust Act 1987 (Commencement) Order 1987

Made - - - - *4th November 1987*

In pursuance of section 3(2) of the Irish Sailors and Soldiers Land Trust Act 1987 (**a**) and the powers therein conferred upon me, I hereby make the following Order:

1. This Order may be cited as the Irish Sailors and Soldiers Land Trust Act 1987 (Commencement) Order 1987.

2. The Irish Sailors and Soldiers Land Trust Act 1987 shall come into force on 4th November 1987.

Geoffrey Howe
Her Majesty's Principal Secretary of State
4th November 1987   for Foreign and Commonwealth Affairs

EXPLANATORY NOTE

(This note is not part of the Order)

This Order brings the Irish Sailors and Soldiers Land Trust Act 1987 into force on 4th November 1987.

(**a**) 1987 c.48.

STATUTORY INSTRUMENTS

1987 No. 1910

HOUSING, ENGLAND AND WALES
HOUSING, SCOTLAND
SOCIAL SECURITY

The Housing Benefit (Implementation Subsidy) Order 1987

Made - - - -	*6th November 1987*
Laid before Parliament	*16th November 1987*
Coming into force -	*7th December 1987*

The Secretary of State for Social Services, with the consent of the Treasury**(a)**, in exercise of the powers conferred on him by section 30(4) of the Social Security Act 1986**(b)**, section 166(1) to (3) of the Social Security Act 1975**(c)** and of all other powers enabling him in that behalf, after consultation in accordance with section 61(7) of the Social Security Act 1986 with organisations appearing to him to be representative of the authorities concerned, hereby makes the following order–

Citation, commencement and interpretation

1.—(1) This Order, which may be cited as the Housing Benefit (Implementation Subsidy) Order 1987, shall come into force on 7th December 1987.

(2) In this Order–

"the Act" means the Social Security Act 1986;

"administration costs" means the costs incurred by an authority in running the housing benefit scheme under Part II of the Social Security and Housing Benefits Act 1982**(d)**, including the costs of staff, staff training, office services, computer software, stationery and publicity materials but excluding the cost of benefit;

"authority" means a rating authority, housing authority or local authority within the meaning of sections 30(1) and 84(1) of the Act;

"estimate" means an estimate submitted to the Secretary of State by an authority on or before 27th April 1987 in the case of an estimate of implementation costs and on or before 31st December 1986 in the case of any other estimate;

"implementation costs" means the costs incurred in the 12 months ending with 31st March 1988 by an authority in implementing the housing benefit scheme under Part II of the Act, including the costs of staff, staff training, office services, computer software, stationery and publicity materials but excluding the cost of benefit;

"proportionate assessment" means an amount calculated under paragraph 2 of the Schedule to this Order;

(a) *See* section 83(5) of the Social Security Act 1986 (c.50).
(b) 1986 c.50.
(c) 1975 c.14; section 166(1) to (3) is applied by section 83(1) of the Social Security Act 1986.
(d) 1982 c.24.

"relevant financial year" means the 12 months ending with 31st March 1987;
"subsidy" means the subsidy payable by the Secretary of State to an authority for the financial year 1987–88 under section 30(4) of the Act in connection with the costs incurred by the authority in implementing the housing benefit scheme.

Calculation of subsidy

2. The Schedule to this Order shall have effect for specifying the manner in which, subject to section 30(9) of the Act, the subsidy payable to an authority is to be calculated.

Signed by authority of the Secretary of State for Social Services.

Michael Portillo
Parliamentary Under-Secretary of State,
29th October 1987   Department of Health and Social Security

We consent,

Mark Lennox-Boyd
Peter Lloyd
6th November 1987   Two of the Lords Commissioners of Her Majesty's Treasury

SCHEDULE

Article 2

CALCULATION OF THE SUBSIDY

1. Subject to paragraph 4 below the amount of subsidy payable to any authority shall be calculated as an amount equal to–
  (a) the estimate of the implementation costs of that authority; or
  (b) the sum which, in the case of that authority, is appropriate under paragraph 3 below;
whichever is the less.

2. For the purposes of paragraphs 3 and 4 below for each authority there shall be calculated a proportionate assessment, based on its estimates for the relevant financial year of its administration costs and of the number of recipients of housing benefit in its area, in accordance with the formula–

$$£25,000,000 \times \left(\frac{0.75A}{B} + \frac{0.25C}{D} \right)$$

where–
  A is the amount of that estimate of administration costs;
  B is the total amount of the estimates of administration costs for that year submitted by all authorities;
  C is the number of recipients in that estimate of the number of recipients of housing benefit;
  D is the total number of such recipients in the estimates for that year of the number of such recipients submitted by all authorities.

3. Where the proportionate assessment calculated for any authority is of an amount specified in any paragraph of column (1) of the Table below, the sum which for the purposes of paragraph 1(b) above is appropriate in the case of that authority is the sum specified opposite in column (2) or, as the case may be, a sum calculated as specified there.

Table

(1) Proportionate Assessment	(2) Sum
(i) £5,000 or less	£5,000
(ii) More than £5,000 but not more than £20,000	£20,000
(iii) More than £20,000 but not more than £200,000	110% of the proportionate assessment rounded down to the nearest pound
(iv) More than £200,000	£220,000 and 15.3% of the amount, rounded down to the nearest pound, by which the proportionate assessment exceeds £200,000

4. The amount of subsidy payable to any authority which has not submitted an estimate of its implementation costs shall–

(a) if the proportionate assessment calculated for that authority is not more than £20,000, be calculated as an amount equal to the sum specified in column (2) of the Table in paragraph 3 above opposite paragraph (i) or (ii), as the case may be, of column (1);

(b) if the proportionate assessment calculated for that authority is more than £20,000, be calculated as an amount equal, subject to rounding down to the nearest £1,000–

(i) to the proportionate assessment, if it is not more than £50,000;

(ii) in any other case, to the aggregate of the sums arrived at by calculating in respect of each portion of that assessment specified in column (1) of the Table below the percentage specified opposite to it in column (2).

Table

(1) Portion of the Proportionate Assessment	(2) Percentage
The first £50,000	100%
Any excess over £50,000 not exceeding £75,000	80%
Any excess over £75,000 not exceeding £100,000	60%
Any excess over £100,000 not exceeding £150,000	40%
Any excess over £150,000 not exceeding £200,000	20%
Any excess over £200,000	10%

EXPLANATORY NOTE

(This note is not part of the Order)

This Order specifies the manner in which the subsidy payable to authorities implementing the housing benefit scheme under Part II of the Social Security Act 1986 is to be calculated.

STATUTORY INSTRUMENTS

1987 No. 1911

CONSUMER PROTECTION

The Approval of Safety Standards Regulations 1987

Made - - - -	*9th November 1987*
Laid before Parliament	*13th November 1987*
Coming into force -	*7th December 1987*

Whereas the Secretary of State has, in accordance with section 11(5) of the Consumer Protection Act 1987(**a**), consulted such organisations as appear to him to be representative of interests substantially affected by these Regulations, such other persons as he considers appropriate and the Health and Safety Commission:

Now, therefore, the Secretary of State, in exercise of the powers conferred upon him by section 11 of the said Act, hereby makes the following Regulations:

1. These Regulations may be cited as the Approval of Safety Standards Regulations 1987 and shall come into force on 7th December 1987.

2. The Secretary of State, if he thinks it appropriate to do so for the purposes of section 10(3) of the Consumer Protection Act 1987, may approve (in whole or in part), or cancel any such approval of, any standard of safety (including any amendment or revision of any such standard).

3. Any such approval or cancellation shall be effected by the publication by the Secretary of State, in such manner as he considers appropriate, of a notice specifying the approval or cancellation together with, in each case, the place where copies of the standard of safety to which the approval or cancellation relates may be obtained.

4. The notice referred to in regulation 3 above shall state the date on which the approval or (as the case may be) cancellation shall take effect.

5. An approval given under these Regulations shall, if it is so stated in the notice referred to in regulation 3 above, cease to have effect at the end of such period as may be specified in the notice.

6. A register of approvals given under these Regulations shall be kept by the Secretary of State at such premises and in such form as he may determine, and shall be open to public inspection.

Francis Maude
Parliamentary Under Secretary of State,
Department of Trade and Industry

9th November 1987

(**a**) 1987 c.43.

EXPLANATORY NOTE

(This note is not part of the Regulations)

These Regulations make provision whereby the Secretary of State may approve standards of safety for the purposes of section 10(3) of the Consumer Protection Act 1987. Under section 10(3), consumer goods are not to be regarded as failing to comply with the general safety requirement (section 10(1) and (2)) in respect of, *inter alia,* any failure to do more in relation to any matter than is required by any standards of safety approved for the purposes of the subsection by or under regulations made under section 11 and imposing requirements with respect to that matter.

The Regulations provide in particular that the Secretary of State may approve, or cancel any approval of, a standard of safety (regulation 2); that an approval or cancellation is to be effected by the publication of a notice by the Secretary of State specifying the approval or cancellation and the place where the relevant standard may be obtained (regulation 3); and that the Secretary of State is to keep a register of approvals given under the Regulations (regulation 6).

It is intended that notices of approvals and cancellations will be published in British Business and BSI News; and that the register of approvals will be made available for public inspection at The Library, Department of Trade and Industry, 1 Victoria Street, London SW1H 0ET.

STATUTORY INSTRUMENTS

1987 No. 1914 (S.131)

POLICE

The Police (Scotland) Amendment (No.2) Regulations 1987

Made - - - -	*3rd November 1987*
Laid before Parliament	*19th November 1987*
Coming into force	*10th December 1987*

The Secretary of State, in exercise of the powers conferred upon him by section 26 of the Police (Scotland) Act 1967(**a**) and of all other powers enabling him in that behalf, after taking into consideration any representations made by the Police Advisory Board for Scotland following the submission of a draft of the Regulations in accordance with section 26(9) of the said Act of 1967, and after taking into consideration the recommendations made by the Police Negotiating Board for the United Kingdom and furnishing the said Police Negotiating Board for the United Kingdom with a draft of the Regulations in accordance with section 2(1) of the Police Negotiating Board Act 1980(**b**), hereby makes the following Regulations:

Citation

1. These Regulations may be cited as the Police (Scotland) Amendment (No.2) Regulations 1987.

Commencement

2. These Regulations shall come into force on 10th December 1987 and shall have effect for the purposes of regulation 8 as from 1st February 1987 and of regulations 10 and 11 as from 1st September 1987.

Interpretation

3. In these Regulations any reference to "the principal Regulations" is a reference to the Police (Scotland) Regulations 1976(**c**).

Amendment of definitions

4. In regulation 1(2)(g) of the principal Regulations (citation, commencement and interpretation) for the definition of "public holiday" there shall be substituted the following definition:–

"'public holiday' means Christmas Day, New Year's Day and each of 6 other days, being as far as is practicable local public holidays and in any year where Christmas Day, 26th December or New Year's Day falls on a Saturday or Sunday the 6 other days shall be increased by 1 for each day on which Christmas Day, 26th December or New Year's day falls on a Saturday or Sunday;".

(**a**) 1967 c.77; section 26(9) was amended by section 2(4) of the Police Negotiating Board Act 1980 (c.10); section 26(1A) and (10) were inserted by section 111 of the Police and Criminal Evidence Act 1984 (c.60).
(**b**) 1980 c.10.
(**c**) S.I. 1976/1073; the relevant amending instruments are S.I. 1978/528, 1980/1050, 1981/67, 1985/111, 1733 and 1987/423.

5. There shall be substituted for regulation 1(2)(h) of the principal Regulations the following:–

"(h) a reference to a police force shall include a reference to the Royal Ulster Constabulary and to a police force maintained under the Police Act 1964(a), so however that nothing in these Regulations shall be construed as relating to the government, administration or conditions of service of the Royal Ulster Constabulary or of such a force as is last mentioned.".

Qualifications for appointment of deputy chief constable, assistant chief constable, superintendent or chief inspector

6. For regulation 7 of the principal Regulations (qualifications for appointment of deputy chief constable, assistant chief constable, superintendent or chief inspector) there shall be substituted the following regulation:–

"Qualifications for appointment of deputy chief constable, assistant chief constable, superintendent or chief inspector

7.—(1) No person shall be qualified for appointment as deputy chief constable or as assistant chief constable in a police force unless–

(a) he has had at least 2 years' experience in the substantive rank of chief superintendent, or in a higher rank, in a police force, as a central police officer or as a constable assigned to duty with the Scottish Crime Squad before the date on which the appointment shall take effect;

(b) he has been certified by a registered medical practitioner approved by the police authority to be in good health, of sound constitution and fitted both physically and mentally to perform the duties of the rank of deputy chief constable or, as the case may be, assistant chief constable.

(2) No person shall be qualified for appointment as superintendent or chief inspector in a police force unless he has had previous police experience in the rank of inspector.".

Qualifications for appointment of chief constable

7. In regulation 8(1) of the principal Regulations (qualifications for appointment of chief constable) for sub-paragraphs (a) and (d) there shall be substituted the following sub-paragraphs:–

"(a) is serving in a police force and has had at least 2 years' experience in the substantive rank of assistant chief constable, or in a higher rank, in a police force other than the force for which the appointment is required, before the date on which the appointment shall take effect;"; and

"(d) has not attained the age of 55 on or before the date on which the appointment shall take effect:

Provided that a person who has attained that age may be appointed if he has served in another police force as chief constable of that force;".

Supplementary rent allowance

8. In regulation 43(3) of the principal Regulations (supplementary rent allowance) for the sum "£8.33" in both places where it occurs there shall be substituted the sum "£13.92".

Removal allowance

9. In regulation 47(1)(d) of the principal Regulations (removal allowance) for the words "not exceeding 13 weeks" there shall be substituted the words "not exceeding 39 weeks".

Scales of pay

10. In Schedule 3 to the principal Regulations (scales of pay) for Table A and Table B there shall be substituted the Table A and the Table B respectively set out in Schedule 1 to these Regulations.

(a) 1964 c.48.

Dog handler's allowance

11. In paragraph 1(1) of Schedule 10 to the principal Regulations (dog handler's allowance) for the sums "£567" and "£771" there shall be substituted the sums "£612" and "£831" respectively.

Revocations

12. The Regulations specified in column 1 of Schedule 2 to these Regulations are revoked to the extent specified in column 3 of that Schedule.

New St. Andrew's House, Edinburgh
3rd November 1987

James Douglas-Hamilton
Parliamentary Under Secretary of State,
Scottish Office

SCHEDULE 1

Regulation 10

TABLE A

Rank	Before completing 1 year of service in the rank £ a year	After 1 year of service in the rank £ a year	After 2 years of service in the rank £ a year	After 3 years of service in the rank £ a year	After 4 years of service in the rank £ a year
Chief Inspector	17,364	17,850	18,336	18,825	19,317
Inspector	15,294	15,771	16,392	16,875	17,364
Sergeant	13,332	13,938	14,427	14,907	15,294

TABLE B

Reckonable service	Annual pay £
Before completing 1 year of service	8,352
After 1 year of service	8,931
After 2 years of service	10,512
After 3 years of service	10,761
After 4 years of service	11,118
After 5 years of service	11,499
After 6 years of service	11,868
After 7 years of service	12,234
After 8 years of service	12,597
After 12 years of service	13,332
After 15 years of service	13,938

Regulation 12

SCHEDULE 2
REVOCATIONS

(Regulations revoked)	(References)	(Extent of revocation)
The Police (Scotland) Amendment Regulations 1978	S.I. 1978/528	The whole Regulations
The Police (Scotland) Amendment Regulations 1980	S.I. 1980/1050	Regulation 6
The Police (Scotland) Amendment Regulations 1981	S.I. 1981/67	Regulation 5
The Police (Scotland) Amendment Regulations 1985	S.I. 1985/111	Regulation 6
The Police (Scotland) Amendment Regulations 1987	S.I. 1987/423	Regulations 6 and 8 and the Schedule

EXPLANATORY NOTE

(This note is not part of the Regulations)

These Regulations further amend the Police (Scotland) Regulations 1976 ("the principal Regulations"). They come into force on 10th December 1987 and have effect for the purposes of regulation 8 as from 1st February 1987 and of regulations 10 and 11 as from 1st September 1987 (retrospection being authorised by section 26(3) of the Police (Scotland) Act 1967).

Regulation 4 amends the definition of "public holiday" to include an extra day or days whenever Christmas Day, 26th December or New Year's Day falls on a Saturday or Sunday.

Regulation 5 amends the definition of a "police force" to include the Royal Ulster Constabulary.

Regulation 6 ensures that candidates for posts at deputy chief constable or assistant chief constable level should have completed two years' service in the rank of chief superintendent or above. It also provides for medical examinations for candidates for deputy chief constable and assistant chief constable posts.

Regulation 7 ensures that candidates for posts at chief constable level should have had at least two years' experience at deputy chief constable or assistant chief constable level in another force; experience as a central police officer or with the Scottish Crime Squad no longer qualifies. The age limit for candidates for chief constable posts who are not already chief constables is also clarified; a candidate is not eligible if, by the date of the appointment, such candidate has attained his 55th birthday.

Regulation 8 increases supplementary rent allowance from £8.33 per week to £13.92 per week.

Regulation 9 extends from 13 weeks to 39 weeks the period during which additional removal expenses may be paid at the discretion of the police authority once the initial period of 13 weeks provided for in the principal Regulations has expired.

Regulations 10 and 11 provide for increases in the rates of pay of police constables, sergeants, inspectors and chief inspectors and in the rates of the dog handler's allowance.

STATUTORY INSTRUMENTS

1987 No. 1915

COAL INDUSTRY

The Opencast Coal (Compulsory Rights and Rights of Way) (Forms) Regulations 1987

Made - - - -	*10th November 1987*
Laid before Parliament	*20th November 1987*
Coming into force	*11th December 1987*

The Secretary of State, in exercise of the powers conferred by sections 4, 15A(1), (5)(c) and (10) and 49(1) of the Opencast Coal Act 1958(**a**) ("the 1958 Act"), sections 7(2), 10(2), 11(1), 12, 15, 22 and 29 of the Acquisition of Land Act 1981(**b**) as applied by section 4(4A) of the 1958 Act(**c**) and paragraphs 2, 3, 6, 13 and 18 of Schedule 1 to the Acquisition of Land (Authorisation Procedure) (Scotland) Act 1947(**d**) as applied by section 4(5) and (8) of, and Part I of Schedule 2 to, the 1958 Act(**e**), and now vested in him(**f**), and of all other powers enabling him in that behalf, hereby makes the following Regulations:–

Citation and commencement

1.—(1) These Regulations may be cited as the Opencast Coal (Compulsory Rights and Rights of Way) (Forms) Regulations 1987.

(2) These Regulations shall come into force on 11th December 1987.

Interpretation

2. In these Regulations–
  (a) "the 1958 Act" means the Opencast Coal Act 1958; and
  (b) any reference to a numbered form includes a reference to a document in substantially the same form.

Prescribed forms: suspension of rights of way

3. Forms 1, 2 and 3 in Part I of the Schedule hereto are the prescribed forms for the purposes of subsections (1), (5)(c) and (10) respectively of section 15A of the 1958 Act.

Prescribed forms: compulsory rights orders

4. The forms set out in Part II of the Schedule hereto are hereby prescribed as follows:–
  (a) in relation to England and Wales–
    (i) forms 4 and 5 are the prescribed forms for the purposes of sections 10(2) and 11(1) respectively of the Acquisition of Land Act 1981;

(**a**) 1958 c.69; section 15A is inserted by the Housing and Planning Act 1986 (c.63) and is set out in Schedule 8 to that Act as is a substituted form of section 15 of the 1958 Act.
(**b**) 1981 c. 67; *see* in particular the definition of "prescribed" in section 29(10).
(**c**) Section 4(4A) is inserted by paragraph 11(2) of Schedule 4 to the 1981 Act.
(**d**) 1947 c. 42.
(**e**) *See* in particular the definition of "prescribed" in paragraph 11 of Schedule 2.
(**f**) *See* the definition of "the Minister" in section 51 of the 1958 Act, S.I. 1969/1498 and 1970/1537.

(ii) form 6 (or in the case of a limited rights order, form 7) is the prescribed form for the purposes of section 12(**a**) of the said 1981 Act; and

(iii) forms 8 and 9 are the prescribed forms for the purposes of sections 15 and 22 respectively of the said 1981 Act;

(b) in relation to Scotland–

(i) forms 4 and 5 are the prescribed forms for the purposes of paragraphs 2 and 3(a) respectively of Schedule 1 to the Acquisition of Land (Authorisation Procedure) (Scotland) Act 1947(**b**);

(ii) form 6 (or, in the case of a limited rights order, form 7) is the prescribed form for the purposes of paragraph 3(b) of that Schedule; and

(iii) forms 8 and 9 are the prescribed forms for the purposes of paragraphs 6 and 13 respectively of that Schedule.

Prescribed particulars

5. The prescribed particulars for the purposes of section 15A(5)(c) of the 1958 Act are the particulars required to be included in a notice in form 2.

Revocation

6. The Opencast Coal (Authorisations and Compulsory Rights Orders) Regulations 1975(**c**) are hereby revoked; but any form prescribed by those regulations shall be deemed to be prescribed by these Regulations where an application or an order as the case may be has been made before the coming into force of these Regulations.

Nicholas Ridley
10th November 1987   One of Her Majesty's Principal Secretaries of State

---

SCHEDULE

Note

The singular has been used throughout these forms: where the plural is required it should be used.

PART I

RIGHTS OF WAY

Regulation 3   FORM 1

NEWSPAPER NOTICE OF AN APPLICATION FOR AN ORDER SUSPENDING A PUBLIC RIGHT OF WAY

OPENCAST COAL ACT 1958

.........RIGHT OF WAY APPLICATION 19... (*a*)

1. Notice is hereby given that the British Coal Corporation in connection with the working of coal by opencast operations propose to apply under section 15 of the Opencast Coal Act 1958 to the Secretary of State for an order suspending a non-vehicular right of way as described in the Schedule below (*b*).

2. Opencast planning permission for the working has been [applied for] [granted] (*c*).

(**a**) Section 12 in its relevant form is set out in section 29 of the said 1981 Act which also amends in relation to compulsory rights orders the relevant provisions of that Act.

(**b**) The provisions of Schedule 1 to the said 1947 Act are modified in their relation to compulsory rights orders by Part I of Schedule 2 to the 1958 Act.

(**c**) S.I. 1975/2054.

3. A copy of the application and of a map showing the right of way can be inspected at *(d)* between the hours of and *(e)* from to *(f)*.

4. [An alternative right of way for use by the public during the period for which the order will be in force will be made available as described in the Schedule below.] [No alternative right of way is to be made available.] *(c)*

5. Written objections, stating the grounds on which objections are made, may be sent by any person to the Secretary of State before *(g)* at *(h)*. If the [district council or county council] [local authority] *(i)* in whose area any part of the right of way lies objects and do not withdraw their objection the Secretary of State must arrange a public inquiry; if any other person objects and does not withdraw his objection he may arrange a public inquiry if he thinks fit.

SCHEDULE

[PART 1] *(j)*

RIGHT OF WAY TO BE SUSPENDED *(b)*

[PART 2

ALTERNATIVE RIGHT OF WAY] *(b)* *(j)*

Dated............................

[Signature of] an officer
authorised by the British
Coal Corporation.

Notes

(a) Insert an appropriate name relating to the location of the right of way.

(b) Give sufficient description for the route of the right of way to be identified without reference to a map.

(c) Use whichever version reflects the position.

(d) The Act requires the place to be "in the locality": it should therefore be within easy reach of people living near the right of way.

(e) Insert reasonable hours during the day.

(f) The dates between which the documents may be inspected should be inserted: it is desirable that the period given should not expire before the end of the period for making objections.

(g) Insert appropriate date: the minimum period is 28 days (i.e. clear days) from the date of the last newspaper notice, whether in the local newspaper or the appropriate Gazette.

(h) Insert address.

(i) Use the first version if the right of way is in England or Wales omitting reference to a county council if the right of way is wholly within a metropolitan county: the second if it is in Scotland.

(j) Omit where no alternative right of way is to be made available.

Regulations 3 and 5   FORM 2

NOTICE OF AN APPLICATION FOR AN ORDER SUSPENDING A PUBLIC RIGHT OF WAY TO BE AFFIXED TO A CONSPICUOUS OBJECT AT EITHER END OF RIGHT OF WAY

OPENCAST COAL ACT 1958

........RIGHT OF WAY APPLICATION 19... (a)

1. Notice is hereby given that the British Coal Corporation in connection with the working of coal by opencast operations propose to apply under section 15 of the Opencast Coal Act 1958 to the Secretary of State for an order suspending a non-vehicular right of way as described in the Schedule below (b).

2. Opencast planning permission for the working has been [applied for] [granted] (c).

3. A copy of the application and of a map showing the right of way can be inspected at   (d) between the hours of   and   (e) from   to   (f).

4. [An alternative right of way for use by the public during the period for which the order will be in force has been made available as described in the Schedule below.] [No alternative right of way is to be made available.] (c)

5. Written objections, stating the grounds on which objections are made, may be sent by any person to the Secretary of State before   (g) at   (h). If the [district council or county council] [local authority] (i) in whose area any part of the right of way lies objects and does not withdraw their objection the Secretary of State must arrange a public inquiry; if any other person objects and does not withdraw his objection he may arrange a public inquiry if he thinks fit.

SCHEDULE

[PART 1] (j)

RIGHT OF WAY TO BE SUSPENDED (b)

[PART 2

ALTERNATIVE RIGHT OF WAY] (b) (j)

Dated.............................   [Signature of] an officer
                                                    authorised by the British
                                                    Coal Corporation.

Notes

(a) Insert an appropriate name relating to the location of the right of way.

(b) Give sufficient description for the route of the right of way to be identified without reference to a map.

(c) Use whichever version reflects the position.

(d) The Act requires the place to be "in the locality": it should therefore be within easy reach of people living near the right of way.

(e) Insert reasonable hours during the day.

(f) The dates between which the documents may be inspected should be inserted: it is desirable that the period given should not expire before the end of the period for making objections.

(g) Insert appropriate date: the minimum period is 28 days (i.e. clear days) from the date of the last newspaper notice, whether in the local newspaper or the appropriate Gazette.

(h) Insert address.

(i) Use the first version if the right of way is in England or Wales omitting reference to a county council if the right of way is wholly within a metropolitan county: the second if it is in Scotland.

(j) Omit where no alternative right of way is to be made available.

FORM 3 Regulation 3

NOTICE OF MAKING OF AN ORDER SUSPENDING A RIGHT OR WAY

OPENCAST COAL ACT 1958

.........ORDER 19... (*a*)

1. Notice is given that on (*b*) the Secretary of State in the exercise of his powers under section 15 of the Opencast Coal Act 1958, on the application of the British Coal Corporation, made the (*a*) Order 19 suspending the right of way described below.

2. The order will come into operation on (*c*) and will suspend the right of way until the Secretary of State revokes the order.

[**2A.** An alternative right of way will be provided as described below.] (*d*)

3. A copy of the order and of the map to which it refers may be inspected at (*e*) between the hours of and (*f*) from to (*g*).

SUSPENDED RIGHT OF WAY (*h*)

[ALTERNATIVE RIGHT OF WAY] (*d*)

Dated............................. [Signature of] an officer
authorised by the British
Coal Corporation.

Notes

(*a*) Insert title of order as made.

(*b*) Give date on which the order was made.

(*c*) Give the date specified in the order.

(*d*) There is no obligation to include this paragraph but it may be included at the option of the British Coal Corporation.

(*e*) The place must be "in the locality": it should therefore be within easy reach of people living near the right of way.

(*f*) Insert reasonable hours during the day.

(*g*) The dates between which the order may be inspected should be inserted: they should allow a reasonable period for inspection, which period ought not to expire before the operative date of the order.

(*h*) Give sufficient description for the route of the right of way to be identified without reference to a map. The description need not be as detailed as on the application.

PART II
COMPULSORY RIGHTS ORDERS

Regulation 4   FORM 4

.........COMPULSORY RIGHTS ORDER 19... (a)

The British Coal Corporation in exercise of their powers under section 4 [and 8(1)] (b) [and 15(6)(d)] (c) of the Opencast Coal Act 1958 hereby make the following Order:–

1.   The British Coal Corporation, for the purpose of facilitating the working of coal by opencast operations, compulsorily acquire with effect from the date of entry specified in accordance with section 5(2) of the Opencast Coal Act 1958 temporary rights [of occupation] (d) and use of the land specified in [the] Schedule [1] hereto and delineated and shown   (e) on the map prepared in duplicate, signed by a duly authorised officer of the Corporation and marked "Map referred to in the   (a) Compulsory Rights Order 19   ".

2.   This Order shall have effect from the date on which it becomes operative for a period of (f) years.

3.   Opencast planning permission [has been applied for] [has been granted] [is deemed to have been granted] (g), at the time of making this Order.

4.   The [permission] [application for permission] (g) relates to land [to which this Order relates (h)] [which is contiguous to the land to which this Order relates (i)] [which is both land to which this Order relates and land which is contiguous to the land over which an alternative right of way is to be provided (j)].

[5.   This Order is limited to the acquisition of the rights specified in Schedule 2 hereto.] (b)

[6.   The land which is described in Schedule [2] [3] (g) hereto and shown   (e) on the map referred to in article 1 of this Order shall be made available during the period for which this Order is to have effect subject to the like rights, trusts and incidents as attach to such of the land referred to in Schedule 1 as forms part of [a common] [an open space] [a fuel or field garden allotment].] (k)

[7.   This Order includes land falling within special categories to which [Part III of the Acquisition of Land Act 1981 as applied by section 4(4A)] [Part III of Schedule 1 to the Acquisition of Land (Authorisation Procedure) (Scotland) Act 1947 as applied by section 4(5) and (8)] of the Opencast Coal Act 1958 applies, namely–

.... Number on map .... Description.] (l)

[8.   This Order includes land to which section 9(4) of the Opencast Coal Act 1958 applies (land formerly requisitioned under emergency powers), namely–

.... Number on map .... Description.] (m)

9.   This Order may be cited as the   (n) Compulsory Rights Order 19   .

Dated..............................   [Signature of] an officer
                                            authorised by the British
                                            Coal Corporation.

SCHEDULE [1]

Numbers on map	Description (extent, situation, category)	Owners or reputed owners	Lessees or reputed lessees	Occupiers and other persons directly concerned
(1)	(2)	(3)	(4)	(5)
(o)	(p)			(q)

[SCHEDULE 2

RIGHTS ACQUIRED] (r)

[SCHEDULE [2] [3]

EXCHANGE LAND] (s)

Notes

(a) Insert an appropriate name relating to the location of the land to be acquired.

(b) Omit except for a limited rights order.

(c) Omit except where the order is used to provide a right of way on land contiguous to the land for which opencast planning permission has been or will be granted.

(*d*) Omit if the order is only to provide a right of way.

(*e*) Refer to the colour or other marking used on the map to identify the land.

(*f*) Give the period not exceeding 20 years.

(*g*) Use the option which reflects the position.

(*h*) Use this option where the deletions have been made under both notes (*b*) and (*c*) indicating that the order is not limited to certain rights and does not acquire rights to grant a right of way.

(*i*) Use only when the order is used solely to provide a right of way as in note (*c*).

(*j*) Use when the order is used to acquire land for mining and contiguous land to provide a right of way as in note (*c*).

(*k*) Use the article only where the order confers rights over land of a description mentioned in the article.

(*l*) Use this article when the order confers rights over land of a special category and insert the appropriate description of the category.

(*m*) Use where the order confers rights over requisitioned land.

(*n*) Insert the name of the order.

(*o*) Column (1) need not be completed where the order relates only to one parcel of land. Where there are two or more parcels they should be numbered 1, 2 etc. on the map and referred to accordingly in column (1).

(*p*) The entry in this column should tell a reader roughly where the land is situated, but without reference to a map. A category should be mentioned where the land is of a description or category calling for the inclusion of article 6 or 7.

(*q*) The words "person directly concerned" are defined in section 5 of the 1958 Act. Anyone within that definition who does not fall to be named in column (3) or (4) should be named in this column.

(*r*) If the order is limited the Schedule should specify which of the rights set out in section 8 of the 1958 Act are conferred by the order.

(*s*) Insert a description of any land to be made available under article 6.

Regulation 4   FORM 5

NEWSPAPER NOTICE OF MAKING OF A COMPULSORY RIGHTS ORDER

OPENCAST COAL ACT 1958

.........COMPULSORY RIGHTS ORDER 19...(*a*)

1.   Notice is hereby given that the British Coal Corporation, in exercise of their powers under section 4 [and 8(1)] (*b*) [and 15(6)(d)] (*b*) of the Opencast Coal Act 1958, have made the   Compulsory Rights Order 19   (*a*).

2.   The Corporation are about to submit the order to the Secretary of State for confirmation and if confirmed the order will confer on the Corporation temporary rights of [occupation and] (*c*) use of the land described below for the purpose of facilitating the working of coal by opencast operations. [The operation of the order is limited to the interests and rights described below] (*b*) [The order [also] provides for an alternative right of way as described below on land contiguous to that to be used for mining for the effective period of the order] (*d*).

3.   A copy of the order and of the accompanying map may be seen between the hours of and   (*e*) from   to   (*f*) at   (*g*). Objections giving the grounds for objection to the order may be made in writing by any person directly concerned to the Secretary of State at   (*h*) before   (*i*).

4.   The order, as made, would have effect from its operative date for a period of   (*j*) years.

DESCRIPTION OF LAND (*k*)

[RIGHTS AND INTERESTS] (*b*)

[ALTERNATIVE RIGHT OF WAY] (*d*)

Dated.............................   [Signature of] an officer
                                          authorised by the British
                                          Coal Corporation.

Notes

(*a*) Insert the name of the order.

(*b*) Omit if not included in the order.

(*c*) Omit if the order is only to provide a right of way.

(*d*) Omit unless the order is used to provide an alternative right of way. Omit "also" from paragraph 2 where the sole purpose is to provide the footpath.

(*e*) Insert reasonable hours during the day.

(*f*) Insert dates giving a reasonable time for inspection: it is desirable that the period given should not expire before the end of the period for making objections.

(*g*) The place must be in the locality: it should therefore be within easy reach of persons living near the site.

(*h*) Give address.

(*i*) The date should be not less than 21 days (i.e. clear days) from the date of the first newspaper notice: it is desirable that this date should tie in with the date given in the notice served on persons directly concerned.

(*j*) Give the period specified in the order.

(*k*) The description should identify and locate the parcel of land.

FORM 6   Regulation 4

NOTICE TO PERSONS DIRECTLY CONCERNED
OF THE MAKING OF A COMPULSORY RIGHTS ORDER
OTHER THAN A LIMITED RIGHTS ORDER

OPENCAST COAL ACT 1958

NOTICE OF MAKING OF .... COMPULSORY RIGHTS ORDER 19... (*a*)

Dear Sir/Madam,

You are informed that the British Coal Corporation have made the   Compulsory Rights Order 19   (*a*) and are about to submit it to the Secretary of State for confirmation. The British Coal Corporation require the powers granted by the order in connection with the working of coal by opencast coal operations.

The effect of the order will be to give the British Coal Corporation rights [to grant a non-vehicular right of way to the public over] (*b*) [similar to those of a [freeholder] [person with dominium utile] (*c*) to enter and occupy] the land described below, in which you are believed to have an interest, [to the exclusion of other persons] (*d*) from the date of entry for the remainder of the period during which the order is effective and to carry out operations for extracting coal. The order will be effective for   (*e*) years from the operative date which unless varied by the Secretary of State [or otherwise determined by section 6 of the Statutory Orders (Special Procedure) Act 1946] (*f*) will be the date when notice of confirmation is first published in a local newspaper in accordance with [section 15 of the Acquisition of Land Act 1981] [paragraph 6 of Schedule 1 to the Acquisition of Land (Authorisation Procedure) (Scotland) Act 1947] (*c*). The rights which the order confers on the Corporation are set out in section 5(4) and (5) of the Opencast Coal Act 1958 (reproduced below).

If you wish to object to the order you may do so by setting out your grounds for objection in writing and sending them to the Secretary of State at   (*g*) before   (*h*)

DESCRIPTION OF LAND OVER WHICH RIGHTS ARE TO BE ACQUIRED (*i*)

Dated..............................   [Signature of] an officer
    authorised by the British
    Coal Corporation.

The text of section 5(4) and (5) of the 1958 Act to be printed here.

Notes

   (*a*) Insert name of order.

   (*b*) Use only where the order provides for an alternative right of way.

   (*c*) Use the first alternative if the land is in England or Wales: the second if it is in Scotland.

   (*d*) Use where the order acquires rights for actual occupation.

   (*e*) Give the period stated in the order.

   (*f*) Omit unless the order relates to land of a description mentioned in one of the variants of paragraph 2 in Form 9.

   (*g*) Insert address.

   (*h*) The date must not be less than 21 days (i.e. clear days) from the service of the notice: it is desirable that this date should tie in with the expiry date for objections given in the newspaper notice.

   (*i*) The description should identify and locate the parcel of land.

Regulation 4   FORM 7

NOTICE TO PERSONS DIRECTLY CONCERNED OF THE MAKING OF A LIMITED COMPULSORY RIGHTS ORDER

OPENCAST COAL ACT 1958

NOTICE OF MAKING OF .... COMPULSORY
RIGHTS ORDER 19... (*a*)

Dear Sir/Madam,

You are informed that the British Coal Corporation have made the   Compulsory Rights Order
19   (*a*) and are about to submit it to the Secretary of State for confirmation. The British Coal
Corporation require the powers granted by the order in connection with the working of coal by opencast
coal operations.

The effect of the order will be to give the British Coal Corporation power to acquire and exercise the
rights set out below over the land described below, in which you are believed to have an interest, from
the date of entry for the remainder of the period during which the order is effective. The order will
be effective for   (*b*) years from the operative date which will be [when notice of its confirmation
is published in a local newspaper] [or otherwise determined by section 6 of the Statutory Orders (Special
Procedures) Act 1946]. (*c*).

If you wish to object to the order you may do so by setting out your grounds in writing and sending
them to the Secretary of State at   (*d*) before   (*e*).

Rights in land to be acquired (*f*)

Land over which rights are to be acquired (*g*)

Dated............................   [Signature of] an officer
                                          authorised by the British
                                          Coal Corporation.

Notes

(*a*) Insert name of order.

(*b*) Give the period stated in the order.

(*c*) Use the first alternative unless the land is subject to special parliamentary procedure.

(*d*) Insert address.

(*e*) The date must not be less than 21 days (i.e. clear days) from the service of the notice: it is desirable
that this date should tie in with the expiry date for objections given in the newspaper notice.

(*f*) Specify the actual rights.

(*g*) The description should identify and locate the parcel of land.

FORM 8 Regulation 4

NEWSPAPER NOTICE
AND NOTICE TO BE SERVED ON PERSONS
DIRECTLY CONCERNED OF CONFIRMATION
OF ORDER

OPENCAST COAL ACT 1958

NOTICE OF CONFIRMATION OF .... COMPULSORY RIGHTS
ORDER 19... (*a*)

1. Notice is hereby given that the Compulsory Rights Order 19 (*a*) which was made by the British Coal Corporation in exercise of their powers under section 4 [and 8(1)] [and 15(6)(d)] (*b*) of the Opencast Coal Act 1958 has been confirmed [with modifications] (*c*) by the Secretary of State under [section 13 of the Acquisition of Land Act 1981] [paragraph 4 of Schedule 1 to the Acquisition of Land (Authorisation Procedure) (Scotland) Act 1947]. (*d*)

2. The order relates to land described below.

3. Copies of the order together with an accompanying map may be seen at (*e*) between and (*f*) from to (*g*).

[**4.** A person aggrieved by the order may, by application to the [High Court] [Court of Session] (*d*) within six weeks from [the date of this notice] (*h*), question its validity on either or both of the following grounds:

(*a*) that the rights granted to the British Coal Corporation by the order are not empowered to be granted;

(*b*) that a relevant statutory requirement has not been complied with.] (*i*)

[**4.** The order as confirmed is subject to special parliamentary procedure and will become operative as provided by the Statutory Orders (Special Procedure) Act 1945. Unless the order is confirmed by Act of Parliament under section 6 of that Act, a person aggrieved by the order may, by application to the [High Court] [Court of Session] (*d*) within six weeks from the operative date of the order, question its validity on either or both of the following grounds:

(*a*) that the rights granted to the British Coal Corporation by the order are not empowered to be granted:

(*b*) that a relevant statutory requirement has not been complied with.]

DESCRIPTION OF LAND TO WHICH THE ORDER RELATES (*j*)

Dated.............................

[Signature of] an officer
authorised by the British
Coal Corporation.

Notes

(*a*) Insert name of order.

(*b*) Follow the form of the order.

(*c*) Omit if no modifications were made by the Secretary of State.

(*d*) Use the first alternative if the land is in England or Wales; the second if it is in Scotland.

(*e*) Ideally this should be the same place where deposits were made on making the order.

(*f*) Insert reasonable hours during the day.

(*g*) Insert a reasonable period.

(*h*) If not the first newspaper publication insert the date of the first publication.

(*i*) Use the first alternative paragraph 4 unless the land is subject to special parliamentary procedure.

(*j*) The description should identify and locate the parcel of land.

Regulation 4   FORM 9

NEWSPAPER NOTICE OF GIVING OF CERTIFICATE UNDER PART III OF THE ACQUISITION OF LAND ACT 1981 OR PART III OF SCHEDULE 1 TO THE ACQUISITION OF LAND (AUTHORISATION PROCEDURE) (SCOTLAND) ACT 1947

OPENCAST COAL ACT 1958

1. The   Compulsory Rights Order 19   (*a*), which has been submitted by the British Coal Corporation to the Secretary of State for confirmation includes the land described in the Schedule below.

[**2.** (*b*)   This land was acquired by   (*c*) for the purposes of their undertaking and the Secretary of State is satisfied that [it is used] [an interest is held in it] (*d*) for the purposes of the carrying on of their undertaking and has certified pursuant to [section 16 of the Acquisition of Land Act 1981] [paragraph 10 of Schedule 1 to the Acquisition of Land (Authorisation Procedure) (Scotland) Act 1947(*e*)] [that it can be purchased and not replaced without serious detriment to the carrying on of the undertaking] [that if purchased it can be replaced by other land belonging to, or available for acquisition by, the undertakers without serious detriment to the carrying on of the undertaking]] (*d*).

[**2.**   This land [is] [forms part of] [a common] [an open space] [a fuel or field garden allotment] (*d*) and the Secretary of State has certified pursuant to [section 19 of the Acquisition of Land Act 1981] [paragraph 11 of Schedule 1 to the Acquisition of Land (Authorisation Procedure) (Scotland) Act 1947] (*e*) that other land (not less in area) and equally advantageous to any persons whose rights are affected and the public will be made available.]

[**2.**   This land [is] [forms part of] [is the site of] (*d*) an ancient monument or other object of archaeological interest and the Secretary of State has certified pursuant to section 20 of the Acquisition of Land Act 1981 that the British Coal Corporation have entered into an undertaking with the Secretary of State to observe such conditions as to the use of the land as are in his opinion requisite having regard to the nature thereof.]

3.   A map showing the land to which the certificate relates and any land proposed to be made available during the period for which the order is to have effect may be inspected at   (*f*) between the hours of   and (*g*) from   to   (*h*).

4.   The certificate becomes operative on the date on which this notice is first published; but a person aggrieved may, by application to the [High Court] [Court of Session] (*e*) within six weeks from that date, question its validity on the grounds that a relevant statutory requirement has not been complied with.

SCHEDULE

LAND TO WHICH THE CERTIFICATE RELATES (*i*)

Dated ....   [Signature of] an officer
                                                   authorised by the British
                                                   Coal Corporation.

Notes

(*a*) Insert the name of the order.

(*b*) Use whichever form of paragraph 2 is appropriate.

(*c*) Name the statutory undertakers.

(*d*) Use whichever form of words is appropriate.

(*e*) Use the first alternative if the land is in England or Wales; the second if it is in Scotland.

(*f*) The place should be "in the locality": it should therefore be within easy reach of persons living in the area affected.

(*g*) Insert reasonable hours during the day.

(*h*) Insert a reasonable period: it is desirable that this should not expire before the end of the period for making an application to Court.

(*i*) Insert description of the land to which the certificates relates.

EXPLANATORY NOTE

(This note is not part of the Regulations)

These Regulations prescribe the forms of certain orders under the Opencast Coal Act 1958 and the forms of the notices and advertisements to be given in connection with making and confirming such orders. The orders in question are orders conferring compulsorily rights of temporary occupation on the British Coal Corporation to facilitate opencast working and orders temporarily suspending non-vehicular rights of way for the same purpose.

The Regulations replace the Opencast Coal (Authorisations and Compulsory Rights Orders) Regulations 1975. The new regulations reproduce with modifications those of the forms prescribed by the 1975 regulations which remain relevant following the amendment of the Opencast Coal Act 1958 by the Housing and Planning Act 1986. Transitional provision is made in Regulation 6 for the continued use of existing forms.

STATUTORY INSTRUMENTS

1987 No. 1916

VALUE ADDED TAX

The Value Added Tax (General) (Amendment) (No. 3) Regulations 1987

Made - - - -	*11th November 1987*
Laid before the House of Commons	*18th November 1987*
Coming into force	*1st January 1988*

The Commissioners of Customs and Excise, in exercise of the powers conferred on them by sections 14(6), 14(9), 16(7), 19(2), paragraph 14 of Schedule 1 and paragraphs 2(1), 2(5) and 6(4) of Schedule 7 to the Value Added Tax Act 1983(**a**) and of all other powers enabling them in that behalf, hereby make the following Regulations:

Citation and commencement

1. These Regulations may be cited as the Value Added Tax (General) (Amendment) (No. 3) Regulations 1987 and shall come into force on 1st January 1988.

Revocations

2. Regulation 12(a) of the Value Added Tax (General) Regulations 1985 (Amendment) Regulations 1985(**b**) and regulation 4 of the Value Added Tax (General) (Amendment) Regulatio s 1986(**c**) are revoked.

3. The Value Added Tax (General) Regulations 1985(**d**) shall be amended in accordance with the following provisions of these Regulations.

4. In regulation 4 –

    (a) in paragraph (1), for the reference to "paragraph 3 or 4 of Schedule 1" there shall be substituted a reference to "paragraph 3(1) or 4(1) of Schedule 1" and for the reference to "paragraph 5 or 11(1)(b) of the said Schedule" there shall be substituted a reference to "paragraph 5, 11(1)(b) or 11A(**e**) of the said Schedule".

    (b) in paragraph (3), in the reference to "paragraph 7, 8, 9 or 10 of Schedule 1" there shall be deleted the reference to "paragraph 8" and for the reference to "21 days" there shall be substituted a reference to "30 days".

(**a**) 1983 c.55; paragraph 6(4) of Schedule 7 was amended by section 16(1) of the Finance Act 1984 (c.43).
(**b**) S.I. 1985/1650.   (**c**) S.I. 1986/71.   (**d**) S.I. 1985/886 was amended by S.I. 1985/1650, 1986/71, 305, 1987/150, 510.   (**e**) Paragraph 11A of Schedule 1 to the Value Added Tax Act 1983 (c.55) was inserted by section 13(4) of the Finance Act 1987 (c.16).

(c) for paragraph (4), there shall be substituted the following:

"(4) Every notification by a registered person under paragraph 7 of Schedule 1 to the Act shall be made in writing to the Commissioners stating the date upon which he ceased to make taxable supplies.".

(d) for paragraph (6), there shall be substituted the following:

"(6) An application under paragraph (5) of this regulation shall constitute notification under paragraph 7 of Schedule 1 to the Act, or a request under paragraph 9 of Schedule 1 to the Act.".

5. Regulations 5, 6 and 7 are revoked.

6. For regulation 8, there shall be substituted the following:

"**8.** Where a person registered under paragraph 5 or 11(1)(b) of Schedule 1 to the Act no longer intends to make taxable supplies in the course or furtherance of his business he shall notify that matter to the Commissioners within 30 days of forming that intention.".

7. In regulation 45(d), after the words "zero-rating provisions" there shall be inserted the words "of subsections (6) and (7) of section 16".

8. In regulation 46(a), for the words "taxable person" there shall be substituted the words "taxable person importing the goods in the course of his business".

9. In regulation 58 –

(a) for paragraph (3), there shall be substituted the following:

"(3) Save as the Commissioners may otherwise allow, where for the purposes of this Part of these Regulations the Commissioners have made a requirement of any person pursuant to regulation 63 –

(a) then the period in respect of which taxable supplies were being made by the person who died or became incapacitated shall end on the day previous to the date when death or incapacity took place; and

(b) a return made on his behalf shall be furnished in respect of that period no later than the last day of the month next following the end of that period; and

(c) the next period shall start on the day following the aforesaid period and it shall end, and all subsequent periods shall begin and end, on the dates previously determined under regulation 58(1).".

(b) in paragraph 4(c), after the reference to "paragraph 11(1)(b)" insert "or paragraph 11A".

10. In regulation 62 –

for paragraph (1), there shall be substituted the following:

"(1) Subject to paragraph (1A) of this regulation and save as the Commissioners may otherwise allow or direct either generally or specially, a person claiming deduction of input tax under section 14(2) of the Act shall do so on the return furnished by him for the prescribed accounting period in which the tax became chargeable.

(1A) At the time of claiming deduction of input tax in accordance with paragraph (1) of this regulation, a person shall, if the claim is in respect of –

(a) a supply from another taxable person, hold the document which is required to be provided under regulation 12;

(b) a supply under section 7(1) of the Act, hold the relative invoice from the supplier;

(c) an importation of goods, hold a document showing the claimant as importer, consignee or owner and showing the amount of tax charged on the goods and authenticated or issued by the proper officer; or

(d) goods which have been removed from warehouse, hold a document authenticated or issued by the proper officer showing the claimant's particulars and the amount of tax charged on the goods;

Provided that where the Commissioners so direct, either generally or in relation to particular cases or classes of cases, a claimant shall hold, instead of the document or invoice (as the case may require) specified in sub-paragraph (a), (b), (c) or (d) above, such other documentary evidence of the charge to tax as the Commissioners may direct.".

11. In regulation 65 –

for paragraph (1), there shall be substituted the following:

"(1) If upon written demand a person neglects or refuses to pay tax, or any amount recoverable as if it were tax, which he is required to pay under the Act or any regulation made thereunder, a Collector or an officer of rank not below that of Senior Executive Officer may distrain on the goods and chattels of that person and by warrant signed by him direct any authorised person to levy such distress, provided that where an amount of tax is due under paragraph 4(9) of Schedule 7 to the Act (other than an amount assessed as due under paragraph 4(1) of the said Schedule upon failure by a person to make a return) no distress shall be levied until 30 days after that amount became due.".

12. In the Schedule to the Regulations –

(a) for the form numbered 1 there shall be substituted the form numbered 1 in the Schedule hereto; and

(b) for the form numbered 3 there shall be substituted the form numbered 3 in the Schedule hereto.

King's Beam House
Mark Lane
LONDON
EC3R 7HE
11th November 1987

Peter Jefferson Smith
Commissioner of Customs and Excise

Form No.1.   **SCHEDULE**   Regulation 4(1)

VALUE ADDED TAX
Application for Registration

HM Customs
and Excise

For official use

Date of receipt	1
Local office code and registration number	
Name	
Trade name	

Taxable turnover	E D R	D	M	Y	Stagger	Status

	Rept	Vol	Oversize name address	Computer user	Group Div	Intg	Overseas

		D	M	Y	
Bn					

You should read the notes opposite
before you answer these questions.
Please write clearly in ink.

Applicant and business

1 Full name

2 Trading name

3 Address

Phone no.

Postcode

4 Status of business

Limited company ☐   Company incorporation certificate no. [   ] and date [day] [month] [19 year]

Sole proprietor ☐   Partnership ☐   Other- specify [   ]

5 Business activity [   ]   Trade classification [   ]

6 Computer user ☐

7 Date of first taxable supply [day] [month] [19 year]   Expected value of taxable supplies in the next 12 months £ [   ]

Repayments of VAT

Bank sorting code and account no.   National Girobank account no.

8 ☐

Compulsory registrations

9 Date from which you have to be registered   day   month   year   [| | 19]

10 Exemption from compulsory registration   [ ]

expected value of zero-rated supplies in the next 12 months   £ [ ]

Other types of registration

11 Taxable supplies below registration limits   [ ]

value of taxable supplies in the last 12 months   £ [ ]

12 No taxable supplies made yet   [ ]

(a) expected annual value of taxable supplies   £ [ ]

(b) expected date of first taxable supply   day   month   year   [| | 19]

Business changes and transfers

13 Business transferred as a going concern   [ ]

(a) date of transfer or change of legal status   day   month   year   [| | 19]

(b) name of previous owner   [ ]

(c) previous VAT registration number (if known)   [ ]

14 Transfer of VAT registration number   [ ]

Related businesses

15 Other VAT registrations   Yes [ ]   No [ ]

Declaration   You must complete this declaration.

16

I _____

(Full name in BLOCK LETTERS)

declare that all the entered details and information in any accompanying documents are correct and complete.

Signature _____ Date _____

Proprietor [ ]   Partner [ ]   Director [ ]   Company Secretary [ ]   Authorised Official [ ]   Trustee [ ]

For official use

Registration	Obligatory	Exemption	Voluntary	Intending	Transfer of Regn. no.
Approved –Initial/Date					
Refused – Initial/Date					
Form Issued – Initial/Date	VAT 9/ Other	VAT 8	VAT 7	Letter	Approval Letter

VAT1 F3733 (FEBRUARY 1986)   Printed in the UK for HMSO   Dd 8858099   5924

Form No.3   Regulation 4(5)

Value Added Tax
Transfer of a Business as a Going Concern
Application for Re-allocation
of a VAT Registration Number

HM Customs
and Excise

Both parts of this application form must be filled in.

Please fill in this part if you are the new owner

Please fill in this part if you are the previous owner

New owner part:

*I/we took over a business as a going concern on

date _____ 19 _____

from _____
                    (name of previous owner)

*I/we *enclose/have already returned Form VAT 1, and apply to use the previous owner's VAT registration number

|___|___|___|___|___|___|___|___|___|

If the application is granted*I/we agree:

• to send *my/our first VAT return to Customs and Excise with all the VAT due for the whole period covered by the return

• to send in any returns due from but not made by the previous owner

• to pay Customs and Excise, when asked, any VAT due on supplies made by the previous owner before the business was transferred - including any VAT on stocks and assets kept by the previous owner

• that any return made in the previous owner's name for a period after the transfer date will be regarded as made by *me/us

• that any payment made by Customs and Excise to the previous owner before the reallocation of the registration number will satisfy any right *I/we have to that money.

Signature(s) _____

_____

(Proprietor, partners, director, company secretary)

date _____ 19 _____

*delete as necessary

Previous owner part:

*I/we transferred a business as a going concern on

date _____ 19 _____

to _____
                    (name of new owner)

From that date *I am/we are no longer liable or eligible to be registered or *I/we withdraw *my/our request for voluntary registration. *I/we agree to the VAT registration number shown opposite being allocated to the new owner.

If the application is granted *I/we declare that:

• the new owner will be entitled to reclaim any input tax which *I/we could have reclaimed if the registration number had not been transferred

• any payment made by Customs and Excise to the new owner will satisfy any right *I/we have to that money

• *I/we have retained stocks and assets valued at £ _____ ,including VAT.

Signature(s) _____

_____

(Proprietor, partners, director, company secretary, executor)

date _____ 19 _____

*delete as necessary

III/1x

EXPLANATORY NOTE

(This note is not part of the Regulations)

These Regulations which come into force on 1st January 1988 amend and consolidate various provisions of the Value Added Tax (General) Regulations 1985.

Regulation 4 which modifies regulations 4(1), 4(3) and 4(4) to reflect amendments to Schedule 1 of the Value Added Tax Act 1983 introduced by section 13, 14 and Schedule 16 of the Finance Act 1987 is designed to simplify the requirements for VAT registration and deregistration. The amendment to regulation 4(6) is for clarification.

Regulation 5 revokes regulations 5, 6 and 7 which became redundant upon the coming into force of the Value Added Tax (General) (Amendment) (No. 2) Regulations 1987 on 1st April 1987.

Regulation 6 amends regulation 8 by introducing a specified time limit of thirty days, consistent with section 14 Finance Act 1987, by which a person who has been granted discretionary registration must notify the Commissioners that he no longer intends to make taxable supplies by way of business.

Regulations 7 and 8 amend regulations 45 and 46 and clarify the entitlement to relief from payment of tax on re-importation of goods by non-taxable and taxable persons.

Regulation 9 amends regulation 58(3) following the repeal of paragraph 12 to Schedule 7 of the Value Added Tax Act 1983 consequent on the coming into force of the Insolvency Act 1985. It also amends regulation 58(4)(c) to reflect the amendment to Schedule 1 of the Value Added Tax Act 1983 introduced by Section 13(4) of the Finance Act 1987.

Regulation 10 amends regulation 62 so as to separate and clarify the provisions regarding the timing and evidence of claims to input tax by virtue of sections 14(6) and 14(9) of the Value Added Tax Act 1983.

Regulation 11 amends and re-enacts regulation 65(1) by consolidating previous amendments and by making it a requirement that the demand to pay tax be written. It also removes the requirement for the demand to be signed.

STATUTORY INSTRUMENTS

1987 No. 1919

INSOLVENCY

COMPANIES

INDIVIDUALS, ENGLAND AND WALES

The Insolvency (Amendment) Rules 1987

Made - - - -	*9th November 1987*
Laid before Parliament	*26th November 1987*
Coming into force -	*11th January 1988*

The Lord Chancellor, in the exercise of his powers under sections 411 and 412 of the Insolvency Act 1986(a), with the concurrence of the Secretary of State, and after consulting the committee existing for that purpose under section 413 of that Act, hereby makes the following Rules:

Citation and commencement

1. These Rules may be cited as the Insolvency (Amendment) Rules 1987 and shall come into force on 11th January 1988, and that day is referred to in these Rules as "the commencement date".

Interpretation

2.—(1) In these Rules references to "the principal Rules" are to the Insolvency Rules 1986(b) and a Rule or Schedule or Form referred to by number means the Rule or Schedule or Form so numbered in the principal Rules.

(2) These Rules shall be read and construed as one with the principal Rules.

Application

3.—(1) Subject to paragraph (2), the principal Rules have effect in relation to insolvency proceedings to which the principal Rules apply by virtue of Rule 13.14 with the amendments set out in the Schedule to these Rules.

(2) The principal Rules as so amended apply to all such proceedings on and after the commencement date whenever those proceedings were commenced.

(3) Rule 4.223-CVL as so amended also applies to any winding up as is mentioned in paragraph 4(1) of Schedule 11 to the Insolvency Act 1986 on and after the commencement date.

(a) 1986 c.45.
(b) S.I. 1986/1925.

Dated 6th November 1987   *Mackay of Clashfern, C.*

I concur,
Dated 9th November 1987   *Francis Maude*
                                            Parliamentary Under-Secretary of State,
                                            Department of Trade and Industry

SCHEDULE   Rule 3(1)

PART 1

AMENDMENT OF THE PRINCIPAL RULES

SECTION 1: AMENDMENT OF INTRODUCTORY PROVISIONS

Amendment of Rule 0.2

1. For Rule 0.2 there shall be substituted the following:–

"Construction and interpretation

0.2.—(1) In these Rules–

"the Act" means the Insolvency Act 1986 (any reference to a numbered section being to a section of that Act);

"the Companies Act" means the Companies Act 1985;

"the Rules" means the Insolvency Rules 1986.

(2) Subject to paragraph (1), Part 13 of the Rules has effect for their interpretation and application.".

Amendment of Rule 0.3

2. In paragraph (2) of Rule 0.3 there shall be inserted at the beginning the words "Rule 3.1 applies to all receivers to whom Part III of the Act applies and the remainder of".

SECTION 2: AMENDMENT OF PART I OF THE RULES

Amendment of Rule 1.10

3. In subparagraph (a) of paragraph (1) of Rule 1.10 after the word "them" there shall be inserted the words ", with the addition, where the company is subject to an administration order, of the names and addresses of the company's preferential creditors (defined in section 4(7)), with the amounts of their respective claims".

Amendment of Rule 1.12

4. In paragraph (3) of Rule 1.12 after the words "Rule 1.3" there shall be inserted the words "(and, where relevant, Rule 1.10)".

Amendment of Rule 1.20

5. In paragraph (1) of Rule 1.20 after the words "one-half" there shall be inserted the words "in value" and there shall be added the following subparagraph:–

"The value of members is determined by reference to the number of votes conferred on each member by the company's articles.".

SECTION 3: AMENDMENT OF PART 2 OF THE RULES

Amendment of Rule 2.6

6. For subparagraph (a) of paragraph (2) of Rule 2.6 there shall be substituted the following:–

"(a) on any person who has appointed, or is or may be entitled to appoint, an administrative receiver of the company;".

Insertion of Rule 2.6A

7. After Rule 2.6 there shall be inserted the following rule:–

"Notice to sheriff, etc

2.6A. The petitioner shall forthwith after filing the petition give notice of its presentation to–

(a) any sheriff or other officer who to his knowledge is charged with an execution or other legal process against the company or its property, and

(b) any person who to his knowledge has distrained against the company or its property.".

Amendment of Rule 2.7

8.—(1) In paragraph (4) of Rule 2.7 there shall be inserted at the beginning the words "Subject to paragraph (4A),".

(2) After paragraph (4) of Rule 2.7 there shall be inserted the following paragraph:–

"(4A) In the case of a person who–
(a) is an authorised institution or former authorised institution within the meaning of the Banking Act 1987,
(b) has appointed, or is or may be entitled to appoint, an administrative receiver of the company, and
(c) has not notified an address for service,
the proper address is the address of an office of that person where, to the knowledge of the petitioner, the company maintains a bank account or, where no such office is known to the petitioner, the registered office of that person, or, if there is no such office, his usual or last known address.".

Amendment of Rule 2.9

9. For subparagraph (c) of paragraph (1) of Rule 2.9 there shall be substituted the following:–
"(c) any person who has appointed, or is or may be entitled to appoint, an administrative receiver of the company;".

Amendment of Rule 2.10

10. For subparagraph (a) of paragraph (3) of Rule 2.10 there shall be substituted the following:–
"(a) to any person who appointed, or is or may be entitled to appoint, an administrative receiver of the company;".

Amendment of Rule 2.11

11.—(1) In paragraph (1) of Rule 2.11 for the word "If" there shall be substituted the word "Where".

(2) In paragraph (4) of Rule 2.11 for the words "instructions for" to the end there shall be substituted the words "the forms required for the preparation of the statement of affairs".

Amendment of Rule 2.16

12.—(1) In Rule 2.16 the existing paragraph shall be numbered (1) and for subparagraph (f) of that paragraph there shall be substituted the following:–
"(f) the manner in which the affairs and business of the company–
(i) have, since the date of the administrator's appointment, been managed and financed, and
(ii) will, if the administrator's proposals are approved, continue to be managed and financed; and".

(2) In Rule 2.16 after the existing paragraph there shall be added the following paragraph:–

"(2) Where the administrator intends to apply to the court under section 18 for the administration order to be discharged at a time before he has sent a statement of his proposals to creditors in accordance with section 23(1), he shall, at least 10 days before he makes such an application, send to all creditors of the company (so far as he is aware of their addresses) a report containing the information required by paragraph (1)(a)–(f)(i) of this Rule.".

Amendment of Rule 2.19

13.—(1) In paragraph (4) of Rule 2.19 the words "At least 21 days'" shall be omitted.

(2) After paragraph (4) of Rule 2.19 there shall be inserted the following paragraph:–
"(4A) Except in relation to a meeting summoned under section 23(1) or 25(2), at least 21 days' notice of the meeting shall be given.".

Amendment of Rule 2.28

14.—(1) In paragraph (1) of Rule 2.28 there shall be inserted at the beginning the words "Subject to paragraph (1A),".

(2) After paragraph (1) of Rule 2.28 there shall be inserted the following paragraph:–

"(1A) Any resolution is invalid if those voting against it include more than half in value of the creditors to whom notice of the meeting was sent and who are not, to the best of the chairman's belief, persons connected with the company.".

Amendment of Rule 2.29

15. For Rule 2.29 there shall be substituted the following:–

"Reports and notices under sections 23 and 25

2.29. Any report or notice by the administrator of the result of a creditors' meeting held under section 23 or 25 shall have annexed to it details of the proposals which were considered by the meeting and of the revisions and modifications to the proposals which were so considered.".

Amendment of Rule 2.33

16. For paragraph (2) of Rule 2.33 there shall be substituted the following:–

"(2) No person may act as a member of the committee unless and until he has agreed to do so and, unless the relevant proxy or authorisation contains a statement to the contrary, such agreement may be given by his proxy-holder or representative under section 375 of the Companies Act present at the meeting establishing the committee.

(2A) The administrator's certificate of the committee's due constitution shall not issue unless and until at least 3 of the persons who are to be members of the committee have agreed to act.".

Amendment of Rule 2.37

17. In paragraph (2) of Rule 2.37 there shall be added at the end the words ", and for this purpose any proxy or any authorisation under section 375 of the Companies Act in relation to any meeting of creditors of the company shall, unless it contains a statement to the contrary, be treated as a letter of authority to act generally signed by or on behalf of the committee-member".

Amendment of Rule 2.43

18. In paragraph (2) of Rule 2.43 for the words from "a statement incorporating" to the end there shall be substituted the words "a copy of any proposed resolution on which a decision is sought, which shall be set out in such a way that agreement with or dissent from each separate resolution may be indicated by the recipient on the copy so sent".

Insertion of Rule 2.46A

19. After Rule 2.46 there shall be inserted the following rule:–

"Formal defects

2.46A. The acts of the creditors' committee established for any administration are valid notwithstanding any defect in the appointment, election or qualifications of any member of the committee or any committee-member's representative or in the formalities of its establishment.".

Amendment of Rule 2.47

20. For paragraph (7) of Rule 2.47 there shall be substituted the following:–

"(7) Where there are joint administrators, it is for them to agree between themselves as to how the remuneration payable should be apportioned. Any dispute arising between them may be referred–
   (a) to the court, for settlement by order, or
   (b) to the creditors' committee or a meeting of creditors, for settlement by resolution.

(8) If the administrator is a solicitor and employs his own firm, or any partner in it, to act on behalf of the company, profit costs shall not be paid unless this is authorised by the creditors' committee, the creditors or the court.".

Amendment of Rule 2.49

21. In paragraph (4) of Rule 2.49 after the word "appearing" in both places where it occurs there shall be inserted the words "or being represented".

Amendment of Rule 2.55

22. In Rule 2.55 for the words "original appointment of an administrator" there shall be substituted the words "administration order".

SECTION 4: AMENDMENT OF PART 3 OF THE RULES

Amendment of Rule 3.1

23. For Rule 3.1 there shall be substituted the following:–

"Acceptance and confirmation of acceptance of appointment

3.1.—(1) Where two or more persons are appointed as joint receivers or managers of a company's property under powers contained in an instrument, the acceptance of such an appointment shall be made by each of them in accordance with section 33 as if that person were a sole appointee, but the joint appointment takes effect only when all such persons have so accepted and is then deemed to have been made at the time at which the instrument of appointment was received by or on behalf of all such persons.

(2) Subject to the next paragraph, where a person is appointed as the sole or joint receiver of a company's property under powers contained in an instrument, the appointee shall, if he accepts the appointment, within 7 days confirm his acceptance in writing to the person appointing him.

(3) Paragraph (2) does not apply where an appointment is accepted in writing.

(4) Any acceptance or confirmation of acceptance of appointment as a receiver or manager of a company's property, whether under the Act or the Rules, may be given by any person (including, in the case of a joint appointment, any joint appointee) duly authorised for that purpose on behalf of the receiver or manager.

(5) In confirming acceptance the appointee or person authorised for that purpose shall state–
    (a) the time and date of receipt of the instrument of appointment, and
    (b) the time and date of acceptance.".

Amendment of Rule 3.2

24. In paragraph (2) of Rule 3.2 for the word "notice" there shall be substituted the words "notices sent to the company and the creditors".

Amendment of Rule 3.3

25.—(1) In paragraph (1) of Rule 3.3 for the word "If" there shall be substituted the word "Where".

(2) In paragraph (4) of Rule 3.3 for the words "instructions for" to the end there shall be substituted the words "the forms required for the preparation of the statement of affairs".

Omission of Rule 3.13

26. Rule 3.13 shall be omitted.

Amendment of Rule 3.17

27. For paragraph (2) of Rule 3.17 there shall be substituted the following:–

"(2) No person may act as a member of the committee unless and until he has agreed to do so and, unless the relevant proxy or authorisation contains a statement to the contrary, such agreement may be given by his proxy-holder or representative under section 375 of the Companies Act present at the meeting establishing the committee.

(2A) The receiver's certificate of the committee's due constitution shall not issue unless and until at least 3 of the persons who are to be members of the committee have agreed to act.".

Amendment of Rule 3.21

28. In paragraph (2) of Rule 3.21 there shall be added at the end the words ", and for this purpose any proxy or any authorisation under section 375 of the Companies Act in relation to any meeting of creditors of the company shall, unless it contains a statement to the contrary, be treated as a letter of authority to act generally signed by or on behalf of the committee-member".

Amendment of Rule 3.27

29. In paragraph (2) of Rule 3.27 for the words from "a statement incorporating" to the end there shall be substituted the words "a copy of any proposed resolution on which a decision is sought, which shall be set out in such a way that agreement with or dissent from each separate resolution may be indicated by the recipient on the copy so sent".

Insertion of Rule 3.30A

30. After Rule 3.30 there shall be inserted the following rule:–

"Formal defects

3.30A. The acts of the creditors' committee established for any administrative receivership are valid notwithstanding any defect in the appointment, election or qualifications of any member of the committee or any committee-member's representative or in the formalities of its establishment.".

Amendment of Rule 3.33

31. In paragraph (1) of Rule 3.33:–
(a) the word "and" shall be omitted at the end of subparagraph (a), and
(b) there shall be added at the end of subparagraph (b) the words:–
"
, and
(c) in any case, to the members of the creditors' committee (if any)".

Amendment of Rule 3.34

32. In Rule 3.34:–
(a) the word "and" shall be omitted at the end of subparagraph (a), and
(b) there shall be added at the end of subparagraph (b) the words:–
"
, and
(c) in any case, to the members of the creditors' committee (if any)".

Amendment of Rule 3.35

33. In paragraph (1) of Rule 3.35 for subparagraph (a) there shall be substituted the following:–
"(a) to the company or, if it is in liquidation, the liquidator, and",
and in subparagraph (b) the words "in any case," shall be omitted.

SECTION 5: AMENDMENT OF PART 4 OF THE RULES

Amendment of Rule 4.1

34.—(1) For paragraph (1) of Rule 4.1 there shall be substituted the following:–

"(1) In a members' voluntary winding up, the Rules in this Part do not apply, except as follows–
(a) Rule 4.3 applies in the same way as it applies in a creditors' voluntary winding up;
(b) Rule 4.72 (additional provisions concerning meetings in relation to Bank of England and Deposit Protection Board) applies in the winding up of authorised institutions or former authorised institutions within the meaning of the Banking Act 1987, whether members' or creditors' voluntary or by the court;
(c) Chapters 9 (proof of debts in a liquidation), 10 (secured creditors), 15 (disclaimer) and 18 (special manager) apply wherever, and in the same way as, they apply in a creditors' voluntary winding up;
(d) Section F of Chapter 11 (the liquidator) applies only in a members' voluntary winding up, and not otherwise;
(e) Section G of that Chapter (court's power to set aside certain transactions; rule against solicitation) applies in any winding up, whether members' or creditors' voluntary or by the court;
(f) Rule 4.182A applies only in a members' voluntary winding up, and not otherwise; and
(g) Rule 4.223-CVL (liquidator's statements) applies in the same way as it applies in a creditors' voluntary winding up.".

(2) After the words "creditors' voluntary" in line 3 of paragraph (2) of Rule 4.1 there shall be inserted the words "winding up".

(3) In paragraph (3) of Rule 4.1–

(a) after the line beginning "Chapter 5" there shall be inserted in a separate line the words "Chapter 11 (Section F)—The liquidator in a members' voluntary winding up;"; and

(b) there shall be added at the end in a separate line the words "Chapter 21 (Section C)—Dissolution after winding up".

Amendment at head of Rule 4.2

35. At the head of Rule 4.2 there shall be inserted the words "(NO CVL APPLICATION)".

Amendment of Rule 4.7

36.—(1) In subparagraph (e) of paragraph (4) of Rule 4.7 for the words from "(i) a recognised bank" to "were licensed" there shall be substituted the words "an authorised institution or former authorised institution within the meaning of the Banking Act 1987".

(2) After paragraph (6) of Rule 4.7 there shall be added the following paragraphs:–

"(7) Where a petition is filed at the instance of a company's administrator the petition shall–

(a) be expressed to be the petition of the company by its administrator,

(b) state the name of the administrator, the number of the petition on which the administration order was made and the date of that order, and

(c) contain an application under section 18 requesting that the administration order be discharged and that the court make any such order consequential upon that discharge as it thinks fit.

(8) Any petition filed in relation to a company in respect of which there is in force an administration order or a voluntary arrangement under Part I of the Act shall be presented to the court which made the administration order or, as the case may be, to which the nominee's report under section 2 was submitted.

(9) Any petition such as is mentioned in paragraph (7) above or presented by the supervisor of a voluntary arrangement under Part I of the Act in force for the company shall be treated as if it were a petition filed by contributories, and Chapter 4 in this Part of the Rules shall apply accordingly.

(10) Where a petition contains a request for the appointment of a person as liquidator in accordance with section 140 (appointment of former administrator or supervisor as liquidator) the person whose appointment is sought shall, not less than 2 days before the return day for the petition, file in court a report including particulars of–

(a) a date on which he notified creditors of the company, either in writing or at a meeting of creditors, of the intention to seek his appointment as liquidator, such date to be at least 10 days before the day on which the report under this paragraph is filed, and

(b) details of any response from creditors to that notification, including any objections to his appointment.".

Amendment of Rule 4.8

37.—(1) For paragraph (4) of Rule 4.8 there shall be substituted the following:–

"(4) If for any reason service at the registered office is not practicable, or the company has no registered office or is an unregistered company, the petition may be served on the company by leaving it at the company's last known principal place of business in such a way that it is likely to come to the attention of a person attending there, or by delivering it to the secretary or some director, manager or principal officer of the company, wherever that person may be found.".

(2) In paragraph (6) of Rule 4.8 after the words "the court may" there shall be inserted the words "approve or".

Amendment of Rule 4.10

38. In paragraph (4) of Rule 4.10 for the words from "a recognised bank" to "were a licensed institution" there shall be substituted the words "an authorised institution or former authorised institution within the meaning of the Banking Act 1987".

Insertion of Rule 4.21A

39. After Rule 4.21 there shall be inserted the following rule:–

"Expenses of voluntary arrangement

4.21A. Where a winding-up order is made and there is at the time of the presentation of the petition in force for the company a voluntary arrangement under Part I of the Act, any expenses properly incurred as expenses of the administration of the arrangement in question shall be a first charge on the company's assets.".

Amendment of Rule 4.22

40.—(1) In paragraph (1) of Rule 4.22 the words "and the nature of the relief which is sought by the petitioner," shall be omitted.

(2) After paragraph (1) of Rule 4.22 there shall be inserted the following paragraph:–

"(1A) No petition shall be filed unless there is produced with it the receipt for the deposit payable on presentation.".

Amendment of Rule 4.24

41.—(1) In Rule 4.24 the word "and" at the end of the line beginning "Rule 4.20" shall be omitted.

(2) At the end of Rule 4.24 there shall be added the words:–
"
                                                                          ; and

Rule 4.21A (expenses of voluntary arrangement)".

Insertion of Rule 4.25A

42. After Rule 4.25 there shall be inserted the following rule:–

"Notice of appointment

4.25A.—(1) Where a provisional liquidator has been appointed the court shall forthwith give notice of the fact to the official receiver.

(2) A copy of that notice shall at the same time be sent by the court to the provisional liquidator where he is not the official receiver.".

Amendment of Rule 4.30

43.—(1) In paragraph (3) of Rule 4.30 for the words from the beginning to "accordingly)" there shall be substituted the words:–

"Without prejudice to any order the court may make as to costs, the provisional liquidator's remuneration (whether the official receiver or another) shall be paid to him, and the amount of any expenses incurred by him (including the remuneration and expenses of any special manager appointed under section 177) reimbursed–

   (a) if a winding-up order is not made, out of the property of the company".

(2) After paragraph (3) of Rule 4.30 there shall be inserted the following paragraph:–

"(3A) Unless the court otherwise directs, in a case falling within paragraph (3)(a) above the provisional liquidator may retain out of the company's property such sums or property as are or may be required for meeting his remuneration and expenses.".

Amendment of Rule 4.31

44. Paragraph (3) of Rule 4.31 shall be omitted.

Amendment of Rule 4.34-CVL

45. For paragraph (3) of Rule 4.34-CVL there shall be substituted the following:–

"(3) Where it is made out by the directors under section 99(1) the statement of affairs shall be delivered by them to the liquidator in office following the creditors' meeting summoned under section 98 forthwith after that meeting has been held; and he shall, within 7 days, deliver it to the registrar of companies.

(4) A statement of affairs under section 99(1) may be made up to a date not more than 14 days before that on which the resolution for voluntary winding up is passed by the company.".

Insertion of Rule 4.34A-CVL

46. After Rule 4.34-CVL there shall be inserted the following rule:–

"Copy statement of affairs

4.34A-CVL. Where a liquidator is nominated by the company at a general meeting held on a day prior to that on which the creditors' meeting summoned under section 98 is held, the directors shall forthwith after his nomination or the making of the statement of affairs, whichever is the later, deliver to him a copy of the statement of affairs.".

Amendment of Rule 4.43

47. In Rule 4.43 the existing paragraph shall be numbered "(1)" and there shall be added after it the following paragraph:–

"(2) The official receiver shall file in court a copy of any report sent under this Chapter.".

Amendment of Rule 4.45

48. In paragraph (1) of Rule 4.45 there shall be inserted after the words "summary of the statement" the words "(if he thinks fit, as amplified, modified or explained by virtue of Rule 4.42)".

Insertion of Rule 4.49A

49. After Rule 4.49-CVL there shall be inserted the following rule:–

"Further information where liquidation follows administration

4.49A. Where under section 140 the court appoints as the company's liquidator a person who was formerly its administrator and that person becomes aware of creditors not formerly known to him in his capacity as administrator, he shall send to those creditors a copy of any statement or report sent by him to creditors under Rule 2.16, so noted as to indicate that it is being sent under this Rule.".

Amendment of Rule 4.50

50. In paragraph (8) of Rule 4.50 for the words from "a recognised bank" to "were a licensed institution" there shall be substituted the words "an authorised institution or former authorised institution within the meaning of the Banking Act 1987".

Amendment of Rule 4.51-CVL

51.—(1) In paragraph (2) of Rule 4.51-CVL for the words "proofs and (if applicable) proxies" there shall be substituted the words "any proxies necessary to entitle them to vote at the meeting".

(2) In paragraph (3) of Rule 4.51-CVL for the words from "a recognised bank" to "were a licensed institution" there shall be substituted the words "an authorised institution or former authorised institution within the meaning of the Banking Act 1987".

Insertion of Rules 4.53A-CVL and 4.53B-CVL

52. After Rule 4.53-CVL there shall be inserted the following rules:–

"Effect of adjournment of company meeting

4.53A-CVL. Where a company meeting at which a resolution for voluntary winding up is to be proposed is adjourned, any resolution passed at a meeting under section 98 held before the holding of the adjourned company meeting only has effect on and from the passing by the company of a resolution for winding up.

Report by director, etc.

4.53B-CVL.—(1) At any meeting held under section 98 where the statement of affairs laid before the meeting does not state the company's affairs as at the date of the meeting, the directors of the company shall cause to be made to the meeting, either by the director presiding at the meeting or by another person with knowledge of the relevant matters, a report (written or oral) on any material transactions relating to the company occurring between the date of the making of the statement of affairs and that of the meeting.

(2) Any such report shall be recorded in the minutes of the meeting kept under Rule 4.71.".

Amendment of Rule 4.56-CVL

53. In paragraph (1) of Rule 4.56-CVL for the words "section 98" there shall be substituted the words "section 95 or 98".

Amendment of Rule 4.63

54.—(1) In paragraph (1) of Rule 4.63 there shall be inserted at the beginning the words "Subject as follows,".

(2) In subparagraph (a) of paragraph (2) of Rule 4.63 there shall be inserted at the beginning the words "subject to paragraph (2A),".

(3) After paragraph (2) of Rule 4.63 there shall be inserted the following paragraph:–

"(2A) In a winding up by the court the support referred to in paragraph (2)(a) must represent a majority in value of all those present (in person or by proxy) at the meeting and entitled to vote. (NO CVL APPLICATION)".

(4) In the second subparagraph of paragraph (4) of Rule 4.63:–

(a) there shall be inserted after the word "person" the words "(whether personally or on his behalf by a proxy-holder)"; and

(b) there shall be substituted for the word "proxy" the word "proxy-holder".

Amendment of Rule 4.65

55.—(1) In paragraph (3) of Rule 4.65 there shall be inserted after the words "Rule 4.113(3)" the words "or, as the case may be, 4.114-CVL(3),".

(2) In paragraph (4) of Rule 4.65 there shall be substituted for the words from "by virtue of this Rule" to the end the words "the chairman may, at his discretion, adjourn the meeting to such time and place as he may appoint".

Omission of Rule 4.66

56. Rule 4.66 shall be omitted.

Amendment of Rule 4.72

57. In paragraph (1) of Rule 4.72 for the words from "— (a) a recognised bank" to the end there shall be substituted the words "an authorised institution or former authorised institution within the meaning of the Banking Act 1987".

Amendment of Rule 4.75

58. In paragraph (1) of Rule 4.75 there shall be inserted at the beginning the words "Subject to Rule 4.73(5),".

Amendment of Rule 4.93

59.—(1) In paragraph (5) of Rule 4.93 there shall be added at the end the words "and for all the purposes of the Act and the Rules shall be chargeable at a rate not exceeding that mentioned in paragraph (6)".

(2) For paragraph (6) of Rule 4.93 there shall be substituted the following:–

"(6) The rate of interest to be claimed under paragraphs (3) and (4) is the rate specified in section 17 of the Judgments Act 1838 on the date when the company went into liquidation.".

Amendment of Rule 4.100

60. For paragraphs (3)–(5) of Rule 4.100 there shall be substituted the following:–

"(3) The liquidator's appointment is effective from the date on which the appointment is certified, that date to be endorsed on the certificate.

(4) The chairman of the meeting (if not himself the official receiver) shall send the certificate to the official receiver.

(5) The official receiver shall in any case send the certificate to the liquidator and file a copy of it in court.".

Amendment of Rule 4.101-CVL

61. In paragraph (2) of Rule 4.101-CVL for the words "is effective from the date of the certificate" there shall be substituted the words "takes effect upon the passing of the resolution for that appointment".

Insertion of Rule 4.101A-CVL

62. After Rule 4.101-CVL there shall be inserted the following rule:–

"Power to fill vacancy in office of liquidator

4.101A-CVL. Where a vacancy in the office of liquidator occurs in the manner mentioned in section 104 a meeting of creditors to fill the vacancy may be convened by any creditor or, if there were more liquidators than one, by the continuing liquidators.".

Amendment of Rule 4.106

63. In paragraph (4) of Rule 4.106 there shall be inserted at the end the words "(NO CVL APPLICATION)".

Amendment of Rule 4.108

64. After paragraph (5) of Rule 4.108 there shall be added the following paragraphs:–

"(6) If there is no quorum present at the meeting summoned to receive the liquidator's resignation, the meeting is deemed to have been held, a resolution is deemed to have been passed that the liquidator's resignation be accepted and the creditors are deemed not to have resolved against the liquidator having his release.

(7) Where paragraph (6) applies any reference in the Rules to a resolution that the liquidator's resignation be accepted is replaced by a reference to the making of a written statement, signed by the person who, had there been a quorum present, would have been chairman of the meeting, that no quorum was present and that the liquidator may resign.".

Amendment of Rule 4.130

65. In paragraph (4) of Rule 4.130 after the word "appearing" in both places where it occurs there shall be inserted the words "or being represented".

Amendment of Rule 4.137

66. For Rule 4.137 there shall be substituted the following:–

**"Notice to official receiver of intention to vacate office
(NO CVL APPLICATION)**

4.137.—(1) Where the liquidator intends to vacate office, whether by resignation or otherwise, he shall give notice of his intention to the official receiver together with notice of any creditors' meeting to be held in respect of his vacation of office, including any meeting to receive his resignation.

(2) The notice to the official receiver must be given at least 21 days before any such creditors' meeting.

(3) Where there remains any property of the company which has not been realised, applied, distributed or otherwise fully dealt with in the winding up, the liquidator shall include in his notice to the official receiver details of the nature of that property, its value (or the fact that it has no value), its location, any action taken by the liquidator to deal with that property or any reason for his not dealing with it, and the current position in relation to it.".

Amendment of Rule 4.138

67. After paragraph (2) of Rule 4.138 there shall be added the following paragraph:–

"(3) Where the liquidator vacates office under section 172(8) (final meeting of creditors), he shall deliver up to the official receiver the company's books, papers and other records which have not already been disposed of in accordance with general regulations in the course of the liquidation. (NO CVL APPLICATION)".

Amendment of Rule 4.142

68. After paragraph (4) of Rule 4.142 there shall be inserted the following paragraph:–

"(4A) If there is no quorum present at the meeting summoned to receive the liquidator's resignation, the meeting is deemed to have been held.".

Insertion of Rule 4.148A

69. After Rule 4.148 there shall be inserted the following rule:–

"Remuneration of liquidator in members' voluntary winding up

4.148A.—(1) The liquidator is entitled to receive remuneration for his services as such.

(2) The remuneration shall be fixed either–

(a) as a percentage of the value of the assets which are realised or distributed, or of the one value and the other in combination, or

(b) by reference to the time properly given by the insolvency practitioner (as liquidator) and his staff in attending to matters arising in the winding up;

and the company in general meeting shall determine whether the remuneration is to be fixed under subparagraph (a) or (b) and, if under subparagraph (a), the percentage to be applied as there mentioned.

(3) In arriving at that determination the company in general meeting shall have regard to the matters set out in paragraph (4) of Rule 4.127.

(4) If not fixed as above, the liquidator's remuneration shall be in accordance with the scale laid down for the official receiver by general regulations.

(5) Rule 4.128 shall apply in relation to the remuneration of the liquidator in respect of the matters there mentioned and for this purpose references in that Rule to "the liquidation committee" and "a meeting of creditors" shall be read as references to the company in general meeting.

(6) If the liquidator considers that the remuneration fixed for him by the company in general meeting, or as under paragraph (4), is insufficient, he may apply to the court for an order increasing its amount or rate.

(7) The liquidator shall give at least 14 days' notice of an application under paragraph (6) to the company's contributories, or such one or more of them as the court may direct, and the contributories may nominate any one or more of their number to appear or be represented.

(8) The court may, if it appears to be a proper case, order the costs of the liquidator's application, including the costs of any contributory appearing or being represented on it, to be paid out of the assets.".

Amendment of Rule 4.152

70. In paragraph (7) of Rule 4.152 for the words "28 of the Banking Act 1979(a)" there shall be substituted the words "58 of the Banking Act 1987".

Amendment of Rule 4.153

71. For paragraph (3) of Rule 4.153 there shall be substituted the following:–

"(3) No person may act as a member of the committee unless and until he has agreed to do so and, unless the relevant proxy or authorisation contains a statement to the contrary, such agreement may be given by his proxy-holder or representative under section 375 of the Companies Act present at the meeting establishing the committee.

(3A) The liquidator's certificate of the committee's due constitution shall not issue before the minimum number of persons (in accordance with Rule 4.152) who are to be members of the committee have agreed to act.".

Amendment of Rule 4.154

72. In paragraph (4) of Rule 4.154 for the words from "substituting" to the end there shall be substituted the words "substituting for the reference in paragraph (3A) of that Rule to Rule 4.152 a reference to this paragraph".

Amendment of Rule 4.159

73. In paragraph (2) of Rule 4.159 there shall be added at the end the words ", and for this purpose any proxy or any authorisation under section 375 of the Companies Act in relation to any meeting of creditors (or, as the case may be, members or contributories) of the company shall, unless it contains a statement to the contrary, be treated as such a letter of authority to act generally signed by or on behalf of the committee-member".

Amendment of Rule 4.167

74. In paragraph (2) of Rule 4.167 for the words from "a statement incorporating" to the end there shall be substituted the words "a copy of any proposed resolution on which a decision is sought, which shall be set out in such a way that agreement with or dissent from each separate resolution may be indicated by the recipient on the copy so sent".

Insertion of Rule 4.172A

75. After Rule 4.172 there shall be inserted the following rule:–

"Formal defects

4.172A. The acts of the liquidation committee established for any winding up are valid notwithstanding any defect in the appointment, election or qualifications of any member of the committee or any committee-member's representative or in the formalities of its establishment.".

Amendment of Rule 4.178

76. In Rule 4.178 for "4.172" there shall be substituted "4.172A".

Amendment of Rule 4.181

77. In Rule 4.181 the existing paragraph shall be numbered "(1)" and there shall be added after it the following paragraph:–

"(2) Paragraph (1) applies whether or not the company is unable to pay its debts.".

Insertion of Rule 4.182A

78. After Rule 4.182 there shall be inserted the following rule:–

**"Distribution in members' voluntary winding up
(NO CVL APPLICATION)**

4.182A.—(1) In a members' voluntary winding up the liquidator may give notice in such newspaper as he considers most appropriate for the purpose of drawing the matter to the attention of the company's creditors that he intends to make a distribution to creditors.

(2) The notice shall specify a date ("the last date for proving") up to which proofs may be lodged. The date shall be the same for all creditors and not less than 21 days from that of the notice.

(3) The liquidator is not obliged to deal with proofs lodged after the last date for proving; but he may do so, if he thinks fit.

(4) A creditor who has not proved his debt before the last date for proving or after that date increases the claim in his proof is not entitled to disturb, by reason that he has not participated in it, either at all or, as the case may be, to the extent that his increased claim would allow, that distribution or any other distribution made before his debt was proved or his claim increased; but when he has proved his debt or, as the case may be, increased his claim, he is entitled to be paid, out of any money for the time being available for the payment of any further distribution, any distribution or distributions which he has failed to receive.

(5) Where the distribution proposed to be made is to be the only or the final distribution in that winding up, the liquidator may, subject to paragraph (6), make that distribution without regard to the claim of any person in respect of a debt not already proved.

(6) Where the distribution proposed to be made is one specified in paragraph (5), the notice given under paragraph (1) shall state the effect of paragraph (5).".

Amendment of Rule 4.218

79. In subparagraphs (m) and (p) of paragraph (l) of Rule 4.218 there shall be substituted for the words "capital gains" the word "corporation".

Amendment of Rule 4.223-CVL

80.—(1) For paragraph (1) of Rule 4.223-CVL there shall be substituted the following:–

"(1) Subject to paragraphs (3) and (3A), the statement which section 192 requires the liquidator to send to the registrar of companies, if the winding up is not concluded within one year from its commencement, shall be sent not more than 30 days after the expiration of that year, and thereafter 6-monthly until the winding up is concluded.".

(2) After paragraph (3) of Rule 4.223-CVL there shall be inserted the following paragraph:–

"(3A) No statement shall be required to be delivered under this Rule where the return of the final meeting in respect of the company under sections 94 or 106 is delivered before the date at which the statement is to be delivered and that return shows that no assets or funds of the company remain unclaimed or undistributed in the hands or under the control of the liquidator or any former liquidator; but where this paragraph applies, the liquidator shall deliver a copy of that return to the Secretary of State.".

Amendment of Rule 4.226

81. At the end of subparagraph (a) of Rule 4.226 the word "and" shall be omitted and at the end of subparagraph (b) of that Rule there shall be added the following words:-
"
, and
(c) apply to all windings up to which section 216 applies, whether or not the winding up commenced before the coming into force of the Rules".

Amendment of Rule 4.229

82. For Rule 4.229 there shall be substituted the following:-

"Second excepted case

4.229.—(1) Where a person to whom section 216 applies as having been a director or shadow director of the liquidating company applies for leave of the court under that section not later than 7 days from the date on which the company went into liquidation, he may, during the period specified in paragraph (2) below, act in any of the ways mentioned in section 216(3), notwithstanding that he has not the leave of the court under that section.

(2) The period referred to in paragraph (1) begins with the day on which the company goes into liquidation and ends either on the day falling six weeks after that date or on the day on which the court disposes of the application for leave under section 216, whichever of those days occurs first.".

SECTION 6: AMENDMENT OF PART 5 OF THE RULES

Amendment of Rule 5.3

83. In subparagraph (c)(iii) of paragraph (2) of Rule 5.3 for the words from the beginning to "(extortionate credit transactions)," there shall be substituted the following:-
"(iii) in Case 1 whether, to the debtor's knowledge, claims have been made under section 339 (transactions at an undervalue), section 340 (preferences) or section 343 (extortionate credit transactions), or there are circumstances giving rise to the possibility of such claims, and in Case 2 whether there are circumstances which would give rise to the possibility of such claims in the event that he should be adjudged bankrupt,".

Amendment of Rule 5.5

84. In paragraph (2) of Rule 5.5 after the words "agrees so to act," there shall be inserted the words "and a copy of the debtor's proposal given to the nominee under that Rule".

Insertion of Rule 5.5A

85. After Rule 5.5 there shall be inserted the following rule:-

"Court in which application to be made

5.5A.—(1) Except in the case of a bankrupt, an application to the court under Part VIII of the Act shall be made to a court in which the debtor would be entitled to present his own petition in bankruptcy under Rule 6.40.

(2) The application shall contain sufficient information to establish that it is brought in the appropriate court.

(3) In the case of a bankrupt such an application shall be made to the court having the conduct of his bankruptcy and shall be filed with those bankruptcy proceedings.".

Amendment of Rule 5.10

86. In paragraph (5) of Rule 5.10 after the words "official receiver" there shall be inserted the words "and (if any) the trustee".

Amendment of Rule 5.13

87. In paragraph (1) of Rule 5.13 the words ", nor more than 28," shall be omitted and at the end there shall be added the words ", nor more than 28 days from that on which that report is considered by the court under Rule 5.12".

Amendment of Rule 5.22

88. In the first sub-paragraph of paragraph (4) of Rule 5.22 there shall be inserted at the end the words "and, in Case 1, the official receiver and (if any) the trustee".

Amendment of Rule 5.23

89. In paragraph (1) of Rule 5.23 for the words "this Part of the Rules" there shall be substituted the words "Rules 5.24, 5.25 and 5.29".

Amendment of Rule 5.25

90. In paragraph (4) of Rule 5.25 for the words "official receiver or the trustee" there shall be substituted the words "trustee, or if there is no trustee, the official receiver".

SECTION 7: AMENDMENT OF PART 6 OF THE RULES

Amendment of Rule 6.8

91. In subparagraph (c) of paragraph (1) of Rule 6.8 there shall be added at the end the words ", provided that such amount or rate must, in the case of a petition based on a statutory demand, be limited to that claimed in that demand".

Amendment of Rule 6.9

92. After paragraph (4) of Rule 6.9 there shall be inserted the following paragraph:–

"(4A) Notwithstanding any other provision of this Rule, where there is in force for the debtor a voluntary arrangement under Part VIII of the Act, the petition shall be presented to the court to which the nominee's report under section 256 was submitted.".

Amendment of Rule 6.10

93.—(1) In subparagraph (a) of paragraph (3) of Rule 6.10 the word "and" shall be omitted and there shall be added at the end of subparagraph (b) of that paragraph the following words:–
"
                                                                                      , and
    (c)   if there is in force for the debtor a voluntary arrangement under Part VIII of the Act, and the petitioner is not the supervisor of the arrangement, one copy for him".

(2) After paragraph (5) of Rule 6.10 there shall be added the following paragraph:–

"(6) Where a petition contains a request for the appointment of a person as trustee in accordance with section 297(5) (appointment of former supervisor as trustee) the person whose appointment is sought shall, not less than 2 days before the day appointed for hearing the petition, file in court a report including particulars of–
    (a) a date on which he gave written notification to creditors bound by the arrangement of the intention to seek his appointment as trustee, such date to be at least 10 days before the day on which the report under this paragraph is filed, and
    (b) details of any response from creditors to that notice, including any objections to his appointment.".

Amendment of Rule 6.11

94.—(1) In paragraph (1) of Rule 6.11 there shall be inserted after the word "affidavit" the words "or affidavits".

(2) In paragraph (2) of Rule 6.11 for the words "The affidavit" there shall be substituted the words "Every affidavit".

(3) In paragraph (5) of Rule 6.11:–
    (a) after the words "applies, the affidavit" there shall be inserted the words "or affidavits";
    (b) after the word "person" where it first appears there shall be inserted the words "or persons"; and
    (c) in subparagraph (a) of that paragraph after the word "demand" there shall be inserted the word "personally".

Amendment of Rule 6.14

95. After paragraph (3) of Rule 6.14 there shall be added the following paragraph:–

"(4) If to the petitioner's knowledge there is in force for the debtor a voluntary arrangement under Part VIII of the Act, and the petitioner is not himself the supervisor of the arrangement, a copy of the petition shall be sent by him to the supervisor.".

Amendment of Rule 6.18

96. In paragraph (3) of Rule 6.18 after the word "debtor" there shall be inserted the words ", the supervisor of any voluntary arrangement under Part VIII of the Act in force for the debtor".

Omission of Rule 6.19

97. Rule 6.19 shall be omitted.

Amendment of Rule 6.39

98. After paragraph (2) of Rule 6.39 there shall be added the following paragraph:–

"(3) If there is at the date of the petition in force for the debtor a voluntary arrangement under Part VIII of the Act, the particulars required by paragraph (2) above shall contain a statement to that effect and the name and address of the supervisor of the arrangement.".

Amendment of Rule 6.40

99. For paragraph (3) of Rule 6.40 there shall be substituted the following:–

"(3) If, in a case not falling within paragraph (1), it is more expedient for the debtor with a view to expediting his petition–

(a) it may in any case be presented to whichever court is specified by Schedule 2 to the Rules as being, in relation to the debtor's own court, the nearest full-time court, and

(b) it may alternatively, in a case falling within paragraph (2)(b), be presented to the court for the insolvency district in which he has resided for the greater part of the 6 months there referred to.

(3A) Notwithstanding any other provision of this Rule, where there is in force for the debtor a voluntary arrangement under Part VIII of the Act the petition shall be presented to the court to which the nominee's report under section 256 was submitted.".

Amendment of Rule 6.42

100.—(1) In paragraph (2) of Rule 6.42 at the beginning there shall be inserted the words "Subject to paragraph (2A),".

(2) After paragraph (2) of Rule 6.42 there shall be inserted the following paragraph:–

"(2A) If the petition contains particulars of a voluntary arrangement under Part VIII of the Act in force for the debtor, the court shall fix a venue for the hearing and give at least 14 days' notice of it to the supervisor of the arrangement; the supervisor may appear and be heard on the petition.".

(3) In subparagraph (b) of paragraph (3) of Rule 6.42 for the words from "retained by the court" to the end there shall be substituted the words "sent by the court to the official receiver; and".

(4) For subparagraph (a) of paragraph (4) of Rule 6.42 there shall be substituted the following:–
"(a) one shall be sent by the court to the official receiver; and".

(5) After paragraph (5) of Rule 6.42 there shall be added the following paragraphs:–

"(6) Where the court hears a petition forthwith, or it will in the opinion of the court otherwise expedite the delivery of any document to the official receiver, the court may, instead of sending that document to the official receiver, direct the bankrupt forthwith to deliver it to him.

(7) Where a petition contains a request for the appointment of a person as trustee in accordance with section 297(5) (appointment of former supervisor as trustee) the person whose appointment is sought shall, not less than 2 days before the day appointed for hearing the petition, file in court a report including particulars of–

(a) a date on which he gave written notification to creditors bound by the arrangement of the intention to seek his appointment as trustee, such date to be at least 10 days before the day on which the report under this paragraph is filed, and

(b) details of any response from creditors to that notice, including any objections to his appointment.".

Amendment of Rule 6.44

101.—(1) In paragraph (2) of Rule 6.44 the words "with one copy," shall be omitted and there shall be added at the end the words ", and a further copy to the official receiver".

(2) Paragraph (4) of Rule 6.44 shall be omitted.

Insertion of Rule 6.46A

102. After Rule 6.46 there shall be inserted the following rule:–

   "Expenses of voluntary arrangement

   6.46A. Where a bankruptcy order is made on a debtor's petition and there is at the time of the petition in force for the debtor a voluntary arrangement under Part VIII of the Act, any expenses properly incurred as expenses of the administration of the arrangement in question shall be a first charge on the bankrupt's estate.".

Amendment of Rule 6.56

103.—(1) In paragraph (3) of Rule 6.56 for the words from the beginning to "accordingly)" there shall be substituted the words:–

   "Without prejudice to any order the court may make as to costs, the interim receiver's remuneration (whether the official receiver or another) shall be paid to him, and the amount of any expenses incurred by him (including the remuneration and expenses of any special manager appointed under section 370) reimbursed–

   (a) if a bankruptcy order is not made, out of the property of the debtor".

(2) After paragraph (3) of Rule 6.56 there shall be added the following paragraph:–

   "(4) Unless the court otherwise directs, in a case falling within paragraph (3)(a) above the interim receiver may retain out of the debtor's property such sums or property as are or may be required for meeting his remuneration and expenses.".

Amendment of Rule 6.57

104. Paragraph (3) of Rule 6.57 shall be omitted.

Amendment of Rule 6.73

105. In Rule 6.73 the existing paragraph shall be numbered "(1)" and there shall be added after it the following paragraph:–

   "(2) The official receiver shall file in court a copy of any report sent under this Chapter.".

Amendment of Rule 6.75

106. In paragraph (1) of Rule 6.75 there shall be inserted after the words "summary of the statement" the words "(if he thinks fit, as amplified, modified or explained by virtue of Rule 6.66 or 6.72)".

Amendment of Rule 6.88

107.—(1) In paragraph (1) of Rule 6.88 there shall be inserted at the beginning the words "Subject as follows,".

(2) In subparagraph (a) of paragraph (2) of Rule 6.88 there shall be added at the end the words ", provided that such support represents a majority in value of all those present (in person or by proxy) at the meeting and entitled to vote".

(3) In the second subparagraph of paragraph (4) of Rule 6.88:–
   (a) there shall be inserted after the word "person" the words "(whether personally or on his behalf by a proxy-holder)"; and
   (b) there shall be substituted for the word "proxy" the word "proxy-holder".

Amendment of Rule 6.91

108. In paragraph (2) of Rule 6.91 there shall be substituted for the words from "by virtue of this Rule" to the end the words "the chairman may, at his discretion, adjourn the meeting to such time and place as he may appoint".

Omission of Rule 6.92

109. Rule 6.92 shall be omitted.

Amendment of Rule 6.97

110. In paragraph (1) of Rule 6.97 there shall be substituted for the words "to be used for the purpose of proving bankruptcy debts" the words "of proof".

Amendment of Rule 6.98

111. In paragraph (1) of Rule 6.98 there shall be inserted at the beginning the words "Subject to Rule 6.96(4),".

Amendment of Rule 6.113

112.—(1) At the end of the first subparagraph of paragraph (3) of Rule 6.113 there shall be added the words "and for all the purposes of the Act and the Rules shall be chargeable at a rate not exceeding that mentioned in paragraph (5)".

(2) For the second subparagraph of paragraph (3) and for paragraph (4) of Rule 6.113 there shall be substituted the following:–

"(4) Interest under paragraph (3) may only be claimed for the period from the date of the demand to that of the bankruptcy order.

(5) The rate of interest to be claimed under paragraphs (2) and (3) is the rate specified in section 17 of the Judgments Act 1838 on the date of the bankruptcy order.".

Amendment of Rule 6.120

113. For paragraphs (3) and (4) of Rule 6.120 there shall be substituted the following:–

"(3) The trustee's appointment is effective from the date on which the appointment is certified, that date to be endorsed on the certificate.

(4) The chairman of the meeting (if not himself the official receiver) shall send the certificate to the official receiver.

(5) The official receiver shall in any case send the certificate to the trustee and file a copy of it in court.".

Amendment of Rule 6.126

114. After paragraph (4) of Rule 6.126 there shall be added the following paragraphs:–

"(5) If there is no quorum present at the meeting summoned to receive the trustee's resignation, the meeting is deemed to have been held, a resolution is deemed to have been passed that the trustee's resignation be accepted and the creditors are deemed not to have resolved against the trustee having his release.

(6) Where paragraph (5) applies any reference in the Rules to a resolution that the trustee's resignation be accepted is replaced by a reference to the making of a written statement, signed by the person who, had there been a quorum present, would have been chairman of the meeting, that no quorum was present and that the trustee may resign.".

Amendment of Rule 6.141

115. In paragraph (4) of Rule 6.141 after the word "appearing" in both places where it occurs there shall be inserted the words "or being represented".

Amendment of Rule 6.145

116. For Rule 6.145 there shall be substituted the following:–

"Notice to official receiver of intention to vacate office

6.145.—(1) Where the trustee intends to vacate office, whether by resignation or otherwise, he shall give notice of his intention to the official receiver together with notice of any creditors' meeting to be held in respect of his vacation of office, including any meeting to receive his resignation.

(2) The notice to the official receiver must be given at least 21 days before any such creditors' meeting.

(3) Where there remains in the bankrupt's estate any property which has not been realised, applied, distributed or otherwise fully dealt with in the bankruptcy, the trustee shall include in his notice to the official receiver details of the nature of that property, its value (or the fact that it has no value), its location, any action taken by the trustee to deal with that property or any reason for his not dealing with it, and the current position in relation to it.".

Amendment of Rule 6.151

117.   For paragraph (3) of Rule 6.151 there shall be substituted the following:–

"(3) No person may act as a member of the committee unless and until he has agreed to do so and, unless the relevant proxy contains a statement to the contrary, such agreement may be given by his proxy-holder present at the meeting establishing the committee.

(3A) The trustee's certificate of the committee's due constitution shall not issue before at least 3 persons elected to be members of the committee have agreed to act.".

Amendment of Rule 6.156

118.—(1) In paragraph (2) of Rule 6.156 the words from "specially" to the end shall be omitted and there shall be substituted the words "specially) and signed by or on behalf of the committee-member, and for this purpose any proxy in relation to any meeting of creditors of the bankrupt shall, unless it contains a statement to the contrary, be treated as such a letter of authority to act generally signed by or on behalf of the committee-member".

(2) After paragraph (6) of Rule 6.156 there shall be added the following paragraph:–

"(7) The acts of the committee are valid notwithstanding any defect in the appointment or qualifications of any committee-member's representative.".

Amendment of Rule 6.162

119.—(1) In paragraph (2) of Rule 6.162 for the words from "a statement incorporating" to the end there shall be substituted the words "a copy of any proposed resolution on which a decision is sought, which shall be set out in such a way that agreement with or dissent from each separate resolution may be indicated by the recipient on the copy so sent".

(2) In paragraph (3) of Rule 6.162 before the word "days" there shall be inserted the word "business".

Amendment of Rule 6.179

120.   After paragraph (6) of Rule 6.179 there shall be added the following paragraph:–

"(7) A notice or copy notice to be served on any person under the age of 18 in relation to the disclaimer of property in a dwelling-house is sufficiently served if sent or given to the parent or guardian of that person.".

Amendment of Rule 6.206

121.—(1) In paragraph (4) of Rule 6.206 the words ", not less than 28 days before the hearing," shall be omitted and there shall be added at the end the words:–
"
                                                                                            –
(a)   where the application is made under section 282(1)(a), in sufficient time to enable them to be present at the hearing, and

(b)   where the application is made under section 282(1)(b), not less than 28 days before the hearing".

(2) After paragraph (4) of Rule 6.206 there shall be added the following paragraph:–

"(5) Where the application is made under section 282(1)(a), paragraph (4) shall additionally be complied with in relation to the person on whose petition the bankruptcy order was made.".

Amendment of Rule 6.208

122.   For paragraph (2) of Rule 6.208 there shall be substituted the following:–

"(2) Except in relation to an application for an order staying all or any part of the proceedings in the bankruptcy, application for an order under this Rule may be made *ex parte*.

(3) Where application is made under this Rule for an order staying all or any part of the proceedings in the bankruptcy, the applicant shall send copies of the application to the official receiver and (if other) the trustee in sufficient time to enable them to be present at the hearing and (if they wish to do so) make representations.

(4) Where the court makes an order under this Rule staying all or any part of the proceedings in the bankruptcy, the rules in this Chapter nevertheless continue to apply to any application for, or other matters in connection with, the annulment of the bankruptcy order.

(5) If the court makes an order under this Rule, it shall send copies of the order to the applicant, the official receiver and (if other) the trustee.".

Amendment of Rule 6.209

123.—(1) In subparagraph (a) of Rule 6.209 after the word "trustee" there shall be inserted the words "or, if no trustee has been appointed, the official receiver".

(2) In subparagraph (b) of Rule 6.209 after the word "trustee" there shall be inserted the words "or, if no trustee has been appointed, the official receiver".

Insertion of Rule 6.212A

124. After Rule 6.212 there shall be inserted the following rule:–

"Annulment under section 261

6.212A. Rules 6.206 to 6.212 apply to an application for annulment under section 261 as they apply to such an application under section 282(1)(a).".

Amendment of Rule 6.213

125. In paragraph (1) of Rule 6.213 after the word "section" there shall be inserted the words "261 or".

Amendment of Rule 6.214

126. In paragraph (1) of Rule 6.214 after the word "section" there shall be inserted the words "261 or".

Amendment of Rule 6.223

127. At the end of Rule 6.223 there shall be added the words "or section 1 of the Criminal Justice (Scotland) Act 1987".

Amendment of Rule 6.232

128. For paragraph (4) of Rule 6.232 there shall be substituted the following:–

"(4) In criminal bankruptcy, forms of proof shall be sent out by the official receiver within 12 weeks from the making of the bankruptcy order, to every creditor who is known to him, or is identified in the bankrupt's statement of affairs.".

Amendment of Rule 6.234

129.—(1) In paragraph (1) of Rule 6.234 for the words "Chapter 11" there shall be substituted the words "Chapter 10".

(2) In paragraph (2) of Rule 6.234 for the words "Chapter 12" there shall be substituted the words "Chapter 11".

Amendment of Rule 6.237

130. In paragraph (6) of Rule 6.237 the following subparagraphs shall be substituted for subparagraphs (d) and (f) respectively:–

"(d) indicate, by reference to any, or the total, amount which is payable otherwise than to the bankrupt out of the estate and of interest on that amount, how the amount of the charge to be imposed is to be ascertained;", and

"(f) identify when any property charged under section 313 shall cease to be comprised in the bankrupt's estate and, subject to the charge (and any prior charge), to vest in the bankrupt.".

SECTION 8: AMENDMENT OF PART 7 OF THE RULES

Amendment of Rule 7.34

131.—(1) For paragraph (1) of Rule 7.34 there shall be substituted the following:–

"(1) Subject as follows, where the costs, charges or expenses of any person are payable out of the insolvent estate, those costs, charges or expenses shall be taxed unless agreed between the responsible insolvency practitioner and the person entitled to payment, and in the absence of such agreement the responsible insolvency practitioner may require taxation by notice in writing requiring that person to deliver his bill of costs to the appropriate taxing officer for taxation; the appropriate taxing officer is that in relation to the court to which the insolvency proceedings are allocated or, where in relation to a company there is no such court, that in relation to any court having jurisdiction to wind up the company.".

(2) In paragraph (3) of Rule 7.34 after the word "taxed" there shall be inserted the words "or fixed by order of the court".

(3) In paragraph (5) of Rule 7.34 there shall be added at the end the words "specified in Rule 12 of Order 62 of the Rules of the Supreme Court".

Amendment of Rule 7.35

132. After paragraph (5) of Rule 7.35 there shall be added the following paragraph:–

"(6) Where costs have been incurred in insolvency proceedings in the High Court and those proceedings are subsequently transferred to a county court, all costs of those proceedings directed by the court or otherwise required to be taxed may nevertheless, on the application of the person who incurred the costs, be ordered to be taxed in the High Court.".

Amendment of Rule 7.49

133. In paragraph (2) of Rule 7.49 there shall be added at the end the words "and any reference to the registrar of civil appeals is replaced by a reference to the registrar of the High Court who deals with insolvency proceedings of the kind involved".

SECTION 9: AMENDMENT OF PART 8 OF THE RULES

Amendment of Rule 8.1

134.—(1) In paragraph (2) of Rule 8.1 after the word "meetings" there shall be inserted the words "summoned or called".

(2) For paragraph (5) of Rule 8.1 there shall be substituted the following:–

"(5) A person given a proxy under paragraph (4) cannot decline to be the proxy-holder in relation to that proxy.

(6) A proxy requires the holder to give the principal's vote on matters arising for determination at the meeting, or to abstain, or to propose, in the principal's name, a resolution to be voted on by the meeting, either as directed or in accordance with the holder's own discretion.".

Amendment of Rule 8.3

135. After paragraph (3) of Rule 8.3 there shall be added the following paragraphs:–

"(4) Where a proxy directs a proxy-holder to vote for or against a resolution for the nomination or appointment of a person as the responsible insolvency practitioner, the proxy-holder may, unless the proxy states otherwise, vote for or against (as he thinks fit) any resolution for the nomination or appointment of that person jointly with another or others.

(5) A proxy-holder may propose any resolution which, if proposed by another, would be a resolution in favour of which by virtue of the proxy he would be entitled to vote.

(6) Where a proxy gives specific directions as to voting, this does not, unless the proxy states otherwise, preclude the proxy-holder from voting at his discretion on resolutions put to the meeting which are not dealt with in the proxy.".

Amendment of Rule 8.5

136. In paragraph (4) of Rule 8.5 for the words "to be used" to the end there shall be substituted the words "(including proofs) sent or given, in accordance with directions contained in any notice convening the meeting, to the chairman of that meeting or to any other person by a creditor, member or contributory for the purpose of that meeting.".

Amendment of Rule 8.6

137.—(1) After paragraph (1) of Rule 8.6 there shall be inserted the following paragraph:–

"(1A) Where a proxy-holder has signed the proxy as being authorised to do so by his principal and the proxy specifically directs him to vote in the way mentioned in paragraph (1), he shall nevertheless not vote in that way unless he produces to the chairman of the meeting written authorisation from his principal sufficient to show that the proxy-holder was entitled so to sign the proxy.".

(2) In paragraph (2) of Rule 8.6 after the word "capacity" there shall be inserted the words "under Rule 8.3".

Amendment of Rule 8.7

138. After paragraph (2) of Rule 8.7 there shall be added the following paragraph:-

"(3) Nothing in this Rule requires the authority of a person to sign a proxy on behalf of a principal which is a corporation to be in the form of a resolution of that corporation.".

SECTION 10: AMENDMENT OF PART 11 OF THE RULES

Amendment of Rule 11.2

139.—(1) In paragraph (1) of Rule 11.2 after the word "creditors" there shall be inserted the words "whose addresses are known to him and".

(2) After paragraph (1) of Rule 11.2 there shall be inserted the following paragraph:-

"(1A) Before declaring a first dividend, the responsible insolvency practitioner shall, unless he has previously by public advertisement invited creditors to prove their debts, give notice of the intended dividend by public advertisement.".

(3) In paragraph (2) of Rule 11.2 for the words "The notice" there shall be substituted the words "Any notice under paragraph (1) and any notice of a first dividend under paragraph (1A)".

Amendment of Rule 11.12

140. In paragraph (2) of Rule 11.12 there shall be added at the end the words "and public advertisement of the intended dividend need only be given if the insolvency practitioner thinks fit".

Amendment of Rule 11.13

141. In paragraph (2) of Rule 11.13 for the words "an amount" there shall be substituted the words "a percentage".

SECTION 11: AMENDMENT OF PART 12 OF THE RULES

Amendment of Rule 12.1

142.—(1) In paragraph (1) of Rule 12.1 for the words "make regulations" there shall be substituted the words ", subject to the Act and the Rules, make regulations with respect to any matter provided for in the Rules as relates to the carrying out of the functions of a liquidator, provisional liquidator, administrator or administrative receiver of a company, an interim receiver appointed under section 286, of the official receiver while acting as receiver or manager under section 287 or of a trustee of a bankrupt's estate, including, without prejudice to the generality of the foregoing, provision".

(2) In paragraph (3) of Rule 12.1 there shall be added at the end the words:-

"
; and
    (d) contain such incidental, supplemental and transitional provisions as may appear to the Secretary of State necessary or expedient".

Amendment of Rule 12.3

143.—(1) In subparagraph (b) of paragraph (2) of Rule 12.3 there shall be added at the end the words "or section 1 of the Criminal Justice (Scotland) Act 1987".

(2) After paragraph (2) of Rule 12.3 there shall be inserted the following paragraph:-

"(2A) The following are not provable except at a time when all other claims of creditors in the insolvency proceedings (other than any of a kind mentioned in this paragraph) have been paid in full with interest under section 189(2) or, as the case may be, section 328(4)-
    (a) in a winding up or a bankruptcy, any claim arising by virtue of—
        (i) section 6(3)(a) of the Financial Services Act 1986, not being a claim also arising by virtue of section 6(3)(b) of that Act, or
        (ii) section 61(3)(a) of that Act, not being a claim also arising by virtue of section 61(3)(b) of that Act;
    (b) in a winding up or a bankruptcy, any claim arising by virtue of section 49 of the Banking Act 1987;

(c) in a winding up, any claim which by virtue of the Act or any other enactment is a claim the payment of which in a bankruptcy or a winding up is to be postponed.".

Insertion of Rule 12.4A

144. After Rule 12.4 there shall be inserted the following rule:–

"Quorum at meeting of creditors or contributories

12.4A.—(1) Any meeting of creditors or contributories in insolvency proceedings is competent to act if a quorum is present.

(2) Subject to the next paragraph, a quorum is–
  (a) in the case of a creditors' meeting, at least one creditor entitled to vote;
  (b) in the case of a meeting of contributories, at least 2 contributories so entitled, or all the contributories, if their number does not exceed 2.

(3) For the purposes of this Rule, the reference to the creditor or contributories necessary to constitute a quorum is to those persons present or represented by proxy by any person (including the chairman) and in the case of any proceedings under Parts I–VII of the Act includes persons duly represented under section 375 of the Companies Act.

(4) Where at any meeting of creditors or contributories–
  (a) the provisions of this Rule as to a quorum being present are satisfied by the attendance of–
   (i) the chairman alone, or
   (ii) one other person in addition to the chairman, and
  (b) the chairman is aware, by virtue of proofs and proxies received or otherwise, that one or more additional persons would, if attending, be entitled to vote,
the meeting shall not commence until at least the expiry of 15 minutes after the time appointed for its commencement.".

Amendment of Rule 12.7

145. For paragraph (3) of Rule 12.7 there shall be substituted the following:–

"(3) Where any form contained in Schedule 4 is substantially the same as one used for a corresponding purpose under either–
  (a) the law and practice obtaining before the coming into force of the Rules; or
  (b) if the form was first required to be used after the coming into force of the Rules, the law and practice obtaining before the making of the requirement,
whichever shall be appropriate in any case, the latter may continue to be used (with the necessary modifications) until 1 March 1988.".

Amendment of Rule 12.10

146. After paragraph (1) of Rule 12.10 there shall be inserted the following paragraph:–

"(1A) A document to be served by post may be sent to the last known address of the person to be served.".

Amendment of Rule 12.11

147. In paragraph (1) of Rule 12.11 after the word "Subject" there shall be inserted the words "to Rule 12.10 and".

Amendment of Rule 12.13

148. After paragraph (3) of Rule 12.13 there shall be added the following paragraph:–

"(4) Nothing in this Rule entitles the insolvency practitioner to decline to allow the inspection of any proof or proxy.".

Amendment of Rule 12.15

149. In Rule 12.15 before the word "Rules" there shall be inserted the words "Act or the".

Insertion of Rule 12.15A

150. After Rule 12.15 there shall be inserted the following rule:–

"Charge for copy documents

12.15A. Where the responsible insolvency practitioner or the official receiver is requested by a creditor, member, contributory or member of a liquidation or creditors' committee to supply copies of any documents he is entitled to require the payment of the appropriate fee in respect of the supply of the documents.".

SECTION 12: AMENDMENT OF PART 13 OF THE RULES

Amendment of Rule 13.13

151. For paragraph (1) of Rule 13.13 there shall be substituted the following:–

"(1) "Business day" has the same meaning as in section 251 of the Act except in Rules 1.7, 4.10, 4.11, 4.16, 4.20, 5.10 and 6.23, where, if the court is the High Court, it has the same meaning as is given in Order 65, Rule 5(4) of the Rules of the Supreme Court, and, in relation to a county court, it means any day on which the court office is open in accordance with Order 2, Rule 2 of the County Court Rules.".

Amendment of Rule 13.14

152. In subparagraph (a) of paragraph (1) of Rule 13.14 the word "administrative" shall be omitted.

PART 2

AMENDMENT OF SCHEDULES TO THE PRINCIPAL RULES

Amendment of Schedule 2

153. Schedule 2 to the principal Rules shall be amended in accordance with Part 3 of this Schedule.

Amendment of Schedule 3

154. For paragraphs 1–3 of Schedule 3 to the principal Rules there shall be substituted the following:–

"**1.** For attendance   £54.00.

2. Per folio of written record   75.4p plus 4p per folio for all copies.

3. Travelling time   £5.67 per hour after first hour of each journey.".

Amendment of the index to Schedule 4

155.—(1) For the entry relating to Form 3.1 (including the form number) in the index to forms in Schedule 4 to the principal Rules there shall be substituted the following:–

"**3.1B** Notice requiring preparation and submission of administrative receivership statement of affairs".

(2) There shall be inserted in that index the following form numbers, titles and headings:–

"**2.4A** Notice to administrator of administration order"

"**3.1** Written acceptance of appointment by receiver

3.1A Notice of appointment of administrative receiver (for newspaper or London Gazette)"

"**4.14A** Notice to official receiver of appointment of provisional liquidator"

"PART 5: INDIVIDUAL VOLUNTARY ARRANGEMENTS

5.1 Order for stay pending hearing of application for interim order

5.2 Interim order of court under section 252 of the Insolvency Act 1986

5.3 Order extending effect of interim order

5.4 Alternative orders to be made at hearing to consider chairman's report"

"**6.24A** Order for substitution of petitioner on creditor's petition

6.24B Change of carriage order"

"**6.79A** Charging order under section 313 of the Insolvency Act 1986".

(3) For the entries relating to the forms shown in the left-hand column below there shall be substituted the words shown on the same line in the right-hand column:–

Form
1.1   "Report of meetings approving voluntary arrangement"

2.5   "Notice of administration order (for newspaper or London Gazette)"

2.8   "Notice requiring preparation and submission of administration statement of affairs"

2.11   "Notice of creditors' meeting in administration proceedings"

2.16   "Notice to court of resignation by administrator under Rule 2.53(1) of the Insolvency Rules 1986"

2.17   "Notice to court of resignation by administrator under Rule 2.53(2) of the Insolvency Rules 1986"

4.16   "Notice requiring preparation and submission of statement of company's affairs"

4.32   "Notice to court of resignation of liquidator following meeting of creditors"

6.1   "Statutory demand under section 268(1)(a) of the Insolvency Act 1986—debt for liquidated sum payable immediately"

6.2   "Statutory demand under section 268(1)(a) of the Insolvency Act 1986—debt for liquidated sum payable immediately following a judgment or order of the court"

6.3   "Statutory demand under section 268(2) of the Insolvency Act 1986—debt payable at future date"

7.9   "Order for production of person arrested under warrant issued under section 134, 236, 364 or 366 of the Insolvency Act 1986"

7.15   "Affidavit in support of application for committal for contempt of court".

(4) The entry relating to Form 7.16 shall be omitted.

References to forms

156.—(1) There shall be inserted in the margin against the principal rules shown in the left-hand column below the form reference shown on the same line in the right-hand column:–

Rule	Form
2.10(1)	"[FORM 2.4A]"
2.19(4)	"[FORM 2.22]"
3.1(3)	"[FORM 3.1]"
3.2(3)	"[FORM 3.1A]"
4.25A	"[FORM 4.14A]"
4.171(3-CVL)	"[FORM 4.50]"
5.7(1)	"[FORM 5.2]"
6.30(2)	"[FORM 6.24A]"
6.31(2)	"[FORM 6.24B]"
6.237(1)	"[FORM 6.79A]"
7.22(a)	"[FORM 7.9]"

(2) In the margin against Rule 3.3(1) for the reference to Form 3.1 there shall be substituted a reference to Form 3.1B.

New forms

157. The forms contained in Part 4 of this Schedule shall be added to Schedule 4 to the principal Rules as Forms 2.4A, 3.1, 3.1A, 4.14A, 5.1, 5.2, 5.3, 5.4, 6.24A, 6.24B and 6.79A.

Amended forms

158.—(1) The forms contained in Section 1 of Part 5 of this Schedule shall be substituted for the forms identically numbered in Schedule 4 to the principal Rules.

(2) The form contained in Section 2 of Part 5 of this Schedule shall be substituted for Form 3.1 in Schedule 4 to the principal Rules.

Omitted form

159. Form 7.16 in Schedule 4 to the principal Rules shall be omitted.

PART 3

AMENDMENT OF SCHEDULE 2

Schedule 2 to the principal Rules shall be replaced by the following:–

"SCHEDULE 2   Rule 6.40(3)

ALTERNATIVE COURTS FOR DEBTORS' PETITIONS IN BANKRUPTCY

Debtor's own county court	*Nearest full-time court*
ABERDARE	CARDIFF
ABERYSTWYTH	CARDIFF
AYLESBURY	LUTON
BANBURY	LUTON or GLOUCESTER or READING
BANGOR	BIRKENHEAD or CHESTER
BARNSLEY	SHEFFIELD
BARNSTAPLE	EXETER
BARROW IN FURNESS	BLACKPOOL or PRESTON
BATH	BRISTOL
BEDFORD	LUTON
BLACKBURN	PRESTON
BLACKWOOD	CARDIFF
BOSTON	NOTTINGHAM
BRIDGEND	CARDIFF
BRIDGWATER	BRISTOL
BURNLEY	BOLTON or PRESTON
BURTON ON TRENT	LEICESTER or DERBY or NOTTINGHAM
BURY ST. EDMUNDS	CAMBRIDGE
CANTERBURY	CROYDON or THE HIGH COURT (LONDON)
CARLISLE	PRESTON or BLACKPOOL
CARMARTHEN	CARDIFF
CHELMSFORD	SOUTHEND or THE HIGH COURT (LONDON)
CHELTENHAM	GLOUCESTER
CHESTERFIELD	SHEFFIELD
COLCHESTER	SOUTHEND or THE HIGH COURT (LONDON)
COVENTRY	BIRMINGHAM
CREWE	STOKE or CHESTER
DARLINGTON	MIDDLESBROUGH
DEWSBURY	LEEDS
DONCASTER	SHEFFIELD
DUDLEY	BIRMINGHAM
DURHAM	NEWCASTLE
EASTBOURNE	BRIGHTON
GREAT GRIMSBY	HULL
GREAT YARMOUTH	NORWICH
GUILDFORD	CROYDON
HALIFAX	LEEDS
HARROGATE	LEEDS
HASTINGS	BRIGHTON
HAVERFORDWEST	CARDIFF
HEREFORD	GLOUCESTER
HERTFORD	LUTON
HUDDERSFIELD	LEEDS
IPSWICH	NORWICH or SOUTHEND
KENDAL	BLACKPOOL or PRESTON
KIDDERMINSTER	BIRMINGHAM
KING'S LYNN	NORWICH or CAMBRIDGE
LANCASTER	BLACKPOOL or PRESTON
LINCOLN	NOTTINGHAM
MACCLESFIELD	STOKE or MANCHESTER
MAIDSTONE	CROYDON or THE HIGH COURT (LONDON)
MEDWAY	CROYDON or THE HIGH COURT (LONDON)
MERTHYR TYDFIL	CARDIFF
MILTON KEYNES	LUTON

"SCHEDULE 2—*continued*

Debtor's own county court	Nearest full-time court
NEATH	CARDIFF
NEWBURY	READING
NEWPORT (GWENT)	CARDIFF
NEWPORT (I.O.W.)	SOUTHAMPTON or PORTSMOUTH
NORTHAMPTON	LUTON
OXFORD	READING
PETERBOROUGH	CAMBRIDGE
PONTYPRIDD	CARDIFF
PORTMADOC	BIRKENHEAD or STOKE or CHESTER
RHYL	BIRKENHEAD or CHESTER
ROCHDALE	OLDHAM or MANCHESTER
SALISBURY	BOURNEMOUTH or SOUTHAMPTON
SCARBOROUGH	YORK or HULL or MIDDLESBROUGH
SCUNTHORPE	HULL or SHEFFIELD
SHREWSBURY	STOKE
ST. ALBANS	LUTON
STAFFORD	STOKE
STOCKTON ON TEES	MIDDLESBROUGH
STOCKPORT	MANCHESTER
STOURBRIDGE	BIRMINGHAM
SUNDERLAND	NEWCASTLE
SWANSEA	CARDIFF
SWINDON	GLOUCESTER or READING
TAMESIDE	MANCHESTER
TAUNTON	EXETER or BRISTOL
TORQUAY	EXETER
TRURO	PLYMOUTH
TUNBRIDGE WELLS	CROYDON
WAKEFIELD	LEEDS
WARRINGTON	CHESTER or LIVERPOOL or MANCHESTER
WARWICK	BIRMINGHAM
WELSHPOOL	STOKE or CHESTER
WEST BROMWICH	BIRMINGHAM
WEYMOUTH	BOURNEMOUTH
WIGAN	BOLTON or MANCHESTER or PRESTON
WINCHESTER	SOUTHAMPTON
WORCESTER	GLOUCESTER
WORKINGTON	PRESTON or BLACKPOOL
WREXHAM	BIRKENHEAD or STOKE or CHESTER
YEOVIL	EXETER or BRISTOL".

PART 4

NEW FORMS

Form 2.4A

Rule 2.10   Notice to Administrator of Administration Order

(TITLE)

(a) Insert name and address of administrator

To: (a)

Order pronounced this _____ day of _____ 19____ by Mr

for an administration order against the under-named company under section 8 of the Insolvency Act 1986.

Name of company:

Registered office of company:

(b) Insert full name, address, telephone number and reference (if any)

Petitioner: (b)

Petitioner's solicitors: (b)

Date of presentation of petition:

Form 3.1

Rule 3.1   Written acceptance of appointment
by Receiver

(TITLE)

(a) Insert name and   To: (a)
address of person
making appointment

(b) Insert full name   (b)
and address of
appointee   hereby accepts appointment as receiver of

(c) Insert name of   (c)
company

(d) Insert date   in accordance with the instrument of appointment received on (d) _____
at (e) _____ hours

(e) Insert time

Date: _____

Time: _____ hours

Signed: _____

Name of signatory: _____
(BLOCK LETTERS)

(by or on behalf of the appointee)

Form 3.1A

Rule 3.2

Notice of appointment of Administrative Receiver
(for newspaper or London Gazette)

(Name of Company)

Registered number _____

(a) Insert any other name(s) with which the company has been registered in the last 12 months

Former company name(s) (a) _____

(b) Insert any trading name(s) used by the company in the last 12 months

Trading name(s) (b) _____

Nature of business _____

(c) Insert the number of the trade classification listed overleaf which most closely relates to the business of the company

Trade classification (c) _____

Date of appointment of administrative receiver(s) _____

Name of person appointing the administrative receiver(s) _____

_____

(d) Insert name(s) of appointee(s)

(d) _____
Administrative Receiver/Joint Administrative Receivers
(office holder no(s)

Address(es)

TRADE CLASSIFICATION

NOTE: This page is *not* part of the advertisement

DIVISION 0
01   AGRICULTURE
02   FORESTRY AND FISHING

DIVISION 1
03   MINING AND ENERGY INDUSTRIES

DIVISION 2
MANUFACTURING INDUSTRIES:—
04   MANUFACTURE OF FOOD, DRINK AND TOBACCO
05   MANUFACTURE OF CHEMICALS
06   METAL MANUFACTURE
07   ENGINEERING AND ALLIED INDUSTRIES
08   TEXTILES AND CLOTHING MANUFACTURE
09   MANUFACTURE OF TIMBER AND FURNITURE
10   PAPER, PRINTING AND PUBLISHING
11   OTHER MANUFACTURE

DIVISION 3
WHOLESALE DISTRIBUTION:—
12   WHOLESALE OF FOOD AND DRINK
13   WHOLESALE OF TEXTILES AND CLOTHING
14   MOTOR VEHICLE WHOLESALERS
15   OTHER WHOLESALE

DIVISION 4
RETAILING:—
16   RETAIL OF FOOD, DRINK AND TOBACCO
17   RETAIL OF TEXTILES AND CLOTHING
18   RETAIL OF BOOKS, PAPERS ETC.
19   MOTOR VEHICLES AND PETROL SALES
20   RETAIL OF FURNITURE
21   RETAIL OF ELECTRICAL GOODS
22   OTHER RETAIL

DIVISION 5
CONSTRUCTION:—
(SIC Division 5)
23   GENERAL CONSTRUCTION AND DEMOLITION
24   HOME IMPROVEMENTS
25   DECORATING AND SMALLWORKS
26   BUILDING REPAIRS
27   ELECTRICAL AND PLUMBING

DIVISION 6
TRANSPORT AND COMMUNICATIONS:—
28   ROAD TRANSPORT
29   AIR TRANSPORT
30   SHIPPING
31   TRAVEL AGENTS
32   OTHER TRANSPORT AND COMMUNICATIONS

DIVISION 7
FINANCE AND BUSINESS SERVICES:—
33   INSURANCE
34   ACCOUNTANTS AND LEGAL SERVICES
35   REAL ESTATE
36   COMPUTER SERVICES
37   MANAGEMENT SERVICES
38   OTHER BUSINESS SERVICES

DIVISION 8
OTHER SERVICES:—
39   RECREATIONAL SERVICES
40   MEDICAL SERVICES
41   EDUCATIONAL SERVICES
42   REPAIRS OF CONSUMER GOODS
43   LAUNDRY
44   HAIRDRESSING AND BEAUTY PARLOURS
45   SCRAP METAL DEALERS
46   OTHER SERVICES

DIVISION 9
HOTELS AND CATERING:—
47   RESIDENTIAL ACCOMMODATION
48   LICENSED PREMISES
49   RESTAURANTS
50   OTHER CATERING

Form 4.14A

ule 4.25A

Notice to Official Receiver of appointment of Provisional Liquidator

(TITLE)

(a) Insert address   To the Official Receiver of the Court (a)

Order pronounced this _____ day of _____ 19____ by Mr

(b) Insert "the official receiver" or, if an isolvency practitioner to be appointed, his ull name and address including name of firm if appropriate)   for the appointment of (b)

as provisional liquidator of the under-named company prior to any winding-up order being made.

Name of company:

Registered office of company:

(c) Insert full name, address, telephone number and reference (if any)   Petitioner: (c)

Petitioner's solicitors: (c)

Section 254   Order granting stay pending hearing of application for Interim
                         Order

                                        (TITLE)

(a) Insert full name and   Upon the application of (a)
    address of applicant

                           And upon hearing

                           And upon reading the evidence

(b) Insert details of any   It is ordered that (b)
    action, execution or
    other legal process to
    be stayed

                           be stayed over the hearing of the application for an interim order pursuant to
                           section 252 of the Insolvency Act 1986, namely the   day of
                                    19   or over any adjournment thereof.

                           Dated _____

Form 5.2

Rule 5.7   Interim Order of Court under section 252 of the Insolvency Act 1986

(TITLE)

(a) Insert full name and address of applicant

Upon the application of (a)

And upon hearing

And upon reading the evidence

(b) Delete as applicable

(b) [And upon the application of   , the nominee, for an extension of the period for which the interim order shall have effect pursuant to section 256(4) of the Insolvency Act 1986,]

(c) 14 days unless an extension is granted on the application of the nominee

It is ordered that during the period of (c) ____ days beginning with the day after the date of this order and during any extended period for which this interim order has effect:

    (i) no bankruptcy petition relating to the above-named (d) _____

(d) Insert name of debtor

    _____ (the debtor) may be presented or proceeded with, and

    (ii) no other proceedings, and no execution or other legal process, may be commenced or continued against the debtor or his property except with the leave of the court.

And it is ordered that the report of the nominee be submitted and delivered by him to the court not later than (e)

(e) Date to be 2 business days before the day on which the report is to be considered

[And it is ordered that (f)   ]

(f) Insert details of any orders made under section 255 (3) and (4) of the Insolvency Act 1986

And it is ordered that

(g) Delete if debtor is not a bankrupt or if he is a bankrupt but the applicant is the official receiver

(g) [And it is ordered that the applicant forthwith serve a copy of this order on the official receiver.]

Date _____

Time _____ hours

Place _____

be appointed for consideration of the nominee's report.

Dated _____

Section 256

Order extending effect of Interim Order

(TITLE)

(a) Insert full name and address of applicant

Upon the application of (a)

And upon hearing

And upon reading the evidence

And the court having this day considered the report of the nominee submitted

(b) Insert date of filing

pursuant to section 256 of the Insolvency Act 1986 and filed on (b)

(c) Insert date

It is ordered that the period for which the interim order made on (c) _____ has effect be extended to (c) _____ to enable a meeting of the debtor's creditors to be summoned to consider the debtor's proposals, such meeting as proposed by the nominee to be held on:—

(d) Date to be not less than 14 days from date of filing of report under Rule 5.13 nor more than 28 days from date of consideration of report under Rule 5.12

Date (d) _____

Time (e) _____ hours

Place _____

(e) Time to be between 10.00 and 16.00 hours on a business day (Rule 5.14(2))

And it is ordered that this application be adjourned to:—

Date _____

Time _____ hours

Place _____

for consideration of the report of the chairman of the creditors' meeting.

Dated _____

Form 5.4

Sections 259, 260 and 261

Alternative orders to be made at hearing to consider chairman's report

(TITLE)

(a) Insert full name and address of applicant

Upon the application of (a)

And upon hearing

(b) Delete as applicable

(b) [And upon reading the report of the chairman of the creditors' meeting that the said meeting had [approved the proposed voluntary arrangement with or without modifications] [declined to approve the debtor's proposal with or without modifications]]

[It is ordered that this application be [adjourned generally with liberty to restore] [adjourned to the   day of   19   to enable an application to be made to extend the time for filing the report of the chairman of the creditors' meeting]]

[And it is ordered that the time for filing the said report be extended to this day.]

[And whereas:
  (i) on the   day of   19   a bankruptcy petition No   of 19   was filed by   against the above-named (the debtor) and
  (ii) by virtue of section 260(5) of the Insolvency Act 1986 the said petition is deemed, unless the court otherwise orders, to have been dismissed

This court makes no further order save that

(i) the registration of the petition as a pending action at the Land Charges Department of HM Land Registry on   under Reference No PA   may be vacated upon the application of the debtor under the Land Charges Rules.

(c) Insert any other orders made in respect of the petition

(ii) (c)   ]

Dated _____

NOTICE TO DEBTOR (where voluntary arrangement approved and there is a pending petition which is deemed to be dismissed).

It is your responsibility and in your interest to ensure that the registration of the petition at HM Land Registry is cancelled.

III/1y*

Form 6.24A

Rule 6.30

Order for substitution of petitioner on creditor's petition

(TITLE)

Upon the hearing of this petition this day

(a) Insert name of creditor who wishes to be substituted as petitioner

and upon the application of (a)

for an order that he be substituted as petitioning creditor therein pursuant to Rule 6.30 of the Insolvency Rules 1986

And upon hearing

(b) Recite details of demand or return of sheriff or bailiff

And upon reading (b)

(c) Insert name of original petitioning creditor

[It is ordered that upon payment by the said (a)   of the statutory deposit to the court the statutory deposit paid by (c)

to the court be repaid to him by the official receiver]

And it is ordered that the said (a)   be substituted as petitioning creditor in place of the said (c)   and that the said (a)   be at liberty to amend the said petition accordingly.
And it is ordered that the said (a)   do within 7 days from the date of this order file an affidavit of truth of statements in the bankruptcy petition and exhibit thereto a sealed copy of the said amended petition and at least 14 days before the date of the adjourned hearing of the petition serve* upon the above-named debtor a sealed copy of the amended petition.
And it is ordered that the hearing of the said amended petition be adjourned to:

*NOTE: In the absence of any order to the contrary, this will involve personal service

Date _____

Time _____ hours

Place _____

It is ordered that the question of the costs of the said (c)
[and of the statutory deposit] be reserved until the final determination of the said amended petition.

Dated _____

Form 6.24B

Rule 6.31   Change of carriage order

(TITLE)

Upon the hearing of this petition this day

And upon the application of (a)   , a creditor of the debtor, for an order

(a) Insert name of
creditor who wishes
to be given carriage
of the petition
giving him carriage of the petition in place of (b)   (the petitioning
creditor) pursuant to Rule 6.31 of the Insolvency Rules 1986

And upon hearing

(b) Insert name of
original petitioning
creditor
And upon reading

It is ordered that the carriage of this petition be given to the said (a)
in place of the said (b)   and that all further proceedings herein be
carried on by the said (a)   in the name of the said (b)

And it is ordered that the said (a)   do within   days from the
date of this order serve upon the said debtor and the said (b)   a
sealed copy of this order

And it is ordered that the said (a)   may rely upon all evidence
previously adduced in these proceedings whether by affidavit or otherwise

And it is ordered that the further hearing of this petition be adjourned to:

Date _____

Time _____ hours

Place _____

And it is ordered that the question of the costs of the said (b)
be reserved until the final determination of this petition.

Dated _____

Form 6.79A

Rule 6.237   Charging Order under section 313 of the Insolvency Act 1986

(TITLE)

(a) Insert full name and   Upon the application of (a)
address of applicant   the trustee in bankruptcy of the above-named bankrupt

And upon hearing

And upon reading the report of

(b) Delete as   And the trustee and the bankrupt having (b) [agreed] [failed to agree] the terms of
applicable   this order,

It is ordered that the interest of the trustee and his successors in title in the
property specified in the Schedule hereto shall stand charged for the benefit of the
bankrupt's estate with:
  (i) £   being the total sum which on present information remains owing
       to unsecured creditors of the bankrupt;
  (ii) all other amounts which are payable otherwise than to the bankrupt out of
        the estate;
  (iii) interest on the said sum and said other amounts at the rate of £   per cent
         per annum as from the date of this order.

(c) Insert details of any   (b) [And it is further ordered (c)   ]
conditions imposed by
the court: see Rule
6.237(6)(e)   And it is ordered that upon the registration of the said charge by the
Superintendent of the Land Charges Department under the Land Charges Act
1972 or the Chief Land Registrar under the Land Registration Acts the said interest
in the property shall cease to be comprised in the bankrupt's estate and shall vest
in the bankrupt subject to the said charge and any prior charge.

The Schedule above referred to.

(d) Insert particulars of   (d)
property

(b) [The title to the property is registered at HM Land Registry and the title number
is _____]

Dated _____

PART 5

AMENDED FORMS

SECTION 1

Form 1.1

Rule 1.24

The Insolvency Act 1986
Report of Meetings
Approving Voluntary Arrangement
**Pursuant to section 4 of the
Insolvency Act 1986**

To the Registrar of Companies

S.4

For official use

Company Number

Name of Company

(a) Insert full name of
company

(a)_____

Limited

(b) Insert full name and
address

I (b)

(c) Insert date

the chairman of meetings held in pursuance of section 4
of the Insolvency Act 1986 on (c)
enclose a copy of my report of the said meetings.

Signed

Date

Presenter's name,
address and reference
(if any):

For Official Use
Liquidation Section   Post Room

Form 2.1

ule 2.1   Petition for Administration Order

(TITLE)

a) Insert title of court   To (a) _____

_____

(b) Insert full name(s)   The petition of (b) _____
and address(es) of
petitioner(s)
_____

_____

(c) Delete if petition   (c) [presented by the directors under section 9 of the Insolvency Act 1986].
not presented by the
company's directors
(d) Insert full name of   1. (d) _____
company subject to
petition   (hereinafter called "the company") was incorporated on (e) _____ under
(e) Insert date of   the Companies Act 19__
incorporation

(f) Insert address of   2. The registered office of the company is at (f) _____
registered office

_____

(g) Insert amount of   3. The nominal capital of the company is (g) £_____ divided into ____ shares of
nominal capital and   £____ each. The amount of the capital paid up or credited as paid up is (h) £____
how it is divided
(h) Insert amount of   4. The principal objects for which the company was established are as follows
capital paid up or
credited as paid up
_____

_____

and other objects set forth in the memorandum of association thereof.

5. The petitioner(s) believe(s) that the company is or is likely to become unable to
pay its debts and that an administration order would be likely to achieve

(j) Delete such as are   (j)   (i) the survival of the company and the whole or some part of its undertaking
inapplicable   as a going concern
                                (ii) the approval of a voluntary arrangement with its creditors under Part 1 of
                                     the Insolvency Act 1986
                               (iii) the sanctioning of a compromise or arrangement between the company
                                     and such persons as are mentioned in section 425 of the Companies Act
                                     1985
                               (iv) a more advantageous realisation of the company's assets than would be
                                     effected on a winding up

for the reasons stated in the affidavit of   filed in support hereof.

6. The petitioner(s) propose(s) that during the period for which the order is in force the affairs, business and property of the company be managed by

(k) Insert full name(s)   (k) _____
and address(es) of
proposed   _____
administrator(s)
                       _____

who is (are) to the best of the petitioner's knowledge and belief qualified to act as (an) insolvency practitioner(s) in relation to the company. The petitioner(s) therefore pray(s) as follows:—

(l) Insert full name of   (1) that the court make an administration order in relation to (l) _____
company
                       _____

(m) Insert name(s) of   (2) that (m) _____
proposed
administrator(s)   be appointed to be the administrator(s) of the said company

(n) Insert details of any (3) (n)
ancilliary orders
sought

                       or

                       (4) that such other order may be made in the premises as shall be just.

                       Note:
                       It is intended to serve this petition on _____

                       _____

                       _____

                       _____

(o) Insert here name,   This petition was issued by (o) _____
address, telephone
number and reference   _____
(if any) of a solicitor
acting for the   _____
petitioner
                       _____ (solicitor for

                       the petitioner(s) whose address for service is:

                       _____

                       _____

                       _____

Form 2.5

Rule 2.10

Notice of Administration Order (for newspaper or London Gazette)

(TITLE)

Registered number _____

Nature of business _____

(a) Insert the number of the trade classification listed overleaf which most closely relates to the business of the company

Trade classification (a) _____

(b) Insert date

Administration order made (b) _____ 19____

_____

Administrator/Joint administrators (office holder no(s)   )

TRADE CLASSIFICATION

NOTE: This page is *not* part of the advertisement

DIVISION 0

01	AGRICULTURE
02	FORESTRY AND FISHING

DIVISION 1

03	MINING AND ENERGY INDUSTRIES

DIVISION 2

MANUFACTURING INDUSTRIES:—

04	MANUFACTURE OF FOOD, DRINK AND TOBACCO
05	MANUFACTURE OF CHEMICALS
06	METAL MANUFACTURE
07	ENGINEERING AND ALLIED INDUSTRIES
08	TEXTILES AND CLOTHING MANUFACTURE
09	MANUFACTURE OF TIMBER AND FURNITURE
10	PAPER, PRINTING AND PUBLISHING
11	OTHER MANUFACTURE

DIVISION 3

WHOLESALE DISTRIBUTION:—

12	WHOLESALE OF FOOD AND DRINK
13	WHOLESALE OF TEXTILES AND CLOTHING
14	MOTOR VEHICLE WHOLESALERS
15	OTHER WHOLESALE

DIVISION 4

RETAILING:—

16	RETAIL OF FOOD, DRINK AND TOBACCO
17	RETAIL OF TEXTILES AND CLOTHING
18	RETAIL OF BOOKS, PAPERS ETC.
19	MOTOR VEHICLES AND PETROL SALES
20	RETAIL OF FURNITURE
21	RETAIL OF ELECTRICAL GOODS
22	OTHER RETAIL

DIVISION 5

CONSTRUCTION:—
(SIC Division 5)

23	GENERAL CONSTRUCTION AND DEMOLITION
24	HOME IMPROVEMENTS
25	DECORATING AND SMALLWORKS
26	BUILDING REPAIRS
27	ELECTRICAL AND PLUMBING

DIVISION 6

TRANSPORT AND COMMUNICATIONS:—

28	ROAD TRANSPORT
29	AIR TRANSPORT
30	SHIPPING
31	TRAVEL AGENTS
32	OTHER TRANSPORT AND COMMUNICATIONS

DIVISION 7

FINANCE AND BUSINESS SERVICES:—

33	INSURANCE
34	ACCOUNTANTS AND LEGAL SERVICES
35	REAL ESTATE
36	COMPUTER SERVICES
37	MANAGEMENT SERVICES
38	OTHER BUSINESS SERVICES

DIVISION 8

OTHER SERVICES:—

39	RECREATIONAL SERVICES
40	MEDICAL SERVICES
41	EDUCATIONAL SERVICES
42	REPAIRS OF CONSUMER GOODS
43	LAUNDRY
44	HAIRDRESSING AND BEAUTY PARLOURS
45	SCRAP METAL DEALERS
46	OTHER SERVICES

DIVISION 9

HOTELS AND CATERING:—

47	RESIDENTIAL ACCOMMODATION
48	LICENSED PREMISES
49	RESTAURANTS
50	OTHER CATERING

Form 2.8

Rule 2.11   Notice Requiring Preparation and Submission of Administration Statement of Affairs

(TITLE)

(a) Insert name of company

Take notice that you are required to prepare and submit to me a statement as to the affairs of (a)

(b) Insert date by which statement must be submitted

by (b)

(c) Insert names and addresses of other persons concerned

A similar notice has been sent to each of the following persons (c)

(d) Delete words in brackets if not applicable

Section 235 of the Insolvency Act 1986 places a duty on you (d) (as an officer of the company) to provide the administrator with information and attend upon him if required; I have to warn you that failure to submit the statement of affairs as required by this notice, or to co-operate with the administrator under section 235 of the Insolvency Act 1986, may make you liable to a fine and, for continued contravention, to a daily default fine.

Under paragraph 10 of Schedule 1 to the Company Directors Disqualification Act 1986 failure to submit a statement of affairs or to co-operate with the administrator under section 235 of the Insolvency Act 1986 are matters which may be taken into account by the court in determining whether a person is unfit to be an officer of or to be involved in the management of a company. Unfit conduct may result in a disqualification order being made by the court.

Dated _____
              Administrator (name and address)

Note:
Forms for the preparation of the statement of affairs
(a) may be obtained from the administrator on request; or
(b) are enclosed.

Rule 2.19   Notice of Creditors' Meetings in
Administration Proceedings

(TITLE)

Notice is hereby given that a meeting of creditors in the above matter is to be held at

_____

_____

on the _____ day of _____ 19__

at _____ hours

(1) to consider my proposals under s.23(1) of the Insolvency Act 1986 and to consider establishing a creditors' committee

Delete whichever is
inapplicable

(2) under s. 14(2)(b) of the Insolvency Act 1986
(3) at the request of creditors under s.17(3)(a) of the Insolvency Act 1986
(4) at the direction of the court under s.17(3)(b) of the Insolvency Act 1986
(5) under s.25(2)(b) of the Insolvency Act 1986

[(2)-(5) only] for the purposes of _____

_____

_____

A proxy form is enclosed which should be completed and returned to me by the date of the meeting if you cannot attend the meeting and wish to be represented. In order to be entitled to vote at the meeting you must give to me, not later than 12.00 hours on the business day before the day fixed for the meeting, details in writing of your claim.

The Administrator

Form 2.12

Rule 2.30

Report of Meeting of Creditors

(TITLE)

I _____

administrator of the company hereby report that [a] [an adjourned] meeting of creditors in the above matter was held at _____

_____

_____

on the _____ day of _____ 19__
at which:

(1) Proposals [Revised proposals] in the form hereto annexed were approved

(2) _____

_____

_____

_____

were nominated to act as members of the creditors' committee

(3) The meeting declined to approve the proposals [revised proposals]

Dated this _____ day of _____ 19___

The Administrator

Form 2.16

Rule 2.53

Notice to Court of Resignation by Administrator Under Rule 2.53(1) of the Insolvency Rules 1986

(TITLE)

(a) Insert full name and address of administrator

I, (a) _____

_____

the administrator of the above company give notice that I am resigning from the

(b) Insert date said office of administrator with effect from (b)

_____

(c) See Rule 2.53(1) for the following reason(s): (c) _____

_____

_____

_____

(d) The date must be at least 7 days before that stated at (b) above

I confirm that on (d) _____

I gave notice to:

(i) _____

(ii) _____

(iii) _____

being persons who under section 13(3) of the Insolvency Act 1986 are entitled to apply for a vacancy in the office of administrator to be filled, of my intention to resign as administrator.

Signed _____

Dated _____

Form 2.17

Rule 2.53

Notice to Court of Resignation by Administrator Under Rule 2.53(2) of the Insolvency Rules 1986

(TITLE)

(a) Insert full name and address of administrator

I, (a) _____

_____

(b) Insert date

the administrator of the above company give notice that on (b) _____, the court gave me leave to resign from the said office of administrator with effect from (b) _____

(c) See Rule 2.53(2)

for the following reason(s): (c) _____

_____

_____

_____

_____

and I hereby resign.

(d) The date must be at least 7 days before application was made to the court for leave to resign.

I confirm that on (d) _____
I gave notice to:

(i) _____

(ii) _____

(iii) _____

being persons who under section 13(3) of the Insolvency Act 1986 are entitled to apply for a vacancy in the office of administrator to be filled, of my intention to apply to the court for leave to resign as administrator.

Signed _____

Dated _____

Rule 4.5

Statutory Demand under section 123(1)(a) or 222(1)(a) of the Insolvency Act 1986

Warning
- This is an **important** document. This demand must be dealt with **within 21 days** after its service upon the company or a winding-up order could be made in respect of the company.
- Please read the demand and notes carefully.

Notes for Creditor
- If the creditor is entitled to the debt by way of assignment, details of the original creditor and any intermediary assignees should be given in part B on page 3.
- If the amount of debt includes interest not previously notified to the company as included in its liability, details should be given, including the grounds upon which interest is charged. The amount of interest must be shown separately.
- Any other charge accruing due from time to time may be claimed. The amount or rate of the charge must be identified and the grounds on which it is claimed must be stated.
- In either case the amount claimed must be limited to that which has accrued due at the date of the demand.
- If signatory of the demand is a solicitor or other agent of the creditor the name of his/her firm should be given.

Demand

To _____

Address _____

_____

This demand is served on you by the creditor:

Name _____

Address _____

_____

The creditor claims that the company owes the sum of £_____ , full particulars of which are set out on page 2.

The creditor demands that the company do pay the above debt or secure or compound for it to the creditor's satisfaction.

Signature of individual _____

Name _____
(BLOCK LETTERS)

Date _____

*Position with or relationship to creditor _____

_____

*Delete if signed by the creditor himself

*I am authorised to make this demand on the creditor's behalf.

Address _____

_____

Tel. No. _____ Ref. _____

N.B. The person making this demand must complete the whole of this page, page 2 and parts A and B (as applicable) on page 3.

Form 4.1 contd.

Particulars of Debt.
These particulars must include (a) when the debt was incurred, (b) the consideration for the debt (or if there is no consideration the way in which it arose) and (c) the amount due as at the date of this demand.)

Notes for Creditor
Please make sure that you have read the notes on page 1 before completing this page.

Note:
If space is insufficient continue on reverse of page 3 and clearly indicate on this page that you are doing so.

PART A

The individual or individuals to whom any communication regarding this demand may be addressed is/are:—

Name _____

(BLOCK LETTERS)

Address _____

_____

Telephone Number _____

Reference _____

PART B

For completion if the creditor is entitled to the debt by way of assignment

	Name	Date(s) of Assignment
Original creditor		
Assignees		

How to comply with a statutory demand

If the company wishes to avoid a winding-up petition being presented it must pay the debt shown on page 1, particulars of which are set out on page 2 of this notice, within the period of **21 days after** its service upon the company. Alternatively, the company can attempt to come to a settlement with the creditor. To do this the company should:

- inform the individual (or one of the individuals) named in part A above immediately that it is willing and able to offer security for the debt to the creditor's satisfaction; or
- inform the individual (or one of the individuals) named in part A immediately that it is willing and able to compound for the debt to the creditor's satisfaction.

If the company disputes the demand in whole or in part it should:

- contact the individual (or one of the individuals) named in part A immediately.

REMEMBER! The company has only 21 days after the date of service on it of this document before the creditor may present a winding-up petition.

Rule 4.20   Order for Winding Up by the Court following upon the Discharge
of an Administration Order

(TITLE)

(a) Delete words in   Upon the petition of the company (a) [by its administrator (b) _____
brackets as applicable   _____] or [(b) _____
(b) Insert name and   _____ a [creditor] [member] of the above-named company] [pursuant
address   to leave of this court by order dated (c) _____] [by agreement with
(c) Insert date   the administrator dated (c) _____]

presented to this court on (c)

And upon hearing

And upon reading the administration order dated (c)

and the evidence

It is ordered that the said administration order be and the same is discharged.

(d) Insert full name of   And it is ordered that the said (d)
company

be wound up by this court under the provisions of the Insolvency Act 1986.

(a) [And it is ordered that _____
be appointed liquidator of the company]

(e) Insert any further   And it is ordered (e)
items of order, eg as
to costs

Dated _____

Form 4.13

Rule 4.20   Notice to Official Receiver of
                      Winding-Up Order

                                    (TITLE)

(a) Insert address   To the Official Receiver of the Court (a)

                      Order pronounced this _____ day of _____ 19__
                      by Mr.

                      for winding up the under-mentioned company under the Insolvency Act 1986

                      Name of company:

                      Registered office of company:

(b) Insert name,   Petitioner or his solicitor(s) (b):
address, telephone
number and reference
(if any)

                      Date of presentation of petition:

Rule 4.22 Petition by Contributory

(TITLE)

(a) Insert title of court To (a)

(b) Insert full name(s) and address(es) of petitioner(s) The petition of (b)

(c) Insert full name of company subject to petition 1. (c)

(hereinafter called "the company") was incorporated on (d) under the Companies Act 19

(d) Insert date of incorporation

(e) Insert address of registered office 2. The registered office of the company is at (e)

3. The nominal capital of the company is £   divided into shares of £   each. The amount of the capital paid up or credited as paid up is £

(f) Delete as applicable The petitioner(s) is/are the holder(s) of shares of £   each. Such shares (f) [were allotted to him/them on the incorporation of the company] [have been registered in his/their name(s) for more than 6 months in the last 18 months] [devolved upon him/them through the death of the former holder of the shares].

4. The principal objects for which the company was established are as follows:—

and other objects stated in the memorandum of association of the company.

(g) Set out the grounds on which the petition is presented 5. (g)

6. In the circumstances it is just and equitable that the company should be wound up.

The petitioner(s) therefore pray(s) as follows:—

(1) that (c)

may be wound up by the court under the provisions of the Insolvency Act 1986

OR

(2) that such other order may be made as the court thinks fit.

Note:
It is intended to serve this petition on:—

ENDORSEMENT

This petition having been presented to the court on _____
let all parties attend before the Registrar in Chambers on

Date _____

Time _____ hours

Place _____
for directions to be given.

The solicitor(s) for the petitioner is/are:

Name _____

Address _____

_____

Telephone No. _____

Reference _____

(h) Delete if London agents not instructed

(h) [Whose London agents are:—

Name _____

Address _____

_____

Telephone No. _____

Reference _____]

Form 4.16

Rule 4.32   Notice Requiring Preparation and Submission of
Statement of Company's Affairs

◄ **Insert name and address
of person required to
submit statement of af-
fairs**

(TITLE)

(a) Insert date   A winding-up order was made against the company on (a)
and under the powers given to the official receiver by section 131 of the
Insolvency Act 1986 I now require you to prepare and submit to me a statement
of the company's affairs, with a copy,

(b) Insert date by   by (b)
which statement must
be submitted
* Amend as necessary   The statement of affairs should be made up as at (a)   , the date of
if statement to be   the winding-up order.*
made up as at a
different date

(c) Insert names and   A similar notice has been sent to each of the following persons:— (c)
addresses of other
persons concerned

(d) Delete words in   Section 235 of the Insolvency Act 1986 places a duty on you (d) (as an officer of
brackets if not   the company) to provide the official receiver with information and attend upon him
applicable   if required; I have to warn you that failure to submit the statement of affairs as
required by this notice, or to co-operate with the official receiver under section
235 of the Insolvency Act 1986, may make you liable to a fine and, for continued
contravention, to a daily default fine.

Under paragraph 10 of Schedule 1 to the Company Directors Disqualification Act
1986 failure to submit a statement of affairs or to co-operate with the official
receiver under section 235 of the Insolvency Act 1986 are matters which may be
taken into account by the court in determining whether a person is unfit to be an
officer of or to be involved in the management of a company. Unfit conduct may
result in a disqualification order being made by the court.

Dated _____
Official Receiver (name and address)

Note:
Forms and instructions for the preparation of the statement of affairs
(a) may be obtained from the official receiver on request; or
(b) are enclosed.

Form 4.53

Rule 4.187, 4.188,   Notice of Disclaimer under section 178
4.189   of the Insolvency Act 1986

(TITLE)

PART 1

(a) Insert name of   I, (a) _____,
liquidator   the liquidator of the above-named company, disclaim all the company's interest in:

(b) Insert full   (b)
particulars of
property*

Dated _____

Signed _____

Name in BLOCK LETTERS _____

Address _____

PART 2   NOTE:

(c) Insert name of   This is a copy of a notice filed at (c)   Court
court

(d) Insert date that on (d)
notice filed in court

Seal of the Court

PART 3

(e) Insert name and   To: (e) _____
address of person to
be sent copy notice   _____
under Rule 4.188 or
4.189   _____

This is a copy of a notice of disclaimer filed by the liquidator in the above matter at
(c)   Court.

NOTE: 1. Part 1 is to be completed by the liquidator and filed in court with a
          copy
          Part 2 is to be completed by the court and returned to the liquidator
          Part 3 is to be completed by or on behalf of the liquidator when
          sending out copy notice under Rule 4.188 or 4.189.
       2. The attention of a recipient of this notice is drawn to sections
          178–182 of the Insolvency Act 1986.
      *3. Where the property concerned consists of land or buildings the nature
          of the interest should also be stated (eg whether leasehold, freehold
          etc).

Form 4.61

Rule 4.211

Order of Public Examination

(TITLE)

Mr Registrar   in chambers

Upon the application of the official receiver

And upon hearing

And upon reading the evidence

(a) Insert full name of person to be examined   It is ordered that (a)

do attend on:

Date _____

Time _____ **hours** _____

Place _____

for the purpose of being publicly examined

Dated _____

Warning to person to be examined

If you fail without reasonable excuse to attend your public examination at the time and place set out in the order above you will be liable to be arrested without further notice (section 134(2) of the Insolvency Act 1986).

You will also be guilty of contempt of court (section 134(1) of the Insolvency Act 1986) and liable to be committed to prison or fined.

Rule 4.214

Order as to Examination of Person who is Suffering from Mental Disorder or Physical Affliction or Disability

(TITLE)

Mr Registrar　　　　　　　　　　　　　　　　　　in chambers

(a) "The official receiver" or insert name and address of applicant and the capacity in which he makes the application

Upon the application of (a)

And upon hearing

And upon reading the evidence

(b) Insert name of examinee

And the court being satisfied that (b)　　　　　　　　　　is suffering from mental disorder or physical affliction or disability and [is unfit to undergo a public examination. It is ordered that the order dated ____ _____ be stayed]

[is unfit to attend the public examination fixed by the order dated ____ _____ It is ordered that the said order be varied as follows

_____

Dated _____

(c) Delete warning where the order for public examination is stayed

Warning to person to be examined (c)

If you fail without reasonable excuse to attend your public examination at the time and place set out in the order above you will be liable to be arrested without further notice (section 134(2) of the Insolvency Act 1986).

You will also be guilty of contempt of court (section 134(1) of the Insolvency Act 1986) and liable to be committed to prison or fined.

Form 4.66

Rule 4.216

Order of Adjournment of Public Examination

(TITLE)

Mr Registrar   in chambers

(a) Delete as applicable
(b) Insert full name of
person to be examined

This being the day appointed for the (a) [further] public examination of (b)
and the said (b)   having submitted
himself for such examination:

Now upon hearing Mr   the official receiver in the above
matter, and upon hearing
and it appearing that

[It is ordered that the public examination be adjourned to:

Date _____

Time _____ hours

Place _____

And it is ordered that the said (b)

shall attend at the above-mentioned time and place, for the purpose of being
further examined]

[It is ordered that the said public examination be adjourned generally]

(c) Set out any further
order or direction of
the court

[And it is further ordered that the said (c)   ]

Dated _____

(d) Delete warning
where the public
examination is not
adjourned to a fixed
date

Warning to person to be examined (d)

If you fail without reasonable excuse to attend your public examination at the time
and place set out in the order above you will be liable to be arrested without further
notice (section 134(2) of the Insolvency Act 1986).

You will also be guilty of contempt of court (section 134(1) of the Insolvency Act
1986) and liable to be committed to prison or fined.

Form 4.67

Rule 4.216

Order Appointing Time for Proceeding with Public Examination Adjourned Generally

(TITLE)

Mr Registrar | in chambers

(a) Delete as applicable | Upon the application of the (a) [official receiver] [examinee] and upon hearing

(b) Insert full name of person to be examined | It is ordered that the public examination of (b) | which was adjourned generally by order of the court dated | will be held on:

Date _____

Time _____ hours

Place _____

And it is ordered that (b) | shall attend at this time and place

[And it is further ordered that the said (c)

(c) Set out any further order or direction by the court

Dated

Warning to person to be examined

If you fail without reasonable excuse to attend your public examination at the time and place set out in the order above you will be liable to be arrested without further notice (section 134(2) of the Insolvency Act 1986).

You will also be guilty of contempt of court (section 134(1) of the Insolvency Act 1986) and liable to be committed to prison or fined.

Form 4.68

Rule 4.223-CVL

The Insolvency Act 1986
Liquidator's Statement of
Receipts and Payments
Pursuant to section 192 of the
Insolvency Act 1986

To the Registrar of Companies

S.192

For official use

Company Number

Name of Company

(a) Insert full name of company

(a)

Limited

(b) Insert full name(s) and address(es)

I/We (b)

the liquidator(s) of the company attach a copy of my/our statement of receipts and payments under section 192 of the Insolvency Act 1986

Signed   Date

Presenter's name, address and reference (if any)

For Official Use

Liquidation Section   Post Room

Statement of Receipts and Payments under section 192 of the Insolvency Act 1986

Name of company
Company's registered number
State whether members' or creditors' voluntary winding up
Date of commencement of winding up
Date to which this statement is brought down
Name and address of liquidator

NOTES
You should read these notes carefully before completing the forms. The notes do not form part of the return to be sent to the registrar of companies.

Form and Contents of Statement
(1) Every statement must contain a detailed account of all the liquidator's realisations and disbursements in respect of the company. The statement of realisations should contain a record of all receipts derived from assets existing at the date of the winding-up resolution and subsequently realised, including balance at bank, book debts and calls collected, property sold, etc, and the account of disbursements should contain all payments for costs, charges and expenses, or to creditors or contributories. Receipts derived from deposit accounts and money market deposits are to be included in the 'balance at bank'. Only actual investments are to be included in the 'amounts invested' section in the analysis of balance on page 5 of the form. Where property has been realised, the gross proceeds of sale must be entered under realisations and the necessary payments incidental to sales must be entered as disbursements. A payment into the Insolvency Services Account is not a disbursement and should not be shown as such; nor are payments into a bank, building society or any other financial institution. However, the interest received on any investment should be shown in the realisations. Each receipt and payment must be entered in the account in such a manner as sufficiently to explain its nature. The receipts and payments must severally be added up at the foot of each sheet and the totals carried forward from one account to another without any intermediate balance, so that the gross totals represent the total amounts received and paid by the liquidator respectively.

Trading Account
(2) When the liquidator carries on a business, a trading account must be forwarded as a distinct account, and the totals of receipts and payments on the trading account must alone be set out in this statement.

Dividends
(3) When dividends, instalments of compositions, etc are paid to creditors or a return of surplus assets is made to contributories, the total amount of each dividend, etc actually paid, must be entered in the statement of disbursements as one sum; and the liquidator must forward separate accounts showing in lists the amount of the claim of each creditor and the amount of dividend, etc payable to each creditor, or contributory.

(4) When unclaimed dividends, etc are paid into the Insolvency Services Account, the total amount so paid in should be entered in the statement of disbursements as one sum. The items to be paid in relation to unclaimed dividends should first be included in the realisations side of the account.

(5) Credit should not be taken in the statement of disbursements for any amount in respect of liquidator's remuneration unless it has been duly allowed by resolutions of the liquidation committee or of the creditors or of the company in general meeting, or by order of the court as the case may require, or is otherwise allowable under the provisions of the Insolvency Rules.

(6) This statement of receipts and payments is required in duplicate.

iquidator's statement of account
nder section 192 of the Insolvency Act 1986

Realisations

Date	Of whom received	Nature of assets realised	Amount
		Brought forward	£
		Carried forward	

te: No balance should be shown on this account but only the total realisations and

Disbursements			
Date	To whom paid	Nature of disbursements	Amount
		Brought forward	£
		Carried forward	

disbursements which should be carried forward to the next account

Analysis of balance

Total realisations   ... .   £
Total disbursements   ... .

                                                                   Balance £

The balance is made up as follows—
1. Cash in hands of liquidator ... .
2. Balance at bank   ... .
3. Amount in Insolvency Services Account ... ...

                                           £

4.* Amounts invested by liquidator   ... ...
     Less: the cost of investments realised   ... ...

        Balance

        Total balance as shown above   ... ...£

[NOTE—Full details of stocks purchased for investment and any realisation of them should be given in a separate statement]

The investment or deposit of money by the liquidator does not withdraw it from the operation of the Insolvency Regulations 1986, and any such investments representing money held for six months or upwards must be realised and paid into the Insolvency Services Account, except in the case of investments in Government securities, the transfer of which to the control of the Secretary of State will be accepted as a sufficient compliance with the terms of the Regulations.

The liquidator should also state—

The amount of the estimated assets and liabilities at the date of the commencement of the winding up—

                                                                      £

Assets (after deducting amounts charged to secured
creditors—including the holders of floating charges) ... ...
Liabilities—Fixed charge creditors   ... ...
            Floating charge holders   ... ...
            Unsecured creditors   ... .

The total amount of the capital paid up at the date of the commencement of the winding up—
            Paid up in cash   ... .
            Issued as paid up otherwise than for cash   ... ...

The general description and estimated value of any outstanding assets (if there is insufficient space here, attach a separate sheet)

Why the winding up cannot yet be concluded

The period within which the winding up is expected to be completed

Form 4.70

Section 89(3)

The Insolvency Act 1986
Members' Voluntary Winding Up
Declaration of Solvency Embodying
a Statement of Assets and Liabilities
Pursuant to section 89(3) of the Insolvency Act 1986

S.89(3)

To the Registrar of Companies

For official use

Company Number

Name of company

(a) Insert full name of
company

(a)

Limited

(b) Insert full name(s)
and address(es)

I/We (b)

attach a declaration of solvency embodying a statement of assets and liabilities

Signed   Date

Presenter's name,
address and reference
(if any)

For Official Use

Liquidation Section   Post Room

Form 4.70 contd.

Section 89(3)

The Insolvency Act 1986
Members' Voluntary Winding Up
Declaration of Solvency
Embodying a Statement of
Assets and Liabilities

Company number _____

Name of company _____

_____ Limited

Presented by _____

Declaration of Solvency

(a) Insert names and addresses

We (a) _____

_____

(b) Delete as applicable

(c) Insert name of company

(d) Insert a period of months not exceeding 12

being (b) [all the] [the majority of the] directors of (c) _____ do solemnly and sincerely declare that we have made a full inquiry into the affairs of this company, and that, having done so, we have formed the opinion that this company will be able to pay its debts in full together with interest at the official rate within a period of (d) _____ months, from the commencement of the winding up.

(e) Insert date

We append a statement of the company's assets and liabilities as at (e) _____, being the latest practicable date before the making of this declaration.

We make this solemn declaration, conscientiously believing it to be true, and by virtue of the provisions of the Statutory Declarations Act 1835.

Declared at _____

this _____ day of _____ 19__

Before me,

Solicitor or Commissioner of Oaths

Statement as at _____ showing assets at estimated realisable values and liabilities expected to rank

Assets and liabilities	Estimated to realise or to rank for payment to nearest £
Assets:	£
Balance at bank	
Cash in hand	
Marketable securities	
Bills receivable	
Trade debtors	
Loans and advances	
Unpaid calls	
Stock in trade	
Work in progress	
Freehold property	
Leasehold property	
Plant and machinery	
Furniture, fittings, utensils etc	
Patents, trade marks etc	
Investments other than marketable securities	
Other property, viz	
Estimated realisable value of assets £	
Liabilities	£
Secured on specific assets, viz	
Secured by floating charge(s)	
Estimated cost of liquidation and other expenses including interest accruing until payment of debts in full	

Unsecured creditors (amounts estimated to rank for payment)

	£	£
Trade accounts		
Bills payable		
Accrued expenses		
Other liabilities		
Contingent liabilities		

Estimated surplus after paying debts in full	£	

Remarks:

Form 6.1

Rule 6.1

Statutory Demand under section 268(1)(a) of the Insolvency Act 1986. Debt for Liquidated Sum Payable Immediately

Notes for Creditor

- If the creditor is entitled to the debt by way of assignment, details of the original creditor and any intermediary assignees should be given in part C on page 3.
- If the amount of debt includes interest not previously notified to the debtor as included in the debtor's liability, details should be given, including the grounds upon which interest is charged. The amount of interest must be shown separately.
- Any other charge accruing due from time to time may be claimed. The amount or rate of the charge must be identified and the grounds on which it is claimed must be stated.
- In either case the amount claimed must be limited to that which has accrued due at the date of the demand.
- If the creditor holds any security the amount of debt should be the sum the creditor is prepared to regard as unsecured for the purposes of this demand. Brief details of the total debt should be included and the nature of the security and the value put upon it by the creditor, as at the date of the demand, must be specified.
- If signatory of the demand is a solicitor or other agent of the creditor the name of his/her firm should be given.

*Delete if signed by the creditor himself

Warning

- This is an **important** document. You should refer to the notes entitled "How to comply with a statutory demand or have it set aside".
- If you wish to have this demand set aside you must make application to do so **within 18 days** from its service on you.
- If you do not apply to set aside **within 18 days** or otherwise deal with this demand as set out in the notes **within 21 days** after its service on you, you could be made bankrupt and your property and goods taken away from you.
- Please read the demand and notes carefully. If you are in any doubt about your position you should seek advice **immediately** from a solicitor or your nearest Citizens Advice Bureau.

Demand

To _____

Address _____

_____

This demand is served on you by the creditor:

Name _____

Address _____

_____

The creditor claims that you owe the sum of £_____ , full particulars of which are set out on page 2, and that it is payable immediately and, to the extent of the sum demanded, is unsecured.

The creditor demands that you pay the above debt or secure or compound for it to the creditor's satisfaction.

[The creditor making this demand is a Minister of the Crown or a Government Department, and it is intended to present a bankruptcy petition in the High Court in London.]
[Delete if inappropriate]

Signature of individual _____

Name _____
(BLOCK LETTERS)

Date _____

*Position with or relationship to creditor _____

_____

*I am authorised to make this demand on the creditor's behalf.
Address _____

_____

Tel. No._____   Ref. _____

N.B. The person making this demand must complete the whole of pages 1, 2 and parts A, B and C (as applicable) on page 3.

Particulars of Debt
(These particulars must include (a) when the debt was incurred, (b) the consideration for the debt (or if there is no consideration the way in which it arose) and (c) the amount due as at the date of this demand.)

Notes for Creditor
Please make sure that you have read the notes on page 1 before completing this page.

Note:
If space is insufficient continue on page 4 and clearly indicate on this page that you are doing so.

Form 6.1 contd.

Part A

Appropriate Court for Setting Aside Demand

Rule 6.4(2) of the Insolvency Rules 1986 states that the appropriate court is the court to which you would have to present your own bankruptcy petition in accordance with Rule 6.40(1) and 6.40(2). In accordance with those rules on present information the appropriate court is [the High Court of Justice] County Court]

(address)

Any application by you to set aside this demand should be made to that court.

Part B

The individual or individuals to whom any communication regarding this demand may be addressed is/are:

Name _____   _____
(BLOCK LETTERS)

Address _____   _____

_____   _____

Telephone Number _____   _____

Reference _____

Part C

For completion if the creditor is entitled to the debt by way of assignment

	Name	Date(s) of Assignment
Original creditor		
Assignees		

How to comply with a statutory demand or have it set aside (ACT WITHIN 18 DAYS)

If you wish to avoid a bankruptcy petition being presented against you, you must pay the debt shown on page 1, particulars of which are set out on page 2 of this notice, within the period of **21 days** after its service upon you. Alternatively, you can attempt to come to a settlement with the creditor. To do this you should:

inform the individual (or one of the individuals) named in part B above immediately that you are willing and able to offer security for the debt to the creditor's satisfaction; or

inform the individual (or one of the individuals) named in part B immediately that you are willing and able to compound for the debt to the creditor's satisfaction.

If you dispute the demand in whole or in part you should:

contact the individual (or one of the individuals) named in part B immediately.

THERE ARE MORE IMPORTANT NOTES ON THE NEXT PAGE

Form 6.1 contd

If you consider that you have grounds to have this demand set aside or if you do not quickly receive a satisfactory written reply from the individual named in part B whom you have contacted you should **apply within 18 days** from the date of service of this demand on you to the appropriate court shown in part A above to have the demand set aside.

Any application to set aside the demand (Form 6.4 in Schedule 4 to the Insolvency Rules 1986) should be made within 18 days from the date of service upon you and be supported by an affidavit (Form 6.5 in Schedule 4 to those Rules) stating the grounds on which the demand should be set aside. The forms may be obtained from the appropriate court when you attend to make the application.

Remember!—From the date of service on you of this document
       (a) you have only 18 days to apply to the court to have the demand set aside, and
       (b) you have only 21 days before the creditor may present a bankruptcy petition

Rule 6.7

Statutory Demand under section 268(1)(a) of the Insolvency Act 1986. Debt for Liquidated Sum Payable Immediately Following a Judgment or Order of the Court

Form 6.2

Notes for Creditor

- If the creditor is entitled to the debt by way of assignment, details of the original creditor and any intermediary assignees should be given in part C on page 3.
- If the amount of debt includes interest not previously notified to the debtor as included in the debtor's liability, details should be given, including the grounds upon which interest is charged. The amount of interest must be shown separately.
- Any other charge accruing due from time to time may be claimed. The amount or rate of the charge must be identified and the grounds on which it is claimed must be stated.
- In either case the amount claimed must be limited to that which has accrued due at the date of the demand.
- If the creditor holds any security the amount of debt should be the sum the creditor is prepared to regard as unsecured for the purposes of this demand. Brief details of the total debt should be included and the nature of the security and the value put upon it by the creditor, as at the date of the demand, must be specified.
- Details of the judgment or order should be inserted, including details of the Division of the Court or District Registry and court reference, where judgment is obtained in the High Court.
- If signatory of the demand is a solicitor or other agent of the creditor the name of his/her firm should be given.

*Delete if signed by the creditor himself

Warning

- This is an **important** document. You should refer to the notes entitled "How to comply with a statutory demand or have it set aside".
- If you wish to have this demand set aside you must make application to do so **within 18 days** from its service on you.
- If you do not apply to set aside **within 18 days** or otherwise deal with this demand as set out in the notes **within 21 days** after its service on you, you could be made bankrupt and your property and goods taken away from you.
- Please read the demand and notes carefully. If you are in any doubt about your position you should seek advice **immediately** from a solicitor or your nearest Citizens Advice Bureau.

Demand

To _____

Address _____

_____

This demand is served on you by the creditor:

Name _____

Address _____

_____

The creditor claims that you owe the sum of £_____ , full particulars of which are set out on page 2, and that it is payable immediately and, to the extent of the sum demanded, is unsecured.

By a Judgment/Order of the _____ court in proceedings entitled (Case) Number _____ between _____

Plaintiff and _____ Defendant it was adjudged/ ordered that you pay to the creditor the sum of £_____ and £_____ for costs.

The creditor demands that you pay the above debt or secure or compound for it to the creditor's satisfaction.

[The creditor making this demand is a Minister of the Crown or a Government Department, and it is intended to present a bankruptcy petition in the High Court in London.] [Delete if inappropriate]

Signature of individual _____

Name _____ (BLOCK LETTERS)

Date _____

*Position with or relationship to creditor _____

_____

*I am authorised to make this demand on the creditor's behalf.

Address _____

_____

Tel. No._____   Ref. _____

N.B. The person making this demand must complete the whole of pages 1, 2 and parts A, B and C (as applicable) on page 3.

Particulars of Debt

(These particulars must include (a) when the debt was incurred, (b) the consideration for the debt (or if there is no consideration the way in which it arose) and (c) the amount due as at the date of this demand.)

Notes for Creditor
Please make sure that you have read the notes on page 1 before completing this page.

Note:
If space is insufficient continue on page 4 and clearly indicate on this page that you are doing so.

Form 6.2 contd.

Part A

Appropriate Court for Setting Aside Demand

Rule 6.4(2) of the Insolvency Rules 1986 states that the appropriate court is the court to which you would have to present your own bankruptcy petition in accordance with Rule 6.40(1) and 6.40(2).

Any application by you to set aside this demand should be made to that court, or, if this demand is issued by a Minister of the Crown or a Government Department, you must apply to the High Court to set aside if it is intended to present a bankruptcy petition against you in the High Court (see page 1).

In accordance with those rules on present information the appropriate court is [the High Court of Justice] County Court]

(address)

Part B

The individual or individuals to whom any communication regarding this demand may be addressed is/are:

Name _____

(BLOCK LETTERS)

Address _____

_____

Telephone number _____

Reference _____

Part C

For completion if the creditor is entitled to the debt by way of assignment

	Name	Date(s) of Assignment
Original creditor		
Assignees		

HERE ARE IMPORTANT NOTES ON THE NEXT PAGE

How to comply with a statutory demand or have it set aside (ACT WITHIN 18 DAYS)

If you wish to avoid a bankruptcy petition being presented against you, you must pay the debt shown on page 1, particulars of which are set out on page 2 of this notice, within the period of **21 days** after its service upon you. However, if the demand follows (includes) a judgment or order of a County Court, any payment must be made to that County Court (quoting the Case No.). Alternatively, you can attempt to come to a settlement with the creditor. To do this you should:

- inform the individual (or one of the individuals) named in part B above immediately that you are willing and able to offer security for the debt to the creditor's satisfaction; or
- inform the individual (or one of the individuals) named in part B immediately that you are willing and able to compound for the debt to the creditor's satisfaction.

If you dispute the demand in whole or in part you should:

- contact the individual (or one of the individuals) named in part B immediately.

If you consider that you have grounds to have this demand set aside or if you do not quickly receive a satisfactory written reply from the individual named in part B whom you have contacted you should **apply within 18 days** from the date of service of this demand on you to the appropriate court shown in part A above to have the demand set aside.

Any application to set aside the demand (Form 6.4 in Schedule 4 to the Insolvency Rules 1986) should be made within 18 days from the date of service upon you and be supported by an affidavit (Form 6.5 in Schedule 4 to those Rules) stating the grounds on which the demand should be set aside. The forms may be obtained from the appropriate court when you attend to make the application.

Remember!——From the date of service on you of this document
  (a) you have only 18 days to apply to the court to have the demand set aside, and
  (b) you have only 21 days before the creditor may present a bankruptcy petition.

Form 6.3

Rule 6.1

Statutory Demand under section 268(2) of the Insolvency Act 1986. Debt Payable at Future Date.

Notes for Creditor
- If the creditor is entitled to the debt by way of assignment, details of the original creditor and any intermediary assignees should be given in part C on page 3.
- If the amount of debt when due includes interest not previously notified to the debtor as included in the debtor's liability, details should be given, including the grounds upon which interest is charged. The amount of interest must be shown separately.
- Any other charge accruing due from time to time may be claimed. The amount or rate of the charge must be identified and the grounds on which it is claimed must be stated.
- In either case the amount claimed must be limited to that which will have accrued due when payment falls due on the date specified.
- If the creditor holds any security the amount of debt should be the sum the creditor is prepared to regard as unsecured for the purposes of this demand. Brief details of the total debt should be included and the nature of the security and the value put upon it by the creditor, as at the date of the demand, must be specified.
- The grounds for the creditor's opinion that the debtor has no reasonable prospects of paying the debt when it falls due must be stated.
- If signatory of the demand is a solicitor or other agent of the creditor the name of his/her firm should be given.

*Delete if signed by the creditor himself

Warning
- This is an **important** document. You should refer to the notes entitled "How to comply with a statutory demand or have it set aside".
- If you wish to have this demand set aside you must make application to do so **within 18 days** from its service on you.
- If you do not apply to set aside **within 18 days** or otherwise deal with this demand as set out in the notes **within 21 days** after its service on you, you could be made bankrupt and your property and goods taken away from you.
- Please read the demand and notes carefully. If you are in any doubt about your position you should seek advice **immediately** from a solicitor or your nearest Citizens Advice Bureau.

Demand

To _____

Address _____

_____

This demand is served on you by the creditor:

Name _____

Address _____

_____

The creditor claims that you will owe the sum of £_____ , full particulars of which are set out on page 2, when payment falls due on _____

The creditor is of the opinion that you have no reasonable prospect of paying this debt when it falls due because

[The creditor making this demand is a Minister of the Crown or Government Department, and it is intended to present a bankruptcy petition in the High Court in London.] [Delete if inappropriate]

Signature of individual _____

Name _____
(BLOCK LETTERS)

Date _____

*Position with or relationship to creditor _____

_____

*I am authorised to make this demand on the creditor's behalf.

Address _____

_____

Tel. No. _____   Ref. _____

N.B. The person making this demand must complete the whole of pages 1, 2 and parts A, B and C (as applicable) on page 3.

Particulars of Debt

(These particulars must include (a) when the debt was incurred, (b) the consideration for the debt (or if there is no consideration the way in which it will arise) and (c) the amount of future debt and the date payment is due.)

Notes for Creditor
Please make sure th
you have read th
notes on page 1 befo
completing this page.

Note:
If space is insuffice
continue on page 4 a
clearly indicate on th
page that you are doi
so.

Form 6.3 contd.

Part A

Appropriate Court for Setting Aside Demand

Rule 6.4(2) of the Insolvency Rules 1986 states that the appropriate court is the court to which you would have to present your own bankruptcy petition in accordance with Rule 6.40(1) and 6.40(2). In accordance with those rules on present information the appropriate court is [the High Court of Justice] [County Court] (address)

Any application by you to set aside this demand should be made to that court.

Part B

The individual or individuals to whom any communication regarding this demand may be addressed is/are:

Name _____

(BLOCK LETTERS)

Address _____

_____

Telephone number _____

Reference _____

Part C

For completion if the creditor is entitled to the debt by way of assignment

	Name	Date(s) of Assignment
Original creditor		
Assignees		

How to comply with a statutory demand or have it set aside (ACT WITHIN 18 DAYS)

If you wish to avoid a bankruptcy petition being presented against you, you must within the period of **21 days** after its service upon you satisfy the creditor that you are able to meet the debt demanded when it is due.

If you dispute that the debt will be due in whole or in part or if you dispute the allegation that you will be unable to pay the debt when it falls due or if you consider that you may be able to offer security for the debt or to compound for it you should:

- contact the individual (or one of the individuals) named in part B immediately.

If you consider that you have grounds to have this demand set aside or if you do not quickly receive a satisfactory written reply from the individual named in part B whom you have contacted you should **apply within 18 days** from the date of service of this demand on you to the appropriate court shown in part A above to have the demand set aside.

THERE ARE MORE IMPORTANT NOTES ON THE NEXT PAGE

Form 6.3 contd.

Any application to set aside the demand (Form 6.4 in Schedule 4 to the Insolvency Rules 1986) should be made within 18 days from the date of service upon you and be supported by an affidavit (Form 6.5 in Schedule 4 to those Rules) stating the grounds on which the demand should be set aside. The forms may be obtained from the appropriate court when you attend to make the application.

Remember!—From the date of service on you of this document
      (a) you have only 18 days to apply to the court to have the demand set aside, and
      (b) you have only 21 days before the creditor may present a bankruptcy petition.

Rule 6.11   **Form 6.11**

Affidavit of Personal Service
of Statutory Demand

(TITLE)

Date of statutory demand _____

(a) Insert name, address and description of person making the oath and whether the creditor or a person acting on his behalf

I, (a) _____

_____

make oath and say as follows:—

(b) Delete 'I' and insert name and address of person who effected service, if applicable

1. (b) [I] [_____]

did on (c) _____ (d) [before] [after]   hours, at (e) _____

(c) Insert date

_____

personally   serve   the   above-named   debtor   with   the   demand   dated _____

(d) Insert time which must be either before or after 16.00 hours Monday to Friday or before or after 12.00 hours Saturday

(f) [2. That on (c) _____ the debtor acknowledged service of the demand by (g) _____]

3. A copy of the demand marked "A" (f) [and the acknowledgement of service marked "B"] is/are exhibited hereto.

(e) Insert address

(f) Delete words in [   ] if no acknowledgement of service has been received

(g) Give particulars of the way in which the debtor acknowledged service of the demand

Sworn at

Rule 6.13, 6.43   **Form 6.14**

Application for Registration of Petition in Bankruptcy against an Individual under Land Charges Act 1972

(TITLE)

Notes	Application is made for registration of a petition in bankruptcy presented this day as a pending action under section 5 of the Land Charges Act 1972 in respect of the following particulars.	**Official Use Only** Seal of Court
This form should be completed in typescript or BLOCK LETTERS in black ink. A separate form should be completed for each debtor and for any alternative name (other than trading name(s)) referred to in the petition. Please tick correct box Insert initials if full forename(s) not known	**Particulars of Debtor:** Forename(s) Surname Male ☐ Female ☐ Not known ☐	**Land Charges Use** **PAB** **BANKS**
Give details of trade, profession or occupation, including any trading name(s) and, in the case of a partnership, the name(s) of the other partner(s)	Occupation	
Include debtor's business address(es) if appropriate. Where there are more than 2 addresses enter the additional addresses on the back page	Address(es) 1. 2.	

Form 6.14 contd.

Enter the key number allocated to the court by the Land Charges Department

Key Number

1	2	3
C	F	/

4	5	6
/	/	/

High Court of Justice } in Bankruptcy

Enter name of court

_____ County Court

Number and date of petition

No. _____ of 19__ Date _____

Please give the full name and address of petitioner, unless the petition is presented by the debtor, in which case insert 'the debtor'

Particulars of Petitioner

Name

_____

Address

_____

_____

_____

Signature of Registrar _____ Date _____

Additional Addresses of Debtor

1. _____

_____

2. _____

_____

3. _____

_____

_____

**The Superintendent
Land Charges Department
Registration (Bankruptcy) Section
Burrington Way
PLYMOUTH PL5 3LP**

Form 6.26

Rule 6.34, 6.46   Application for Registration of a Bankruptcy Order
against an Individual under
Land Charges Act 1972

(TITLE)

Notes		Land Charges Use
This form should be completed in typescript or BLOCK LETTERS in black ink. A separate form should be completed for each bankrupt and for any alternative name (other than trading name(s)) referred to in the bankruptcy order. Please tick correct box Insert initials if full forename(s) not known	Application is made for registration of a bankruptcy order in the register of writs and orders under section 6 of the Land Charges Act 1972 in respect of the following particulars.	**WOB**
	Particulars of Bankrupt: Forename(s)	
	Surname	**BANKS**
	Male ☐ Female ☐ Not known ☐	
Give details of trade, profession or occupation, including any trading name(s) and, in the case of a partnership, the name(s) of the other partner(s)	Occupation	
Include bankrupt's business address(es) if appropriate. Where there are more than 2 addresses enter the additional addresses on the back page	Address(es) 1. 2.	

Form 6.26 contd.

Enter the key number allocated to the court by the Land Charges Department

Key Number

1	2	3
C	F	

4	5	6

High Court of Justice   in Bankruptcy

Enter name of court   _____ County Court

Number of petition   No. _____ of 19____

Particulars of Petitioner

Please give the full name and address of petitioner, unless the petition is presented by the debtor, in which case insert 'the debtor'

Name

_____

Address

_____

_____

Date of Bankruptcy Order

Signature of Official Receiver_____ Date _____

Address _____

_____

Additional Addresses of Bankrupt

1.

_____

_____

2.

_____

3.

_____

_____

**The Superintendent
Land Charges Department
Registration (Bankruptcy) Section
Burrington Way
Plymouth PL5 3LP**

Form 6.30

Rule 6.45, 6.48   Bankruptcy Order on Debtor's Petition

(TITLE)

(a) Insert date   Upon the petition of the above-named debtor, which was presented on (a)

And upon hearing

(b) Delete words in   (b) [and upon considering the report of (c)
square brackets if no
appointment made
under section 273(2)   appointed under section 273(2) of the Insolvency Act 1986]

(c) Insert name of   And upon reading the petition and statement of affairs
insolvency practitioner
appointed under
section 273(2)   It is ordered that (d)

(d) Insert full
description of debtor
as set out in the   be adjudged bankrupt.
petition

(e) Delete if no   (e) [And it is certified that the estate of the bankrupt be administered in a summary
certificate of summary   manner]
administration is
issued under section   [And it is ordered that (f)   be appointed trustee of the
275   bankrupt's estate].

(f) Only to be
completed where a   [And it is also ordered that   ]
trustee is appointed
under section 297(3),
(4) or (5) of the
Insolvency Act 1986
on the making of the   Date _____
bankruptcy order
Time _____ hours

Important Notice to Bankrupt

*Delete as appropriate   *[The] [One of the] official receiver(s)* attached to the court is by virtue of this
order receiver and manager of the bankrupt's estate. You are required to attend
(g) Insert address of   upon the Official Receiver of the court at (g) _____
official receiver's
office

immediately after you have received this order.

The Official Receiver's offices are open Monday to Friday (except on holidays)
from 10.00 to 16.00 hours.

(h) Order to be
endorsed where
debtor is represented
by a solicitor

Endorsement on Order (h)

The solicitor to the debtor is:—

Name _____

Address _____

Telephone No. _____

Reference _____

Form 6.55

Rule 6.172

Order for Public Examination of Bankrupt

(TITLE)

Mr Registrar   in chambers

Upon the application of the official receiver

And upon hearing

And upon reading the evidence

It is ordered that the above-named bankrupt do attend on:

Date _____

Time _____ hours

Place _____

for the purpose of being publicly examined

Dated _____

Warning to Bankrupt

If you fail without reasonable excuse to attend your public examination at the time and place set out in the order above you will be liable to be arrested without further notice (section 364(1) of the Insolvency Act 1986).

You will also be guilty of contempt of court (section 290(5) of the Insolvency Act 1986) and liable to be committed to prison or fined.

Form 6.57

le 6.174

Order as to Examination of Bankrupt who is Suffering from Mental Disorder or Physical Affliction or Disability

(TITLE)

Mr Registrar   in chambers

(a) "The official receiver" or insert ame and address of applicant and the capacity in which he akes the application

Upon the application of (a)

And upon hearing

And upon reading the evidence

And the court being satisfied that the bankrupt is suffering from mental disorder or physical affliction or disability and [is unfit to undergo a public examination. It is ordered that the order dated   be stayed]

OR

[is unfit to attend the public examination fixed by the order dated   . It is ordered that the said order be varied as follows:—

                                      ]

Insert details of any further order in the matter

[And it is ordered (b)

                                      ]

Dated _____

(c) Delete warning where the order for ublic examination is stayed

Warning to Bankrupt (c)

If you fail without reasonable excuse to attend your public examination at the time and place set out in the order above you will be liable to be arrested without further notice (section 364(1) of the Insolvency Act 1986).

You will also be guilty of contempt of court (section 290(5) of the Insolvency Act 1986) and liable to be committed to prison or fined.

III/1aa

Rule 6.176

Order of Adjournment of Public Examination of Bankrupt

(TITLE)

Mr Registrar   in chambers

(a) Delete as applicable   This being the day appointed for the (a) [further] public examination of the above-named bankrupt and the above-named bankrupt having submitted himself for such examination:

Now upon hearing Mr   the official receiver in the
above matter, and upon hearing   and it appearing that

It is ordered that the public examination be adjourned to:

Date _____

Time _____ hours

Place _____

And it is ordered that the above-named bankrupt shall attend at the above-mentioned time and place, for the purpose of being further examined as to his affairs, dealings and property

OR

It is ordered that the public examination be adjourned generally

(b) Set out any further   [And it is further ordered that the said (b)
order or direction of
the court

Dated _____

(c) Delete warning   **Warning to Bankrupt (c)**
where the public
examination is not   If you fail without reasonable excuse to attend your public examination at the time
adjourned to a fixed   and place set out in the order above you will be liable to be arrested without further
date   notice (section 364(1) of the Insolvency Act 1986).

You will also be guilty of contempt of court (section 290(5) of the Insolvency Act 1986) and liable to be committed to prison or fined.

Form 6.60

Rule 6.176

Order Appointing Time for Proceeding with Public Examination of Bankrupt Adjourned Generally

(TITLE)

Mr Registrar   in chambers

(a) Delete as applicable   Upon the application of the (a) [official receiver] [above-named bankrupt]

And upon hearing

It is ordered that the public examination of the above-named bankrupt which was adjourned generally by order of the court dated   will be held on:

Date _____

Time _____ hours

Place _____

And it is ordered that the above-named bankrupt shall attend at this time and place

(b) Set out any further   [And it is further ordered that the said (b)
order or direction of
the court

]

Dated _____

Warning to Bankrupt

If you fail without reasonable excuse to attend your public examination at the time and place set out in the order above you will be liable to be arrested without further notice (section 364(1) of the Insolvency Act 1986).

You will also be guilty of contempt of court (section 290(5) of the Insolvency Act 1986) and liable to be committed to prison or fined.

Rule 6.178
6.179, 6.180

Notice of Disclaimer under section 315
of the Insolvency Act 1986

(TITLE)

PART 1

(a) Insert name of trustee

I, (a) _____ ,
the trustee of the above-named bankrupt's estate, disclaim all my interest in:

(b) Insert full particulars of property*

(b)

Dated _____

Signed _____

Name in BLOCK LETTERS _____

Address _____

PART 2

(c) Insert name of court

(d) Insert date that notice filed in court

NOTE:

This is a copy of a notice filed at (c)   Court

on (d)

Seal of the Court

PART 3

(e) Insert name and address of person to be sent copy notice under Rule 6.179 or 6.180

To: (e) _____

_____

This is a copy of a notice of disclaimer filed by the trustee in the above matter at (c)
Court.

NOTE: 1. Part 1 is to be completed by the trustee and filed in court with a copy
          Part 2 is to be completed by the court and returned to the trustee
          Part 3 is to be completed by or on behalf of the trustee when sending
          out copy notice under Rule 6.179 or 6.180

      2. The attention of a recipient of this notice is drawn to sections
          315–321 of the Insolvency Act 1986.

   *3. Where the property concerned consists of land or buildings the nature
          of the interest should also be stated (eg whether leasehold, freehold,
          etc).

Form 6.78

Section 334(2)   ## Notice to Existing Trustee of the Presentation of a Petition for a Later Bankruptcy

(TITLE)

(a) Insert name and address of existing trustee

To (a)

(b) Insert date

Please note that a bankruptcy petition was presented to the court on (b)

(c) Insert bankrupt's full title as appearing in the petition

against (c)

who was previously adjudged bankrupt on (b)

and of whose estate you are trustee.

Any property covered by section 334(3) of the Insolvency Act 1986 which you have not yet distributed, should now be retained by you pending:—
  (a) the dismissal of the above petition, or
  (b) the making of a further bankruptcy order.

If a bankruptcy order is made, the trustee appointed will contact you in due course, with regard to the recovery of such property, any distribution or disposition of which shall, from the giving of this notice, be void, unless made with the consent of the court.

Dated _____

Signed _____

Name in BLOCK LETTERS _____

Description and Address _____

_____

Form 7.9

Rule 7.22, 7.23

Order for Production of Person Arrested under Warrant Issued under sections 134, 236, 364 or 366 of the Insolvency Act 1986

(TITLE)

The court having been notified that

(a) Insert full name of person arrested

(a)

has been

(b) Insert date

arrested under a warrant issued by this court on (b)

(c) Insert name of prison

It is ordered that the Governor of (c)   Prison
have (a)

brought in custody for examination before this court sitting at:

Date _____

Time _____ hours

Place _____

and that in the meantime he be detained and afterwards, if the court directs, be taken back to prison and detained pursuant to the warrant.

Dated _____

Form 7.15

Affidavit in support of application for committal for contempt of court

(TITLE)

(a) Insert full name and address of applicant
    I(a)

(b) Insert capacity of relevant insolvency practitioner or official receiver
    (b)   make oath and say as follows:—

(c) Insert full name and address of person against whom committal is sought
    (1) That (c)

(d) Insert details of person's failure to comply with the relevant provisions of the Act or the Rules
    (d)

(e) Insert date of service of notice, if applicable
    [(2) That on (e)   (f)

(f) Insert name
    was duly served with a notice requiring him to (g)

(g) Insert details of any requirement under relevant provisions of the Act or the Rules

a copy of which is exhibited hereto and marked "A" and without reasonable excuse he has failed to comply with the terms of the notice.]

OR

(1) That the above-named person failed to comply with the order of this court

(h) Insert date
    made on (h)   directing him to

(j) Set out terms of order
    (j)

(k) Insert date of service of order
    (2) That on (k)   the above-named person was [personally] served with a copy of the said order

Sworn at _____

Date _____

Before me _____

_____

A solicitor or Commissioner of Oaths

SECTION 2

AMENDED FORM 3.1B

Form 3.1B

Notice Requiring Preparation and Submission of Administrative Receivership Statement of Affairs

(TITLE)

(a) Insert name of company — Take notice that you are required to prepare and submit to me a statement as to the affairs of (a)

(b) Insert date by which statement must be submitted — by (b)

(c) Insert names and addresses of other persons concerned — A similar notice has been sent to each of the following persons (c)

(d) Delete words in brackets if not applicable — Section 235 of the Insolvency Act 1986 places a duty on you (d) (as an officer of the company) to provide the administrative receiver with information and attend upon him if required; I have to warn you that failure to submit the statement of affairs as required by this notice, or to co-operate with the administrative receiver under section 235 of the Insolvency Act 1986, may make you liable to a fine and, for continued contravention, to a daily default fine.

Under paragraph 10 of Schedule 1 to the Company Directors Disqualification Act 1986 failure to submit a statement of affairs or to co-operate with the administrative receiver under section 235 of the Insolvency Act 1986 are matters which may be taken into account by the court in determining whether a person is unfit to be an officer of or to be involved in the management of a company. Unfit conduct may result in a disqualification order being made by the court.

Dated _____

Administrative Receiver (name and address)

Note:
Forms for the preparation of the statement of affairs
   (a) may be obtained from the administrative receiver on request; or
   (b) are enclosed.

III/1aa*

EXPLANATORY NOTE

(This note is not part of the Rules)

These Rules make detailed amendments to the Insolvency Rules 1986, which set out detailed procedures for the conduct of all company and individual insolvency proceedings in England and Wales under the Insolvency Act 1986. These Rules apply to all insolvency proceedings to which the Insolvency Rules 1986 apply on and after 11th January 1988, whether or not those proceedings were commenced before, on or after that date.

Rule 3(3) also applies Rule 4. 223-CVL of the Insolvency Rules 1986 as amended to those insolvency proceedings specified in paragraph 4(1) of Schedule 11 to the Insolvency Act 1986.

1987 No. 1920

CONSUMER PROTECTION

The Cosmetic Products (Safety) (Amendment) Regulations 1987

Made - - - -	*10th November 1987*
Laid before Parliament	*23rd November 1987*
Coming into force (except as provided in regulation 1)	*21st December 1987*

Whereas the Secretary of State has, in accordance with section 11(5) of the Consumer Protection Act 1987(**a**), consulted such organisations as appear to him to be representative of interests substantially affected by these Regulations, such other persons as he considers appropriate and the Health and Safety Commission;

And whereas the Secretary of State is a Minister designated(**b**) for the purposes of section 2 of the European Communities Act 1972(**c**) in relation to measures for safety and consumer protection as respects cosmetic products and any provisions concerning the composition, labelling, marketing, classification or description of cosmetic products and in relation to indication of origin on imported goods;

Now, therefore, the Secretary of State in exercise of powers conferred on him by section 11 of the said Act of 1987 and by section 2 of the said Act of 1972 and of all other powers enabling him in that behalf hereby makes the following Regulations:

1.—(1) These Regulations may be cited as the Cosmetic Products (Safety) (Amendment) Regulations 1987 and except as provided by paragraph (2) below, shall come into force on 21st December 1987.

(2) Regulation 2(y), regulation 2(bb) insofar as it relates only to entry Number 52 in Schedule 1 to these Regulations, regulation 2(cc), regulation 2(ee) and regulation 2(ff) shall come into force–

    (a) in relation to the supply, offering to supply, agreeing to supply, exposing for supply or possessing for supply of cosmetic products by the manufacturer in or importer into the United Kingdom or, in the case of cosmetic products, manufactured in or imported into the United Kingdom on behalf of another person, by that other person, on 1st January 1988, except where the cosmetic products are supplied, agreed to be supplied, exposed for supply or possessed for supply by retail in which case they shall come into force on 1st January 1989; and

    (b) in all other cases, on 1st January 1989.

(**a**) 1987 c.43.   (**b**) S.I. 1972/1811, 1975/1707.   (**c**) 1972 c.68.

2. The Cosmetic Products (Safety) Regulations 1984(**a**) are hereby amended–

(a) in regulation 4(1), in the definition of "the Directive", by the omission of the word "and" between "Council Directive No. 83/574/EEC" and "Commission Directive No. 83/496/EEC" and by the addition of the words "Commission Directive No. 84/415/EEC(j), Commission Directive No. 85/391/EEC(k), Commission Directive No. 85/490/EEC(l), Commission Directive No. 86/179/EEC(m) and Commission Directive No. 86/199/EEC(n)" and by the insertion as footnotes at the foot of the relevant page of the following–

"(j) O.J. L228, 25.8.84, p.31

(k) O.J. L224, 22.8.85, p.40

(l) O.J. L295, 7.11.85, p.30

(m) O.J. L138, 24.5.86, p.40

(n) O.J. L149, 3.6.86, p.38";

(b) in regulation 5(2) by the insertion after the word "manufacturer" of the word "in";

(c) in regulation 6(3) by the substitution for the words "3, 4 and 5" of the words "3, 4, 5 and (in the case of Part II) 7".

(d) in regulation 6 by the substitution for paragraph (4) of the following paragraph–

"(4) A cosmetic product shall not contain–

(a) any colouring agent listed in columns 1 and 2 of Schedule 3 unless–

(i) the requirements in columns 3 and 4 of Part I of that Schedule in relation to that colouring agent are satisfied; or

(ii) the requirements in columns 3 and 4 of Part II of that Schedule in relation to that colouring agent are satisfied and the cosmetic product in question is supplied on or before the date specified in column 5 of that Part;

(b) any colouring agent which is not listed in that Schedule and which is intended to come into contact with the mucous membrane;"

(e) in regulation 6 by the omission of paragraph (5);

(f) in regulation 6(6) by the substitution for sub-paragraph (a) of the following sub-paragraph–

"(a) any preservative listed in column 2 of Schedule 5 unless–

(i) the requirements in columns 3, 4 and 5 of Part I of that Schedule in relation to that preservative are satisfied; or

(ii) the requirements in columns 3, 4 and 5 of Part II of that Schedule in relation to that preservative are satisfied and the preservative in question is supplied on or before the date specified in column 7 of that Part;"

(g) in regulation 6(6) by the omission of the word "and" between sub-paragraphs (a) and (b) and by the addition of the following sub-paragraph–

"(c) any preservative listed in column 2 of Part II of Schedule 5 after the date specified in column 7 of that Schedule";

(h) in regulation 6(7) by the omission of the word "and" between sub-paragraphs (a) and (b);

(i) in regulation 9 by the substitution for paragraph (2) of the following paragraph–

"(2) Regulations 5, 6 and 8 above do not apply in any case in which the cosmetic product is supplied, offered for supply, agreed to be supplied, exposed or possessed for supply for the purposes of exporting that product to any country which is not a member State of the European Economic Community";

(j) in Schedule 1 by the substitution for the words in column 2 of entry Number 24 of the words–

"4-(or *p*-)Aminobenzoic acid esters except glycerol 1-(4-aminobenzoate) when provisionally permitted for use as a UV filter in accordance with the requirements specified at Item 4 of Part II of Schedule 6";

(**a**) S.I. 1984/1260, amended by S.I. 1985/2045.

(k) in Schedule 1 by the substitution in column 2 of entry Number 64 for the letter "B" of the symbol "*";

(l) in Schedule 1 by the substitution for the words in column 2 of entry Number 85 of the words "4-Benzyloxyphenol";

(m) in Schedule 1 by the insertion in column 4 of entry Number 148A of the figure "366";

(n) in Schedule 1 by the substitution in column 2 of entry Number 212 for the words "column 4 of Part II of Schedule 2" of the words "column 5 of Part II of Schedule 2";

(o) in Schedule 1 by the substitution in column 2 of entry Number 213 for the words "column 4 of Part II of Schedule 2" of the words "column 5 of Part II of Schedule 2";

(p) in Schedule 1 by the insertion after entry Number 285 of the following entry–
"285A – 4-ethoxyphenol 348 178";

(q) in Schedule 1 by the substitution in column 2 of entry Number 348 for the words "Hydroquinone monobenzyl ether" of the words "Hydroquinone monobenzyl, monoethyl and monomethyl ethers";

(r) in Schedule 1 by the insertion in column 3 of entry Number 348 after the figure "431" of the figures "285A, 411A";

(s) in Schedule 1 by the substitution in column 2 of entry Number 395 for the words "Part II of Schedule 5" of the words "Part I of Schedule 5";

(t) in Schedule 1 by the substitution in column 2 of entry Number 397 for the words "column 4 of Part II of Schedule 2" of the words "column 5 of Part II of Schedule 2";

(u) in Schedule 1 by the insertion after entry Number 411 of the following entry–
"411A 4-methoxyphenol 348 178";

(v) in Schedule 1 by the substitution in column 2 of entry Number 562 for the words "Selenium and its compounds" of the words "Selenium and its compounds except when permitted under the restrictions laid down against entry Number 50 in Part I of Schedule 2";

(w) in Schedule 1 by the substitution in column 2 of entry Number 603 for the words "column 4 of Part II of Schedule 2" of the words "column 5 of Part II of Schedule 2";

(x) in Schedule 1 entry number 645A by the insertion in column 4 of the figure "366";

(y) in Schedule 1 by the renumbering and appropriate relocation in numerical order of entry Number 675 (Aristolochic acid and its salts) as entry Number 56A and by the insertion after entry Number 674 of following–

"676 2, 3, 7, 8-Tetrachlorodibenzo-p-dioxin – 367

677 2, 6-Dimethyl-1, 3-dioxan-4-yl acetate (Dimethoxane) – 368

678 Pyrithione sodium (INNM) – 369";

(z) in Part I of Schedule 2 by the substitution in column 3 of entry Number 11 for the words "use other than as a preservative (see also Part II of Schedule 5)" of the words "all purposes and products";

(aa) in Part I of Schedule 2 by the substitution for entry Number 45 of the following–

"45	1, 3-Bis (hydroxymethyl) imidazolidiene-2-thione	(a) Hair-care preparations	2 per cent	Not to be used in aerosol dispensers (sprays)	Contains 1, 3-Bis (hydroxymethyl) imidazolidine-2-thione
		(b) Nail-care preparations	2 per cent	pH as applied value must be less than 4";	

(bb) in Part I of Schedule 2 by the insertion after entry Number 49 of the additional entries set out in Schedule 1 to these Regulations;

(cc) in Schedule 2 by the substitution for Part II of Schedule 2 of the Part set out in Schedule 2 to these Regulations;

(dd) in Part III of Schedule 2 by the substitution in column 3 of entry number 4 for the words "(See also Part II of Schedule 5)" of the words "(See also Part I of Schedule 5)";

(ee) by the substitution for Schedule 3 of the Schedule set out in Schedule 3 to these Regulations and by the omission of Schedule 4;

(ff) by the substitution for Schedule 5 of the schedule set out in Schedule 4 to these Regulations;

(gg) in Schedule 7 by the insertion in paragraph 1 after the words "Commission Directive No. 83/514/EEC;" of the words " "Annex D" means the Annex to Commission Directive No. 85/490/EEC*(a)*" and by the insertion as a footnote at the foot of the relevant page of "(a) O.J. No. L295, 7.11.85, p.30."

(hh) in Schedule 7 by the insertion after entry Number 6(26) of the following–

"(27) Any test for the identification and determination of the amount of glycerol 1-(4-aminobenzoate) in a cosmetic product shall be carried out in accordance with that part of Annex D which is headed "Identification and determination of glycerol 1-(4-aminobenzoate)".

(28) Any test to determine the amount of chlorobutanol in a cosmetic product shall be carried out in accordance with that part of Annex D which is headed "Determination of chlorobutanol".

(29) Any test for the identification and determination of the amount of quinine in a cosmetic product shall be carried out in accordance with that part of Annex D which is headed "Identification and determination of quinine".

(30) Any test for the identification and determination of inorganic sulphites and hydrogen sulphites in a cosmetic product shall be carried out in accordance with that part of Annex D which is headed "Identification and determination of inorganic sulphites and hydrogen sulphites".

(31) Any test for the identification and determination of chlorates of the alkali metals in a cosmetic product shall be carried out in accordance with that part of Annex D which is headed "Identification and determination of chlorates of the alkali metals".

(32) Any test for the identification and determination of sodium iodate in a cosmetic product shall be carried out in accordance with that part of Annex D which is headed "Identification and determination of sodium iodate".".

Francis Maude
Parliamentary Under-Secretary of State,
Department of Trade and Industry

10th November 1987

Regulation 2(bb)

SCHEDULE 1

Column 1	Column 2	Column 3	Column 4	Column 5	Column 6
Reference Number	Name of substance	Purpose of substance or type of product	Maximum concentration of substance in product	Other requirements	Required information
50	Selenium disulphide	Anti-dandruff shampoos	1 per cent		Contains selenium disulphide. Avoid contact with eyes or damaged skin
51	Aluminium zirconium chloride hydroxide complexes $Al_xZr(OH)_y$ CL_z and the aluminium zirconium chloride hydroxide glycine complexes	Anti-perspirants	20 per cent as anhydrous aluminium zirconium chloride hydroxide 5.4 per cent as zirconium	The ratio of the number of aluminium atoms to that of zirconium atoms must be between 2 and 10 The ratio of the number of (Al + Zr) atoms to chlorine atoms must be between 0.9 and 2.1. Not to be used in aerosol dispensers (sprays)	Do not apply to irritated or damaged skin
52	Quinolin–8–ol and bis (8–hydroxyquinolinium) sulphate	Stabilizer for hydrogen peroxide in rinse-off hair-care preparations	0.3 per cent calculated as base		

Regulation 2(cc)

SCHEDULE 2

PART II

SUBSTANCES LISTED IN ANNEX IV, PART I OF THE DIRECTIVE AS SUBSTANCES PROVISIONALLY ALLOWED

Column 1 Reference Number	Column 2 Name of substance	Column 3 Purpose of substance or type of product	Column 4 Maximum concentration of substance in product	Column 5 Other requirements	Column 6 Required information	Column 7 Permitted for use until
1	Methanol	Denaturant for ethanol and isopropyl alcohol	5 per cent calculated as a percentage of ethanol and isopropyl alcohol	—	—	31.12.1987
2	1,1,1–Trichloroethane (methyl chloroform)	Aerosol spray	35 per cent (When mixed with dichloromethane total concentration must not exceed 35 per cent)	—	Do not spray on a naked flame or any incandescent material	31.12.1987
3	3,4′,5–Tribromosalicylanilide (Tribromsalan)	Deodorant soaps	1 per cent	Purity of the 3,4′,5–Tribromosalicylanilide: must be not less than 98.5 per cent Other bromosalicylanilides: not to exceed 1.5 per cent 4′,5–dibromosalicylanilide: not to exceed 0.1 per cent Inorganic bromide: not to exceed 0.1 per cent expressed as NaBr	Contains tribromosalicylanilide	31.12.1987
4	2,2′–Dithiobis (pyridine 1–oxide), addition product with magnesium sulphate trihydrate	Rinsed off hair care products	1 per cent	—	—	31.12.1987
5	1–Phenoxypropan–2–ol	–Rinse-off products only –Prohibited in oral hygiene products	2 per cent	For preservative use see Schedule 5 – Part II – No 11	—	31.12.1987

SCHEDULE 3   Regulation 2(ee)

SCHEDULE 3   Regulation 6(4)

COLOURING AGENTS

In this Schedule the colouring agents referred to in regulation 6(4)(a) are–

    (i) those identified either by name or by colour index number (the colour index numbers being those specified in the third edition of The Colour Index published in 1971 by the Society of Dyers and Colourists);

    (ii) lakes or salts of these colouring agents which do not use substances prohibited under Annex II or which are excluded under Annex V from the scope of the Cosmetics Directive (76/768/EEC).

In the case of colouring agents identified by the addition of (*) to the name or colour index number, the insoluble barium, strontium and zirconium lakes, salts and pigments of these colouring agents shall also be permitted. They must pass the test for insolubility which will be determined by the procedure laid down in Article 8 of the Directive.

Colouring agents whose number is preceded by the letter 'E' in accordance with the EEC Directive of 23 October 1962 on the approximation of the rules of Member States concerning foodstuffs and colouring matters(a), as amended,(b) and adapted(c) must fulfil the purity requirements laid down in those Directives. They continue to be subject to the general criteria set out in Annex III to the 1962 Directive concerning colouring matters where the letter 'E' has been deleted therefrom.

(a) O.J. No. 115, 11.11.1962, p. 2645.
(b) Council Directives Nos. 65/469/EEC, 67/653/EEC, 68/419/EEC, 70/758/EEC, 76/399/EEC and 78/144/EEC (O.J. Nos. L178, 26.10.1965, p. 2793; L263, 30.10.1967, p. 4; L309, 24.12.1968, p. 24; L157, 18.7.1970, p. 36; L108, 26.4.1976, p. 19; L44, 15.2.1978, p. 20).
(c) Annexes I and VII to the Act of Accession of 22 January 1972, as adjusted by the Council Decision of 1 January 1973 (O.J. No. L2, 1.1.1973, p. 1).

PART I
COLOURING AGENTS LISTED IN ANNEX III PART 2 OF THE DIRECTIVE AS COLOURING AGENTS ALLOWED FOR USE IN COSMETIC PRODUCTS

Field of application

In column 3 of this Schedule, the entry "x" in a sub-column means that the colouring agent must not be used other than as follows–

Sub-column 1 = Colouring agents allowed in all cosmetic products;

Sub-column 2 = Colouring agents allowed in all cosmetic products except those intended to be applied in the vicinity of the eyes, in particular eye make-up and eye make-up remover;

Sub-column 3 = Colouring agents allowed exclusively in cosmetic products intended not to come into contact with the mucous membranes;

Sub-column 4 = Colouring agents allowed exclusively in cosmetic products intended to come into contact only briefly with the skin.

Column 1	Column 2	Column 3				Column 4
Name or colour index number	Colour	Type of product Field of application				Other requirements
		1	2	3	4	
10006	Green				X	
10020	Green			X		
10316*	Yellow		X			
11680	Yellow			X		
11710	Yellow			X		
11725	Orange				X	
11920	Orange	X				
12010	Red			X		
12075*	Orange	X				
12085*	Red	X				3 per cent maximum concentration in the finished product
12120	Red				X	
12150	Red	X				
12370	Red				X	
12420	Red				X	
12480	Brown				X	
12490	Red	X				
12700	Yellow				X	See also Part 2
13015	Yellow	X				E 105
13065	Yellow				X	See also Part 2
14270	Orange	X				E 103
14700	Red	X				
14720	Red	X				E 122
14815	Red	X				E 125
15510*	Orange		X			
15525	Red	X				
15580	Red	X				

Column 1	Column 2	Column 3				Column 4
Name or colour index number	Colour	Type of product Field of application				Other requirements
		1	2	3	4	
15585*	Red		X			
15620	Red				X	
15630*	Red	X				3 per cent maximum concentration in the finished product
15800	Red			X		See also Part 2
15850*	Red	X				
15865*	Red	X				
15880	Red	X				
15980	Orange	X				E 111
15985*	Yellow	X				E 110
16035	Red	X				
16185	Red	X				E 123
16230	Orange			X		
16255*	Red	X				E 124
16290	Red	X				E 126
17200	Red	X				
18050	Red			X		
18130	Red				X	
18690	Yellow				X	
18736	Red				X	
18820	Yellow				X	
18965	Yellow	X				
19140*	Yellow	X				E 102
20040	Yellow				X	Maximum 3, 3′–dimethylbenzidine concentration in the colouring agent : 5 ppm
20170	Orange			X		
20470	Black				X	See also Part 2
21100	Yellow				X	Maximum 3, 3′–dichloro-benzidine concentration in the colouring agent : 5 ppm
21108	Yellow				X	Maximum 3, 3′–dichloro-benzidine concentration in the colouring agent : 5 ppm
21230	Yellow			X		
24790	Red				X	
27290*	Red				X	
27755	Black	X				E 152
28440	Black	X				E 151
40215	Orange				X	

| Column 1 | Column 2 | Column 3 | | | | Column 4 |
| Name or colour index number | Colour | Type of product Field of application | | | | Other requirements |
		1	2	3	4	
40800	Orange	X				
40820	Orange	X				E 160 e
40825	Orange	X				E 160 f
40850	Orange	X				E 161 g
42045	Blue				X	See also Part 2
42051*	Blue	X				E 131
42053	Green	X				
42080	Blue				X	
42090	Blue	X				
42100	Green				X	
42170	Green				X	See also Part 2
42510	Violet			X		
42520	Violet				X	5 ppm max concentration in the finished product
42640	Violet	X				
42735	Blue			X		
44045	Blue				X	See also Part 2
44090	Green	X				E 142
45100	Red				X	
45170*	Red	X				
45170:1			X			
45190	Violet				X	See also Part 2
45220	Red				X	
45350	Yellow	X				6 per cent max concentration in the finished product
45370*	Orange	X				Not more than 1 per cent 2–(6–hydroxy–3–oxo–3H–xanthen–9–yl) benzoic acid and 2 per cent 2–(bromo–6–hydroxy–3–oxo–3H–xanthen–9–yl) benzoic acid
45380*	Red	X				as immediately above
45396	Orange	X				When used in lipstick, the colouring agent is allowed only in free acid form and in a maximum concentration of 1 per cent
45405	Red		X			Not more than 1 per cent 2–(6–hydroxy–3–oxo–3H–xanthen–9–yl) benzoic acid and 2 per cent 2–(bromo–6–hydroxy–3–oxo–3H–xanthen–9–yl) benzoic acid
45410*	Red	X				as immediately above

Column 1	Column 2	Column 3				Column 4
Name or colour index number	*Colour*	*Type of product Field of application*				*Other requirements*
		1	*2*	*3*	*4*	
45425	Red	X				Not more than 1 per cent 2–(6–hydroxy–3–oxo–3H–xanthen–9–yl) benzoic acid and 3 per cent 2–(iodo–6–hydroxy–3–oxo–3H–xanthen–9–yl) benzoic acid
45430*	Red	X				as immediately above E 127
47000	Yellow			X		See also Part 2
47005	Yellow	X				E 104
50325	Violet				X	
50420	Black		X			
51319	Violet				X	
58000	Red	X				
59040	Green		X			
60724	Violet				X	
60725	Violet	X				
60730	Violet		X			
61565	Green	X				
61570	Green	X				
61585	Blue				X	
62045	Blue				X	
69800	Blue	X				E 130
69825	Blue	X				
71105	Orange		X			
73000	Blue	X				
73015	Blue	X				E 132
73360	Red	X				
73385	Violet	X				
73900	Violet				X	See also Part 2
73915	Red				X	
74100	Blue				X	
74160	Blue	X				
74180	Blue				X	See also Part 2
74260	Green		X			
75100	Yellow	X				
75120	Orange	X				E 160 b
75125	Yellow	X				E 160 d
75130	Orange	X				E 160 a
75135	Yellow	X				E 161 d
75170	White	X				

Column 1	Column 2	Column 3				Column 4
Name or colour index number	*Colour*	*Type of product Field of application*				*Other requirements*
		1	*2*	*3*	*4*	
75300	Yellow	X				E 100
75470	Red	X				E 120
75810	Green	X				E 140 and E 141
77000	White	X				E 173
77002	White	X				
77004	White	X				
77007	Blue	X				
77015	Red	X				
77120	White	X				
77163	White	X				
77220	White	X				E 170
77231	White	X				
77266	Black	X				
77267	Black	X				
77268:1	Black	X				E 153
77288	Green	X				Free from chromate ions
77289	Green	X				Free from chromate ions
77346	Green	X				
77400	Brown	X				
77480	Brown	X				E 175
77489	Orange	X				E 172
77491	Red	X				E 172
77492	Yellow	X				E 172
77499	Black	X				E 172
77510	Blue	X				Free from cyanide ions
77713	White	X				
77742	Violet	X				
77745	Red	X				
77820	White	X				E 174
77891	White	X				E 171
77947	White	X				
Lactoflavin	Yellow	X				E 101
Caramel	Brown	X				E 150
Capsanthin, capsorubin	Orange	X				E 160 c
Beetroot red	Red	X				E 162
Anthocyanins	Red	X				E 163
Aluminium, zinc, magnesium and calcium stearates	White	X				

Column 1	Column 2	Column 3				Column 4
Name or colour index number	*Colour*	*Type of product Field of application*				*Other requirements*
		1	*2*	*3*	*4*	
Bromothymol blue	Blue				X	
Bromocresol green	Green				X	

PART II

COLOURING AGENTS LISTED IN ANNEX IV PART 2 OF THE DIRECTIVE AS COLOURING AGENTS PROVISONALLY ALLOWED FOR USE IN COSMETIC PRODUCTS

Field of application

In column 3 of this Schedule the entry "X" in a sub-column means that the columns agent must not be used other than as follows–

Sub-column 1 = Colouring agents allowed in all cosmetic products;

Sub-column 2 = Colouring agents allowed in all cosmetic products except those intended to be applied in the vicinity of the eyes, in particular eye make-up and eye make-up remover;

Sub-column 3 = Colouring agents allowed exclusively in cosmetic products intended not to come into contact with the mucous membranes;

Sub-column 4 = Colouring agents allowed exclusively in cosmetic products intended to come into contact only briefly with the skin.

Column 1	Column 2	Column 3				Column 4	Column 5
Name or colour index number	*Colour*	*Type of product Field of application*				*Other requirements*	*Authorization valid until*
		1	*2*	*3*	*4*		
12700	Yellow			X		See also Part I	31.12.1987
13065	Yellow			X		See also Part I	31.12.1987
15800	Red	X				See also Part I	31.12.1988
19120	Yellow				X		31.12.1988
20470	Black			X		See also Part I	31.12.1988
21110	Orange				X	Maximum 3,3'–dichloro-benzidine concentration in the colouring agent: 5 ppm	31.12.1987
21115	Orange				X	as immediately above	31.12.1988
26100	Red	X					31.12.1988
42045	Blue			X		See also Part I	31.12.1988
42170	Green			X		See also Part I	31.12.1988
42535	Violet			X			31.12.1987
44025	Green				X		31.12.1987
44045	Blue			X		See also Part I	31.12.1987
45190	Violet			X		See also Part I	31.12.1988
47000	Yellow	X				See also Part I	31.12.1988
61554	Blue			X		Only in hair-care preparations in a maximum concentration of 50 ppm	31.12.1987
73312	Red				X		31.12.1987
73900	Violet			X		See also Part I	31.12.1987
73905	Red				X		31.12.1988
74180	Blue			X		See also Part I	31.12.1988
75660	Yellow				X		31.12.1988
Acid red 195	Red			X			31.12.1987

Regulation 2(ff)

SCHEDULE 4

Regulations 6(6) and 8(1)

SCHEDULE 5

PRESERVATIVES

In this Schedule, the matters specified in columns 3, 4, 5 and 6 which apply to a particular substance are those set out to the right of its name as mentioned in column 2; and the matters specified in columns 4, 5 and 6 which apply in any particular case are those set out to the right of the matter specified in column 3 which applies in that case. The substance may not be used or contained other than in the types of product specified in column 3. The concentration of the substance, when it is used as a preservative, in a product may not exceed the limit set out in column 4. Where a product is intended to be mixed with another product in specified proportions before use, the level of concentration shall be calculated by reference to the mixture. Other requirements are specified in column 5.

In column 4 of this Schedule, "A" indicates that the concentration of the substance in a product may exceed the limit set out in that column provided that–

(a) the presence of any excess of the substance in a product over the concentration so set out is not for the primary purpose of inhibiting the development of micro-organisms; and

(b) the purpose for which any such excess is present in the product is apparent from the labelling of the product.

In this Schedule–

"salts" means salts of the cations sodium, potassium, calcium, magnesium, ammonium and ethanolamines and of the anions chloride, bromide, sulphate and acetate;

"esters" means esters of methyl, ethyl, propyl, isopropyl, butyl, isobutyl and phenyl.

In column 4 of this Schedule, the percentage concentration is measured by reference to mass (m/m) unless a contrary intention appears.

All preservative substances containing formaldehyde or any substances named in this Schedule which release formaldehyde must be labelled with the warning "contains formaldehyde" when the concentration of formaldehyde in the final product exceeds 0.05 per cent.

PART I

PRESERVATIVES LISTED IN ANNEX VI, PART I OF THE DIRECTIVE AS PRESERVATIVES ALLOWED

Column 1	Column 2	Column 3	Column 4	Column 5	Column 6
Reference Number	Name of substance	Purpose of substance or type of product	Maximum concentration of substance in product	Other requirements	Required information
1	Benzoic acid, its salts and esters	All products	0.5 per cent (acid) A	—	—
2	Propionic acid and its salts	All products	2 per cent (acid) A	—	—
3	Salicylic acid and its salts	All products	0.5 per cent (acid) A	Not to be used in preparations for children under three years of age except for shampoos	Not to be used for children under three years of age (Solely for products which might be used for children under three years of age and which remain in prolonged contact with the skin)
4	Sorbic acid (hexa–2,4–dienoic acid) and its salts	All products	0.6 per cent (acid) A	—	—
5	Formaldehyde and paraformaldehyde	Oral hygiene products / Other products (see also Part I of Schedule 2)	0.1 per cent (expressed as free formaldehyde) / 0.2 per cent (expressed as free formaldehyde)	Not to be used in aerosol dispensers (sprays)	—
6	Hexachlorophene (INN)	All products	0.1 per cent	–Not to be used in products for children less than three years old or in personal hygiene products. –Purity criterion: absence of 2,3,7,8–tetrachlorodibenzo–p–dioxin	Not to be used for children under three years of age. Contains hexachlorophene
7	Biphenyl–2–ol (o–phenylphenol) and its salts	All products	0.2 per cent expressed as the phenol A	—	—
8	Pyrithione zinc (INN)	Products rinsed off after use	0.5 per cent A	Not to be used in oral hygiene products	—
9	Inorganic sulphites and hydrogen sulphites	All products	0.2 per cent expressed as free SO_2 A	—	—

Column 1	Column 2	Column 3	Column 4	Column 5	Column 6
Reference Number	Name of substance	Purpose of substance or type of product	Maximum concentration of substance in product	Other requirements	Required information
10	Sodium iodate	Products rinsed off after use	0.1 per cent	—	—
11	Chlorobutanol (INN)	All products	0.5 per cent	Not to be used in aerosol dispensers (sprays)	Contains chlorobutanol
12	4–Hydroxybenzoic acid and its salts and esters	All products	0.4 per cent (acid) for 1 ester, 0.8 per cent (acid) for mixtures of esters A	—	—
13	3–Acetyl–6–methylpyran–2,4 (3H)–dione (Dehydracetic acid) and its salts	All products	0.6 per cent (acid)	Not to be used in aerosol dispensers (sprays)	—
14	Formic acid	All products	0.5 per cent (acid) A	—	—
15	3,3'–Dibromo–4,4' –hexamethylene –dioxydibenzamidine (Dibromohexamidine) and its salts (including isethionate)	All products	0.1 per cent	—	—
16	Thiomersal (INN)	Eye make-up and eye make-up remover	0.007 per cent calculated as mercury. When mixed with other authorised mercury compounds total mercury concentration must not exceed 0.007 per cent	—	Contains thiomersal
17	Phenylmercuric salts (including borate)	Eye make-up and eye make-up remover	0.007 per cent calculated as mercury. When mixed with other authorised mercury compounds total mercury concentration must not exceed 0.007 per cent	—	Contains phenylmercuric compounds
18	Undec–10–enoic acid and its salts	All products	0.2 per cent (acid) A	See also Schedule 5, Part II, Item 8	—
19	Hexetidine (INN)	Rinse-off products only	0.1 per cent A	See also Schedule 5, Part II, Item 15	—
20	5–Bromo–5–nitro–1, 3–dioxane	Rinse-off products only	0.1 per cent	Avoid formation of nitrosamines See Schedule 5, Part II, No. 7	—

Column 1	Column 2	Column 3	Column 4	Column 5	Column 6
Reference Number	Name of substance	Purpose of substance or type of product	Maximum concentration of substance in product	Other requirements	Required information
21	Bronopol (INN)	All products	0.1 per cent	A	Avoid formation of nitrosamines	—
22	2,4-Dichlorobenzyl alcohol	All products	0.15 per cent	A	—	—
23	Triclocarban (INN)	All products	0.2 per cent	A	Purity criteria: 3,3',4,4'-Tetrachloroazobenzene 1 ppm; 3,3',4,4'-Tetrachloroazoxybenzene 1 ppm	—
24	4-Chloro-m-cresol	Not to be used in products intended to come into contact with mucous membranes	0.2 per cent	A	—	—
25	Triclosan (INN)	All products	0.3 per cent	A	—	—
26	4-Chloro-3,5-xylenol	All products	0.5 per cent	A	—	—
27	3,3'-Bis(1-hydroxymethyl-2,5-dioxoimidazolidin-4-yl)-1,1'-methylenediurea ("Imidazolidinyl urea")	All products	0.6 per cent	A	—	—
28	Poly(1-hexamethylenebiguanide hydrochloride)	All products	0.3 per cent	A	—	—
29	2-Phenoxyethanol	All products	1.0 per cent	A	—	—
30	Hexamethylenetetramine (methenamine (INN))	All products	0.15 per cent	A	—	—
31	Methenamine 3-chloroallylochloride (INNM)	All products	0.2 per cent	A	—	—
32	1-(4-Chlorophenoxy)-1-(imidazol-1-yl)-3,3-dimethylbutan-2-one	All products	0.5 per cent	A	—	—
33	1,3-Bis(hydroxymethyl)-5,5-dimethylimidazolidine-2,4-dione	All products	0.6 per cent	A	—	—

Column 1	Column 2	Column 3	Column 4	Column 5	Column 6
Reference Number	Name of substance	Purpose of substance or type of product	Maximum concentration of substance in product	Other requirements	Required information
34	Benzyl alcohol	All products (See also Schedule 2 Part I, No. 46)	1.0 per cent A	—	—
35	1–Hydroxy–4–methyl–6–(2,4,4–trimethylpentyl)–2–pyridone and its monoethanolamine salt	Rinse-off products only	1.0 per cent A	—	—
		For other products	0.5 per cent A		
36	1,2–Dibromo–2,4–dicyanobutane	All products	0.1 per cent	Not to be used in cosmetic sunscreen products	—
37	6,6–Dibromo–4,4–dichloro–2,2′–methylenediphenol (Bromochlorophen)	All products	0.1 per cent A	—	—
38	4–Isopropyl–m–cresol	All products	0.1 per cent	—	—
39	Mixture of 5–Chloro–2–methylisothiazol–3($2H$)–one and 2–methylisothiazol–3($2H$)–one with magnesium chloride and magnesium nitrate	All products	0.003 per cent of a mixture in the ratio 3:1 of 5–chloro–2–methylisothiazol–3($2H$)–one and 2–methylisothiazol–3($2H$)–one	—	—

PART II

PRESERVATIVES LISTED IN ANNEX VI PART 2 OF THE DIRECTIVE AS PRESERVATIVES PROVISIONALLY ALLOWED

Column 1 *a* Reference Number	Column 2 *b* Name of substance	Column 3 Type of product	Column 4 *c* Maximum concentration of substance in product	Column 5 *d* Other limitations and requirements	Column 6 *e* Required information Conditions of use and warnings which must be printed on the label	Column 7 *f* Allowed until
1	Boric acid	(a) Products for oral hygiene	0.5 per cent A	—	—	31.12.1988
		(b) Other products (see also Schedule 2 Part 1, No. 1)	3.0 per cent A			
2	Chlorphenesin (INN)	All products	0.5 per cent A	—	—	31.12.1987
3	Dibromopropamidine (INN) and its salts (including isethionate (INN))	All products	0.1 per cent	—	—	31.12.1988
4	Alkyl (C12–C22) trimethyl–ammonium bromide and chloride (including Cetrimonium bromide (INN))	All products	0.1 per cent A	—	—	31.12.1988
5	3–Heptyl–2–(3–heptyl–4–methyl–4–thiazolin–2–ylidenemethyl)–4–methyl–thiazolinium iodide	Creams, toilet lotions and shampoos	0.002 per cent	—	—	31.12.1988
6	4,4–Dimethyl–1,3–oxazolidine	Products rinsed off after use	0.1 per cent	The pH of the finished product shall not be lower than 6	—	31.12.1989
7	5–Bromo–5–nitro–1,3–dioxane	Non rinse-off products	0.1 per cent	Avoid formation of nitrosamines (See Schedule 5–Part I, No. 20)	—	31.12.1987

Column 1 a	Column 2 b	Column 3	Column 4 c	Column 5 d	Column 6 e	Column 7 f
Reference Number	Name of substance	Type of product	Maximum concentration of substance in product	Other limitations and requirements	Required information Conditions of use and warnings which must be printed on the label	Allowed until
8	Undec–10–enoic acid: esters, the amide, the mono–and bis(2–hydroxethyl) amides and their sulphosuccinates	All products (See Schedule 5–Part I, No. 18)	0.2 per cent (acid) A	—	—	31.12.1987
9	Clorofene (INN)	All products	0.2 per cent	—	—	31.12.1987
10	2–Chloro–N–(hydroxymethyl) acetamide	Products rinsed off after use	0.3 per cent expressed as the chloracetamide	—	—	31.12.1987
11	1–Phenoxypropan–2–ol	Products rinsed off after use	1.0 per cent	For other uses see Schedule 2–Part II–No. 5	—	31.12.1987
12	Benzethonium chloride (INN)	Not to be used in products intended to come into contact with mucous membranes	0.1 per cent A	—	—	31.12.1988
13	Benzalkonium chloride (INN) bromide and saccharinate	All products	0.25 per cent A	—	—	31.12.1987
14	1–[1,3–Bis(hydroxymethyl)–2,5– dioxoimidazolidin–4– yl]1,3–bis(hydroxymethyl) urea	All products	0.5 per cent	—	—	31.12.1987
15	Hexetidine (INN)	All products (See also Schedule 5, Part I, No. 19)	0.1 per cent	—	—	31.12.1987
16	4–Hydroxybenzoic acid benzyl ester	All products	0.1 per cent (acid)	—	—	31.12.1988
17	Hexamidine (INN) and its salts (including isethionate and 4–hydroxybenzoate)	All products	0.1 per cent A	—	—	31.12.1988

Column 1	Column 2	Column 3	Column 4	Column 5	Column 6	Column 7
a	*b*		*c*	*d*	*e*	*f*
Reference Number	Name of substance	Type of product	Maximum concentration of substance in product	Other limitations and requirements	Required information Conditions of use and warnings which must be printed on the label	Allowed until
18	Benzylformal (a 1:1 mixture of benzyloxymethanol and (benzyloxymethoxy) methanol)	All products	0.2 per cent	—	—	31.12.1987
19	2–Chloroacetamide	All products	0.3 per cent	—	Contains chloroacetamide	31.12.1987
20	Chlorhexidine (INN) and its digluconate, diacetate and dihydrochloride	All products	0.3 per cent	A	—	31.12.1987
21	1,3,5–Tris(2–hydroxyethyl) hexahydro–1,3,5 triazine	Products rinsed off after use	0.2 per cent	—	Contains 1,3,5–Tris(2–hydroxyethyl) hexahydro–1,3,5 triazine	31.12.1988

EXPLANATORY NOTE

(This note is not part of the Regulations)

These Regulations amend the Cosmetic Products (Safety) Regulations 1984 ("the Principal Regulations") as amended by the Cosmetic Products (Safety) (Amendment) Regulations 1985, and implement Commission Directives No. 85/391/EEC (O.J. L224, 22.8.85, p. 40), No. 85/490/EEC (O.J. L295, 7.11.85, p. 30), No. 86/179/EEC (O.J. L138, 24.5.86 p. 40) and No. 86/199/EEC (O.J. L149, 3.6.86 p. 38) on cosmetic products, and as permitted by the Directives impose certain additional requirements on the composition of cosmetic products. The Regulations are made under the Consumer Protection Act 1987 and the European Communities Act 1972.

The main changes are–

(1) the deletion of Schedules 3 and 4 of the principal Regulations and their replacement by the Schedule set out in Schedule 3 to these Regulations. The replacement Schedule lists colouring agents which are acceptable throughout the European Community and take account of the review of provisionally approved colourants undertaken to satisfy Article 5 of the Cosmetics Directive (76/768/EEC) (regulation 2(ee));

(2) the replacement of Schedule 5 of the principal Regulations by the Schedule set out in Schedule 4 to the Regulations. The Schedule lists the preservatives which may be used in cosmetic products and takes account of the review of provisionally approved preservatives undertaken to satisfy Article 5 of the Cosmetics Directive (76/768/EEC) (regulation 2(ff));

(3) the amendment of the wording of regulations 5(2) and 9(2) to make it clear that the controls over supply also apply to products exported to other member States of the European Economic Community (regulation 2(b) and (i));

(4) the prohibition of the use of 2,3,7,8–tetrachlorodibenzo–p–dioxin, dimethoxane, pyrithione sodium and heightened versions of hydroquinone (regulation 2 (q) and (y));

(5) the restriction of the use of selenium disulphide, aluminium zirconium hydroxides, quinolin–8–ol and bis (8–hydroxyquinolinium) sulphate, 2, 2′ diothiobis (pyridine 1–oxide), addition product with magnesium sulphate trihydrate and 1–phenoxypropan–2–ol and the modification of the restriction on the use of 1,3–Bis (Hydroxymethyl) imidazolidene–2–thione (regulation 2(aa) (bb) and (cc));

(6) the specification of methods in certain cases for identifying and in all cases for determining the presence in cosmetic products of glycerol 1–(4 aminobenzoate);, chlorobutanol, quinine, inorganic sulphites and hydrogen sulphites, chlorates of the alkali metal and sodium iodate (regulation 2(hh)).

STATUTORY INSTRUMENTS

1987 No. 1921 (S.132)

INSOLVENCY

COMPANIES

The Insolvency (Scotland) Amendment Rules 1987

Made - - - -	*9th November 1987*
Laid before Parliament	*24th November 1987*
Coming into force	*11th January 1988*

The Secretary of State, in exercise of the powers conferred on him by section 411 of the Insolvency Act 1986(**a**), and of all other powers enabling him in that behalf, hereby makes the following Rules:

Citation and commencement

1. These Rules may be cited as the Insolvency (Scotland) Amendment Rules 1987 and shall come into force on 11th January 1988.

Interpretation

2. In these Rules, "the principal Rules" means the Insolvency (Scotland) Rules 1986(**b**) and, unless the context otherwise requires, any reference to a Rule or Schedule or form is a reference to that Rule or Schedule or form in the principal Rules.

Amendment and application

3.—(1) Subject to paragraphs (2) and (3) the principal Rules shall be amended in accordance with the provisions of the Schedule to these Rules.

(2) The principal Rules as so amended shall apply on and after the date on which these Rules come into force to all insolvency proceedings to which the principal Rules apply, whenever such proceedings have commenced.

(3) Any form which is substituted by a form ("a new form") contained in Part III of the Schedule to these Rules may continue to be used instead of the new form for the purpose for which it was prescribed, and with such variations as circumstances require, until 1st March 1988.

Department of Trade and Industry
1 Victoria Street, London
9th November 1987

Francis Maude
Parliamentary Under Secretary of State

(**a**) 1986 c.45.
(**b**) S.I. 1986/1915.

Rule 3   **SCHEDULE**

PART I

AMENDMENT OF THE PRINCIPAL RULES

Rule 0.2

1. In paragraph (1) of Rule 0.2 after the definition "the Companies Act" there shall be inserted the following definition:-

""the Banking Act" means the Banking Act 1987(**a**);",

and after the definition of "insolvency proceedings", there shall be inserted the following definition:–

""proxy-holder" shall be construed in accordance with Rule 7.14;".

Rule 1.10

2. In paragraph (1)(a) of Rule 1.10 after the word "them" there shall be inserted the words "with, in addition, where the company is subject to an administration order, the names and addresses of the company's preferential creditors (defined in section 386), with the amounts of their respective claims,".

Rule 1.12

3. In paragraph (3) of Rule 1.12, for the words from "Rule 1.3" to the end there shall be substituted the words "Rule 1.10".

Rule 2.2

4. In paragraph (1) of Rule 2.2 for the words "to the person" there shall be substituted the words "to any person".

Rule 2.3

5. For paragraph (3)(a) of Rule 2.3 there shall be substituted the following:–

"(a) any person who has appointed, or is or may be entitled to appoint, an administrative receiver;".

Rule 2.7

6.—(1) In Rule 2.7 there shall be inserted at the beginning of the Rule the word "(1)".

(2) For paragraph (f) of that Rule there shall be substituted the following:–

"(f) the manner in which the affairs and business of the company–

(i) have, since the date of the administrator's appointment, been managed and financed, and

(ii) will, if the administrator's proposals are approved, continue to be managed and financed; and".

(3) At the end of that Rule there shall be inserted the following paragraph:–

"(2) Where the administrator intends to apply to the court under section 18 for the administration order to be discharged at a time before he has sent a statement of his proposals to creditors, in accordance with section 23(1), he shall, at least 10 days before he makes such an application, send to all creditors of the company of whom he is aware, a report containing the information required by paragraph (1)(a) to (f)(i) of this Rule.".

Rule 2.13

7. For Rule 2.13 there shall be substituted the following:–

"**Report and notice of meetings**

2.13.   Any report or notice by the administrator of the result of creditors' meetings held under section 23(1) or 25(2) shall have annexed to it details of the proposals which were considered by the meeting in question and of any revisions and modifications to the proposals which were also considered.".

Rule 2.20

8. In Rule 2.20, for the words "original appointment of an administrator" there shall be substituted the words "administration order".

(**a**) 1987 c.22.

Rule 4.1

9. In Rule 4.1 there shall be inserted at the beginning of the Rule the word "(1)" and there shall be inserted at the end of the Rule the following paragraph:–

"(2) The court shall be satisfied that a person has caution for the proper performance of his functions as provisional liquidator if a statement is lodged in court or it is averred in the winding-up petition that the person to be appointed is an insolvency practitioner, duly qualified under the Act to act as liquidator, and that he consents so to act.".

Rule 4.5

10.—(1) In paragraph (3) of Rule 4.5, for the words from the beginning of the paragraph to "accordingly" there shall be substituted the following:

"(3) Without prejudice to any order of the court as to expenses, the provisional liquidator's remuneration shall be paid to him, and the amount of any expenses incurred by him (including the remuneration and expenses of any special manager appointed under section 177) reimbursed–

(a) if a winding up order is not made, out of the property of the company".

(2) After paragraph (3) of that Rule there shall be inserted the following paragraph:–

"(4) Unless the court otherwise directs, in a case falling within paragraph (3)(a) above, the provisional liquidator may retain out of the company's property such sums or property as are or may be required for meeting his remuneration and expenses.".

Rule 4.6

11. In Rule 4.6(2) the words from "and, without prejudice to the power of the court" to the end of the Rule shall be deleted.

Rule 4.10

12. After paragraph (3) of Rule 4.10, there shall be inserted the following paragraph:–

"(4) Any person appointed as liquidator of a company under section 140(1) who, following such appointment becomes aware of creditors of the company of whom he was not aware when he was acting as the administrator of the company, shall send to such creditors a copy of any statement or report which was sent by him to creditors under Rule 2.7, with a note to the effect that it is being sent under this Rule.".

Rule 4.11

13. In Rule 4.11, for the words "at 6 monthly intervals" there shall be substituted the words "not more than 30 days after the end of each accounting period which ends after that year".

Rule 4.12

14.—(1) In paragraph (1) of Rule 4.12, for the words "section 138(3)" there shall be substituted "section 138(3) or (4)" and after the words "contributories of the company" there shall be inserted the words "or, as the case may be, a meeting of the creditors".

(2) After paragraph (2) of that Rule, there shall be inserted the following paragraph:–

"(2A) Any meetings of creditors or contributories under section 138(3) or (4) shall be summoned for a date not later than 42 days after the date of the winding up order or such longer period as the court may allow.".

Rule 4.16

15. In paragraph (2) of Rule 4.16–

(a) for the word "Company" in Column 2 there shall be substituted the words "The company or, in the application of section 49(6) of the Bankruptcy Act, any member or contributory of the company"; and

(b) for the words "Debtor's assets" in Column 1 there shall be substituted the words "Debtor's estate".

Rule 4.18

16. In Rule 4.18(5), there shall be inserted after the word "shall" the following:–

"state whether a liquidation committee has been established by a meeting of creditors or contributories, and, if this is not the case, he shall–".

Rule 4.19

17.—(1) In paragraph (3) of Rule 4.19 for the words from "shall be effective" to "meeting of the contributories", there shall be substituted the words "takes effect upon the passing of the resolution for his appointment" and for the words "this date" there shall be substituted the words "the date of his appointment".

(2) In paragraph (6) of that Rule for the words "company meeting" there shall be substituted the words "a meeting of contributories".

Rule 4.22

18. For Rule 4.22 there shall be inserted the following:–

"Taking possession and realisation of the company's assets

4.22—(1) The liquidator shall—

    (a) as soon as may be after his appointment take possession of the whole assets of the company and any property, books, papers or records in the possession or control of the compamy or to which the company appears to be entitled; and

    (b) make up and maintain an inventory and valuation of the assets which he shall retain in the sederunt book.

(2) The liquidator shall be entitled to have access to all documents or records relating to the assets or the property or the business or financial affairs of the company sent by or on behalf of the company to a third party and in that third party's hands and to make copies of any such documents or records.

(3) If any person obstructs a liquidator who is exercising, or attempting to exercise, a power conferred by sub-section (2) above, the court, on the application of the liquidator, may order that person to cease so to obstruct the liquidator.

(4) The liquidator may require delivery to him of any title deed or other document or record of the company, notwithstanding that a right of lien is claimed over the title deed or document or record, but this paragraph is without prejudice to any preference of the holder of the lien.

(5) Section 39(4) and (7) of the Bankruptcy Act shall apply in relation to a liquidation of a company as it applies in relation to a sequestration of a debtor's estate, subject to the modifications specified in Rule 4.16(2) and to any other necessary modifications.".

Rule 4.24

19. In sub-paragraph (a) of paragraph (1) of Rule 4.24 before the words "to the registrar of companies" there shall be inserted the words "a copy of the certificate" and in sub-paragraph (b) of that paragraph for the word "it" there shall be substituted the words "a copy of the certificate".

Rule 4.29

20. After paragraph (5) of Rule 4.29, there shall be inserted the following paragraphs:–

"(6) If there is no quorum present at the meeting summoned to receive the liquidator's resignation, the meeting is deemed to have been held, a resolution is deemed to have been passed that the liquidator's resignation be accepted, and the creditors are deemed not to have resolved against the liquidator having his release.

(7) Where paragraph (6) applies–

    (a) the liquidator's resignation is effective as from the date for which the meeting was summoned and that date shall be stated in the notice given by the liquidator under paragraph (3), and

    (b) the liquidator is deemed to have been released as from that date.".

Rule 4.31

21. In Rule 4.31, there shall be inserted at the end of paragraph (6) the following:–

"subject to the modifications that in Rule 4.25(3) sub-paragraph (a) shall apply with the word "new" replaced by the word "former" and sub-paragraph (b) shall not apply".

Rule 4.34

22. In paragraph (4) of Rule 4.34, after the word "appearing" in both places where it occurs, there shall be inserted the words "or being represented".

Rule 4.41

23.—(1) In paragraph (1)(b) of Rule 4.41, there shall be inserted after the word "decides," the word "of".

(2) In paragraph (6) of that Rule, for the words "section 28 of the Banking Act 1979" there shall be substituted the words "section 58 of the Banking Act".

Rule 4.42

24. In paragraph (3) of Rule 4.42, there shall be inserted after the words "agreed to do so", the following:–

"and, unless the relevant proxy or authorisation contains a statement to the contrary, such agreement may be given on behalf of the member by his proxy-holder or any representative under section 375 of the Companies Act who is present at the meeting at which the committee is established".

Rule 4.43

25. In paragraph (4) of Rule 4.43, for the words from "with the substitution" to the end of that paragraph there shall be substituted the words "with the substitution of the reference to Rule 4.41 in paragraph (3) of that Rule by a reference to this paragraph".

Rule 4.48

26. In paragraph (2) of Rule 4.48, there shall be added at the end the following:–

", and for this purpose any proxy or authorisation under section 375 of the Companies Act in relation to any meeting of creditors (or, as the case may be, members or contributories) of the company shall, unless it contains a statement to the contrary, be treated as such a mandate to act generally signed by or on behalf of the committee-member".

Rule 4.53

27. In paragraph (2) of Rule 4.53, for the reference to "Rule 4.41(1)" there shall be substituted a reference to "Rule 4.43(4)".

Rule 4.55

28. In paragraph (2) of Rule 4.55, for the words from "a statement incorporating" to the end of the paragraph, there shall be substituted the following:–

"a copy of any proposed resolution on which a decision is sought, which shall be set out in such a way that agreement with or dissent from each separate resolution may be indicated by the recipient on the copy so sent".

Rule 4.59A

29. After Rule 4.59, there shall be inserted the following new Rule:–

"Formal defects

4.59A. The acts of the liquidation committee established for any winding up are valid notwithstanding any defect in the appointment, election or qualifications of any member of the committee or any committee - member's representative or in the formalities of its establishment.".

Rule 4.65

30. In Rule 4.65, for the reference to "Rules 4.44 to 4.59" there shall be substituted a reference to "Rules 4.44 to 4.59A".

Rule 4.66

31.—(1) In paragraph (1) of Rule 4.66, there shall be inserted, before sub-paragraph (b), the following sub-paragraph:–

"(aa) Where the court makes a winding up order in relation to a company and, at the time when the petition for winding up was first presented to the court, there was in force in relation to the company a voluntary arrangement under Part 1 of the Act, any expenses properly incurred as expenses of the administration of that arrangement;".

(2) In paragraph (6)(b) of that Rule, for the words "the permanent trustee" there shall be substituted the words "the liquidator" and, for the words from "section 38(4)" to the end of the paragraph, there shall be substituted the words "Rule 4.22(4)".

Rule 4.67

32. In paragraph (1)(i) of Rule 4.67, for the words "capital gains" there shall be substituted the word "corporation".

Rule 4.78

33. At the end of paragraph (a) of Rule 4.78, the word "and" shall be omitted and at the end of paragraph (b) of that Rule there shall be inserted the following:–

"

, and

(c) apply to all windings up to which section 216 applies, whether or not the winding up commenced before or after the coming into force of the Insolvency (Scotland) Amendment Rules 1987.".

Rule 4.81

34. For Rule 4.81 there shall be substituted the following:–

"Second excepted case

4.81.—(1) Where a person to whom section 216 applies as having been a director or shadow director of the liquidating company applies for leave of the court under that section not later than 7 days from the date on which the company went into liquidation, he may, during the period specified in paragraph (2) below, act in any of the ways mentioned in section 216(3), notwithstanding that he has not the leave of the court under that section.

(2) The period referred to in paragraph (1) begins with the day in which the company goes into liquidation and ends either on the day falling 6 weeks after that date or on the day on which the court disposes of the application for leave under section 216, whichever of those days occurs first.".

Rule 7.3

35.—(1) In paragraph'(2) of Rule 7.3, the word "and" after sub-paragraph (b) shall be deleted and at the end of sub-paragraph (c) there shall be inserted a new sub-paragraph as follows:–

"

; and

(d) a meeting of creditors or contributories under section 138(3) or (4).".

(2) After paragraph (3) of that Rule there shall be inserted the following paragraph:–

"(3A) Any notice under this paragraph shall be published not less than 21 days or, in cases to which paragraph (2) above applies, 14 days before the meeting.".

(3) There shall be inserted after paragraph (6) of that Rule the following paragraph:–

"(7) The provisions of this Rule shall not apply to a meeting of creditors summoned under section 95 or 98 but any notice advertised in accordance with section 95(2)(c) or 98(1)(c) shall give not less than 7 days' notice of the meeting.".

Rule 7.4

36. For paragraph (1) of Rule 7.4 there shall be substituted the following:–

"(1) This Rule applies where a company goes, or proposes to go, into liquidation and it is an authorised institution or a former authorised institution within the meaning of the Banking Act.".

Rule 7.5

37. In paragraph (1) of Rule 7.5 there shall be inserted–

(a) after the words "insolvency proceedings" the words ", other than at a meeting of creditors summoned under section 98,", and

(b) after the word "or" the words "except at a meeting of creditors summoned under section 95".

Rule 7.6

38.—(1) For paragraph (1) of Rule 7.6 there shall be substituted the following:–

"(1) Subject to paragraph (8), this Rule applies to any request by a creditor or creditors–

(a) to–

(i) an administrator under section 17(3), or

(ii) a liquidator under section 171(3) or 172(3),

for a meeting of creditors; or

(b) to a liquidator under section 142(3) for separate meetings of creditors and contributories, or for any other meeting under any other provision of the Act or the Rules.".

(2) In paragraph (4) of that Rule after the word "administrator" there shall be inserted the words "or, as the case may be, the liquidator".

Rule 7.7

39. After paragraph (2) of Rule 7.7, there shall be inserted the following paragraph:–

"(3) Where at any meeting of creditors or contributories–

    (a) the provisions of this Rule as to a quorum being present are satisfied by the attendance of–

        (i) the chairman alone, or

        (ii) one other person in addition to the chairman, and

    (b) the chairman is aware, by virtue of claims and proxies received or otherwise, that one or more additional persons would, if attending, be entitled to vote,

the meeting shall not commence until at least the expiry of 15 minutes after the time appointed for its commencement.".

Rule 7.8

40.—(1) In paragraph (5) of Rule 7.8–

    (a) the words "(1) or (2)" shall be replaced by the words "(2) or (3)"; and

    (b) there shall be inserted at the end of that paragraph the words "and notice of the adjourned meeting may be given by the chairman".

(2) After paragraph (6) of that Rule, there shall be inserted the following paragraph:–

"(7) Where a company meeting at which a resolution for voluntary winding up is to be proposed is adjourned without that resolution having been passed, any resolution passed at a meeting under section 98 held before the holding of the adjourned company meeting only has effect on and from the passing by the company of a resolution for winding up.".

Rule 7.12

41. In paragraph (4) of Rule 7.12–

    (a) there shall be inserted after the words "by a person" the words "(whether personally or on his behalf by a proxy-holder)," and

    (b) there shall be substituted for the word "proxy" the words "proxy-holder".

Rule 7.14

42. In paragraph (4) of Rule 7.14 there shall be inserted at the end of the paragraph the words "and any person to whom such a proxy is given cannot decline to be the proxy-holder in relation to that proxy".

Rule 7.16

43. After paragraph (3) of Rule 7.16, there shall be added the following paragraphs:–

"(4) Where a proxy directs a proxy-holder to vote for or against a resolution for the nomination or appointment of a person to be the responsible insolvency practitioner, the proxy-holder may, unless the proxy states otherwise, vote for or against (as he thinks fit) any resolution for the nomination or appointment of that person jointly with another or others.

(5) A proxy-holder may propose any resolution which, if proposed by another, would be a resolution in favour of which he would be entitled to vote by virtue of the proxy.

(6) Where a proxy gives specific directions as to voting, this does not, unless the proxy states otherwise, preclude the proxy-holder from voting at his discretion on resolutions put to the meeting which are not dealt with in the proxy.".

Rule 7.18

44. In paragraph (4) of Rule 7.18 for the words "to be used" to the end there shall be substituted the following:–

"(including claims)–

    (a) to be used in connection with that meeting, or

    (b) sent or given to the chairman of that meeting or to any other person by a creditor, member or contributory for the purpose of that meeting, whether or not they are to be used at it.".

Rule 7.19

45.—(1) After paragraph (1) of Rule 7.19 there shall be inserted the following paragraph:–

"(1A) Where a proxy-holder has signed the proxy as being authorised to do so by his principal and the proxy specifically directs him to vote in the way mentioned in paragraph (1), he shall nevertheless not vote in that way unless he produces to the chairman of the meeting written authorisation from his principal sufficient to show that the proxy-holder was entitled so to sign the proxy.".

(2) In paragraph (2) of Rule 7.19:–

(a) after the word "capacity" there shall be inserted the words "in accordance with Rule 7.16(3)", and

(b) for the words "in its application to him" there shall be substituted "in the application of this Rule to any such person".

Rule 7.20

46. After paragraph (2) of Rule 7.20 there shall be added the following paragraph:–

"(3) Nothing in this Rule requires the authority of a person to sign a proxy on behalf of a principal which is a corporation to be in the form of a resolution of that corporation.".

Rule 7.21

47. In paragraph (2) of Rule 7.21 there shall be inserted before the word "Rules" the words "Act or the".

Rule 7.22

48. In Rule 7.22 after paragraph (1) there shall be inserted the following paragraph:–

"(1A) Any document to be sent by post may be sent to the last known address of the person to whom the document is to be sent.".

Rule 7.26

49. After paragraph (2) of Rule 7.26 there shall be inserted the following paragraph:–

"(2A) Where the responsible insolvency practitioner is requested by a creditor, member, contributory or by a member of a liquidation committee or of a creditors' committee to supply a copy of any document, he is entitled to require payment of the appropriate fee in respect of the supply of that copy.".

Rule 7.27

50. After paragraph (3) of Rule 7.27 there shall be inserted the following paragraph:–

"(4) Nothing in this Rule entitles the responsible insolvency practitioner to decline to allow inspection of any claim or proxy.".

Rule 7.33

51. At the end of Rule 7.33 there shall be inserted the following paragraphs:–

"(5) Without prejudice to paragraph (3), the responsible insolvency practitioner shall retain, or shall make arrangements for retention of, the sederunt book for a period of ten years from the relevant date.

(6) Where the sederunt book is maintained in non-documentary form it shall be capable of reproduction in legible form.

(7) In this Rule "the relevant date" has the following meanings:–
(a) in the case of a company voluntary arrangement under Part I of the Act, the date of final completion of the voluntary arrangement;
(b) in the case of an administration order under Part II of the Act, the date on which the administration order is discharged;
(c) in the case of a receivership under Part III of the Act, the date on which the receiver resigns and the receivership terminates without a further receiver being appointed; and
(d) in the case of a winding-up, the date of dissolution of the company.".

Rule 7.34

52. After Rule 7.33 there shall be inserted the following Rule:–

"Disposal of company's books, papers and other records

7.34.—(1) Where a company has been the subject of insolvency proceedings ("the original proceedings") which have terminated and other insolvency proceedings ("the subsequent proceedings") have commenced in relation to that company, the responsible insolvency practitioner appointed in relation to the original proceedings, shall, before the expiry of the later of–
(a) the period of 30 days following a request to him to do so by the responsible insolvency practitioner appointed in relation to the subsequent proceedings, or
(b) the period of 6 months after the relevant date (within the meaning of Rule 7.33),
deliver to the responsible insolvency practitioner appointed in relation to the subsequent proceedings the books, papers and other records of the company.

(2) In the case of insolvency proceedings, other than winding up, where–

    (a) the original proceedings have terminated, and

    (b) no subsequent proceedings have commenced within the period of 6 months after the relevant date in relation to the original proceedings,

the responsible insolvency practitioner appointed in relation to the original proceedings may dispose of the books, papers and records of the company after the expiry of the period of 6 months referred to in sub-paragraph (b), but only in accordance with directions given by–

    (i) the creditors' committee (if any) appointed in the original proceedings,

    (ii) the members of the company by extraordinary resolution, or

    (iii) the court.

(3) Where a company is being wound up the liquidator shall dispose of the books, papers and records of the company either in accordance with–

    (a) in the case of a winding up by the court, directions of the liquidation committee, or, if there is no such committee, directions of the court;

    (b) in the case of a members' voluntary winding up, directions of the members by extraordinary resolution; and

    (c) in the case of a creditors' voluntary winding up, directions of the liquidation committee, or, if there is no such committee, of the creditors given at or before the final meeting under section 106,

or, if, by the date which is 12 months after the dissolution of the company, no such directions have been given, he may do so after that date in such a way as he deems appropriate.".

Schedule 1

Paragraph 4 (Rule 4.7)

53. In paragraph 4 of Schedule 1–

    (a) after paragraph (3) of Rule 4.7, as substituted by that paragraph, there shall be inserted the following paragraph:–

        "(3A) Where a liquidator is nominated by the company at a general meeting held on a day prior to that on which the creditors' meeting summoned under section 98 is held, the directors shall forthwith after his nomination or the making of the statement of affairs, whichever is the later, deliver to him a copy of the statement of affairs."; and

    (b) at the end of the said Rule 4.7 there shall be inserted the following paragraphs:–

        "(5) The statement of affairs under section 99(1) shall be made up to the nearest practicable date before the date of the meeting of creditors under section 98 or to a date not more than 14 days before that on which the resolution for voluntary winding up is passed by the company, whichever is the later.

        (6) At any meeting held under section 98 where the statement of affairs laid before the meeting does not state the company's affairs as at the date of the meeting, the directors of the company shall cause to be made to the meeting, either by the director presiding at the meeting or by another person with knowledge of the relevant matters, a report (written or oral) on any material transactions relating to the company occurring between the date of the making of the statement of affairs and that of the meeting and any such report shall be recorded in the report of the meeting kept under Rule 7.13.".

Paragraph 9 (Rule 4.15)

54. In paragraph 9 of Schedule 1, there shall be inserted at the beginning the word "(1)" and at the end the following sub-paragraph:–

    "(2) In paragraph (6) there shall be inserted at the end the following:–

    "and to the director who presides over any meeting of creditors as provided by section 99(1)".".

Paragraph 12 (Rule 4.19)

55. In paragraph 12 of Schedule 1–

    (a) in Rule 4.19(2), as substituted by that paragraph, for the words "is effective from the date of the certificate" there shall be substituted the words "takes effect on the passing of the resolution for his appointment"; and

    (b) at the end of the said paragraph there shall be inserted the following sub-paragraph:–

        "(4) After paragraph 6 there shall be inserted the following paragraph:–

            "(7) Where a vacancy in the office of liquidator occurs in the manner mentioned in section 104, a meeting of creditors to fill the vacancy may be convened by any creditor or, if there were more liquidators than one, by any continuing liquidator".".

Paragraph 18 (Rule 4.31)

56. In paragraph 18 of Schedule 1, at the end of paragraph (4) of Rule 4.31, as substituted by that paragraph, there shall be inserted the following:–

"subject to the modifications that in Rule 4.25(3) sub-paragraph (a) shall apply with the word "new" replaced by the word "former" and sub-paragraph (b) shall not apply".

Schedule 2

Paragraph 3 (Rule 4.11)

57. In paragraph 3 of Schedule 2, there shall be inserted at the end the following:–

"subject to the modifications that for the words "accounting period" where they occur, there shall be substituted the words "period of twenty six weeks".

Paragraph 5 (Rule 4.19)

58. In paragraph 5(2) of Schedule 2, in Rule 4.19(2), as substituted by that paragraph, for the words "is effective from the date of the certificate" there shall be substituted the words "takes effect on the passing of the resolution for his appointment".

Paragraph 9 (Rule 4.28)

59. In paragraph 9(4) of Schedule 2, after paragraph (6) of Rule 4.28 as amended by the said paragraph 9(4) there shall be inserted the following paragraph:–

"(7) If there is no quorum present at the meeting summoned to receive the liquidator's resignation the meeting is deemed to have been held.".

Forms

60.—(1) The form contained in Part II of this Schedule shall be added to Schedule 5 to the principal Rules as Form 4.29 (Scot).

(2) The forms contained in Part III of this Schedule shall be substituted for the forms bearing the identical numbers in Schedule 5 to the principal Rules.

PART II

Para 60(1)

NEW FORM

Rule 7.15   **The Insolvency Act 1986**   **Form 4.29 (Scot)**

Proxy

Pursuant to Rules 7.14 and 7.15 of the Insolvency (Scotland) Rules 1986

(a) Insert name of
the company

(b) Insert nature of
Insolvency
proceedings

(a) _____

(b) _____

Name of Creditor/Member _____

Address_____

_____

_____ (hereinafter called "the principal").

(c) Insert the name
and address of
the proxy-holder
and of any
alternatives. A
proxy-holder
must be an
individual aged
over 18.

Name of proxy-holder (c) 1. _____

Address_____

_____

whom failing 2. _____

_____

_____

whom failing 3. _____

_____

_____

I appoint the above person to be the principal's proxy-holder at

*Delete as
appropriate

*[all meetings in the above Insolvency proceedings relating to the above company]

*[the meeting of *creditors/members of the above Company to be held on _____ or at any adjournment of that meeting].

Voting Instructions

The proxy-holder is authorised to vote or abstain from voting in the name, and on behalf, of the principal in respect of any matter*/s, including resolution*/s, arising for determination at said meeting*/s and any adjournment*/s thereof and to propose any resolution*/s in the name of the principal, either

    (i) in accordance with instructions given below or,
    (ii) if no instructions are given, in accordance with his/her own discretion.

(d) Complete only if you wish to instruct the proxy-holder to vote for a specific person as liquidator

(d) 1. To *propose/support a resolution for the appointment of

_____

of_____

whom failing _____

_____

as liquidator of the company.

(e) Delete if the proxy-holder is only to vote as directed in (1).

(e) [in the event of a person named in paragraph (1) withdrawing or being eliminated from any vote the proxy-holder may vote or abstain in any further ballot at *his/her discretion.]

(f) Set forth any voting instructions for the proxy-holder. If more room is required attach a separate sheet

2. (f) _____

_____

_____

_____

Signed _____ Date _____

Name in BLOCK LETTERS _____

Position of signatory in relation to the *creditor/or member or other authority for signing.

_____

_____

Notes for the Principal and Proxy-holder

1. The chairman of the meeting who may be nominated as proxy-holder, will be the insolvency practitioner who is presently *liquidator/receiver/administrator/ nominee under the voluntary arrangement or a director of the company.

2. All proxies must be in this form or a form substantially to the same effect with such variations as circumstances may require. (Rules 7.15(3) and 7.30).

3. To be valid the proxy must be lodged at or before the meeting at which it is to be used. (Rule 7.16(2)).

4. Where the chairman is nominated as proxy-holder he cannot decline the nomination. (Rule 7.14(4)).

5. The proxy-holder may vote for or against a resolution for the appointment of a named person to be liquidator jointly with another person, unless the proxy states otherwise. (Rule 7.16(4)).

6. The proxy-holder may propose any resolution in favour of which he could vote by virtue of this proxy. (Rule 7.16(5)).

7. The proxy-holder may vote at his discretion on any resolutions not dealt with in the proxy, unless the proxy states otherwise. (Rule 7.16(6)).

8. The proxy-holder may not vote in favour of any resolution which places him, or any associate of his, in a position to receive remuneration out of the insolvent estate unless the proxy specifically directs him so to vote. (Rule 7.19(1)).

9. Unless the proxy contains a statement to the contrary the proxy-holder has a mandate to act as representative of the principal on the creditors' or liquidation committee. (Rule 4.48).

PART III
SUBSTITUTED FORMS

Rule 2.18   **The Insolvency Act 1986**   **Form 2.13 (Scot)**

Notice to Court of Resignation of Administrator

Pursuant to section 19(1) of the Insolvency Act 1986 and Rule 2.18 of the Insolvency (Scotland) Rules 1986

(a) Insert name of the company

(a) _____

(b) Insert full name and address of administrator

I, (b) _____

_____

_____

the administrator of the above company give notice that I am resigning from the said office of administrator

(c) Insert date

with effect from (c) _____

_____

(d) See Rule 2.18

For the following reason(s): (d)_____

_____

_____

_____

(e) The date must be at least 7 days before that stated at (c) above

(f) See section 13(3) and Rule 2.18

I confirm that on (e) _____
I gave notice to (f):
  (i) _____
  (ii) _____
(iii) _____

being persons who under section 13(3) of the Insolvency Act 1986 are entitled to apply for a vacancy in the office of administrator to be filled, of my intention to resign from the said office of administrator.

Signed _____

Dated _____

The Insolvency Act 1986   **Form 4.1 (Scot)**

Statutory Demand for Payment of Debt

Pursuant to Section 123(1)(a) or Section 222(1)(a) of the Insolvency Act 1986

Warning

● This is an important document. This demand must be dealt with within 21 days of its service upon the company or a winding up order could be made in respect of the company

● Please read the demand and the notes carefully

● There are additional notes on the two following pages

Demand

To _____

Address _____

_____

This demand is served by the creditor:

Name _____

Address _____

_____

The creditor claims that the company owes

the sum of | £ _____ |

Full particulars of the debt/s claimed to be owed by the company are set out on page 2 of this Demand.

The creditor demands that the company pays the above sum or secures or compounds for it to the creditor's satisfaction

Signature _____

Name _____
          (BLOCK LETTERS)

Position with or relationship to creditor ____
_____ duly authorised

Address _____

_____

Tel. No. _____

Ref. _____

N.B. The person making this demand must complete the whole of this page and Parts A and B on page 3.

Notes for Creditors

● This demand can only be used by the creditor to demand a sum exceeding £750.

● If the creditor is entitled to the debt by way of assignation, details of the original creditor and any intermediate assignees should be given in Part B on page 3.

● If the amount of debt includes interest, details should be given including the grounds upon which interest is charged. The amount of interest must be shown separately.

● Any other charge payable from time to time may be claimed. The amount or rate of the charge must be identified and the grounds on which it is claimed must be stated.

● In either case the amount claimed must be limited to that which has accrued and is due at the date of the demand.

● If the signatory of the demand is a solicitor or other agent of the creditor the name of his/her firm should be given.

Particulars of Debts. (These particulars must include (a) the date or dates when the debt/s was/were incurred, (b) the grounds of claim and (c) the amount due as at the date of this demand.)

Notes for Creditor

Please make sure that you have read the notes on page 1 before completing this page.

Note:

If the space is insufficient continue on reverse of page 3 and clearly indicate on this page that you are doing so.

Part A

The person or persons to whom any communication regarding this demand should be addressed is/are

Name _____

(BLOCK LETTERS)

Address _____

_____

Tel. No. _____

Reference _____

Part B

For completion if the creditor is entitled to the debt by way of assignation

	Name	Date(s) of Assignation
Original creditor		
Assignees		

How to comply with a statutory demand

If the company wishes to avoid a winding-up petition being presented it must pay the sum shown on page 1 and of which particulars are set out on page 2 of this Demand within the period of 21 days of its service upon the company.

Alternatively, the company may attempt to reach a settlement with the creditor. To do this the company should:

inform the person (or one of them, if more than one) named in Part A above immediately that it is willing and able to offer security for the debt to the creditor's satisfaction; or

inform the person (or one of them) named in Part A immediately that it is willing and able to compound for the debt to the creditor's satisfaction.

If the company disputes the demand in whole or in part it should:

contact the person (or one of them) named in Part A immediately.

REMEMBER! The company has only 21 days from the date of service on it of this document before the creditor may present a winding-up petition

Rule 4.15   **The Insolvency Act 1986**   Form 4.7 (Scot)

Statement of Claim by Creditor

Pursuant to Rule 4.15(2)(a) of the Insolvency (Scotland) Rules 1986

WARNING

It is a criminal offence

● for a creditor to produce a statement of claim, account, voucher or other evidence which is false, unless he shows that he neither knew nor had reason to believe that it was false; or

● for a director or other officer of the company who knows or becomes aware that it is false to fail to report it to the liquidator within one month of acquiring such knowledge.

On conviction either the creditor or such director or other officer of the company may be liable to a fine and/or imprisonment.

Notes

(a) Insert name of company

(a) _____
_____
_____
_____

(b) Insert name and address of creditor

(b) _____
_____
_____
_____

(c) Insert name and address, if applicable, of authorised person acting on behalf of the creditor

(c) _____
_____
_____
_____

(d) Insert total amount as at the due date (see note (e) below) claimed in respect of all the debts, the particulars of which are set out overleaf.

I submit a claim of *(d)* £_____ in the liquidation of the above company and certify that the particulars of the debt or debts making up that claim, which are set out overleaf, are true, complete and accurate, to the best of my knowledge and belief.

(e) The due date in the case of a company

    (i) which is subject to a voluntary arrangement is the date of a creditors' meeting in the voluntary arrangement;

    (ii) which is in administration is the date of the administration order;

    (iii) which is in receivership is the date of appointment of the receiver; and

    (iv) which is in liquidation is the commencement of the winding up.

The date of commencement of the winding up is

    (i) in a voluntary winding up the date of the resolution by the company for winding up (section 86 or 98); and

    (ii) in a winding up by the court, the date of the presentation of the petition for winding up unless it is preceded by a resolution for voluntary winding up (section 129).

Signed_____
Creditor/person acting on behalf of creditor

Date_____

Rule 4.15   **Form 4.7 (Scot)**
                                                      (contd)

PARTICULARS OF EACH DEBT

Notes

*A separate set of particulars should be
made out in respect of each debt.*

1. *Describe briefly the debt, giving details of
   its nature, the date when it was incurred
   and when payment became due.*

   *Attach any documentary evidence of the
   debt, if available.*

2. *Insert total amount of the debt, showing
   separately the amount of principal and
   any interest which is due on the debt as
   at the due date (see note (e)). Interest
   may only be claimed if the creditor is
   entitled to it. Show separately the V.A.T.
   on the debt and indicate whether the
   V.A.T. is being claimed back from H.M.
   Customs and Excise.*

3. *Insert the nature and amount of any
   preference under Schedule 6 to the Act
   claimed in respect of the debt.*

4. *Specify and give details of the nature of
   any security held in respect of the debt
   including—*
   *(a) the subjects covered and the date
   when it was given;*
   (b) the value of the security.

   *Security is defined in section 248(b) of
   the Insolvency Act 1986 as meaning "any
   security (whether heritable or moveable),
   any floating charge and any right of lien
   or preference and any right of retention
   (other than a right of compensation or
   set off)". For claims in administration
   procedure security also includes a
   retention of title agreement, hire
   purchase agreement, agreement for the
   hire of goods for more than three
   months and a conditional sale agreement
   (see Rules 2.11 and 2.12).*

   *In liquidation only the creditor should state
   whether he is surrendering or undertakes to
   surrender his security; the liquidator may at
   any time after 12 weeks from the date of
   commencement of the winding up (note (e))
   require a creditor to discharge a security or
   to convey or assign it to him on payment of
   the value specified by the creditor.*

5. *In calculating the total amount of his
   claim in a liquidation, a creditor shall
   deduct the value of any security as
   estimated by him unless he surrenders it
   (see note 4). This may apply in
   administration (see Rule 2.11).*

1. **Particulars of debt**

2. **Amount of debt**

3. **Preference claimed for debt**

4. **Security for debt**

5. **Total amount of the debt**

Rules 4.2
4.18
4.19
4.27

The Insolvency Act 1986

Notice of Appointment of Liquidator

Pursuant to Rules 4.2, 4.18, 4.19 and 4.27 of the Insolvency (Scotland) Rules 1986

Form 4.9 (Scot)

R4.19

For official use

To the Registrar of Companies

(a) To the Court

Company number

(a) Delete except where the liquidator is appointed by a meeting of creditors or contributories

Name of Company

(b) Insert name of company

(b)

(c) Insert full name(s) and address(es)

I/We (c)

(d) Insert date

* Delete whichever does not apply

give notice that on (d) _____ *I/We *was/were appointed *liquidator(s)/provisional liquidator(s) of

(b) _____

by *an order of the court dated (d) _____

   or

*a resolution of a meeting of the *creditors/contributories on

(d) _____

(e) Leave in and complete only where liquidator is appointed to succeed a former liquidator

(f) Insert name and address of former liquidator

(e) *I/We *was/were appointed to succeed as liquidator

(f) _____

who *was removed/resigned from office as liquidator on

(d) _____ and who *has/has not been released.

(g) Delete or complete in accordance with Rule 4.18(5)

(g) A liquidation committee was established by a meeting of *creditors/and contributories on

(d) _____

(h) Delete if (g) applies

(h) I *intend/do not intend to summon a meeting of *creditors only/creditors and contributories for the purpose of establishing a liquidation committee.

Date _____

Signed _____
     (by each liquidator if more than one)

Name in BLOCK LETTERS _____

Presentor's name, address and reference:

For official use

Liquidation Section	Post Room

EXPLANATORY NOTE

(This note does not form part of the Rules)

These Rules make certain amendments to the Insolvency (Scotland) Rules 1986 ("the principal Rules") which set out the detailed procedures for the conduct of insolvency proceedings under the Insolvency Act 1986 relating to companies which the courts in Scotland have jurisdiction to wind up.

These Rules come into force on 11th January 1988 and apply to all insolvency proceedings to which the principal Rules apply on and after that date whether or not those proceedings have commenced before, on or after that date.

STATUTORY INSTRUMENTS

1987 No. 1933

PENSIONS

The Personal Pension Schemes (Deferment of Commencement) Regulations 1987

Made - - - -	*12th November 1987*
Laid before Parliament	*24th November 1987*
Coming into force -	*15th December 1987*

The Secretary of State for Social Services, in exercise of the powers conferred upon him by sections 1(1), (2), (4), (5), (9), (10) and (11), 2(1), (2) and (5), 3(1)(b), (2) and (5), 12(1) and 84(1) of the Social Security Act 1986**(a)**, and of all other powers enabling him in that behalf, by this instrument, which is made before the end of a period of 12 months from the commencement of the enactments under which it is made, makes the following Regulations:–

Citation and commencement

1. These Regulations may be cited as the Personal Pension Schemes (Deferment of Commencement) Regulations 1987 and shall come into force on 15th December 1987.

Revocation

2. The Personal Pension Schemes (Appropriate Schemes) Regulations 1987**(b)** are hereby revoked.

Amendment of the Pension Schemes (Voluntary Contributions Requirements and Voluntary and Compulsory Membership) Regulations 1987

3. Regulation 2(2) of the Pension Schemes (Voluntary Contributions Requirements and Voluntary and Compulsory Membership) Regulations 1987**(c)** shall be amended by substituting for the date "4th January 1988" the date "1st July 1988".

Amendment of the Personal and Occupational Pension Schemes (Incentive Payments) Regulations 1987

4. Sub-paragraphs (2)(b) and (3)(b) of regulation 2 of the Personal and Occupational Pension Schemes (Incentive Payments) Regulations 1987**(d)** shall be amended in each case by substituting for the date "3rd January 1988" the date "5th April 1988".

(a) 1986 c.50; *see* definitions of "prescribed" and "regulations" in section 84(1).
(b) S.I. 1987/1109.
(c) S.I. 1987/1108.
(d) S.I. 1987/1115.

Signed by authority of the Secretary of State for Social Services.

Nicholas Scott
Minister of State,
12th November 1987   Department of Health and Social Security

---

EXPLANATORY NOTE

(This note is not part of the Regulations)

These Regulations are made under the Social Security Act 1986 ("the 1986 Act") before the expiry of the period of 12 months beginning with the bringing into force of the sections under which they are made.

Consequently, by virtue of section 61(5) of the 1986 Act, the provisions of section 61(2) and (3) of the Social Security Pensions Act 1975 (c.60) (which, as amended by section 86(1) of, and paragraph 94 of Schedule 10 to, the 1986 Act, require reference to the Occupational Pensions Board of, and a report by the Board on, proposals to make regulations for the purpose of Part I of the 1986 Act), do not apply to them.

The Regulations revoke the Personal Pension Schemes (Appropriate Schemes) Regulations 1987 and make consequential amendments to the Pension Schemes (Voluntary Contributions Requirements and Voluntary and Compulsory Membership) Regulations 1987 and the Personal and Occupational Pension Schemes (Incentive Payments) Regulations 1987.

STATUTORY INSTRUMENTS

1987 No. 1936

TOWN AND COUNTRY PLANNING, ENGLAND AND WALES

The Town and Country Planning (British Coal Corporation) (Amendment) Regulations 1987

Made - - - -	*12th November 1987*
Laid before Parliament	*20th November 1987*
Coming into force	*11th December 1987*

The Secretary of State for the Environment in exercise of the powers conferred on him by section 273 of the Town and Country Planning Act 1971(a) and the Secretary of State for Energy in exercise of powers conferred by the said section 273 now vested in him(b) and of all other powers enabling them in that behalf and with the consent of the Treasury hereby make the following Regulations:

Citation and commencement

1. These Regulations may be cited as the Town and Country Planning (British Coal Corporation) (Amendment) Regulations 1987 and shall come into force on 11th December 1987.

Compensation for British Coal Corporation

2. In Schedule 1 to the Town and Country Planning (National Coal Board) Regulations 1974(c), in relation to section 237 of the Town and Country Planning Act 1971, add in column (2):–

"1A After subsection (1)(a) insert:

"Provided that the British Coal Corporation shall not be entitled to compensation in respect of the refusal, or the grant subject to conditions, of planning permission for the working of coal by opencast operations;".".

10th November 1987	*Nicholas Ridley* Secretary of State for the Environment

12th November 1987	*Cecil Parkinson* Secretary of State for Energy

---

(a) 1971 c.78.
(b) S.I. 1974/692.
(c) S.I. 1974/1006; for references in these Regulations to the National Coal Board, references to the British Coal Corporation were substituted, as respects any time after March 5th 1987, by section 1(3) of the Coal Industry Act 1987 (c.3).

We Consent,

Tony Durant
David Lightbown
Two of the Lords Commissioners of Her Majesty's Treasury

12th November 1987

EXPLANATORY NOTE

(This note is not part of the Regulations)

These Regulations amend the Town and Country Planning (British Coal Corporation) Regulations 1974 (formerly the Town and Country Planning (National Coal Board) Regulations 1974).

Under the Opencast Coal Act 1958 (c.69) opencast working by the British Coal Corporation required Ministerial authorisation and the Minister had power to grant deemed planning permission for the working. Section 2(5) of that Act excluded compensation under the Town and Country Planning Act 1971 in respect of various orders and decisions including orders revoking or modifying planning permission for opencast working, and the refusal of such planning permission or its grant subject to conditions.

The Housing and Planning Act 1986 (c.63) brings opencast working within general planning procedures by abolishing the authorisation requirement and deemed permission. It also repeals section 2(5). These repeals are brought into force by the Housing and Planning Act 1986 (Commencement No. 9) Order 1987 (S.I. 1987/1939) on 11th December 1987.

The repeal of section 2(5) would make the Corporation eligible for compensation on the same basis as statutory undertakers by virtue of the Town and Country Planning (British Coal Corporation) Regulations 1974 which apply section 237 of the 1971 Act to the Corporation.

These Regulations have the effect of amending the 1971 Act to prevent the British Coal Corporation from being eligible for compensation in respect of the refusal of planning permission for opencast working or its grant subject to conditions. They will be entitled to compensation for revocation or modification of planning permission. Where the Corporation are entitled to compensation, the amount of compensation is calculated on the same basis as the compensation for statutory undertakers.

STATUTORY INSTRUMENTS

1987 No. 1937 (S.133)

TOWN AND COUNTRY PLANNING, SCOTLAND

The Town and Country Planning (British Coal Corporation) (Scotland) Amendment Regulations 1987

Made - - -	*12th November 1987*
Laid before Parliament	*20th November 1987*
Coming into force	*11th December 1987*

The Secretary of State for Scotland, in exercise of the powers conferred on him by section 259 of the Town and Country Planning (Scotland) Act 1972(**a**), and the Secretary of State for Energy, in exercise of the powers conferred by the said section 259 and now vested in him(**b**), and of all other powers enabling them in that behalf, hereby with the consent of the Treasury make the following Regulations:

Citation and commencement

1. These Regulations may be cited as the Town and Country Planning (British Coal Corporation) (Scotland) Amendment Regulations 1987 and shall come into force on 11th December 1987.

Compensation for British Coal Corporation

2. In Schedule 1 to the Town and Country Planning (National Coal Board) (Scotland) Regulations 1975(**c**), in column (2) of the entry relating to section 226 of the Town and Country Planning (Scotland) Act 1972, there shall be inserted after paragraph 1–

"**1A.** After subsection (1)(a) insert:

"Provided that the British Coal Corporation shall not be entitled to compensation in respect of the refusal, or the grant subject to conditions, of planning permission for the working of coal by opencast operations;".".

James Douglas-Hamilton
Parliamentary Under Secretary of State,
9th November 1987
Scottish Office

Cecil Parkinson
12th November 1987
Secretary of State for Energy

We consent,

Tony Durant
D. Lightbown
12th November 1987   Two of the Lords Commissioners of Her Majesty's Treasury

---

(**a**) 1972 c.52.
(**b**) S.I. 1974/692.
(**c**) S.I. 1975/1280. (For references in these Regulations to the National Coal Board, references to the British Coal Corporation were substituted, as respects any time after 5th March 1987, by section 1(3) of the Coal Industry Act 1987 (c.3).)

EXPLANATORY NOTE

(This note is not part of the Regulations)

These Regulations amend the Town and Country Planning (National Coal Board) (Scotland) Regulations 1975.

Under the Opencast Coal Act 1958 (c.69) opencast working by the British Coal Corporation required Ministerial authorisation and the Secretary of State had power to grant deemed planning permission for the working. Section 2(5) of that Act excluded compensation under the Town and Country Planning (Scotland) Act 1972 in respect of various orders and decisions including orders revoking or modifying planning permission for opencast working, and the refusal of such planning permission or its grant subject to conditions.

The Housing and Planning Act 1986 brings opencast working within general planning procedures by abolishing the authorisation requirement and the provision for deemed planning permission. It also repeals section 2(5). The relevant provisions of the 1986 Act are brought into force on 11th December 1987 by the Housing and Planning Act 1986 (Commencement No.9) Order 1987 (S.I. 1987/1939).

The repeal of section 2(5) would make the Corporation eligible for compensation on the same basis as statutory undertakers by virtue of the Town and Country Planning (National Coal Board) (Scotland) Regulations 1975 which apply section 226 of the 1972 Act to the Corporation.

These Regulations have the effect of amending the 1972 Act in its application to the British Coal Corporation to prevent the Corporation from being eligible for compensation in respect of the refusal of planning permission for opencast working or its grant subject to conditions. They will be entitled to compensation for revocation or modification of planning permission. Where the Corporation are entitled to compensation, the amount of compensation will be calculated on the same basis as the compensation for statutory undertakers.

STATUTORY INSTRUMENTS

1987 No. 1939 (C.58)

HOUSING, ENGLAND AND WALES
TOWN AND COUNTRY PLANNING, ENGLAND AND WALES
TOWN AND COUNTRY PLANNING, SCOTLAND
COAL INDUSTRY

The Housing and Planning Act 1986
(Commencement No. 9) Order 1987

Made - - - - *16th November 1987*

The Secretary of State for the Environment, as respects England, the Secretary of State for Wales, as respects Wales, and the Secretary of State for Scotland, as respects Scotland, in the exercise of the powers conferred on them by section 57(2) of the Housing and Planning Act 1986**(a)** and of all other powers enabling them in that behalf, hereby make the following Order:–

1. This Order may be cited as the Housing and Planning Act 1986 (Commencement No. 9) Order 1987.

2. The provisions of the Housing and Planning Act 1986 listed below shall come into force on 11th December 1987–

section 18 (except insofar as it gives effect to paragraph 10 of Schedule 4 to the Act),

section 24(3) insofar as it repeals the provisions specified in the Schedule to this Order, Part V.

10th November 1987
Nicholas Ridley
Secretary of State for the Environment

12th November 1987
Peter Walker
Secretary of State for Wales

16th November 1987
James Douglas-Hamilton
Parliamentary Under Secretary of State, Scottish Office

(a) 1986 c.63.

SCHEDULE

Chapter	Short title	Extent of repeal
1980 c.51.	Housing Act 1980	Section 140.
1980 c.65.	Local Government, Planning and Land Act 1980.	Section 156(3)
1985 c.51.	Local Government Act 1985.	In Schedule 13, in paragraph 14, sub-paragraph (d) and the word "and" preceding it. In Schedule 14, paragraph 58(e).

EXPLANATORY NOTE

(This note is not part of the Order)

This Order brings into force on 11th December 1987 certain provisions of the Housing and Planning Act 1986.

In Part I (housing) of the Act the provisions brought into force are–

section 18, which gives effect to Schedule 4 to the Act. Schedule 4 amends the Leasehold Reform Act 1967 (c.88), the Rent (Agriculture) Act 1976 (c.80) and the Rent Act 1977 (c.42) in relation to shared ownership leases; it also contains consequential amendments to other statutes, one of which (paragraph 10) is not brought into force by the Order;

section 24(3) so far as it effects repeals consequent upon section 18. The repealed provisions are set out in the Schedule to the Order.

Part V (opencast coal) of the Act is also brought into force. In conjunction with Part I of Schedule 8 and Part II of Schedule 12 (which also come into effect) Part V repeals and amends certain provisions of the Opencast Coal Act 1958 (c.69). The principal effect is that the specific authorisation of the Secretary of State will no longer be necessary before the British Coal Corporation carry out particular opencast working.

NOTE AS TO EARLIER COMMENCEMENT ORDERS

(This note is not part of the Order)

The following provisions of the Act have been brought into force by commencement orders made before the date of this Order–

Provision	Date of commencement	S.I. No.
sections 1 to 4 sections 10 to 14 sections 16 and 17 sections 19 and 20 sections 22 and 23 section 24 (partially) Part III (ss. 27–29) Part VI (partially)	7th January 1987	1986/2262
section 49(1) (partially)	2nd March 1987	1987/304
section 40 section 49(2) (partially)	1st April 1987	1987/348
section 9	13th May 1987	1987/754
section 24(1) (partially)	1st September 1987	1987/1554
sections 26, 50 and 51	1st October 1987	1987/1607
section 25 section 41 section 49(1) (partially) section 49(2) (partially)	2nd November 1987	1987/1759

STATUTORY INSTRUMENTS

1987 No. 1940

LANDLORD AND TENANT

The Housing Association Shared Ownership Leases (Exclusion from Leasehold Reform Act 1967 and Rent Act 1977) Regulations 1987

Made - - - -	*13th November 1987*
Laid before Parliament	*20th November 1987*
Coming into force	*11th December 1987*

The Secretary of State for the Environment, as respects England, and the Secretary of State for Wales, as respects Wales, in exercise of the powers conferred upon them by paragraph 5 of Schedule 4A to the Leasehold Reform Act 1967 **(a)** and section 5A(3) of the Rent Act 1977 **(b)** and of all other powers enabling them in that behalf, hereby make the following Regulations:

1. These Regulations may be cited as the Housing Association Shared Ownership Leases (Exclusion from Leasehold Reform Act 1967 and Rent Act 1977) Regulations 1987 and shall come into force on 11th December 1987.

2. The requirements or circumstances prescribed, for the purposes of the conditions in paragraph 3(2)(c), (e) and (f) of Schedule 4A ("Schedule 4A") to the Leasehold Reform Act 1967 and the conditions in section 5A(2)(c), (e) and (f) of the Rent Act 1977, are those set out in Schedule 1 to these Regulations.

3. The matters prescribed for the purposes of paragraph 4 of Schedule 4A are those set out in Schedule 2.

Nicholas Ridley
Secretary of State for the Environment

9th November 1987

Peter Walker
Secretary of State for Wales

13th November 1987

(a) 1967 c.88; Schedule 4A was inserted by paragraph 6 of Schedule 4 to the Housing and Planning Act 1986 (c.63).
(b) 1977 c.42; section 5A was inserted by paragraph 1 of Schedule 4 to the Housing and Planning Act 1986.

SCHEDULE 1

Article 2

SHARED OWNERSHIP LEASES (GENERAL)

Definition

1. In this Schedule "market value price" means the amount agreed between or determined in a manner agreed between the parties or, in default of such agreement or determination, determined by an independent expert agreed between the parties or, in default of agreement, appointed on the application of either party by or on behalf of the President of the Royal Institution of Chartered Surveyors, as the amount which the interest of the tenant would fetch, if sold on the open market by a willing vendor, on the assumption that the tenant had previously purchased 100 per cent. of the shares in the dwelling-house, disregarding the following matters–

    (i) any mortgage of the tenant's interest;

    (ii) any interest in or right over the dwelling-house created by the tenant;

    (iii) any improvement made by the tenant or any predecessor in title of his;

    (iv) any failure by the tenant or any predecessor in title to carry out any repairing obligations under the lease.

Requirements relating to Condition (c)

2. The requirements as to the provision for the tenant to acquire additional shares in the dwelling-house are that–

    (a) the tenant is to be entitled to acquire additional shares up to a maximum of 100 per cent., in instalments of 25 per cent. or such lesser percentage, if any, as may be specified in the lease;

    (b) the tenant is to be able to exercise this entitlement by serving notice in writing on the landlord at any time during the term of the lease, stating the additional shares he proposes to acquire;

    (c) the price for the additional shares is to be an amount no greater than the same percentage of the market value price at the date of service of the tenant's notice under sub-paragraph (b) above, as the percentage of the additional shares;

    (d) the rent payable by the tenant under the lease (excluding any amount payable, directly or indirectly, for services, repairs, maintenance, insurance or management costs) is to be reduced, upon the purchase of any additional shares, in the same proportion as the reduction in the percentage of shares remaining unpurchased by the tenant.

Circumstances relating to Condition (e)

3.—(1) If the lease enables the landlord to require payment for the outstanding shares in the dwelling-house, the circumstances in which the landlord is entitled so to do shall be that–

    (a) there has been a disposal, other than an exempt disposal, of any interest in the dwelling-house by the tenant;

    (b) the amount payable by the tenant is an amount no greater than the same percentage of the market value price at the date of the disposal as the percentage of the shares in the dwelling-house remaining unpurchased by the tenant.

(2) In sub-paragraph (1) above, "exempt disposal" means–

    (a) a disposal under a will or intestacy;

    (b) a disposal under section 24 of the Matrimonial Causes Act 1973 **(a)** or section 2 of the Inheritance (Provision for Family and Dependants) Act 1975 **(b)** ;

    (c) a grant of a sub-tenancy in respect of which a notice has been given under section 52(1)(b) of the Housing Act 1980 **(c)** (notice that a tenancy is to be a protected shorthold tenancy) or of a kind mentioned in any of Cases 11 to 18 or 20 in Schedule 15 to the Rent Act 1977 **(d)** ;

    (d) a grant of a sub-tenancy of part of the dwelling-house, if any other part of the dwelling-house remains in the possession of the tenant;

    (e) a grant of a mortgage.

(a) 1973 c.18.   **(b)** 1975 c.63.   **(c)** 1980 c.51.
(d) 1977 c.42. Case 11 was amended by the Housing Act 1980 (c.51) and the Rent (Amendment) Act 1985 (c.24). Case 12 was amended by and Case 20 inserted by the Housing Act 1980.

Requirements relating to Condition (f)

4. The provision in the lease of a house for the tenant to acquire the landlord's interest shall–

(a) be exercisable at any time by the tenant by giving notice in writing, to take effect not before he has acquired 100 per cent. of the shares in the dwelling-house;

(b) require the landlord's interest to be transferred, as soon as practicable after the coming into effect of the notice mentioned in sub-paragraph (a) above, to the tenant or to such other person as the tenant may direct;

(c) not entitle the landlord to make any charge for the conveyance or assignment of his interest.

Article 3

SCHEDULE 2

LEASES FOR THE ELDERLY

Definition

1. In paragraph 4 of Schedule 4A and in this Schedule, "lease for the elderly" means a lease to a person of or over the age of 55 at the date of the grant of the lease.

Requirements as respects leases for the elderly

2. The prescribed requirements for the purposes of the condition in paragraph 4(2)(b) of Schedule 4A are that a lease for the elderly–

(a) shall contain a covenant by the landlord to provide the tenant with facilities which consist of or include access to the services of a warden and a system for calling him;

(b) shall contain an absolute covenant by the tenant not to underlet the whole or part of the demised premises;

(c) shall contain a covenant by the tenant not to assign or part with possession of the whole or part of the demised premises except–

　(i) subject to such conditions as the lease may specify, to a person of or over the age of 55 at the date of the assignment; or

　(ii) where the assignment is–

　　(a) by an executor or administrator of a deceased tenant to that tenant's spouse if residing there at the date of the tenant's death, or to a person residing there with the tenant at that date who is of or over the age of 55 at the date of the assignment; or

　　(b) if the lease so provides and subject to such conditions as the lease may specify, by a mortgagee or chargee exercising his power of sale;

(d) shall not provide for the tenant to acquire the interest of the landlord under an option to purchase.

EXPLANATORY NOTE

(This note is not part of the Regulations)

Schedule 4 to the Housing and Planning Act 1986 introduces amendments to the Leasehold Reform Act 1967, the Rent (Agriculture) Act 1976 (c.80) and the Rent Act 1977, whereby certain shared ownership leases are excluded from the provisions of those Acts. Leases granted by housing associations, which fulfil the conditions respectively set out in paragraphs 3(2) and 4(2) of Schedule 4A to the 1967 Act and section 5A(2) of the 1977 Act (or that section as modified by the 1976 Act) are so excluded. Those conditions relate to the terms of the leases in question and provide for certain additional requirements and circumstances to be prescribed in regulations made by the Secretary of State. No other percentage is prescribed for the purposes of paragraph 3(2)(b) of Schedule 4A to the 1967 Act or section 5A(2)(b) of the 1977 Act.

These Regulations prescribe the necessary additional requirements and circumstances. They also prescribe the meaning of the expression "lease for the elderly" used in paragraph 4 of Schedule 4A.

STATUTORY INSTRUMENTS

1987 No. 1941

SPORTS GROUNDS AND SPORTING EVENTS

The Safety of Sports Grounds Regulations 1987

Made - - - -	*16th November 1987*
Laid before Parliament	*25th November 1987*
Coming into force -	*1st January 1988*

In exercise of the powers conferred upon me by sections 6(1) and (4) and 10A(1) and (2) of the Safety of Sports Grounds Act 1975(**a**), and after such consultation as is mentioned in section 18(4) of that Act, I hereby make the following Regulations:

Citation, commencement and extent

1.—(1) These Regulations may be cited as the Safety of Sports Grounds Regulations 1987 and shall come into force on 1st January 1988.

(2) These Regulations do not extend to the Isles of Scilly.

Revocation

2. The Safety of Sports Grounds Regulations 1976(**b**), the Safety of Sports Grounds (Scotland) Regulations 1976(**c**) and the Safety of Sports Grounds (Amendment) Regulations 1986(**d**) are hereby revoked, except for the purposes of any appeal to which paragraph 6 of Schedule 5 to the Fire Safety and Safety of Places of Sport Act 1987 (transitional provisions as respects appeals about safety certificates)(**e**) applies.

Interpretation

3. For the purposes of these Regulations "the 1975 Act" means the Safety of Sports Grounds Act 1975.

Applications

4.—(1) An application for a safety certificate shall be in the form contained in the Schedule to these Regulations or a form to the like effect.

(2) An application for the amendment, replacement or transfer of a safety certificate shall be made in writing and any such application shall set out the names and addresses of any persons who to the applicant's knowledge will or may be concerned in ensuring compliance with the terms and conditions of the safety certificate as amended, replaced or transferred.

Notices by local authority

5.—(1) As soon as practicable after a local authority have decided—

(a) to issue a safety certificate (including an issue by way of replacement of a safety certificate); or

(b) to amend a safety certificate; or

(c) to refuse to amend or replace a safety certificate,

(**a**) 1975 c.52; section 6(1)(c) was substituted by section 22(7) of the Fire Safety and Safety of Places of Sport Act 1987 (c.27) and section 10A was inserted by section 24 of that Act.

(**b**) S.I. 1976/1263.   (**c**) S.I. 1976/1300.   (**d**) S.I. 1986/1045.   (**e**) 1987 c.27.

they shall serve on every interested party notice in writing of their decision setting out the information referred to in paragraph (4) below, together, in the case of a refusal, with their reasons for it.

(2) Where on an application for a special safety certificate a local authority have determined to refuse that application on grounds other than the one referred to in section 5(1) of the 1975 Act, they shall as soon as practicable after that refusal serve on the applicant notice in writing of their decision, together with their reasons for it.

(3) Where on an application for the transfer of a safety certificate a local authority—

(a) determine that the person to whom it is proposed to transfer the certificate is not a qualified person, they shall, in addition to the notice referred to in section 5(1) of the 1975 Act, serve on the holder of the certificate a copy of that notice;

(b) determine that the person to whom it is proposed to transfer the certificate is a qualified person but decide not to transfer the certificate, they shall serve on that person and the holder of the certificate notice in writing of their decision together with their reasons for it.

(4) A notice served under paragraph (1) above shall state that a copy of the safety certificate and a copy of any application in respect of which the local authority's decision was taken is available for inspection at a place and at the times specified in the notice.

(5) A soon as may be after the decision referred to in paragraph (1) above, the local authority shall cause to be published in a newspaper circulating in the locality of the sports ground to which the safety certificate relates a notice setting out that decision and the information referred to in paragraph (4) above.

(6) In this regulation " interested party " means—

(a) the holder of a safety certificate whose application to have it amended or replaced has been refused;

(b) any other person known to the local authority to be or likely to be concerned in ensuring compliance with the terms and conditions of the safety certificate;

(c) the chief officer of police; and

(d) where the local authority is in Greater London or a metropolitan county, the fire authority or, in any other case, the building authority.

Appeals under section 5 of the 1975 Act

6.—(1) An appeal under section 5 of the 1975 Act(a) shall be brought (in accordance with subsection (3A) or, as the case may be, subsection (3B) of section 5 of that Act(b)) in the case of an appeal in respect of—

(a) a general safety certificate, not later than twenty-eight days, and

(b) a special safety certificate, not later than seven days,

after the relevant date.

(2) In paragraph (1) above " relevant date " means—

(a) in the case of a person to whom a safety certificate is issued, the date of the receipt by him of that certificate;

(b) in the case of a person on whom a notice is served under section 4(1) (a) or 5(1) of the 1975 Act or regulation 5(1), (2) or (3) above, the date of the receipt by him of that notice; and

(c) in the case of any other person, the date of the publication of the notice required by regulation 5(5) above.

(a) Section 5 was amended by paragraph 7(1) of Schedule 8 to the Local Government Act 1985 (c.51) and by section 22 of the Fire Safety and Safety of Places of Sport Act 1987.

(b) Subsections (3A) and (3B) of section 5 were inserted by section 22(3) of the Fire Safety and Safety of Places of Sport Act 1987.

Appeals under section 10A of the 1975 Act

7.—(1) An appeal by an aggrieved person against a prohibition notice under section 10A(1) of the 1975 Act**(a)** shall be brought (in accordance with subsection (3) or, as the case may be, subsection (4) of section 10A of that Act) not later than twenty-one days after the day on which the notice was served on him under section 10(1) of the 1975 Act**(b)**.

(2) An appeal by an aggrieved person against an amendment to a prohibition notice under section 10A(1) of the 1975 Act (as extended by section 10A(2) of that Act) shall be brought (in accordance with subsection (3) or, as the case may be, subsection (4) of section 10A of that Act) not later than twenty-one days after the day on which the notice amending the prohibition notice was served on him under section 10(9) of the 1975 Act.

Fees

8. A local authority may determine the fee to be charged in respect of an application for the issue, amendment, replacement or transfer of a safety certificate but such a fee shall not exceed an amount commensurate with the work actually and reasonably done by or on behalf of the local authority in respect of the application.

Home Office
16th November 1987

Douglas Hurd
One of Her Majesty's Principal Secretaries of State

SCHEDULE Regulation 4(1)

SAFETY OF SPORTS GROUNDS ACT 1975
APPLICATION FOR A SAFETY CERTIFICATE

When completed, this form should be sent to the Chief Executive of:

  (a) *the county council where the sports ground is situated in a non-metropolitan county in England or Wales; or*

  (b) *the borough council where the sports ground is situated in Greater London; or*

  (c) *the district council where the sports ground is situated in a metropolitan county in England; or*

  (d) *the regional/islands council where the sports ground is situated in Scotland.*

To be completed in all cases

I hereby apply for a *[general] [special] safety certificate in respect of the sports ground described below to be issued to ....

I make the application *[on behalf of] [as] ....

of † ....

Date .... Signed ....

Address ....

.... Tel. No. ....

* Delete as appropriate

† *If applying on behalf of a sports club, company or some other person, insert status (e.g. secretary).*

Under the provisions of section 3(1) of the Safety of Sports Grounds Act 1975, a local authority receiving an application for a safety certificate have to determine whether the person to whom the certificate may be issued is likely to be in a position to prevent contravention of the terms and conditions of the certificate. The applicant should therefore furnish below the information required so as to enable the local authority to make such a determination. Under section 3(4) of the Act the local authority may also require the applicant to submit plans and further information.

(a) Section 10A was inserted by section 24 of the Fire Safety and Safety of Places of Sport Act 1987.
(b) Section 10 was substituted by section 23(1) of the Fire Safety and Safety of Places of Sport Act 1987.

1. (a) Name and address of sports ground

. . . .

. . . .

(b) Name of the occupier . . . .

Name and address of the owner . . . .

. . . .

(c) Names and addresses of any persons other than the proposed holder of the certificate who to his knowledge will or may be concerned in ensuring compliance with the terms and conditions of the safety certificate for which this application is being made.

. . . .

. . . .

. . . .

. . . .

Complete Part I only for an application for a general safety certificate (to cover activities held over an indefinite period).

Complete Part II only for an application for a special safety certificate (to cover one occasion or a series of occasions).

PART I: GENERAL SAFETY CERTIFICATES

2. List activities to be covered by general safety certificate

. . . .

. . . .

3. Give the approximate date of the construction of the spectator accommodation on the sports ground and details of any subsequent extension, major alteration or re-construction of the spectator accommodation on the sports ground, together with relevant dates.

. . . .

. . . .

. . . .

4. Give particulars of current fire certificates covering any premises on any part of the sports ground:

(a) name of issuing fire authority . . . .

(b) name of holder of fire certificate . . . .

(c) date of issue of fire certificate . . . .

(d) description of premises covered by the fire certificate . . . .

5. Give particulars of any current statutory licences granted in respect of the sports ground or parts of it:

(a) name of issuing licensing authority . . . .

(b) name of licensee . . . .

(c) type of licence (liquor, gaming etc.) . . . .

(d) date of expiry . . . .

(e) description of the part or parts of the sports ground covered by the licence . . . .

. . . .

6.—(1) State maximum capacity for which spectator accommodation at the sports ground is intended:

    (a) seated spectators. . . . .

    (b) standing spectators . . . .

(2) State any restrictions on that capacity:

    (a) seated spectators. . . . .

    (b) standing spectators . . . .

7. Set out separately for each of the last three years the total number of seated spectators and the total number of standing spectators for each activity other than reserve team matches, practice sessions or community use, held at the sports ground. Each activity (other than those excluded) should be named, together with the number of occasions on which each activity took place during each of those years.

8. Set out separately for each activity the total number of seated spectators and the total number of standing spectators attending at the occasion during the last three years when that activity took place which attracted the highest number of spectators. Give the date of that event and the name of the activity taking place.

PART II: SPECIAL SAFETY CERTIFICATES

9. Name event for which special safety certificate is required

    . . . .

10. Give date(s) of event . . . .

11. Give the number of occasions on which this special event has taken place at the sports ground during the last three years . . . .

12. Set out separately the total number of seated spectators and the total number of standing spectators at any similar event held within the last three years at the sports ground, giving the name of the event and the date on which it was held.

EXPLANATORY NOTE

(This note is not part of the Regulations)

These Regulations, which apply throughout Great Britain (except the Isles of Scilly), replace the Safety of Sports Grounds Regulations 1976 (" the 1976 Regulations ") and the Safety of Sports Grounds (Amendment) Regulations 1986 (which apply in England and Wales, except the Isles of Scilly) and the Safety of Sports Grounds (Scotland) Regulations 1976 (" the 1976 Scottish Regulations ").

Regulations 8 to 13 of the 1976 Regulations and regulations 9 and 10 of the 1976 Scottish Regulations made provision for the procedure for appeals to the Secretary of State in respect of safety certificates under section 5 of the Safety of Sports Grounds Act 1975 (" the 1975 Act "). When the amendments made by section 22 of the Fire Safety and Safety of Places of Sport Act 1987 (" the 1987 Act ") come into force, those appeals will be made to magistrates' courts in England and Wales and by summary application in Scotland and regulations 8 to 13 of the 1976 Regulations and regulations 9 and 10 of the 1976 Scottish Regulations will no longer be necessary. By virtue of the Fire Safety and Safety of Places of Sport Act 1987 (Commencement No. 1) Order 1987 (S.I. 1987/1762), Part II of the 1987 Act (in which section 22 is contained) comes into force on 1st January 1988, the same date as the coming into force of these Regulations. Accordingly, these Regulations no longer include provision corresponding to regulations 8 to 13 of the 1976 Regulations and regulations 9 and 10 of the 1976 Scottish Regulations (the enabling power for which is, in any event, replaced by section 22 (7) of the 1987 Act) but provide instead (in regulation 6) for the time within which an appeal must be brought before a magistrates' court in England and Wales or by summary application in Scotland.

These Regulations also differ from the 1976 Regulations and the 1976 Scottish Regulations in that they no longer prescribe a minimum time before the event for which the application is made for the submission of an application for a special safety certificate. They also do not require the local authority to have made decisions in respect of such applications by specified periods.

Regulation 5 of these Regulations requires certain notices to be given to interested parties (as defined) and a newspaper notice to be published. Regulation 8 of these Regulations differs from regulation 14 of the 1976 Regulations and regulation 11 of the 1976 Scottish Regulations in that it allows local authorities to charge fees in respect of applications for the replacement and transfer of safety certificates as well as for applications for their issue and amendment.

These Regulations also differ from the 1976 Regulations (as amended) and the 1976 Scottish Regulations in that they refer only to sports grounds and not to sports stadia in consequence of the amendments made to the 1975 Act by section 19 of, and Schedule 2 to, the 1987 Act (which provisions also come into force on 1st January 1988 by virtue of the Commencement Order referred to above).

Regulation 7 of these Regulations is a new provision which prescribes the period within which appeals in respect of prohibition notices (and amendments to those notices) issued under section 10 of the 1975 Act (as substituted by section 23 (1) of the 1987 Act) must be brought under section 10A (1) and (2) of the 1975 Act (as inserted by section 24 of the 1987 Act).

STATUTORY INSTRUMENTS

1987 No. 1942

BUILDING SOCIETIES

The Building Societies (Business Premises) Order 1987

Made - - - -	*13th November 1987*
Laid before Parliament	*1st December 1987*
Coming into force -	*31st December 1987*

The Building Societies Commission, with the consent of the Treasury, in exercise of the powers conferred on it by section 17(7) of the Building Societies Act 1986(a) and of all other powers enabling it in that behalf hereby makes the following Order:

Citation and commencement

1. This Order may be cited as the Building Societies (Business Premises) Order 1987 and shall come into force on 31st December 1987.

Interpretation

2. In this Order–

"the Act" means the Building Societies Act 1986;

"group member" means, in relation to a society, the society and each associated body of the society;

"outsider" means, in relation to a society, a person who is not a group member;

"relevant time" means, in relation to a society, any day which is, or is treated for any purpose by or under the Act as, the last day of its financial year;

"society" means a building society;

"the society's business area" means, in relation to premises of a society, the net internal area of each part of the premises which–

    (a) is occupied by a group member for the purpose of conducting its business, or

    (b) is intended by a group member to be occupied by it, for the purpose of conducting its business, from a date no later than the date two years after the date of acquisition of the premises by the society;

"total area", in relation to premises, means–

    (a) where the premises comprise a building or floors within a building, the net internal area of that building or, as the case may be, those floors;

    (b) where the premises include land which is not built on, the aggregate of any net internal area to which subparagraph (a) of this definition refers and the area of any of such land which is let for gain; and

"valuer" means a person who is competent to value premises of a society to which this Order applies (whether or not that person is employed by the society).

(a) 1986 c.53.

Business Premises

3.—(1) Where at a relevant time premises are held under section 6 of the Act (which gives a society the power to hold land for the purposes of its business or that of a subsidiary or other associated body) by virtue of subsection (5) of that section, those premises shall be treated at that time in their entirety as land held under section 17 of the Act (which gives a society the power to hold and develop land as a commercial asset) for the purposes of the requirements of Part III of the Act for the structure of commercial assets unless–

    (a) at that time the society holds, or is treated by paragraph (2) below as holding, a current valuer's certificate which states, in relation to those premises as at a date specified in the certificate, either–

        (i) that the society's business area is not less than 30 per cent of the total area, or

        (ii) that, following calculations in accordance with the Schedule below, the open market value of the society's business area is not less than 30 per cent of the open market value of the entirety of the premises, and

    (b) if at the relevant time no part of the premises is or has been occupied by a group member, the society acquired the premises no more than two years before the relevant time.

(2) For the purposes of paragraph (1) above a valuer's certificate, received by the society within two months after the relevant time and which relates to the premises as at a date specified in the certificate (being no later than the relevant time), shall be treated as held by the society at the relevant time.

(3) For the purposes of paragraph (1) above, a valuer's certicate shall no longer be current where either–

    (a) the society's business area has decreased, or

    (b) in the case of a certificate given under paragraph (1)(a)(ii) above, the use (or, where the premises are not yet occupied, the intended use) of the premises, or of any part of the premises, has changed,

since the date specified for the purposes of paragraph (1)(a) above in the certificate.

In witness whereof the common seal of the Building Societies Commission is hereunto fixed, and is authenticated by me, a person authorised under paragraph 14 of Schedule 1 to the Building Societies Act 1986, on 6th November 1987.

D. B. Severn
Secretary to the Commission

We consent to this Order.

Michael Neubert
David Lightbown
13th November 1987   Two of the Lords Commissioners of Her Majesty's Treasury

---

Article 3(1)(a)(ii)   **SCHEDULE**

CALCULATION OF OPEN MARKET VALUES

1. In calculating the open market value of the entirety of premises and of a society's business area within the premises–

    (a) it shall be assumed that, where an outsider occupies an area which forms part of the society's business area, the occupation of that part (and the interest of the outsider in that part) has terminated, and

    (b) subject to subparagraph (a) above–

(i) the open market value of the entirety of the premises shall be treated as the aggregate of the open market values of all calculable interests in the premises and each part of the premises, and

(ii) the open market value of the society's business area shall be treated as the open market value of the entirety of the premises less the aggregate of the open market values of all calculable interests of outsiders taken into account in paragraph (i) above.

2. For the purposes of paragraph 1 above, the interest of the society is a calculable interest and so is the interest of each person occupying the premises or any part of the premises whose interest can be derived from that of the society.

EXPLANATORY NOTE

(This note is not part of the Order)

This Order provides that business premises held by a building society, in circumstances where less than 30 per cent of the area of the premises is occupied for business purposes by the society or a subsidiary or other associated body of the society, are treated as held under section 17 of the Building Societies Act 1986 and are thus classified among class 3 assets unless it is certified by a valuer that the value of that area is not less than 30 per cent of the value of the entirety of the premises. By virtue of section 20 of that Act class 3 assets may not exceed 5 per cent of the total commercial assets of a society.

STATUTORY INSTRUMENTS

1987 No. 1945

MUSEUMS AND GALLERIES

The Armed Forces Museums (Designation of Institutions) Order 1987

Made - - - -	*11th November 1987*
Laid before Parliament	*18th November 1987*
Coming into force	*11th December 1987*

Whereas the institution specified in this Order is of a kind mentioned in section 30(1) of the National Heritage Act 1983(a) ("the 1983 Act") and was immediately before the making of this Order, staffed by persons at least one of whom was employed in the civil service of the State:

Now, therefore, the Secretary of State, in exercise of the powers conferred on him by section 31(1) of the 1983 Act hereby makes the following Order:

Citation and commencement

1. This Order may be cited as the Armed Forces Museums (Designation of Institutions) Order 1987 and shall come into force on the 11th December 1987.

Designation of institutions

2. For the purposes of section 31 of the 1983 Act there is hereby designated, as an institution in relation to which Schedule 2 of that Act shall have effect, the following institution:

> The charity established by the deed dated 19th August 1976 and made by Major-General David Crichton Alexander C.B., Major Alfred George Brown M.B.E., Major Alastair John Donald and Major Peter Michael Thompson for providing and maintaining the Royal Marines Corps Museum.

George Younger
One of Her Majesty's Principal
Secretaries of State

11th November 1987

(a) 1983 c.47.

EXPLANATORY NOTE

(This note is not part of the Order)

By Schedule 2 to the National Heritage Act 1983 the governing body of an institution, which has been duly designated by the Secretary of State under that Act, is required to offer, by such date as the Secretary of State may determine, employment to each person who was immediately before the date of designation employed in the civil service of the State for the purposes of that institution.

The terms of employment offered have to be such, that taken as a whole they are no less favourable to the employee than those held by him in the civil service, and the offer has to remain open for 3 months. If the person does so change his employment he then enjoys continuity of employment and his employment with the designated institution is included as one to which a scheme under section 1 of the Superannuation Act 1972 (c.11) can apply, and the Schedule to that Act is accordingly construed as if it included a reference to the institution. Disputes as to whether terms taken as a whole are less favourable may be referred to the industrial tribunal.

The institution may not be designated unless it satisfies the conditions provided for by section 31 of the Act that it has as a main object the collection, exhibition or retention of articles relating to the history and traditions of some section of the armed forces of the Crown, and that immediately prior to designation at least one of its staff was employed in the civil service.

This Order effects the necessary designation in the case of the Royal Marines Museum.

STATUTORY INSTRUMENTS

1987 No. 1948

AGRICULTURE

The Farm Business Specification Order 1987

Made - - - -	*13th November 1987*	
Laid before Parliament	*18th November 1987*	
Coming into force	*1st January 1988*	

The Minister of Agriculture, Fisheries and Food, the Secretary of State for Scotland and the Secretary of State for Wales, acting jointly, in exercise of the powers conferred on them by section 28(1) of the Agriculture Act 1970(**a**) and of all other powers enabling them in that behalf, hereby make the following Order:

Citation, commencement and extent

1.—(1) This Order may be cited as the Farm Business Specification Order 1987 and shall come into force on 1st January 1988.

(2) This Order shall apply to Great Britain.

Interpretation

2. In this Order, unless the context otherwise requires–

"agriculture" and cognate expressions shall be construed, except in relation to Scotland, in accordance with section 109 of the Agriculture Act 1947(**b**) and, in relation to Scotland, in accordance with section 86 of the Agriculture (Scotland) Act 1948(**c**);

"agricultural business" means a business consisting in, or such part of any business as consists in, the pursuit of agriculture, and includes any business of a type specified in the Schedule to this Order where that business is carried on by a person also carrying on a business consisting in or partly in the pursuit of agriculture and is carried on on the same or adjacent land;

"farm-based industry" means–

(a) the manufacture of craft items and tourist souvenirs;

(b) food processing and the purification, carbonation and bottling of spring water;

(c) the processing of timber;

(d) the processing of agricultural produce for purposes other than human or animal consumption; or

(e) the repair and renovation of agricultural machinery;

"farm shop" means a shop primarily used for the sale of the produce of the agricultural business of which the shop forms part;

"food processing" means the application of any process or treatment to agricultural produce for the purposes of human consumption but does not include–

(a) the cleaning and trimming of raw fruit and vegetables to which no further process or treatment is applied and the packaging of such fruit and vegetables;

(**a**) 1970 c. 40. Section 28 was amended by section 22 of the Agriculture Act 1986 (c. 49).
(**b**) 1947 c. 48.
(**c**) 1948 c. 45.

(b) the slaughter of livestock and the skinning and gutting of animal carcases;

(c) any process or treatment applied for the purposes of the manufacture of wine; or

(d) any process or treatment applied to cow's milk for the purposes of the liquid consumption of that milk or for the purposes of the manufacture of any milk-based drink as defined in regulation 3 of the Milk-based Drinks (Hygiene and Heat Treatment) Regulations 1983(a) and regulation 3 of the Milk-based Drinks (Scotland) Regulations 1983(b), and any process or treatment applied to any such milk-based drink;

"livery" means the provision of accommodation and care for horses and ponies;

"provision of accommodation", in relation to persons, includes provision of facilities for camping and caravanning;

"sports" means any game or exercise other than field sports, horse riding and sports involving the use of motor vehicles, firearms or crossbows.

Specified farm businesses

3. The businesses described in the Schedule to this Order are hereby specified pursuant to section 28(1) of the Agriculture Act 1970 (Interpretation of provisions relating to Capital and other Grants) as businesses which (when carried on by a person also carrying on a business consisting in or partly in the pursuit of agriculture on the same or adjacent land) are included in the definition of "agricultural business" set out in that subsection.

In witness whereof the Official Seal of the Minister of Agriculture, Fisheries and Food is hereunto affixed on 10th November 1987.

John MacGregor
Minister of Agriculture, Fisheries and Food

10th November 1987

Sanderson of Bowden
Minister of State, Scottish Office

13th November 1987

Peter Walker
Secretary of State for Wales

(a) S.I. 1983/1508.
(b) S.I. 1983/1514; the relevant amending instrument is S.I. 1986/790.

Article 3   **SCHEDULE**

                              SPECIFIED FARM BUSINESSES

1. Farm-based industry.

2. Farm shops.

3. Direct sale to farm visitors of fruit and vegetables which the visitors pick themselves.

4. Provision of accommodation, food and drink.

5. Provision of facilities for sports and recreation.

6. Provision of educational facilities relating to farming and the countryside and to farm-based industry.

7. Provision of livery.

8. Provision of horses and ponies for hire.

9. Letting of any land, building or buildings for the purposes of the carrying on of any business of a type specified above.

EXPLANATORY NOTE

(This note is not part of the Order)

This Order specifies certain businesses which, when carried on by a person also carrying on a business consisting in or partly in the pursuit of agriculture on the same or adjacent land, are included in the definition of "agricultural business" in section 28(1) of the Agriculture Act 1970. The specified businesses may thus become eligible for farm capital grants which under section 29(1) of that Act may be made in connection with the carrying on or establishment of an agricultural business.

STATUTORY INSTRUMENTS

1987 No. 1949

AGRICULTURE

The Farm Diversification Grant Scheme 1987

Approved by both Houses of Parliament.

Made - - - -	*16th November 1987*
Laid before Parliament	*18th November 1987*
Coming into force -	*1st January 1988*

The Minister of Agriculture, Fisheries and Food, the Secretary of State for Scotland and the Secretary of State for Wales, acting jointly, in exercise of the powers conferred on them by sections 28 and 29 of the Agriculture Act 1970(a), and of all other powers enabling them in that behalf, with the approval of the Treasury, hereby make the following Scheme:

Citation, commencement and extent

1.—(1) This Scheme may be cited as the Farm Diversification Grant Scheme 1987 and shall come into force on 1st January 1988.

(2) This Scheme shall apply to Great Britain.

Interpretation

2.—(1) In this Scheme, unless the context otherwise requires–

"agriculture" and cognate expressions shall be construed, except in relation to Scotland, in accordance with section 109 of the Agriculture Act 1947(b) and, in relation to Scotland, in accordance with section 86 of the Agriculture (Scotland) Act 1948(c);

"agricultural business" means a business consisting in, or such part of any business as consists in, the pursuit of agriculture, and includes any ancillary farm business;

"ancillary farm business" means any business of a type specified in the Schedule to the Farm Business Specification Order 1987(d) where that business is carried on by a person also carrying on a business consisting in or partly in the pursuit of agriculture on the same or adjacent land;

"the appropriate Minister means–

(a) in relation to England, the Minister of Agriculture, Fisheries and Food;

(a) 1970 c.40. Section 28 was amended by section 22 of the Agriculture Act 1986 (c.49).
(b) 1947 c.48.
(c) 1948 c.45.
(d) S.I. 1987/1948. The list of farm businesses specified in the Schedule to that Order is the same as items 1–9 in column 1 of the Schedule to this Scheme.

(b) in relation to Scotland, the Secretary of State;

(c) in relation to Wales, the Secretary of State;

"approved" means approved by the appropriate Minister and "approve" and "approval" shall be construed accordingly;

"contractor" means any person who enters into an agreement to supply agricultural work or services in connection with agricultural land;

"designated maps" means–

(a) in relation to England, the 3 volumes of maps numbered 1 to 3, each such volume being marked "volume of maps of less-favoured farming areas in England" and with the number of the volume, dated 3rd April 1984, signed and sealed by the Minister of Agriculture, Fisheries and Food and deposited at the offices of the Ministry of Agriculture, Fisheries and Food at Great Westminster House, Horseferry Road, London SW1P 2AE;

(b) in relation to Wales, the 2 volumes of maps numbered 1 and 2, both volumes being marked "volume of maps of less-favoured farming areas in Wales" and with the number of the volume, dated 29th March 1984, signed by the Secretary of State for Wales and deposited at the offices of the Welsh Office Agriculture Department at Plas Crug, Aberystwyth, Dyfed SY23 1NG;

(c) in relation to Scotland, the 4 maps numbered 1 to 4, each such map being marked "map of less-favoured farming areas in Scotland" and with the number of the map, dated 2nd April 1984, signed by the Secretary of State for Scotland and deposited at the offices of the Department of Agriculture and Fisheries for Scotland at Chesser House, Gorgie Road, Edinburgh EH11 3AW;

"eligible person" has the meaning assigned to that expression in paragraph 3;

"farm-based industry" means–

(a) the manufacture of craft items and tourist souvenirs;

(b) food processing and the purification, carbonation and bottling of spring water;

(c) the processing of timber;

(d) the processing of agricultural produce for purposes other than human or animal consumption; or

(e) the repair and renovation of agricultural machinery;

"farm diversification plan" has the meaning assigned to that expression in paragraph 4;

"farm shop" means a shop primarily used for the sale of the produce of the agricultural business of which the shop forms part;

"food processing" means the application of any process or treatment to agricultural produce for the purposes of human consumption but does not include–

(a) the cleaning and trimming of raw fruit and vegetables to which no further process or treatment is applied and the packaging of such fruit and vegetables;

(b) the slaughter of livestock and the skinning and gutting of animal carcases;

(c) any process or treatment applied for the purposes of the manufacture of wine; or

(d) any process or treatment applied to cow's milk for the purposes of the liquid consumption of that milk or for the purposes of the manufacture of any milk-based drink as defined in regulation 3 of the Milk-based Drinks (Hygiene and Heat Treatment) Regulations 1983(a) and regulation 3 of the Milk-based Drinks (Scotland) Regulations 1983(b), and any process or treatment applied to any such milk-based drink;

"less-favoured area" means land which is within the area shaded blue or pink on the designated maps;

(a) S.I. 1983/1508.
(b) S.I. 1983/1514; the relevant amending instrument is S.I. 1986/790.

"livery" means the provision of accommodation and care for horses and ponies;

"provision of accommodation", in relation to persons, includes provision of facilities for camping and caravanning;

"sports" means any game or exercise other than field sports, horse riding and sports involving the use of motor vehicles, firearms or crossbows.

(2) Any reference in this Scheme to a numbered paragraph or "the Schedule" shall, unless the context otherwise requires, be construed as a reference to the paragraph bearing that number in this Scheme or the Schedule to this scheme.

Eligible persons

3.—(1) Subject to the provisions of this paragraph, the following classes of person shall be eligible for grant under this Scheme–

(a) an individual carrying on an agricultural business if the appropriate Minister is satisfied that that individual or, as the case may be, the farm manager or other person through whom the business is carried on–

(i) derives more than half of his annual income calculated in accordance with sub-paragraph (2) below from that business; and

(ii) spends not less than 1,100 hours per year in agricultural activities relating to that business; and

(iii) possesses sufficient agricultural skill and competence, in that he holds an appropriate certificate issued by a teaching establishment recognised for this purpose by that Minister or has been engaged in agricultural activities for not less than five years,

and if the individual carrying on that agricultural business submits a farm diversification plan in accordance with paragraph 4, and undertakes, if that plan is approved, to carry it out;

(b) any person representing a body carrying on an agricultural business if–

(i) the appropriate Minister is satisfied that the main purpose of that business is the pursuit of agriculture and that the farm manager or other person through whom the business is carried on satisfies the requirements as to income, hours spent in agricultural activities and as to agricultural skill and competence, as specified in sub-paragraph (1)(a) above, and

(ii) the said person representing the said body submits on behalf of the said body a farm diversification plan in accordance with paragraph 4 and undertakes, if that plan is approved, to carry it out;

(c) persons carrying on an agricultural business in partnership if–

(i) the appropriate Minister is satisfied that the farm manager or other person through whom the business is carried on satisfies the requirements as to income, hours spent in agricultural activities and as to agricultural skill and competence as specified in sub-paragraph (1)(a) above, and

(ii) a farm diversification plan is submitted in accordance with paragraph 4 and the undertaking required of an individual by sub-paragraph (1)(a) above is given on behalf of the partnership;

(d) the owner of land occupied for the purposes of the pursuit of agriculture who submits a farm diversification plan relating to such land or to adjacent land jointly with one of the kinds of person eligible for grant under sub-paragraph (a), (b) or (c) above.

(2) For the purposes of this paragraph, a person's annual income shall be calculated in each case by reference to such year or years within the three years immediately preceding the day on which the farm diversification plan is submitted as the appropriate Minister shall determine, being a year or years which he is satisfied gives or give a fair indication of the normal amount of income of that person and the normal amount of income derived by that person from the agricultural business.

(3) Where a person eligible for grant under sub-paragraph (1) above is a contractor, it shall be a further condition of eligibility that he has entered into a written agreement with the occupier of the land in connection with which the contractor supplies agricultural work or services which is expressed to continue in force for a period of not less than

seven years from the day immediately preceding the day on which the farm diversification plan is submitted.

Farm diversification plans

4.—(1) The appropriate Minister shall not approve any proposed expenditure for the purposes of grant under this scheme unless a farm diversification plan relating to that expenditure is submitted for the approval of that Minister and is approved by him.

(2) A farm diversification plan submitted for approval shall be set out in such form as the appropriate Minister may from time to time require and the person submitting it shall furnish all such particulars and information relating thereto as the appropriate Minister may require, and in particular–

(a) sufficient information to show that the person undertaking to carry out the plan is an eligible person and that the plan relates to the carrying on or establishment of an ancillary farm business;

(b) details of the agricultural business of which the ancillary farm business forms or will form part at the time of submission of the plan for approval and of any other business carried out on the same land as the agricultural business;

(c) a description of the land and buildings to which the plan relates;

(d) an indication of the measures to be taken, and in particular of the investments to be made and the timing of such investments in order to achieve the aim of the plan;

(e) a description of the ancillary farm business to which the plan relates on completion of the plan in the form of an estimated budget and an estimate of the implications of the completion of the plan for the economic situation of the agricultural business of which that ancillary farm business forms or will form part, including the number of persons gainfully employed in the carrying on of that agricultural business.

(3) The duration of a farm diversification plan shall be such period as is specified in the plan, being a period not exceeding six years from the date of approval of the plan.

Restrictions on approval of farm diversification plans

5.—(1) The appropriate Minister shall not approve a farm diversification plan under this Scheme unless he is satisfied that in the absence of financial assistance under this Scheme the plan could not, or could not appropriately, be realised and that–

(a) on completion of the plan the ancillary farm business to which the plan relates will be capable of being carried on as a profit-making enterprise; or

(b) the completion of the plan will bring about a lasting improvement in the economic situation of the agricultural business of which the ancillary farm business forms or will form part.

(2) The appropriate Minister shall not approve for the purposes of grant a farm diversification plan in so far as it includes–

(a) proposed expenditure amounting in aggregate to less than £750 or more than £35,000;

(b) proposed expenditure which, in the opinion of the appropriate Minister, would in any six-year period exceed £35,000 when added to other expenditure which has been incurred in the six-year period in question in relation to the same agricultural business and which is included in any previous farm diversification plan approved under this scheme;

(c) proposed expenditure in relation to the provision of horses and ponies for hire outside a less-favoured area;

(d) proposed expenditure in relation to the purchase of land or buildings.

(3) The appropriate Minister shall not approve a farm diversification plan under this Scheme in relation to any ancillary farm business where the agricultural business of which that ancillary farm business forms or will form part–

(a) is affected by a current farm diversification plan approved under this Scheme, or

(b) is affected by a current improvement plan approved under the Agriculture

Improvement Regulations 1985(a) and that improvement plan includes proposed expenditure in connection with any work, facility or transaction of a kind specified in paragraph 12 or 13 in column 1 of the Schedule to those Regulations.

(4) The appropriate Minister may make the approval of a farm diversification plan under this Scheme subject to such conditions as he sees fit and in particular may require that the person undertaking to carry out the plan shall for the duration of the plan furnish to that Minister in such form as he may determine accounts relating to the ancillary farm business to which the plan relates and to the agricultural business of which that ancillary farm business forms or will form part.

Closing date for approval of farm diversification plans

6. The appropriate Minister shall not approve any farm diversification plan for the purposes of grant under this Scheme after 30th November 1994.

Variation and withdrawal of farm diversification plans

7.—(1) The appropriate Minister may, on the written request of the person currently responsible for carrying out a farm diversification plan, vary or withdraw the approval of that plan.

(2) The appropriate Minister shall not vary a farm diversification plan more than once in the period of twelve months following the approval of that plan or more than once in any subsequent period of twelve months.

Farm diversification grants

8.—(1) Subject to the provisions of this Scheme, the appropriate Minister may make to any eligible person a grant towards expenditure incurred by him for the purposes of, or in connection with, the carrying on or establishment of an ancillary farm business, being expenditure which–
   (a) has been incurred in respect of any work, facility or transaction of a kind specified in column 2 of the Schedule in relation to an ancillary farm business of a kind specified in column 1 of the Schedule; and
   (b) appears to the appropriate Minister to be of a capital nature or to have been incurred in connection with expenditure of a capital nature, and
   (c) is included in, and appears to the appropriate Minister to be necessary or appropriate for the purposes of, an approved farm diversification plan in respect of that business and to be the responsibility of that person.

(2) The appropriate Minister may make the payment of grant under sub-paragraph (1) above subject to such conditions as that Minister sees fit, and in particular may require that the person currently responsible for the carrying on of the ancillary farm business in respect of which expenditure has been incurred shall furnish to that Minister copies of the accounts relating to that business and of the agricultural business of which it forms part in such form as that Minister may determine for a period not exceeding two years after the completion of the farm diversification plan.

(3) Where it appears to the appropriate Minister that expenditure in respect of which grant is claimed under sub-paragraph (1) above has been incurred partly for purposes which are eligible for grant under that sub-paragraph and partly for purposes which are not so eligible, that Minister may for the purposes of grant under that sub-paragraph treat as having been incurred for the purposes which are so eligible so much of that expenditure as appears to that Minister to be referable to those eligible purposes.

Amounts of grant

9.—(1) Subject to the provisions of this paragraph and to paragraph 12, the amount of any grant payable under paragraph 8(1) towards expenditure in respect of any work,

(a) S.I. 1985/1266.

facility or transaction of a kind specified in column 2 of the Schedule, shall be twenty-five per cent of that expenditure.

(2) In the case of expenditure which is incurred by–
   (a) a young farmer who fulfils the requirements specified in sub-paragraph (3) below; or
   (b) a young farmers' partnership in respect of which the requirements specified in sub-paragraph (4) below are fulfilled;
the amount of grant so payable shall be thirty-one and one quarter per cent.

(3) The requirements in relation to a young farmer are that he–
   (a) is less than forty years of age on the date on which he submits a farm diversification plan to the appropriate Minister;
   (b) is at that date the sole owner or sole tenant of the land on which he carries on his agricultural business, including the land on which he carries on or intends to carry on the ancillary farm business to which the plan relates;
   (c) submits a farm diversification plan to the appropriate Minister within five years of the date on which he became sole owner or sole tenant of the land on which he carries on his agricultural business, including the land on which he carries on or intends to carry on the ancillary farm business to which the plan relates;
   (d) has not previously been responsible for carrying out a farm diversification plan under this Scheme as an individual carrying on an agricultural business or a person carrying on an agricultural business in partnership or an owner of land occupied for the purposes of the pursuit of agriculture; and
   (e) holds an appropriate certificate relating to the possession of agricultural skill and competence issued by a teaching establishment recognised for that purpose by the appropriate Minister.

(4) The requirements in relation to a young farmers' partnership are that–
   (a) a partner in that partnership fulfils the requirements set out in sub-paragraph (3) (d) and (e) above and submits a farm diversification plan to the appropriate Minister within five years of the date on which he became sole or joint owner or sole or joint tenant of the land on which he carries on an agricultural business in partnership, including the land on which he carries on or intends to carry on the ancillary farm business to which the plan relates;
   (b) all the partners in the partnership are less than forty years of age on the date on which the farm diversification plan is submitted to the appropriate Minister; and
   (c) the partnership exists for the purposes of carrying on the agricultural business of which the ancillary farm business to which the plan relates forms or will form part.

Standard costs

10. In such cases, and subject to such conditions as the appropriate Minister may from time to time determine, the cost of any work, facility or transaction or the amount of any other cost or expenditure shall, if the claimant so elects, be taken for the purpose of determining the amount of any grant payable under this Scheme as such standard cost or amount as that Minister may from time to time fix with the approval of the Treasury.

Claims for grant

11. Any claims for grant under this scheme shall be made in such form and manner and at such time as the appropriate Minister may from time to time require, and the claimant for grant shall furnish all such particulars and information relating to the claim and copies of such documents and records relating thereto as that Minister may require.

Reduction or withholding of grant

12.—(1) The appropriate Minister may reduce or withhold any grant payable under this Scheme in any case where–

(a) assistance in respect of expenditure towards which such grant is claimed has been given otherwise than under this Scheme, or

(b) the carrying out or provision of the work, facility or transaction towards the expenditure on which such grant is claimed appears to that Minister to frustrate the purpose served by assistance previously given out of money provided by Parliament or the European Economic Community, or

(c) he considers that the expenditure towards which such grant is claimed is excessive having regard to the work, facility or transaction carried out or provided to which the claim relates, or

(d) the carrying out of the work, facility or transaction towards the expenditure on which such grant is claimed has been effected in a way which appears to that Minister to have destroyed or damaged the natural beauty and amenity of the countryside to an extent which cannot be justified by any resulting benefit to any agricultural business.

(2) Before reducing or withholding any grant under the provisions of sub-paragraph (1)(c) or (d) above the appropriate Minister shall–

(a) give to any person whose grant it is proposed to reduce or withhold a written notification of the reasons for the action proposed to be taken by that Minister, and

(b) afford that person an opportunity of appearing before and being heard by a person appointed for the purpose by the appropriate Minister, and

(c) consider the report by a person so appointed and supply a copy of that report to the person mentioned in sub-paragraph (a) above.

In Witness whereof the Official Seal of the Minister of Agriculture, Fisheries and Food is hereunto affixed on 10th November 1987.

John MacGregor
Minister of Agriculture, Fisheries and Food

10th November 1987

Sanderson of Bowden
Minister of State, Scottish Office

13th November 1987

Peter Walker
Secretary of State for Wales

We approve,

16th November 1987

Mark Lennox-Boyd
David Lightbown
Two of the Lords Commissioners of Her Majesty's Treasury

Paragraphs 8(1) and 9(1)　　SCHEDULE

Column 1	Column 2
Kind of ancillary farm business.	*Kind of work or facility or transaction for which grant may be paid.*
1. Farm-based industry.	**1.** Provision, alteration, enlargement or reconditioning of permanent buildings.
	2. Works of a capital nature relating to workshops, office accommodation, stores and processing rooms, including the provision or improvement of toilet and washing facilities.
	3. Provision, replacement and installation of fixed equipment and machinery.
	4. Provision or improvement of facilities for the supply of gas, electricity, heating oil and water.
	5. Provision or improvement of drainage, including facilities for the disposal of rain and surface water and facilities for the treatment and disposal of foul waste.
	6. Provision or improvement of roads, paths, fences, hard standings and car parks.
2. Farm shops.	**1.** Provision, alteration, enlargement or reconditioning of permanent buildings.
	2. Works of a capital nature relating to shop premises, office accommodation and stores, including the provision or improvement of toilet and washing facilities.
	3. Provision or improvement of facilities for the supply of gas, electricity, heating oil and water.
	4. Provision or improvement of drainage, including facilities for the disposal of rain and surface water and facilities for the treatment and disposal of foul waste.
	5. Provision or improvement of roads, paths, fences, hard standings and car parks.
3. Direct sale to farm visitors of fruit and vegetables which the visitors pick themselves.	**1.** Provision or improvement of roads, paths, fences, hard standings and car parks.
	2. Provision or improvement of toilet facilities.
4. Provision of accommodation, food and drink.	**1.** Provision, alteration, enlargement or reconditioning of permanent buildings.
	2. Works of a capital nature relating to tourist accommodation, including the provision or improvement of catering, drying, washing and toilet facilities.
	3. Provision and installation of fixed equipment and machinery.
	4. Provision or improvement of facilities for the supply of gas, electricity, heating oil and water.
	5. Provision or improvement of drainage, including facilities for the disposal of rain and surface water and facilities for the treatment and disposal of foul waste.
	6. Provision or improvement of roads, paths, fences, hard standings and car parks.

Column 1	Column 2
Kind of ancillary farm business.	*Kind of work or facility or transaction for which grant may be paid.*

5. Provision of facilities for sports and recreation.

   1. Provision, alteration, enlargement or reconditioning of permanent buildings.

   2. Works of a capital nature relating to office and clubhouse accommodation, including fixed seating and shelter for spectators, and the provision or improvement of drying, washing and toilet facilities.

   3. Provision and installation of fixed equipment.

   4. Provision or improvement of facilities for the supply of gas, electricity, heating oil and water.

   5. Provision or improvement of drainage, including facilities for the disposal of rain and surface water and facilities for the treatment and disposal of foul waste.

   6. Provision or improvement of roads, paths, fences, hard standings and car parks.

   7. Works of a capital nature relating to the establishment of sports grounds and recreational areas, including–
     (a) field drainage;
     (b) land levelling and grading;
     (c) re-seeding and regeneration of amenity grassland;
     (d) laying of turf and of hard surfaces;
     (e) the establishment of ponds for recreational fishing.

6. Provision of educational facilities relating to farming and the countryside and to farm-based industry.

   1. Provision, alteration, enlargement or reconditioning of permanent buildings.

   2. Works of a capital nature relating to lecture hall accommodation and the establishment of display and exhibition areas, including fixed seating and shelters, viewing galleries, notices and signs, and the provision or improvement of toilet and washing facilities.

   3. Provision or improvement of facilities for the supply of gas, electricity, heating oil and water.

   4. Provision or improvement of drainage, including facilities for the disposal of rain and surface water and facilities for the treatment and disposal of foul waste.

   5. Provision or improvement of roads, paths, fences, hard standings and car parks.

   6. Works of a capital nature relating to the establishment of nature trails, including–
     (a) the establishment of ponds and wet areas;
     (b) the clearance of obstacles (other than trees or shrubs);
     (c) the re-grading of land;
     (d) the provision and planting of trees, shrubs and other plants.

Column 1	Column 2
Kind of ancillary farm business.	*Kind of work or facility or transaction for which grant may be paid.*
7. Provision of livery.	1. Provision, alternation, enlargement or reconditioning of permanent buildings.
8. Provision of horses and ponies for hire*.	2. Provision and installation of fixed equipment. 3. Provision or improvement of toilet facilities and facilities for the supply of electricity and water. 4. Provision or improvement of drainage, including facilities for the disposal of rain and surface water and facilities for the treatment and disposal of foul waste. 5. Provision or improvement of car parks, hard standings and associated fences.
9. Letting of any land, building or buildings for the purposes of the carrying on of any business of a type specified above.	Any work, facility or transaction of a type specified above in respect of which grant is payable in relation to the type of business for the purposes of which the land, building or buildings is or are to be let.
10. Any business of a type specified above.	1. Any work, facility, or transaction (including conservation or amenity works) incidental to the carrying out of any work, facility or transaction specified above or necessary or proper in carrying it out or providing it or securing the full benefit thereof. 2. Preparation of farm diversification plans.

* In accordance with paragraph 5(2)(c), grant in relation to the provision of horses and ponies for hire is only available in a less-favoured area.

EXPLANATORY NOTE

(This note is not part of the Scheme)

This Scheme, which applies to Great Britain and operates from 1st January 1988, makes provision for aid for the diversification of agricultural businesses in the form of grants in respect of expenditure of a capital nature incurred in connection with the establishment or carrying on of ancillary farm businesses (paragraph 8(1)). The works, facilities or transactions eligible for grant, and the types of ancillary farm business in relation to which those works, facilities or transactions may be performed or provided, are set out in the Schedule.

The rate of grant payable generally under the Scheme is twenty-five per cent, and a higher rate of thirty-one and one quarter per cent is available in relation to agricultural businesses carried on by young farmers or young farmers' partnerships (paragraph 9). Grant in relation to the provision of horses and ponies for hire is only available in less-favoured areas (paragraph 5(2)(c)). Less-favoured areas are defined by reference to designated maps which are available for inspection during normal office hours at the addresses specified in the definition of designated maps (paragraph 2(1)). Copies of the maps may also be inspected during normal office hours at any Regional or Divisional Office of the Ministry of Agriculture, Fisheries and Food, at any Divisional Office of the Welsh Office Agriculture Department and at any Area Office of the Department of Agriculture and Fisheries for Scotland.

The classes of person which may benefit from grant are defined (paragraph 3). To benefit from assistance, an applicant must submit a farm diversification plan for approval by the appropriate Minister (paragraph 4). The plan must show that on its completion the ancillary farm business to which it relates will be capable of being carried on as a profit-making enterprise, or that its completion will bring about a lasting improvement in the economic situation of the agricultural business of which the ancillary farm business forms part (paragraph 5(1)).

The Scheme also–

(a) imposes certain restrictions on approval of farm diversification plans (paragraph 5);

(b) provides for the variation and withdrawal of plans (paragraph 7);

(c) provides for standard costs (paragraph 10);

(d) provides for the reduction or withholding of grant in certain circumstances where it would otherwise be payable (paragraph 12);

(e) sets a closing date of 30th November 1994 for the approval of farm diversification plans (paragraph 6).

STATUTORY INSTRUMENTS

1987 No. 1950

AGRICULTURE

HORTICULTURE

The Agriculture Improvement (Amendment) Regulations 1987

Made - - - -	*13th November 1987*
Laid before Parliament	*18th November 1987*
Coming into force	*1st January 1988*

The Minister of Agriculture, Fisheries and Food and the Secretary of State, acting jointly, being Ministers designated for the purposes of section 2(2) of the European Communities Act 1972(**a**) in relation to the common agricultural policy of the European Economic Community(**b**), in exercise of the powers conferred on them by the said section 2(2) and of all other powers enabling them in that behalf, hereby make the following Regulations:

1. These Regulations may be cited as the Agriculture Improvement (Amendment) Regulations 1987 and shall come into force on 1st January 1988.

2. The Agriculture Improvement Regulations 1985(**c**) shall be amended in accordance with the following provisions of these Regulations.

3. For regulation 7 thereof (closing date for submission of improvement plans) there shall be substituted the following regulation—

"**7.**—(1) Subject to paragraph (2) below, the appropriate Minister shall not approve an improvement plan under these regulations where the plan is received by him after 31st December 1994 or such later date as that Minister may in special circumstances permit.

(2) The appropriate Minister shall not approve an improvement plan under these regulations which includes proposed expenditure in connection with any work, facility or transaction of a kind specified in paragraph 12 or 13 of column 1 of the Schedule where that plan is received by him after 1st January 1988.".

4. For regulation 8 thereof (variation and withdrawal of improvement plans) there shall be substituted the following regulation–

"**8.**—(1) Subject to paragraph (2) below, the appropriate Minister may, on the written request of the person currently responsible for the carrying on of an agricultural business to which an improvement plan relates, vary or withdraw the approval of that plan, where the request is made at least two years after the original approval of the plan.

(2) The appropriate Minister may, on the written request of the person currently responsible for the carrying on of an agricultural business to which an improvement plan relates,

---

(**a**) 1972 c. 68.
(**b**) S.I. 1972/1811.
(**c**) S.I. 1985/1266. By S.R. (N.I.) 1987 No. 156 the Agriculture Improvement Regulations 1985 were revoked in so far as they formed part of the law of Northern Ireland.

vary or withdraw the approval of that plan at any time after the original approval of the plan, provided that–

    (a) the plan includes proposed expenditure in connection with any work, facility or transaction of a kind specified in paragraph 12 or 13 of column 1 of the Schedule;

    (b) the request for variation or withdrawal of approval of the plan is received by the appropriate Minister before 1st July 1988;

    (c) the person who requests variation or withdrawal of approval of the plan has submitted a farm diversification plan for approval under the Farm Diversification Grant Scheme 1987(**a**).".

In Witness whereof the Official Seal of the Minister of Agriculture, Fisheries and Food is hereunto affixed on 10th November 1987.

John MacGregor
Minister of Agriculture, Fisheries and Food

13th November 1987

Peter Walker
One of Her Majesty's Principal Secretaries of State

EXPLANATORY NOTE

(This note is not part of the Regulations)

These Regulations amend the Agriculture Improvement Regulations 1985 in two respects as regards farm improvement plans which include proposed expenditure in connection with on-farm craft and tourism projects:–

    (1) The closing date for receipt of applications for approval of such farm improvement plans is brought forward to 1st January 1988 (regulation 3);

    (2) Ministers are empowered, on written request, to vary or withdraw approval of such plans at any time after the date of original approval provided that the request is received by 1st July 1988 and the person making the request has submitted a farm diversification plan under the Farm Diversification Grant Scheme 1987 (regulation 4).

In future, grant aid for on-farm craft and tourism projects will be available under the Farm Diversification Grant Scheme 1987.

(**a**) S.I. 1987/1949.

STATUTORY INSTRUMENTS

1987 No. 1957 (S.135)

FOOD

FOOD HYGIENE

The Slaughterhouse Hygiene (Scotland) Amendment Regulations 1987

Made - - - -	*11th November 1987*
Laid before Parliament	*25th November 1987*
Coming into force	*31st December 1987*

The Secretary of State, in exercise of the powers conferred on him by sections 13(1) and 56 of the Food and Drugs (Scotland) Act 1956(a) and of all other powers enabling him in that behalf, and having in accordance with section 56(6) of that Act consulted with such organisations as appear to him to be representative of interests substantially affected by these Regulations, hereby makes the following Regulations:

Citation and commencement

1. These regulations may be cited as the Slaughterhouse Hygiene (Scotland) Amendment Regulations 1987 and shall come into force on 31st December 1987.

Amendment of the Slaughterhouse Hygiene (Scotland) Regulations 1978

2. The Slaughterhouse Hygiene (Scotland) Regulations 1978(b) are hereby amended as follows:–

  (a) in regulation 2(1) (Interpretation)–

    (i) in the definition of "animal" for the words "and horses" there shall be substituted the words ", horses and farmed deer";

    (ii) after the definition of "equipment" there shall be inserted the following definition:–

      ""farmed deer" means any deer which–

        (a) are kept by any person by way of business on land enclosed by a deer-proof barrier;

        (b) are conspicuously marked in such a way as to identify them as his; and

        (c) are kept by him–

          (i) primarily for the purpose of the production of meat or other foodstuffs or skins or other by-products; or

          (ii) primarily for breeding deer to be kept as mentioned in head (i) above;";

(a) 1956 c.30; section 56(8) was amended by, and section 56(8A) inserted by, paragraph 8 of Schedule 15 to the Criminal Justice Act 1982 (c.48); section 56(8A) was amended by the Law Reform (Miscellaneous Provisions) (Scotland) Act 1985 (c.73), section 41 and is to be read with section 289G of the Criminal Procedure (Scotland) Act 1975 (c.21) and S.I. 1984/526; section 56(8) was also amended by the Weights and Measures Act 1963 (c.31), Schedule 9, Part II.

(b) S.I. 1978/1273; the relevant amending instruments are S.I. 1984/842, 1985/1856 and 1986/1808.

(b) for paragraph (b) of the proviso to regulation 36(6) (which provides for a derogation from the requirement to skin sheep heads) there shall be substituted–

"(b) that the heads of sheep and goats need be skinned only if the said heads are intended for human consumption, and where heads are not to be skinned the head, including the tongue and the brains, shall be discarded at the time of skinning the carcase.";

(c) for regulation 49 there shall be substituted the following regulation:–

"**49.** No person shall–

(a) smoke, chew tobacco or take snuff in any lairage, slaughterhall or workroom; and

(b) urinate, defecate or spit except in a sanitary convenience.".

New St. Andrew's House, Edinburgh
11th November 1987

Sanderson of Bowden
Minister of State,
Scottish Office

EXPLANATORY NOTE

(This note is not part of the Regulations)

These Regulations further amend the Slaughterhouse Hygiene (Scotland) Regulations 1978 which regulate the construction, equipment and operation of slaughterhouses in order to secure the hygienic handling of meat therein.

In particular, the Regulations–

(a) extend the 1978 Regulations to farmed deer (regulation 2(a));

(b) make permanent a derogation from the requirement of regulation 36(6) of the 1978 Regulations to skin the heads of sheep in circumstances where the heads are not to be used for human consumption (regulation 2(b)); and

(c) amend the regulation governing personal conduct and hygiene in slaughterhouses (regulation 2(c)).

STATUTORY INSTRUMENTS

1987 No. 1959

INSOLVENCY

COMPANIES
INDIVIDUALS, ENGLAND AND WALES

The Insolvency (Amendment) Regulations 1987

Made - - - -	*12th November 1987*
Laid before Parliament	*25th November 1987*
Coming into force	*11th January 1988*

The Secretary of State, in exercise of the powers conferred on him by Rule 12.1 of the Insolvency Rules 1986(**a**), hereby makes the following Regulations:–

Citation and Commencement

1. These Regulations may be cited as the Insolvency (Amendment) Regulations 1987 and shall come into force on 11th January 1988, and that date shall be referred to in these Regulations as "the commencement date".

Interpretation

2.—(1) In these Regulations references to "the principal Regulations" are to the Insolvency Regulations 1986(**b**) and a Regulation or Schedule or Form referred to by number means the Rule or Schedule or Form so numbered in the principal Regulations.

(2) These Regulations shall be read and construed as one with the principal Regulations.

Application

3.—(1) Subject to paragraph (2), the principal Regulations have effect in relation to insolvency proceedings to which the principal Regulations apply by virtue of Regulation 2(5) with the amendments set out in the Schedule to these Regulations.

(2) The principal Regulations as so amended apply to all such proceedings on and after the commencement date, whether or not those proceedings were commenced before or after the commencement date.

Francis Maude
Parliamentary Under-Secretary of State,
Department of Trade and Industry

12th November 1987

(**a**) S.I. 1986/1925.   (**b**) S.I. 1986/1994.

SCHEDULE Regulation 3(1)

Amendment of Regulation 2

1. In paragraph (1) of Regulation 2 –
    (a) before the words '"creditors' committee"' there shall be inserted the words '"bank" means any authorised institution in England and Wales within the meaning of the Banking Act 1987;';
    (b) for the words '"local bank" means any recognised bank in England and Wales within the meaning of the Banking Act 1979(**a**)' there shall be substituted the words '"local bank" means any bank'; and
    (c) before the words '"responsible insolvency practitioner"' there shall be inserted the words '"payment instrument" means cheque or payable order;'.

Amendment of Regulation 5

2. In paragraph (4) of Regulation 5 for the words "cheques, money orders or payable orders" there shall be substituted the words "payment instruments".

Insertion of Regulation 10A

3. After Regulation 10 there shall be inserted the following regulation:–

    "Retention and delivery of records

    10A.—(1) All records kept by a responsible insolvency practitioner under Regulations 8 and 9 and any such records received by him from a predecessor in that office shall be retained by him for a period of 6 years following his vacation of that office, unless he delivers them to another responsible insolvency practitioner who succeeds him in office.

    (2) Where a responsible insolvency practitioner is succeeded in office by another responsible insolvency practitioner, the records referred to in paragraph (1) above shall be delivered to that successor forthwith following his appointment, unless the winding up or bankruptcy, as the case may be, is for practical purposes complete and the successor is the official receiver, in which case the records are only to be delivered to the official receiver if the latter so requests.".

Amendment of Regulation 15

4. (1) In paragraph (1) of Regulation 15 for the words "payable order on H.M Paymaster General" there shall be substituted the words "payment instruments".

(2) In paragraph (2) of Regulation 15:–
    (a) for the words "payable order" there shall be substituted the words "payment instrument"; and
    (b) for the word "debts" there shall be substituted the word "debt".

(3) In paragraph (3) of Regulation 15 for the words "payable order" there shall be substituted the words "payment instruments".

(4) In paragraph (5) of Regulation 15 after the word "invalid" there shall be inserted the words "and any cheques which have not been delivered".

(5) In paragraph (7) of Regulation 15 there shall be inserted at the end the words "and any cheques which have not been delivered after endorsing them with the word "cancelled"."

Amendment of Regulation 20

5. For Tables 1 and 2 in paragraph (3) of Regulation 20 there shall be substituted the following:–

(**a**) 1979 c.37.

"Table 1

Grade or Status of Official	Total hourly rate £
Official Receiver	35
Deputy Official Receiver	29
Senior Examiner	24
Senior Executive Officer	22
Examiner (D)	22
Higher Executive Officer	19
Examiner (E)	17
Executive Officer	16
Administrative Officer	13
Administrative Assistant	11

Table 2

Grade or Status of Official	Total hourly rate £
Official Receiver	24
Deputy Official Receiver	20
Senior Examiner	20
Examiner (D)	18
Senior Executive Officer	17
Higher Executive Officer	15
Examiner (E)	14
Executive Officer	13
Administrative Officer	10
Administrative Assistant	8".

Insertion of Regulation 28A

6.   After Regulation 28 there shall be inserted the following regulation:–

"**Retention and delivery of records**

28A.—(1) All records kept by a liquidator under Regulations 26 and 27 and any such records received by him from a predecessor in such office shall be retained by him for a period of 6 years following his vacation of that office, unless he delivers them to another liquidator who succeeds him in office.

(2) Where a liquidator is succeeded in office by another liquidator the records referred to in paragraph (1) above shall be delivered to that successor forthwith following his appointment.".

Amendment of the Schedule

7.   In the Schedule to the principal Regulations in Form 2 for the words "payable orders" in both places where they occur there shall be substituted the words "payment instruments".

EXPLANATORY NOTE

(This note is not part of the Regulations)

These Regulations amend the Insolvency Regulations 1986 (S.I. 1986/1994), which regulate matters which are of an administrative and not of a judicial character in the conduct of company and individual insolvency proceedings. In particular they:–

(a) permit the issuing of cheques in addition to payable orders from the Insolvency Services Account in relation to windings up by the court and bankruptcies;

(b) alter the rates for remuneration payable to the official receiver in certain cases;

(c) impose obligations as regards the length of time insolvency practitioners must keep records of insolvency cases;

(d) effect amendments consequential upon the enactment of the Banking Act 1987.

These Regulations apply to all insolvency proceedings to which the Insolvency Regulations 1986 apply on and after 11th January 1988, whether or not those proceedings were commenced before, on or after that date.

STATUTORY INSTRUMENTS

1987 No. 1960

EDUCATION, ENGLAND AND WALES

The Education Support Grants (Amendment) Regulations 1987

Made - - - -	*17th November 1987*
Coming into force	*1st December 1987*

In exercise of the powers conferred on the Secretary of State by sections 1(2) to (4) and (7) and 3(4) of the Education (Grants and Awards) Act 1984(**a**), and after consulting, in accordance with section 3(5) of the Act, such bodies representing local educational authorities as appear to them to be appropriate, the Secretary of State for Education and Science, as respects England, and the Secretary of State for Wales, as respects Wales, hereby make the following regulations, a draft of which has been laid before Parliament and has been approved by resolution of each House of Parliament pursuant to section 3(2) of that Act:–

1.　These Regulations may be cited as the Education Support Grants (Amendment) Regulations 1987 and shall come into force on 1st December 1987.

2.　The Education Support Grants (Amendment) Regulations 1985(**b**), the Education Support Grants (Amendment) (No.2) Regulations 1985(**c**) and the Education Support Grants (Amendment) Regulations 1986(**d**) are hereby revoked.

3.　In regulation 4 of the Education Support Grants Regulations 1984(**e**) ("the principal regulations") for the figure "70" there shall be substituted the figure "50" and there shall be added after the word "approved" in the second place where it appears the following words–

"in the case of item No. 4(a) in the Schedule hereto and 70 per cent of the expenditure so approved in any other case.".

4.　After regulation 4 of the principal regulations there shall be inserted the following regulation–

"**Condition of Grant**

4A.Where at the time of approving expenditure for the purpose of these Regulations, the Secretary of State requests information in respect of any purpose or pilot project listed in the Schedule hereto, payment of grant in respect of that purpose or pilot project shall be conditional on that information being included in the authority's application for payment of grant.".

5.　For the Schedule to the principal regulations (which specifies the purposes for or on connection with which education support grants are payable) there shall be substituted the following Schedule–

(**a**) 1984 c. 11.
(**b**) S.I. 1985/1070.
(**c**) S.I. 1985/2028.
(**d**) S.I. 1986/1031.
(**e**) S.I. 1984/1098.

"SCHEDULE   Regulation 2(1)

PURPOSES FOR OR IN CONNECTION WITH WHICH GRANTS ARE PAYABLE

1. The management and appraisal of school teachers.

2. The teaching of mathematics in schools.

3. The teaching of science and technology as part of primary education.

4. A pilot project devised with one of the following objectives:
   (a) to provide records of achievement for pupils in secondary schools or students at further education establishments;
   (b) to improve the quality of education provided in primary schools in urban areas;
   (c) to improve the quality or the range of the curriculum provided in primary schools in rural areas;
   (d) to meet the educational needs of persons from ethnic minorities, to promote harmony between different racial groups or in other ways to prepare persons for life in a multi-ethnic society;
   (e) to improve the use of the spoken word by pupils of compulsory school age;
   (f) to promote social responsibility in children;
   (g) to broaden the range of languages learnt by pupils in secondary schools as their first foreign language.

5. The provision of re-training and up-dating courses directed towards the needs of industry and commerce.

6. The development of the use of information technology at further education establishments, by providing equipment, preparing or providing course material and computer software, or training teachers employed at such establishments.

7. The planning, development and co-ordination of provision to meet the educational needs (including the need for guidance) of persons who are unemployed (excluding those currently receiving full-time education).

8. Where provision to meet the need of the unemployed for educational guidance is being planned, developed and co-ordinated, the planning, development and co-ordination of the provision of such guidance for other adult persons.

9. The provision of data-processing equipment, and accessories and software for such equipment, for use in the management of further education establishments.

10. Developing the knowledge and appreciation, among pupils in schools in Wales, of the heritage, culture and language of Wales.

11. The development, provision and appraisal of courses of initial training for school governors.

12. The provision of support for parents in the teaching of children under the age of 5 with special educational needs.

13. The provision of computerised learning aids and associated software at further education establishments for use by students with special educational needs.

14. The employment of staff to strengthen links between further education establishments and employers in order to improve the quality and relevance of further education courses.

15. Combatting, through education, the misuse of drugs.

16.   Securing the supervision of pupils in schools at midday.

17.   The provision to schools and further education establishments of books and equipment for use on courses leading to an examination for the General Certificate of Secondary Education.

18.   The organisation in urban areas of leisure-time activities of vocational benefit to young persons mainly between the ages of 14 and 21.

19.   The development and support of methods of learning which do not require regular attendance at educational establishments including activities connected with the Open College.

20.   The provision of computer-aided engineering equipment for engineering courses in further education establishments.

21.   The development of the use of information technology in primary and secondary schools through the provision of staff and computer hardware.".

Kenneth Baker
Secretary of State for Education and Science

16th November 1987

Wyn Roberts
Minister of State, Welsh Office

17th November 1987

EXPLANATORY NOTE

(This note is not part of the Regulations)

These Regulations further amend the Education Support Grants Regulations 1984 by an amendment to regulation 4 to reduce the rate of grant payable on one of the purposes in the Schedule for or in connection with which grants are payable and by the addition of a new regulation (regulation 4A) to make payment of grant conditional upon such information as the Secretary of State may request in respect of a purpose or pilot project at the time of approving expenditure being included in the authority's application for payment of grant (regulations 3 and 4 respectively). Further, the original Schedule is replaced by a revised Schedule which consolidates earlier amendments, omits item 4 of the original Schedule (the provision of micro-electronic equipment for use by children with special educational needs), adds one further pilot project to those eligible for support under what is now item 4 (at item 4(g)), amends item 10 to include the Welsh language and item 17 to add further education establishments, and adds as items 18 to 21 four further purposes for or in connection with which grants are payable by the Secretary of State to local education authorities (regulation 5). This has enabled earlier amending regulations made in 1985 and 1986 to be revoked (regulation 2).

STATUTORY INSTRUMENTS

1987 No. 1961

MERCHANT SHIPPING

The Merchant Shipping (Pilot Ladders and Hoists) Regulations 1987

Made - - - -	*18th November 1987*
Laid before Parliament	*27th November 1987*
Coming into force	*1st January 1988*

The Secretary of State for Transport, after consultation with the persons referred to in section 22(2) of the Merchant Shipping Act 1979(**a**), in exercise of the powers conferred on him by subsections (1)(a) and (b) and (3) to (6) of section 21 and section 22(1) of that Act and of all other powers enabling him in that behalf, hereby makes the following Regulations:

Citation, revocation and interpretation

1.—(1)   These Regulations may be cited as the Merchant Shipping (Pilot Ladders and Hoists) Regulations 1987 and shall come into force on 1st January 1988.

(2) The Merchant Shipping (Pilot Ladders and Hoists) Regulations 1980(**b**) and the Merchant Shipping (Pilot Ladders and Hoists) (Amendment) Regulations 1981(**c**) are hereby revoked.

2.—(1) In these Regulations:–

"associated equipment" includes manropes, safety lines and harnesses, lifebuoys with self igniting lights, heaving lines, lighting, and when required by regulation 7(8), stanchions and bulwark ladders;

"existing ship" means a ship the keel of which was laid or which was at a similar stage of construction before 25th May 1980;

"Merchant Shipping Notice" means a Notice described as such issued by the Department of Transport and any reference to a particular Merchant Shipping Notice includes a reference to any document amending or replacing that Notice which is considered by the Secretary of State to be relevant from time to time and is specified in a Merchant Shipping Notice.

(2) Any reference in these Regulations to a numbered regulation is a reference to the regulation of that number in these Regulations.

Application and classification of ships

3.   These Regulations apply in relation to:

(a) sea-going United Kingdom ships; and

(b) other sea-going ships while they are within the United Kingdom or the territorial waters thereof:

(**a**) 1979 c. 39; section 21 was amended by the Safety at Sea Act 1986 (c.23), section 11, and section 21(6) was amended by the Criminal Justice Act 1982 (c.48), section 49(3).
(**b**) S.I. 1980/543.
(**c**) S.I. 1981/581.

Provided that these Regulations shall not apply to a ship which is not a United Kingdom ship flying the flag of a State which is not a party to the International Convention for the Safety of Life at Sea 1974 by reason of her being within the United Kingdom or within the territorial waters thereof if she would not have been there but for stress of weather or any other circumstances which could not have been prevented by the master, the owner or the charterer (if any).

4. For the purpose of these Regulations the ships to which these Regulations apply shall be arranged in the same classes in which ships are arranged for the purposes of the Merchant Shipping (Life-Saving Appliances) Regulations 1980(**a**) and any reference in these Regulations to a ship of any class shall be construed accordingly.

Provision of pilot ladders, accommodation ladders, hoists and associated equipment.

5.—(1) Every ship of
  (i) Classes, I, II, II(A), VII, VII(T), VII(A), VIII, VIII(T), VIII(A), and VIII(A)(T);
  (ii) Class X where the distance in normal operating conditions, from the water to the point of access to the vessel exceeds 2.5 metres; and
  (iii) Classes III to VI(A) inclusive and of IX, IX(A), IX(A)(T), XI, and XII, when engaged on a voyage during the course of which a pilot is likely to be employed;

shall be provided by the owner with a pilot ladder and associated equipment complying with the requirements of regulation 7(3) to (10) and, when required by regulation 5(2)(b), an accommodation ladder or ladders complying with the requirements of regulation 7(2).

(2) The owner shall ensure that–
  (a) suitable positions are available on each side of the ship to enable the master to comply with the requirements of regulation 7(1) and 7(2);
  (b) in every ship to which paragraph (1) above applies, where the distance from the sea level to the point of access to the ship is more than 9 metres, accommodation ladders sited on each side of the ship, are provided: Provided however that a single accommodation ladder capable of being transferred, or other equally safe and convenient means, may be provided instead.
  (c) all mechanical pilot hoists (hereinafter referred to as "hoists") if fitted, comply with regulations 8 and 9.

Pilot ladders, accommodation ladders, hoists and associated equipment

6. The master shall ensure that–
  (a) each pilot ladder, accommodation ladder and associated equipment meets the requirements of regulation 7, as appropriate, and is efficient for the purpose of enabling pilots, officials and other persons to embark and disembark safely;
  (b) each pilot ladder, accommodation ladder, hoist and associated equipment is properly maintained and stowed and regularly inspected to ensure that, so far as is reasonably practicable, each is safe to use;
  (c) each pilot ladder is used only for the embarkation and disembarkation of pilots and by officials and other persons while a ship is arriving at or leaving a port;
  (d) the rigging of the pilot ladder, accommodation ladder, hoist and associated equipment used for the transfer of pilots and the embarkation and disembarkation of persons thereby is supervised by a responsible officer of the ship.

7.—(1) Every pilot ladder shall be so positioned and secured–
  (a) that it is clear of any possible discharges from the ship;
  (b) that it is within the parallel body length of the ship and, as far as is practicable, within the mid-ship half section of the ship taking into consideration paragraphs 7 and 8 of Merchant Shipping Notice No. 898;

(**a**) S.I. 1980/538, as amended by S.I. 1986/1072.

(c) that each step rests firmly against the ship's side, and, if belting is fitted in way of this position, such belting shall be cut back sufficiently to comply with this requirement;

(d) that the person using it can gain safe and convenient access to the ship after climbing not less than 1.5 metres and not more than 9 metres.

(2)(a) Where an accommodation ladder is provided for the purpose of regulation 5(2) it shall be so sited that, when used in conjunction with a pilot ladder for embarking or disembarking pilots, officials and other persons, the lower end of the accommodation ladder rests firmly against the side of the ship within the parallel body length of the ship and, as far as is practicable, within the mid-ship half section and leading aft. Precautions shall be taken to bowse-in such accommodation ladder falls against the roll of the ship.

(b) Whenever an accommodation ladder is used in conjuction with a pilot ladder the pilot ladder shall be rigged immediately adjacent to the lower platform of the accommodation ladder so that the pilot ladder's upper end extends at least 2 metres above the accommodation ladder's lower platform.

(3) A single length of pilot ladder shall be used capable of reaching the water from the point of access to or egress from the ship and due allowance shall be made for all conditions of loading and trim of the ship. The securing strongpoints, shackles and securing ropes shall be at least as strong as the side ropes specified in paragraph (5) below.

(4) The steps of the pilot ladder shall–

(a) be made of ash, oak, elm, or teak or other hardwood or other material of equivalent strength, stiffness and durability. The four lowest steps may be of rubber or other material of equivalent strength, stiffness and durability;

(b) be made in one piece, and in the case of wooden steps free of knots;

(c) have an efficient non-slip surface;

(d) be not less than 480 millimetres long, 115 millimetres wide and 25 millimetres in depth, excluding any non-slip device or grooving;

(e) be equally spaced not less than 300 millimetres nor more than 380 millimetres apart; and

(f) be secured in such a manner that each will remain horizontal;

Provided that–

(i) no pilot ladder shall have more than two replacement steps which are secured in position by a method different from that used in the original construction of the ladder, and any steps so secured shall be replaced as soon as reasonably practicable by steps secured in position by the method used in the original construction of the pilot ladder; and

(ii) when any replacement step is secured to the side ropes of the pilot ladder by means of grooves in the sides of the step, such grooves shall be in the longer sides of the step.

(5) The side ropes of the pilot ladder shall consist of two manila ropes not less than 18 millimetres in diameter on each side. Each rope shall be left uncovered by any other material, and shall be continuous with no joins below the top step.

(6)   (i) Two man-ropes of not less than 20 millimetres in diameter properly secured to the ship shall be provided; and

(ii) a safety line and harness for rescue purposes shall be kept at hand ready for use; and

(iii) a lifebuoy equipped with a self-igniting light shall be kept at hand ready for use; and

(iv) a heaving line shall be kept at hand ready for use.

(7) Spreaders between 1.80 metres and 2.00 metres long, made of ash, oak, elm or teak or other hardwood or other material of equivalent strength, stiffness and durability, made in one piece, and in the case of wooden spreaders, free of knots, shall be provided at such intervals as will prevent the ladder from twisting. The lowest spreader shall be on the fifth step from the bottom of the ladder, and the interval between any spreader and the next shall not exceed nine steps.

(8)(a) Means shall be provided to ensure safe and convenient passage for any person embarking on or disembarking from the ship between the head of the pilot ladder, or of any accommodation ladder or other appliance provided pursuant to paragraph (2) above and the ship's deck.

(b) Where such passage is by means of a gateway in the rails or bulwark, adequate handholds shall be provided.

(c) Where such passage is by means of a bulwark ladder, such ladder shall be securely attached to the bulwark rail or landing platform. Two hand-hold stanchions shall be fitted at the point of embarking on or disembarking from the ship on each side which shall be not less than 700 millimetres nor more than 800 millimetres apart. Each stanchion shall be rigidly secured to the ship's structure at or near its base and also at a higher point, shall be not less than 40 millimetres in diameter and shall extend not less than 1.20 metres above the top of the bulwarks. Stanchions or handrails shall not be attached to the bulwark ladder.

(9) Lighting shall be provided such that both the pilot ladder overside and also the position where any person embarks or disembarks on the ship shall be adequately lit.

(10) Means shall be provided to enable the pilot ladder to be used, in accordance with the requirements of this regulation, on either side of the ship.

Hoists

8.—(1) The owner shall ensure that a hoist, if provided, and its ancillary equipment, is of a type approved by the Secretary of State. It shall be of such design and construction as to ensure that any person can be embarked and disembarked in a safe manner, including a safe access from the hoist to the deck and from the deck to the hoist. The hoist shall be used solely for the embarkation and disembarkation of pilots, and of officials and other persons while a ship is arriving at or leaving a port.

(2) The hoist shall be so located that it is within the parallel body length of the ship and, as far as is practicable, within the mid-ship half section of the ship taking into consideration Merchant Shipping Notice No. M898.

(3) From a standing position at the control point it shall be possible for the operator to have the hoist under observation continuously between its highest and lowest working positions.

(4) The owner and master shall ensure that in respect of the hoist there is on board a copy of the manufacturer's maintenance manual, approved by the Secretary of State, which contains a maintenance log book. The hoist shall be maintained in accordance with the maintenance manual.

(5) A record of maintenance and repairs of the hoist shall be entered in the maintenance log book by the officer responsible for its maintenance.

(6) Notwithstanding the previous provisions of this regulation, in the case of existing ships, any hoists which are fitted and were manufactured before 20th November 1973, may be carried, if they have been modified in accordance with Merchant Shipping Notice No. M898.

(7) Any approval given pursuant to this regulation shall be given in writing and shall specify the date when it is to come into force and the conditions (if any) on which it is given.

Construction of hoist

9.—(1) The working load of a hoist shall be the sum of the weight of the hoist ladder and falls in the fully lowered condition and the maximum number of persons which the hoist is designed to carry, the weight of each person being taken as 150 kg. The maximum complement a hoist is permitted to carry shall be clearly and permanently marked on the hoist.

(2) Every hoist shall be of such construction that, when operating under the working load determined in accordance with paragraph (1) above, each component shall have an adequate factor of safety having regard to the material used, the method of construction and the nature of its duty.

(3) In selecting the materials of construction, regard shall be paid to the conditions under which the hoist will be required to operate.

(4) The hoist shall consist of the following main parts–

  (a) a mechanically powered winch;

  (b) two separate falls;

  (c) a ladder consisting of two parts–

    (i) a rigid upper part for the transportation of any person upwards or downwards;

    (ii) a flexible lower part, consisting of a short length of pilot ladder, which enables any person to climb from the pilot launch or tender to the rigid upper part of the ladder and vice versa.

(5) *Mechanically powered winch*

  (a) The source of power for the winches shall be electrical, hydraulic or pneumatic. In the case of a pneumatic system, an exclusive air supply shall be provided with adequate arrangements to control its quality. In the case of ships engaged in the carriage of flammable cargoes, the source of power shall not be such as to cause a hazard to the ship. All systems shall be capable of efficient operation under the conditions of vibration, humidity and range of temperature likely to be experienced in the ship in which they are installed.

  (b) The winch shall include a brake or other equally effective arrangement (such as a properly constructed worm drive) which is capable of supporting the working load in the event of power failure. The brake or other arrangement shall be capable of supporting the working load when the hand gear is in use.

  (c) Efficient hand gear shall be provided to lower or recover, at a reasonable speed, the person carried in the event of power failure.

  (d) Any crank handle provided for manual operation shall, when engaged, be so arranged that the power supply is automatically cut off.

  (e) Hoists shall be fitted with automatic safety devices in order to cut off the power supply when the ladder comes against any stop so as to avoid overstressing the falls or any other part of the hoist: provided that in the case of hoists operated by pneumatic power, the safety cut-out device may be omitted if the maximum torque available from the air motor cannot result in overstressing of the falls or other parts of the hoist.

  (f) All hoist controls shall incorporate an emergency stop to cut off the power supply and an emergency stop switch within easy reach of the person carried by means of which he may cut off the power.

  (g) The winch controls shall be clearly and durably marked to indicate "Hoist", "Stop" and "Lower". The manner in which these controls operate shall correspond to the manner in which the hoist operates and shall automatically return to the "Stop" position when released.

  (h) Efficient arrangements shall be provided to ensure that the falls wind evenly on to the winch-drums.

  (i) The hoist shall be securely attached to the structure of the ship. Attachment shall not be solely by means of the ship's side rails. Proper and strong attachment points shall be provided for the hoists of the portable type on each side of the ship.

  (j) The winch shall be capable of hoisting or lowering the safe working load (determined in accordance with regulation 9(1)) at a speed of between 15 and 30 metres per minute.

  (k) There shall be safe means of access between the ladder at its upper limit and the deck and vice versa; such access shall be gained directly by a platform securely guarded by handrails.

  (l) An electrical appliance associated with the ladder section of the hoist shall not be operated at a voltage exceeding 25 volts.

(6) *Falls*

  (a) The falls shall be made of flexible steel wire rope of adequate strength and resistant to corrosion in a salt-laden atmosphere.

(b) The falls shall be securely attached to winch-drums and the ladder. These attachments shall be capable of withstanding a proof load of not less than 2.2. times the load on such attachments. The falls shall be maintained at a sufficient relative distance from one another, so as to reduce the possibility of the ladder becoming twisted.

(c) The falls shall be of sufficient length to allow for all conditions of freeboard likely to be encountered in service and to retain at least three turns on the winch-drums with the hoist in its lowest position.

(7)   *Ladder section*

(a) The rigid part shall be not less than 2.50 metres in length and be equipped in such a way that the person carried can maintain a safe position whilst being hoisted or lowered. Such part shall be provided with–

    (i) a sufficient number of steps complying with sub-paragraph (c) of this paragraph to provide a safe and easy access to and from the platform referred to in paragraph (5)(k) of this regulation;

    (ii) safe handholds capable of being used under all conditions including extremes of temperature, together with non-slip steps;

    (iii) a spreader at the lower end of not less 1.80 metres. The ends of the spreader shall be provided with rollers which shall roll freely on the ship's side during the whole operation of embarking or disembarking;

    (iv) an effective guard ring, suitably padded, so positioned as to provide physical support for the person carried without hampering movement;

    (v) adequate means for communication between the person carried and the operator and/or the responsible officer who supervises the embarkation or disembarkation of the person carried;

    (vi) an emergency stop switch within easy reach of the person carried by means of which he may cut off the power.

(b) Below the rigid part mentioned in sub-paragraph (a) above, a section of flexible ladder comprising eight steps shall be provided, constructed in accordance with the following requirements–

The steps of the flexible ladder shall–

    (i) be made of ash, oak, elm or teak or other hardwood or other material of equivalent strength, stiffness and durability. The four lowest steps may be of rubber or other material of equivalent strength, stiffness and durability;

    (ii) be made in one piece, and in the case of wooden steps, free of knots;

    (iii) have an efficient non-slip surface;

    (iv) be not less than 480 millimetres long, 115 millimetres wide, and 25 millimetres in depth, excluding any non-slip device or grooving;

    (v) be equally spaced not less than 300 millimetres nor more than 380 millimetres apart; and

    (vi) be secured in such a manner that each will remain horizontal;

    Provided that–

    (aa) No flexible ladder section shall have more than two replacement steps which are secured in position by a method different from that used in the original construction of the flexible ladder section and any steps so secured shall be replaced as soon as reasonably practicable by steps secured in position by the method used in the original construction of the flexible ladder. When any replacement step is secured to the side ropes of the ladder by means of grooves in the sides of the step, such grooves shall be in the longer sides of the step; and

    (bb) the side ropes of the flexible ladder section shall consist of two manila ropes not less than 18 millimetres in diameter on each side. Each rope shall be left uncovered by any other material and shall be continuous with no joins below the top step.

(c) The steps of the flexible ladder section and those of the rigid ladder section shall be in the same vertical line, of the same width, spaced vertically equidistant and placed as close as practicable to the ship's side. The handholds of both parts of the ladder section shall be aligned as closely as possible.

(d) If belting is fitted in the way of the hoist position, such belting shall be cut back sufficiently to allow the hoist to be placed as close as practicable to the ship's side.

(8) *Operation of the hoist*

(a) The master shall ensure that rigging and testing of the hoist pursuant to paragraph (9) below and the embarkation and disembarkation of any person is supervised by a responsible officer of the ship. Any person engaged in rigging and operating the hoist shall be instructed in the rigging and operating procedures to be adopted and the equipment shall be tested prior to the embarkation or disembarkation of any person.

(b) The master shall ensure that lighting is provided so that the hoist overside, its controls and the position where the person carried embarks or disembarks on the ship is adequately lit; and that the equipment specified in regulation 7(6)(ii), (iii), and (iv) is kept at hand ready for use if required.

(c) The master shall ensure that a pilot ladder complying with the provisions of regulation 7 is rigged adjacent to the hoist and available for immediate use so that access to it is available from the hoist during any point of its travel; and that the pilot ladder is capable of reaching the sea level from its own point of access to the ship.

(d) The position on the ship's side where the hoist will be lowered shall be indicated.

(e) An adequately protected stowage position shall be provided for the hoist. In very cold weather the master shall ensure that the hoist is rigged in adequate time having regard to the danger of ice formation.

(9) *Testing*

(a) Every new hoist shall be subjected to an overload test of 2.2 times the working load. During this test the load shall be lowered a distance of not less than 5 metres and the brake applied to stop the hoist drum. Where a winch is not fitted with a brake, and depends upon an equally effective arrangement as prescribed in regulation 9(5)(b) to support the load in the event of power failure, the load shall be lowered at the maximum permitted lowering speed and a power failure shall be simulated to show that the hoist will stop and support the load.

(b) An operating test of 10 per cent overload shall be carried out after installation on board the ship.

(c) Subsequent examinations of the hoists under working conditions shall be made at each annual or intermediate and renewal survey for the vessel's safety equipment certificate.

(d) (i) The master shall ensure that, in addition to the testing required in sub-paragraphs (a), (b) and (c) of this paragraph, regular test rigging and inspection, including a load test to at least 150 kg, shall be carried out by designated ship's personnel at intervals of not more than six months.

(ii) A record to that effect shall be made by the master in the ship's official logbook.

(iii) In ships not required to keep an official logbook, a record to that effect shall be made by the master or person responsible for maintaining such records and be retained on board for a period of not less than 12 months.

Equivalents

10. Where these Regulations require that a particular fitting, material, appliance or apparatus or type thereof, shall be fitted or carried in a ship, or that any particular provision shall be made, the Secretary of State may permit any other fitting, material, appliance or apparatus, or type thereof to be fitted or carried, or any other provision to be made in that ship if he is satisfied after trial thereof or otherwise that such other fitting, material, appliance or apparatus, or type thereof, or provision, is at least as effective as that required by these Regulations.

Penalties

11.—(1) A master of a ship who contravenes any provision of regulations 6, 8(4) or 9(8)(a), (b), (c), (e) or (9)(d)(i) shall be guilty of an offence and liable on summary conviction to a fine not exceeding £1000 or, on conviction on indictment, to imprisonment for a term not exceeding two years and a fine.

(2) An owner of a ship who contravenes regulations 5 or 8(1) or (4) shall be guilty of an offence and liable on summary conviction to a fine not exceeding £1000 or, on conviction on indictment, to imprisonment for a term not exceeding two years and a fine.

(3) An officer who fails to supervise as instructed by the master and required by regulations 6(d) or 9(8)(a) shall be guilty of an offence and liable on summary conviction to a fine not exceeding £500 or on conviction on indictment to imprisonment for a term not exceeding one year and a fine.

(4) An officer responsible for the maintenance of the hoist who fails to keep a record as required by regulation 8(5) shall be guilty of an offence and liable on summary conviction to a fine not exceeding £500.

(5) Any person who fails to comply with regulation 9(9)(d)(ii) or (iii) shall be guilty of an offence and liable on summary conviction to a fine not exceeding £50.

(6) It shall be a defence for a person charged with an offence under these Regulations to prove that he took all reasonable steps and exercised all due diligence to ensure that the Regulations were complied with.

Power to detain

12. If a ship to which these Regulations apply carries a pilot ladder or hoist which does not conform to the specified requirements of these Regulations, the ship shall be liable to be detained and section 692(1)–(3) of the Merchant Shipping Act 1894 (**a**) (which relates to the detention of a ship) shall have effect in relation to the ship, subject to the modification that for the words "this Act" wherever they appear, there were substituted "the Merchant Shipping (Pilot Ladders and Hoists) Regulations 1987".

Signed by authority of the Secretary of State.

David B. Mitchell
Minister of State,
18th November 1987   Department of Transport

EXPLANATORY NOTE

(This note is not part of the Regulations)

These Regulations revoke and re-enact, with amendments, the Merchant Shipping (Pilot Ladders and Hoists) Regulations 1980. The major amendments are:

1. The owner is required to provide associated equipment and accommodation ladder (when applicable) in addition to the pilot ladder and to ensure that suitable positions are provided for securing the pilot ladder.

2. The master is required to ensure that the associated equipment and the pilot ladder, accommodation ladder and hoist are in good order, efficient and used correctly.

3. Provision of a defence to ensure that a person will not be liable to conviction of a criminal offence if he has done what he can to avoid committing the offence.

(**a**) 1894 c.60.

STATUTORY INSTRUMENTS

1987 No. 1963

CUSTOMS AND EXCISE

The General Betting Duty Regulations 1987

Made - - - -	*19th November 1987*
Laid before the House of Commons	*27th November 1987*
Coming into force	*20th December 1987*

The Commissioners of Customs and Excise, in exercise of the powers conferred on them by section 12(2) of, and paragraph 2 of Schedule 1 to, the Betting and Gaming Duties Act 1981(a) and of all other powers enabling them in that behalf, hereby make the following Regulations:

PART I

PRELIMINARY

Citation and commencement

1. These Regulations may be cited as the General Betting Duty Regulations 1987 and shall come into force on 20th December 1987.

Interpretation

2.—(1) In these Regulations, unless the context otherwise requires –

"the Act" means the Betting and Gaming Duties Act 1981;

"Collector" means the Collector of Customs and Excise, Manchester;

"duty" means general betting duty chargeable under section 1 of the Act;

"month" means a calendar month or such other period as the Commissioners allow;

"occupier" includes –

(a) any person who provides or intends to provide facilities on any track for any persons engaging or proposing to engage in any activity by reason of which they are or may be or may become liable for the payment of duty;

(b) any person who permits or intends to permit any such activity on any track; and

(c) any organiser of a meeting;

"officer" means the proper officer of Customs and Excise;

"off-course bet" means a bet which is not an on-course bet;

(a) 1981 c.63; paragraph 2 of Schedule 1 was amended by the Finance Act 1987 (c. 16), section 3(3).

"off-course bookmaker" means a person who intends to carry on or is carrying on bookmaking other than at a meeting;

"on-course bookmaker" means a person who intends to carry on or is carrying on bookmaking at a meeting.

(2) In these Regulations any reference to a form prescribed in the Schedule to these Regulations includes a reference to a form to the like effect which has been approved by the Commissioners.

Revocation and savings

3.—(1) Subject to paragraph (2) below, the General Betting Duty Regulations 1986(a) and the General Betting Duty (Amendment) Regulations 1987(b) are hereby revoked.

(2) The revoked Regulations, insofar as they relate to accounting periods, returns and payments of duty shall continue to apply to periods partly completed at the date of revocation.

PART II

OFF-COURSE BOOKMAKERS

Records

4.—(1) An off-course bookmaker shall not accept a bet unless –
   (a) in the case of a bettor in person, the particulars are recorded on a slip at the time that the bet is made;
   (b) in the case of a bet made by letter or other method involving the delivery or print out of paper bearing details of the bet, he retains the letter or other paper; and
   (c) in the case of a bet made by telephone, or any other method not covered by sub-paragraphs (a) and (b) above, he records particulars of it on a slip, or in such other manner as the Commissioners allow.

(2) Slips, letters and other papers recording a bet made with an off-course bookmaker on any day shall, unless the Commissioners otherwise allow –
   (a) immediately be marked or be caused to be marked by the bookmaker with the first unused number from a consecutive series starting with 1 and ending with not less than 9,999;
   (b) be kept by the bookmaker on the premises on which the bets to which they relate are made; and
   (c) be kept by the bookmaker for a period of 6 months intact and separate from those recording bets made on any other day and shall be produced or delivered on demand to an officer.

Vouchers

5. In the case of a bet by a bettor in person, the off-course bookmaker shall immediately issue to the bettor a voucher bearing the same number as in regulation 4(2)(a) above.

Returns and payments

6.—(1) Every off-course bookmaker shall complete and sign a return and shall furnish such return to the Collector.

(2) A return under this regulation shall be made monthly in the form numbered 1 in the Schedule to these Regulations and such return shall be furnished not later than the 15th day following the end of the month to which it relates.

(a) S.I. 1986/400.   (b) S.I. 1987/312.

(3) At the time of making the return required by this regulation the off-course bookmaker shall pay to the Collector the amount of duty due.

Accounts – off-course

7.—(1) Save as the Commissioners otherwise allow, every off-course bookmaker shall keep a betting duty account in the form numbered 2 in the Schedule to these Regulations.

(2) Every off-course bookmaker shall, by noon on the first working day following the day on which the bets were made, indelibly complete the daily account contained in the betting duty account.

(3) Every off-course bookmaker shall, at the time payment is due under regulation 6 above, indelibly complete the summary account contained in the betting duty account.

(4) Every off-course bookmaker shall upon demand produce his betting duty account to an officer; and that betting duty account, whether in the hands of the bookmaker or another person, shall be and remain the property of the Commissioners.

(5) No-one shall make any alteration or addition to a betting duty account except in accordance with this regulation or except as directed by an officer.

PART III

ON-COURSE BOOKMAKERS

Notification

8. An on-course bookmaker shall not accept an off-course bet unless he has given the Commissioners 7 clear days' notice in writing that he intends to accept such bets.

Field books

9.—(1) Save as the Commissioners otherwise allow, every on-course bookmaker shall –

   (a) keep a field book and retain it for a period of 6 years after the last entry made therein; and

   (b) keep his current field book at his stand during the time he is carrying on bookmaking and on demand produce it to an officer.

(2) Every field book shall –

   (a) be a volume with permanently bound pages; and

   (b) indelibly bear the name and betting duty reference number of the bookmaker; and

   (c) have each page consecutively and indelibly numbered.

Entries in field books

10.—(1) Every on-course bookmaker shall, on receipt of a bet, immediately enter in his field book –

   (a) the date and amount of the bet;

   (b) the event and the contingency which are the subjects of the bet;

   (c) in respect of a bet received by telephone the letter "T";

   (d) in respect of an off-course bet the word "OFF"; and

   (e) in respect of a bet placed by a bookmaker, the name of that bookmaker.

(2) Every on-course bookmaker shall, immediately after each event, enter in his field book the total amount of off-course bets received by him in respect of that event.

(3) Save as the Commissioners otherwise allow, every on-course bookmaker shall, within 7 days of receiving a bet placed by a bookmaker, enter in his field book the betting duty reference number of that bookmaker.

(4) Save as the Commissioners otherwise allow, all entries in field books shall be made indelibly.

Returns and payments

11. Every on-course bookmaker who accepts an off-course bet shall comply with regulation 6 above (returns and payments) as if he were an off-course bookmaker, but shall declare only off-course bets.

Accounts – off-course

12. Every on-course bookmaker who accepts an off-course bet shall comply with regulation 7 above (accounts) as if he were an off-course bookmaker, but shall enter only details of off-course bets.

PART IV

TRACK OCCUPIERS

Notice of meeting

13. Every track occupier shall give notice in writing to the Commissioners 7 days before the date of any meeting specifying the date and the time of the meeting.

Changes to meetings

14. Save as the Commissioners otherwise allow, the track occupier shall, if he intends to make either of the following changes, give notice in writing of the change to the Commissioners 7 days before the change takes place –

(a) in the occupation of the track by its transfer to any other person; or

(b) in the days or times when meetings are to be held.

Notice of irregularities

15. A track occupier shall, immediately it is known to him, bring to the notice of the Commissioners or of an officer any contravention or attempted contravention of these Regulations by a bookmaker.

PART V

GENERAL

Security

16. The Commissioners may require a bookmaker to provide security for the payment of any duty which is or may become due from him.

King's Beam House,
Mark Lane,
London EC3R 7HE
19th November 1987

Bryce Knox
Commissioner of Customs and Excise

Form No. 1   **SCHEDULE**   (Regulation 6)

General Betting Duty

BD 211

Bookmaker's Monthly Return

H M Customs
and Excise

For the period   **to**
(These dates must not be altered without the agreement of Customs and Excise)

Fold here

Period	
Due to reach BDCC by	

- You must ensure that the completed form and any duty payable are received no later than the due date by the Collector, BDCC, Custom House, Trafford Road, Salford M5 2RD. Allow for delays in the post.
- Envelopes have been provided for your use.
- Nil returns are required.
- Make cheques and postal orders payable to 'HM Customs and Excise' and crossed 'account payee'. Do not send cash. If you must send cash, in your own interest use registered post.

Betting Duty Reference No.

		£	p
Amount of stakes taken in the above period	1		
Amount of duty due on the above stakes	2		
Deduct any overdeclaration made on previous return(s) (except those notified in writing by Customs and Excise)	3		
Add any underdeclaration made on previous return(s) (except those notified in writing by Customs and Excise)	4		
Net amount of duty due	5		

Declaration by Signatory

....
(Full name in BLOCK LETTERS)

...eclare that the information given above is true and complete.

...\ remittance for the duty due is enclosed.

...iigned ....

...\)ate ....

Warning

...\)ailure to furnish a return, the furnishing of a return which is false
...\n any material particular or failure to pay duty by the due date are
...)ffences which may involve heavy penalties.

FOR OFFICIAL USE			
Amount Received		£	p

Remittance Code	Ø	1	3	5	7

Initials

Post Opening Serial No.

Form No. 2 (Regulation 7)

Month .... Year ....

Daily Account

Date	Amount of bets made (Daily Total) £	p
Total B / F		
Total		

Date	Amount of bets made (Daily Total) £	p
Total C/F		

	£	p
(1) Total stakes for month		
(2) Uplift Poundage / any to come		
Total liable for duty (1 + 2)		
Amount of duty due		
Previous over-declarations / under declarations		
Amount paid		
Date paid		

Month .... Year ....

Daily Account

Date	Amount of bets made (Daily Total) £	p
Total B / F		
Total		

Date	Amount of bets made (Daily Total) £	p
Total C/F		

Summary Account

	£	p
(1) Total stakes for month		
(2) Uplift Poundage / any to come		
Total liable for duty (1 + 2)		
Amount of duty due		
Previous over-declarations / under declarations		
Amount paid		
Date paid		

EXPLANATORY NOTE

(This note is not part of the Regulations)

These Regulations replace the General Betting Duty Regulations 1986, with modifications which reflect the abolition of the on-course rate of general betting duty by section 3 of the Finance Act 1987. The main changes are as follows: –

    (a) ON-COURSE BOOKMAKERS (PART III)

        (i) before dutiable off-course bets can be accepted by an on-course bookmaker, 7 clear days' notice must be given in writing of the intention to accept such bets (regulation 8);

       (ii) on-course bookmakers who accept off-course bets are required to furnish duty returns and pay duty (regulation 11);

      (iii) on-course bookmakers continue to be required to keep field books (Regulations 9 and 10); but the recording of stake totals after each event and the keeping of a betting duty account now applies only to bookmakers accepting dutiable off-course bets (regulations 10(2) and 12);

      (iv) on-course bookmakers are no longer required to possess and produce an authority before commencing bookmaking at a track and to number bets and issue betting tickets;

    (b) TRACK OCCUPIERS (PART IV)

      Track occupiers are no longer required to hold and furnish track registers, require production of authorities and signature of track attendance registers.

    (c) TOTALISATOR OPERATORS

      Totalisator operators are no longer required to make returns and payments or keep a betting duty account.

The Regulations come into force on the 20th December 1987.

STATUTORY INSTRUMENTS

1987 No. 1964

INDUSTRIAL TRAINING

The Industrial Training Levy (Road Transport) Order 1987

Made - - - -	19th November 1987
Laid before Parliament	30th November 1987
Coming into force	1st August 1988

Whereas proposals made by the Road Transport Industry Training Board for the raising and collection of a levy have been submitted to, and approved by, the Manpower Services Commission under section 11(1) of the Industrial Training Act 1982(a) ("the 1982 Act") and have thereafter been submitted by the said Commission to the Secretary of State under that subsection;

And whereas in pursuance of section 11(3) of the 1982 Act the said proposals include provision for the exemption from the levy of employers who, in view of the small number of their employees, ought in the opinion of the Secretary of State to be exempted from it;

And whereas the Secretary of State estimates that the amount which, disregarding any exemptions, will be payable by virtue of this Order by any employer in the road transport industry, does not exceed an amount which the Secretary of State estimates is equal to one per cent. of the relevant emoluments being the aggregate of the emoluments and payments intended to be disbursed as emoluments which have been paid or are payable by any such employer to or in respect of persons employed in the industry, in respect of the period specified in the said proposals as relevant, that is to say the period hereafter referred to in this Order as "the twenty-second base period";

And whereas the Secretary of State is satisfied that proposals published by the said Board in pursuance of section 13 of the 1982 Act provide for exemption certificates relating to the levy in such cases as he considers necessary;

Now, therefore, the Secretary of State in exercise of the powers conferred on him by sections 11(2), 12(3) and 12(4) of the 1982 Act, and of all other powers enabling him in that behalf, hereby makes the following Order:–

Citation and commencement

1. This Order may be cited as the Industrial Training Levy (Road Transport) Order 1987 and shall come into force on 1st August 1988.

2.—(1) In this Order unless the context otherwise requires:–

    (a) "assessment" means an assessment of an employer to the levy;

    (b) "the Board" means the Road Transport Industry Training Board;

    (c) "business" means any activities of industry or commerce;

(a) 1982 c.10.

(d) "employer" means a person who is an employer in the road transport industry at any time in the twenty-second levy period;

(e) "exemption certificate" means a certificate issued by the Board under section 14 of the Industrial Training Act 1982;

(f) "the industrial training order" means the Industrial Training (Road Transport Board) Order 1966(a);

(g) "the levy" means the levy imposed by the Board in respect of the twenty-second levy period;

(h) "notice" means a notice in writing;

(i) "road transport establishment" means an establishment in Great Britain engaged in the twenty-second base period wholly or mainly in the road transport industry for a total of twenty-seven or more weeks or, being an establishment that commenced to carry on business in the twenty-second base period, for a total number of weeks exceeding one-half of the number of weeks in the part of the said period commencing with the day on which business was commenced and ending on the last day thereof;

(j) "the road transport industry" does not include any activities which have been transferred from the industry of the Board to the industry of another industrial training board by one of the transfer orders but save as aforesaid means any one or more of the activities which, subject to the provisions of paragraph 2 of Schedule 1 to the industrial training order, are specified in paragraph 1 of that Schedule as the activities of the road transport industry or, in relation to an establishment whose activities have been transferred to the industry of the Board by one of the transfer orders, any activities so transferred;

(k) "the twenty-second base period" means the period of twelve months that commenced on 6th April 1987;

(l) "the twenty-second levy period" means the period commencing with the day upon which this Order comes into force and ending on 31st July 1989;

(m) "the transfer orders" means:–

   (i) the Industrial Training (Transfer of the Activities of Establishments) (No. 2) Order 1974(b),

   (ii) the Industrial Training (Transfer of the Activities of Establishments) (No. 2) Order 1975(c),

   (iii) the Industrial Training (Transfer of the Activities of Establishments) Order 1976(d),

   (iv) the Industrial Training (Transfer of the Activities of Establishments) (No. 3) Order 1976(e),

   (v) the Industrial Training (Transfer of the Activities of Establishments) Order 1977(f),

   (vi) the Industrial Training (Transfer of the Activities of Establishments) Order 1978(g),

   (vii) the Industrial Training (Transfer of the Activities of Establishments) (No. 2) Order 1978(h),

   (viii) the Industrial Training (Transfer of the Activities of Establishments) Order 1979(i),

   (ix) the Industrial Training (Transfer of the Activities of Establishments) Order 1980(j),

   (x) the Industrial Training (Transfer of the Activities of Establishments) (No. 2) Order 1980(k),

   (xi) the Industrial Training (Transfer of the Activities of Establishments) Order 1981(l), and

---

(a) S.I. 1966/1112, amended by S.I. 1982/664.   (b) S.I. 1974/1495.   (c) S.I. 1975/1157.
(d) S.I. 1976/396.   (e) S.I. 1976/2110.   (f) S.I. 1977/1951.
(g) S.I. 1978/448.   (h) S.I. 1978/1225.   (i) S.I. 1979/793.
(j) S.I. 1980/586.   (k) S.I. 1980/1753.   (l) S.I. 1981/1041.

(xii) the Industrial Training (Transfer of the Activities of Establishments) Order 1985(**a**).

(2) Any reference in this Order to an establishment that commences to carry on business or that ceases to carry on business shall not be taken to apply where the location of the establishment is changed but its business is continued wholly or mainly at or from the new location, or where the suspension of activities is of a temporary or seasonal nature.

Imposition of the levy

3. The levy to be imposed by the Board on employers in respect of the twenty-second levy period shall be assessed in accordance with the provisions of the Schedule to this Order.

Assessment notices

4.—(1) The Board shall serve an assessment notice on every employer assessed to the levy.

(2) The amount payable under an assessment notice shall be rounded down to the nearest £1.

(3) An assessment notice shall state the Board's address for the service of a notice of appeal or of an application for an extension of time for appealing.

(4) An assessment notice may be served on the person assessed to the levy either by delivering it to him personally or by leaving it, or sending it to him by post, at his last known address or place of business in the United Kingdom or, if that person is a corporation, by leaving it, or sending it by post to the corporation at such address or place of business or at its registered or principal office.

Payment of levy

5.—(1) Subject to the provisions of this Article and of Articles 6 and 7, the amount of the levy payable under an assessment notice served by the Board shall be due and payable to the Board in two instalments, as follows –

(a) the first instalment, being that portion of the levy from which, in accordance with paragraph 4 of the Schedule to this Order, exemption certificates are not to exempt any employer in the industry, shall be due and payable on 1st September 1988, or one month after the date of the assessment notice, whichever is the later;

(b) the second instalment, being the remainder, if any, of the levy, shall be due and payable on 1st December 1988, or one month after the date of the assessment notice, whichever is the later.

(2) The amount of an assessment shall not be recoverable by the Board until there has expired the time allowed for appealing against the assessment by Article 7(1) of this Order and any further period or periods of time that the Board or an industrial tribunal may have allowed for appealing under paragraph (2) or (3) of that Article or, where an appeal is brought, until the appeal is decided or withdrawn.

Withdrawal of assessment

6.—(1) the Board may, by a notice served on the person assessed to the levy in the same manner as an assessment notice, withdraw an assessment if that person has appealed against that assessment under the provisions of Article 7 of this Order and the appeal has not been entered in the Register of Appeals kept under the appropriate Regulations specified in paragraph (5) of that Article.

(2) The withdrawal of an assessment shall be without prejudice to the power of the Board to serve a further assessment notice on the employer.

(**a**) S.I. 1985/1662.

Appeals

7.—(1) A person assessed to the levy may appeal to an industrial tribunal against the assessment within one month from the date of the service of the assessment notice or within any further period or periods of time that may be allowed by the Board or an industrial tribunal under the following provisions of this Article.

(2) The Board by notice may for good cause allow a person assessed to the levy to appeal to an industrial tribunal against the assessment at any time within the period of four months from the date of the service of the assessment notice or within such further period or periods as the Board may allow before such time as may then be limited for appealing has expired.

(3) If the Board shall not allow an application for extension of time for appealing, an industrial tribunal shall upon application made to the tribunal by the person assessed to the levy have the like powers as the Board under the last foregoing paragraph.

(4) If the Board shall not allow an application for extension of time for appealing, an industrial tribunal shall upon application made to the tribunal by the person assessed to the levy have the like powers as the Board under the last foregoing paragraph.

(5) In the case of an assessment that has reference to an establishment that ceases to carry on business in the twenty-second levy period on any day after the date of the service of the assessment notice, the foregoing provisions of this Article shall have effect as if for the period of four months from the date of the service of the assessment notice mentioned in paragraph (2) of this Article there were substituted the period of six months from the date of the cessation of business.

(6) An appeal or an application to an industrial tribunal under this Article shall be made in accordance with the Industrial Tribunals (England and Wales) Regulations 1965(a) except where the assessment relates to persons employed at or from one or more establishments which are wholly in Scotland and to no other persons in which case the appeal or application shall be made in accordance with the Industrial Tribunals (Scotland) Regulations 1965(b).

(7) The powers of an industrial tribunal under paragraph (3) of this Article may be exercised by the President of the Industrial Tribunals (England and Wales) or by the President of the Industrial Tribunals (Scotland) as the case may be.

Evidence

8.—(1) Upon the discharge by a person assessed to the levy of his liability under an assessment the Board shall if so requested issue to him a certificate to that effect.

(2) The production in any proceedings of a document purporting to be certified by the Secretary of the Board to be a true copy of an assessment or other notice issued by the Board or purporting to be a certificate such as is mentioned in the foregoing paragraph of this Article shall, unless the contrary is proved, be sufficient evidence of the document and of the facts stated therein.

Signed by order of the Secretary of State

Patrick Nicholls
Parliamentary Under Secretary of State,
Department of Employment

19th November 1986

(a) S.I. 1965/1101; relevant amending instruments are S.I. 1967/301, 1977/1473.　(b) S.I. 1965/1157; relevant amending instruments are S.I. 1967/302, 1977/1474.

Article 3   SCHEDULE

1.—(1) In this Schedule unless the context otherwise requires –

(a) "business" means any activities of industry or commerce;

(b) "emoluments" means all emoluments assessable to income tax under Schedule E of the Income and Corporation Taxes Act 1970(**a**) (other than pensions), being emoluments from which tax under that Schedule is deductible, whether or not tax in fact falls to be deducted from any particular payment thereof;

(c) "the relevant date" means the 5th April 1988;

(d) "the relevant establishment" means the road transport establishment of an employer other than one which is an establishment of an employer who is exempted by virtue of paragraph 3 of this Schedule;

(e) other expressions have the meanings assigned to them respectively by paragraph 3 or 4 of Schedule 1 to the industrial training order or by Article 2 of this Order.

(2) For the purposes of this Schedule no regard shall be had to the emoluments of any person employed as follows:–

(a) wholly in agriculture;

(b) wholly as a registered dock worker on dock work; or

(c) wholly in the supply of food or drink for immediate consumption.

2. Subject to the provisions of this Schedule, the levy shall be assessed by the Board in respect of each employer and the amount thereof shall be equal to 0.8 per cent. of the sum of the emoluments of all the persons employed by the employer in the twenty-second base period at or from the relevant establishment or establishments.

3. There shall be exempt from the levy an employer –

(a) in whose case the sum of the emoluments of all the persons employed by him in the twenty-second base period at or from his road transport establishment or establishments is £26,500 or less (£24,500 or less in the case of an employer wholly or mainly engaged on the relevant date in any of the activities comprised in Group 1 of the Appendix to this Schedule, or £35,000 or less in the case of an employer wholly or mainly engaged on the relevant date in any of the activities comprised in Group 2 of the said Appendix);

(b) who was wholly or mainly engaged on the relevant date in giving instruction by way of business in the driving of heavy goods vehicles.

4. Exemption certificates issued by the Board shall not exempt any employer in the industry from that portion of the levy which equals 0.2 per cent. of the sum of the emoluments upon which the levy is to be assessed under paragraph 2 above.

5. Where any persons whose emoluments are taken into account for the purpose of the preceding paragraphs of this Schedule were employed at or from an establishment that ceases to carry on business in the twenty-second levy period, the sum of the emoluments of those persons shall, for the purposes only of paragraph 2 above, be reduced in the same proportion as the number of days between the commencement of the said levy period and the date of cessation of business (both dates inclusive) bears to the number of days in the said levy period.

APPENDIX

Column 1	Column 2
Group No.	Description of activities
1	The carriage or haulage of goods by goods vehicles on roads for hire or reward.
	The removal of furniture by way of business.
2	Repair of or dealing in motor cycles.
	The letting out on hire (without the services of a driver) of motor vehicles designed to convey eight passengers or less or (with or without the services of a driver) goods vehicles for the carriage or haulage of goods.
	Dealing (not being selling by retail) in components, replacements, spare parts or accessories (not being tyres) for motor vehicles or goods vehicles.

(**a**) 1970 c.10.

EXPLANATORY NOTE

(This note is not part of the Order)

This Order, which comes into force on 1st August 1988, gives effect to proposals of the Road Transport Industry Training Board which were submitted to and approved by the Manpower Services Commission, and thereafter submitted by the Manpower Services Commission to the Secretary of State. The proposals are for the imposition of a levy on employers in the road transport industry for the purpose of raising money towards meeting the expenses of the Board.

The levy is to be imposed in respect of the twenty-second levy period commencing with the day upon which this Order comes into force and ending on 31st July 1989. The levy will be assessed by the Board and there will be a right of appeal against an assessment to an industrial tribunal.

STATUTORY INSTRUMENTS

1987 No. 1965

NATIONAL HEALTH SERVICE, ENGLAND AND WALES

The National Health Service (General Dental Services) Amendment (No. 3) Regulations 1987

Made - - - -	*18th November 1987*
Laid before Parliament	*30th November 1987*
Coming into force	*21st December 1987*

The Secretary of State for Social Services, in exercise of powers conferred on him by sections 35(1) and 36(1) of the National Health Service Act 1977(**a**) and of all other powers enabling him in that behalf, hereby makes the following Regulations:

Citation and commencement

1. These Regulations may be cited as the National Health Service (General Dental Services) Amendment (No. 3) Regulations 1987 and shall come into force on 21st December 1987.

Amendment of regulations

2. In regulation 23(1) of the National Health Service (General Dental Services) Regulations 1973(**b**) (Statement of Remuneration) –

(a) in column 1 (Determination) below "V", there shall be inserted "VA"; and

(b) in column 2 (subject matter of determination), there shall be inserted, so as to relate to determination VA, "Allowances in respect of a dentist undergoing a period of training;".

Signed by authority of the Secretary of State for Social Services.

Edwina Currie
18th November 1987   Parliamentary Under-Secretary of State,
Department of Health and Social Security

(**a**) 1977 c.49; section 35 was substituted by the Family Practitioner Committees (Consequential Modifications) Order 1985 (S.I. 1985/39), article 7(9). Section 36 was amended by the Health and Social Security Act 1984 (c.48), Schedule 3, paragraph 5 and by S.I. 1985/39, article 7(10). For the definition of "regulations", *see* section 128(1) of the National Health Service Act 1977.   (**b**) S.I. 1973/1468; the relevant amending instrument is S.I. 1980/986.

EXPLANATORY NOTE

(This note is not part of the Regulations)

These Regulations amend the National Health Service (General Dental Services) Regulations 1973 which concern arrangements under which dentists provide general dental services under the National Health Service in England and Wales by providing for the Statement of Dental Remuneration (distributed to those providing general dental services), to include allowances in respect of dentists undergoing training.

STATUTORY INSTRUMENTS

1987 No. 1967

SOCIAL SECURITY

The Income Support (General) Regulations 1987

Made - - - -	*20th November 1987*
Coming into force -	*11th April 1988*

ARRANGEMENT OF REGULATIONS

PART I
General

PART II
Conditions of Entitlement

PART III

Membership of a family

PART IV

Applicable amounts

PART V

Income and capital

CHAPTER I: GENERAL

CHAPTER II: INCOME

CHAPTER III: EMPLOYED EARNERS

PART VI

*Applicable amounts and assessment of income and
capital in urgent cases*

70. Urgent cases

71. Applicable amounts in urgent cases

72. Assessment of income and capital in urgent cases

SCHEDULES

Whereas a draft of this instrument was laid before Parliament in accordance with section 83(3) of the Social Security Act 1986 and approved by resolution of each House of Parliament:

Now, therefore, the Secretary of State for Social Services, in exercise of the powers conferred by sections 20(1), (3)(d), (4), (9), (11) and (12), 22(1), (2), (4) and (5) to (9), 23(1), (3) and (5), 51(1)(n) and 84(1) of the Social Security Act 1986(a) and sections 114, 166(1) to (3A) of the Social Security Act 1975(b) and of all other powers enabling him in that behalf by this instrument, which is made before the end of a period of 12 months from the commencement of the enactments under which it is made, hereby makes the following Regulations:

Citation and commencement

1. These Regulations may be cited as the Income Support (General) Regulations 1987 and shall come into force on 11th April 1988.

Interpretation

2.—(1) In these Regulations, unless the context otherwise requires—

" the Act " means the Social Security Act 1986;

" attendance allowance " means—

(a) an attendance allowance under section 35 of the Social Security Act(c);

(a) 1986 c.50; section 84(1) is an interpretation provision and is cited because of the meanings assigned to the words "prescribed" and "regulations".

(b) 1975 c.14; section 114 is applied by section 52(3)(b) of the Social Security Act 1986 (c.50); section 166(3A) is inserted by section 62 of that Act and section 166(1) to (3A) is applied by section 83(1) of that Act.

(c) Section 35 was amended by the National Health Service Act 1977 (c.49), Schedule 15, paragraph 63, by the Social Security Act 1979 (c.18) section 2 and by the Social Security Act 1980 (c.30), Schedule 1, Part II, paragraph 8.

(b) an increase of disablement pension under section 61 or 63 of that Act(a);

(c) a payment under regulations made in exercise of the power conferred by section 159(3)(b) of that Act;

(d) an increase of an allowance which is payable in respect of constant attendance under section 5 of the Industrial Injuries and Diseases (Old Cases) Act 1975(b);

(e) a payment by virtue of article 14, 15, 16, 43 or 44 of the Personal Injuries (Civilians) Scheme 1983(c) or any analogous payment; or

(f) any payment based on need for attendance which is paid as part of a war disablement pension;

" benefit week " has the meaning prescribed in paragraph 4 of Schedule 7 to the Social Security (Claims and Payments) Regulations 1987(d);

" claimant " means a person claiming income support;

" close relative " means a parent, parent-in-law, son, son-in-law, daughter, daughter-in-law, step-parent, step-son, step-daughter, brother, sister, or the spouse of any of the preceding persons or, if that person is one of an unmarried couple, the other member of that couple;

" concessionary payment " means a payment made under arrangements made by the Secretary of State with the consent of the Treasury which is charged either to the National Insurance Fund or to a Departmental Expenditure Vote to which payments of benefit under the Act, the Social Security Act or the Child Benefit Act 1975(e) are charged;

" co-ownership scheme " means a scheme under which a dwelling is let by a housing association and the tenant, or his personal representative, will, under the terms of the tenancy agreement or of the agreement under which he became a member of the association, be entitled, on his ceasing to be a member and subject to any condition stated in either agreement, to a sum calculated by reference directly or indirectly to the value of the dwelling;

" couple " means a married or an unmarried couple;

" course of study " means any full-time course of study or sandwich course whether or not a grant is made for attending it;

"Crown tenant " means a person who occupies a dwelling under a tenancy or licence where the interest of the landlord belongs to Her Majesty in right of the Crown or to a government department or is held in trust for Her Majesty for the purposes of a government department, except (in the case of an interest belonging to Her Majesty in right of the Crown) where the interest is under the management of the Crown Estate Commissioners;

" dwelling occupied as the home " means the dwelling together with any garage, garden and outbuildings, normally occupied by the claimant as his home including any premises not so occupied which it is impracticable or unreasonable to sell separately, in particular, in Scotland, any croft land on which the dwelling is situated.

" earnings " has the meaning prescribed in regulation 35 or, as the case may be, 37;

" employed earner " shall be construed in accordance with section 2(1)(a) of the Social Security Act;

" housing association " has the meaning assigned to it by section 1(1) of the Housing Associations Act 1985(f);

" housing benefit expenditure " means expenditure of a kind for which housing benefit may be granted;

(a) Subsections (3) and (4) of section 61 were added by the Social Security Act 1986 (c.50), section 39 and Schedule 3, paragraph 6.
(b) 1975 c.16.
(c) S.I. 1983/686; the relevant amending instruments are S.I. 1983/1164 and 1984/1675.
(d) S.I. 1987/1968.
(e) 1975 c.61.
(f) 1985 c.69.

"invalid carriage or other vehicle" means a vehicle propelled by petrol engine or by electric power supplied for use on the road and to be controlled by the occupant;

"liable relative" has the meaning prescribed in regulation 54;

"lone parent" means a person who has no partner and who is responsible for, and a member of the same household as, a child or young person;

"long tenancy" means a tenancy granted for a term of years certain exceeding twenty one years, whether or not the tenancy is, or may become, terminable before the end of that term by notice given by or to the tenant or by re-entry, forfeiture (or, in Scotland, irritancy) or otherwise and includes a lease for a term fixed by law under a grant with a covenant or obligation for perpetual renewal unless it is a lease by sub-demise from one which is not a long tenancy;

"mobility allowance" means an allowance under section 37A of the Social Security Act(**a**);

"mobility supplement" means any supplement under article 26A of the Naval, Military and Air Forces etc (Disablement and Death) Service Pensions Order 1983(**b**) including such a supplement by virtue of any other scheme or order or under Article 25A of the Personal Injuries (Civilians) Scheme 1983(**c**);

"net earnings" means such earnings as are calculated in accordance with regulation 36;

"net profit" means such profit as is calculated in accordance with regulation 38;

"non-dependant" has the meaning prescribed in regulation 3;

"non-dependant deduction" means a deduction that is to be made under regulation 17(e) and paragraph 11 of Schedule 3;

"nursing home" has the meaning prescribed in regulation 19(3);

"occupational pension" means any pension or other periodical payment under an occupational pension scheme but does not include any discretionary payment out of a fund established for relieving hardship in particular cases;

"partner" means where a claimant—

    (a) is a member of a married or an unmarried couple, the other member of that couple;

    (b) is married polygamously to two or more members of his household, any such member;

"payment" includes a part of a payment;

"period of study" means—

    (a) in the case of a course of study for one year or less, the period beginning with the start of the course to the end;

    (b) in the case of a course of study for more than one year, in the first or, as the case may be, any subsequent year of the course, the period beginning with the start of the course or, as the case may be, that year's start and ending with either—

        (i) the day before the start of the next year of the course in a case where the student's grant is assessed at a rate appropriate to his studying throughout the year, or, if he does not have a grant, where it would have been assessed at such a rate had he had one; or

        (ii) in any other case the day before the start of the normal summer vacation appropriate to his course,

and, for the purposes of this definition, any period of attendance at the educational establishment which is outside the period of the course shall be treated as part of the period of study;

(**a**) Section 37A was inserted by section 22(1) of the Social Security Pensions Act 1975 (c.60) and amended by the National Health Service Act 1977 (c.49), Schedule 15, paragraph 64, the Social Security Act 1979 (c.18), section 3 and by sections 71 and 86 and Schedule 11 of the Social Security Act 1986 (c.50).
(**b**) S.I. 1983/883; article 26A was added by S.I. 1983/1116 and amended by S.I. 1983/1521 and 1986/592.
(**c**) S.I. 1983/686, amended by S.I. 1983/1164, 1540 and 1986/628.

"policy of life insurance" means any instrument by which the payment of money is assured on death (except death by accident only) or the happening of any contingency dependent on human life, or any instrument evidencing a contract which is subject to payment of premiums for a term dependent on human life;

"polygamous marriage" means any marriage where there is more than one spouse and the ceremony of marriage as between the spouses took place under the law of a country which permits polygamy;

"relative" means close relative, grand-parent, grand-child, uncle, aunt, nephew or neice;

"relevant enactment" has the meaning prescribed in regulation 16(8)(a);

"remunerative work" has the meaning prescribed in regulation 5;

"residential accommodation" has the meaning prescribed in regulation 21(3);

"residential care home" has the meaning prescribed in regulation 19(3);

"self-employed earner" shall be construed in accordance with section 2(1)(b) of the Social Security Act;

"single claimant" means a claimant who neither has a partner nor is a lone parent;

"Social Security Act" means the Social Security Act 1975**(a)**;

"student" has the meaning prescribed in regulation 61;

"supplementary benefit" means a supplementary pension or allowance under section 1 or 4 of the Supplementary Benefits Act 1976**(b)**;

"terminal date" in respect of a claimant means the terminal date in his case for the purposes of regulation 7 of the Child Benefit (General) Regulations 1976**(c)**;

"training allowance" means an allowance (whether by way of periodical grants or otherwise) payable—

(a) out of public funds by a Government department or by or on behalf of the Manpower Services Commission;

(b) to a person for his maintenance or in respect of a member of his family; and

(c) for the period, or part of the period, during which he is following a course of training or instruction provided by, or in pursuance of arrangements made with, that department or approved by that department in relation to him or so provided or approved by or on behalf of that Commission,

but it does not include an allowance paid by any Government department to or in respect of a person by reason of the fact that he is following a course of full-time education or is training as a teacher;

"year of assessment" has the meaning prescribed in section 526(5) of the Income and Corporation Taxes Act 1970**(d)**;

"young person" has the meaning prescribed in regulation 14.

(2) In these Regulations, unless the context otherwise requires, a reference—

(a) to a numbered Part is to the Part of these Regulations bearing that number;

(b) to a numbered regulation or Schedule is to the regulation in or Schedule to these Regulations bearing that number;

(c) in a regulation or Schedule to a numbered paragraph is to the paragraph in that regulation or Schedule bearing that number;

(d) in a paragraph to a lettered or numbered sub-paragraph is to the sub-paragraph in that paragraph bearing that letter or number.

(3) Unless the context requires otherwise, any reference to the claimant's family or, as the case may be, to a member of his family, shall be construed for the purposes of these Regulations as if it included in relation to a polygamous marriage a reference to any partner and to any child or young person who is treated as the responsibility of the claimant or his partner, where that child or young person is a member of the claimant's household.

(a) 1975 c.14.
(b) 1976 c.71, as amended by section 6(1) of, and Part I of Schedule 2 to, the Social Security Act 1980 (c.30).
(c) S.I. 1976/965; the relevant amending instruments are S.I. 1980/1054, 1982/470 and 1987/357.
(d) 1970 c.10.

Definition of non-dependant

3.—(1) In these Regulations, " non-dependant " means any person, except someone to whom paragraph (2) applies, who normally resides with a claimant.

(2) This paragraph applies to—

(a) any member of the claimant's family;

(b) a child or young person who is living with the claimant but who is not a member of his household by virtue of regulation 16 (membership of the same household);

(c) a person who jointly occupies the claimant's dwelling;

(d) subject to paragraph (3), any person who is liable to make payments in respect of his occupation of the dwelling to the claimant or the claimant's partner;

(e) a person who lives with the claimant in order to care for him or a partner of his and who is engaged by a charitable or voluntary body (other than a public or local authority) which makes a charge to the claimant or his partner for the services provided by that person.

(3) A person, other than one to whom sub-paragraph (a) to (c) or (e) of paragraph (2) applies, who lives in board and lodging accommodation or a hostel within the meaning of regulation 20(2) (applicable amounts for persons in board and lodging accommodation and hostels)shall be a non-dependant.

(4) For the purposes of this regulation a person resides with another only if they share any accommodation except a bathroom, a lavatory or a communal area.

(5) In this regulation " communal area " means any area (other than rooms) of common access (including halls and passageways) and rooms of common use in sheltered accommodation.

PART II

CONDITIONS OF ENTITLEMENT

Temporary absence from Great Britain

4.—(1) Where a claimant is entitled to income support for a period immediately preceding a period of temporary absence from Great Britain, his entitlement to income support shall continue during the first four weeks of that period of temporary absence only in the circumstances specified in paragraph (2).

(2) The circumstances in which a claimant's entitlement to income support is to continue during the first four weeks of a temporary absence from Great Britain are that—

(a) the period of absence is unlikely to exceed 52 weeks; and

(b) while absent from Great Britain, the claimant continues to satisfy the other conditions of entitlement to income support; and

(c) any one of the following conditions applies—

(i) the claimant is not required to be available for employment under regulation 8(1) and Schedule 1 other than paragraph 5, 10, 18 to 20 of that Schedule (persons not required to be available for employment); or

(ii) he is not required to be available for employment under regulation 8(1) and paragraph 5 of Schedule 1 (incapacity for work) and his absence from Great Britain is for the sole purpose of receiving treatment from an appropriately qualified person for the incapacity by reason of which he is not required to be so available; or

(iii) he is in Northern Ireland; or

(iv) he is a member of a couple and he and his partner are both absent from Great Britain, and a premium referred to in paragraph 9, 10, 11 or 13 of Schedule 2 (applicable amounts) is applicable in respect of his partner.

Persons treated as engaged in remunerative work

5.—(1)Subject to the following provisions of this regulation, for the purposes of section 20(3)(c) of the Act (conditions of entitlement to income support), remunerative work is work in which a person is engaged, or, where his hours of work fluctuate, he is engaged on average, for not less than 24 hours a week being work for which payment is made or which is done in expectation of payment.

(2) The number of hours for which a person is engaged in work shall be determined—

  (a) where no recognisable cycle has been established in respect of a person's work, by reference to the number of hours or, where those hours are likely to fluctuate, the average of the hours, which he is expected to work in a week;

  (b) where the number of hours for which he is engaged fluctuate, by reference to the average of hours worked over—

    (i) if there is a recognisable cycle of work, the period of one complete cycle (including, where the cycle involves periods in which the person does no work, those periods but disregarding any other absences);

    (ii) in any other case, the period of five weeks immediately before the date of claim or the date of review, or such other length of time as may, in the particular case, enable the person's average hours of work to be determined more accurately.

(3) A person shall be treated as engaged in remunerative work during any period for which he is absent from work referred to in paragraph (1) if the absence is either without good cause or by reason of a recognised, customary or other holiday.

(4) A person who makes a claim and to whom or whose partner section 23 of the Act (trade disputes) applies shall, for the period of seven days following the date on which the stoppage of work due to a trade dispute at his or his partner's place of work commenced or, if there is no stoppage, the date on which he or his partner first withdrew his labour in furtherance of a trade dispute, be treated as engaged in remunerative work.

(5) A person who was, or was treated as being, engaged in remunerative work and in respect of that work earnings to which regulation 35(1)(b) to (d) (earnings of employed earners) applies are payable shall be treated as being engaged in remunerative work for the period for which those earnings are taken into account in accordance with Part V.

Persons not treated as engaged in remunerative work

6. A person shall not be treated as engaged in remunerative work if—

  (a) he is mentally or physically disabled and his earning capacity is, by reason of that disability, reduced to 75 per cent or less of what he would, but for that disability, be reasonably expected to earn;

  (b) he is engaged in child minding in his home;

  (c) he is engaged by a charity or voluntary body or is a volunteer where the only payment received by him or due to be paid to him, is a payment which is to be disregarded under regulation 40(2) and paragraph 2 of Schedule 9 (sums to be disregarded in the calculation of income other than earnings);

  (d) he is engaged on a scheme for which a training allowance is being paid; or

  (e) subject to regulation 5(4) (persons treated as engaged in remunerative work) he is a person to whom section 23 of the Act (trade disputes) applies; or

  (f) he is a person who is not required to be available for employment because regulation 8 and paragraph 4 of Schedule 1 (person caring for another) applies to him.

Meaning of employment

7. For the purposes of section 20(3)(d) of the Act (conditions of entitlement to income support) only work in employed earner's employment within the meaning of the Social Security Act—

  (a) which the claimant can reasonably be expected to do;

  (b) for which payment is made or which is done in expectation of payment; and

(c) for which he would normally be engaged for not less than 24 hours a week or, if he is mentally or physically disabled, such lesser number of hours as, having regard to his disability, he is usually capable of working,

shall be treated as employment.

Persons not required to be available for employment

8.—(1) A person, other than one to whom regulation 10(1)(h) applies (circumstances in which a person is to be treated as available for employment), to whom any paragraph of Schedule 1 (persons not required to be available for employment) applies in any week shall not be required to be available for employment in that week.

(2) A person, other than one to whom regulation 10(1)(h) applies, to whom none of the provisions of Schedule 1 other than paragraph 5 applies, shall, where—

(a) a medical practitioner to whom the question of that person's incapacity for work by reason of some disease or bodily or mental disablement has been referred under regulation 8 of the Social Security (Adjudication) Regulations 1986**(a)** (medical references) is of the opinion that the person is not so incapable; and

(b) that person's medical practitioner continues to supply evidence of his incapacity for work in accordance with regulation 2 of the Social Security (Medical Evidence) Regulations 1976**(b)** (evidence of incapacity for work); and

(c) that person has made and is pursuing an appeal against the determination of an adjudication officer that he is not so incapable; and

(d) that person, were he required to be available for employment, would not be treated as so available under regulation 9(1) (persons treated as available for employment),

not be required to be available for employment pending the determination of his appeal.

Persons treated as available for employment

9.—(1) Except in a case to which regulation 10 (circumstances in which claimants are not to be treated as available for employment) applies, a claimant shall be treated as available for employment if, and only if—

(a) he is available to be employed within the meaning of section 17(1)(a)(i) of the Social Security Act**(c)** or Regulations made under it (requirement to be available to be employed for the purposes of unemployment benefit) in employment to which regulation 7 applies (meaning of employment); or

(b) he is normally engaged for less than the number of hours prescribed in paragraph (c) of regulation 7 in respect of him in employment to which that regulation applies, and he is available, within the meaning of section 17(1)(a)(i) or Regulations made under it, for such further number of hours which would, in aggregate with the number of hours for which he is normally engaged, be not less than the number of hours prescribed in paragraph (c) of regulation 7 for his case; or

(c) he satisfies the conditions in paragraph (2) and is attending—

(i) a course of education at an establishment recognised by the Secretary of State as being, or as comparable to, a school or college; or

(ii) a course of training or instruction analogous to a course for which a training allowance would be payable,

and, in either case, he is prepared to terminate the course immediately a suitable vacancy becomes available to him.

(a) S.I. 1986/2218, to which there are no relevant amending instruments.
(b) S.I. 1976/615; the relevant amending instruments are S.I. 1982/699 and 1987/409.
(c) 1975 c.14; section 17(1) was amended by the Social Security (No. 2) Act 1980 (c.39), sections 3(1), 7(6) and the Schedule.

(2) the conditions referred to in paragraph (1)(c) are that either—

(a) the claimant was, for a continuous period of not less than three months falling immediately before the commencement date,—

(i) in receipt of a qualifying benefit; or

(ii) on a course of training or instruction organised by or on behalf of the Manpower Services Commission as part of the Youth Training Scheme; or

(b) during the period of six months falling immediately before the commencement date the claimant was—

(i) for a period, or periods in aggregate, of not less than three months in receipt of a qualifying benefit or on a course of training or instruction organised by or on behalf of the Manpower Services Commission as part of the Youth Training Scheme; and

(ii) after the period referred to in head (i) of this sub-paragraph or, in the case of periods in aggregate, after the first such period and throughout the remainder of the six months for which that head did not apply to him, engaged in appropriate work;

and that the period of three months referred to in sub-paragraph (a) or, as the case may be, the period of six months referred to in sub-paragraph (b) fell wholly after the terminal date.

(3) In this regulation—

" appropriate work " means remunerative work for the purpose of section 20(3)(c) of the Act (conditions of entitlement to income support) or other work the emoluments from which are such as to disentitle the person engaged in it from a qualifying benefit;

" commencement date " means the date on which the claimant first attended the course of education or course of training or instruction;

" course " means a course in the pursuit of which the time spent receiving instruction or tuition, undertaking supervised study, examination or practical work or taking part in any exercise, experiment or project for which provision is made in the curriculum of the course does not, subject to paragraph (4), exceed 21 hours a week;

" qualifying benefit " means unemployment benefit or sickness benefit under the Social Security Act(a) or, in the case of a claimant who is required to be available for employment under section 20(3)(d) of the Act (conditions of entitlement to income support) or who is not so required under paragraph 5 of Schedule 1 (persons not required to be available by reason of sickness or incapacity), income support.

(4) In calculating the time spent in pursuit of a course for the purpose of this regulation, no account shall be taken of time occupied by meal breaks or spent on unsupervised study, whether undertaken on or off the premises of the educational establishment or place of instruction or training.

Circumstances in which claimants are not to be treated as available for employment

10.—(1) A claimant shall not be treated as available for employment if he is a person to whom any one of the following sub-paragraphs applies—

(a) after a situation in any suitable employment has been properly notified to him as vacant or about to become vacant he has without good cause refused or failed to apply for that situation or refused to accept that situation when offered to him, and that situation is still vacant or open to application;

(b) he has neglected to avail himself of a reasonable opportunity of suitable employment and that opportunity is still available to him;

(c) he has failed to avail himself of a reasonable opportunity of short-term work which is available in the area in which he lives, and—

(i) he is aged 18 or over but under 45;

(a) *See* sections 12(1)(a) and (b) and 14 of the Social Security Act 1975 (c.14); section 12(1)(a) and (b) was amended by the Social Security (No. 2) Act 1980 (c.39), section 7(6) and the Health and Social Security Act 1984 (c.48), Schedule 5, paragraph 2; section 14 was amended by the Social Security Pensions Act 1975 (c.60), sections 18(1) and 65, Schedule 4, paragraph 39, the Social Security Act 1979 (c.18) and section 21(4), Schedule 3, paragraph 6, the Social Security and Housing Benefits Act 1982 (c.24), sections 39(3) and 48, Schedule 4, paragraph 9; the Social Security (No. 2) Act 1980 (c.39), section 7 and the Schedule and the Social Security Act 1986 (c.50), section 86, Schedule 10, paragraph 83.

(ii) his partner, if any, is aged under 45;

(iii) there is no child or young person who is a member of his family;

(iv) his partner or, as the case may be, the claimant herself is not pregnant; and

(v) neither he nor his partner, if any, is mentally or physically disabled;

(d) he has placed restrictions on the nature, hours, rate of remuneration or locality or other conditions of employment which he is prepared to accept and as a consequence of those restrictions he has no reasonable prospects of securing employment; but this sub-paragraph shall not apply where—

    (i) he is prevented from having reasonable prospects of securing employment consistent with those restrictions only as a result of adverse industrial conditions in the locality or localities concerned which may reasonably be regarded as temporary, and, having regard to all the circumstances, personal and other, the restrictions which he imposes are reasonable; or

    (ii) the restrictions are nevertheless reasonable in view of his physical condition; or

    (iii) the restrictions are nevertheless reasonable having regard both to the nature of his usual occupation and also to the time which has elapsed since he became unemployed;

(e) having failed to comply with a written notice given or sent to him by or on behalf of the Secretary of State or the Manpower Services Commission requesting him to report at a specified time, place and date to an officer of the Department of Health and Social Security, the Department of Employment, the Manpower Services Commission or a local education authority for an interview in connection with his prospects of employment, he fails without good cause to comply with the requirements of a further notice given or sent to him within 14 days of the date specified in the first notice by or on behalf of the Secretary of State or, as the case may be, the Manpower Services Commission and requesting him to report as aforesaid at a time, place and date specified in the further notice for the purpose of such an interview;

(f) he has been disallowed unemployment benefit on the ground that he failed to claim in the manner prescribed by regulation 4 of the Social Security (Claims and Payments) Regulations 1987(a) (making a claim for benefit) by virtue of the fact that the form approved by the Secretary of State for the purpose of claiming was not duly completed so far as it related to his availability for employment; or

(g) he is a share fisherman within the meaning of the Social Security (Mariners' Benefits) Regulations 1975(b) who is not entitled to unemployment benefit under the Social Security Act because he has failed to satisfy the additional condition for receipt of that benefit in paragraph (5) or (8) of regulation 8 of those Regulations (that he performed no work as a sea-going or on-shore share fisherman and that he has not neglected to avail himself of a reasonable opportunity of employment as a fisherman);

(h) he is a student during the period of study other than one to whom paragraph 1, 2, 7 or 20 of Schedule 1 applies (persons not required to be available for employment) but in the case of paragraph 20 only where the student is a person to whom regulation 70(3)(a) applies (certain persons from abroad).

(2) A determination that a claimant is not to be treated as available for employment—

(a) under paragraph (1)(a), shall apply for a period not exceeding—

    (i) the period during which the situation in question remains vacant; or

    (ii) 13 weeks,

whichever is the shorter;

(b) under paragraph (1)(b), shall apply for a period not exceeding—

    (i) the period during which the opportunity is still available to him; or

    (ii) 13 weeks,

whichever is the shorter;

(a) S.I. 1987/1968.
(b) S.I. 1975/529.

III/1ee*

(c) under paragraph (1)(c)—

  (i) shall not apply until the claimant has been given 14 days' notice in writing and that period has expired, and then

  (ii) shall apply for a period not exceeding the period during which the opportunity is still available to him or, if shorter, the period of 13 weeks;

(d) under paragraph (1)(d), shall apply for so long as the claimant has no reasonable prospect of employment as a consequence of the restrictions referred to in that paragraph;

(e) under paragraph (1)(e), shall apply on the day specified in the further notice and any subsequent day falling before the day on which the claimant reports to an officer of the Department of Health and Social Security, the Department of Employment, the Manpower Services Commission or a local education authority at the place specified in the notice and there attends an interview in connection with his prospects of employment or before the day on which the Secretary of State or, as the case may be, the Manpower Services Commission rescinds the further notice, whichever event first occurs;

(f) under paragraph (1)(f), shall apply for so long as the claimant fails to claim in the manner referred to in that paragraph;

(g) under paragraph (1)(g) or (h), shall apply for so long as that paragraph continues to apply to him.

(3) In this regulation—

(a) employment shall not be deemed to be employment suitable in the case of any claimant if it is employment to which subsection (4) of section 20 of the Social Security Act (employment not to be deemed suitable for purposes of that section) applies;

(b) " properly notified " means notified by an officer acting on behalf of the Secretary of State, or by the Manpower Services Commission, a local education authority or some other recognised agency, or by or on behalf of an employer.

Registration for employment

11.—(1) Subject to paragraph (2), a claimant who—

(a) is aged less than 18; and

(b) is required to be available for employment for the purposes of section 20(3)(d)(i) of the Act (conditions of entitlement to income support);

must also be registered for employment in accordance with paragraph (3).

(2) A claimant other than one to whom regulation 10(1)(h) (circumstances in which claimants are not to be treated as available for employment) applies and who would, but for this paragraph, be required to be registered for employment in accordance with paragraph (3), shall not be required so to register for employment if—

(a) a medical practitioner to whom the question of the claimant's incapacity for work by reason of some disease or bodily or mental disablement has been referred under regulation 8 of the Social Security (Adjudication) Regulations 1986(a) (medical references) is of the opinion that he is not so incapable; and

(b) the claimant's medical practitioner continues to supply evidence of his incapacity for work in accordance with regulation 2 of the Social Security (Medical Evidence) Regulations 1976(b) (evidence of incapacity); and

(c) the claimant has made and is pursuing an appeal against the determination of an adjudication officer that he is not so incapable.

(3) A claimant to whom paragraph (1) applies shall, except where the Secretary of State decides otherwise, be registered for employment by registering with the Manpower Services Commission or a local education authority.

(a) S.I. 1986/2218, to which there are no relevant amending instruments.
(b) S.I. 1976/615; the relevant amending instruments are S.I. 1982/699 and 1987/409.

Relevant Education

12. For the purposes of these Regulations a child or young person is to be treated as receiving relevant education if, and only if—

(a) he is receiving full-time education not being advanced education for the purposes of section 2 of the Child Benefit Act 1975**(a)** (meaning of child); or

(b) although he is not receiving such full-time education he is treated as a child for the purposes of that section of that Act,

except that, in a case to which paragraph (b) applies, he shall not be treated as receiving relevant education beyond the terminal date in his case.

Circumstances in which persons in relevant education are to be entitled to income support

13.—(1) Notwithstanding that a person is to be treated as receiving relevant education under regulation 12 (relevant education) he shall, if paragraph (2) applies to him and he satisfies the other conditions of entitlement to income support, be entitled to income support.

(2) This paragraph applies to a young person who—

(a) is the parent of a child for whom he is treated as responsible under regulation 15 (circumstances in which a person is to be treated as responsible or not responsible for another) and who is treated as a member of his household under regulation 16 (circumstances in which a person is to be treated as being or not being a member of the household); or

(b) is severely mentally or physically handicapped and because of that he would be unlikely, even if he were available for employment, to obtain employment within the next 12 months; or

(c) has no parent nor any person acting in the place of his parents; or

(d) is living away from and is estranged from his parents or any person acting in place of his parents; or

(e) is living away from his parents and any person acting in the place of his parents in a case where his parents are or, as the case may be, that person is unable financially to support him and—

　(i) chronically sick or mentally or physically disabled; or

　(ii) detained in custody pending trial or sentence upon conviction or under a sentence imposed by a court; or

　(iii) prohibited from entering or re-entering Great Britain; or

(f) is attending a course of education to which regulation 9 (persons treated as available for employment) applies and satisfies the other conditions of that regulation; or

(g) has completed or terminated such a course and while attending that course satisfied the other conditions of that regulation; or

(h) is a person to whom paragraph 16 of Schedule 1 (refugees not required to be available for employment) applies.

(3) In this regulation—

(a) any reference to a person acting in the place of a young person's parents includes—

　(i) for the purposes of paragraph (2)(c) and (d), a reference to a local authority or voluntary organisation where the young person is in their care under a relevant enactment, or to a person with whom the young person is boarded out by a local authority or voluntary organisation whether or not any payment is made by them; and

　(ii) for the purposes of paragraph (2)(e), any person with whom the young person is so boarded out;

(a) 1975 c.61, as amended by sections 4, 8 and 21 of, and Schedule 5, Part I to, the Social Security Act 1980 (c.30) and by section 70 of the Social Security Act 1986 (c.50).

(b) "chronically sick or mentally or physically disabled" means, in relation to a person to whom that expression refers, a person—

 (i) in respect of whom the condition specified in paragraph 12(1) of Schedule 2 (additional condition for the higher pensioner and disability premiums) is satisfied; or

 (ii) in respect of whom an amount under article 26 of the Naval, Military and Air Forces etc (Disablement and Death) Service Pensions Order 1983(a) (provision of expenses in respect of appropriate aids for disabled living) is payable in respect of the cost of providing a vehicle, or maintaining a vehicle to a disabled person; or

 (iii) who is substantially and permanently disabled.

PART III

MEMBERSHIP OF THE FAMILY

Persons of a prescribed description

14.—(1) Subject to paragraph (2), a person of a prescribed description for the purposes of section 20(11) of the Act as it applies to income support (definition of the family) and section 23(1) and 3 of the Act (trade disputes) is a person aged 16 or over but under 19 who is treated as a child for the purposes of section 2 of the Child Benefit Act 1975 (meaning of child), and in these Regulations such a person is referred to as a " young person ".

(2) Paragraph (1) shall not apply to a person who is entitled to income support or would, but for section 20(9) of the Act (provision against dual entitlement of members of family), be so entitled.

Circumstances in which a person is to be treated as responsible or not responsible for another

15.—(1) Subject to the following provisions of this regulation a person shall be treated as responsible for a child or young person for whom he has primary responsibility.

(2) Where a child or young person spends equal amounts of time in different households, or where there is a question as to who has primary responsibility for him, the child or young person shall be treated for the purposes of paragraph (1) as being the primary responsibility of—

(a) the person who is receiving child benefit in respect of him; or

(b) if there is no such person—

 (i) where only one claim for child benefit has been made in respect of him, the person who made that claim; or

 (ii) in any other case the person who in the opinion of the adjudication officer has the primary responsibility for him.

(3) Where regulation 16(6) (circumstances in which a person is to be treated as being or not being a member of the household) applies in respect of a child or young person, that child or young person shall be treated as the responsibility of the claimant for that part of the week for which he is under that regulation treated as being a member of the claimant's household.

(4) Except where paragraph (3) applies, for the purposes of these Regulations a child or young person shall be treated as the responsibility of only one person in any benefit week and any person other than the one treated as responsible for the child or young person under this regulation shall be treated as not so responsible.

(a) S.I. 1983/883.

Circumstances in which a person is to be treated as being or not being a member of the household

16.—(1) Subject to paragraphs (2) to (5), the claimant and any partner and, where the claimant or his partner is treated as responsible under regulation 15 (circumstances in which a person is to be treated as responsible or not responsible for another) for a child or young person, that child or young person and any child of that child or young person shall be treated as members of the same household where any of them is absent from the dwelling occupied as his home.

(2) Paragraph (1) shall not apply in respect of any person referred to therein who is not treated as occupying a dwelling as his home because he fails to satisfy the conditions in sub-paragraph (8) of paragraph 4 of Schedule 3 (housing costs).

(3) Paragraph (1) shall not apply in respect of any member of a couple or of a polygamous marriage where—

(a) one, both or all of them are patients detained in a hospital provided under section 4 of the National Health Service Act 1977(a) (special hospitals) or section 90(1) of the Mental Health (Scotland) Act 1984(b) (provision of hospitals for patients requiring special security); or

(b) one, both or all of them are detained in custody pending trial or sentence upon conviction or whilst serving a sentence imposed by a court; or

(c) one of them is in accommodation and, if the accommodation is accommodation provided under the provisions referred to in paragraph (a) of the definition of residential accommodation in regulation 21(3) (special cases), the couple, or as the case may be, the members of the polygamous marriage are not entitled to income support and they have insufficient income to meet the minimum charge for that accommodation; or

(d) the claimant is abroad and does not satisfy the conditions of regulation 4 (temporary absence from Britain); or

(e) one of them is permanently in residential accommodation or a residential care home or a residential nursing home.

(4) A child or young person shall not be treated as a member of the claimant's household where he is—

(a) boarded out with the claimant or his partner under a relevant enactment; or

(b) boarded out with the claimant or his partner prior to adoption; or

(c) placed for adoption with the claimant or his partner pursuant to a decision under the Adoption Agencies Regulations 1983(c) or the Adoption Agencies (Scotland) Regulations 1984(d).

(5) Subject to paragraph (6), paragraph (1) shall not apply to a child or young person who is not living with the claimant and he—

(a) has been continuously absent from Great Britain for a period of more than four weeks commencing—

(i) where he went abroad before the date of claim for income support, with that date;

(ii) in any other case, with the date on which he went abroad; or

(b) has been an in-patient or in residential accommodation for a continuous period of more than 12 weeks commencing—

(i) where he became an in-patient or, as the case may be, entered that accommodation before the date of the claim for income support, with that date; or

(ii) in any other case, with the date on which he became an in-patient or entered that accommodation,

and, in either case, has not been in regular contact with either the claimant or any member of the claimant's household; or

(c) is in the care of a local authority under a relevant enactment; or

(a) 1977 c.49; section 4 was amended by section 148, Schedule 4, paragraph 47 of the Mental Health Act 1983 (c.20).
(b) 1984 c.36.
(c) S.I. 1983/1964.
(d) S.I. 1984/988.

(d) has been boarded out with a person other than the claimant prior to adoption; or

(e) has been placed for adoption pursuant to a decision under the Adoption Agencies Regulations 1983 or the Adoption Agencies (Scotland) Regulations 1984; or

(f) is detained in custody pending trial or sentence upon conviction or under a sentence imposed by a court.

(6) A child or young person to whom any of the circumstances mentioned in sub-paragraphs (c) or (f) of paragraph (5) applies shall be treated as being a member of the claimant's household only for that part of any benefit week where that child or young person lives with the claimant.

(7) Where a child or young person for the purposes of attending the educational establishment at which he is receiving relevant education is living with the claimant or his partner and neither one is treated as responsible for that child or young person that child or young person shall be treated as being a member of the household of the person treated as responsible for him and shall not be treated as a member of the claimant's household.

(8) In this regulation—

(a) " relevant enactment " means the Army Act 1955(a), the Air Force Act 1955(b), the Naval Discipline Act 1957(c), the Adoption Act 1958(d), the Matrimonial Proceedings Children Act 1958(e), the Children Act 1958(f), the Social Work (Scotland) Act 1968(g), the Family Law Reform Act 1969(h), the Children and Young Persons Act 1969(i), the Matrimonial Causes Act 1973(j), the Guardianship Act 1973(k), the Children Act 1975(l), the Domestic Proceedings and Magistrates' Courts Act 1978(m), the Adoption (Scotland) Act 1978(n), the Child Care Act 1980(o), and the Foster Children Act 1980(p);

(b) " voluntary organisation " has the meaning assigned to it in the Child Care Act 1980 or, in Scotland, the Social Work (Scotland) Act 1968.

PART IV

APPLICABLE AMOUNTS

Applicable amounts

17. Subject to regulations 18 to 22 and 70 (applicable amounts in other cases and reductions in applicable amounts and urgent cases), a claimant's weekly applicable amount shall be the aggregate of such of the following amounts as may apply in his case:

(a) an amount in respect of himself or, if he is a member of a couple, an amount in respect of both of them, determined in accordance with paragraph 1 (1), (2) or (3), as the case may be, of Schedule 2;

(b) an amount determined in accordance with paragraph 2 of Schedule 2 in respect of any child or young person who is a member of his family, except a child or young person whose capital, if calculated in accordance with Part V in like manner as for the claimant, except where otherwise provided, would exceed £3,000;

(c) if he is a member of a family of which at least one member is a child or young person, an amount determined in accordance with Part II of Schedule 2 (family premium);

(d) the amount of any premiums which may be applicable to him, determined in accordance with Parts III and IV of Schedule 2 (premiums);

(e) any amounts determined in accordance with Schedule 3 (housing costs) which may be applicable to him in respect of mortgage interest payments or such other housing costs as are prescribed in that Schedule.

(a) 1955 c.18.   (b) 1955 c.19.   (c) 1957 c.53.   (d) 1958 c.5.   (e) 1958 c.40.   (f) 1958 c.65.   (g) 1968 c.49.
(h) 1969 c.46.   (i) 1969 c.54.   (j) 1973 c.18.   (k) 1973 c.29.   (l) 1975 c.72.   (m) 1978 c.22.   (n) 1978 c.28.
(o) 1980 c.5.   (p) 1980 c.6.

Polygamous marriages

18. Subject to regulations 19 to 22 and 70 (applicable amounts in other cases and reductions in applicable amounts and urgent cases), where a claimant is a member of a polygamous marriage his weekly applicable amount shall be the aggregate of such of the following amounts as may apply in his case:

(a) the highest amount applicable to him and one of his partners determined in accordance with sub-paragraph (3) of paragraph 1 of Schedule 2 as if he and that partner were a couple;

(b) an amount equal to the difference between the amounts specified in sub-paragraphs (3)(b) and (1)(c) of paragraph 1 of Schedule 2 in respect of each of his other partners;

(c) an amount determined in accordance with paragraph 2 of Schedule 2 (applicable amounts) in respect of any child or young person for whom he or a partner of his is responsible and who is a member of the same household except a child or young person whose capital, if calculated in accordance with Part V in like manner as for the claimant, except where otherwise provided, would exceed £3,000;

(d) if he or another partner of the polygamous marriage is responsible for a child or young person who is a member of the same household, the amount specified in Part II of Schedule 2 (family premiums);

(e) the amount of any premiums which may be applicable to him determined in accordance with Parts III and IV of Schedule 2 (premiums);

(f) any amounts determined in accordance with Schedule 3 (housing costs) which may be applicable to him in respect of mortgage interest payments or such other housing costs as are prescribed in that Schedule.

Applicable amounts for persons in residential care and nursing homes

19.—(1) Subject to regulation 22 (reduction of applicable amounts) where—

(a) the claimant lives in a residential care home or nursing home; or

(b) if he is a member of a family—
  (i) he and the members of his family live in such a home; or
  (ii) he and the members of his family normally live in such a home and, where there is a period of temporary absence from the home of any member of the family, provided that the claimant or his partner lives in the home during that absence,

his weekly applicable amount shall except in a case to which regulation 21 (applicable amounts in special cases) or Part II of Schedule 4 (persons to whom regulation 19 does not apply) applies, be calculated in accordance with Part I of that Schedule.

(2) Where—

(a) a claimant immediately before 27th July 1987 was in receipt of supplementary benefit as a boarder in a residential care home which was not required to register under Part I of the Registered Homes Act 1984 because section 1(4) of that Act (registration) applied to it; and

(b) immediately before 11th April 1988 his appropriate amount fell to be determined, by virtue of regulation 3 of the Supplementary Benefit (Requirements and Resources) Amendment Regulations 1987**(a)** (transitional provisions), in accordance with paragraph 1 of Schedule 1A to the Supplementary Benefit Requirements Regulations 1983**(b)** (maximum amounts for residential care homes) or would have been so determined but for his temporary absence from the home,

his weekly applicable amount shall be calculated in accordance with Part I of Schedule 4 (applicable amounts of persons in residential care homes or nursing homes) as if the home was a residential care home within the meaning of this regulation if, and for so long as, the claimant remains resident in the same home apart from any temporary absence, and the home continues to provide accommodation with board and personal care for the claimant by reason of his old age, disablement, past or present dependence on alcohol or drugs or past or present mental disorder.

(a) S.I. 1987/1325.
(b) S.I. 1983/1399; the relevant amending instruments are S.I. 1985/1835 and 1986/1292.

(3) In this regulation and Schedule 4—

" nursing home " means—

(a) premises which are a nursing home or mental nursing home within the meaning of the Registered Homes Act 1984 **(a)** and which are either registered under Part II of that Act or exempt from registration under section 37 thereof (power to exempt Christian Science Homes); or

(b) any premises used or intended to be used for the reception of such persons or the provision of such nursing or services as is mentioned in any paragraph of subsection (1) of section 21 or section 22 (1) of the Registered Homes Act 1984 (meaning of nursing home or mental nursing home) or, in Scotland, as are mentioned in section 10 (2) of the Nursing Homes Registration (Scotland) Act 1938 **(b)** (interpretation) and which are maintained or controlled by a body instituted by special Act of Parliament or incorporated by Royal Charter;

(c) in Scotland,

(i) premises which are a nursing home within the meaning of section 10 of the Nursing Homes Registration (Scotland) Act 1938 which are either registered under that Act or exempt from registration under section 6 or 7 thereof (general power to exempt homes and power to exempt Christian Science Homes); or

(ii) premises which are a private hospital within the meaning of section 12 of the Mental Health (Scotland) Act 1984 **(c)** (private hospitals), and which are registered under that Act;

" residential care home " means an establishment "—

(a) registered under Part I of the Registered Homes Act 1984; or

(b) which provides residential accommodation with both board and personal care for persons in need of personal care by reason of old age, disablement, past or present dependence on alcohol or drugs, or past or present mental disorder for fewer than four persons, excluding persons carrying on or intending to carry on the home or employed or intended to be employed there and their relatives, but only if—

(i) at least two employed or self-employed persons (referred to in this paragraph as responsible persons) are each engaged in providing personal care to residents of the establishment for a minimum of 35 hours a week and those persons are not engaged in any other remunerative work; and

(ii) each of those responsible persons has at least one year's relevant experience in caring for persons in need of the category of personal care for which the establishment provides such care; and

(iii) at least one responsible person is available throughout the day to care for residents of the establishment; and

(iv) at least one responsible person is on call throughout the night to care for residents of the establishment; and

(v) all residents have free access to the premises at all times; or

(c) run by the Abbeyfield Society including all bodies corporate or incorporate which are affiliated to that Society; or

(d) managed or provided by a body incorporated by Royal Charter or constituted by Act of Parliament other than a local social services authority; or

(e) in Scotland, which is a home registered under section 61 of the Social Work (Scotland) Act 1968 **(d)** or is an establishment provided by a housing association registered with the Housing Corporation established by the Housing Act 1964**(e)** which provides care equivalent to that given in residential accommodation provided under Part IV of the Social Work (Scotland) Act 1968;

(a) 1984 c.23.

(b) 1938 c.73; section 10 was amended by section 15 of the Mental Health (Scotland) Act 1960 (c.61), and that amendment is preserved notwithstanding the repeal of that 1960 Act by section 126(1)(a) of the Mental Health (Scotland) Act 1984 (c.36). Section 10 was also amended by Schedule 7 of the National Health Service (Scotland) Act 1972 (c.58), Schedules 7 and 8 of the Nurses, Midwives and Health Visitors Act 1979 (c.36) and by Schedule 7 of the Health Services Act 1980 (c.53) and subsection (2) of that section 10 was added by section 26 of, and paragraph 14 of Schedule 4 to, the Health Services Act 1980 (c.53).

(c) 1984 c.36.

(d) 1968 c.49; section 61 was amended by the Criminal Procedure (Scotland) Act 1975 (c.21), section 289C and G and Schedule 7C.

(e) 1964 c.56.

" temporary absence " means—

(a) in the case of a person who is over pensionable age, 52 weeks;

(b) in any other case, 13 weeks.

(4) In Schedule 4 the expressions " old age ", " mental disorder ", " mental handicap ", " drug or alcohol dependence " and " disablement " have the same meanings as those expressions have for the purposes of the Registered Homes Act 1984 and Regulations made thereunder.

Applicable amounts for persons in board and lodging accommodation and hostels

20.—(1) Subject to regulation 22 (reductions of applicable amounts) where—

(a) the claimant lives in board and lodging accommodation or a hostel; or

(b) if he is a member of a family,

(i) he and the members of his family live in such accommodation; or

(ii) he and the members of his family normally live in such accommodation and, where there is a period of absence from the accommodation of any member of the family, provided that the claimant or his partner lives in the accommodation during that absence,

his weekly applicable amount shall, except in a case to which regulation 21 (special cases) or Part II of Schedule 5 (persons to whom regulation 20 does not apply) applies, be calculated in accordance with Part I of that Schedule.

(2) In this regulation and Schedule 5—

" board and lodging accommodation " means—

(a) accommodation provided to the claimant or, if he is a member of a family, to him or any other members of his family, for a charge which is inclusive of the provision of that accommodation and at least some cooked or prepared meals which are both prepared and consumed in that accommodation or associated premises; or

(b) accommodation provided in a hotel, guest-house, lodging-house or some similar establishment;

" board and lodging area " means the area numbered in column (1) of Schedule 6 (board and lodging areas) and described in column (2) thereof and for the purposes of this regulation and Schedule 5 any place not included in the description of a board and lodging area in Schedule 6 shall be treated as forming part of the board and lodging area nearest to it;

" hostel " means a building not being a residential care home or nursing home—

(a) in which there is provided for persons generally or for a class of persons, residential accommodation, otherwise than in separate and self-contained premises, and either board or facilities for the preparation of food adequate to the needs of those persons, or both and—

(b) which is

(i) managed by a housing association registered with the Housing Corporation established by the Housing Act 1964; or

(ii) operated other than on a commercial basis and in respect of which funds are provided wholly or in part by a government department or agency or a local authority; or

(iii) managed by a voluntary body or charity and provides care, support or supervision with a view to assisting those persons to be rehabilitated or resettled within the community; or

(iv) for the purposes of any particular case, such other establishment of like nature as the Secretary of State may, in his discretion, determine.

Special cases

21.—(1) Subject to regulation 22 (reductions in applicable amounts) in the case of a person to whom any paragraph in column (1) of Schedule 7 applies (applicable amounts in special cases), the amount included in the claimant's weekly amount in respect of him shall be the amount prescribed in the corresponding paragraph in column (2) of that Schedule; but no amount shall be included in respect of a child or young person if the capital of that child or young person calculated in accordance with Part V in like manner as for the claimant, except where otherwise provided, would exceed £3,000.

(2) In Schedule 7, for the purposes of paragraph 1, 2, 3 or 18 (patients), where a person has been a patient for two or more distinct periods separated by one or more intervals each not exceeding 28 days, he shall be treated as having been a patient continuously for a period equal in duration to the total of those distinct periods.

(3) In Schedule 7—

" person from abroad " means a person, who—

(a) has a limited leave as defined in section 33(1) of the Immigration Act 1971**(a)** (hereinafter referred to as "the 1971 Act") to enter or remain in the United Kingdom which was given in accordance with any provision of the immigration rules (as defined in that section) which refers to there being, or to there needing to be, no recourse to public funds or to there being no charge on public funds during that limited leave; but this sub-paragraph shall not apply to a person who is a national of a Member State, a state which is a signatory to the European Convention on Social and Medical Assistance (done in Paris on 11th December 1953)**(b)**, the Channel Islands or the Isle of Man; or

(b) having a limited leave (as defined in section 33(1) of the 1971 Act) to enter or remain in the United Kingdom, has remained without further leave under that Act beyond the time limited by the leave; or

(c) is the subject of a deportation order being an order under section 5(1) of the 1971 Act (deportation) requiring him to leave and prohibiting him from entering the United Kingdom; or

(d) is adjudged by the immigration authorities to be an illegal entrant (as defined in section 33(1) of the 1971 Act) who has not subsequently been given leave under that Act to enter or remain in the United Kingdom; or

(e) has been allowed temporary admission to the United Kingdom by virtue of paragraph 21 of Schedule 2 to the 1971 Act; or

(f) has been allowed temporary admission to the United Kingdom by the Secretary of State outside any provision of the 1971 Act; or

(g) has not had his immigration status determined by the Secretary of State;

" patient " means a person (other than a prisoner) who is regarded as receiving free in-patient treatment within the meaning of the Social Security (Hospital In-Patients) Regulations 1975**(c)**.

" prisoner " means a person who is detained in custody pending trial or sentence upon conviction or under a sentence imposed by a court other than a person whose detention is under the provisions of the Mental Heath Act 1983**(d)** or Mental Health (Scotland) Act 1984;

" residential accommodation " means, subject to paragraph (4), accommodation for a person whose stay in the accommodation has become other than temporary which is accommodation provided—

(a) 1971 c.77, as amended by the British Nationality Act 1981 (c.61), section 39 and Schedule 4.
(b) Cmnd 9512.
(c) S.I. 1975/555; the relevant amending instruments are S.I. 1977/1693 and 1987/1683.
(d) 1983 c.72.

(a) under sections 21 to 24 and 26 of the National Assistance Act 1948**(a)** (provision of accommodation); or

(b) in Scotland, for the purposes of section 27 of the National Health Service (Scotland) Act 1947**(b)** (prevention of illness and after-care) or under section 59 of the Social Work (Scotland) Act 1968**(c)** (provision of residential and other establishments) other than in premises which are registered under section 61 of that Act (registration) and which are used for the rehabilitation of alcoholics or drug addicts; or

(c) under section 7 of the Mental Health (Scotland) Act 1984 (functions of local authorities); or

(d) under section 21 of, and paragraph 1 or 2 of Schedule 8 to, the National Health Service Act 1977**(d)** (care of mothers and young children, prevention, care and aftercare) by a local social services authority other than—

    (i) such accommodation where full board is not available to the person; or

    (ii) accommodation provided under the said section 21 and paragraph 2 which is registered under the provisions of Part I of the Registered Homes Act 1984 where the premises are used for the rehabilitation of alcoholics or drug users; or

    (iii) a hostel within the meaning of regulation 20(2) (applicable amounts for persons in board and lodging accommodation or hostels).

(4) A person who would, but for this paragraph, be in residential accommodation within the meaning of paragraph (3) shall not be treated as being in residential accommodation if he is a person—

(a) who is under the age of 18 and in the care of a local authority under Part II or III of the Social Work (Scotland) Act 1968 (promotion of social welfare of children in need of care), or

(b) who is staying in a residential care home as defined in regulation 19(3) (applicable amounts for persons in residential care and nursing homes) under the provisions referred to in sub-paragraph (b) to (d) of paragraph (3) where—

    (i) the weekly cost of such accommodation exceeds the maximum amount provided for under regulation 19 and paragraphs 6, 8, 9, 10 and 11 of Schedule 4 (applicable amounts of persons in residential care and nursing homes) in respect of such accommodation; and

    (ii) the local authority accepts responsibility for the making of arrangements for the provision of such accommodation for that person in the light of that person being entitled to such maximum amount as a person in a residential care home under and by virtue of that regulation, provided that in the case of a person over pensionable age the local authority had accepted such responsibility for a period of not less than 2 years immediately before that person attained pensionable age.

(5) A claimant to whom paragraph 19 of Schedule 7 (disability premium) applies shall be entitled to income support for the period in respect of which that paragraph applies to him notwithstanding that his partner was also entitled to income support for that same period.

(a) 1948 c.29; section 21 was amended by the Local Government Act 1972 (c.70), Schedule 23, paragraphs 1 and 2 and Schedule 30; the National Health Service Reorganisation Act 1973 (c.32), Schedule 4, paragraph 44 and Schedule 5; the Housing (Homeless Persons) Act 1977 (c.48), Schedule; the National Health Service Act 1977 (c.49), Schedule 15, paragraph 5; the Health Services Act 1980 (c.53), Schedule 1, Part I, paragraph 5. Section 22 was amended by the Social Work (Scotland) Act 1968 (c.49), section 87(4) and Schedule 9, Part I; the Supplementary Benefits Act 1976 (c.71), Schedule 7, paragraph 3; the Housing (Homeless Persons) Act 1977 (c.48), Schedule; the Social Security Act 1980 (c.30), section 20, Schedule 4, paragraph 2(1) and Schedule 5, Part II and the Health and Social Services and Social Security Adjudications Act 1983 (c.41), section 20(1)(a). Section 24 was amended by the National Assistance (Amendment) Act 1959 (c.30), section 1(1); the National Health Service (Scotland) Act 1972 (c.58), Schedule 6, paragraph 82; the Local Government Act 1972 (c.70), Schedule 23, paragraph 2; the National Health Service Reorganisation Act 1973 (c.32), Schedule 4, paragraph 45 and the Housing (Homeless Persons) Act 1977 (c.48), Schedule. Section 26 was amended by the Health Services and Public Health Act 1968 (c.46), section 44 and Schedule 4 and the Social Work (Scotland) Act 1968 (c.49), Schedule 9, Part I and applied by section 87(3); the Local Government Act 1972 (c.70), Schedule 23, paragraph 2; the Housing (Homeless Persons) Act 1977 (c.48), Schedule and the Health and Social Services and Social Security Adjudications Act 1983 (c.41), section 20(1)(b).

(b) 1947 c.27, as applied by section 1(4)(c) of the Social Work (Scotland) Act 1968 (c.49); section 27 for the purposes of section 1(4)(c) of the 1968 Act is continued in force by paragraph 15 of Schedule 15 to the National Health Service (Scotland) Act 1978 (c.29).

(c) 1968 c.49.

(d) 1977 c.49; paragraph 1(2) and 2(5) of Schedule 8 were repealed by section 30 of, and Schedule 10 to, the Health and Social Services and Social Security Adjudications Act 1983, and paragraph 2(1) and (3) of Schedule 8 were amended by section 148 of, and Schedule 4 to, the Mental Health Act 1983 (c.20).

Reductions in applicable amounts in certain cases of actual or notional unemployment benefit disqualification

22.—(1) The weekly applicable amount of a claimant to whom paragraph (4) or (5) applies shall, subject to paragraph (2), be reduced by a sum equal to 40 per cent of the following amount (hereinafter referred to as the " relevant amount ")—

(a) in the case of a person to whom regulation 17 or 18 or paragraph 4 to 6, 9 to 12, 16, 17(c)(i) or (d)(i) of Schedule 7 applies—

   (i) where he is a single claimant aged less than 18 or a member of a couple or a polygamous marriage where all the members, in either case, are less than 18, the amount specified in paragraph 1(1)(a) of Schedule 2 (applicable amounts);

   (ii) where he is a single claimant aged not less than 18 but less than 25, the amount specified in paragraph 1(1)(b) of that Schedule;

   (iii) where he is a single claimant aged not less than 25 or a member of a couple or a polygamous marriage at least one of whom is aged not less than 18, the amount specified in paragraph 1(1)(c) of that Schedule;

(b) in the case of a person to whom regulation 19 or 20 (applicable amounts for persons in residential care or nursing homes or board and lodging accommodation or hostels) or paragraph 14 or 15 of Schedule 7 (applicable amounts in special cases) applies, the amount allowed for personal expenses for him specified in paragraph 13 of Schedule 4 or, as the case may be, paragraph 11(b) of Schedule 5.

(2) Where—

(a) the claimant's capital calculated in accordance with Part V (including any capital treated as his) does not exceed £200; and

(b) he or any member of his family is either pregnant or seriously ill,

his weekly applicable amount shall be reduced by a sum equal to 20 per cent of the relevant amount in his case.

(3) A reduction under paragraph (1) or (2) shall, if it is not a multiple of 5p, be rounded to the nearest such multiple or, if it is a multiple of 2·5p but not of 5p, to the next lower multiple of 5p.

(4) This paragraph applies to a claimant—

(a) whose weekly applicable amount is calculated otherwise than in accordance with regulation 21 and paragraph 1 to 3, 8(b), 13, 16 and 18 of Schedule 7; and

(b) whose right to income support is, under section 20(3)(d)(i) of the Act (conditions of entitlement to income support), subject to the condition of availability for employment; and

(c) who—

   (i) is disqualified for receiving unemployment benefit under section 20(1) of the Social Security Act**(a)** (disqualifications etc); or

   (ii) has made a claim for unemployment benefit which has not been determined by an adjudication officer and in respect of which, in the opinion of an adjudication officer, a question as to disqualification under that section arises; or

   (iii) has not made a claim for unemployment benefit or has had such a claim disallowed other than by reason of section 20(1) and, in either case, would be so disqualified if he were to make such a claim or it had not been so disallowed.

(5) This paragraph applies to a claimant who is not required to be available for employment by virtue of regulation 8(2) (persons not required to be available for employment) or a person to whom regulation 11(2) applies (exemption from requirement to register for employment).

(a) 1975 c.14; subsection (1) was amended and subsection (1A) was added by the Social Security Act 1986 (c.50), section 43.

(6) This regulation shall apply—

    (a) in a case to which head (i) of paragraph (4)(c) applies, for the period of the disqualification;

    (b) in a case to which head (ii) of paragraph (4)(c) applies, for a period of 13 weeks except that where, on subsequent determination of the claim for unemployment benefit—

        (i) disqualification is not imposed, any reduction imposed under paragraph (1) or (2), as the case may be, shall be withdrawn,

        (ii) disqualification is imposed but for a period of less than 13 weeks, the period of such reduction shall be adjusted to correspond with the period of disqualification;

    (c) in a case to which head (iii) of paragraph (4)(c) applies, for the period for which the claimant would be disqualified if he were to make a claim for unemployment benefit or if such a claim had not been disallowed for other reasons.

    (d) in a case to which paragraph (5) applies, for so long as that paragraph continues so to apply.

PART V

INCOME AND CAPITAL

CHAPTER I

GENERAL

Calculation of income and capital of members of claimant's family and of a polygamous marriage

23.—(1) The income and capital of a claimant's partner and, subject to paragraph (2) and to regulation 44 (modifications in respect of children and young persons), the income of a child or young person which by virtue of section 22(5) of the Act is to be treated as income and capital of the claimant, shall be calculated in accordance with the following provisions of this Part in like manner as for the claimant; and any reference to the "claimant" shall, except where the context otherwise requires, be construed, for the purposes of this Part, as if it were a reference to his partner or that child or young person.

(2) Regulations 36(2) and 38(2), so far as they relate to paragraphs 1 to 10 of Schedule 8 (earnings to be disregarded) and regulation 41(1) (capital treated as income) shall not apply to a child or young person.

(3) Where a claimant or the partner of a claimant is married polygamously to two or more members of his household—

    (a) the claimant shall be treated as possessing capital and income belonging to each such member and the income of any child or young person who is one of that member's family; and

    (b) the income and capital of that member or, as the case may be, the income of that child or young person shall be calculated in accordance with the following provisions of this Part in like manner as for the claimant or, as the case may be, as for any child or young person who is a member of his family.

Treatment of charitable or voluntary payments

24.—(1) Subject to paragraph (5), any charitable or voluntary payment, other than one which is or is due to be made at regular intervals or is one to which regulation 44(2) (modifications in respect of children and young persons) applies, made to the claimant on or after the date of claim shall be calculated in accordance with the following provisions of this regulation; and for the purposes of this regulation any such payment made to a member of the claimant's family or to a person whose income and capital he is treated as possessing under regulation 23(3) (calculation of income and capital of members of claimant's family and of a polygamous marriage) shall be treated as a payment made to the claimant and shall be disregarded in calculating the income or capital of that member or that person.

(2) The first £250, whether in aggregate or otherwise, of any such payments made in the period of 52 weeks beginning with the first day of the benefit week in which the first payment is made shall be taken into account under Chapter VI of this Part as capital and to the extent that it is not a payment of capital shall be treated as capital.

(3) Any such payments in the period of 52 weeks in excess of £250 shall be taken into account under Chapter V of this Part as income and to the extent that it is not a payment of income shall be treated as income.

(4) In the case of a claimant who continues to be in receipt of income support at the end of the period of 52 weeks, the foregoing provisions of this regulation shall continue to apply thereafter with the modification that any subsequent period of 52 weeks shall begin with the first day of the benefit week in which the first payment is made after the end of the previous period of 52 weeks.

(5) This regulation shall not apply to a person to whom section 23 of the Act (trade disputes) applies or to a member of his family for so long as that section applies to that person.

Liable relative payments

25. Regulations 29 to 44, 46 to 52 and Chapter VIII of this Part shall not apply to any payment which is to be calculated in accordance with Chapter VII thereof (liable relatives).

Calculation of income and capital of students

26. The provisions of Chapters II to VI of this Part (income and capital) shall have effect in relation to students and their partners subject to the modifications set out in Chapter VIII thereof (students).

Disregard of fractions

27. Where any income or capital calculated in accordance with this Part includes a fraction of a penny that fraction shall be disregarded.

CHAPTER II

INCOME

Calculation of income

28.—(1) For the purposes of section 20(3) of the Act (conditions of entitlement to income support) the income of a claimant shall be calculated on a weekly basis—

(a) by determining in accordance with this Part, other than Chapter VI, the weekly amount of his income; and

(b) by adding to that amount the weekly income calculated under regulation 53 (calculation of tariff income from capital).

(2) For the purposes of paragraph (1) "income" includes income derived under regulations 24 and 41 to 43 (treatment of charitable or voluntary payments, capital treated as income, notional income and notional earnings of seasonal workers).

Calculation of earnings derived from employed earner's employment and income other than earnings

29.—(1) Except where regulation 33 applies (weekly amount of charitable or voluntary payment) earnings derived from employment as an employed earner and income which does not consist of earnings shall be taken into account over a period determined in accordance with the following paragraphs and at a weekly amount determined in accordance with regulation 32 (calculation of weekly amount of income).

(2) Subject to paragraph (3), the period over which a payment is to be taken into account shall be—

(a) in a case where it is payable in respect of a period, a period equal to the length of that period;

(b) in any other case, a period equal to such number of weeks as is equal to the number obtained (and any fraction shall be treated as a corresponding fraction of a week) by dividing the net earnings, or in the case of income which does not consist of earnings, the amount of that income by the amount of income support which would be payable had the payment not been made plus an amount equal to the total of the sums which would fall to be disregarded from that payment under Schedule 8 or, as the case may be, 9 (earnings and other income to be disregarded) as is appropriate in the claimant's case,

and that period shall begin on the date on which the payment is treated as paid under regulation 31 (date on which income is treated as paid).

(3) Where earnings not of the same kind are derived from the same source and the periods in respect of which those earnings would, but for this paragraph, fall to be taken into account—

(a) overlap, wholly or partly, those earnings shall be taken into account over a period equal to the aggregate length of those periods;

(b) and that period shall begin with the earliest date on which any part of those earnings would otherwise be treated as paid under regulation 31 (date on which income is treated as paid).

(4) In a case to which paragraph (3) applies, any payment to which regulation 35(1)(b) or (c) (earnings of employed earners) applies shall be taken into account before a payment to which regulation 35(1)(d) applies but after any earnings normally derived from the employment.

(5) For the purposes of this regulation the claimant's earnings and income which does not consist of earnings shall be calculated in accordance with Chapters III and V respectively of this Part.

Calculation of earnings of self-employed earners

30.—(1) Except where paragraph (2) applies, where a claimant's income consists of earnings from employment as a self-employed earner the weekly amount of his earnings shall be determined by reference to his average weekly earnings from that employment—

(a) over a period of 52 weeks; or

(b) where the claimant has recently become engaged in that employment or there has been a change which is likely to affect the normal pattern of business, over such other period of weeks as may, in any particular case, enable the weekly amount of his earnings to be determined more accurately.

(2) Where the claimant's earnings consist of royalties or sums paid periodically for or in respect of any copyright those earnings shall be taken into account over a period equal to such number of weeks as is equal to the number obtained (and any fraction shall be treated as a corresponding fraction of a week) by dividing the earnings by the amount of income support which would be payable had the payment not been made plus an amount equal to the total of the sums which would fall to be disregarded from the payment under Schedule 8 (earnings to be disregarded) as is appropriate in the claimant's case.

(3) For the purposes of this regulation the claimant's earnings shall be calculated in accordance with Chapter IV of this Part.

Date on which income is treated as paid

31.—(1) Except where paragraph (2) applies, a payment of income to which regulation 29 (calculation of earnings derived from employed earner's employment and income other than earnings) applies shall be treated as paid—

(a) in the case of a payment which is due to be paid before the first benefit week pursuant to the claim, on the date on which it is due to be paid;

(b) in any other case, on the first day of the benefit week in which it is due to be paid or the first succeeding benefit week in which it is practicable to take it into account.

(2) Income support, unemployment benefit, sickness or invalidity benefit, or severe disablement allowance under the Social Security Act(**a**) shall be treated as paid on the day of the benefit week in respect of which it is paid.

Calculation of weekly amount of income

32.—(1) For the purposes of regulation 29 (calculation of earnings derived from employed earner's employment and income other than earnings), subject to paragraphs (2) to (5) and regulation 34 (incomplete benefit weeks), where the period in respect of which a payment is made—

(a) does not exceed a week, the weekly amount shall be the amount of that payment;

(b) exceeds a week, the weekly amount shall be determined—

(i) in a case where that period is a month, by multiplying the amount of the payment by 12 and dividing the product by 52;

(ii) in a case where that period is three months, by multiplying the amount of the payment by 4 and dividing the product by 52;

(iii) in a case where that period is a year by dividing the amount of the payment by 52;

(iv) in any other case by multiplying the amount of the payment by 7 and dividing the product by the number equal to the number of days in the period in respect of which it is made.

(2) Where a payment for a period not exceeding a week is treated under regulation 31(1)(a) (date on which income is treated as paid) as paid before the first benefit week and a part is to be taken into account for some days only in that week (the relevant days), the amount to be taken into account for the relevant days shall be calculated by multiplying the amount of the payment by the number equal to the number of relevant days and dividing the product by the number of days in the period in respect of which it is made.

(3) Where a payment is in respect of a period equal to or in excess of a week and a part thereof is to be taken into account for some days only in a benefit week (the relevant days), the amount to be taken into account for the relevant days shall, except where paragraph (4) applies, be calculated by multiplying the amount of the payment by the number equal to the number of relevant days and dividing the product by the number of days in the period in respect of which it is made.

(4) In the case of a payment of—

(a) unemployment benefit, sickness or invalidity benefit, or severe disablement allowance under the Social Security Act, the amount to be taken into account for the relevant days shall be the amount of benefit paid in respect of those days;

(b) income support, the amount to be taken into account for the relevant days shall be calculated by multiplying the weekly amount of the benefit by the number of relevant days and dividing the product by seven.

(5) Except in the case of a payment which it has not been practicable to treat under regulation 31(1)(b) as paid on the first day of the benefit week in which it is due to be paid, where a payment of income from a particular source is or has been paid regularly and that payment falls to be taken into account in the same benefit week as a payment of the same kind and from the same source, the amount of that income to be taken into account in any

(**a**) *See* sections 12(1)(a) to (c), 14 to 16 and 36 of the Social Security Act 1975 (c.14); section 12(1)(a) and (b) was amended by the Social Security (No. 2) Act 1980 (c.39), section 7(6) and the Health and Social Security Act 1984 (c.48), Schedule 5, paragraph 2; section 14 was amended by the Social Security Pensions Act 1975 (c.60), section 18(1) and 65, Schedule 4, paragraph 39, the Social Security Act 1979 (c.18) section 21(4), Schedule 3, paragraph 6, the Social Security and Housing Benefits Act 1982 (c.24) sections 39(3) and 48, Schedule 4, paragraph 9; the Social Security (No. 2) Act 1980 (c.39) section 7 and the Schedule and the Social Security Act 1986 (c.50) section 86 Schedule 10 paragraph 83; section 15 was amended by the Social Security Pensions Act 1975 section 65, Schedule 4, paragraph 40, the Social Security Act 1979 section 21, Schedule 1, paragraph 1, Schedule 3, paragraph 7, the Social Security and Housing Benefits Act 1982 section 48, Schedule 4 paragraph 10; and the Social Security Act 1986 (c.50) section 86 Schedule 10 Part V paragraph 83; section 15A was inserted by section 18(3) of the Social Security Act 1985 (c.53); section 16 was amended by the Social Security Act 1979, Schedule 1, paragraph 10 and the Social Security Act 1985 section 9(1) and modified for certain purposes by the Social Security Act 1986 (c.50) section 4; section 36 was substituted by the Health and Social Security Act 1984, section 11 and subsection 4A was added by the Social Security Act 1985 Schedule 4, paragraph 3.

one benefit week shall not exceed the weekly amount determined under paragraph (1)(a) or (b), as the case may be, of the payment which under regulation 31(1)(b) (date on which income is treated as paid) is treated as paid first.

(6) Where the amount of the claimant's income fluctuates and has changed more than once, or a claimant's regular pattern of work is such that he does not work every week, the foregoing paragraphs may be modified so that the weekly amount of his income is determined by reference to his average weekly income—

  (a) if there is a recognisable cycle of work, over the period of one complete cycle (including, where the cycle involves periods in which the claimant does no work, those periods but disregarding any other absences);

  (b) in any other case, over a period of five weeks or such other period as may, in the particular case, enable the claimant's average weekly income to be determined more accurately.

Weekly amount of charitable or voluntary payment

33.—(1) Subject to paragraph (2), the weekly amount of any charitable or voluntary payment which is to be treated as income under regulation 24(3) (treatment of charitable or voluntary payments) shall be determined as follows—

  (a) in a case where the first such payment exceeds the annual limit of £250, the excess shall be divided by 52; and the resulting amount treated as weekly income for a period of 52 weeks beginning on the date on which that payment was made;

  (b) in a case where any subsequent payment in aggregate with earlier payments first exceeds that limit, the excess shall be divided by the number equal to the number of weeks (including any part of a week) in the interval beginning with the date of that payment to the end of the period of 52 weeks; and the resulting amount treated as weekly income for each week in that interval; and

  (c) any payment made after that in either sub-paragraph (a) or (b) shall be divided by the number equal to the number of weeks (including any part of a week) in the interval beginning with the date of that payment to the end of the period of 52 weeks; and the resulting amount treated as weekly income for each week in that interval.

(2) Where the date on which the payment is made is not the first day of the benefit week in which it is made it shall be treated as paid on the first day of that benefit week or the first succeeding benefit week in which it is practicable to take the weekly amount of the payment into account.

Incomplete weeks of benefit

34.—(1) Where a claim for income support is made for a period (the relevant period) which is not a complete benefit week and a payment of income is to be taken into account in that period, for the purposes of calculating the amount to be taken into account—

  (a) the claimant shall be treated as if he had a benefit week beginning seven days before the end of the relevant period; and

  (b) except where paragraph (2) or (3) applies, the amount to be taken into account in the relevant period shall be determined—

    (i) by multiplying the weekly amount of the payment determined under regulation 32(1) (calculation of weekly amount of income) less any sum which would fall to be disregarded from that amount under Schedule 8 or, as the case may be, 9 (earnings and other income to be disregarded) by the number equal to the number of days in the relevant period; and

    (ii) by dividing the product by 7.

(2) Where entitlement to income support would otherwise end before the last day of a benefit week (the relevant week) and a payment of income is to be taken into account in that week, for the purposes of calculating the amount to be taken into account in the relevant week—

  (a) the claimant shall be treated as if he had a benefit week beginning seven days before the last day of the relevant week; and

(b) except where paragraph (3) applies, the amount to be taken into account shall be determined—

  (i) by multiplying the weekly amount of the payment determined under regulation 32(1) less any sum which would fall to be disregarded from that amount under Schedule 8 or, as the case may be, 9 by the number equal to the number of days in the relevant week in respect of which there is entitlement to income support; and

  (ii) by dividing the product by 7.

(3) The amount of any unemployment benefit, sickness or invalidity benefit, or severe disablement allowance under the Social Security Act to be taken into account under paragraph (1) or (2) shall be the amount of benefit payable in respect of those days for which income support is payable.

CHAPTER III

EMPLOYED EARNERS

Earnings of employed earners

35.—(1) Subject to paragraph (2) "earnings" means in the case of employment as an employed earner, any remuneration or profit derived from that employment and includes—

(a) any bonus or commission;

(b) any payment in lieu of remuneration except any periodic sum paid to a claimant on account of the termination of his employment by reason of redundancy;

(c) any payment in lieu of notice or any lump sum payment intended as compensation for the loss of employment but only in so far as it represents loss of income;

(d) any holiday pay except any payable more than four weeks after the termination or interruption of employment but this exception shall not apply to a claimant to whom, and for so long as, section 23 of the Act (trade disputes) applies;

(e) any payment by way of a retainer;

(f) any payment made by the claimant's employer in respect of expenses not wholly, exclusively and necessarily incurred in the performance of the duties of the employment, including any payment made by the claimant's employer in respect of—

  (i) travelling expenses incurred by the claimant between his home and place of employment;

  (ii) expenses incurred by the claimant under arrangements made for the care of a member of his family owing to the claimant's absence from home;

(g) any award of compensation made under section 68(2) or 71(2)(a) of the Employment Protection (Consolidation) Act 1978**(a)** (remedies for unfair dismissal and compensation);

(h) any such sum as is referred to in section 18(2) of the Social Security (Miscellaneous Provisions) Act 1977**(b)** (certain sums to be earnings for social security purposes).

(2) "Earnings" shall not include—

(a) any payment in kind;

(b) any remuneration paid by or on behalf of an employer to the claimant who for the time being is unable to work due to illness or maternity;

(c) any payment in respect of expenses wholly, exclusively and necessarily incurred in the performance of the duties of the employment;

(d) any occupational pension.

(a) 1978 c.44; section 68(2) was amended by the Employment Act 1982 (c.46), section 21, Schedule 3, paragraph 21; section 71(2) was amended by the Employment Act 1982 (c.46), sections 5 and 21, Schedule 3, paragraph 22 and Schedule 4.

(b) 1977 c.5; section 18(2) was amended by section 159, Schedule 16, paragraph 29 of the Employment Protection (Consolidation) Act 1978 (c.44) and by section 86(2) of, and Schedule 10, Part IV, paragraph 75 and Schedule 11 to, the Social Security Act 1986 (c.50).

Calculation of net earnings of employed earners

36.—(1) For the purposes of regulation 29 (calculation of earnings of employed earners) the earnings of a claimant derived from employment as an employed earner to be taken into account shall, subject to paragraph (2), be his net earnings.

(2) There shall be disregarded from a claimant's net earnings, any sum, where applicable, specified in paragraphs 1 to 13 of Schedule 8.

(3) For the purposes of paragraph (1) net earnings shall be calculated by taking into account the gross earnings of the claimant from that employment less—

(a) any amount deducted from those earnings by way of—

(i) income tax;

(ii) primary Class 1 contributions under the Social Security Act**(a)**; and

(b) one-half of any sum paid by the claimant by way of a contribution towards an occupational or personal pension scheme.

CHAPTER IV

SELF-EMPLOYED EARNERS

Earnings of self-employed earners

37.—(1) Subject to paragraph (2), "earnings", in the case of employment as a self-employed earner, means the gross receipts of the employment and shall include any allowance paid under section 2 of the Employment and Training Act 1973**(b)** to the claimant for the purpose of assisting him in carrying on his business.

(2) "Earnings" shall not include, where a claimant is employed in providing board and lodging accommodation for which a charge is payable, any payment by way of such a charge except where the claimant is a seasonal worker to whom regulation 43 (notional earnings of seasonal workers) applies and the payment is due during the period of his normal employment.

Calculation of net profit of self-employed earners

38.—(1) For the purposes of regulation 30 (calculation of earnings of self-employed earners), the earnings of a claimant to be taken into account shall be—

(a) in the case of a self-employed earner who is engaged in employment on his own account, the net profit derived from that employment;

(b) in the case of a self-employed earner whose employment is carried on in partnership or is that of a share fisherman within the meaning of the Social Security (Mariners' Benefits) Regulations 1975**(c)**, his share of the net profit derived from that employment less—

(i) an amount in respect of income tax and of social security contributions payable under the Social Security Act calculated in accordance with regulation 39 (deduction of tax and contributions for self-employed earners); and

(ii) one-half of any qualifying premium payable.

(2) There shall be disregarded from a claimant's net profit any sum, where applicable, specified in paragraphs 1 to 13 of Schedule 8.

(a) *See* sections 1(2) and 4 of the Social Security Act 1975 (c.14); section 1 was amended by the Employment Protection Act 1975 (c.71), section 40, the Social Security (Miscellaneous Provisions) Act 1977 (c.5), section 24 and Schedule 2, the Social Security (Contributions) Act 1982 (c.2) section 2, the Social Security Act 1985 (c.53) section 29 and Schedule 5, paragraph 5, the Social Security Act 1986 (c.50), section 86 and Schedule 11 and S.I. 1987/48; section 4 was amended by the Social Security Pensions Act 1975 (c.60), Schedule 4, paragraph 36, the Education (School-Leaving Dates) Act 1976 (c.5), section 2(4), the Social Security Act 1979 (c.18), section 14(1), the Social Security and Housing Benefits Act 1982 (c.24), Schedule 5, the Social Security Act 1985 (c.53) sections 7(1) and (2) and 8(1) the Social Security Act 1986 (c.50) sections 74(1)(a) and (2) and 86 and Schedule 10, paragraph 104, article 2 of S.I. 1986/25 and article 2 of S.I. 1987/46.

(b) 1973 c.50; section 2 was amended by sections 9 and 11 and Schedule 2 Part II paragraph 9 and Schedule 3 of the Employment and Training Act 1981 (c.57).

(c) S.I. 1975/529.

(3) For the purposes of paragraph (1)(a) the net profit of the employment shall, except where paragraph (9) applies, be calculated by taking into account the earnings of the employment over the period determined under regulation 30 (calculation of earnings of self-employed earners) less—

    (a) subject to paragraphs (5) to (7), any expenses wholly and exclusively defrayed in that period for the purposes of that employment;

    (b) an amount in respect of—

       (i) income tax; and

      (ii) social security contributions payable under the Social Security Act,

    calculated in accordance with regulation 39 (deduction of tax and contributions for self-employed earners); and

    (c) one-half of any qualifying premium payable.

(4) For the purposes of paragraph (1)(b), the net profit of the employment shall be calculated by taking into account the earnings of the employment over the period determined under regulation 30 less, subject to paragraphs (5) to (7), any expenses wholly and exclusively defrayed in that period for the purposes of that employment.

(5) Subject to paragraph (6), no deduction shall be made under paragraph (3)(a) or (4) in respect of—

    (a) any capital expenditure;

    (b) the depreciation of any capital asset;

    (c) any sum employed or intended to be employed in the setting up or expansion of the employment;

    (d) any loss incurred before the beginning of the period determined under regulation 30 (calculation of earnings of self-employed earners);

    (e) the repayment of capital on any loan taken out for the purposes of the employment;

    (f) any expenses incurred in providing business entertainment.

(6) A deduction shall be made under paragraph (3)(a) or (4) in respect of the repayment of capital on any loan used for—

    (a) the replacement in the course of business of equipment or machinery; and

    (b) the repair of an existing business asset except to the extent that any sum is payable under an insurance policy for its repair.

(7) An adjudication officer shall refuse to make a deduction in respect of any expenses under paragraph (3)(a) or (4) where he is not satisfied that the expense has been defrayed or, having regard to the nature of the expense and its amount, that it has been reasonably incurred.

(8) For the avoidance of doubt—

    (a) a deduction shall not be made under paragraph (3)(a) or (4) in respect of any sum unless it has been expended for the purposes of the business;

    (b) a deduction shall be made thereunder in respect of—

       (i) the excess of any VAT paid over VAT received in the period determined under regulation 30 (calculation of earnings of self-employed earners);

      (ii) any income expended in the repair of an existing asset except to the extent that any sum is payable under an insurance policy for its repair;

     (iii) any payment of interest on a loan taken out for the purposes of the employment.

(9) Where a claimant is engaged in employment as a child minder the net profit of the employment shall be one-third of the earnings of that employment, less—

    (a) an amount in respect of—

       (i) income tax; and

      (ii) social security contributions payable under the Social Security Act,

    calculated in accordance with regulation 39 (deduction of tax and contributions for self-employed earners); and

    (b) one-half of any qualifying premium payable.

(10) Notwithstanding regulation 30 (calculation of earnings of self-employed earners) and the foregoing paragraphs, an adjudication officer may assess any item of a claimant's income or expenditure over a period other than that determined under regulation 30 as may, in the particular case, enable the weekly amount of that item of income or expenditure to be determined more accurately.

(11) For the avoidance of doubt where a claimant is engaged in employment as a self-employed earner and he is also engaged in one or more other employments as a self-employed or employed earner any loss incurred in any one of his employments shall not be offset against his earnings in any other of his employments.

(12) In this regulation "qualifying premium" means any premium or other consideration payable under an annuity contract for the time being approved by the Board of Inland Revenue as having for its main object the provision for the claimant of a life annuity in old age or the provision of an annuity for his partner or for any one or more of his dependants and in respect of which relief from income tax may be given.

Deduction of tax and contributions for self-employed earners

39.—(1) The amount to be deducted in respect of income tax under regulation 38 (1) (b) (i), (3) (b) (i) or (9) (a) (i) (calculation of net profit of self-employed earners) shall be calculated on the basis of the amount of chargeable income and as if that income were assessable to income tax at the basic rate of tax less only the personal relief to which the claimant is entitled under sections 8 (1) and (2) and 14 (1) (a) and (2) of the Income and Corporation Taxes Act 1970 (personal relief)**(a)** as is appropriate to his circumstances; but, if the period determined under regulation 30 (calculation of earnings of self-employed earners) is less than a year, the amount of the personal relief deductible under this paragraph shall be calculated on a *pro rata* basis.

(2) The amount to be deducted in respect of social security contributions under regulation 38(1)(b)(i), (3)(b)(ii) or (9)(a)(ii) shall be the total of—

(a) the amount of Class 2 contributions payable under section 7 (1) or, as the case may be, (4) of the Social Security Act**(b)** except where the claimant's chargeable income is less than the amount for the time being specified in section 7 (5) of that Act**(c)** (small earnings exception); and

(b) the amount of Class 4 contributions (if any) which would be payable under section 9 of that Act**(d)** (contributions recoverable under Taxes Acts) in respect of profits or gains equal to the amount of that income.

(3) In this regulation "chargeable income" means—

(a) except where sub-paragraph (b) applies, the earnings derived from the employment less any expenses deducted under paragraph (3) (a) or, as the case may be, (4) of regulation 38;

(b) in the case of employment as a child minder, one-third of the earnings of that employment.

(a) 1970 c.10; section 8 (1) was amended by the Finance Act 1971 (c.68) section 37 Schedule 6 paragraphs 1 and 5, and the Finance Act 1985 (c.54) section 36, subsection (1A) was added by the Finance (No.2) Act 1975 (c.45) section 31 and amended by the Finance Act 1977 (c.36) section 22. Subsection (1B) was added by the Finance (No.2) Act 1975 section 31. Section 8(2) was amended by the Finance Act 1971 section 37 Schedule 6 paragraphs 1 and 5 and article 2 of S.I. 1985/430; sub-paragraph (b) was substituted by the Finance (No.2) Act 1979 (c.47) section 12 Schedule 2 paragraph 1; sub-paragraph (b) (i) and (ii) were amended by the Finance Act 1981 (c.35) section 139 Schedule 19 Part VI and the Finance Act 1982 (c.39) section 157 Schedule 22 Part IV; sub-paragraph (b) (iii) was added by the Finance Act 1981 (c.35) section 27 and sub-paragraph (b) (iv) by the Finance Act 1987 (c.16) section 27. Section 14 (1) was amended by the Finance Act 1970 (c.24) section 14 Schedule 8 Part VI; section 14 (2) was amended by the Finance Act 1976 (c.40) section 36, the Finance (No.2) Act 1979 (c.47) section 11 Schedule 1 paragraph 2 and the Finance Act 1980 (c.48) section 24.

(b) Section 7 (1) was amended by section 2 (4) of the Education (School-leaving Dates) Act 1976 (c.5), section 17 (1) of the Health and Social Security Act 1984 (c.48), article 3 of S.I. 1986/25 and article 3 of S.I. 1987/46.

(c) Section 7 (5) was amended by article 3 of S.I. 1986/25 and 1987/46.

(d) Section 9 was amended by sections 4 and 65 of, and Schedule 5 to, the Social Security Pensions Act 1975 (c.60), the Social Security (Contributions) Act 1982 (c.2) section 1 and by S.I. 1986/25.

CHAPTER V

OTHER INCOME

Calculation of income other than earnings

40.—(1) For the purposes of regulation 29 (calculation of income other than earnings) the income of a claimant which does not consist of earnings to be taken into account shall, subject to paragraphs (2) and (3), be his gross income and any capital treated as income under regulations 24(3), 41 and 44 (treatment of charitable and voluntary payments, capital treated as income and modifications in respect of children and young persons).

(2) There shall be disregarded from the calculation of a claimant's gross income under paragraph (1), any sum, where applicable, specified in Schedule 9.

(3) Where the payment of any benefit under the benefit Acts**(a)** is subject to any deduction by way of recovery the amount to be taken into account under paragraph (1) shall be the gross amount payable.

(4) For the avoidance of doubt there shall be included as income to be taken into account under paragraph (1) any payment to which regulation 35(2) or 37(2) (payments not earnings) applies.

Capital treated as income

41.—(1) Any capital payable by instalments which are outstanding on the first day in respect of which income support is payable or the date of the determination of the claim, whichever is earlier, or, in the case of a review, the date of any subsequent review shall, if the aggregate of the instalments outstanding and the amount of the claimant's capital otherwise calculated in accordance with Chapter VI of this Part exceeds £6,000, be treated as income.

(2) Any payment received under an annuity shall be treated as income.

(3) In the case of a person to whom section 23 of the Act (trade disputes) applies and for so long as it applies, any payment under section 1 of the Child Care Act 1980**(b)** (duty of local authorities to promote welfare of children) or, as the case may be, section 12 of the Social Work (Scotland) Act 1968**(c)** (general social welfare) shall be treated as income.

Notional income

42.—(1) A claimant shall be treated as possessing income of which he has deprived himself for the purpose of securing entitlement to income support or increasing the amount of that benefit.

(2) Except in the case of—

(a) a discretionary trust;

(b) a trust derived from a payment made in consequence of a personal injury;

(c) unemployment benefit under the Social Security Act which may be payable to a claimant who is not required to be available for employment; or

(d) an increase of child benefit payable to a claimant under regulation 2(2) of the Child Benefit and Social Security (Fixing and Adjustment of Rates) Regulations 1976**(d)** (rates of child benefit),

income which would become available to the claimant upon application being made but which has not been acquired by him shall be treated as possessed by him but only from the date on which it would be so acquired.

(3) Except in the case of a discretionary trust, or a trust derived from a payment made in consequence of a personal injury, any income which is due to be paid to the claimant but—

(a) has not been paid to him;

(a) The benefit Acts are specified in section 84(1) of the Social Security Act 1986 (c.50).
(b) 1980 c.5.
(c) 1968 c.49.
(d) S.I. 1976/1267; relevant amending instruments are S.I. 1980/110, 1986/1172 and 1987/45.

(b) is not a payment prescribed in regulation 9 or 10 of the Social Security (Payments on Account, Overpayment and Recovery) Regulations 1987**(a)** (duplication and prescribed payments or maintenance payments) and not made on or before the date prescribed in relation to it,

shall be treated as possessed by the claimant.

(4) Any payment of income made—

(a) to a third party in respect of a member of the family (but not a member of the third party's family) shall be treated—

(i) in a case where that payment is derived from a payment of any benefit under the benefit Acts, a war disablement pension or war widow's pension, as possessed by that member if it is paid to any member of that family;

(ii) in any other case, as possessed by that member to the extent that it is used for the food, clothing, footwear, fuel, rent or rates for which housing benefit is payable, or any housing costs to the extent that they are met under regulations 17(e) or 18(f) (housing costs), of any member of that family;

(b) to a member of the family in respect of a third party (but not in respect of another member of that family) shall be treated as possessed by that member to the extent that it is kept by him or used by or on behalf of any member of the family;

but, except where sub-paragraph (a)(i) applies and in the case of a person to whom section 23 of the Act (trade disputes) applies, this paragraph shall not apply to any payment in kind.

(5) Where a claimant's earnings are not ascertainable at the time of the determination of the claim or of any subsequent review the adjudication officer shall treat the claimant as possessing such earnings as is reasonable in the circumstances of the case having regard to the number of hours worked and the earnings paid for comparable employment in the area.

(6) Where—

(a) a claimant performs a service for another person; and

(b) that person makes no payment of earnings or pays less than that paid for a comparable employment in the area,

the adjudication officer shall treat the claimant as possessing such earnings (if any) as is reasonable for that employment unless the claimant satisfies him that the means of that person are insufficient for him to pay or to pay more for the service; but this paragraph shall not apply to a claimant who is engaged by a charitable or voluntary body or is a volunteer if the adjudication officer is satisfied that it is reasonable for him to provide his services free of charge.

(7) Where a claimant is treated as possessing any income under any of paragraphs (1) to (4) the foregoing provisions of this Part shall apply for the purposes of calculating the amount of that income as if a payment had actually been made and as if it were actual income which he does possess.

(8) Where a claimant is treated as possessing any earnings under paragraph (5) or (6) the foregoing provisions of this Part shall apply for the purposes of calculating the amount of those earnings as if a payment had actually been made and as if they were actual earnings which he does possess except that paragraph (3) of regulation 36 (calculation of net earnings of employed earners) shall not apply and his net earnings shall be calculated by taking into account the earnings which he is treated as possessing, less—

(a) an amount in respect of income tax equivalent to an amount calculated by applying to those earnings the basic rate of tax in the year of assessment less only the personal relief to which the claimant is entitled under sections 8(1) and (2) and 14(1)(a) and (2) of the Income and Corporation Taxes Act 1970 (personal relief) as is appropriate to his circumstances; but, if the period over which those earnings are to be taken into account is less than a year, the amount of the personal relief deductible under this paragraph shall be calculated on a *pro rata* basis;

(b) an amount in respect of primary Class 1 contributions payable under the Social Security Act in respect of those earnings; and

---

(a) S.I. 1987/491.

(c) one-half of any sum payable by the claimant by way of a contribution towards an occupational or personal pension scheme.

Notional earnings of seasonal workers

43.—(1) Where the claimant is a seasonal worker or, if he is one of a couple, he or his partner is a seasonal worker (but not both), and—

(a) a claim for income support is made in respect of any day in the claimant's off-season or, as the case may be, in his partner's off-season; and

(b) his or, as the case may be, his partner's net earnings in his last period of normal employment less any earnings for any week in that period which have been taken into account in calculating entitlement to income support, exceeded three times the total of the amounts for that period specified in head (i) or, as the case may be, (ii) of sub-paragraph (a) and, where applicable, sub-paragraph (b) of paragraph (2),

the amount by which those earnings exceeded that total shall be divided by the number equal to the number of weeks (including any part of a week) in his or, as the case may be, his partner's off-season and the amount so obtained shall be treated as earnings possessed by the claimant or his partner in each of those weeks.

(2) The amounts specified for the purposes of paragraph (1)(b) are—

(a) either—

  (i) in a case where the claimant is one of a couple, the personal allowance for a couple; or

  (ii) in a case where he is not one of a couple, the personal allowance for a single claimant not less than age 25; and

(b) in respect of each child or young person who is a member of the claimant's family, the amount which is equal to the applicable amount for a child under age 11.

(3) Where the claimant and his partner are seasonal workers and both have started their, or only one has started his, off-season paragraph (1) shall apply to the claimant or, where his partner is the only one whose off-season has started, to his partner as if he were the only seasonal worker until the end of his off-season and thereafter to the other member subject to the modifications in paragraphs (4) to (6).

(4) The other member's last period of normal employment shall be—

(a) in a case where that member's normal employment has ceased, the period beginning with the start of the employment of that member and ending with the last day of that employment;

(b) in a case where that member's normal employment has not ceased, the period beginning with the start of the employment of that member and ending with—

  (i) the day before the start of the off-season of his partner; or

  (ii) the date of claim for income support,

  whichever is the later;

(5) The period of the other member's off-season shall be—

(a) in a case where that member's normal employment has ceased, the period beginning with the start of his off-season and ending with the day before he is to resume normal employment; or

(b) in a case where that member's normal employment has not ceased, the period beginning with the date on which the off-season of either member first starts or, as the case may be, the date of claim for income support whichever is later and ending with the day before that on which either member is first to resume normal employment.

(6) The other member's net earnings in his last period of normal employment as determined under paragraph (4), less

(a) any earnings for any week in that period which have been taken into account in calculating entitlement to income support; and

(b) in so far as any week in that period—

(i) does not coincide with a week in his partner's period of normal employment, 3 times the total of the amounts for that week specified for the purposes of paragraph (1)(b);

(ii) does coincide with a week in his partner's period of normal employment, the extent (if any) by which the amount so specified has not been taken into account in the calculation of his partner's notional earnings,

shall be divided by the number equal to the number of weeks (including any part of a week) in that member's off-season as determined under paragraph (5) and the amount so obtained shall be treated as earnings possessed by that member in each of those weeks.

(7) In this regulation, the expressions "normal employment", "off-season" and "seasonal worker" have the meanings assigned to those expressions in regulation 21 of the Social Security (Unemployment, Sickness and Invalidity Benefit) Regulations 1983(a) (additional condition with respect to receipt of unemployment benefit) except that the expression "employment" in that regulation shall be construed as if it included a reference to employment as a self-employed earner.

(8) Where a claimant or his partner is treated as possessing any earnings under this regulation the foregoing provisions of this Part, except regulation 38(2) in so far as it applies to paragraph 3 of Schedule 8 (earnings to be disregarded), shall apply for the purposes of calculating those earnings as if a payment had actually been made and as if they were actual earnings which he does possess.

Modifications in respect of children and young persons

44.—(1) Any capital of a child or young person payable by instalments which are outstanding on the first day in respect of which income support is payable or at the date of the determination of the claim, whichever is earlier, or, in the case of a review, the date of any subsequent review shall, if the aggregate of the instalments outstanding and the amount of that child's or young person's other capital calculated in accordance with Chapter VI of this Part in like manner as for the claimant, except where otherwise provided, would exceed £3,000, be treated as income.

(2) In the case of a child or young person who is residing at an educational establishment at which he is receiving relevant education—

(a) any payment made to the educational establishment, in respect of that child's or young person's maintenance, by or on behalf of a person who is not a member of the family or by a member of the family out of funds contributed for that purpose by a person who is not a member of the family, shall be treated as income of that child or young person but it shall only be taken into account over periods during which that child or young person is present at that educational establishment; and

(b) if a payment has been so made, for any period in a benefit week in term-time during which that child or young person returns home, he shall be treated as possessing an amount of income in that week calculated by multiplying the amount of personal allowance and disabled child premium, if any, applicable in respect of that child or young person by the number equal to the number of days in that week in which he was present at his educational establishment and dividing the product by seven; but this sub-paragraph shall not apply where the educational establishment is provided under section 8 of the Education Act 1944(b) (duty of local authority to secure primary and secondary schools) by a local education authority or where the payment is made under section 49 or 50 of the Education (Scotland) Act 1980(c) (power of education authority to assist persons).

(a) S.I. 1983/1598.

(b) 1944 c.31; section 8 was amended by the Education (Miscellaneous Provisions) Act 1948 (c.40), section 3, the Education Act 1980 (c.20) section 38 and Schedule 7 and by the Education Act 1981 (c.60), section 2.

(c) 1980 c.44; section 50 was amended by the Education (Scotland) Act 1981 (c.58), section 2.

(3) Where a child or young person—

    (a) is resident at an educational establishment and he is wholly or partly maintained at that establishment by a local education authority under section 8 of the Education Act 1944; or

    (b) is maintained at an educational establishment under section 49 or 50 of the Education (Scotland) Act 1980,

he shall for each day he is present at that establishment be treated as possessing an amount of income equal to the sum obtained by dividing the amount of personal allowance and disabled child premium, if any, applicable in respect of him by seven.

(4) Where the income of a child or young person who is a member of the claimant's family calculated in accordance with the foregoing provisions of this Part exceeds the amount of the personal allowance and disabled child premium, if any, applicable in respect of that child or young person, the excess shall not be treated as income of the claimant.

(5) Where the capital of a child or young person if calculated in accordance with Chapter VI of this Part in like manner as for the claimant, except where otherwise provided, would exceed £3,000, any income of that child or young person shall not be treated as income of the claimant.

(6) In calculating the net earnings or net profit of a child or young person there shall be disregarded, (in addition to any sum which falls to be disregarded under paragraphs 11 to 13), any sum specified in paragraphs 14 and 15 of Schedule 8 (earnings to be disregarded).

(7) Any income of a child or young person which is to be disregarded under Schedule 9 (income other than earnings to be disregarded) shall be disregarded in such manner as to produce the result most favourable to the claimant.

(8) Where a child or young person is treated as possessing any income under paragraphs (2) and (3) the foregoing provisions of this Part shall apply for the purposes of calculating that income as if a payment had actually been made and as if it were actual income which he does possess.

CHAPTER VI

CAPITAL

Capital limit

45. For the purposes of section 22 (6) of the Act as it applies to income support (no entitlement to benefit if capital exceeds prescribed amount), the prescribed amount is £6,000.

Calculation of capital

46.—(1) For the purposes of Part II of the Act as it applies to income support, the capital of a claimant to be taken into account shall, subject to paragraph (2), be the whole of his capital calculated in accordance with this Part and any income treated as capital under regulations 24 (2) and 48 (treatment of charitable or voluntary payments and income treated as capital).

(2) There shall be disregarded from the calculation of a claimant's capital under paragraph (1) any capital, where applicable, specified in Schedule 10.

Disregard of capital of child or young person

47. The capital of a child or young person who is a member of the claimant's family shall not be treated as capital of the claimant.

Income treated as capital

48.—(1) Any annual bounty derived from employment to which paragraph 7 of Schedule 8 applies shall be treated as capital.

(2) Except in the case of an amount to which section 23(5)(a)(ii) of the Act (refund of tax in trade disputes cases) applies, any amount by way of a refund of income tax deducted from profits or emoluments chargeable to income tax under Schedule D or E shall be treated as capital.

(3) Any holiday pay which is not earnings under regulation 35(1)(d) (earnings of employed earners) shall be treated as capital.

(4) Except any income derived from capital disregarded under paragraph 1, 2, 4, 6, or 12 of Schedule 10, any income derived from capital shall be treated as capital but only from the date it is normally due to be credited to the claimant's account.

(5) Subject to paragraph (6), in the case of employment as an employed earner, any advance of earnings or any loan made by the claimant's employer shall be treated as capital.

(6) For so long as section 23 of the Act (trade disputes) applies to a person, paragraph (5) shall not apply to him and, if he is a person to whom sub-section (8) of that section applies, that paragraph shall not apply until the end of the period specified in that sub-section.

(7) Any payment under section 30 of the Prison Act 1952 **(a)** (payments for discharged prisoners) or allowance under section 17 of the Prisons (Scotland) Act 1952 **(b)** (allowances to prisoners on discharge) shall be treated as capital.

(8) Any payment made by a local authority which represents arrears of payments under section 34(6) or, as the case may be, section 50 of the Children Act 1975 **(c)** (contributions to a custodian towards the cost of accommodation and maintenance of a child) shall be treated as capital.

Calculation of capital in the United Kingdom

49. Capital which a claimant possesses in the United Kingdom shall be calculated—

(a) except in a case to which sub-paragraph (b) applies, at its current market or surrender value, less—

(i) where there would be expenses attributable to sale, 10 per cent; and

(ii) the amount of any incumbrance secured on it;

(b) in the case of a National Savings Certificate—

(i) if purchased from an issue the sale of which ceased before 1st July last preceding the first day on which income support is payable or the date of the determination of the claim, whichever is the earlier, or in the case of a review, the date of any subsequent review, at the price which it would have realised on that 1st July had it been purchased on the last day of that issue;

(ii) in any other case, at its purchase price.

Calculation of capital outside the United Kingdom

50. Capital which a claimant possesses in a country outside the United Kingdom shall be calculated—

(a) in a case in which there is no prohibition in that country against the transfer to the United Kingdom of an amount equal to its current market or surrender value in that country, at that value;

(b) in a case where there is such a prohibition, at the price which it would realise if sold in the United Kingdom to a willing buyer,

less, where there would be expenses attributable to sale, 10 per cent and the amount of any incumbrance secured on it.

Notional capital

51.—(1) A claimant shall be treated as possessing capital of which he has deprived himself for the purpose of securing entitlement to income support or increasing the amount of that benefit.

(a) 1952 c.52; section 30 was substituted by section 66(3) of the Criminal Justice Act 1967 (c.80).
(b) 1952 c.61.
(c) 1975 c.72, as amended by section 64 of the Domestic Proceedings and Magistrates' Courts Act 1978 (c.22).

(2) Except in the case of—

(a) a discretionary trust;

(b) a trust derived from a payment made in consequence of a personal injury; or

(c) any loan which would be obtainable only if secured against capital disregarded under Schedule 10,

any capital which would become available to the claimant upon application being made but which has not been acquired by him shall be treated as possessed by him but only from the date on which it would be so acquired.

(3) Any payment of capital made

(a) to a third party in respect of a member of the family (but not a member of the third party's family) shall be treated—

(i) in a case where that payment is derived from a payment of any benefit under the benefit Acts, a war disablement pension or a war widow's pension, as possessed by that member if it is paid to any member of the family;

(ii) in any other case, as possessed by that member to the extent that it is used for the food, clothing, footwear, fuel, rent or rates for which housing benefit is payable, or any housing costs to the extent that they are met under regulation 17 (e) and 18 (f) (housing costs), of any member of that family;

(b) to a member of the family in respect of a third party (but not in respect of another member of the family) shall be treated as possessed by that member to the extent that it is kept by him or used on behalf of any member of the family.

(4) Where a claimant stands in relation to a company in a position analogous to that of a sole owner or partner in the business of that company, he shall be treated as if he were such sole owner or partner and in such a case—

(a) the value of his holding in that company shall, notwithstanding regulation 46 (calculation of capital), be disregarded; and

(b) he shall, subject to paragraph (5), be treated as possessing an amount of capital equal to the value or, as the case may be, his share of the value of the capital of that company and the foregoing provisions of this Chapter shall apply for the purposes of calculating that amount as if it were actual capital which he does possess.

(5) For so long as the claimant undertakes activities in the course of the business of the company, the amount which he is treated as possessing under paragraph (4) shall be disregarded.

(6) Where a claimant is treated as possessing capital under any of paragraphs (1) to (4), the foregoing provisions of this Chapter shall apply for the purposes of calculating its amount as if it were actual capital which he does possess.

Capital jointly held

52. Except where a claimant possesses capital which is disregarded under regulation 51 (4) (notional capital), where a claimant and one or more persons are beneficially entitled in possession to any capital asset they shall be treated as if each of them were entitled in possession to the whole beneficial interest therein in an equal share.

Calculation of tariff income from capital

53.—(1) Where the claimant's capital calculated in accordance with this Part exceeds £3,000 it shall be treated as equivalent to a weekly income of £1 for each complete £250 in excess of £3,000 but not exceeding £6,000.

(2) Notwithstanding paragraph (1), where any part of the excess is not a complete £250 that part shall be treated as equivalent to a weekly income of £1.

(3) For the purposes of paragraph (1), capital includes any income treated as capital under regulations 24 (2), 48 and 60 (charitable or voluntary payments, income treated as capital and liable relative payments treated as capital).

CHAPTER VII

LIABLE RELATIVES

Interpretation

54. In this Chapter, unless the context otherwise requires—

" claimant " includes a young claimant;

" liable relative " means—

   (a) a spouse or former spouse of a claimant or of a member of the claimant's family;

   (b) a parent of a child or young person who is a member of the claimant's family or of a young claimant;

   (c) a person who has not been adjudged to be the father of a child or young person who is a member of the claimant's family or of a young claimant where that person is contributing towards the maintenance of that child, young person or young claimant and by reason of that contribution he may reasonably be treated as the father of that child, young person or young claimant;

   (d) a person liable to maintain another person by virtue of section 26(3)(c) of the Act (liability to maintain) where the latter is the claimant or a member of the claimant's family,

and, in this definition, a reference to a child's, young person's or young claimant's parent includes any person in relation to whom the child, young person or young claimant was treated as a child or a member of the family;

" payment " means a periodical payment or any other payment made by or derived from a liable relative including, except in the case of a discretionary trust, any payment which would be so made or derived upon application being made by the claimant but which has not been acquired by him but only from the date on which it would be so acquired; but it does not include any payment—

   (a) arising from a disposition of property made in contemplation of, or as a consequence of—

     (i) an agreement to separate; or

     (ii) any proceedings for judicial separation, divorce or nullity of marriage;

   (b) made after the death of the liable relative;

   (c) made by way of a gift but not in aggregate or otherwise exceeding £250 in the period of 52 weeks beginning with the date on which the payment, or if there is more than one such payment the first payment, is made; and, in the case of a claimant who continues to be in receipt of income support at the end of the period of 52 weeks, this provision shall continue to apply thereafter with the modification that any subsequent period of 52 weeks shall begin with the first day of the benefit week in which the first payment is made after the end of the previous period of 52 weeks;

   (d) to which regulation 44(2) applies (modifications in respect of children and young persons);

   (e) made—

     (i) to a third party in respect of the claimant or a member of the claimant's family; or

     (ii) to the claimant or to a member of the claimant's family in respect of a third party,

   where having regard to the purpose of the payment, the terms under which it is made and its amount it is unreasonable to take it into account;

   (f) in kind;

   (g) to, or in respect of, a child or young person who is to be treated as not being a member of the claimant's household under regulation 16 (circumstances in which a person is to be treated as being or not being a member of the same household);

   (h) which is not a periodical payment, to the extent that any amount of that payment—

     (i) has already been taken into account under this Part by virtue of a previous claim or determination; or

(ii) has been recovered under section 27(1) of the Act (prevention of duplication of payments) or is currently being recovered; or

(iii) at the time the determination is made, has been used by the claimant except where he has deprived himself of that amount for the purpose of securing entitlement to income support or increasing the amount of that benefit;

"periodical payment" means—

(a) a payment which is made or is due to be made at regular intervals in pursuance of a court order or agreement for maintenance;

(b) in a case where the liable relative has established a pattern of making payments at regular intervals, any such payment;

(c) any payment not exceeding the amount of income support payable had that payment not been made;

(d) any payment representing a commutation of payments to which sub-paragraphs (a) or (b) of this definition applies whether made in arrears or in advance,

but does not include a payment due to be made before the first benefit week pursuant to the claim which is not so made;

"young claimant" means a person aged 16 or over but under 19 who makes a claim for income support.

Treatment of liable relative payments

55. Except where regulation 60(1) (liable relative payments to be treated as capital) applies a payment shall—

(a) to the extent that it is not a payment of income, be treated as income;

(b) be taken into account in accordance with the following provisions of this Chapter.

Period over which periodical payments are to be taken into account

56.—(1) The period over which a periodical payment is to be taken into account shall be—

(a) in a case where the payment is made at regular intervals, a period equal to the length of that interval;

(b) in a case where the payment is due to be made at regular intervals but is not so made, such number of weeks as is equal to the number (and any fraction shall be treated as a corresponding fraction of a week) obtained by dividing the amount of that payment by the weekly amount of that periodical payment as calculated in accordance with regulation 58(4) (calculation of the weekly amount of a liable relative payment);

(c) in any other case, a period equal to a week.

(2) The period under paragraph (1) shall begin on the date on which the payment is treated as paid under regulation 59 (date on which a liable relative payment is to be treated as paid).

Period over which payments other than periodical payments are to be taken into account

57.—(1) Subject to paragraph (2), the number of weeks over which a payment other than a periodical payment is to be taken into account shall be equal to the number (and any fraction shall be treated as a corresponding fraction of a week) obtained by dividing that payment by—

(a) where the payment is in respect of the claimant or the claimant and any child or young person who is a member of the family, the aggregate of £2 and the amount of income support which would be payable had the payment not been made;

(b) where the payment is in respect of one or more than one child or young person who is a member of the family the amount prescribed in Schedule 2 (applicable amount) in respect of each child or young person and any family and lone parent premium;

(2) Where a liable relative makes a periodical payment and any other payment concurrently and the weekly amount of that periodical payment, as calculated in accordance with regulation 58 (calculation of the weekly amount of a liable relative payment), is less than—

(a) in a case where the periodical payment is in respect of the claimant or the claimant and any child or young person who is a member of the family, the aggregate of £2 and the amount of income support which would be payable had the payments not been made; or

(b) in a case where the periodical payment is in respect of one or more than one child or young person who is a member of the family, the aggregate of the amount prescribed in Schedule 2 in respect of each such child or young person and any family and lone parent premium,

that other payment shall, subject to paragraph (3), be taken into account over a period of such number of weeks as is equal to the number obtained (and any fraction shall be treated as a corresponding fraction of a week) by dividing that payment by an amount equal to the extent of the difference between the amount referred to in sub-paragraph (a) or (b), as the case may be, and the weekly amount of the periodical payment.

(3) If—

(a) the liable relative ceases to make periodical payments, the balance (if any) of the other payment shall be taken into account over the number of weeks equal to the number (and any fraction shall be treated as a corresponding fraction of a week) obtained by dividing that balance by the amount referred to in sub-paragraph (a) or (b) of paragraph (1), as the case may be;

(b) the amount of any subsequent periodical payment varies, the balance (if any) of the other payment shall be taken into account over a period of such number of weeks as is equal to the number obtained (and any fraction shall be treated as a corresponding fraction of a week) by dividing that balance by an amount equal to the extent of the difference between the amount referred to in sub-paragraph (a) or (b) of paragraph (2) and the weekly amount of the subsequent periodical payment.

(4) The period under paragraph (1) or (2) shall begin on the date on which the payment is treated as paid under regulation 59 (date on which a liable relative payment is treated as paid) and under paragraph (3) shall begin on the first day of the benefit week in which the cessation or variation of the periodical payment occurred.

Calculation of the weekly amount of a liable relative payment

58.—(1) Where a periodical payment is made or is due to be made at intervals of one week, the weekly amount shall be the amount of that payment.

(2) Where a periodical payment is made or is due to be made at intervals greater than one week and those intervals are monthly, the weekly amount shall be determined by multiplying the amount of the payment by 12 and dividing the product by 52.

(3) Where a periodical payment is made or is due to be made at intervals and those intervals are neither weekly nor monthly, the weekly amount shall be determined by dividing that payment by the number equal to the number of weeks (including any part of a week) in that interval.

(4) Where a payment is made and that payment represents a commutation of periodical payments whether in arrears or in advance, the weekly amount shall be the weekly amount of the individual periodical payments so commutated as calculated under paragraphs (1) to (3) as is appropriate.

(5) The weekly amount of a payment to which regulation 57 applies (period over which payments other than periodical payments are to be taken into account) shall be equal to the amount of the divisor used in calculating the period over which the payment or, as the case may be, the balance is to be taken into account.

Date on which a liable relative payment is to be treated as paid

59.—(1) A periodical payment is to be treated as paid—

(a) in the case of a payment which is due to be made before the first benefit week pursuant to the claim, on the day in the week in which it is due to be paid which corresponds to the first day of the benefit week;

(b) in any other case, on the first day of the benefit week in which it is due to be paid unless, having regard to the manner in which income support is due to be paid in the particular case, it would be more practicable to treat it as paid on the first day of a subsequent benefit week.

(2) Subject to paragraph (3), any other payment shall be treated as paid—

(a) in the case of a payment which is made before the first benefit week pursuant to the claim, on the day in the week in which it is paid which corresponds to the first day of the benefit week;

(b) in any other case, on the first day of the benefit week in which it is paid unless, having regard to the manner in which income support is due to be paid in the particular case, it would be more practicable to treat it as paid on the first day of a subsequent benefit week.

(3) Any other payment paid on a date which falls within the period in respect of which a previous payment is taken into account, not being a periodical payment, is to be treated as paid on the first day following the end of that period.

Liable relative payments to be treated as capital

60.—(1) Subject to paragraph (2), where a liable relative makes a periodical payment concurrently with any other payment, and the weekly amount of the periodical payment as calculated in accordance with regulation 58(1) to (4) (calculation of the weekly amount of a liable relative payment), is equal to or greater than the amount referred to in sub-paragraph (a) of regulation 57(2) (period over which payments other than periodical payments are to be taken into account) less the £2 referred to therein, or sub-paragraph (b) of that regulation, as the case may be, the other payment shall be treated as capital.

(2) If, in any case, the liable relative ceases to make periodical payments, the other payment to which paragraph (1) applies shall be taken into account under paragraph (1) of regulation 57 but, notwithstanding paragraph (4) thereof, the period over which the payment is to be taken into account shall begin on the first day of the benefit week following the last one in which a periodical payment was taken into account.

CHAPTER VIII

STUDENTS

Interpretation

61.　In this Chapter, unless the context otherwise requires—

" a course of advanced education " means—

(a) a full-time course leading to a postgraduate degree or comparable qualification, a first degree or comparable qualification, a diploma of higher education, a higher national diploma, a higher national diploma of the Business & Technician Education Council or the Scottish Vocational Education Council or a teaching qualification; or

(b) any other full-time course which is a course of a standard above ordinary national diploma, a national diploma of the Business & Technician Education Council or the Scottish Vocational Education Council, a general certificate of education (advanced level) a Scottish certificate of education (higher grade) or a Scottish certificate of sixth year studies;

" contribution " means any contribution in respect of the income of any other person which a Minister of the Crown or an education authority takes into account in assessing the amount of the student's grant and by which that amount is, as a consequence, reduced;

" covenant income " means the income net of tax at the basic rate payable to a student under a Deed of Covenant by a person whose income is, or is likely to be, taken into account in assessing the student's grant or award;

"education authority" means a government department, a local education authority as defined in section 114(1) of the Education Act 1944(a) (interpretation), an education authority as defined in section 135(1) of the Education (Scotland) Act(b) (interpretation), an education and library board established under Article 3 of the Education and Libraries (Northern Ireland) Order 1986(c), any body which is a research council for the purposes of the Science and Technology Act 1965(d) or any analogous government department, authority, board or body, of the Channel Islands, Isle of Man or any other country outside Great Britain.

"grant" means any kind of educational grant or award and includes any scholarship, studentship, exhibition, allowance or bursary;

"grant income" means—

(a) any income by way of a grant;

(b) in the case of a student other than one to whom sub-paragraph (c) refers, any contribution which has been assessed whether or not it has been paid;

(c) in the case of a student to whom paragraph 1, 2 or 7 of Schedule 1 applies (lone parent or disabled student), any contribution which has been assessed and which has been paid;

and any such contribution which is paid by way of a covenant shall be treated as part of the student's grant income.

"period of study" means—

(a) in the case of a course of study for one year or less, the period beginning with the start of the course to the end;

(b) in the case of a course of study for more than one year, in the first or, as the case may be, any subsequent year of the course, the period beginning with the start of the course or, as the case may be, that year's start and ending with either—

(i) the day before the start of the next year of the course in a case where the student's grant is assessed at a rate appropriate to his studying throughout the year, or, if he does not have a grant, where it would have been assessed at such a rate had he had one; or

(ii) in any other case the day before the start of the normal summer vacation appropriate to his course;

"periods of experience" has the meaning prescribed in paragraph 1(1) of Schedule 5 to the Education (Mandatory Awards) Regulations 1987(e);

"sandwich course" has the meaning prescribed in paragraph 1(1) of Schedule 5 to the Education (Mandatory Awards) Regulations 1987;

"standard maintenance grant" means—

(a) except where paragraph (b) applies, in the case of a student attending a course of study at the University of London or an establishment within the area comprising the City of London and the Metropolitan Police District, the amount specified for the time being in paragraph 2(2)(a) of Schedule 2 to the Education (Mandatory Awards) Regulations 1987 for such a student;

(b) in the case of a student residing at his parents' home the amount specified in paragraph 3(2) thereof;

(c) in any other case, the amount specified in paragraph 2(2) other than in sub-paragraph (a) or (b) thereof;

"student" means a person aged less than 19 who is attending a full-time course of advanced education or, as the case may be, a person aged 19 or over but under pensionable age who is attending a full-time course of study at an educational establishment; and for the purposes of this definition—

(a) 1944 c.31, as amended by S.I. 1974/595, article 3(22), Schedule 1, Part I and by S.I. 1977/293, article 4(1).
(b) 1980 c.44.
(c) S.I. 1986/594 (N.I. 3).
(d) 1965 c.4.
(e) S.I. 1987/1261.

(a) a person who has started on such a course shall be treated as attending it throughout any period of term or vacation within it, until the end of the course or such earlier date as he abandons it or is dismissed from it;

(b) a person on a sandwich course shall be treated as attending a full-time course of advanced education or, as the case may be, of study;

" year " in relation to a course, means the period of 12 months beginning on 1st January, 1st April or 1st September according to whether the academic year of the course in question begins in the spring, the summer or the autumn respectively.

Calculation of grant income

62.—(1) The amount of a student's grant income to be taken into account shall, subject to paragraph (2), be the whole of his grant income.

(2) There shall be disregarded from the amount of a student's grant income any payment—

(a) intended to meet tuition fees or examination fees;

(b) intended to meet the cost of special equipment for a student on a course which began before 1st September 1986 in architecture, art and design, home economics, landscape architecture, medicine, music, ophthalmic optics, orthoptics, physical education, physiotherapy, radiography, occupational therapy, dental hygiene, dental therapy, remedial gymnastics, town and country planning and veterinary science or medicine;

(c) intended to meet additional expenditure incurred by a disabled student in respect of his attendance on a course;

(d) intended to meet additional expenditure connected with term time residential study away from the student's educational establishment;

(e) on account of the student maintaining a home at a place other than that at which he resides while attending his course but only to the extent that his rent or rates is not met by housing benefit;

(f) on account of any other person but only if that person is residing outside of the United Kingdom and there is no applicable amount in respect of him;

(g) intended to meet the cost of books and equipment (other than special equipment) or if not so intended an amount equal to £210 towards such costs;

(h) intended to meet travel expenses incurred as a result of his attendance on the course.

(3) A student's grant income shall be apportioned—

(a) subject to paragraph (4), in a case where it is attributable to the period of study, equally between the weeks in that period;

(b) in any other case, equally between the weeks in the period in respect of which it is payable.

(4) In the case of a student on a sandwich course, any periods of experience within the period of study shall be excluded and the student's grant income shall be apportioned equally between the remaining weeks in that period.

Calculation of covenant income where a contribution is assessed

63.—(1) Where a student is in receipt of income by way of a grant during a period of study and a contribution has been assessed, the amount of his covenant income to be taken into account for that period and any summer vacation immediately following shall be the whole amount of his covenant income less, subject to paragraph (3), the amount of the contribution.

(2) The weekly amount of the student's covenant income shall be determined—

(a) by dividing the amount of income which falls to be taken into account under paragraph (1) by 52 or, if there are 53 benefit weeks (including part weeks) in the year, 53; and

(b) by disregarding from the resulting amount, £5.

(3) For the purposes of paragraph (1), the contribution shall be treated as increased by the amount, if any, by which the amount excluded under regulation 62(2)(h) (calculation of grant income) falls short of the amount included in the standard maintenance grant to meet travel expenses.

Covenant income where no grant income or no contribution is assessed

64.—(1) Where a student is not in receipt of income by way of a grant the amount of his covenant income shall be calculated as follows—

(a) any sums intended for any expenditure specified in regulation 62(2)(a) to (f), (calculation of grant income) necessary as a result of his attendance on the course, shall be disregarded;

(b) any covenant income, up to the amount of the standard maintenance grant, which is not so disregarded, shall be apportioned equally between the weeks of the period of study and there shall be disregarded from the covenant income to be so apportioned the amount which would have been disregarded under regulation 62(2)(g) and (h) (calculation of grant income) had the student been in receipt of the standard maintenance grant;

(c) the balance, if any, shall be divided by 52 or, if there are 53 benefit weeks (including part weeks) in the year, 53 and treated as weekly income of which £5 shall be disregarded.

(2) Where a student is in receipt of income by way of a grant and no contribution has been assessed, the amount of his covenant income shall be calculated in accordance with sub-paragraphs (a) to (c) of paragraph (1), except that—

(a) the value of the standard maintenance grant shall be abated by the amount of his grant income less an amount equal to the amount of any sums disregarded under regulation 62(2)(a) to (f); and

(b) the amount to be disregarded under paragraph (1)(b) shall be abated by an amount equal to the amount of any sums disregarded under regulation 62(2)(g) and (h).

Relationship with amounts to be disregarded under Schedule 9

65. No part of a student's covenant income or grant income shall be disregarded under paragraph 15 of Schedule 9 (charitable and voluntary payments) and any other income shall only be disregarded thereunder if, and to the extent that, the amount disregarded under regulation 63(2)(b) (calculation of covenant income where a contribution is assessed) or, as the case may be, 64(1)(c) (covenant income where no grant income or no contribution is assessed) is less than £5.

Other amounts to be disregarded

66.—(1) For the purposes of ascertaining income other than grant income and covenant income, any amounts intended for any expenditure specified in regulation 62(2) (calculation of grant income) necessary as a result of his attendance on the course shall be disregarded but only if, and to the extent that, the necessary expenditure exceeds or is likely to exceed the amount of the sums disregarded under regulation 62(2), 63(3) and 64(1)(a) or (b) (calculation of grant income and covenant income) on like expenditure.

(2) Where a claim is made in respect of any period in the normal summer vacation and any income is payable under a Deed of Covenant which commences or takes effect after the first day of that vacation, that income shall be disregarded.

Disregard of contribution

67. Where the claimant or his partner is a student and the income of one has been taken into account for the purpose of assessing a contribution to the student's grant, an amount equal to the contribution shall be disregarded for the purpose of calculating the income of the one liable to make that contribution.

Income treated as capital

68. Any amount by way of a refund of tax deducted from a student's income shall be treated as capital.

Disregard of changes occurring during summer vacation

69. In calculating a student's income an adjudication officer shall disregard any change in the standard maintenance grant occurring in the recognised summer vacation appropriate to the student's course, if that vacation does not form part of his period of study, from the date on which the change occurred up to the end of that vacation.

PART VI

URGENT CASES

Urgent cases

70.—(1) In a case to which this regulation applies, a claimant's weekly applicable amount and his income and capital shall be calculated in accordance with the following provisions of this Part.

(2) Subject to paragraph (4), this regulation applies to—

 (a) a claimant to whom paragraph (3) (certain persons from abroad) applies;

 (b) a claimant who is treated as possessing income under regulation 42 (3) (notional income);

 (c) a claimant who or whose partner is a seasonal worker treated as possessing earnings under regulation 43 (seasonal workers).

(3) This paragraph applies to a person from abroad within the meaning of regulation 21 (3) (special cases) who—

 (a) having, during any one period of limited leave of a kind referred to in sub-paragraph (a) of that definition (including any period as extended), supported himself without recourse to public funds other than any such recourse by reason of the previous application of this sub-paragraph, is temporarily without funds during that period of leave because remittances to him from abroad have been disrupted provided that there is a reasonable expectation that his supply of funds will be resumed;

 (b) is awaiting the determination of an application made under section 3 of the 1971 Act(**a**) (general provisions for regulation and control) for his leave to remain in the United Kingdom to be varied so as to be leave under any provision in the immigration rules which does not refer to there being, or to there needing to be, no recourse to public funds or to there being no charge on public funds during that limited leave;

 (c) is awaiting the outcome of an appeal made under Part II of the 1971 Act (including any period for which the appeal is treated as pending under section 33 (4) of that Act);

 (d) is a person to whom sub-paragraph (b) of that definition applies who has applied for leave within the meaning of the 1971 Act to remain in the United Kingdom, being leave under any provision in the immigration rules which does not refer to there being, or to there needing to be, no recourse to public funds or to there being no charge on public funds during that leave and is awaiting the determination of that application;

 (e) is a person to whom sub-paragraph (c) of that definition applies but whose removal from the United Kingdom has been deferred in writing by the Secretary of State;

(**a**) 1971 c.77, as amended by the British Nationality Act 1981 (c.61), section 39 and Schedule 4.

(f) is a person, other than someone to whom sub-paragraph (c) of that definition applies, who has been granted permission to remain in the United Kingdom pending the removal of a person to whom sub-paragraph (e) applies;

(g) is a person who has no or no further right of appeal under the 1971 Act but has been allowed to remain in the United Kingdom while an application so to remain is, or representations on his behalf are, being considered by the Secretary of State;

(h) is a person to whom sub-paragraph (d) of that definition applies and who has been allowed to remain in the United Kingdom with the consent in writing of the Secretary of State;

(i) is a person to whom sub-paragraph (e), (f) or (g) of that definition applies and whose applicable amount, but for this sub-paragraph, would if calculated in accordance with regulation 21 (special cases) be nil;

(j) is a person other than one to whom sub-paragraph (e) applies who is subject to a direction for his removal from the United Kingdom, but whose removal has been deferred in writing by the Secretary of State.

(4) This regulation shall only apply to a person to whom paragraph (2) (b) or (c) applies, where the income or earnings he is treated as possessing by virtue of regulation 42(3) (notional income) or regulation 43 (notional earnings of seasonal workers) is not readily available to him; and

(a) the amount of income support which would be payable but for this Part is less than the amount of income support payable by virtue of the provisions of this Part; and

(b) the adjudication officer is satisfied that, unless the provisions of this Part are applied to the claimant, the claimant or his family will suffer hardship.

Applicable amounts in urgent cases

71.—(1) For the purposes of calculating any entitlement to income support under this Part—

(a) except in a case to which sub-paragraph (b) or (c) applies, a claimant's weekly applicable amount shall be the aggregate of—

(i) 90 per cent of the amount applicable in respect of himself or, if he is a member of a couple or of a polygamous marriage, of the amount applicable in respect of both of them under paragraph 1 (1), (2) or (3) of Schedule 2 or, as the case may be, the amount applicable in respect of them under regulation 18 (polygamous marriages); and where regulation 22 (reduction in applicable amounts in certain cases of actual or notional unemployment benefit disqualification) applies, the reference in this head to 90 per cent of the amount applicable shall be construed as a reference to 90 per cent of the relevant amount under that regulation reduced by the percentage specified in paragraph (1) or (2), as the case may be, of that regulation;

(ii) the amount applicable under paragraph 2 of Schedule 2 in respect of any child or young person who is a member of his family except a child or young person whose capital, if calculated in accordance with Part V in like manner as for the claimant, except where otherwise provided, would exceed £3,000;

(iii) the amount, if applicable, specified in paragraph 15 (2) or (3) of Schedule 2 (pensioner premiums); and

(iv) any amounts applicable under regulation 17 (e) or 18 (f) (housing costs);

(b) where the claimant is a resident in board and lodging accommodation, a hostel, a residential care home or a nursing home, his weekly applicable amount shall be the aggregate of—

(i) 90 per cent of the amount of the allowance for personal expenses prescribed in paragraph 13 (a) of Schedule 4 (applicable amounts of persons in residential care and nursing homes) or paragraph 11 (b) of Schedule 5 (applicable amounts of persons in board and lodging accommodation or hostels) whichever is appropriate in respect of him or, if he is a member of a couple or of a polygamous marriage, of the amount applicable in respect of both or all of them; and where regulation 22 (reduction in applicable amounts in certain cases of actual or notional unemployment benefit disqualification) applies, the reference in this head to 90 per cent of the amount so reduced shall be construed as a reference to 90 per cent of the relevant amount under that regulation reduced by the percentage specified in paragraph (1) or (2), as the case may be, of that regulation;

(ii) the amount applicable under paragraph 13 (b) to (e) of Schedule 4 or paragraph 11 (c) to (f) of Schedule 5, whichever is appropriate, in respect of any child or young person who is a member of his family except a child or young person whose capital, if calculated in accordance with Part V in like manner as for the claimant, except where otherwise provided, would exceed £3,000;

(iii) the amount in respect of the weekly charge for his accommodation calculated in accordance with regulation 19 and Schedule 4 or regulation 20 and Schedule 5 whichever is appropriate except any amount in respect of a child or young person who is a member of the family and whose capital, if calculated in accordance with Part V in like manner as for the claimant, except where otherwise provided, would exceed £3,000.

(c) where the claimant is resident in residential accommodation, his weekly applicable amount shall be the aggregate of—

(i) 90 per cent of the amount in respect of personal expenses as is referred to in column (2) of paragraph 13 (a) to (c) and (e) of Schedule 7 (applicable amounts in special cases) applicable to him;

(ii) the amount applicable under column (2) of paragraph 13 (d) of Schedule 7, in respect of any child or young person who is a member of his family except a child or young person whose capital, if calculated in accordance with Part V in like manner as for the claimant, except where otherwise provided, would exceed £3,000;

(iii) the amount, being 80 per cent of the sum referred to in column (2) of paragraph 13 (a) to (c) and (e) of Schedule 7 (applicable amounts in special cases), in respect of the cost of the residential accommodation.

(2) The period for which a claimant's weekly applicable amount is to be calculated in accordance with paragraph (1) where paragraph (3) of regulation 70 (urgent cases) applies shall be—

(a) in a case to which sub-paragraph (a) of paragraph (3) of that regulation applies, any period, or the aggregate of any periods, not exceeding 42 days during any one period of leave to which that regulation applies;

(b) in a case to which sub-paragraph (b) of paragraph (3) of that regulation applies—

(i) the period ending not later than the date on which that determination is sent to the claimant; or

(ii) if he has a right to appeal against the determination under Part II of the 1971 Act, the period ending not later than 28 days after the date on which that determination is sent to him;

(c) in a case to which sub-paragraph (c) of paragraph (3) of that regulation applies, the period ending not later than the end of the period for which that appeal is treated as pending under section 33 (4) of the 1971 Act;

(d) in a case to which sub-paragraph (d) of paragraph (3) of that regulation applies, the period ending not later than—

(i) where the application referred to in that regulation is successful, the date on which that determination is sent to the claimant; or

(ii) where that application is refused, the date on which he is removed from the United Kingdom;

(e) in any case to which sub-paragraph (e), (f), (g), (h) or (j) of paragraph (3) of that regulation applies, the period ending not later than—

(i) the date on which the claimant is removed from the United Kingdom; or

(ii) where given leave (within the meaning of section 33 of the 1971 Act) to remain in the United Kingdom, or otherwise permitted in writing by the Secretary of State to remain in the United Kingdom, the date on which that leave was given;

(f) in a case to which sub-paragraph (i) of paragraph (3) of that regulation applies, the period ending not later than the date on which—

(i) leave (within the meaning of section 33 of the 1971 Act) is granted; or

(ii) he is removed from the United Kingdom; or

(iii) his immigration status is determined by the Secretary of State,

Assessment of income and capital in urgent cases

72.—(1) The claimant's income shall be calculated in accordance with Part V subject to the following modifications—

(a) any income possessed or treated as possessed by him shall be taken into account in full notwithstanding any provision in that Part disregarding the whole or any part of that income;

(b) any income to which regulation 53 (calculation of tariff income from capital) applies shall be disregarded;

(c) income treated as capital by virtue of regulations 24 (1) and (2) (treatment of charitable or voluntary payments) and 48 (1), (2) and (3) (income treated as capital) shall be taken into account as income;

(d) in a case to which paragraph (2) (b) of regulation 70 (urgent cases) applies, any income to which regulation 42 (3) (notional income) applies shall be disregarded;

(e) in a case to which paragraph (2) (c) of regulation 70 applies, any income to which regulation 43 (seasonal workers) applies shall be disregarded.

(2) The claimant's capital calculated in accordance with Part V, but including any capital referred to in paragraphs 3 and, to the extent that such assets as are referred to in paragraph 6 consist of liquid assets, 6 and 7 and 9 (b) of Schedule 10 (capital to be disregarded) shall be taken into account in full and the amount of income support which would, but for this paragraph be payable under this regulation, shall be payable only to the extent that it exceeds the amount of that capital.

Signed by authority of the Secretary of State for Social Services.

Nicholas Scott

20th November 1987   Minister of State, Department of Health and Social Security

---

SCHEDULE 1   Regulation 8

PERSONS NOT REQUIRED TO BE AVAILABLE FOR EMPLOYMENT

Lone parents

1. A person who is a lone parent and responsible for a child who is a member of his household.

Single persons looking after foster children

2. A single claimant or a lone parent with whom a child is boarded out by a local authority or voluntary organisation within the meaning of the Child Care Act 1980(**a**) or, in Scotland, the Social Work (Scotland) Act 1968(**b**).

(**a**) 1980 c.5.
(**b**) 1968 c.49.

Persons temporarily looking after another person

3. A person who is—

(a) looking after a child because the parent of that child or the person who usually looks after him is ill or is temporarily absent from his home; or

(b) looking after a member of the family who is temporarily ill.

Persons caring for another person

4. A person who is regularly and substantially engaged in caring for another person if—

(a) the person doing the caring is in receipt of an invalid care allowance under section 37 of the Social Security Act(a); or

(b) the person being cared for is in receipt of attendance allowance under section 35 of that Act; or

(c) the person being cared for has claimed attendance allowance under that section but only for the period up to the date of determination of that claim, or the period of 26 weeks from the date of that claim, whichever date is the earlier.

Persons incapable of work

5. A person who, by reason of some disease or bodily or mental disablement, is incapable of work.

Disabled workers

6. A person who is mentally or physically disabled and whose earning capacity is, by reason of that disability, reduced to 75 per cent or less of what he would, but for that disability, be reasonably expected to earn.

Disabled students

7. A person who is a student and who, by reason of any mental or physical disability, would, in comparison with other students, be unlikely to obtain employment within a reasonable period of time.

Blind persons

8. A person who is a blind person registered in a register compiled by a local authority under section 29 of the National Assistance Act 1948(b) (welfare services) or, in Scotland, who has been certified as blind in a register maintained by or on behalf of a regional or islands council, but a person who has ceased to be so registered on regaining his eyesight shall nevertheless be treated as so registered for a period of 28 weeks following the date on which he ceased to be so registered.

Pregnancy

9. A woman who—

(a) is incapable of work by reason of pregnancy; or

(b) is or has been pregnant but only for the period commencing 11 weeks before her expected week of confinement and ending seven weeks after the date on which her pregnancy ends.

Persons in education

10. A person to whom any provision of regulation 13(2)(a) to (e) (persons receiving relevant education who are parents, persons severely handicapped, orphans and persons estranged from their parents or guardian) applies.

Training allowances

11. A person who is in receipt of a training allowance.

Open University students

12. A person who is following an Open University course and is attending, as a requirement of that course, a residential course.

(a) 1975 c.14; subsection (3) of section 37 was amended by sections 37, 86 and Schedule 11 of the Social Security Act 1986 (c.50).

(b) 1948 c.29; section 29 was amended by section 1(2) of the National Assistance (Amendment) Act 1959 (c.30); the Mental Health (Scotland) Act 1960 (c.61), sections 113 and 114 and Schedule 4; the Local Government Act 1972 (c.70), Schedule 23, paragraph 2; the Employment and Training Act 1973 (c.50), Schedule 3, paragraph 3; the National Health Service Act 1977 (c.49), Schedule 15, paragraph 6; and the Health and Social Services and Social Security Adjudication Act 1983 (c.41), Schedule 10, Part I.

Persons within 10 years of pensionable age

13. A person who is within 10 years of attaining pensionable age and—

(a) has not been in remunerative work during the previous 10 years; and

(b) has no prospect of future employment in remunerative work; and

(c) during that period has not been required to be available for employment in accordance with section 20(3)(d)(i) of the Act (conditions of entitlement to income support), or would not have been so required had a claim to income support been made by or in respect of him.

Persons aged 60

14. A person aged not less than 60.

Allowances under the Job Release Act 1977

15. A person who is in receipt of an allowance under the Job Release Act 1977**(a)**.

Refugees

16. Notwithstanding that he would otherwise be a student, a person who is a refugee within the definition in Article 1 of the Convention relating to the Status of Refugees done at Geneva on 28th July 1951**(b)** as extended by Article 1(2) of the Protocol relating to the Status of Refugees done at New York on 31st January 1967**(c)** and who—

(a) is attending for more than 15 hours a week a course for the purpose of learning English so that he may obtain employment; and

(b) on the date on which that course commenced, had been in Great Britain for not more than 12 months,

but only for a period not exceeding nine months.

Persons required to attend court

17. A person who is required to attend court for any period exceeding two days as a justice of the peace, a party to any proceedings, a witness or a juror.

Discharged prisoners

18. A person who has been discharged from detention in a prison, remand centre or youth custody institution but only for the period of seven days commencing with the date of his discharge.

Persons affected by a trade dispute

19. A person to whom section 23 of the Act (trade disputes) applies or in respect of whom section 20(3) of the Act (conditions of entitlement to income support) has effect as modified by section 23(8) of the Act (persons affected by a trade dispute and such persons returning to work for the first 15 days).

Persons from abroad

20. A person to whom regulation 70(3) (applicable amount of certain persons from abroad) applies.

Persons in custody

21. A person remanded in, or committed in, custody for trial or for sentencing.

(a) 1977 c.8.
(b) Cmnd. 9171.
(c) Cmnd. 3906.

Regulations 17 and 18	**SCHEDULE 2**

APPLICABLE AMOUNTS

Regulations 17(a) and (b) PART I
and 18(a) (b) and (c)

PERSONAL ALLOWANCES

1. The weekly amounts specified in column (2) below in respect of each person or couple specified in column (1) shall be the weekly amounts specified for the purposes of regulations 17(a) and 18(a) and (b) (applicable amounts and polygamous marriages).

Column (1)	Column (2)
Person or Couple	*Amount*
(1) Single claimant aged—	
(a) less than 18;	(1) (a) £19·40;
(b) not less than 18 but less than 25;	(b) £26·05;
(c) not less than 25.	(c) £33·40.
(2) Lone parent aged—	
(a) less than 18;	(2) (a) £19·40;
(b) not less than 18.	(b) £33·40.
(3) Couple—	
(a) where both members are aged less than 18;	(3) (a) £38·80;
(b) where at least one member is aged not less than 18.	(b) £51·45.

2. The weekly amounts specified in column (2) below in respect of each person specified in column (1) shall be the weekly amounts specified for the purposes of regulations 17(b) and 18(c).

Column (1)	Column (2)	
Child or Young Person	*Amount*	
Person aged—		
(a) less than 11;	(a)	£10·75;
(b) not less than 11 but less than 16;	(b)	£16·10;
(c) not less than 16 but less than 18;	(c)	£19·40;
(d) not less than 18.	(d)	£26·05.

Regulations 17(c) and 18(d) PART II

FAMILY PREMIUM

3. The weekly amount for the purposes of regulations 17(c) and 18(d) in respect of a family of which at least one member is a child or young person shall be £6·15.

Regulations 17(d) and 18(e) PART III

PREMIUMS

4. Except as provided in paragraph 5, the weekly premiums specified in Part IV of this Schedule shall, for the purposes of regulations 17(d) and 18(e), be applicable to a claimant who satisfies the condition specified in paragraphs 8 to 14 in respect of that premium.

5. Subject to paragraph 6, where a claimant satisfies the conditions in respect of more than one premium in this Part of this Schedule, only one premium shall be applicable to him and, if they are different amounts, the higher or highest amount shall apply.

6.—(1) The severe disability premium to which paragraph 13 applies may be applicable in addition to either the higher pensioner premium to which paragraph 10 applies or the disability premium to which paragraph 11 applies.

(2) The disabled child premium to which paragraph 14 applies may be applicable in addition to any other premium which may apply under this Schedule.

7. For the purposes of this Part of this Schedule, once a premium is applicable to a claimant under this Part, a person shall be treated as being in receipt of any benefit—

(a) in the case of a benefit to which the Social Security (Overlapping Benefits) Regulations 1979(a) applies, for any period during which, apart from the provisions of those Regulations, he would be in receipt of that benefit; and

(b) for any period spent by a person in undertaking a course of training or instruction provided or approved by the Manpower Services Commission under section 2 of the Employment and Training Act 1973(b).

Lone Parent Premium

8. The condition is that the claimant is a member of a family but has no partner.

Pensioner Premium

9. The condition is that the claimant—

(a) is a single claimant or lone parent aged not less than 60 but less than 80; or

(b) has a partner and is, or his partner is, aged not less than 60 but less than 80.

Higher Pensioner Premium

10.—(1) Where the claimant is a single claimant or a lone parent, the condition is that—

(a) he is aged not less than 80; or

(b) he is aged less than 80 but not less than 60, and

(i) the additional condition specified in paragraph 12(1)(a) is satisfied; or

(ii) he was entitled to income support and the disability premium was applicable to him in respect of a benefit week within eight weeks of his 60th birthday and he has, subject to sub-paragraph (3), remained continuously entitled to income support since attaining that age.

(2) Where the claimant has a partner, the condition is that—

(a) he or his partner is aged not less than 80; or

(b) he or his partner is aged less than 80 but not less than 60 and either—

(i) the additional condition specified in paragraph 12(1)(a) is satisfied by whichever of them is aged not less than 60; or

(ii) he was entitled to income support and the disability premium was applicable to him in respect of a benefit week within eight weeks of his 60th birthday and he has, subject to sub-paragraph (3), remained continuously entitled to income support since attaining that age.

(3) For the purposes of this paragraph and paragraph 12—

(a) once the higher pensioner premium is applicable to a claimant, if he then ceases, for a period of eight weeks or less, to be entitled to income support, he shall, on becoming re-entitled to income support, thereafter be treated as having been continuously entitled thereto;

(b) in so far as sub-paragraphs (1)(b)(ii) and (2)(b)(ii) are concerned, if a claimant ceases to be entitled to income support for a period not exceeding eight weeks which includes his 60th birthday, he shall, on becoming re-entitled to income support, thereafter be treated as having been continuously entitled thereto.

Disability Premium

11. The condition is that—

(a) where the claimant is a single claimant or a lone parent, he is aged less than 60 and the additional condition specified in paragraph 12 is satisfied; or

(a) S.I. 1979/597.
(b) 1973 c.50, as amended by sections 9 and 11 and Schedule 2, Part II paragraph 9 and Schedule 3 of the Employment and Training Act 1981 (c.57).

(b) where the claimant has a partner, either—

    (i) the claimant is aged less than 60 and the additional condition specified in paragraph 12(1)(a) or (b) is satisfied by him; or

    (ii) his partner is aged less than 60 and the additional condition specified in paragraph 12(1)(a) is satisfied by his partner.

Additional condition for the Higher Pensioner and Disability Premiums

12.—(1) Subject to sub-paragraph (2) and paragraph 7 the additional condition referred to in paragraphs 10 and 11 is that either—

(a) the claimant or, as the case may be, his partner—

    (i) is in receipt of one or more of the following benefits: attendance allowance, mobility allowance, mobility supplement, invalidity pension under section 15 of the Social Security Act(**a**), or severe disablement allowance under section 36 of that Act(**b**); or

    (ii) is provided by the Secretary of State with an invalid carriage or other vehicle under section 5(2) of the National Health Service Act 1977(**c**) (other services) or, in Scotland, under section 46 of the National Health Service (Scotland) Act 1978(**d**) (provision of vehicles) or receives payments by way of grant from the Secretary of State under paragraph 2 of Schedule 2 to that 1977 Act (additional provisions as to vehicles) or, in Scotland, under that section 46; or

    (iii) is registered as blind in a register compiled by a local authority under section 29 of the National Assistance Act 1948(**e**) (welfare services) or, in Scotland, has been certified as blind and in consequence he is registered as blind in a register maintained by or on behalf of a regional or islands council; or

(b) the claimant is and has, in respect of a period of not less than 28 weeks, been treated as having been incapable of work for the purposes of one or more of the provisions of the Social Security Act or Part I of the Social Security and Housing Benefits Act 1982(**f**) or, if he was in Northern Ireland for the whole or part of that period, was treated as having been incapable of work for the purposes of one or more of the comparable Northern Irish provisions; or

(c) the claimant or, as the case may be, his partner was in receipt of either—

    (i) mobility allowance or invalidity pension under section 15 of the Social Security Act when entitlement to that benefit ceased solely on account of the maximum age for its payment being reached and the claimant has since remained continuously entitled to income support and, if the mobility allowance or invalidity pension was payable to his partner, the partner is still alive; or

    (ii) except where paragraph 1(a), (b), (c)(ii) or (d)(ii) of Schedule 7 (patients) applies, attendance allowance which is no longer in payment solely on account of the claimant or, as the case may be, his partner having undergone or having been treated as undergoing treatment for a period of more than four weeks by virtue of regulation 5 of the Social Security (Attendance Allowance) (No. 2) Regulations 1975(**g**),

and, in either case, the higher pensioner premium or disability premium has been applicable to the claimant or his partner.

(2) For the purposes of sub-paragraph (1)(a)(iii), a person who has ceased to be registered as blind on regaining his eyesight shall nevertheless be treated as blind and as satisfying the additional condition set out in that sub-paragraph for a period of 28 weeks following the date on which he ceased to be so registered.

(3) For the purposes of sub-paragraph (1)(b), once the disability premium is applicable to a claimant by virtue of his satisfying the condition specified in that provision, if he then ceases, for a period of eight weeks or less, to be treated as incapable of work for the purposes of the provisions specified in that provision he shall, on again becoming so incapable of work, immediately thereafter be treated as satisfying the condition in sub-paragraph (1)(b).

(**a**) Section 15 was amended by the Social Security Pensions Act 1975 (c.60), Schedule 4 paragraph 40, the Social Security Act 1979 (c.18) section 21, Schedule 1, paragraph 1 and Schedule 3 paragraph 7, the Social Security and Housing Benefits Act 1982 (c.24), Schedule 4, Part I, paragraph 10 and the Social Security Act 1986 (c.50), Schedule 10, Part V, paragraph 83.

(**b**) Section 36 was substituted by the Health and Social Security Act 1984 (c.48), section 11; and subsection (4A) of that section inserted by the Social Security Act 1985 (c.53), Schedule 4, paragraph 3.

(**c**) 1977 c.49; section 5(2) amended and subsection (2A) added by section 1 of the Public Health Laboratory Service Act 1979 (c.23) and subsection (2B) added by section 9 of the Health and Social Security Act 1984 (c.48).

(**d**) 1978 c.29.

(**e**) 1948 c.29; section 29 was amended by section 1(2) of the National Assistance (Amendment) Act 1959 (c.30); the Mental Health (Scotland) Act 1960 (c.61) sections 113 and 114 and Schedule 4; the Local Government Act 1972 (c.70) Schedule 23 paragraph 2; the Employment and Training Act 1973 (c.50) Schedule 3 paragraph 3; the National Health Service Act 1977 (c.49) Schedule 15 paragraph 6; and the Health and Social Services and Social Security Adjudications Act 1983 (c.41) Schedule 10 Part I.

(**f**) 1982 c.24.

(**g**) S.I. 1975/598; the relevant amending instrument is S.I.1983/1015.

(4) For the purpose of sub-paragraph (1)(c), once the higher pensioner premium is applicable to the claimant by virtue of his satisfying the condition specified in that provision, if he then ceases, for a period of eight weeks or less, to be entitled to income support, he shall on again becoming so entitled to income support, immediately thereafter be treated as satisfying the condition in sub-paragraph (1)(c).

Severe Disability Premium

13.—(1) The condition is that the claimant is a severely disabled person.

(2) For the purposes of sub-paragraph (1), a claimant shall be treated as being a severely disabled person if, and only if—

(a) in the case of a single claimant or a lone parent—

    (i) he is in receipt of attendance allowance, and

    (ii) subject to sub-paragraph (3), he has no non-dependants aged 18 or over residing with him, and

    (iii) no-one is in receipt of an invalid care allowance under section 37 of the Social Security Act**(a)** in respect of caring for him;

(b) if he has a partner—

    (i) he is in receipt of attendance allowance; and

    (ii) his partner is also in receipt of such an allowance or, if he is a member of a polygamous marriage, all the partners of that marriage are in receipt thereof; and

    (iii) subject to sub-paragraph (3), he has no non-dependants aged 18 or over residing with him,

and, either there is someone in receipt of an invalid care allowance in respect of caring for only one of the couple or, in the case of a polygamous marriage, for one or more but not all the partners of the marriage, or, as the case maybe, there is no one in receipt of such an allowance in respect of caring for either member of the couple or any partner of the polygamous marriage.

(3) For the purposes of sub-paragraph (2)(a)(ii) and (2)(b)(iii) no account shall be taken of—

(a) a person receiving attendance allowance; or

(b) a person to whom regulation 3(3) (non-dependants) applies; or

(c) subject to sub-paragraph (4), a person who joins the claimant's household for the first time in order to care for the claimant or his partner and immediately before so joining the claimant or his partner was treated as a severely disabled person.

(4) Sub-paragraph (3)(c) shall apply only for the first 12 weeks following the date on which the person to whom that provision applies first joins the claimant's household.

Disabled Child Premium

14. The condition is that a child or young person for whom the claimant or a partner of his is responsible and who is a member of the claimant's household—

(a) has no capital or capital which, if calculated in accordance with Part V in like manner as for the claimant, except where otherwise provided, would not exceed £3,000; and

(b) is in receipt of attendance allowance or mobility allowance or both or is no longer in receipt of that allowance because he is a patient provided that the child or young person continues to be a member of the family; or

(c) is blind or treated as blind within the meaning of paragraph 12(1)(a)(iii) and (2).

PART IV

WEEKLY AMOUNTS OF PREMIUMS SPECIFIED IN PART III

Premium	Amount
15.—(1) Lone parent premium.	(1) £3·70.
(2) Pensioner premium—	
(a) where the claimant satisfies the condition in paragraph 9(a);	(2) (a) £10·65;
(b) where the claimant satisfies the condition in paragraph 9(b).	(b) £16·25.

(a) Section 37 was amended by the Social Security (Miscellaneous Provisions) Act 1977 (c.5), section 22(2).

Premium	*Amount*
(3) Higher Pensioner Premium—	
(a) where the claimant satisfies the condition in paragraph 10(1)(a) or (b);	(3) (a) £13·05;
(b) where the claimant satisfies the condition in paragraph 10(2)(a) or (b);	(b) £18·60.
(4) Disability Premium—	
(a) where the claimant satisfies the condition in paragraph 11(a);	(4) (a) £13·05;
(b) where the claimant satisfies the condition in paragraph 11(b).	(b) £18·60.
(5) Severe Disability Premium—	
(a) where the claimant satisfies the condition in paragraph 13(2)(a);	(5) (a) £24·75;
(b) where the claimant satisfies the condition in paragraph 13(2)(b)—	
(i) if there is someone in receipt of an invalid care allowance;	(b) (i) £24·75.
(ii) if no-one is in receipt of such an allowance.	(ii) £49·50.
(6) Disabled Child Premium.	(6) £6·15 in respect of each child or young person in respect of whom the condition specified in paragraph 14 is satisfied.

PART V

ROUNDING OF FRACTIONS

16. Where income support is awarded for a period which is not a complete benefit week and the applicable amount in respect of that period results in an amount which includes a fraction of a penny that fraction shall be treated as a penny.

Regulations 17(e) and 18(f)

SCHEDULE 3

HOUSING COSTS

Eligible Housing Costs

1. Subject to the following provisions of this Schedule, the amounts which may be applicable to a person in respect of mortgage interest payments or other prescribed housing costs under regulation 17(e) or 18(f) (applicable amounts) are—

(a) mortgage interest payments;

(b) interest on loans for repairs and improvements to the dwelling occupied as the home;

(c) payments by way of rent, ground rent or, in Scotland, feu duty, relating to a long tenancy;

(d) payments under a co-ownership scheme;

(e) payments under or relating to a tenancy or licence of a Crown tenant;

(f) service charges;

(g) where the dwelling occupied as the home is a tent, payments in respect of the tent and the site on which it stands;

(h) payments analogous to those mentioned in this paragraph.

Basic condition of entitlement to housing costs

2. Subject to the following provisions of this Schedule, the housing costs referred to in paragraph 1 shall be met where the claimant, or if he is one of a family, he or any member of his family is treated as responsible for the expenditure to which that cost relates in respect of the dwelling occupied as the home which he or any member of his family is treated as occupying.

Circumstances in which a person is treated as responsible for housing costs

3.—(1) A person is to be treated as responsible for the expenditure which relates to housing costs where—

(a) he or his partner is liable to meet those costs other than to a member of the same household;

(b) because the person liable to meet those costs is not doing so, he has to meet those costs in order to continue to live in the dwelling occupied as the home and either he was formerly the partner of the person liable, or he is some other person whom it is reasonable to treat as liable to meet the cost;

(c) he in practice shares those costs with other members of his household, other than close relatives of his or his partner, at least one of whom either is responsible under the preceding provisions of this paragraph or has an equivalent responsibility for housing benefit expenditure and for which it is reasonable in the circumstances to treat him as sharing responsibility.

(2) Where any one or more, but not all, members of the claimant's family are affected by a trade dispute, the housing costs shall be treated as those of those members of the family not so affected.

Circumstances in which a person is or is not to be treated as occupying a dwelling as his home

4.—(1) Subject to the following provisions of this paragraph, a person shall be treated as occupying as his home the dwelling normally occupied as his home by himself or, if he is a member of a family, by himself and his family and he shall not be treated as occupying any other dwelling as his home.

(2) In determining whether a dwelling is the dwelling normally occupied as the claimant's home for the purposes of sub-paragraph (1) regard shall be had to any other dwelling occupied by the claimant or by him and his family whether or not that dwelling is in Great Britain.

(3) Subject to sub-paragraph (4) where a single claimant or a lone parent is a student or is on a training course and is liable to make payments (including payments of mortgage interest or, in Scotland, payments under heritable securities or, in either case, analogous payments) in respect of either (but not both) the dwelling which he occupies for the purpose of attending his course of study or his training course or, as the case may be, the dwelling which he occupies when not attending his course, he shall be treated as occupying as his home the dwelling in respect of which he is liable to make payments.

(4) A full-time student shall not be treated as occupying a dwelling as his home for any week of absence from it, other than an absence occasioned by the need to enter hospital for treatment, outside the period of study, if the main purpose of his occupation during the period of study would be to facilitate attendance on his course.

(5) Where a claimant has been required to move into temporary accommodation by reason of essential repairs being carried out to the dwelling normally occupied as his home and he is liable to make payments (including payments of mortgage interest or, in Scotland, payments under heritable securities or, in either case analogous payments) in respect of either (but not both) the dwelling normally occupied or the temporary accommodation, he shall be treated as occupying as his home the dwelling in respect of which he is liable to make payments.

(6) Where a person is liable to make payments in respect of two (but not more than two) dwellings, he shall be treated as occupying both dwellings as his home only—

(a) where he has left and remains absent from the former dwelling occupied as the home through fear of violence in that dwelling or by a former member of his family and it is reasonable that housing costs should be met in respect of both his former dwelling and his present dwelling occupied as the home; or

(b) in the case of a couple or a member of a polygamous marriage where a partner is a student or is on a training course and it is unavoidable that he or they should occupy two separate dwellings and reasonable that housing costs should be met in respect of both dwellings;

(c) in the case where a person has moved into a new dwelling occupied as the home, except where sub-paragraph (5) applies, for a period not exceeding four benefit weeks if his liability to make payments in respect of two dwellings is unavoidable.

(7) Where—

(a) a person has moved into a dwelling and was liable to make payments in respect of that dwelling before moving in; and

(b) had claimed income support before moving in and either that claim has not yet been determined or it has been determined but an amount has not been included under this Schedule and if the claim has been refused a further claim has been made within four weeks of the date on which the claimant moved into the new dwelling occupied as the home; and

(c) the delay in moving into the dwelling in respect of which there was liability to make payments before moving in was reasonable and—

      (i) that delay was necessary in order to adapt the dwelling to meet the disablement needs of the claimant or any member of his family; or

      (ii) the move was delayed pending the outcome of an application under Part III of the Act for a social fund payment to meet a need arising out of the move or in connection with setting up the home in the dwelling and either a member of the claimant's family is aged five or under or the claimant's applicable amount includes a premium under paragraph 9, 10, 11, 13 or 14 of Schedule 2; or

      (iii) the person became liable to make payments in respect of the dwelling while he was a patient or in residential accommodation,

he shall be treated as occupying the dwelling as his home for any period not exceeding four weeks immediately prior to the date on which he moved into the dwelling and in respect of which he was liable to make payments.

(8) A person shall be treated as occupying a dwelling as his home for a period not exceeding 52 weeks while he is temporarily absent therefrom only if—

    (a) he intends to return to occupy the dwelling as his home; and

    (b) the part of the dwelling normally occupied by him has not been let or, as the case may be, sub-let; and

    (c) the period of absence is unlikely to exceed 52 weeks, or, in exceptional circumstances, (for example where the person is in hospital or otherwise has no control over the length of his absence) is unlikely substantially to exceed that period.

(9) In this paragraph—

    (a) " patient " means a person who is undergoing medical or other treatment as an in-patient in any hospital or similar institution;

    (b) " residential accommodation " means accommodation—

      (i) provided under sections 21 to 24 and 26 of the National Assistance Act 1948**(a)** (provision of accommodation); or

      (ii) provided under section 21(1) of, and paragraph 1 or 2 of Schedule 8 to, the National Health Service Act 1977**(b)** (prevention, care and after-care); or

      (iii) provided under section 59 of the Social Work (Scotland) Act 1968**(c)** (provision of residential and other establishments) where board is available to the claimant; or

      (iv) which is a residential care home within the meaning of that expression in regulation 19(3) (persons in residential care or nursing homes) other than sub-paragraph (b) of that definition; or

      (v) which is a nursing home;

    (c) " training course " means such a course as is referred to in sub-paragraph (c) of the definition of training allowance in regulation 2(1) (interpretation).

Circumstances in which no amount of housing costs may be met

5. No amount may be met under the provisions of this Schedule—

    (a) in respect of housing benefit expenditure; or

    (b) where the claimant is in accommodation to which either regulation 19 (applicable amounts for persons in residential care or nursing homes) or 20 (applicable amounts for persons in board and lodging accommodation or hostels) applies, unless his absence from the dwelling occupied as his home in such accommodation is only temporary within the meaning of paragraph 4(8).

(a) 1948 c.29; section 21 was amended by the Local Government Act 1972 (c.70), Schedule 23 paragraphs 1 and 2 and Schedule 30; the National Health Service Reorganisation Act 1973 (c.32), Schedule 4 paragraph 44 and Schedule 5; the Housing (Homeless Persons) Act 1977 (c.48), Schedule; the National Health Service Act 1977 (c.49), Schedule 15 paragraph 5; the Health Services Act 1980 (c.53), Schedule 1 Part I paragraph 5. Section 22 was amended by the Social Work (Scotland) Act 1968 (c.49), section 87(4) and Schedule 9 Part I; the Supplementary Benefits Act 1976 (c.71) Schedule 7 paragraph 3; the Housing (Homeless Persons) Act 1977 (c.48), Schedule; the Social Security Act 1980 (c.30), section 20, Schedule 4 paragraph 2(1) and Schedule 5 Part II and the Health and Social Services and Social Security Adjudications Act 1983 (c.41), section 20(1)(a). Section 24 was amended by the National Assistance (Amendment) Act 1959 (c.30), section 1(1); the National Health Service (Scotland) Act 1972 (c.58), Schedule 6 paragraph 82; the Local Government Act 1972 (c.70), Schedule 23 paragraph 2; the National Health Service Reorganisation Act 1972 (c.32), Schedule 4 paragraph 45 and the Housing (Homeless Persons) Act 1977 (c.48), Schedule. Section 26 was amended by the Health Services and Public Health Act 1968 (c.46), section 44 and Schedule 4 and the Social Work (Scotland) Act 1968 (c.49) Schedule 9 Part I and applied by section 87(3); the Local Government Act 1972 (c.70), Schedule 23 paragraph 2; the Housing (Homeless Persons) Act 1977 (c.48), Schedule and the Health and Social Services and Social Security Adjudications Act 1983 (c.41), section 20(1)(b).
(b) 1977 c.49.
(c) 1968 c.49.

Apportionment of housing costs

6.—(1) Where—

    (a) for the purposes of section 48(5) of the General Rate Act 1967**(a)** (reduction of rates on dwellings), it appears to a rating authority or it is determined in pursuance of sub-section (6) of that section 48 that the hereditament including the dwelling occupied as the home is a mixed hereditament and that only a proportion of the rateable value of the hereditament is attributable to use for the purpose of a private dwelling; or

    (b) in Scotland, an assessor acting pursuant to section 45(1) of the Water (Scotland) Act 1980**(b)** (provision as to valuation roll) has apportioned the net annual value of the premises including the dwelling occupied as the home between the part occupied as a dwelling and the remainder,

the amounts applicable under this Schedule shall be such proportion of the amounts applicable in respect of the hereditament or premises as a whole as is equal to the proportion of the rateable value of the hereditament attributable to the part of the hereditament used for the purposes of a private tenancy or, in Scotland, the proportion of the net annual value of the premises apportioned to the part occupied as a dwelling house.

(2) Where responsibility for expenditure which relates to housing costs met under this Schedule is shared, the amounts applicable shall be calculated by reference to the appropriate proportion of that expenditure for which the claimant is responsible.

Interest on loans to acquire an interest in the dwelling occupied as the home

7.—(1) Subject to sub-paragraphs (2) to (9), the following amounts shall be met under this paragraph—

    (a) if the claimant or, if he is a member of a couple, or if a member of a polygamous marriage, he or any partner of his is aged 60 or over, 100 per cent of the eligible interest in his case;

    (b) if the claimant or, if he is a member of a couple, or if a member of a polygamous marriage, he and any partner of his are aged under 60—

        (i) where the claimant has been in receipt of income support in respect of a continuous period of not less than 16 weeks, 100 per cent of the eligible interest in his case;

        (ii) in any other case, 50 per cent of the eligible interest in that case.

(2) Where in a case to which sub-paragraph (1)(b)(ii) applies—

    (a) either—

        (i) the claim for income support is refused; or

        (ii) an award of income support is terminated on appeal or review,

    solely because the claimant's income exceeds his applicable amount by virtue of the fact that only 50 per cent of the eligible interest in his case is to be met under sub-paragraph (1)(b)(ii); and

    (b) the claimant or any partner of his makes a further claim no later than 20 weeks after—

        (i) where the original claim for income support was refused, the date of that claim; or

        (ii) where an award of income support was terminated on appeal or review, the date of the claim in respect of which that award was made,

the amount to be met under this paragraph commencing on a date not before the expiry of 16 weeks from the date specified in (i) or (ii) above, as the case may be, shall be 100 per cent of the eligible interest in that case and until that date shall be the amount specified in sub-paragraph (1)(b)(ii).

(3) Subject to sub-paragraphs (4) to (6), in this paragraph " eligible interest " means the amount of interest on a loan, whether or not secured by way of a mortgage or, in Scotland, under a heritable security, taken out to defray money applied for the purpose of—

    (a) acquiring an interest in the dwelling occupied as the home; or

    (b) paying off another loan but only to the extent that interest on that other loan would have been eligible interest had the loan not been paid off.

(4) Subject to sub-paragraphs (5) and (6) and paragraph 6, the amount of eligible interest in any case shall be the amount, calculated on weekly basis, of—

    (a) where, or in so far as, section 26 of the Finance Act 1982**(c)** (deduction of tax from certain loan interest) applies to the payments of interest on the loan, the interest which is payable

---

(a) 1967 c.9; sections 48(5) and (6) were amended by the Local Government, Planning and Land Act 1980 (c.65) section 33; section 48(6) was also amended by the Rates Act 1984 (c.33) section 16 Schedule 1 paragraph 10.

(b) 1980 c.45.

(c) 1982 c.39.

after deduction of a sum equal to income tax thereon at the basic rate for the year of assessment in which the payment of interest becomes due;

(b) in any other case the interest which is payable on the loan without deduction of such a sum.

(5) Where a loan is applied only in part for the purpose specified in sub-paragraph (3), only such proportion of the interest thereon as is equal to the proportion of the loan applied for that purpose shall qualify as eligible interest.

(6) Where, under the terms of a loan taken out for a purpose specified in sub-paragraph (3), interest is payable on accumulated arrears of interest (whether or not those arrears have been consolidated with the outstanding capital), the amount of such interest shall be met under this paragraph as if it were eligible interest but only in so far as it represents interest on arrears incurred during any period—

(a) when sub-paragraph (1)(b)(ii) applied in that case; or

(b) when the claimant was not entitled to income support which fell within the period of 20 weeks specified in sub-paragraph (2)(b),

and, in either case, only to the extent that arrears do not exceed 50 per cent of the eligible interest that otherwise would have been payable during the period in question.

(7) Where a person who was formerly one of a couple or a polygamous marriage—

(a) has taken out, either solely or jointly with his former partner, a loan secured on the dwelling occupied as the home for a purpose other than one specified in sub-paragraph (3); and

(b) has left the dwelling occupied as the home and either cannot or will not pay the interest on the loan,

and, if that person's former partner has to pay the interest on the loan in order to continue to live in the dwelling occupied as the home, there shall be met in respect of the former partner under this paragraph the amount of interest on the loan calculated as if it were a loan taken out for a purpose specified in sub-paragraph (3).

(8) Where an amount is met under this paragraph, if, notwithstanding that the amount of interest payable is reduced by virtue of—

(a) a reduction in interest rates; or

(b) a reduction in the amount of loan capital outstanding,

the amount of instalments which the borrower is liable to pay remains constant, the amount met shall not be adjusted to take account of the new amount of interest payable except where a determination is subsequently reviewed under section 104(1)(b) of the Social Security Act(a) (review of decisions).

(9) For the purpose of sub-paragraph (1)—

(a) a person shall be treated as being in receipt of income support during the following periods—

(i) any period in respect of which it was subsequently held, on appeal or review, that he was so entitled; and

(ii) any period of eight weeks or less in respect of which he was not in receipt of income support and which fell immediately between periods in respect of which he was in receipt thereof or to which (i) above applies;

(b) a person shall be treated as not being in receipt of income support during any period other than a period to which (a)(ii) above applies in respect of which it is subsequently held on appeal or review that he was not so entitled;

(c) where the claimant—

(i) was a member of a couple or a polygamous marriage; and

(ii) his partner was, in respect of a past period, in receipt of income support for himself and the claimant; and

(iii) the claimant is no longer a member of that couple or polygamous marriage; and

(iv) the claimant made his claim for income support within eight weeks of ceasing to be a member of that couple or polygamous marriage,

he shall be treated as having been in receipt of income support for the same period as his former partner had been or had been treated, for the purposes of sub-paragraph (1), as having been;

(d) where the claimant's partner's applicable amount was determined in accordance with paragraph 1(1) (single claimants) or paragraph 1(2) (lone parent) of Schedule 2 (applicable amounts) in respect of a past period, provided that the claim was made within eight weeks of the claimant and his partner becoming one of a couple or polygamous marriage, the claimant shall be treated as having been in receipt of income support for the same period as his partner had been or had been treated, for the purposes of sub-paragraph (1), as having been;

(a) Section 104 is applied by section 52(3) of the Social Security Act 1986 (c.50); sub-section (1) was substituted by section 52 of, and paragraph 10 of Schedule 5 to, the Social Security Act 1986.

(e) where the claimant is a member of a couple or a polygamous marriage and his partner was, in respect of a past period in receipt of income support for himself and the claimant, and the claimant has become in receipt as a result of an election by the members of the couple or polygamous marriage, he shall be treated as having been in receipt of income support for the same period as his partner had been or had been treated, for the purposes of sub-paragraph (1), as having been.

Interest on loans for repairs and improvements to the dwelling occupied as the home

8.—(1) Subject to sub-paragraph (2), there shall be met under this paragraph an amount in respect of interest payable on a loan which is taken out, with or without security, for the purpose of—

(a) carrying out repairs or improvements to the dwelling occupied as the home; or

(b) paying off another loan but only to the extent that interest on that other loan would have been met under this paragraph had the loan not been paid off,

and which is used for that purpose or is to be so used within six months of the date of receipt or such further period as is reasonable, and the amount to be met under this paragraph shall be calculated as if the loan were a loan to which paragraph 7 applied.

(2) Subject to sub-paragraph (4), where the claimant has capital in excess of £500, the excess shall be set against the amount or the aggregate of the amounts borrowed and interest allowed only by reference to any balance.

(3) In this paragraph "repairs and improvements" means major repairs necessary to maintain the fabric of the dwelling occupied as the home and any of the following measures undertaken with a view to improving its fitness for occupation—

(a) installation of a fixed bath, shower, wash basin, sink or lavatory, and necessary associated plumbing;

(b) damp proofing measures;

(c) provision or improvement of ventilation and natural lighting;

(d) provision of electric lighting and sockets;

(e) provision or improvement of drainage facilities;

(f) improvement in the structural condition of the dwelling occupied as the home;

(g) improvements to the facilities for storing, preparing and cooking food;

(h) provision of heating, including central heating;

(i) provision of storage facilities for fuel and refuse;

(j) improvements to the insulation of the dwelling occupied as the home;

(k) other improvements which are reasonable in the circumstances.

(4) For the purposes of sub-paragraph (2) no account shall be taken of capital which is disregarded by virtue of paragraph 1, 2, 4 to 6, 8(b), 9(a), 10 to 18 or 20 of Schedule 10 (capital to be disregarded).

Other housing costs

9.—(1) Subject to sub-paragraph (5), there shall be met under this paragraph the amounts, calculated on a weekly basis, in respect of the housing costs specified in paragraph 1(c) to (h) subject to the deductions specified in sub-paragraph (2).

(2) Subject to sub-paragraph (3), the deductions to be made from the weekly amounts to be met under this paragraph are—

(a) where the costs are inclusive of any of the items mentioned in paragraph 5(2) to Schedule 1 of the Housing Benefit (General) Regulations 1987**(a)** (payment in respect of fuel charges), the deductions prescribed in that paragraph unless the claimant provides evidence on which the actual or approximate amount of the service charge for fuel may be estimated, in which case the estimated amount;

(b) where the costs are inclusive of ineligible service charges within the meaning of paragraph 1 to Schedule 1 of the Housing Benefit (General) Regulations 1987 (ineligible service charges) the amounts attributable to those ineligible service charges or where that amount is not separated from or separately identified within the housing costs to be met under this paragraph, such part of the payments made in respect of those housing costs which are fairly attributable to the provision of those ineligible services having regard to the costs of comparable services.

(3) Where arrangements are made for the housing costs mentioned in paragraph 1(c) to (g), payable for a year, to be paid for 53 weeks, or irregularly, or so that no such costs are payable for or

---

(a) S.I. 1987/1971.

collected in certain periods, or so that the costs for different periods in the year are of different amounts, the weekly amount shall be the amount payable for the year divided by 52.

(4) Where as compensation for work carried out by way of reasonable repairs or redecoration which are not normally the responsibility of the claimant or other member of his family, payment of the costs mentioned in paragraph 1(c) to (g) are waived, they shall, for a period not exceeding eight weeks, be treated as payable.

(5) Where an amount calculated on a weekly basis in respect of housing costs specified in paragraph 1(e) (Crown tenants) includes amounts in respect of water charges or eligible rates (or both) within the meaning of regulation 9 of the Housing Benefit (General) Regulations 1987(a), that amount shall be reduced by—

(a) where the amount payable is known—

(i) in respect of water charges, that amount;

(ii) in respect of eligible rates, 20 per cent of that amount calculated on a weekly basis;

(b) in any other case—

(i) in respect of water charges, the amount which would be the likely charge had the property not been occupied by a Crown tenant;

(ii) in respect of eligible rates, 20 per cent of the amount which would be the likely eligible rates had the property not been occupied by a Crown tenant,

calculated on a weekly basis.

(6) For the purposes of paragraph (5) " water charges " means charges or rates in respect of water and, except in Scotland, of sewerage and allied environmental services.

Restriction on meeting housing costs under this Schedule

10.—(1) Subject to sub-paragraph (2), where—

(a) the dwelling occupied as the home is occupied with security of tenure, that is to say—

(i) under a protected or statutory tenancy for the purposes of the Rent Act 1977(b) or the Rent (Scotland) Act 1984(c), excluding any case in which the tenant has been given a notice to which any Case in Part II of Schedule 15 to the Act of 1977 or, as the case may be, Part II of Schedule 2 to the Act of 1984 (cases in which Court must order possession where dwelling-house subject to regulated tenancy) applies;

(ii) under a secure tenancy for the purposes of Chapter II of Part I of the Housing Act 1980(d) or Part II of the Tenants' Rights Etc (Scotland) Act 1980(e) (security of tenure of public sector tenants);

(iii) where the tenant is a protected occupier or statutory tenant for the purposes of the Rent (Agriculture) Act 1976(f); or

(iv) under a crofting tenancy for the purposes of the Crofters (Scotland) Acts 1955 and 1961(g);

(b) the claimant or, if he is a member of a family, any member of the family acquires some other interest in the dwelling occupied as the home; and

(c) in consequence of the acquisition the aggregate of any amounts which would, but for this paragraph, be applicable under paragraphs 7, 8 and 9 exceed the amount of the eligible rent for the purposes of regulation 10 of the Housing Benefit (General) Regulations 1987 (rent) immediately before the acquisition,

the aggregate amount so applicable shall initially be restricted to the amount of the eligible rent immediately before the acquisition and shall be increased subsequently only to the extent that this is necessary to take account of any increase, after the date of the acquisition, in expenditure on any housing costs.

(2) Sub-paragraph (1)—

(a) shall not apply where the claimant or the member of the family became liable to complete the acquisition at a time when income support was not payable in respect of him;

(b) shall cease to apply if its application becomes inappropriate by reason of any major change in the circumstances of the family affecting their ability to meet expenditure on housing costs;

(a) S.I. 1987/1971.
(b) 1977 c.42; Part II of Schedule 15 was amended by the Housing Act 1980 (c.51) sections 55, 66, 67 and by the Rent (Amendment) Act 1985 (c.24), section 2.
(c) 1984 c.58.
(d) 1980 c.51.
(e) 1980 c.52.
(f) 1976 c.80.
(g) 1955 c.21, 1961 c.58.

(c) shall cease to apply where income support ceases to be payable in respect of the claimant or his family except that it shall reapply wherever income support again becomes payable within a period of eight weeks or less.

(3) Where the amounts to be met under paragraphs 7 to 9 and, subject to any deduction applicable under paragraph 11 are excessive, they shall be subject to restriction in accordance with sub-paragraphs (4) to (6).

(4) Subject to sub-paragraphs (5) and (6), the amounts to be met shall be regarded as excessive and shall be restricted and the excess not allowed, if and to the extent that—

(a) the dwelling occupied as the home, excluding any part which is let or is normally occupied by persons in board and lodging accommodation, is larger than is required by the claimant and his family and any child or young person to whom regulation 16(4) applies (foster children) and any other non-dependants having regard, in particular, to suitable alternative accommodation occupied by a household of the same size; or

(b) the immediate area in which the dwelling occupied as the home is located is more expensive than other areas in which suitable alternative accommodation exists; or

(c) the outgoings of the dwelling occupied as the home in respect of which the amounts to be met under paragraphs 7 to 10 are higher than the outgoings of suitable alternative accommodation in the area.

(5) Where, having regard to the relevant factors, it is not reasonable to expect the claimant and his family to seek alternative cheaper accommodation no restrictions shall be made under this paragraph.

(6) Where sub-paragraph (5) does not apply and the claimant (or other member of the family) was able to meet the financial commitments for the dwelling occupied as the home when these were entered into, no restriction shall be made under this paragraph during the first six months of any period of entitlement to income support nor during the next six months if and so long as the claimant uses his best endeavours to obtain cheaper accommodation.

(7) In this paragraph " the relevant factors " are—

(a) the availability of suitable accommodation and the level of housing costs in the area; and

(b) the circumstances of the family including in particular the age and state of health of its members, the employment prospects of the claimant and, where a change in accommodation is likely to result in a change of school, the effect on the education of any child or young person who is a member of his family, or any child or young person who is not treated as part of his family by virtue of regulation 16(4) (foster children).

Non-dependant deductions

11.—(1) Subject to the following provisions of this paragraph, the following deductions from the amount to be met under the preceding paragraphs of this Schedule in respect of housing costs shall be made in respect of a non-dependant—

(a) in respect of a non-dependant aged 18 or more who is in remunerative work or is a person to whom regulation 3(3) applies (non-dependants)—

(i) where the claimant or his partner is a Crown tenant and paragraph 9(5)(a)(ii) or (b)(ii) applies, £11·20;

(ii) in any other case, £8·20.

(b) in respect of a non-dependant aged 18 or more to whom (a) does not apply—

(i) where the claimant or his partner is a Crown tenant and paragraph 9(5)(a)(ii) or (b)(ii) applies, £6·45;

(ii) in any other case, £3·45.

(2) In the case of a non-dependant aged 18 or more to whom sub-paragraph (1)(a) applies because he is in remunerative work, where the claimant satisfies the adjudication officer that the non-dependant's gross weekly income is less than £49·20, the deduction to be made under this paragraph shall be the deduction specified in sub-paragraph (1)(b) appropriate in his case.

(3) Only one deduction shall be made under this paragraph in respect of a couple or, as the case may be, the members of a polygamous marriage, and where a different amount or no amount would, but for this sub-paragraph, fall to be deducted in respect of the members of the couple or polygamous marriage as individuals, the higher deduction shall be made.

(4) In applying the provisions of sub-paragraph (2) in the case of a couple or, as the case may be, a polygamous marriage, regard shall be had, for the purpose of sub-paragraph (2) to the couple's or, as the case may be, all the members of the polygamous marriage's, joint weekly income.

(5) Where a person is a non-dependant in respect of more than one joint occupier of a dwelling (except where the joint occupiers are a couple or members of a polygamous marriage), the deduction in respect of that non-dependant shall be apportioned between the joint occupiers (the amount so

apportioned being rounded to the nearest penny) having regard to the number of joint occupiers and the proportion of the housing costs in respect of the dwelling occupied as the home payable by each of them.

(6) No deduction shall be made in respect of any non-dependants occupying the dwelling occupied as the home of the claimant, if the claimant or any partner of his is—

    (a) blind or treated as blind by virtue of paragraph 12 of Schedule 2 (additional condition for the higher pensioner and disability premiums); or

    (b) receiving an attendance allowance.

(7) No deduction shall be made in respect of a non-dependant—

    (a) if, although he resides with the claimant, it appears to the adjudication officer that the dwelling occupied as his home is normally elsewhere; or

    (b) if he is in receipt of a training allowance paid in connection with a Youth Training Scheme established under section 2 of the Employment and Training Act 1973(a) and he is not a person to whom regulation 3(3) applies (persons in board and lodging accommodation or hostels); or

    (c) if he is a full-time student during a period of study and he is not a person to whom regulation 3(3) applies; or

    (d) if he is aged under 25 and in receipt of income support and he is not a person to whom regulation 3(3) applies; or

    (e) in respect of whom a deduction in the calculation of a rent rebate or allowance falls to be made under regulation 63 of the Housing Benefit (General) Regulations 1987 (non-dependant deductions).

Rounding of fractions

12. Where any calculation made under this Schedule results in a fraction of a penny, that fraction shall be treated as a penny.

Regulation 19   **SCHEDULE 4**

PART I

APPLICABLE AMOUNTS OF PERSONS IN RESIDENTIAL CARE AND NURSING HOMES

1.—(1) Subject to sub-paragraph (2), the weekly applicable amount of a claimant to whom regulation 19 applies shall be the aggregate of—

    (a) subject to paragraph 3, the weekly charge for the accommodation, including all meals and services, provided for him or, if he is a member of a family, for him and his family increased, where appropriate, in accordance with paragraph 2 but, except in a case to which paragraph 12 applies, subject to the maximum determined in accordance with paragraph 5; and

    (b) a weekly amount for personal expenses for him and, if he is a member of a family, for each member of his family determined in accordance with paragraph 13; and

    (c) where he is only temporarily in such accommodation any amount applicable under regulation 17(e) or 18(f) (housing costs) in respect of the dwelling normally occupied as the home.

(2) No amount shall be included in respect of any child or young person who is a member of the claimant's family if the capital of that child or young person calculated in accordance with Part V in like manner as for the claimant, except where otherwise provided, would exceed £3,000.

2.—(1) Where, in addition to the weekly charge for accommodation, a separate charge is made for the provision of heating, attention in connection with bodily functions, supervision, extra baths, laundry or a special diet needed for a medical reason, the weekly charge for the purpose of paragraph 1(1)(a) shall be increased by the amount of that charge.

(2) Where the weekly charge for accommodation does not include the provision of all meals, it shall, for the purpose of paragraph 1(1)(a), be increased in respect of the claimant or, if he is a member of a family, in respect of each member of his family by the following amount:

    (a) if the meals can be purchased within the residential care or nursing home, the amount equal to the actual cost of the meals, calculated on a weekly basis; or

(a) 1973 c.50, as amended by sections 9 and 11 and Schedule 2, Part II, paragraph 9 and Schedule 3 of the Employment and Training Act 1981 (c.57).

(b) if the meals cannot be so purchased, the amount calculated on a weekly basis—

    (i) for breakfast, at a daily rate of £1·10;

    (ii) for a midday meal, at a daily rate of £1·55; and

    (iii) for an evening meal, at a daily rate of £1·55;

except that, if some or all of the meals are normally provided free of charge or at a reduced rate, the amount shall be reduced to take account of the lower charge or reduction.

3. Where any part of the weekly charge for the accommodation is met by housing benefit, an amount equal to the part so met shall be deducted from the amount calculated in accordance with paragraph 1(1)(a).

4. Where a payment is to be made in respect of a period of less than one benefit week, the applicable amount of the claimant under regulation 19 and this Schedule shall include the weekly amount to which paragraph 1(1)(a) applies, other than the increase for meals met under paragraph 2(2) which shall be met only in respect of the number of days falling in that period, if the weekly charge for the accommodation falls to be paid during that period.

5.—(1) Subject to paragraph 12 the maximum referred to in paragraph 1(1)(a) shall be—

    (a) in the case of a single claimant, the appropriate amount in respect of that claimant specified in or determined in accordance with paragraphs 6 to 11;

    (b) where the claimant is a member of a family, the aggregate of the following amounts—

        (i) in respect of each member of the family aged under 11, 1½ times the amount specified in paragraph 2(a) of Schedule 2; and

        (ii) in respect of each other member of the family, the appropriate amount specified in or determined in accordance with paragraphs 6 to 11.

(2) The maximum amount in respect of a member of the family aged under 11 calculated in the manner referred to in sub-paragraph (1) (b) (i) shall be rounded to the nearest multiple of 5p by treating an odd amount of 2·5p or more as 5p and by disregarding an odd amount of less than 2·5p.

Residential care homes

6.—(1) Subject to sub-paragraph (2) and paragraphs 8 to 11, where the accommodation provided for the claimant is a residential care home for persons in need of personal care by virtue of—

    (a) old age, the appropriate amount shall be £130·00 per week;

    (b) past or present mental disorder but excluding mental handicap, the appropriate amount shall be £130·00 per week;

    (c) past or present drug or alcohol dependence, the appropriate amount shall be £130·00 per week;

    (d) mental handicap, the appropriate amount shall be £160·00 per week;

    (e) physical disablement, the appropriate amount shall be—

        (i) in the case of a person to whom paragraph 8 applies, £190.00 per week, or

        (ii) in any other case £130·00 per week; or

    (f) any condition not falling within sub-paragraphs (a) to (e) above, the appropriate amount shall be £130·00 per week.

(2) Where the claimant is over pensionable age and—

    (a) he is blind; or

    (b) there is in respect of him a certificate, issued by the Attendance Allowance Board under section 35(2) of the Social Security Act**(a)**, which states that he has satisfied or is likely to satisfy both the conditions mentioned in section 35(1) of that Act; or

    (c) he is in receipt of any payment based on need for attendance which is payable—

        (i) under section 61 of the Social Security Act**(b)**, or

        (ii) by virtue of article 14 of the Naval, Military and Air Forces etc (Disablement and Death) Service Pensions Order 1983**(c)** or article 14 of the Personal Injuries (Civilians) Scheme 1983**(d)**,

the appropriate amount shall, except where sub-paragraph (1)(d) or (e)(i) applies, be £155·00 per week.

(a) 1975 c.14; section 35(2) was amended and subsection (2A) was added by the Social Security Act 1979 (c.18) section 2. Subsections (3) and (4) of section 61 were added by the Social Security Act 1986 (c.50) section 39, Schedule 3 paragraph 6.

(b) Subsections (3) and (4) of section 61 were added by the Social Security Act 1986 (c.50) section 39, Schedule 3, paragraph 6.

(c) S.I. 1983/883.

(d) S.I. 1983/686.

Nursing homes

7. Subject to paragraphs 8 to 11, where the accommodation provided for the claimant is a nursing home for persons in need of personal care by virtue of—

  (a) past or present mental disorder but excluding mental handicap, the appropriate amount shall be £185·00 per week;

  (b) mental handicap, the appropriate amount shall be £200·00 per week;

  (c) past or present drug or alcohol dependence, the appropriate amount shall be £185·00 per week;

  (d) physical disablement, the appropriate amount shall be—

   (i) in the case of a person to whom paragraph 8 applies, £230·00 per week, or

   (ii) in any other case, £185·00 per week;

  (e) terminal illness, the appropriate amount shall be £230·00 per week; or

  (f) any condition not falling within sub-paragraphs (a) to (e), the appropriate amount shall be £185·00 per week.

8. For the purposes of paragraphs 6(e) and 7(d) this paragraph applies to a person under pensionable age or a person over pensionable age who, before attaining pensionable age, had become physically disabled.

9. The appropriate amount applicable to a claimant in a residential care home or nursing home shall, subject to paragraph 10, be determined—

  (a) where the home is a residential care home registered under Part I of the Registered Homes Act 1984(a), by reference to the particulars recorded in the register kept by the relevant registration authority for the purposes of that Act; or

  (b) where the home is a residential care home not so registered or a nursing home, by reference to the type of care which, taking into account the facilities and accommodation provided, the home is providing to the claimant.

10.—(1) Where more than one amount would otherwise be applicable, in accordance with paragraph 9, to a claimant in a residential care home or a nursing home, the appropriate amount in any case shall be determined in accordance with the following sub-paragraphs.

(2) Where the home is a residential care home registered under Part I of the Registered Homes Act 1984 and where the personal care that the claimant is receiving corresponds to the care received by a category of residents for whom the register indicates that the home provides accommodation, the appropriate amount shall be the amount, in paragraph 6 or 8, as the case may be, as is consistent with that personal care.

(3) Where the home is a residential care home which is so registered but where the personal care that the claimant is receiving does not correspond to the care received by a category of residents for whom the register indicates that the home provides accommodation, the appropriate amount shall be the lesser or least amount, in paragraphs 6 or 8, as the case may be, as is consistent with those categories.

(4) In any case not falling within sub-paragraph (2) or (3), the appropriate amount shall be whichever amount of the amounts applicable in accordance with paragraphs 6 or 7 and 9 is, having regard to the types of personal care that the home provides, most consistent with the personal care being received by the claimant in that accommodation.

11.—(1) Where the accommodation provided for the claimant is a residential care home or a nursing home which is, in either case, situated in the Greater London area and the actual charge for that accommodation exceeds the appropriate amount in his case by virtue of the preceding paragraphs of this Schedule, that amount shall be increased by any excess up to £17·50.

(2) In sub-paragraph (1), " the Greater London area " means all those areas specified as being within Area 53 in Schedule 6.

Circumstances in which the maximum is not to apply

12.—(1) Where a claimant who satisfies the conditions in sub-paragraph (2) has been able to meet the charges referred to in paragraphs 1 and 2 without recourse to income support or supplementary benefit, the maximum determined in accordance with paragraph 5 shall not apply for the period of 13 weeks or, if alternative accommodation is found earlier, such lesser period following the date of claim except to the extent that the claimant is able to meet out of income disregarded for the purposes of Part V the balance of the actual charge over the maximum.

(a) 1984 c.23.

(2) The conditions for the purposes of sub-paragraph (1) are that—

(a) the claimant has lived in the same accommodation for more than 12 months; and

(b) he was able to afford the charges in respect of that accommodation when he took up residence; and

(c) having regard to the availability of suitable alternative accommodation and to the circumstances mentioned in paragraph 10(7)(b) of Schedule 3 (housing costs), it is reasonable that the maximum should not apply in order to allow him time to find alternative accommodation; and

(d) he is not a person who is being accommodated—

(i) by a housing authority under Part III of the Housing Act 1985(a) (housing the homeless), or

(ii) by a local authority under section 1 of the Child Care Act 1980(b) (duty of local authorities to promote welfare of children) or, in Scotland, section 12 of the Social Work (Scotland) Act 1968(c) (general welfare); and

(e) he is seeking alternative accommodation and intends to leave his present accommodation once alternative accommodation is found.

(3) Where—

(a) the claimant was a resident in a residential care home or nursing home immediately before 29 April 1985 and has continued after that date to be resident in the same accommodation, apart from any period of temporary absence; and

(b) immediately before that date, the actual charge for the claimant's accommodation was being met either wholly or partly out of the claimant's resources, or, wholly or partly out of other resources which can no longer be made available for this purpose; and

(c) since that date the local authority have not at any time accepted responsibility for the making of arrangements for the provision of such accommodation for the claimant; and

(d) the Secretary of State, in his discretion, has determined that this sub-paragraph shall have effect in the particular case of the claimant in order to avoid exceptional hardship,

the maximum amount shall be the rate specified in sub-paragraph (4) if that rate exceeds the maximum which, but for this sub-paragraph, would be determined under paragraph 5.

(4) For the purposes of sub-paragraph (3) the rate is either—

(a) the actual weekly charge for the accommodation immediately before 29 April 1985 plus £10; or

(b) the aggregate of the following amounts—

(i) the amount estimated under regulation 9(6) of the Supplementary Benefit (Requirements) Regulations 1983(d) as then in force as the reasonable weekly charge for the area immediately before that date;

(ii) £26.15; and

(iii) if the claimant was entitled at that date to attendance allowance under section 35 of the Social Security Act at the higher rate £28·60 or, as the case may be, at the lower rate, £19·10,

whichever is the lower amount.

Personal allowances

13.   The allowance for personal expenses for the claimant and each member of his family referred to in paragraph 1(1)(b) shall be—

(a) for the claimant £9·55; and, if he has a partner, for his partner, £9.55;

(b) for a young person aged 18, £9·55;

(c) for a young person aged under 18 but over 16, £6·20;

(d) for a child aged under 16 but over 11, £5·30;

(e) for a child aged under 11, £3·45.

(a) 1985 c.68.
(b) 1980 c.5.
(c) 1968 c.49.
(d) S.I. 1983/1399.

PART II

PERSONS TO WHOM REGULATION 19 DOES NOT APPLY

14. A claimant and his family whose accommodation and meals (if any) are provided in whole or in part by a close relative of any member of the family or other than on a commercial basis.

15. A person who is on holiday and during a period which has not continued for more than 13 weeks is absent from his home or from a hospital or similar institution in which he is normally a patient.

16. A person who has entered a residential care or nursing home for the purpose of receiving an amount of income support to which he would not otherwise be entitled.

17. A person aged 16 or over but under 19 who is in the care of a local authority under a relevant enactment except someone who is personally liable to pay the cost of his accommodation and maintenance direct to someone other than a local authority.

Regulation 20

SCHEDULE 5

PART I

APPLICABLE AMOUNTS OF PERSONS IN BOARD AND LODGING ACCOMMODATION OR HOSTELS

1.—(1) Subject to sub-paragraph (2), the weekly applicable amount of a claimant to whom regulation 20 applies shall be the aggregate of—

(a) subject to paragraph 3, the weekly charge for the accommodation including all meals and services provided for him or, if he is a member of a family, for him and his family increased where appropriate in accordance with paragraph 2 but, except in a case to which paragraph 10 applies, subject to the maximum determined in accordance with paragraph 5; and

(b) a weekly amount for personal expenses for him and, if he is a member of a family, for each member of his family determined in accordance with paragraph 11; and

(c) where he is only temporarily in such accommodation any amount applicable under regulation 17 (e) or 18 (f) (housing costs) in respect of the dwelling normally occupied as the home.

(2) No amount shall be included in respect of any child or young person who is a member of the claimant's family if the capital of that child or young person calculated in accordance with Part V in like manner as for the claimant, except where otherwise provided, would exceed £3,000.

2. Where the weekly charge for accommodation does not include the provision of all meals, it shall, for the purpose of paragraph 1 (1) (a) be increased in respect of the claimant or, if he is a member of a family, in respect of each member of his family by the following amount—

(a) if the meals can be purchased within the board and lodging accommodation or hostel, the amount equal to the actual cost of the meals, calculated on a weekly basis; or

(b) if the meals cannot be so purchased, the amount calculated on a weekly basis—

　(i) for breakfast, at a daily rate of £1·10;

　(ii) for a midday meal, at a daily rate of £1·55;

　(iii) for an evening meal, at a daily rate of £1·55;

except that, if some or all of the meals are normally provided free of charge or at a reduced rate, the amount shall be reduced to take account of the lower charge or reduction.

3. Where any part of the weekly charge for the accommodation is met by housing benefit, an amount equal to the part so met shall be deducted from the amount calculated in accordance with paragraph 1 (1) (a).

4. Where a payment is to be made in respect of a period of less than one week, the applicable amount of the claimant under regulation 20 and this Schedule shall include the weekly amount to which paragraph 1 (1) (a) applies, other than the increase for meals met under paragraph 2 which shall be met only in respect of the number of days falling in that period, if the weekly charge for the accommodation falls to be paid during that period.

5. Subject to paragraphs 6 and 7 the maximum referred to in paragraph 1 (1) (a) shall be—

(a) in the case of a single claimant—

    (i) in board and lodging accommodation, the appropriate amount in respect of that claimant specified in column (3) of Schedule 6 in respect of the board and lodging area in which his accommodation is situated; or

    (ii) in a hostel £70·00 per week;

(b) where the claimant is a member of a family, in respect of each member of the family aged under 11, 1½ times the amount specified in paragraph 2 (a) of Schedule 2, and either

    (i) if he is residing in board and lodging accommodation, in respect of each other member of the family, the appropriate amount specified in column (3) of Schedule 6 in respect of the board and lodging area in which the family's accommodation is situated; or

    (ii) if he is residing in a hostel, in respect of each other member of the family, £70·00 per week.

6. The maximum amount applicable in respect of a member of the family aged under 11 calculated in the manner referred to in paragraph 5 (b) (i) shall be rounded to the nearest multiple of 5p by treating an odd amount of 2·5p or more as 5p and by disregarding an odd amount of less than 2·5p.

7. Except as provided by paragraph 9, the maximum amount specified in paragraph 5 shall be increased by any excess of the actual charge made to the claimant or, if he is a member of a family, made in respect of the family up to £17·50 in a case to which paragraph 8 applies or, if the claimant is one of a couple and paragraph 8 (a) or (c) (i) or (ii) applies, up to £35·00.

8. The increase referred to in paragraph 7 shall apply in the case of—

(a) a claimant who has attained a pensionable age or, if one of a couple or polygamous marriage either member of that couple or any member of that marriage is aged 65 or over;

(b) a claimant or any other member of the family who is infirm by reason of physical or mental disability;

(c) a claimant in respect of whom one or more of the following conditions are satisfied:—

    (i) he or his partner is a person suffering from a mental disorder within the meaning of the Mental Health Act 1983**(a)** or the Mental Health (Scotland) Act 1984**(b)** in respect of whom a local social services authority has, under section 21 of, and paragraph 2 of Schedule 8 to, the National Health Service Act 1977**(c)** (prevention, care and after-care), made arrangements for the provision of residential accommodation in a private household or in premises which are not required to be registered under the Registered Homes Act 1984**(d)**;

    (ii) he or his partner is a person who is resident in premises which are used for the rehabilitation of alcoholics or drug addicts and is so resident for the purposes of such rehabilitation.

9. Only one increase under paragraph 7 shall be applicable in respect of the claimant or any member of his family and the amount payable by virtue of that paragraph in respect of a claimant and his partner shall not exceed £35·00 and, if the claimant or any of his family who are in board and lodging accommodation or in a hostel is in receipt of an attendance allowance the increase shall only be payable to the extent that the excess of the actual charge for board and lodging accommodation or the hostel over the maximum amount is more than the amount of the attendance allowance in payment but only up to the amount specified for the time being as the higher rate of attendance allowance for the purposes of section 35 (3) of the Social Security Act.

10.—(1) Where the claimant satisfies the conditions in sub-paragraph (2), the maximum referred to in paragraph 1 (1) (a) shall not apply for a period of 13 weeks or, if alternative accommodation is found earlier, such lesser period following date of claim except to the extent that the claimant is able to meet out of income disregarded for the purposes of Part V the balance of the actual charge for the board and lodging accommodation over the maximum.

(2) For the purposes of sub-paragraph (1) the conditions are that—

(a) the claimant has lived in the same accommodation for more than 12 months; and

(b) he was able to afford the charges in respect of that accommodation when he took up residence; and

---

(a) 1983 c.20.
(b) 1984 c.36.
(c) 1977 c.49; paragraph 2 of Schedule 8 was amended by section 148 of, and Schedule 4 to, the Mental Health Act 1983 and section 30 of, and Schedule 10 to, the Health and Social Services and Social Security Adjudications Act 1983 (c.41).
(d) 1984 c.23.

(c) having regard to the availability of board and lodging accommodation or hostels and to the circumstances mentioned in paragraph 10(7)(b) of Schedule 3 (housing costs), it is reasonable for the maximum referred to in paragraph 5 not to apply for the said period in order to allow the claimant time to find alternative accommodation; and

(d) he is not a person who is being accommodated—

   (i) by a housing authority under Part III of the Housing Act 1985**(a)** (housing the homeless), or

   (ii) by a local authority under section 1 of the Child Care Act 1980**(b)** (duty of local authorities to promote welfare of children), or, in Scotland, section 12 of the Social Work (Scotland) Act 1968**(c)** (general welfare); and

(e) he is seeking alternative accommodation and intends to leave his present accommodation once alternative accommodation is found.

11. The allowance for personal expenses for the claimant and each member of his family referred to in paragraph 1(1)(b) shall be—

(a) for the claimant and for his partner where—

   (i) at least one member of the family is a child or young person, £11·50;

   (ii) he or his partner satisfies the conditions specified in Part III of Schedule 2 (applicable amounts) for the applicability of any of the premiums specified in that Part, £11·50;

(b) in any other case—

   (i) for the claimant, £10·30, and

   (ii) for his partner, £10·30;

(c) for a young person aged 18, £10·30;

(d) for a young person aged 16 or over but under 18, £6·20;

(e) for a child aged 11 or over but under 16, £5·30;

(f) for a child aged under 11, £3·45.

PART II

PERSONS TO WHOM REGULATION 20 AND PART I OF THIS SCHEDULE IS NOT TO APPLY

12. A claimant and his family whose accommodation and meals (if any) are provided in whole or in part by a close relative of any member of that family or other than on a commercial basis.

13. A person who is on holiday and during a period which has not continued for more than 13 weeks is absent from the home or from a hospital or similar institution in which he is normally a patient.

14. A person who has entered into arrangements for board and lodging accommodation for the purpose of receiving an amount of income support to which he would not otherwise be entitled.

15. A person aged 16 or over but under 19 who is in the care of a local authority under the provisions of a relevant enactment, except where he is personally liable to pay the cost of his accommodation and maintenance direct to someone other than a local authority.

16.—(1) Subject to sub-paragraphs (2) to (5) below, a person who—

(a) is aged 16 or over but under 25, and, if one of a couple, whose partner is also 16 or over but under 25; and

(b) is required to be available for employment.

(2) Sub-paragraph (1) above shall not have effect in respect of such a person before the beginning of, and during, the initial period (including that period as extended under sub-paragraph (5) below) shown as applicable in column (4) of Schedule 6 in respect of the board and lodging area in which that person's accommodation is situated.

(3) Without prejudice to sub-paragraph (4) below, sub-paragraph (1) above shall not have effect in respect of a claimant who was in receipt of supplementary benefit as a boarder on 24th November 1985.

(a) 1985 c.68.
(b) 1980 c.5.
(c) 1968 c.49.

(4) Sub-paragraph (1) above shall not have effect also where such a person—

(a) is treated as responsible for a child or young person; or

(b) is in a hostel; or

(c) is, or has a partner who is, pregnant; or

(d) is, or has a partner who is, chronically sick, mentally handicapped, physically disabled or suffering from a mental disorder or was, or has a partner who was, suffering from a mental disorder and it is unreasonable to expect him or his partner to be in accommodation other than board and lodging accommodation; or

(e) had, or has a partner who had, prior to the date of claim been in the accommodation for six months whilst either in employment and not in receipt of supplementary allowance under the Supplementary Benefit Act 1976 or income support, or, if not in employment and in receipt of such an allowance or income support, was not required to be available for employment; or

(f) has, or has a partner who has, entered that accommodation as part of a programme of rehabilitation or resettlement under guidance from a government department, health authority, local authority, voluntary organisation or the probation service; or

(g) is a student, during his normal summer vacation provided he occupies the same accommodation as he occupied when attending his course of study; or

(h) has, or has a partner who has, been in the care of a local authority under a relevant enactment and twelve months has not elapsed since he or his partner ceased to be in care; or

(i) is aged 16 or over but under 19 and—

(i) has no parent and there is no person acting in the place of his parent; or

(ii) has had to leave his family home because he was in physical or moral danger; or

(iii) is in the care of the local authority under the provisions of a relevant enactment, being a person who is personally liable to pay the cost of his accommodation and maintenance direct to someone other than a local authority; or

(j) is in the same accommodation as that of his or of his partner's parents or step-parents who are in board and lodging accommodation; or

(k) is in the same accommodation as that of the persons with whom he or his partner has been previously boarded out by a local authority under the provisions of a relevant enactment; or

(l) is, or has a partner who is, remanded on bail, or is, or has a partner who is, in compliance with a court order, under the supervision of a probation officer, a local social services authority or, in Scotland, a social work department; or

(m) would, or has a partner who would, suffer exceptional hardship if sub-paragraph (1) above were to apply; and any question as to whether any person comes within this sub-paragraph shall be determined by the Secretary of State in his discretion and his decision of such questions—

(i) shall be given in relation to particular cases only;

(ii) may be revised from time to time as he considers appropriate;

(iii) may be given so as to have effect for a specified period; and

(iv) shall be conclusive for the purposes of this Schedule.

(5) Where during an initial period a person becomes employed and is not in receipt of income support or he is no longer required to be available for employment and is in receipt of income support, that initial period shall be extended by the period during which that person is employed or is no longer required to be available for employment provided he is in the same board and lodging area.

17.—(1) A person who was for a period one to whom regulation 20 and Part II of this Schedule applied because of sub-paragraph (2) of paragraph 16 (during an initial period) and in respect of whom the relevant period has not elapsed.

(2) For the purposes of this paragraph "the relevant period" means the period of 26 weeks beginning with the first day of the benefit week following the date of the adjudication officer's decision involving a determination that that person is a person to whom regulation 20 and Part II of this Schedule applies because of paragraph 16 (2).

18. In this Schedule "initial period" means that period provided by paragraph 16 (2) consisting of a week or multiple of weeks beginning with the first day of the benefit week following the date of the adjudication officer's decision involving a determination that the person concerned is a person in board and lodging accommodation because of paragraph 16 (2), being a week or multiple of weeks that correspond to benefit weeks during which the person is required to be available for employment.

Regulation 20(2)   **SCHEDULE 6**
paragraph 5 of Schedule 5
                              BOARD AND LODGING AREAS

                                      PART I

                      WALES AND SOUTH WESTERN REGION

Column (1)	Column (2)	Column (3)	Column (4)
Number of Area	*Description of Area*	*Appropriate Amount (£)*	*Initial Period (number of weeks)*
Area 1	In the County of CORNWALL	45	2
	Comprises: The Borough of RESTORMEL The District of CARRICK The District of KERRIER The District of PENWITH		
	The ISLES OF SCILLY		
	Part District of CARADON		
	Consisting of the parishes of: Boconnoc, Broadoak, Duloe, Lanreath, Lansallos, Lanteglos, Looe, Morval, Pelynt, St Keyne, St Martin, St Pinnock, St Veep, St Winnow.		
	Part District of NORTH CORNWALL		
	Consisting of the parishes of: Bodmin, Egloshayle, Lanhydrock, Lanivet, Padstow, St Breock, St Ervan, St Eval, St Issey, St Merryn, Wadebridge, Withiel.		
Area 2	In the County of CORNWALL	50	2
	Comprises: Part District of CARADON		
	Consisting of the parishes of: Antony, Botusfleming, Callington, Calstock, Landrake with St Erney, Landulph, Linkinhorne, Liskeard, Maker with Rame, Menheniot, Millbrook, Pillaton, Quethiock, St Cleer, St Dominic, St Germans, St Ive, St John, St Mellion, St Neot, Saltash, Sheviock, South Hill, Torpoint, Warleggan.		
	Part District of NORTH CORNWALL		
	Consisting of the parishes of: Advent, Altarnun, Blisland, Boyton, Bude Stratton, Camelford, Cardinham, Davidstow, Egloskerry, Forrabury and Minster, Helland, Jacobstow, Kilkhampton, Laneast, Launcells, Launceston, Lawhittan Rural, Lesnewth, Lewannick, Lezant, Marhamchurch, Michaelstow, Morwenstow, Northhill, North Petherwin, North Tamerton, Otterham, Poundstock, St Breward, St Clether, St Endellion, St Gennys, St Juliot, St Kew, St Mabyn, St Minver Highlands, St Minver Lowlands, St Stephens by Launceston Rural, St Teath, St Thomas the Apostle Rural, St Tudy South Petherwin, Stock Climsland, Tintagel, Tremaine, Trenegloss, Tresmeer, Trevalga, Trewen, Warbstow, Week St Mary, Werrington, Whitstone.		

Column (1)	Column (2)	Column (3)	Column (4)
Number of Area	*Description of Area*	*Appropriate Amount (£)*	*Initial Period (number of weeks)*

In the County of DEVON

Comprises: The Borough of PLYMOUTH
Part District of SOUTH HAMS

Consisting of the parishes of: Aveton Gifford, Bigbury, Bickleigh, Blackawton, Brixton, Buckland-tout-Saints, Charleton, Chivelstone, Churchstow, Cornwood, East Allington, East Portlemouth, Ermington, Harford, Holbeton, Ivybridge, Kingsbridge, Kingston, Loddiswell, Malborough, Modbury, Newton and Noss, Ringmore, Salcombe, Shaugh Prior, Sherford, Slapton, South Huish, South Milton, South Pool, Sparkwell, Stoke Fleming, Stokenham, Strete, Thurlestone, Ugborough, Wembury, West Alvington, Woodleigh, Yealmpton.

Part District of TORRIDGE

Consisting of the parishes of: Abbots Bickington, Ashwater, Black Torrington, Bradford, Bradworthy, Bridgerule, Broadwoodwidger, Clawton, Cookbury, Halwill, Hollacombe, Holsworthy, Holsworthy Hamlets, Luffincott, Milton Damerel, Northcott, Pancrasweek, Pyworthy, St Giles on the Heath, Sutcombe, Tetcott, Thornbury, Virginstow, West Putford.

Part District of WEST DEVON
Consisting of the parishes of: Bere Ferrers, Bradstone, Brentor, Buckland Monachorum, Chillaton, Coryton, Dunterton, Horrabridge, Kelly, Lamerton, Lewtrenchard, Lifton, Lydford, Marystow, Mary Tavy, Meavy, Milton Abbot, Peter Tavy, Sampford Spiney, Sheepstor, Stowford, Sydenham Damerel, Tavistock, Tavistock Hamlets, Thrushelton, Walkhampton, Whitchurch.

Area 3	In the County of DEVON	50	2

Comprises: The District of NORTH DEVON
Part District of TORRIDGE

Consisting of the parishes of: Abbotsham, Alverdiscott, Alwington, Ashreigney, Atherington, Beaford, Bideford, Buckland Brewer, Buckland Filleigh, Bulkworthy, Clovelly, Dolton, Dowland, East Putford, Frithelstock, Great Torrington, Hartland, High Bickington, Huish, Huntshaw, Landcross, Langtree, Littleham, Little Torrington, Merton, Monkleigh, Newton St Petrock, Northam, Parkham, Peters Marland, Petrockstow, Roborough, St Giles in the Wood, Shebbear, Sheepwash, Weare Giffard, Welcombe, Winkleigh, Woolfardisworthy, Yarnscombe.

Area 4	In the County of DEVON	50	2

Comprises: The Borough of TORBAY

Part District of SOUTH HAMS

Consisting of the parishes of: Ashprington, Berry Pomeroy, Cornworthy, Dartington, Dartmouth, Dean Prior, Diptford, Dittisham, Halwell,

Column (1)	Column (2)	Column (3)	Column (4)
Number of Area	Description of Area	Appropriate Amount (£)	Initial Period (number of weeks)

Harberton, Holne, Kingswear, Littlehempston, Marldon, Moreleigh, North Huish, Rattery, South Brent, Staverton, Stoke Gabriel, Totnes, West Buckfastleigh.

Part District of TEIGNBRIDGE

Consisting of the parishes of: Ashburton, Bickington, Bishopsteignton, Bovey Tracey, Broadhempston, Buckfastleigh, Buckland in the Moor, Chudleigh, Coffinswell, Dawlish, Haccombe and Combe, Hennock, Ideford, Ilsington, Ipplepen, Kerswell, Kingsteignton, Lustleigh, Manaton, Moretonhampstead, Newton Abbot, North Bovey, Ogwell, Teigngrace, Teignmouth, Torbryan, Trusham, Widecombe in the Moor, Woodland.

Area 5	In the County of DEVON	55	2

Comprises: The Borough of EXETER
The District of EAST DEVON
The District of MID DEVON

Part District of TEIGNBRIDGE

Consisting of the parishes of: Ashcombe, Ashton, Alphington, Bridford, Christow, Doddiscombsleigh, Dunchideock, Dunsford, Exminster, Holcombe Burnell, Ide, Kenn, Kenton, Mamhead, Powderham, Shillingford St George, Tedburn St Mary, Trusham, Whitestone.

Part District of WEST DEVON

Consisting of the parishes of: Ashbury, Beaworthy, Belstone, Bondleigh, Bratton Clovelly, Bridestowe, Broadwoodkelly, Chagford, Drewsteignton, Exbourne, Germansweek, Gidleigh, Hatherleigh, Highampton, Iddesleigh, Inwardleigh, Jacobstowe, Meeth, Monkokehampton, Northlew, North Tawton, Okehampton, Okehampton Hamlets, Sampford Courtnay, Sourton, South Tawton, Spreyton, Throwleigh.

Area 6	In the County of SOMERSET	55	2

Comprises: The District of
TAUNTON DEANE
The District of WEST SOMERSET

Part District of SOUTH SOMERSET

Consisting of the parishes of: Aller, Ashill, Barrington, Beercrocombe, Broadway, Buckland St Mary, Chaffcombe, Chard, Chillington, Combe St Nicholas, Crewkerne, Cricket St Thomas, Cudworth, Curry Mallet, Curry Rivel, Dawlish Wake, Dinnington, Donyatt, Drayton, Fivehead, Hinton St George, High Ham, Huish Episcopi, Illminster, Illminster Without, Ilton, Isle Abbots, Isle Brewers, Kingsbury Episcopi, Kingstone, Knowle St Giles, Langport, Lopen, Merriott, Misterton, Muchelney, Pitney, Puckington, Seavington St Mary, Seavington St Michael,

Column (1)	Column (2)	Column (3)	Column (4)
Number of Area	*Description of Area*	*Appropriate Amount (£)*	*Initial Period (number of weeks)*

Shepton Beauchamp, Stocklinch, Wambrook, Wayford, West Crewkerne, Whitelackington, Whitestaunton, Winsham.

| Area 7 | In the County of DORSET | 55 | 2 |

Comprises: The Borough of WEYMOUTH
AND PORTLAND
Part District of NORTH DORSET
Consisting of the parishes of: Anderson, Blandford Forum, Blandford St Mary, Bryanston, Charlton Marshall, Chettle, Child Okeford, Durwenston, Farnham, Fifehead Magdalen, Fifehead Neville, Glanvilles Wootton, Hammon, Hanford, Hazelbury Bryan, Hilton, Hinton St Mary, Ibberton, Iwerne Courtney or Shroton, Iwerne Stepleton, Langton, Long Blandford, Lydlinch, Manston Mappowder, Marnhull, Milborne St Andrew, Milton Abbas, Okeford Fitzpaine, Pimperne, Pulham, Shillingstone, Spetisbury, Stalbridge, Stoke Wake, Stourpaine, Stourton Candle, Sturminster Newton, Tarrant Crawford, Tarrant Gunville, Tarrant Hinton, Tarrant Keyneston, Tarrant Launceston, Tarrant Monkton, Tarrant Rawston, Tarrant Rushton, Turnworth, Winterborne Clewston, Winterborne Houghton, Winterborne Kingston, Winterborne Stickland, Winterborne Whitchurch, Winterborne Zelstone, Woolland.
Part District of WEST DORSET
Consisting of the parishes of: Abbotsbury, Allington, Alton Pancras, Askerswell, Athelhampton, Beaminster, Bettiscombe, Bincombe, Bothenhampton, Bradford Peverell, Bradpole, Bridport, Broadmayne, Broadwindsor, Buckland Newton, Burleston, Burstock, Burton Bradstock, Catherston Leweston, Cattistock, Cerne Abbas, Charminster, Charmouth, Chedington, Cheselbourne, Chickerell, Chideock, Chilcombe, Chilfrome, Compton Valence, Corscombe, Dewlish, Dorchester, East Chelborough, Evershot, Fleet, Frampton, Frome St. Quintin, Frome Vauchurch, Godmanstone, Halstock, Hooke, Kingston Russell, Langton Herring, Littlebredy, Litton Cheney, Loders, Long Bredy, Lyme Regis, Maiden Newton, Mapperton, Marshwood, Melbury Sampford, Melcombe Horsey, Minterne Magna, Mosterton, Netherbury, Nether Cerne, North Poorton, Osmington, Owermoigne, Piddlehinton, Piddletrenthide, Pilsdon, Portesham, Powerstock, Poxwell, Puddletown, Puncknowle, Rampisham, Seaborough, Shipton Gorge, South Perrott, Stanton St. Gabriel, Stinsford, Stoke Abbot, Stratton, Swyre, Sydling St Nicholas, Symondsbury, Thorncombe, Tincleton, Toller Fratrum, Toller Procorum, Tolpuddle, Up Cerne, Warmwell, Watercombe, West Chelborough, West Compton, West Knighton, West Stafford, Whitcombe, Whitechurch Canonicorum, Winterborne Came, Winterborne Herringston, Winterborne Monkton, Winterborne St Martin, Winterbourne Abbas, Winterbourne Steepleton, Woodsford, Wooton Fitzpaine, Wraxall, Wynford Eagle.

Column (1)	Column (2)	Column (3)	Column (4)
Number of Area	*Description of Area*	*Appropriate Amount (£)*	*Initial Period (number of weeks)*

Area 8   In the County of DORSET   55   2

Comprises: The Borough of CHRISTCHURCH
The District of BOURNEMOUTH
The District of POOLE
The District of PURBECK
The District of WIMBORNE

Area 9   In the County of AVON   50   2

Comprises: The Borough of BATH
Part District of WANSDYKE

Consisting of the parishes of: Bathampton, Batheaston, Bathford, Cameley, Camerton, Charlcombe, Chelwood, Chew Magna, Chew Stoke, Chitton, Claverton, Combe Hay, Compton Dando, Compton Martin, Corston, Dunkerton, East Harptree, Englishcombe, Farmborough, Farrington Gurney, Freshford, High Littleton, Hinton Blewett, Hinton Charterhouse, Kelston, Keynsham, Marksbury, Monkton Combe, Nempnett Thrubwell, Newton St Loe, North Stoke, Norton Malreward, Norton Radstock, Peasedown St John, Priston, Publow, St Catherine, Shoscombe, Southstoke, Stanton Drew, Stowey-Sutton, Swainswick, Timsbury, Ubley, Wellow, West Harptree.

Part District of WOODSPRING

Consisting of the parishes of: Banwell, Blagdon, Bleadon, Burrington, Butcombe, Churchill, Congresbury, Hewish, Hutton, Kewstoke, Langford, Locking, Loxton, Puxton, Redhill, St. Georges, Sandford, Weston-Super-Mare, Wick St Lawrence, Winscombe, Worle, Wrington.

In the County of SOMERSET

Comprises: The District of SEDGEMOOR

Part District of MENDIP

Consisting of the parishes of: Ashwick, Baltonsborough, Batcombe, Binegar, Butleigh, Chewton Mendip, Chilcompton, Cranmore, Croscombe, Dinder, Ditcheat, Doulting, Downhead, East Pennard, Emborough, Evercreech, Glastonbury, Godney, Holcombe, Lamyat, Litton, Lydford-on-Fosse, Meare, Milton Clevedon, North Wootton, Pilton, Priddy, Pylle, Rodney Stoke, St Cuthbert Out, Sharpham, Shepton Mallet, South Easton, Stoke St Michael, Stratton-on-the-Fosse, Street, Walton, Wells, West Bradley, Westbury, West Pannard, Wookey.

Area 10   In the County of DORSET   55   4

Comprises: Part District of NORTH DORSET

Consisting of the parishes of: Ashmore, Bourton, Buckhorn Weston, Cann, Compton Abbas, East Orchard, East Stour, Fontmell Magna, Gillingham, Iwerne Minister, Kington Magna, Margaret Marsh, Melbury Abbas, Motcombe, Shaftesbury, Silton, Stour Provost, Sutton Waldron, Todber, West Orchard, West Stour.

Column (1)	Column (2)	Column (3)	Column (4)
Number of Area	*Description of Area*	*Appropriate Amount (£)*	*Initial Period (number of weeks)*

Part District of WEST DORSET

Consisting of the parishes of: Batcombe, Beer Hackett, Bishops Caundle, Bradford Abbas, Castleton, Caundle, Caundle Marsh, Chetnole, Clifton Maybank, Folke, Goathill, Haydon, Hermitage, Hillfield, Holnest, Holwell, Leigh, Leweston, Lillington, Longburton, Melbury Bubb, Melbury Osmond, Nether Compton, North Wootton, Oborne, Over Compton, Poyntington, Purse Caundle, Ryme Intrinsica, Sandford Orcas, Sherborne, Stockwood, Thornford, Trent, Yetminster.

In the County of SOMERSET

Comprises: Part District of MENDIP

Consisting of the parishes of: Beckington, Berkley, Buckland Dinham, Coleford, Elm, Frome, Hemington, Kilmersdon, Leigh-on-Mendip, Lullington, Mells, Norton St Philip, Nunney, Rode, Selwood, Tellisford, Trudoxhill, Upton Noble, Wanstow, Whatley, Witham Friary.

Part District of SOUTH SOMERSET

Consisting of the parishes of: Abbas and Templecombe, Alford, Ansford, Ash, Babcary, Barton St David, Barwick, Bratton Seymour, Brewham, Bruton, Brympton, Castle Cary, Charlton Horethorne, Charlton Mackrell, Charlton Musgrove, Chilthorne Domer, Chilton Cantelo, Chiselborough, Closworth, Compton Dundon, Compton Pauncefoot, Corton Denham, Cucklington, East Chinnock, East Coker, Hardington Mandeville, Haselbury, Henstridge, Holton, Horsington, Ilchester, Keinton Mandeville, Kingsdon, Kingweston, Limington, Longload, Long Sutton, Lovington, Mandeville, Maperton, Martock, Milborne Port, Montacute, Mudford, North Barrow, North Cadbury, North Cheriton, North Perrott, Norton Sub Hamdon, Odcombe, Penselwood, Pitcombe, Plucknett, Queen Camel, Shepton Montague, Somerton, South Barrow, South Cadbury, South Petherton, Sparkford, Stoke Sub Hamdon, Stoke Trister, Tintinhull, West Camel, West Chinnock, West Coker, Wincanton, Yarlington, Yeovil, Yeovilton, Yeovil Without.

In the County of WILTSHIRE

Comprises: The District of SALISBURY
The District of WEST WILTSHIRE

Part District of KENNET

Consisting of parishes of: Alton Barnes, Alton Priors, Burbage, Charlton, Chute, Chute Forest, Collingbourne Ducis, Collingbourne Kingston, Easton, Enford, Eveleigh, Fittleton, Huish, Ludgershall, Manningford, Milton Lilbourne, Netheravon, North Newnton, North Tidworth, Pewsey, Rushall, Upavon, Wilcot, Wilsford, Woodborough, Wootton Rivers.

III/1gg**

Column (1)	Column (2)	Column (3)	Column (4)
Number of Area	*Description of Area*	*Appropriate Amount (£)*	*Initial Period (number of weeks)*
Area 11	In the County of WILTSHIRE	60	4
	Comprises: The Borough of THAMESDOWN		
	The District of NORTH WILTSHIRE		
	Part District of KENNET		
	Consisting of the parishes of: Aldbourne Allcannings, Avebury, Baydon, Beechingstoke, Berwick Bassett, Bishops Cannings, Broad Hinton, Bromham, Buttermere, Cheverell Magna, Cheverell Parva, Chilton Foliat, Chirton, Devizes, Easterton, East Kennet, Erlestock, Etchilhampton, Froxfield, Fyfield, Grafton, Great Bedwyn, Ham, Little Bedwyn, Marden, Market Lavington, Marlborough, Marston, Mildenhall, Ogbourne St Andrew, Ogbourne St George, Patney, Potterne, Poulshot, Preshute, Ramsbury, Roundway, Rowde, Savernake, Seend, Shalbourne, Stanton St Bernard, Stert, Tidcombe and Fosbury, Urchfont, West Lavington, West Overton, Winterbourne Bassett, Winterbourne Monkton, Worton.		
Area 12	In the County of AVON	55	4
	Comprises: The Borough of BRISTOL		
	The District of KINGSWOOD		
	The District of NORTHAVON		
	Part District of WANSDYKE		
	Consisting of the parish of: Whitchurch		
	Part District of WOODSPRING		
	Consisting of the parishes of: Abbots Leigh, Backwell, Barrow Gurney, Brockley, Clapton-in-Gordano, Cleve, Clevedon, Dundry, Easton-in-Gordano, Flax Bourton, Kenn, Kingston Seymour, Long Ashton, Nailsea, North Weston, Portbury, Portishead, Tickenham, Walton-in-Gordano, Weston-in-Gordano, Winford, Wraxall, Yatton.		
Area 13	In the county of GLOUCESTERSHIRE	55	4
	Comprises: The Borough of CHELTENHAM		
	The Borough of GLOUCESTER		
	The Borough of TEWKESBURY		
	The District of COTSWOLD		
	The District of FOREST DEAN		
	The District of STROUD		
Area 14	WALES	55	4
	In the County of GWENT		
	Comprises: The Borough of NEWPORT		
	The Borough of TORFAEN		
	The District of ISLWYN		
	The District of MONMOUTH		
	Part District of BLAENAU GWENT		
	Consisting of the communities of: Abertillery, Nantyglo and Blaina.		

Column (1)	Column (2)	Column (3)	Column (4)
Number of Area	*Description of Area*	*Appropriate Amount (£)*	*Initial Period (number of weeks)*

In the County of MID GLAMORGAN

Comprises: The Borough of
    MERTHYR TYDFIL
    The Borough of OGWR
    The Borough of RHONDDA
    The Borough TAFF-ELY
    The District of
    CYNON VALLEY
    The District of
    RHYMNEY VALLEY

In the County of POWYS

Comprises: Part District of BRECKNOCK

Consisting of the community of: Ystradfelte.

In the County of SOUTH GLAMORGAN

Comprises: The Borough of CARDIFF
    The Borough of the VALE OF
    GLAMORGAN

Area 15

In the County of DYFED   55   4

Comprises: The District of LLANELLI

In the County of POWYS

Comprises: Part District of BRECKNOCK

Consisting of the communities of: Glyntawe, Ystradgynlais Lower, Ystradgynlais Higher.

In the County of WEST GLAMORGAN

Comprises: The Borough of AFAN
    The Borough of LLIW VALLEY
    The Borough of NEATH
    The Borough of SWANSEA

Area 16

In the County of DYFED   55   2

Comprises: The District of CARMARTHEN
    The District of DINEFWR

Area 17

In the County of DYFED   50   4

Comprises: The District of PRESELI
    The District of SOUTH
    PEMBROKESHIRE

Area 18

In the County of POWYS   50   4

Comprises: Part District of BRECKNOCK

Consisting of the communities of: Aberllynfi, Aberyscir, Battle, Brecon, Bronllys, Cantref, Cathedene, Cray, Crickhowell, Fennifach, Garthbrengy, Glyn, Glynfach, Hay, Hay Rural, Llanbedr Ystradwy, Llanddetty, Llandefaelog Fach, Llandeilo'r Fan, Llandefalle, Llanddew, Llanelieu, Llanfigan, Llanfihangel Cwmdu, Llanfihangel Fechan, Llanfihangel Nant Bran,

Column (1)	Column (2)	Column (3)	Column (4)
Number of Area	Description of Area	Appropriate Amount (£)	Initial Period (number of weeks)

Llanfilo, Llanfrynach, Llangasty-Talyllyn, Llangattock, Llangenny, Llangorse, Llangynidr, Llanhamlach, Llanigon, Llansantffraed, Llanspyddid, Llanwern, Llyswen, Maescar, Merthyr Cynog, Modrydd, Partrishaw, Penpont, Pipton, St David Without, Senny, Talgarth, Talachddu, Traianglos, Traianmawr, Trallong, Tregoyd and Velindre, Ysclydach.

In the County of GWENT

Comprises: Part District of
BLAENAU GWENT

Consisting of the communities of: Brynmawr, Ebbw Vale, Lanelly, Tredegar.

Area 19	In the County of POWYS	50	4

Comprises: The District of MONTGOMERY
The District of RADNOR

Part District of BRECKNOCK

Consisting of the communities of: Allemawr, Builth Wells, Crickadarn, Gwarafog, Gwenddwr, Isygarreg, Llanafanfechan, Llanafanfawr, Llanddewi Abergwesyn, Llanddewi'r Cwm, Llandulas, Llanfihangel Abergwesyn, Llanfihangel Brynpabuan, Llanganten, Llangynog, Llanlleonfel, Llanwrthwl, Llanwrtyd Wells, Llanwrtyd Without, Llanynis, Llysdinam, Mochynleth, Maesmynis, Penbault, Rhosferig, Treflys.

Area 20	In the County of DYFED	55	2

Comprises: The District of CEREDIGION

Area 21	In the County of CLWYD	50	4

Comprises: The Borough of WREXHAM
MAELOR
The District of ALYN AND
DEESIDE

Part District of DELYN

Consisting of the communities of: Flint (that part South of Lead Brook), Leeswood, Mold, Mold Rural (that part which lies South of the A5116 and A494), Nercwys, Northop (that part which lies South of Northop Brook and the A5116).

Part District of GLYNDWR

Consisting of the communities of: Bettws-Gwerfi-Goch, Bryneglwys (that part which lies South of the A5104), Chirk, Corwen, Glyntraian, Gwyddelwern, Llanarmon Dyffryn Ceiriog, Llanarmon Mynydd Mawr, Llarmon-yn-Lal (that part which lies to the East of the A494), Llandegla (that part which lies to the East of the A494 to its intersection with the A525, to the North of the A525 to its intersection with

Column (1)	Column (2)	Column (3)	Column (4)
Number of Area	*Description of Area*	*Appropriate Amount (£)*	*Initial Period (number of weeks)*

the A5104 to the South of the A5104), Llandrillio, Llanferres (that part which lies to the East of the A494), Llangadwaladr, Llangar, Llangedwyn, Llangollen, Llangollen Ruual, Llanrhaeadr-yn-Mochnant, Llansantffraid-Glynceiriog, Llansantffraid Glyndyfrdwy, Llansilin, Llantysilio.

Area 22 In the County of CLWYD   55   2

Comprises: The Borough of RHUDDLAN
Part District of COLWYN

Consisting of the communities of: Abergele, Abergele Rural, Betws-yn-Rhos, Bylchau, Cefn, Cerrigydrudion, Gwytherin, Llanefydd, Llangernyw, Llangwm, Llanfair Talhaiarn, Llanfihangel Glyn Myfyr, Llansannan, Pentrefoelas, Trefnant.

Part District of DELYN

Consisting of the communities of: Caerwys Brynford, Flint (that part North of Lead Brook), Gilcain, Gwaenysgor, Halkyn, Holywell, Llanasa, Mold Rural (that part which lies North of the A5116 and A494), Nannerch, Northop (that part which lies North of Northop Brook and the A5116), Trelawnyd, Whitford, Ysceifiog.

Part District of GLYNDWR

Consisting of the communities of: Aberwheeler, Bryneglwys (that part which lies North of the A5104), Glocaenog, Cyfflliog, Denbigh, Derwen, Efenechtyd, Llanarmon-yn-Ila (that part which lies West of the A494), Llanbedr, Llandegla (that part which lies West of the A494 to its intersection with the A525, South of the A525 to its intersection with the A5104, North of the A5104), Llandyrnog, Llanelidan, Llanfair-Dyffyn-Clwyd, Llanferres (that part which lies to the west of the A494), Llanfwrog Rural, Llanrhaedr-yng-Nghinmerch, Llanynys Rural, Nantglyn, Ruthin.

Area 23 In the County of GWYNEDD   55   2

Comprises: The District of DWYFOR
The District of MEIRIONNYDD

Area 24 In the County of CLWYD   45   2

Comprises: Part District of COLWYN

Consisting of the communities of: Colwyn Bay, Llanelian-yn-Rhos.

In the County of GWYNEDD

Comprises: The District of ABERCONWY

Area 25 In the County of GWYNEDD   50   2

Comprises: The District of ARFON

Area 26 In the County of GWYNEDD   55   2

Comprises: The District of YNYS MON
(ISLE OF ANGLESEY)

PART II

LONDON SOUTH REGION

Column (1) Number of Area	Column (2) Description of Area	Column (3) Appropriate Amount (£)	Column (4) Initial Period (number of weeks)
Area 27	In the County of ISLE OF WIGHT	60	2
	Comprises: The Borough of MEDINA The District of SOUTH WIGHT		
Area 28	In the County of HAMPSHIRE	60	4
	Comprises: The Borough of EASTLEIGH The Borough of SOUTHAMPTON Part Borough of WINCHESTER		
	Consisting of the parishes of: Abbots Barton, Beauworth, Bighton, Bishops Sutton, Bramdean, Cheriton, Chilcombe, Colden Common, Compton, Crawley, Headbourne Worthy, Hursley, Itchen Stoke and Ovington, Itchen Valley, Kilmiston, Kings Worthy, Littleton, Micheldever, New Alresford, Northington, Old Alresford, Olivers Battery, Otterbourne, Owlesbury, Sparsholt, Tichborne, Twyford, Winchester, Wonston.		
	The District of NEW FOREST The District of TEST VALLEY		
Area 29	In the County of HAMPSHIRE	55	4
	Comprises: The Borough of FAREHAM The Borough of GOSPORT The Borough of HAVANT The Borough of PORTSMOUTH Part Borough of WINCHESTER		
	Consisting of the parishes of: Bishops Waltham, Boarhunt, Colemore and Priors Dean, Corhampton and Meonstoke, Curdridge, Denmead, Droxford, Durley, Exton, Greatham, Hambledon, Sarisbury, Shedfield, Soberton, Southwick and Widley, Swanmore, Upham, Warnford, West Meon, Wickham.		
	Part District of EAST HAMPSHIRE		
	Consisting of the parishes of: Buriton, Clanfield, Colemore and Priors Dean, East Meon, Froxfield, Greatham, Hawkley, Horndean, Langrish, Liss, Petersfield, Rowlands Castle, Steep.		
Area 30	In the County of EAST SUSSEX	55	2
	Comprises: The Borough of BRIGHTON The Borough of HOVE The District of LEWES Part District of MID SUSSEX		
	Consisting of the parishes of: Albourne, Burgess Hill, Clayton, Cuckfield, Fulking, Haywards Heath, Hurstpierpoint, Keymer, Lindfield Rural, Newtimber, Poynings, Pyecombe, Twineham.		
	In the County of WEST SUSSEX		
	Comprises: The Borough of WORTHING The District of ADUR The District of ARUN The District of CHICHESTER		
	Part District of HORSHAM		

Column (1) *Number of Area*	Column (2) *Description of Area*	Column (3) *Appropriate Amount (£)*	Column (4) *Initial Period (number of weeks)*
	Consisting of the parishes of: Amberley, Ashington, Ashurst, Bramber, Coldwaltham, Henfield, Parham, Pulborough, Shermanbury, Storrington, Steyning, Sullington, Thakeham, Upper Beeding, Washington, West Chiltington, Wiston, Woodmancote.		
Area 31	In the County of EAST SUSSEX Comprises: The Borough of EASTBOURNE The Borough of HASTINGS The District of ROTHER The District of WEALDEN	55	2
Area 32	In the County of KENT Comprises: The District of CANTERBURY The District of DOVER The District of SHEPWAY The District of THANET	55	2
Area 33	In the County of KENT Comprises: The Borough of ASHFORD The District of SWALE	55	2
Area 34	In the County of KENT Comprises: The Borough of GILLINGHAM The District of DARTFORD The District of GRAVESHAM The District of MAIDSTONE The District of MEDWAY The District of SEVENOAKS The District of TONBRIDGE AND MALLING The District of TUNBRIDGE WELLS	55	4
Area 35	In the County of SURREY Comprises: The Borough of EPSOM AND EWELL The Borough of GUILDFORD The Borough of REIGATE AND BANSTEAD The Borough of WAVERLEY The Borough of WOKING The District of MOLE VALLEY The District of RUNNYMEDE The District of TANDRIDGE Part Borough of ELMBRIDGE Consisting of the parishes of: Walton on Thames, Weybridge. Part Borough of RUSHMORE Consisting of the parishes of: Ash, Sandy Hill. Part Borough of SURREY HEATH Consisting of the parishes of: Bisley, Chobham, West End, Windlesham.	60	4

Column (1)	Column (2)	Column (3)	Column (4)
Number of Area	*Description of Area*	*Appropriate Amount (£)*	*Initial Period (number of weeks)*

In the County of WEST SUSSEX

Comprises: The Borough of CRAWLEY

   Part District of HORSHAM

Consisting of the parishes of: Billingshurst, Cowfold, Horsham, Horsham Rural, Itchingfield, Lower Beeding, Nuthurst, Rudgwick, Rusper, Shipley, Slinfold, Warnham, West Grinstead.

   Part District of MID SUSSEX

Consisting of the parishes of: Ardingly, Balcombe, Bolney, Cuckfield Rural, East Grinstead, Horsted Keynes, Slaugham, West Hoathly, Worth.

Area 36   In the County of HAMPSHIRE   60   4

Comprises: The District of BASINGSTOKE
   The District of HART
   The District of RUSHMORE

   Part Borough of SURREY HEATH

Consisting of the areas of: Camberley, Frimley, Mytchett.

   Part District of
   EAST HAMPSHIRE

Consisting of the parishes of: Alton, Bentley, Bentworth, Binstead, Bramshott, Chawton, East Tisted, Faringdon, Four Marks, Froyle, Grayshott, Headley, Kingsley, Lasham, Medstead, Newton Valence, Ropley, Selborne, Shalden, West Tisted, Whitehill, Wield, Worldham.

Area 37   In the County of BERKSHIRE   60   4

Comprises: The District of NEWBURY
   The District of READING

In the County of OXFORDSHIRE

Comprises: Part District of SOUTH
   OXFORDSHIRE

Consisting of the parishes of: Benson, Bix, Blewbury, Brightwell-cum-Sotwell, Checkendon, Childrey, Cholsey, Crowmarsh, Didcot, East Hagbourne, Ewelme, Eye and Dunsden, Goring, Goring Heath, Harpsden, Henley on Thames, Highmoor, Ipsden, Kidmore End, Mapledurham, Moulsford, Nettlebed, North Moreton, Nuffield, Pishill with Stoner, Rotherfield Grays, Rotherfield Peppard, Shiplake, Sonning Common, South Moreton, South Stoke, Stoke Row, Swynncombe, Wallingford, West Hagbourne, Whitchurch, Woodcote.

   Part District of VALE OF WHITE
   HORSE

Consisting of the parishes of: Ardington, Ashbury, Aston Tirrold, Aston Upthorpe, Bourton, Chilton, Compton, Compton Beauchamp, East Challow, East Hendred, Grove, Harwell, Kingston Lisle, Letcombe Bassett, Letcombe Regis, Lockinge, Sparsholt, Uffington, Upton, Wantage, West Challow, West Hendred, Woolstone.

Column (1) Number of Area	Column (2) Description of Area	Column (3) Appropriate Amount (£)	Column (4) Initial Period (number of weeks)
Area 38	In the County of BERKSHIRE Comprises: The Borough of SLOUGH The Borough of WINDSOR AND MAIDENHEAD The District of BRACKNELL The District of WOKINGHAM	65	4

PART III

LONDON NORTH REGION

Column (1) Number of Area	Column (2) Description of Area	Column (3) Appropriate Amount (£)	Column (4) Initial Period (number of weeks)
Area 39	In the County of OXFORDSHIRE Comprises: The Borough of OXFORD The District of CHERWELL The District of WEST OXFORDSHIRE Part District of SOUTH OXFORDSHIRE Consisting of the parishes of: Adwell, Aston Rowant, Beckley and Stowood, Berrick Salome, Brightwell Baldwin, Britwell, Chalgrove, Chinnor, Clifton Hampden, Crowell, Cuddeston and Denton, Culham, Cuxham with Easington, Dorchester, Drayton St Leonard, Elsfield, Forest Hill with Shotover, Garsington, Great Haseley, Great Milton, Holton, Horspath, Little Milton, Littlemore, Little Wittenham, Lewknor, Long Wittenham, Marsh Baldon, Marston, Newington, Nuneham Courtney, Pyrton, Risinghurst and Sandhills, Sandford on Thames, Shirburn, Stadhampton, Stanton St John, Stoke Talmage, Sydenham, Tetsworth, Thame, Thomley, Tiddington-with-Albury, Toot Baldon, Towersey, Watlington, Warborough, Waterperry, Waterstock, Wheatfield, Wheatley, Woodeaton. Part District of VALE OF WHITE HORSE Consisting of the parishes of: Abingdon, Appleford, Appleton with Eaton, Baulking, Besselsleigh, Buckland, Buscot, Charney Basset, Coleshill, Cumnor, Denchworth, Drayton, East Hanney, Eaton Hastings, Fernham, Frilford, Fyfield and Tubney, Garford, Goosey, Great Coxwell, Great Faringdon, Hatford, Hinton Waldrist, Kennington, Kingston Bagpuize with Southmoor, Little Coxwell, Littleworth, Longcot, Longworth, Lyford,	65	4

Column (1)	Column (2)	Column (3)	Column (4)
Number of Area	*Description of Area*	*Appropriate Amount (£)*	*Initial Period (number of weeks)*
	Marcham, Milton Steventon, North Hinksey, Pusey, Radley, St Helen Without, Shellingford, Shrivenham, South Hinksey, Stanford in the Vale, Sunningwell, Sutton Courtney, Watchfield, West Hanney, Wooton, Wytham.		
Area 40	In the County of BUCKINGHAMSHIRE	60	4
	Comprises: The District of BEACONSFIELD The District of CHILTERN The District of WYCOMBE		
	The District of AYLESBURY VALE		
Area 41	In the County of HERTFORDSHIRE	60	4
	Comprises: The Borough of WATFORD The District of DACORUM The District of NORTH HERTFORDSHIRE The District of ST ALBANS The District of THREE RIVERS		
	Part District of HERTSMERE		
	Consisting of the parishes of: Bushey and Aldenham.		
	Part District of WELWYN HATFIELD		
	Consisting of the parishes of: Essendon, Hatfield, Northaw, North Mimms.		
Area 42	In the County of ESSEX	55	4
	Comprises: The District of HARLOW Part District of EPPING FOREST		
	Consisting of the parishes of: Abbess Beauchamp and Berners Roding, Bobbingworth, Epping, Epping Upland, Fyfield, High Laver, High Ongar, Lambourne, Little Laver, Magdalen Laver, Matching, Moreton, Nazeing, North Weald Bassett, Ongar, Roydon, Sheering, Stapleford Tawney, Theydon Bois, Theydon Garnon, Theydon Mount, Willingale.		
	In the County of HERTFORDSHIRE		
	Comprises: The Borough of STEVENAGE The District of EAST HERTFORDSHIRE The District of NORTH HERTFORDSHIRE		
	Part Borough of BROXBOURNE		
	Consisting of: that part which lies North of Cheshunt Park and Slipe Lane including Hoddersdon and Wormley.		
	Part District of WELWYN HATFIELD		
	Consisting of the parishes of: Ayot St Lawrence, Ayot St Peter, Welwyn, Welwyn Garden City.		

Column (1)	Column (2)	Column (3)	Column (4)
Number of Area	*Description of Area*	*Appropriate Amount (£)*	*Initial Period (number of weeks)*
Area 43	In the County of ESSEX	55	4
	Comprises: The Borough of THURROCK The District of BASILDON The District of BRENTWOOD The District of CASTLEPOINT		
Area 44	In the County of ESSEX	55	2
	Comprises: The Borough of SOUTHEND-ON-SEA The District of ROCHFORD		
Area 45	In the County of ESSEX	60	2
	Comprises: Part District of TENDRING		
	Consisting of the parishes of: Beamont-cum–Moze, Clacton-on-Sea, Frinton and Walton, Little Clacton, St Osyth, Tendring, Thorpe-le-Soken, Weeley.		
Area 46	In the County of ESSEX	60	4
	Comprises: The Borough of COLCHESTER The District of BRAINTREE The District of CHELMSFORD The District of MALDON The District of UTTLESFORD		
	Part District of TENDRING		
	Consisting of the parishes of: Alresford, Ardleigh, Bradfield, Brightlingsea, Elmstead, Frating, Great Bentley, Great Bromley, Great Oakley, Harwich, Lawford, Little Bentley, Little Bromley, Little Oakley, Manningtree, Mistley, Ramsey, Thorrington, Wix, Wrabness.		
Area 47	In the County of BEDFORDSHIRE	60	4
	Comprises: The Borough of LUTON The District of BEDFORD The District of MID BEDFORDSHIRE The District of SOUTH BEDFORDSHIRE		
	In the County of BUCKINGHAMSHIRE		
	Comprises: The Borough of MILTON KEYNES		
Area 48	In the County of CAMBRIDGESHIRE	65	4
	Comprises: The District of CAMBRIDGE The District of EAST CAMBRIDGESHIRE The District of HUNTINGDON The District of PETERBOROUGH The District of SOUTH CAMBRIDGESHIRE		

Column (1)	Column (2)	Column (3)	Column (4)
Number of Area	*Description of Area*	*Appropriate Amount (£)*	*Initial Period (number of weeks)*

Part District of FENLAND

Consisting of the parishes of: Benwick, Chatteris, Doddington, Manea, March, Whittlesey, Wimblington.

Area 49	In the County of SUFFOLK	55	4

Comprises: The District of BABERGH
The District of FOREST HEATH
The District of IPSWICH
The District of
ST EDMONDSBURY
The District of SUFFOLK
COASTAL

Part District of MID SUFFOLK

Consisting of the parishes of: Badwell Ash, Benton, Drinkstone, Elmswell, Felsham, Gedding, Great Ashfield, Hessett, Hinderclay, Hunston, Langham, Norton, Rattlesden, Rickinghall Inferior, Stowlangtoft, Thurston, Tostock, Walsham-le-Willows, Wattisfield, Woolpit.

Area 50	In the County of NORFOLK	55	2

Comprises: The District of GREAT
YARMOUTH

Part District of BROADLAND

Consisting of the parishes of: Acle, Beighton, Burlingham, Cantley, Freethorpe, Halvergate, Reedham, South Walsham, Upton with Fishley.

Part District of
NORTH NORFOLK

Consisting of the parishes of: Catfield, Hersey, Hickling, Higham, Ludham, Potter Heigham, Sea Palling, Sutton, Tunstead.

In the County of SUFFOLK
Part District of WAVENEY

Consisting of the parishes of: Ashby, Barnby, Barsham, Beccles, Benacre, Blundeston Flixton, Blyford, Brampton, Carlton Colville, Corton, Covehithe, Easton Bavents, Ellough, Frostenden, Gisleham, Halesworth, Henham, Henstead with Hulver Street, Herringfleet, Holton, Kessingland, Lound, Lowestoft, Mettingham, Mutford, North Cove, Oulton, Redisham, Reydon, Ringsfield, Rumburgh, Rushmere, St Andrew Ilketshaw, St John Ilketshall, St Lawrence Ilketshall, St Margaret Ilkershall, Shadingfield, Shipmeadow, Somerleyton, Sotherton, Sotterley, South Cove, Southwold, Spexhall, Stoven, Uggeshall, Wangford, Westhall, Weston, Willingham St Mary, Wissett, Worlingham, Wrentham.

Column (1) *Number of Area*	Column (2) *Description of Area*	Column (3) *Appropriate Amount (£)*	Column (4) *Initial Period (number of weeks)*
Area 51	In the County of NORFOLK	60	4

Comprises: The Borough of NORWICH
The District of
SOUTH NORFOLK

Part District of BRECKLAND

Consisting of the parishes of: Attleborough,
Banham, Besthorpe, Blo'Norton, Brettenham,
Bridgham, Carbrooke, Caston, Croxton,
Garboldisham, Great Ellingham, Griston,
Harling, Kenninghall, Kilverston, Little
Ellingham, Merton, New Buckenham, North
Lopham, Old Buckenham, Ovington,
Quidenham, Riddlesworth, Rocklands, Roundham,
Scoulton, Shropham, Snetterton, South Lopen,
Stow Bedon, Thetford, Thompson,
Tottington, Walton, Wretham.

Part District of BROADLAND

Consisting of the parishes of: Alderford,
Attlebridge, Aylsham, Beeston St Andrew,
Beeston St Lawrence, Belaugh, Blickling,
Blofield, Booton, Brampton, Brandiston, Brundall,
Buxton with Lammas, Catton, Cawston,
Coltishall, Crostwich, Drayton, Felthorpe,
Foulsham, Frettenham, Great Plumstead, Great
Witchingham, Guestwick, Hainford,
Hautbois, Haveringland, Hellesdon,
Hemblington, Hevingham, Heydon, Honingham,
Horsford, Horsham St Faith, Horstead with
Stanninghall, Lenwade, Little Plumstead,
Little Witchingham, Marsham, Morton on the
Hill, Newton St Faith, Oulton, Postwick,
Rackheath, Reepham, Ringland, Salhouse, Sall,
Sco Ruston, Spixworth, Sprowston, Stratton
Strawless, Strumpshaw, Swannington,
Taverham, Themelthorpe, Thorpe St Andrew,
Tuttington, Weston Longville, Witton
Woodbastick, Wood Dalling, Wroxham.

Part District of
NORTH NORFOLK

Consisting of the parishes of: Alby with Thwaite,
Aldborough, Antingham, Ashmanhaugh,
Aylmerton, Baconsthorpe, Bacton, Barton Turf,
Beeston Regis, Bodham Brumstead, Cley next
the sea, Colby, Corpusty, Cromer, Dilham, East
Beckham, East Runton, East Ruston, Eccles,
Edgefield, Edingthorpe, Erpingham, Felbrigg,
Felmingham, Gimingham, Gresham,
Hanworth, Happisburgh, Hempstead, Holt,
Honing, Horning, Hoveton, Ingham,
Ingworth, Itteringham, Kelling, Knapton,
Lessingham, Letheringsett with Glandford, Little
Barningham, Matlaske, Mundesley, Neatishead,
Northrepps, North Walsham, Overstrand,
Paston, Plumstead, Ridlington, Roughton,
Salthouse, Saxthorpe, Scottow, Sheringham,
Sidestrand, Skeyton, Sloley, Smallburgh,
Southrepps, Stalham, Stody Suffield, Sustead,
Swafield, Swanton Abbott, Thornage, Thorpe

Column (1)	Column (2)	Column (3)	Column (4)
Number of Area	*Description of Area*	*Appropriate Amount (£)*	*Initial Period (number of weeks)*

Market, Thurgarton, Trimingham, Trunch, Tunstead, Upper Sheringham, Walcott, West Beckham, West Runton, Westwick, Weybourne, Wickmere, Witton, Worstead.

In the County of SUFFOLK

Comprises: Part District of MID SUFFOLK

Consisting of the parishes of: Aspall, Athelington, Bacton, Bedfield, Bedingfield, Botesdale, Braiseworth, Brockford, Brome, Brundish, Burgate, Cotton, Denham, Eye, Finningham, Fressingfield, Gislingham, Horham, Hoxne, Kenton, Laxfield, Mellis, Mendham, Mendlesham, Metfield, Monk Soham, Oakley, Occold, Palgrave, Redgrave, Redlingfield, Rickinghall Superior, Rishangles, Southolt, Stoke Ash, Stradbroke, Stuston, Syleham, Tannington, Thorndon, Thornham, Magna, Thornham Parva, Thranderton, Thwaite, Westhorpe, Wexheringsett-cum-Brockford, Weybread, Wickham Sketh, Wilby, Wingfield, Witherscale, Worlingworth, Wortham, Wyverstone, Yaxley.

Part District of WAVENEY

Consisting of the parishes of: Bungay, Flixton, South Elmham All Saints and St Nicholas, South Elmham St Cross, South Elmham St James, South Elmham St Margeret, South Elmham St Mary otherwise Homersfield, South Elmham St Michael, South Elmham St Peter.

Area 52	In the County of CAMBRIDGESHIRE Part District of FENLAND	55	2

Consisting of the parishes of: Elm, Leverington, Newton, Outwell, Parson Drove, Tydd St Giles, Upwell, Wisbech, Wisbech St Mary.

In the County of NORFOLK

Comprises: The District of WEST NORFOLK

Part District of BRECKLAND

Consisting of the parishes of: Ashill, Bawdesewell, Beachamwell, Beeston with Bittering, Beetley, Billingford, Bintree, Bradenham, Brisley, Bylaugh, Cockley Cley, Colkirk, Cranwich, Cranworth, Didlington, East Dereham, East Tuddenham, Elsing, Foulden, Foxley, Fransham, Garveston, Gately, Gooderstone, Great Cressingham, Great Dunham, Gressenhall, Guist, Hardingham, Hilborough, Hockering, Hoe, Holme Hale, Horningtoft, Ickburgh, Kempstone, Lexham, Litcham, Little Cressingham, Little Dunham, Longham, Lynford, Lyng, Mattishall, Mileham, Mundford, Narborough, Narford, Necton, Newton by Castle Acre, North Elmham, North Pickenham, North Tuddenham, Oxborough, Rougham, Saham Toney, Scarning, Shipdham, South Acre, South Pickenham, Sparham, Sporle with Palgrage, Stanfield, Stanford, Swaffham, Swanton Moreley, Tittleshall, Twyford,

Column (1)	Column (2)	Column (3)	Column (4)
Number of Area	*Description of Area*	*Appropriate Amount (£)*	*Initial Period (number of weeks)*

Weasenham All Saints, Weasenham St Peter, Weeting with Broomhill, Wellingham, Wendling, Whinburg, Whissonsett, Yaxham.

Part District of NORTH NORFOLK

Consisting of the parishes of: Binham, Blakeley, Briningham, Brinton, Briston, Dunton, Fakenham, Field Dalling, Fulmodeston, Great Ryburgh, Great Snoring, Great Walsingham, Gunthorpe, Helhoughton, Hempton, Hindolveston, Hindringham, Holkham, Kettlestone, Laugham, Little Ryburgh, Little Snoring, Little Walsingham, Melton Constable, Morston, Pudding Norton, Raynham, Sculthorpe, Stibbard, Stiffkey, Swanton Novers, Tattersett, Thurning, Thursford, Warham, Wells-next-the-Sea, Wighton, Wiveton, Wood Norton.

Area 53 In the GREATER LONDON Area   70   8

Comprises: The Boroughs of:

BARKING	HOUNSLOW
BARNET	ISLINGTON
BEXLEY	KENSINGTON AND
BRENT	CHELSEA
BROMLEY	KINGSTON-UPON-
CAMDEN	THAMES
CITY OF	LAMBETH
WESTMINSTER	LEWISHAM
CROYDON	MERTON
EALING	NEWHAM
ENFIELD	REDBRIDGE
GREENWICH	RICHMOND-UPON-
HACKNEY	THAMES
HARINGEY	SOUTHWARK
HAMMERSMITH	SUTTON
HARROW	TOWER HAMLETS
HAVERING	WALTHAM FOREST
HILLINGDON	WANDSWORTH

The CITY OF LONDON

In the County of ESSEX

Comprises: Part District of EPPING FOREST

Consisting of the parishes of: Chigwell, Waltham Holy Cross.

In the County of HERTFORDSHIRE

Comprises: Part Borough of BROXBOURNE

That part which lies South of Cheshunt Park and includes Slipe Lane.

Part District of HERTSMERE

Consisting of the parishes of: Elstree, Ridge, Shenley, South Mimms.

In the County of SURREY

Comprises: The Borough of SPELTHORNE
Part Borough of ELMBRIDGE

Consisting of that part which was previously administered by the old Esher Urban District Council.

PART IV

MIDLANDS REGION

Column (1)	Column (2)	Column (3)	Column (4)
Number of Area	Description of Area	Appropriate Amount (£)	Initial Period (number of weeks)
Area 54	In the County of NORTHAMPTONSHIRE	50	4
	Comprises: The Borough of WELLINGBOROUGH The District of CORBY The District of EAST NORTHAMPTONSHIRE The District of KETTERING		
Area 55	In the County of NORTHAMPTONSHIRE	55	4
	Comprises: The Borough of NORTHAMPTON The District of DAVENTRY The District of SOUTH NORTHAMPTONSHIRE		
Area 56	In the County of LEICESTERSHIRE	55	4
	Comprises: The City of LEICESTER The Borough of HINCKLEY AND BOSWORTH The Borough of OADBY AND WIGSTON The District of BLABY The District of CHARNWOOD The District of HARBOROUGH The District of MELTON The District of NORTH WEST LEICESTERSHIRE The District of RUTLAND		
Area 57	In the County of WARWICKSHIRE	55	4
	Comprises: The Borough of RUGBY Part District of STRATFORD-ON-AVON		
	Consisting of the parishes of: Admington, Alderminster, Atherstone on Stour, Avon Dassett, Barcheston, Barton-on-Heath, Bearley, Beaudesert, Billesley, Binton, Bishop's Itchington, Burmington, Burton Dassett, Butlers Marston, Brailes, Chadshunt, Chapel Ascote, Charlecote, Cherington, Chesterton and Kingston, Claverdon, Clifford Chambers, Combrook, Compton Wynyates, Dorsington, Ettington, Farnborough, Fenny Compton, Fulbrook, Gaydon, Great Wolford, Halford, Hampton Lucy, Harbury, Henley in Arden, Hodnell, Honington, Idlicote, Ilmington, Kineton, Ladbroke, Langley, Lighthorne, Little Compton, Little Wolford, Long Compton, Long Itchington, Long Marston, Lower Radbourne, Lower Shuckburgh, Loxley, Luddington, Milcote, Moreton-Morrell, Napton on the Hill, Newbold Pacey, Old Stratford and Drayton, Oxhill, Pillerton Hersey, Pillerton Priors, Preston Bagot, Preston on Stour, Priors Hardwicke, Priors Marston, Quinton, Radway, Ratley and		

Column (1)	Column (2)	Column (3)	Column (4)
Number of Area	*Description of Area*	*Appropriate Amount (£)*	*Initial Period (number of weeks)*

Upton, Shipston on Stour, Shotteswell, Snitterfield, Southam, Stockton, Stoneton, Stourton, Stratford-upon-Avon, Stretton on Fosse, Sutton under Brailes, Tanworth in Arden, Tidmington, Temple Grafton, Tredington, Tysoe, Ufton, Ullenhall, Upper Radbourne, Upper Schuckburg, Warmington, Watergall, Welford on Avon, Wellesbourne, Weston on Avon, Wills Pastures, Whatcote, Whichford, Whitchurch, Wolverton, Wootton Wawen, Wormleighton.

Part District of WARWICK

Consisting of the parishes of: Ashow, Baddesley, Barford, Beauscale, Bishop's Tachbrook, Blackdown, Budbrooke, Bushwood, Clinton, Cubbington, Eathorpe, Guy's Cliffe, Haseley, Hatton, Honiley, Hunningham off Church, Kenilworth, Lapworth, Leek Wootton, Norton Lindsey, Old Milverton, Radford Semele, Rowington, Royal Leamington Spa, Sherbourne, Shrewley, Wappenbury, Warwick, Wasperton, Weston under Wetherley, Whitnash, Wroxall.

Area 58

In the County of WARWICKSHIRE — 55 — 4

Comprises: The Borough of NORTH WARWICKSHIRE
The Borough of NUNEATON

Part District of WARWICK

Consisting of the parishes of: Baginton, Bubbenhall, Stoneleigh.

In the County of WEST MIDLANDS

Comprises: The Borough of COVENTRY

Area 59

In the County of WEST MIDLANDS — 55 — 8

Comprises: The Borough of SOLIHULL
The District of BIRMINGHAM

Area 60

In the County of STAFFORDSHIRE — 55 — 4

Comprises: Part District of SOUTH STAFFORDSHIRE

Consisting of the parishes of: Bilbrook, Bobbington, Brewood, Codsall, Enville, Himley, Kinver, Lower Penn, Pattingham and Patshull, Perton, Swindon, Trysull and Seisdon, Wombourne.

In the County of WEST MIDLANDS

Comprises: The Borough of DUDLEY
The Borough of SANDWELL
The Borough of WALSALL
The Borough of WOLVERHAMPTON

Area 61

In the County of HEREFORD and WORCESTER — 55 — 4

Comprises: The District of BROMSGROVE

Part District of LEOMINSTER

Consisting of the parishes of: Bayton, Bockleton, Eastham, Hanley, Knighton on Teme, Kyre,

Column (1)	Column (2)	Column (3)	Column (4)
Number of Area	Description of Area	Appropriate Amount (£)	Initial Period (number of weeks)

Lindridge, Mamble, Pensax, Rochford, Stanford
with Orleton, Stockton on Teme, Stoke Bliss,
Tenbury.

The District of REDDITCH
The District of WORCESTER
The District of WYCHAVON
The District of WYRE FOREST

Part District of MALVERN HILLS

Consisting of the parishes of: Alfrick, Abberley,
Astley, Berrow, Birtsmorton, Bransford,
Broadheath, Broadwas, Bushley, Castlemorton,
Clifton upon Teme, Cotheridge, Croome D'Abitot,
Doddenham, Earls Croome, Eldersfield, Great
Malvern, Great Witley, Grimley, Guarlford,
Hallow, Hanley Castle, Hill Croome, Hillhampton,
Holdfast, Holt, Kempsey, Kenswick, Knightwick,
Leigh, Little Malvern, Little Witley, Longdon,
Lower Sapey, Lulsey, Madresfield, Martley,
Newland, Pendrock, Powick, Queenhill, Ripple,
Rushwick, Severn Stoke, Shelsley Beauchamp,
Shelsley Kings, Shelsley Welsh, Shrawley,
Suckley, Upton upon Severn, Welland, Wichenford.

In the County of WARWICKSHIRE

Part District of
STRATFORD-UPON-AVON

Consisting of the parishes of: Alcester, Arrow,
Aston, Cantlow, Bidford-upon-Avon, Coughton,
Exhall, Great Alme, Haselor, Kinwarton,
Morton Bagot, Oldberrow, Salford Priors,
Sambourne, Spernall, Studley, Weethley, Wiford.

Area 62	In the County of HEREFORD and WORCESTER	55	4

Comprises: The Borough of HEREFORD
The District of SOUTH
HEREFORDSHIRE

Part District of LEOMINSTER

Consisting of the parishes of: Adforton, Almeley,
Aymestrey, Birley Bishopstone, Blackmere,
Bodenham, Brampton Bryan, Bridge Sollers,
Brilley, Brimfield, Brinsop, Brobury, Buckton and
Coxall, Burrington, Byford, Byton, Canon Pyon,
Combe, Croft, Docklow, Downton, Dilwyn,
Eardisland, Eardisley, Elton, Eye Moreton and
Ashton, Eyton, Ford, Hampton Wafer, Hatfield,
Hope under Dinmore, Humer, Huntington,
Kimbolton, Kingsland, Kings Pyon, Kington,
Kington Rural, Kinnersley, Kinsham, Knill, Laysters,
Leinthalstarkes, Leintwardine, Leominster, Letton,
Lingen, Little Hereford, Lower Harpton, Lucton,
Luston, Lyonshall, Mansell Gamage, Mansell Lacy,
Middleton-on-the-Hill, Moccas, Monkland,
Monnington-on-Wye, Newton, Norton Canon,
Orleton, Pembridge, Pipe Aston, Preston-on-Wye,
Pudlestone, Richard Castle (Hereford), Rodd Nash
and Little Brampton, Sarnesfield, Shobdon,
Stapleton, Staunton-on-Arrow, Staunton-on-Wye,
Stoke Prior, Streatford, Titley, Walford Letton

Column (1)	Column (2)	Column (3)	Column (4)
Number of Area	*Description of Area*	*Appropriate Amount (£)*	*Initial Period (number of weeks)*

and Newton, Weobly, Whitney, Wigmore, Willersley, Willey, Winforton, Wormsely, Yarpole, Yazor.

Part District of
MALVERN MILLS

Consisting of the parishes of: Acton Beauchamp, Ashperton, Avenbury, Aylton, Bishops Frome, Bosbury, Bredenbury, Brockhampton, Bromyard, Caddington, Canon Frome, Castle Frome, Collington, Colwall, Cradley, Donnington, Eastnor, Edvin Loach, Edwyn Ralph, Eggleton, Evesbatch, Felton, Grendon Bishop, Hampton Charles, Ledbury Rural, Ledbury Town, Linton, Little Cowarne, Little Marcle, Mathon Rural, Moreton Jeffries, Much Cowarne, Much Marcle, Munsley, Norton Saltmarshe, Ocle Pychard, Pencombe with Grendon Warren, Pixley, Putley, Stanford Biship, Stoke Lacy, Stretton Grandison, Tarrington, Tedstone Delamere, Tedstone Wafre, Thornbury, Ullingswick, Upper Sapey, Wacton, Wellington Heath, Whitbourne, Winslow, Wolferlow, Woolhope, Yorkhill.

Area 63	In the County of SHROPSHIRE	55	4

Comprises: The Borough of OSWESTRY
The Borough of SHREWSBURY and ATCHAM
The District of BRIDGNORTH
The District of NORTH SHROPSHIRE
The District of SOUTH SHROPSHIRE
The District of THE WREKIN

Area 64	In the County of STAFFORDSHIRE	55	4

Comprises: The Borough of TAMWORTH
The District of CANNOCK CHASE
The District of LICHFIELD

Part District of SOUTH STAFFORDSHIRE

Consisting of the parishes of: Acton Trussell, Bednall and Reddesley Hay, Blymhill, Cheslyn Hay, Dunston with Coppenhall, Essington, Featherstone, Great Wyrley, Hatherton, Hilton, Huntington, Lapley, Penkridge, Saredon, Shareshill, Stretton, Weston-Under-Lizard.

Part District of STAFFORD

Consisting of the parishes of: Adbaston, Barlaston, Berkswich, Bradley, Brocton, Castle Church, Chebsey, Church Eaton, Colwich, Coton, Creswell, Derrington, Eccleshall, Ellenhall, Forton, Fradswell, Fulford, Gayton, Gnosall, Haughton, High Offley, Hilderstone, Hopton, Ingestre, Marston, Milwich, Moreton, Noirbury, Ranton, Salt and Enson, Sandon, Seighford, Stafford, Stone, Stone Rural, Stowe, Tixall, Weston, Whitgreave.

Column (1)	Column (2)	Column (3)	Column (4)
Number of Area	*Description of Area*	*Appropriate Amount (£)*	*Initial Period (number of weeks)*
Area 65	In the County of STAFFORDSHIRE	50	4
	Comprises: The Borough of NEWCASTLE-UNDER-LYME The District of STAFFORDSHIRE MOORLANDS The District of STOKE-ON-TRENT		
	Part District of STAFFORD		
	Consisting of the parishes of: Standon, Swynnerton.		
Area 66	In the County of DERBYSHIRE	50	4
	Comprises: The District of DERBY The District of EREWASH The District of SOUTH DERBYSHIRE		
	Part District of AMBER VALLEY		
	Consisting of the parishes of: Alderwasley, Ashleyhay, Belper, Crich, Denby, Dethick Lea and Holloway, Duffield, Hazelwood, Heanor, Holbrook, Horsley, Horsley Woodhouse, Idridgehay and Alton, Kedleston, Kilburn, Kirk Langley, Mackworth, Mapperley, Pentrich, Quarndon, Ravensdale Park, Ripley, Shipley, Shottle and Postern, Smalley, South Wingfield, Turnditch, Weston Underwood, Windley.		
	Part District of WEST DERBYSHIRE		
	Consisting of the parishes of: Alkmonton, Ashbourne, Atlow, Ballidon, Biggin, Boylestone, Bradbourne, Bradley, Brailsford, Brassington, Callow, Carsington, Clifton and Compton, Cubley, Doveridge, Eaton and Alsop, Edlaston, Fenny Bently, Hartington Nether Quarter, Hartington Town Quarter, Hognaston, Hollington, Hopton, Hulland, Hulland Ward, Hungry Bently, Ible, Kirk Ireton, Kniveton, Lea Hall, Longford, Mapleton, Marston Montgomery, Marcaston, Newton Grange, Norbury and Roston, Offcote and Underwood, Osmaston, Parwich Rodsley, Shirley, Snelston, Somersal Herbert, Sudbury, Thorpe, Tissington, Wyaston, Yeaveley, Yeldersley.		
	In the County of NOTTINGHAMSHIRE		
	Comprises: Part District of BROXTOWE		
	Consisting of the parishes of: Awsworth, Brinsley, Cossall, Eastwood, Greasley, Kimberley, Trowell.		
	In the County of STAFFORDSHIRE		
	Comprises: The District of EAST STAFFORDSHIRE		

Column (1)	Column (2)	Column (3)	Column (4)
Number of Area	*Description of Area*	*Appropriate Amount (£)*	*Initial Period (number of weeks)*

Area 67	In the County of DERBYSHIRE	55	4

Comprises: The Borough of CHESTERFIELD
The District of BOLSOVER
The District of NORTH EAST DERBYSHIRE

Part District of AMBER VALLEY

Consisting of the parishes of: Alfreton, Ironville, Leabrooks, Riddings, Somercoats, Swannick.

Part District of WEST DERBYSHIRE

Consisting of the parishes of: Aldwark, Ashford in the Water, Bakewell, Baslow and Bubnell, Beeley, Birchover, Blackwell, Bonsall, Brushfield, Calver, Chatsworth, Chelmorton, Cromford and Scarthin, Darley Dale, Earl Sterndale, Edensor, Elton, Eyam, Flagg, Foolow, Froggatt, Gratton, Great Hucklow, Great Longstone, Grindlow, Hackney, Harthill, Hartington Middle Quarter, Hassop, Hazelbadge, Hurdlow, Ironbrook Grange, Little Hurdlow, Little Longstone, Litton, Matlock, Middleton by Wirksworth, Middleton and Smerrill, Monyash, Nether Haddon, Over Haddon, Pilsey, Rowland, Rowsley, Sheldon, Stanton, Stoke, Stoney Middleton, Taddington, Tansley, Tideswell, Wardlow, Wensley and Snitterton, Wheston, Winster, Wirksworth, Youlgreave.

In the County of NOTTINGHAMSHIRE

Comprises: The District of BASSETLAW
The District of MANSFIELD

Part District of ASHFIELD

Consisting of the parishes of:
Ashfield, Felly, Selston.

Part District of NEWARK and SHERWOOD

Consisting of the parishes of: Averham, Bathley, Bilsthorpe, Bleasby, Blidworth, Boughton, Bulcote, Carlton-on-Trent, Caunton, Caythorpe, Clipstone, Cromwell, Eakring, Edingley, Edwinstowe, Egmanton, Epperstone, Farnsfield, Fiskerton-cum-Morton, Gonalston, Grassthorpe, Gunthorpe, Hallam, Halloughton, Haywood Oaks, Hockerton, Hoveringham, Kelham, Kersall, Kirton, Kneesall, Laxton, Lindhurst, Lowdham, Maplebeck, North Muskham, Norwell, Ollerton, Ompton, Ossington, Oxton, Perlthorpe cum Budby, Rolleston, Rufford, South Muskham, Southwell, Staythorpe, Sutton-on-Trent, Thurgarton, Upton, Walesby, Wellow, Weston, Winkburn.

Area 68	In the County of NOTTINGHAMSHIRE	55	4

Comprises: The Borough of GEDLING
The Borough of NOTTINGHAM
The Borough of RUSHCLIFFE

Part District of ASHFIELD

Consisting of the parishes of: Annesley, Hucknall.

Column (1)	Column (2)	Column (3)	Column (4)
Number of Area	Description of Area	Appropriate Amount (£)	Initial Period (number of weeks)

	Part District of BROXTOWE		
	Consisting of the parishes of: Nuthall, Strelley.		
Area 69	In the County of LINCOLNSHIRE	55	2
	Comprises: The District of BOSTON The District of SOUTH HOLLAND		
Area 70	In the County of LINCOLNSHIRE	50	2
	Comprises: Part District of EAST LINDSEY		
	Consisting of the parishes of: Addlethorpe, Alford, Anderby, Asgarby, Ashby by Partney, Aswardby, Bilsby, Bratoft, Brinkhill, Burgh-le-Marsh, Calceby, Candlesby, Carrington, Chapel St Leonards, Claxby, Claxby Pluckacre, Coningsby, Croft, Cumberworth, Dalby, Driby, East Keal, East Kirkby, Eastville, Farlesthorpe, Firsby, Friskney, Frithville, Great Steeping, Gunby, Hagnaby, Hagworthingham, Haltham, Halton Holegate, Hammeringham, Hareby, Harrington, Hogsthorpe, Huttoft, Ingoldmells, Irby in the Marsh, Kirkby-on-Bain, Kirkstead, Langriville, Langton by Spilsby, Little Steeping, Lusby, Mareham-le-Fen, Marham-on-the-Hill, Markby, Mavis Enderby, Midville, Miningsby, Moorby, Mumby, New Leake, Old Bolingbroke, Orby, Raithby Hundleby, Revesby, Rigsby with Ailby, Roughton, Sausthorpe, Scremby, Scrivelsby, Sibsey, Skegness, Skendleby South Ormsby cum Ketsby, Spilsby, Stickford, Stickney, Tattershall, Tattershall Thorpe, Thornton-le-Fen, Thorpe St Peter, Toynton All Saints, Toynton St Peter, Tumby, Ulceby with Fordington, Wainfleet All Saints, Wainfleet St Mary, Well, Welton-le-Marsh, West Fen, West Keal, Westville, Wildmore, Willoughby with Sloothby, Winceby, Wood Enderby.		
Area 71	In the County of LINCOLNSHIRE	50	4
	Comprises: The District of NORTH KESTEVEN The District of SOUTH KESTEVEN		
	Part District of EAST LINDSEY		
	Consisting of the parishes of: Asterby, Baumber, Belchford, Benniworth, Bucknall, Cawkwell, East Barkwirth, Edlington, Fulletby, Gautby, Goulceby, Great Sturton, Greetham, Hatton, Hemingby, High Toynton, Horncastle, Horsington, Langton, Langton by Wragby, Low Toynton, Market Stainton, Minting, Panton, Ranby, Salmonby, Scamblesby, Somersby, Sotby, Stixwould, Tetford, Thimbleby, Thornton, Tupholme, Waddingworth, West Ashby, West Barkwirth, West Torrington, Wispington, Woodhall, Woodhall Spa, Wragby.		

Column (1)	Column (2)	Column (3)	Column (4)
Number of Area	*Description of Area*	*Appropriate Amount (£)*	*Initial Period (number of weeks)*

Part District of WEST LINDSEY

Consisting of the parishes of: Aisthorpe, Apley, Barlings, Blyborough, Blyton, Brampton, Brattleby, Broxholme, Bullington, Burton, Caenby, Cammeringham, Cherry Willingham, Cold Hanworth, Corringham, Dunholme, East Ferry, East Stockwith, Faldingworth, Fenton, Fillingham, Fiskerton, Friesthorpe, Fulnetby, Gainsborough, Gate Burton, Glentworth, Goltho, Grange-de-Lings, Grayingham, Greetwell, Hackthorn, Hardwick, Harpswell, Heapham, Hemswell, Holton cum Beckering, Ingham, Kettlethorpe, Kexby, Knaith, Laughton, Lea, Marton, Morton, Nettleham, Newball, Newton-on-Trent, Normanby by Spital, North Carlton, Northorpe, Owmby, Pilham, Rand, Reepham, Riseholme, Saxby, Saxilby with Ingleby, Scampton, Scothern, Scotter, Scotton, Snarford, Snelland, South Carlton, Spridlington, Springthorpe, Stainfield Bardney, Stainton by Langworth, Stow, Sturton by Stow, Sudbrooke, Thorpe in the Fallows, Thonock, Torksey, Upton, Walkerwith, Welton, West Firsby, Wickenby, Wildsworth, Willingham, Willoughton.

The City of LINCOLN

In the County of NOTTINGHAMSHIRE

Comprises: Part District of NEWARK

Consisting of the parishes of: Alverton, Balderton, Barnby-in-the-Willows, Besthorpe, Broadholme, Caddington, Collingham, Cotham, East Stoke, Elston, Farndon, Girton, Harby, Hawton, Holme, Kilvington, Langford, Meering, Newark-on-Trent, North Clifton, South Clifton, South Scarle, Spalford, Staunton, Sverston, Thorney, Thorpe, Wigsley.

PART V

NORTH WESTERN REGION

Column (1)	Column (2)	Column (3)	Column (4)
Number of Area	*Description of Area*	*Appropriate Amount (£)*	*Initial Period (number of weeks)*
Area 72	In the County of CHESHIRE	55	4
	Comprises: The District of CHESTER The District of CONGLETON The District of CREWE and NANTWICH Part District of VALE ROYAL		
	Consisting of the parishes of: Alvanley, Frodsham, Helsby, Manley, Rushton, Tarporley, Utkinton.		

Column (1)	Column (2)	Column (3)	Column (4)
Number of Area	*Description of Area*	*Appropriate Amount (£)*	*Initial Period (number of weeks)*
Area 73	In the County of CHESHIRE	60	4
	Comprises: Part Borough of MACCLESFIELD		
	Consisting of the parishes of: Adlington, Bollington, Bosley, Chelford, Eaton, Gasworth, Henbury, Hurdsfield, Kettleshulme, Lyme Handley, Macclesfield, Macclesfield Forest, Marton, North Rode, Pott Shrigley, Poynton-with-Worth, Prestbury, Rainow, Siddington, Snelson, Sutton, Wildboarclough, Wincle, Withington.		
	In the County of DERBYSHIRE		
	Comprises: Part Borough of HIGH PEAK		
	Consisting of the parishes of: Buxton, Buxworth and Brownside, Chapel-en-le-Frith, Chinley, Green Fairfield, Hartington Upper Quarter, King Sterndale, Peak Forest, Whaley Bridge, Wormhill.		
Area 74	In the County of CHESHIRE	55	8
	Comprises: Part Borough of MACCLESFIELD		
	Consisting of the parish of: Disley.		
	In the County of DERBYSHIRE		
	Comprises: Part Borough of HIGH PEAK		
	Consisting of the parishes of: Charlesworth, Chisworth, Glossop, Hayfield, New Mills, Tintwistle.		
	In the County of LANCASHIRE		
	Comprises: Part Borough of BLACKBURN		
	Consisting of the parish of: Turton North.		
	IN GREATER MANCHESTER		
	Comprises: The Boroughs of: BOLTON SALFORD BURY STOCKPORT MANCHESTER TAMESIDE OLDHAM TRAFFORD ROCHDALE WIGAN		
Area 75	In the County of CHESHIRE	50	4
	Comprises: The Borough of HALTON The Borough of WARRINGTON		
	Part Borough of MACCLESFIELD		
	Consisting of the parishes of: Agden, Alderley Edge, Ashley, Aston by Budworth, Bexton, Bollington, Chorley, Great Warford, High Leigh, Knutsford, Little Warford, Marthall, Mere, Millington, Mobberley, Mottram St Andrew, Nether Alderley, Ollerton, Over Alderley, Peover Inferior, Peover Superior, Pickmere, Plumley, Rostherne, Tabley Inferior, Tabley Superior, Tatton, Toft.		
	Part District of VALE ROYAL		
	Consisting of the parishes of: Acton Bridge, Allostock, Anderton, Antrobus, Aston, Barnton, Bostock, Byley, Comberbach, Crowton, Cuddington, Darnhall, Davenham, Delamere, Dutton, Great Budworth, Hartford, Lach-Dennis, Little		

Column (1)	Column (2)	Column (3)	Column (4)
Number of Area	*Description of Area*	*Appropriate Amount (£)*	*Initial Period (number of weeks)*

Budworth, Little Leigh, Lostock Gralam, Marbury, Marston, Marton, Moulton, Nether Peover, Norley, Northwich, Oakmere, Rudheath, Sandiway, Sproston, Stanthorne, Sutton, Weaverham, Whatcroft, Whitegate, Whitley, Wimboldsley, Wincham, Winsford.

In the County of MERSEYSIDE

Comprises: part Borough of KNOWSLEY

Consisting of the parishes of: Cronton, Tarbock.

Part Borough of ST HELENS

Consisting of that part which lies to the East of Black Brook which includes Haydock and Newton-le-Willows.

Area 76	In the County of CHESHIRE	50	4
	Comprises: The Borough of ELLESMERE PORT AND NESTON		
	In the County of MERSEYSIDE		
	Comprises: The Borough of WIRRAL		

Area 77	In the County of MERSEYSIDE	50	4

Comprises: The District of LIVERPOOL
Part Borough of KNOWSLEY

Consisting of the parishes of: Halewood, Kirkby, Roby and Prescot, Simonswood, Whiston.

Part Borough of ST HELENS

Consisting of the parishes of: Billinge Chapel End, Bold, Eccleston, Rainford, Rainhill, St Helens (that part which lies West of Black Brook), Seneley Green, Windley.

Part District of SEFTON

Consisting of the parishes of: Aintree, Altcar, Ince, Blundell, Lydiate, Maghull, Melling, Netherton and Bootle, Sefton, Thornton, Liverpool postal districts of: 9, 10, 20, 21, 22, 23, 30, 31.

Area 78	In the County of MERSEYSIDE	50	2
	Comprises: Part Borough District of SEFTON		
	Consisting of the parish of: Southport.		

Area 79	In the County of LANCASHIRE	55	2
	Comprises: The Borough of BLACKPOOL The Borough of FYLDE Part Borough of WYRE		

Consisting of the parishes of: Great Eccleston, Hambleton, Knott-End-on-Sea, Inskip-with-Sowerby, Out Rawcliffe, Pilling, Preesall, St Michaels on Wyre, Stalmine-with-Staynall, Upper Rawcliffe-with-Tarnacre and the towns of Fleetwood and Thornton Cleveleys.

Area 80	In the County of LANCASHIRE	55	2
	Comprises: The Borough of LANCASTER Part Borough of WYRE		

Consisting of the parishes of: Cabus, Forton, Nether Wyresdale, Winmarleigh.

Column (1)	Column (2)	Column (3)	Column (4)
Number of Area	Description of Area	Appropriate Amount (£)	Initial Period (number of weeks)
Area 81	In the County of LANCASHIRE	50	4
	Comprises: The Borough of CHORLEY The Borough of PRESTON The Borough of SOUTH RIBBLE The District of WEST LANCASHIRE		
	Part Borough of BLACKBURN		
	Consisting of the parishes of: Blackburn and Darwen, Eccleshill, Livesey, Pick Up Bank, Pleasington, Tockholes, Yate.		
	Part Borough of RIBBLE VALLEY		
	Consisting of the parishes of: Aighton Bailey and Chaigley, Balderstone, Billington, Bowland-with-Leagram, Chipping, Clayton-le-Dale, Dinckley, Dutton, Hothersall, Longridge, Mellor, Osbaldeston, Ramsgreave, Ribchester, Salesbury, Thornley-with-Wheatley, Wilpshire.		
	Part Borough of WYRE		
	Consisting of the parishes of: Barnacre-with-Bonds, Bilsborrow, Bleasdale, Catterall, Claughton, Garstang, Kirkland, Myerscough, Nateby.		
Area 82	In the County of LANCASHIRE	55	4
	Comprises: The Borough of BURNLEY The Borough of ROSSENDALE The District of HYNDBURN The District of PENDLE Part Borough of RIBBLE VALLEY		
	Consisting of the parishes of: Bashall Eaves, Bolton by Bowland, Bowland Forest High, Bowland Forest Low, Chatburn, Clitheroe, Downham, Easington, Great Mitton, Gisburn Forest, Grindleton, Horton Gisburn, Little Mitton, Mearley, Middop, Newsholme, Newton, Paythorne, Pendleton, Read, Rimmington, Sabden, Sawley, Slaidburn, Twiston, Waddington, West Bradford, Whalley, Wiswell, Worston.		
Area 83	In the County of CUMBRIA	55	2
	Comprises: Part District of SOUTH LAKELAND		
	Consisting of the parishes of: Arnside, Barbon, Beetham, Burton, Casterton, Crook, Crosthwaite and Lyth, Dalton, Dent, Dillicar, Docker, Fawcett Forest, Firbank, Garsdale, Gayrigg, Helsington, Heversham, Hincaster, Holme, Hugill, Hutton Roof, Kendal, Kentmere, Killington, Kirby Lonsdale, Lakes, Lambrigg, Levens, Longsledale, Lupton, Mansergh, Meathop and Ulpha, Middleton, Milnthorpe, Natland, Nether Staveley, New Hutton, Old Hutton and Holescales, Over Staveley, Patton, Preston Patrick, Preston Richard, Scaithwaiterigg, Sedbergh, Sedgwick, Skelsmergh, Stainton, Strickland Ketel, Strickland Roger, Underbarrow and Bradleyfield, Whinfell, Whitwell and Selside, Windermere, Witherslack.		

Column (1)	Column (2)	Column (3)	Column (4)
Number of Area	*Description of Area*	*Appropriate Amount (£)*	*Initial Period (number of weeks)*
Area 84	In the County of CUMBRIA	55	2
	Comprises: The District of EDEN		
Area 85	In the County of CUMBRIA	55	4
	Comprises: The Borough of CARLISLE Part District of ALLERDALE		
	Consisting of the parishes of: Aikton, Allhallows, Allonby, Aspatria, Blennerhasset and Torpenhow, Boltons, Bowness, Bromfield, Caldbeck, Dundraw, Hayton and Mealo, Holme Abbey, Holme East Waver, Holme Lowe, Holme St Cuthbert, Ireby, Kirkbampton, Kirkbridge, Sebergham, Silloth, Thursby, Waverton, Westnewton, Westward, Wigton, Woodside.		
Area 86	In the County of CUMBRIA	55	2
	Comprises: Part District of ALLERDALE		
	Consisting of the parishes of: Above Derwent, Bassenthwaite, Bewaldeth and Snittlegarth, Blindbothel, Blindcrake, Borrowdale, Bothel and Threapland, Bridekirk, Brigham, Broughton, Broughton Moor, Buttermere, Camerton, Cockermouth, Crosscanonby, Dean, Dearham, Embleton, Flimby, Gilcrux, Great Clifton, Greysouthen, Harrington, Keswick, Little Clifton, Lorton, Loweswater, Maryport, Oughterside and Allerby, Papcastle, Plumbland, St Johns Castlerigg and Wythburn, Seaton, Setmurthy, Underskiddaw, Winscales, Workington, Wythop.		
Area 87	In the County of CUMBRIA	55	2
	Comprises: Part District of COPELAND		
	Consisting of the parishes of: Arlecdon and Frizington, Bootle, Cleator Moor, Distington, Drigg and Carleton, Egremont, Ennerdale and Kinniside, Eskdale, Gosforth, Irton with Santon, Lamplugh, Lowca, Lowside Quarter, Moresby, Muncaster, Nether Wasdale, Parton, Ponsonby, St Bees, St John Beckermet, Seascale, Waberthwaite, Weddicar, Whitehaven.		
Area 88	In the County of CUMBRIA	55	2
	Comprises: The District of BARROW-IN-FURNESS Part District of COPELAND		
	Consisting of the parishes of: Millom, Millom Without, Ulpha, Wincham.		
	Part District of SOUTH LAKELAND		
	Consisting of the parishes of: Aldingham, Angerton, Blawith, Broughton East, Broughton West, Cartmel Fell, Claife, Colton, Coniston, Dunnerdale with Seathwaite, Egton with Newland, Grange-over-Sands, Haverthwaite, Hawkshead, Kirkby Ireleth, Lower Allithwaite, Lower Holker, Lowick, Mansriggs, Osmotherley, Pennington, Satterthwaite, Skelwith, Staveley, Subberthwaite, Torver, Ulverston, Upper Allithwaite, Urswick.		

PART VI

NORTH EASTERN REGION

Column (1)	Column (2)	Column (3)	Column (4)
Number of Area	*Description of Area*	*Appropriate Amount (£)*	*Initial Period (number of weeks)*

Area 89 — In the County of HUMBERSIDE — 60 — 2

Comprises: The Borough of GRIMSBY
The District of CLEETHORPES

In the County of LINCOLNSHIRE

Comprises: Part District of EAST LINDSEY

Consisting of the parishes of: Aby with Greenfield, Alvingham, Authorpe, Beesby in the Marsh, Belleau, Binbrook, Brackenborough, Burgh on Bain, Burwell, Calcethorpe, Claythorpe, Conisholme, Covenham St Bartholomew, Covenham St Mary, Donington on Bain, East Wykeham, Fotherby, Fulstow, Gayton le Marsh, Gayton le Wold, Grainsby, Grainthorpe, Great Carlton, Grimoldby, Hainton, Hallington, Hannah cum Hagnaby, Haugh, Haugham, Holton le Clay, Keddington, Kelstern, Legbourne, Little Carlton, Little Cawthorpe, Little Grimsby, Louth, Ludborough, Ludford, Mablethorpe and Sutton, Maidenwell, Maltby le Marsh, Manby, Marsh Chapel, Muckton, North Coates, North Cockerington, North Elkington, North Ormsby, North Reston, North Somercotes, North Thoresby, Raithby cum Maltby, Saleby with Thoresthorpe, Saltfleetby All Saints, Saltfleetby St Clement, Saltfleetby St Peter, Skidbrooke with Saltfleet Haven, South Cockerington, South Elkington, South Reston, South Somercotes, South Thoresby, South Willingham, Stenigot, Stewton, Strubby with Woodthorpe, Swaby, Tathwell, Tetney, Theddlethorpe All Saints, Theddlethorpe St Helen, Tothill, Utterby, Waithe, Walmsgate, Welton-le-Wold, Withcall, Withern with Stain, Wyham cum Cadeby, Yarburgh.

Part District of WEST LINDSEY

Consisting of the parishes of: Bigby, Bishop Norton, Brocklesby, Buslingthorpe, Cabourne, Caistor, Claxby, Glentham, Grasby, Great Limber, Holton le Moor, Keelby, Kirmond le Mire, Legsby, Linwood, Lissington, Market Rasen, Middle Rasen, Nettleton, Normanby le Wold, North Kelsey, North Willingham, Osgodby, Owersby, Riby, Rothwell, Searby cum Owmby, Sixhills, Snitterby, Somerby, South Kelsey, Stainton le Vale, Swallow, Swinhope, Tealby, Thoresway, Thornganby, Toft Newton, Waddingham, Walesby, West Rasen.

Area 90 — In the County of HUMBERSIDE — 55 — 4

Comprises: The Borough of BEVERLEY
The District of HOLDERNESS
The District of KINGSTON
UPON HULL

Column (1)	Column (2)	Column (3)	Column (4)
Number of Area	*Description of Area*	*Appropriate Amount (£)*	*Initial Period (number of weeks)*
Area 91	In the County of HUMBERSIDE Comprises: The Borough of GLANFORD The District of SCUNTHORPE	55	4
Area 92	In the County of HUMBERSIDE Comprises: The Borough of EAST YORKSHIRE In the County of NORTH YORKSHIRE Comprises: The Borough of SCARBOROUGH Part District of RYEDALE Consisting of the parishes of: Aislaby, Allerston, Ampleforth, Appleton le Moors, Arden with Ardenside, Barugh (Great and Little), Beadlam, Bilsdale West Side, Bransdale, Byland with Wass, Cawthorne, Cawton, Cold Kirby, Coulton, Cropton, Dale Town, Ebberston, East Newton and Laysthorpe, Fadmoor, Farndale East, Farndale West, Foxholes, Ganton, Gillamoor, Gilling East, Great Edstone, Grimstone, Harome, Hartoft, Hawnby, Helmsley, Hutton le Hole, Kingthorpe, Kirby Misperton, Kirkbymoorside, Laskill Pasture, Lastingham, Levisham, Little Edstone, Lockton, Luttons, Marishes, Marton, Middleton, Murton, Muscoates, Nawton, Newton, Normanby, North Holme, Nunnington, Old Byland, Oldstead, Oswaldkirk, Pickering, Pockley, Rievaulx, Rosedale East Side, Rosedale West Side, Salton, Scawton, Sherburn, Sinnington, Skiplam, Snilesworth, Spaunton, Sproxton, Stonegrave, Thornton Dale, Thornton Riseborough, Thorpe le Willows, Weaverthorpe, Welburn, Willerby, Wilton, Wombleton, Wrelton.	50	2
Area 93	In the County of WEST YORKSHIRE Comprises: Part Borough of LEEDS Consisting of the parishes of: Garforth, Great and Little Preston, Ledsham, Ledston, Methley, Micklefield, Mickletown, Oulton, Stourton Grange, Swillington. Part District of WAKEFIELD Consisting of the parishes of: Castleford, Darrington, East Hardwick, Featherstone, Normanton, Pontefract. In the County of NORTH YORKSHIRE Comprises: Part District of SELBY Consisting of the parishes of: Balne, Beal, Birkin, Brotherton, Burton Salmon, Byram cum Sutton, Cridling Stubbs, Eggborough, Fairburn, Heck, Hensall, Hillam, Huddleston with Newthorpe, Kellington, Kirk Smeaton, Little Smeaton, Monk Fryston, Sherburn in Elmet, South Milford, Stapleton, Walden Stubbs, Whitley, Womersley.	55	4

Column (1)	Column (2)	Column (3)	Column (4)
Number of Area	Description of Area	Appropriate Amount (£)	Initial Period (number of weeks)
Area 94	In the County of NORTH YORKSHIRE	55	4
	Comprises: The Borough of HARROGATE The Borough of YORK		
	Part District of RYDALE		
	Consisting of the parishes of: Acklam, Airyholme with Howthorpe and Baxter Howe, Amotherby, Appleton le Street with Easthorpe, Barton le Street, Barton le Willows, Bickerton, Bilton in Ainsty, Birdshall, Brawby, Broughton, Bulmer, Burythorpe, Buttercrambe with Bossall, Butterwick with Newsham, Claxton, Clifton Without, Coneysthorpe, Cowthorpe, Crambe, Duggleby, Earswick, Firby, Flaxton, Fryton, Ganthorpe, Gate Helmsley, Great Habton, Harton, Haxby, Heslerton, Hessay, Hildenley, Holtby, Hovingham, Howsham, Huntington, Hutton Wandesley, Huttons Ambo, Kennisthorpe, Kirby Grindalythe, Knapton, Langton, Leavening, Leppington, Lillings Ambo, Little Habton, Long Marston, Malton, Moor Monkton, Murton, Nether Poppleton, New Earswick, Newton, Newton on Derwent, North Grimston, Norton on Derwent, Nun Monkton, Osbaldwick, Rawcliffe, Rillington, Rufforth, Ryton, Sand Hutton, Scackleton, Scagglethorpe, Scampston, Scrayingham, Settrington, Skelton, Slingsby, South Holme, Stittenham, Stockton on the Forest, Strensall, Swinton, Terrington with Wiganthorpe, Thixendale, Thornton le Clay, Thorpe Bassett, Tockwith with Wilstrop, Towthorpe, Upper Helmsley, Upper Poppleton, Warthill, Wath, Welburn, Westow, Wharram le Street, Whitwell on the Hill, Widdington, Wiggington, Wighill, Wintringham, Yeddingham.		
	Part District of SELBY		
	Consisting of the parishes of: Acaster Malbis, Acaster Selby, Angram, Appleton Roebuck, Askham Bryan, Askham Richard, Barkston Ash, Barlby, Barlow, Biggin, Bilbrough, Bishopthorpe, Bolton Percy, Brayton, Burn, Camblesforth, Carlton, Catterton, Cawood, Chapel Haddlesey, Church Fenton, Cliffe, Colton, Copmanthorpe, Deighton, Drax, Dunnington, Elvington, Escrick, Fulford, Gateforth, Grimston, Hambleton, Healaugh, Hemingbrough, Heslington, Hirst Courtney, Kelfield, Kexby, Kirby Wharfe with North Milford, Lead, Little Fenton, Long Drax, Naburn, Newlands, Newton Kyme cum Toulston, North Duffield, Osgodby, Oxton, Riccall, Ryther cum Ossendyke, Saxton with Scarthingwell, Selby, Skipwith, South Duffield, Steeton, Stillingfleet, Stutton with Hazelwood, Tadcaster East, Tadcaster West, Temple Hirst, Thorganby, Thorpe Willoughby, Towton, Ulleskelf, West Haddlesey, Wheldrake, Wistow.		
Area 95	In the County of WEST YORKSHIRE	55	4
	Comprises: Part Borough of LEEDS		
	Consisting of: Central Leeds postal districts 1 to 20 and 28, the parishes of Aberford, Armley, Arthington, Barwick in Elmet and Scholes, Bramhope, Bramley,		

Column (1)	Column (2)	Column (3)	Column (4)
Number of Area	*Description of Area*	*Appropriate Amount (£)*	*Initial Period (number of weeks)*
	Calverly, Carlton, Drighlington, East Ardsley, Farnley, Farsley, Gildersome, Guiseley, Harewood, Hawksworth Village, Horsforth, Lotherton cum Aberford, Morley, Otley, Parlington, Pool, Pudsey, Rawdon, Rodley, Scarcroft, Stanningley, Thorner, Tysersal, West Ardsley, Wortley, Yeadon; including areas West of the A642 from a point at the Borough Boundary Northwards to the junction with the A63.		
Area 96	In the County of WEST YORKSHIRE	55	4
	Comprises: Part Borough of KIRKLEES		
	Consisting of the area bounded: from the junction with the Southern boundary of Bradford City Boundary follow the North Western and North Eastern boundaries of Spenborough Metropolitan Borough, the North Eastern boundary of Batley Metropolitan Borough and then the Eastern Boundary of Ossett Metropolitan Borough to the junction with the Northern boundary of Horbury Urban District; proceed generally Westward on the Southern boundaries of Ossett Metropolitan Borough and Dewsbury County Borough to the junction with Mirfield Urban District at Falhouse Green (inclusive); from Falhouse Green follow the Western boundaries of Mirfield Urban District and Spenborough Metropolitan Borough to the junction with the Southern boundary of Bradford City Boundary.		
	Part District of WAKEFIELD		
	Consisting of the parishes of: Ackworth, Badsworth, Crigglestone, Crofton, Havercroft with Cold Hiendley, Hemsworth, Hessle and Hill Top, Huntwick with Foulby and Nostell, Newland with Woodhouse Moor, North Elmsall, Notton, Ossett, Ryhill, Sharlston, Sitlington, South Elmshall, South Hiendly, South Kirkby, Stanley, Thorpe Audlin, Upton, Wakefield, Warmfield Cum Heath, West Bretton, West Hardwick, Woolley.		
Area 97	In the County of WEST YORKSHIRE	55	4
	Comprises: The Borough of CALDERDALE Part Borough of KIRKLEES		
	Consisting of the parishes of: Denby Dale, Holmfirth, Huddersfield, Kirkburton, Meltham including the area covered by the former Colne Valley Urban District Council.		
Area 98	In the County of NORTH YORKSHIRE	60	4
	Comprises: The District of CRAVEN		
	In the County of WEST YORKSHIRE		
	Comprises: The Borough of BRADFORD		
Area 99	In the County of NORTH YORKSHIRE	45	4
	Comprises: The District of HAMBLETON The District of RICHMONDSHIRE		

Column (1)	Column (2)	Column (3)	Column (4)
Number of Area	Description of Area	Appropriate Amount (£)	Initial Period (number of weeks)
Area 100	In the County of CLEVELAND	55	4
	Comprises: The Borough of HARTLEPOOL The District of MIDDLESBROUGH The District of STOCKTON ON TEES		
Area 101	In the County of CLEVELAND	55	2
	Comprises: The Borough of LANGBAURGH		
Area 102	In the County of DURHAM	55	4
	Comprises: The District of EASINGTON Part District of SEDGEFIELD		
	Consisting of the parishes of: Butterwick and Oldacres, Embleton, Trimdon.		
	In the County of TYNE AND WEAR		
	Comprises: The Borough of SUNDERLAND The Borough of SOUTH TYNESIDE		
Area 103	In the County of TYNE AND WEAR	55	2
	Comprises: Part Borough of NORTH TYNESIDE		
	Consisting of the area bounded by: from the coast running Westwards along the River Tyne to the Tyne Tunnel then running Northwards along the centre of Spine Road to the District Boundary line, then along the District Boundary line to the coast.		
Area 104	In the County of NORTHUMBERLAND	60	4
	Comprises: Part District of CASTLE MORPETH		
	Consisting of the parishes of: Heddon on the Wall, Matfen, Stamfordham. The District of CASTLEWARD		
	In the County of TYNE AND WEAR		
	Comprises: Part Borough of GATESHEAD		
	Consisting of: the District of Gateshead		
	Comprises: The Borough of NEWCASTLE UPON TYNE Part Borough of NORTH TYNESIDE		
	Consisting of the area bounded to the East by: from the River Tyne at the Tyne Tunnel running Northerly along the centre of Spine Road to the District boundary line.		

Column (1)	Column (2)	Column (3)	Column (4)
Number of Area	*Description of Area*	*Appropriate Amount (£)*	*Initial Period (number of weeks)*
Area 105	In the County of DURHAM	60	4
	Comprises: The Borough of DURHAM		
	The District of CHESTER-LE-STREET		
	In the County of TYNE AND WEAR		
	Comprises: Part Borough of GATESHEAD		
	Consisting of the parishes of: Birtley, Lamesley.		
Area 106	In the County of NORTHUMBERLAND	55	4
	Comprises: The Borough of BLYTH VALLEY		
	The District of ALNWICK		
	Part District of CASTLE MORPETH		
	Consisting of the parishes of: Cresswell, East Chevington, Ellington, Hartburn, Hebron, Hepscott, Longhirst, Longhorsley, Lynemouth, Meldon, Mitford, Morpeth, Netherwitton, Pegswood, Thirston, Trittlington, Ulgham, Wallington Demesne, West Chevington, Widdrington.		
	The District of WANSBECK		
Area 107	In the County of NORTHUMBERLAND	55	2
	Comprises: The District of BERWICK UPON TWEED		
Area 108	In the County of DURHAM	55	4
	Comprises: The Borough of DARLINGTON		
	Part District of SEDGEFIELD		
	Consisting of the parishes of: Bishop Middleham, Bradbury and the Isle, Chilton, Cornforth, Elstob, Ferryhill, Fishburn, Foxton and Shotton, Great Aycliffe, Mainsforth, Morden, Preston le Skerne, Sedgefield, Shildon, Spennymoor, Stillington, Windlestone, Woodham.		
	The District of TEESDALE		
	The District of WEAR VALLEY		
Area 109	In the County of DURHAM	55	4
	Comprises: The District of DERWENTSIDE		
	In the County of NORTHUMBERLAND		
	Comprises: The District of TYNEDALE		
	In the County of TYNE AND WEAR		
	Part Borough GATESHEAD		
	Consisting of the parishes of: Blackhall Mill, Chopwell, Highfield, High Spen, Rowlands Gill.		
Area 110	In the County of HUMBERSIDE	55	4
	Comprises: The District of BOOTHFERRY		
	In the County of SOUTH YORKSHIRE		
	Comprises: The CENTRAL DONCASTER Districts of:		
	Balby, Belle Vue, Bessacar, Hexthorpe, Hyde Park, St Georges, St Johns, Townfields, Westfield, Wheatley, Woodfield.		

Column (1)	Column (2)	Column (3)	Column (4)
Number of Area	*Description of Area*	*Appropriate Amount (£)*	*Initial Period (number of weeks)*
	The parishes of: Adwick le Street, Armthorpe, Auckley, Austerfield, Barnburgh, Barnby Dun with Kirk Sandall, Bawtry, Bentley with Arksey, Blaxton, Braithwell, Brodsworth, Cadeby, Cantley, Clayton with Frickley, Conisbrough Parks, Edenthorpe, Edlington, Finningley, Fishlake, Hatfield, Hickleton, High Melton, Hooton Pagnell, Kirk Bramwith, Loversall, Marr, Rossington, Sprotborough, Stainforth, Stainton, Sykehouse, Thorne, Thorpe in Balne, Tickhill, Wadworth, Warmsworth.		
Area 111	In the County of SOUTH YORKSHIRE Comprises: The District of BARNSLEY The District of ROTHERHAM Part District of DONCASTER Consisting of the parishes of: Adwick-on-Dearne, Conisbrough, Denaby, Mexborough.	55	4
Area 112	In the County of DERBYSHIRE Comprises: Part Borough of HIGH PEAK Consisting of the parishes of: Ashapton, Aston, Bamford, Brough and Shatton, Castleton, Derwent, Edale, Hope, Hope Woodlands, Mytham Bridge, Shatton, Thornhill. Part District of WEST DERBYSHIRE Consisting of the parishes of: Abney and Abney Grange, Bradwell, Eyam Woodlands, Grindleford, Hathersage, Highlow, Nether Padley, Offerton, Outseats, Padley. In the County of SOUTH YORKSHIRE Comprises: The District of SHEFFIELD	55	4

PART VII

SCOTLAND

Column (1)	Column (2)	Column (3)	Column (4)
Number of Area	*Description of Area*	*Appropriate Amount (£)*	*Initial Period (number of weeks)*
Area 113	In the GRAMPIAN REGION Comprises: Part District of BANFF and BUCHAN Consisting of the parishes of: Aberdour, Auchterless, Crimond, Cruden, Fraserburgh, Fyvie, Inverkeithny, King Edward, Longside, Lonmay, Monquhitter, New Deer, Old Deer, Peterhead, Pitsligo, Rathen, St Fergus, Strichen, Turriff, Tyrie.	60	4

Column (1)	Column (2)	Column (3)	Column (4)
Number of Area	*Description of Area*	*Appropriate Amount (£)*	*Initial Period (number of weeks)*
Area 114	In the GRAMPIAN REGION	55	4
	Comprises: The District of MORAY		
	Part District of BANFF and BUCHAN		
	Consisting of the parishes of: Alvah, Banff, Boyndie, Fordyce, Forglen, Marnoch, Ordhiquhill.		
	In the HIGHLAND REGION		
	Comprises: The District of BADENOCH and STRATHSPEY The District of INVERNESS The District of LOCHALSH The District of NAIRN The District of ROSS and CROMARTY		
	Part District of SUTHERLAND		
	Consisting of the parish of: Kincardine.		
Area 115	In the HIGHLAND REGION	55	4
	Comprises: The District of CAITHNESS		
	Part District of SUTHERLAND		
	Consisting of the parishes of: Assynt, Clyne, Creich, Dornoch, Durness, Eddrachilles, Farr, Golspie, Kildonnan, Lairg, Loth, Rogart, Tongue.		
	In the ISLANDS Area		
	Comprises: The ORKNEY ISLANDS Area		
Area 116	In the ISLANDS Area	55	4
	Comprises: The WESTERN ISLES ISLANDS Area		
Area 117	In the ISLANDS Area	60	4
	Comprises: The SHETLAND ISLANDS Area		
Area 118	In the HIGHLAND REGION	60	4
	Comprises: The District of LOCHABER The District of SKYE		
Area 119	In the STRATHCLYDE REGION	60	4
	Comprises: Part District of ARGYLL and BUTE		
	Consisting of the parishes of: Ardchattan and Muckairn, Coll, Colonsay and Oronsay, Craignish, Glenorchy and Inishail, Inverary, Kilbrandon and Kilchattan, Kilchrenan and Dalavich, Kilfinichen and Kilvickeon, Kilmartin, Kilmichael Glassary, Kilmore and Kilbride, Kilninian and Kilmore, Kilniver and Kilmelford, Lismore and Appin, North Knapdale, South Knapdale, Tiree, Torosay.		
Area 120	In the TAYSIDE REGION	65	4
	Comprises: The District of ANGUS		

III/1hh*

Column (1)	Column (2)	Column (3)	Column (4)
Number of Area	Description of Area	Appropriate Amount (£)	Initial Period (number of weeks)
Area 121	In the DUMFRIES AND GALLOWAY REGION	60	4
	Comprises: The District of WIGTOWN		
Area 122	In the DUMFRIES AND GALLOWAY REGION	60	4
	Comprises: The District of ANNANDALE and ESKDALE The District of NITHSDALE The District of STEWARTRY		
	In the STRATHCLYDE REGION		
	Comprises: Part District of LANARK		
	Consisting of the village of: Leadhills contained within the area defined by a line leaving the Regional Boundary at Wanlock Dod, proceeding North to Water Head, South East to Glen Ea's Hill and South West to Stake Hill to rejoin the Regional Boundary.		
Area 123	In the BORDERS REGION	55	4
	Comprises: The District of BERWICKSHIRE The District of ETTRICK and LAUDERDALE The District of ROXBURGH The District of TWEEDDALE		
Area 124	In the STRATHCLYDE REGION	60	4
	Comprises: Part District of ARGYLL and BUTE		
	Consisting of the parishes of: Campbeltown, Gigha and Cara, Jura, Kilarow and Kilmany, Kilcalmonell, Kilchoman, Kildaton and Oa, Killearn and Kilchenzie, Saddell and Skipness, Southend.		
Area 125	In the CENTRAL REGION	60	4
	Comprises: The District of FALKIRK		
	In the LOTHIAN REGION		
	Comprises: The District of CITY OF EDINBURGH The District of EAST LOTHIAN The District of MID LOTHIAN The District of WEST LOTHIAN		
	In the STRATHCLYDE REGION		
	Comprises: Part District of MOTHERWELL		
	Consisting of the area bounded from a point on the West Lothian District Boundary where the River Almond meets the boundary just South of Harthill, West by this river to the junction with the Motherwell District Boundary at Easter Baton (inclusive) and then by this District Boundary Northwards to its junction with the West Lothian District Boundary just West of Bogend Farm (inclusive).		

Column (1)	Column (2)	Column (3)	Column (4)
Number of Area	*Description of Area*	*Appropriate Amount (£)*	*Initial Period (number of weeks)*
Area 126	In the CENTRAL REGION	60	4
	Comprises: The District of CLACKMANNAN The District of STIRLING		
Area 127	In the FIFE REGION	60	4
	Comprises: The District of DUNFERMLINE The District of KIRKCALDY		
	Part District of NORTH EAST FIFE		
	Consisting of the parishes of: Abdie, Aberdour, Anstruther Easter, Anstruther Wester, Auchterderran, Auchtermuchtis, Auchtertool, Ballingry, Bowhill, Cardenden, Carnbee, Ceres, Collessie, Cowdenbeath, Crail, Crossgates, Crosshill, Cults, Cupar, Dunbog, Elie, Falkland, Flisk, Glencraig, Hill of Beath, Kelby, Kemback, Kennoway, Kettle, Kilconquhar, Kilrenny, Largo, Lochgelly, Lochore, Monimal, Newburgh, Newburn, Pittenweem, Scoonie, St Monance, Strathmiglo.		
	In the TAYSIDE REGION		
	Comprises: The District of PERTH and KINROSS		
Area 128	In the STRATHCLYDE REGION	60	8
	Comprises: Part District of ARGYLL and BUTE		
	Consisting of the parishes of: Dunoon and Kilmun, Inverchaolin, Kilfinan, Kilmodan, Kingarth, Lochgoilhead, North Bute, Rothesay, Strachur, Strathlachan.		
	The District of BEARSDEN AND MILNGAVIE The District of CITY OF GLASGOW The District of CLYDEBANK The District of CUMBERNAULD		
	Part District of CUNNINGHAME		
	Consisting of the parishes of: Beith, Cumbrae, Dalry, Kilbirnie, Largs.		
	The District of DUMBARTON The District of EAST KILBRIDE The District of EASTWOOD The District of HAMILTON The District of INVERCLYDE The District of LANARK		
	except that part consisting of the village of Leadhills contained within the area defined by a line leaving the Regional Boundary at Wanlock Dod proceeding North to Waterhead, South East to Glen Ea's Hill and South West to Stake Hill to rejoin the Regional Boundary.		
	The District of MONKLANDS The District of MOTHERWELL		
	except that part consisting of the area bounded from a point on the West Lothian District Boundary		

Column (1)	Column (2)	Column (3)	Column (4)
Number of Area	*Description of Area*	*Appropriate Amount (£)*	*Initial Period (number of weeks)*
	where the River Almond meets the boundary just South of Harthill, West by this river to the junction with the Motherwell District Boundary at Easter Baton (inclusive) and then by this District Boundary Northwards to its junction with the West Lothian District Boundary just West of Bogend Farm (inclusive).		
	The District of RENFREW The District of STRATH KELVIN		
Area 129	In the STRATHCLYDE REGION	60	4
	Comprises: The District of CUMNOCK AND DOON VALLEY		
	Part District of CUNNINGHAME		
	Consisting of the parishes of: Ardrossan, Dreghorn, Hunterston, Island of Arran, Irvine, Kilwinning, Saltcoats, Seamill, Springside, Stevenston, West Kilbride.		
	The District of KILMARNOCK AND LOUDON The District of KYLE AND CARRICK		
Area 130	In the GRAMPIAN REGION	65	4
	Comprises: The District of CITY OF ABERDEEN The District of GORDON The District of KINCARDINE AND DEESIDE		
Area 131	In the TAYSIDE and FIFE REGION	65	4
	Comprises: The District of CITY OF DUNDEE		
	Part District of NORTH EAST FIFE		
	Consisting of the parishes of: Balmerino, Cameron, Creich, Dairsie, Dunino, Ferry Port on Craig, Forgan, Kilmany, Kingsbarns, Leuchars, Logie, Moonzie, St Andrew's and St Leonard's.		

Regulation 21

SCHEDULE 7

APPLICABLE AMOUNTS IN SPECIAL CASES

Column (1)	Column (2)

Patients

1. Subject to paragraphs 2, 3 and 18, a person who has been a patient for a period of more than six weeks and who is—

    (a) a single claimant;

    (b) a lone parent;

1. (a) £8·25 plus any amount applicable under regulation 17(e);

    (b) £8·25 plus any amounts applicable to him under regulation 17(b), (c) or (e) or under regulation 17(d) because of paragraph 8 or 14 of Schedule 2 (applicable amounts);

Column (1)	Column (2)

(c) a member of a couple—
  (i) where only one of the couple is a patient or, where both members of the couple are patients but only one has been a patient for that period;

  (ii) where both members of the couple have been a patient for that period;

(d) a member of a polygamous marriage—
  (i) where at least one member of the polygamous marriage is not a patient or has not been a patient for more than that period;

  (ii) where all the members of the polygamous marriage have been patients for more than that period.

(c) (i) the amount applicable in respect of both of them under regulation 17 reduced by £8·25;

  (ii) £16·50 plus any amounts which may be applicable under regulation 17(b), (c) or (e) or under regulation 17(d) because of paragraph 14 of Schedule 2;

(d) (i) the applicable amount under regulation 18 (polygamous marriages) shall be reduced by £8·25 in respect of each such member who is a patient;

  (ii) the applicable amount shall be £8·25 in respect of each member plus any amounts applicable under regulation 18(c) or (d) or (f) or (e) because of his satisfying the condition specified in paragraph 3 or 14 of Schedule 2.

2. A single claimant who has been a patient for a continuous period of more than 52 weeks, where—
  (a) the following conditions are satisfied—
    (i) a person has been appointed to act for him under regulation 33 of the Social Security (Claims and Payments) Regulations 1987**(a)** (persons unable to act); and
    (ii) his income support is payable to an administrative officer of the hospital or other institution either as or at the request of the person so appointed; and
    (iii) a registered medical practitioner treating him certifies that all or part of his income support cannot be used by him or on his behalf; or
  (b) those conditions are not satisfied.

2. (a) Such amount (if any) not exceeding £8·25 as is reasonable having regard to the views of the hospital staff and the patient's relatives if available as to the amount necessary for his personal use;

(b) £8·25.

3. Subject to paragraph 18—
  (a) a claimant who is not a patient and who is a member of a family of which another member is a child or young person who has been a patient for a period of more than 12 weeks; or

  (b) where the person is a member of a family and paragraph 1 applies to him and another member of the family who is a child or young person has been a patient for a period of more than 12 weeks.

3. (a) The amount applicable to him under regulation 17 or 18 except that the amount applicable under regulation 17(b) or 18(c) in respect of the child or young person referred to in Column (1) of this paragraph shall be £8·25 instead of an amount determined in accordance with paragraph 2 of Schedule 2; or

(b) the amount applicable to him under paragraph 1 except that the amount applicable under regulation 17(b) or 18(c) in respect of the child or young person referred to in Column (1) of this paragraph shall be £8·25 instead of an amount determined in accordance with paragraph 2 of Schedule 2.

(a) S.I. 1987/1968.

Column (1)	Column (2)
4. Subject to paragraph 18 a claimant who is a member of a family, where one or more members of that family is a patient and one or more members of that family temporarily enter into board and lodging accommodation within the meaning of regulation 20(2) (persons in board and lodging accommodation) in order to be near to the member who is a patient.	**4.** The amount applicable to the family in accordance with regulation 17 or 21 as the case may be plus, except in a case to which any of paragraphs 12 to 15 of Schedule 5 applies, the weekly charge for the board and lodging accommodation calculated in accordance with paragraph 1(1)(a) of that Schedule except that no increase shall be included in respect of meals under paragraph 2 of that Schedule.
5. A claimant who is a member of a polygamous marriage, where one or more members of that marriage or any child or young person for whom any member of that marriage is treated as responsible for by virtue of regulation 15 (circumstances in which a person is to be treated as responsible or not responsible for another) temporarily enter into board and lodging accommodation in order to be near to the partner, child or young person who is a patient.	**5.** The amount applicable to the family in accordance with regulation 18 or 21 as the case may be plus, except in a case to which any of paragraphs 12 to 15 of Schedule 5 applies, the weekly charge for the board and lodging accommodation calculated in accordance with paragraph 1(1)(a) of that Schedule except that no increase shall be included in respect of meals under paragraph 2 of that Schedule.

Claimants without accommodation

6. A claimant who is without accommodation.	**6.** The amount applicable to him under regulation 17(a) only.

Members of religious orders

7. A claimant who is a member of and fully maintained by a religious order.	**7.** Nil.

Prisoners

8. A person—	**8.** (a) Nil;
(a) except where sub-paragraph (b) applies, who is a prisoner;	
(b) who is detained in custody pending trial or sentence following conviction by a court.	(b) only such amount, if any, as may be applicable under regulation 17(e).

Specified cases of temporarily separated couples

9. A claimant who is a member of a couple and who is temporarily separated from his partner where one of them is living in the home while the other member is—	**9.** Either—
(a) not a patient but is resident in a nursing home; or	(a) the amount applicable to him as a member of a couple under regulation 17; or
(b) resident in a residential care home; or	(b) the aggregate of his applicable amount and that of his partner assessed under the provisions of these Regulations as if each of them were a single claimant, or a lone parent,
(c) in accommodation referred to in sub-paragraphs (a) to (d) of the definition of residential accommodation in regulation 21(3) (special cases); or	whichever is the greater.
(d) resident in premises used for the rehabilitation of alcoholics or drug addicts; or	
(e) attending a course of training or instruction provided or approved by the Manpower Services Commission where the course requires him to live away from home; or	
(f) in a probation or bail hostel approved for the purpose by the Secretary of State.	

Column (1)	Column (2)

Polygamous marriages where one or more partners are temporarily separated

10. A claimant who is a member of a polygamous marriage and who is temporarily separated from a partner of his, where one of them is living in the home while the other member is—

    (a) not a patient but is resident in a nursing home; or

    (b) resident in a residential care home; or

    (c) in accommodation referred to in sub-paragraphs (a) to (d) of the definition of residential accommodation in regulation 21(3) (special cases); or

    (d) resident in premises used for the rehabilitation of alcoholics or drug addicts; or

    (e) attending a course of training or instruction provided or approved by the Manpower Services Commission where the course requires him to live away from home; or

    (f) in a probation or bail hostel approved for the purpose by the Secretary of State.

10. Either—

    (a) the amount applicable to the members of the polygamous marriage under regulation 18; or

    (b) the aggregate of the amount applicable for the members of the polygamous marriage who remain in the home under regulation 18 and the amount applicable in respect of those members not in the home calculated as if each of them were a single claimant, or a lone parent,

whichever is the greater.

Couples where one member is abroad

11. A claimant who is a member of a couple and whose partner is temporarily not present in Great Britain.

11. For the first four weeks of that absence, the amount applicable to them as a couple under regulation 17, or 19 to 21 as the case may be and thereafter the amount applicable to the claimant in Great Britain under regulation 17 or 19 to 21 as the case may be as if the claimant were a single claimant or, as the case may be, a lone parent.

Polygamous marriages where any member is abroad

12. A claimant who is a member of a polygamous marriage and who, or whose partner, is temporarily not present in Great Britain.

12. For the first four weeks of that absence, the amount applicable to them as members of a polygamous marriage under regulations 18 to 21 as the case may be and thereafter the amount applicable to the claimant in Great Britain under regulations 18 to 21 as the case may be as if the member not in Great Britain were not a member of the marriage.

Persons in residential accommodation

13.—(1) Subject to sub-paragraph (2), a person in or only temporarily absent from residential accommodation who is—

    (a) a single claimant;

    (b) a lone parent;

    (c) one of a couple;

    (d) a child or young person;

13.—(1)

    (a) £41·15 of which £32·90 is in respect of the cost of the residential accommodation and £8·25 for personal expenses;

    (b) the amount specified in sub-paragraph (a) of this column;

    (c) twice the amount specified in sub-paragraph (a) of this column;

    (d) the appropriate amount in respect of him prescribed in paragraph 2 of Schedule 2 (applicable amounts);

Column (1)	Column (2)
(e) a member of a polygamous marriage.	(e) the amount specified in sub-paragraph (a) of this column multiplied by the number of members of the polygamous marriage in or only temporarily absent from that accommodation;
(2) A single claimant who has become a patient and whose residential accommodation was provided by and managed by a local authority.	(2) £8·25.

Polish Resettlement

14. A claimant for whom accommodation is provided under section 3 and Part II of the Schedule to the Polish Resettlement Act 1947**(a)** (provision of accommodation in camps).	**14.** The weekly amount of the charge payable in respect of the claimant and his family under section 3(6) of, and Part II of the Schedule to, that Act plus the amounts prescribed in paragraph 11(a) (ii) (whether or not the conditions referred to therein are satisfied) and 11(c) to (f) of Schedule 5 (applicable amounts for persons in board and lodging accommodation or hostels) as are appropriate in his case, in respect of personal expenses.

Resettlement Units

15. Claimant being afforded temporary board and lodging in a resettlement unit under section 30 of and paragraph 2 of Schedule 5 to the Supplementary Benefits Act 1976**(b)** (reception centres).	**15.** The weekly amount of any charge for board and lodging made by the Secretary of State under that section 30 plus the amount prescribed in paragraph 11(a) or (b) of Schedule 5 whichever is appropriate in respect of personal expenses.

Persons temporarily absent from board and lodging accommodation or a hostel, residential care or nursing home

16. Where a person has to pay a retaining fee for accommodation which, but for his temporary absence from it, regulation 19 or 20 (persons in residential care or nursing homes) (persons in board and lodging accommodation or hostels would apply and—	**16.** The amount otherwise applicable to him under these Regulations may be increased to take account of the retaining fee by an amount not exceeding 80 per cent of the applicable amount referred to in paragraph 1(1)(a) of Schedule 4 (applicable amounts of persons in residential care or nursing homes) or paragraph 1(a) of Schedule 5 (applicable amounts of persons in board and lodging accommodation or hostels) as the case may be and—
(a) he is a person in accommodation referred to in any of sub-paragraphs (a) to (d) of regulation 21(3) (special cases) and paragraph 13 does not apply to him by reason only that his stay in that accommodation has not become other than temporary; or	(a) in a case to which sub-paragraph (a) or (b) of Column 1 applies any such increase shall not be for a continuous period of more than 52 weeks;
(b) he is a person to whom paragraph 1 to 3 or 18 (patients) applies; or	(b) in a case of a person to whom only sub-paragraph (c) of Column 1 applies, any such increase shall not be for a continuous period of more than four weeks.
(c) he is absent for a period of at least one week from that accommodation being accommodation either in a residential care home or nursing home and he is not required to be available for employment.	

(a) 1947 c.19, as amended by Schedule 4 of the Social Security Act 1980 (c.30) and by S.I. 1951/174 and 1968/1699.

(b) 1976 c.71, as amended by section 6 of, and Schedule 2 and Schedule 65, Part II to, the Social Security Act 1980 and by section 102 and Schedule 17 of the Local Government Act 1985 (c.51).

Column (1)	Column (2)

Persons from abroad

17. Except in relation to a person from abroad to whom regulation 70(3) applies (urgent cases)—

(a) a person from abroad who is a single claimant;

17. (a) Nil;

(b) a lone parent—

   (i) where he is a person from abroad;

   (b) (i) nil;

   (ii) where he is not a person from abroad but one or more members of his family are persons from abroad;

   (ii) the amount applicable to him under regulation 17(a) plus in respect of any members of his family not a person from abroad, any amounts applicable to him under regulation 17(b), (c) or (d) plus the amount applicable to him under regulation 17(e) or, as the case may be, regulation 19, 20, or 21;

(c) a member of a couple—

   (i) where the claimant is not a person from abroad but his partner is such a person, whether or not regulation 70 applies to that partner;

   (c) (i) the amount applicable in respect of him only under regulation 17(a) plus in respect of any child or young person who is a member of his family and who is not a person from abroad, any amounts which may be applicable to him under regulation 17(b), (c) or (d) plus the amount applicable to him under regulation 17(e); or as the case may be regulation 19, 20 or 21;

   (ii) where the claimant is a person from abroad but his partner is not such a person;

   (ii) nil;

   (iii) where the claimant and his partner are both persons from abroad;

   (iii) nil;

(d) where regulation 18 (polygamous marriages) applies and—

   (i) the claimant is not a person from abroad but one or more but not all of his partners are persons from abroad;

   (d) (i) the amounts determined in accordance with that regulation or regulation 19, 20 or 21 in respect of the claimant and any partners of his and any child or young person for whom he or any partner is treated as responsible, who are not persons from abroad;

   (ii) the claimant is a person from abroad, whether or not one or more of his partners are persons from abroad;

   (ii) nil;

   (iii) the claimant and all his partners are persons from abroad;

   (iii) nil;

(e) where any amount is applicable to the claimant under regulation 17(d) because of Part III of Schedule 2 because he or his partner satisfies the conditions prescribed therein and he or his partner as the person so satisfying the condition is a person from abroad.

(e) no amount shall be applicable under regulation 17(d) because of Part III of Schedule 2.

Persons in residential care or nursing homes, board and lodging accommodation or hostels who become patients

18. A claimant to whom regulation 19 (persons in residential care or nursing homes) or

Column (1)	Column (2)
regulation 20 (persons in board and lodging accommodation or hostels) applies immediately before he or a member of his family became a patient where—	
(a) he or any member of his family has been a patient for a period of six weeks or less and the claimant—	
(i) continues to be liable to meet the weekly charge for the accommodation without reduction in respect of himself or that member of his family who is a patient;	**18.** (a) (i) The amount which would be applicable under regulation 19 or 20, as the case may be, as if the claimant or the member of the family who is a patient were resident in the accommodation to which regulation 19 or 20 applies;
(ii) continues to be liable to meet the weekly charge for the accommodation but at a reduced rate;	(ii) the amount which would be applicable under regulation 19 or 20, as the case may be, having taken into account the reduced charge, as if the claimant or the member of the family who is a patient were resident in the accommodation to which regulation 19 or 20 applies;
(iii) is a single claimant and is likely to return to the accommodation, but has ceased to be liable to meet the weekly charge for that accommodation; or	(iii) the amount applicable to him (if any) under paragraph 2(2) of Schedule 4, or, as the case may be, paragraph 2 of Schedule 5 (meal allowances) plus the amount in respect of him as an allowance for personal expenses under paragraph 13 of Schedule 4 or paragraph 11 of Schedule 5, as the case may be, as if he were residing in the accommodation to which regulation 19 or 20 applies;
(iv) is a single claimant who ceases to be liable to meet the weekly charge for the accommodation and who is unlikely to return to that accommodation;	(iv) the amount which would be applicable to him under regulation 17;
(b) he or his partner has been a patient for a period of more than six weeks and the patient is—	
(i) a single claimant;	(b) (i) £8·25 plus either the amount prescribed in paragraph 16 in respect of any retaining fee he is liable to pay for the accommodation or the amount applicable by virtue of regulation 17(e), but not both;
(ii) a lone parent;	(ii) where one or more children or young persons remain in the accommodation, the amount applicable to the family as if regulation 19 or, as the case may be, 20, having taken into account any reduction in charge, continued to apply to all the members of the family except that where the lone parent is the patient no amount shall be applicable in respect of him under paragraph 2(2) of Schedule 4 or paragraph 2 of Schedule 5 (meals allowances) and for the amount in respect of the allowance for personal expenses prescribed by either

Column (1)	Column (2)
	paragraph 13 of Schedule 4 or, as the case may be, paragraph 11 of Schedule 5, there shall be substituted the amount £8·25;
	—where all the children or young persons are absent from the accommodation, £8·25 plus any amounts applicable to him under regulation 17(b), (c) or (d) plus, if appropriate, either the amount applicable under Column 2 of paragraph 16(a) or the amount applicable by virtue of regulation 17(e) (housing costs) but not both;
	—where one or more children or young persons are also patients and have been so for more than 12 weeks, in respect of those children and young persons remaining in the accommodation and the lone parent patient the amount specified in case one of Column (2) of sub-paragraph (b)(iii) save that the child or young person who has been a patient for more than 12 weeks shall be disregarded as a member of the family in assessing the amount applicable under regulation 19 or 20 as the case may be, and in respect of each such child or young person there shall be added the amount of £8·25;
(iii) one of a couple or polygamous marriage and one of that couple or marriage is not a patient or has been a patient for six weeks or less;	(iii) where the members of the family not patients remain in the accommodation, the amount applicable to the family as if regulation 19 or, as the case may be, regulation 20, having taken into account any reduction in charge, continued to apply to all the members of the family except that in respect of the member of the couple or polygamous marriage who has been a patient for more than six weeks no amount shall be applicable in respect of him under paragraph 2(2) of Schedule 4 or paragraph 2 of Schedule 5, as the case may be, and for the amount in respect of the allowance for personal expenses prescribed by either paragraph 13 of Schedule 4 or paragraph 11 of Schedule 5, there shall be substituted the amount of £8·25;
	—where one or more children or young persons are also patients and have been so for more than 12 weeks, in respect of those children and young persons and the member of the couple or polygamous marriage remaining in the accommodation the amount specified in case one of Column (2) of sub-paragraph (b)(ii) save that the child or young person who has been a patient for more than 12 weeks shall be disregarded as a

Column (1)	Column (2)
	member of the family in assessing the amount applicable under regulation 19 or 20 as the case may be, and in respect of each such child or young person there shall be added the amount of £8·25;
(iv) one of a couple or polygamous marriage where all the members of that couple or marriage are patients and have been so for more than six weeks;	(iv) where there is no child or young person in the family £8·25 in respect of each member of the couple or polygamous marriage plus either the amount prescribed in paragraph 16 in respect of any retaining fee for the accommodation he is liable to pay or the amount applicable by virtue of regulation 17(e) or 18(f), but not both;
	—where there is a child or young person remaining in the accommodation, the amount which would be applicable in respect of the family as if regulation 19 or, as the case may be, 20 having taken into account any reduction in charge continued to apply to all the members of the family except that in respect of a member of the couple or polygamous marriage no amount shall be applicable in respect of him under paragraph 2(2) of Schedule 4 or paragraph 2 of Schedule 5, as the case may be, and for the amount in respect of the allowance for personal expenses prescribed by either paragraph 13 of Schedule 4 or paragraph 11 of Schedule 5 in respect of that member there shall be substituted the amount of £8·25;
	—where there is a child or young person in the family but no child or young person remains in the accommodation, the amount applicable under paragraph 1(c) or 1(d) as is appropriate plus either the amount applicable under Column 2 of paragraph 16(a) or the amount applicable by virtue of regulation 17(e) or 18(f) but not both;
	—where one or more children or young persons are also patients and have been so for more than 12 weeks, in respect of those children and young persons and the member of the couple or polygamous marriage remaining in the accommodation and the lone parent patient the amount specified in case two of Column (2) of sub-paragraph (b)(iv) save that the child or young person who has been a patient for more than 12 weeks shall be disregarded as a member of the family in assessing the amount applicable under regulation 19 or 20 as the case may be, and in respect of each such child or young person there shall be added the amount of £8·25;

Column (1)	Column (2)
(c) a child or young person who has been a patient for a period of more than 12 weeks.	(c) the amount applicable under regulation 19 or, as the case may be, regulation 20 as if that child or young person was not a member of the family plus an amount of £8·25 in respect of that child or young person.

Claimants entitled to the disability premium for a past period

19. A claimant—	**19.** The amount only of the disability premium applicable by virtue of paragraph 11(b) of Schedule 2 as specified in paragraph 15(4)(b) of that Schedule.
(a) whose time for claiming income support has been extended under regulation 19(2) of the Social Security (Claims and Payments) Regulations 1987(a) (time for claiming benefit); and	
(b) whose partner was entitled to income support in respect of the period beginning with the day on which the claimant's claim is treated as made under paragraph 6(4) of Schedule 7 to those Regulations and ending with the day on which the claim is actually made; and	
(c) who satisfied the condition in paragraph 11(b) of Schedule 2 and the additional condition referred to in that paragraph and specified in paragraph 12(1)(b) of that Schedule in respect of that period.	

Rounding of fractions

20. Where any calculation under this Schedule or as a result of income support being awarded for a period less than one complete benefit week results in a fraction of a penny that fraction shall be treated as a penny.

SCHEDULE 8

Regulations 36(2), 38(2) and 44(6)

SUMS TO BE DISREGARDED IN THE CALCULATION OF EARNINGS

1. In the case of a claimant who has been engaged in remunerative work as an employed earner—
  (a) any earnings paid or due to be paid on termination of his employment—
    (i) by way of retirement but only if on retirement he is entitled to a retirement pension under the Social Security Act, or would be so entitled if he satisfied the contribution conditions;
    (ii) otherwise than by retirement except earnings to which regulation 35(1)(b) to (e) and (g) and (h) applies (earnings of employed earners);
  (b) any earnings paid or due to be paid on the interruption of his employment except earnings to which regulation 35(1)(d) and (e) applies; but this sub-paragraph shall not apply where the claimant has been suspended from his employment.

2. In the case of a claimant who has been engaged in part-time employment as an employed earner immediately before he made a claim for income support, any earnings paid on termination or interruption of that employment except any payment to which regulation 35(1)(e) applies (earnings of employed earners); but this paragraph shall not apply where the claimant has been suspended from his employment.

(a) S.I. 1987/1968.

3. In the case of a claimant who has been engaged in remunerative work or part-time employment as a self-employed earner and who has ceased to be so employed, from the date of the cessation of his employment any earnings derived from that employment except earnings to which regulation 30(2) (royalties etc.) applies.

4.—(1) If the calculation of the claimant's applicable amount—

(a) includes, or but for his being an in-patient or in accommodation in a residential care home, nursing home, hostel, board and lodging accommodation or in residential accommodation would include, an amount by way of a disability premium under Schedule 2 (applicable amounts), or

(b) (i) includes, or but for his being an in-patient or in accommodation in a residential care home, nursing home, hostel, board and lodging accommodation or in residential accommodation would include, an amount by way of the higher pensioner premium under Schedule 2; and

(ii) he or his partner has attained the age of 60 and immediately before attaining that age either was engaged in employment and the claimant was or but for his being an in-patient or in accommodation in a residential care home, nursing home, hostel or board and lodging accommodation or in residential accommodation would have been, entitled under sub-paragraph (a) to a disregard of £15; and

(iii) either he or his partner has continued in part-time employment,

£15; but, notwithstanding regulation 23 (calculation of income and capital of members of claimant's family and of a polygamous marriage), if this paragraph applies to a claimant it shall not apply to his partner except where, and to the extent that, the earnings of the claimant which are to be disregarded under this paragraph are less than £15.

(2) For the purposes of sub-paragraph (1)(b)(iii) no account shall be taken of any period not exceeding eight consecutive weeks occurring on or after the date on which the claimant or his partner attained the age of 60 during which either ceased to be engaged in employment or the claimant ceased to be entitled to income support.

5. If an amount by way of a lone parent premium under Schedule 2 (applicable amounts) is, or but for the pensioner premium being applicable to him or for his accommodation in a residential care home, nursing home, hostel, board and lodging accommodation or in residential accommodation would be, included in the calculation of the claimant's applicable amount, £15.

6.—(1) In a case where paragraph 4 does not apply, if the claimant is one of a couple and both members of that couple are under age 60 and one of the couple has for a continuous period of two years been in receipt of income support in respect of a couple (whether or not the same couple) and during that period—

(a) neither member has been engaged in remunerative work; or

(b) neither member has been receiving full-time education;

for a period exceeding eight consecutive weeks, £15; but, notwithstanding regulation 23 (calculation of income and capital of members of claimant's family and of a polygamous marriage), if this paragraph applies to one of the couple it shall not apply to the other except where, and to the extent that, the earnings of the one which are to be disregarded under this paragraph are less than £15;

(2) For the purposes of this paragraph—

(a) in determining whether a period is continuous no account shall be taken of any period not exceeding eight weeks during which the claimant ceased to be a member of a couple or to be in receipt of income support;

(b) in determining whether one of a couple has been in receipt of income support for a continuous period of two years, consecutive periods during which either member was in receipt of income support shall be treated as periods during which one of that couple had been so in receipt.

(3) For the purposes of this paragraph—

(a) any period beginning before the commencement of these regulations during which the claimant or the other member of the couple was in receipt of supplementary benefit in respect of a couple, and immediately preceding the receipt of income support, is to be taken into account as if it were a period of income support except where during that period either the claimant or the other member was engaged in remunerative work or receiving relevant education within the meaning of section 6 of the Supplementary Benefits Act 1976(a);

(b) any period during which the claimant or the other member of the couple is in receipt of income support under the Social Security (Northern Ireland) Order 1986(b) or was in receipt of supplementary benefit under the Supplementary Benefit (Northern Ireland) Order 1977(a) and immediately preceding the receipt of income support is to be taken into account as if it were a period of income support;

and in determining whether any such period is continuous sub-paragraph (2) hereof shall apply by analogy.

7.—(1) In a case to which none of paragraphs 4 to 6 applies to the claimant, £15 of earnings derived from one or more employments as—

(a) a part-time fireman in a fire brigade maintained in pursuance of the Fire Services Acts 1947 to 1959(b);

(b) an auxiliary coastguard in respect of coast rescue activities;

(c) a person engaged part time in the manning or launching of a lifeboat;

(d) a member of any territorial or reserve force prescribed in Part I of Schedule 3 to the Social Security (Contributions) Regulations 1979(c);

but, notwithstanding regulation 23 (calculation of income and capital of members of claimant's family and of a polygamous marriage), if this paragraph applies to a claimant it shall not apply to his partner except to the extent specified in sub-paragraph (2).

(2) If the claimant's partner is engaged in employment—

(a) specified in sub-paragraph (1) so much of his earnings as would not in aggregate with the amount of the claimant's earnings disregarded under this paragraph exceed £15;

(b) other than one specified in sub-paragraph (1) so much of his earnings from that employment up to £5 as would not in aggregate with the claimant's earnings disregarded under this paragraph exceed £15.

8. Where the claimant is engaged in one or more employments specified in paragraph 7(1) but his earnings derived from such employments are less than £15 in any week and he is also engaged in any other part-time employment so much of his earnings from that other employment up to £5 as would not in aggregate with the amount of his earnings disregarded under paragraph 7 exceed £15.

9. In a case to which none of paragraphs 4 to 8 applies to the claimant, £5.

10. Notwithstanding paragraph 6, 7, or 9, where two or more payments of the same kind and from the same source are to be taken into account in the same benefit week, there shall be disregarded from each payment the sum specified in that paragraph; but this paragraph shall only apply in the case of a payment which it has not been practicable to treat under regulation 31(1)(b) (date on which income treated as paid) as paid on the first day of the benefit week in which it is due to be paid.

11. Any earnings derived from employment which are payable in a country outside the United Kingdom for such period during which there is a prohibition against the transfer to the United Kingdom of those earnings.

12. Where a payment of earnings is made in a currency other than sterling, any banking charge or commission payable in converting that payment into sterling.

13. Any earnings which are due to be paid before the date of claim and which would otherwise fall to be taken into account in the same benefit week as a payment of the same kind and from the same source.

14. Any earnings of a child or young person except earnings to which paragraph 15 applies.

15. In the case of earnings of a person treated as receiving relevant education under regulation 12(b) (relevant education) and who is engaged in remunerative work, if—

(a) an amount by way of a disabled child premium under Schedule 2 (applicable amounts) is, or but for his accommodation in a residential care home, nursing home, hostel or board and lodging accommodation would be, included in the calculation of his applicable amount and his earning capacity is not, by reason of his disability, less than 75 per cent of that which he would, but for that disability normally be expected to earn, £15;

(b) in any other case, £5.

16. In this Schedule " part-time employment " means employment in which the person is not to be treated as engaged in remunerative work under regulation 5 or 6 (persons treated, or not treated, as engaged in remunerative work).

(a) S.I. 1977/2156 (N.I. 27); the relevant amending instruments are S.I. 1980/870 (N.I. 8), 1987/464 (N.I. 8).
(b) 1947 c.41, 1951 c.27, 1959 c.44.
(c) S.I. 1979/591; Part I of Schedule 3 was substituted by S.I. 1980/1975.

Regulation 40 (2)   **SCHEDULE 9**

SUMS TO BE DISREGARDED IN THE CALCULATION OF INCOME OTHER THAN EARNINGS

1. Any amount paid by way of tax on income which is taken into account under regulation 40 (calculation of income other than earnings).

2. Any payment in respect of any expenses incurred by a claimant who is—

(a) engaged by a charitable or voluntary body; or

(b) a volunteer,

if he otherwise derives no remuneration or profit from the employment and is not to be treated as possessing any earnings under regulation 42 (6) (notional income).

3. In the case of employment as an employed earner, any payment in respect of expenses wholly, exclusively and necessarily incurred in the performance of the duties of the employment.

4. In the case of a payment of statutory sick pay under Part I of the Social Security and Housing Benefits Act 1982 or statutory maternity pay under Part V of the Act or any remuneration paid by or on behalf of an employer to the claimant who for the time being is unable to work due to illness or maternity—

(a) any amount deducted by way of primary Class 1 contributions under the Social Security Act;

(b) one-half of any sum paid by the claimant by way of a contribution towards an occupational or personal pension scheme.

5. Any housing benefit.

6. Any mobility allowance.

7. Any concessionary payment made to compensate for the non-payment of—

(a) any payment specified in paragraph 6 or 9;

(b) income support.

8. Any mobility supplement or any payment intended to compensate for the non-payment of such a supplement.

9. Any attendance allowance but, where the claimant is in a residential care home or nursing home, only to the extent that it exceeds the amount for the time being specified as the higher rate for the purposes of section 35 (3) of the Social Security Act**(a)**.

10. Any payment to the claimant as holder of the Victoria Cross or George Cross or any analogous payment.

11. Any sum in respect of a course of study attended by a child or young person payable by virtue of regulations made under section 81 of the Education Act 1944**(b)** (assistance by means of scholarships and otherwise), or by virtue of section 2 (1) of the Education Act 1962 **(c)** (awards for courses of further education) or section 49 of the Education (Scotland) Act 1980**(d)** (power to assist persons to take advantage of educational facilities).

12. In the case of a claimant to whom regulation 9 (1) (persons treated as available for employment) applies, any sums intended for any expenditure specified in paragraph (2) of regulation 62 (calculation of grant income) necessary as a result of his attendance on his course.

13. In the case of a claimant attending a training course provided under the Adult and Youth Training Programme established under section 2 (1) of the Employment and Training Act 1973 **(e)** or a course at an employment rehabilitation centre established under that section—

(a) any travelling expenses reimbursed to the claimant;

(b) any living away from home allowance under section 2 (2) (d) of that Act but only to the extent that his rent or rates payable in respect of accommodation not normally occupied by him as his home are not met by housing benefit;

(a) 1975 c.14; section 35 (3) was amended by section 2 of the Social Security Act 1979 (c.18).

(b) 1944 c.31; section 81 was amended by S.I. 1964/490.

(c) 1962 c.12; section 2 (1) was substituted by section 19 of, and Schedule 5 to, the Education Act 1980 (c.20).

(d) 1980 c.44.

(e) 1973 c.50; section 2 was amended by sections 9 and 11, Schedule 2, Part II, paragraph 9 and Schedule 3 of the Employment and Training Act 1981 (c.57).

but this paragraph does not apply to any part of any allowance under section 2(2)(d) of that Act expressed to be a personal allowance.

14. Any Job Start Allowance payable pursuant to arrangements made under section 2(1) of the Employment and Training Act 1973.

15. Except in the case of a person to whom section 23 of the Act (trade disputes) applies and for so long as it applies, subject to paragraphs 36 and 37, £5 of any charitable payment or of any voluntary payment made or due to be made (whether or not so made) at regular intervals other than a payment which is made by a person for the maintenance of any member of his family or his former partner or of his children; and, for the purposes of this paragraph, where a number of such charitable or voluntary payments fall to be taken into account in any one week they shall be treated as though they were on one such payment.

16. Subject to paragraphs 36 and 37, £5 of any of the following, namely—

(a) a war disablement pension or war widow's pension or a payment made to compensate for the non-payment of such a pension;

(b) a pension paid under the social security scheme of a country outside Great Britain and which either—

   (i) is analogous to a war disablement pension; or

   (ii) is paid to a war widow in respect of a person's death but is otherwise analogous to such a pension.

(c) a pension paid under any special provision made by the law of the Federal Republic of Germany or any part of it or of the Republic of Austria, to victims of National Socialist persecution.

17. Where a claimant receives income under an annuity purchased with a loan which satisfies the following conditions—

(a) that the loan was made as part of a scheme under which not less than 90 per cent of the proceeds of the loan were applied to the purchase by the person to whom it was made of an annuity ending with his life or with the life of the survivor of two or more persons (in this paragraph referred to as "the annuitants") who include the person to whom the loan was made;

(b) that the interest on the loan is payable by the person to whom it was made or by one of the annuitants;

(c) that at the time the loan was made the person to whom it was made or each of the annuitants had attained the age of 65;

(d) that the loan was secured on a dwelling in Great Britain and the person to whom the loan was made or one of the annuitants owns an estate or interest in that dwelling; and

(e) that the person to whom the loan was made or one of the annuitants occupies the accommodation on which it was secured as his home at the time the interest is paid,

the amount, calculated on a weekly basis equal to—

   (i) where, or in so far as, section 26 of the Finance Act 1982**(a)** (deduction of tax from certain loan interest) applies to the payments of interest on the loan, the interest which is payable after deduction of a sum equal to income tax on such payments at the basic rate for the year of assessment in which the payment of interest becomes due;

   (ii) in any other case the interest which is payable on the loan without deduction of such a sum.

18. Any payment made to the claimant by a member of his houshold which is a contribution towards his living and accommodation costs except a payment to which paragraph 19 or 20 applies.

19. Where the claimant occupies a dwelling as his home which is also occupied by a person other than one to whom paragraph 18 refers or one who is provided with board and lodging accommodation and that person is contractually liable to make payments in respect of his occupation of the dwelling to the claimant—

(a) £4 of any payment made by that person; and

(b) a further £6·70, where that payment is inclusive of an amount for heating.

20. Where a claimant is employed in providing board and lodging accommodation for which a charge is payable, £35 of the weekly charge paid by each person provided with such accommodation.

21. Except where regulation 42(4)(a)(i) (notional income) applies or in the case of a person to whom section 23 of the Act (trade disputes) applies and for so long as it applies, any income in kind.

(a) 1982 c. 39.

22.—(1) Any income derived from capital to which the claimant is or is treated under regulation 52 (capital jointly held) as beneficially entitled but, subject to sub-paragraph (2), not income derived from capital disregarded under paragraph 1, 2, 4, 6 or 12 of Schedule 10.

(2) Income derived from capital disregarded under paragraph 2 or 4 of Schedule 10 but only to the extent of any mortgage repayments and payment of rates made in respect of the dwelling or premises in the period during which that income accrued.

23. Any income which is payable in a country outside the United Kingdom for such period during which there is prohibition against the transfer to the United Kingdom of that income.

24. Where a payment of income is made in a currency other than sterling, any banking charge or commission payable in converting that payment into sterling.

25.—(1) Any payment made to the claimant in respect of a child or young person who is a member of his family—

(a) in accordance with a scheme approved by the Secretary of State under section 50(4) of the Adoption Act 1958**(a)** or as the case may be, section 51 of the Adoption (Scotland) Act 1978**(b)** (schemes for payments of allowances to adopters);

(b) which is a payment made by a local authority in pursuance of section 34(6) or, as the case may be, section 50 of the Children Act 1975**(c)** (contributions to a custodian towards the cost of the accommodation and maintenance of a child);

to the extent specified in sub-paragraph (2).

(2) In the case of a child or young person—

(a) to whom regulation 44(5) (capital in excess of £3,000) applies, the whole payment;

(b) to whom that regulation does not apply, so much of the weekly amount of the payment as exceeds the applicable amount in respect of that child or young person and where applicable to him any amount by way of a disabled child premium.

26. Any payment made by a local authority to the claimant with whom a person is boarded out by virtue of arrangements made under section 21(1)(a) of the Child Care Act 1980**(d)** or, as the case may be, section 12 of the Social Work (Scotland) Act 1968**(e)** or by a voluntary organisation under section 61 of the 1980 Act or by a care authority under regulation 9 of the Boarding Out and Fostering of Children (Scotland) Regulations 1985**(f)** (provision of accommodation and maintenance for children in care).

27. Any payment made by a health authority, local authority or voluntary organisation to the claimant in respect of a person who is not normally a member of the claimant's household but is temporarily in his care.

28. Except in the case of a person to whom section 23 of the Act (trade disputes) applies and for so long as it applies, any payment made under section 1 of the Child Care Act 1980 (duty of local authorities to promote welfare of children) or, as the case may be, section 12 of the Social Work (Scotland) Act 1968 (general welfare).

29.—(1) Any payment received under an insurance policy, taken out to insure against the risk of being unable to maintain repayments on a loan to which paragraph 7 or 8 of Schedule 3 applies (interest on loans to acquire an interest in the dwelling, or for repairs and improvements to the dwelling, occupied as the home) and used to meet such repayments, to the extent that it does not exceed—

(a) subject to sub-paragraph (2), the amount, calculated on a weekly basis, of any interest which is excluded under that paragraph;

(b) the amount of the payment, calculated on a weekly basis, due on the loan attributable to the repayment of capital; and

(c) the amount, calculated on a weekly basis, of the premium due on that policy.

(2) The amount to which sub-paragraph (1)(a) refers shall be taken into account in calculating the amount to be excluded under this paragraph only for such period during which there is applicable to the claimant 50 per cent of his eligible interest under paragraph 7 of Schedule 3.

(a) 1958 (7 & 8 Eliz.2) c.5; section 50(4) was added by the Children Act 1975 (c.72), section 32.
(b) 1978 c.28.
(c) 1975 c.72, as amended by section 64 of the Domestic Proceedings and Magistrates' Courts Act 1978 (c.22).
(d) 1980 c.5, amended by section 9, Schedule 2, paragraph 49 of the Health and Social Services and Social Security Adjudication Act 1983 (c.41).
(e) 1968 c.49.
(f) S.I. 1985/1799.

30. Except where paragraph 28 applies, any payment made to the claimant which is intended and used as a contribution towards—

(a) the amount of eligible interest which is not met under paragraph 7 or 8 of Schedule 3 (interest on loans to acquire an interest in the dwelling, or for repairs and improvements to the dwelling, occupied as the home);

(b) the capital repayments—

  (i) where the loan is one specified in paragraph 7(3)(a) or 8(1)(a) of Schedule 3; or

  (ii) where the loan is one specified in paragraph 7(3)(b) or 8(1)(b) of Schedule 3 only to the extent that the capital outstanding on that loan represents the capital balance outstanding on the previous loan at the time when the loan was taken out;

(c) any payment or charge specified in paragraph 1 of Schedule 3 to the extent that that payment or charge has not been met;

(d) his rent in respect of the dwelling occupied by him as his home but only to the extent that it is not met by housing benefit; or his accommodation charge but only to the extent that the actual charge for the accommodation exceeds the amount determined in accordance with regulation 19 or 20 (board and lodging, hostels, residential care and nursing homes).

31. Any social fund payment.

32. Any payment of income which under regulation 48 (income treated as capital) is to be treated as capital.

33. Any payment under paragraph 2 of Schedule 6 to the Act (pensioner's Christmas bonus).

34. In the case of a person to whom section 23 of the Act (trade disputes) applies and for so long as it applies, any payment up to the amount of the relevant sum within the meaning of subsection 6 of that section made by a trade union; but, notwithstanding regulation 23 (calculation of income and capital of members of claimant's family and of a polyamous marriage) if this paragraph applies to a claimant it shall not apply to his partner except where, and to the extent that, the amount to be disregarded under this paragraph is less than the relevant sum.

35. Any payment which is due to be paid before the date of claim which would otherwise fall to be taken into account in the same benefit week as a payment of the same kind and from the same source.

36. The total of a claimant's income or, if he is a member of a family, the family's income and the income of any person which he is treated as possessing under regulation 23(3) (calculation of income and capital of members of claimant's family and of a polygamous marriage) to be disregarded under regulation 63(2)(b) and 64(1)(c) (calculation of covenant income where a contribution assessed) and paragraphs 15 and 16 shall in no case exceed £5 per week.

37. Notwithstanding paragraph 36 where two or more payments of the same kind and from the same source are to be taken into account in the same benefit week, there shall be disregarded from each payment the sum which would otherwise fall to be disregarded under this Schedule; but this paragraph shall only apply in the case of a payment which it has not been practicable to treat under regulation 31(1)(b) (date on which income treated as paid) as paid on the first day of the benefit week in which it is due to be paid.

SCHEDULE 10

Regulation 46(2)

CAPITAL TO BE DISREGARDED

1. The dwelling occupied as the home but, notwithstanding regulation 23 (calculation of income and capital of members of claimant's family and of a polygamous marriage), only one dwelling shall be disregarded under this paragraph.

2. Any premises acquired for occupation by the claimant which he intends to occupy within 26 weeks of the date of acquisition or such longer period as is reasonable in the circumstances to enable the claimant to obtain possession and commence occupation of the premises.

3. Any sum directly attributable to the proceeds of sale of any premises formerly occupied by the claimant as his home which is to be used for the purchase of other premises intended for such occupation within 26 weeks of the date of sale or such longer period as is reasonable in the circumstances to enable the claimant to complete the purchase.

4. Any premises occupied in whole or in part by—

    (a) a partner or relative of any member of the family where that person is aged 60 or over or is incapacitated;

    (b) the former partner of a claimant where the claimant is not to be treated as occupying a dwelling as his home; but this provision shall not apply where the former partner is a person from whom the claimant is estranged or divorced.

5. Any reversionary interest.

6. The assets of any business owned in whole or in part by the claimant and for the purposes of which he is engaged as a self-employed earner or, if he has ceased to be so engaged, for such period as may be reasonable in the circumstances to allow for disposal of any such asset.

7. Any arrears of, or any concessionary payment made to compensate for arrears due to the non-payment of—

    (a) any payment specified in paragraph 6, 8 or 9 of Schedule 9 (other income to be disregarded);

    (b) an income-related benefit or supplementary benefit, family income supplement under the Family Income Supplements Act 1970(**a**) or housing benefit under Part II of the Social Security and Housing Benefits Act 1982;

but only for a period of 52 weeks from the date of the receipt of the arrears or of the concessionary payment.

8. Any sum—

    (a) paid to the claimant in consequence of damage to, or loss of the home or any personal possession and intended for its repair or replacement; or

    (b) acquired by the claimant (whether as a loan or otherwise) on the express condition that it is to be used for effecting essential repairs or improvements to the home,

and which is to be used for the intended purpose, for a period of 26 weeks from the date on which it was so paid or acquired or such longer period as is reasonable in the circumstances to enable the claimant to effect the repairs, replacement or improvements.

9. Any sum—

    (a) deposited with a housing association as defined in section 1(1) of the Housing Associations Act 1985(**b**) or section 338(1) of the Housing (Scotland) Act 1987(**c**) as a condition of occupying the home;

    (b) which was so deposited and which is to be used for the purchase of another home, for the period of 26 weeks or such longer period as is reasonable in the circumstances to complete the purchase.

10. Any personal possessions except those which had or have been acquired by the claimant with the intention of reducing his capital in order to secure entitlement to supplementary benefit or income support or to increase the amount of that benefit.

11. The value of the right to receive any income under an annuity and the surrender value (if any) of such an annuity.

12.—(1) Where the funds of a trust are derived from a payment made in consequence of any personal injury to the claimant the value of the trust fund and the value of the right to receive any payment under that trust, for a period of two years or such longer period as is reasonable in the circumstances beginning—

    (a) if, at the date of the payment the claimant or his partner is in receipt of an income-related benefit, on that date;

    (b) in any other case, on the date on which an income-related benefit is first payable to the claimant or his partner after the date of that payment,

but, for the purposes of regulation 17, 18, 21, 44(5) and 71 and Schedules 4 and 5 (applicable amounts and modifications in respect of children and young persons) in calculating the capital of a child or young person there shall be no limit as to the period of disregard under this paragraph.

(2) For the purposes of sub-paragraph (1) any reference to an income-related benefit shall be construed as if it included a reference to supplementary benefit.

13. The value of the right to receive any income under a life interest or from a liferent.

(**a**) 1970 c.55.
(**b**) 1985 c.69.
(**c**) 1987 c.26.

14. The value of the right to receive any income which is disregarded under paragraph 11 of Schedule 8 or paragraph 23 of Schedule 9 (earnings or other income to be disregarded).

15. The surrender value of any policy of life insurance.

16. Where any payment of capital falls to be made by instalments, the value of the right to receive any outstanding instalments.

17. Except in the case of a person to whom section 23 of the Act (trade disputes) applies and for so long as it applies, any payment made under section 1 of the Child Care Act 1980 (duty of local authorities to promote welfare of children) or, as the case may be, section 12 of the Social Work (Scotland) Act 1968 (general welfare).

18. Any social fund payment.

19. Any refund of tax which falls to be deducted under section 26 of the Finance Act 1982**(a)** (deductions of tax from certain loan interest) on a payment of relevant loan interest for the purpose of acquiring an interest in the home or carrying out repairs or improvements in the home.

20. Any capital which under regulations 41 and 44(1) (capital treated as income and modifications in respect of children and young persons) is to be treated as income.

21. Where a payment of capital is made in a currency other than sterling, any banking charge or commission payable in converting that payment into sterling.

EXPLANATORY NOTE

(This note is not part of the Regulations)

These Regulations provide for various matters concerning entitlement to, and the amount of, income support.

Part I contains general provisions affecting the citation, commencement and interpretation of the Regulations (regulations 1 to 3).

Part II prescribes the circumstances in which a person's entitlement is to continue notwithstanding his absence from Great Britain; provide for what is to be treated as remunerative work and relevant education; specifies the circumstances in which a person is not required to be available for employment, or is to be treated or not treated as in remunerative work, available for employment, or in relevant education; and also provides for a person under the age of 18 to be registered for employment (regulations 4 to 13).

Part III makes provision in respect of children and young persons and prescribes, for the purpose of determining the members of a family, the circumstances in which a person is to be treated as responsible for another or as a member of the same household (regulations 14 to 17).

Part IV provides for a claimant's applicable amount (by reference to which the amount of his income support is calculated) to consist of the following: a personal allowance for the claimant and members of his family; where applicable, a family, lone parent, pensioner or disability premium and an amount in respect of mortgage interest payments or other prescribed housing costs. It also makes special provision in the case of polygamous marriages, boarders, certain cases of disqualification from unemployment benefit, and other special cases (regulations 17 to 22).

Part V contains provisions for the calculation of income and capital. Chapters II to V make provision for income not expressly disregarded to be taken into account on a weekly basis; define earnings and prescribe the manner in which earnings and other income are to be calculated; they also prescribe the circumstances in which capital is to be treated as income and a person is to be treated as possessing income which he in fact does not possess.

(a) 1982 c.39.

Chapter VI makes provision for the calculation of capital; sets the capital limit over which a person is not to be entitled to benefit at £6,000 and provides for a weekly tariff income on capital over £3,000 and under that limit at a rate of £1 for every £250. Chapters VII and VIII make special provision in relation to the calculation of payments made by liable relatives and in respect of students (regulations 23 to 69).

Part VI makes provision for persons from abroad and for persons who are treated as possessing earnings who could not otherwise qualify for income support to be entitled to income support in cases of hardship; and for determining their applicable amount and income and capital (regulations 70 to 72).

These regulations are made before the expiry of 12 months from the commencement of provisions under which they are made: they are accordingly exempt, by section 61(5) of the Social Security Act 1986, from reference to the Social Security Advisory Committee and have not been so referred.

STAFFORDSHIRE
COUNTY COURT HOUSE
L
H
STOKE-ON-TRENT